The World

ARCTIC OCEAN

180°
160°W
140° West Longitude
80°N
120°W
100°W

Greenland
(DENMARK)

Arctic Circle   Alaska
(U.S.)
60°N
CANADA

Aleutian Islands

NORTH AMERICA

ATLANTIC OCEAN

40°North Latitude   UNITED STATES

PACIFIC OCEAN

Azores
(PORT.)

Midway Islands
(U.S.)
Bermuda
(U.K.)

Tropic of Cancer
MEXICO
BAHAMAS
Puerto Rico (U.S.)

20°N   Hawaii (U.S.)
CUBA
DOMINICAN
REPUBLIC   ST. CHRISTOPHER AND NEVIS
ANTIGUA-BARBUDA
HAITI   DOMINICA
JAMAICA   Virgin Is. (U.S.-U.K.)   ST. VINCENT AND
BELIZE   THE GRENADINES
GUATEMALA   ST. LUCIA
HONDURAS   BARBADOS
EL SALVADOR   NICARAGUA   GRENADA   TRINIDAD AND TOBAGO

CAPE VERDE

COSTA RICA   VENEZUELA   GUYANA
PANAMA   SURINAME
COLOMBIA   FR. GUIANA
(FRANCE)

P
O
L
Y
N
E
S
I
A

KIRIBATI

0°   Equator
Galapagos
Islands
(ECUADOR)
ECUADOR

SOUTH AMERICA

PERU

WESTERN
SAMOA   American
Samoa (U.S.)
BRAZIL

TONGA

BOLIVIA

20°S   French
Polynesia
(FRANCE)
Tropic of Capricorn
PARAGUAY

Easter Island
(CHILE)
CHILE

PACIFIC OCEAN
URUGUAY

40°S
ARGENTINA

Falkland Islands
(U.K.)

South Georgia
(Falkland Is.)

60°S

Antarctic Circle
80°S   **ANTARCTICA**
160°W   140°   120°   100°   80°   60°

Central America and the Caribbean

30°N   110°W   100°W   90°W   80°   180°   160°W   140°W

UNITED STATES

Gulf of California

70°W

Tropic of
Cancer   **NORTH AMERICA**
20°N   MEXICO

Gulf of Mexico
BAHAMAS
ATLANTIC OCEAN
60°W
50°W

CUBA
DOMINICAN
REPUBLIC   Puerto Rico
(U.S.)
Virgin Is. (U.S.)
HAITI   ANTIGUA-BARBUDA
Guadeloupe (Fr.)
JAMAICA   ST. CHRISTOPHER   DOMINICA
AND NEVIS   Martinique (Fr.)
BELIZE   *West Indies*   ST. LUCIA
HONDURAS   ST. VINCENT AND   BARBADOS
THE GRENADINES
GUATEMALA   *CARIBBEAN SEA*
EL SALVADOR   GRENADA
NICARAGUA   TRINIDAD
AND TOBAGO
PACIFIC OCEAN   **Central
America**
N
10°N   Panama
Canal
W   E
COSTA   S
RICA   VENEZUELA
GUYANA
PANAMA   COLOMBIA   **SOUTH AMERICA**   SURINAME

0   500 Miles
0   500 Kilometers

America
and
Its People

Volume Two from 1865

Second Edition

America and Its People

Volume Two from 1865

Second Edition

James Kirby Martin
University of Houston

Randy Roberts
Purdue University

Steven Mintz
University of Houston

Linda O. McMurry
North Carolina State University

James H. Jones
University of Houston

HarperCollins*College*Publishers

For Our Students

Executive Editor: Bruce Borland
Developmental Editor: Barbara Chernow
Project Editor: Shuli Traub
Design Supervisor: Dorothy Bungert
Text Design: Lucy Lesiak Design/MN'O Production
Services
Cover Design: Jaye Zimet
Cover Art: Steve Karchin
Photo Researcher: Leslie Coopersmith
Production Manager: Willie Lane
Compositor: Waldman Graphics, Inc.
Printer and Binder: R. R. Donnelley & Sons Company
Cover Printer: The Lehigh Press Inc.

America and Its People, Second Edition
Copyright © 1993 by James Kirby Martin, Randy
Roberts, Steven Mintz, Linda O. McMurry, and
James H. Jones

America and its people / James Kirby Martin . . .
[et al.].—2nd ed.
    p. cm.
    Includes bibliographical references and indexes.
    Contents: v. 1. To 1877—v. 2. From 1865.
    ISBN 0–673–46364–8 (v. 1).—
    ISBN 0–673–46365–6 (v. 2)
    1. United States—History.   I. Martin, James
Kirby, 1943–
  E178.1.A4886 1993b   92–28837
                              CIP

92 93 94 95 9 8 7 6 5 4 3 2 1

# rief Contents

etailed Contents

16   The Nation Reconstructed: North, South, and the West, 1865–1877   514

17   Emergence as an Economic Power   550

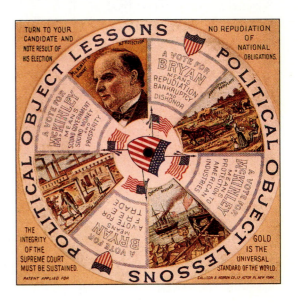

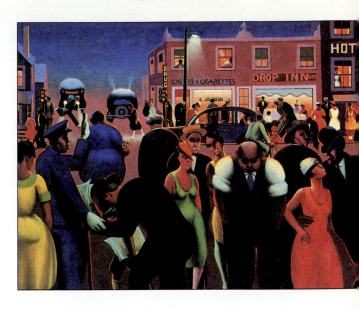

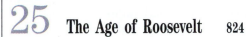

25 The Age of Roosevelt   824

26 The End of Isolation: America Faces the World, 1920–1945   860

$\mathcal{T}$ables and Figures

Preface

The survey textbook in U.S. history is an essential learning instrument. It must do much more than present a chronological rendering of names, dates, and facts. It must gain the attention of students and engage them, and it must challenge students intellectually. It must not deal in caricature but show real people confronting real problems, complete with their triumphs and failures. It must offer historical perspectives on the lives of diverse groups of peoples as well as on the tumultuous affairs of nations. It must increase the tolerance of students for differing interpretations of formative historical change. As such, it must encourage thinking in historical perspective while seeking to enhance such fundamental skills as the recognition of key issues and the solving of difficult problems. The U.S. survey history text, in sum, must function as a work of synthesis that will assist course instructors in making history interesting and meaningful for students.

This is not an easy set of assignments for any textbook. In our increasingly technocratic culture, students have been repeatedly advised to concentrate their academic energies in courses that will ensure them steady incomes as workers in society. An exciting, intelligently conceived history textbook, we are convinced, can help course instructors challenge this mentality by demonstrating that history functions as a central laboratory for learning about life and for acquiring knowledge and skills essential for successful living.

As instructors actively involved in teaching U.S. survey history, we began the development of *America and Its People* with these thoughts in mind. The most compelling works of history, we concluded, focus on people, both the great and the ordinary. They establish the importance of time, place, and circumstance in comprehending the varieties of human endeavor. They do not smooth over but highlight the dramatic conflict among individuals and groups that has so often produced meaningful historical change. They frame their themes rigorously, and they tell their story with a strong narrative pulse. The most effective works of history, we believe, encourage readers to comprehend their own times and themselves more clearly in the light of what has come before them. In this sense, studying the past provides broadened perspective, if not greater tolerance and understanding about the human condition, not only about the past but also for the formulation of present and future realities.

In writing *America and Its People* we have followed these guidelines. We have sought to impart to today's generation of college students our enthusiasm for the value of historical inquiry and our sense of which fundamentals a well-educated person needs to know about the American experience. In our opinion, the story of the United States—of colonization, Indian removal, the Revolution, slavery, social reform, the Civil War, global expansion, the Great Depression and New Deal, and the more recent civil rights and women's liberation movements—is best told by focusing on the dilemmas and struggles faced by passing generations of Americans. Thus our "people-centered" approach encourages students to grasp and evaluate the difficult choices human beings have made in molding the texture of life in the modern United States.

Besides structuring the book's contents to encourage student involvement, we have worked to keep the needs of history faculty members very much in mind. The text's structure conforms to the course outlines used by most history instructors. *America and Its People* also places a premium on chronological flow, an essential organizational element for college students grappling with the complexities of U.S. history. It also provides a clear narrative rendering of essential political, diplomatic, cultural, social, intellectual, and military history and concisely identifies major historical concepts and themes.

Finally, we have taken great care to present a text offering both breadth and balance. We have found that the often-expressed dichotomies between political and diplomatic history and social and cultural history disappear when history is people-centered from its inception. Materials on ethnicity, gender, and race belong at the core of the historical narrative, not as adjunct information, and we have attempted to include the important findings and insights of both traditional and newer historical subjects. It is our hope that we have achieved a sensitive and compelling presentation.

FEATURES

The book's structure is organized to heighten and sustain student interest. To borrow a phrase associated with computers, we have aimed at the production of a "user-friendly" text. Each chapter begins with an **outline of contents** and a carefully selected **anecdote** or **incident** that frames the chapter's themes while drawing students into the material. A chronological and topical narrative follows, building toward a **chapter conclusion** highlighting and reinforcing essential points. In addition, each chapter contains a **chronology of key events**; a **bibliography of suggested readings**; and a **special feature essay** designed to offer students an in-depth look at a significant topic in one of the following people-oriented categories that illustrate change over time: Aspects of Family Life, Sports and Leisure, The American Mosaic, Medicine, The Human Toll of Combat, and Perspectives on Lawbreaking. For this new edition we have developed two important new special feature categories: **America and the World** and **Primary Source Essays**.

Other features of the text include an extensive **full-color map**, **photo**, and **figure art program** including four full-page battlefield picture maps with accompanying essays; a **multidimensional timeline** at the front of the book that is replete with high interest items; and valuable tables, charts, graphs, and maps in the **Appendix**.

NEW TO THIS EDITION

As authors we are grateful for the extremely positive reception accorded the first edition of *America and*

Its People. As with all books, however, there is always room for improvement, and we have worked very hard to make our text even more balanced in this new edition. One objective was to clarify numerous small points along the way. A second was to update our interpretations according to the latest findings in particular subfields. A third was to enhance coverage of political, diplomatic, and intellectual history. Users will find that we have taken Chapter 7, formerly entitled "Shaping the New Nation, 1789–1815," and expanded it into two chapters: Chapter 7, "Shaping the New Nation, 1789–1800," and Chapter 8, "The Jeffersonians in Power, 1800–1815." This expansion has allowed us to deepen and enrich our narrative of key political and diplomatic events in the young American republic from Washington's presidential administration through the War of 1812.

We have also included new materials on key intellectual trends, such as the flowering of a distinct American literature in antebellum America (Chapter 11), and major developments in science and technology (Chapter 9). With respect to diplomatic and intellectual history, we direct attention to the two new categories of special feature essays, which provide supplementary coverage of pivotal subjects ranging from America's first encounters with Japan to Benjamin Franklin's impressions of George Whitefield as presented in Franklin's *Autobiography*.

Still another objective in this revision was to enhance the chronological flow of our presentation. A number of reviewers suggested that we move the chapter focusing on urbanization and city culture to follow directly the chapter on immigration. Thus the sequence of chapters covering the late nineteenth century is as follows: Chapter 18, "Immigrants and Workers in Industrial America"; Chapter 19, "The Rise of an Urban Society and City People"; Chapter 20, "Imperial America, 1870–1900"; and Chapter 21, "End of the Century Crisis." In addition, in Volume II, we have increased the coverage of Native Americans (Chapter 18), added new material in the Vietnam War (Chapter 29), and refocused the last chapter (Chapter 31) to deal with the economic conditions of the late 1980s and early 1990s and to cover in detail the changes in the United States and the world. The collapse of the Soviet Union and the dramatic conclusion of the Cold War both receive extended discussion.

Finally, we have written new opening vignettes for several of the chapters in order to focus more directly on the chapter's themes. Chapter 7, for example, now begins with a discussion of the United States' first census in 1790; the opening vignette in Chapter 18 deals with Chinese immigrants and the building of the transcontinental railroad; and Chapter 30 opens with a discussion of consumer advocate Ralph Nader. Chapters 4, 8, 11, and 31 also feature new opening vignettes.

ACKNOWLEDGMENTS

Any textbook project is very much a team effort. We would like to thank the many individuals who have worked with us on this project, beginning with the talented historians who have served as reviewers and whose valuable critiques greatly strengthened the final product: Joe S. Anderson, Azusa Pacific University; Larry Balsamo, Western Illinois University; Lois W. Banner, University of Southern California; Robert A. Becker, Louisiana State University; Delmar L. Beene, Glendale Community College; Nancy Bowen, Del Mar College; Blanche Brick, Blinn College; Larry Burke, Dodge City Community Junior College; Frank L. Byrne, Kent State University; Colin G. Calloway, University of Wyoming; Albert Camarillo, Stanford University; Clayborne Carson, Stanford University; Jay Caughtry, University of Nevada at Las Vegas; Raymond W. Champagne, Jr., University of Scranton; John P. Crevelli, Santa Rosa Junior College; Shannon J. Doyle, University of Houston; David Glassberg, University of Massachusetts; James P. Gormly, Washington and Jefferson College; Elliott Gorn, Miami University; Neil Hamilton, Brevard Community College; Nancy Hewitt, Duke University; Alphine W. Jefferson, Southern Methodist University; David R. Johnson, University of Texas at San Antonio; Ellen K. Johnson, Northern Virginia Community College; George W. Knepper, University of Akron; Steven F. Lawson, University of South Florida; Barbara LeUnes, Blinn College; James McCaffrey, University of Houston, Downtown; James McMillan, Arizona State University; Myron Marty, Drake University; Otis Miller, Belleville Area College; William Howard Moore, University of Wyoming; Peter Myers, Palo Alto College; Roger L. Nichols, University of Arizona; Michael Perman, University of Illinois at Chicago; Paula Petrik, University of Maine; Robert Pierce, Foothill College; George Rable, Anderson College; Max Reichard, Delgado Community College; Leonard R. Riforgiato, Pennsylvania State University, Shenango Valley Campus; Marilyn Rinehart, North Harris County College; John Ray Skates, University of Southern Mississippi; Sheila Skemp, University of Mississippi; Kathryn Kish Sklar, SUNY at Binghamton; James Strandberg, University of Wisconsin—Stout; Robert Striplin, American River College; J. K. Sweeney, South Dakota State University; Alan Taylor, Boston University; Phillip Vaughn, Rose State College; Peter H. Wang, Cabrillo Community College; Valdenia Winn, Kansas City Kansas Community College; Bill Worley, Sterling College; and Eli Zaretsky, University of Missouri.

The dedicated staff at HarperCollins provided us with great support and expert guidance. From the beginning, Bruce Borland has been a very special friend to this project. We also wish to thank Barbara Chernow, Betty Slack, Shuli Traub, Dorothy Bungert, Leslie Coopersmith, and Willie Lane. To all of them, we offer our sincere gratitude and appreciation.

Each author received invaluable help from friends, colleagues, and family. James Kirby Martin thanks Larry E. Cable, Don R. Gerlach, Joseph T. Glatthaar, Karen Guenther, David M. Oshinsky, Jeffrey T. Sammons, Hal T. Shelton, and Karen Martin, whose talents as an editor and critic are too often overlooked. Randy Roberts thanks Terry Bilhartz and Joan Randall, and especially James S. Olson and Suzy Roberts. Steven Mintz thanks Susan Kellogg for her encouragement, support, and counsel. Linda O. McMurry thanks Joseph P. Hobbs, John David Smith, Richard McMurry, and William C. Harris. James H. Jones thanks James S. Olson, Terry Rugeley, Laura B Auwers, and especially Linda S. Auwers, who contributed both ideas and criticisms. All of the authors thank Gerard F. McCauley, whose infectious enthusiasm for this project has never wavered. And above all else, we wish to thank our students to whom we have dedicated this book.

SUPPLEMENTS

A comprehensive and up-to-date supplements package accompanies *America and Its People*.

For Instructors

AMERICA THROUGH THE EYES OF ITS PEOPLE: A COLLECTION OF PRIMARY SOURCES

Prepared by Carol Brown, of Houston Community College, this one-volume collection of primary documents portraying the rich and varied tapestry of American life contains documents of Native Americans, women, African-Americans, Hispanics, and others who helped to shape the course of U. S. history. Designed to be duplicated by instructors for student use, the documents have accompanying student exercises.

"THIS IS AMERICA" IMMIGRATION VIDEO

Produced by the Museum of Immigration, these two 20-minute videos tell the story of immigrant America and the personal stories and accomplishments of immigrants. By showing how the richness of our culture is due to the contributions of millions of immigrant Americans, the videos make the point that America's strength lies in the ethnically and culturally diverse backgrounds of its citizens.

INSTRUCTOR'S RESOURCE MANUAL

This extensive resource by Mark Newman of the University of Illinois, Chicago, begins with essays on teaching history through maps, film, and primary sources. Each chapter contains a synopsis, sample discussion questions, lecture supplements called "Connections and Extensions," and instructional flowcharts. The manual includes a special reproducible set of map exercises by James Conrad of Nichols College, designed to teach basic geographic literacy.

DISCOVERING AMERICAN HISTORY THROUGH MAPS AND VIEWS

Created by Gerald Danzer, University of Illinois, Chicago, the recipient of the AHA's 1989 James Harvey Robinson Award for his work in the development of map transparencies, this set of 140 four-color acetates is a unique instructional tool. It contains an introduction on teaching history through maps and a detailed commentary on each transparency. The collection includes cartographic and pictorial maps, views and photos, urban plans, building diagrams, and works of art.

VIDEO LECTURE LAUNCHERS

Each 2 to 5 minutes in duration, these lecture launchers cover key issues in American history, from 1877 to the present. The launchers are accompanied by an Instructor's Manual.

VISUAL ARCHIVES OF AMERICAN HISTORY

This video laser disc provides over 500 photos, and 29 minutes of film clips of major events in American history. Each photo or film clip may be instantly accessed, making this collection ideal for classroom use.

TEXT MAP TRANSPARENCIES

A set of 30 four-color transparencies from the maps in the text.

TEST BANK

Created by Ken Weatherbie of Del Mar College, this test bank features approximately 45 multiple-choice, 10 essay, and 5 map items per chapter. Multiple-choice items are referenced by topic, text page number, and type (factual or interpretive).

TESTMASTER COMPUTERIZED TESTING SYSTEM

This flexible, easy-to-master computer test bank includes all the test items in the printed Test Bank. The TestMaster software allows you to edit existing questions and add your own items. Tests can be printed in several different formats and can include figures such as graphs and tables. Available for IBM and Macintosh computers.

GRADES

A grade-keeping and classroom management software program that maintains data for up to 200 students.

For Students

LEARNING TO THINK CRITICALLY: FILMS AND MYTHS ABOUT AMERICAN HISTORY

Randy Roberts and Robert May of Purdue University use well-known films such as *Gone with the Wind* and *Casablanca* to explore some common myths about America and its past. Many widely held assumptions about our country's past come from or are perpetuated by popular films. Which are true? Which are patently not true? And how does a student of history approach documents, sources, and textbooks with a critical and discerning eye? This short handbook subjects some popular beliefs to historical scrutiny to help students develop a method of inquiry for approaching the subject of history in general.

STUDY GUIDE AND PRACTICE TESTS

Each chapter of this study guide, by Ken Chiaro of Pima Community College, contains a student introduction, reading comprehension and geography exercises, true-false, completion, and multiple-choice "Practice Tests."

SUPERSHELL COMPUTERIZED TUTORIAL

This interactive program for IBM computers helps students learn the major facts and concepts through drill and practice exercises and diagnostic feedback. SuperShell provides immediate correct answers and the text page number on which the material is discussed. Missed questions appear with greater frequency; a running score of the student's performance is maintained on the screen throughout the session.

MAPPING AMERICAN HISTORY: STUDENT ACTIVITIES

Written by Gerald Danzer of the University of Illinois, Chicago, this free map workbook for students features exercises designed to teach students to interpret and analyze cartographic materials as historical documents. The instructor is entitled to a free copy of the workbook for each copy of the text purchased from HarperCollins.

TIMELINK COMPUTER ATLAS OF AMERICAN HISTORY

This atlas, compiled by William Hamblin of Brigham Young University, is an introductory software tutorial and textbook companion. This Macintosh program presents the historical geography of continental United States from colonial times to the settling of the West and the admission of the last continental state in 1912. The program covers territories in different time periods, provides quizzes, and includes a special Civil War module.

The Authors

About the Authors

JAMES KIRBY MARTIN is a member of the Department of History at the University of Houston. A graduate of Hiram College in Ohio, he earned his Ph.D. degree at the University of Wisconsin in 1969, specializing in Early American history. His interests also include American social and military history. Among his publications are *Men in Rebellion* (1973), *In the Course of Human Events* (1979), *A Respectable Army* (1982), and *Drinking in America: A History*, rev. ed. (1987), the latter two volumes in collaboration with Mark E. Lender. Martin serves as general editor of the *American Social Experience* series, New York University Press. He recently was a senior fellow at the Philadelphia Center for Early American Studies, University of Pennsylvania, as well as scholar-in-residence at the David Library of the American Revolution, Washington Crossing, Pennsylvania. He is completing a biography of Benedict Arnold.

RANDY ROBERTS earned his Ph.D degree in 1978 from Louisiana State University. His areas of specialization include modern U.S. history and the history of American popular culture and sports. He is a member of the Department of History at Purdue University, where he recently won the Murphy Award for outstanding undergraduate teaching. His publications include *Jack Dempsey: The Manassa Mauler* (1979), *Papa Jack: Jack Johnson and the Era of White Hopes* (1983), and, in collaboration with James S. Olson, *Playing for Keeps: Sports and American Society, 1945 to the Present* (1989) and *Where the Domino Fell: America and Vietnam, 1945–1990* (1991). Roberts serves as co-editor of the *Studies in Sports and Society* series, University of Illinois Press, and is on the editorial board of the *Journal of Sports History*. His current research and writing interests include a biographical investigation of Hollywood actor John Wayne.

STEVEN MINTZ graduated from Oberlin College in Ohio before earning his Ph.D. degree at Yale University in 1979. His special interests include American social history with particular reference to families, women, children, and communities. Mintz is a member of the Department of History at the University of Houston. From 1989 to 1990 he was a vis-

iting scholar at Harvard University's Center for European Studies, and has served as a consultant to the Smithsonian Institution's National Museum of American History. His books include *A Prison of Expectations: The Family in Victorian Culture* (1983), and, in collaboration with Susan Kellogg, *Domestic Revolutions: A Social History of American Family Life* (1988). Mintz is an editor of the *American Social Experience* series, New York University Press, and is completing a book on pre-Civil War American reform.

LINDA O. McMURRY is a member of the Department of History at North Carolina State University. She completed her undergraduate studies at Auburn University, where she also earned her Ph.D. degree in 1976. Her fields of specialization include nineteenth- and twentieth-century U.S. history with an emphasis on the African-American experience and the New South. A recipient of a Rockefeller Foundation Humanities fellowship, she has written *George Washington Carver: Scientist and Symbol* (1981), and *Recorder of the Black Experience: A Biography of Monroe Nathan Work* (1985). McMurry has been active as a consultant to public television stations and museums on topics relating to black history, and is currently completing a study of biracial organizations in the South from the Reconstruction era to World War II.

JAMES H. JONES earned his Ph.D. degree at Indiana University in 1972. His areas of specialization include modern U.S. history, the history of medical ethics and medicine, and the history of sexual behavior. A member of the Department of History at the University of Houston, Jones has been a senior fellow of the National Endowment for the Humanities, a Kennedy fellow at Harvard University, a senior research fellow at the Kennedy Institute of Ethics, Georgetown University, and a Rockefeller fellow at the University of Texas Medical Branch, Galveston. His published writings include *Bad Blood: The Tuskegee Syphilis Experiment* (1981), and he is currently finishing a book on Alfred C. Kinsey and the emergence of scientific research dealing with human sexual behavior.

COMPARATIVE CHRONOLOGIES

POLITICAL/DIPLOMATIC	SOCIAL/ECONOMIC	CULTURAL

30,000 B.C.–1450

300–900 Mayan civilization flourishes in present-day Mexico and Guatemala. **c.900** Toltecs rise to power in the Valley of Mexico and later conquer the Maya. **c.1000** Vikings led by Leif Ericson reach Labrador and Newfoundland. **1095** European Christians launch the Crusades to capture the Holy Lands from Muslims. **c.1100** Inca civilization emerges in what is now Peru.	**30,000–20,000 B.C.** First people arrive in North America from Asia across what is now the Bering Strait. **8000–5000 B.C.** Central American Indians begin to practice agriculture.	**1271** Marco Polo begins a 20-year journey to China. **1347–1353** "Black Death" kills one-third of Europe's population. **1420s** Prince Henry of Portugal sends out mariners to explore Africa's western coast. **c.1450** Johannes Gutenberg, a German printer, develops movable type, the basis of modern printing.

1450–1550

1494 Treaty of Tordesillas divides the New World between Portugal and Spain. **1497–1498** John Cabot's voyages to Newfoundland and Cape Breton Island lay the basis of English claims to North America. **1519** Hernando Cortés and 600 Spanish conquistadores begin the conquest of the Aztec empire. **1531** Francisco Pizarro and 180 Spanish soldiers start the conquest the Inca empire.	**1492** Columbus makes the first of his voyages to the Americas. **1496** Columbus introduces cattle, sugarcane, and wheat to the West Indies. **1501** Spain authorizes the first shipment of African slaves to the Caribbean. **1507** The New World is named America after Florentine navigator Amerigo Vespucci. **1508** First sugar mill is built in the West Indies. **1517** Coffee is introduced in Europe. **1542** Spain outlaws the *encomienda* system and the enslavement of Indians.	**1517** Martin Luther's public protest against the sale of indulgences (pardons of punishment in purgatory) marks the beginning of the Protestant Reformation. **1518** Bartolomé de Las Casas proposes that Spain replace Indian laborers with African slaves. **1527** Henry VIII of England begins to sever ties with the Roman Catholic church. **1539** First printing press in the New World is established in Mexico City.

1550–1650

1607 English adventurers establish first permanent English settlement at Jamestown in Virginia. **1608** Samuel de Champlain claims Quebec for France. **1610** Spanish found Santa Fe, New Mexico. **1619** First representative assembly in English North America meets in Jamestown. **1620** Pilgrims arrive at Cape Cod on the *Mayflower* and establish a colony at Plymouth.	**1553** Europeans learn about the potato. **1576** Some 40,000 slaves brought to Latin America. **1585–1587** Sir Walter Raleigh sponsors England's first North American settlements at Roanoke Island, along the coast of present-day North Carolina. **1616** Chicken pox wipes out most New England Indians. **1617** England begins transporting criminals to Virginia as punishment.	**1584** Richard Hakluyt's *Discourse of Western Planting* encourages English exploration, conquest, and colonization. **1613** Pocahontas becomes the first Indian in Virginia to convert to Christianity. **1636** Harvard College founded. **1637–1638** Anne Hutchinson convicted of heresy in Massachusetts and flees to Rhode Island. **1640** The first book is published in the colonies, the *Bay Psalm Book*.

POLITICAL/DIPLOMATIC	SOCIAL/ECONOMIC	CULTURAL
		1550–1650
1624 New York is settled by the Dutch and named New Netherland.	**1619** Cargoes of Englishwomen begin to arrive in Virginia.	**1647** Massachusetts Bay Colony adopts the first public school law in the colonies.
1630 The Puritans establish Massachusetts Bay Colony.	**1619** A Dutch ship brings the first Africans to Virginia.	**1649** Maryland's Act of Toleration affirms religious freedom for all Christians in the colony.
1632 Maryland, the first proprietary colony, is established as a refuge for Roman Catholics.	**1624** Cattle are introduced into New England.	
1638 Delaware is settled by Swedes and is named New Sweden.	**1630** Colonial population totals about 5700.	
1649 Charles I of England beheaded.		
		1650–1750
1660, 1663 Parliament passes Navigation Acts to ensure that the colonies trade exclusively with England.	**1670** Colonial population totals about 114,500, including 4535 slaves.	**1650** Anne Bradstreet, New England's first poet, publishes *The Tenth Muse*.
1664 Dutch settlers in New Netherlands surrender to the English, who rename the colony New York.	**1673** Regular mail service between Boston and New York begins.	**1692** Witchcraft scare in Salem, Massachusetts, results in the execution of 20 men and women.
1676 Bacon's Rebellion in Virginia.	**1699** Parliament outlaws the export of woolen products from the colonies.	**1731** Benjamin Franklin founds first circulating library in Philadelphia.
1681–1682 William Penn founds Pennsylvania as a "holy experiment" in which diverse groups can live together in harmony.	**1714** Tea is introduced in the colonies.	**1732** Benjamin Franklin begins publishing *Poor Richard's Almanac*.
1688–1689 The English drive James II from the throne in the Glorious Revolution and replace him with William and Mary.	**1739** Stono slave uprising occurs in South Carolina.	**1735** John Peter Zenger acquitted on charge of seditious libel on ground that truth can be no libel.
1733 Georgia founded as a haven for debtors and a buffer against Spanish Florida.	**1749** Benjamin Franklin invents the lightning rod.	**1739** George Whitefield begins preaching tours, turning local revivals into the Great Awakening.
		1750
1750 Parliament passes the Iron Act, which prohibits colonists from expanding the production of finished iron or steel products.	**1750** The flatboat and the Conestoga wagon appear in Pennsylvania.	**1755** A British army surgeon, Dr. Richard Schuckburg, composes *Yankee Doodle* during the French and Indian war.
1754 Albany Congress draws up a plan to unite the 13 colonies under a single government.	**1756** Stagecoach line is established between New York and Philadelphia.	**1756** Wolfgang Amadeus Mozart born in Salzburg, Austria.
1754–1763 French and Indian War.		
1759 British forces under General James Wolfe conquer Quebec.		

POLITICAL/DIPLOMATIC	SOCIAL/ECONOMIC	CULTURAL

1760

1760 George III becomes king of England.

1763 Pontiac leads an unsuccessful Indian rebellion on the western frontier.

1763 The Proclamation of 1763 forbids white settlement west of the Appalachian Mountains.

1764 The Sugar Act levies new duties on coffee, indigo, sugar, and wine.

1764 Currency Act prohibits colonial governments from issuing paper money and requires all taxes and debts to British merchants to be paid in British currency.

1765 Quartering Act requires colonists to provide barracks, candles, bedding, and beverages to soldiers stationed in their area.

1765 Stamp Act, which requires stamps to be affixed to all legal documents, almanacs, newspapers, pamphlets, and playing cards, among other items, provokes popular protests.

1766 Parliament repeals the Stamp Act, but asserts its authority to tax the colonists in the Declaratory Act.

1767 Townshend Duties Act imposes taxes on imported glass, lead, paint, paper, and tea to defray the cost of colonial administration.

1760 Colonial population numbers about 1.6 million, including 325,000 slaves.

1763 English surveyors Charles Mason and Jeremiah Dixon set the boundary between Pennsylvania and Maryland—the Mason-Dixon line.

1765 The first medical school in the colonies is established in Philadelphia.

1766 Mastodon bones are discovered along the Ohio River.

1767 Daniel Boone undertakes his first exploration west of the Appalachian Mountains.

1759 Touro Synagogue in Newport, Rhode Island, is designed. It is the first synagogue in the 13 colonies.

1761 *The Complete Housewife*, a cookbook, is published in New York City.

1766 Robert Rogers writes the first play on a Native American subject, *Ponteach, or the Savages of America*.

1770

1770 The Boston Massacre leaves five colonists dead and others wounded.

1770 Townshend Duties are repealed, except the tax on tea.

1772 Parliament declares that the crown will pay the salaries of royal governors and colonial judges.

1773 Tea Act allows the East India Company to sell tea directly to American retailers.

1773 Boston Tea Party occurs when a band of "Indians" boards three British vessels and dumps 342 chests of tea into Boston Harbor.

1774 The Coercive Acts close the port of Boston; modify the Massachusetts charter; provide for trials outside colonies when royal officials are accused of serious crimes; and call for billeting of troops in unoccupied private homes.

1770 Colonial population is about 2.2 million.

1773 Harvard College announces that it will no longer rank students in order of social prominence.

1774 Mother Ann Lee, founder of the Shakers in America, lands in New York City.

1771 Historical painter Benjamin West renders *Death of Wolfe* and *Penn's Treaty with the Indians*.

1773 Phillis Wheatley, the slave of a Boston merchant, publishes *Poems on Various Subjects*.

1776 Thomas Paine publishes *Common Sense*, urging immediate separation from England.

POLITICAL/DIPLOMATIC	SOCIAL/ECONOMIC	CULTURAL
		1770
1775 The shot "heard 'round the world"— the first military clashes between British troops and patriots take place at Lexington and Concord. **1775** George III issues declarations that a state of rebellion exists in the colonies. **1776** Continental Congress adopts the Declaration of Independence. **1778** Benjamin Franklin negotiates an American alliance with France.		
		1780
1781 Lord Cornwallis surrenders to George Washington at Yorktown. **1781** The states approve the nation's first constitution, the Articles of Confederation. **1783** The Treaty of Paris is signed, ending the American Revolution. **1787** Congress passes the Northwest Ordinance, forever barring slavery north of the Ohio River. **1787** Constitutional convention convenes in Philadelphia. **1788** Constitution is ratified. **1789** Electoral College names George Washington the first president.	**1780** U.S. population is about 2,780,400. **1783** Benjamin Franklin invents bifocals. **1784** The *Empress of China* inaugurates sea trade with China. **1786** Western Massachusetts farmers, led by Daniel Shays, close county courthouses to protest low farm prices and high state taxes. **1787** Levi Hutchins, a Concord, New Hampshire, clockmaker invents the alarm clock.	**1782** J. Hector St. John de Crèvecoeur publishes *Letters from an American Farmer*. **1786** Virginia legislature enacts separation of church and state. **1786** Charles Willson Peale opens the first art gallery in Philadelphia. **1789** William Hill Brown's *The Power of Sympathy* is the first novel published in the United States.
		1790
1790 Congress adopts Hamilton's proposal to fund the national debt at full value and to assume state debts from the revolutionary war. **1791** Bank of the United States established. **1791** The Bill of Rights becomes part of the Constitution. **1794** General Anthony Wayne defeats an Indian alliance at the Battle of Fallen Timbers, opening Ohio to white settlement. **1796** Washington issues a Farewell Address, warning against political factionalism and foreign entanglements. **1798** Congress adopts the Alien and Sedition acts. **1798–1799** Kentucky and Virginia resolutions declare the Alien and Sedition acts unconstitutional.	**1790** U.S. population is 3,929,214. **1790** Samuel Slater opens the first textile factory in the United States. **1793** Eli Whitney invents the cotton gin. **1794–1795** The Whiskey Rebellion, protesting the federal excise tax on whiskey, is put down.	**1793** Louis XVI of France sent to the guillotine. **1794** Thomas Paine publishes *The Age of Reason*. **1798** Charles Brockden Brown publishes *Wieland*.

POLITICAL/DIPLOMATIC	SOCIAL/ECONOMIC	CULTURAL

1800

POLITICAL/DIPLOMATIC	SOCIAL/ECONOMIC	CULTURAL
1800 House of Representatives selects Thomas Jefferson as third president. **1801** Jefferson sends eight ships to enforce a blockade of Tripoli. **1803** Thomas Jefferson purchases Louisiana Territory from Napoleon for $15 million or 4 cents an acre. **1803** *Marbury* v. *Madison* upholds the principle of judicial review. **1804** Vice president Aaron Burr kills Alexander Hamilton in a duel. **1807** Jefferson imposes a trade embargo in order to pressure Britain and France to respect American rights. **1807** Congress votes to prohibit the African slave trade. **1809** Embargo Act repealed. **1809** Non-Intercourse Act prohibits trade with Britain and France.	**1800** U.S. population is 5,308,483, including 896,849 slaves. **1800** John Chapman, better known as Johnny Appleseed, passes out religious tracts and apple seeds throughout the Ohio Valley. **1804** Lewis and Clark expedition sets out from St. Louis to explore the Louisiana Purchase. **1807** Seth Thomas and Eli Terry begin to manufacture clocks out of interchangeable parts. **1807** Robert Fulton proves the practicality of the steamboat by sailing the *Clermont* from New York City to Albany in 32 hours.	**1800** Mason Locke Weems publishes his *Life of Washington*, the source of the legend about Washington chopping down the cherry tree. **1806** Noah Webster's *Compendious Dictionary of the English Language* is published.

1810

POLITICAL/DIPLOMATIC	SOCIAL/ECONOMIC	CULTURAL
1812 Congress declares war against Britain. **1813–1814** Creek War. **1814** United States and Britain sign Treaty of Ghent, which ends the War of 1812. **1816** Second Bank of the United States chartered. **1818** United States and Britain agree to joint occupation of Oregon. **1819** Spain cedes Florida to the United States. **1819** "A Firebell in the Night." A crisis over slavery erupts after Missouri applies for admission to the Union as a slave state.	**1810** U.S. population is 7,239,881. **1814** The first totally mechanized factory producing cotton cloth from raw cotton opens in Waltham, Massachusetts. **1817** American Colonization Society is founded to colonize free blacks in Africa. **1819** Panic of 1819. **1819** An asylum for the deaf, dumb, and blind opens in Hartford, Connecticut, inaugurating a new era of humanitarian concern for the handicapped. **1819** The *Savannah* becomes the first steamship to cross the Atlantic. **1819** *Dartmouth* v. *Woodward* upholds the sanctity of contracts. *McCulloch* v. *Maryland* upholds the constitutionality of the second Bank of the United States.	**1814** Francis Scott Key writes the lyrics to "The Star-Spangled Banner" during the British assault on Fort McHenry, Maryland. **1818** Washington Irving publishes *Rip Van Winkle*. **1819** William Ellery Channing helps found American Unitarianism.

POLITICAL/DIPLOMATIC	SOCIAL/ECONOMIC	CULTURAL
		1820

1820 Missouri Compromise prohibits slavery in the northern half of the Louisiana Purchase; Missouri enters the union as a slave state and Maine as a free state.

1821 Mexico declares independence from Spain.

1823 President James Monroe opposes any further European colonization or interference in the Americas, establishing the principle now known as the Monroe Doctrine.

1820 U.S. population is 9,638,453.

1820 Land Act reduces the price of public land to $1.25 per acre.

1822 Stephen F. Austin founds the first American colony in Texas.

1822 Liberia founded as a colony for free blacks.

1825 Erie Canal opens.

1827 *Freedom's Journal*, the first black newspaper, begins publication in New York City.

1828 The *Cherokee Phoenix*, the first Indian newspaper, begins publication.

1829 The first U.S. school for the blind opens in Boston.

1821 Emma Willard founds the Troy Female Seminary, one of the first academies to offer women a higher education.

1823 John Howard Payne and Henry Bishop compose the song "Home, Sweet Home."

1823 James Fenimore Cooper publishes *The Pioneers*, the first of his Leatherstocking tales.

1827 James Audubon publishes *Birds of America*, consisting of 435 lifelike paintings of birds.

1829 David Walker issues his militant "Appeal to the Colored Citizens of the World."

1830

1830 Indian Removal Act provides funds to purchase Indian homelands in exchange for land in present-day Oklahoma and Arkansas.

1832 Jackson vetoes the bill to recharter the second Bank of the United States.

1832 South Carolina nullifies the federal triff.

1836 Texans under Sam Houston defeat the Mexican army at the Battle of San Jacinto.

1837 Panic of 1837 begins.

1830 U.S. population is 12,866,020.

1830 Joseph Smith, Jr., founds the Church of Jesus Christ of Latter-Day Saints.

1830 America's first commercially successful steam locomotive, the *Tom Thumb*, loses a race against a horse.

1831 William Lloyd Garrison begins publishing the militant abolitionist newspaper *The Liberator*.

1831 Oberlin College opens its doors as the nation's first coeducational college. In 1835, it becomes the first American college to admit blacks.

1831 Nat Turner's slave insurrection occurs in Southampton County, Virginia.

1832 Samuel F. B. Morse invents the telegraph.

1835 The Liberty Bell cracks as it tolls the death of Chief Justice John Marshall.

1837 Horace Mann becomes Massachusetts's first superintendent of education.

1839 Liberty party founded.

1839 Charles Goodyear successfully vulcanizes rubber.

1831 Samuel Francis Smith composes the words to the song "America."

1834 *A Narrative of the Life of David Crockett* is published.

1836 William Holmes McGuffey publishes his first and second *Reader*.

1838 Sarah Grimké publishes *Letters on the Equality of the Sexes and the Condition of Women*, one of the earliest public defenses of sexual equality.

POLITICAL/DIPLOMATIC	SOCIAL/ECONOMIC	CULTURAL

1840

POLITICAL/DIPLOMATIC	SOCIAL/ECONOMIC	CULTURAL
1846 Britain and the United States divide Oregon along the 49th parallel.	**1840** U.S. population is 17,069,453.	**1841** Edgar Allan Poe publishes "Murders in the Rue Morgue," the first modern detective story.
1846 The United States declares war on Mexico.	**1841** The first wagon train arrives in California.	**1843** New word *millionaire* coined to describe Pierre Lorillard, tobacco magnate.
1848 Treaty of Guadalupe Hidalgo ends the Mexican War.	**1842** The Massachusetts Supreme Court upholds workers' right to organize.	**1848** Karl Marx and Friedrich Engels publish the *Communist Manifesto*.
	1845 A potato blight strikes Ireland.	
	1846 Elias Howe patents the first reliable sewing machine.	
	1846 William Morton, a Boston dentist, uses an anesthetic for the first time during a surgical operation.	
	1846–1847 Brigham Young leads the Mormons to the Great Salt Lake Valley.	
	1848 Alexander T. Stewart opens the first department store in New York City.	
	1848 Gold is discovered at Sutter's Mill in California.	
	1848 The first women's rights convention is held in Seneca Falls, New York.	
	1849 Elizabeth Blackwell becomes the first woman physician in the United States.	

1850

POLITICAL/DIPLOMATIC	SOCIAL/ECONOMIC	CULTURAL
1850 Compromise of 1850 is enacted.	**1850** U.S. population is 23,191,876.	**1850** Nathaniel Hawthorne publishes *The Scarlet Letter*.
1854 Abolitionist William Lloyd Garrison publicly burns the U.S. Constitution, calling it an "agreement with hell and a covenant with death."	**1850** U.S. Navy outlaws flogging.	**1851** Herman Melville publishes *Moby Dick*.
1854 Stephen A. Douglas introduces the Kansas-Nebraska Act. Opponents of the act form the new Republican party.	**1851** The Young Men's Christian Association opens its first American chapter in Boston.	**1852** Harriet Beecher Stowe's *Uncle Tom's Cabin* sells a million copies in its first year and a half.
1854 Commodore Matthew Perry negotiates a treaty opening Japan to American trade.	**1857** Elisha Graves Otis installs the first passenger elevator in a New York City department store.	**1854** Henry David Thoreau publishes *Walden*.
1859 John Brown's raid fails at Harpers Ferry.	**1859** Edwin L. Drake drills the first commercial oil well at Titusville, Pennsylvania.	**1855** Walt Whitman publishes *Leaves of Grass*.
		1859 Charles Darwin publishes *Origin of Species*.

POLITICAL/DIPLOMATIC	SOCIAL/ECONOMIC	CULTURAL

1860 Abraham Lincoln is elected sixteenth president.

1860 South Carolina secedes from the Union.

1861 Confederate States of America formed.

1863 President Lincoln signs the Emancipation Proclamation.

1865 John Wilkes Booth assassinates President Lincoln at Ford's Theater in Washington, D.C.; Andrew Johnson becomes seventeenth president.

1865 Thirteenth Amendment ratified, abolishing slavery.

1867 Russia sells Alaska to the United States for $7.2 million, or less than 2 cents an acre.

1868 House of Representatives impeaches Andrew Jackson; he escapes conviction in the Senate by one vote.

1860 U.S. population is 31,443,321.

1860 The Pony Express begins carrying mail between St. Joseph, Missouri, and Sacramento, California.

1862 To help raise revenue for the Civil War, the first federal income tax goes into effect.

1863 New York City draft riots.

1865 The Ku Klux Klan is founded in Pulaski, Tennessee.

1866 The potato chip is invented by a Saratoga, New York, chef.

1866 Cyrus W. Field lays the first permanent trans-Atlantic telegraph cable.

1867 Christopher Latham Sholes and Carlos Glidden invent the first practical typewriter.

1869 William Finley Semple of Mount Vernon, Ohio, receives a patent for chewing gum.

1869 First transcontinental railroad is completed.

1860 Erastus and Irwin Beadle issue the first dime novels, featuring such figures as Daniel Boone and Kit Carson.

1865 Mark Twain publishes his first story, "The Celebrated Jumping Frog of Calaveras County."

1870 Senator Hiram R. Revels of Mississippi becomes the first black U.S. senator.

1875 Civil Rights Act forbids racial discrimination in public accommodations and public transportation and guarantees black Americans the right to serve on juries.

1877 Electoral Commission awards disputed electoral votes to Republican Rutherford Hayes, who is inaugurated nineteenth president.

1877 Hayes withdraws the last federal troops from the South, ending Reconstruction.

1878 Bland-Allison Act requires the U.S. Treasury to buy $2 to $4 million of silver each month in order to inflate the currency.

1870 U.S. population is 39,818,449.

1871 Great Chicago fire claims 300 lives, destroys 17,500 buildings, and leaves 100,000 people homeless.

1873 Comstock Act bans obscene materials, including rubber prophylactics, from the mails.

1875 The first Kentucky Derby.

1876 Custer's Last Stand.

1876 Twenty-nine-year-old Alexander Graham Bell patents the telephone.

1876 The nation celebrates its centennial with a $10 million exposition in Philadelphia.

1879 Congress votes to allow women to argue cases before the Supreme Court.

1879 Thomas Edison, 32, invents the light bulb.

1879 Frank W. Woolworth establishes his first successful 5-and-10-cent store in Lancaster, Pennsylvania.

1871 P. T. Barnum opens his circus, which he calls "The Greatest Show on Earth."

1871 James Whistler paints "Arrangement in Gray and Black No. 1," better known as "Whistler's Mother."

1875 Mary Baker Eddy publishes *Science and Health*, the basic text of Christian Science.

1876 Mark Twain publishes *The Adventures of Tom Sawyer*.

1876 Baseball's National League founded.

1879 Henry George publishes *Progress and Poverty*.

POLITICAL/DIPLOMATIC	SOCIAL/ECONOMIC	CULTURAL

1880

1881 President James A. Garfield mortally wounded at a Washington train station; Chester Arthur becomes twenty-first president.

1882 Chinese Exclusion Act suspends Chinese immigration for ten years; extended in 1892 and 1902.

1883 Civil Service Act classifies approximately 15,000 federal jobs as civil service positions to be awarded only after a competitive examination.

1883 Supreme Court declares Civil Rights Act of 1875 unconstitutional.

1887 Congress establishes the Interstate Commerce Commission, the first federal regulatory commission, to regulate railroads.

1887 Dawes Allotment Act subdivides all Indian reservations into individual plots of land of 160 to 320 acres and opens "surplus" land to white settlers.

1880 U.S. population is 50,155,783.

1881 Clara Barton founds the American Red Cross.

1883 U.S. railroads adopt four standard time zones.

1886 Supreme Court extends protection of due process to corporations.

1886 The Statue of Liberty is unveiled.

1886 The American Federation of Labor founded in Columbus, Ohio.

1886 Pharmacist James S. Pemberton invents Coca-Cola.

1888 The first incubators are used for premature infants.

1889 The Johnstown flood kills almost 2300 people.

1881 Helen Hunt Jackson publishes *A Century of Dishonor* describing mistreatment of American Indians.

1883 "Buffalo Bill" Cody organizes his first Wild West Show.

1884 Mark Twain publishes *The Adventures of Huckleberry Finn*.

1888 Edward Bellamy publishes *Looking Backward*, describing life in Boston in the year 2000.

1890

1890 Congress passes the Sherman Anti-trust Act, forbidding restraints on trade.

1891 Separate Federal Courts of Appeal are created to relieve the Supreme Court's case load.

1896 William McKinley defeats William Jennings Bryan for the presidency.

1897 President Cleveland vetoes a literacy requirement for adult immigrants.

1898 Spanish-American War begins.

1898 United States acquires Guam, the Philippines, and Puerto Rico, and annexes Hawaii.

1899 Emilio Aguinaldo leads a rebellion against the United States to win Philippine independence.

1899 United States annexes Wake Island.

1890 U.S. population is 62,947,714.

1890 The U.S. Bureau of the Census announces that the western frontier is now closed.

1890 Sequoia and Yosemite National parks in California established.

1891 Basketball is invented by Dr. James A. Naismith in Springfield, Massachusetts.

1892 Ellis Island opens as a center to screen immigrants.

1893 Chlorine is first used to treat sewage in Brewster, New York.

1895 *Pollack* v. *Farmers Loan and Trust Company* declares a federal income tax unconstitutional.

1896 *Plessy* v. *Ferguson* decision rules that the principle of "separate but equal" does not deprive blacks of civil rights guaranteed under the Fourteenth Amendment.

1897 A high society ball, costing $370,000, is held at New York's Waldorf Astoria Hotel despite a serious economic depression.

1890 Jacob A. Riis publishes *How the Other Half Lives*.

1896 The first comic strip appears in Joseph Pulitzer's *New York World*.

1896 Billy Sunday begins his career as an evangelist.

1899 Composer Scott Joplin's "Maple Leaf Rag" helps popularize ragtime.

1899 In *The School and Society*, John Dewey outlines his ideas about "progressive education."

POLITICAL/DIPLOMATIC	SOCIAL/ECONOMIC	CULTURAL
		1900
1902 Oregon, South Dakota, and Utah become first states to adopt initiative and recall.	**1900** U.S. population is 75,994,575.	**1900** Theodore Dreiser publishes his first novel, *Sister Carrie*.
1903 Wisconsin becomes the first state to adopt primary elections.	**1900** Great Galveston, Texas, hurricane kills 6000.	**1900** L. Frank Baum publishes *The Wonderful Wizard of Oz*.
1904 Construction of Panama Canal begins.	**1903** The Wright Brothers make the first piloted flight in a powered airplane.	**1903** W. E. B. Du Bois publishes *The Souls of Black Folk*, declaring that "the problem of the twentieth century is the color line."
1907 President Theodore Roosevelt dispatches 16 battleships ("the great white fleet") on an around-the-world cruise.	**1904** The ice-cream cone and iced tea are introduced at the St. Louis World's Fair.	**1903** Edwin S. Porter's *The Great Train Robbery* is the first American film to tell a story.
	1906 The Great San Francisco earthquake leaves 452 people dead and 225,000 homeless.	**1906** Upton Sinclair's *The Jungle* exposes unsanitary conditions in the meat-packing industry.
	1908 Henry Ford introduces the Model T.	
	1908 Jack Johnson becomes the first black heavyweight boxing champion.	
	1909 The National Association for the Advancement of Colored People formed to press for equal rights for black Americans.	
	1909 Explorers Robert E. Peary and Matthew Henson reach the North Pole.	
		1910
1913 Sixteenth Amendment gives Congress the power to levy an income tax.	**1910** U.S. population is 91,972,266.	**1913** The first crossword puzzle appears in a U.S. newspaper.
1914 World War I begins in Europe.	**1911** Female garment workers (145) lose their lives in a fire at New York's Triangle Shirtwaist Company.	**1914** Edgar Rice Burroughs publishes *Tarzan of the Apes*.
1917 United States enters the war.	**1912** The *Titanic* sinks on its maiden voyage, and 1500 of the ship's 2200 passengers drown.	**1915** Margaret Sanger is arrested in New York City for teaching methods of contraception.
1917 Jeannette Rankin becomes first woman elected to Congress.	**1914** President Wilson proclaims the first Mother's Day.	**1918** Post Office confiscates copies of *The Little Review* on grounds of obscenity. It contains a part of James Joyce's *Ulysses*.
	1918 Influenza epidemic claims more than 20 million lives worldwide.	
		1920
1920 Palmer Raids to arrest suspected Communists.	**1920** U.S. population is 105,710,620.	**1920** F. Scott Fitzgerald publishes his first novel, *This Side of Paradise*.
1920 National Prohibition begins.	**1920** A Chicago grand jury indicts eight Chicago "Black Sox" players for throwing the 1919 World Series.	**1921** The first bathing beauty pageant is held in Atlantic City, New Jersey.
1920 Nineteenth Amendment grants women the right to vote.	**1923** Colonel Jacob Schick receives patent for first electric shaver.	**1922** Tomb of Egyptian Pharaoh Tutankhamen ("King Tut") discovered.
1920 The Panama Canal declared officially opened.	**1924** Clarence Birdseye develops the first packaged frozen foods.	**1925** Scopes trial, the celebrated "Monkey Trial," involving the teaching of evolution in public schools, takes place in Tennessee.
1928 Kellogg-Briand Treaty renounces war "as an instrument of national policy."		

POLITICAL/DIPLOMATIC	SOCIAL/ECONOMIC	CULTURAL
1920		
	1926 National Broadcasting Company becomes the first nationwide radio network. **1927** Charles Lindbergh completes 33-hour solo flight from New York to Paris. **1929** Stock market crashes.	**1927** The first talking motion picture, *The Jazz Singer*, starring Al Jolson, opens. **1928** Walt Disney releases first Mickey Mouse cartoon.
1930		
1933 Adolf Hitler is appointed Chancellor of Germany. **1935** Italy invades Ethiopia. **1935** Huey Long is assassinated. **1936** Civil War breaks out in Spain. **1938** Munich Pact hands over a third of Czechoslovakia to Nazi Germany. **1939** Soviet Union and Germany sign a nonaggression pact. **1939** World War II begins following Germany's invasion of Poland.	**1930** U.S. population is 122,775,046. **1933** Twenty-first Amendment repeals prohibition. **1934** Public Enemy Number One, John Dillinger, is shot and killed by FBI agents at a Chicago movie theater. **1935** Wagner Act guarantees workers' right to bargain collectively. **1936** The last public hanging in the United States takes place in Owenboro, Kentucky. **1937** Following a 44-day sit-down strike, General motors recognizes the United Automobile Workers. **1938** Patent issued for nylon.	**1931** CBS inaugurates the first regular schedule of TV broadcasts. **1935** Charles Darrow, an unemployed engineer, markets a new board game, Monopoly. **1936** Jesse Owens wins four gold medals at the Berlin Olympics. **1937** Ther German zeppelin *Hindenberg* bursts into flames at Lakehurst, New Jersey, killing 35 passengers. **1938** Action Comics #1 presents the Man of Steel, Superman. **1938** Orson Welles's broadcasts reports of a Martian invasion. **1939** John Steinbeck publishes *The Grapes of Wrath*.
1940		
1941 Japan attacks Pearl Harbor, killing nearly 2000 U.S. soldiers and sailors. **1942** Nazis begin their "final solution" to the Jewish problem. **1942** President Franklin D. Roosevelt authorizes internment of 112,000 West Coast Japanese-Americans. **1944** D-Day. **1945** V-E Day. **1945** Atomic bombs dropped on Hiroshima and Nagasaki, Japan. **1945** V-J Day. **1946** Winston Churchill declares that "an iron curtain" had descended across Europe. **1948** State of Israel is proclaimed. **1949** Mao Ze-dong's Communist forces win China's civil war.	**1940** U.S. population is 131,669,275. **1942** Physicist Enrico Fermi sets off the first atomic chain reaction. **1942** Gasoline rationing goes into effect. **1943** A race riot in Detroit leaves 25 blacks and 9 whites dead. **1944** GI Bill of Rights provides educational benefits for veterans. **1945** The transistor is invented. **1946** ENIAC, the first electronic computer, begins service. **1947** Air Force Captain Charles Yeager becomes the first pilot to fly faster than the speed of sound. **1947** Twenty-eight-year-old Jackie Robinson becomes the first black player in major league baseball.	**1948** Alfred Kinsey publishes *Sexual Behavior in the Human Male*, followed five years later by *Sexual Behavior in the Human Female*. **1948** The first successful long-playing record is developed. **1949** French fashion designers introduce the bikini bathing suit.

POLITICAL/DIPLOMATIC	SOCIAL/ECONOMIC	CULTURAL

1950

1950 North Korean troops cross the 38th parallel, beginning the Korean War.

1950 Senator Joseph McCarthy claims that 205 State Department employees are members of the Communist party.

1951 Ethel and Julius Rosenberg are sentenced to death for atomic espionage.

1954 The French garrison at Dien Bien Phu falls to Vietnamese nationalists led by Ho Chi Minh.

1954 *Brown* v. *Board of Education* decision holds that "separate educational facilities are inherently unequal."

1959 Fidel Castro leads Cuban revolution against the regime of Fulgencio Batista.

1950 U.S. population is 150,697,361.

1952 United States detonates the first hydrogen bomb.

1954 Dr. Jonas Salk develops a vaccine against polio.

1955 The birth control pill is invented.

1955 Black seamstress Rosa Parks refuses to give up her seat on a Montgomery, Alabama, city bus, sparking a year-long bus boycott.

1957 Nine black students enter Central High School in Little Rock, Arkansas under the protection of 1000 army paratroopers.

1957 Soviet Union rockets *Sputnik*, the first artificial satellite, into space.

1958 European Common Market is formed.

1950 Charles Schulz creates the cartoon strip "Peanuts."

1951 J. D. Salinger publishes *Catcher in the Rye*.

1952 Ralph Ellison publishes *The Invisible Man*.

1956 Elvis Presley's first hit, "Heartbreak Hotel," is released.

1957 Jack Kerouac's *On the Road* is published.

1957 Dr. Seuss publishes *The Cat in the Hat*.

1960

1960 U-2 spy plane is shot down over the Soviet Union.

1961 Cuban exiles stage abortive invasion of Cuba at Bay of Pigs.

1961 Cuban missile crisis erupts.

1963 United States and Soviet Union agree to ban nuclear tests in the atmosphere.

1963 President Kennedy is assassinated; Lyndon Johnson becomes thirty-sixth president.

1964 Civil Rights Act bans discrimination in jobs and public facilities.

1965 United States begins regular bombing missions over North Vietnam and sends American ground combat troops into South Vietnam.

1968 Martin Luther King, Jr., and Robert F. Kennedy are assassinated.

1960 U.S. population is 179,323,175.

1960 First civil rights sit-in takes place in Greensboro, North Carolina.

1961 Russian cosmonaut Yuri Gagarin becomes the first human to orbit the earth.

1964 Martin Luther King, Jr., receives the Nobel Peace Prize.

1965 Congress requires cigarette packages and ads to carry health warnings.

1969 Astronaut Neil Armstrong becomes the first person to walk on the moon.

1960 A House subcommittee accuses disk jockeys of accepting "payola" to play certain records on the air.

1961 FCC Chairman Newton Minow describes TV as a "vast wasteland."

1963 Betty Friedan publishes *The Feminine Mystique*, helping launch a new feminist movement.

1967 The musical *Hair* with its nudity brings controversy to the Broadway stage.

1969 Half a million young people attend a four-day rock concert near Woodstock, New York.

POLITICAL/DIPLOMATIC	SOCIAL/ECONOMIC	CULTURAL

1970

POLITICAL/DIPLOMATIC	SOCIAL/ECONOMIC	CULTURAL
1972 Five burglars are arrested for breaking into Democratic National Headquarters at Washington's Watergate Office Complex. **1973** United States ends direct military involvement in Vietnam. **1973** Vice President Spiro Agnew pleads no contest to a charge of income tax evasion and resigns his office. **1974** Richard Nixon becomes the first president to resign from office. **1975** Vietnam War ends as Communist troops occupy Saigon. **1978** Jimmy Carter mediates Egyptian-Israeli peace settlement. **1979** Iranian militants seize American hostages. **1979** Soviet Union invades Afghanistan.	**1970** U.S. population is 203,235,175. **1971** Twenty-sixth Amendment gives 18-year-olds the right to vote. **1973** Arab oil embargo begins; oil prices quadruple. **1977** United States ends a ten-year moratorium on capital punishment. **1979** The nation's most serious nuclear power accident occurs at Pennsylvania's Three Mile Island nuclear plant. **1979** Oil price climbs from $10 to $20 a barrel.	**1970** Satirical comic strip *Doonesbury* begins appearing in 30 newspapers. **1971** Controversial situation comedy "All in the Family" debuts. **1977** Record television audiences watch the dramatization of Alex Haley's black family history *Roots*. **1977** The film *Saturday Night Fever* popularizes disco dance music.

1980

POLITICAL/DIPLOMATIC	SOCIAL/ECONOMIC	CULTURAL
1981 Ronald W. Reagan inaugurated as fortieth president; minutes later, Iran releases American hostages after 444 days of captivity. **1981** Sandra Day O'Connor becomes the first female Supreme Court Justice. **1984** Democrats make Geraldine Ferraro the first female vice-presidential nominee of a major party. **1985** Mikhail S. Gorbachev becomes leader of the Soviet Union. **1985** United States begins secret arms-for-hostages negotiations with Iran. **1986** Profits from Iranian arms sales are diverted to Nicaraguan contras. **1988** George Bush is elected forty-first president. **1989** Communist regimes collapse in Eastern Europe.	**1980** U.S. population is 226,545,805. **1981** Doctors diagnose the first cases of AIDS. **1981** President Reagan dismisses 15,000 striking air traffic controllers. **1982–1983** The nation's worst post–World War II recession raises unemployment to 10.2 percent, but reduces inflation and interest rates. **1986** Crack, a highly addictive form of cocaine, appears in U.S. cities. **1987** The Dow Jones Industrial Average plummets a record 509 points in a single day.	**1987** *Platoon*, a highly sympathetic account of the plight of U.S. troops in Vietnam, wins the Academy Award for best picture. **1987** The publication of Allan Bloom's *The Closing of the American Mind* triggers widespread debate about American education. **1987** Baby M case raises moral and ethical issues involved in surrogate parenting.

POLITICAL/DIPLOMATIC	SOCIAL/ECONOMIC	CULTURAL

POLITICAL/DIPLOMATIC	SOCIAL/ECONOMIC	CULTURAL
1990 Iraqi troops invade and occupy Kuwait. **1990** Margaret Thatcher steps down as prime minister of Great Britain. **1990** President Bush and Soviet President Mikhail S. Gorbachev sign agreements to cut stockpiles of long-range nuclear arms and eliminate most chemical weapons. **1991** U.S., Western European, and Arab forces eject Iraq from Kuwait by force. **1991** Attempted coup in the Soviet Union fails. **1991** Israel and its Arab neighbors begin peace talks. **1992** Bill Clinton is elected forty-second president.	**1990** The two Germanys are reunited after 45 years. **1991** Confirmation hearings of Clarence Thomas for the Supreme Court focus attention on the issue of sexual harassment. **1992** Riots erupt in Los Angeles following the "not guilty" verdict in the Rodney King case. **1992** *Roe* v. *Wade* is upheld, with modifications.	**1990** Soviet President Mikhail S. Gorbachev wins the Nobel Peace Prize for promoting political liberalization in Eastern Europe and ending the Cold War. **1990** Emperor Akihito is enthroned in Japan, the 125th occupant of the Chrysanthemum Throne.

America
and
Its People

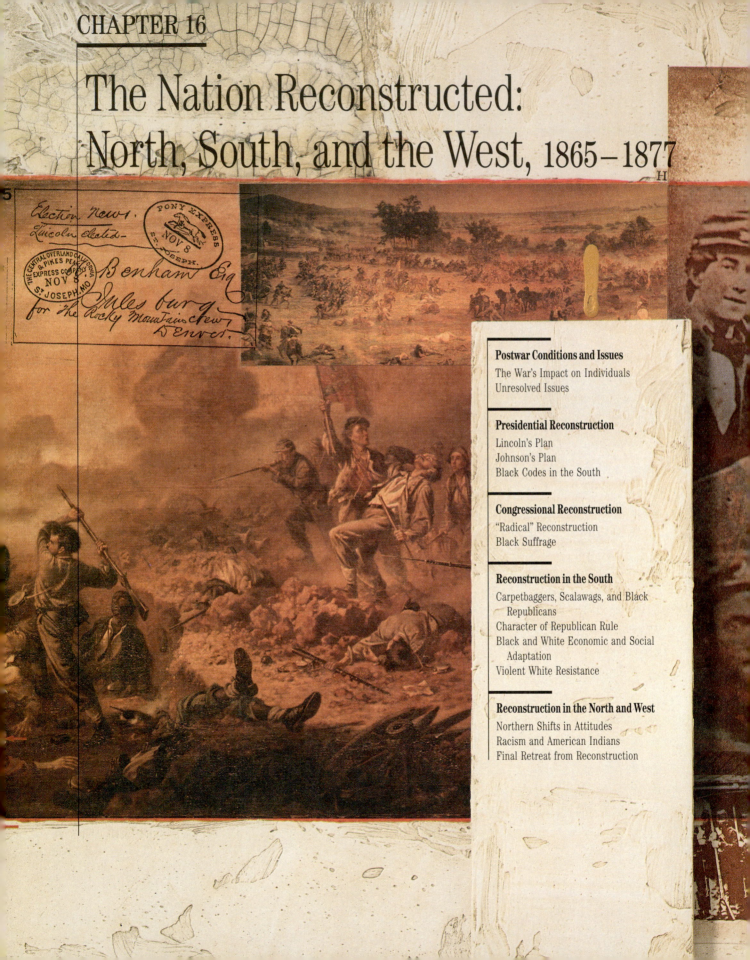

CHAPTER 16

The Nation Reconstructed: North, South, and the West, 1865–1877

As Thomas Pinckney approached El Dorado, his plantation on the Santee River in South Carolina, he felt a quiver of apprehension. Pinckney, a captain in the defeated Confederate army, had stayed the night with neighbors before going to reclaim his land. "Your negroes sacked your house," they reported, "stripped it of furniture, bric-a-brac, heirlooms, and divided these among themselves. They got it in their heads that the property of whites belongs to them." Pinckney remembered the days when his return home had been greeted with slaves' chants of "Howdy do, Marster! Howdy do, Boss!" Now he was welcomed with an eerie silence. He did not even see any of his former slaves until he went into the house. There, a single servant seemed genuinely glad to see him, but she pleaded ignorance as to the whereabouts of the other freedmen. He lingered about the house until after the dinner hour. Still no one appeared, so he informed the servant that he would return in the morning and expected to see all his former slaves.

On his ride back the next day, Pinckney nostalgically recalled his days as a small boy when the slaves had seemed happy to see him as he accompanied his mother on her Saturday afternoon rounds. He could not believe he had any reason to fear his "own people" whom he "could only remember as respectful, happy and affectionate." He probably mistook their previous displays of submissiveness as expressions of a genuine affection that would not be altered by freedom. Yet he was armed this time, and after summoning his former slaves, he quickly noticed that they too were armed. Their sullen faces reflected their defiant spirits.

Pinckney told them, "Men, I know you are free. I do not wish to interfere with your freedom. But I want my old hands to work my lands for me. I will pay wages." The freedmen remained silent as he gave further reassurances. Finally one responded, "O yes, we gwi wuk! We gwi wuk fuh ourse'ves. We ain' gwi wuk fuh no white man." Pinckney was confused and asked how they expected to support themselves and where they would go. They quickly informed him that they intended to stay and work "right here on de lan' whar we wuz bo'n an' whar belongs tuh us." One former slave, dressed in a Union army uniform, stood beside his cabin, brought his rifle down with a crash, and declared, "I'd like tuh see any man put me outer dis house."

Pinckney had no intention of allowing the freedman to work the land for themselves. He joined with his neighbors in an appeal to the Union commander at Charleston, who sent a company of troops and addressed the blacks himself. They still refused to work under his terms, so Pinckney decided to "starve" them into submission. He denied them access to food and supplies. Soon his head plowman begged food for his hungry family, claiming he wanted to work, "But de other niggers dee won' let me wuk." Pinckney held firm, and the man returned several days later saying, "Cap'n, I come tuh ax you tuh lemme wuk fuh you, suh." Pinckney pointed him to the plow and let him draw his rations. Slowly, his other former slaves drifted back to work. "They had suffered," he later recalled, "and their ex-master had suffered with them."

All over the South this scenario was acted out with variations, as former masters and former slaves sought to define their new relationships. Whites tried to keep the freedmen a dependent labor source; African-Americans struggled to win as much independence as possible. Frequently Union officials were called upon to arbitrate; the North had a stake in the final outcome. At the same time the other sections of the nation faced similar problems of determining the status of heterogeneous populations whose interests were sometimes in conflict with the majority. The war had reaped a costly harvest of death and hostility, but at the same time it accelerated the modernization of the economy and society. Western expansion forced Americans to deal with the often hostile presence of the Plains Indians; the resumption of large-scale immigration raised issues of how to adapt to an increasingly pluralistic society made up of many different ethnic and religious groups. More and more the resolution of conflicting interests became necessary: farmer versus industrialist, whites versus blacks, Republicans versus Democrats, Indians versus settlers, North versus South, management versus labor, immigrant versus native born, men

Although freedmen hoped that emancipation would release them from supervised gang labor in cotton fields, many were forced to sign yearly labor contracts and work under conditions similar to slavery.

versus women, one branch of government versus another. Complicating these issues were unresolved questions about federal authority, widespread racial prejudice in both North and South, and strongly held beliefs in the sanctity of property rights.

Reconstruction offered an opportunity to balance conflicting interests with justice and fairness. In the end, however, the government was unwilling to establish ongoing programs and permanent mechanisms to protect the rights of minorities. As on Pinckney's plantation, economic power usually became the determining factor in establishing relationships. Authorities sacrificed the interests of both African-Americans and the Indians of the West to the goals of national unity and economic growth. In 1865 a planter predicted the outcome, using a reference to the black Shakespearean character Othello. "Where shall Otello go? Poor elk—poor bufaloe—poor Indian—poor Nigger—this is indeed a white man country." Yet in the ashes of failure were left two cornerstones on which the future could be built—the Fourteenth and Fifteenth amendments to the Constitution.

POSTWAR CONDITIONS AND ISSUES

General William T. Sherman proclaimed, "War is all hell." Undoubtedly it was for most soldiers and civilians caught up in the actual throes of battle and for the families of the 360,000 Union and 258,000 Confederate soldiers who would never return home. The costs of war, however, were not borne equally. Many segments of the Northern economy were stimulated by wartime demands, and with the once powerful Southern planters no longer there, Congress enacted programs to aid industrial growth. Virtually exempt from the devastation of the battlefield, the North built railroads and industries and increased agricultural production at the same time that torn-up Southern rails were twisted around trees, Southern factories were put to the torch, and Southern farmland lay choked with weeds.

In 1865 Southerners were still reeling from the bitter legacy of total war. General Philip Sheridan announced that after his troops had finished in the Shenandoah Valley even a crow would have to carry rations to fly over the area.

One year after the war, Carl Schurz noted that along the path of Sherman's march the countryside still "looked for many miles like a broad black streak of ruin and desolation." Southern cities suffered the most. A Northern reporter described Columbia, South Carolina, as a "wilderness of ruins . . . blackened chimneys and crumbling walls." Atlanta, Richmond, and Charleston shared the same fate. Much of what was not destroyed was confiscated, and emancipation divested Southerners of another $2 billion to $4 billion in assets. The decline of Southern wealth has been estimated at more than 40 percent during the four years of war.

The War's Impact on Individuals

Returning soldiers and their wives had to reconstruct relationships disrupted by separation—and the assumption of control by the women on farms and plantations. War widows envied them that adjustment. While the homeless wandered, one plantation mistress moaned, "I have not one human being in the wide world to whom I can say 'do this for me.'" Another noted, "I have never even so much as washed out a pocket handkerchief with my own hands, and now I have to do all my work." Southerners worried about how to meet their obligations; Confederate currency and bonds were worthless except as collectors' items—and even as collectors' items, they were too plentiful to have much value. One planter remarked drily that his new son "promises to suit the times, haveing remarkably large hands as if he might one day be able to hold plough handles." Many white Southerners, rich and poor, suffered a self-induced paranoia. They imagined the end of slavery would bring a nightmare of black revenge, rape, and pillage unless whites retained social control.

For four million former slaves, emancipation had come piecemeal, following the course of the Northern armies. It was not finalized until the ratification of the Thirteenth Amendment in December 1865. By then most border states had voluntarily adopted emancipation, but the amendment destroyed the remnants of slavery in Delaware and Kentucky. Most slaves waited patiently for the day of freedom, continuing to work the plantations but speaking up more boldly. Sometimes the Yankees came, proclaimed them free, and then left them to the mercy of their masters. Most, therefore, reacted cautiously to test the limits of their new freedom.

Many African-Americans had to leave their plantations, at least for a short time, to feel liberated. A few were confused as to the meaning of freedom and thought they would never have to work again. Soon, most learned they had gained everything—and nothing. As Frederick Douglass, the famous black abolitionist, noted, the freedman "was free from the individual master but a slave of society. He had neither money, property, nor friends. He was free from the old plantation, but he had nothing but the dusty road under his feet. He was free from the old quarter that once gave him shelter, but slave to the rains of summer and the frosts of winter. He was turned loose, naked, hungry, and destitute to the open sky."

The wartime plight of homeless and hungry blacks as well as whites impelled Congress to take unprecedented action, establishing on March 3, 1865, the Bureau of Refugees, Freedmen, and Abandoned Lands, within the War Department. The bureau was to provide "such issues of provisions, clothing, and fuel" as were needed to relieve "destitute and suffering refugees and their wives and children." Never before had the national government assumed responsibility for relief. Feeding and clothing the population had not been deemed its proper function. Considered drastic action, warranted only by civil war, the bureau was supposed to operate for just a year.

Under Commissioner Oliver O. Howard, the bureau had its own courts to deal with land and labor disputes. Agents in every state provided rations and medical supplies and helped to negotiate labor contracts between freedmen and landowners. The quality of the service rendered to the freedmen depended on the ability and motivation of the individual agents. Some courageously championed the freedmen's cause; others sided with the former masters. One of the most lasting benefits of the Freedmen's Bureau was the schools it established, frequently in cooperation with such Northern agencies as the American Missionary Association. During and after the war, African-Americans of all ages flocked to these schools to taste the previously forbidden fruit of education. The freedmen shrewdly recognized the keys to the planters' power—land, literacy, and the vote. The white South legally denied all three to African-Amerians in slavery, and many freedmen were determined to have them all.

Some former bondsmen had a firmer grasp of reality than their "liberators." Southern whites had long claimed to "know our Negroes" better than outsiders could. Ironically, this was proven false, but the reverse *was* true. Ex-slaves knew their ex-masters very well. One freedman pleaded, "Gib us our own land and we can take care ourselves; but widout land, de ole massas can hire us or starve us, as dey please." The events on Pinckney's plantation proved the wisdom of that statement.

Later generations have laughed at the widespread rumor among freedmen that they were to receive "forty acres and a mule" from the government, but the rumor did have some basis.

During the war, General Sherman was plagued with swarms of freedmen following his army, and in January 1865 he issued Special Field Order 15 setting aside a strip of abandoned coastal lands from Charleston, South Carolina, to Jacksonville, Florida, for the exclusive use of freedmen. African-Americans were to be given "possessory titles" to 40-acre lots. Three months later, the bill establishing the Freedmen's Bureau gave the agency control of thousands of acres of abandoned and confiscated lands to be rented to "loyal refugees and freedmen" in 40-acre plots for three-year periods with an option to buy at a later date. By June 1865, 40,000 African-Americans were cultivating land. In the Sea Islands and elsewhere, they proved they could be successful independent farmers. Yet land reform was not a popular cause among whites. Although a few congressmen continued to advocate land confiscation and redistribution, the dream of "forty acres and a mule" was a casualty of the battle for control of Reconstruction when Andrew Johnson's pardons returned most confiscated lands. Indeed, the is-

(Text continues on p. 522)

Freedmen realized that education was one key to real freedom and flocked to schools opened by the Freedmen's Bureau, the American Missionary Association, and various religious and rights groups.

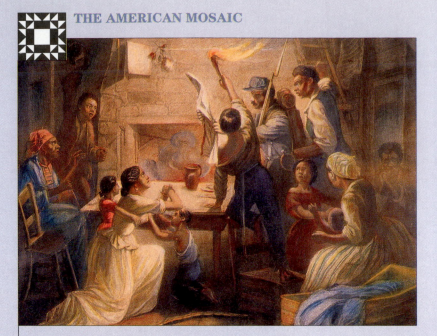

DAY OF JUBILO:
SLAVES CONFRONT EMANCIPATION

Rooted in Africa, the oral tradition became one of the tools slaves used to maintain a sense of self-worth. Each generation heard the same stories, and story-telling did not die with slavery. The day that slaves first learned of their emancipation remained vivid in their own minds and later in those of their descendants. The great-grandchildren of a strong-willed woman named Caddy relished the family account of her first taste of freedom:

> Caddy threw down that hoe, she marched herself up to the big house, then she looked around and found the mistress. She went over to the mistress, she flipped up her dress and told the white woman to do something. She said it mean and ugly. This is what she said: *Kiss my ass!*

Caddy's reaction was not typical. There was no typical response. Reminiscences of what was called the "Day of Jubilo" formed a tapestry as varied as the range of personality. Some, however, seem to have occurred more frequently than others. Many freedmen echoed one man's description of his and his mother's action when their master announced their emancipation: "Jes like tarpins or turtles after 'mancipation. Jes stick our heads out to see how the land lays."

Caution was a shrewd and realistic response. One of the survival lessons in slavery had been not to trust whites too much. This had been reinforced during the war when Union troops moved through regions proclaiming emancipation only to depart, leaving blacks at the mercy of local whites. One elderly slave described the aftermath to a Union correspondent. "Why, the day after you left, they jist had us all out in a row and told us they was going to shoot us, and they did hang two of us; and Mr. Pierce, the overseer, knocked one with a fence rail and he died the next day. Oh, Master! we seen stars in de day time."

Environment played a role in slaves' reactions to the Day of Jubilo. Urban slaves frequently enjoyed more freedom than plantation slaves. Even before emancipation such black social institutions as schools and churches emerged in many cities. When those cities were liberated, organized celebrations occurred quickly. In Charleston 4000 black men and women paraded before some 10,000 spectators. Two black women sat in one mule-drawn cart while a mock auctioneer shouted, "How much am I offered?" In the next cart a black-draped coffin was inscribed with the words "Slavery is Dead." Four days after the fall of Richmond blacks there held a mass rally of some 1500 people in the First African Church.

Knowledge of their freedom came in many forms to the slaves. Rural slaves were less likely to enjoy the benefits of freedom as early as urban slaves. Many heard of the Emancipation Proclamation through the slave grapevine or from Union soldiers long before its words became reality for them. Masters sometimes took advantage of the isolation of their plantations to keep their slaves in ignorance or to make freedom seem vague and frightening. Their ploys usually failed, but learned patterns of deference made some freedmen unwilling to challenge their masters. Months after emancipation one North Carolina slave continued to work without compensation, explaining to a Northern correspondent, "No, sir; my mistress never said anything to me that I was to have wages, nor yet that I was free; nor I never said anything to her. Ye see I left it to her honor to talk to me about it, because I was afraid she'd say I was insultin' to her and presumin', so I wouldn't speak first. She ha'n't spoke yet." There were, however, limits to his patience; he intended to ask her for wages at Christmas.

Numerous freedmen described the exuberance they felt. One elderly Virginia black went to the barn, jumped from one stack of straw to another, and "screamed and screamed!" A Texas man remembered, "We all felt like horses" and "everybody went wild." Other blacks recalled how slave songs and spirituals were updated, and "purty soon ev'ybody fo' miles around was singin' freedom songs."

Quite a few slaves learned of freedom when a Union officer or Freedmen's Bureau agent read them the Emancipation Proclamation—often over the objections of the master. "Dat one time," Sarah Ford declared, "Massa Charley can't open he mouth, 'cause de captain tell him to shut up, dat he'd do the talkin'." Some masters, however, still sought to have the last word. A Louisiana planter's wife announced immediately after the Union officer departed, "Ten years from today I'll have you all back 'gain."

Fear did not leave all slaves as soon as their bondage was lifted. Jenny Proctor of Alabama recalled that her fellow slaves were stunned by the news. "We didn' hardly know what he means. We jes' sort of huddle 'round together like scared rabbits, but after we knowed what he mean, didn' many of us go, 'cause we didn' know where to of went." James Lucas, a former slave of Jefferson Davis, explained, "folks dat ain' never been free don' rightly know de *feel* of bein' free. Dey don' know de meanin' of it."

Freedmen quickly learned that one could not eat or wear freedom. "Dis livin' on liberty," one declared, "is lak young folks livin' on love after they gits married. It just don't work." They searched for the real meaning of liberty in numerous ways. Some followed the advice of a black Florida preacher, "You ain't none 'o you, gwinter feel rale free till you shakes de dus ob de Ole Plantashun offen you feet," and moved. Others declared their independence by legalizing their marriages and taking new names or publicly using surnames they had secretly adopted while in slavery. "We had a real sho' nuff weddin' wid a preacher," one recalled. "Dat cost a dollar." When encouraged to take his old master's surname, a black man declared, "Him's nothing to me now. I don't belong to he no longer, an' I don't see no use in being called for him." Education was the key for others. "If I nebber does do nothing more while I live," a Mississippi freedman vowed, "I shall give my children a chance to go to school, for I considers education next best ting to liberty."

Most came to a good understanding of the benefits and limits of their new status. One explained, "Why, sar, all I made before was Miss Pinckney's, but all I make now is my own." Another noted, "You could change places and work for different men." One newly freed slave wrote his brother, "I's mightly well pleased tu git my eatin' by de 'sweat o' my face, an all I ax o' ole masser's tu jes' keep he hands off o' de Lawd Almighty's property, fur *dat's me*." A new sense of dignity was cherished by many. An elderly South Carolina freedman rejoiced, "Don't hab me feelins hurt now. Used to hab me feelins hurt all de times. But don't hab em hurt now, no more." Charlie Barbour exulted over the fact "dat I won't wake up some mornin' fer fin' dat my mammy or some ob de rest of my family am done sold." Most agreed with Margrett Millin's answer when she was asked decades later whether she had liked slavery or freedom better. "Well, it's dis way. In slavery I owns nothin'. In freedom I's own de home and raise de family. All dat cause me worryment and in slavery I has no worryment, but I takes de freedom."

sue of economic security for the freedman was obscured by other questions that seemed more important to whites.

Unresolved Issues

At war's end some issues had been settled, but at a terrible cost. As historian David Potter noted, "slavery was dead, secession was dead, and six hundred thousand men were dead." A host of new problems had arisen from the nature of civil war and the results of that war as well as the usual postwar dislocations. Many questions remained unanswered. Reconstruction was shaped by the unresolved issues.

The first of these concerned the status of the freedmen. They were indeed free, but were they citizens? The Dred Scott decision (1857) had denied citizenship to all African-Americans. Even if it were decided that they were citizens, what rights were conferred by that citizenship? Would they be segregated as free blacks in the antebellum North had often been? Also, citizenship did not automatically confer suffrage; women were proof of that. Were the freedmen to be given the ballot? These weighty matters were complicated by racial prejudice as well as constitutional and partisan questions.

The Constitution had been severely tested by civil war, and many felt it had been twisted by the desire to save the Union. Once the emergency was over, how were constitutional balance and limits to be restored? Except during the terms of a few strong presidents, Congress had been the most powerful branch of government during the nation's first 70 years. Lincoln had assumed unprecedented powers, and Congress was determined to regain its ascendency. The ensuing battle directly influenced Reconstruction policies and their implementation.

Secession was dead, but what about states' rights? Almost everyone agreed that a division of power between the national and state governments was crucial to the maintenance of freedom. The fear of centralized tyranny remained strong. There was reluctance to enlarge federal power into areas traditionally controlled by the states, even though action in some of those areas was essential to craft the kind of peace many desired. Hesitation to reduce states' rights produced timid and compromised solutions to such issues as suffrage. Also troubling many was federal action in the realm of social welfare—an idea so new that it failed to win lasting acceptance by that generation.

Another constitutional question concerned the status of the former Confederate states and how they were to be readmitted to the Union. There was no constitutional provision for failed secession, and many people debated whether the South had actually left the Union or not. The query reflected self-interest rather than an intellectual inquiry. Ironically, Southerners and their Democratic sympathizers now argued that the states had never legally separated from the rest of the nation, thus denying validity to the Confederacy in order to quickly regain their place in the Union. Extremists on the other side—Radical Republicans—insisted that the South had reverted to the status of conquered territory, forfeiting all rights as states. Under territorial governments, Representative Thaddeus Stevens declared, Southerners could "learn the principles of freedom and eat the fruit of foul rebellion." Others, including Lincoln, believed that the Confederate states had remained in the Union but had forfeited their rights. This constitutional hair-splitting grew out of the power struggle between the executive and legislative branches to determine which had the power to readmit the states and on what terms. It also reflected the hostility of some Northerners toward the "traitorous rebels" and the unwillingness of some Southerners to accept the consequences of defeat.

Republican Representative Thaddeus Stevens of Pennsylvania was among those who thought that the Southern states had forfeited their rights. He believed they should revert to the status of territories and be required to reapply for statehood in the Union.

Lingering over all these questions were partisan politics. Although not provided for in the Constitution, political parties had played a major role in the evolving American government. The road to war had disrupted the existing party structure—killing the Whig party, dividing the Democratic party, and creating the Republican party. The first truly sectional party, the Republican party had very few adherents in the South. Its continued existence was dubious in the face of the probable reunion of the Northern and Southern wings of the Democratic party. Paradoxically, the political power of the South, and in turn the Democratic party, was increased by the abolition of slavery. As freedmen, all African-Americans would be counted for representation; as slaves only three-fifths of them had been counted. Thus the Republican party's perceived need to make itself a national party also colored the course of Reconstruction.

PRESIDENTIAL RECONSTRUCTION

Early in the conflict, questions regarding the reconstruction of the nation were secondary to winning the war—without victory there would be no nation to reconstruct. Nonetheless, Lincoln had to take some action as Union forces pushed into the South. Authority had to be imposed in the reclaimed territory, so the president named military governors for Tennessee, Arkansas, and Louisiana in 1862 after federal armies occupied most of those states. He also began formulating plans for civilian government for those states and future Confederate areas as they came under the control of Union forces. The result was a Proclamation of Amnesty and Reconstruction issued in December of 1863 on the constitutional basis of the president's power to pardon.

Lincoln's Plan

Called the 10 percent plan, Lincoln's provisions were incredibly lenient. Rebels could receive presidential pardon by merely swearing their future allegiance to the Union and their acceptance of the end of slavery. In other words, former Confederates were not required to say they were sorry—only to promise they would be good in the future. A few people were excluded from pardons: Confederate military and civilian officers; United States judges, congressmen, and military officers who had resigned their posts to serve the Confederacy; and those accused of failing to treat captured black Union soldiers as prisoners of war. Nevertheless, Lincoln did not require the new state governments to bar such people from future voting or office-holding. Moreover after only 10 percent of the number who had voted in 1860 had taken the oath, a state could form a civilian government. When such states produced a constitution outlawing slavery, Lincoln promised to recognize them as reconstructed. He did not demand any provisions for protecting black rights or allowing black suffrage.

Tennessee, Arkansas, and Louisiana met Lincoln's requirements and soon learned they had only cleared the first barrier in what became a long obstacle course. Radical Republicans, such as Representative Thaddeus Stevens of Pennsylvania and Senator Charles Sumner of Massachusetts, were outraged by the president's generosity. They thought the provisions did not adequately punish Confederate treason, restructure Southern society, protect the rights of African-Americans, or aid the Republican party. The Radicals were in a minority, but many moderate Republicans were also dismayed by Lincoln's leniency, and shared the Radical view that Reconstruction was a congressional, not a presidential, function. As a result Congress recognized neither the three states' elected congressmen nor their electoral votes in the 1864 election.

After denying the president's right to reconstruct the nation, Congress drew up a plan for reconstruction: the Wade-Davis Bill. Its terms were much more stringent, yet not unreasonable. A majority, rather than 10 percent, of each states' voters had to declare their allegiance in order to form a government. Only those taking "ironclad" oaths of their past Union loyalty were allowed to participate in the making of new state constitutions. Barely a handful of high-ranking Confederates, however, were to be permanently barred from political participation. The only additional requirement imposed by Congress was the repudiation of the Confederate debt; Northerners did not want Confederate bondholders to benefit from their "investment in treason" at a cost to loyal taxpayers. Congress would determine when a state had met these requirements.

Constitutional collision was postponed by Lincoln's pocket veto of the bill and his assassination on April 14, 1865. While most of the nation mourned, some Radicals rejoiced at the results of John Wilkes Booth's action. Lincoln had been a formidable opponent and had articulated his position on the South in his second inaugural address. Calling for "malice toward none" and "charity for all," he proposed to "bind the nation's wounds" and achieve "a just and lasting peace." His successor, Andrew Johnson, on the other hand, had announced, "Treason is a crime, and crime must be punished." Johnson was a Tennessee Democrat and Unionist; he had been the only Southerner to remain in the Senate after his state seceded. Placed on the 1864 Republican "Union" ticket as a gesture of unity, Johnson's political affiliation was less

Andrew Johnson, a former governor and a senator from North Carolina, was the only senator from a seceding state to remain loyal to the Union. In 1862 Lincoln appointed him military governor of Tennessee, and in 1864 Johnson was selected as Lincoln's running mate.

than clear, but some considered him a weaker opponent than Lincoln. Radical Senator Benjamin Wade proclaimed, "By the gods there will be no trouble now in running this government."

Radicals found comfort in, but miscalculated, Johnson's hatred of the planters. He hated them for their aristocratic domination of the South, not for their slaveholding. Born of humble origins in Raleigh, North Carolina, and illiterate until adulthood, Johnson entered politics in Tennessee as a successful tailor. A champion of the people, he called the planters a "cheap purse-proud set . . . not half as good as the man who earns his bread by the sweat of his brow." Favoring free public education and a homestead act, Johnson was elected mayor, congressman, governor, and senator, before being appointed military governor of Tennessee and then becoming vice president. Although he shared the Radicals' hatred and distrust of the planters, he was a firm believer in black inferiority and did not support the Radical aim of black legal equality. He also advocated strict adherence to the Constitution and strongly supported states' rights.

Johnson's Plan

In the end Johnson did not reverse Lincoln's lenient policy. Congress was not in session when Johnson became president so he had about eight months to pursue policies without congressional interference. He issued his own proclamation of amnesty in May 1865 that barred everyone with taxable property worth more than $20,000. Closing one door, he opened another by providing for personal presidential pardons for excluded individuals. By year's end he had issued about 13,000 pardons. The most important aspect of the pardons was Johnson's claim that they restored all rights, including property rights. Thus many freedmen with crops in the ground suddenly found their masters back in charge—a disillusioning first taste of freedom that foreclosed further attempts at widespread land redistribution.

Johnson's amnesty proclamation did not immediately end the Radicals' honeymoon period with him, but his other proclamation issued on the same day caused deep concern. In it, he announced plans for the reconstruction of

North Carolina—a plan that would set the pattern for all Southern states. A native Unionist was named provisional governor with the power to call a constitutional convention elected by loyal voters. Omitting Lincoln's 10 percent provision, Johnson did eventually require ratification of the Thirteenth Amendment, repudiation of Confederate debts, and state constitutional provisions abolishing slavery and renouncing secession. He also recommended limited black suffrage, primarily to stave off congressional attempts to give the vote to all black males.

The presidential plan fell short of the Radicals' hopes, but many moderates might have accepted it if the South had complied with the letter and the spirit of Johnson's proposals. Instead, Southerners seemed determined to ignore their defeat, even to make light of it. The state governments, for the most part, met the minimum requirements (Mississippi and South Carolina refused to repudiate the debt and Mississippi declined to ratify the Thirteenth Amendment). Their apparent acceptance, however, grew out of a belief that very little had actually changed, and Southerners proceeded to show almost total disregard for Northern sensibilities. Presenting themselves, like prodigal sons, for admission to Congress were four Confederate generals, six Confederate cabinet officials, and as the crowning indignity, Confederate Vice President Alexander H. Stephens. Most Northerners were not exceedingly vindictive. Although Union soldiers had sung, "We'll hang Jeff Davis in a sour apple tree," he, and only he, served more than a few months in prison, and the only execution was not for treason, but for alleged war crimes at the Confederate prison camp in Andersonville, Georgia. Still the North did expect some sign of change and hoped for some indication of repentence by the former rebels.

Black Codes in the South

At the very least, Northerners expected adherence to the abolition of slavery, and the South was blatantly forging new forms of bondage. African-Americans were to be technically free, but Southern whites expected them to work and live as they had before emancipation. To accomplish this, the new state governments enacted a

The freedom of ex-slaves was sharply curtailed through Black Codes and vagrancy laws. This sketch shows the provost guard in New Orleans rounding up vagrant blacks in 1864.

series of laws known as the Black Codes. This legislation granted certain rights denied to slaves. Freedmen had the right to marry, own property, sue and be sued, and testify in court. Complex legalisms, however, often took away what was apparently given. Black Codes in all states prohibited racial intermarriage. Some forbade freedmen to own certain types of property, such as alcoholic beverages and firearms. Most so tightly restricted black legal rights that they were practically nonexistent. Black Codes imposed curfews on African-Americans, segregated them, and outlawed their right to congregate in large groups.

The Black Codes did more than merely provide means of racial control; they also sought to fashion a labor system as close to slavery as possible. Some required that African-Americans obtain special licenses for any job except agricultural labor or domestic service. Most mandated the signing of yearly labor contracts, which sometimes required African-Americans to call the landowner "master" and allowed withholding wages for minor infractions. To accomplish the same objective, Mississippi prohib-

Southern whites frequently vented their frustrations on blacks. In the New Orleans riot of July 30, 1866, 37 blacks and three white sympathizers were killed after a Radical Republican meeting.

ited black ownership or even rental of land. Mandatory apprenticeship programs took children away from their parents, and vagrancy laws allowed authorities to arrest blacks "wandering or strolling about in idleness" and use them on chaingangs or rent them out to planters for as long as a year.

When laws failed, some Southern whites resorted to violence. In Memphis, whites resented the presence of black troops at nearby Fort Pickering. A local paper asserted "the negro can do the country more good in the cotton field than in the camp" and chastised "the dirty, fanatical, nigger-loving Radicals of this city." In May 1866 a street brawl erupted between white policemen and recently discharged black soldiers. That night, after the soldiers had returned to the fort, white mobs attacked the black section of the city, with the encouragement of the police and local officials, one of whom urged the mob to "go ahead and kill the last damned one of the nigger race." The reign of terror lasted over 40 hours and left 46 blacks and 2 whites dead. This and other outbreaks of violence disgusted Northern voters.

Most Northerners would not have insisted on black equality or suffrage, but the South had regressed too far. Some Black Codes were even identical to the old slave codes, with the word negro substituted for slave. At the same time, reports of white violence against blacks filtered back to Washington. It is no wonder that upon finally reconvening in December 1865, Congress refused to seat the representatives and senators from the former Confederate states and instead proceeded to investigate conditions in the South.

CONGRESSIONAL RECONSTRUCTION

To discover what was really happening in the South, Congress established the Joint Committee on Reconstruction, which conducted inquiries and interviews that provided graphic and chilling examples of white repression and brutality toward African-Americans. Prior to the committee's final report, even moderates were convinced that action was necessary. In early 1866 Congress passed a bill to extend the life of the Freedmen's Bureau. The bill also granted the agency new powers to establish special courts for disputes concerning freedmen and to promote black education. Johnson vetoed it, claiming that the bureau was constitutional only in wartime conditions. Now, he claimed, the country had returned "to a state of peace and industry."

At first Johnson prevailed; his veto was not overridden. Then he made a mistake. In an impromptu speech on Washington's birthday, Johnson launched into a bitter attack on the Joint Committee on Reconstruction. Even moderates were offended. In mid-March 1866 Congress passed the Civil Rights Act. It declared that "all persons born in the United States and not subject to any foreign power, excluding Indians not taxed," were citizens and entitled to "full and equal benefit of all laws." Congress was responding to the Black Codes, but Johnson deemed the bill both unconstitutional and unwise. He vetoed it. This time, however, Congress overrode the veto. It then passed a slightly revised Freedmen's Bureau bill in July and enacted it over Johnson's veto. Even though the South had ignored much of Johnson's advice, such as granting limited suffrage to blacks, he stubbornly held to his conviction that reconstruction was complete and labeled his congressional opponents as "traitors."

His language did not create a climate of cooperation. Congress was concerned about the constitutional questions he raised and his challenge to congressional authority. To protect its handiwork and establish an alternate program of reconstruction, it drafted the Fourteenth Amendment. Undoubtedly the most significant legacy of Reconstruction, the first article of the amendment defined citizenship and its basic rights. Every person born in the United States and subject to its jurisdiction is declared a citizen. It also forbids any state from abridging "the privileges and immunities" of citizenship, from depriving any person of "due process of law," and from denying citizens the "equal protection of the laws." Although 100 years passed before its provisions were enforced as intended, the amendment has been interpreted to mean that states as well as the federal government are bound by the Bill of Rights—an important con-

TABLE 16.1

Reconstruction Amendments, 1865–1870			
Amendment	Main Provisions	Congressional Passage (⅔ majority in each house required)	Ratification Process (¾ of all states including ex-Confederate states required)
13	Slavery prohibited in United States	January 1865	December 1865 (27 states, including 8 southern states)
14	1. National citizenship 2. State representation in Congress reduced proportionally to number of voters disfranchised 3. Former Confederates denied right to hold office	June 1866	Rejected by 12 Southern and border states, February 1867 Radicals make readmission of Southern states hinge on ratification Ratified July 1868
15	Denial of franchise because of race, color, or past servitude explicitly prohibited	February 1869	Ratification required for readmission of Virginia, Texas, Mississippi, Georgia Ratified March 1870

stitutional change that paved the way for the civil rights decisions and laws of the twentieth century.

The remaining four sections of the amendment spelled out Congress's minimum demands for postwar change and was the South's last chance for a lenient peace. A creation of the congressional moderates, the amendment did not require black suffrage but reduced the "basis of representation" proportionately for those states not allowing it. Former Confederate leaders were also barred from holding office unless pardoned by Congress—not the president. Finally, neither Confederate war debts nor compensation to former slaveholders were ever to be paid. The amendment, which passed Congress in June 1866, was then sent to the states for ratification.

President Johnson bridled at this assault on his perceived powers and urged the Southern states not to ratify the amendment. All but Tennessee decided to take his advice and wait for further congressional action. They and Johnson miscalculated; both hoped that the public would repudiate the amendment in the 1866 congressional elections. Johnson hit the campaign trail, urging people to oust the Radicals. His "swing around the circle" was met with heckling and humiliation. The campaign was vicious, characterized by appeals to racial prejudice by the Democrats and charges of Democratic treason by the Republicans. Although few elections are referenda on any single issue, the Republicans won overwhelming victories, which they interpreted as a mandate for congressional reconstruction.

"Radical" Reconstruction

The election results along with Southern intransigence finally gave the Radicals an upper hand. In 1867 Congress passed the Military Reconstruction Act that raised the price of readmission. The act declared all existing "Johnson governments," except Tennessee's, void and divided the South into five military districts headed by military governors granted broad powers to govern. Delegates to new constitutional conventions were to be elected by all qualified voters—a group that by congressional

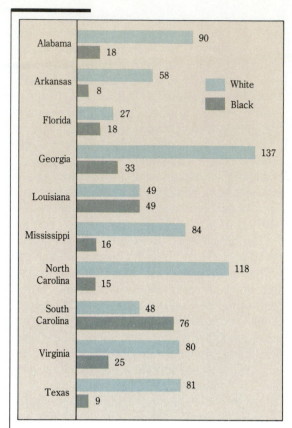

Figure 16.1
Composition of state constitutional conventions under congressional reconstruction

stipulation included black males and excluded former Confederate leaders. Following the ratification of a new state constitution providing for black suffrage, elections were to be held and the state would be required to ratify the Fourteenth Amendment. When that amendment became part of the Constitution and Congress approved the new state constitutions, the states would be granted representation in Congress once again.

Obviously, Johnson was not pleased with the congressional plan; he vetoed it, only to see his veto overridden. Nevertheless, as commander-in-chief he reluctantly appointed military governors, and by the end of 1867 elections had been held in every state except Texas. Because many white Southerners boycotted the elections, the South came under the control of Republicans supported by Union forces. In a way, however, Southerners had brought more radical measures upon themselves by their inflexibility. As the *Nation* declared in 1867,

> Six years ago, the North would have rejoiced to accept any mild restrictions upon the spread of slavery as a final settlement. Four years ago, it would have accepted peace on the basis of gradual emancipation. Two years ago, it would have been content with emancipation and equal civil rights for the colored people without the extension of suffrage. One year ago, a slight extension of the suffrage would have satisfied it.

Congress realized the plan it had enacted was unprecedented and subject to challenge by the other two branches of government. To check Johnson's power to disrupt, Congress took two other actions on the same day it passed the Military Reconstruction Act. The Command of the Army Act limited presidential military power. The Tenure of Office Act required Senate consent for the removal of any official whose appointment had required the Senate's confirmation. It was meant in part to protect Secretary of War Edwin M. Stanton, who supported the Radicals.

The Supreme Court had also shown its willingness to challenge Reconstruction actions in two important cases of 1866. In *Ex parte Milligan* the justices struck down the conviction of a civilian by a military tribunal in an area where civil courts were operating. Another decision ruled as void a state law barring ex-Confederates from certain professions on the basis that the act was *ex post facto*. Nevertheless, other decisions reflected a hesitation to tackle some of the thornier issues of Reconstruction. Important cases were pending, and Congress acted in March 1868 to limit the court's power to review cases. Because the congressional action was clearly constitutional, the Supreme Court acquiesced and in *Texas* v. *White* (1869) even acknowledged congressional power to reframe state governments.

President Johnson was not so accommodating. He sought to sabotage military reconstruction by continuing to pardon former Confederates, removing military commanders who were Radical sympathizers, and naming former Confederates to federal positions. Congress was

angry but could not find adequate grounds for impeachment. Johnson did not attempt to mend fences. In August 1867, during a congressional recess, he tried to replace Secretary of War Stanton with Ulysses S. Grant. When the Senate refused confirmation, however, Grant returned the office to Stanton. Johnson did not surrender; on February 21 he named Lorenzo Thomas to the cabinet position. Stanton also refused to surrender and barricaded himself in his office. On February 24 the House voted impeachment.

The Senate was given 11 articles of impeachment for its trial of the president. Eight related to the violation of the Tenure of Office Act and another to a violation of the Command of the Army Act. Only the last 2 reflected the real reasons for congressional action. Those articles accused Johnson of "inflammatory and scandalous harangues" against Congress and of "unlawfully devising and contriving" to obstruct congressional will. The heated and bitter trial lasted from March 5 to May 26. Johnson did not attend, but his lawyers made a good legal case that he had not technically violated the Tenure of Office Act since Stanton had been appointed by Lincoln. They tried to keep the trial focused on indictable offenses. Radical prosecutors continued to argue that Johnson had committed "high crimes and misdemeanors," but they also asserted that a president could be removed for political reasons, even without being found legally guilty of crimes—a position James Madison had supported during the drafting of the Constitution.

Andrew Johnson was the only president of the United States to be impeached. His successful defense centered on the legitimate uses of his executive powers.

The vote for conviction fell one short of the required two-thirds majority, when seven Republicans broke ranks and voted against conviction. This set the precedent that a president must be guilty of serious misdeeds to be removed from office. The outcome was a political blow to the Radicals, costing them some support. The action, however, did make Johnson more cooperative for the last months of his presidency.

Black Suffrage

In the 1868 presidential election, the Republicans won with Ulysses S. Grant, whose Civil War victories made his name a household word. He ran on a platform that endorsed congressional reconstruction, urged repayment of the national debt, and defended black suffrage in the South as necessary but supported the right of each Northern state to restrict the vote. His slogan, "Let us have peace," was appealing, but his election was less than a ringing endorsement for Radical policies. The military hero who had seemed invincible barely won the popular vote in several key states.

While Charles Sumner and a few other Radicals had long favored national black suffrage, only after the Republicans' electoral close call in 1868 did the bulk of the party begin to consider a suffrage amendment. Many were swayed by the political certainty that the black vote would be theirs and might give them the margin of victory in future close elections. Others were embarrassed by the hypocrisy of forcing black suffrage on the South while only 7 percent of Northern African-Americans could vote. Still others believed that granting African-Americans the vote would relieve whites of any further responsibility to protect black rights.

Suffrage supporters faced many objections to such an amendment. One was based on the lack of popular support. At that time only seven Northern states granted blacks the right to vote, and since 1865, referendum proposals for black suffrage in eight states had been voted down. In fact, only in Iowa and Minnesota (both containing minuscule black populations) had voters supported the extension of the vote. The amendment was so unpopular that, ironically, it could never have won adoption without its ratification by the Southern states, where black suffrage already existed.

A more serious challenge was the question of whether Congress could legislate suffrage at all. Before Reconstruction the national government had never taken any action regarding the right to vote; suffrage had been considered not a right but a privilege which only the states could confer. The Radical answer was that the Constitution expressly declared that "the United States shall guarantee to every State in this Union a republican form of government." Charles Sumner further asserted that "anything for human rights is constitutional" and that black rights could only be protected by black votes.

Senator George Vickers sarcastically asked, "does not the doctrine of human rights asserted by the senator apply as well to females as to males?" Although he was "no advocate for woman suffrage," he noted that "if the Congress of the United States had been composed exclusively of women we should have had no civil war. We might have had a war of words, but that would have been all." When one senator did propose female suffrage, a colleague informed him that "to extend the right of suffrage to negroes in this country I think is necessary for their protection; but to extend the right of suffrage to women is not necessary."

Some women, such as Elizabeth Cady Stanton and Susan B. Anthony, did not want to rely upon their fathers, brothers, or husbands to protect their rights. As leaders of the Women's Loyal League, both had worked hard for the adoption of the Thirteenth Amendment, only to be rewarded by inclusion of the word "male" in the Fourteenth Amendment of the Constitution—the first time that word appears. Some women, such as Lucy Stone of the American Woman Suffrage Association, accepted the plea of long-time woman suffrage supporter Frederick Douglass that it was the "Negro's hour," and worked for ratification. Anthony, however, vowed to "cut off this right arm of mine before I will ever work for or demand the ballot for the Negro and not the woman." Such differences played a role in splitting the women's movement in 1869 between those working for a national suffrage amendment and those who concentrated their efforts on the state level. Anthony and Stanton founded the National Woman Suffrage Association to battle for a constitutional amendment and other feminist reforms. Others

Susan B. Anthony (left) moved from temperance work to join with Elizabeth Cady Stanton in 1869 to form the National Woman Suffrage Association.

became disillusioned with that approach and established the American Woman Suffrage Association, which focused on obtaining suffrage on a state-by-state basis.

Actually, women did not lose much by not being included in the Fifteenth Amendment. To meet the various objections, compromise was necessary. The resulting amendment did not grant the vote to anyone. It merely stated that the vote could not be denied "on account of race, color, or previous condition of servitude." Suffrage was still essentially to be controlled by the states, and other bases of exclusion were not deemed unconstitutional. These loopholes would eventually allow white Southerners to make a mockery of the amendment.

Although congressional reconstruction was labeled "Radical," compromise had instead produced another essentially moderate plan. What Congress did *not* do is as important as what it did. It did not even guarantee the right to vote. There was only one execution for war crimes and only Jefferson Davis was imprisoned for more than a few months. For all but a handful, ex-Confederates were not permanently barred from voting or holding office. By 1872 only about 200 were still denied the right to hold office. Most local Southern governments were undisturbed. Land as well as rights were restored to former rebels, eliminating the possibility of extensive land redistribution. Most areas that had traditionally been the states' domain remained so, free from federal meddling. For example, no requirements were placed on the states to provide any education to freedmen. The only attempt by the national government to meet the basic needs of its citizens was the temporary Freedmen's Bureau—justified only as an emergency measure. The limited nature of Reconstruction doomed it as an opportunity to provide means for the protection of minority rights.

Such congressional moderation reflected the spirit of the age. Enduring beliefs in the need for strict construction of the Constitution and in states' rights presented formidable barriers to truly radical changes. Property rights were considered sacrosanct—even for "traitors." Cherished ideals of self-reliance and the conviction that a person determined his or her own destiny led many to support Horace Greeley's so-called root, hog, or die approach to the black problem. By ending the threat of slavery, he argued, "we may soon break up our Freedmen's Bureaus and all manner of coddling devices and let the negroes take care of themselves." Few agreed with Charles Sterns who argued that even a hog could not root without a snout—that there could be no equality of opportunity where one group had long been allowed an unfair advantage. Many instead sided with an editorialist for the *New York Herald* who wrote of the bill to extend the life of the Freedmen's Bureau: "The bill ought to be called an act to support the negroes in idleness by the honest labor of white people, or an act to establish a gigantic and corrupt political machine for the benefit of the radical faction and a swarm of officeholders." Clearly the idea of affirmative action or even equal opportunity had even less support then than it did 100 years later.

Tainting every action was the widespread conviction that African-Americans were not equal to whites. Many Northerners were more concerned with keeping blacks in the South than with abstract black rights. In 1866, for example, New York Senator Roscoe Conkling catered to the Northern fear of black immigration while calling for support of the Fourteenth Amendment:

> Four years ago mobs were raised, passions were aroused, votes were given, upon the idea that emancipated negroes were to burst in hordes upon the North. We then said, give them liberty and rights in the South, and they will stay there and never come into a cold climate. We say so still, and we want them let alone, and that is one thing that this part of the amendment is for.

Even Radical Representative George Julian admitted to his Indiana constituents, "the real trouble is that *we hate the negro*. It is not his ignorance that offends us, but his color."

Northerners who engaged in politics in the South before or after the war were called carpetbaggers. This cartoon shows Grant and Union soldiers propping up carpetbag rule with bayonets, while the "Solid South" staggers under the weight.

The plan for Reconstruction evolved fitfully, buffeted first one way and then another by the forces of the many unresolved issues at war's end. If permanent changes were very limited, nonetheless precedents had been set for later action, and for a brief time congressional reconstruction brought about the most democratic governments the South had ever seen—or would see for another hundred years.

RECONSTRUCTION IN THE SOUTH

Regardless of the specific details hammered out in Washington, any dictated peace would probably have been unpalatable to Southern whites. They were especially leery of any action that seemed to threaten white supremacy—whether or not that was the intended result. Even before the war, suspicion greeted every Northern move. Southerners continued to see a radical abolitionist behind every bush.

The Freedmen's Bureau established during the last year of the war operated for five years in the South. Most Southerners criticized and condemned the bureau from its first day to its last. Many believed its agents were partial to African-Americans. As one Mississippi planter declared, "The negro is a sacred animal. The Yankees are about negroes like the Egyptians were about cats." Actually there was a great diversity in the background and goals of bureau agents. Some were idealistic young New Englanders who, like the Yankee schoolmarms, came south to aid in the transition to freedom. Others were army officers whose first priority was to maintain order—often by siding with the landowners. All were overworked, underpaid, and under pressure.

The results of bureau actions were mixed in regard to conditions for African-Americans. The agents helped to negotiate labor contracts that African-Americans were forced to sign to obtain rations. Frequently the wages were well below the rate at which slaves had been hired out by their owners before the war. While it should be remembered that money was scarce at the time, these contracts helped to keep African-Americans on the farm—someone else's farm. On the other hand, between 1865 and

1869 the bureau issued over 21 million rations, of which about 5 million went to whites. Thus it showed that the government could establish and administer a massive relief program, as it would again do during the depression of the 1930s. The bureau also operated more than 40 hospitals, opened hundreds of schools, and accomplished the herculean task of resettling some 30,000 people displaced by the war.

Carpetbaggers, Scalawags, and Black Republicans

Until the passage of the Reconstruction Acts in 1867, Southern governments were much the same as they had been before the war. Afterwards, however, Republican officeholders joined bureau agents in directing the course of Reconstruction. Despised by many whites, these men, depending on their origins, were derisively labeled "carpetbaggers," "scalawags," and "nigrahs." Opponents considered all three groups despicable creatures whose "black and tan" governments were tyrannizing native whites, while engaged in an orgy of corruption. Myths created about Southern Republicans lingered long after the restoration of Democratic party rule.

Northerners who came to the South during or after the war and became engaged in politics were called carpetbaggers. They supposedly arrived with a few meager belongings in their carpetbags, which would expand to hold ill-gotten gains from looting an already devastated South. Probably what most infuriated whites was the carpetbaggers' willingness to cooperate with African-Americans. Calling them "a kind of political dry-nurse for the negro population," native whites accused the carpetbaggers of cynically exploiting the freedmen for their own gain. Many agreed with the charge that the carpetbaggers were standing "right in the public eye, stealing and plundering, many of them with both arms around negroes, and their hands in their rear pockets, seeing if they cannot pick a paltry dollar out of them."

White Southerners who voted for Republicans were labeled scalawags. The term, said to be derived from Scalloway, "a district in the Shetland Islands where small, runty cattle and horses were bred," had been used previously as a "synonym for scamp, loafer, or rascal." Thus Southern white Republicans were depicted as people "paying no taxes, riding poor horses, wearing dirty shirts, and having no use for soap." Such men were said to have "sold themselves for office" and become a "subservient tool and accomplice" of the carpetbaggers.

Most detested by white Southerners were the black Republicans. Having long characterized African-Americans as inferior creatures dependent on white management for survival, Southerners loathed the prospect of blacks in authority. They feared that the former slaves would exact payment for their years of bondage. Democrats also knew that racism was their best rallying cry to regain power. Thus Reconstruction governments were denounced for "Ethiopian minstrelsy, Ham radicalism in all its glory." Whites claimed ignorant freedmen, incapable of managing their own affairs, were allowed to run the affairs of state with disastrous results. A former governor of South Carolina observed, "All society stands now like a cone on its Apex, with base up."

Such legends persisted for a long time, despite contrary facts. Southern whites had determined even before Reconstruction began that it would be "the most galling tyranny and most stupendous system of organized robbery that is to be met with in history." The truth was, as W. E. B. Du Bois later wrote, "There is one thing that the white South feared more than negro dishonesty, ignorance, and incompetency, and that was negro honesty, knowledge, and efficiency." To a surprising degree they got what they most feared.

Black voters were generally as fit to vote as the millions of illiterate whites enfranchised by Jacksonian democracy. Black officials as a group were as qualified as their white counterparts. In South Carolina two-thirds of them were literate, and in all states most of the acknowledged leaders were well educated and articulate. They usually had been members of the Northern or Southern free black elite or part of the slave aristocracy of skilled artisans and household slaves. Hiram Revels, a U.S. senator from Mississippi, was the son of free blacks who had sent him to college in the North. James Walker Hood,

In a historic first, seven African-Americans were elected to the Forty-first and Forty-second Congresses. Between 1869 and 1901, two African-Americans became senators and 20 served in the House.

the presiding officer of the North Carolina constitutional convention of 1867, was a black carpetbagger from Pennsylvania who came to the state as an African Methodist Episcopal Zion missionary. Some, such as Francis Cardoza of South Carolina, were the privileged mulatto sons of white planters. Cardoza had been educated in Scottish and English universities. During Reconstruction 14 such men served in the U.S. House of Representatives and 2 in the Senate. By 1901 6 others were elected to the House, before Southern black political power was effectively demolished.

Even if black Republicans had been incompetent, they could hardly be held responsible for the perceived abuses of so-called black reconstruction. Only in South Carolina did African-Americans have a majority of the delegates to the constitutional convention provided for by the Reconstruction Acts. Neither did they dominate the new governments; only for a two-year period in South Carolina did blacks control both houses of the legislature. None were elected governor, although P. B. S. Pinchback, the lieutenant governor of Louisiana, did serve as acting governor for a short time. When the vote was restored to ex-Confederates, African-Americans comprised only one-third of the voters of

the South, and only in two states did they have a majority.

Actually, carpetbaggers dominated most Republican governments to an extent not warranted by their numbers. They accounted for less than one percent of the party's voters but held a third of the offices. Their power was especially obvious in the higher offices. Over half of all Southern Republican governors and almost half of the Republican congressmen and senators were former Northerners. Although some carpetbaggers did resemble their stereotypes, most did not. Many had come south before black enfranchisement and could not have predicted political futures based on black votes. Most were Union veterans whose wartime exposure to the region convinced them that they could make a good living there without having to shovel snow. Some brought with them much needed capital for investment in their new home. A few came with a sense of mission to educate blacks and reform Southern society.

Obviously, if African-Americans constituted only a third of the population and carpetbaggers less than one percent, those two groups had to depend on the votes of a sizable number of native white Southerners to obtain office in some regions of the South. Those men came from diverse backgrounds. Some scalawags were members of the old elite of bankers, merchants, industrialists, and even some planters who, as former Whigs, favored the "Whiggish" economic policies of the Republican party and hoped to control and use the black vote for their own purposes. On discovering their inability to dominate the Republican governments, most of these soon drifted into alliance with the Democrats. The majority of Southern white Republican voters were yeoman farmers and poor whites from areas where slavery had been unimportant. They had long resented planter domination and had opposed secession.

To win their vote the Republicans appealed to class interests. In Georgia they proclaimed, "Poor White men of Georgia: Be a Man! Let the Slave-holding aristocracy no longer rule you. Vote for a constitution which educates your children free of charge; relieves the poor debtor from his rich creditor; allows a liberal homestead for your families; and more than all, places you on a level with those who used to boast that for every slave they were entitled to three-fifths of a vote in congressional representation." Many accepted such arguments and joined African-Americans to put Republicans into office. The coalition, however, was always shaky, given the racism of poor whites. The scalawags actually represented a swing vote that finally swung toward the Democratic party of white supremacy later in the 1870s.

Character of Republican Rule

While the coalition lasted, the Republican governments became the most democratic that the South had ever had. More people could vote for more offices, all remaining property requirements for voting and officeholding were dropped, representation was made fairer through reapportionment, and more offices became elective rather than appointive. Salaries for public officials made it possible to serve without being wealthy. Most important, universal male suffrage was enacted with the support of black legislators. Ironically, by refusing to deny Southern whites what had been denied to them—the vote—African-Americans sowed the seeds of their own destruction.

The Republican state constitutions, which brought the South firmly into the mainstream of national reform, often remained in effect years after the end of Reconstruction. Legislatures abolished automatic imprisonment for debt and reduced the use of the death penalty. More institutions for the care of the indigent, orphans, mentally ill, deaf, and blind were established. Tax structures were overhauled, reducing head taxes and increasing property taxes to relieve somewhat poorer taxpayers. At the same time, Southern railroads, harbors, and bridges were rebuilt.

Reforms also affected the status of women, increasing their rights in the possession of property and divorce. Although giving women legal control of their property was mainly intended to protect the families of their debt-ridden husbands, African-Americans in particular pushed for more radical changes. When William Whipper's motion to give South Carolina women the

African-Americans eagerly participated in politics when allowed. In this 1867 election in the nation's capital, they served as polling place judges and lined up as early as 2 A.M. to vote.

vote did not receive a second, he persevered and declared:

> However frivolous you may think it, I know the time will come when every man and woman in this country will have the right to vote. I acknowledge the superiority of woman. There are large numbers of the sex who have an intelligence more than equal to our own. Is it right or just to deprive these intelligent beings of the privileges which we enjoy? The time will come when you will have to meet this question. It will continue to be agitated until it must ultimately triumph.
>
> However derisively we may treat these noble women, we shall yet see them successful in the assertion of their rights.

The area in which black legislators had the most success was laying the foundations for public education. Antebellum provisions for

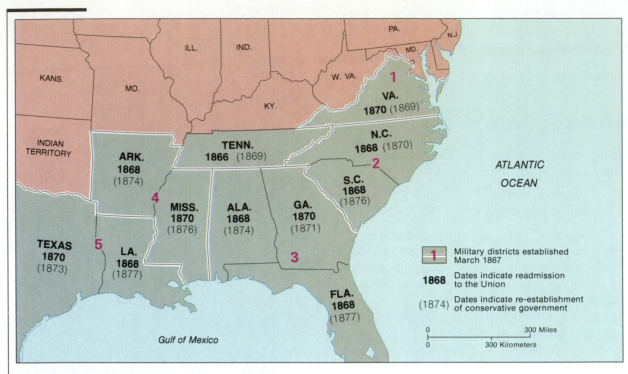

Reconstruction and Redemption

public schools below the Mason-Dixon line were meager to nonexistent. In every state African-Americans were among the main proponents of state-supported schools, but most accepted segregated facilities as necessary compromises. Some black parents did not even desire integration; they believed their children could not flourish in environments tainted by white supremacy. By 1877 some 600,000 blacks were in schools, but only the University of South Carolina and the public schools of New Orleans were integrated.

As desirable as many of the new social services were, they required money and money was scarce. The war had destroyed not only railroads and bridges but also much of the Southern tax base. The necessary tax increases were bound to be unpopular, as were soaring state debts. Both were blamed on corruption, with some justification. Louisiana governor Henry C. Warmouth netted some $100,000 dollars in a year in which his salary was only $8000. A drunken South Carolina governor signed an issue of state bonds for a woman in a burlesque show.

One black man was paid $9000 to repair a bridge with an original cost of only $500. Contracts for rebuilding and expanding railroads, subsidies to industries, and bureaucracies for administering social services offered generous opportunities for graft and bribery. When these occurred, Southern whites loudly proclaimed that they knew it would happen if shifty former slaves were given the keys to the till.

Actually, although African-Americans received a large share of the blame, they received little of the profit. A smaller percentage of blacks than whites were involved in the scandals. Also the corruption that the Democrats denounced at every turn was rather meager compared with the shenanigans of such contemporary Northern Democratic regimes as the Boss Tweed Ring of New York. There seemed to be an orgy of national corruption that infected both parties. Indeed, in the South a Democratic state treasurer who came to office after Reconstruction deserves the dubious distinction of being the largest embezzler of the era.

The "tyranny" that so distressed Southern whites did not include wholesale disfranchisement or confiscation of their lands. In fact, the demands of most African-Americans were quite reasonable and moderate. Their goals were expressed by the declarations of the many postwar black conventions, such as a Virginia one in 1865 that declared, "All we ask is an *equal chance* with the white *traitors* varnished and japanned with the oath of amnesty."

Black and White Economic and Social Adaptation

Just as the ex-slaves on Thomas Pinckney's plantation had learned, freedmen everywhere soon realized that the economic power of whites had diminished little. If anything, land became more concentrated in the hands of a few. In one Alabama county, the richest 10 percent of landowners increased their share of landed wealth from 55 to 63 percent between 1860 and 1870. Some African-Americans, usually through hard work and incredible sacrifice, were able to obtain land. The percentage of blacks owning property increased from less than 1 to 20 percent. Indeed, African-Americans seemed to fare better than poor whites. One observer noted, "The negro, bad as his condition is, seems to me, on the whole, to accommodate himself more easily than the white to the change of situation." The truth of his assertion is reflected in the fact that the percentage of whites owning land dropped from 80 to 67 percent. Increasingly, poor blacks and whites became agricultural laborers on someone else's land.

The black landless farmers, like the slaves before them, were not mere pawns. If they could not control their destinies, at least they could shape them. As one Northern observer wrote, "They have a mine of strategy to which the planter sooner or later yields." Through strikes and work slowdowns, African-Americans resisted contract and wage labor because working in gangs under white supervision smacked too much of slavery. When they could not own land, they preferred to rent it, but the few who had the cash to do so found few Southern whites would risk the wrath of their neighbors by breaking the taboo against renting to blacks.

Sharecropping emerged both as a result of black desire for autonomy and whites' lack of cash. Landowners gave blacks as well as poor whites a plot of land to work in return for a share of the crops. Freedom from white supervision was so desirable to freedmen that they sometimes hitched mule teams to their old slave cabins and carried them off to their assigned acres. To put distance between themselves and slavery, many black men would not allow their wives and children to work in the fields.

Sharecropping at first seemed to be a good bargain for African-Americans because they frequently negotiated their way to a half share of the crops. Their portion of the profits from Southern agriculture, including all provisions, rose from 22 percent under slavery to 56 percent by the end of Reconstruction. Moreover, they were making more for working less. Fewer family members worked and black men labored shorter hours; as a group African-Americans worked one-third fewer hours than under slavery. Per capita black income increased quickly after the war to about one-half that of whites, but then it stagnated.

African-Americans obtained a little more freedom to control working conditions under the sharecropping system, but their poverty limited their ability to acquire machinery. Many relied on "human power" for plowing.

Sharecropping later proved to be disastrous for most blacks and poor whites. They needed more than land to farm; they also required seeds, fertilizers, and provisions to live on until they harvested their crops. To obtain these they often borrowed against their share of the crops. Falling crop prices, high credit rates, and sometimes cheating by creditors left many to harvest a growing burden of debt with each crop. In many states, when the Democrats regained power, laws favoring creditors were passed. These led to debt peonage for many sharecroppers.

If most freedmen did not win economic freedom, they benefited from freedom in other ways. It was no longer illegal to learn to read and write, and African-Americans pursued education with much zeal. Many even paid as much as 10 percent of their limited incomes for tuition. They began to learn the fundamentals, and a growing number also sought higher education. Between 1860 and 1880 over 1000 African-Americans earned college degrees. Some went north to college, but most went to 1 of the 13 Southern colleges established by the American Missionary Association or by black and white churches with the assistance of the Freedmen's Bureau. Such schools as Howard and Fisk were a permanent legacy of Reconstruction.

African-Americans were also able to enjoy and expand their rich cultural heritage. Religion was a central focus for most, just as it had been in slavery. Withdrawing from white congregations with segregated pews and self-serving sermons on the duty of servants to their masters, freedmen everywhere established separate black churches. The membership in such antebellum denominations as the African Methodist Episcopal soared. In essence, black Christians declared their religious independence, and their churches became centers of political and social activities as well as religious ones. As one carpetbagger noted, "The colored preachers are *the great power* in controlling and uniting the colored vote." The churches also functioned as vehicles for self-help and sources of entertainment.

Most African-Americans desired racial intermingling no more than whites. Many could not feel free until they had removed themselves and their children as far as possible from white arrogance. They created separate congregations and acquiesced to segregated schooling. Nevertheless, they did not want to be publicly humiliated by such measures as separate railroad cars. They frequently used their limited political power to protect civil rights through clauses in state constitutions and legislation, as well as by appeals for the enforcement of national laws. Consequently, black Southerners did enjoy the use of public facilities to a greater degree than they would during the 75 years following Reconstruction.

The very changes that gave African-Americans hope during Reconstruction distressed poor whites. Black political equality rankled them, but much more serious was their own declining economic status. As their landownership declined, more whites became dependent on sharecropping and low wage jobs, primarily in the textile industry. Even these meager opportunities were eagerly greeted; as one North Carolina preacher proclaimed, "Next to God, what this town needs is a cotton mill." Economic competition between poor whites and blacks was keen, but their common plight also favored cooperation based on class interest. The economic pressures applied by the white elite frequently hurt both groups as well as middle-class yeoman farmers, and for brief periods during Reconstruction they warily united in politics. Invariably, however, these attempts were shattered by upper-class appeals to white supremacy and racial unity.

Ironically, although poor whites were perceived by nearly everyone as the group most hostile to blacks, the two shared many aspects of a rich Southern cultural heritage. Both groups developed colorful dialects. For each, aesthetic expression was based on utility—reflecting their need to use wisely what little they had. Their quilts were not merely functional but often quite beautiful. In religion and recreation, their experiences were similar. At camp meetings and revivals, poor whites practiced a highly emotional religion, just as many black Southerners did. Both groups spun yarns and sang songs that reflected the perils of their existence and provided folk heroes. They also shared many superstitions as well as useful folk remedies. Race, however, was a potent wedge between them that upper-class whites frequently exploited for their own political and economic goals.

Planters no longer dominated the white elite; sharecropping turned them and others into absentee landlords. The sons of the old privileged families joined the growing ranks of lawyers, railroad entrepreneurs, bankers, industrialists, and merchants. In some ways, the upper and middle classes began to merge, but in many places the old elite and their sons still enjoyed a degree of deference and political leadership. Their hostility toward African-Americans was not as intense, largely because they possessed means of control. When their control slipped, however, they also became ranting racists.

So strongly were all Southern whites imbued with a belief in white superiority that most could not imagine total black equality. A Freedmen's Bureau agent reported in 1866 that "a very respectable old citizen . . . swore that, if he could not thrash a negro who insulted him, he would leave the country." White attitudes toward blacks were as irrational as they were generalized. Most whites exempted the blacks they knew from such generalizations. As an Alabama planter declared in 1865, "If all were like some of mine I wouldn't say anything. They're as intelligent and well behaved as anybody. But I can't stand free niggers anyhow!"

Violent White Resistance

Large numbers of whites engaged in massive resistance to Reconstruction. Unlike the resistance of Southern blacks 100 years later, however, this brand of resistance was not passive but very aggressive. In 1866, some bored young men in Pulaski, Tennessee, organized a social club with all the trappings of fraternal orders—secret rituals, costumes, and practical jokes. They soon learned that their antics intimidated African-Americans; thenceforth the Ku Klux Klan grew into a terrorist organization, copied all over the South under various names. A historian of the Klan asserts that it "whipped, shot, hanged, robbed, raped, and otherwise outraged Negroes and Republicans across the South in the name of preserving white civilization." A major goal of the Klan was to intimidate Republican voters and restore Democrats to office.

The Ku Klux Klan and other white terrorist groups used violence to eliminate black gains. This 1874 cartoon and others like it helped arouse the public to demand action against the Klan.

In South Carolina, when blacks working for a scalawag began to vote, Klansmen visited the plantation and "whipped every nigger man they could lay their hands on." The group's increasing lawlessness alarmed many people and led to congressional action. The Klan was broken up by three Enforcement Acts (1870–1871) that gave the president the right to suspend habeas corpus against "armed combinations" interfering with any citizen's right to vote. In 1871 Grant did so in nine South Carolina counties. Disbanding the Klan, however, did little to decrease Southern violence or the activities of similar terrorist groups.

Some blacks Southerners were probably never allowed to vote freely. At the peak of Reconstruction, fewer than 30,000 federal troops were stationed in the entire South—hardly enough to protect the rights of 4.5 million African-Americans. As troops were being withdrawn, Democrats sought to regain control of their states. They made appeals to white supremacy and charged the Republicans with corruption. Without secret ballots landowners could threaten sharecroppers with eviction for "improper" voting. In addition to economic intimidation, violence against freedmen escalated in most states as the Democrats increased their political power. When victory seemed close, Democrats justified any means to the desired end that they called "redemption." A South Carolina Democratic campaign plan in 1876 urged, "Never threaten a man individually. If he deserves to be threatened, the necessities of the times require that he should die. A dead Radical is very harmless." One Democratic candidate for governor in Louisiana proclaimed, "We shall carry the next election if we have to ride saddle-deep in blood to do it." In six heavily black counties in Mississippi such tactics proved highly successful—reducing Republican votes from more than 14,000 in 1873 to only 723 in 1876. Beginning with Virginia and Tennessee in 1869, by 1876 all but three states—Louisiana, Florida, and South Carolina—had Democratic "Redeemer" governments. The final collapse of Reconstruction became official the following year with the withdrawal of federal troops from the three unredeemed states.

RECONSTRUCTION IN THE NORTH AND WEST

In the end, the South could be said to have lost the war but won the peace. After 1877 Southern whites found little resistance to their efforts to forge new institutions to replace both the economic benefits and racial control of slavery. By 1910 they had devised a system of legalized repression that gave whites many of the benefits of slavery without all the responsibilities. Surely this was not what the North had envisioned after Appomattox. How did it happen? Much of the answer is found in events occurring in the North and West.

Northern Shifts in Attitudes

The basic cause for the decline of Reconstruction can be seen in an 1874 conversation between two Northern Republicans during which one declared that the people were "tired out with this wornout cry of 'Southern Outrages!!!' Hard times and heavy taxes make them wish the

... 'everlasting nigger' were in [hell] or Africa. ... It is amazing the change that has taken place in the last two years in the public sentiment." A shifting political climate, economic hard times, increasing preoccupation with other issues, and continued racism combined to make most Northerners wash their hands of the responsibility for the protection of black rights.

When Grant won the presidency in 1868, the nation appeared to reject the Democratic charge that the Republican Congress had "subjected ten states, in the time of profound peace, to military despotism and Negro supremacy." In reality the voters had chosen a war hero who had no political record or experience. They voted not so much for a program, but for Grant's campaign slogan: "Let us have peace."

The victorious general proved to be a poor choice for the presidency. Not only was he politically inexperienced, but he also lacked a taste for politics. Haunted by a fear of failure and socially insecure, Grant was too easily influenced by men of wealth and prestige. He made some dismal appointments and remained loyal to individuals who did not merit his trust. The result was a series of scandals. Grant was not personally involved, but his close association with the perpetrators blemished both his and his party's image. The first major scandal involved Crédit Mobilier, a dummy construction company used to milk money from railroad investors in order to line the pockets of a few insiders, including Vice President Schuyler Colfax and a number of other prominent Republicans. Later, bribes and kickback schemes surfaced that involved Indian trading posts, post office contracts, and commissions for tax collection. Such revelations as well as the corruption in some Southern Republican governments did little to enhance the public image of the party, and Democrats were quick to make corruption a major issue in both the North and the South.

Although by the 1872 presidential election, there had only been a hint of scandal, some Republicans were disenchanted. In that election the Republican party was split; a number, calling themselves Liberal Republicans, formed a separate party. They supported their own candidate, *New York Tribune* editor Horace Greeley, rather than Grant. Among Greeley's campaign pledges was a more moderate Southern policy. Even with the Democrats also nominating Greeley, Grant easily won reelection, but the fear of disgruntled Republicans merging with Democrats remained. By 1874 Republicans were becoming aware that the black vote would not save them. That year the Democrats captured the House and gained in the Senate, following further revelations of Republican corruption.

At least as detrimental to Republican political fortunes was a depression that followed the panic of 1873, which was caused by overinvestment in railroads and risky financial deals. Lasting six years, it was the most serious economic downturn the nation had yet experienced. Whatever their cause, depressions usually result in "voting the rascals out." Democratic fortunes were bound to rise as the people's fell. Yet economic distress had an even wider impact on Reconstruction. People's attention became focused on their pocketbooks rather than on abstract ideals of equality and justice. Economic scrutiny brought such issues as currency and tariffs to the forefront. As the depression deepened, many questioned Republican support for "sound money" backed by gold and the retirement of the legal tender "greenback" paper money that had been issued during the war.

Those greenbacks had increased the money supply needed to finance postwar economic expansion. Yet many Republicans were suspicious of any money not backed by specie—that is, gold or silver. One of the last actions of the Republican-controlled Congress was to pass the Resumption Act of 1875. It provided for the gradual redemption of greenbacks in gold. The resulting deflation favored creditors over debtors because debtors were forced to repay loans with money that was worth more than it had been when they borrowed it. Many Americans, especially farmers, were in debt, and deflation coupled with a depression brought economic distress.

Actually, the panic of 1873 merely brought into clearer focus the vast changes occurring in the North during Reconstruction. The South had never had the undivided attention of the rest of the nation. Such events as the comple-

tion of the first transcontinental railroad in 1869 often overshadowed reports of "Southern outrages." The United States was experiencing the growing pains of economic modernization and western expansion. The Republican platform of 1860 had called for legislation favoring both of these as well as stopping the expansion of slavery. Comprised of diverse interest groups, the party went through a battle for its soul during Reconstruction. For a while the small abolitionist faction had gained some ascendancy due to postwar developments. By the late 1870s, however, the Republican party had foresaken its reformist past to become a protector of privilege rather than a guarantor of basic rights. In effect, Republicans and Democrats joined hands in conservative support of railroad and industrial interests.

Racism and American Indians

The major reason for the decline of Reconstruction was the pervasive belief in white supremacy. There could be little determination to secure equal rights for those who were considered unequal in all other respects. Reconstruction became a failed opportunity to resolve justly the status of one minority, and the climate of racism almost ensured failure for others as well. Western expansion not only diverted attention from Reconstruction but also raised the question of what was to be done about the Plains Indians. They, too, were considered inferior to whites. William H. Seward, who later became secretary of state, spoke for most white Americans when in 1860 he described blacks as "a foreign and feeble element like the Indians, incapable of assimilation." Indeed, while Reconstruction at first offered hope to African-Americans, for the American Indian hope was fading.

In the end, African-Americans were oppressed; Native Americans were exterminated or separated into shrinking reservations. From the white viewpoint the reason was obvious. As a so-called scientific treatise of the 1850s explained, "The *Barbarous* races of America . . . although nearly as low in intellect as the Negro races, are essentially untameable. Not merely have all attempts to civilize them failed, but also every endeavor to enslave them. Our Indian tribes submit to extermination, rather than wear the yoke under which our negro slaves fatten and multiply." Because most Africans, like Europeans, depended on agriculture rather than hunting, they adapted more easily to agricultural slavery. Black labor was valuable, if controlled; Indians were merely barriers to expansion.

When settlers first began moving onto the Great Plains, they encountered about 250,000 Plains Indians and 13 million buffalo. Some tribes, including the Zuni, Hopi, Navaho, and Pawnee, were fairly settled and depended on gardening and farming. Such tribes as the Sioux, Apache, and Cheyenne, however, were nomadic hunters who followed the buffalo herds over vast tracts of land. These herds played a crucial role in most Plains Indians' culture— providing almost all the basic necessities. Indians ate the buffalo meat, made clothing and tepees out of the hides, used the fats for cosmetics, fashioned the bones into tools, made thread from the sinews, and even burned dried buffalo droppings as fuel. To settlers, however, the buffalo were barriers to western expansion. The herds interfered with construction, knocked over telegraph poles and fences, and could derail trains during stampedes.

Other cultural differences caused misunderstandings between settlers and Native Americans. Among Anglo-Americans, capitalism fostered competition and frontier living promoted individualism. On the other hand, Plains Indians lived in tribes based on kinship ties. As members of an extended family that included distant cousins, Indians were taught to place the welfare of the group over the interests of the individual. The emphasis within a tribe was on cooperation rather than competition. Some tribes might be richer than other tribes, but there was seldom a large gap between the rich and the poor within a tribe.

Power as well as wealth was usually shared. Tribes were loosely structured rather than tightly organized. Chiefs seldom had much individual power. The Cheyenne, for example, had a council of 44 to advise the chief. Instead of having a lot of political power, chiefs were generally religious and ceremonial leaders. Anglo-Americans did not always understand their limited power. Whites incorrectly believed that an individual Indian could make decisions and sign agreements that would be considered legal by their fellow Indians.

Another major cultural difference between the newly arriving settlers and the Plains Indians was their attitudes toward the land. Most Indians had no concept of private property. Chief Joseph of the Nez Percé eloquently expressed the Indian view: "The earth was created by the assistance of the sun, and it should be left as it was. . . . The country was made without lines of demarcation, and it is no man's business to divide it."

Chief Joseph of the Nez Percé expressed the views of Native Americans who had no concept of owning the earth. He proclaimed, "The earth and myself are of one mind."

The Indians refused to draw property lines and borders because of how they viewed the place of people in the world. Whites tended to see land, plants, and animals as resources to be exploited. Indians, on the other hand, stressed the unity of all life—and its holiness. As Chief Joseph said, "The earth and myself are of one mind." Thus people were not meant to dominate the rest of nature; they were a part of it.

Most of the Plains Indians believed that land could be utilized, but never owned. The idea of /owning land was as absurd as owning the air people breathed. To some, the sacredness of the land made farming against their religion. Chief Somohalla of the Wanapaun explained why his people refused to farm. "You ask me to plow the ground! Shall I take a knife and tear my mother's bosom? . . . You ask me to cut grass and make hay and sell it, and be rich like white men! But how dare I cut off my mother's hair?"

Indians had great reverence for all land. In addition, some particular pieces of land were considered especially sacred or holy. Certain bodies of water were seen as sources of healing and sites for worship. Some areas were burial grounds, where the spirits of ancestors were believed to reside. White settlers had little understanding of or respect for such Indian sentiments. The results could be tragic where interests collided.

From the white viewpoint, the most significant characteristic of many of the Plains Indian tribes, such as the Cheyenne, Sioux, and Arapaho, was their ability as mounted warriors. Using horses introduced by the Spanish, they had resisted white encroachment for two centuries. Most had no desire for assimilation; they merely wanted to be left alone. "If the Indians had tried to make the whites live like them," one Sioux declared, "the whites would have resisted, and it was the same way with the Indians."

Although some tribes could coexist peacefully with settlers, the nomadic tribes had a way of life that was incompatible with miners, railroad developers, cattle ranchers, and farmers. To Anglo-Americans the Indians were barriers to expansion. They agreed with Theodore

Roosevelt that the West was not meant to be "kept as nothing but a game reserve for squalid savages." Thus U.S. Indian policy focused on getting more territory for white settlement. Prior to Reconstruction this was done by signing treaties that divided land between Indians and settlers and restricted the movement of each on the lands of the other. Frequently Indian consent was fraudulently obtained, and white respect for Indian land depended on how desirable it was for settlement. As the removal of the Southern Cherokees to Oklahoma had shown in the 1830s, compatibility of cultures did not protect Native Americans from the greed of whites.

During the Civil War, Sioux, Cheyenne, and Arapaho braves rejected the land cessions made by their chiefs. Violence against settlers erupted as frontier troop strength was reduced to fight the Confederacy. The war also provided an excuse to nullify previous treaties and pledges with the tribes resettled in Oklahoma by Andrew Jackson's Indian removal. Some did sup-

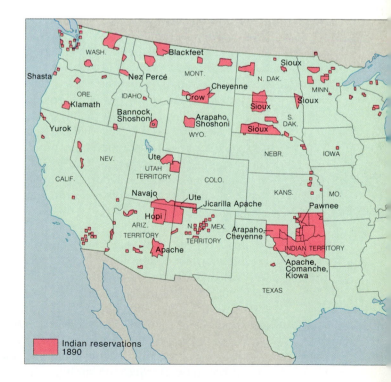

Indian Battles and Reservations

port the Confederacy, but all suffered the consequences of Confederate defeat. Settlers moved into the most desirable land, pushing the Indians farther south and west. Some Indians began to resist.

By the close of the Civil War, Indian hostility had escalated, especially after an 1864 massacre. The territorial governor of Colorado persuaded most of the warring Cheyennes and Arapahoes to come to Fort Lyon on Sand Creek, promising them protection. Colonel J. M. Chivington's militia, however, attacked an Indian camp flying a white flag and the American flag and killed hundreds of Indian men, women, and children. The following year Congress established a committee to investigate the causes of conflict. Its final report in 1867 led to the creation of an Indian Peace Commission charged with negotiating settlements. At two conferences in 1867 and 1868, Indian chiefs were asked to restrict their tribes to reservations in the undesirable lands of Oklahoma and the Black Hills of the Dakotas in return for supplies and assistance from the government.

Most Indians did not consider the offer very generous. Some acquiesced and others resisted, but in the end federal authorities subdued or killed them all. Several factors made their resistance unsuccessful. Railroads had penetrated the West, bringing in both settlers and federal troops more rapidly. Most important, however, was the destruction of the buffalo herds. Just as modern Americans would be helpless without oil or electricity, the Plains Indians' culture could not survive the near extinction of the buffalo by professional and sport hunters. In 1872 the Indian commissioner accurately forecasted that in a few years the "most powerful and hostile bands of today" would be "reduced to the condition of supplicants for charity."

In 1876, the final year of Reconstruction, Lieutenant Colonel George A. Custer's defeat at Little Bighorn called attention to the "Indian problem." The stage was set for this confrontation with Chief Sitting Bull's Sioux warriors and their Cheyenne allies two years earlier when gold was discovered in the Black Hills. The territory suddenly became tempting, and miners began pouring into the lands guaranteed to the Indians only five years before. "The white man is in the Black Hills just like maggots," one Indian lamented.

Despite Sitting Bull's victory, the die had been cast during Reconstruction. All that remained were "mopping up" exercises. Federal authorities solved the Indian problem by reducing the number of Indians to a level that posed no threat. Still, white Americans would not leave the Indians alone. The exact nature of the Indians' status, like that of African-Americans, would be determined after Reconstruction was over. The treatment of both, as well as of immigrants, would be justified by the increasingly virulent racism of whites, which was given "scientific" support by the scholars of the late nineteenth century. One thing was clear in 1876: Northerners who believed that the only good Indian was a dead Indian could hardly condemn Southern whites for their treatment of African-Americans. The patriotism engendered by the 1876 centennial of the Declaration of Independence also fostered a desire for unity among white Americans at the expense of nonwhites.

Final Retreat from Reconstruction

By 1876, fewer Americans championed black rights than had at the close of the war. Some of the old abolitionist Radicals had grown tired of what had become a protracted and complex problem. They therefore justified their withdrawal from the fight by the failures of some Southern Reconstruction governments. Those least likely to do so, such as Thaddeus Stevens and Charles Sumner, were dead. Until his death in 1874, Sumner had struggled to get Congress to pass a civil rights act that would spell out more specifically the guarantees of the Fourteenth Amendment. He proposed that segregation of all public facilities, including schools, be declared illegal and the right of African-Americans to serve on juries specified. After his death, in part as a tribute to him but mostly as one provision of a larger political bargain, Congress enacted the Civil Rights Act of 1875. The act did not include Sumner's clause on schools and did not provide any means of enforcement. For African-Americans it was a paper victory that marked an end of national action on their behalf. Never effectively enforced, the act was

In this 1898 watercolor, an Indian participant in the Battle of Little Bighorn depicts its aftermath. As Sitting Bull and others stand watching, Sioux and Cheyenne warriors ride horseback over the corpses of Custer (left center) and his troops.

rendered totally impotent by Supreme Court decisions of the late nineteenth century.

By 1876 all the elements were present for a national retreat on Reconstruction: the distraction of economic distress, a deep desire for unity among whites, the respectability of racism, a frustrated weariness with black problems by former allies, a growing conservatism on economic and social issues, a changing political climate featuring a resurgence of the Democratic party, and finally a general public disgust with the failure of Reconstruction. The presidential election of that year sealed the fate of Reconstruction and brought about an official end to it.

Corruption was a major issue in the 1876 election and the Democrats chose Samuel J. Tilden, a New Yorker whose claim to fame was breaking up the notorious Boss Tweed Ring. The Republicans nominated Rutherford B. Hayes, a man who had offended few—largely by doing little. Although Hayes had been elected governor of Ohio three times, to one observer he was "a third rate nonentity, whose only rec-

ommendation is that he is obnoxious to no one." As would become typical of most elections during the decades following Reconstruction, the campaign did not focus on any burning issues. The Democrats ran against Republican corruption. The Republicans ran against Democratic violence in the South. "Our strong ground," Hayes wrote, "is the dread of a solid South, *rebel rule*, etc., etc. . . . It leads people away from 'hard times'; which is our deadliest foe."

The election itself was so riddled with corruption and violence that no one can ever know what would have happened in a fair election. One thing is certain. The Democrats gained strength. Tilden won the popular vote and led Hayes in undisputed electoral votes 184 to 165. However, 185 votes were needed for election, and 20 votes were disputed—19 of them from Louisiana, Florida, and South Carolina. They were the only Southern states still under Republican rule with the backing of federal troops. In each, rival election boards sent in different returns.

With no constitutional provision for such an occurrence, the Republican Senate and Democratic House established a special commission to decide which returns were valid. The 15-member Electoral Commission had 5 members each from the House, the Senate, and the Supreme Court. At first it was evenly divided with 7 Republicans and 7 Democrats; politically independent Supreme Court Justice David Davis was the swing vote. Illinois Democrats then made a mistake and selected Davis as their senator. Thus, a Republican justice was appointed to replace him on the Electoral Commission, which proceeded to vote along party lines, 8 to 7, to give all the disputed votes to Hayes. Democrats were outraged, and a constitutional crisis seemed in the making if a united Democratic front in the House voted to reject the commission's findings.

A series of agreements between Hayes's advisors and Southern Democratic congressmen averted the crisis. In what came to be called the "Compromise of 1877," Hayes agreed to support federal aid for Southern internal improvements, especially a transcontinental railroad. He also promised to appoint a Southern Democrat to his cabinet and to allow Southern Democrats a say in the allocation of federal offices in their region. Most important, however, was his pledge to remove the remaining federal troops from the South. In return Southern Democrats promised to protect black rights and to support the findings of the Electoral Commission. On March 2, the House voted to accept the report and declare Hayes the presidential winner by an electoral vote of 185 to 184. After taking office, Hayes removed the troops, and the remaining Republican governments in the South soon collapsed.

Scholars once considered the Compromise of 1877 an important factor in the end of Reconstruction. Actually, its role was more symbolic than real; it merely buried the corpse. The battle for the Republican party's soul had been lost by its abolitionist faction well before the election of 1876. The Democratic party had never sought to extend or protect blacks' rights. The Supreme Court began to interpret the Fourteenth and Fifteenth amendments very narrowly, stripping them of their strength. Thus African-Americans were left with a small number of allies, and one by one many of their rights were lost during the next four decades.

CONCLUSION

As the Civil War ended, many unresolved issues remained. The most crucial involved the status of the freedmen and of the former Confederate states. The destinies of both were inextricably intertwined. Anything affecting the status of either influenced the fate of the other. Quick readmission of the states with little change would doom black rights. Enforced equality of African-Americans under the law would create turbulence and drastic change in the South. This difficult problem was further complicated by constitutional, economic, and political considerations, ensuring that the course of Reconstruction would be chaotic and contradictory.

Presidential Reconstruction under both Lincoln and Johnson favored rapid reunification

UNCONTESTED ELECTORAL VOTE	ELECTORAL TOTAL		POPULAR VOTE
REPUBLICAN			
Rutherford B. Hayes 165	185	🟢	4,034,311
DEMOCRATIC			
Samuel J. Tilden 184	184	🟠	4,288,546
GREENBACK			
Peter Cooper —	—		75,973
	349		8,398,830

*Contested Result.
Settled by Special Election
Commission in favor of Hayes.

Election of 1876

CHRONOLOGY
OF KEY EVENTS

1863 Lincoln proclaims 10 percent plan for Reconstruction, which requires states to abolish slavery and have 10 percent of the citizens who had voted in the 1860 election subscribe to an oath to support the Constitution and the Union

1864 Lincoln vetoes Wade-Davis Bill on grounds that it imposes too severe conditions on the readmission of the seceded states; Sand Creek Massacre of Indians in Colorado

1865 Congress establishes Freedmen's Bureau to aid former slaves and refugees; Confederate army surrenders at Appomattox; John Wilkes Booth assassinates Lincoln at Ford's Theater in Washington, D.C.; Andrew Johnson becomes seventeenth president; Thirteenth Amendment is ratified, abolishing slavery

1866 Civil Rights Act provides that all persons born in the United States are citizens and possess equal legal and property rights; Fourteenth Amendment is proposed

1867 Reconstruction Act, passed over Johnson's veto, divides the South into five military districts, each governed by an army general. Requires each state to adopt a constitution disqualifying former Confederate officials from holding office; grant black citizens the right to vote; and ratify the Fourteenth Amendment

1868 House of Representatives impeaches President Johnson; he escapes conviction in the Senate by one vote; Fourteenth Amendment is ratified; it guarantees citizenship to black Americans; Indian peace conference leads to establishment of reservations in Oklahoma and the Black Hills of the Dakotas; Ulysses S. Grant is elected eighteenth president

1870 Fifteenth Amendment is ratified; outlaws the exclusion from voting on the basis of race

1870–1871 Ku Klux Klan Acts are passed, which outlaw use of force to prevent people from voting and authorize use of federal troops to enforce the laws; Tweed Ring in New York City is exposed

1872 Crédit Mobilier scandal is exposed

1876 Custer is defeated at Little Bighorn; disputed presidential election between Tilden and Hayes

1877 Electoral commission awards disputed ballots to Republican Rutherford B. Hayes, who becomes nineteenth president

and white unity more than changes in the racial structure of the South. The South, however, refused to accept a meaningful end of slavery, as was blatantly demonstrated by the Black Codes. Congressional desire to reestablish legislative supremacy and the Republican need to build a national party combined with this Southern intransigence to unite Radical and moderate Republicans on the need to protect black rights and to restructure the South. What emerged from congressional reconstruction were Repub-

lican governments that expanded democracy and enacted needed reforms but were deeply resented by many Southern whites. At the core of that resentment was not disgust over incompetence or corruption but hostility to black political power in any form.

Given the pervasiveness of racial prejudice, what is remarkable is not that the Freedmen's Bureau, the constitutional amendments, and the civil rights legislation did not produce permanent change but that these actions were taken at all. Cherished ideas of property rights, limited government, and self-reliance, as well as an almost universal belief in black inferiority, almost guaranteed that the experiment would fail. The first national attempt to resolve fairly and justly the question of minority rights in a pluralistic society was abandoned in less than a decade. Indians, blacks, and women saw the truth of the Alabama planter's words of 1865: "Poor elk—poor buffaloe—poor Indian—poor Nigger—this is indeed a white man country." Nevertheless, less than a century later seeds planted by the amendments would finally germinate, flower, and be harvested.

SUGGESTIONS FOR FURTHER READING

OVERVIEWS AND SURVEYS

Eric Anderson and Alfred A. Moss, Jr., *The Facts of Reconstruction: Essays in Honor of John Hope Franklin* (1992); Mary Francis Berry and John W. Blassingame, *Long Memory: The Black Experience in America* (1982); Eric Foner, *Reconstruction: America's Unfinished Revolution, 1863–1877* (1988); Jay R. Mandle, *Not Slave, Not Free: The African-American Experience Since the Civil War* (1992); James McPherson, *Ordeal by Fire* (1982); James G. Randall and David Donald, *The Civil War and Reconstruction*, 2d ed. (1969); Kenneth M. Stampp, *The Era of Reconstruction, 1865–1877* (1965).

POSTWAR CONDITIONS AND ISSUES

Herman Belz, *Emancipation and Equal Rights: Politics and Constitutionalism in the Civil War Era* (1976); John H. Cox and LaWanda Cox, *Politics, Principles, and Prejudice* (1963); W. E. B. DuBois, *Black Reconstruction* (1935); John Hope Franklin, *Reconstruction After the Civil War* (1961); Peter Kolchin, *First Freedom: The Responses of Alabama's Blacks to Emancipation and Reconstruction* (1972); J. Morgan Kousser and James McPherson, eds., *Region, Race, and Reconstruction* (1982); Leon Litwack, *Been in the Storm So Long* (1979); Rembert W. Patrick, *Reconstruction of the Nation* (1967); James Roark, *Masters Without Slaves* (1977); Willie Lee Rose, *Rehearsal for Reconstruction* (1964); James Sefton, *The United States Army and Reconstruction, 1865–1877* (1967); Ted Tunnell, *Crucible of Reconstruction* (1984).

PRESIDENTIAL RECONSTRUCTION

Richard H. Abbott, *The Republican Party and the South, 1855–1877: The First Southern Strategy* (1986); Michael Les Benedict, *A Compromise of Principle* (1974); William R. Brock, *An American Crisis* (1963); LaWanda Cox, *Lincoln and Black Freedom* (1981); David Donald, *The Politics of Reconstruction* (1965); William B. Hesseltine, *Lincoln's Plan of Reconstruction* (1960); Peyton McCrary, *Abraham Lincoln and Reconstruction* (1978); Eric McKitrick, *Andrew Johnson and Reconstruction* (1960); James M. McPherson, *The Struggle for Equality: Abolitionists and the Negro in the Civil War and Reconstruction* (1964); Patrick W. Riddleberger, *1866: The Critical Year Revisited* (1979); Hans L. Trefousse, *The Radical Republicans* (1969).

CONGRESSIONAL RECONSTRUCTION

Michael Les Benedict, *The Impeachment of Andrew Johnson* (1973); Ellen DuBois, *Feminism and Suffrage* (1978); William Gillette, *The Right to Vote* (1969); Harold M. Hyman, *A More Perfect Union* (1973); Joseph James, *The Framing of the Fourteenth Amendment* (1956); Stanley I. Kutler, *The Judicial Power and Reconstruction Politics* (1968); Hans L. Trefousse, *The Impeachment of a President* (1975).

RECONSTRUCTION IN THE SOUTH

Dan T. Carter, *When the War Was Over: The Failure of Self-Reconstruction in the South, 1865–1867* (1985); Stephen J. DeCanio, *Agriculture in the Postbellum South* (1974); Paul D. Escott, *Many Excellent People* (1985); Barbara Jeanne Fields, *Slavery and Freedom on the Middle Ground: Maryland During the Nineteenth Century* (1985); Eric Foner, *Nothing but Freedom* (1983); Herbert G. Gutman, *The Black Family in Slavery and Freedom* (1976); Steven Hahn, *The Roots of Southern Populism* (1983); William C. Harris, *The Day of the Carpetbagger* (1979); Thomas Holt, *Black over White* (1977); Gerald Jaynes, *Branches Without Roots: Genesis of the Black Working Class in the American South, 1862–1882* (1986); Jay R. Mandle, *The Roots of Black Poverty* (1978); Robert C. Morris, *Reading, 'Riting and Reconstruction* (1981); Otto H. Olsen, ed., *Reconstruction and Redemption in the South* (1980); Michael Perman, *The Road to Redemption: Southern Politics, 1869–1879* (1984); Lawrence N. Powell, *New Masters: Northern Planters During the Civil War and Reconstruction* (1980); Howard Rabinowitz, *Race Relations in the*

Urban South (1978); George C. Rable, *But There Was No Peace: The Role of Violence in the Politics of Reconstruction* (1984); Peter J. Rachleff, *Black Labor in the South: Richmond, Virginia, 1865–1890* (1984); Roger L. Ransom and Richard Sutch, *One Kind of Freedom: The Economic Consequences of Emancipation* (1977); Joe Gray Taylor, *Louisiana Reconstructed* (1974); Allen Trelease, *White Terror* (1971); Ted Tunnell, *Crucible of Reconstruction* (1984); Jonathan M. Wiener, *Social Origins of the New South: Alabama, 1860–1885* (1978); Sarah Woolfolk Wiggins, *The Scalawag in Alabama Politics* (1977); Joel Williamson, *After Slavery: The Negro in South Carolina During Reconstruction* (1965), and *A Rage for Order: Black-White Relations in the American South Since Emancipation* (1986).

RECONSTRUCTION IN THE NORTH AND WEST

Ralph K. Andrist, *The Long Death: The Last Days of the Plains Indians* (1964); Robert F. Berkhofer, *The White Man's Indian* (1978); Eugene H. Berwanger, *The West and Reconstruction* (1981); Charles Fairman, *Reconstruction and Reunion*, 2 vols. (1971–1987); David A. Gerber, *Black Ohio and the Color Line, 1860–1915* (1976); William Gillette, *Retreat from Reconstruction* (1979), and *The Right to Vote* (1969); Norris Handley, Jr., ed., *The American Indian* (1974); Nell Irvin Painter, *The Exodusters* (1977); Keith Ian Polakoff, *The Politics of Inertia* (1973); Francis Paul Prucha, *American Indian Policy in Crisis* (1975); Ronald T. Takaki, *Iron Cages* (1979); Mark W. Summers, *Railroads, Reconstruction and the Gospel of Prosperity* (1984); Wilcomb E. Washburn, *The Indian in America* (1975), and *Red Man's Land/White Man's Law* (1971); C. Vann Woodward, *Reunion and Reaction* (1951).

BIOGRAPHIES

Fawn M. Brodie, *Thaddeus Stevens* (1959); David Donald, *Charles Sumner and the Rights of Man* (1970); Erik S. Lunde, *Horace Greeley* (1980); William S. McFeely, *Yankee Stepfather: General O. O. Howard and the Freedmen* (1968), and *Grant: A Biography* (1981), and *Frederick Douglass* (1990); John G. Neihardt, *Black Elk Speaks* (1932); Hans L. Trefousse, *Andrew Johnson* (1989).

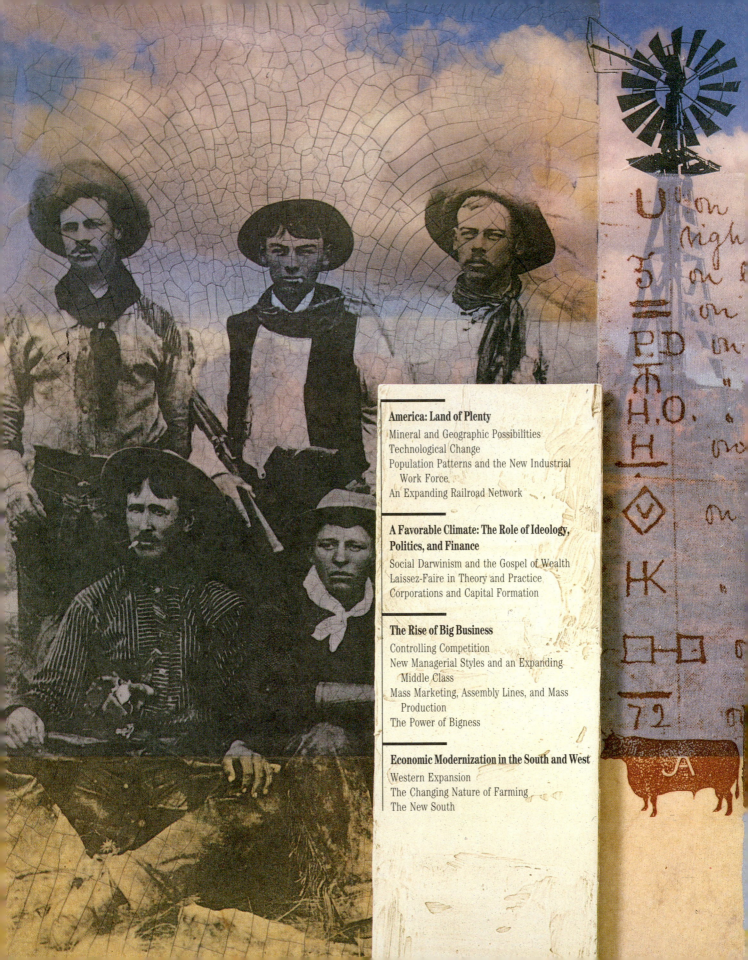

Emergence as an Economic Power

Fig. 1

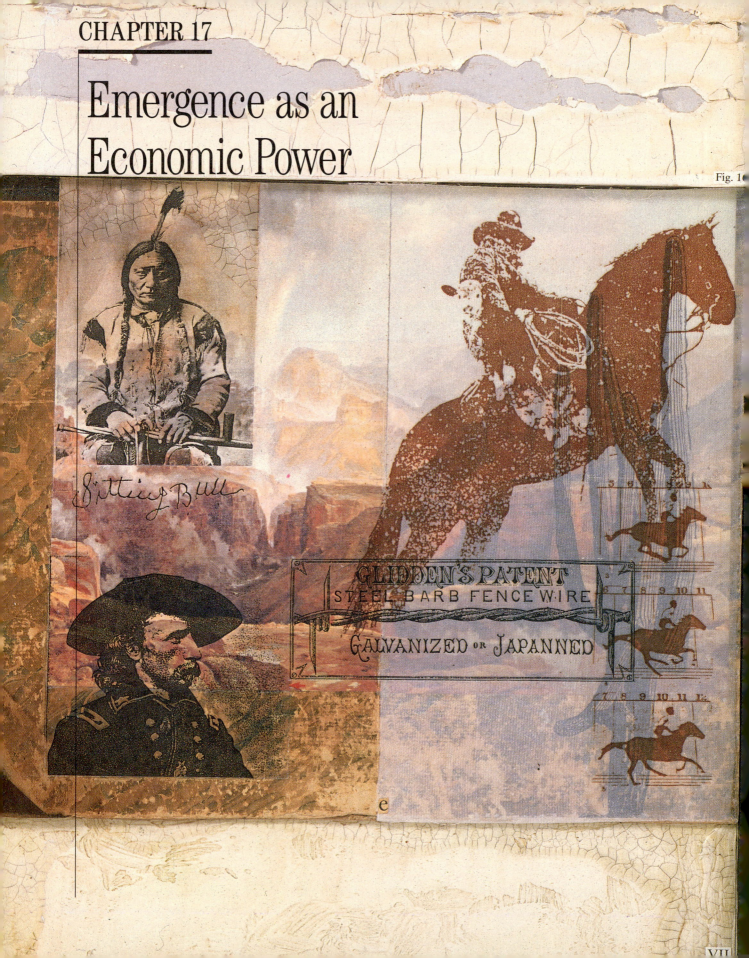

Sitting Bull

GLIDDEN'S PATENT
STEEL BARB FENCE WIRE

GALVANIZED or JAPANNED

On a cold winter's night in December 1900, 75 of the richest, most influential American businessmen gathered at the New York University Club. They met for a dinner to honor Charles Schwab, president of Carnegie Steel Company. Seated to the honoree's right was J. P. Morgan, the powerful investment banker and consolidator of industry. He had been placed there so that he would not miss a word of Schwab's speech. When Schwab finally rose, he delivered a veiled threat instead of a speech. With pretended innocence he rhapsodized over a bright future of low prices and stability for the steel industry. This future was to be ushered in by the formation of a scientifically integrated firm—one that combined all phases of the industry from the production of raw steel to the manufacture of finished products.

Morgan did not miss the point. Previously, Carnegie Steel had limited its operations to making raw steel. For several years Morgan and others had been busily creating trusts among the producers of such finished steel products as tubes and wire. Trusts were attempts to unite smaller competing firms in order to control market and raise prices. Trusts often used their combined power to put remaining competitors out of business. The steel products trusts, however, had a problem. Andrew Carnegie's company was the largest supplier of raw steel and he hated trusts. Thus when American Tin Plate Company threatened to cancel its orders with Carnegie unless he refused to sell to its competitors, he decided to beat them at their own game. He joined several informal arrangements to fix prices, known as "pools," only to sabotage them from within. Morgan and his cohorts soon realized that depending on Carnegie for raw steel would doom their consolidation schemes. Consequently, in July 1900 National Tube, American Steel and Wire, and American Hoop canceled all their contracts with Carnegie. They were going to produce their own steel or buy it from others—and put Carnegie out of business.

Rather than surrender, Carnegie telegraphed instructions to his company's officers: "Crisis has arrived, only one policy open; start at once hoop, wire, nail mills . . . Extend coal and coke roads, announce these; also tubes . . .

Have no fear as to result, victory certain. Spend freely for finishing mills, railroads, boat lines." By continuing his policy of spending money to make money, Carnegie knew he could produce superior products at cheaper prices. After Schwab assured him that they could manufacture tubes at a price $10 a ton cheaper than National Tube, he decided to pay no dividends on common stock and began plans to build a $12 million tube plant.

The antiquated and scattered plants of his competitors would have been no match for Carnegie's new ones. Panicked promoters scurried to J. P Morgan in the weeks before the testimonial dinner. Few doubted Federal Steel president Elbert Gary's assertion that Carnegie could "have driven entirely out of business every steel company in the United States." Carnegie, however, wanted to retire. Schwab's speech was aimed at producing a bargain, not a war. After the dinner Morgan fired dozens of questions at Schwab. Later they held an all-night session at Morgan's house. In the early hours of the next day Morgan finally said, "Well, if Andy wants to sell, I'll buy. Go find his price."

Schwab approached Carnegie on the golf course, where he might be more inclined to cooperate. Carnegie listened and asked Schwab to return the next day for an answer. At that time Carnegie handed him a slip of paper with his asking price of $480 million written in pencil. When Schwab gave Morgan the offer, he glanced at it and replied, "I accept the price." A few days later Morgan stopped by Carnegie's office, shook hands on the deal and stated, "Mr. Carnegie, I want to congratulate you on being the richest man in the world."

Two of the best had locked in combat, and both were victors. Carnegie had his millions to endow libraries, and anything else that struck his fancy. Morgan founded United States Steel Corporation. A colossus even among the existing giants of American industry, it was capitalized at $1.4 billion, a figure three times larger than the annual budget of the United States. The fates of Carnegie and Morgan reflected the momentous changes after the Civil War. Moving from the ranks of second-rate industrial powers, by 1900 the nation was the leader—with a manufacturing output exceeding the combined total of Great Britain, France, and Germany. The speed with which this happened seems more suited to fairy tales than reality. As Andrew Carnegie exclaimed in 1886, "The old nations of the earth creep on at a snail's pace; the Republic thunders past with the rush of an express."

Many yardsticks supported his assertion. Between 1870 and 1914 railroad mileage increased from 53,000 to 250,000—more than the combined mileage of the rest of the world. Almost every sector of the economy grew in multiples of two or more from the 1860s to 1900. Land under agricultural production doubled; the gross national product was six times larger; the amount of manufactured goods per person tripled.

This phenomenal growth resulted from the foundations laid by antebellum industrial development, the abundance of the land and its people, technological breakthroughs, and a favorable business climate—ideologically, financially, legally, and politically. The rapidity of change produced chaotic conditions, which led to new managerial styles and finally to economic consolidation and the rise of such supercorporations as United States Steel.

The forces of economic modernization swept through all sections and all segments of the economy. The results were profound alterations of the social order that touched virtually every aspect of life. Much of what is now commonplace—electric lights, petroleum, the telephone, the skyscraper, the hand-held camera, the typewriter—was largely unknown prior to the Civil War. The natures of work and marketing were drastically transformed, affecting all social relationships. The new order produced a few big winners, such as Carnegie and Morgan, but there were losers, too.

AMERICA: LAND OF PLENTY

In 1847 Walt Whitman boasted, "Yankeedoodledom is going ahead with the resistless energy of a sixty-five-hundred-horse-power steam engine. . . . Let the Old World wag on under its cumbersome load of form and conservatism; we are of a newer, fresher race and land. And all we have to say is, to point to fifty years hence

Lavish displays of wealth were common in the business world, as in this 1901 dinner meeting of officials of the Carnegie Steel Company to celebrate the formation of U.S. Steel.

and say, 'Let those laugh who win.'" By 1897 Americans were laughing. Their victory was facilitated by the abundance of the nation's new land, new people, and new ideas.

Mineral and Geographic Possibilities

Explorers and early settlers in what would become the United States were disappointed not to find an abundance of gold and silver such as had enriched their Spanish neighbors to the south. Only in the nineteenth century did Americans begin to realize the vast wealth that their expansion had brought. Most spectacular was the discovery of gold in California in the 1840s. It sparked frenzied prospecting all through the West. Each new discovery led to "rushes," creating mining towns almost overnight. Between 1850 and the 1880s thousands of men and women of almost every ethnic background helped create makeshift social institutions whenever and wherever strikes were made in California, Nevada, Montana, Idaho, Colorado, and the Black Hills of the Dakotas.

Wherever it moved, the mining frontier tended to follow the same pattern. Adventurous optimists searched for the elusive glint of precious metals. After living weeks or months at subsistence level, many went home poorer. A few, however, did strike it rich—usually as discoverers rather than miners. Inexpensive and inefficient placer mining (washing loose ore from gravel) quickly exhausted the easily obtainable supplies of precious metals. Extracting ore from beneath the ground and in veins of quartz was expensive. It required large capital investments best raised by mining syndicates, which were frequently financed by eastern and European investors. Prospectors usually sold their claims to these companies for a fraction of their value.

As mining became an organized business, its focus moved to less exotic but more useful minerals such as copper, lead, talc, zinc, quartz, and oil. These fed the growing demands of the industrializing East. By the 1880s mining no longer represented easy riches for pioneering individuals; it had become an integrated part of the modernizing, industrial economy of the nation.

The extraction of the nation's mineral resources played an important role in the rise of basic industry. Prior to the Civil War, manufacturing centered mainly on such consumer goods as textiles, paper, and flour, which were processed from farm or forest materials. Emerging basic industries such as steel, petroleum, and electric power depended on large supplies of various minerals, which seemed to become available as needed. Sometimes new deposits were found; other times new uses for minerals spurred the mining of known deposits.

Iron working was extensive prior to the war, and major deposits were found from 1850 onward in Michigan and Minnesota. Wrought iron could be forged into plows and other implements. It was limited, however, by its lack of durability and could be used successfully only on farms and in small businesses. Then Andrew Carnegie and others employed new technology to produce large quantities of relatively cheap and durable steel. The availability of steel opened new manufacturing vistas, and between 1870 and 1900 the output of steel grew from 850,000 tons to over 10.5 million tons.

The same pattern developed in the mining of other minerals. Copper had been found in Michigan prior to the war and in Arizona in the 1870s. A much richer copper deposit was discovered in Butte, Montana, in 1881. At first mainly used for household products, copper became a key ingredient in such new fields as oil refining, electrical generation and conduction, and telephone communications. Most went into the miles and miles of wiring that electrified the cities. The new uses for copper modernized America and increased demand for the mineral. Its output grew from 8000 tons in 1860 to 800,000 tons in 1914, and by 1900 the annual value of copper production almost equaled that of gold and silver combined.

Coal mining had also been a minor enterprise before 1850, but its production grew from about a half million tons in 1860 to 270 million tons in 1900. Its spectacular rise was generated by the increased use of coal-burning steam engines to power machinery and locomotives. In 1876 visitors to the Philadelphia Centennial Exhibition were awed by the massive Corliss reciprocating engine with its 30-foot fly wheel. Its size was no more impressive than the change it symbolized. As late as 1869 almost half of all power used in manufacturing came from water wheels; by 1900 coal-burning steam engines supplied 80 percent of such power. Earlier dependence on water supplies had forced manufacturers to locate along rivers—often in rather sparsely populated rural areas. The steam engine, and later gasoline engines and electric motors, allowed new freedom in selecting plant sites, and manufacturing began to move to the cities that supplied both workers and transportation connections.

Even more dramatic was the rise of the importance of petroleum. Many people were aware of large reserves in Pennsylvania, which seeped into streams and springs. Demand, however, was mainly limited to such uses as patent medicines of dubious value. In 1855 Pennsylvania businessman George Bissell decided to explore other possible uses. He sent a sample to a Yale professor who hailed its potential use as both a lighting source and lubricating oil. Encouraged by that report, Bissell funded drilling efforts, and in 1859 his employee, Edwin L. Drake, tapped the first oil well in Titusville,

Pennsylvania. Commonly labeled "Drake's folly," it marked the beginning of another growing industry. Oil was needed to lubricate the increasing number of machine parts, and in the 1870s about 20 million barrels were being produced annually. After John D. Rockefeller and others began refining oil into kerosene, it also provided a popular form of illumination, displacing candles before being replaced by electricity.

An officer in Rockefeller's Standard Oil Company is reputed to have volunteered to drink all the oil ever found outside of Pennsylvania. He was fortunate that no one held him to his word. Although for the rest of the century most of the nation's oil continued to come from the Appalachian area and the Midwest, growing demand led to the search for "liquid gold" in the Southwest. In 1901 a well shot a 160-foot stream of oil into the air at Spindletop, Texas. New sources were thus available for the development of the gasoline engine in the twentieth century. Abundant natural resources and technology often interacted—each shaping the evolution of the other.

Technological Change

Seldom has a single generation experienced such rapid change as in the late nineteenth century. Technology dramatically transformed much of people's lives. Bewildering as the changes sometimes were, the public generally welcomed new inventions with wide-eyed awe. Some of the most important public events were like mass rituals to the new god of technology. Completion of the first transcontinental railway at Promontory Point, Utah, on May 10, 1869, was greeted with parades and thanksgiving services as well as the ringing of the Liberty Bell. Awed sightseers crammed expositions celebrating "progress." At the Philadelphia Centennial Exposition, visitors confronted for the first time not only the Corliss engine but also bicycles, the typewriter, the elevator, Alexander Graham Bell's telephone, and even the "floor covering of the future"—linoleum. By the time of the World's Columbian Exposition at Chicago in 1893, the Corliss engine was obsolete, and many of the miracles of 1876 were commonplace "necessities." At the 1893 exposition

Called "Drake's folly," the first oil well was drilled in Titusville, Pennsylvania, in 1859. Edwin Drake (in top hat) got his inspiration from watching salt-well drilling operations.

everything was powered by electricity, including 5000 arc lamps and 100,000 incandescent bulbs.

These mass rituals reflected a nationalistic pride, voiced by the commissioner of patents in 1892: "America has become known the world around as the home of invention." The patent record definitely supported his contention. Whereas only 276 inventions had been recorded during the Patent Office's first decade in the 1790s, during the single year of the Columbian Exposition 22,000 patents were issued.

The impact of new inventions was enormous. In 1889 an economist wrote that to catalog "what the world did not have half a century ago is almost equivalent to enumerating all those things which the world now regards as constituting the dividing lines between civilization and barbarism." Technological change af-

The Columbian Exposition of 1893 in Chicago celebrated the enormous technological progress of the late nineteenth century. In the Palace of Electricity many visitors saw their first electric lamp.

fected the lives of individuals far more than any political or philosophical development of the era. Even a select list of late-nineteenth-century inventions would fill numerous pages. Offices became mechanized with the invention of the typewriter in 1867 and the development of a practical adding machine in 1888. As clerical work became more needed as well as requiring less skill, it was classed as women's work with lower pay scales. Numerous inventions such as George Westinghouse's airbrake, which made longer, faster trains possible, revolutionized railroad transportation. Later, electric street-cars profoundly changed the character of urban development by accelerating the move to the suburbs.

Along with transportation changes, communication innovations welded a unified nation from a collection of island communities. Links with the rest of the world also increased when an Atlantic telegraphic cable was completed in 1866. New inventions in the field of printing made popular newspapers with wide circulations a reality—along with mass advertising.

Photographic advances culminated in George Eastman's Kodak hand-held camera in 1888. However, few, if any, inventions rivaled the importance of Bell's 1876 "toy." Telephones rapidly became necessities—more than one and one-half million were installed by 1900.

Increasingly, new inventions such as the telephone relied on cheap and efficient sources of electricity. Here the name of Thomas Edison stands above the rest. Beginning his career at an early age by peddling candy and newspapers on trains, he soon became a telegrapher and invented various improvements. The success of his ideas convinced him to go into the "invention business." Establishing a research lab at Menlo Park, New Jersey, in 1876, he promised to produce "a minor invention every ten days and a big thing every six months or so." He pretty much kept his promise, inventing the phonograph in 1877 and the incandescent light bulb in 1879, as well as hundreds of other devices such as a better telephone, the dictaphone, the mimeograph, the dynamo, motion pictures, and electric transmission. With backing from banker J. P. Morgan, he created the first electric company in 1882 in New York City and formed the Edison General Electric Company in 1888 to produce light bulbs.

As in all research, Edison followed a number of blind alleys, but his only serious mistake was the choice of direct electrical current. This limited the range of transmission to a radius of about two miles. George Westinghouse's development of an alternating current system in 1886 soon supplanted direct current, forcing even Edison's companies to make the switch. Westinghouse also acquired and improved an electric motor that had been invented by a Croatian immigrant named Nikola Tesla in 1888.

While a handful of inventors struck it rich, more often inventions paved the way to vast fortunes for such entrepreneurs as Carnegie. The success of most of the captains of industry came from their effective exploitation of new technology. Carnegie invented no new product but utilized such advances as the Bessemer and open-hearth processes to produce cheap and plentiful steel. In like manner, Rockefeller built his industrial empire on new refining methods, and Gustavus Swift's meat-packing operation depended on the invention of the refrigerated railroad car. Eventually machine-made, interchangeable parts revolutionized every industry engaged in mass production.

The course of U.S. industrialization was profoundly influenced by both the relative abundance of natural resources and scarcity of manpower. In the beginning, Americans burned wood extravagantly. Later, seemingly inexhaustible supplies of coal and metal ores continued the bias toward labor-saving and material-consuming technology. Thus while population only tripled, industrial output grew nine times larger between 1860 and 1914. Population changes and growth, however, played an important role in the expanding economy.

Population Patterns and the New Industrial Work Force

Technology produced machines that displaced many skilled craftspeople and farmers, but paid employment also increased. For example, by the 1890s mechanization allowed one farmer to harvest 18 times as much wheat as he had done by hand in 1830. Nevertheless, the needs of a rapidly expanding population created so many new markets that the agricultural work force still grew by 50 percent. At the same time nonagricultural employment rose 300 percent. As early as 1880 the number of people employed in manufacturing, transportation, and construction grew to 5 million from only 1.5 million a generation earlier. During the next decade, farmers became a minority for the first time, and by 1900 six out of every ten Americans made their living outside of agriculture.

Those not engaged in farming increasingly concentrated in the cities. Between 1860 and 1900 urban residents increased from 6 million to 24 million. This clustering of population was essential to the expansion of industry—both feeding it and being fed by it. Some economic historians contend that of all the factors spurring industrial growth none was more important than the rise of an American mass market. Both the urban population boom and the transportation revolution created markets unparalleled in vastness and accessibility.

Mass markets would not have inevitably led to mass production and mass marketing without the public's acceptance of standardized goods.

In his Menlo Park, New Jersey, laboratory, Thomas Edison aimed at practicality in his inventions. He eventually obtained over 1000 patents. Here he is listening to his phonograph in 1888.

Many people were lured to the cities with the promise of excitement, modern conveniences, and better, higher-paying jobs.

Several factors made Americans more receptive than Europeans to such goods. Class distinctions, though not absent, were more blurred and became increasingly so with the availability of ready-made clothing. Also, physical mobility broke down many of the local loyalties so prevalent in Europe. Such factors created opportunities that modern mass advertising exploited. Nowhere were changes greater than in the food industry. Food processors originally produced limited quantities for nearby markets. As transportation advances widened distribution areas, producers first relied on wholesale merchants and agents to sell their goods to the public. Then the marketing of consumer goods underwent a remarkable transformation. The communication revolution allowed manufacturers to peddle their wares directly to the consumer. Rather than selling nonperishable foods by the barrel to wholesalers, they now packaged them in smaller containers of standard size and weight. By 1900, $90 million was being spent annually to convince Americans of the advantages of specific brand names; modern advertising had embarked on its persistent quest to shape the tastes of the public.

Advertising increased demand for many products, creating more industrial jobs for urban consumers. The dramatic expansion of this industrial workforce was fed mainly by massive migration to the cities. Although more people were being born than were dying in American cities, the natural increase of the urban population accounted for no more than one-fifth of its growth. This was true for several reasons. A declining birthrate reduced the number of children produced by the average woman from over 7 in 1800 to 3.6 in 1900, and this decline was most pronounced in the cities, where more women worked outside the home and had access to birth control information. Also, infectious disease led to higher death rates in the cities; an 1890 report revealed that 24 percent of the babies born in cities died in their first year.

Four-fifths of the new city residents moved there. Some 8 or 9 million of the 18 million of them were probably migrants from rural America. They came to cities for a variety of reasons. One was an increasing surplus of young men and women in the countryside. Rural birthrates remained high while mechanization decreased the number of hands needed to produce a crop. Such surpluses naturally "pushed" people from rural areas, but the cities also "pulled" them with the promise of more excitement, variety, and modern conveniences. Urban jobs also paid more; in 1890 clerical workers earned more than three times as much as farm laborers. While the average agricultural laborer earned $244 a year, clerical workers averaged $848.

Internal migration, however, did little to meet the fivefold increase in demand for industrial labor. Even before the Civil War native-born Americans could no longer be lured in sufficient numbers to work in factories. Rural white Americans more frequently joined the growing ranks of white-collar workers. Rural African-Americans would have gladly taken even the lowest factory job. However, because of the persistent notions of black inferiority, they were passed over in favor of foreign workers. Thus in 1890 only 7 percent of black males worked in factories, and as late as 1900 about 90 percent of African-Americans remained in the South—the least urbanized section of the nation.

Unlike industrializing European nations, therefore, the United States did not rely primarily on its own population to produce its industrial work force. Instead large numbers of immigrants manned the factories. The "pull" of job opportunities combined with factors "pushing" Europeans out of their native countries to produce a virtual flood of immigration. Some European villages lost half their residents as millions of people came to the United States. The large numbers facilitated industrialization but eventually produced a backlash from native-born Americans (see Chapter 18).

An Expanding Railroad Network

Americans developed a love/hate relationship with the railroads. The same locomotive that inspired Walt Whitman's rhapsody to its "fierce throated beauty" was described by Frank Norris in 1901 as "the leviathan, with tentacles of steel clutching into the soil, the soulless Force, the iron-hearted Power, the Master, the Colossus, the Octopus." There might be differing visions, but no one doubted the importance of the railroads. "The generation between 1865 and 1895 was already mortgaged to the railroads," Henry Adams wrote, "and no one knew it better than the generation itself."

The railroads provoked strong emotions because of their crucial role in forging a new society. More than anything else, railroads transformed a continent of isolated communities into a unified nation with an interdependent economy. Their rails brought raw materials to population centers, making possible large factories that mass produced goods. Those goods could then be shipped to national mass markets over the same rails. Changes were required, however, before railroads could meet the needs of an expanding economy.

The early railroads were strictly local affairs. By 1865 there were already 35,000 miles of rails, but few linked up in any rational way. Eleven different gauges of rail caused both goods and passengers to be unloaded from one set of cars and reloaded on another set—sometimes at a depot on the opposite side of town. Between New York and Chicago, cargo had to be unloaded and reloaded as many as six times. In some cases the inefficiency was intentional. Many small antebellum roads purposely

adopted different gauges and conflicting schedules to prevent being swallowed up by larger, powerful competitors.

Unlike many European rail systems, American railroads grew with little advance planning or regulation by government. Their development was far from orderly, and they sprouted like weeds in populous areas where immediate profits could be made. Especially in the antebellum South, too many small lines serviced the same places. Four hundred companies sprang up—each with an average track length of a mere 40 miles. Twenty competing lines provided service between Atlanta and St. Louis.

While too many railroads served some sections in the East, prior to 1869 no transcontinental lines linked the East and West coasts. Financing their construction was the major problem. The construction of the railroads of the East required large amounts of capital, but a return on the investment came quickly. This was not true in the West. There railroads often preceded settlement and, therefore, traffic for their lines. Because of the need for transcontinental routes, land grants became the solution.

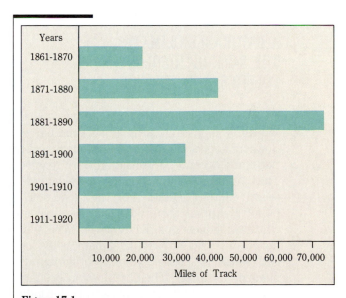

Figure 17.1
Railroad construction, 1861–1920. By 1865 there were 35,000 miles of railroad, but few lines connected in any logical way to provide direct routes from one location to another. Source: U.S. Bureau of the Census, 1975.

Contemporary and later analysts have questioned the size of those grants, but they undoubtedly had the desired effect. By the turn of the century there were five transcontinental routes.

At the same time, after some fierce competitive battles, a few eastern railroad companies gained control of many of the numerous local lines. When the dust settled, there were four main trunklines in the Northeast and five in the Southeast. The average track length of a railroad grew from a mere 100 miles in 1865 to over 1000 in two decades. Seven major groups controlled over two-thirds of the nation's railroad mileage. Gauges were standardized and a more efficient rail system emerged.

America's "newer, fresher race and land" provided the material basis for economic expansion. The "Land of Plenty" produced resources, people, and machinery in seemingly inexhaustible amounts and railroads tied them together. Nevertheless, even such wealth does not adequately explain the phenomenal mushrooming of American industry or the rise of large corporations. Less tangible developments nurtured the fantastic growth rate.

A FAVORABLE CLIMATE: THE ROLE OF IDEOLOGY, POLITICS, AND FINANCE

People, materials, and machinery were the "seeds" of industrialization. For a good harvest, however, good soil, favorable climatic conditions, and adequate fertilization were required. The bountiful economic harvest of the late nineteenth century depended on the "good soil" of popular support fostered by intellectual and cultural justifications. Favorable governmental policies created a desirable climate, while legal and financial developments provided the needed "fertilizer." The combination produced not only more industries but also larger industries. In 1870 shops and factories employed an average of 8 workers. Thirty years later the average work force was four times as large, and approximately 1450 factories employed 500 or more workers.

Social Darwinism and the Gospel of Wealth

Expanding economic opportunities fostered cutthroat competition from which fewer and fewer winners emerged. The road to wealth taken by the new captains of industry was strewn with ruined competitors and broken labor movements. Ruthlessness not only became increasingly necessary, it was also transformed into a virtue by the twin ideologies of Social Darwinism and the Gospel of Wealth.

For such men as Andrew Carnegie the works of Social Darwinists Herbert Spencer and William Graham Sumner helped to relieve any unwelcome guilt. "I remember that light came as in a flood and all was clear," Carnegie later recalled about his reaction to Spencer's writings. Spencer and his followers applied the biological concepts of Charles Darwin to the workings of society. Just as competition for survival ensured that the fittest of a species would live longer and produce more offspring, a similar process of natural selection in society was said to cause the fittest individuals to survive and flourish in the marketplace. Survival of the fittest supposedly enriched not only the winners but also society as a whole. Human evolution would produce what Spencer called "the ultimate and inevitable development of the ideal man" through a culling process. "If [individuals] are sufficiently complete to live, they do live," he wrote, "and it is well that they should live. If they are not sufficiently complete to live, they die and it is best they should die."

According to the Social Darwinists, poverty and slums were as inevitable as the concentration of wealth in the hands of the "fittest." Spencer pleaded that "there should not be a forcible burdening of the superior for the support of the inferior." His disciple Sumner declared, "If we do not like the survival of the fittest, we have only one possible alternative, and that is the survival of the unfittest." In other words, governmental or charitable intervention to improve the conditions of the poor was said to interfere with the functioning of natural law and prolonged the life of "defective gene pools" to the detriment of society as a whole.

The so-called fittest naturally greeted "scientific" endorsement of their elite positions with eagerness. John D. Rockefeller told his Baptist Sunday school class, "The growth of large business is merely the survival of the fittest. This is not an evil tendency in Business. It is merely the working out of a law of nature and a law of God." His statement illustrates that the captains of industry did not rely solely on science for justification; they also looked to religion. Indeed, although some business leaders used the jargon of Darwinism, Andrew Carnegie was one of the few actually to read and understand the dense, obtuse writings of Spencer.

Few business leaders were intellectuals, and some who understood Darwinist principles found the ruthlessness of the theory an unpalatable justification for their ruthless actions. They sought their solace in religious rationales for the accumulation of great wealth. Since colonial times, the Protestant work ethic had denounced idleness and viewed success as evidence of being among the "elect"—God's chosen people. Building upon this base, apologists constructed the "Gospel of Wealth." Some simply and boldly announced God's sanction of their wealth; Rockefeller asserted, "God gave me my riches." Not surprisingly, Carnegie was the one to produce a written, logically argued rationale. "Not evil, but good, has come to the race," he wrote, "from the accumulation of wealth by those who have the ability and energy that produces it." The masses would waste extra income "on the indulgence of appetite." On the other hand, "Wealth, passing through the hands of the few," Carnegie wrote, "can be a much more potent force for the elevation of our race than if it had been distributed in small sums to the people themselves." In other words, the "fittest" at the top could decide for people what they needed better than they could decide for themselves. In Carnegie's case, he took that responsibility seriously, distributing some $300 million to such philanthropic causes as founding libraries.

Among the most effective apologists for the wealthy, however, were religious leaders of the era. In 1901 Bishop William Lawrence proclaimed, "Godliness is in league with riches." Not only did the elite deserve their riches, but the poor also were responsible for their status. The eminent preacher Henry Ward Beecher argued that "no man suffers from poverty unless it be more than his fault—unless it be his sin." Perhaps the most popular evangelist for the Gospel of Wealth was Russell Conwell, who delivered his celebrated "Acres of Diamonds" speech approximately 6000 times between 1861 and 1925. In it he declared that anyone could get rich and asserted, "I say that you ought to get rich, and it is your duty to get rich." To those preaching sacrifice and vows of poverty, Conwell proclaimed, "It is a mistake of these pious people to think you must be awfully poor in order to be pious." Instead he asserted,

> Money is power, and you ought to be reasonably ambitious to have it. You ought because you can do more good with it than you could without it. Money printed your Bible, money builds your churches, money sends your missionaries, and money pays your preachers. . . . The man who gets the largest salary can do the most good with the power that is furnished to him.

Thus the maldistribution of wealth was not only inevitable but also desirable according to both scientific and religious thought. Probably more important was the support provided by popular culture. *McGuffey Readers* continued to stress the virtue of hard work and its inevitable rewards in poems such as "Try, Try Again." Novelist Horatio Alger penned many stories whose heroes rose from poverty to comfortable middle-class status through a combination of diligence and good luck. Thus popular literature reinforced the idea that success always came to those who deserved it in America, the land of opportunity. Finally, economic theory also lent respectability to greed and to the idea that government should not intervene in the economy.

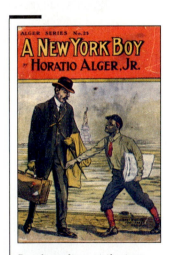

Popular culture at the turn of the century reinforced the American dream. In the Horatio Alger stories, the hero always escapes poverty through hard work and good fortune and joins the middle class.

Laissez-Faire in Theory and Practice

In 1776 Adam Smith's *The Wealth of Nations* presented arguments that would long be used to explain the workings of a free economy and to prescribe government's role in that economy. Smith asserted that the market was directed and controlled by an "invisible hand" composed of a multitude of individual choices. If government did not meddle, competition engendered by an unregulated market naturally led to the production of desired goods and services at reasonable prices. Short supply of a good in demand increased the price of that good, thereby encouraging more people to produce it in order to reap large profits. This increased production eventually caused the price to fall as supply equaled or even exceeded demand. In short, if everyone were left free to act according to self-interest, the result would be an economy best suited to meet the needs of general society.

Acceptance of the "invisible hand" of supply and demand economic theory naturally led to a policy called "laissez-faire." Government's proper role was to leave the economy alone. Apologists maintained that any governmental interference inevitably disrupted the operation of the natural forces that ordered the economy—thus producing a disorderly, inefficient market. Business leaders naturally endorsed the theory's rejection of governmental regulation. At the same time, however, they saw no contradiction in asking for government aid and subsidies to foster industrialization. To a large extent the industrialists got what they wanted—a laissez-faire policy that left them alone, except to help. Ironically, this distortion of theory helped to produce an economy where business consolidation wreaked havoc

Following the Civil War, government did little to regulate business. As a result, no laws protected consumers from fraudulent services or products like this claim for patent medicine.

upon the very competition needed for natural regulation of the economy.

Absolute free enterprise never really existed. There was plenty of governmental activity—just not in the area of regulation. Indeed the freedom of action given to businesspeople following the Civil War boggles the modern mind. No laws protected the consumer from adulterated foods, spurious claims for ineffective or even dangerous patent medicines, the sale of stock in nonexistent companies, or unsafe and overpriced transportation services. No national regulating agency existed prior to the establishment of the Interstate Commerce Commission in 1887. The proclamation "Let the buyer beware" asked people to make decisions and choices without adequate access to the information needed to protect their interests.

While denying support and protection to consumers or workers, government at all levels aided businesspeople. Alexander Hamilton's vision of an industrializing nation fostered by favorable governmental action never entirely died and was rejuvenated by the Republican party. Among the party's many promises in 1860 were pledges to enact higher tariffs, to subsidize the completion of a transcontinental railroad, and to establish a stable national banking system. The victory of Republican ideology undoubtedly helped to create a favorable environment for rapid industrialization. There was no sharp break with the past, however; nor was there a great victory by business over agriculture. The pattern of governmental aid to business was, as one historian has noted, "like certain kinds of embroidery . . . boldly visible but not of simple design." No form of aid was without antebellum precedents. Many concessions to business had wide public support that crossed party lines, often because other groups also benefited. Both the motives behind many actions and their results were mixed. In addition, the gains from some probusiness legislation were larger on paper than in practice. At the same time, agriculture was far from unrepresented and powerless, as can be seen by the passage of the Homestead and Morrill Land Grant acts, which provided free land to settlers and financed agricultural education.

Tariffs had a long history. Two days before Lincoln took office, Democratic President Buchanan signed the Morrill Tariff, marking the first tariff increase since 1842. That inaugurated an upward, practically uninterrupted, rise in tariff rates for the remainder of the century. At first, such American industries as steel needed to be protected from European competition to survive. Yet even after Carnegie and others were able to greatly reduce the cost of steel production, the tariff remained—allowing higher profits at the expense of consumers. As the average rate approached 50 percent, the duties on some commodities exceeded 80 percent of foreign manufacturers' prices. Without foreign competition, businesspeople were able to charge more for goods. Consumers came to resent these higher prices. Such bonanzas should not, however, obscure the fact that tariffs were widely viewed as serving the national interest by fostering economic independence from the British and others.

Additional forms of subsidy were also meant to serve the public good. Dwarfing all others were the land grants to railroads. In 1862 and 1864 Congress granted 20 square miles of public land in alternating sections for each mile of track laid by the Union Pacific and Central Pacific railroads in order to speed the completion of a transcontinental route. Only the scale of these grants was new; prior to the war railroads had already received nearly 20 million acres of federal land. By the time the grants ended, a total of 130 million acres of federal land went to various railroads, along with some 51 million acres of state land. Congress gave all those acres to a handful of people—creating some of America's wealthiest families. Nevertheless, as the 1869 celebrations of the completion of the first transcontinental line reflected, the public was not outraged. After all, even that incredible number of acres constituted less than 7 percent of the national domain in the West. In return the government paid only half fare to move troops and supplies. In addition, the value of the remaining land increased, and the uniting of the East and West spurred the entire economy. Only a decade after the grants' ceased were they denounced.

Business also benefited from favorable labor and financial legislation as well as low-interest loans. Individuals exploited these policies for personal gain, and the results were not uniformly positive. Aid to business, however, was never unlimited or unrestricted, and it enjoyed wide public support at first. Indeed nationalism and patriotism accompanied the process of industrialization. Many Americans took pride in the nation's growing economic power. When John D. Rockefeller explained his business activities by saying, "I wanted to participate in the work of making our country great," his words fell on sympathetic ears. Only after the problems of industrialization became more apparent did the public begin to cry "foul."

Corporations and Capital Formation

Such governmental aid as high tariffs, land grants, low interest loans, and lack of regulation provided rich fertilizer for economic expansion. The harvest brought both blessings and problems. The same is true of the rise of the corporation and decline of individual ownership and partnerships.

Corporations were certainly not new; they had long been used to finance ventures too expensive or too risky for a single individual to undertake—such as the English colonization of the New World. There were many advantages to incorporation for large-scale enterprises. By selling "shares" to a multitude of individual investors, the great sums of capital needed by modern industry could be amassed. Corporations did not risk the disruption of operation due to death of a partner or arguments between partners. Individuals could also hedge their bets. Rather than using all one's capital to buy a single ship, for example, one could buy a 10 percent interest in ten ships. Thus a hurricane or pirates could not wipe out one's investment with a bout of bad luck.

Despite the long history of corporations, changes dating from the Jacksonian period paved the way for their postwar domination of the economy. The first of these changes was the shift from the old practice of states issuing individual charters to each corporation. Under that system a corporation had to apply to a state legislature for a charter. New standard corporation laws allowed businesspeople to incorporate on their own, provided they met the requirements of the laws. Following the Civil War, courts also began to affirm the principle of "limited liability." Previously, bankruptcy could bring not only the loss of one's investment but also seizure of personal property by creditors. A corporation's liability finally became limited to its assets—making investment a safer and more desirable venture. One knew just how much could be lost.

One favorable court decision, *Santa Clara County* v. *The Southern Pacific Railroad* (1886), was a perversion of the Fourteenth Amendment. The Supreme Court ruled that a corporation was a legal "person" and therefore entitled to all the protections granted by the amendment. States could not deny corporations "equal protection of the law" or deprive them of their rights or property without "due process" of the law. In other words, all regulations had to apply equally to flesh-and-blood persons and to corporations. Corporations were eventually granted the "right" to "reasonable" profits—to be determined by the courts, not the state.

Instead of receiving "equal protection," corporations actually became privileged members of society. Real people whose rights were protected by the Constitution were also held personally responsible for illegal activities. There were no handcuffs or jail cells large enough for "corporate persons." Punishing individuals for corporate crimes was also difficult because corporate directors acted merely as employees of the company. A popular saying noted that a corporation had neither a soul to be damned nor a body to be kicked. Such advantages helped to spur the growth of corporations; by 1904 almost 70 percent of all manufacturing employees worked for corporations.

Perhaps the greatest advantage of corporations remained the ability to raise large amounts of capital. The expansion of industry in the late nineteenth century required big infusions of money. Every sector of the economy demanded capital: Farmers needed new machinery to increase productivity; manufacturers needed new plants to utilize the latest technology; cities needed new construction to service the needs of the urban population.

From where was all this money to come? Some, of course, was generated by the rising gross national product—the total value of goods and services produced in one year—which grew from $225 per person in 1870 to nearly $500 in 1900. New technology increased productivity and put more money into the hands of people—"extra money" not required to meet physical needs. Their collective decision on its use laid the foundations for the modern American economy. Many chose to use their extra money, or capital, to make more money by investment. The result was "capital deepening." An increasing share of the national income was invested rather than spent for personal consumption. Indeed the proportion of income going to capital formation almost doubled from 15 percent at the time of the Civil War to 29 percent in the 1880s.

Increasing amounts of this capital were invested in manufacturing. One reason was that investment bankers, such as J. P. Morgan, marketed corporate stocks and bonds. Foreign investment was also important; by 1900 Europeans had $3.4 billion invested in the United States, which represented approximately one-third of the almost $10 billion invested in manufacturing. This was rich fertilizer indeed for growth.

The net result of the favorable conditions of the late nineteenth century was industrial supremacy. Americans reveled in their nation's transformation to a colossus outproducing the entire world. Vast mineral wealth, technological breakthroughs, population changes, railroads, popular support, beneficial government policies, liberal corporation laws, and the availability of capital fostered this transformation. Many of these factors influenced not only the speed and size of the industrial "harvest" but also the nature of the fruit. At first the favorable conditions worked like overfertilized land—producing too many plants for the available space and resources. In this overgrown industrial garden competition created chaos until such entrepreneurs as Andrew Carnegie found ways to prune away their rivals.

THE RISE OF BIG BUSINESS

"You might as well endeavor to stay the formation of clouds, the falling of rains, the flowing of streams, as to attempt . . . to prevent the or-

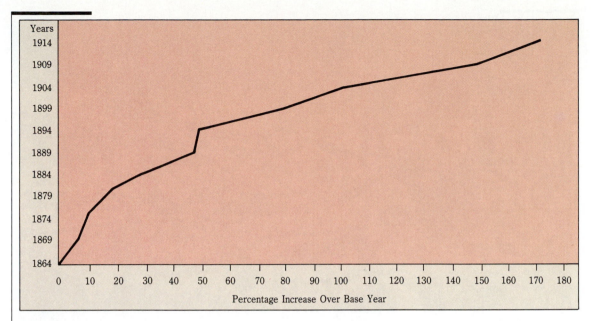

Figure 17.2
Index of manufacturing production, 1864–1914

ganization of industry." These words of John D. Rockefeller's attorney described what he considered to be the inevitable domination of entire industries by large corporations such as U.S. Steel. In industry after industry men like Rockefeller, Morgan, and Carnegie eliminated competitors and controlled markets. Methods of domination were refined and perfected over the course of time. The impact of this consolidation of industry was enormous. As companies grew larger, new management styles and more white-collar workers were needed. Mass production began to rise—profoundly changing the nature of work for industrial laborers. Also giant corporations amassed great power over production, people, and politics.

Controlling Competition

Most business leaders did not really advocate free enterprise fueled by competition. To them competition meant chaos, and they sought to eliminate it. J. P. Morgan, one historian wrote, "felt that the American economy should ideally be like a company organizational chart, with each part in its proper place, and the lines of authority clearly designated. He did not really believe in the free enterprise system, and like

most ardent socialists, he hated the waste, duplication, and clutter of unrestrained competition." To men like Morgan too many companies glutted the markets—producing chaos and cutthroat competition.

As America's first big business, the railroad industry was the first to confront the problems of competition. Most incurred gigantic debts to finance construction costs and expensive machinery. Debt payments were "fixed costs" that stayed the same regardless of how much business they received. As the 20 separate lines between Atlanta and St. Louis indicate, in many areas too many companies were after the same traffic. Thus railroads desperately sought to woo shippers to their lines by giving lower rates for bulk shipments and long hauls. To some preferred customers they also gave "rebates"—secret kickbacks below their published prices. They sought to make up for the lost revenue by overcharging smaller shippers.

Such tactics did not really solve the railroads' problems, especially when rate wars broke out. In the 1870s some railroad managers tried cooperation as a cure for competition. They formed regional federations to divide traffic equitably and to raise rates to increase profits. Such "pools," however, were not legally

After a period of intense competition in the railroad industry, a few rail barons consolidated lines by often using unscrupulous methods, seemingly carving up the nation at will.

enforceable. Greed frequently overcame scruples, dooming many such agreements.

For the railroads consolidation rather than cooperation became the key to controlling competition. Ruthless tactics sometimes accompanied consolidation. The former shipping magnate Cornelius Vanderbilt gained control of the New York Central Railroad in 1867 by buying two key lines that connected with it. He then refused to accept any rail cars going to or from the Central. His embargo worked but was much criticized. Vanderbilt's response was, "Can't I do what I want with my own?" He proceeded to acquire more lines to connect New York with Chicago and beyond. The net result of his ruthlessness was a personal fortune and an efficient, well-constructed railway system. Elsewhere buyouts and mergers eventually reduced the number of competitors—especially after depressions in the 1870s and 1890s.

Another weapon in the arsenal against competition was the "trust." John D. Rockefeller developed this device because the oil industry suffered from similar problems as the railroads. The relatively low cost of drilling oil wells at first encouraged the proliferation of so many small companies that output and prices fluctuated dramatically. After entering the oil business in 1862, John D. Rockefeller founded the Standard Oil Company of Ohio in 1870. This giant corporation was capitalized at $41 million. Competition, however, still created chaos, and Rockefeller lamented that "the butcher, the baker, and the candlestick maker began to refine oil."

Before creating the trust, Rockefeller tried a combination of pooling and rebates. In 1872 he organized the South Improvement Company. It was a combination of oil refiners and railroad directors aimed at dividing the oil carriage trade

John D. Rockefeller used ruthless techniques to eliminate competition and consolidate the oil-refining industry.

between the railroads. In return for a guaranteed share of the shipments, Rockefeller convinced the railroads to give rebates. Eventually Rockefeller was able to obtain rebates not only on the oil he shipped but also on the shipments of his competitors. Thus Rockefeller could undersell his competitors, whom he often bought out during times of economic depression.

Such techniques allowed Rockefeller to control 90 percent of the oil business, but legal problems arose from Standard Oil's far-flung holdings. His solution was the trust. In 1882 he convinced the major stockholders in a number of refineries to surrender their stock to a board of nine trustees. In return they received trust certificates that entitled them to a share of the joint profits of all the refineries. The benefits of this device were readily apparent. Pools had no legal standing and could be manipulated by some members to the detriment of other members. In a trust, however, competitive actions were of no benefit. Everyone shared all losses and gains.

Soon trusts began popping up like crabgrass throughout the economy. By 1888 a corporate lawyer wrote:

It is currently reported and believed that the "Trust" monopolies have drawn within their grasp not only kerosene oil and cotton seed oil, but sugar, oatmeal, starch, white corn meal, straw paper, . . . whiskey, rubber, steel, . . . wrought iron, pipes, iron nuts, stoves, lead, copper, envelopes, paper bags, paving pitch, cordage, coke, reaping and binding and mowing machines, plows, glass, and water works. And the list is growing day by day. Millions of dollars, in cash and property, are being drawn into the vortex.

Andrew Carnegie disliked pools and trusts, but found other ways to gain a competitive edge. One of these was "vertical integration." Buying the sources of his raw materials—iron ore and coke—he both lowered their cost to him and controlled his supplies. Not content merely with this "backward integration," he also practiced "forward integration" by acquiring many of the transportation facilities needed to distribute his product. This vertical integration lowered final prices by cutting out profit-taking by suppliers and shippers.

The key to Carnegie's success was his ability to cut costs without lowering quality. He used such traditional measures as wage cuts and increased hours for workers, but he also constantly explored new methods to increase productivity. When told that a plant had broken all records the previous week, he replied, *"Congratulation! Why not do it every week?"* By not focusing on short-term profits, he was willing to invest in expensive new technology to lower long-term costs of production. Reportedly, he opened one board meeting with the question, "Well, what shall we throw away this year?"

Carnegie often boasted that he knew almost nothing about steel. He hired experts to do that. What he did know was how to run a company and make money. His shrewdness took all variables into account. For example, he built his steel mill in Homestead—just outside the Pittsburgh city limits—which unlike the city was serviced by two railroads. He could therefore wrangle over rates, an opportunity not shared by his competitors in the city.

Carnegie effectively used all the economies of scale available to large firms. Soon he was able to undersell and destroy most of the dozens of steel companies that had blossomed

Andrew Carnegie rose from an immigrant textile mill worker to control the U.S. steel industry.

in response to the increased demand by railroads and industry. He also was a master at exploiting downturns in the business cycles. Most of his acquisitions were made during depressions, when prices were lower.

Competitors and labor movements suffered from Carnegie's actions, but the result was better steel at cheaper prices. As Carnegie once noted, "Two pounds of ironstone mined upon Lake Superior and transported nine hundred miles to Pittsburgh; one pound and one half of coal, mined and manufactured into coke, and transported to Pittsburgh; a small amount of manganese ore mined in Virginia and brought to Pittsburgh . . . these four pounds of materials [are] manufactured into one pound of steel, for which the consumer pays one cent." Such cheap steel aided the expansion of the railroads and the rise of other industries.

Of course, Carnegie was well-paid for these benefits—receiving almost a half billion dollars when he sold Carnegie Steel to J. P. Morgan. That sale illustrates another factor in consolidation: the role of bankers. Morgan and other bankers often stepped in during economic panics to reorganize bankrupt companies. They chewed up failing companies and railroads and spat them out as single supercorporations. The result was a more orderly economy, but at the price of centralizing vast economic power into the hands of a few unelected individuals. As one wit quipped when U. S. Steel was formed, "God created the world in 4004 B.C. and J. P. Morgan reorganized it in 1901."

New Managerial Styles and an Expanding Middle Class

The consolidation of companies into giant corporations created the need for new management techniques. Again, the railroads pioneered. As railroad companies grew larger, their activities covered hundreds of miles and employed thousands of workers. Safety and market conditions also required the entire system to operate as a single unit under a tight schedule. These conditions caused managerial problems. In the beginning, as one railroad expert wrote, "management had been personal and autocratic; the superintendent, a man

gifted with energy and clearness of perception, molded the property to his own will. But as the properties grew, he found himself unable to give his personal attention to everything. Undaunted, he sought to do everything and do it well. He ended by doing nothing."

Railroad management required a level of coordination previously unknown in business. In the 1850s Erie Railroad employee Daniel McCallum sought answers. For the longer roads, he asserted, "I am fully convinced that in the want of system lies the true secret of their failure." Seeking to create system by establishing a formal administrative structure, he knew he was breaking new ground. "We have no precedent or experience upon which we can fully rely." The result was the first organizational table for an American company. McCallum drew up a chart with a chain of command moving from local train agents through five branches representing main operating divisions to the president and board of directors. Responsibilities were divided on a functional basis. Top management was separate from daily operations.

Better accounting procedures were also needed to keep track of the monies collected and paid out by numerous conductors as well as station and freight agents. On the Baltimore and Ohio railroad the management and accounting of funds were given to new divisions: the controller's office and the treasurer's office. Later the Louisville and Nashville Railroad adopted a cost-accounting system to provide accurate data to judge the performance of their lines.

Other large-scale businesses began to adopt the accounting methods, hierarchical administrative structures, and divisions of responsibilities pioneered by the railroads. The result was the creation of "middle management," who coordinated the operations of far-flung local plants and reported to the top executives. Big businesses were now run by bureaucracies staffed by white-collar workers, who had no role in founding the companies they served but who began to work their way up the bureaucratic ladder.

A profound consequence of the new economic order was the expansion of the middle

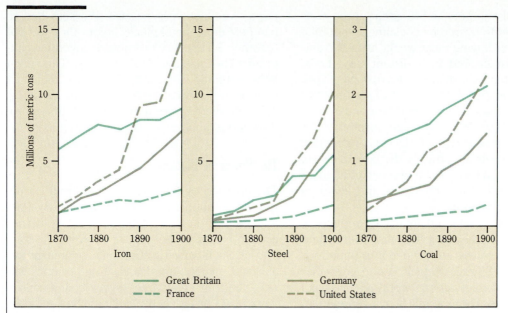

Figure 17.3
Iron, coal, and steel production, 1870–1900. Source: Carl N. Degler, *The Age of Economic Revolution.*
Copyright © 1977 by Scott, Foresman and Co.

class. Corporations needed accountants, middle managers, clerical workers, and sales representatives. The urban growth that accompanied industrialization also created demands for the services of professionals, shopkeepers, and government employees. The earnings of the middle class rose nearly 30 percent between the Civil War and the 1890s. By 1900 more than a third of urban families owned their homes. Although its members were sometimes dissatisfied with the new economic order, the middle class clearly derived benefits from and had a stake in it.

Mass Marketing, Assembly Lines, and Mass Production

Drastic transformations occurred in consumer industries as well as basic industry, as can be seen in the meat-packing business. There the interplay of new technology and new organization also ushered in new marketing techniques. Once again, the railroads played a key role by opening up the grazing ranges of the Great Plains. Because of its rail network, Chicago quickly became the major funnel through which

cattle were distributed from West to East. From its Union Stock Yards, cattle were shipped to abattoirs, or slaughterhouses, on the outskirts of eastern cities. The meat from the slaughtered animals was then distributed through local butchers to city residents.

There were several problems with such a distribution system, chief of which was the deterioration of the stock during long train journeys. Until the development of the refrigerated car, however, the only alternative was pickling or curing meat—processes that had already made Chicago the pork-packing center, but which were not as well suited to beef. Cattle dealer Gustavus Swift realized the possibilities opened up by refrigerated cars. Not only could fresh beef and pork be shipped more safely, but by centralizing slaughtering, waste products could be utilized. Profits were increased by making horns into buttons and hooves into glue. Eventually Swift formed glue, fertilizer, soap, and glycerine factories. People said that Swift used every part of a pig except the squeal.

Local butchers and wholesalers usually lacked refrigerated storage facilities, so Swift established his own warehouses, bypassing wholesale distributors and their cut of the profits. Swift had to overcome consumer resistance to the idea of buying meat weeks after the animal was slaughtered in a distant city. Local butchers often fed consumer distrust; New York shops frequently displayed signs reading "No Chicago beef sold here." Swift responded with a major advertising campaign stressing the superiority of western beef. His mass-marketing tactics proved successful. By the late 1890s six packers supplied almost 90 percent of all meat shipped in interstate commerce, and abattoirs virtually disappeared.

Swift also pioneered in mass production, employing assembly lines. The slaughtering and packing process was subdivided into numerous distinct jobs. Workers repeated one particular action as carcasses moved along on overhead conveyor belts. There was little wasted motion, and, as one of Swift's superintendents noted, "If you need to turn out a little more, you speed up the conveyor a little and the men speed up to keep pace."

Motion picture star Charlie Chaplin later parodied such tactics in the movie *Modern Times*. In it, a too-rapid conveyor created comic chaos. The waste of time, however, was no laughing matter to industrial managers. Engineer Frederick W. Taylor laid the foundations of "scientific management" with his time-and-motion studies. Stopwatch in hand, Taylor observed the workers and then divided the manufacturing process into units that allowed for little wasted motion. He believed his ideas would benefit labor as well as management. Instead, his aim "to induce men to act as nearly like machines as possible" promoted monotony and displaced workers—especially higher paid skilled ones.

In meat packing, machinery did not replace workers; their work was merely subdivided to increase efficiency. In other industries, after the work had been broken down into simple, repetitive tasks, machines were created to replace hand labor. Mass production by machine worked best on products made from standardized, interchangeable parts. The idea of standardized parts was not new; they had been used before the Civil War to make such products as guns. The early machines that cut the

parts were not very precise. Workers had to hand file most metal pieces before they were fit together. As in other businesses, inventions improved the machine tool industry. The turret lathe automatically made a series of complex cuts in metal with great speed and accuracy. The ingredients were now in place to mass produce large numbers of standardized goods.

The Power of Bigness

The creation of the gigantic U.S. Steel Corporation was not an isolated occurrence. By 1904 a single firm in each of 50 different industries accounted for 60 percent or more of the total output. Such concentrations of economic power alarmed many Americans. Competition was never entirely eliminated, however, and consolidation did bring such benefits as lower prices and higher standards of living. Nevertheless, the transition from local, independently owned shops and factories to giant national corporations with impersonal boards of directors dramatically altered the work and leisure time of the American people (Chapter 18). The transition was often painful for individuals and not always smooth. The economy experienced a frightening cycle of boom and bust. Three se-

Because the emergence of gigantic trusts concentrated economic power into relatively few hands, many people saw the trusts as the real "bosses of the Senate."

This portrait of the family of William Astor illustrates the lavish life-style of the rich. Parties of the wealthy were especially ostentatious; at one, guests smoked cigarettes rolled in one hundred dollar bills after drinking coffee.

vere depressions (1873–1879, 1882–1885, and 1893–1897) rocked the nation, causing widespread unemployment and business failures.

Big business also created a class of millionaires who flaunted ostentatious homes and lavish life-styles. For example, during the depression in 1897 Mr. and Mrs. Bradley Martin decided to give a costume ball. They invited most of the richest people in New York to the Waldorf-Astoria Hotel, which was redecorated to resemble the palace at Versailles in France. The hostess dressed as Mary Queen of Scots and wore an enormous ruby necklace that had once adorned Queen Marie Antoinette. One guest came in a $10,000 suit of armor inlaid with gold. Those few hours of entertainment cost the Martins $369,000.

When one realizes that in 1890 about 11 million of the 12.5 million families in the United States averaged less than $380 a year in income, it is obvious that all did not share equally in the economic expansion of the era. Wealth had al-

ways been concentrated and industrialization continued the trend. In 1890 the richest 9 percent of Americans owned nearly three-quarters of the nation's wealth.

Many people resented or envied the life-styles such wealth provided, but they feared the power it produced. Big business grew while government and organized labor remained relatively small. Thus business leaders wielded enormous power over many phases of American life. Some actions benefited the nation but were taken in a high-handed manner. For example, before the 1880s each location determined its time by the position of the sun. Even in cities fairly close together clocks were set differently; New York City and Boston were 12 minutes apart. To simplify schedules, in 1883 railroad owners established four time zones—without consulting any branch of government.

Such arbitrary power alarmed the American public. Some of the freewheeling railroad barons aggravated fears. Vanderbilt once re-

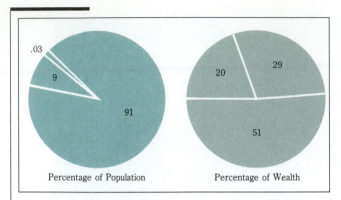

Figure 17.4
Distribution of wealth, 1890. The bulk of the wealth was concentrated in less than 10 percent of the population, while 0.03 percent of the population controlled 20 percent of the wealth. Source: George K. Holmes, "The Concentration of Wealth," *Political Science Quarterly*, vol. 8, no. 4, December 1893, p. 593.

marked, "What do I care about the law? Hain't I got the power?" Another time a member of the Pennsylvania legislature reportedly said, "Mr. Speaker, I move we adjourn unless the Pennsylvania Railroad has some more business to conduct." The railroad industry pioneered the accumulation and use of economic power. Others followed in its footsteps, often corrupting politics. Popular outcries eventually forced congressional action to curb their excesses (Chapter 21).

ECONOMIC MODERNIZATION IN THE SOUTH AND WEST

Although most industrialization occurred in the Northeast, all regions experienced profound changes as a national, interdependent economy emerged. In that process a world based on personal relationships was displaced by a more impersonal world based on contractual relationships. Just as the local cobbler was replaced by large factories mass producing shoes, the largely self-sufficient farmer who sold a little surplus locally to buy the cobbler's shoes gave way to cash-crop farmers who bought factory-made shoes by mail-order catalog—never

seeing the people who made or sold them. At the same time, his crops went to feed urban masses hundreds of miles away—none of whom he knew personally.

Some of the forces feeding the growth of industry also fueled agricultural expansion. Rural population kept growing, although not as rapidly as urban population. Both the number of farms and farmers more than doubled at the same time that farmers became a minority of the population. Most of these new farmers were in the West, which was being tamed and exploited in the late nineteenth century. Demand by the urban masses for food sparked a farming revolution based on mechanization and scientific agriculture. One region, however, did not share equally in the benefits of economic modernization. For a variety of reasons, the South failed to keep pace with the rest of the nation. Despite numerous efforts to forge a "New South," the region slipped further and further behind.

Western Expansion

The transcontinental railroads were not originally meant to "open up" the West. They were laid across what was called the "Great American Desert" in order to link the East and West coasts. The perceived worthlessness of the Plains was reflected in the willingness to give much of it away—to the Indians and later to the railroads. The mining frontier first altered perceptions of the region's value. Confrontations between miners and Indians foreshadowed the expulsion of the Indians from land that had been "given" them "forever" before whites realized its real worth.

Miners starred in the first act of the drama of western expansion and were followed by other casts of actors. The railroads played a significant role in creating new ways to exploit the land. In addition to mineral wealth, the region had two other plentiful resources: grass and cattle. Railroads provided the means to get the cattle to eastern cities, where urban residents wanted more meat to eat. The result was the birth of western ranching.

At first, ranching, like placer mining, did not require much capital. Both the cows and the grass were free. By 1860 some five million head of wild Texas longhorns had descended from cattle imported by Spanish colonists. They displaced the buffaloes that were being hunted to virtual extinction. In fact, cattle were so plentiful that they were considered almost worthless in the West. However, steers sold for $30 to $50 a head in Chicago. All that was needed was a way to get them there.

Joseph G. McCoy realized the potential for profit and established the first "cowtown" at Abilene, Kansas, where he built stock pens and loading chutes. Cowboys drove cattle there for shipment by rail to Chicago. Other cowtowns arose as some six million head of cattle endured the "long drive" to those sites between 1866 and 1888.

As longhorns could not be easily captured or herded on foot, the methods of the Mexican vaquero were copied and the American cowboy was born. Herding cattle while mounted on horses was hard, dirty work. One participant wrote, "It was tiresome grimy business for the attendant punchers, who travelled over in a cloud of dust, and heard little but the constant chorus from the crackling of hoofs and ankle joints, from the bellows, lows, and bleats of the trudging animals." Romantic stories both whitened as well as glorified the cowboy. At least one-third were Mexicans and African-Americans. Actually, the heyday of the cowboy was rather brief, for ranching, like mining, was soon transformed into an organized business.

Profits from a successful drive were very good—about 40 percent. This naturally attracted eastern investors, and soon the long drives declined as better methods were found. The lean, rangy longhorns were better suited to enduring the long drive than to producing choice, juicy steaks. They became even less desirable after being herded long distances. As the rail network expanded into Texas, ranchers switched from rounding up stray cattle to raising and breeding the longhorns with superior imported stock to improve the quality of the beef.

The cattle breeders needed large tracts of grassland for grazing and usually just appropriated land from the public domain. Most centered their operations around stream banks and claimed all the adjoining grasslands. During this open-range era, high profits attracted even

(Text continues on p. 576)

In the heyday of the open range, thousands of wild cattle were rounded up to be driven to cowtowns for shipment to the East.

$5,000 REWARD

JESSE JAMES
For Train Robbery

THE WILD WEST

At 6 P.M. April 5, 1892, a mysterious train, its shades tightly drawn, pulled out of Cheyenne, Wyoming, the state capital, bound for Casper, 200 miles to the northwest. Aboard the trains were 46 heavily armed vigilantes who carried an impressive array of weapons including army rifles, dynamite, and strychnine. The train had been chartered by Wyoming's cattle kings. The vigilantes' mission: to kill Johnson County settlers suspected of cattle rustling.

For more than two decades, the cattlemen had accused homesteaders of land grabbing and cattle theft. Juries refused to convict the small stockmen, and the cattle barons responded by taking the law into their own hands. In one incident,

on the night of July 20, 1889, 10 cattlemen captured 2 homesteaders and hanged them from a stunted pine tree. Altogether 6 or 7 suspected rustlers were shot or hanged. Despite lynchings and shootings, rustling continued, and in the summer of 1891, the cattle barons decided to launch an armed invasion of Johnson County and kill the most notorious rustlers. Members of the Wyoming Stock Growers' Association were asked to provide names of suspected rustlers. They compiled a list of 70 purported cattle thieves.

On Saturday, April 9, 1892, the vigilantes shot and killed 2 suspected rustlers at K C Ranch near the southern edge of Johnson County. Word of the killings quickly

spread to Buffalo, Wyoming, the county seat, 46 miles to the north. There, 200 small stockmen formed a posse to avenge the murders. At the T A Ranch, 14 miles south of Buffalo, the posse surrounded the vigilantes.

Before the invaders could be captured, however, Wyoming's acting governor and the state's senators sent frantic telegrams to President Benjamin Harrison declaring that a state of insurrection existed in Johnson County and asking that the U.S. cavalry be sent in to quell the disturbances. Early on Wednesday, April 13, the cavalry rode to the rescue and escorted the invaders out of Johnson County. The vigilantes, who included several federal marshals and state officials, were charged with first degree murder, but the charges eventually were dropped. The Johnson County war was over.

Today, it is commonly assumed that the roots of violence in American society lie in our frontier heritage of violence and lawlessness. According to popular mythology—disseminated by dime novels, pulp newspapers, and television and movie westerns—the frontier was a lawless land populated by violent men: outlaws, stagecoach robbers, gunslingers, highwaymen, vigilantes, claim jumpers, cattle rustlers, horse thieves, Indian fighters, border ruffians, and mule skinners.

How violent was the Wild West? Certain forms of violence and lawlessness were indeed common: warfare between Indians and whites, attacks on Chinese and Mexican minorities, vigilantism, rowdyism, drunkenness, opium addiction, gambling, vigilante executions, stagecoach robberies, and gunfights. Racially motivated acts of brutality represented the ugliest side of frontier violence. In 1871, in one of the most gruesome incidents, ranchers in California's Sacramento Valley tracked 30 Digger Indians into a cave and shot them, saving the children for last because they "could not bear to kill them with [a] 56-calibre Spencer rifle. 'It tore them up so bad.'" Instead, they were shot with a 38-calibre Smith and Wesson revolver.

Chinese immigrants faced particular hostility. In Los Angeles, on October 24, 1871, a white mob stormed the city's Chinatown district and murdered between 20 and 25 Chinese men and women. In Rock Springs, Wyoming Territory, on September 2, 1885, a heavily armed white mob attacked the town's Chinatown, set fire to the Chinese coal miners' shacks, and fired bullets at fleeing workers, killing 50, 10 percent of the town's Chinese population. A few days later, in Seattle, Washington Territory, a mob killed Chinese hop pickers while they were asleep in their tents. In November, a Tacoma mob routed Chinese immigrants out of their dwellings and loaded them into wagons and dumped them outside of town.

African-Americans and Hispanics also encountered frontier violence. In 40 Texas counties, at least 373 black freedmen were lynched or murdered between June 1865 and June 1868. In California, some 15,000 Mexican, Chilean, and Peruvian gold hunters were driven out of the gold fields by threats of lynching, branding, whippings, and ear croppings. Said one white miner: "Give 'em a fair jury trial and rope 'em with all the majesty of the law."

Vigilante lynchings represented another widespread form of frontier violence. The lack of courts of law and police forces in the West gave rise to committees of vigilance—extralegal committees organized to suppress and punish crime summarily—in frontier regions. These committees banded together to punish murderers, counterfeiters, corrupt government officials, and horse and cattle thieves. In a single year in California, 1855, 47 people were executed by mobs, 9 by legal tribunals, and 10 by sheriffs or police officers. Between 1865 and 1890, 27 vigilante movements arose in Texas pursuing outlaws like John Wesley Hardin. A final wave of vigilantism originated in rural southern Indiana in 1887. Known as the White Cap movement, local rural committees flogged drunks, prostitutes, and men who failed to support their families.

The most notorious perpetrators of frontier violence were the outlaws and gunmen, like Belle Starr, Billy the Kid, Black Bart, Frank and Jesse James, John Wesley Hardin, the Younger brothers, Butch Cassidy and the Sundance Kid, and the Dalton Gang, who held up stagecoaches and trains, robbed banks, and stole horses and cattle. Hardin and the Jameses—who ironically were the sons of ministers—as well as the Younger brothers learned outlaw strategy as Confederate guerrillas during the Civil War. Hardin, who was probably the most prolific murderer, shot and killed over 20 men between 1868, when he was 15, and 1878, when he was finally captured and incarcerated in a Texas prison. Frank and Jesse James, America's most renowned bank and train robbers, staged at least 26 daring robberies between 1866 and 1881 in Missouri, taking in half a million dollars. Black Bart (born Charles E. Boles) robbed 27 stagecoaches in 28 attempts in California between 1875 and 1882, using an empty shotgun as his only weapon.

Most popular accounts of Western banditry, however, appear to be grossly exaggerated and romanticized. Bat Masterson, who, according to legend, killed 30 men in gunfights, actually killed 3. Billy the Kid, who supposedly killed 1 man for each of his 21 years of life, also apparently killed 3.

Kansas's cattle towns, legend holds, witnessed a killing every night. But in fact in Abilene, Caldwell, Dodge City, Ellsworth, and Wichita, a grand total of 45 homicides took place during a 15-year span, 1.5 homicides per cattle trading season, never exceeding 5 in one year. In Deadwood, South Dakota, where Wild Bill Hickok was shot in the back while playing poker in 1876, only four homicides—and no lynchings—took place in the town's most violent year. And in Tombstone, Arizona, the "town too tough to die" and the site of the shootout at the OK Corral, where Marshall Virgil Earp and his brothers Wyatt and Morgan, backed up by gambler Doc Holliday, hurled the Clanton brothers "into eternity in the duration of a moment," only 5 men were killed during the city's deadliest year.

Despite the omnipresence of rifles, knives, and revolvers and the prevalence of saloons, gambling houses, and bordellos, rape, robbery, and burglary were relatively rare. "We could go to sleep in our cabins," wrote one miner, "with our bag of gold dust under our pillows minus locks, bolts or bars, and feel a sense of absolute security."

more investors. Eventually the ranchers joined other segments of the economy that were outproducing demand. As the Plains became overgrazed, beef prices dropped from $30 to $10 a head in 1885 and 1886. Poorer producers were driven out by these low prices, challenges to their land claims by sheepherders and farmers, and bad weather. A winter of terrible blizzards following the scorching summer in 1886 led to the death of 90 percent of western cattle.

After sometimes bloody battles for supremacy between these economic competitors, the "Wild West" was largely tamed by the 1890s. Ranchers who remained established legal title to their grazing lands, fenced them in with barbed wire, and practiced scientific breeding and feeding of their stock. The forces of economic consolidation had reached ranching—making it a business requiring large amounts of capital.

Land legislation of the era aided the monopolization of ranching by a relatively few "cattle barons." Large tracts of public lands were given away or sold cheaply through such acts as the Homestead Act of 1862, the Timber Culture Act of 1873, and the Desert Land Act of 1877. Enacted to promote socially desirable goals, all had large loopholes that were exploited by cattlemen and land speculators. To promote settlement, the Homestead Act gave 160 free acres to those who would cultivate it for five years. The Desert Land Act granted 640 acres at $1.25 an acre to anyone who would irrigate the land. The Timber Culture Act, based on the theory that the trees increased rainfall, awarded 160 acres to anyone who would plant trees on a quarter of the land. Cattlemen and speculators fraudulently claimed to have met the terms of the grants or hired dummy entrymen to stake claims for them. A bucket of water was sometimes the only basis for claims of irrigation. Lumber barons in California, Nevada, Oregon, and Washington similarly utilized other land-granting laws. Thus much of the newly discovered wealth of the West ended up in hands of a few winners in the great land lottery.

While the mining, cattle, and lumber frontiers offered some quick, easy riches before being transformed into capital-intensive businesses, the farming frontier required more patience to make any profits. By the time farmers

arrived in the new West, much of the best land had already been appropriated. Most of the 274 million acres distributed under the terms of the Homestead Act were eventually purchased by bona fide settlers from speculators and cattlemen. Other farmers bought land from the railroads, which promoted settlement to increase traffic in isolated areas. To lure settlers railroad companies often provided easy credit terms and extolled western opportunities in flyers and speeches.

Many farming pioneers soon learned that railroad propaganda sometimes overstated the promise of the West. When they arrived, they discovered a shortage of wood and water but an overabundance of severe weather, insects, and social isolation. The houses they built of "bricks" cut from thick prairie sod were functional but bleak. At first, many farmers managed only to eke out a bare subsistence. Eventually, however, western farmers were caught up in the forces of change that transformed agriculture as dramatically as other sectors of the economy.

The Changing Nature of Farming

When Congress passed the Homestead Act in 1862, most of the arable land east of the Mississippi was already taken. The established farmers of the Old Northeast adapted fairly well to the changing economy and were generally prosperous. Most did not try to compete with the new wheat and corn areas of the West. Instead they turned their efforts to supplying the rapidly growing urban areas with fresh vegetables, dairy products, poultry, and pigs. They also profited from rising land values by selling extra acres to residential and industrial developers at high prices. Although they may not have liked all the changes, most received a reasonable share of the fruits of economic expansion. The same could not be said for many farmers in the West and South.

The challenges of farming were much greater in the West, and when they were finally met, overproduction depressed prices. Cultivation of the West required new agricultural techniques and adaptations to the environment. The scarcity of trees not only dictated the building of sodhouses but also made the cost of fencing prohibitive. Until the development of barbed

Because of the scarcity of trees on the Plains, settlers built homes from "bricks" of sod. With walls 2 to 3 feet thick, the houses were gloomy but provided cozy and solid protection from the elements.

wire in 1874, crops were not easily protected from the millions of roaming cattle.

A more serious problem was the lack of water. Farmers came to believe they had found solutions by using new varieties of seed, pumping water from far below the ground surface with windmills, and using cultivation techniques known as "dry farming." In reality their success resulted mainly from abnormally wet summers in the 1870s, as they learned when conditions returned to normal. During the good times, however, optimism flourished. As one Kansas official noted: "Most of us crossed the Mississippi with no money but with a vast wealth of hope and courage. Haste to get rich has made us borrowers, and the borrowing has made booms, and the booms have made men wild, and Kansas became a vast asylum covering 50,000 square miles." Then came the droughts. By 1900 two-thirds of the homesteaders had failed, and farmers returned east with signs saying, "In God We Trusted; in Kansas We Busted."

In the South, the Civil War brought several changes that crippled agriculture. Wartime devastation destroyed half the region's farm equipment and killed one-third of its draft animals. The death of slavery also ended the plantation system, and replacements had to be found. The number of farms doubled from 1860 to 1880, but the number of landowners remained the same. The size of the average farm dropped from 347 acres to 156 acres, as sharecropping and tenancy rose. The farms were not only smaller but also frequently worked by people who did not own them. In other words, at the very time the rest of the economy was consolidating, Southern agriculture was marching off in the opposite, less efficient direction. Another problem was a shortage of cash, which forced Southern farmers to borrow against future crops. Crop liens and high credit costs kept a lot of black and white farmers trapped in a cycle of debt and poverty.

Many Plains and Southern farmers became losers in the economic modernization of agriculture. Nevertheless, both the winners and the losers were playing essentially the same game. That game was the commercialization of farming. Most of the rules were the same as those for manufacturers: specialization, new technology, mechanization, expanded markets, heavier capital investment, and reliance on interstate transportation. Most of these changes were wholeheartedly embraced by farmers of that generation until they fell behind their industrial cousins in the expanding economy.

Most farmers agreed with a farm journal's assertion: "Agriculture, like all other business, is better for its subdivision, each one growing that which is best suited for his soil, climate, and market." Specialization became apparent in the decline of subsistence farming and the growing importance of cash crops. Although general farming continued, most farmers planted more of their acreage in the single crop best suited for their land and market. Outside of the South, cash crops were usually supplemented by small gardens and stock raising. In Dixie cotton reigned supreme, and tenant farmers were often forced by landowners and merchants to plant all available acres with cotton. Most, however, specialized by choice.

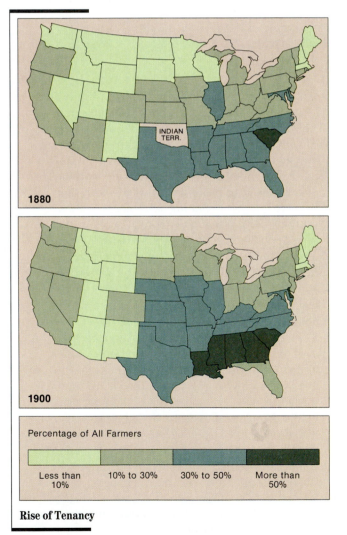

1880

1900

Percentage of All Farmers

Less than 10% | 10% to 30% | 30% to 50% | More than 50%

Rise of Tenancy

Technology and mechanization also revolutionized agriculture. Inventions came to the farms as rapidly as to the factories and increased productivity just as dramatically. After the mechanization of wheat farming, the hours required to farm an acre dropped from 61 to 3, and the per acre cost of production fell from $3.65 to $0.66. Machines entered every phase of agriculture, and by 1890 some 900 companies were manufacturing such items as hay loaders, cord binders, seeders, rotary plows, mowers, and combines. Farmers began to learn "scientific agriculture" at land-grant colleges that Congress established under the Morrill Land Grant Act of 1862. Agricultural researchers explored ways to increase production and found new uses for overabundant crops at agricultural experiment stations funded by the Hatch Act of 1887. Obviously, farmers were not opposed to all government aid to the economy.

As in manufacturing, mechanization brought economies of scale to agriculture, but they were not as easily exploitable. Although some bonanza farmers in the Dakotas cultivated 100,000 acres and more, the average farm remained 150 acres. The farms of the West were usually much larger than average because dry-farming techniques produced low yields per acre. To succeed, a western farmer needed more acres, and to work those acres he needed more machines; both cost money. Thus, like businesspeople, farmers needed access to capital. Unable to sell shares in their enterprise, most obtained personal loans using their land, machinery, and crops as collateral. Unfortunately, as production increased, prices fell, and to counteract lower profits farmers further expanded production in a self-defeating downward spiral. Mortgage indebtedness grew 2.5 times faster than agricultural wealth.

One solution to overproduction was to expand markets, which required cheap and reliable transportation facilities. Railroads, therefore, had as much impact in agriculture as in industry. Instead of selling surplus food to the local cobbler, American farmers fed distant urban masses at home and abroad; 20 percent of agricultural production was exported. This also meant that farmers' profits hinged on many factors beyond their control—such as the size of harvests in Argentina. Marketing became a key to success. One farm editor declared: "The work of farming is only half done when the crop is out of the ground."

Most farmers realized and, at first, even celebrated their status as businesspeople. Agricultural expansion was as dramatic as that of industry, yet farmers began to lose ground. In 1860 farmers owned 50 percent of the nation's wealth and received 30 percent of the national income. By 1910 those figures had dropped to 20 and 18 percent, respectively. At the same time farmers were becoming a minority of the population. When they discovered that they could not adapt as well as industrialists to the new economic order, they began to assert the superiority of rural culture. They stressed farmers' ties to the soil and heralded individualism and self-sufficiency as truly American characteristics. Their ties to a specific farm, however, were not very binding; in 1910 more than half of all farmers had lived less than five years on the land they were farming. Most farms were indeed individually owned and operated, but if farmers retained the outward forms of economic individualism, their functions were far removed from that of the independent, self-sufficient yeoman farmer.

The New South

Like the farmers, many Southerners wholeheartedly endorsed the new economic order at first. Some even saw the South's salvation in the destruction of slavery. In 1870, South Carolinian Edwin DeLeon proclaimed "a New South, whose wants and wishes, ends and aims, plans and purposes, are as different from those of 1860, as though a century instead of a decade only, divided the two." The most prominent advocate of this "New South" was Henry W. Grady, the editor of the *Atlanta Constitution*. He wrote and traveled extensively to proclaim the region's unlimited opportunities. Grady envisioned three major changes from the Old South: diversified farming, industrialization, and racial accommodation and cooperation. To win support for these changes, New South spokesmen linked the new order to the virtues of romanticized versions of the Old South and the "Lost Cause" of the Confederacy. Confederate heroes were named to boards of directors and appeals

At Tuskegee Institute in Alabama blacks received instruction in agriculture and the trades to prepare them for advancement in the "New South." Here, black women learn both upholstery and mattress making.

to Southern nationalism were made. The defeated South was encouraged to take up a new battle—for industrial supremacy. As one historian wrote, the "romance of the past was used to underwrite the materialism of the present."

Many shared Grady's vision. At the Cotton States Exposition of 1895 in Atlanta, a black spokesman for the New South emerged. Booker T. Washington, principal of Tuskegee Normal and Industrial Institute in Macon County, Alabama, was asked by the exposition's white organizers to give an address. His speech, which came to be called the "Atlanta Compromise," rivaled those of Grady in its optimistic appraisal of Southern potential. It also outlined a basis for racial cooperation. If whites would allow blacks educational and economic opportunity, Washington promised that blacks "will buy your surplus land, make blossom the waste places in your fields, and run your factories." He urged blacks to make themselves economically indispensable to whites and forego agitation for political and social rights. Their economic importance would bring them white acceptance—and the rights they desired.

Booker T. Washington, on his last southern tour in 1915, addresses an enthusiastic crowd in Louisiana. A firm believer in industrial training for blacks, Washington was opposed by a number of black intellectuals, who viewed his approach as a guarantee of continued black servility.

ducer of raw steel, and by 1890 Southern steel and iron made up almost 20 percent of the national total. At the same time Southern agriculture was recovering. Cotton production exceeded prewar records by the 1870s.

The tobacco and textile industries especially seemed to be bringing the dream to life. Both were based on major Southern crops. In the 1880s, James B. Duke introduced the cigarette industry to the region and followed a path similar to other captains of industry. Duke was a North Carolina tobacco grower when he encountered a machine that rolled cigarettes in 1881. He bought the patent and proceeded to change American tastes to suit his purposes. Prior to then most tobacco users either chewed the weed or smoked pipes or cigars. Duke enclosed "trading cards" featuring pictures and stories of popular heroes in packs of cigarettes to lure youngsters into smoking. At the same time Duke was buying out competitors and in 1890 created a trust through which he controlled 150 companies in an almost perfect monopoly until 1911 federal antitrust actions disbanded the trust.

Though entirely homegrown, Duke's enterprise had no distinctly Southern characteristics. The same was not true of the textile industry. Its development was flavored with a kind of regional revivalism and paternalism. Textile mills were seen as the key to economic salvation; investing in them was said to be a Southerner's religious duty. A good example was the founding of Salisbury Cotton Mills. In 1887 the town of Salisbury, North Carolina, had done little to recover from the war. It was poor, dirty, and full of saloons. Then a lean, intense Tennessee preacher named Mr. Pearson came to town. A big tent was erected for a revival meeting that lasted a month. Pearson drew huge crowds from the town and countryside as he preached that Salisbury needed to go to work. Idleness had bred corruption; building a cotton mill was the most Christian act his hearers could perform. The result was Salisbury Cotton Mills.

The evangelical appeal of the cotton mill crusade tended to create a myth that the mills were mainly built and run to aid the lower classes. The creation of "mill towns" helped to promote the image of mill owners as "fathers" to their employees. In these mill towns, the

Washington practiced what he preached. Tuskegee was a model New South institution, focusing on industrial education and promoting diversified farming. It boasted the only all-black agricultural experiment station. As its director, George Washington Carver advocated the utilization of undeveloped Southern resources and sought to expand markets for such crops as peanuts and sweet potatoes.

The New South optimism was based on dramatic changes taking place in the region. Railroad development increased at a rate greater than in the nation at large. The textile, timber, and tobacco industries boomed. Birmingham grew into a major pro-

George Washington Carver urged Alabama planters to raise peanuts and sweet potatoes, plants that would replenish the soil, rather than cotton, which depleted the soil and left it worthless.

company built houses, stores, schools, and even churches for the workers. In reality, many mill owners proved not to be such good "fathers." By local custom African-Americans were excluded from the textile mills. The workers were drawn from poor whites, and often the entire family worked in the mills. They worked an average of 12 hours a day. Wages were as low as 50 cents a day and were usually not paid in cash, but in "trade checks." These trade checks were accepted to pay rent in company houses or buy goods in company stores. Elsewhere merchants and landlords would not accept the checks at face value. Thus some mill workers never saw any cash, merely turning their trade checks back over to the mill owners in return for supplies and housing. It is no wonder that profits were high for mill owners. Those high profits caused a textile boom in the South, and the number of mills grew from 161 in 1880 to 400 in 1900.

Despite all the signs of progress major obstacles prevented the South's economy from keeping pace with the rest of the nation. Southern agriculture remained trapped in the inefficient sharecropping system and single-crop agriculture. Increased cotton production was accompanied by falling crop prices. By 1900 over half of the region's white farmers and three-quarters of black farmers were tenants. Most barely made enough to feed and clothe their families; few had the money to improve farming techniques or try new crops. By 1880 the South was not growing enough food to feed its people. Poor nutrition added bad health and disease to the region's problems.

The persistent ideology of white supremacy not only doomed Booker T. Washington's vision of black advancement but also helped keep the South mired in poverty. Race relations actually worsened in the 1890s as white Southerners struggled to keep black Southerners "in their place" (Chapter 21). In 1896 the Supreme Court ruled in the *Plessy* v. *Ferguson* decision that separate accommodations for African-Americans did not violate the Fourteenth Amendment if the facilities were substantially equal in quality. The effect was to legalize segregation—a disaster for both black and white Southerners. Accommodations were never really equal, and African-Americans suffered from inferior

schools and services. At the same time, keeping most of the black third of the Southern population in ignorance and poverty depressed wage scales and the tax base needed to support public education and other services.

Another key to the South's relative poverty was its shortage of capital, which was rooted in the slave system and the Civil War. Reliance on slavery and cotton had enriched the Old South but helped to impoverish the New South. Using slaves to grow cotton produced good profits, so that much of the Old South's capital had been spent buying slaves. In the five chief cotton states—Alabama, Louisiana, South Carolina, Georgia, and Mississippi—about 60 percent of the agricultural wealth was invested in slaves. Less than one-third of Southern farmers' assets were spent buying land and machinery.

While the North was using its capital to build canals, railroads, cities, and factories, the South used its profits to buy more slaves. Emancipation meant that as much as $4 billion that had been invested in slaves were lost. In addition, the war was largely fought on Southern soil. Railroads had been torn up, factories and cities were burned down. Fields were overgrown with weeds, tools were worn out, and a third of all farm animals had disappeared. Before the Civil War the South had seen little reason to use its capital to build factories and cities. After the war, the region no longer had the capital to do those things.

Forced to rely on capital from the North and Europe, Southerners sought to attract outside investment in many ways. At industrial expositions and in hundreds of publications and speeches, the South's rich natural resources and cheap labor supply were portrayed as avenues to quick riches. To attract manufacturers, several Southern state governments offered tax exemptions, land grants, and even cheap labor from "convict-lease" systems. In other words, states rented out their prisoners (often black) to private interests, providing a cheap labor source that often displaced paid labor.

In the late nineteenth century, Northern dollars did flow south, replacing Sherman's armies. In the 1880s Northerners increased their investments in the cotton industry sevenfold. They also provided most of the capital to rebuild and expand Southern railroads and to start the

Iron furnaces at Rockwood, Tennessee, c. 1874. Northern capital helped finance the fledgling iron and steel industry of the new South.

region's steel industry. However, the use of Northern capital in most industries also meant that the profits went to Northerners as well. A good example of how this worked is found in the story of the timber industry. In the postwar era, over 60 percent of the nation's forests were located in the South. A growing demand for lumber to build cities made timber the region's leading industry and number one employer. Yet in the end, the South was probably left poorer rather than richer by the exploitation of its timber.

Corrupt state governments allowed Northerners and foreigners to obtain vast tracts of timber land at costs far below their actual value. Temporary logging camps were set up and manned mainly by low-paid black workers. In the words of one visitor, these workers were "single, homeless, and possessionless." Once an area was stripped of its trees, the camp moved on to a new one. The overcutting of Southern forests destroyed many of them and created erosion and flooding problems. Most of the timber was turned into raw lumber at sawmills and sold to Northern factories to be made into fin-

ished products. Only in North Carolina did a significant furniture industry develop. The South therefore remained in a colonial economic position. In other words, for the most part the region supplied unfinished raw materials, such as lumber, for which prices were rather low. After these products were converted into manufactured goods in the North, the South had to buy those goods at higher prices than it had received for the raw materials.

For all these reasons the progress that was made did not alter the South's position at the bottom of the economic ladder. Although the South's share of national manufacturing doubled between 1880 and 1920, it rose only to 10 percent of the total—roughly the same percent it had at the start of the Civil War. Per capita income increased 21 percent, but fell from 60 percent of that of the North in 1860 to 40 percent in 1900. As happened in the West, the South's reliance on Northern capital kept the majority of profits going elsewhere. By the late 1880s farmers in both regions would unite to oppose the changes brought by industrial capitalism.

HRONOLOGY
OF KEY EVENTS

1856 Bessemer steelmaking process is invented

1859 Edwin Drake drills the first commercial oil well in Titusville, Pennsylvania

1861 Morrill Tariff is passed; first of a series of high protective tariffs

1862 Homestead Act gives 160 acres of free public land to those who would cultivate it for five years; Morrill Land Grant Act establishes many technical and agricultural colleges

1866 Cyrus W. Field lays the first permanent trans-Atlantic telegraph cable

1869 First transcontinental railroad is completed

1870 John D. Rockefeller founds Standard Oil Company

1873 Timber Culture Act awards 160 acres of public land to those who would plant trees on a quarter of the land

1876 Alexander Graham Bell invents the telephone

1877 Thomas Edison invents the phonograph; Desert Land Act grants 640 acres at $1.25 per acre to anyone who would irrigate the land

1879 Edison invents the incandescent light bulb

1883 Country is divided into time zones

1885 George Westinghouse promotes the development of alternating current

1886 *Santa Clara County* v. *Southern Pacific Railroad* rules that a corporation is a legal entity entitled to constitutional protection

1888 George Eastman produces the first handheld camera

1895 Booker T. Washington's "Atlanta Compromise" speech advocates that blacks focus on achieving economic success, rather than social and political equality

1896 *Plessy* v. *Ferguson* decision rules that the principle of "separate but equal" does not deprive blacks of civil rights guaranteed under the Fourteenth amendment

1901 Andrew Carnegie sells his steel company for almost $500 million to a group that was forming U.S. Steel

CONCLUSION

In one generation the United States became the economic colossus of the world. After a heated period of intense competition, the merger movement forged supercorporations that controlled the majority of their industries. There were many positive benefits of this economic expansion and consolidation. In some cases people were able to buy superior goods at cheaper prices. As Edwin Atkinson noted in 1886, "Did Vanderbilt keep any of you down by saving you two dollars and seventy-five cents on a barrel of flour, while he was making fourteen cents?"

Social mobility did increase. Although some skilled artisans slipped downward on the social ladder, upward mobility rates usually doubled the downward rates. Of course not all shared equally. Few made the transition from rags to riches that Carnegie accomplished. Most industrial leaders instead came from rather privileged backgrounds. The majority were relatively well-educated Protestants of native birth.

Average annual incomes also rose steadily for almost all classes of workers. On the other hand those wage increases rarely equaled the rising cost of living. Nevertheless, most families' standard of living improved because more members of the family worked for wages. Items that had been considered luxuries soon became viewed as necessities.

At the same time, individuals paid huge social costs for these advances. Some people paid a disproportionate share of these costs. Patterns of working and living dramatically changed. Many workers found themselves in a new status that imperiled their independence. Personal relationships were being replaced by impersonal, contractual arrangements. Shady corporate practices corrupted public morality. As Henry Demarest Lloyd noted in 1881, Standard Oil "has done everything with the Pennsylvania legislature except refine it." In short, all aspects of life underwent profound transformation, and the story of the late nineteenth century is the story of adaptation and adjustment to the new social and economic order.

SUGGESTIONS FOR FURTHER READING

OVERVIEWS AND SURVEYS

Daniel Boorstin, *The Americans: The Democratic Experience* (1973); Sean Dennis Cashman, *America in the Gilded Age* (1984); Carl N. Degler, ed., *The Age of the Economic Revolution* (1977); John A. Garraty, *The New Commonwealth, 1877–1890* (1968); Ray Ginger, *The Age of Excess, 1877–1914* (1963); Morton Keller, *Affairs of State: Public Life in Late Nineteenth Century America* (1977); Edward C. Kirkland, *Industry Comes of Age* (1961); Nell Irvin Painter, *Standing at Armageddon: The United States, 1877–1919* (1987); Alan Trachtenberg, *The Incorporation of America: Culture and Society in the Gilded Age* (1982); Robert Wiebe, *The Search for Order, 1877–1920* (1968).

AMERICA: LAND OF PLENTY

George M. Daniels, *Science and Society in America* (1971); Sigfried Giedion, *Mechanization Takes Command* (1948); Samuel P. Hays, *The Response to Industrialism, 1885–1914* (1957); Robert Higgs, *The Transformation of the American Economy* (1971); Leo Marx, *The Machine in the Garden* (1964); Elting E. Morison, *From Know-How to Nowhere: The Development of American Technology* (1974), and *Men, Machines, and Modern Times* (1966); D. F. Noble, *America by Design* (1977); Nathan Rosenberg, *Technology and American Economic Growth* (1972).

A FAVORABLE CLIMATE: THE ROLE OF IDEOLOGY, POLITICS, AND FINANCE

Robert Bannister, *Social Darwinism* (1979); W. Elliot Brownlee, *Dynamics of Ascent*, 2d ed. (1988); Thomas C. Cochran, *Business in American Life* (1972); Sidney Fine, *Laissez-faire and the General Welfare State* (1956); Milton Friedman and Anna J. Schwartz, *Monetary History of the United States, 1867–1960* (1963); Louis Galambos, *The Public Image of Big Business in America* (1975); Richard Hofstadter, *Social Darwinism in American Thought*, rev. ed. (1955); T. Jackson Lears, *No Place of Grace: Antimodernism and the Transformation of American Culture* (1981); Robert McCloskey, *American Conservatism in the Age of Enterprise* (1951); Daniel T. Rodgers, *The Work Ethic in Industrial America, 1850–1920* (1978); Martin Sklar, *The Corporate Reconstruction of American Capitalism, 1890–1916* (1988); John L. Thomas, *Alternative America: Henry George, Edward Bellamy, Henry Demarest Lloyd, and the Adversary Tradition* (1983); Christopher L. Tomlins, *The State and the Unions: Labor Relations, Law, and the Organized Labor Movement in America, 1880–1960* (1985); James Weinstein, *The Corporate Ideal in the Liberal State* (1968).

THE RISE OF BIG BUSINESS

Alfred D. Chandler, *The Visible Hand: The Managerial Revolution in American Business* (1977); Thomas Cochran, *Railroad Leaders, 1845–1890* (1953); Francis L. Eames, *The New York Stock Exchange* (1894); Jonathan Hughes, *The Vital Few* (1966); Matthew Josephson, *The Robber Barons* (1934); Daniel Nelson, *Managers and Workers: Origins of the New Factory System in the United States, 1880–1920* (1975); Glenn Porter, *The Rise of Big Business, 1865–1920*, 2d ed. (1992); John F. Stover, *American Railroads* (1961); George R. Taylor and Irene D. Neu, *The American Railroad Network, 1861–1890* (1956); Peter Temin, *Iron and Steel in Nineteenth Century America* (1964); Daniel Yergin, *The Prize: The Epic Quest for Oil, Money and Power* (1991); Olivier Zunz, *Making America Corporate, 1870–1920* (1990).

ECONOMIC MODERNIZATION IN THE SOUTH AND WEST

Lewis Atherton, *The Cattle Kings* (1961); Gunther Barth, *Instant Cities: Urbanization and the Rise of San Francisco and Denver* (1975); Ray A. Billington, *Westward Expansion*, 5th ed. (1982); Allan

G. Bogue, *From Prairie to Corn Belt* (1963); Orville Vernon Burton and Robert C. McMath, Jr., eds., *Towards a New South?: Post-Civil War Southern Communities* (1982); David L. Carlton, *Mill and Town in South Carolina, 1880–1920* (1982); Thomas D. Clark, *Frontier America*, 2d ed. (1969), with Albert D. Kirwan, *The South Since Appomattox* (1967); William C. Culberson, *Vigilantism: Political History of Private Power in America* (1990); Edward E. Dale, *The Range Cattle Industry, 1865 to 1925*, rev. ed. (1969); Pete Daniel, *Breaking the Land: The Transformation of Cotton, Tobacco, and Rice Cultures Since 1880* (1985); David Dary, *Cowboy Culture* (1981); Everett Dick, *The Sod-House Frontier, 1854–1890* (1937); Philip Durham and E. L. Jones, *The Negro Cowboys* (1965); Robert R. Dykstra, *The Cattle Towns* (1968); John S. Ezell, *The South Since 1865*, 2d ed. (1975); Gilbert C. Fite, *The Farmer's Frontier, 1865–1900* (1966); Paul Gaston, *The New South Creed* (1970); P. W. Gates, *History of Public Land Law Development* (1968); Dewey Grantham, Jr., *The Democratic South* (1963); Melvin Greenhut and W. Tate Whitman, eds., *Essays in Southern Economic Development* (1964); William S. Greever, *Bonanza West: Western Mining Rushes* (1963); Steven Hahn, *The Roots of Southern Populism: Yeoman Farmers and the Transformation of the Georgia Upcountry, 1850–1890* (1983); Robert Higgs, *Competition and Coercion: Blacks in the American Economy, 1865–1914* (1977); Robert V. Hine, *The American West*, 2d ed. (1984); W. Eugene Hollon, *Frontier Violence: Another Look* (1974); Julie Roy Jeffrey, *Frontier Women* (1979); Terry G. Jordan, *Trails to Texas: Southern Roots of Western Cattle Ranching* (1981); J. Morgan Kousser, *The Shaping of Southern Politics* (1974); Howard R. Lamar, *The Far Southwest, 1846–1912* (1966); Patricia Nelson Limerick, *The Legacy of Conquest: The Unbroken Past of the American West* (1987); Roger D. McGrath, *Gunfighters, Highwaymen, and Vigilantes: Violence on the Frontier* (1984); Melton A. McLaurin, *Paternalism and Protest: Southern Cotton Mill Workers and Organized Labor* (1971); Rodman W. Paul, *Mining Frontiers of the Far West, 1848–1880* (1963); Earl Pomeroy, *The Pacific Slope* (1965); Roger Ransom and Richard Sutch, *One Kind of Freedom: The Economic Consequences of Emancipation* (1977); R. M. Robbins, *Our Landed Heritage* (1942); J. M. Shagg, *The Cattle Trading Industry* (1973); Fred A. Shannon, *The Farmer's Last Frontier* (1945); Duane M. Smith, *Rocky Mountain Mining Camps* (1967); Henry Nash Smith, *Virgin Land: The West as Symbol and Myth* (1950); Frederick Jackson Turner, *The Frontier in American History* (1920); C. Vann Woodward, *Origins of the New South, 1877–1913* (1951), and *The Strange Career of Jim Crow*, 3d ed. (1974); Gavin Wright, *Old South, New South* (1986).

BIOGRAPHIES

Andy Adams, *Log of a Cowboy* (1927); Frederick Lewis Allen, *The Great Pierpont Morgan* (1949); Robert V. Bruce, *Bell: Alexander Graham Bell and the Conquest of Solitude* (1973); Alfred D. Chandler, Jr., *Pierre S. du Pont and the Making of the Modern Corporation* (1971); Robert F. Durden, *The Dukes of Durham* (1975); Julius Grodinsky, *Jay Gould* (1957); Louis R. Harlan, *Booker T. Washington: The Making of a Black Leader, 1856–1901* (1972), and *Booker T. Washington: The Wizard of Tuskegee, 1901–1915* (1983); David F. Hawke, *John D.: Founding Father of the Rockefellers* (1950); Maury Klein, *The Life and Legend of Jay Gould* (1986); Harold C. Livesay, *Andrew Carnegie and the Rise of Big Business* (1975); Allan Nevins, *Study in Power: John D. Rockefeller*, 2 vols. (1953); Raymond B. Nixon, *Henry W. Grady: Spokesman of the New South* (1943); Andrew Sinclair, *Corsair: The Life of J. Pierpont Morgan* (1981); Robert M. Utley, *Billy the Kid* (1989); Joseph F. Wall, *Andrew Carnegie* (1970), and *Alfred I. du Pont: The Man and His Family* (1990); George Wheeler, *Pierpont Morgan and Friends* (1973).

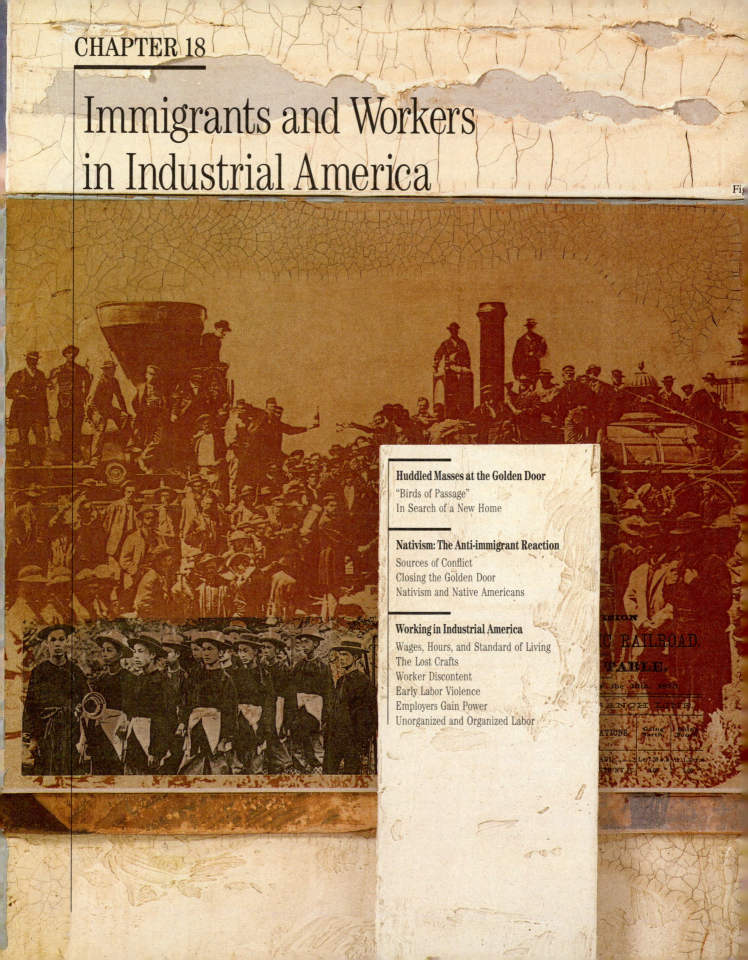

CHAPTER 18

Immigrants and Workers in Industrial America

In 1862, while the nation was locked in the grip of a terrible Civil War, Congress authorized the most ambitious building project that the country had ever contemplated: construction of a transcontinental railroad. The price tag was staggering: $136 million, more than twice the federal budget of 1861. The challenge was enormous: 1800 miles across arid plains and desert and the rugged granite walls of the Sierra Nevada and the Rocky Mountains.

Two companies undertook the actual construction: The Union Pacific began laying track westward from Omaha, Nebraska, and the Central Pacific commenced eastward from Sacramento, California. Of the two companies, the Central Pacific faced the more arduous task. It had to carve a rail bed through the high Sierra Nevadas. It also faced the more severe labor shortages. Managers constantly complained that they had too few workers and that too many of the few they had were unreliable.

In early 1865, the Central Pacific decided to dip into a new labor pool. Charles Crocker, chief of construction, persuaded his company to employ Chinese immigrants, arguing that the people who built the Great Wall of China and invented gunpowder could help build a railroad. Although the Chinese were paid less than white laborers, they fully vindicated Crocker's decision, earning reputations as tireless and extraordinarily reliable workers. Within two years, 12,000 of the Central Pacific's 13,500 employees were Chinese immigrants. Often working with pickaxes, hammers, and crowbars, the workers labored high in the mountains and inside tunnels. Explosions, avalanches, and other accidents left an estimated 1200 Chinese workers dead.

Despite their heroic labors, California's Chinese immigrants faced discrimination and racial violence. White Americans criticized their attachment to their homeland and questioned their loyalty to the United States. Perhaps Charles Wolcott Brooks, who spent several years in China, best articulated the views of Californian authorities. He was asked: "Do you think they have any particular love for our [American] institutions?" He replied:

"I don't think they have any at all. They come purely as a matter of gain—as a matter of dollars and cents. If it is profitable, they will come. If it is not profitable, they will not come. The very fact of their retaining their own dress and customs, and keeping themselves so entirely separate, as a people, shows that they have not. . . . The Chinese come abroad not to spend, but to accumulate. They maintain their own customs and language. . . . The Chinese . . . hate us most cordially."

Many Chinese may not have developed any emotional attachment to America or its institutions. After all, most never planned to stay in the United States. They loved the villages that they left behind, and they valued their own ageless Chinese customs. In America they sought the opportunity to work—not voting rights, education, or assimilation—and no work was beneath them. They resignedly accepted the most menial jobs in the mines, on the railroad construction gangs, and in the booming western cities.

For a large portion of the Chinese immigrants in the United States, home was always thousands of miles away. Since they only came to America to accumulate money, the Chinese immigrants lived as inexpensively as possible. They slept in huge halls, where as many as 1000 men could sleep on matted floors. Often 3 men would share one mat, sleeping in 8-hour shifts. By this method, a Chinese man could reduce the cost of his room to 10 cents a month. When not sleeping, he worked, and he sent most of his earnings back to his family in China, to whom he intended to return someday.

The majority left their wives in China. In America, there were 20 Chinese men for every Chinese woman. Occasionally the men would return to China long enough to impregnate their wives, but then it was back to America again for more "coolie" labor and Yankee dollars. If a Chinese man survived this difficult existence until he was 50 or 60 years old, he would return to China for good, respected by his family and village. If, as often happened, he died young in America, his bones would be sent back to China, and they too would be respected by his family and village.

Immigration, then, could in no way be interpreted as a rejection of China. In reality, it was a defense of the Chinese way of life, for the money sent home helped preserve the tradi-

Scorned and ridiculed for their "different" looks and customs, Chinese laborers demonstrated remarkable strength, courage, and endurance in helping build the railroads crisscrossing the country in the late nineteenth century.

tional order. America was not a sacred idea, but a means to an end, and, of course, sometimes a very lonely country. It was no wonder that opium, prostitution, and suicide were shadowy attractions of San Francisco's Chinatown.

Americans failed to understand the mind of the Chinese immigrant. To them, the Chinese were just non-Western, non-Christian, and non-white aliens. Although railroad builders and mine owners regarded the Chinese as good, inexpensive laborers, native-born American workers believed they brought down wages for all workers. Every major American labor organizer of the period, from T. V. Powderly and Samuel Gompers to Eugene V. Debs and Henry George, called for federal action to restrict Chinese immigration. Some leaders charged that the "coolies" so depressed wages that women in white

working families had to resort to prostitution to avoid starvation.

Labor leaders were joined by Irish-American politicians, the Catholic church, Eastern editorialists, and California workers in their crusade against Chinese laborers. All agreed, the Chinese should—*must*—be excluded from the United States as undesirable, unassimilable aliens. In 1882, Congress responded with the Chinese Exclusion Act, which suspended Chinese immigration. It was the first time that America closed its doors to any immigrants for ethnocultural reasons.

Later, other immigrant groups shared experiences similar to the Chinese. Native-born Americans saw other ethnic groups as beyond reform, as not having the "right stuff" to become Americans. Again and again labor leaders, religious authorities, and old-line Americans joined forces in opposition to certain groups of immigrants. The entire process toward restriction culminated in 1924 with the passage of the National Origins Act.

Yet immigrants contributed greatly to the growth of industrial America. They and their fellow workers—native-born white and black Americans—built the railroads that crisscrossed the country; mined the gold and silver that made other men rich; and labored in the oilfields, steel mills, coal pits, packing plants, and factories that made such names as Rockefeller, Carnegie, Swift, and Westinghouse famous. Without these men and their companions, there would have been no industrialization. In the process they made the United States an ethnically rich nation.

HUDDLED MASSES AT THE GOLDEN DOOR

On October 28, 1886, President Grover Cleveland traveled to New York Harbor to watch the unveiling of the Statue of Liberty. A gift from France, Frederic Auguste Bartholdi's grand statue was meant to symbolize solidarity between the two republics, but that was not how Americans and incoming immigrants interpreted the sculpture. For them it was a simple symbol of welcome, with the statue's torch lighting the path to a better future. A poem, written by Emma Lazarus and eventually placed at the base of the statue, emphasized the promise of America:

> Give me your tired, your poor,
> Your huddled masses yearning to breathe free,
> The wretched refuse of your teeming shore.
> Send these, the homeless, tempest-tossed to me,
> I lift my lamp beside the golden door!

In popular theory, the promise of America exerted a powerful pull on Europe and Asia. The United States stood for political freedom, social mobility, and economic opportunity. Since the first settlers landed in Jamestown, millions of immigrants had responded to the American magnet. At no time was immigration as great as in the late nineteenth and early twentieth centuries. Between 1860 and 1890, more than 10 million immigrants arrived on America's shores. Between 1890 and 1920 over 15 million more arrived.

America was not the only country to lure immigrants from Europe. Millions more immigrated to Australia, New Zealand, South Africa, Canada, Brazil, Argentina, and other underpopulated areas of the globe. In truth, seen in its worldwide context, the United States' pull was less powerful than Europe's push. During the nineteenth century, almost every European country experienced a dramatic population increase. Advances in medicine and public health standards reduced infant mortality rates and increased life expectancies, but available land and food could not increase to meet the new population demands. Almost every European country, from Ireland in the northwest to Greece in the southeast, experienced the same phenomenon. First came a population boom; 20 years later, when the baby boomers reached maturity, emigration increased sharply.

Historians have divided immigration to the United States into two categories: old and new. The source of the old immigration was northern and western Europe—England, Ireland, France, Germany, and Scandinavia. The immigrants were mostly Protestants (except for the Irish Catholics) and always white; a majority were literate and had lived under constitutional forms of government. Assimilation for them was a relatively easy process. The new immigration came from eastern and southern Europe. Greeks, Poles, Russians, Italians, Slavs, Turks—these people found assimilation more difficult. Politically, religiously, and culturally, they differed greatly from both the earlier immigrants and native-born Americans.

The shift from "old" to "new" occurred during the 1880s. For example, in 1882, when 788,992 immigrants arrived in America, most were German, British, and Scandinavian; 87 percent came from northern and western Europe. By 1907 this pattern had changed. That year when 1,285,349 immigrants landed in America, more than 80 percent were from southern and eastern Europe.

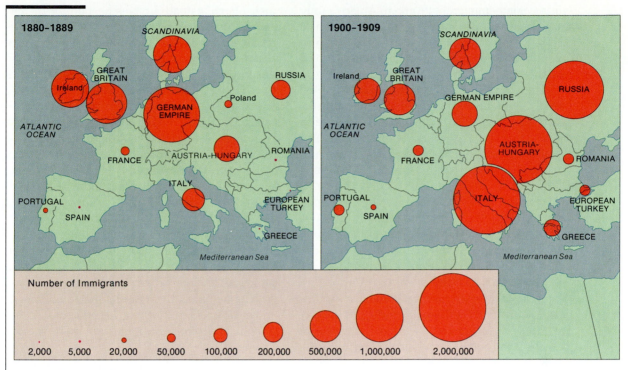

Immigration, 1880–1889 and 1900–1909

The source of old immigration was primarily northern and western Europe—England, Ireland, Germany, and Scandinavia. By the late 1890s a wave of new immigrants began to arrive from eastern and southern Europe.

Certainly, a geographic shift in origin of immigration to the United States took place, but more than geography differentiated the old and the new immigrants. Their reasons for leaving Europe, visions of America, settlement patterns, and occupational choices varied dramatically.

By the late nineteenth century, the motives and the opportunity to immigrate to America were present in southern and eastern Europe. With the abolition of serfdom, peasants were free to emigrate; and with the rise in population, young men faced job, land, and food shortages. Finally, railroads and steamships made travel faster and less expensive. During the 1880s, British and German steamships carried immigrants across the Atlantic for as little as $8, and by the turn of the century the trip only took five and a half days. In short, the conditions were right for the push to America.

"Birds of Passage"

Essentially two types of immigrants came to America. Permanent immigrants formed one group; migrant workers comprised the other. The people in the second group, often called birds of passage, were like the Chinese. They never intended to make the United States their home. Unable to earn a livelihood in their home countries, they came to America, worked and saved, and then returned home. Most were young men in their teens and twenties. They left behind their parents, young wives, and children, indications that their absence would not be too long. Before 1900, an estimated 78 percent of Italian immigrants and 95 percent of Greek immigrants were men. Many of them traveled to America in the early spring, worked until the late fall, and then returned to the warmer climates of their southern European homes for the winter. Some immigrants came to America fully intending to return home, but for one reason or another—love, hardship, early death—did not. Overall, 20 to 30 percent of all immigrants did return home.

The activity of the birds of passage can be clearly seen in Italian immigration patterns. Starting in the 1870s, Italian birthrates began to rise and mortality rates fell. Population pressure became severe, especially in *Il Mezzogiorno*, the southern and poorest provinces of Italy. Known as "the land that time forgot," the social customs and family patterns of *Il Mezzogiorno* seemed timeless. Life revolved around *la famiglia* (the family), and *l'ordine della famiglia* (the rules of family behavior and responsibility) was a sacred code. Unfortunately for the people in *Il Mezzogiorno*, the central government, dominated by northerners and concerned only with northern interests, did not forget the impoverished southern provinces. Heavily taxed and hurt by high protective tariffs on northern industrial goods, southern Italians sank deeper into poverty. Cynically, but realistically, they noted the sad truth of the old expression "*la legge va contra i cristiani*" (the law works against the people).

The law and population pressures already worked against the region; soon nature also joined the opposition. Natural disasters rocked southern Italy during the first decade of the twentieth century. Earthquakes caused untold devastation in the provinces of Basilicata and Calabria. Vesuvius erupted and buried a town near Naples. Then Etna erupted. The most cruel blow came in 1908 when an earthquake and tidal wave swept through the Strait of Messina between Sicily and the Italian mainland. The disaster destroyed hundreds of villages and killed hundreds of thousands of people. In the city of Messina alone, more than 100,000 people perished.

The kinds of jobs that Italian men sought reflected their attitude toward America. They did not look for careers. Occupations that provided opportunity for upward economic mobility were alien to them. Unlike most of the earlier immigrants to America, they did not want to farm in America or even own land, both of which implied a permanence that did not figure in their plans. Instead, Italians headed for the cities, where labor was needed and wages were relatively good. Few jobs were beneath them. Native-born Americans commented that the Italian birds of passage readily accepted "work no white man could stand." Expecting their stay in America to be short, they lived as inexpensively as possible under conditions that native-born families considered intolerable.

Italians were particularly attracted to heavy construction jobs. One study of Italians in America noted in 1905 that Italians gravitated toward "work that is simple and monotonous . . . that can be performed by men disposed in a gang, under the more or less military supervision of a foreman, so that the worker becomes himself like a part of a machine." Contracted out by a professional labor broker known as a *padrone*, Italians supplied the muscle that dug tunnels and canals, laid railroad tracks, and constructed bridges and roads. So important were they to

Most of the miners from Pennsylvania to California were immigrants from Europe and Asia. Anxious to improve their standard of living in their homeland, these immigrants would accept dangerous, but high-paying jobs.

the construction business that in 1905 the Industrial Commission concluded that "it would be a difficult thing . . . to build a railroad of any considerable length without Italian labor." As early as 1890, 90 percent of New York's public works employees and 99 percent of Chicago's street workers were Italian.

While they received good wages, their homes in Italy were seldom forgotten. One nostalgic Italian admitted, "Doctor, we brought to America only our brains and our arms. Our hearts stayed there in the little house in the beautiful fields of our Italy." And for women, adjustment to America was even more difficult. They often wore black clothing, an old country practice that symbolized self-sacrifice, misery, and determination. Edward Corsi, the son of immigrants who became President Franklin Roosevelt's commissioner of immigration, recalled that his mother never adjusted to America: "She loved quiet, and hated the noise and confusion. . . . She spent her days, and the waking hours of the nights, sitting at one outside window staring up at the little patch of sky above the tenements. She was never happy here, though she tried."

Italians were not the only birds of passage. The same forces—population pressure, unemployment, hunger, and the breakdown of agrarian societies—sent Greeks, Slavs, Chinese, Japanese, Mexicans, French Canadians, and inhabitants of scores of other nations to the United States. Seeking neither permanent homes nor citizenship, they desired only an opportunity to work for a living, hoping to save enough money to return to a better life in the country of their birth. Always the land they coveted was some distant home not in the United States.

Slavs, and especially Poles, dramatized this pattern of temporary migration—the desire to use America as a means of improving their lot in their home country. Strong and determined, they preferred the work that paid the best— usually the most dangerous and physically exhausting. After disembarking at East Coast ports, Slavs generally headed directly to the mill and mining towns of Pennsylvania and the Midwest. They found the wages they were after in the stockyards of Chicago, the coal mines of Scranton, and the steel mills of Pittsburgh and Buffalo. In 1910 a Pittsburgh steel worker earned between $2.28 and $2.41 for a 12-hour day; a miner in the same area earned between $2.40 and $3.00 for 8 hours of work. For an unskilled laborer, who usually made less than a dollar a day for other jobs, that was considered good pay.

Unlike the Italians who preferred to work in sociable gangs and above ground, Poles readily accepted the hard lonely labor of the mines and steel mills. The extra money was enough compensation for the danger of underground or indoor work. Employers quickly noted this Slavic inclination. In 1909 a Pittsburgh newspaper advertisement solicited "Tinners, Catchers, and Helpers. To work in open shops. Syrians, Poles, and Romanians Preferred." Such an advertisement attracted hundreds of hardy Slavs in search of good wages and the fast route home.

In Search of a New Home

In contrast to the birds of passage, several million other immigrants came to America with no intention of ever returning to the land of their birth. These were the permanent immigrants, for whom America offered political and religious freedom as well as economic opportunity. The promise of America was especially appealing to members of ethnic and religious minorities who were persecuted, abused, and despised in their homelands. Germans from Slavic countries, Greeks from Romania, Serbs from Hungary, Turks from Bulgaria, Poles from Russia—for these men and women home held few warm associations.

A fine case in point is Czarist Russia, a country notoriously and historically inhospitable to many minorities. In 1907, 250,000 "Russians" emigrated from Russia. But who were these "Russians?" More than 115,000 were Jews, and another 73,000 were Poles. Others were Finns, Germans, and Lithuanians. Only a small percentage of the Russian emigrants were of Russian ethnic stock. In short, emigration from Russia was generally an alternative for minorities.

The Jews were the prototypical true immigrants. Like the Irish Catholics a generation before, they fled nearly unbearable hardships.

Hester Street, 1907, on New York City's Lower East Side was home to thousands of Jewish immigrants from Russia and eastern Europe. The immigrants crowded into the tenements lining the street, which bustled with peddlers and pedestrians.

From the thirteenth century, millions of Jews had maintained a relatively stable communal life in Poland. Then during the eighteenth century Russia, Prussia, and Austria conquered and divided Poland. Most of the Polish Jews lived under Russian rule, and the quality of their lives took an immediate, drastic, downward turn. Russian authorities drove Jews out of commerce and forced them into an area known as the Pale of Settlement, where over 90 percent of Russian Jews lived. There they toiled as farmers of the poor soil of the steppes or earned a living as artisans or craftsmen in impoverished villages. There, too, Russian officials burned their books, disrupted their religious practices, and occasionally even broke up their families. Particularly painful were the Russian conscription laws, which took thousands of boys between the ages of 12 and 18 for periods of military service up to 25 years.

Starting in 1881, when the liberal Russian Czar Alexander II was assassinated, conditions for Jews in Russia rapidly deteriorated from bad to worse to intolerable. Laws restricted Jewish businesses, prevented Jewish land ownership, and limited Jewish education. Pogroms, a form of legally sanctioned mob attack against Jews, killed and injured thousands of persons. Sometimes at the whim of authorities, Russian Cossacks burned Jewish houses and destroyed Jewish possessions.

For Jews, then, emigration offered a chance for a far better life than existed for them in the Pale of Settlement. Dr. George M. Price, one of the several million Jews who left Russia for America during the late nineteenth century, expressed the feelings of these immigrants for their homeland. In his diary he wrote: "Sympathy for Russia? How ironical it sounds! Am I not despised? Am I not urged to leave? Do I not hear the word zhid (Jew) constantly? Can I even think that some consider me a human capable of thinking and feeling like others? Do I not rise daily with the fear lest the hungry mob attack me? . . . It is impossible . . . that a Jew should regret leaving Russia." He voiced his feelings for America, his new home, in his booklet *Yidn in America* (1891) where he described the Atlantic crossing as "a kind of hell that cleanses a man of his sins before coming to the land of Columbus." Compared to Russia, the United States seemed like heaven to Price.

Because they came to the United States to stay, the form of Jewish immigration differed substantially from that of the birds of passage. For them, immigration was not simply a young man's alternative. Jews, as all other permanent immigrants, tended to come to America in family units. Men and women, young and old—they were all represented. They brought their life savings and most valuable possessions with them, never expecting to see again what they left behind. As a result, the move to America was financially and physically taxing. And once in America, whole families had more expenses than the young male birds of passage.

Since America was now their home, Jewish men looked for jobs offering future opportunities rather than simply the opportunity to work for wages. They were not drawn to the steel mills and mines or even to jobs in construction. They desired skilled, not unskilled, labor. Many Jews had skills, for the uncertain life of the Russian Pale had taught them not to depend on land or commerce. In the Pale a Jew's greatest possession was the ability to do something that could not be taken away. This meant a skilled craft. In the Pale and in America, Jews were tailors and seamstresses, cigar makers and toy makers, tanners and butchers, carpenters, joiners, roofers, and masons, coppersmiths and blacksmiths. They had the knowledge and ability to perform the thousands of skilled tasks needed in an urban environment. The available statistical evidence reinforces this point. Where 75 percent of Italians and Poles entering the United States between 1899 and 1910 were unskilled laborers or farmers, 67 percent of all Jews were skilled workers.

NATIVISM: THE ANTI-IMMIGRANT REACTION

Sometimes an isolated event, by itself not historically important, can illuminate like a flash of lightning the social landscape and beliefs of a particular time. Certainly this is true with the *Hennessy* case. In 1890 a feud between gangs on the New Orleans docks turned violent. Joe and Pete Provenzano were arrested and tried for attempting to massacre the rival gang. The trial took a sensational turn when David Hennessy, the New Orleans superintendent of police, asserted in 1891 that he had evidence that a secret Sicilian organization known as the Mafia was involved in the affair. Shortly after Hennessy made his bold charges, five armed men gunned him down. Before he died, Hennessy was heard to say, "The dagos shot me."

The crime raised a hue and cry against Sicilians, and local police arrested scores, urged on by Mayor Joseph Shakespeare's instructions to "arrest every Italian you come across, if necessary." The mayor told the public, "We must teach these people a lesson that they will not forget for all time." Eleven Sicilians were brought to trial, but a jury failed to convict them. Undaunted, a local mob promptly took matters into its own hands and shot or clubbed to death nine and hanged two of the suspects. As far as most natives of New Orleans were concerned, justice had been done.

Many Americans seemed to agree. Editorialists praised the mob action and damned the vile "un-American" Italians. Soon the affair sent ripples across diplomatic waters. Italy protested the mob assault, but Washington refused to take any action. Anti-Italian rhetoric became ugly, and wild rumors ricocheted like bullets. Some said that the Italian fleet was headed toward America's east coast; others claimed that uniformed Italians were going through military drills in the streets of New York City. One thing was clear, noted an editorialist in the *Review of Reviews*, Congress had to pass immigration legislation to keep out "the refuse of the murder-breeds of Southern Europe."

The *Hennessy* case soon faded from the front pages of American newspapers. Italy did not attack the United States, and Congress did not immediately push through a restrictive immigration policy. But the emotions it generated and revealed were very real. Native-born Americans harbored deep suspicions of and resentments toward immigrants, especially those from southern and eastern Europe. If American industrialists saw in the immigrants a bottomless pool of dependable inexpensive labor, other Americans saw something far different and much less promising. Workers saw competition. Protestants saw Catholics and Jews. Educators saw illiterate hordes. Politicians saw peasants, unfamiliar with the workings of republicanism, democracy, and constitutionalism, and, what was even worse, perhaps contaminated by a belief in socialism, communism, or anarchism. Social Darwinists saw a mass of dark-skinned, thick-browed, bent-backed people who were far "below" northern and western Europeans on the evolutionary ladder. In short, native-born Americans, heirs of a different culture, religion, and complexion, saw something alien and inferior, perhaps even dangerous.

They reacted accordingly. They posted signs: "No Jews or Dogs Allowed." They called the Chinese "coolies," and the Mexicans "bean heads." Overall, they created an atmosphere of hostility that too often spilled over into open violence. In 1891 in a New Jersey mill town, 500 tending boys in a glassworks rioted when the management hired 14 young Russian Jews. During an 1895 labor conflict in the southern Colorado coal fields, a group of American miners killed 6 Italians. When Slavic coal miners went on strike in 1897 in eastern Pennsylvania, local citizens massacred 21 Polish and Hungarian workers. On the West Coast, Chinese workers were subject to regular and vicious attacks. Especially during economic hard times, native-born Americans lashed out against the new immigrants.

Sources of Conflict

Nativism, as this anti-immigrant backlash was called, took many forms. Racial nativism, the subject of thousands of books and articles, is the best remembered. University professors such as Wisconsin's Edward Alsworth Ross and popular writers such as Madison Grant decried the new immigrants as biologically less advanced than the Americans who traced their ancestry back to northern and western Europe. "Observe immigrants," Ross wrote in *The Old World in the New*, "in their gatherings, washed, combed, and in their Sunday best. You are struck by the fact that from ten to twenty percent are hirsute, low-browed, big-faced persons of obviously low mentality. . . . These ox-like men are descendants of those who always stayed behind." Using such criteria as complexion, size of cranium, length of forehead, and slope of shoulders, the immigrants from southern and eastern Europe were judged inferior to most native-born Americans. That university professors and scientists accepted such theories of innate racial and ethnic inferiority gave credibility to these notions. And popular writers readily accepted these stereotypes. Jacob Riis, a Danish immigrant who became an urban reformer in America and wrote the popular book *How the Other Half Lives* (1890), characterized Italians as "born gamblers" who lived destitute and disorderly lives; Chinese as secretive and addicted to every vice; and Jews as "enslaved" by their pursuit of gold and living amidst filth.

Religious differences reinforced ethnic variations. Overwhelmingly Catholic and Jewish, the new immigrants challenged the Protestant orthodoxy in America. Anti-Catholicism, noted a leading student of nativism, "blossomed spectacularly" during the late nineteenth century. Many Americans regarded the pope as the anti-Christ and Catholics as his evil minions. And it was widely believed that the authoritarian bent of the Catholic mind made it incompatible with democratic institutions. As the Reverend Josiah Strong observed in his best-selling book, *Our Country: Its Possible Future and the Present Crisis* (1885), there was "an irreconcilable difference between papal principles and the fundamental principles of our free institutions."

Native-born Americans viewed Jews with even greater suspicion, attributing the characteristics of Shakespeare's Shylock to Jews as a whole. "Money is their God," wrote leading journalist and social critic Jacob Riis. Other writers commented that Jews were tactless, tasteless, and pushy. Eventually many social clubs, country clubs, hotels, and universities excluded Jews, arguing that money alone could not purchase respectability.

The *Leo Frank* case painfully demonstrated the ubiquitous anti-Semitism in American society. Frank, a Cornell University graduate and a son of a wealthy New York merchant, managed an Atlanta pencil factory. In 1914 one of the factory hands, Mary Phagan, was found murdered on the premises. Frank was tried and convicted on flimsy evidence, but the case soon became an international cause célèbre. After reviewing the case, the governor of Georgia commuted Frank's death sentence to life imprisonment. The decision outraged native Georgian whites. They boycotted Jewish merchants and clamored for Frank's blood. Finally, a group of citizens from Mary Phagan's home town took Leo Frank from a state prison, transported him 175 miles across the state, and coldly hanged him. As news of the hanging spread, people gathered to gaze at the sight and shout "Now we've got you! We've got you now!" In the 1980s, new evidence in the Phagan case proved Frank innocent, and Georgia's Board of Pardon's granted him a posthumous pardon. But dispassionate justice was scarce in the weeks after Frank's death.

Orators used the *Leo Frank* case as an object lesson. Tom Watson, the fiery Georgia politician, warned listeners, "From all over the world, the Children of Israel are flocking to this country, and plans are on foot to move them from Europe *en masse* . . . to empty upon our shores the very scum and dregs of the *Parasite Race*." Like Josiah Strong and Edward Alsworth Ross, Tom Watson believed that Congress should stop the flow of immigrants before America was flooded by the waves of eastern and southern Europeans.

Many congressmen agreed with Watson. They too harbored strong suspicions of the new immigrants. For them, political fears mixed naturally with racial and religious misgivings. They tended to equate immigration with radicalism and suspected that every boat that docked at Ellis Island contained a swarm of socialists, communists, and anarchists prepared to foment revolution. As unfounded as their fears were, they could always point to isolated cases of radicalism among immigrants. They drew attention, for example, to Leon Czolgosz, born only months after his eastern European immigrant parents arrived in America. Discontented and unable to adjust to American life, Czolgosz became a convert to revolutionary anarchism. On September 6, 1901, he attended the Pan-American Exposition in Buffalo and waited patiently in a receiving line to shake hands with President William McKinley. When he reached McKinley, Czolgosz smiled, lifted up a gun, and shot the president twice through his tuxedo vest. Questioned about his action, Czolgosz confessed, "I don't believe in the Republican form of government and I don't believe we should have any rulers. It is right to kill them." Such actions and statements seemed to confirm the worst fears of antiradical nativists.

The strongest resentments against the new immigrants, however, were purely economic. American workers, particularly the unskilled, believed that the immigrants depressed wages by their willingness to "work cheap." An iron worker complained, "Immigrants work for almost nothing and seem to be able to live on wind—something which I can not do." Even skilled workers maintained that the birds of passage immigrants were unwilling to support any union efforts to improve working conditions in America. Samuel Gompers, head of the American Federation of Labor, said that the immigration problem in America was "appalling." He believed that the immigrants from eastern and southern Europe and from Asia were ignorant, unskilled, and unassimilable. Calling for strong restrictive legislation, he said, "Some way must be found to safeguard America."

In short, by the 1890s, when a terrible depression had disrupted the normal economic and social course of America, the new immigrants became a convenient scapegoat for the nation's myriad ills. Americans were swept along by a wave of xenophobic fear. It was a time when people elevated racial prejudice and rumors to universal truths. Native-born Americans blamed crime on Italians and prostitution on the Chinese; they claimed that the social ills of America's expanding cities—corruption, poor sanitation, violence, crime, disease, pollution—were the fault of the new immigrants.

In 1882 Congress passed the Chinese Exclusion Act, which barred Chinese laborers from entering the United States for ten years.

And they looked to the federal government for relief and protection.

Closing the Golden Door

The first immigrants attacked were those who were the most different from native-born Americans and the most unskilled—the Chinese. Between 1868 and 1882, more than 160,000 Chinese entered the United States. They laid down railroad tracks and mined for gold, silver, and coal. Unlike native-born Americans and most members of other immigrant groups, they did not consider cooking, washing, and ironing as "women's work," and in these areas they were particularly successful. Perhaps even too successful.

Lee Chew, who as a boy in China dreamed of obtaining wealth in "the country of the American wizards," immigrated as a young man to the United States. In America he found opportunity. He worked and saved and sacrificed. In America he also discovered that the Chinese were subject to the worst forms of exploitation and abuses. As they did with blacks in the South and Indians in the West, white Americans cheated and sometimes violently attacked the Chinese. "Americans are not all bad," Lee noted, "nor are they wicked wizards. Still . . . their treatment of us is outrageous."

During the depression of the mid-1870s the Chinese came under increasingly bitter and violent attack. At the forefront of the nativistic onslaught were the Irish, themselves recent immigrants, who competed with the Chinese for unskilled jobs. Irish political leaders in America demanded an end to Chinese immigration into the United States. But by the provisions of the Burlingame Treaty (1868) with China, the Chinese were free to immigrate and to establish American citizenship.

Eventually Congress responded to the pressure for restriction. In 1880, China gave the United States the right "to regulate, limit or suspend," though not to prohibit, the immigration of workers. Quickly the golden door slammed shut. In 1882 the Chinese Exclusion Act suspended Chinese immigration for ten years and drastically restricted the rights of the Chinese already in the United States. In 1892 Congress extended the act for another ten years, and then in 1902 extended it indefinitely. The legislation established a precedent for the future exclusion of other immigrants. By the 1890s most Americans agreed that the country should restrict "undesirable" immigrants. But how, for example, could Congress close America's door to southern and eastern Europeans while leaving it open for northern and western Europeans? To achieve this end, politicians advocated a literacy test. As early as the late 1880s economist Edward W. Bemis proposed that the United States exclude all male adults who could not read and write their own language. He maintained that such a law would effectively stop the flow of eastern and southern Europeans into America. The idea soon had the backing of the influential Republican Senator Henry Cabot Lodge of Massachusetts and the equally important Immigration Restriction League.

In 1896 Lodge pushed through Congress a literacy test bill, which would have excluded any adult immigrant unable to read 40 words in his language. Lodge's timing was poor. The bill reached the desk of Democratic President Grover Cleveland two days before his second term expired. Cleveland promptly vetoed the measure. The bill, Cleveland suggested, tested prior opportunities and America stood for open opportunities. In short, the bill fell pitifully below American ideals.

Cleveland's veto did not end the demand for restrictive legislation, nor did it even kill the idea of a literacy test. Presidents William Howard Taft and Woodrow Wilson vetoed similar pieces of legislation. In 1917, on the eve of America's entry into World War I, Wilson vetoed a literacy test bill on the grounds that it was "not a test of character, of quality, or of personal fitness." Nevertheless Congress passed the act over Wilson's veto.

World War I chilled an already cold climate for immigrants from southern and eastern Europe. Those who were born in the polyglot Austro-Hungarian Empire were now considered the enemy. Others were watched with deep suspicion. This was especially true after the 1917 Bolshevik Revolution in Russia. Once again American authorities regarded Jews from Russia as potential revolutionaries. Responding to this fear, in 1918 and 1920 Congress passed legislation to exclude or deport anarchists and other "dangerous radicals."

The generation-long battle over restriction ended with a clear victory for nativism. In the early 1920s Congress discovered its own solution: the quota system. The Emergency Quota Act (1921) limited immigration according to a nation-based quota system. It provided that no more than 3 percent of any given nationality in America in 1910 could annually immigrate to the United States. In 1924 the National Origins Act lowered the quota to 2 percent of each nationality residing in America in 1890. By using 1890 as the base year, the act was clearly aimed at restricting eastern and southern Europeans, for there were far fewer of the new immigrants

in America in 1890 than in 1910. Although in 1927 the base year was changed to 1920, the National Origins Act had achieved its desired result. The golden door was no longer fully open to eastern and southern Europeans, and it was completely closed to Asians. An important era in American history had ended.

Nativism and Native Americans

Immigrants were not the only people affected by nativist impulses. In a cruel irony, American Indians also felt the impact of nativist theories and prejudices. During the 1860s, 1870s, and 1880s, Indians were forced onto reservations by the federal government. The process was not peaceful. At almost every step Indian tribes resisted. From Texas and the Great Plains to California and the Pacific Northwest, Indian tribes clashed with federal troops in bloody confrontations. Occasionally the Indians won small victories in individual battles. But after the Battle of the Little Bighorn (1876), where Sitting Bull and Crazy Horse joined forces to annihilate Lieutenant Colonel George A. Custer and 264 of his men (see Chapter 16), Indian victories were few and small.

The last major bloody confrontation occurred during the cold December of 1890 on the Pine Ridge Reservation (Sioux) in South Dakota. Poorly fed and supplied on the reservation, dissatisfied with their present, and longing for the glories of their past, members of the Teton Sioux took up the "Ghost Dance," a harmless ritual that promised the faithful the mystical disappearance of the whites and the return of their lands. An inept government agent overreacted, calling in troops to suppress the Ghost Dance and arrest the Sioux leader Sitting Bull, who the government considered the focal point of Indian resistance. When Indian police killed Sitting Bull, some Sioux took up arms and left the reservation. Near Wounded Knee Creek, U.S. soldiers, armed with rapid-fire Hotchkiss guns, attempted to disarm the Indians. When one Indian resisted, soldiers opened fire, killing more than 300 men, women, and children. The Battle of Wounded Knee, which resembled more a slaughter than a battle, ended the violent era of Indian and white relations.

At the Cheyenne/Arapaho Reservation in Darlington, Oklahoma, Arapaho followers of the Ghost Dance religion, some in a trance, perform the Circle Dance.

The violent confrontations caused Americans to search for a solution to the "Indian problem." Most believed that the Indians had to be removed from rich American land. An editor for the *New York Herald* claimed, "It is inconsistent with our civilization and with common sense to allow the Indian to roam over a country as fine as that around the Black Hills, preventing its development in order that he may shoot game and scalp his neighbors. That can never be. The region must be taken from the Indian." Others had even more radical solutions. L. Frank Baum, who in 1900 became famous for writing *The Wizard of Oz*, noted in the Aberdeen *Saturday Pioneer* in 1890 that the "nobility of the Redskin is extinguished" and that the whites "are masters of the American continent." To end any lingering problems, Baum proposed "the total annihilation of the few remaining Indians . . . Their glory has fled, their spirits broken, their manhood effaced; better that they should die than live the miserable wretches that they are."

By the time of Wounded Knee, however,

the U.S. government had embarked on its own solution to the Indian problem, one which emphasized ethnocide rather than genocide. An assault on tribalism, ethnocide—the calculated destruction of a culture—was an attempt by white Americans to force Indian Americans to assimilate into their culture. Although not as bloody as the Indian wars, ethnocide was even more destructive to Indian societies.

At the heart of this new policy was the destruction of the reservation system. Reservations encouraged tribal unity, and, as such, distinctiveness from white American society. Congress believed that the solution was to treat Indians less like members of individual tribes and more like autonomous individuals. As a first step, in 1871 Congress had ruled that no Indian tribe "shall be acknowledged or recognized as an independent nation, tribe or power, with whom the United States may contract by treaty." Then in an attempt to destroy Indian culture, in 1887 Congress passed the Dawes Severalty Act, which authorized the president to divide tribal lands and redistribute the lands among tribal members, giving 160 acres to each head of a family and lesser amounts to bachelors, women, and children. Although the plots would be held in trust for 25 years to prevent Indians from immediately selling the land, the object of the legislation was to make Indians individual landowners. In addition, all Indians receiving land grants were also made citizens of the United States.

Dawes was motivated by what he believed were the best interests of the Indians. Like other reformers, he believed that the most effective solution to the Indian problem was to assimilate Indians into mainstream white American culture. To this end, other reformers opened Indian schools to teach Indian children to be mechanics and farmers and to train them for citizenship. Richard Pratt, an army officer who founded the Carlisle Indian Industrial School in Pennsylvania in 1879, maintained that the fastest and surest way to assimilate Indians was to remove Indian children from reservations and send them to boarding schools in the East. By 1905 there were 25 boarding schools patterned after Carlisle. The schools emphasized ruthless assimilation. The "Rules for Indian Schools" called for compulsory observation of the Christian Sabbath, all formal and casual conversation in English, and instruction in "the sports and games enjoyed by white youth, such as baseball, hopscotch, croquet, marbles, bean bags, dominoes, checkers." Even more boarding schools were established on reservations to serve the same ends. What surprised reformers the most, however, was the failure of these schools to break tribal loyalties or destroy Indian culture.

While the reformers opened schools, Congress continued its efforts to break up the reservations. The Curtis Act of 1898 ended tribal sovereignty in Indian Territory, voiding tribal control of mineral rights, abolishing tribal laws and courts, and imposing the laws and courts of the United States on the Indians. The Dead Indian Act (1902) permitted Indians to sell allotted lands they had inherited, thereby circumventing the 25 year trust period imposed by the Dawes Act. Four years later, Congress continued its assault on the trust period with the Burke Act, which eliminated the trust period altogether and allowed the secretary of interior to decide when Indians were competent to manage their own affairs. Finally, in 1924 Congress enacted the Snyder Act, which granted all Indians born in the United States full citizenship. As far as Congress was concerned, the United States had now assimilated its true natives.

Reformers believed that these acts would end the tribal system and lead to assimilation. The legislation, however, served only the land interests of white Americans. By 1932 the allotment program had taken 90 million acres of land away from tribal control, and as late as 1981 a U.S. district court decision branded the program "probably one of the best-intended grievous errors in the history of American policymaking." Far from being assimilated, Indians saw their own culture attacked and partially destroyed, while at the same time they were never fully accepted into the dominant American culture.

WORKING IN INDUSTRIAL AMERICA

If during the 1920s advocates of immigration restrictions and Indian assimilation won an important battle, they lost their self-proclaimed war. They longed for a rural, white, Protestant, ethnically homogeneous America, but the war they waged took the form more of a rear guard action than an offensive. Between 1870 and 1920 America had changed dramatically. It became a richly complex, ethnically diverse, industrial country. In fact, even before 1900 its cities were the most cosmopolitan in the world. In 1880 more than 87 percent of the inhabitants of Chicago were immigrants and their children. In other major American cities the statistics were similar: Milwaukee and Detroit, 84 percent; New York and Cleveland, 80 percent; St. Louis and San Francisco, 78 percent. By contrast, 94 percent of the inhabitants of London in 1910 came from England and Wales.

These new immigrants provided the muscle for America's spectacular industrial growth. They laid railroad tracks, built bridges and roads, mined coal, silver, and gold, and made steel. Once again, statistics tell at least part of the story. In 1919 more than 90 percent of the anthracite coal miners were immigrants from eastern and southern Europe. Of the 14,359 workers in Carnegie's steel plants in the Pittsburgh area, 11,694 were eastern and southern Europeans. Indeed, without immigrant labor American industrialization would have moved forward at a far slower pace.

Wages, Hours, and Standard of Living

Was it worth it after all? Was the price paid by native-born and immigrant labor for industrialization worth the benefits they received? This is not a simple question to answer; in fact, each laborer might have answered it differently. But in their answers there would have been common themes. Unquestionably industrialization extracted a heavy toll from the laborers, who suffered psychologically and emotionally in industrial America. It changed not only how, when, and where they worked but also how they regarded work and how they perceived themselves. Equally unquestionably, however, industrialization transformed the United States into the most prosperous country in the world. To some degree, laborers shared in that prosperity and increase in material comfort.

Wages played an important role in a laborer's attitude toward work. In general, wages rose and prices fell during the late nineteenth and early twentieth centuries. Exactly how much is a question of heated historical debate. Clarence Long, an economic historian, in his study of wages and earnings in the late nineteenth century, estimated that when adjusted for changes in the price level, real daily wage rates rose from about $1 in 1860 to $1.50 in 1890, and real annual earnings increased from approximately $300 in 1860 to more than $425 in 1890. Other students of the subject believe Long's estimates are overly optimistic and that wages tended to stagnate, especially in the large textile industries. Even Long, however, admits that the pace of wages and earnings lagged well behind the spectacular growth in the American economy.

Even with the modest improvements in wages, laborers fought a continual battle with poverty. More often than not, the prosperity of a family depended on how many members of that family worked. Carroll D. Wright, chief of the Massachusetts Bureau of the Statistics of Labor, expressed the matter plainly in 1882: "A family of workers can always live well, but the man with a family of small children to support, unless his wife works also, has a small chance of living properly."

Take, for example, the case of 2 coal miners studied in 1883 by agents for the Illinois Bureau of Labor Statistics. Both were hardworking union men who earned wages of $1.50 per day. The first worked only 30 weeks in 1883, and his total income was $250. He lived with his wife and five children in a $6 per month, 2-room tenement apartment. During the year, he spent only $80 on food, mainly bread, salted meat, and coffee. His apartment was crowded but neat, and his children attended public school. In 1883, at least, he made barely enough to allow his family to maintain a minimal standard of living. His existence was precarious. Strikes, layoffs, sickness, or injury could easily throw him and his family into abject poverty.

The second miner worked full time in 1883 and earned $420. He had a wife and four children, 3 of whom were also miners, and they brought home an additional $1000. They lived comfortably in their own 6-room house perched on an acre of land. They ate well, spending $900 a year on food. Steak, butter, potatoes, bacon,

and coffee comprised a typical breakfast. They bought books and enjoyed a full leisure life. The material quality of life, then, often depended on circumstances other than occupation or wages.

The most important factor in determining the economic well-being of a working-class family was how many members of the family worked. Fathers and sons, mothers and daughters, and often aunts, uncles, and grandparents—all contributed to the "family economy." To be sure, the nature of the family economy created concern. Carroll D. Wright in the United States Census of 1880 warned, "the factory system necessitates the employment of women and children to an injurious extent, and consequently its tendency is to destroy family life and ties and domestic habits, and ultimately the home."

In truth, the opposite was probably true. Without the income earned by wives and children, families faced greater threats to their unity. Economically, families worked as a single entity; the desires of any particular individual often had to be sacrificed for the good of the family. This meant that women and children worked, families took in boarders, and all earnings were used for a common end. Far from destroying the family, the family economy often strengthened it.

During the first decade of the twentieth century, social workers conducted numerous studies to determine how much a family or a single individual needed to sustain a typical working-class existence for a year. Estimates for New York City ranged between $800 and $876 for a family of four, $505 for a single man, and $466 for a working woman. Many of New York's laborers fell painfully below the recommended minimum. Single women lived particularly difficult lives. A New York study concluded that women earned about half as much as men, and that the majority made less than $300 per year. One woman worker described her meager existence: "I didn't live, I simply existed. I couldn't live that [which] you could call living. . . . It took me months and months to save up money to buy a dress or a pair of shoes. . . . I had the hardest struggle I ever had in my life."

What was true for women was equally valid for blacks, Asians, and Mexicans in America. They were given the most exhausting and dan-

The family economy was an important part of survival in America. This family earned extra money by arranging artificial flowers at home.

gerous work, paid the least, and were fired first during economic hard times. For a black share-cropper farming a patch of worked-over soil in Mississippi, or a Chinese miner carrying nitro-glycerin down a hole in a Colorado mountain, or a Mexican working on a Texas ranch, $300 per year would have seemed a kingly sum.

There were clear divisions even among workers. At the top ranks were the highly skilled laborers. Mostly English-speaking, generally Protestant, and almost exclusively white, they were paid well, had good job security, and con-sidered themselves elite craftsmen. Below them were the semiskilled and unskilled workers. Most were immigrants from southern and east-ern Europe, spoke halting if any English, and were Catholics or Jews. They lacked job secu-rity and had to struggle for a decent existence. At the bottom of the semiskilled and unskilled category were the nonwhite and women work-ers, for whom even a decent existence was nor-mally out of reach.

Like wages, hours varied widely. The cen-tral question workers asked was, "How much of a person's life should be devoted to work?" Long hours were not a new phenomenon tied to in-dustrial America. Farm workers and artisans often labored from sunup to sundown, but the tempo and quality of their labor was different. Farm work was governed by the season and the weather. During summer months and harvest, work was intense, but it slowed down during the shorter days of winter. There was always time for fishing, horse racing, visiting, and tavern-going. The rhythms of the preindustrial work-shop similarly mixed work with fellowship. If the work days were long, they were also sociable. As they worked, laborers talked, joked, laughed, and even drank. In fact, laborers considered rum drinking an integral aspect of work. As Richard O'Flynn recalled, "The rum barrel was always near the work—ready for distribution, by this means they kept the men hard at work all day."

Nor was time measured out in teaspoons for the preindustrial laborer. Punctuality was not the golden virtue it became during industriali-zation. In the early nineteenth century, house-

(Text continues on p. 606)

HOUSEWORK IN VICTORIAN AMERICA

Housework in nineteenth-century America was harsh physical labor. Preparing even a simple meal was a time- and energy-consuming chore. Prior to the twentieth century, cooking was performed on a coal- or wood-burning stove. Unlike an electric or a gas range, which can be turned on with the flick of a single switch, cast-iron and steel stoves were exceptionally difficult to use.

Ashes from an old fire had to be removed. Then, paper and kindling had to be set inside the stove, dampers and flues had to be carefully adjusted, and a fire lit. Since there were no thermostats to regulate the stove's temperature, a woman had to keep an eye on the contraption all day long. Any time the fire slackened, she had to adjust a flue or add more fuel.

Throughout the day, the stove had to be continually fed with new supplies of coal or wood—an average of 50 pounds a day. At least twice a day, the ash box had to be emptied, a task which required a woman to gather ashes and cinders in a grate and then dump them into a pan below. Altogether, a housewife spent four hours every day sifting ashes, adjusting dampers, lighting fires, carrying coal or wood, and rubbing the stove with thick black wax to keep it from rusting.

It was not enough for a housewife to know how to use a cast-iron stove. She also had to know how to prepare unprocessed foods for consumption. Prior to the 1890s, there were few factory-prepared foods. Shoppers bought poultry that was still alive and then had to kill and pluck the birds. Fish had to have scales removed. Green coffee had to be roasted and ground. Loaves of sugar had to be pounded, flour sifted, nuts shelled, and raisins seeded.

Cleaning was an even more arduous task than cooking. The soot and smoke from coal- and wood-burning stoves blackened walls and dirtied drapes and carpets. Gas and kerosene lamps left smelly deposits of black soot on furniture and curtains. Each day, the lamp's glass chimneys had to be wiped and wicks trimmed or replaced. Floors had to scrubbed, rugs beaten, and windows washed. While a small minority of well-to-do families could afford to hire cooks at $5 a week, waitresses at $3.50 a week, laundresses at $3.50 a week, and cleaning women and choremen for $1.50 a day, in the overwhelming majority of homes, all household tasks had to be performed by a housewife and her daughters.

Housework in nineteenth-century America was a full-time job. Gro Svendsen, a Norwegian immigrant, was astonished by how hard the typical American housewife had to work. As she wrote her parents in 1862:

> We are told that the women of America have much leisure time but I haven't yet met any woman who thought so! Here the mistress of the house must do all the work that the cook, the maid and the housekeeper would do in an upper class family at home. Moreover, she must do her work as well as these three together do it in Norway.

Before the end of the nineteenth century, when indoor plumbing became common, chores that involved the use of water were particularly demanding. Well-to-do urban families had piped water or a private cistern, but the overwhelming majority of American families got their water from a hydrant, a pump, a well, or a stream located some distance from their house. The mere job of bringing water into the house was exhausting. According to calculations made in 1886, a typical North Carolina housewife had to carry water from a pump or a well or a spring eight to ten times each day. Washing, boiling, and rinsing a single load of laundry used about 50 gallons of water. Over the course of a year she walked 148 miles toting water and carried over 36 tons of water.

Homes without running water also lacked the simplest way to dispose of garbage: sinks with drains. This meant that women had to remove dirty dishwater, kitchen slops, and, worst of all, the contents of chamberpots from their house by hand.

Laundry was the household chore that nineteenth-century housewives detested most. Rachel Haskell, a Nevada housewife, called it "the Herculean task which women all dread" and "the great domestic dread of the household."

On Sunday evenings, a housewife soaked clothing in tubs of warm water. When she woke up the next morning, she had to scrub the laundry on a rough washboard and rub it with soap made from lye, which severely irritated her hands. Next, she placed the laundry in big vats of boiling water and stirred the clothes about with a long pole to prevent the clothes from developing yellow spots. Then she lifted the clothes out of the vats with a washstick, rinsed the clothes twice, once in plain water and once with bluing, wrung the clothes out, and hung them out to dry. At this point, clothes would be pressed with heavy flatirons and collars would be stiffened with starch.

The last years of the nineteenth century witnessed a revolution in the nature of housework. Beginning in the 1880s, with the invention of the carpet sweeper, a host of new "labor-saving" appliances were introduced. These included the electric iron (1903), the electric vacuum cleaner (1907), and the electric toaster (1912). At the same time, the first processed and canned foods appeared. In the 1870s, H. J. Heinz introduced canned pickles and sauerkraut; in the 1880s,

Franco-American Co. introduced the first canned meals; and in the 1890s, Campbell's sold the first condensed soups. By the 1920s, the urban middle class enjoyed a myriad of new household conveniences, including hot and cold running water, gas stoves, automatic washing machines, refrigerators, and vacuum cleaners.

Yet despite the introduction of electricity, running water, and "labor-saving" household appliances, time spent on housework did not decline. Indeed, the typical full-time housewife today spends just as much time on housework as her grandmother or great-grandmother. In 1924, a typical housewife spent about 52 hours a week in housework. Half a century later, the average full-time housewife devoted 55 hours to housework. A housewife today spends less time cooking and cleaning up after meals, but she spends just as much time as her ancestors on housecleaning and even more time on shopping, household management, laundry, and childcare.

How can this be? The answer lies in a dramatic rise in the standards of cleanliness and childcare expected of a housewife. As early as the 1930s, this change was apparent to a writer in the *Ladies Home Journal*:

> Because we housewives of today have the tools to reach it, we dig every day after the dust that grandmother left to spring cataclysm. If few of us have nine children for a weekly bath, we have two or three for a daily immersion. If our consciences don't prick us over vacant pie shelves or empty cookie jars, they do over meals in which a vitamin may be omitted or a calorie lacking.

hold clocks were rare and many of them possessed only a single hand. Large-scale production of household clocks did not begin in America until the 1830s, and it was not until the Civil War that cheap, mass-produced pocket watches became readily available. Certainly the idea of punching a time clock exactly on time was alien to the preindustrial worker, who might think in terms of hours but not in terms of minutes.

Preindustrial labor, then, had a more relaxed atmosphere. This is not meant to romanticize it. Farm work and shop labor could be hard and dangerous, but there were not sharp lines between labor and leisure. Gambling, storytelling, singing, debating, and drinking formed a crucial part of the work day. Thrift, regularity, sobriety, orderliness, punctuality—hallmarks of an industrial society—were virtues not rigorously observed.

The new concept of time changed not only how people worked, but also how they regarded labor. The great architectural feature of nineteenth- and early twentieth-century New England mill towns was the giant, looming bell towers of the factories. At George Pullman's model factory outside Chicago, the bell tower was a solid Victorian structure whose clock face reflected in a pool in front of it. Before clocks and watches, the bell towers served a utilitarian function. They told the laborers when to get out of bed, be at work, eat lunch, and go home. The importance of time was literally drilled home in a brochure prepared by the International Harvester Corporation to teach Polish laborers the English language. "Lesson One" read:

I hear the whistle. I must hurry.
I hear the five minute whistle.
It is time to go into the shop.
I take my check from the gate board and hang it
    on the department board.
I change my clothes and get ready to work.
The starting whistle blows.
I eat my lunch.
It is forbidden to eat until then.
The whistle blows at five minutes of starting
    time.
I get ready to go to work.
I work until the whistle blows to quit.
I leave my place nice and clean.
I put all my clothes in the locker.
I must go home.

The lesson perfectly describes the ideal industrial worker. He is at work on time, labors continuously until a whistle tells him to eat, keeps himself and his workplace clean, and goes straight home after work. In short, he is punctual, hardworking, clean, and sober. He does not show up at work late, retire to a saloon for lunch, and gamble his weekly pay on Saturday night.

Given this new standard of work and time demanded by factory owners, laborers were reluctant to work the preindustrial dawn-to-dusk day. In 1889 hundreds of trade unionists paraded through the streets of Worcester, Massachusetts, behind a banner which read: "Eight Hours for Work, Eight Hours for Rest, Eight Hours for What We Will." That was their goal, and a popular song of the day captured the ideal.

We mean to make things over;
We're tired of toil for naught;
We may have enough to live on,
But never an hour for thought.

We want to feel the sunshine,
We want to smell the flowers;
We are sure that God has willed it,
And we mean to have eight hours.

The reality, however, fell far short of the ideal. It is difficult to generalize about hours because they varied considerably from occupation to occupation. In 1890, for example, bakers averaged over 65 hours a week, steelworkers over 66, and canners nearly 77. Working in a steel mill blast furnace was a 12-hour-a-day, 7-day-a-week job, including one 24-hour continuous shift and 1 day off every 2 weeks. Even as late as 1920, skilled workers still averaged 50.4 hours a week and the unskilled 53.7 hours. Before the 1930s, workers regarded the idea of an 8-hour day or even a 10-hour day as an unattainable dream.

For women, the new ideals of industrial America created even more work. The increased emphasis on cleanliness led to a greater demand for tidy homes. As a result, women devoted more time to cleaning, dusting, and scrubbing. In addition, the growing availability of washable cotton fabrics increased the amount of laundering housewives performed. Finally, more varied diets meant women spent more

Factory owners demanded standards of work, behavior, and punctuality that left the industrial worker little leisure time. During the late nineteenth century, workers campaigned unsuccessfully for an eight-hour workday.

more than 4000; and in 1916 the plant housed 15,000 workers. During that latter year, the Ford Motor Company works at Highland Park, Michigan, employed 33,000 workers. Increasingly, giant industries dominated the American economy.

These huge plants demanded an organized, disciplined work force. The informality of the preindustrial workshop, with only a handful of employees, was an inevitable casualty. During those earlier times, for example, a cigar maker might go to the shop early in the morning, sip his *café con leche*, and roll 50 cigars, including a few smokes for himself. At noon he retired to a saloon and played pinochle while eating a leisurely lunch and then returned to his bench for another four hours. There he talked and joked with his fellow workers with the hum of the other voices and the click of the cutting blade as background. In the industrial factories workers were carefully regulated to ensure maximum productivity. Work became formalized and structured, and between the owner and the worker several levels of bureaucrats emerged.

Mechanization of work led to both the large factories and the incredible boom in productivity. It also caused an erosion of certain skilled trades. Imaginative inventors designed machines that performed tasks previously done by skilled artisans. A simple cigar mold, for example, allowed an unskilled worker to bunch cigar tobacco, a job once handled by a skilled tobacco roller. Where once a single tailor took a piece of cloth, cut it, fashioned it, sewed it, and made it into a pair of pants, by 1859 a Cincinnati clothing factory had divided the process into 17 different semiskilled jobs. The replacement of highly skilled workers by semiskilled laborers was a characteristic of the factory system. As one historian has observed, "the typical factory hand became a machine operator or fractionated workman, toiling at a single bit of the manufacturing process."

By the end of the century, it appeared to many observers that all work was being mechanized and moving toward the factory mode. Even farmers followed the mechanization march. By the early 1880s, one Dakota Territory wheat farm—or "food factory" as a critic called it—stretched over 30,000 acres, used 20 reapers and 30 steam-powered threshers, and em-

time plucking feathers from chickens, soaking and blanching hams, roasting coffee beans, grinding whole spices and sugar, and cooking meals. By 1900 the typical housewife worked 6 hours a day on just 2 tasks: meal preparation and cleaning. This was in addition to the time they spent on other household tasks.

The Lost Crafts

Although workers complained regularly about wages and hours, they were equally disturbed by several other results of industrialization. The late-nineteenth-century industries differed from the preindustrial workshop in four important areas: size, discipline, mechanization, and displacement of skill. The new factories were huge; they employed hundreds, even thousands, of laborers. In 1850 the McCormick reaper plant in Chicago employed about 150 workers; in 1900 the work force had grown to

Workers at Swift's meat-packing plant wield huge cleavers as they impassively go about their tasks. A slip of the cleaver could mean the loss of a limb or even death for a worker.

ployed 1000 field hands. Workers did not know their bosses, but this impersonality of labor was offset by a remarkable increase in output.

Worker Discontent

In the long run, industrialization brought much to many. Between 1860 and 1920 the volume of manufactured goods increased almost 14-fold. Consumer goods, which once only the rich could afford, came into the purchasing range of the middle class. Newspapers and magazines advertised, and department stores displayed, a wide variety of factory products.

From a worker's perspective, however, industrialization was often an inhumane process. Factory labor tended to be monotonous, and machines made work more dangerous. Industrial accidents were alarmingly common, and careless or tired workers sacrificed their fingers, hands, arms, and sometimes even lives. Describ-

ing the hazards of work in the Chicago stockyards, one historian noted, "Each job had its own dangers: the dampness and cold of the packing rooms and hide cellar; the sharp blade of the beef boner's knife; the noxious dust of the wool department and fertilizer plant; the wild charge of a half-crazed steer on the killing floor." Frequent speedups increased the chances of injury. In one year at Armour's meat-packing plant in Chicago, 22,381 workers were injured or became ill.

To make matters even worse, owners often assumed an uncaring attitude toward their laborers. Concerned with production quotas and cost efficiency, owners seemed insensitive to workers' needs; and in fact, many *were* insensitive. As one factory manager proclaimed, "I regard my people as I regard my machinery. So long as they can do my work for what I choose to pay them, I keep them, getting out of them all I can. What they do or how they fare outside my walls I don't know, nor do I consider it my business to know. They must look out for themselves as I do myself."

Where once workers determined their production and work pace, now factory managers with stopwatches made laborers account for their time by seconds. Workers particularly resented scientific time-motion experts who strove to get the maximum production out of every laborer. One worker expressed the feelings of many others: "We don't want to work as fast as we are able to. We want to work as fast as we think it's comfortable for us to work. We haven't come into existence for the purpose of seeing how great a task we can perform through a lifetime."

Workers did not passively accept industrialization and the changes caused by that enormous process. At almost every step they resisted change, and they had formidable weapons at their disposal. On one level, resistance entailed a simple, individual decision not to change completely. Factory managers demanded a steady, dependable work force, but they were plagued by chronic absenteeism. Immigrant workers refused to labor on religious holidays, and in some towns factories had to shut down on the day the circus arrived. Across America, heavy drinking on Sunday led to "blue Mondays," a term used to described absenteeism.

Another form of individual protest was simply quitting. Most industrial workers changed jobs at least every three years, and in many industries the annual turnover rate was over 100 percent. Some quit because they were bored, "forced to work too hard," or because they were struck by spring wanderlust and simply wanted to move. Others quit because of severe discipline, unsafe working conditions, or low wages. Compulsive quitting was a clear indication that perhaps 20 percent of the work force never came to terms with industrialization.

Quick to quit, workers were similarly quick to take collective action. The late nineteenth century witnessed the most sustained and violent industrial conflict in the nation's history. Strikes were as common as political corruption during the period. Between 1881 and 1890, the Bureau of Labor Statistics estimated that 9668

strikes and lockouts had occurred. In 1886, 1432 strikes and 140 lockouts involved 610,024 workers. Although most of the conflicts were relatively peaceful, some were so violent that citizens across the nation feared that America was moving toward another revolution.

Early Labor Violence

An examination of several conflicts indicates clearly the relative power of industrialists and workers. An early violent conflict occurred in the anthracite coal region of eastern Pennsylvania. The late 1860s and early 1870s were troubled times for this socially and ethnically divided area. Mine owners competed ruthlessly against each other, and they all distrusted the miners and their union, the Workingmen's Benevolent Association (WBA). Added to economic and class tensions, the area was torn by ethnic conflicts. American-born and Protestant Scots-Irishmen owned most of the mines, and Welshmen and Englishmen served as mine superintendents. Increasingly, however, the miners were Irish-Catholic immigrants. Old World prejudices thus mingled with New World economics.

Matters became worse when the depression of the mid-1870s hit the area. Led by Franklin B. Gowen, president of the Reading Railroad, a company that owned considerable mining land and made a large profit hauling coal to market, the mine owners came together and agreed to observe common policies regarding prices, wages, and union negotiations. Competition thus reduced, the owners cut wages and increased workloads. This sort of oppression was nothing new to the Irish, and they responded much as they had in the Old Country. More important than the WBA were the Ancient Order of Hibernians, a secret fraternal society of Irish immigrants, and its inner circle, the Molly Maguires. While the WBA battled the owners at the negotiation table, the Molly Maguires waged a violent guerrilla war. They disrupted the operation of several mines and attacked a handful of mining officials.

Because it was secretive, little is known about the Mollies. However, Gowen and the owners were able to infiltrate the group with a secret agent, James McParlan. McParlan was one of Ireland's own. Born in County Armagh, he was a Catholic who had been raised to hate informers. But he agreed to inform on his fellow Irishmen for the Pinkerton agency. While McParlan was gathering information, the WBA went on strike. Disorder and violence followed. Using the local press, Gowen convinced much of the community that a direct link existed between the WBA, the Mollies, and the bloodshed. His tactic worked and the strike was broken.

A short time later, Gowen used McParlan's testimony to destroy both the Mollies and the WBA. Altogether, 20 Mollies were convicted and executed. Throughout their sensational trials, Gowen again linked Molly activities with the WBA. It was a scenario that industrialists would use again and again. The greatest weapon against strikers was the community's fear of violence. If an industrialist could convince the public that unions promoted violence, then they could characterize their own union-busting tactics as a sincere defense of law and order. Gowen used the tactic successfully in 1875 and 1876.

The same depression that convulsed the Pennsylvania coal fields shook the rest of the country as well. To keep from going under, many businessmen cut rates and attempted to recoup their losses by reducing labor costs. This was true especially in the highly competitive railroad business. Repeatedly, workers suffered wage cuts, and usually unskilled wages were slashed more than the skilled. Workingmen, one railroad worker declared in 1877, "know what it is to bring up a family on ninty cents a day, to live on beans and cornmeal week in and week out, to run in debt at the stores until you cannot get trusted any longer, to see the wife breaking down under privation and distress, and the children growing up sharp and fierce like wolves day after day because they don't get enough to eat." And that knowledge drove many workers to desperate lengths.

During the dog days of mid-July 1877, the Baltimore and Ohio Railroad (B&O) announced its third consecutive 10 percent wage cut. Angry, frustrated, hot, hungry, and led by the new Trainmen's Union, railroad workers along the line went on strike. When trouble followed, Baltimore and Ohio workers seized an important

The Great Railroad Strike, 1877
The spontaneous uprising that followed the railroad strike of 1877 paralyzed two-thirds of the nation's trackage for two weeks and destroyed millions of dollars worth of railroad property.

junction at Martinsburg, West Virginia. The state militia and local sheriffs sympathized with the workers and could not end the strike. As a result, President Rutherford B. Hayes sent in federal troops to protect an army of strikebreakers.

From Martinsburg the strike spread north and west. Railroad workers walked off their jobs, and trains, which were vital to the American economy and the very symbols of progress during the nineteenth century, sat unused and deserted. The strike paralyzed transportation in the Midwest and much of the industrial northeast. It seemed there was violence and destruction everywhere. In Baltimore the state militia shot into a mob and killed ten persons; in Pittsburgh rioters burned 2000 freight cars, looted stores, and torched railroad buildings; in Buffalo, Chicago, and Indianapolis workers and police engaged in bloody battles.

When local police and state militiamen failed to quell the problems, President Hayes ordered more federal troops to do the job. Eventually, superior force restored peace and the trains started rolling again, but not before more than a hundred strikers were killed. Like most spontaneous strikes, the Great Strike of 1877 failed. But the anger it revealed frightened America. Although some authorities labeled the disturbances as the work of communist agitators, more thoughtful observers realized it was caused by legitimate grievances. For owners and workers alike, the strike was a lesson. Owners learned that workers were not merely passive partners in the industrial process. Labor learned that when pressed, the federal government was not neutral—it would side with capital.

Employers Gain Power

Between 1877 and 1886 industrialists grew in organizational and economic power. In the steel, oil, coal, railroad, and meat industries, ruthless competition and consolidation produced industrial giants. Workers could not match the power of Rockefeller, Carnegie, and Swift, who controlled their industries and were the victors in the competitive industrial wars. They were confident men who believed that they knew what was best for themselves and their workers, and their confidence bred arrogance. A sense of superiority and self-righteousness ran through their public statements. For example, one textile company manager confidently declared, "There is such a thing as too much education for working people . . . I have seen cases where young people were spoiled for labor by being educated to a little too much refinement."

The power of industrialists can be seen in the famous Haymarket Square riot of 1886. In 1885, skilled molders won a 15 percent pay increase after a strike at McCormick Harvester Machine Company in Chicago. Reacting angrily to the union's activities, McCormick introduced pneumatic molders that could be run by unskilled workers. Again in 1886, the skilled workers went on strike, but this time the result was different. The combined forces of McCormick and local police ensured the safety of an army of strikebreakers and the plant's output continued until the strike was broken.

Tempers, however, remained high, and violence resulted. In May, after the strike ended, police and workers clashed once again, and a handful of laborers were killed and wounded. Disturbed by the violent force used by police in defense of industrialists' positions, August Spies, a Chicago anarchist and labor agitator who edited the radical newspaper *Arbeiter Zeitung*, called for a protest meeting in Haymarket Square, a location that could hold 20,000 persons. The meeting was held on May 4 under rainy skies and before a small and generally unenthusiastic crowd of about 3000 labor supporters. The speeches were dull and the listeners were peaceful. But as the meeting was breaking up, local police unexpectedly charged the crowd. Then somebody—to this day no one knows who—threw a bomb into the melee, killing police and protesters alike. Surrounded by the fog of confusion and anger, the police opened fire, shooting protesters and even, accidentally, each other.

Industrialists, city officials, ministers, and the local press convinced a bewildered public that the bombing was a prelude to anarchistic revolution. Police arrested eight local radicals, including Spies, and charged them with conspiracy. There was no real evidence against them, but the mood of the authorities was so biased that no evidence was needed. The eight were tried and convicted, and seven were sentenced to be hanged. One man committed suicide in his cell and three were eventually pardoned, but Spies and three others were executed. For radicals, labor agitators, and unionists, the message was clear: Police and public opinion were on the side of the industrialists.

The excessive violence of the Molly Maguires, the great strike of 1877, and the Haymarket Square riot was not necessarily typical of disputes between labor and management. Although labor violence continued unabated in the 1890s, with such dramatic episodes as the Homestead strike and the Pullman strike (see Chapter 20), often late-nineteenth-century labor disputes were settled peacefully. In most cases, however, management won the conflicts. Only in small towns, where prolabor and antiindustrial sentiment knew no class lines, did labor battle management on anything approaching even terms.

Unorganized and Organized Labor

Historians have used the term "robber barons" to characterize late-nineteenth-century industrialists. Whether "robber" is accurate or not is debatable, but "baron" is a fitting description. They controlled their industries as medieval barons ruled their fiefs. Their word was usually final, and such a modern concept as democracy found an unsympathetic environment inside factory walls. A Pennsylvania coal miner described accurately what workers experienced behind those walls: "They find monopolies as strong as government itself. They find capital as rigid as absolute monarchy. They find their so-called independence a myth, and that their subjection to power is as complete as when their forefathers were part and parcel of the baronial estate."

Unfortunately, during the last third of the nineteenth century, labor was unable to form an organization powerful enough to deal with cap-

ital on equal terms. Before 1900, most unions were weak, and their goals were often out of touch with the changing American economy. In addition, the labor force itself was divided along ethnic, racial, gender, and craft lines. It was during this period, then, that labor attempted to overcome its own divisions and fumbled its way toward a clearer vision of what were its own best interests.

Before the 1870s most American unions were locally rooted, craft-based organizations. They were geared to the small Jacksonian workshop, not to the large modern factory. The first union to attempt to organize all workers was the short-lived National Labor Union (NLU). Founded in Baltimore in 1866, the NLU was a consciously national organization. Its program was ambitious. Besides shorter hours and

The famous Haymarket Square riot of 1886 began as a peaceful protest meeting but ended in violence. The arrest of eight local radicals without real evidence sent a message to workers that the police and public opinion sided with the industrialists.

higher wages, it supported women's and blacks' rights, monetary reform, and worker-owned industries. As one of their leaders said, the "only way by which the toiling masses can protect themselves against the unjust claims and soul-crushing tyranny of capital" was for "themselves to become capitalists." It disdained the emerging industrial capitalism. Referring to capital, its leader, William Sylvis, wrote to Karl Marx: "We have made war upon it, and we mean to win it. If we can we will win through the ballot box; if not, we will resort to sterner means. A little bloodletting is sometimes necessary in desperate cases." Rich in ideas and solutions, the NLU was poor in organization and finances. The NLU, whose reach exceeded its grasp, died during the depression of the mid-1870s.

The vision of the NLU was carried on by the Noble and Holy Order of the Knights of Labor. Begun in 1869 as a secret fraternal order as well as a union, the Knights remained small and unimportant until 1878 when it went public. Led by Terence V. Powderly, a machinist and former mayor of Scranton, Pennsylvania, in 1881 the Knights opened its membership not only to "any person working for wages but to anyone who had at any time worked for wages." The Knights excluded only bankers, lawyers, liquor dealers, speculators, and stockbrokers, whom they viewed as money manipulators and exploiters.

Complete worker solidarity was the Knights' goal. "An injury to one is an injury to all," they proclaimed. They welcomed and spoke for all laborers—women and men, black and white, immigrant and native, unskilled and skilled. Like the NLU, the Knights rejected industrial capitalism and favored cooperatively owned industries. "The aim of the Knights of Labor," Powderly emphasized, "is to make each man his own employer." Although critics at the time labeled the Knights "wild-eyed, utopian visionaries," they are best understood in the context of exploited workers searching for a less exploitive alternative to industrial capitalism. If their statements were extreme, their suffering was real.

Powderly was an able leader, who had a clear view of the future and was able to express the fears and ambitions of American labor. He called for reforms of the currency system, the abolition of child labor, regulation of trusts and monopolies, an end to alien contract labor networks, and government ownership of public utilities. By nature a diplomatic, good-natured man, he favored peaceful arbitration of labor disputes and opposed strikes. He also opposed the formation of narrow trade unions, instead advocating that skilled workers should assist the unskilled. Harmony and fellowship ultimately dominated his vision of America's future. Consensus, not conflict, was his goal.

The Knights' rhetoric found sympathetic listeners among American workers. During the early 1880s membership rolls grew. Then came 1884, the beginning of what labor historians have called "the great upheaval." Strikes erupted in the coal fields of Pennsylvania and Ohio and the railroad yards of Missouri and Illinois. The labor conflicts continued into 1885 and 1886. Labor won some, but by no means all, of the strikes. Although its role was small, the Knights were associated with several of the important labor victories. By mid-1886 perhaps 750,000 workers had joined the Knights.

From that high point, however, the decline was rapid. From the start, the Knights could not weld together its diverse rank and file. Administrative and organizational problems surfaced, and Powderly's relatively conservative leadership was opposed by more radical members, who fully accepted strikes and conflict. In 1886, the Haymarket Square bombing branded all unions as un-American and violent in the public mind. By 1893, when Powderly was driven from office, the Knights' membership had declined alarmingly. Weakened and divided, it failed to survive the depression of the mid-1890s.

Unlike the Knights and the NLU, the American Federation of Labor (AFL) did not aspire to remake society. Its leaders accepted industrial capitalism and rejected partisan politics and the dreams of radical visionaries. Instead they concentrated on practical, reachable goals—higher wages, shorter work days, and improved working conditions. Most importantly, they only recruited skilled laborers, recognizing that easily replaceable unskilled workers were in a poor position to negotiate with employers.

Formed in 1886 by the coming together of skilled trade unions, the AFL was led ably by

CHRONOLOGY
OF KEY EVENTS

1866 National Labor Union is founded in Baltimore

1871 Congress declares that no Indian tribe "shall be acknowledged . . . as an independent nation, tribe or power"; Knights of Labor is founded

1877 Great railroad strike; 20 Molly Maguires are convicted and executed for terrorism in the Pennsylvania coal fields

1882 Chinese Exclusion Act suspends Chinese immigration for ten years; extended in 1892 and 1902

1886 Statue of Liberty is unveiled; Haymarket Square riot in Chicago; American Federation of Labor is founded in Columbus, Ohio

1887 Dawes Severalty Act authorizes the president to redistribute Indian lands among tribal members and gives U.S. citizenship to all Indians receiving land grants

1890 U.S. soldiers kill more than 300 Sioux Indians near Wounded Knee Creek in South Dakota

1892 Homestead, Pennsylvania, strike

1894 Pullman strike

1896 President Cleveland vetoes literacy requirement for adult immigrants

1915 Leo Frank lynching

1921 Emergency Quota Act provides that no more than 3 percent of a nationality in America in 1910 could immigrate annually to the United States

1924 National Origins Act lowers the immigration quota to two percent of each nationality residing in the United States in 1890; Snyder Act grants all Indians born in the United States full citizenship

As head of the American Federation of Labor (AFL), Samuel Gompers worked for higher wages, shorter hours, industrial safety, and the right of skilled workers to organize.

Samuel Gompers, a Jewish immigrant from England who had been the president of a New York cigar makers' union. Like many cigar makers, Gompers was well, if informally, educated. Cigar-rolling was a quiet job, and the rollers often employed one of their number as a reader. As a boy Gompers not only learned a skill, but he absorbed the leading political, economic, and literary ideas of his day. "In fact," Gompers later wrote, "these [readings and] discussions in the shops were more like public debating societies or . . . 'labor forums.'"

The workers discussed the works of Marx and Engels, and Gompers even learned German so that he could fully understand German socialists—but he never joined the socialist movement. He maintained that the transition from capitalism to socialism would be glacially slow. Far better, he felt, to strive for the attainable than talk, dream, and wait for the utopian.

As the head of the AFL for almost 40 years, Gompers used his considerable "moral power" and organizational ability to fight for achievable goals. American laborers were divided over religious, racial, ethnic, gender, and political issues, but they all desired higher wages, more leisure time, and greater liberty. Working out of his eight-by-ten office, and using tomato boxes for filing cases, Gompers battled for those unifying issues. He focused on the world around him, not the best of all possible worlds. For this reason, he opposed "theorizers" and "intellectuals" in the labor movement. Once effectively organized, he maintained, labor could deal with capital on equal terms.

Gompers's approach toward working with capital and organizing labor proved successful in the long run. Before 1900, however, the AFL was not more successful than the Knights or the NLU. In fact, workers benefited little from unions before the turn of the century. All together fewer than 5 percent of American workers joined trade unions, and the major areas of industrial growth were the least unionized. Nevertheless, the experimentation during the late nineteenth century taught workers valuable lessons. To combat the power of capital, labor needed equal power. During the twentieth century labor would move closer to that power.

CONCLUSION

In 1986 the Statue of Liberty was given a good cleaning. Its copper was shined as much as copper turned green can be shined, and its structure was refortified. America celebrated, and television newscasters recited once again Emma Lazarus's poem "The New Colossus"—or as one commentator called it "her 'huddled masses' poem." Few asked the question, "What are we celebrating?"

What America celebrated was nothing less than the emergence of modern America. In 1876 when France shipped the Statue of Liberty to the United States, the country, despite a recent civil war, was remarkably uniform. Most Americans traced their ancestry to Great Britain, worshiped in a Protestant church, and lived on farms or in small villages. If they were divided, it was along political and economic lines, not along ethnic and religious ones. The United States was not a world leader. Its navy was small, its diplomats uninfluential, and its industry still largely underdeveloped.

By 1900 America had changed radically. Unprecedented immigration had transformed the country into the most diverse nation in the world. Italians, Slavs, Serbs, Greeks, Chinese— a host of immigrants crowded into American cities. Catholics and Jews worked alongside Protestants in the country's expanding industries. For some it was an exciting, hopeful time; for others a painful, disillusioning one. Old America gave way to a New America with startling speed. In fact, most Americans in 1900 had not yet adjusted to the massive changes. What role would the new immigrants play in American life? What rights did workers have in the large industries? These and other questions would be answered in the next century.

SUGGESTIONS FOR FURTHER READING

OVERVIEWS AND SURVEYS

Thomas J. Archdeacon, *Becoming American: An Ethnic History* (1983); John Bodnar, *The Transplanted: A History of Immigrants in Urban America* (1985); Roger Daniels, *Coming to America: A History of Immigration and Ethnicity in American Life* (1990); Leonard Dinnerstein and David Reimers, *Ethnic Americans* (1975); Harold U. Faulkner, *Politics, Reform, and Expansion* (1959); John Garraty, *The New Commonwealth* (1968); Ray Ginger, *The Age of Excess* (1965); Oscar Handlin, *The Uprooted*, 2d ed. (1973); Samuel Hays, *The Response to Industrialism, 1885–1914* (1957); Jacqueline Jones, *The Dispossessed: America's Underclasses from the Civil War to the Present* (1992); Maldwyn Allen Jones, *American Immigration*, 2d ed. (1992); Alan M. Kraut, *The Huddled Masses* (1982); James S. Olson, *The Ethnic Dimension in American History* (1979); Rudolph J. Vecoli and Suzanne M. Sinke, eds., *A Century of European Migrations, 1830–1930* (1991); Robert Wiebe, *The Search for Order, 1877–1920* (1967).

HUDDLED MASSES AT THE GOLDEN DOOR

Rodolfo Acuña, *Occupied America: A History of Chicanos*, 3d ed. (1988); Josef J. Barton, *Peasants and Strangers* (1975); Rowland Berthoff, *British Immigrants in Industrial America, 1790–1950* (1953); John W. Briggs, *The Italian Passage* (1978); Jack Chen, *The Chinese of America* (1980); Alexander DeConde, *Half Bitter, Half Sweet: An Excursion into Italian-American History* (1971); Hasia R. Diner, *Erin's Daughters in America: Irish Immigrant Women in the Nineteenth Century* (1983); John Duff, *The Irish in the United States* (1971); David M. Emmons, *The Butte Irish* (1989); Elizabeth Ewen, *Immigrant Women in the Land of Dollars: Life and Culture on the Lower East Side* (1985); Richard Gambino, *Blood of My Blood* (1974); Mario García, *Desert Immigrants* (1981); Susan A. Glenn, *Daughters of the Shtetl: Life and Labor in the Immigrant Generation* (1990); Caroline Golab, *Immigrant Destinations* (1977); Irving Howe, *World of Our Fathers* (1976); Yuji Ichioka, *The Issei: The World of the First Generation Japanese Americans, 1885–1924* (1988); Maldwyn Allen Jones, *American Immigration* (1960), and *Destination America* (1976); Thomas Kessner, *The Golden Door* (1977); Harry Kitano, *Japanese Americans*, 2d ed. (1976); Helen Znaniecka Lopata, *Polish Americans* (1976); Joseph Lopreato, *Italian Americans* (1970); Carey McWilliams, *North from Mexico* (1948); Ande Manners, *Poor Cousins* (1972); Kerby A. Miller, *Emigrants and Exiles: Ireland and the Irish Exodus to North America* (1985); Charles C. Moskos, Jr., *Greek Americans*, 2d ed. (1989); Cecyle S. Neidle, *America's Immigrant Women* (1975); Humbert Nelli, *Italians in Chicago, 1880–1930* (1970), and *The Business of Crime* (1976); William Petersen, *Japanese Americans* (1971); Moses Rischin, *The Promised City: New York's Jews, 1870–1914* (1962); Andrew Rolle, *The Immigrant Upraised* (1968), and *The Italian Americans* (1980); Theodore Saloutos, *The Greeks in the United States* (1964); Philip Taylor, *The Distant Magnet* (1971); Stephan Thernstrom, *Poverty and Progress* (1964), and *The Other Bostonians* (1973); Maurice Violette, *The Franco Americans* (1976); Sydney Weinberg, *The World of Our Mothers: Lives of Jewish Immigrant Women* (1988); Joseph Wytrawal, *America's Polish Heritage* (1961), and *The Poles in America* (1969); Virginia Yans-McLaughlin, *Family and Community: Italian Immigrants in Buffalo, 1880–1930* (1977); Olivier Zunz, *The Changing Face of Inequality* (1982).

NATIVISM: THE ANTI-IMMIGRANT REACTION

David H. Bennett, *The Party of Fear: From Nativist Movements to the New Right in American History* (1988); Robert Carlson, *The Quest for Conformity* (1975); Leonard Dinnerstein, *The Leo Frank Case* (1968); Milton M. Gordon, *Assimilation in American Life* (1964); Mark Haller, *Eugenics* (1963); Leo Hershkowitz, *Tweed's New York* (1977); John Higham, *Strangers in the Land* (1955); Gerd Korman, *Industrialism, Immigrants, and Americanizers* (1967); Richard M. Linkh, *American Catholicism and European Immigrants, 1900–1924* (1975); Seymour Mandelbaum, *Boss Tweed's New York* (1965); Paul McBride, *Culture Clash* (1975); Stuart Creighton Miller, *The Unwelcome Immigrant* (1969); Thomas J. Pavlak, *Ethnic Identification and Political Behavior* (1976); Diane Ravitch, *The Great School Wars* (1974); Alexander Saxton, *The Indispensable Enemy* (1971).

WORKING IN INDUSTRIAL AMERICA

Paul Avrich, *The Haymarket Tragedy* (1984); James R. Barrett, *Work and Community in the Jungle: Chicago's Packinghouse Workers, 1894–1922* (1987); Susan Porter Benson, *Counter Cultures: Saleswomen, Managers, and Customers in American Department Stores, 1890–1940* (1986); John Bodnar, *Immigration and Industrialization* (1977); Jeanne Boydston, *Home and Work: Housework, Wages, and the Ideology of Labor in the Early Republic* (1990); Paul Boyer, *Urban Masses and Moral Order in America, 1820–1920* (1978); David Brody, *Steelworkers in America* (1960); Wayne G. Broehl, Jr., *The Molly Maguires* (1964); Robert V. Bruce, *1877: Year of Violence* (1959); John R. Commons, et al., *History of Labour in the United States*, 4 vols. (1918–1935); Ruth Schwartz Cowan, *More Work for Mother: The Ironies of Household Technology* (1983); Melvyn Dubofsky, *Industrialism and the American Worker*, 2d ed. (1985), and *We Shall Be All: A History of the Industrial Workers of the World* (1969); Leon Fink, *Workingmen's Democracy: The Knights of Labor and American Politics* (1983); Victor Greene, *The Slavic Community on Strike* (1968); Gerald Grob, *Workers and Utopia* (1961); Herbert Gutman, *Work, Culture, and Society in Industrializing America* (1976); Jacqueline Hall, et al., *Like a Family: The Making of a Southern Cotton Mill World* (1987); Tamara Hareven and Randolph Langenbach, *Amoskeag: Life and Work in an American Factory-City* (1979) and Hareven, *Family, Time, and Industrial Timer* (1982); Alice Kessler-Harris, *Out to Work: A History of Wage-Earning Women in the United States* (1982); William H. Harris, *The Harder We Run: Black Workers Since the Civil War* (1982); David Katzman, *Seven Days a Week: Women and Domestic Service in Industrializing America* (1978); Stuart B. Kaufman, *Samuel Gompers and the Origins of the AFL* (1973); Susan Kennedy, *If All We Did Was to Weep at Home: A History of White Working-Class Women in America* (1979); S. J. Kleinberg, *The Shadow of the Mills: Working-Class Families in Pittsburgh, 1870–1907* (1989); Susan Levine, *Labor's True Woman, Carpet Weavers, Industrialization, and Labor Reform in the Gilded Age* (1984); Harold Livesay, *Samuel Gompers and Organized Labor in America* (1978); Glenna Matthews, *"Just a Housewife": The Rise and Fall of Domesticity in America* (1987); David Montgomery, *Beyond Equality* (1967), *Workers' Control in America* (1979), and *The Fall of the House of Labor, 1865–1925* (1987); Stephen H. Norwood, *Labor's Flaming Youth: Telephone Operators and Worker Militancy, 1878–1923* (1990); Annegret S.

Ogden, *The Great American Housewife: From Helpmate to Wage Earner* (1986); Daniel T. Rodgers, *The Work Ethic in Industrial America, 1850–1920* (1978); Gerald Rosenblum, *Immigrant Workers* (1973); Roy A. Rosenzweig, *Eight Hours for What We Will* (1983); Nick Salvatore, *Eugene V. Debs, Citizen and Socialist* (1982); David Shannon, *The Socialist Party of America* (1955); Peter Shergold, *Working-Class Life* (1982); Susan Strasser, *Never Done: A History of American Housework* (1982); Sharon Hartman Strom, *Beyond the Typewriter: Gender, Class, and the Origins of Modern American Office Work* (1992); Leslie W. Tentler, *Wage-Earning Women* (1979); Daniel J. Walkowitz, *Worker City, Company Town: Iron and Cotton-Worker Protest in Troy and Cohoes, New York, 1855–84* (1978); Norman Ware, *The Labor Movement in the United States, 1860–1895* (1929).

Fig. 16

CHAPTER 19

The Rise of an Urban Society and City People

Andrew Borden had, as the old Scotch saying goes, short arms and long pockets. He was cheap, not because he had to be frugal but because he hated to spend money. He had dedicated his entire life to making and saving money, and tales of his unethical and parsimonious business behavior were legendary in his home town of Fall River, Massachusetts. Local gossips maintained that as an undertaker he cut off the feet of corpses so that he could fit them into undersized coffins that he had purchased at a very good price. Andrew, however, was not interested in rumors or the opinions of other people; he was concerned with his own rising fortunes. By 1892 he had amassed over half a million dollars, and he controlled the Fall River Union Savings Bank as well as serving as the director of the Globe Yard Mill Company, the First National Bank, the Troy Cotton and Manufacturing Company, and the Merchants Manufacturing Company.

Andrew was rich, but he did not live like a wealthy man. Instead of living alongside the other prosperous Fall River citizens in the elite neighborhood known as The Hill, Andrew resided in an area near the business district called the flats. He liked to save time as well as money, and from the flats he could conveniently walk to work. For his daughters Lizzie and Emma, whose eyes and dreams focused on The Hill, life in the flats was an intolerable embarrassment. Their house was a grim, boxlike structure that lacked comfort and privacy. Since Andrew believed that running water on each floor was a wasteful luxury, the only washing facilities were a cold-water faucet in the kitchen and a laundry room water tap in the cellar. Also in the cellar was the only toilet in the house. To make matters worse, the house was not connected to the Fall River gas main. Andrew preferred to use kerosene to light his house. Although it did not provide as good light or burn as cleanly as gas, it was less expensive. To save even more money, he and his family frequently sat in the dark.

The Borden home was far from happy. Lizzie and Emma, ages 32 and 42 in 1892, strongly disliked their stepmother Abby and resented Andrew's penny-pinching ways. Lizzie especially felt alienated from the world around her.

Although Fall River was the largest cotton-manufacturing town in America, it offered few opportunities for the unmarried daughter of a prosperous man. Society expected a woman of Lizzie's social position to marry, and while she waited for a proper suitor, her only respectable social outlets were church and community service. So Lizzie taught a Sunday School class and was active in the Women's Christian Temperance Union, the Ladies' Fruit and Flower Mission, and other organizations. She kept herself busy, but she was not happy.

In August, 1892, strange things started to happen in the Borden home. They began after Lizzie and Emma learned that Andrew had secretly changed his will. Abby became violently ill. In time so did the Borden maid Bridget Sullivan and Andrew himself. Abby told a neighborhood doctor that she had been poisoned, but Andrew refused to listen to her wild ideas. Shortly thereafter, Lizzie went shopping for prussic acid, a deadly poison she said she needed to clean her sealskin cape. When a Fall River druggist refused her request, she left the store in an agitated state. Later in the day, she told a friend that she feared an unknown enemy of her father's was after him. "I'm afraid somebody will do something," she said.

On August 4, 1892, Bridget awoke early and ill, but she still managed to prepare a large breakfast of johnnycakes, fresh-baked bread, ginger and oatmeal cookies with raisins, and some three-day-old mutton and hot mutton soup. After eating a hearty meal, Andrew left for work. Bridget also left to do some work outside. This left Abby and Lizzie in the house alone. Then somebody did something very specific and very grisly. As Abby was bent over making the bed in the guest room, someone moved into the room unobserved and killed her with an ax.

Andrew came home for lunch earlier than usual. He asked Lizzie where Abby was, and she said she did not know. Unconcerned, Andrew, who was not feeling well, lay down on the parlor sofa for a nap. He never awoke. Like Abby, he was slaughtered by someone with an ax. Lizzie "discovered" his body, still lying on the sofa. She called Bridget, who had taken the back stairs to her attic room: "Come down quick; father's dead; somebody came in and killed him."

Preconceived notions of Victorian femininity saved Lizzie Borden from being convicted of murdering her father and stepmother.

Experts have examined and reexamined the crime, and most have reached the same conclusion: Lizzie killed her father and stepmother. In fact, Lizzie was tried for the gruesome murders. Despite a preponderance of evidence, however, an all male jury found her not guilty. Their verdict was unanimous and was arrived at without debate or disagreement. A woman of Lizzie's social position, they affirmed, simply could not have committed such a terrible crime.

Even before the trial began, newspaper and magazine writers had judged Lizzie innocent for the same reasons. As historian Kathryn Allamong Jacob, an expert on the case, noted, "Americans were certain that well-brought up daughters could not commit murder with a hatchet on sunny summer mornings." Criminal women, they believed, originated in the lower classes and even looked evil. A criminologist writing in the *North American Review* commented, "[The female criminal] has coarse black hair and a good deal of it. . . . She has often a long face, a receding forehead, overjutting brows, prominent cheek bones, an exaggerated frontal angle as seen in monkeys and savage races, and nearly always square jaws." They did not look like round-faced Lizzie, and did not belong to the Ladies' Fruit and Flower Mission.

Jurors and editorialists alike judged Lizzie according to their preconceived notions of Victorian womanhood. They believed that such a woman was gentle, docile, and physically frail, short on analytical ability but long on nurturing instincts. "Women," wrote an editorialist for *Scribner's*, "are merely large babies. They are shortsighted, frivolous and occupy an intermediate stage between children and men." Too uncoordinated and weak to accurately swing an ax and too gentle and unintelligent to coldly plan a double murder, women of Lizzie's background simply had to be innocent because of their basic innocence.

Even as Lizzie was being tried and found innocent, Victorian notions were being challenged. In the larger cities of America, a new culture was taking form, one based on freedoms, not restraints. In this new climate, anything was possible, or so at least some people claimed. Immigrants could become millionaires and women could vote and hold office. Rigid Victorian concepts crumbled under the weight of new ideas; but the new freedoms came with a high price. In both the cities and the culture that flourished within them, a new order had to be constructed out of the chaos of freedom.

NEW CITIES AND NEW PROBLEMS

Transforming the Walking City

Andrew Borden's life was a throwback to older urban residential patterns. He would have felt comfortable with the physical layout of the mid-nineteenth-century walking city. In an age before reliable mass transportation, when only the rich could afford a carriage, the majority of city dwellers had to walk to and from work. This simple fact dictated the type of cities that emerged in America. They were compact and crowded, their sizes normally limited to about two miles radius from center city or the distance a person could walk in half an hour. Even America's largest cities—New York, Philadelphia, and Boston—conformed to these standards.

Inside these cities, houses, businesses, and factories were strewn about willy-nilly. Tightly packed near the waterfront were shops, banks, warehouses, and business offices, and not far away were the residences of the people who owned those enterprises or worked in them. There was little residential segregation. If the rich occupied the finest houses in the center city, the poor lived in the alleys and dirty streets close by. In city life, people dealt with people in this congested, highly personalized world. Rich and poor, native-born and immigrant, black and white—they all walked along the same streets and worked in the same area.

Booming industrialization during the last third of the century shattered this arrangement. As industrialists built their new plants in or near existing cities, urban growth accelerated at an alarming rate. Like twin children, factories and cities grew and matured together, each helping the other to reach its physical potentials. In 1860, before America's industrial surge, 20 percent of the population lived in cities. By 1900 almost 40 percent of the population lived in cities or towns, and that figure climbed to over 50 percent in 1920. At the same time, the numbers of large cities (those with a population of over 100,000) increased at an even faster rate. In 1860, America had only 9 large cities. The numbers rose to 38 in 1900 and 68 in 1920.

Immigrant as well as native sources fueled the urban explosion. Although most of the late-nineteenth-century immigrants came from rural communities, they settled in America's industrial heartland (see Chapter 18). In 1920, 87 percent of Irish immigrants, 89 percent of the Russians, 84 percent of Italians and Poles, 80 percent of Hungarians, and 75 percent of Aus-

trians, British, and Canadians lived in cities. Added to these were the native-born migrants who moved from poor rural areas to the cities. For every industrial worker who moved to the countryside, 20 farmers moved to urban America. Just as in Europe and Asia, rural opportunities in the United States were dwindling at the same time that the rural population was growing. Thus 10 farm sons moved to the cities for each son who became a farm owner.

Black migration from the rural South to the urban North further expanded the labor pool in the industrial cities. Slow at first, it increased each decade, as blacks left the land of their bondage determined to forge a better life for themselves and their families in the northern cities. Between 1897 and 1920 almost one million blacks left the South, and of those, 85 percent settled in the urban North.

City Technology

Even the largest of the walking cities was unprepared to meet the demands the newcomers placed on it. Cities were already crowded, and construction technology was not yet sufficiently advanced to accommodate the recent arrivals. But in time, engineers and scientists discovered ways to expand cities. During the half century after 1870, horizontal and vertical growth changed the skyline and living conditions of urban America.

Better transportation facilities solved the basic limitation of the walking city. As early as the 1830s, the horse-drawn omnibus permitted a handful of wealthier urbanites to escape life in the crowded center city. Usually pulled by one or two horses, an omnibus carried 12 to 20 passengers along a fixed route for between 6 and 12 cents. Faster than walking, it was also expensive, certainly beyond the means of an unskilled laborer who earned less than one dollar a day. Similarly the commuter railroads, which also dated back to the 1830s and 1840s and cost between 12 and 25 cents to ride, served only the wealthier classes. Constructed and owned by entrepreneurs, omnibuses and commuter railways existed only for the comfort of people who could pay.

The horse railway expanded the city for the middle-class urbanites, white-collar workers,

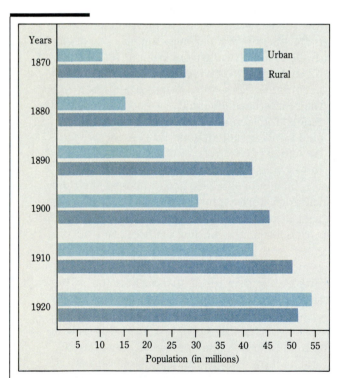

Figure 19.1
Urban and rural population, 1870–1920. Immigrants and native-born migrants from rural areas contributed to the urban population explosion.

During the early decades of the twentieth century, hundreds of thousands of African-Americans fled the rural South for the cities of the industrial North.

and skilled workers. For 5 cents, these horse-drawn omnibuses carried passengers over steel rails at a speed of 6 to 8 miles per hour. In the southern and border towns, the mules, which tended to live longer, pulled the omnibuses. By the 1880s, over 300 American cities and towns had constructed horsecar lines, and they significantly expanded the size of cities. Now a person could live 5 miles from his or her place of work and still travel there in less than an hour. The age of walking was almost over.

The horsecar was not always as safe or as comfortable as its developers planned. Travelers complained about pickpockets, tobacco juice, and overcrowding. Describing the activity of pickpockets, one passenger suggested, "Before boarding a car, prudent persons leave their purses and watches in the safe deposit company and carry bowie knives and derringers." Entrepreneurial conductors often overloaded their cars, occasionally packing 80 persons into a car designed for 25, a situation which made the

pickpocket's task easier. Novelist William Dean Howells observed, "Men and women are indecently crushed without regard for the personal dignity we prize."

Drivers and horses suffered even worse fates. Underfed, overworked horses struggled day after day until they dropped from exhaustion, at which point they were unhitched and left to die. The drivers fared little better. In New York City during the early 1880s they worked 16-hour days for $12 a week. Exposed to the weather in the front or rear of the cars, they suffered terribly in the winter as cold winds whipped their faces and froze their fingers around the reins. One streetcar conductor, hardened by years of work, remarked, "I feel that I could almost digest cobble stones." When the conductors demanded a 12-hour day, a young New York assemblyman and future president, Theodore Roosevelt, labeled them "communistic" and suggested that no men who asked to be so coddled were worthy of their sex.

For hillier cities like San Francisco and Pittsburgh, the cable car, introduced during the 1870s, proved a blessing for humans and horse alike. Utilizing steam power, cable cars were faster and cleaner than transportation that depended on horses. Even relatively flat cities such as Kansas City and Chicago installed cable cars. Pulled by a moving underground cable, engineers believed it would be the public transportation of the future—but its problems were considerable. Expensive to install and quick to break down, the cable car soon became a victim of the electric trolley, which was cheaper to run and more dependable.

In 1888, former naval engineer Frank Sprague converted the horsecar network of Richmond, Virginia, to electricity. Employing the electrical current in overhead wires, trolleys could operate in stop-and-go traffic and travel at average speeds of 10 to 12 miles per hour. American cities quickly climbed aboard the electric bandwagon. By 1902, 97 percent of urban transit mileage had been electrified. Trolleys connected not only city with suburb, but also city with city. By 1920 a person could travel from Boston to New York entirely by trolleys known as interurbans.

Called "one of the most rapidly accepted innovations in the history of technology," trolleys were not without their problems. The overhead wires gave cities a weblike appearance, and in the winter the electric wires snapped from the cold and created serious dangers. In addition, they sometimes frightened horses and thus worsened traffic problems. Altogether, by the 1890s, the mixture of horsecars, cable cars, and trolleys jostling each other and pedestrians on city streets created immense traffic jams. English science fiction writer H. G. Wells found Chicago streets in 1906 "simply chaotic—one hoarse cry for discipline."

Clogged streets inspired engineers to search for other transportation solutions. Looking above and below ground, they designed elevated railway lines and subways. Electricity powered both, and each helped to ease mass transportation for the masses. The Chicago "el" (elevated railway) and the New York City subway satisfied the minds of urban traffic engineers and even occasionally stirred the souls of artists. W. Louis Sonntag, Jr., painted a beautiful watercolor of New York City's Bowery in 1896, capturing the wonder of the age of electricity. Illuminated by electric lights, an el and a trolley pass in the night.

While mass transportation allowed cities to spread miles beyond their cores, steel and glass permitted cities to reach for the sky. At midcentury, few buildings, were higher than five stories. Church spires still dominated the urban skyline. Buildings, like cities themselves, were personal; they did not dwarf the individual. That, however, soon changed. As a real estate columnist wrote in the *Chicago Tribune* in 1888: "In real estate calculations, Chicago has thus far had but three directions, north, south, and west, but there are indications now that a fourth is to be added and that it is to cut a larger figure in the coming decade than all the others. The new direction is zenithward. Since water hems in the business center on three sides and a nexus of railroads on the south, Chicago must grow upward."

Using traditional brick-and-masonry construction, architects could not design buildings much higher than ten stories. In 1885 New York architect William LeBaron Jenney solved the problem by using cast iron and steel, the product that was transforming America into an industrial giant. Using light masonry over an iron and steel skeleton, Jenney built the Home Insurance Building in Chicago, which although only ten stories was the first true skyscraper in history. Steel, light masonry, and eventually glass revolutionized building construction, and the use of electric elevators made skyscrapers functional.

Louis Henri Sullivan, who had once worked for Jenney, demonstrated the architectural possibilities of the skyscraper. Working in Chicago, a town that had been almost totally destroyed by the great fire in 1871, Sullivan became the leading exponent of skyscraper technology, turning his back on classical models and preaching the doctrine that "form follows function." Quick-tempered and difficult to work with, Sullivan nonetheless designed many of the most beautiful and practical skyscrapers in America, including the Wainwright Building in St. Louis and the Transportation Building in Chicago.

Skyscrapers changed the profile of American cities as surely as industrialism altered the American landscape. Returning to America from Europe in 1906, novelist Henry James observed "the multitudinous skyscrapers standing up to the view . . . like extravagant pins in a cushion already overplanted, and stuck in as in the dark, anywhere and anyhow." What disturbed James's sensibilities excited most Americans. The skyscraper, many reasoned, was America out to prove that its reach did not exceed its grasp. In fact, businesspeople and industrialists even used skyscrapers to glorify their own accomplishments. Bigger was best, and the race to the sky was on. In 1913, President Woodrow Wilson pressed the button that lit up the Woolworth Building. At 792 feet, it was the largest building in America, a monument to five-and-ten-cents king Frank Woolworth. This hauntingly beautiful structure, which freely adapted aspects of Gothic and Moorish construction, truly was "the Cathedral of Commerce."

The Segregated City

With the outward and upward growth of cities came an end to the more personal walking city. Mass transportation freed the upper and middle classes from having to live in the city core. Voicing their opinion with their feet, they scampered for the "streetcar suburbs," where popular theory held that the water was purer, the trees fuller, and the air fresher. They commuted to work and no longer mixed daily with their economic inferiors.

The working class moved into areas and even houses deserted by wealthier families. In New York City the large stately brownstone homes that had served the upper classes were divided into small apartments that satisfied the new demand for inexpensive housing. Of course, architects had not designed the houses to be used as multiunit apartments, and numerous problems resulted. Heatless, sunless, and poorly ventilated rooms became increasingly common.

Ethnic groups and races, like economic classes, tended to stake out neighborhoods in the new, larger cities. In addition, real estate

This watercolor of New York City's Bowery at night by W. Louis Sonntag, Jr., shows how steam, steel, and electricity played a major part in transforming cities.

brokers and landlords restricted blacks and immigrants to particular areas. For the first time, black ghettos emerged in the major northern cities, and in Chicago, New York, Boston, and Philadelphia, English became a foreign language in ethnic neighborhoods. These neighborhoods reproduced in their finer details Old World conditions. Familiar faces, foods, churches, and speech patterns comforted lonely immigrants. Even Old World prejudices survived in the ethnic neighborhoods. Greeks from Athens continued to regard Spartans as stupid and pugnacious, and northern Italians maintained their belief that southern Italians were lazy and untrustworthy.

Since members of the ethnic working class were too poor for even moderately priced mass transit, they tended to settle close to their places of work. Only on a bitterly cold winter day would workers pay the nickle or dime it cost to ride a streetcar or a horse-pulled omnibus. In New York City, Jews and Italians lived within walking distance of the Lower East Side garment factories. In Chicago, the Poles and Lithuanians who worked in the meat-packing industry awoke in the morning and went to sleep at night close to the sound of dying animals and the stench of stockyard filth.

Just as new residential trends separated rich and poor, the central business district underwent important changes. Prices for central city real estate shot up at an incredible rate, sometimes as much as 1000 percent a decade in the late nineteenth century. Only businesses and industries could afford the new prices, and the central cities were turned over to high-income businesses, banks, warehouses, railroad terminals, and the recently developed department stores. It became an area where money was made, not where people lived.

The Problems of Growth

By the 1890s, British observers despaired over what had become of the once small American cities. The uncontrolled growth, they suggested, had created ugliness on an almost unprecedented scale. English traveler Charles Philips Trevelyan graphically described the horrors of industrial Pittsburgh:

> A cloud of smoke hangs over it by day. The glow of scores of furnaces light the river banks by night. It stands at the junction of two great rivers, the Monongahela which flows down in a turbid yellowish stream, and the Allegheny which is blackish . . . All nations are jumbled up here, the poor living in tenement dens or wooden shanties thrown up or dumped down with little reference to roads or situation, whenever a new house is wanted. It is the most chaotic city, and as yet there is no public spirit or public consciousness to make conditions healthy or decent.

Rudyard Kipling sounded a similar note after visiting Chicago. Although he had seen the suffering and overcrowded conditions of Bombay and Cairo, Kipling was appalled by the Windy City: "This place is the first American city I have encountered . . . Having seen it, I urgently desire never to see it again."

Trevelyan's and Kipling's judgments were not the rantings of anti-American foreigners. Numerous American observers echoed their opinions. American cities were unprepared for the incredible growth they experienced during the late nineteenth century. Housing, clean water, competent police, and adequate public services were all in short supply. To make matters worse, the people who moved to the cities usually came from rural areas and were uninitiated in the ways of city life. Finally, health standards were low everywhere and scientists had barely begun to study the problems and diseases created by crowded urban conditions.

High crime rates plagued rich and poor. Pickpockets, robbers, con artists, and violent gangs roamed the streets and alleyways of American cities. Urban officials had established police forces in the 1830s and 1840s. In the 1850s, police were outfitted with uniforms and badges and allowed to carry clubs and revolvers. Still, the police could not control or seriously curtail urban crime. In fact, during this earlier period, police were often expected to clean streets, inspect boilers, or run poorhouses as well as prevent crime and maintain public order. In addition, police corruption was as common as purse snatchings. Police took bribes from saloon keepers and streetwalkers to overlook illegal activities, and it was not uncommon to find policemen serving the ends of robbers or intimidating voters on election day. They owed their loyalty to the political boss who appointed them, not to some abstract public. Not until the end of the century would there be successful attempts to bring professionalism and civil service reform to police departments.

Housing presented an even more pressing problem. The immigrants disembarking at the ports of entry and the farmers arriving at the train depots had to have some place to live. The situation created opportunities as well as problems. The building industry was one of the great urban boom industries, and its leaders largely determined the shape and profile of the modern city. Like the other businesspeople, they worked in an essentially unregulated economic world, bent on maximizing their profits and equipped with a lofty disregard of public opinion.

In urban housing money talked. The rich could afford good housing. In New York City, the

Tenement life on the Lower East Side of New York was overcrowded, filthy, and dangerous. For the wealthy, city life could be quite luxurious, as the rooms of Alexander T. Stewart's Fifth Avenue mansion show.

wealthy built opulent mansions up Fifth Avenue along Central Park. Moving up Fifth Avenue from Forty-second Street to Ninety-second Street, the "homes" of the leaders of New York's—and often the nation's—society, business, commerce, and industry shouldered each other for their place in the sun. Dubbed the Gold Coast, there were "French" chateaux, "castles on the Rhine," and Cornelius Vanderbilt's block-long Gothic palace. High ceilings, European furnishings, and spacious rooms were commonplace, and even the new apartments of the upper classes were designed and constructed by gifted architects and artisans. Along Central Park West at Seventy-second Street, the Dakota Apartments still stand as a standard for "the good life." Like the Woolworth Building, they are one of the beautiful architectural triumphs of the period.

Tenements, built to minimal codes but overcrowded and undermaintained, greeted urban newcomers without money. They were de-

signed to cram the largest number of people into the smallest amount of space. Like skyscrapers, they made use of vertical space by piling family upon family into small, poorly lighted, badly ventilated apartments. By 1900 portions of the Jewish Tenth Ward in the New York's Lower East Side had reached population density levels of 500,000 persons to one square mile and as many as one person per square foot of land in the most crowded areas. This was perhaps the highest density in world history. To be in the land of tenements, noted writer William Dean Howells, "is to inhale the stenches of the neglected streets, and to catch the yet fouler and dreadfuller poverty-smell which breathes from the open doorways. . . . It is to see the work-worn look of mothers, the squalor of the babies, the haggish ugliness of the old women, and the slovenly frowziness of the young girls."

Dumbbell tenements were the most notorious examples of exploitative urban housing. Each building had an indentation in the middle—thus giving it the famous dumbbell shape—that allowed for better ventilation. Architectural critic Lewis Mumford claimed they "raised bad housing into an art." Although they conformed to the Tenement Reform Law of 1879, which required all rooms to have access to light and air, they made maximum use of standard 25- by 100-feet urban lots. The problems inherent in the dumbbell tenement were obvious from the first, but the design was not outlawed in New York until 1901. In fact, dumbbell apartments spread east to Boston and west to Cincinnati and Cleveland.

Street conditions, unlike housing, were more democratic in that they plagued rich and poor alike. People dumped their trash and horses unloaded their own particular pollution onto the dirty city thoroughfares. Spring rains turned them into fetid quagmires, and winter freezes left them with hard deep ruts. In addition, well into the 1870s, pigs roamed the streets of most cities, rooting for food in the garbage and further polluting the environment. Indeed, when trolleys began to replace horses as the primary form of urban transportation, editorialists predicted that the age of air pollution would soon come to an end. Yet as late as 1900, there were still 150,000 horses in New York City, each producing between 20 and 30 pounds of manure a day. Even in a smaller city such as Rochester, New York, health officials estimated that in 1900 the city's 15,000 horses produced enough excrement to fill a hole one acre in area and 175 feet deep.

Waste not dumped onto the streets often found its way into the rivers that flowed through the major cities or the harbors that bordered them. By the turn of the century, 13 million gallons of sewage were emptied each day into the Delaware River, the major source for Philadelphia's drinking water. In Baltimore, according to H. L. Mencken, the bay smelled like a "billion polecats." This paled in comparison to Pittsburgh's rivers. The Golden Triangle, where the Allegheny and Monongahela rivers meet to form the Ohio River, could have just as aptly been dubbed the black triangle because of the industrial waste poured into it.

The establishment of dump sites did little to solve the terrible garbage problem. The Reverend Hugh Miller Thompson described the conditions in a New Orleans dump to a meeting of the American Public Health Association in 1879: "Thither were brought the dead dogs and cats, the kitchen garbage and the like, and duly dumped. This festering rotten mess was picked over by rag-pickers and wallowed over by pigs, pigs and humans contesting for a living in it, and as the heaps increased, the odors increased also, and the mass lay corrupting under a tropical sun, dispersing the pestilential fumes where the winds carried them."

Between 1880 and 1914, the years of the greatest amount of immigration, the garbage problem worsened. According to a 1905 study, Americans produced more trash than any other people. An American city dweller, for example, produced an average 860 pounds of mixed rubbish each year, compared to 450 pounds per capita in English cities and 319 pounds in German cities. Viewed in a more graphic way, one 1912 report noted that if the year's refuse of New York City was gathered in one place, "the resulting mass would equal in volume a cube about one eighth of a mile on an edge. This surprising volume is over three times that of the great pyramid of Gizeh, and would accommodate one hundred and forty Washington monuments with ease."

Overcrowded housing, polluted streets and rivers, uncollected garbage—these problems and others contributed to the notoriously unhealthy urban environment. Unfortunately advances in medicine and public health lagged behind technological and industrial progress. Diseases ranging from yellow fever and smallpox to diphtheria and typhoid claimed victims by the thousands. In 1878 a yellow fever epidemic moved along the Mississippi River; 5150 people died in Memphis and another 3977 in New Orleans. Known as the American Plague, the disease struck without warning and often led to a rapid but painful death. Walter Reed's discovery in 1900 that the disease was carried by the *Aedes aegypti* mosquito led to a cure for the dreaded scourge.

The smallpox virus proved a more persistent problem. Although not as deadly as yellow fever, it struck more people and left millions of faces scarred by pockmarks. Like diphtheria and scarlet fever, smallpox flourished in the overcrowded and garbage-strewn cities. During the late nineteenth century, health wardens unsuccessfully tried to limit the diseases. Often party hacks, they owed their jobs to their political loyalty rather than their knowledge of public health. Asked to define "hygiene," one worthy health official replied, "It is a mist rising from wet ground."

Death, suffering, and massive inconvenience prodded city officials to move toward a more systematic approach to their problems. It was a slow transition, involving the replacement of political appointees with trained experts. Yet during the late nineteenth century remarkable progress was made, particularly after the discovery of the germ theory in the 1880s, which linked contagious disease to environmental conditions.

Health officials and urban engineers vigorously attacked the sewage and water problems. Discussing the importance of a good sewer system, one Baltimore engineer noted in 1907 that Paris is "the center of all that is best in art, literature, science, and architecture, and is both clean and beautiful. In the evolution of this ideal attainment, its sewers took at least a leading part." Without good sewers and clean drinking water, urban civilization was almost a contradiction of terms. To improve conditions, cities replaced cesspools and backyard privies with modern sewer systems, and most large cities turned to filtration and chlorination to assure pure water supplies.

From Private City to Public City

In housing, pure water, and clean streets, the battle lines in most cities were drawn between individual profits and public need. Individual entrepreneurs shaped the modern American city. They laid the horsecar and trolley lines, constructed the skyscrapers, apartments, and tenements, and provided water for the growing urban populations. Like their industrial counterparts, they worked, planned, and invested, fully expecting to earn huge profits. Their pocketbooks came before their civic responsibilities. The result was that they provided good housing and services for only those city dwellers who could pay.

Historians have termed this type of city the "private city." Allowing the profit motive to de-

termine urban growth created numerous problems. It led to such waste and inefficiency as competing trolley lines, where promoters could turn a profit, and such inconveniences as poorly cleaned streets, where there was little money to be made. But most important, it stood contrary to planned urban growth. Urban entrepreneurs were generally unconcerned about the city as a whole. They regarded parks as uneconomic use of real estate and battled against the idea of zoning. In the end, they contributed to the ugliness and problems of Pittsburgh, New York, Chicago, and other American cities.

By the turn of the century, urban engineers and other experts began calling for planned urban growth and more concern for city services. Advocates of the "public city," they wanted efficient, clean, healthy cities where rich and poor could enjoy a decent standard of life. They formed a professional class. Most were college educated, and they brought knowledge, administrative expertise, and a taste for bureaucracy to government service. After 1900 they would increasingly dominate the quest for better services and public responsibility, but in many cities their voices were heard too late. The scars of the private city remained on the urban landscape.

CITY CULTURE

Nightlife

It was almost like magic. At 3:00 P.M. on September 4, 1882, Thomas Edison's chief electrician threw the switch on the inventor's Pearl Street station. Four hundred electric lights went on. Wall Street buildings were for the first time illuminated by the clearest of all artificial lighting. "It was not until 7 o'clock, when it began to be dark that the electric light made itself known and showed how bright and steady it was," commented a *New York Times* reporter. In the *Times* offices, where 52 Edison lights illuminated the night, "it seemed almost like writing by daylight." Just as trolleys spelled the end for the horse car, electric lights eventually replaced gaslights, candles, kerosene, and oil lamps.

Electricity soon bathed America's leading cities in white light, making night day and giving it a timeless quality. In the rural regions life revolved around the sun. Farmers awoke with the sun, labored during the hours of daylight, and went to sleep soon after the sun disappeared over the horizon. Although one's labor changed depending on the season, the order of one's day was changeless. In cities and industries, however, night became more than just a time to rest. Labor and leisure claimed their share of the night.

This new nightlife fired the imaginations of urbanites. If nighttime labor proved a plague for the working class, nighttime leisure animated the lives of the wealthy. For Broadway's "fast set," the real fun began after the theaters closed. They moved down the Great White Way, stopping at one of the exclusive restaurants for a late-night dinner. Surrounded by electric lights and mirrors, they dined on meals available only in urban centers. They ate shrimp mornay, beef marguery, canape of crab meat, bisque de creme, and other such exotic dishes. At restaurants like Delmonico's, eating became a refined pleasure and not just a physical necessity.

City eating habits, as much as electric lights, demonstrated the yawning gap between the values of an older rural America and those of the emerging urban society. In 1840, critics of presidential candidate Martin Van Buren attacked him for his eating habits. William Henry Harrison, his opponent who subsisted on "raw beef without salt," ridiculed Van Buren's taste for strawberries, raspberries, celery, cauliflower, and French cooking, claiming that democratic virtue thrived only on crude, tasteless food. The American diet, however, expanded along with the nation's cities. Lorenzo Delmonico, the Swiss immigrant who founded New York's most famous restaurant, popularized ices and green vegetables and cooked food that rivaled the best in Paris.

City dwellers not only consumed different

Late in the century, when electricity and steel came into wide use, the face of American cities was greatly altered. Here Herald Square is illuminated at night.

types of food. The middle and upper classes consumed more of everything. Like the new diet, this shift in consumption patterns signaled a break with the past. The traditional Victorian ethos emphasized production and values—thrift, self-control, delayed gratification, and hard work—that encouraged production. But with industrial success came a general fear of overproduction, and increasingly advertisers and economic advisors attempted to transform Americans from "savers" to "spenders." In various ways, they told people to abandon traditional laissez-faire economic thinking, which viewed scarcity as an inevitable and fundamental fact of life, and to give in to their desire for luxury.

In large American cities, not only restaurants but also department stores and hotels fostered this new attitude. John Wanamaker in Philadelphia, Marshall Field in Chicago, and Rowland H. Macy in New York opened department stores that catered to and pampered the middle and upper classes by offering an unequaled range of products and quality service. Architecture and interior decoration of the department stores, with their emphasis on grand entrances, marble staircases, chandeliers, stained glass, plush carpets, and wood paneling, inspired extravagance. Spending came easily when the shopper was made to feel like royalty. Grand hotels, like the Waldorf Astoria in New York and the Palmer House in Chicago, trafficked in the same luxury. Inside the giant hotels and department stores, the austerity doctrines of the early nineteenth century were easily forgotten.

It is difficult to imagine the impression electric lights, fruit salads, department stores, and grand hotels made on the people who lived in or visited American cities. They underscored a style of life clearly different from what existed in rural America. City life presented a strange new world that inspired American writers, painters, and musicians with feelings of excitement and revulsion. This ambivalent reaction formed the basis of a new urban culture. A culture, which like a mixed salad, combined the energies and experiences of all city people—black and white, male and female, immigrant and native-born.

From the Genteel Tradition to Realism and Naturalism

Frank Norris was born in Chicago, grew up in San Francisco, and lived for a time in Paris. He restlessly moved about the world looking for action. As a reporter he traveled to Cuba to cover the Spanish-American War, and to South Africa to chronicle the Boer War. In his journalism and in his novels, he told the truth, and he fed his readers bloody slices of the real world. He battled "false views of life, false characters, false sentiments, false morality, false history, false philosophy, false emotions, false heroism." Shortly before he died at 32 of appendicitis in 1902, he boasted, "I never truckled. I never took off the hat to fashion and held it out for pennies. I told them the truth. They liked it or they didn't like it. What had that to do with me? I told them the truth."

The truth. How literature had changed during the previous generation! At the end of the Civil War, the American literary tradition had little to do with harsh truth. Controlled by a literary aristocracy in Boston, literature conformed to the "genteel tradition." Great writers endeavored to reinforce morality, not portray reality. Real life was too sordid, corrupt, and mean; it was far too coarse, violent, and vulgar. Literature, these arbiters decided, should transcend the real and anchor to the ideal. James Russell Lowell, one of the leaders of the genteel tradition, spoke for other genteel writers when he commented that no man should describe any activity that would make his wife or daughter blush. Sex, violence, and passion were taboo.

Out of rural America came the first challenge to the genteel tradition. Such local colorists as Bret Harte, who set his stories in the rough mining camps of the West, emphasized regional differences and used regional dialects to capture the flavor of rural America. In their own way, the local colorists were as confined by their approaches to writing as the defenders of the genteel tradition. Although their characters used real American speech, they were hardly realistically presented. Humor and innocence were the hallmarks of local colorists.

Only Mark Twain, whose real name was Samuel Langhorne Clemens, transcended the

Samuel Langhorne Clemens, better known as Mark Twain, wrote novels that were both humorous and insightful about problems in nineteenth-century rural America. In the novel *The Adventures of Huckleberry Finn*, for example, he addressed the issue of racism.

jured. "No'm," Huck responds. "Killed a nigger." Relieved, she replies, "Well, it's lucky; because sometimes people do get hurt."

The greatest success and failure of Mark Twain is that he never outgrew his obsession with life on the Mississippi River. Except perhaps in his *Connecticut Yankee*, the impact of industrialism and city life on the American character did not much interest Twain. It did, however, fascinate most of the other great writers of his generation. Equipped with camera eyes and critical minds, they wanted to show American life in all its harsh and sordid reality. Realism, the name of their movement, soon replaced the genteel sentimentality of the previous generation. Defined as "the truthful treatment of material" by its leader William Dean Howells, realism centered on average individuals dealing with concrete ethical choices in realistic circumstances. Even style became secondary. "Who cares for a fine style," Norris wrote in 1899. "Tell your yarn and let your style go to the devil. We don't want literature, we want life."

As realism matured in the largely unregulated and highly competitive cities, it turned into naturalism. A more pessimistic movement, naturalism portrayed the individual as a helpless victim, battered defenseless by natural forces beyond a person's control. Influenced by the writings of Charles Darwin, Karl Marx, and eventually Sigmund Freud, naturalists described a world in which biological, social, and psychological forces determined a person's fate. They were particularly interested in how the uncaring forces of industrialization and urbanization determined the course of individual lives. Even when they wrote about the problems of rural America, the power of factory and city worked in the shadows.

Describing the Urban Jungle

The premier naturalistic writer was Theodore Dreiser. Unlike most earlier American novelists, he was not the product of Protestant, Anglo-Saxon, middle-class respectability. His German-Catholic immigrant father's life was the flip side of the American success story. After a promising beginning, he and his family slid deeper and deeper into poverty. As a boy and a young man,

genre. Like a local colorist, he used regional dialects, humor, and sentimentality in all his novels, but he also explored the darker impulses of human nature. *The Adventures of Huckleberry Finn* (1884), his classic work, exposes the greed, violence, corruption, alcoholism, and racism in American society. As Huck and runaway slave Jim travel down the Mississippi River toward freedom, they encounter a society based on a perversion of Christian ethics and the Golden Rule. Nowhere is Twain more insightful than when he deals with American racism. In one scene, Huck invents a story about a riverboat explosion. A woman asks if anyone was in-

Theodore knew what it was like to subsist on potatoes and fried mush, and all his life he dreaded winter, which reminded him of his most painful days of poverty. Sympathetic to those who had suffered similarly, he wrote, "Any form of distress—a wretched, down-at-heels neighborhood, a poor farm, an asylum, a jail, or an individual or group of individuals anywhere that seemed to be lacking in the means of subsistence or to be devoid of the normal comforts of life—was sufficient to set up in me thoughts and emotions, which had a close kinship to actual and severe physical pain."

Novelist Theodore Dreiser, writing in a style called naturalism, described urban social problems, often portraying characters as helpless victims of their environment.

Dreiser left home at 16 and went to Chicago, where he became first a journalist and then a novelist. Unlike better educated writers, Dreiser had no genteel tradition to shed or rebel against. With his plodding style and atrocious English, Dreiser lacked every writing tool except genius. His first novel, *Sister Carrie* (1900), unflinchingly describes the effect of modern urban society on the lives of one woman and one man. Carrie travels to Chicago from the countryside in search of happiness, which she equates with material possessions, but she discovers only poverty, exploitation, and hardship. Like the course of Dreiser's own family, the likeable, friendly Carrie sinks ever deeper into physical and moral despair.

Although Frank Norris praised the novel, it shocked most readers accustomed to the genteel tradition. Doubleday, Page and Company published *Sister Carrie* but did not advertise it. As a result it sold only 456 copies, and Dreiser's royalties amounted only to a depressing $68.40. With time, however, Americans recognized Dreiser's genius and read his novels as realistic treatments of modern industrial society.

Like Dreiser, Stephen Crane was also interested in the effects poverty and urban life had on individual character. His first novel, *Maggie: A Girl of the Streets* (1893), traces the life of a girl raised in a New York City slum. In rapid order, she loses her innocence, her virginity, and her life. It was not a story of a character being rewarded or punished. Maggie was an honest, cheerful person, but that was not the issue. She was a victim of her environment, and issues of personal good or evil were at best irrelevant. Poverty determined Maggie's, and later Carrie's, fate.

Taken together, naturalistic writers challenged the traditional idea that individuals had the power to control their own destinies. Rugged individualism, that cherished frontier ideal, seemed poor protection against the forces of urban poverty and industrial exploitation. Carrie was no match for the sweatshop owner, and Maggie's innocence was merely a target in her environment. Although neither *Maggie* nor *Sister Carrie* was a blueprint for reform, both suggested a pressing need for change. The same private city that offered opportunity for the wealthy held little promise for the poor.

Painting Urban Reality

During the 1830s and 1840s nationalistic Americans began to develop a truly national culture. Unlike Europe, America did not have proud literary, artistic, or musical traditions. America had produced no Parthenon, no Rembrandt, no Beethoven. What America did have was land, thousands of square miles of wild land. It was an asset that became the basis of American culture. Writers wrote about it, and artists painted it. James Fenimore Cooper created Natty Bumppo, the virtuous frontier hero. Artist Thomas Cole endowed the American wilderness with a religious quality. Indeed, after visiting Europe, Cole reported that plowed fields and mountain castles had ruined the Old World landscape. "American scenery," he wrote, "has features, and glorious ones, unknown to Europe. The most distinctive, and perhaps the most impressive, characteristic of American scenery is its wildness."

American artists shared with American writers and social critics a general aesthetic and philosophical dislike of the city. As Americans moved west, artists continued to focus on the landscape. Albert Bierstadt exaggerated the drama of the Rocky Mountains, but his pictures thrilled eastern and western Americans alike. Even the great, late-nineteenth-century realists—Winslow Homer, Thomas Eakins, and John LaFarge—harbored a suspicion, if not an outright fear, of the city. To be sure, Eakins's work demonstrated a profound respect for the machine, but his admiration did not extend to the city.

By the end of the century, however, the varied urban landscape began to intrigue artists. Steel bridges, colorful immigrant costumes, smoke-filled, congested streets, clashing boxers, washed clothes hanging between tenements, pigeons soaring over flat apartment roofs—each demonstrated the everyday beauty of the city. The energy, conflict, and power of the city seemed to explode with artistic possi-

bilities. When a critic noted that in George Bellows's *Stag at Starkey's* the fighters' faces are hidden, Bellows replied, "Who cares what a prize fighter looks like. It's his muscles that count."

Appropriately enough, the center of this new movement was New York City. The leader of the school—often described as "ashcan" because of its urban orientation—was Robert Henri, an artistic and political radical. Skyscrapers thrilled him, and he saw beauty in the most squalid slum. He was joined by such other artists who shared his love of city life and political radicalism as John Sloan, George Luks, Maurice Prendergast, Everett Shinn, W. J. Glackens, and Ernest Lawson. Their paintings were generally in the impressionistic style, which concentrated on using unmixed primary colors and quick brush strokes to produce a general impression of a scene. But they were more concerned with content than technique. As George Luks sneered at a critic, "Technique, did you say? My slats! Say, listen, you—it's in you or it isn't. Who taught Shakespeare technique? Guts! Guts! Life! Life! That's my technique."

Like Theodore Dreiser, who admired the ashcan school, Henri and his followers used their talent to show problems in the growing cities. Bellow's *Cliff Dwellers* portrayed teeming life but also overcrowded tenement conditions. His *Steaming Streets* underscored the problems of urban traffic. And George Luks's *Hester Street* illuminated the excitement but also the packed conditions of the Jewish section of Lower New York.

Maturing along with the ashcan painters was a second school of artists that also gained inspiration from the urban landscape. Labeled modernists, they championed the pure freedom of nonrepresentational abstract painting. Their intellectual leader was Alfred Stieglitz, whose studio at 291 Fifth Avenue in New York was used to exhibit the modernist paintings of Georgia O'Keeffe, Marsden Hartley, John Marin, Max Weber, and Arthur Dove. Like the ashcanners, they too were drawn to the conflict and power of the city. Describing the city as the theme for abstract art, John Marin observed, "I see great forces at work, great movements, the large buildings and the small buildings, the warring of the great and the small. . . . While these powers

Everett Shinn's *The Laundress* presents American urban life in an impressionistic style.

John Sloan's *Sunday, Women Drying Their Hair*, 1912, an urban portrait typical of the ashcan school, so named because the artists associated with it preferred to paint the unglamorous, everyday aspects of city life.

are at work . . . I can hear the sound of their strife, and there is great music being played."

In 1913 the ashcanners and the modernists participated in the most important art exhibition in American history. Held at the Sixty-ninth Regiment Armory in New York, the show also included works by Cézanne, Van Gogh, Picasso, Marcel Duchamp, Georges Braque, and Juan Gris, the leaders of the European post-impressionists. The Armory Show drew some sharp criticism; Duchamp's cubist *Nude Descending a Staircase* was called "an explosion in a shingle factory." Other critics and collectors maintained that the exhibition marked a new age for American art. "The members of this association have shown you that American artists—young American artists, that is—do not dread . . . the ideas or the culture of Europe," noted leading collector John Quinn. "This exhibition will be epoch-making." Its more impor-

tant result was to fuse European and American art movements. It further signaled the ascendancy of the modernists, who dominated the next generation of American art. Perhaps poet Harry Kemp, who was both excited and confused by the show, best captured the reaction to the radical paintings:

> I cannot shake their wild control;
> Their colors still go roaring through my soul, . . .
> Strange cubes evolving into half-guessed forms,
> Cyclones of green, and purple rainbow-storms.
> Thus artists on some huge Jupiter might paint
> (Or some mad star beyond earth's constraint) . . .
> You go out with a whirlwind in your head.
> The thing, at least, is not inert or dead;
> There's life and motion there, and rending force,
> Color-Niagaras thundering on their course,
> Power that breaks like a great wave in spray—
> And what it means we'll let To-morrow say!

The Sounds of the City

Modern American music began in the nation's large cities, and from the very first was the language of the oppressed. Before the late nineteenth century, critics regarded American music as decidedly inferior to European music. America had produced no great classical composers in the European tradition, and what music it did create was largely the sounds of work and worship. Uninfluenced by European traditions, American blacks adapted the rhythms and melodies of Africa to meet American conditions. Out of this marriage came the work songs of Mississippi slaves, the street cries of Charleston fish and fruit vendors, and the religious spirituals. Unlike European music, which was based on a 12-note scale, African music centered on rhythmical complexity and used notes that did not conform to the standard scale. Repetition, call and response, and strong beat became the hallmarks of black American music. Stephen Foster and minstrel shows helped to popularize the music with white audiences.

The two traditions, African and European, existed independently in the United States until the 1890s, when they were suddenly thrown together in New Orleans. As in most southern cities, Jim Crow laws passed during the 1890s legally and forcefully separated the races in New Orleans. For the history of American music this process had unexpected results. It forced together blacks from very different backgrounds. Before the 1890s wealthy half-white, half-black Creoles had lived in the affluent downtown section of New Orleans and followed European musical traditions. Segregation, however, forced them uptown, where poorer blacks who followed African musical traditions lived. Although Creoles and poor blacks did not mix socially, they did forge new musical styles.

The result was jazz, a musical form based on improvisation within a structured band format, which used both African and European traditions. Such early New Orleans jazz bands as Buddy Bolden's Classic Jazz Band and Joe "King" Oliver's Creole Jazz Band pioneered the style. Playing in an era before recorded music,

Jazz combined European and African-American music styles into a new musical form. Here King Oliver's Creole Jazz Band poses for a rare picture.

Bolden was considered to be particularly talented. He had lived in the uptown region even before segregation, where Baptist churches stood next to voodoo parlors and music provided the background for prayer, work, and play. Bolden's style was characterized by a powerful, moody grace that mesmerized audiences. But Bolden's music came from the soul of a troubled man. Plagued by syphilis and alcoholism, in 1907 he went berserk during a street parade and spent the rest of his life in a mental hospital.

Storyville, the New Orleans red-light district, provided employment for the jazz musicians. Freed from manual labor during the day, they honed their musical skills and explored the possibilities of their instruments. Charlie "Sweet Lovin" Galloway, Ferdinand "Jelly Roll" Morton, Robert "Baby" Dodds, Bunk Johnson, Sidney Bechet, Alphonse Picou, and, especially, Louis Armstrong entertained Storyville customers. Called the "Gibraltar of commercialized human degradation and lust," Storyville was also the mecca of jazz musicians.

The black musicians who worked in Storyville made far more than even skilled laborers. On an average night, 50 musicians played in Storyville; during carnival season as many as 75 worked. The very best " professors," who played in the most exclusive houses, made between $90 and $1000 a week. Band members' earnings ranged from $30 to $100 a week. Alphonse Picou recalled the days before Storyville was officially closed with fond nostalgia: "Those were happy days, man, happy days. Buy a keg of beer for one dollar and a bag of food for another. . . . Talking 'bout wild and wooly! There were two thousand registered girls and must have been ten thousand unregistered. And all crazy about clarinet blowers."

Jazz flourished in Storyville, but so too did ragtime and the blues. Ragtime, a syncopated piano style, needed only one performer and was therefore popular as cafe and bordello entertainment. Tony Jackson, Scott Joplin, and Jelly Roll Morton played ragtime piano with style and grace. Joplin, a Texas-born black who had formal musical training, wrote several scores of popular rags, and his "Maple Leaf Rag" (1899) probably sold a million copies in sheet music

form. Morton also advanced ragtime, developing the piano swing beat. Blues musicians, mostly blacks raised outside of European traditions and from the Mississippi Delta region, performed in cheap saloons and expressed the pain of life in an hostile world.

During World War I, government officials closed Storyville, charging it was a health hazard. As the houses of prostitution closed their doors, the talented black musicians headed north—to St. Louis, Chicago, Memphis, Kansas City, and New York. They continued to play jazz and the form continued to evolve. White musicians, trained in the European tradition, soon put their imprint on the American musical form. Bix Beiderbecke from Davenport, Iowa, for example, formed a Chicago-based jazz band. He used more instruments, replaced the African banjo with the guitar, and moved away from improvisation.

Although larger jazz bands dominated music during the next generation, they were an outgrowth of the New Orleans sound. It was also the result of the mixture of European and African traditions. It could only have happened in the fertile atmosphere of the cities, where old and new, black and white, immigrant and native-born combined to create new literary, artistic, and musical forms.

ENTERTAINING THE MULTITUDES

City sports, like city music, were loud and raucous. They moved to the beat of the trolley cars and steel wheels on steel tracks, not horses' hooves on dusty farm roads. Before the urbanization of the late nineteenth century, the sports and games that Americans played tended to be informal and participant oriented. Rules varied from region to region, and few people even considered the standardization of rules desirable. By 1900 this cozy informality had changed dramatically. Entertainment became a major industry, and specialized performers competed for the right to entertain the multitudes.

The emergence of commercialized entertainment was the result of changes in both American technology and values. Transportation improvements allowed professional entertainers and sports teams to move across America more easily and cheaply, and technological advances in the popular press, telegraph, and telephone allowed the results of games and entertainment news to be quickly spread throughout the country. Added to this was the decline in the Victorian notion that entertainment was somehow suspect. Drawing on Puritan criticisms of play and recreation and a Republican ideology that was hostile to luxury, hedonism, and extravagance, American Victorians tended to associate theaters, dance halls, circuses, and organized sports with such vices as gambling, swearing, drinking, and immoral sexual behavior. They judged popular entertainments guilty by association.

In the second half of the nineteenth century, however, a new outlook challenged Victorian prejudices. Members of the Victorian counterculture revered play, gratification, and revelry more than hard work, punctuality, delayed gratification, and self-control. At first, members of the counterculture tended to be immigrants and bachelors. Unlike Anglo-Americans, Irish, German, and eastern and southern European immigrants brought with them to America a culture that was at odds with Victorian notions of work and play. In addition, immigrants tended to marry later than native-born Americans; even at midcentury 40 percent of men between the ages of 25 and 35 were unmarried. These men formed a "bachelor subculture" that centered around saloons, gambling halls, race tracks, boxing rings, billiard rooms, and cockpits. Toward the end of the century as the Victorian economic and social order began to crumble, upper-class and then middle-class Americans became interested in the activities of the bachelor subculture. The result was a new attitude toward sport and leisure.

Of Fields and Cities

"Baseball," wrote Mark Twain, "is the very symbol, the outward and visible expression of the drive and push and struggle of the raging, tearing, booming nineteenth century." It captured the bustle and hustle of city life. More than any other sport of the period, baseball was an urban game. All of the early professional teams were located in cities and most of the paid players were products of the cities.

The mythology of the sport, however, harkened back to America's past. The myth still lingers that Abner Doubleday "invented" baseball in 1839, when he laid out the first baseball diamond in the pastoral village of Cooperstown, New York, The United States Post Office gave semiofficial recognition to the myth in 1939 when it issued a commemorative stamp honoring the centennial anniversary of the event. In fact, if anyone can be said to have invented a sport that actually evolved, it was Alexander J. Cartwright, Jr., a New York City stationery bookstore owner who in 1845 set down the first written rules for the game.

The symbols of the game also recalled America's rural past. Unlike most modern sports, no clock governed the pace of a baseball game. In crowded, dirty cities, baseball was played on open, grassy fields with such bucolic names as Sportsman Park, Ebbets Field, and the Polo Grounds. (Yankee Stadium, opened in 1923, was the first baseball enclosure to veer from the rural tradition.) The field even had fences and bullpens, and the game was played during the planting and harvesting seasons of spring, summer, and fall.

If the symbols and mythology of baseball were rural, the game itself was very urban. Team managers, like their industrialist counterparts, preached the values of hard work, punctuality, thrift, sobriety, and self-control to their players. Baseball, they emphasized, was like modern life, ruthlessly competitive and demanding sacrifice for the "good of the team." As Mr. Clayton, a character in an 1891 baseball novel, explained, "We can't work and we can't play, we can't learn and we can't make money without getting some of other people's help." Like modern corporate society, then, modern sports reinforced the ideal of teamwork.

During the last third of the nineteenth century, as men like Rockefeller and Carnegie struggled to bring order to their industrial empires, modern baseball took form. Rules were standardized. In the early years of baseball, a base runner could be thrown out by hitting him with the ball as he ran between the bases. Organizers outlawed such violent relics of the past.

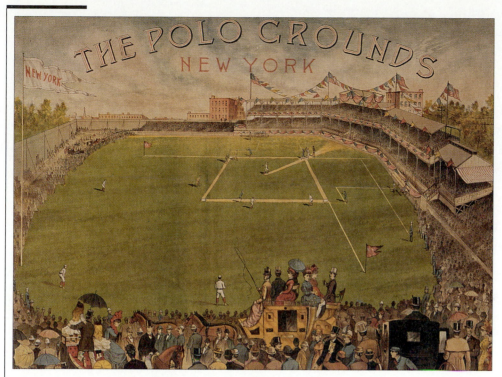

Baseball was the leading sport of the late nineteenth century. It brought a sense of America's rural past into the country's urban present.

Owners attempted to make the sport suitable for the urban middle class. They banned the spitball, arranged games to fit the urban professionals' schedules, fined players for using profanity, and encouraged women to attend the games.

Most important, they formed competitive professional leagues centered in the industrial cities of America. In 1869 Harry Wright took his all-professional Cincinnati Red Stockings on a barnstorming tour. Traveling on the recently completed Transcontinental Railroad, they played teams from New York City to San Francisco and compiled a record of 57 wins, no losses, and 1 tie. Over 23,000 fans watched their 6-game series in New York, and almost 15,000 spectators attended a single game they played in Philadelphia. In Washington, D.C., President Ulysses S. Grant commended them on their accomplishments. During the year the team traveled 11,877 miles by rail, stage, and boat, and entertained more than 200,000 spectators.

The Cincinnati club taught the rest of America, as one journalist commented, that "steady, temperate habits and constant training are all conditions precedent to all first class professional organizations." It also demonstrated to entrepreneurs that there was money to be made in professional sports. In 1876 William A. Hulbert and several associates formed the National League, which was organized around owners and clubs, not players. In business terms, the league was a loosely organized cartel designed to eliminate competition among franchises for players. Eventually, league officials devised the "reserve clause," which effectively bound a player to the team that held the rights to him. This further undermined the ability of a player to negotiate for higher salary. Although the National League was known as a "rich man's" league because it charged a 50-cents admission price, it was certainly not a rich player's league.

In 1890 the players revolted and formed the Players' League. Headed by lawyer and star player John Montgomery Ward, the Players'

(Text continues on p. 642)

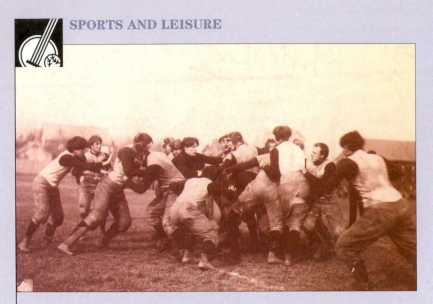

COLLEGE FOOTBALL WARS

Although the year was 1905, the story is hauntingly familiar. It deals with colleges, football, and corruption. Henry Beach Needham in an article in *McClure's* charged that college football had become a professional endeavor, that players were paid performers who cared little for their studies. Take, for example, James J. Hogan, Yale's captain and star player who knew how to make the most out of an "amateur" sport. At the age of 27, he agreed to play football for Yale. In return, Yale paid his tuition, gave him a $100 a year scholarship, housed him in rooms at its most luxurious dormitory, and fed him at the University Club. In addition, Hogan and two other players received all the profits from the sale of game programs, and Hogan was appointed the American Tobacco Company's agent in New Haven and received a commission on every package of cigarettes sold in the area. Finally, after each season—

but during the school term—Hogan was given a ten-day vacation trip to Cuba.

Hogan's case was by no means unique. In an age of unregulated football competition, it was each school for itself, each player for himself. Money talked and school spirit was for the students in the stands. Players were more mercenaries than students; their loyalty was constantly on the auction block. Andrew Smith demonstrated this principle in 1902. On October 4, Smith played an exceptional game for Pennsylvania State University against a powerhouse Penn team. By that next Monday he had transferred schools and was practicing with Penn, a college that had also "drafted" players from Middlebury, Colorado College, Lafayette, and Peddie. Of course, at least Lafayette College had little cause for complaint. Fielding H. Yost, who coached the University of Michigan for three decades, recalled his undergraduate

days at West Virginia. During one season, an undefeated Lafayette had "hired" Yost to play against the also unbeaten Penn. After the game, Yost "transferred" back to West Virginia.

Critics charged that football was undermining the very ethics that college professors were laboring to instill into students. As early as 1893, E. L. Godkin, editor of the influential *Nation*, noted that the leading colleges were losing their educational orientation and becoming "huge training grounds for young gladiators, around whom as many spectators roar as roared in the Flavian amphitheatre." More than a decade later, Charles W. Eliot, president of Harvard, complained bitterly that each fall undergraduates at his university seemed totally obsessed by football, talking about or thinking about little else. Godkin and Eliot found a kindred spirit in John S. Mosby, who had led the Confederate Mosby's Raiders during the Civil War. Although he had been suspended from Virginia in 1853 for shooting a fellow student, Mosby continued to think of the school as his alma mater. In 1909 the old Raider wrote, "I do not think football should be tolerated where the youth of the country are supposed to be taught literature, science and humanity. The game seems to overshadow everything else at the University."

Mosby's letter was prompted by another football problem—violence. By the turn of the century, the number of athletes killed or injured in football games had reached an alarming level. In 1909 Virginia halfback Archer Christian died shortly after being injured in a game against Georgetown. As Mosby asked, "I believe that cock-fighting is unlawful in Virginia: Why should better care be taken of a game chicken than a school boy?" Other critics pondered the same question, for during the 1909 season 30 boys were killed and 216 seriously injured in football games.

The most publicized death of that season was Army's captain Eugene Byrne. He was fatally injured in a game against Harvard. The event was so shocking that the game was immediately halted, and the Army-Navy game of that year was canceled. Buried with full military honors, thousands mourned Byrne's senseless death and questioned the place of college football in American society.

Football brutality was a serious problem. The nature of the game emphasized violence. Unlike today when the team with the ball has four plays to make a 10-yard first down, during the late-nineteenth and early twentieth centuries the offensive team had three plays to make a 5-yard first down. In addi-tion, passing was severely restricted both by the rules and by tradition. As a result, coaches emphasized "mass plays" that directed the maximum amount of force against one isolated player or point on the field. The flying wedge was the most notorious mass play. The play entailed players grouping themselves in a V formation and starting to run before the ball was put into play. Then at the last moment the ball was snapped and passed to a player within the wall of the wedge. The wedge of runners then crashed into their stationary opponents. Given that equipment was crude—players often played without helmets and no helmet had a facemask—this brute use of a massed force injured hundreds of players each year.

If the flying wedge and other mass plays were not bad enough, referees rarely enforced rules against slugging, kicking, and piling on. Victory was the supreme object; and any method seemed justified in the pursuit of that goal. One Princeton player confessed to a reporter that he and his teammates were coached to eliminate dangerous opponents during the early-minutes of a game. A writer for the *Nation* believed this ruthless drive for victory illustrated a fundamental American characteristic: "The spirit of the American youth, as of the American man, is to win, 'to get there,' by fair means or foul; and the lack of moral scruple which pervades the struggles of the business world meets with temptations equally irresistible in the miniature contests of the football field."

By the end of the terribly brutal 1905 season many educators, journalists, and politicians had decided that college football served no educational good and did considerable harm. Professor Shailer Mathews of Chicago's Divinity School labeled football "a social obsession—a boy-killing, education-prostituting, gladiatorial sport." Even though President Theodore Roosevelt stepped in and tried to clean up the game and officials altered the rules of the sport, a number of universities chose to drop football from their athletic programs. Columbia, Union, Northwestern, Stanford, and California led the abolitionist movement.

Between 1905 and 1910 critics continued to level charges of brutality, commercialism, and corruption against football. The 1905 rules had not lessened the violence, and death continued to shock concerned Americans. In 1910 the rules of football were once again altered. In the most important change, the forward pass as we know it today was legalized. Although football conservatives continued for several years to ignore the new offensive weapon, in 1913 the pass came into its own. That year a highly regarded Army team filled an open date in its schedule with a small Indiana school called Notre Dame. During the game Notre Dame quarterback Charley Dorais threw perfectly timed passes to his favorite end Knute Rockne. The result was a 35–13 upset by the Irish of Notre Dame. By the end of the season other teams had adopted the new tactic and passes filled the autumn air. The age of the mass play was over.

Passing made football even more exciting, and after 1913 criticism of the sport generated little support. Of course, brutality, commercialism, and corruption continued, but such scandals led more to attacks on individual schools than against football as a college sport. Indeed, by 1917 football reigned unrivaled as college's supreme sport and public spectacle.

League was an experiment in workers' control of an industry. In words similar to those used by workers in other industries, the players' "manifesto" of 1889 claimed, "There was a time when the [National] League stood for integrity and fair dealing. Today it stands for dollars and cents. . . . Players have been bought, sold, and exchanged, as though they were sheep, instead of American citizens . . . by a combination among themselves, stronger than the strongest trusts, they [the owners] were able to enforce the most arbitrary measures, and the player had either to submit or get out of the profession in which he had spent years in attaining a proficiency." Lofty in ideals, the Players' League was badly managed and lasted only one year.

With the failure of the Players' League, the National League increased its control over professional baseball. It either crushed rival leagues or absorbed them. In 1903, for example, after a short business war the National League entered into a partnership with the American League. The only losers were the players, whose salaries decreased with the absence of competition. Nevertheless, the popularity of the sport soared. By 1909, when William Howard Taft established the practice of the president opening each season by throwing out the first ball, baseball had become the national pastime.

"I Can Lick Any Sonofabitch in the House"

Only boxing rivaled baseball in popularity during the late nineteenth century. Like baseball, boxing began the period as a largely unstructured sport, but by 1900 entrepreneurs had reorganized the activity into a profitable business. Although boxing remained illegal in most parts of America, it produced some of the first national sports heroes.

Bare knuckle boxing, the forerunner of modern boxing, was a brutal, bloody sport. It involved two men fighting bare-fisted until one could not continue. A round lasted until one of the men knocked or threw down his opponent. At that point both men rested for 30 seconds and then started to fight again. Fights could and often did last over 100 rounds and as long as 7 or 8 hours. After such a fight it took months for the men to recover.

Boxers, unlike baseball players, often emerged from poor immigrant families. Irish-Americans dominated the sport during the late nineteenth century, and they used boxing as a means of social mobility in American life. Such men as John Morrissey, James C. Heenan, and John L. Sullivan became national legends during the period. Morrissey, for instance, was born in Ireland, lived in poverty in Troy, New York, gained fame as a prizefighter, and eventually became a leading New York gambler and politician. By the time he died, he had served two terms in Congress and made a fortune.

The Great John L. (John L. Sullivan), however, eclipsed Morrissey in popularity. He became the greatest known American athlete during the nineteenth century. "Excepting General Grant," one newspaperman wrote, "no American has received such ovations as Sullivan." Born in Boston of Irish immigrant parents, Sullivan was a loud boastful man who loved to fight. He often walked into a saloon and claimed he could outfight and outdrink "any sonofabitch in the house." After he won the bare-knuckle world heavyweight title in 1882, tales of his punching power and his unrestrained attacks on Victorian morality spread across the country. Politicians, actors, writers, and merchants avidly followed his exploits, but Sullivan never lost touch with his immigrant, working-class origin. In Irish Boston, Sullivan's elevated standing went unquestioned. Comparing the Boston of old and new America, one poet wrote:

> Just fancy what mingled emotions
> Would fill the Puritan heart
> To learn what renown was won for his town
> By means of the manly art!
> Imagine a Winthrop or Adams
> In front of the bulletin board,
> Each flinging his hat at the statement that
> The first blood was by Sullivan scored.

During the 1880s, Sullivan watched his sport move toward greater respectability. Boxing, like baseball, underwent a series of reforms. The traditional challenge system for arranging fights was replaced by modern promotional techniques pioneered by New Orleans athletic clubs. Fighters deserted bare-fisted combat and started wearing gloves. Most important of all, professional boxers adopted the Marquis of Queensberry Rules, which standardized a round at three minutes, allowed a one-minute rest period between rounds, and outlawed all wrestling throws and holds. The new rules also replaced the fight to the finish with a fight to a decision over a specified number of rounds. Although the new rules did not reduce the violence of the sport, they did provide for more orderly bouts.

The Queensberry Rules resembled the recently adopted factory innovations. Just as workers lost control of the pace of work, fighters no longer could determine the pace of the action. Under the old rules prizefighters could tacitly agree to slow down the action in order to catch their breath or simply exchange boasts and oaths. Now a bell and a referee told them when to fight and when to rest. The factory system had effectively invaded boxing.

John L. Sullivan won the last bare-knuckle championship contest. In 1889 he defeated Jake Kilrain in a fight held near Richburg, Mississippi. It was an illegal fight, but it attracted spectators from all social classes. Bat Masterson, the gunfighter and gambler, served as timekeeper, and he was joined at ringside by wealthy sons of southern aristocrats, gamblers, and sporting men of every variety. The fight lasted for 75 rounds, and both boxers drank whiskey between rounds. After winning the epic fight, Sullivan gained even greater fame.

Sullivan lost the title in 1892 to James J. Corbett in a legal gloved contest fought in New Orleans. Nicknamed "Gentleman Jim," Corbett's scientific boxing style and smooth manners outside the ring demonstrated that boxing had gained increased respectability. In fact, by the 1890s boxing was no longer a working-class sport. Like baseball, it had become an organized, structured, and profitable business. All that was left of the older sport was the legend of the Great John L.—the boisterous, crude, lovable, man-child. As he told future novelist Theodore Dreiser shortly after the Corbett fight: "I'm ex-champion of the world, defeated by that little dude from California, but I'm still John L. Sullivan—ain't that right. Haw! Haw! They can't take that away from me, can they? Haw! Haw! Have some more champagne boy."

The Excluded Americans

Although promoters talked about the democratic nature of sports, this was far from the case. To be sure, a number of Irish and German men—often immigrants or sons of immigrants— prospered in professional sports. Far more Americans were excluded from the world of sports.

In large cities the lines between social classes tended to blur, much to the discomfort of the wealthy who struggled to separate themselves from the hoi polloi. The rich moved to the suburbs and employed other methods of residential segregation to isolate themselves. Another tactic to protect their exclusive status was to allow their children only to marry within their narrow group of acquaintances. They also used sports and athletic clubs to set themselves apart. "Gentlemen and ladies," as they styled themselves, they only wanted to compete against opponents of similar dress, speech, education, and wealth.

One way to exclude the masses was to engage in sports that only the very rich could play. Yachting and polo demanded nearly unlimited free time, expensive equipment, and a retinue of hired helpers. The New York Yacht Club was founded in 1884 and was soon joined by a "succession of gentlemen ranking high in the social and financial circles" of the city. By the 1890s every major eastern seaboard city had its exclusive yacht club, and each summer the richest yacht owners sailed their splendid vessels to Newport, Rhode Island, the most exclusive of the summer colonies.

Athletic clubs devoted to track and field, golf, and tennis were similarly exclusive. The members of Shinnecock Hills, one of the oldest golf clubs in America, prided themselves on the beauty of their course as well as their own social standing. Such exclusive clubs catered to more than the members' athletic concerns. Each club had an elaborate social calendar filled with dress balls and formal dinners. When they did schedule sporting events, participation and the privilege of watching were normally on an invitation only basis.

To prevent the various social classes from mixing too freely in athletics, wealthy patrons advocated the code of amateurism, which separated the greedy professionals—who often came from the poorer classes—from the more prosperous athletes who participated in a sport simply for the love of the game. The constitution of the British Amateur Rowing Association, for example, defined an amateur as a person who had never rowed for a stake or money; who had never knowingly rowed with or against a professional; who had never taught any form of athletics for money; who had never "been employed in or about boats, or in manual labour, for money or wages"; and who was not "by trade or employment for wages a mechanic, artisan or labourer, or engaged in any menial duty." The revival of the Olympic Games in 1896 strengthened the amateur code. Thus when it was discovered that Jim Thorpe, an Oklahoma Indian who had attended the Carlisle Indian School and who won the decathlon and the pentathlon in the 1912 Stockholm Games, had played baseball for a minor league professional team during the summer of 1909, the International Olympic Committee stripped him of his medals.

Although amateurism was a subtle attack on the working class, sports leaders moved more forcefully against blacks. During the 1870s and 1880s, blacks and whites competed in sports against each other on a fairly regular basis. A number of blacks even rose to become world champions. Marshall W. "Major" Taylor was hailed as the "Fastest Bicycle Rider in the World"; Isaac Murphy rode horses to three Kentucky Derby victories; and George Dixon and other blacks won boxing titles. During the 1890s, however, blacks and whites were segregated in most sports.

Jim Crow laws came to boxing during this period. John L. Sullivan steadfastly refused to fight black boxers. In 1892 he issued his famous challenge to fight all contenders: "In this challenge I include all fighters—first come, first served—who are white. I will not fight a Negro. I never have and I never shall." True to his word, the Boston Strong Boy never did. The same year, lightweight champion George Dixon administered a frightful beating to white challenger Jack Skelly in New Orleans. After the fight, the editor of the *New Orleans Times-Democrat* wrote that it was "a mistake to match a negro and a white man, a mistake to bring the two races together on any terms of equality, even in the prize ring." After 1892 the number of "mixed bouts" declined rapidly.

Organized baseball also excluded blacks during the 1890s. During the 1880s several owners integrated their professional baseball teams, but the trend toward segregation that led to the landmark court case, *Plessy* v. *Ferguson* (1896), overtook baseball. In 1889 baseball's *Sporting News* announced that "race prejudice exists in professional baseball ranks to a marked degree, and the unfortunate son of Africa who makes his living as a member of a team of white professionals has a rocky road to travel." The observation was accurate. By 1892 major league baseball was all white, and it would remain so until Jackie Robinson broke the "color barrier" in 1946.

Cultural expectations and stereotypes also limited the development of women athletes. Scientists spoke and wrote confidently about women's "arrested evolution." Compared to men, they were considered weak and uncoordinated, athletically retarded because of their narrow sloping shoulders, broad hips, underdeveloped muscles, and short arms and legs. Although they might ride a bicycle or gently swing a croquet mallet, men ridiculed women who were interested in serious competitive athletics. The cult of domesticity, which idealized women as nurturers and maintained that women's proper sphere was the home, also militated against female participation in competitive sports.

Even during the 1890s, when the tall, commanding Gibson Girl became the physical ideal and women became more interested in sports and exercise, women's athletics developed along different lines than men's. Male and female physical educators considered women to be uncompetitive and decided that women's sports should serve a utilitarian function. Sports, they emphasized, should promote a woman's physical and mental qualities and thus make her more attractive to men. They also believed that sports and exercise would sublimate female sexual drives. As renowned physical educator Dudley A. Sargent noted: "No one seems to realize that there is a time in the life of a girl when it is better for her and for the community to be something of a boy rather than too much of a girl."

In the late nineteenth century, bicycling was one of the few sports considered appropriate for women.

But tomboyish behavior had to stop short of abrasive competition. Lucille Eaton Hill, director of physical training at Wellesley College, urged women to "avoid the evils which are so apparent . . . in the conduct of athletics for men." She and her fellow female physical educators encouraged widespread participation rather than narrow specialization. In short, women left spectator and professional sports to the men. Indeed, not until 1924 were women allowed to compete in Olympic track and field events, and even then on a limited basis.

From Central Park to Coney Island

Like sports, parks changed to satisfy new urban demands. Mid-nineteenth-century park designers felt uneasy about the urban environment. In parks they saw an antidote for the tensions and anxieties caused by living in cities. Frederick Law Olmsted, the most famous park architect, believed cities destroyed community ties and fostered ruthless competition. He designed

Central Park to serve as a rural retreat in the midst of New York. Surrounded by rolling hills and quiet lakes, city dwellers would be moved toward greater sociability. "No one who has closely observed the conduct of the people who visit [Central] Park," Olmsted declared, "can doubt that it exercises a distinctly harmonizing and refining influence upon the most unfortunate and most lawless classes of the city—an influence favorable to courtesy, self-control, and temperance." But while Olmsted believed in the social function of parks, he was occasionally upset by the behavior of a "certain class" of visitors who believed "that all trees, shrubs, fruit and flowers are common property" and who refused to behave according to Olmsted's ideal.

Olmsted's vision of a quiet, orderly park was shared by other leaders of Victorian culture. They believed that culture and leisure activities should serve society by smoothing the rough edges of the urban masses. Instead of supporting baseball and boxing, they built parks, libraries, and museums. In 1870, for example, both the Metropolitan Museum of Art in New York and the Museum of Fine Arts in Boston were opened. Visitors to these repositories of culture were expected to behave in an orderly, quiet, respectful manner. Laughing, talking, coughing, shouting, and loud demonstrations of enthusiasm were frowned on by museum officials.

The quiet world offered by Central Park and the new museums, however, was too tame for many urbanites. They wanted more excitement. This was clearly seen at the World's Columbian Exposition of 1893 in Chicago. The most popular area of the World's Fair was the Midway, the center of commercial amusements. Visitors eagerly rode the Ferris wheel, visited the "40 Ladies from 40 Nations" exhibition, and watched "Little Egypt" perform her exotic dances. Parks and entertainment that amuse, not soothe, attracted the most people.

Entrepreneurs were quick to satisfy the public's desire for entertainment. During the 1890s a series of popular amusement parks opened in Coney Island. Unlike Central Park, which was constructed as a rural retreat, the Coney Island parks glorified the sense of adventure and excitement of the cities. They offered exotic, dreamland landscapes; wonderful, novel machines; and a free, loose social environment.

Coney Island provided a temporary escape from the pressures of urban life. Its sense of informality and sheer excitement attracted people of every class.

At Coney Island men could remove their coats and ties, and both sexes could enjoy a rare personal freedom. As one immigrant claimed, for the young "privacy could be had only in public."

Coney Island also encouraged new values. If, as Olmsted believed, Central Park reinforced self-control, sobriety, and delayed gratification, Coney Island stressed the emerging consumer-oriented values of extravagance, gaiety, abandon, revelry, and instant gratification. It attracted working-class Americans who longed for at least a taste of the "good life." If a person could never hope to own a mansion in Newport, he could for a few dimes experience the exotic pleasures of Luna Park or Dreamland Park.

Even the rides in the amusement parks were designed to create illusions and break down reality. Mirrors distorted people's images and rides threw them off balance. At Luna Park, the "Witching Waves" simulated the bobbing of a ship at high sea, and the "Tickler" featured spinning circular cars that threw riders to-

gether. "Such rides," wrote a student of Coney Island, "served in effect as powerful hallucinogens, altering visitors' perceptions and transforming their consciousness, dispelling everyday concerns in the intense sensations of the present moment. They allowed customers the exhilaration of whirlwind activity without physical exertion, of thrilling drama without imaginative effort."

The Magic of the Flickering Image

Coney Island showed workers that machines could liberate as well as enslave. It offered an escape from an oppressive urban landscape to an exotic one. The motion picture industry, however, offered a less expensive, more convenient escape. During the early twentieth century it developed into a major popular culture form, one that reflected the hopes and ambitions, fears and anxieties of an urban people.

In 1887 when Thomas Edison moved his research laboratory from Menlo Park to Orange, New Jersey, he gave William K. L. Dickson, one of his leading inventors, the task of developing a motion picture apparatus. Edison envisioned a machine "that should do for the eye what the phonograph did for the ear." Working closely with Edison, Dickson developed the Edison kinetophonograph, a machine capable of showing film in synchronization with a phonograph record. The idea of talking pictures, however, was not as popular as the moving pictures themselves. After further refinements by Edison and other inventors, silent moving pictures became a commercial reality.

The first movies, as the new form was soon called, presented brief vaudeville turns or glimpses of everyday life. Such titles as *Fred Ott's Sneeze*, *Chinese Laundry*, *The Gaiety Girls Dancing*, *Dentist Scene*, and *Highland Dance* tell the full content of each 3- or 4-minute film. Still the movies attracted considerable interest, and filmmakers began to experiment with such new techniques as editing and intercutting separate "shots" to form a dramatic narrative. In 1903 the release of Edwin S. Porter's *The Great Train Robbery*, the first western and the first film to exploit the violence of armed robbery, fully demonstrated the commercial possibilities of the invention. Although *The Great Train Robbery* ran only 12 minutes, it mesmerized audiences.

During the early twentieth century, movies developed a strong following in ethnic, working-class neighborhoods. Local entrepreneurs converted stores and saloons into nickelodeons and introduced immigrants to a silent world of promise. Movies provided inexpensive and short escapes from the grimmer realities of urban life. Describing the experience of visiting a nickelodeon, Abraham Cahan, editor of the *Jewish Daily Forward*, wrote in 1906: "People must be entertained and five cents is little to pay. A movie lasts half an hour. If it isn't too busy you can see it several times. They open in the afternoon and customers, mostly men and women, eat fruit and have a good time." In addition, since the movies were silent, they required no knowledge of English to be enjoyed.

Ministers, politicians, and other guardians of traditional Victorian morality criticized the new form of entertainment. Movies, said Nebraska's superintendent of schools Joseph R. Fulk, "engendered idleness and cultivated careless spending" at the "expense of earnest and persistent work." Worse yet, they stirred "primitive passions," encourage "day-dreaming," and fostered "too much familiarity between boys and girls." Fulk's fears—of idleness, careless spending, and sexual temptation—express perfectly the Victorian view of movies. Soon local boards of censorship formed to protect innocent boys and girls, and perhaps not so innocent men and women, from being corrupted by movies.

In the cities, censorship movements ultimately failed. Furthermore, attempts by white, native-born American entrepreneurs to control the new industry similarly failed. Ironically, while films were beginning to attract middle-class audiences, control of the industry shifted to immigrant entrepreneurs, most of whom were Jewish and had come to America from eastern Europe. They proved better able than native-born businessmen to develop the possibilities of the medium. They emerged from a

Early nickelodeons were cramped and uncomfortable, but they provided endless leisure enjoyments for immigrants and native-born Americans.

Swashbuckling hero Douglas Fairbanks and "America's Sweetheart" Mary Pickford in a scene from *The Taming of the Shrew*, a United Artists film of 1929. In 1919, Fairbanks and Pickford, who married the following year, joined Charlie Chaplin and D. W. Griffith to form United Artists Corporation.

cape union difficulties. While such "stars" as Charlie Chaplin, Douglas Fairbanks, and Mary Pickford captured the hearts of America, producers such as Adolph Zukor, William Fox, Louis B. Mayer, Carl Laemmle, and Harry Warner forged a multimillion-dollar industry.

The Agony of Painless Escape

Coney Island and movie theaters provided one form of escape, and the criticism of both was fairly uniform. James Gibbons Huneker, a leading cultural critic of the period, feared the surrender of reason and repression that Coney Island encouraged. "Unreality," he commented, "is as greedily craved by the mob as alcohol by the dipsomaniac; indeed, the jumbled nightmares of a morphine eater are actually realized at Luna Park." And Maxim Gorky, the Russian writer and revolutionary who visited America in 1906, suggested that mass amusement acted as an opiate of the people. At the same time as popular culture was exploring the theme of mechanized instant gratification, however, Americans were seeking escape in other, more ominous forms.

Like the whirring machines at Coney Island and the flickering images on the silent, silver screen, the mindless escape of narcotics attracted millions of Americans. During the late nineteenth and early twentieth centuries, as the nation underwent the trauma of industrialization and urbanization, Americans took drugs in unprecedented amounts. Apologists blamed this development on the Civil War. They claimed that soldiers became addicted to morphine after using the drug as a pain killer. Yet France, Germany, Great Britain, Russia, and Italy also fought wars in the second half of the nineteenth century, and their drug addiction rates were far below those of the United States.

Part of the problem was that before 1915 there were few restrictions on the importation and use of opium, its derivatives, and cocaine. Physicians prescribed opiates for a wide range of ailments, and patent medicine manufacturers used morphine, laudanum, cocaine, or heroin in their concoctions. William Hammond, former surgeon general of the army, swore by cocaine and drank a glass of a cocaine drink with each meal. The Hay Fever Association officially rec-

culture that valued laughter, cooperation, and entertainment. These attitudes allowed them to make movies that appealed to Americans.

Committed to giving the people what they wanted, they were less committed to the traditional Victorian code of morality. As Samuel Goldwyn, one of the best immigrant filmmakers, observed, "If the audience don't like a picture, they have a good reason. The public is never wrong. I don't go for all this thing that when I have a failure, it is because the audience doesn't have the taste or education, or isn't sensitive enough. The public pays the money. It wants to be entertained. That's all I know." To better entertain the public, film moguls started producing feature length films and moved the industry from the East Coast to sunny Hollywood, where they could shoot outdoors and incidentally, es-

ommended cocaine as an effective remedy. Coca-Cola used cocaine as one of its secret ingredients, and the Parke Davis Company produced coca-leaf cigarettes, cheroots, and a Coca Cordial. Vin Mariani, a wine product containing cocaine and endorsed by Pope Leo XIII, was advertised as "a perfectly safe and reliable diffusable stimulant and tonic; a powerful aid to digestion and assimilation; admirably adapted for children, invalids, and convalescents."

Cocaine in particular was regarded as a wonder drug. One manufacturer claimed that it could take "the place of food, make the coward brave, the silent eloquent, free the victims of the alcohol and opium habits from their bondage, and, as an anesthetic, render the sufferer insensitive to pain." But by the late 1890s its harmful effects had become obvious. Journalists and government officials linked it to urban crime and racial unrest in the South. Eventually, angry citizens and the federal and state governments launched the first great American crusade against cocaine. It culminated with the Harrison Anti-Narcotic Act in 1914, which controlled the distribution of opiates and cocaine; but drug addiction remained a problem in cities well into the 1920s.

Robert Louis Stevenson's *Dr. Jekyll and Mr. Hyde*, which he wrote under the influence of cocaine, described the dangers of challenging society's standards and altering one's personality, but in America's cities a new culture had taken shape. It opposed Victorian restraints, glorified the freedoms of urban life, and at the same time worried about the implications of a liberated life-style. Social, as well as economic, freedom came with a price. By the 1890s many Americans believed some new form of regulations was needed to check the social and economic freedom unleashed in urban America.

CONCLUSION

On January 17, 1906, Marshall Field, the dry-goods merchant and founder of the large Chicago department store that bears his name, died. "The first as well as the richest citizen" in Chicago, noted the *New York Sun*, Field left his children over $140 million. Americans questioned how one man could accumulate such a

fortune. "No man could earn a million dollars honestly," said politician William Jennings Bryan. Another critic suggested that Field's fortune was made at the expense of his more than 10,000 employees, 95 percent of whom earned $12 dollars a week or less: "The female sewing-machine operators, who make the clothes which are sold in the Field establishment, get $6.75 per week. . . . The makers of socks and stockings are paid: finishers, $4.75 per week of fifty-nine working hours . . . knitters, $4.75 per week of fifty-nine and one-half working hours."

Most Americans, however, focused on what Field offered shoppers more than what he paid his employees. Field's, A. T. Stewart, Rowland H. Macy, John Wanamaker—their very names conjured visions of miles and miles of consumer goods. They brought order to shopping and emphasized standardization of products. In their department stores in New York, Chicago, and Philadelphia, customers could purchase ready-made clothes, jewelry, toys, sheet music, cutlery, and a wide range of other products. Serving urban markets and satisfying urban desires, they provided a safe haven for urban shoppers. Inside one of the great department stores, consumers isolated themselves from the garbage in the streets, the filth in the air, and the sounds of traffic and commerce that dominated the outside world. They chose not to think about the workers who made the goods they purchased.

Both the orderly world of the department store and the chaotic one of the streets were the products of urban entrepreneurs who fashioned the modern cities. In pursuit of profits they were capable of producing dazzling monuments to commerce and terrible tributes to greed. The same spirit that built the Woolworth Building and the Dakota Apartments also constructed dumbbell tenements. By 1900, their days of absolute dominance were numbered. Although they would remain a vital part of American capitalism, in the future they would be rivaled by governmental planners—people who wanted to extend the smooth, efficient order of the department store to the outside streets.

The emergence of the great cities changed American life. To be sure, they exerted an economic domination, but their influence was still greater. Eventually, they came to dominate the American imagination. In the cities, the clash of

CHRONOLOGY
OF KEY EVENTS

1869 First professional baseball team, the Cincinnati Red Stockings, begins a barnstorming tour of America

1870 The Metropolitan Museum of Art in New York and the Museum of Fine Arts in Boston open

1871 Great Chicago fire claims 300 lives, destroys 17,500 buildings, and leaves 100,000 people homeless

1873 San Francisco introduces the cable car

1878 Yellow fever epidemic causes 5150 deaths in Memphis and 3977 in New Orleans

1879 New York City adopts Tenement Reform Law requiring all rooms to have access to light and air

1882 Electric lighting comes into widespread use for the first time in New York City

1884 Mark Twain's *The Adventures of Huckleberry Finn* is published

1885 William LeBaron Jenney erects the Home Insurance Building in Chicago, the first true skyscraper

1887 W. K. L. Dickson and Thomas Edison develop motion pictures

1888 Richmond, Virginia, introduces the electric-power trolley

1892 James J. Corbett wins heavyweight boxing title from John L. Sullivan; Stephen Crane publishes his first novel, *Maggie: A Girl of the Streets*

1899 Scott Joplin composes "Maple Leaf Rag"

1900 Theodore Dreiser publishes his first novel, *Sister Carrie*

1903 Edwin S. Porter's *The Great Train Robbery* is the first American film to tell a story

1912 Jim Thorpe, an Oklahoma Indian, wins the decathlon and pentathlon at the 1912 Olympic Games in Stockholm

1913 Artists from the ashcan and modernist schools participate in the Armory Show in New York City

1914 Harrison Anti-Narcotic Act controls the distribution of opiates and cocaine

ideas and beliefs, of peoples and traditions created an exciting, new heterogeneous culture. The result was evident at places such as Coney Island and the Armory Show, it was visible in many of the movies, and it was audible at a New Orleans jazz cafe. As the nineteenth century drew to a close, a new culture was clearly emerging. It would add a new element to the new century.

SUGGESTIONS FOR FURTHER READING

OVERVIEWS AND SURVEYS

Daniel J. Boorstin, *The Americans: The Democratic Experience* (1973); Sean Dennis Cashman, *America in the Gilded Age* (1984); Howard P. Chudacoff, *The Evolution of American Urban Society* (1975); Charles N. Glaab and A. Theodore Brown, *A History of Urban America*, 3d ed. (1983); David R. Goldfield

and Blaine A. Brownell, *Urban America* (1979); Raymond A. Mohl, *The New City* (1985); Lewis Mumford, *The City in History* (1961); Benjamin Rader, *American Sports* (1990); Robert H. Walker, *Life in the Age of Enterprise, 1865–1900* (1967); Sam Bass Warner, Jr., *The Urban Wilderness* (1972); Robert H. Wiebe, *The Search for Order, 1877–1920* (1967).

NEW CITIES AND NEW PROBLEMS

John M. Allswang, *Bosses, Machines and Urban Voters* (1977); Andrew Alpern, *Apartments for the Affluent* (1975); Nelson M. Blake, *Water for the Cities* (1956); Charles W. Cheape, *Moving the Masses* (1980); Howard P. Chudacoff, *Mobile Americans: Residential and Social Mobility in Omaha, 1880–1920* (1972); Dean R. Esslinger, *Immigrants and the City* (1975); David M. Fine, *The City, The Immigrant and American Fiction, 1880–1920* (1977); Robert M. Fogelson, *Big-City Police* (1977); Kenneth Fox, *Better City Government* (1977); Frederic Cople Jaher, *The Urban Establishment* (1982); Maury Klein and Harvey A. Kantor, *Prisoners of Progress: American Industrial Cities, 1850–1920* (1976); Roger Lane, *Policing the City: Boston, 1822–1885* (1967), and *Violent Death in the City* (1979); Blake McKelvey, *American Urbanization* (1973); Clay McShane, *Technology and Reform* (1974); Harold M. Mayer and Richard C. Wade, *Chicago* (1969); Martin V. Melosi, *Garbage in the Cities* (1982), and (ed.) *Pollution and Reform in the American Cities, 1870–1930* (1980); Gilbert Osofsky, *Harlem: The Making of a Ghetto* (1966); Harold L. Platt, *The Electric City: Energy and the Growth of the Chicago Area, 1880–1930* (1991); Bradley R. Rice, *Progressive Cities* (1977); Christine M. Rosen, *The Limits of Power: Great Fires and the Process of City Growth in America* (1986); Martin J. Schiesl, *The Politics of Efficiency* (1977); Allan H. Spear, *Black Chicago* (1967); John Stilgoe, *Borderland: Origins of the American Suburb, 1820–1939* (1988); Joel A. Tarr, "Transportation Innovation and Changing Spatial Patterns in Pittsburgh, 1850–1934" in *Essays in Public Works History* (1978); Jon C. Teaford, *The Municipal Revolution in America* (1975), *City and Suburb* (1979), and *The Unheralded Triumph: City Government in America, 1870–1900* (1984); David Ward, *Cities and Immigrants* (1971); Sam Bass Warner, Jr., *Streetcar Suburbs* (1962); William S. Worley, *J. C. Nichols and the Shaping of Kansas City* (1991).

CITY CULTURE

Lois W. Banner, *Women in Modern America* (1974), and *American Beauty* (1983); Gunther Barth, *City People* (1980); Susan P. Benson, *Counter Cultures: Saleswomen, Managers, and Customers in American Department Stores, 1890–1940* (1986); Burton J. Bledstein, *The Culture of Professionalism* (1976); Paul Boyer, *Urban Masses and Moral Order in America, 1820–1920* (1978); Carl W. Condit, *The Chicago School of Architecture* (1964), and *The Rise of the Skyscraper* (1952); Carl N. Degler, *At Odds: Women and the Family in America from the Revolution to the Present* (1980); Blanche H. Gelfant, *The American City Novel* (1954); James Gilbert, *Perfect Cities: Chicago's Utopias of 1893* (1991); Alfred Kazin, *On Native Grounds* (1942); Neil Leonard, *Jazz and the White Americans* (1962); Lawrence W. Levine, *Highbrow/Lowbrow: the Emergence of Cultural Hierarchy in America* (1988); William L. O'Neill, *Divorce in the Progressive Era* (1967); David J. Pivar, *Purity Crusade: Sexual Morality and Social Control, 1868–1900* (1973); W. J. Rorabaugh, *The Alcoholic Republic* (1979); Sheila M. Rothman, *Woman's Proper Place*

(1978); Lewis O. Saum, *The Popular Mood of America, 1860–1890* (1990); William J. Schafer and Johannes Riedel, *The Art of Ragtime* (1973); Thomas J. Schlereth, *Victorian America* (1991); Vincent Scully, *American Architecture and Urbanism* (1969); Larzer Ziff, *The American 1890s* (1966).

ENTERTAINING THE MULTITUDES

Melvin L. Adelman, *A Sporting Time* (1986); Reid Badger, *The Great American Fair* (1979); David F. Burg, *Chicago's White City of 1893* (1976); Dominick Cavallo, *Muscles and Morals: Organized Playgrounds and Urban Reform, 1880–1920* (1981); John E. DiMeglio, *Vaudeville U.S.A.* (1973); Perry Duis, *The Saloon* (1983); Lewis A. Erenberg, *Steppin' Out: New York Nightlife and the Transformation of American Culture, 1890–1930* (1981); Charles E. Funnell, *By the Beautiful Sea* (1975); Warren Goldstein, *Playing for Keeps: A History of Early Baseball* (1989); Elliott Gorn, *The Manly Art* (1986); Allen Guttmann, *A Whole New Ball Game: An Interpretation of American Sports* (1988); Stephen Hardy, *How Boston Played: Sport, Recreation, and Community, 1865–1915* (1982); John F. Kasson, *Amusing the Millions, Coney Island at the Turn of the Century* (1978), and *Rudeness & Civility: Manners in Nineteenth-Century Urban America* (1990); T. J. Jackson Lears, *No Place of Grace: Antimodernism and the Transformation of American Culture, 1880–1920* (1981); Lary May, *Screening Out the Past: The Birth of Mass Culture and the Motion Picture Industry* (1980); Donald J. Mrozek, *Sport and American Mentality, 1880–1910* (1983); James D. Norris, *Advertising and the Transformation of American Society, 1865–1920* (1990); Russel B. Nye, *The Unembarrased Muse* (1970); Kathy Peiss, *Cheap Amusements: Working Women and Leisure in Turn-of-the-Century New York* (1986); Steven A. Riess, *Touching Base: Professional Baseball and American Culture in the Progressive Era* (1980); Robert Sklar, *Movie-Made America* (1975); Dale A. Somers, *The Rise of Sports in New Orleans, 1850–1900* (1972).

BIOGRAPHIES

Neil Harris, *Humbug: The Art of P. T. Barnum* (1973); Michael T. Isenberg, *John L. Sullivan and His America* (1988); Justin Kaplan, *Mr. Clemens and Mark Twain* (1966); Peter Levine, *A. G. Spalding and the Rise of Baseball* (1985); Randy Roberts, *Papa Jack: Jack Johnson and the Era of White Hopes* (1983), and *Jack Dempsey: The Manassa Mauler* (1979); Laura Wood Roper, *FLO: A Biography of Frederick Law Olmsted* (1973); Elizabeth Stevenson, *Park Maker: A Life of Frederick Law Olmsted* (1977).

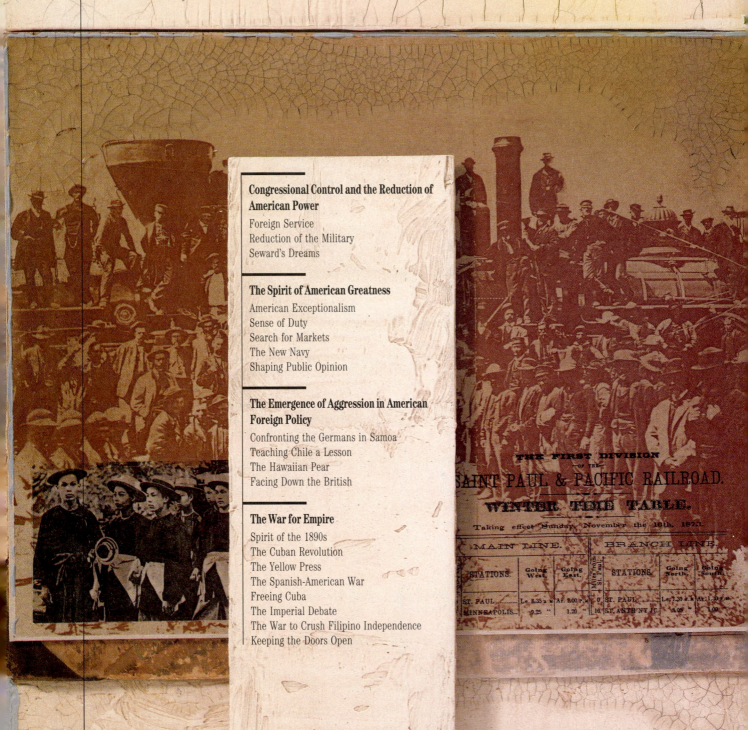

Imperial America, 1870–1900

THE FIRST DIVISION
OF THE
SAINT PAUL & PACIFIC RAILROAD.
WINTER TIME TABLE.
Taking effect Sunday, November the 16th, 1873.

MAIN LINE.				BRANCH LINE.		
STATIONS.	Going West.	Going East.	Miles from St. Paul	STATIONS.	Going North.	Going South.
ST. PAUL	Le. 8.35 a m	Ar. 2.00 p m	0	ST. PAUL	Le. 7.30 a m	Ar. 1.30 p m
MINNEAPOLIS	9.25 "	1.20 "	10	ST. ANTHONY JC.	8.05 "	1.00 "

a

XXII. No. 1. THE EN

Dreams of expansion came easily to Americans during the nineteenth century. For most of the century they expanded westward, moving into Texas and Kansas, pushing across the Great Plains, and occupying California and the Pacific Northwest. But they did not restrict their dreams to the millions of acres between Mexico and Canada. They cast covetous eyes toward Central America and the islands of the Caribbean and the Pacific. Plans to annex Nicaragua, Cuba, Santo Domingo, the Virgin Islands, Hawaii, and Samoa fired politicians' imaginations. Before the Civil War, the debate over slavery blocked these larger expansionist efforts. Once the Union was preserved, however, expansionists returned to their plans with revived energy and enthusiasm.

President Ulysses S. Grant had a pet expansionist project of his own. He eyed the Dominican Republic, the eastern two-thirds of the Caribbean island of Santo Domingo. Annexation, he maintained, would benefit America in a number of ways. The island was rich in mineral resources, possessed an important natural harbor, and its inhabitants were eager to buy American products. Most importantly for Grant, who was ever mindful of America's race problem, the Dominicans were black. The island could serve as a frontier for black Americans, a retreat from Ku Klux Klan harassment.

With so much to gain, Grant put his full political weight behind annexation. His conduct was less than presidential. First, he sent his personal secretary and close friend Orville Babcock to Santo Domingo on a "fact finding" mission. Unimpressed by the islanders, Babcock reported: "The people are indolent and ignorant. The best class of people are the American Negroes who have come here from time to time." But Babcock was convinced that the Dominican Republic was a commercial and strategic prize worthy of annexation. What was more, Buenaventura Baez, the unscrupulous president of the republic, was anxious to sell his country. With the money he would make from the transaction, Baez hoped to move and establish residence in Paris or Madrid, because, as Babcock noted, the Dominican Republic was "a dull country."

Unrest at home added fuel to Baez's willingness to sell. His government was threatened both by neighboring Haiti and a strong force of Dominican rebels. So difficult was Baez's position that Babcock had to order a United States Navy ship to protect the Baez government during the annexation negotiations, which were completed in the late fall of 1869. The promise of American dollars had convinced Baez that his country should belong to the United States.

Grant was pleased. The treaty of annexation, however, would have to be ratified by the Senate, a body more difficult to satisfy than Baez's government. An informal man, Grant decided to forgo presidential protocol and personally visit Charles Sumner, the chairman of the Senate Foreign Relations Committee. On the evening of January 2, 1870, Grant made an unannounced call at Sumner's Washington home on Lafayette Park. Later Sumner recalled that Grant was drunk. Drunk or sober, Grant was certainly in earnest. He energetically discussed the need to annex the Dominican Republic. Sumner listened then replied: "Mr. President, I am an Administration man, and whatever you do will always find in me the most careful and candid consideration." Grant departed for his short walk back to the White House believing he had won Sumner's full support. In fact, he had only won the powerful Massachusetts senator's "candid consideration."

After consideration and considerable investigation, Sumner decided that the entire annexation scheme was distasteful. He was disturbed by Babcock's and Baez's unethical financial dealings and was enraged that the United States Navy had been used to keep the Dominican president in power. Sumner was not a man to mince words. Labeled "probably the most intolerant man that American history has ever known," he accused Grant of being "a colossus of ignorance." Finally by a vote of 5 to 2, the Foreign Relations Committee voiced its disapproval of the treaty of annexation.

Grant was furious. His son later recalled, "I never saw Father so grimly angry." Known for his bulldog tenacity during the Civil War, Grant was not about to quit. He hinted that if the United States did not take the Dominican Republic, one of the European powers would, and he reported the results of a rigged plebiscite in which the Dominicans supposedly supported annexation by the suspiciously lopsided vote of 15,169 to 11, but Grant's efforts failed. On June 30, 1870, the Senate rejected the treaty. Defining America's duty toward the island, Sumner said, "Our duty is as plain as the Ten Commandments. Kindness, beneficence, assistance, aid, help, protection, all that is implied in good neighborhood, these we must give freely, bountifully, but their independence is as sacred to them as is ours to us."

The failed attempt to annex the Dominican Republic is important for the themes it underscored. It demonstrated both the desire for expansion by the president and his advisors and the power of Congress in foreign affairs. During the remainder of the century the scenario would be repeated again and again, often with different results. Gradually during this period, presidents wrested more control over foreign affairs from Congress. And Congress, for its part, accepted a more expansionist foreign policy. As presidents and Congress found common ground, America expanded outward into the Caribbean and the Pacific. The expansion took different forms. Sometimes the United States annexed countries outright. Other times America remained content to exercise less forceful control over nominally independent countries. The results were the same. The United States ultimately acquired an overseas empire and expanded its influence over the Western Hemisphere.

Area of Grant's Expansionist Scheme

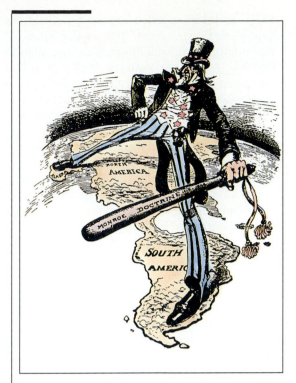

During the turn of the century, the United States increasingly tried to influence world affairs. Here, Uncle Sam assumes a forceful attitude.

retary of state as great a prize as it had been. Once regarded as a stepping-stone to the presidency, politicians increasingly viewed the post as a reward for outstanding party men or the refuge for defeated presidential aspirants. Even the diplomats themselves did not escape criticism. One newspaper editor said the diplomatic service was too often used as "gilt edged pigeon holes for filing away Americans, more or less illustrious, who are no longer particularly wanted at home."

The irreverent treatment of the State Department reflected a congressional and national mood. Concerns over the currency, civil service reform, Reconstruction, taxation, the tariff, Indian fighting, and railroad building dwarfed interest in foreign affairs. As late as 1889, Henry Cabot Lodge, whose interests in foreign affairs were great, could write: "Our relations with foreign nations today fill but a slight place in American politics, and excite . . . a languid interest. We have separated ourselves so completely from the affairs of other people." During the

CONGRESSIONAL CONTROL AND THE REDUCTION OF AMERICAN POWER

Foreign Service

In 1869 when Grant took office, congressmen and other Americans held the State Department and the diplomatic service in low esteem. No majestic building housed the State Department. Instead the department was headquartered in a former orphan asylum. Nor was the post of sec-

1870s and 1880s, when a powerful Congress largely dictated foreign policy, the spirit of Washington's Farewell Address and the Monroe Doctrine guided the country. Washington had counseled America to steer clear of foreign entanglements and Monroe had made isolationism a national obsession. Separated from a powerful Europe by the cold North Atlantic, Congress saw no reason to spend time or money on the State Department or foreign affairs.

Using its control over the budget as a sword, Congress trimmed the State Department to the bone. In 1869, Congress allowed the State Department a paltry 31 clerks; by 1881 presidential efforts had succeeded in raising that number to a still inadequate 50. Politicians who considered the foreign service "a nursery of snobs" viewed diplomats as an expensive, nearly useless luxury. A few reformers even advocated the abolition of the foreign service. They argued that two oceans protected America and they could hire international lawyers to handle really serious international crises.

Reduction of the Military

The sword that trimmed the State Department was also used on America's army and navy. When the Civil War ended and peace returned to the country, Congress quickly reduced America's military might. The result made the United States a weaker country. In 1865 America had the largest and perhaps the most powerful navy in the world. To be sure, it was a ragtag navy, composed of just about any vessel that would float. Ranging from the powerful *Monitor*-class ironclads to modest yachts, the United States Navy numbered 971 vessels. Within nine months of Appomattox, the fleet was reduced to 29.

As Congress watched unconcerned, the navy declined intellectually as well as physically. To begin with, there were far too many officers. Although after the post–Civil War reductions America's navy was less than one-tenth as large as Great Britain's, it contained over half as many officers. With promotions based strictly upon length of service, any officer who lived long enough could become an admiral. The system almost guaranteed poor leadership. While the world's best navies converted to steel and steam, American naval leaders remained tied to wood and sails. As one American officer from the period recalled, "To burn coal was so grievous an offense in the eyes of the authorities that for years the coal-burning captain was obliged to enter in the logbook in *red ink* his reasons for getting up steam and starting the engines." Quickly the American navy became a joke. In 1881 authorities claimed, with some justification, that a single modern ship of the Chilean navy could destroy the entire United States fleet.

The men appointed as the secretaries of the navy did nothing to help matters. They were mostly political appointees who knew little and cared less about ships. One historian noted that Richard W. Thompson of Indiana, whom Rutherford B. Hayes appointed secretary of the navy, was "so densely ignorant of naval affairs as to express surprise upon learning that ships were hollow."

The power and effectiveness of the army were similarly reduced. On May 23, 1865, with the Civil War just ended, Union bluecoats marched down Pennsylvania Avenue in a victory parade. There were over 100,000 soldiers. It took an hour for General Meade's cavalry to pass the reviewing stand. "Marching twelve abreast, the general's infantry consumed another five hours." The next day thousands of General Sherman's men repeated the performance, marching briskly "like the lords of the world!"

The sight would not be repeated for over 50 years. Demobilization occurred quickly and haphazardly. In May 1865 the army contained 1,034,064 volunteers; by November 1866 only 11,043 remained in uniform. Eventually Congress slashed the number of even the regular troops. By the end of Reconstruction, Congress had reduced the army to a distant echo of its former self. In 1876 the maximum strength stood at 27,442 troops.

Certainly in 1876 the United States did not need an active foreign service and a powerful army and navy to secure its borders. No countries threatened America. Geography defended the United States, and the European balance of power discouraged foolish European designs on any part of the Western Hemisphere. At the same time, the relative weakness of America's foreign service, army, and navy discouraged the United States from attempting to extend its influence beyond its own borders. All in all, most congressmen were entirely happy with the situation.

Seward's Dreams

Not everyone in government agreed with congressional leadership in foreign affairs. Regularly during the 1860s and 1870s, presidents or their secretaries of state called for a more forceful, expansionist foreign policy. William Henry Seward of New York, who served as secretary of state for Lincoln and Johnson, was such a man. A cold and vain man with a weak chin and a prominent nose, Seward dreamed of an American empire that would dominate the Pacific and Caribbean basins. During his term as secretary of state, he advocated a vigorous expansionism. He negotiated with Denmark to purchase the Danish West Indies (Virgin Islands), with Russia to buy Alaska, and with Santo Domingo for the Dominican harbor of Samana Bay. In addition, his plan for an American empire encompassed Haiti, Cuba, Iceland, Greenland, Honduras's Tigre Island, and Hawaii.

Congress balked. It did not share Seward's vision. During Seward's term, America did acquire the Midway Islands in the middle of the Pacific Ocean, but few Americans even noticed the addition. The purchase of Alaska in 1867 drew more comments, most of which were negative. Congressmen grumbled over the treaty. Some senators claimed that $7.2 million was too much money for a frozen wasteland that only Eskimos and seals could love. Others cracked jokes about "Johnson's Polar Bear Garden" and "Frigidia." But in the end the Senate, influenced by a few well-placed bribes, reluctantly ratified the treaty.

Articulate and aggressive anti-imperialists blocked the remainder of Seward's dreams. During the late 1860s and the 1870s congressional power was at a high tide. Seward and President Andrew Johnson were no match for Sumner and Thaddeus Stevens and their colleagues in Congress. Congressmen consistently

Congress and most Americans did not share Secretary of State William Henry Seward's expansionist ambitions. Only a few well-placed bribes convinced the Senate to purchase Alaska in 1867. The purchase became known as "Seward's Folly."

found other issues more pressing than foreign affairs. Some pushed for money to enact a fair Reconstruction policy. Others freely gave money to railroad construction companies and Union veterans; such gifts contributed significantly to their reelection. But they drew America's purse strings tight when confronted with most expansionist schemes.

THE SPIRIT OF AMERICAN GREATNESS

Although Congress was reluctant to endorse expansionist schemes, during the last third of the nineteenth century many other citizens had become convinced that the United States had to adopt a more aggressive and forceful foreign policy. Their reasons varied. Some believed expansion would be good for American business. Others felt America had a duty to spread its way of life to less fortunate countries. Still others maintained that economic and strategic security required that the country acquire overseas bases. Behind all the arguments, however, rested a common assumption: The United States was a great and important country, and it should start acting the part.

American Exceptionalism

For many Americans it started with God's plan. The idea of American exceptionalism—that the nation houses God's chosen people—has deep roots in the country's history. Puritan concepts of "a city upon the hill" mixed easily with talk of the greatness of republicanism and democracy and the manifest destiny of America. The teachings of Social Darwinists added "scientific proof" to the concept of American exceptionalism. With such Darwinian phrases as "natural selection" and "survival of the fittest," American intellectuals praised the course of American history. Even Charles Darwin himself was not immune to the lure of American exceptionalism. In *The Descent of Man* (1871), he wrote: "There is apparently much truth in the belief that the wonderful progress of the United States, as well as the character of the people, are the results of natural selection; the more energetic, restless, and courageous men from all parts of Europe have emigrated during the last ten or twelve generations to that great country."

Such ideas found warm reception in America. Darwin's theories were more readily accepted in the United States than they were in England. There was, however, a dark side to American exceptionalism, and this too many Americans were quick to endorse: If white Anglo-Saxon Americans were biologically superior, then other races and other nations had to be inferior. During the late nineteenth century, such Social Darwinists as Herbert Spencer in England and John Fiske in the United States helped to make racism intellectually acceptable. Catering to Anglo-Saxon audiences, Social Darwinists advanced one pseudo-scientific theory after another to "prove" the superiority of Anglo-Saxons.

From the idea of superiority to the acceptance of domination was a short step. If Americans were God's and Darwin's chosen people, why shouldn't they dominate and uplift less fortunate countries and peoples? This was the question that advocates of a more aggressive American foreign policy asked their audiences. Senator Albert J. Beveridge of Indiana spoke for many Americans when he told Congress,

> God has not been preparing the English-speaking and Teutonic peoples for a thousand years for nothing but vain and idle self-admiration. No! He has not made us the master organizers of the world to establish a system where chaos reigns. . . . He has given us the spirit of progress to overwhelm the forces of reaction throughout the earth. He has made us adept in government that we may administer government among savage and senile peoples.

Sense of Duty

Religious leaders also noted the duty that American exceptionalism implied. Talk of the "White Man's Burden" was rife during the period. Protestant missionaries carried their faith and beliefs to the far corners of the world. The benefits of their message extended well beyond preaching salvation and saving souls. They also extolled the virtues of American civilization, which included everything from democracy and rule by law to sanitation, material progress, sewing machines, and cotton underwear. Defining good and bad, progress and savagery by American standards, they attempted to alter native customs and beliefs to conform to a single American model.

Many foreign missionaries sought to unite the people of the world by extolling the virtues of American civilization.

Popular writer and religious leader Reverend Josiah Strong voiced what other missionaries and true believers acted upon. In 1885 Strong published *Our Country: Its Possible Future and Present Crisis*, a book that quickly sold 170,000 copies and was translated into dozens of languages. "The Anglo-Saxon," Strong wrote, "is the representative of two great ideas . . . civil liberty [and] a pure *spiritual* Christianity." These two ideas, he added, are destined to elevate all mankind, and "the Anglo-Saxon . . . is divinely commissioned to be . . . his brother's keeper." He firmly believed that it was America's destiny and duty to expand and spread its influence. Quoting the Bible while speaking to Anglo-Saxon Americans, he intoned, "Prepare ye the way of the Lord!"

Search for Markets

Strong's message was not lost on the business leaders of America. They fully agreed that missionaries should preach the benefits of American material progress as well as the glories of the Protestant faith. Looking south toward Latin America and west toward Asia, American businesspeople and farmers saw vast virgin markets for their industrial and agricultural surpluses as well as endless sources of raw materials. Sensing that American markets, filled with low paid workers, offered few new opportunities, they entertained fabulous visions of hungry Latin Americans and shoeless Chinese. They fully agreed with the able American diplomat John A. Kasson who warned the readers of the *North American Review* in 1881: "We are rapidly utilizing the whole of our continental territory. We must turn our eyes abroad, or they will soon look inward upon discontent."

During the late nineteenth century, Kasson's words seemed particularly apt. Although the United States became the leading industrial and agricultural country in the world, domestic consumption did not keep pace with the galloping production. In addition, throughout the period the government pursued tight-money policies, and the real income of laborers made only modest gains. The result was a boom and bust economy that witnessed spectacular growth as well as severe depressions. In fact, in the 25 years after 1873, the country suffered through depressions during 1873–1878, 1882–1885, and 1893–1897.

In part, the United States was a victim of its own spectacular success. Increased production without increased consumption led only to glutted markets and falling prices. For example, in 1870 Americans produced 4.3 million bales of cotton; by 1891 that figure had grown to 9 million. In 1871 a pound of cotton sold for 18 cents; by 1891 the price had dropped to 7 cents. The story was the same for wheat, meat, tobacco, and corn. Increasingly, farmers—and industrialists—looked toward foreign markets. Too often, export trade spelled the difference between prosperity and bankruptcy. Although American businesspeople and bankers had yet to develop overseas marketing networks and foreign branch banks to market their goods and finance sales, they clearly saw the need for such additions. The future of America, many economic leaders believed, would be determined by the ability of the government to find and secure overseas trade.

During the depression years, the lure of foreign trade proved particularly strong. Depressions meant farm foreclosures and industrial unemployment, problems that led to social unrest. The Grange and Populist movements, the two largest agrarian revolts, originated in cotton and wheat areas during depression years. And such labor confrontations as the violent railroad strikes of 1877, Chicago's Haymarket riot of 1886, and the Pullman strike of 1894 occurred during lean economic times. For many Americans the issue was simple: The United States must acquire foreign markets or face economic hardship and revolution at home. As one industrial spokesman put it: The time has come for the United States to pursue "an intelligent and spirited foreign policy," one in which the government would "see to it" that the country has adequate foreign markets. If force proved necessary, then so be it.

The State Department was in full agreement. William Henry Seward and Hamilton Fish, Johnson's and Grant's secretaries of state, believed firmly that America needed new markets. Seward called the potentially bottomless markets of Asia "the prize," and he wanted the

As this advertisement for Ford in Paris suggests, by the early twentieth century, American business had found new markets abroad.

United States to acquire islands in the Pacific as stepping-stones toward that prize. He similarly believed that the United States should extend its economic control to include Canada and Latin America. Hamilton Fish agreed with the hoarse-voiced, cigar-chewing Seward. Although like Seward he had to contend with a cautious, isolationist Congress, Fish made several important strides toward the Asia markets. During his term as secretary of state, the United States signed treaties and established more formal relations with Hawaii and Samoa, two Pacific island groups that would later become part of the American empire.

During the late 1870s and 1880s, economic hard times quickened the search for new markets. William Evarts, Rutherford B. Hayes's secretary of state, valued a good story. He once told a British minister that George Washington had been able to throw a dollar across the Rappahannock River because a dollar went farther in those days. Evarts also valued dollars, and he felt Americans needed far more of them. As secretary of state, he worked toward an American commercial empire. "The vast resources of our country need an outlet," he told the nation. He hoped that unexploited Asian and Latin American markets would guarantee continual economic growth and social tranquility for all Americans.

James G. Blaine and Frederick T. Frelinghuysen, who served as secretaries of state for James Garfield and Chester Arthur, concentrated their efforts on Latin American markets. Blaine later recounted that during his short stay in the State Department in 1881 he followed two principles: "first, to bring about peace . . . ; second, to cultivate such friendly commercial relations with all American countries as would lead to a large increase in the export trade of the United States." When Blaine was forced out of office after Garfield's assassination, Frelinghuysen continued his policies. He successfully negotiated bilateral reciprocity treaties with many Latin American countries. These treaties lowered tariffs and thus stimulated trade between the United States and Latin America.

By the mid-1880s, efforts in favor of expansion combined with economic and social problems at home convinced Congress to reevaluate its isolationist policies. The West was settled, the Indians defeated, the Union reconstructed, and the railroads built. It was now time to look at our oceans not as defensive barriers but as paths toward new markets and increased prosperity. A final problem, however, remained. America's navy and merchant marine seemed woefully unfit for the challenge.

The New Navy

By 1880 the United States Navy was a sad joke. Ill-informed officers commanded obsolete wooden ships. Both men and vessels should have been retired years before. The English writer and wit Oscar Wilde was close to the truth when he had one of his fictional characters reply to an American woman who complained that her country had no ruins and no curiosities: "No ruins! No curiosities! You have your Navy and your manners!"

If America hoped to compete for world markets, it had to upgrade its navy. During the 1880s and early 1890s advocates of a New Navy moved Congress to action. The transformation from a "heterogeneous collection of naval trash" to a great navy occurred in two stages. The face-lift began in 1883, during the administration of Chester A. Arthur. Prodded by the president, Congress passed an act providing for three small cruisers and a dispatch boat. These ships were the beginning of the famous White Squadron. More vessels soon followed. Under the direction of President Grover Cleveland and his able secretary of the navy, William Whitney, the White Squadron grew in size and naval bureaucracy and fleet personnel improved.

By 1890 great gains had been made, but serious problems remained. The White Squadron was not a world-class navy. The ships built were lightly armored, fast cruisers, ideal for hit-and-run missions but inadequate for any major naval engagement. While England and Germany were building large, heavily armored battleships capable of bombarding and damaging coastal cities, the United States continued to think of naval warfare in terms of commerce raiding.

Benjamin F. Tracy, Benjamin Harrison's secretary of war, was determined to change American naval thinking. Although careful to note that he wanted a fleet not for "conquest, but defense," Tracy had a very modern view of what defense entailed. To adequately defend America's interests, Tracy called for ships which could "raise blockades" and attack an enemy's coast, "for a war, though defensive in principle, may be conducted most effectively by being offensive in its operations." In fact, Tracy maintained that proper defense might even include shooting first: "The nation that is ready to strike the first blow will gain an advantage which its antagonist can never offset." Such a first-strike definition of defense meant one thing: The United States needed to build modern, armored battleships. Tracy wanted two battleship fleets, one for the Atlantic and another for the Pacific.

Personal tragedy momentarily sidetracked Tracy. In February 1890 his wife and youngest daughter burned to death in a fire that destroyed Tracy's Washington home. But Tracy's program was kept alive in Congress by such "Big Navy" advocates as Senator Eugene Hale of Maine and Representative Henry Cabot Lodge of Massachusetts. They found Congress in the mood to act. As one senator said, "You can not negotiate without a gun." In 1890, Congress appropriated money for the construction of three first-class battleships and a heavy cruiser. It was the beginning of a new, very much offensive navy for the United States. Reviewing his accomplishments in 1891, Tracy boasted: "The sea will be the future seat of empire. And we shall rule it as certainly as the sun doth rise."

Talk of empire, navy, trade, and national greatness came together in 1890 in the publication of a monumentally important book, *The Influence of Sea Power upon History*, by Captain Alfred Thayer Mahan. Mahan, who was attached to the Naval War College, was more comfortable around books than on ships. Although he had served throughout the world, he had the look, temperament, and inclinations of a college don. His masterpiece set forward the simple thesis that naval power was the key to national greatness. Taking Greece, Rome, and England as examples, he attempted to demonstrate that countries rise to world power through expanding their foreign commerce and protecting that commerce with a strong navy. Without a powerful navy, Mahan emphasized, a nation can never enjoy full prosperity and security. Without a strong navy, in short, no nation could ever hope to be a world power.

Shaping Public Opinion

Mahan's writings and Tracy's proposal were applauded by American politicians and business-people who felt it was time for the United States to assume the rights and responsibilities of world power status. These were important men —men of wealth, education, and influence. Some like Whitelaw Reid, editor of the *New York Tribune*, helped shape public opinion through their editorials. Others like Henry Cabot Lodge, Theodore Roosevelt, Albert J. Beveridge, and John Hay were powerful politicians and administrators. They were vocal nationalists who believed that the United States was destined to be the greatest of world powers. Increasingly after 1890, these and other men of like mind dominated and shaped America's foreign policy, and "public opinion" followed their lead. "After all," noted Secretary of State Walter Q. Gresham in 1893, "public opinion is made and controlled by the thoughtful men of the country."

These expansionists often shared common experiences and beliefs. Most were prosperous

Republicans from old-line American families, and most had traveled abroad widely. Anglo-Saxon by heritage, they tended to be ardent Anglophiles, full of praise for Great Britain's imperial efforts. They believed that the United States should join "Mother England" in administering to the "uncivilized" corners of the globe. As Beveridge noted, without the work of Anglo-Saxons "the world would relapse into barbarism and night . . . We are trustees of the world's progress, guardians of its righteous place."

Lodge and other expansionists called for a bold foreign policy, what they termed the "large policy." They advocated the construction of a canal through Central America to allow American ships to move between the Atlantic and Pacific oceans more rapidly. To protect the canal, the United States would have to exert control over Cuba and the other strategically located Caribbean islands. Next America would have to acquire coaling stations and naval bases across the Pacific. Secure bases in Hawaii, Guam, Wake Island, and the Philippines would allow the United States to exploit the seemingly limitless China market. Finally, a powerful navy would have to protect the entire American empire.

In the end, then, all of their plans returned to the theme of a strong navy. Like his friend Mahan, priggish Lodge was a student of history. "It is the sea power which is essential to the greatness of every splendid people," he said. It had enabled Rome to crush the Carthaginians, England to defeat Napoleon, and the North to win the Civil War. Without the power of a strong navy, Lodge believed that America could never experience real peace and security: "All the peace the world has ever had has been obtained by fighting, and all the peace that any nation . . . can ever have, is by readiness to fight if attacked." For Lodge as for Tracy, thoughts of peace and war often ran together and appeared in the same sentences.

THE EMERGENCE OF AGGRESSION IN AMERICAN FOREIGN POLICY

Proponents of the New Navy and the "large policy" talked loudly about peace. But their talk of peace, like their foreign policy and naval ambi-

tions, was couched in aggressive language. "To be prepared for war is the most effectual means to promote peace," said Theodore Roosevelt. The more they talked about peace, the closer war seemed. It is not surprising that the United States launched a more belligerent foreign policy at the same time it was building and launching more powerful ships. The two developments originated from the same source: a ready acceptance of force as the final arbiter of international disputes. Before the turn of the century, the acceptance of force would lead to the Spanish-American War of 1898, and between 1885 and 1897, during the presidencies of Benjamin Harrison and Grover Cleveland, the same attitudes almost caused several other wars. The Spanish-American War was not an aberrant event. Rather it was the result of a more aggressive American foreign policy, one aimed at acquiring both world respect and an empire.

Confronting the Germans in Samoa

Changing American attitudes toward foreign policy were first seen in Samoa, a group of 14 volcanic islands lying 4000 miles from San Francisco along the trade route to Australia. Throughout the nineteenth century, American whalers stopped in Samoa, and its two splendid natural harbors, Apia and Pago Pago, had often provided refuge for ships caught in Pacific storms. If the natives were quarrelsome among themselves, they were exceptionally friendly with Americans.

American interest in Samoa was decidedly more mercenary. In 1872 an American negotiated a treaty with a tribal chief to grant the United States rights to a naval station at Pago Pago. Although an antiexpansionist Senate took no action on the treaty, expansionists kept trying. In 1878 the Senate did ratify a similar treaty, which formally committed the United States to Samoa. Unfortunately for the United States, Germany and England were also determined to influence events on the islands.

America's chief rival for Samoa was Germany. Like the United States, Germany was just beginning to think in terms of empire. German Chancellor Otto von Bismarck decided that Samoa should belong to Germany, and as a result of the intricacies of European politics, England sided with the "iron chancellor." President Cleveland and his secretary of state, Thomas F. Bayard, firmly disagreed. Germany and the United States were set on a collision course.

When a conference between the three countries held in Washington in 1887 failed to solve the problem, war seemed closer still. Neither Germany nor the United States had much money invested in the islands, but both felt their national pride was at stake. "We must show sharp teeth," remarked Bismarck. Cleveland decided to show part of America's new White Squadron. He dispatched three warships to Samoa. Nature, however, had the most powerful weapon. On the morning of March 16, 1889, a typhoon swept across Samoa, destroying the American and German warships anchored in Apia harbor.

The violent winds seemed to calm the ruffled emotions of the United States and Germany. "Men and nations," wrote the *New York World*, "must bow before the decrees of nature." The same year as the typhoon, Germany, the United States, and England met for another conference, this one in Berlin. Without consulting the Samoans, they decided to partition the islands. Everyone seemed satisfied—except the Samoans who were deprived of their independence and saddled with an unpopular king. The plan lasted until 1899, when Germany and the United States ended the facade of Samoan independence and officially made colonies of the islands. The United States was granted Tutuila, with the harbor of Pago Pago, and several smaller islands. Many expansionists believed that America's aggressive stand against Germany had paid handsome dividends.

Teaching Chile a Lesson

American expansionists had something to gain from their confrontation with Germany over Samoa. Pago Pago was, after all, "the most perfectly landlocked harbor that exists in the Pacific Ocean." It was an ideal coaling station for ships running between San Francisco and Australia. American troubles with Chile, however, are more difficult to understand. Trade and strategic policy played small roles. More than

MORE BLUSTER THAN BLOOD.

America's attempt to gain the Samoan Islands as coaling stations along the route to Australia led to a diplomatic crisis with Germany.

anything else, touchy pride and jingoism pushed the United States toward war with Chile.

Had people not died, the background to the confrontation would have been amusing. In 1891 a revolutionary faction, which the United States had opposed, gained control of the Chilean government and initiated a foreign policy that was unfriendly toward America. Shortly thereafter, on October 16, 1891, an American cruiser, the *Baltimore*, anchored off the coast of Chile, sent about 100 members of its crew ashore on leave at Valparaiso. Many of the sailors did what sailors normally do on leave: They retired to a local saloon—in this particular case, to the True Blue Saloon—and drank. An officer who arrived on the scene later said that the men had gone ashore "for the purpose of getting drunk" and that by evening they were "probably drunk, properly drunk." As the men left the saloon, a riot broke out. An angry, anti-American mob attacked the sailors, killing 2 and injuring 16. To make matters worse, the Chilean police,

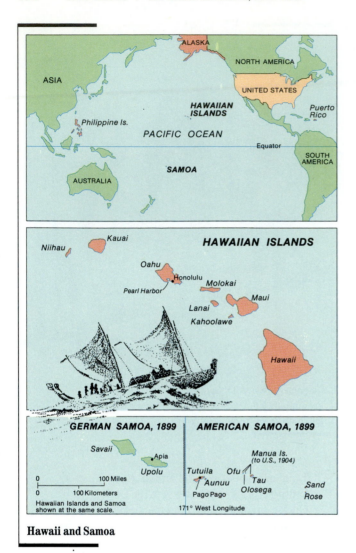

Hawaii and Samoa

who had done nothing to halt the fighting, carried the surviving Americans off to jail.

It was an unfortunate affair, and the United States loudly protested, demanding a formal apology and "prompt and full reparation." The Chilean government refused. President Harrison, a former general who had worn Union blue during the Civil War and who prided himself on his patriotism and was easily swayed by jingoism, threatened to break off diplomatic relations—a serious step toward war—unless the United States received an immediate apology. When his secretary of state, James G. Blaine, tried to counsel moderation, Harrison angrily replied, "Mr. Secretary, that insult was to the uniform of United States sailors."

Public opinion sided with Harrison. The *New York Sun* commented that "we must teach men who will henceforth be called snarling whelps of the Pacific that we cannot be snapped at with impunity." And angry young Theodore Roosevelt insisted, "For two nickels he would declare war himself . . . and wage it sole." Finally the Chilean government backed down. It apologized for the attack on the sailors and paid an indemnity of $75,000.

The threat of force had again carried the day. Advocates of the New Navy and aggressively nationalistic Americans cheered Harrison's actions. The foreign policy of the United States was becoming increasingly belligerent and strident. Few Americans heeded Edwin L. Godkin, editor of the influential *Nation*, who wrote, "The number of men and officials in this country who are now ready to fight somebody is appalling. Navy officers dream of war and talk and lecture about it incessantly. The Senate debates are filled with predictions of impending war and with talk of preparing for it at once. . . . Most truculent and bloodthirsty of all, jingo editors keep up a din day after day about the way we could cripple one country's fleet and destroy another's commerce, and fill heads of boys and silly men with the idea that war is the normal state of a civilized country."

The Hawaiian Pear

Throughout the late nineteenth century, Hawaii figured prominently in American foreign policy planning. Earlier in the century, the islands had been a favorite place for American missionaries. Many went to Hawaii to spread Christianity and ended up settling and raising their families in the tropical paradise. More important still was the location of the islands. Not only were they ideally situated along the trade routes to Asia, but they offered a perfect site for protecting the Pacific sea lanes to the American west coast and the potential locations of an isthmus canal. In Hawaii, missionary, economic, and strategic concerns met in complete harmony.

By the mid-1880s, Congress was willing to accept expansionists' dreams for Hawaii. In 1884 a treaty between Hawaii and the United States set aside Pearl Harbor for the exclusive use of the American navy. After some debate the Senate ratified the treaty in 1887, and Hawaii officially became part of American strategic planning. By that time the islands were already economically tied to the United States. An 1875 treaty had allowed Hawaiians to sell their sugar in the United States duty-free, giving them a two cents per pound advantage over other foreign producers. The legislation encouraged American speculators to invest in Hawaiian sugar and to import Chinese and Japanese laborers to the islands to work on the large plantations. The investments returned incredibly high dividends, and for a time business boomed.

Problems arose suddenly in 1890. The McKinley Tariff Act removed all tariffs on foreign sugar and protected domestic sugar producers by awarding American sugar a bounty of two cents per pound. Hawaiian sugar prices plummeted. The American minister in Honolulu estimated that the McKinley Tariff cost Hawaiian producers $12 million. In addition, in 1891 the government of the islands changed. Queen Liliuokalani ascended the throne. A poet and a composer, she expressed interest in humanitarian work and initiated a strongly anti-American policy. She wanted to purge American influences in Hawaii and disfranchise all white men except those married to native women.

The white population in Hawaii reacted quickly. On January 17, 1893, three days after the queen dismissed the legislature and proclaimed a new constitution, white islanders overthrew her government. Supported by the American minister in Honolulu, John L. Stevens, and aided by American sailors and marines, the revolution was fast, almost bloodless, and successful. Stevens then proclaimed Hawaii an American protectorate and wired his superiors in Washington that "the Hawaiian pear is now fully ripe, and this is the golden hour for the United States to pluck it."

The revolutionaries in Hawaii favored prompt American annexation of the islands. In Washington, the Harrison administration, which was due to leave office on March 4, agreed. It negotiated a treaty of annexation with "indecent haste" and sent it to the Senate for ratification. Public sentiment cheered Harrison's actions, and the cry, "Liliuokalani give us your little brown hannie!" swept the country.

Before the Senate could ratify the treaty, Cleveland took office. An anti-imperialist, Cleveland had grave misgivings about the revolution, America's reaction, and the treaty. Five days after his inauguration, he recalled the treaty from the Senate and sent a special agent, James H. Blount of Georgia, to Hawaii to investigate the entire affair. After a careful investigation, Blount reported to Cleveland that the majority of native Hawaiians opposed annexation and that on moral and legal grounds the treaty was unjustified. Cleveland accepted Blount's report and killed the treaty.

This did not end the controversy. A white American minority continued to govern Hawaii. To correct the situation, Cleveland sent another representative, Albert S. Willis, to Hawaii to convince the new government to step down and allow Queen Liliuokalani to return to the throne. Willis failed in his mission. "Queen Lil" refused to promise full amnesty for the revolutionaries if she were returned to power. "My decision would be," she said, "as the law directs, that such persons should be beheaded." In addition, President Sanford B. Dole, head of a large Hawaiian pineapple corporation, refused to leave office. In the end, Cleveland washed his hands of the entire matter, and the revolutionaries proclaimed an independent Hawaiian republic on July 4, 1894. Four years and three days later, during the Spanish-American War, the United States finally annexed Hawaii.

Facing Down the British

Potentially the most serious conflict America faced during the 1890s originated in a dispute over a strip of land in a South American jungle. Venezuela and British Guiana shared a common border; the dispute was over exactly where that border was located. Both sides claimed land the other side said was theirs. For almost 50 years this dispute remained peacefully unsettled, but the discovery of gold in the region in the 1880s increased the importance of the issue. It was a rich deposit—the largest nugget ever discovered, 509 ounces, was found there—and both Britain and Venezuela wanted it for their own. In response to Venezuelan requests for help, several times the United States offered to arbi-

Queen Liliuokalani assumed the Hawaiian throne in 1891. Strongly nationalistic, she sought to purge white influence from Hawaii. She was overthrown by white islanders with the aid of American sailors and marines.

trate the matter, and each time Britain refused the offer.

By June 1895 Cleveland and his new secretary of state, Richard Olney, had decided that Britain's actions were in violation of the spirit, if not the letter, of the Monroe Doctrine. Both men were short tempered. Ever since a cancer operation had left him with an artificial jaw of vulcanized rubber, Cleveland had been irritable. And Olney, who had persuaded Cleveland to use federal troops to put down the Pullman strike in Chicago the year before, was a man of strong ideas who did not shrink from the use of force. In a strongly worded message to Great Britain, Olney warned, "Today the United States is practically sovereign on this continent, and its fiat is law upon the subjects to which it confines its interposition." Olney demanded that Britain submit the dispute to arbitration, hinting that the United States might intervene militarily if its wishes were not honored.

Lord Salisbury, Britain's prime minister, foreign secretary, and consummate aristocrat, waited four months to reply to Olney's note, and

then answered, in effect, that the dispute did not involve either the United States or the Monroe Doctrine and would America kindly mind its own business. Olney was furious. Americans throughout the country felt insulted. Cleveland, who was duck hunting in North Carolina when Salisbury's response was received in Washington, returned to the capital, read the message, and became "mad clean through." In a special message to Congress, he asked for funds to establish a commission to determine the actual Venezuelan boundary, and he insisted that he would use force if necessary to maintain that boundary against any aggressors. Both houses of Congress unanimously approved Cleveland's request. The excitement of war was in the air. Although he was in London during much of the controversy, Senator Henry Cabot Lodge captured the mood of America when he wrote a friend, "War is a bad thing no doubt, but there are worse things both for nations and for men."

The violence of America's reaction surprised Salisbury and British officials. England certainly did not want war, particularly at that time when it was becoming involved in a conflict in South Africa. Salisbury reversed his position and allowed a commission to arbitrate the dispute. In the end, the arbitral tribunal gave Britain most of the land it claimed.

America, however, felt it was the real winner. Cleveland had faced the British lion and won. The Monroe Doctrine and American prestige soared to new heights. More important for the future, Cleveland's actions, coupled with his handling of the Hawaiian revolution, significantly increased the power of the president over foreign affairs. Relations between the United States and Britain would quickly improve, and relations between America and Venezuela would rapidly deteriorate, but future presidents would not soon relinquish their control over foreign policy.

THE WAR FOR EMPIRE

Spirit of the 1890s

During the Venezuela crisis many Americans seemed to openly invite and look forward to the prospect of war. Theodore Roosevelt, who was determined to atone for the failure of his father to fight in the Civil War and be the first in war even if he were the last in peace, wrote: "Let the fight come if it must; I don't care whether our sea coast cities are bombarded or not; we would take Canada." For Roosevelt, war would be an ennobling experience. It would test and validate American greatness. "All the great masterful races," Roosevelt wrote, "have been fighting races; and the minute that a race loses the hard fighting virtues, then . . . it has lost its proud right to stand as the equal of the best."

Throughout the 1890s other Americans echoed Roosevelt's war cries. Viewed as a whole, it was a decade of strident nationalism and aggressive posturing. It was also a troubled and violent decade. Racked by the depression of 1893, frustrated by the problems created by monopolies and overproduction, and plagued by internal strife, Americans turned on each other, often with violent results. Strikes in Pullman, Illinois, and Homestead, Pennsylvania, saw laborers battle federal and state authorities. Populist protest dramatized the widening gulf between city and country, rich and poor. Anarchists and socialists talked about the need for violent solutions to complex problems.

Popular culture in America reflected this aggressive mood. As Roosevelt denounced "the soft spirit in the cloistered life" and "the base spirit of gain," Americans looked to arenas of conflict for their heroes. They glorified boxers like the great John L. Sullivan, who held the heavyweight championship of the world between 1882 and 1892. They cheered as violence increased on the Ivy League football fields. They admired bodybuilders like Bernarr Macfadden and Eugene Sandow, who was heralded as the most perfectly developed man in the world. In the first issue of *Physical Culture*, Macfadden declared, "Weakness Is a Crime." In saloons across the country, Sullivan defiantly boasted, "I can lick any sonofabitch in the house." And in the parlors of the wealthy, Roosevelt stressed, "Cowardice in a race, as in an individual, is the unpardonable sin." Between Sullivan and Roosevelt, and the Americans that admired both men, was a bond forged by the love of violence and power.

This attitude led to the glorification of war and jingoistic nationalism. During the mid-1890s a remarkable interest in Napoleon gripped the nation; between 1894 and 1896, 28 books were written about the Corsican general. In public schools throughout the country, administrators instituted daily flag salutes and made the recitation of the new pledge of allegiance mandatory. Even the popular music of the day had a particularly martial quality. Such marches as John Philip Sousa's "Stars and Stripes Forever" (1897) and "A Hot Time in the Old Town" (1896) captured the aggressive, patriotic, and boisterous mood of the country.

As the disputes with Germany, Chile, and Great Britain demonstrated, neither the American people nor its leaders feared war. The horrors of the Civil War were dying with the generation that had known them. A younger generation of men, filled with romantic and idealized conceptions of battle and heroism, now openly sought a war of their own. In Washington some politicians even began to view war as a way to unite the country, to quell the protests of angry farmers and laborers.

The Cuban Revolution

Oftentimes the mood of a nation governs the reaction to and interpretation of events. Such was the case with America's attitude toward the Cuban Revolution. In 1895, while Sousa was writing energetic marches and Americans were cheering new boxing heroes, an independence revolt broke out in Cuba. It was not the first time the Cubans took up arms in pursuit of independence. During the Ten Years' War (1868–1878) Cuban patriots had unsuccessfully fought for their independence against their Spanish rulers. The war was bloody and violent, and Cubans actively sought American support; but the United States, guided by a policy of isolationism, steered clear.

By 1895, however, cautious isolationism was out of step with Sousa's and Roosevelt's aggressive tempo. From the start, Americans expressed far more than casual interest in the rebellion. To be sure, American business was concerned. Americans had invested over $50 million in Cuba, and the annual trade between the two countries totaled almost $100 million. Once the revolution started, insurgents burned crops in the fields, and the trade between Cuba and the United States slowed to a trickle. Overall, however, economics played a relatively unimportant role in forming America's attitude toward the revolution.

Humanitarianism was a far more important factor. Americans cheered the underdog. In Cuba's valiant fight, they saw a reenactment of their own war for independence. And the resourceful Cubans made sure that Americans stayed well supplied with stories of Spanish atrocities and Cuban heroism. The Cuban junta—central revolutionary committee—established bases in New York City and Tampa, Florida, and daily provided American newspapers with stories aimed at sympathetic American hearts.

Not all the stories were false. The Cuban—and Spanish—suffering was real enough. Unable to defeat the Spanish army in the field, Cuban revolutionaries resorted to guerrilla tactics. They burned sugarcane fields and blew up mills. They destroyed railroad tracks and bridges. They vowed to win their independence or destroy Cuba in the process. One of their leaders, General Maximo Gomez, aptly stated the guerrillas' and Cuba's position: "The chains of Cuba have been forged by her own richness, and it is precisely this which I propose to do away with soon." Supported by the populace, the guerrillas succeeded in turning Cuba into an economic and military nightmare for Spanish officials.

In 1896 Spain sent Governor-General Valeriano Weyler y Nicolau to Cuba to crush the rebellion. A man of ruthless clarity, he understood the nature of guerrilla warfare. Guerrillas could not be defeated by conventional engagements. Their generals did not imitate the tactics of Napoleon; they were not concerned with flanking maneuvers and cavalry charges. Their weapons were patience and endurance and popular support. Weyler knew this, and he decided to fight the guerrillas on their own terms.

His first plan was to rob the guerrillas of their base of support, the rural villages and the sympathetic peasants. He divided the island into military districts and relocated Cubans into guarded camps. It was a policy that the United States would later use to fight guerrillas in the Philippines and Vietnam, but Weyler was brutal in his execution of it. He forced over a half million Cubans from their homes and crowded them into shabbily constructed and unsanitary camps. The food was bad, the water worse. Disease spread with frightful speed and horrifying results. Perhaps 200,000 Cubans died in the camps as Weyler earned the sobriquet "the Butcher." After inspecting the camps, Senator Renfield Proctor of Vermont reported on the plight of the Cuban people to Congress: "Torn from their homes, with foul earth, foul air, foul water, and foul food or none, what wonder that one-half have died and that one-quarter of the living are so diseased that they cannot be saved? . . . Little children are still walking about with arms and chest terribly emaciated, eyes swollen, and abdomens bloated to three times the natural size."

The Yellow Press

In the United States reports of the suffering Cuban masses filled the front pages of newspapers. In New York City, William Randolph Hearst's *New York Journal* and Joseph Pulitzer's *New York World* used the junta's lurid stories as ammunition in a newspaper war. Newspaper reporters freely engaged in "yellow journalism," exaggerating conditions that were in truth depressingly sad and inhumane. Most stories had a sensational twist. One particularly incendiary drawing by Frederic Remington, the famous western artist sent to Cuba by Hearst, pictured three leering Spanish officials searching a nude Cuban woman. Hearst ran the picture five columns wide on the second page of the *Journal*, and the edition sold close to one million copies, the largest newspaper run in history until then. Neither the picture nor the story, however, mentioned that Spanish women—not men—conducted the search, although men had conducted other such searches. Such coverage biased American opinion against Spain. It also sold newspapers. When Hearst bought the *Journal* in 1895 it had daily circulation of 77,000 copies; by the summer of 1898 sales had increased to over 1.5 million daily.

"Yellow journalism" persuaded many Americans to call for U.S. intervention in the Cuban Revolution. Grover Cleveland, however, was not easily moved by newspaper reports. His admin-

This *New York Journal* sketch by Frederick Remington of Spanish officials searching a woman on an American steamer shocked the nation. Such "yellow journalism," or exaggeration of the facts, played an important role in persuading Americans to call for intervention in the Cuban Revolution.

istration wanted to protect American interests in Cuba but was dead set against any sort of military intervention in the conflict. Without recognizing the revolutionaries, he worked to convince Spain to grant "home rule." Spain was unconvinced. But Cleveland was unprepared to move beyond vague warnings. When he left office in early 1897, the revolution in Cuba raged as violently as ever. Cleveland passed the Cuban problems to his successor William McKinley. Like Cleveland, McKinley deplored war. He had fought bravely in the Civil War, and he knew the horrors of war firsthand. For McKinley, arbitration was the civilized way to settle disputes. War was a poor and wasteful alternative. Before he would even consider military intervention, McKinley was determined to exhaust every peaceful alternative.

McKinley displayed strength and patience. As many influential Americans called for U.S. intervention, McKinley worked diplomatically to end the fighting. Rather than inflame public opinion, he attempted to remove the issue from public debate. In his inaugural address, for example, he did not even mention Cuba. For a time it appeared that his efforts would succeed. In October 1897 a new government in Spain moved toward granting more autonomy to Cuba. It removed Weyler and promised to end his hated reconcentration program. Spain, said McKinley, was following "honorable paths." Patience and cool heads, he hoped, would carry the day.

Spain moved with glacial slowness. Some of its reforms were half-hearted, others were merely designed to calm American emotions. In Cuba the bloodshed continued. As Spanish officials and Cuban revolutionaries ignored or denounced Spain's "honorable paths," pressure on McKinley to take stronger action mounted. In May 1897 he dispatched his trusted political friend William J. Calhoun of Ohio to Cuba to provide him with an independent report on the conditions on the island. Calhoun's report confirmed the grim picture presented in American newspapers. "The country outside of the military posts was practically depopulated," Calhoun noted. "Every house had been burned, banana trees cut down, cane fields swept with fire, and everything in the shape of food destroyed. . . . I did not see a house, a man, woman or child; a horse, mule or cow, not even a dog; I did not see a sign of life, except an occasional vulture or buzzard sailing through the air. The country was wrapped in the stillness of death and the silence of desolation." By January of 1898 the president looked as defeated as his diplomatic efforts. He had to take drugs to sleep, his skin was pasty, and his dark eyes seemed to be sinking farther back into his head. During February two events would end any hope of a diplomatic solution and lead to the Spanish-American War.

William Randolph Hearst had often told his reporters: "Don't wait for things to turn up. Turn them up!" He did just that in early February 1898. With the help of the Cuban junta, Hearst acquired a private letter from Enrique Dupuy de Lôme, the Spanish minister in the United States, to a Spanish friend of his in Cuba. The letter contained de Lôme's unguarded and undiplomatic opinion of McKinley. Reprinted on the front page of the *Journal* on February 9, 1898, Hearst labeled the letter: "Worst insult to the United States in Its History." De Lôme called McKinley "weak and a bidder for the admiration of the crowd." He accused the American president of being a hypocrite and a "would-be politician." Even worse, De Lôme suggested that Spain's new peace policy was mere sham and propaganda.

The letter hit the American public like a bombshell. Although de Lôme resigned, America was in no mood to forget and forgive. Former Secretary of State Richard Olney wrote his old boss Grover Cleveland, "I confess [that] some expressions of his letter stagger me and, if they . . . mean that Spain has been tricking us as regards autonomy and other matters incidental to it, I should have wanted the privilege of sending him his passports before he had any chance to

be recalled or resign." Olney expressed the mood of the nation. As one of the leaders of the Cuban junta noted, "The de Lôme letter is a great thing for us."

Less than one week later a second event rocked America. On the still evening of February 15, an explosion ripped apart the *Maine*, a U.S. battleship anchored in Havana harbor. The ship quickly sank, killing over 250 officers and men. An investigation in 1898 ruled that an external explosion had sunk the *Maine*. In a 1976 study, Admiral Hyman G. Rickover blamed the sinking on an internal explosion. In truth, no one knows the who, how, and why answers. Americans at the time, however, were not in an impartial or philosophical mood. They blamed Spain. One diplomatic historian commented, "'Remember the *Maine*!' became a national watch word . . . In a Broadway bar a man raised his glass and said solemnly, 'Gentlemen, re-

(Text continues on p. 675)

The sinking of the *Maine* was one of the major events leading to the Spanish-American War. It is still uncertain who or what caused the explosion that sank the ship.

PRIMARY SOURCE ESSAY

WILLIAM RANDOLPH HEARST AND THE SINKING OF THE *MAINE*

If William Randolph Hearst (1863–1951) did not invent "yellow journalism," he certainly perfected the genre. The only child of wealthy parents, Hearst started life with every advantage. Throughout his life, his primary goal was the acquisition of power. The newspaper world offered him his first taste of power. In 1887 he became the proprietor of his father's *San Francisco Examiner*. His style became readily apparent. He bought the best equipment, hired the best writers, and emphasized sensationalism and emotionalism in reporting the news. "Truth in the news," Hearst's leading biographer noted, "was never of great importance" to him; "he was essentially a showman and propagandist, not a newsman." But if he was not a great newsman, he was a powerful one. In 1895 he bought the *New York Journal* and employed yellow journalism to build its circulation. In later years he extended his publishing empire to Chicago, Boston, Los Angeles, Atlanta, Omaha, Pittsburgh, Rochester, and other cities. He also bought magazines as well as newspapers. It seem clear that Hearst planned to use his strength in publishing to support his political ambitions. But he was never a successful politician. Bashful in public, his high-pitched voice and cold eyes gave him a weak public presence. In addition, his tempestuous private life was a decided political disadvantage. Nevertheless, his publishing empire gave him power, and if it could not make him president, it could make him a feared political enemy.

William Randolph Hearst. This photo was taken in 1906, when Hearst was a member of Congress.

NEW YORK JOURNAL, FEBRUARY 17, 1898

ONE WORD WOULD PRECIPITATE WAR.

Nation Awaits a Verdict on the Great Disaster.

TREACHERY SUSPECTED.

General Belief That the Spaniards Blew Up the Maine.

WAS THERE A TORPEDO?

Officials Generally Believe That the Awful Wreck Was the Result of One.

The clearest report from Havana indicates that the explosion was too far forward for boilers, or coal bunkers, or magazines; that the vessel seemed to lift in the front and then its forecastle was filled with flames.

A Submarine Mine Probably Did the Work.

All theories of accident, explosion from within, having been discussed, we will now take up the external causes.

THE HARBOR OF HAVANA IS UNDOUBTEDLY MINED AND PLOTTED OUT IN SQUARES SO THAT ALL THAT IS NECESSARY TO DESTROY A VESSEL IS TO SEE WHAT SQUARE SHE IS IN, MAKE NECESSARY CONNECTION AND PRESS A BUTTON. THE TORPEDO DOES THE REST. The vessel, swinging to the tide may have accidentally fouled a submarine mine, which exploded.

As the marine sentry, on the forecastle, did not see any boat, none but a submarine torpedo could have approached her without being observed. Either one of these could have done the deed.

A bomb, disguised to look like a lump of coal, might have been used, but the explosion was evidently far forward of the boilers.

This method caused the loss of the steamer Sultana, on the Mississippi River in 1865. This vessel's boilers were exploded by a bomb placed in the fuel, and hundreds of Iowa soldiers, who had just been released from Anersonville Prison, were killed, maimed and drowned. The vessel blew up, and then burned just like the Maine.

Where the explosion came from, can be settled when divers examine the wreck. If the plates are bulged in, the explosion came from without. If they are bulged out, the explosion came from within.

Raising of the *Maine*, 1911. Upon examination, it was determined that the ship had been sunk by an outside explosion.

$50,000 REWARD.—WHO DESTROYED THE MAINE?—$50,000 REWARD.

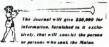

EDITION FOR GREATER NEW YORK

NEW YORK JOURNAL
AND ADVERTISER.

The Journal will give $50,000 for information, furnished to it exclusively, that will convict the person or persons who sank the Maine.

NO. 5,572.   Copyright, 1898, by W. R. Hearst—NEW YORK, THURSDAY, FEBRUARY 17, 1898.—16 PAGES.   PRICE ONE CENT

DESTRUCTION OF THE WAR SHIP MAINE WAS THE WORK OF AN ENEMY.

$50,000!
$50,000 REWARD!
For the Detection of the
Perpetrator of
the Maine Outrage!

Assistant Secretary Roosevelt
Convinced the Explosion of
the War Ship Was Not
an Accident.

The Journal Offers $50,000 Reward for the
Conviction of the Criminals Who Sent
258 American Sailors to Their Death.
Naval Officers Unanimous That
the Ship Was Destroyed
on Purpose.

$50,000!
$50,000 REWARD!
For the Detection of the
Perpetrator of
the Maine Outrage!

NAVAL OFFICERS THINK THE MAINE WAS DESTROYED BY A SPANISH MINE.

Hidden Mine or a Sunken Torpedo Believed to Have Been the Weapon Used Against the American Man-of-War---Officers
and Men Tell Thrilling Stories of Being Blown Into the Air Amid a Mass of Shattered Steel and Exploding
Shells---Survivors Brought to Key West Scout the Idea of Accident---Spanish Officials Pro-
test Too Much---Our Cabinet Orders a Searching Inquiry---Journal Sends
Divers to Havana to Report Upon the Condition of the Wreck.
Was the Vessel Anchored Over a Mine?

The *New York Journal's* inflammatory but unsubstantiated report of the sinking of the *Maine* fueled
anti-Spanish sentiment and catapulted the United States into war.

It was an easy matter for the Spaniards to have destroyed the Maine. She lay not far from a magazine in Havana, and wires from the shore to a hidden mine, filled with high explosive could easily have been arranged. The utmost vigilance of the American officers could not have guarded against a concealed mine. . . .

On the evening of February 15, 1898, the *Maine*, a 24-gun battleship, rested quietly in Havana harbor. Captain Charles D. Sigsbee, commander of the ship, sat in his cabin writing a letter to his wife. Then, at 9:40 P.M., an explosion rocked the ship. Sigsbee was unhurt, but 260 of the ship's 350 officers and men died in the explosion. As survivors jumped off the side of the *Maine*—and the ship sank into the mud of Havana harbor—Spaniards in Havana helped Americans in the dangerous rescue efforts.

That same evening William Randolph Hearst had enjoyed the nightlife—theater and late dinner—of New York. When he returned to Worth House, his fashionable Twenty-fifth Street residence, his valet was waiting up for him with a message. Hearst was to telephone his *New York Journal* offices at once. It was over the phone that his editor told him that the *Maine* had sunk. "Good heavens, what have you done with the story," Hearst asked. "We have put it on the first page, of course," his editor replied. "Have you put anything else on the front page." "Only the other big news." "There is not any other big news," Hearst responded. "Please spread the story all over the page. This means war."

Without knowing the facts of the episode, Hearst knew the slant his paper would take on the news: Spain sank the *Maine*. To this day there is no evidence that Spain was at fault. Indeed during the previous year Spain had gone to great lengths, accepted painful national insults, in order to avoid conflict with the United States. It is inconceivable that Spain would have destroyed the *Maine* as an act of national policy. It is inconceivable that a poor nation of 18 million people would have courted war with a prosperous nation of 75 million citizens.

But truth and political realities were of marginal interest to Hearst. He was determined to use the sinking of the *Maine* to push the United States toward war. During the week after the tragedy the *New York Journal* ran headlines that were total lies. On February 17, for example, the *Journal's* headline read: THE WARSHIP MAINE WAS SPLIT IN TWO BY AN ENEMY'S SECRET INFERNAL MACHINE. This was pure fabrication. There was no infernal machine (underwater mine), no secret enemy plot. But such stories captured the imagination of the *Journal's* readers and moved America closer to war. In less than a month President McKinley reluctantly asked Congress for a declaration of war. Hearst labeled the conflict "the *Journal's* war," and W. A. Swanberg, Hearst's biographer, asserts that "there would have been no war" had Hearst not inflamed public opinion.

member the *Maine*!' Through the streets of American cities went the cry, 'Remember the *Maine*! To Hell with Spain!' "

War was in the air, and it is doubtful if McKinley or any other president could have long preserved peace. Congress was ready for war. On March 6, McKinley told a leading congressman, "I must have money to get ready for war." Congress responded on March 8 by passing the "Fifty Million Bill" (the amount of McKinley's request) without a single dissenting vote. Although McKinley continued to work for a diplomatic solution to the crisis, his efforts lacked his earlier energy and optimism. By early April, diplomacy had reached its end.

On April 11, an exhausted McKinley sent a virtual war message to Congress. He asked for authority to use force to end the Cuban war. His message mixed talk of commerce with lofty humanitarianism. America must take up the "cause of humanity," he wrote, and stop the "very serious injury to the commerce, trade, and business of our people, and the wanton destruction of property."

On April 19 Congress officially acted. It proclaimed Cuba's independence, called for Spain's evacuation, and authorized McKinley to use the army and navy to achieve those ends. In the Teller Amendment, Congress added that the United States had no intention of annexing Cuba for herself. As Senator John C. Spooner of Wisconsin said, "We intervene not for conquest, not for aggrandizement, not because of the Monroe Doctrine; we intervene for humanity's sake." For some Americans it was a great and noble decision. Senator Albert Beveridge, one of the great speakers of his day, intoned: "At last, God's hour has struck. The American people go forth in a warfare holier than liberty—holy as humanity." For the men and boys who would have to fight the battles, the war would soon seem considerably less noble.

The Spanish-American War

There is no simple explanation for the Spanish-American War. Economics and imperial ambitions certainly played a part, but no more so than did humanitarianism and selfless concern for the suffering of others. McKinley tried to find a peaceful solution, but he failed. Some historians and many of his contemporaries have viewed McKinley as a weak, hollow president, a messenger boy for America's financial community. A Washington joke in the late 1890s ran, "Why is McKinley's mind like a bed?" Answer: "Because it has to be made up for him everytime he wants to use it." Such was not the case. McKinley did have a vision—a peaceful vision—of America's role in world affairs. But the unpredictability of events and the mood of the nation were more powerful than the president.

In theory America had prepared for war with Spain. In 1897 the Navy Department had drawn up contingency plans for a war against Spain for the liberation of Cuba. It had envisioned a war centered mainly in the Caribbean, but the navy had plans to attack the Philippine Islands, which belonged to Spain, and even the coast of Spain, if necessary. In the Caribbean, the navy planned to blockade Cuba and assist an army invasion of the island. On paper, neatly written and soundly reasoned, America was well prepared for a war that seemed more of a military exercise than a deadly struggle.

In reality, the military was not physically ready for war. The process of mobilizing troops was chaotic and the training given volunteers was inadequate. In addition, the army faced severe supply shortages. Volunteers suffered the most. They were herded into camps, often without such basic equipment as tents and mess kits. Long before they ever faced enemy guns or even saw Cuba, they battled wet uniforms, bad food, and deadly sanitary conditions. Far more volunteers died in stateside camps than were killed by Spanish bullets.

For black troops, regular and volunteers, racism exasperated already difficult conditions. They too were plagued by spoiled beef, thick wool uniforms, and unsanitary conditions. Also, since most of the large camps were located in the South—in places such as Tampa, New Orleans, Mobile, and Chickamauga Park, Tennessee—they also had to battle Jim Crow laws and other forms of racial hostility. They saw signs that proclaimed "Dogs and niggers not allowed" and were pelted by rocks. Once in the camps, they were given the lowest military assignments. George W. Prioleau, a black chaplain,

All black troops fighting in Cuba were commanded by white officers, much to the dissatisfaction of the black soldiers.

noted: "Talk about fighting and freeing poor Cuba and of Spain's brutality; of Cuba's murdered thousands, and starving reconcentradoes. Is America any better than Spain?"

While the agony of mobilization was taking place, the navy moved into action. During the tense weeks before the United States went to war against Spain, Theodore Roosevelt, then acting secretary of the navy, wired his friend Commodore George Dewey, leader of America's Asiatic Squadron: "KEEP FULL OF COAL. IN THE EVENT OF DECLARATION OF WAR [WITH] SPAIN, YOUR DUTY WILL BE TO SEE THAT THE SPANISH SQUADRON DOES NOT LEAVE THE ASIATIC COAST, AND THEN OFFENSIVE OPERATIONS IN PHILIPPINE ISLANDS." Dewey had been anxiously waiting for just that order. He was a warrior, and he looked forward to war. One historian remarked that "Dewey looked like a resplendent killer falcon, ready to bite through wire, if necessary, to get at a prey."

Biting through wire was not necessary. He only had to sail to Manila Bay. At the break of light on the morning of May 1, 1898, he struck. In a few hours of fighting, he destroyed Spain's Asiatic fleet. It was a stunning victory. Only one American died, and he of heat prostration manning a ship's overworked boiler. "You have made a name for the nation, and the Navy, and yourself," Roosevelt wrote Dewey. Americans rejoiced in the quick victory. Newspapers were filled with stories of American heroics and poems praised Dewey. One not-very-accomplished poet captured the public mood:

> Oh, dewey was the morning
> Upon the first of May,
> And Dewey was the Admiral,
> Down in Manila Bay.
> And dewey were the Spaniard's eyes,
> Them orbs of black and blue;
> And dew we feel discouraged?
> I do not think we dew.

Not every victory came so easily. Closer to home in the Caribbean theater, the war was much more prosaic. The main Spanish forces in Cuba were in control of the strategically important Santiago Bay. To defeat the Spanish it would take the combined efforts of the army and the navy. With this in mind, McKinley ordered Major General William R. Shafter, commander of the 5th Corps, from Tampa to Santiago. The trip to Cuba set the tone for the entire expedition. Delays, confused orders, and other problems slowed the process. Some 17,000 American troops were forced to spend 19 days on crowded transports, sweating in their woolen uniforms, eating unappetizing travel rations, and thinking about what lay ahead. Finally, toward the end of June, and with the help of Cuban rebels, American troops landed at the ports of Daiquiri and Siboney.

From there they moved toward Santiago. The distance was not great. Santiago Bay was only about 15 miles from the coastal town of Siboney. But the road to Santiago was little more than a rutted, dirt trail. When it rained, wagons became mired in the mud, streams swelled and made fording treacherous, and the troops suffered in the jungle humidity. Slowly the army moved forward, more concerned with broken wagons and tropical diseases than Spanish soldiers.

On July 1, American soldiers learned first hand the horrors of battle. Between the American position and Santiago were Spanish troops in the tiny hamlet of El Caney and along the San Juan Heights, a ridge to the east of Santiago. From the first, American plans broke down in the face of stiff Spanish opposition. There were no romantic charges, no idealized warfare. The American troops that struggled up Kettle and San Juan hills moved very slowly and suffered alarming casualties. Although outnumbered more than ten to one, Spanish soldiers made U.S. troops pay for every foot they advanced. After America finally secured the enemy positions, correspondent Richard H. Davis wrote, "Another such victory as that of July 1 and our troops must retreat."

General Shafter was frankly worried and even considered retreat. Grossly overweight and gout-ridden, Shafter had neither the disposition nor the ability to lead an energetic campaign. Fortunately for him, Spain's forces in Cuba were even less ready to fight. In Santiago, Spanish soldiers faced shortages of food, water, and ammunition. On July 3, the Spanish squadron tried to break an American blockade and force its way out of Santiago Bay. The act was a suicidal move. American guns destroyed the Spanish fleet and killed some 500 Spanish sailors. Only one American died in the decisive engagement. When his men broke out in a yell of joy, Captain Philip of the *Texas* said, "Don't cheer, men, the poor devils are dying."

Little fighting remained. On July 17 the leading Spanish general in Cuba surrendered to Shafter. Timid in war, Shafter was petty in victory. He refused to permit any naval officers to sign the capitulation document, nor would he allow any Cubans to participate in the surrender negotiations and ceremonies. It was a sad moment. The Cubans who had fought so long and bravely for their independence were denied the glory of their success.

Before the full Spanish surrender, the United States extended its influence in the Caribbean. In late July, General Nelson A. Miles invaded Puerto Rico, Spain's other Caribbean colony. Without any serious resistance, U.S. forces took the island. Finally, on August 12, Spain surrendered, granting Cuban independence and ceding Puerto Rico and Guam to the United States. Both countries agreed to settle the fate of the Philippines at a postwar peace conference to be held in Paris.

For America, it had been a short, successful war. Spanish bullets killed only 379 Americans, the smallest number in any of America's declared wars. Disease and other problems cost over 5000 more lives. If the army's mobilization had been chaotic, its troops had performed heroically under fire. And the navy, which took most of the credit for winning the war, demonstrated the wisdom of its planners. Finally, the war served to bring the North and South closer together as the two sections fought alongside

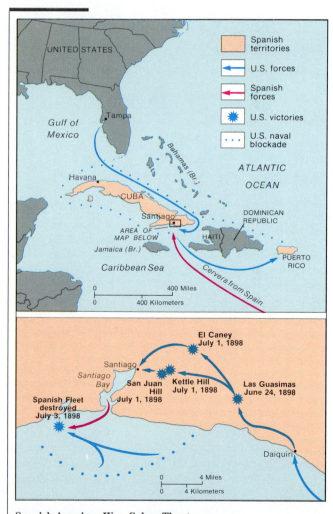

Spanish-American War, Cuban Theater

(Text continues on p. 680)

THEODORE ROOSEVELT AND THE ROUGH RIDERS

Aboard the *Yucatan*, anchored off the coast of Cuba, Theodore Roosevelt (TR) received the news on the evening of June 21, 1898. He and his men, a volunteer cavalry regiment dubbed the Rough Riders, had received their orders to disembark from the safety of the ship and join the fighting ashore. It was a welcomed invitation, celebrated with cheers, war dances, songs, boasts, and toasts. "To the Officers— may they get killed, wounded or promoted," urged one toast that captured the mood aboard the ship.

Roosevelt and many men of his generation looked forward to war, greedily anticipating the chance to prove their mettle in battle. They had been raised on stories of the Civil War, stories that over the years had taken on the golden gloss of time. Tales of Shiloh, Chancellorsville, Antietam, and Gettysburg; of Robert E. Lee, Ulysses S. Grant, and Stonewall Jackson; of battles won and causes lost had fired their imaginations. The Spanish-American War was their chance to experience firsthand what they had long only heard about from their fathers' and uncles' lips.

Few men wanted the war more than Roosevelt. Son of a wealthy New York family, he was competitive by nature and enjoyed all physical sports. He also loved history, writing books about American wars and heroic deeds. And for Roosevelt there was perhaps even a deeper motivation. During the Civil War his father, the man he admired above everyone else, had hired a substitute soldier to serve for him. Thousands of other wealthy men had done the same, but for Theodore such a course was unmanly. During the war, he believed, able-bodied men should be in a uniform, not dressed in mufti. He would not repeat his father's mistake. When the Spanish-American War was declared, TR quickly resigned his post as assistant secretary of the navy and joined the fray. In his own mind, he could do nothing else. In *The Rough Riders*, his memoirs of the war, he quoted a poem by Bret Harte, whose last verse was:

"But when won the coming battle,
What of profit springs therefrom?
What if conquest, subjugation,
Even greater ills become?"
But the drum
Answered, "Come!"

And come Roosevelt did.

The men who followed him were kindred spirits. They were rough riders, the men who with Roosevelt formed the First United States Volunteer Cavalry regiment. Some were Ivy Leaguers from Harvard, Yale, and Princeton who belonged to the most exclusive clubs in Boston and New York City. Many had been college athletes, stars in football, tennis, and track and field, men for whom war was a grand playing field. Others were Westerners—cowboys, hunters, frontier sheriffs, Indian fighters, Texas Rangers, prospectors—"a splendid set of men," wrote Roosevelt, "tall and sinewy, with resolute, weather-beaten faces, and eyes that looked a man straight in the face without flinching." Such men were accustomed to riding horses, shooting rifles, and living off the land.

Bucky O'Neill was something of a Rough Rider ideal. Indian fighter and sheriff of Prescott, Arizona, Bucky could shoot with the hunters, exchange stories with the prospectors, and philosophize with the college graduates. Roosevelt once overheard Bucky and Dr. Robb Church, the former Princeton football player who served as the surgeon for the Rough Riders, "discussing Aryan word roots together, and then sliding off into a review of the novels of Balzac, and a discussion as to how far Balzac could be said to be the founder of the modern realistic school of fiction." Once when Bucky and Roosevelt were leaning on the ship's railing searching the Caribbean sky for the Southern Cross, the old Indian fighter asked, "Who would not risk his life for a star?" TR agreed that great risk was part of greatness.

Brimming with enthusiasm, perhaps a bit innocent in their naiveté, the Rough Riders viewed Cuba as a land of stars, a place to win great honors or die in the pursuit. Like many of his men, TR believed "that the nearing future held . . . many chances of death, of honor and renown." And he was ready. Dressed in a Brooks Brothers uniform made especially for him and with several extra pairs of spectacles sewn in the lining of his Rough Rider hat, Roosevelt prepared to meet his destiny.

In a land of beauty, death often came swiftly. As the Rough Riders and other soldiers moved inland toward Santiago, snipers fired upon them. The high-speed Mauser bullets seemed to come out of nowhere, making a *z-z-z-z-z-eu* as they moved through the air or a loud *chug* as they hit flesh. Since the Spanish snipers used smokeless gunpowder, no puffs of smoke betrayed their positions.

During their first day in Cuba, the Rough Riders experienced the "blood, sweat, and tears" of warfare. Dr. Church looked "like a kid who had gotten his hands and arms into a bucket of thick red paint." Some men died, and others, dying, lay where they had been shot. The reality of war strikes different men differently. It horrifies some, terrifies others, and enrages still others. Sheer exhilaration was the best way to describe Roosevelt's response to the death and danger. Even sniper fire could not keep TR from jumping up and down with excitement.

On July 1, 1898, the Rough Riders faced their sternest task. Moving from the coast toward Santiago along the Camino Real, the main arm of the U.S. forces encountered an entrenched enemy. Spread out along the San Juan Heights, Spanish forces commanded a splendid position. As American troops emerged from a stretch of jungle, they found themselves in a dangerous position. Once again the sky seemed to be raining Mauser bullets and shrapnel. Clearly, the Heights had to be taken. Each hour of delay meant more American casualties.

The Rough Riders were deployed to the right to prepare to assault Kettle Hill. Once in position, they faced an agonizing wait for orders to charge. Most soldiers hunched behind cover. Bucky O'Neill, however, casually strolled up and down in front of his troops, chain-smoked cigarettes, and shouted encouragement. A sergeant implored him to take cover. "Sergeant," Bucky remarked, "the Spanish bullet isn't made that will kill me." Hardly had he finished the statement when a Mauser bullet ripped into his mouth and burst out of the back of his head. Even before he fell, Roosevelt wrote, Bucky's "wild and gallant soul had gone out into the darkness."

Finally the orders came. On foot the Rough Riders moved up Kettle Hill toward the Spanish guns. It was a slow, painful, heroic charge. Bullets, sounding "like the ripping of a silk dress," cut down a number of Roosevelt's men. But unable to stop the push of the American forces, the Spanish gave way, leaving their fortified positions and running for safety.

From the heights of Kettle Hill, Roosevelt watched another U.S. attack on nearby San Juan Hill. Once again feeling the wolf rising in his heart, he led his men toward the new objective. Again the fighting was difficult. But again the Spanish gave way. By the end of the day, American forces had taken the San Juan Heights. Before them was Santiago and victory. "The great day of my life," as TR called it, was over.

"Another such victory like that of July 1," wrote Richard Harding Davis, "and our troops must retreat." Indeed, casualties ran high, and the Rough Riders suffered the heaviest losses. But the fighting helped to break the Spanish resistance. It was the last really difficult day of fighting in the war. Perhaps more importantly, the day made Roosevelt a national hero. Aided by his ability at self-promotion, TR used the event as a political stepping-stone. "I would rather have led the charge," he later wrote, "than served three terms in the U.S. Senate."

each other rather than against each other. All in all, many Americans agreed with U.S. Ambassador to England John Hay that it had been a "splendid little war."

There was nothing little about the consequences of the war. With the Spanish-American War the United States became an imperial power. The war increased America's appetite for overseas territories. The McKinley administration used the war to annex Hawaii and part of Samoa. In addition, at the Paris Peace Conference the United States wrested the Philippines, Puerto Rico, and Guam from Spain. Although the United States paid Spain $20 million for the Philippines, there was no question that Spain was forced to negotiate under duress. These new imperial possessions gave the United States strategic bases in the Caribbean and along the trade routes to Asia.

Freeing Cuba

Many Americans favored the annexation of Cuba. In the land grab that ended the war, the idealism of the Teller Amendment and the war's beginning was all but forgotten. When the war ended, U.S. troops stayed in Cuba, and the country was ruled by an American-run military government. Particularly under General Leonard Wood, the military government helped Cuba recover from its terrible conflict with Spain. Wood restored the Cuban economy and promoted reforms in the legal system, education, sanitation, and health care. Neither Wood nor McKinley, however, was willing to grant Cuba its immediate independence. In his annual message of December 1898, McKinley noted that American troops would stay in Cuba until "complete tranquility" and a "stable government" existed on the island.

In 1903 the United States finally recognized Cuban independence. But it was a limited independence. According to the Platt Amendment to the Army Appropriation Bill of 1901, Cuba could exercise self-government, but it could sign no treaties that might limit its independence. Should, in the judgment of the United States, Cuban independence ever be threatened, the Platt Amendment authorized the United States to intervene in Cuba's internal and external affairs. The amendment was also written into the 1901 Cuban constitution. In short, for Cuba, independence had the look and feel of an American protectorate.

The Imperial Debate

Compared to the Philippines, Cuba was a minor problem. McKinley's decision to annex the Philippines pleased some Americans and angered many more. Businessmen who dreamed of the rich China markets applauded McKinley's decision. Naval strategists similarly believed it was a wise move. They argued that if the United States failed to take the Philippines, then one of the other major powers probably would. Germany, Japan, and England had already expressed interest in the strategically located islands. Finally, Protestant missionaries favored annexation to facilitate their efforts to Christianize the Filipinos. That the Filipinos already favored Roman Catholicism did not seem to dampen the fervor of the Protestant missionaries.

Opposed to the annexation of the Philippines was a heterogeneous group of Americans who called themselves anti-imperialists. The group included such notable Americans as agrarian leader William Jennings Bryan, steel magnate Andrew Carnegie, labor organizer Samuel Gompers, writers Mark Twain and William Dean Howells, reformers Lincoln Steffens and Jane Addams, university presidents Charles W. Eliot of Harvard and David Starr Jordan of Stanford, and politicians George Frisbie Hoar of Massachusetts and "Pitchfork Ben" Tillman of South Carolina.

Their reasons for being anti-imperialists were as varied as their occupations and backgrounds. Some were high-minded idealists who believed that the Filipinos had the right to govern themselves. Others had more selfish reasons for opposing annexation. Samuel Gompers, for example, feared that annexation would lead to an influx of Filipino workers into the United States and hurt the American labor movement. Still others opposed annexation for base racial grounds. Vividly remembering the difficulties of Reconstruction, many Southerners and Northerners believed that annexation would only lead to renewed racial problems. The annexation of "dependencies inhabited by ignorant and inferior races," noted the *Nation* editor E. L. Godkin, could only lead to trouble.

During early 1899 the imperial debate raged. Journalists editorialized, speakers pontificated, and humorists detailed the absurdities of both sides. Mark Twain asked, "Shall we . . . go on conferring our Christianity upon the peoples that sit in darkness, or shall we give those poor things a rest? Shall we bang right ahead in our old-time, loud, pious way . . . or shall we sober up and sit down and think it over first?" Twain's thoughtful questions about all the uproar changed very few opinions. Even Andrew Carnegie's offer to write a personal check for $20 million to buy the independence of the Philippines failed to end the debate. Ultimately, imperialists and anti-imperialists had different visions for America, and no bridge could span the gulf between.

The issue was settled on February 6, 1899, when the Senate voted on the Treaty of Paris. Strained tempers were evident in the tense atmosphere. Imperialist Senator Henry Cabot Lodge called the treaty fight the "closest, most bitter, and most exciting I have ever known, or ever expect to see in the Senate." For a time it appeared that the imperialists would not be able to muster the two-thirds majority needed to ratify the treaty. Anti-imperialist and titular leader of the Democratic party William Jennings Bryan ironically saved the imperialist cause. Not wanting to prolong the war by rejecting the treaty, he urged Democratic anti-imperialists to vote for ratification. In the close vote of 57 to 27 the Senate ratified the treaty. Undoubtedly Bryan hoped to use the issue of Philippine independence to capture the presidency in 1900, but such was not the case. With ratification of the treaty, the issue lost its sense of urgency and Americans grew tired of the debate.

The War to Crush Filipino Independence

Filipino independence, however, was not an abstract debate in the Philippines. Imperialist arguments about duty, destiny, defense, and dollars were lost on independence-minded Filipinos, led by Emilio Aguinaldo, who had fought bravely against the Spanish both before and after Dewey arrived in Manila. They had battled for their own independence, not to replace Spain with the United States as their colonial master. When it was clear that the United States did not have Filipino interests at heart, Aguinaldo and his followers resumed their fight for independence. Like the Cubans, freedom was a cause they held dear. Like the Spanish, the United States was not willing to grant that freedom.

Between 1899 and 1902 American troops and Filipino revolutionaries fought an ugly and destructive colonial war. Mark Twain's *The War Prayer* captured the mood of the fighting: "O Lord our God, help us to tear their soldiers to bloody shreds with our shells . . . , blast their hopes, blight their lives, protract their bitter pilgrimage." American soldiers faced a difficult task. Some did not know what they were fighting for, whose interests they were defending, or what rights they were protecting. Others regarded the Filipinos as subhuman. They referred to them as "niggers" and "gugus," and they regarded the notion of Philippine independence as a joke.

Black American troops fighting to destroy Filipino freedom faced an even greater and more painful dilemma. Many black soldiers readily identified with Filipino aspirations. Some white officers even suspected, as journalist Stephen Bonsel noted in 1902, that "the negro soldiers were in closer sympathy with the aims of the native populations than they were with those of their white leaders and the policy of the United States." Although the majority of black troops professionally followed the orders of their white officers, an unusually large number deserted. Once again, Bonsel suggested the reason. The white soldier "deserted because he was lazy and idle and found service irksome"; blacks deserted "for the purpose of joining the insurgents," with whose struggle they identified.

For black and white soldiers alike, however, the actual fighting was bloody and frustrating. Aguinaldo's men were efficient guerrilla warriors. They fought only when victory was certain, usually ambushing small patrols. They burned bridges, destroyed railroads, sniped,

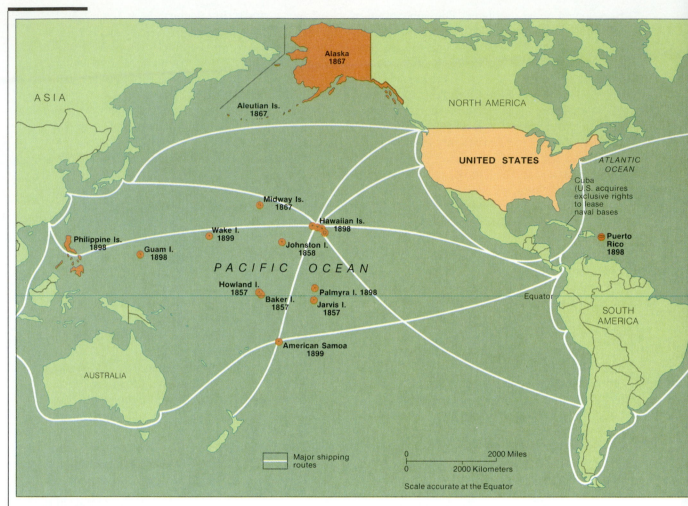

American Empire

With the Treaty of Paris, the United States gained an expanded colonial empire that included Puerto Rico, Alaska, Hawaii, parts of Samoa, Guam, the Philippines, and a chain of Pacific islands.

and sabotaged. They filled pits with sharpened stakes and tortured prisoners. Some American captives had their ears cut off, and many Filipinos who supported the United States were hacked to death with bolos or buried alive. Aguinaldo's hope was that eventually the game would not be worth the prize, and that the American president would call his troops home.

McKinley was not about to do any such thing, and American troops proved just as vicious as the Filipino insurgents. Atrocities committed by American soldiers became alarmingly common. Americans used the "water cure" to

obtain information. This entailed forcing a prisoner to drink gallons of water and then emptying his stomach quickly with a kick or a punch. In one especially violent campaign General Jacob H. Smith ordered his subordinates to take no prisoners: "I wish you to kill and burn . . . the more you kill and burn the better it will please me. I want all persons killed who are capable of bearing arms in actual hostilities against the United States." In the last category he included any male 10 years or older.

In another campaign, American leaders used the same tactics that had made the Spanish General Weyler infamous in Cuba. They tried to destroy the guerrilla base by herding more than 300,000 civilians into concentration zones. Death, disease, starvation, and suffering increased in the concentration centers. "Suburbs of hell" was what one American commander called them. For many observers, the difference between Spanish actions in Cuba and American actions in the Philippines was a matter of degree and not kind. Philosopher William James wrote, "We are destroying the lives of these islanders by the thousands, their villages and their cities. . . . No life shall you have, we say, except as a gift from our philanthropy after your unconditional surrender to our will. . . . Could there be a more damning indictment of that whole bloated ideal termed 'modern civilization' than this amounts to?" Along the same line, industrialist and anti-imperialist Andrew Carnegie told a U.S. peace commissioner in the Philippines, "You seem to have about finished your work of civilizing the Filipinos. About 8000 of them have been completely civilized and sent to Heaven."

Aguinaldo hoped that Bryan would defeat McKinley for the presidency in 1900 and thereby install an anti-imperialist in the White House. The November election dashed Aguinaldo's hopes. Five months later American troops captured the Filipino leader. This coupled with American reform efforts designed to improve transportation, education, and public health in the Philippines doomed the Philippine independence movement. On July 4, 1902, the war was officially ended. The American victory was complete. However, approximately 4200 Americans and over 20,000 Filipino soldiers had died. Perhaps another 200,000 Filipino civilians died of famine, disease, and war-related incidents. The United States paid Spain $20 million for the Philippines, which it had won control of after the cease-fire. But it cost another $400 million to crush the Philippine independence movement.

Keeping the Doors Open

The struggle against the Filipinos led to congressional investigations and shocked many Americans. Political and business leaders, how-

ever, continued to believe that the Philippines were worth the fight because the islands were of strategic importance both as a military base and a stepping-stone toward the Asian markets. Yet policy makers understood the popular mood; they knew that the American public would be hostile to any U.S. military venture into China *just* to support trade.

To prevent other countries from carving up China, in 1899 Secretary of State John Hay issued an "open door" note. Hay believed that imperial competition in China was dangerous and economically inefficient. It stimulated costly anticolonial resistance and rebellion and gave no incentive to European countries to improve their economic efficiency. Hay's Open Door note was an attempt to prevent further European partitioning of the Manchu empire and to protect the principle of open trade in China. Under the terms of the Open Door Policy, all countries

After the United States acquired the Philippine islands through conquest and purchase, Emilio Aguinaldo led the struggle for Philippine independence. Filipino resistance to the U.S. presence in the Philippine islands continued through mid-1902, even after Aguinaldo's capture by U.S. troops in 1901.

American soldiers stand guard over captured Filipino guerrillas in 1899. Expansionism raised questions of whether the native peoples of acquired lands had the same rights as American citizens.

active in China would respect each other's trading rights by imposing no discriminating duties and closing no ports within their spheres of influence. Although most European countries expressed little interest in Hay's Open Door Policy—which, after all, benefited the United States the most—in 1900 Hay announced that the European powers had accepted his proposal.

The Chinese themselves had other plans. In the late spring of 1900 a group of Chinese nationalists, known as Boxers, besieged the Legation Quarter in Peking, calling for the expulsion or death of all westerners in China. The Boxers, whose Chinese name better translates as "Righteous and Harmonious Fists," were a quasi-religious organization that believed deeply in magic and maintained that all its members were impervious to western bullets. As a joint European and American rescue force proved, bullets could and would kill Boxers. By late summer, 1900, westernizers had crushed the Boxer Rebellion.

Additional troops in China threatened Hay's Open Door Policy. On July 3, 1900, during the tensest moment of the Boxer Rebellion, he issued a second Open Door note, calling on all western powers to preserve "Chinese territorial and administrative entity" and uphold "the principle of equal and impartial trade with all parts of the Chinese Empire." Once again, few European countries paid attention to Hay's Open Door Policy. Mutual distrust and the fear of provoking a general European war—more than any American plan—prevented the major European powers from dismembering China. Out of Hay's Open Door Policy notes came the idea, held mostly in America, that the United States was China's protector. It was another example of the increasingly active role the United States had taken in world affairs.

CONCLUSION

Thirty-two years separated the inauguration of Ulysses S. Grant and the assassination of William McKinley, but during that generation, America and the presidency changed radically. Part of the change can be attributed to

CHRONOLOGY OF KEY EVENTS

1867 Russia sells Alaska to the United States for $7.2 million, or less than 2 cents an acre

1870 Senate rejects President Grant's attempt to annex the Dominican Republic

1889 Britain, Germany, and the United States agree to share control of Samoa

1890 Captain Alfred Thayer Mahan's *The Influence of Sea Power upon History* asserts that naval power is the key to national greatness

1893 Americans organize the overthrow of Queen Liliuokalani of Hawaii and, with the help of U.S. marines, set up a new government

1895 Venezuela border dispute; Cuban revolt against Spain begins

1898 The battleship *Maine* explodes in Havana harbor; Spanish-American War begins; Dewey sinks Spanish fleet in Manila Bay; Battle of San Juan Hill; destruction of Spanish fleet in Santiago harbor ends Spanish resistance in Cuba; Hawaii is annexed

1899 Aguinaldo leads a rebellion against the United States to win Philippine independence; John Hay, McKinley's secretary of state, issues an Open Door note to prevent further partitioning of China by European powers and to protect the principle of free trade

1900 Boxer Rebellion, a Chinese nationalist revolt against foreigners, erupts

1901 Platt Amendment gives the United States the right to maintain two naval stations on Cuba and to send troops to the island to preserve order

1902 United States crushes Philippine revolt

growth—industry boomed, the population swelled, agricultural production increased. The growth was also psychological. Perhaps a more appropriate term would be maturation. During those years many Americans achieved a new sense of confidence, and their vision broadened. After 250 years of looking westward across America's seemingly limitless acres of land, they began to look toward the oceans and consider the possibilities of a new form of expansion. They also began to follow the imperial examples of England, France, Italy, and Germany. Talk of world power, world outlook, world responsibilities colored their rhetoric.

This outward thrust was accompanied and enhanced by the growth of presidential power.

Grant worked hard for the annexation of the Dominican Republic, but Congress blocked his efforts. By the turn of the century, however, Congress clearly expected the president to lead the nation in the area of foreign affairs. Harrison, Cleveland, and McKinley, as well as their advisors, firmly guided America's foreign affairs. Although the presidents pursued different policies, they agreed that America should have a greater influence in world affairs. None questioned the fundamental fact that the United States was and should be a world power.

Many questions, nevertheless, remained unanswered. What were the rights of a world power? What were its responsibilities? What were its duties? Neither Harrison, Cleveland, nor McKinley gained much experience in running a colonial administration. The limits and possibilities of American power had yet to be defined and explored. The next three presidents—Roosevelt, Taft, and Wilson—would help to define how America would use its new power.

SUGGESTIONS FOR FURTHER READING

OVERVIEWS AND SURVEYS

William H. Becker and Samuel F. Wells, Jr., eds, *Economics and World Power: An Assessment of American Diplomacy Since 1789* (1984); Robert L. Beisner, *From the Old Diplomacy to the New, 1865–1900* (1975), and *Twelve Against Empire* (1968); Charles S. Campbell, Jr., *Transformation of American Foreign Relations, 1865–1900* (1976); Warren I. Cohen, ed., *New Frontiers in American-East Asian Relations* (1983); B. Franklin Cooling, *Gray Steel and Blue Water Navy* (1979); Alexander DeConde, *A History of American Foreign Policy* (1963); Foster R. Dulles, *Prelude to World Power: American Diplomatic History, 1860–1900* (1965); Robert H. Ferrell, *American Diplomacy* (1965); David F. Healy, *U.S. Expansionism: Imperialist Urge in the 1890s* (1970), and *Drive to Hegemony: The United States in the Caribbean* (1988); Thomas Hietala, *Manifest Design* (1985); Richard Hofstadter, *The Paranoid Style in American Politics and Other Essays* (1965); Michael Hunt, *The Making of a Special Relationship* (1983); Walter LaFeber, *The New Empire: An Interpretation of American Expansion* (1963); R. W. Leopold, *The Growth of American Foreign Policy* (1962); Thomas G. Paterson, et al., *American Foreign Policy*, 2 vols., 3d ed. (1988), and Paterson and Stephen C. Rabe, *Imperial Surge: The United States Abroad* (1992); Milton Plesur, *America's Outward Thrust* (1971); Robert H. Wiebe, *The Search for Order, 1877–1920* (1967); William A. Williams, *The Tragedy of American Diplomacy*, 2d ed. (1972), and *The Roots of the Modern American Empire* (1969).

CONGRESSIONAL CONTROL AND THE REDUCTION OF AMERICAN POWER

Charles S. Campbell, Jr., *Special Business Interests and the Open Door Policy* (1951); Allan R. Millett and Peter Maslowski, *For the Common Defense: A Military History of the United States of America* (1984); David Pletcher, *The Awkward Years* (1963); Tom E. Terrill, *The Tariff, Politics, and American Foreign Policy, 1874–1901* (1973).

THE SPIRIT OF AMERICAN GREATNESS

Henry Blumenthal, *France and the United States* (1970); Alexander E. Campbell, *Great Britain and the United States, 1895–1903* (1960); Warren I. Cohen, *America's Response to China*, 3d ed. (1990); John Dobson, *America's Ascent: The United States Becomes a Great Power, 1880–1914* (1978); James A. Field, Jr., *America and the Mediterranean World, 1776–1882* (1969); Thomas J. McCormick, *China Market* (1967); Bradford Perkins, *The Great Rapprochement: England and the United States, 1895–1914* (1968); Emily Rosenberg, *Spreading the American Dream* (1982); Paul A. Varg, *The Making of a Myth: The United States and China, 1897–1912* (1968); Marilyn B. Young, *Rhetoric of Empire: American China Policy, 1895–1901* (1968).

THE EMERGENCE OF AGGRESSION IN AMERICAN FOREIGN POLICY

David Anderson, *Imperialism and Idealism: American Diplomats in China, 1861–1898* (1985); William R. Braisted, *The United States Navy in the Pacific, 1897–1909* (1958); Phillip Darby, *Three Faces of Imperialism* (1987); R. P. Gilson, *Samoa 1830 to 1900* (1970); John A. S. Grenville, *Lord Salisbury and Foreign Policy* (1964); Kenneth J. Hagan, *American Gunboat Diplomacy and the Old Navy, 1877–1889* (1973); Walter R. Herrick, *The American Naval Revolution* (1966); Michael Hunt, *Ideology and U.S. Foreign Policy* (1987); Akira Iriye, *Across the Pacific* (1967); Thomas J. Osborne, *Empire Can Wait: American Opposition to Hawaiian Annexation, 1893–1898* (1981); William A. Russ, Jr., *The Hawaiian Revolution* (1959); Harold Sprout and Margaret Sprout, *The Rise of American Naval Power* (1939); Merze Tate, *The United States and the Hawaiian Kingdom* (1965).

THE WAR FOR EMPIRE

Frank Freidel, *The Splendid Little War* (1958); John M. Gates, *Schoolbooks and Krags* (1973); Willard B. Gatewood, Jr., *"Smoked Yankees" and the Struggle for Empire* (1971), and *Black Americans and the White Man's Burden, 1898–1903* (1975); Lewis L. Gould, *The Presidency of William McKinley* (1980); David Healy, *U.S. Expansionism* (1970); Gerald F. Linderman, *The Mirror of War: American Society and the Spanish-American War* (1974); Ernest R. May, *Imperial Democracy* (1961), and *American Imperialism* (1968); Stuart C. Miller, *"Benevolent Assimilation": The American Conquest of the Philippines, 1899–1903* (1982);

H. Wayne Morgan, *From Hayes to McKinley* (1969), ed. *The Gilded Age*, rev. ed. (1970), and *America's Road to Empire* (1965); Louis Pérez, Jr., *Cuba under the Platt Amendment, 1902–1934* (1986); Julius W. Pratt, *Expansionists of 1898* (1936); Goran Rystad, *Ambiguous Imperialism* (1975); Daniel B. Schirmer, *Republic or Empire* (1972); E. Berkeley Tompkins, *Anti-Imperialism in the United States* (1970); David F. Trask, *The War with Spain in 1898* (1981); Richard E. Welch, Jr., *Response to Imperialism* (1979); Leon Wolff, *Little Brown Brother* (1961).

BIOGRAPHIES

David Donald, *Charles Sumner and the Rights of Man* (1970); John A. Garraty, *Henry Cabot Lodge* (1953); H. Wayne Morgan, *William McKinley and His America* (1963); Allan Nevins, *Grover Cleveland* (1932), and *Hamilton Fish*, rev. ed. (1957); Ernest N. Paolino, *The Foundations of the American Empire: William Henry Seward and U. S. Foreign Policy* (1973); Ronald Spector, *Admiral of the New Empire: The Life and Career of George Dewey* (1974); John M. Taylor, *William Henry Seward* (1991).

End of the Century Crisis

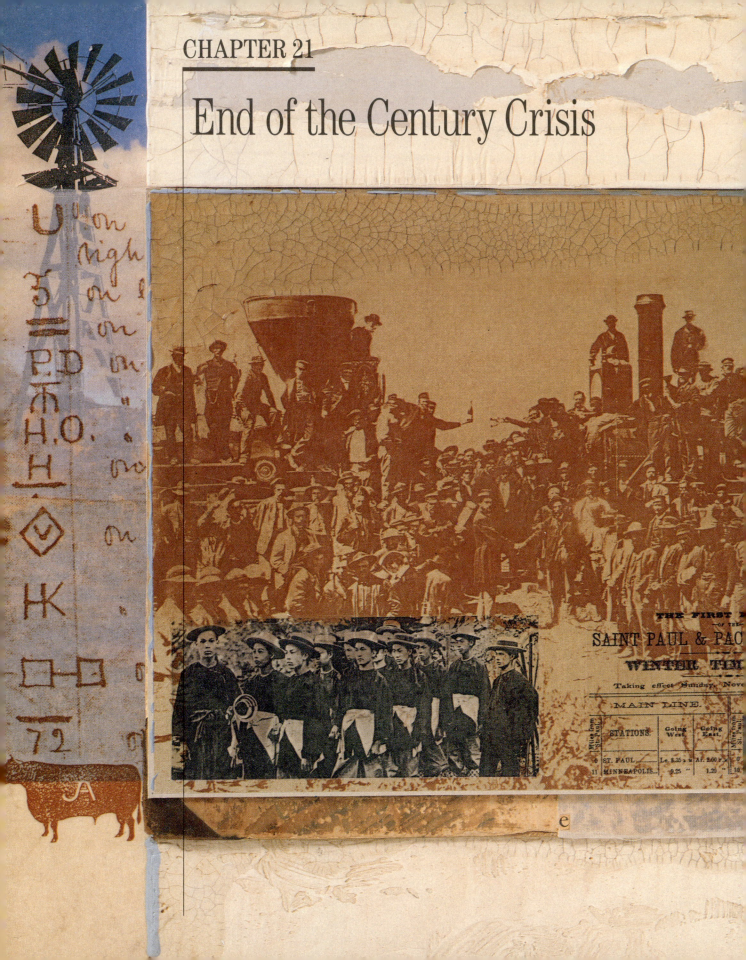

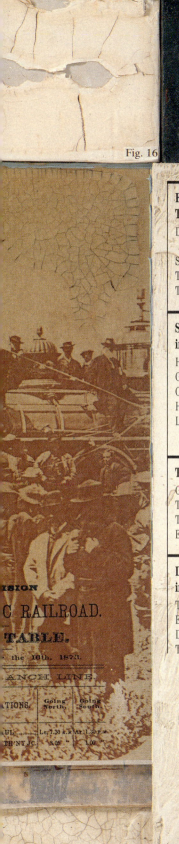

On July 9, 1896, William Jennings Bryan rose to speak to the delegates at the Democratic National Convention in Chicago. "I thought I had never seen a handsomer man," a reporter wrote, "young, tall, powerfully built, clear-eyed, with a mane of black hair which he occasionally thrust back with his hand." Thirty-six years old, Bryan was the son of a circuit court judge. His father was a Baptist deacon and his mother was a devout Methodist. Steeped in both religion and politics from an early age, Bryan was elected to Congress from Nebraska in 1890.

As the cry for "free silver" swept the rural areas of the West and South, Bryan took up the cause. "I don't know anything about free silver," he admitted. "The people of Nebraska are for free silver and I am for free silver. I will look up the arguments later." In the 1890s the slogan referred to expanding the amount of money in circulation by coining more silver dollars. Farmers believed such inflation of the currency would raise crop prices and alleviate their heavy debt burdens. Many rural residents felt the national government had not been responsive to their needs—that both political parties had been captured by industrialists, railroad owners, and bankers. In 1896 silver was a symbol for popular grievances. Among other things, silver represented rural values, the common people, and a growing discontent with northeastern political domination.

By the time of the Democratic convention the Republicans had nominated William McKinley and adopted a platform calling for the gold standard—or currency backed entirely by gold supplies in the federal treasury. The Democrats were divided between the "silverites" and the "Gold Democrats," monetary conservatives who supported President Grover Cleveland. Control of the party by the northeast was being challenged by southern and western delegates when Bryan finally rose to speak.

Called "the Great Commoner," Bryan voiced the frustrations of farmers with the failure of traditional politicians to meet their needs. "We have petitioned," he cried, "and our petitions have been scorned; we have entreated, and our entreaties have been disregarded; we have begged, and they have mocked when our calamity came. We beg no longer; we entreat no more; we petition no more. We defy them!"

He enthralled the crowd from the beginning, but his closing words created pandemonium. "We will answer the demand for a gold standard," he roared, "by saying to them: 'You shall not press down upon the brow of labor this crown of thorns, you shall not crucify mankind upon a cross of gold.'" As he spoke his fingers first traced the course of imaginary trickles of blood from his temples. He closed with his arms outstretched as if he were nailed to a cross.

When he dropped his arms, he had won the Democratic nomination and cinched the victory of the party's silverites. The Cleveland supporters left Chicago unwilling to accept Bryan's "foul pit of repudiation, socialism, [and] anarchy," as one declared. Another said, "I am a Democrat still—very still." Because many party regulars deserted him and nearly half the Democratic newspapers opposed him, Bryan was only able to raise the meager sum of about $500,000. Taking his campaign directly to the people, he appealed to sectional and class animosities: "Probably the only passage in the Bible read by some financiers is that about the wise men of the East. They seem to think that wise men have been coming from that direction ever since."

Low on funds, Bryan relied on his oratorical genius and electrifying charisma. Between August and November he had traveled more than 18,000 miles, visiting 27 states and giving 600 speeches. His youth sustained him as he made his own travel arrangements, bought his own tickets, carried his own bags, rode in public cars, and walked from train stations to hotels late at night. He was often called upon to give unscheduled speeches; when one Indiana crowd awakened him, he spoke in his nightshirt.

With a Republican campaign fund of more than $3.5 million, McKinley wisely refused to follow Bryan's course. "I might just as well put up a trapeze in my front lawn and compete with some professional athlete as to go out speaking against Bryan," he said. Between June and November, McKinley left his home in Canton, Ohio, for only three days. Railroads provided cheap excursion rates to Canton so that every day except Sunday, crowds of up to 50,000 thronged

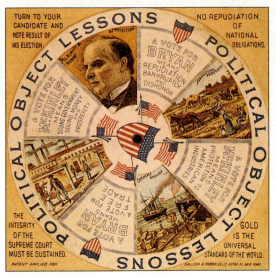

In the 1896 election, Republicans sought to convince voters that Bryan was a radical who threatened American values and institutions, while McKinley (shown in the campaign poster above) would guarantee stability, order, and integrity.

to McKinley's lawn. There he conducted his "front porch" campaign. The gatherings were hardly spontaneous. His staff organized the groups by occupation or interest, screened each delegation's remarks, and planned each event in detail down to brass bands and banners.

Unlike Bryan's speeches, McKinley's were calm and dispassionate, stressing national unity rather than division. "We are all dependent on each other, no matter what our occupation may be," he declared. "All of us want good times, good wages, good markets; and then we want good money always." From his front porch he addressed some 750,000 people from 30 states. The Republicans also spent more for printing than Bryan raised for his entire campaign. By the campaign's end Republicans sent 200 million pamphlets in several languages to 15 million voters and some 250 paid speakers toured 27 states.

On election day Bryan and his wife rose at 6:30 A.M. and voted at a local fire station in Omaha, Nebraska. He then gave seven speeches in his hometown before collapsing, exhausted, in bed that evening. McKinley walked to his poll-

ing place and stood in line to vote. He then returned home to wait for the returns—his lawn and porch in worse shape than he was. All over the nation politicians and just plain people waited to find out which man and party would preside over the dawning of the twentieth century.

The election came in a decade of turbulence that saw violence toward the labor movement, rising racial tensions, militant farmers, and discontented unemployed workers—all of which intensified after a major depression began in 1893. The social fabric seemed to be unraveling rapidly, which is why the election of 1896 was considered so important. For the first time since the 1870s voters were given a clear choice between two very different candidates and platforms.

Following Reconstruction, national politics were colorful but not very significant. No important policy differences separated the two major parties, the campaigns revolved around personalities, gimmicks, emotional slogans, and local issues. As elections were trivialized, they also became a major source of entertainment, and voters turned out in record numbers. This triumph of style over substance in politics, as well as culture, caused the era to be labeled the "Gilded Age." By 1890 both the Democratic and Republican parties had lost touch with the sentiments of large blocks of voters. The losers in the great national race toward economic modernization began to question its assumptions. Their voices rose in the 1890s, but unable to unite around a viable agenda, they failed to win many battles at that time. The issues they raised, however, appeared regularly on political agendas in the twentieth century.

EQUILIBRIUM AND INERTIA: THE NATIONAL POLITICAL SCENE

American politics have often seemed odd to Europeans. Never was this more true than in the closing decades of the nineteenth century. American political parties bewildered them. In his 1898 book, *The American Commonwealth*, Lord James Bryce wrote that "neither party has any principles, any distinctive tenets. Both have traditions. Both claim to have tendencies. Both have certainly war cries, organizations, interests enlisted in their support. But those interests are in the main the interests of getting or keeping the patronage of government. . . . All has been lost, except office or the hope of it."

Patronage, or the granting of political favors and offices, became more important than issues to the two major parties for many reasons. Close elections caused the parties to be careful not to alienate potential supporters. Most people also believed in limited government. Political parties were therefore organized more to win offices than to govern. The result was a failure by government to deal effectively with the enormous changes wrought by industrialization and urbanization.

Divided Power: The Parties and the Federal Government

After Reconstruction both the Democratic and Republican parties emerged with sizable and stable constituencies. For the 20 years between 1876 and 1896 they shared a rare equality of political power. Elections were so close that until 1896 no president won office with a majority of the popular vote. Two (Hayes and Harrison) even entered the presidency without a plurality. The average popular vote margin was 1.5 percent. Republicans occupied the White House for 12 years, Democrats for 8. Only during three 2-year periods did the same party control the presidency and both houses of Congress— Democrats once and Republicans twice. Most of the time Congress itself was split, with Democrats generally taking the House and the Republicans the Senate. Very few seats shifted parties in any given election.

The party division of Congress inevitably weakened the presidents of the era. None was elected to consecutive terms. Calling them "the lost Americans," one observer noted that "their gravely vacant and bewhiskered faces mixed, melted, swam together" in the public mind. Lord Bryce claimed none of them "would have been remembered had he not been President." To be fair, all were competent men, some with distinguished war records, most with considerable public service. One reason they were so forgettable was the era's concept of the presidency. Many agreed with Cleveland's assertion that the office "was essentially executive in nature." "I did not come here to legislate," he said. Presidents were only supposed to implement efficiently and honestly laws passed by Congress—occasionally vetoing ill-advised legislation. Even though these presidents were able to turn back many of the encroachments on presidential authority that began in Andrew Johnson's term, none considered it his duty to propose legislation.

Some found the office frustrating. After James Garfield moved from leadership roles in the House of Representatives to the presidency, he lamented, "I have heretofore been treating of the fundamental principles of government, and here I am considering all day whether A or B should be appointed to this or that office." Even representatives and senators were frequently frustrated, however, because congressional action was often stalemated. In the House, outdated, complex rules hampered action. Party discipline was practically impotent in both houses, and since neither controlled both houses for more than a two-year term, there was little possibility of formulating and enacting any coherent legislative program.

The lack of legislative action did not seem to be a serious problem at the start of the Gilded Age. Most people rejected the idea of an activist government. Widely accepted doctrines of laissez-faire and Social Darwinism limited what people expected of government. The Social Darwinist William Graham Sumner once proclaimed that government had "at bottom . . . two chief things . . . with which to deal. They are the property of men and the honor of women. These it has to defend against crime." Both parties basically accepted a narrow vision of federal responsibility. When vetoing a small appropriation for drought relief in Texas, Democrat Cleveland asserted that "though the people support the Government, the Government should not support the people." Republican leader Roscoe Conkling claimed that the only duty of government was "to leave every class and every individual free and safe in the exertions and pursuits of life."

Such antigovernment sentiment tended to increase the power of the judicial branch. Many saw the courts as a bastion against governmental interference in the economy, and they certainly fulfilled that role. On the basis of the Fourteenth Amendment, judges were especially active in striking down state laws to regulate business. The courts narrowly interpreted the Constitution on federal authority—ruling that the power to tax did not extend to personal incomes and that the power to regulate interstate commerce applied only to trade, not manufacturing. Congress also indirectly gave judges more power by enacting vague laws that relied upon the courts for both definition and enforcement.

Subtle Differences: The Bases of Party Loyalty

One consequence of the equality of power shared by the Democrats and Republicans was the reluctance of either party to chance losing voters by taking clear positions on most contemporary issues. Perhaps this reluctance was also based on the memories of the divisive 1860 election and its devastating impact on party and national unity. In addition, during the early

stages few Americans criticized industrialization and economic modernization, and there was widespread agreement on many issues.

Most members of both parties did not question the pace or cost of industrialization. They also saw little need for the federal government to play a major role in regulating the economy. When a Democratic president replaced a Republican one in 1893, one of Andrew Carnegie's managers wrote him, "I cannot see that our interests are going to be affected one way or another by the change in administration." Indeed business leaders had so little to fear from either party that they contributed generously to both.

Until 1896 the parties did share numerous similarities. Both were led by wealthy men but still tried to appeal to wage earners and farmers as well as merchants and manufacturers. Most members of both parties believed in protective tariffs and "sound currency." Both rejected economic radicalism and positive programs to aid workers. Presidents of both parties sent federal troops to break up strikes.

Ironically, for all their similarities the parties evoked fierce loyalty from a heterogeneous mix of people. One reason party platforms were so innocuous as to be interchangeable is that both parties were composed of factions and coalitions of "strange bedfellows." Because of its past and abolitionist connection the Republican party retained the support of activist reformers, idealists, and African-Americans. Yet most Republicans came from established "old stock" families. The more wealth a man had, the more likely he was to vote Republican. The party therefore was a curious combination of "insiders" and "outsiders."

The Democrats were even more mixed. The party's constituents sometimes seemed united mainly by opposition to the Republicans on various grounds. One Republican leader complained, "The Republican party does things, the Democratic party criticizes; the Republican party achieves, the Democratic party finds fault." Several generations later humorist Will Rogers quipped, "I don't belong to an organized party; I'm a Democrat." His words were certainly true of the Gilded Age. The party contained such disparate elements as Southern whites, immigrants, Catholics, and Jews.

For historical and cultural reasons, party

loyalty was frequently determined by the three factors of region, religion, and ethnic origin. The regional factor was most evident in the support white Southerners gave to the Democratic party. To vote for the party of abolition and Reconstruction was considered treason and a threat to white supremacy. On the other hand, the Republicans could count on heavy support from New England for the opposite reasons. To New Englanders, the Democrats were members of the party of traitorous rebellion against the Union. Because the Republicans could not expect to receive southern white votes, this was one issue they did need to tiptoe around. They frequently "waved the bloody shirt," reminding Northerners that the Democrats had caused the Civil War. In 1876 one Republican declared, "Every man that tried to destroy this nation was a Democrat. . . . Soldiers, every scar you have on your heroic bodies was given you by a Democrat."

For various reasons immigrants had long gravitated toward the Democratic party. Many were members of the poorest classes, which traditionally voted Democratic. In the 1850s anti-immigration Know Nothing party members joined the Republican ranks, reinforcing immigrants' ties to the Democrats. Most of the "new immigrants" of the Gilded Age settled in cities controlled by Democratic political machines that won their loyalty by meeting the immigrants' needs. As immigration swelled, increasing Democratic strength, Republicans became more and more restrictionist. In fact, immigration policy was one of the very few substantive issues on which the parties took clearly different stands.

Religious affiliations also helped determine party loyalty—partly because of the positions on immigration. Many of the late-nineteenth-century immigrants were Catholics and Jews who were suspicious of the Protestant-dominated Republican party. There were also fundamental differences in the religious orientation of most Republicans and Democrats. Republicans tended to belong to *pietistic* sects that based salvation on good works and moral behavior. Democrats, on the other hand, leaned toward *ritualistic* religions based on faith and observance of church rituals. Pietistic Republi-

cans frequently sought to legislate morality, supporting prohibition of alcohol and enforcement of Sunday blue laws, which barred various activities on the sabbath—including baseball. Many Democrats did not believe that personal morality could or should be a matter of state concern. A Chicago Democrat explained, "A Republican is a man who wants you t' go t' church every Sunday. A Democrat says if a man wants t' have a glass of beer on Sunday he can have it."

The roots and constituencies of the parties created differences in their outlooks. The Republicans became the "party of morality," the Democrats the "party of personal liberty." Democrats not only rejected government interference in their personal life; in the nineteenth century, they were also more suspicious of government action of any sort. Some quoted Democrat Albert Gallatin's dictum: "We are never doing as well as when we are doing nothing."

Because of their mixed constituencies, however, the differences and divisions *within* parties were as great, and sometimes greater, than those between them. Democrats could count on the South for all its electoral votes, but southern Democrats frequently broke party ranks when voting on legislation. They sometimes voted with western Republicans on acts favorable to farmers. They were, however, fundamentally conservative men of whiggish tendencies who usually voted with northern Republicans on financial and economic issues, as well as on immigration restriction. In a bizarre political arrangement, southern Democrats also voted with northern Republicans at times in order to receive a share of the patronage.

The Republicans were even more deeply divided into factions. One group, led by Roscoe Conkling of New York, was labeled the "Stalwarts." Followers of James G. Blaine of Maine were called "Half-breeds." The only significant item of dispute between the two was who would receive the numerous jobs appointed by the president. The distribution of patronage was a prime function of both parties of the era. Thus the division was bitter. When Conkling was asked if he intended to campaign for Blaine for president in 1884, he snapped that he did not engage in criminal activities.

There was one faction of the Republican party that did have some ideological basis. It was composed of reformers whose primary concern was honest and effective government. They had bolted the party in 1872 because of the corruption of the Grant regime, and they bolted again in 1884. Party regulars ridiculed them, calling them "goo-goos" for their idealistic good government crusade. They were finally labeled "Mugwumps," and a joke asserted that they had their "mugs" on one side of the fence and their "wumps" on the other.

The divisions in the Republican party reflected the fact that the politicians of the day were less concerned with issues and ideology than with winning office and distributing patronage. Lord Bryce observed that American politicians could be distinguished from European ones by the fact "that their whole time is frequently given to political work, that many of them draw an income from politics . . . that . . . they are proficient in the acts of popular oratory, of electioneering, and of party management."

The Business of Politics: Party Organization

Gilded Age politicians were very serious about their careers. They worked hard at both "party management" and "electioneering." The result was the largest voter turnout in the nation's history. In the elections from 1860 to 1900 an average of 78 percent of eligible voters cast ballots. Outside of the South (where blacks were increasingly prevented from voting and where the Democratic nomination determined the general election), the turnout sometimes reached 90 percent.

Party organization was geared to get out the vote. The parties were structured like pyramids with ward or precinct meetings at the base. At these all party members were allowed to attend. They generally elected representatives to county committees, which then sent members to the state committees that conducted the ongoing business of the party and nominated state candidates for office. At the top were the national committees. National conventions, where representation was based on the electoral votes of the states, met every four years to select na-

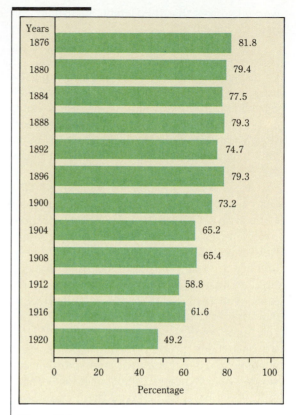

Figure 21.1
Voter participation in presidential elections, 1876–1920

tional candidates, draft platforms, and vote on party rules.

There was one main difference in Republican and Democratic party organization. Republicans generally depended on strong state organizations, and Democrats tended to rely on urban political machines to win and control votes. Since city governmental structures did not keep pace with the huge population increases, machines based on ward captains provided many of the services for which government would later be held responsible. The machine also helped immigrants and rural migrants to adjust to city life. One ward boss noted: "There's got to be in every ward somebody that any bloke can come to—no matter what he's done—and get help. Help, you understand, none of your law and justice, but help." The politicians were paid in votes from the people, bribes from legal and illegal businesses, and graft from contractors. The system worked so well that the Democrats usually carried the big cities.

For both parties recruiting and maintaining party voters was a game for professionals. In Pennsylvania, Republican workers compiled a list of 800,000 voters with notations as to their reliability as voters. Politics was also a rough and frequently corrupt game. Conkling warned, "Parties are not built by deportment, or by ladies' magazines, or gush." In 1888 when Benjamin Harrison proclaimed, "Providence has given us the victory," Republican party boss Matt Quay snorted, "Providence hadn't a damn thing to do with it." Quay then added that Harrison "would never know how close a number of men were impelled to approach the gates of the penitentiary to make him president." Electoral corruption was not limited to one party. In the same year a Mississippi Democrat admitted: "It is no secret that there has not been a full vote and a fair count in Mississippi since 1875, that we have been preserving the ascendancy of white people by revolutionary methods. In other words, we have been stuffing ballot boxes, committing perjury, and here and there in the state carrying the elections by fraud and violence."

Gilded Age politics was not dull. One could almost claim that the business of politics was entertainment. One observer remarked, "What the theatre is to the French, or the bull fight . . . to the Spanish . . . [election campaigns] and the ballot box are to *our* people." The drama of emotional tent meetings rivaled circuses. The pageantry of parades also provided excitement. Almost everyone got caught up in the elections, frequently displaying such paraphernalia as buttons, handkerchiefs, hats, banners, and posters emblazoned with their party's symbol or slogan. In 1888 one tobacco company enclosed pictures similar to baseball cards of the 25 presidential hopefuls in its packages. Politics was undoubtedly the prime form of mass entertainment.

Many politicians surely must have enjoyed their status as "media stars" and folk heroes. For some, whose ethnic or class backgrounds closed conventional doors of opportunity, politics provided a vehicle of upward social mobility, similar to professional entertainment and athletics or trade union leadership. Yet politics as a vocation offered other rewards. Elected and appointed officials not only received salaries but also openly accepted gifts from lobbyists and free passes from railroads. They sometimes used their governmental status to promote their private interests. James G. Blaine of Maine expressed no qualms about accepting stock concessions from an Arkansas railroad that he had aided in getting a federal land grant. One quip claimed that the United States had the best Congress money could buy.

The Struggle for Inclusion: Women and Politics

Politics could be a rough and dirty business—one that many considered an inappropriate activity for women. Increasingly women disagreed and sought inclusion. After an 1869 split in the suffrage movement, the National Woman Suffrage Association, (NWSA) led by Elizabeth Cady Stanton and Susan B. Anthony, fought for the vote on the national level through the courts and a proposed constitutional amendment. At the same time the American Woman Suffrage Association (AWSA) sought victories at the state level.

By 1890, when the groups merged to form the National American Woman Suffrage Association (NAWSA), the victories of both groups were limited. NWSA lost an 1874 Supreme

Gimmicks in Gilded Age political campaigns, such as this Bryan donkey, stirred public interest, resulting in the highest voter turnouts in the nation's history.

Court decision resulting from a suit filed by Virginia Minor against a St. Louis registrar for denying her the right to vote. The Court ruled that citizenship did not automatically confer the vote and that suffrage could be denied specific groups, such as criminals, the insane, and women. In 1878 Anthony did succeed in getting a constitutional amendment introduced into the Senate that stated that "the right to vote shall not be denied or abridged by the United States or by any state on account of sex." It continued to be submitted for the next 18 years but was usually killed in committee and only rarely reached the floor of the Senate.

There was more success on the state and local level. By 1890 19 states allowed women to vote on school issues, and 3 states extended women the franchise on tax and bond issues. Referenda were held in 11 states, but only the territory of Wyoming had granted women full political equality. Three states—Colorado, Utah, and Idaho—adopted women's suffrage during the 1890s, but then the movement seemed to lose steam. As male resistance mounted, no other state acted until 1910. Many men agreed with a Texas senator that "equal suffrage is a repudiation of manhood."

In 1869 Wyoming became the first territory to allow women to vote in all territorial elections. It later refused to enter the Union without women's suffrage.

STYLE OVER SUBSTANCE: GOVERNMENT IN THE GILDED AGE, 1877–1892

Politics provided great entertainment, but there were always people who wanted more. Often local political activity was considerably more vibrant than the political inertia at the national level. As discontent arose, many problems were first tackled on the city, county, and state levels before becoming a part of the national agenda. Such issues as the currency and tariffs could only be solved at the national level. Others such as demands for clean government were undertaken at all levels. On the whole, the states responded more vigorously than the national government to the problems created by economic changes—only to have the Supreme Court sometimes tie their hands. People began to look to Washington for solutions. The presidents and Congress responded timidly. National elections

still focused mainly on trivial issues. When backed to the wall, Congress would enact laws to quiet popular cries for action, but such laws were often limited in scope and unenforceable. Style triumphed over substance, and most problems remained unsolved.

Hayes and the "Money Question"

After the disputed election of 1876 almost created a constitutional crisis, the presidency was snatched from Democrat Samuel J. Tilden and given to Rutherford B. Hayes. A series of bargains was needed for the acceptance of the 8 to 7 vote of the electoral commission that named Hayes president. Thus from the start, his administration was tainted with snide references to him as "His Fraudulence" and "Old 8 to 7." He was actually honest, competent, and did much to establish the Republican party as the "party of morality" after the corruption of the Grant regime. His wife also helped to link Republicans with morality by refusal to serve strong drinks—earning her the label of "Lemonade Lucy." One guest at a White House party remarked in disgust that "the water flowed like champagne."

Hayes is now probably best remembered for removing the remaining federal troops from the South—marking the end of Reconstruction. At the time, however, economics rather than race relations occupied the public's mind. Hayes came into office more than three years into an economic depression that began with the panic of 1873. That depression raised the "money question" and the currency issue would continue to crop up for more than two decades. The issue was as complex as it was heated.

At its root was a long period of deflation following the Civil War. The level of prices dropped because the production of goods was growing faster than the supply of money. More goods than the money with which to buy them reduced prices. Farmers are not necessarily hurt by a general deflation if all prices fall

equally and their debt level is low. Wheat, corn, and cotton prices, however, declined more than other prices in the late nineteenth century. Farmers had also borrowed heavily to expand production, and they were caught in a debt squeeze with their mortgage payments remaining high while the prices they received fell. For example, a farmer who borrowed $1000 to buy a farm in 1868 on a 25-year mortgage found that he had to produce over twice as much cotton to make the mortgage payment in 1888. Although he received virtually nothing for doubling his efforts, his creditor received not only interest for the use of his money but also an additional bonanza—dollars worth twice as much as the ones he lent.

Debtors of all occupations began blaming their problems on deflation and saw inflation of the currency as the cure. For them inflation was a moral issue—a question of justice. One way this could happen was to increase the number of legal tender paper "greenbacks" first issued during the war. Supporters of that solution or-

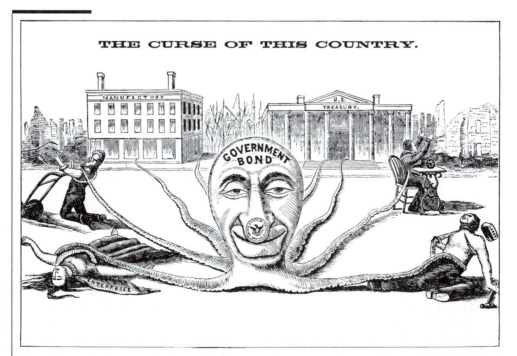

In this Greenback party cartoon from the 1870s, a gold-nosed government octopus puts a stranglehold on U.S. farmers, laborers, and small businesses. Greenbackers, who organized with the aim of distributing more money to more of the American people, opposed specie (gold) payments on bonds.

ganized the Greenback party in 1874. Instead, two years before Hayes entered the White House, Congress enacted the Resumption Act of 1875 to eliminate paper money not backed by gold or silver.

With the defeat of greenbackism, some inflationists turned their attention to silver. Before the issuance of greenbacks, the nation had been on a bimetallic standard since the 1790s. The dollar was based on both gold and silver, and for years dollars were coined at a 16 to 1 mint ratio. In other words a dollar contained 16 times as much silver as gold. By the 1870s this ratio did not reflect the market prices of the metals. Silver prices were so high that producers sold it on the open market rather than take it to the mint to be coined. Unable to buy silver at that ratio, Congress had passed the Coinage Act of 1873 that halted the minting of silver dollars.

Soon after, the discovery of large deposits of silver drove prices down. Then it was in the interest of both silver miners and inflationists to return to the coining of silver at 16 to 1. Together they formed a large lobby that wrested minor concessions from Congress. The Bland-Allison Act of 1878 required the government to buy between $2 and $4 million worth of silver each month. Like much of the legislation of the Gilded Age, the Bland-Allison Act proved to be a cosmetic answer to popular demands. It neither raised silver prices nor inflated the currency significantly. Thus inflationists remained unhappy, and the Greenback party nominated James B. Weaver in the 1880 election.

Garfield, Arthur, and the Patronage Issue

In the 1880 election neither of the two major parties focused on substantial issues but instead relied upon slogans and gimmicks to win votes. The battle for the Republican nomination was between the Half-Breed and Stalwart factions. Hayes had sought to set some standards for federal officeholders; his actions, however, mainly alienated fellow Republicans, and he refused to run for a second term in 1880. Stalwarts hoped to run Grant again, but the Republican convention became deadlocked. On the thirty-sixth ballot the party picked James A. Garfield, a veteran but relatively unknown Ohio congressman.

To conciliate the Stalwarts, Chester A. Arthur, a Conkling henchman, became the vice-presidential nominee.

The Democrats nominated an even more obscure figure, General Winfield Scott Hancock, whose only claim to fame was being a hero of the Battle of Gettysburg. He was described as "a good man weighing 250 pounds." Garfield was also bland, but he had the advantage of a log cabin birth and a brief career on a canal towpath—which gave rise to a popular Republican campaign slogan, "From the towpath to the White House." The 1880 election was one of the closest of the century in popular vote. Garfield received a mere 39,000 vote plurality out of almost 10 million ballots cast. Greenback nominee Weaver came in a distant third, gaining only 3.4 percent of the popular vote.

The currency question was overshadowed by the issue of patronage because of returning prosperity and a tragic event. Only four months after Garfield's inauguration he was shot twice by a deranged office seeker named Charles Guiteau, who explained, "I am a Stalwart. Arthur is now President of the United States." A native of Vermont, Arthur attended Union College, became an abolitionist lawyer, and then held a series of appointed offices. Considered by many to be a party hack, Arthur surprised them by becoming a champion of governmental reform.

The mugwumps and others had become increasingly concerned with corruption in government. In an 1873 novel that gave the era its label of the Gilded Age, Mark Twain and Charles Dudley Warner wrote, "The present era of indelible rottenness is not Democratic, it is not Republican, it is national. Politics are not going to cure more ulcers like these, nor the decaying body they fester upon." Because of the pervasiveness of the corruption, some saw no way out. "All being corrupt together," E. L. Godkin, editor of *The Nation*, wrote, "what is the use of investigating each other?"

Some reformers believed that one answer to the problem of corruption was reforming the "spoils system" of patronage. Since the early 1800s government jobs had been considered the "spoils" of political victory to be awarded to loyal party workers regardless of their qualifications. Problems grew between 1865 and 1891 as federal positions tripled, from 53,000 to

Charles Guiteau shoots President Garfield as Secretary of State Blaine looks on in horror. After suffering for two and a half months, the President died on September 19, 1881. Guiteau, whose behavior during his trial suggested insanity, was convicted on January 25, 1882, and hanged on June 30.

166,000. Indeed, presidents spent much of their time making some 100,000 appointments—most of which were in the postal service. That number of jobs provided incentives to precinct and ward bosses to get out the vote, but such inventions as the typewriter required government workers to have skills other than getting people to vote.

Hayes's actions to improve the quality of political appointees lost him his party's support, and not until after the revulsion at Garfield's assassination did Congress finally take action. With the support and encouragement of President Arthur, Congress enacted the Pendleton Act in 1883. It outlawed political contributions by appointed officeholders and established competitive examinations for federal positions to be given by the Civil Service Commission. The act was rather timid—only applying to about 10 percent of government employees. It was also not passed from purely unselfish motives. Since it was to apply only to future appointees and protect incumbents, the Democrats called it "a bill to perpetuate in office the

Republicans who now control the patronage of the Government." In the same manner, every president after its enactment increased the number of positions protected from political removal—usually to prevent his appointees from being removed. The political system was becoming modernized, but some questioned whether it was being improved.

Cleveland, the Railroads, and Tariffs

When 1884 brought the next presidential election, Arthur's actions had won him more favor from the public than from his party. The Republicans bypassed him and nominated James G. Blaine, who was far from bland. He was so handsome and charismatic that a colleague's wife once remarked, "Had he been a woman, people would have rushed off to send expensive flowers." Indeed, Blaine had almost all the qualities of a successful presidential candidate: a phenomenal memory for names and faces, eloquent oratory, and a quick wit. He was, however, a tainted political commodity. While in

Congress he had become very rich without any visible means of outside income. Copies of letters circulated that seemed to indicate Blaine was up for sale to the railroads. He was more than the mugwumps could stomach and they could not support him.

Realizing the potential advantage of a mugwump defection, the Democrats selected Grover Cleveland, a reform governor of New York. He was neither physically attractive nor charismatic. He did have one appealing quality, however. He was honest. As one supporter explained, "We love him for the enemies he has made." Yet Cleveland and Blaine did not disagree on the major issues. Therefore, their campaign revolved around personalities and became one of the most scurrilous in the nation's history.

Blaine's tainted past was obvious fodder for the Democrats' campaign. At torchlit rallies Democrats chanted: "Blaine! Blaine! James G. Blaine! Continental liar from the state of Maine!" Unable to find a shred of evidence to challenge Cleveland's honesty, Republicans publicized a more personal scandal. As a bachelor, Cleveland had supported an illegitimate child since 1874, even though his paternity was questionable. Thus Republicans countered Democratic chants with "Ma! Ma! Where's my pa? Going to the White House? Ha! Ha! Ha!" In the end Cleveland's victory may have come as the result of an indiscretion by a Blaine supporter who labeled the Democrats as the party of "rum, Romanism, and rebellion." Even though Blaine's mother was Catholic, Democrats were able to rally Catholic voters to win key states.

The major legislation of Cleveland's first presidency came as the result of public pressure and actions of the courts. The power and discriminatory rates of the railroads scared and angered many Americans, and actions to regulate the railroads had started at the state level. Beginning with the establishment of a regulatory commission in Massachusetts in 1869, 14 states had railroad commissions by 1880. The most active advocate of regulation was the Patrons of Husbandry—a farmers' group organized into local chapters called "granges." The Grangers and their allies, especially in the Midwest, got stronger legislation enacted that set maximum rates and charges within their states.

The railroad men naturally attacked these so-called Granger laws through the courts. At first they lost. In the 1877 *Munn* v. *Illinois* decision, the Supreme Court ruled that when "private property is affected with a public interest it . . . must submit to be controlled by the public for the common good." Nevertheless, it was difficult for states to regulate railroads chartered by other states and doing business across state lines. Then in the 1886 *Wabash, St. Louis & Pacific Railway Company* v. *Illinois* case the Supreme Court took away their rights to even try by ruling that only Congress had the right to regulate interstate commerce.

Pressure began to build for federal action, and Congress responded to the demands with the Interstate Commerce Act, which Grover Cleveland signed in February 1887. It prohibited pools, rebates, and rate discriminations; provided that all charges by the railroads should be "reasonable and just"; and established the Interstate Commerce Commission (ICC). The commission was significant as the first federal regulatory agency, but its power was woefully limited. It could investigate charges against the railroads and issue "cease and desist" orders, which could only be enforced by the courts.

In this cartoon, Grover Cleveland's illegitimate child is used to impugn "Grover the Good's" well-known political integrity.

Public anger over railroad power finally pushed Congress to pass the Interstate Commerce Act in 1887.

Conservative courts soon nullified 90 percent of the commission's orders, and between 1887 and 1905 the Supreme Court decided against the ICC in 15 of 16 cases. By 1892 railroad attorney Richard S. Olney wrote, "The Commission, as its functions have now been limited by the Courts, is, or can be made of great use to the railroads. It satisfies the popular clamor for a government supervision of railroads, at the same time that such supervision is almost entirely nominal . . . It thus becomes a sort of protection against hasty and crude legislation hostile to railroad interests. . . . The part of wisdom is not to destroy the Commission but to utilize it." One railroad executive admitted, "There is not a road in the country that can be accused of living up to the rules of the Interstate Commerce Commission."

The Interstate Commerce Act temporarily satisfied "popular clamor" without alienating railroad owners. It therefore did not become a partisan issue for either party. However, during Cleveland's term, a major issue on which Democrats and Republicans actually differed emerged: the tariff. Both parties supported these taxes on imports in order to raise revenue and to protect American products from being undersold by foreign competitors. The question was merely how high these tariffs should be. Regardless of party, congressmen voted their constituents' interests, which made few of them consistent on the issue. "I am a protectionist for every interest which I am sent here by my constituents to protect," one Democratic senator explained. Supporters of protectionism were those who sold on the domestic markets; opponents depended on foreign markets. Both groups included some farmers and manufacturers from every region.

Like most Democrats, Cleveland had long been less enthusiastic about high tariffs than Republicans. While in office he found that existing tariff rates were producing treasury surpluses that tempted congressmen to propose programs and appropriations which he considered dangerous expansions of federal activities. A moralistic man, Cleveland was deeply opposed to governmental involvement in the economy and social issues. Thus he became an advocate of tariff reduction. In 1887 at his urging, the Democratic House enacted moderate reductions, but the Republican Senate blocked the bill. Cleveland then proceeded to make the tariff a focus of his reelection bid in 1888.

Harrison and Big Business

In 1888 the Democrats renominated Cleveland and wrote tariff reduction into their platform. The Republicans chose Benjamin Harrison and cheerfully picked up the gauntlet—denouncing Cleveland's "free trade" as unpatriotic. They also promised generous pensions to veterans. Voters at last were given some choice on a real issue. The result was a viciously corrupt and close election. Harrison's campaign chairman, Matt Quay, proceeded to "put the manufacturers of Pennsylvania under the fire and fry all the fat out of them." He asked them to make large contributions to the Republican party as insurance premiums against lowered tariff rates. When Cleveland lost, many blamed his defeat on taking too clear a stand on an issue. Republicans erroneously interpreted his narrow defeat as a mandate for protectionism. Congress then enacted the McKinley Tariff, which raised the average duties to the highest level yet. The Republicans misread public sentiment; the McKinley Tariff was very unpopular.

Both high tariffs and trusts were becoming distasteful to many Americans. Popular demand for legislative action against trusts had been growing during the 1880s. Again action started on the state level; 15 southern and western states had passed antitrust legislation by the mid-1880s. Of course, companies simply incorporated in more sympathetic states. The laws were both ineffective and likely to be overturned by federal courts, but they did reflect popular distaste for the monopolies. Congress responded to these rumblings by enacting the Sherman Antitrust Act in 1890. On the surface it seemed to doom the trusts, prohibiting any "contract, combination in the form of trust or otherwise, or conspiracy in restraint of trade or commerce." As with the Interstate Commerce Act appearances were deceiving, but not to all the congressmen who passed it. One senator explained that the congressmen had wanted to pass "some bill headed 'A bill to Punish Trusts' with which to go to the country" to aid their reelection.

Until 1901 the act was virtually unenforced; the Justice Department instituted only 14 suits and failed to get convictions in most of them. The Supreme Court also emasculated the law in *United States* v. *E. C. Knight Co.* (1895), ruling that it applied to commerce but not manufacturing. Thus the subject of the suit, a sugar trust controlling 98 percent of the industry, was not in violation. Indeed, the only effective use made of the act in its first decade was as a tool to break up labor strikes by court injunctions.

The Sherman Antitrust Act of 1890 was designed to quiet "public clamor." In that same year popular pressure led to further action on the currency question. Following the Bland-Allison Act of 1878, the money supply continued to grow too slowly for the expanding economy. By 1890 pressure to coin more silver was growing, and Congress responded with the Sherman Silver Purchase Act. It required the government to buy 4.5 million ounces of silver

each month at the unrealistic ratio of 16 to 1. Paper money to pay for the purchases was redeemable in gold or silver, keeping the inflationary impact minimal. The act was a compromise that satisfied no one; the silver issue grew more heated in the 1890s.

During Harrison's presidency Congress was more active than previously—passing the McKinley Tariff, the Sherman Antitrust Act, the Sherman Silver Purchase Act, and the first billion dollar budget. At the same time the Republican party was becoming alienated from its abolitionist past and more closely tied to big business.

Legislative Activity on Minority Rights and Social Issues

To African-Americans the Republicans remained the party of black rights, but following the election of 1876 the party did less and less to earn that label. By 1890, however, conditions finally moved some Republicans to action. Dismayed by increasing southern assaults on the black vote, Senator Henry Cabot Lodge and others drafted a federal elections bill. The Lodge Bill sought to protect voter registration and guarantee fair congressional elections by establishing mechanisms to investigate charges of voting fraud and to deal with disputed elections.

Southern white response was rapid and bitter. The *Florida Times-Union* charged: "The gleam of federal bayonets will again be seen in the South." The *Mobile Register* warned that the bill "would deluge the South in blood." Northern Democrats lent their support to southern outrage. Cleveland exclaimed, "It is a dark blow at the freedom of the ballot." Although in 1890 Republicans controlled both houses of Congress, they finally bartered away the Lodge Election Bill to gain support for the McKinley Tariff. Protection of manufacturers was more important to them than the protection of African-Americans.

In that same year Republicans also let the Blair Education Bill die. It would have provided federal aid to schools, mostly black, that did not get a fair share of local and state funds. The Blair Bill marked the last glimpse of the party's dying abolitionist roots as well as the dethronement of party idealism. The Fifty-first Congress was seeking to alleviate treasury surpluses to protect tariffs, but in the end the only group to receive substantial aid was Union Army veterans, who were voted pensions by the so-called Billion Dollar Congress in 1890.

Other measures of the era affected minorities—but usually in a negative way. Southern white Democrats enacted discriminatory legislation against blacks at the local and state level. A movement for immigration restriction, usually initiated by Republicans, led to the Chinese Exclusion Act of 1882 and other legislation banning certain categories of immigrants and giving the federal government control of overseas immigration. In 1887 the Dawes Act attacked the tribal roots of American Indian culture by trying to make Native Americans homesteading farmers, and resulted unintentionally in making them dependent wards of the state.

Although most social issues received short shrift at the federal level, at the local and state level some received passionate attention. The two main ones—education and prohibition—were essentially Republican issues. An Iowa Republican slogan called for "a school house on every hill, and no saloon in the valley." Many were alarmed by the increased use of alcohol—annual consumption of beer rose from 1.6 to 6.9 gallons per capita from 1850 to 1880. Republicans moved beyond the educative temperance movement to attempt to make drinking alcohol a crime. They also sought to increase compulsory school attendance, but their efforts were often linked to moves to undermine parochial schools and schools that taught immigrants in their native tongues. In most areas these Republican actions backfired, losing more voters than they gained. For example, Republicans had once predicted "Iowa will go Democratic when Hell goes Methodist," but in 1890 the state fell to their opponents.

By 1890 very little effective legislation had been adopted to deal with the problems arising from a pluralistic society experiencing rapid social and economic change. This resulted partly from a political equilibrium that bred inertia. At the same time concepts of the limited nature of governmental responsibility did not provide impetus for action. Nevertheless, public demands

for change were growing. No group challenged the status quo more than the farmers.

THE FARMERS REVOLT

Cries for change naturally came from the losers in the new economic order. Among the greatest losers were American farmers. Their failure to thrive in the expanding economy convinced many that the cards had been stacked against them. After seeking various solutions to their problems, farmers turned to politics—taking up Populist leader Mary E. Lease's cry "to raise less corn and more hell." Their success was limited, but they led the first American mass movement to reject Social Darwinism and laissez-faire. They also promoted the "radical" idea that "it is the duty of government to protect the weak, because the strong are able to protect themselves." Some even questioned basic tenets of industrial capitalism.

Grievances: Real and Imagined

In 1887 North Carolina editor Leonidas L. Polk summed up the views of many farmers: "There is something radically wrong in our industrial system. There is a screw loose. . . . The railroads have never been so prosperous, and yet agriculture languishes. The banks have never done a better . . . business, and yet agriculture languishes. Manufacturing enterprises never made more money, . . . and yet agriculture languishes. Towns and cities flourish and 'boom,' . . . and yet agriculture languishes."

The basic cause of the farmers' problems was the decline of agricultural prices—primarily because of overproduction. Farmers had a hard time believing, however, that they could produce too much. Kansas governor Lorenzo Dow Lewelling wondered how "there were hungry people . . . because there was too much bread" and "so many . . . poorly clad . . . because there was too much cloth."

Overproduction was an abstract, invisible enemy; many farmers sought more tangible, personal villains—the railroads, bankers, and monopolists. As "Sockless" Jerry Simpson claimed, "It is a struggle between the robbers

By the late 1880s many farmers were already suffering from severe economic dislocation. This 1889 cartoon shows a poor, hungry farmer gazing at a banquet for tariff-gorged industrialists while Congressman McKinley pours whiskey.

and the robbed." Farmers believed they were being robbed by high freight and credit costs, an unfair burden of taxation, middlemen who exploited their marketing problems, and an inadequate currency.

Although there was no conspiracy by the "monopolists" to fleece the farmers, their grievances did contain a germ of truth. Freight rates were higher for farmers in the West because of the long distances to markets and the scattered and seasonal nature of grain shipments. Although western farmers generally paid the same interest rates as easterners, they were more dependent on mortgages to finance their operations than the corporations. They could not market stocks and bonds to raise needed capital. Southern farmers also paid dearly through higher credit prices for goods obtained by crop liens. Their large debts increased farmers' marketing problems. All the crops in a region were usually harvested at the same time, and farmers

had to sell them immediately to pay off loans. Middlemen took advantage of the glutted markets—buying the crops at low prices and selling them after the prices rose. Sometimes their profit margin was greater than that of the farmer who had gotten up before dawn and worked long hours to produce the goods. The unfairness of this galled farmers because they lived dreary lives, isolated from the excitement and modern conveniences of the city. The isolation was especially hard on the women, who were, as one writer noted, "not much better than slaves. It is a weary, monotonous round of cooking and washing and mending and as a result the insane asylum is $\frac{1}{3}$d filled with wives of farmers."

Governmental policy also seemed to hurt more than help. Property taxes hit farmers hard because they had lots of land but little income. The tariffs generally hurt most farmers by both raising the prices they paid for goods and mak-

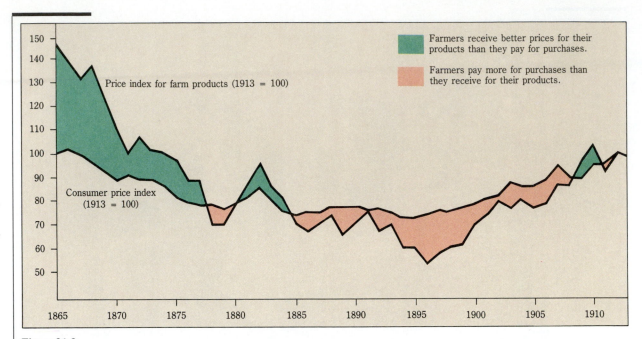

Figure 21.2
Price indexes for consumer and farm products, 1865–1913

ing it harder for them to sell their crops on the international market. The deflationary policy of the federal government especially hurt the farmers because of their great indebtedness. Every economic downturn brought a wave of farm foreclosures and frustration. Thousands of dreams died slowly, as one Kansas farmer's letter reveals.

> At the age of 52 years, after a long life of toil, economy and self-denial, I find myself and family virtually paupers. With hundreds of cattle, hundreds of hogs, scores of good horses, and a farm that rewarded the toil of our hands with 16,000 bushels of golden corn, we are poorer by many dollars than we were years ago. What once seemed a neat little fortune and a house of refuge for our declining years . . . has been rendered valueless.

The Farmers Organize

In the age of economic consolidation farmers realized early the need to unite and cooperate. They were never able, however, to do so as effectively as the industrialists and railroad mag-

nates, due to their greater geographic separation as well as a frontier-bred individualism. The first national farm organization was the Patrons of Husbandry. It was founded in 1867 by Oliver Kelley, a U.S. Department of Agriculture employee. His action illustrated that the federal government was not totally insensitive to farm problems. Organized into local granges that sponsored lectures, dances, and picnics, the group met a deep hunger for social interaction, and the membership grew to more than one million by 1874.

The Grangers soon moved beyond their social functions to address the economic grievances of the farmers. Grangers' actions focused on railroad regulation and cooperatives, both of which met with some success. They were responsible for numerous state laws that established railroad commissions to oversee and regulate railroad operations. Grangers viewed cooperatives as one solution to the high prices paid by farmers and the low prices paid to farmers. Buying cooperatives were formed to purchase in bulk directly from manufacturers, eliminating retail markups. In some places granges established cooperative banks, grain elevators, cotton gins, insurance companies, processing plants, and even plants to manufacture farm implements. Sales cooperatives aimed at increasing crop prices by joint marketing.

Granger victories and successes were generally short-lived and limited. The Supreme Court nullified the Granger laws that regulated railroads in the *Wabash* case of 1886. Most of the cooperatives were short on capital and skilled management and were hampered by the continued individualism of many farmers. They were no match against the unrelenting attacks by private business. In the late 1870s the granges began to decline and revert to rural social clubs but continued to operate some cooperative stores.

Economic grievances remained, and the farmers' organizational response shifted to the Alliance movement. Milton George, the editor of the Chicago-based *Western Rural* organized a northwestern Alliance in 1880. Never very ef-

fective, by the late 1880s it was mainly a paper organization. In the South, however, the Alliance movement was more radical and more successful. Started in 1877 as a frontier farmers' club in Lampasas County, Texas, it grew into the Grand State Alliance in 1879. Beginning in 1886, under the new leadership of Dr. Charles W. Macune, the southern Alliance spread rapidly by organizing new locals and absorbing existing farm groups in the South and other regions. At the same time a separate Colored Alliance was established. By 1890 the southern Alliance was a national organization with about 1.5 million members—and an additional 1 million members in its African-American affiliate.

Like the Grangers, Alliancemen sought to establish cooperatives, mostly without long-term success. They also conducted wider social and educational programs and boasted about 1000 affiliated newspapers. Self-help, however, proved inadequate; in 1890 they turned to po-

A Grange meeting at a schoolhouse in Illinois. The Grange worked for farmers' interests by opposing monopolies, advocating lower standard freight and passenger rates on railroads, urging the founding of agricultural schools, and forming buying cooperatives.

litical action. In the 1890 elections southern Alliancemen tried to capture their state Democratic parties rather than supplant them. In the Northwest and Great Plains farmers were not burdened with such intense party loyalty or the complication of the racial issue. Thus they established independent third parties. Regardless of the form of the organization, Alliancemen sought political solutions to their problems.

The Agrarian Agenda

The demands of the farmers mixed rhetoric, radicalism, and realism. Their words expressed an anger that had flared white-hot after years of smouldering resentment. No one voiced that anger better than Kansas homesteader Mary E. Lease.

> Wall Street owns the country. It is no longer a government of the people, by the people and for the people, but a government of Wall Street, by Wall Street and for Wall Street. The great common people of this country are slaves, and monopoly is the master. The West and South are bound and prostrate before the manufacturing East. . . . Our laws are the output of a system which clothes rascals in robes and honesty in rags. The parties lie to us and the political speakers mislead us. We were told two years ago to go to work and raise a big crop, that was all we needed. We went to work and plowed and planted; the rains fell, the sun shone, nature smiled, and we raised the big crop that they told us to; and what came of it? Eight-cent corn, ten-cent oats, two-cent beef and no price at all for butter and eggs—that's what came of it.

Kansas homesteader and radical activist Mary E. Lease urged farmers to "raise less corn and more hell."

Farmer's words rang with a rejection of aspects of capitalism that in retrospect seems radical. They spoke in a language that divided the nation into "haves" and "have-nots." "There are but two sides," one manifesto proclaimed. "On the one side are the allied hosts of monopolies, the money power, great trusts and railroad corporations. . . . On the other are the farmers, laborers, merchants and all the people who produce wealth. . . . Between those two there is no middle ground." To farmers, government either stood by idly or actively aided the monopolists as the "fruits of the toil of millions are stolen to build up colossal fortunes for a few." The result was that from "the same prolific womb of governmental injustice we breed the two great classes—tramps and millionaires." They also saw a division between the toiling masses who produced wealth and the parasitic capitalists who exploited it. In response they proclaimed that "wealth belongs to him who creates it."

Their rhetoric earned scorn from critics who labeled the leaders "hayseed socialists." There were some unsavory aspects to the movement. A few agrarians espoused simplistic and often anti-Semitic conspiracy theories. Other flamboyant demagogues such as "Pitchfork Ben" Tillman of South Carolina exploited rural anger for their personal political ambitions. Thus, with a mixture of contempt and fear, critics called the rural reformers "crackpot radicals."

By Gilded Age standards farmer demands were indeed radical even though most have been adopted in the twentieth century. Their most socialistic ideas called for government ownership and operation of the railroads and the telegraph and telephone. These demands, however, did not reflect a desire for state ownership of all productive property. As landowners, farmers rejected socialism, but some did believe that these transportation and communication facilities were "natural monopolies" that could only be run efficiently under centralized management and were too important to the public welfare to be in the hands of private monopolies for profit.

The remainder of the agrarian political agenda reflected a rather realistic and moderate response to the farmers' problems. To ease their credit crisis they advocated an inflated, more flexible currency and the subtreasury plan. Considered by the Alliancemen to be the keystone of their program, subtreasuries (federal warehouses) were to be constructed as places where farmers could store their crops and receive treasury notes amounting to 80 percent of the crops' market value. Relieved from the pressure to sell immediately, farmers could wait for prices to rise to sell their crops and then pay back their subtreasury advances plus small interest and storage fees. Farmers saw the plan as a solution to the twin evils of the crop lien and depressed prices at harvest time. To finance government programs farmers called for a graduated income tax based upon the ability to pay.

Farmers believed that many of their ailments could be relieved by a more responsive, activist government. They therefore proposed political changes to "restore the government of the Republic to the hands of 'the plain people,' with which class it originated." Among the proposed changes were initiative and referendum, direct primaries, the direct election of the United States senators, and the use of a secret ballot.

Initiative and referendum would allow people to propose legislation through petitions and enact laws by popular vote—thereby bypassing the state legislatures that seemed unwilling to act on their grievances. Direct primaries would let "the people" vote on political party candidates rather than having party leaders pick the candidates. In the same manner, people would directly elect senators instead of allowing state legislatures to select them. All of these proposals were intended to give citizens more control over their government. To make those changes effective a secret ballot was needed to protect voters from economic intimidation by employers and creditors or physical intimidation by threats of violence.

Although the farmers failed to address the fundamental problem of overproduction, adoption of the agrarian demands could have relieved somewhat the agricultural distress fueling their anger. Thus the farmers became increasingly involved in political organization.

Emergence of the Populist Party

In 1890 Alliancemen entered politics in the West and the South with remarkable success. Under independent party banners, western Alliancemen elected a governor in Kansas, gained control of 4 state legislatures, and sent U.S. senators from Kansas and Nebraska. Working through the existing Democratic state parties,

southern Alliancemen elected 4 governors, 44 congressmen, and several senators.

Western Alliancemen interpreted this success as a mandate to establish a national third party. At a May 1891 meeting in Cincinnati they failed to convince the southern Alliancemen to join them. By 1892, however, the Southerners were disillusioned with Alliance-backed Democrats who failed to support the subtreasury system. They soon overcame their apprehension of third parties, and the Alliances joined hands in St. Louis to create the People's or Populist party. In July 1892 the Populist party's national convention in Omaha drafted a platform and gave its presidential nomination to James B. Weaver of Iowa, a former Union general and greenback supporter and presidential candidate. To symbolize the unity of the party they nominated former Confederate officer James G. Field for vice president. The Populist platform included all the agrarian agenda: the subtreasury plan; an income tax; free coinage of silver to inflate the currency; government ownership of railroads, telephone, and telegraph; and the political reforms intended to restore government to "the hands of the people."

The majority of the Populists were small-scale farmers in the South and West whose farms were minimally mechanized. Most relied on a single cash crop, had unsatisfactory access to credit, and lived in social isolation some distance from towns and railroads. In other words their existence was marginal in all respects. The majority owned some land, but sizable numbers of sharecroppers and tenant farmers joined the party. Prosperous, large-scale, diversified farmers found little appeal in the party's platforms or activities.

The Populists realized the need to broaden the base of their constituency. Therefore, the Omaha platform included planks to appeal to urban workers. They advocated an eight-hour day, immigration restriction, and the abolition of the Pinkerton system that supplied strike breakers to management. One plank promised "fair and liberal" pensions to veterans. In the South some Populists, such as Tom Watson of Georgia, sought to woo black voters. "You are kept apart," he told audiences of black and white farmers, "that you may be separately fleeced of your earnings. You are made to hate

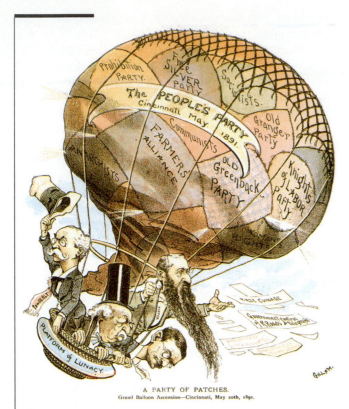

A PARTY OF PATCHES.
Grand Balloon Ascension—Cincinnati, May 20th, 1891.

The Populist party was a coalition of western and southern farm organizations, urban laborers, Grangers, and Greenbackers. This hostile cartoonist ridiculed the Populist platforms of free coinage of silver; government ownership of railroads, telephone, and telegraph; a graduated income tax; restrictions on immigration; an eight-hour workday; popular election of U.S. senators; and the secret ballot as platforms "of lunacy."

each other because upon that hatred is rested the keystone of the arch of financial despotism which enslaves you both."

The Populists conducted colorful campaigns, which one Nebraska Democrat called a blend of "the French Revolution and a western religious revival." Their anger fostered a revolutionary spirit that appealed to large numbers of farmers. In 1892 Weaver became the first third-party candidate to win over one million votes. He also carried Kansas, Colorado, Idaho, and Nevada for a total of 22 electoral votes. Populist strength in such mining states as Colorado reflected the appeal to silver miners of the party's demand for inflation by means of the free and unlimited coinage of silver at 16 to 1. On the other hand, the Populists failed to carry

a single southern state, largely because of voting fraud and the Democrats' cries of white supremacy and ability to control a large number of black votes through economic intimidation. Nevertheless, it was a remarkable showing for a new party, revealing the extent of popular discontent. The next year brought the panic of 1893, which produced more discontent and gave the Populists great hopes for the election of 1896.

DEPRESSION AND TURBULENCE IN THE 1890s

Social harmony became somewhat strained in the late 1880s with such violent episodes as the Haymarket Square riot of 1886. Economic "losers," mainly workers and farmers, were already becoming restless. The depression following the panic of 1893 intensified their suffering. Naturally, turbulence increased, setting the stage for the election of 1896, where an attempt was to be made to unite the losers in a quest for political power.

The Roots and Results of the Depression

While the Populists made their bid for office in the election of 1892, the two major parties featured a rerun of the election of 1888. Once again Cleveland and Harrison faced each other over the issue of the tariff. The unpopular McKinley Tariff created a different outcome, and Cleveland entered the White House—just in time for the panic of 1893.

The depression started in Europe and spread to the United States as overseas buyers reduced their purchases of American goods as well as their American investments. Their unloading of some $300 million of investments caused American gold to leave the country to pay for these securities. Thus supplies of currency dropped—leading rapidly to falling prices. There had also been serious overexpansion of the economy, especially in railroad construction. Confidence faltered, the stock market crashed, and banks failed.

The panic ushered in a depression in which unemployment reached 20 percent of the work force. Farm prices dropped to new lows, and farm foreclosures reached new highs. Sharp wage cuts and massive layoffs took place in virtually every industry. Henry Adams lamented, "Men died like flies under the strain, and Boston grew suddenly old, haggard, and thin." Still opposed to direct federal aid, President Cleveland's only response to the suffering was repeal of the Sherman Silver Purchase Act and the sale of lucrative federal bonds to a banking syndicate, headed by J. P. Morgan, aimed at protecting the nation's gold reserves.

The Democrats did act on their campaign issue, passing the Wilson-Gorman Tariff that reduced the rates by 10 percent. Reformers were disappointed with the moderate cuts but were appeased by a provision placing a 2 percent tax on incomes. That provision, however, was declared unconstitutional in *Pollock* v. *The Farmer's Loan and Trust Co.* in 1895. In the face of massive suffering, many people wanted the government to do more.

Expressions of Worker Discontent

Violence had begun to escalate in labor-management relations in the late 1880s and continued into the 1890s. In 1892, for example, Andrew Carnegie and the Amalgamated Association of Iron and Steel Workers clashed at Carnegie's Homestead plant outside of Pittsburgh.

In an effort to crush the union, Carnegie slashed wages, and, expecting a confrontation, he fortified his steel mills, hired strikebreakers, and employed the Pinkerton Agency to protect them. This done, Carnegie departed for Scotland on a fishing trip and left his manager, Henry Clay Frick, to do battle with organized labor.

On July 5, strikers and Pinkerton agents fought their first battle. The smoke from cannons, rifles, dynamite, and burning oil filled the hot summer air. Ten men were killed and another 70 were wounded, but the workers won this first engagement. Frick appealed to the governor of Pennsylvania for help; the governor dispatched 8000 militiamen to Homestead "to protect law and order"—a phrase normally synonymous with defense of industrialists' property.

The fighting continued until late July when an anarchist from Chicago named Alexander Berkman decided to take matters into his own hands. He went to Frick's office, shot the manager twice, and stabbed him seven times before being subdued. Frick lived and police arrested Berkman. Although Berkman had no connections with the steel union, the local and national press linked unionism with radicalism. Shortly afterward, strikebreakers went to work and the union was defeated and destroyed by the powerful forces of capital, government, and press.

Striking workers from Carnegie's Homestead plant outside Pittsburgh used guns and dynamite to try to stop the Pinkerton guards approaching the plant on barges from a nearby river.

During the depression, employers frequently cut wages to preserve profits. In 1894 the workers in the Pullman plant at Chicago found their wages reduced several times while their rent for company-owned housing remained the same. When management refused to negotiate with the union, members of the American Railway Union (ARU) refused to handle any cars made in the Pullman plant. The boycott totally disrupted railroad traffic in the Midwest. Railroad executives appealed to Illinois Governor John Altgeld for help, but the liberal politician refused to interfere. The executives then turned to U.S. Attorney General Richard Olney, a former railroad corporation lawyer. Olney and President Cleveland responded quickly. They used the excuse of protecting the mails to come to the aid of the railroad managers. Over Altgeld's protest, the government sent 2000 troops to the Chicago area, and a federal court issued a blanket injunction that virtually ordered union leaders to discontinue the strike. When ARU president Eugene V. Debs defied the injunction, he was imprisoned. Only after federal troops arrived did violence occur. Within two days, bitter fighting had broken out, railcars were burned, and over $340,000 worth of damage had been done to railroad property. Force—absolute, final, and federal—crushed the Pullman strike.

Such unified repressive force drove some workers to the political left. Prior to 1894, the Socialist Labor party had been miniscule in membership. Badly divided, it was led by the abrasive Daniel DeLeon. After the Pullman strike Eugene V. Debs emerged from prison a socialist and made socialism more respectable. Born in Indiana in 1855, the balding Debs had the common touch and delivered with a Hoosier twang a version of socialism based upon distinctly American values. The movement thus acquired a fiery and effective orator. "Many of you think you are competing," Debs would declare. "Against whom? Against Rockefeller? About as I would if I had a wheelbarrow and competed with the Santa Fe [railroad]." Around the nucleus of his personality the larger and stronger Socialist party of America began to form and directly challenge unrestrained capitalism.

The mass suffering during the depression

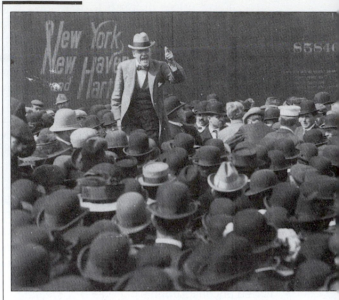

Eugene V. Debs was the Socialist Party of America's presidential nominee four times. Here Debs addresses a crowd of railroad workers during one of his campaigns.

also provoked some to ask the federal government to provide work for the unemployed. One such person was Jacob S. Coxey, a short, quiet Ohio businessman who advocated putting men to work on the roads. They were to be paid by the printing of $500 million in legal tender paper money, which would also help to inflate the currency. He organized the Army of the Commonwealth of Christ to march to Washington and demand action. When about 500 of the marchers straggled into the capital on May 1, 1894, their leader was arrested for walking on the grass. Federal authorities beat and arrested his troops. Although "Coxey's Army" fell far short of his dream of a demonstration of 400,000 jobless workers, their actions did get the attention of the public. Forty-three newspaper reporters accompanied them, reporting almost every detail of the march. One journalist quipped, "Never in the annals of insurrection has so small a company of soldiers been accompanied by such a phalanx of recording angels."

Deteriorating Race Relations

The turbulent 1890s was also one of the worst decades of racial violence in the nation's history.

That violence stemmed from class as well as race conflict. Following Reconstruction, southern "Redeemer" Democrats in some states had forged a rather strange alliance with black Republicans. In return for the protection of the Redeemers and a share of the lesser offices, African-Americans helped those conservative, elitist whites to beat back challenges from lower-class whites, who called the Redeemer Democrats "Bourbons," after the French royal line. Tom Watson was right when he told black and white farmers that the Bourbons were using race as a wedge to keep them apart.

The Bourbon-black alliance could work only so long as it was in the interests of upper-class whites to support black rights and votes. There were few external pressures to do so as the Republican party and all three branches of government deserted African-Americans. Although the Populists failed to unite blacks and whites on the basis of class interests, the attempt led to considerable bloodshed. Whites shed white blood, but more frequently they spilled black blood. Lynching became a tool for controlling both black votes and actions. Under the pretext of "maintaining law and order" vigilante mobs hanged, mutilated, and burned African-Americans in increasing numbers. During the decade of the 1890s an average of two to three black Southerners were lynched each week.

It is probably not coincidental that attempts to limit black voting began in earnest precisely at the time that farmer unrest arose. Mississippi led the way in finding ways to skirt the Fifteenth Amendment. Without mentioning "race, color, or previous condition of servitude," the 1890 Mississippi constitution established poll taxes, literacy tests, and residency requirements aimed at reducing black voting. A key element of the literacy tests was a requirement that voters be able to explain what they read to the satisfaction of the voter registrars; African-Americans found registrars extremely hard to satisfy. The Supreme Court displayed its disregard for black rights by upholding the so-called Mississippi Plan in *Williams* v. *Mississippi*. Other states soon adopted similar measures. Later, to woo lower-class white voters, grandfather clauses were added—providing exemptions from these requirements based on voting eligibility prior to the Reconstruction Acts.

These clauses applied to all adult white males and to no African-Americans.

Once whites stripped away black political power other black rights toppled. With no need to cater to black voters, whites soon began to pass discriminatory legislation. Most wanted segregation as a means of racial control, but the Fourteenth Amendment raised constitutional questions. The Supreme Court removed that barrier. After several rulings that limited constitutional protection of black rights, in the 1896 *Plessy* v. *Ferguson* decision the Court finally ruled that public accommodations for blacks could be "separate but equal." With segregation legalized, for the next two decades southern states frantically passed legislation—known as "Jim Crow" laws—to legally require the separation of the races. When the frenzy stopped, some states had even passed laws prohibiting interracial checker playing and requiring textbooks used in black schools to be stored in separate rooms from those used in white schools.

Segregation and the exclusion of African-Americans from public facilities had long ex-

Jacob S. Coxey led his army of unemployed workers into Washington, D.C., where he was arrested and his army dispersed by club-wielding police.

(Text continues on p. 716)

"RISE, BROTHERS!": THE BLACK RESPONSE TO JIM CROW

African-Americans had long struggled against white prejudice and repression. During Reconstruction constant vigilance was needed to protect and expand newly won rights. Some efforts were in vain, but black successes had helped to curb the growth of segregation. For example, blacks in Savannah, Georgia, succeeded in desegregating their city's streetcar system in 1872 by boarding the so-called white cars, threatening legal action, and boycotting the Jim Crow cars. Beginning in the 1890s, however, a rising tide of virulent white racism eventually confounded black attempts to resist being made into second-class citizens. With a new determination white Southerners stripped blacks of the right to vote, passed segregation laws, and lynched blacks who refused to cooperate.

Once whites had won the battle and the smoke had cleared from the battlefields, a mythology of black submission and acceptance arose. Booker T. Washington became a symbol of black cooperation and accommodation. Selected passages of his 1895 Atlanta address were heralded as the "will of blacks." Other voices were ignored. Few quoted the words of John Hope in the year following the "Atlanta Compromise." Then a professor at a black college in Nashville, Hope exhorted his fellow blacks:

> Rise, Brothers! Come let us possess this land. Never say "Let well enough alone." Cease to console yourself with adages that numb the moral sense. Be discontented. Be dissatisfied.... Be restless as the tempestuous billows on the boundless sea. Let your dissatisfaction break mountain-high against the walls of prejudice and swamp it to the very foundation. Then we shall not have to plead for justice nor on bended knee crave mercy; for we shall be men. Then and not until then will liberty in its highest sense be the boast of our Republic!

Instead of passive acceptance, the response of many blacks to the new wave of discrimination was to employ every available tactic to protest the loss of their rights. Before disfranchisement was completed, black officeholders made impassioned speeches and lobbied their white colleagues in opposition to discriminatory legislation. Activists organized local "Negro Rights," "Emancipation," and "Colored Uplift" groups that wrote strongly worded resolutions and organized petition drives. Individuals and groups launched legal challenges in the courts. Some tested the new laws by breaking them. Protest meetings were held. Boycotts of newly segregated facilities occurred in such diverse southern cities as New Orleans, Savannah, Jacksonville, and Richmond. The black press often fearlessly attacked white actions; a Bay Minette, Alabama, paper counseled, "The best remedy for lynching is a good Winchester rifle." Finally, a few engaged in the ultimate protest—armed resistance.

Two examples illustrate the nature and results of black protest at the turn of the century. The first, a Savannah streetcar boycott in 1906, enjoys many similarities to the Montgomery bus boycott of 1955—the main exception being the outcome. The second, the story of Robert Charles, indicates that this early civil rights movement had its share of martyrs, as did the movement a half century later.

At the beginning of the twentieth century whites and blacks of Savannah were proud that their city had been immune to the lynching virus. By 1906 it was also one of the few southern cities without a single Jim Crow law on its books. Race relations were better than average but not ideal. Although 54 percent of the city's 72,000 residents were black, the white minority exercised a firm, if benevolent, control over the black majority. There were only three black public officials, and they held positions allotted to blacks by law. Nevertheless, the black community had spawned a leadership class that commanded some respect from the white establishment and enjoyed some political clout. Thus they had been able to turn back all previous attempts to enact segregation.

The year 1906, however, brought increased racial tension throughout the South with several outbreaks of violence in such places as Brownsville, Texas, and Atlanta, Georgia. In Georgia white prejudice was aroused by the bitter gubernatorial campaign of Hoke Smith. Savannah whites began to urge their leaders to get into the "new order of things" and exclude blacks from both politics and social contact with whites. On September 12, 1906, the city adopted a law that required separate seating in streetcars and empowered the police to arrest anyone sitting in the wrong place.

The black elite of the leading black ministers, physicians, and businessmen had already formed a committee to lobby against the ordinance. Once the law was passed, they immediately organized a boycott. In the churches, ministers urged compliance, and the black *Savannah Tribune* declared: "Let us walk! walk! and save some nickels . . . Do not trample on your pride by being 'jim crowed.' Walk!" Black

hackmen reduced their fares for boycotters from 25 cents to 10 cents. One group attempted to form the United Transportation Company to compete with white lines. Those rich enough to own wagons drove themselves and friends to town.

Many who could get no other transportation heeded the words of the leaders and walked. It was reported that the mayor's secretary had given his maid carfare to bring two large suitcases from his home to city hall. When she arrived late and soaked with perspiration, he discovered that she had followed the advice of her minister and refused to ride the streetcar. The local white paper noted that trolley after trolley went by with the back seats vacant. The boycott was almost total.

City authorities responded much like those of Montgomery did in 1955. They cracked down on unlicensed hacks and harassed licensed ones. Blacks remained firm for some time—even after it became apparent that the boycott was not going to change white minds. As late as May 1908, two years after the start of the boycott, the streetcar line admitted that no more than 80 percent of blacks had returned to the cars. Without action by the federal government, even economic loss could not persuade whites to abandon segregation.

While Savannah blacks suffered inconvenience to protest the enfringement of their rights, Robert Charles paid a much higher price. In his twenties in 1900, he was a quiet, intense young man who worked at odd jobs and supported black emigration to Africa as a response to white prejudice in the South. He read a lot and collected weapons, but broke no laws. One night in July he sat on a front porch

in New Orleans talking quietly with a friend. Close to midnight three police officers arrived with drawn pistols and flailing billy clubs to announce his arrest.

Charles responded to the unjust arrest by drawing his gun and shooting one of the officers. Wounded himself, he then fled— not to safety but to rearm. Grabbing a rifle, Charles moved from one hiding place to another. Along his trail he left five dead police officers and a dozen wounded ones. A mob of over one thousand joined police in the manhunt, frequently firing indiscriminately into the black community. Finally surrounded, Charles was burned out of his hiding place and immediately riddled with bullets. As was customary, the mob then badly mutilated the body. They killed the man but not the spirit. Newspaper woman Ida Wells-Barnett investigated the incident and ended her report with the words: "The white people of this county may charge that he was a desperado, but to the people of his own race Robert Charles will always be regarded as the 'hero of New Orleans.' " Later his willingness to fight police brutality with retaliatory violence would be renewed by the Black Panthers in the 1960s.

Even heroic actions failed to protect black rights from the onslaught of discrimination at the dawn of the new century. Nevertheless these men and women added to the heritage of black protest that would reap rewards a half century later—when sympathetic media coverage changed public opinion and the federal government finally decided that it was in the national interest to protect the rights of all citizens.

In the 1896 *Plessy* v. *Ferguson* decision, the U.S. Supreme Court ruled that enforced separation of the races and "separate but equal" public facilities for black Americans were not discriminatory, as prohibited by the Fourteenth Amendment. Facilities were certainly separate, as in this black school near Henderson, Kentucky, but rarely equal.

isted in a haphazard way based upon custom. Converting this informal and inconsistent arrangement into a legalized system of repression spawned violence, and no one stepped in to protect African-Americans. The popularity of Booker T. Washington's 1895 "Atlanta Compromise" with its plea for racial cooperation is easily understandable under the conditions it was delivered. Both whites and blacks were eager to find a way out of the bloodshed.

Fissures seemed to be opening up along quite a number of the seams in American society. The turbulence was enough to provoke one of the major parties to respond somewhat to popular demands in 1896; and that created a dilemma for the Populists.

The Tide Is Turned: The Election of 1896

After the Republicans nominated William McKinley and the Democrats chose William Jennings Bryan, the Populists were left with an impossible choice. When Bryan and the Democrats endorsed silver, the Populists had their thunder stolen. They had hoped to ride silver to power because of the growing popularity of the issue. William. H. Harvey's pro-silver book *Coin's Financial School* had become a best-seller in

1894. Rather than picking up silverite bolters from the major parties, as the Populists expected, however, they were faced with a real problem. To nominate someone else would split the silver votes and ensure a victory for McKinley. Yet to nominate Bryan meant a loss of their identity and momentum.

Many Populists argued fervently against "fusion" with the Democrats, who focused almost exclusively on silver at the expense of the rest of the Populist demands. Watson and others viewed the obsession with silver as "a trap, a pitfall, a snare, a menace, a fraud, a crime against common sense and common honesty." In the end Populists bit the bullet and nominated Bryan for president but chose Tom Watson for vice president rather than the Democratic choice, Arthur Sewall.

"God's in his Heaven, all's right with the world!" Republican campaign manager Mark Hanna wired McKinley when he learned of the Republican victory. McKinley carried the popular vote 7.1 million to 6.5 million and the electoral votes 271 to 176. The defeat of Bryan and the silver forces brought an end to political equilibrium. Millions of Democrats left their party, and the Republican party became the majority party. Republicans won the presidency in

HRONOLOGY
OF KEY EVENTS

1867 The Grangers, first national farmers' organization, is founded

1873 "Crime of '73": Coinage Act declares that gold alone would be minted to back paper money

1877 Southern Farmers' Alliance is founded in Texas; *Munn* v. *Illinois* upholds the constitutionality of state regulation of railroads

1878 Bland-Allison Act requires the U.S. Treasury to buy $2 to $4 million of silver a month in order to inflate the currency

1881 President James A. Garfield mortally wounded at a Washington, D.C., train station; Chester Arthur becomes twenty-first president

1883 Pendleton Act classifies approximately 15,000 federal jobs as civil service positions to be awarded only after a competitive examination

1886 *Wabash, St. Louis, & Pacific Railway Company* v. *Illinois* reverses *Munn* v. *Illinois* and states that only Congress can regulate commerce between states

1887 Congress establishes the Interstate Commerce Commission, the first federal regulatory commission, to regulate railroads

1890 Founding of the National American Woman Suffrage Association; Congress passes Sherman Antitrust Act, forbidding restraints on trade; Sherman Silver Purchase Act increases amount of silver that had to be purchased annually and allows the Treasury to issue paper money based on silver; Mississippi becomes first southern state to adopt poll taxes, literacy tests, and residency requirements to restrict black voting

1892 Populist party is formed, and receives over a million votes; Homestead, Pennsylvania, steel strike

1893 Severe economic depression begins

1894 Pullman strike; Coxey's Army marches on Washington, D.C., to protest unemployment and to urge a public works program to relieve unemployment

1895 *United States* v. *E. C. Knight Co.* weakens Sherman Antitrust Act by stating that law does not apply to companies that operated exclusively in one state; *Pollock* v. *Farmer's Loan and Trust Co.* declares a federal income tax unconstitutional

1896 *Plessy* v. *Ferguson* decision rules that the principle of "separate but equal" does not deprive blacks of civil rights guaranteed under the Fourteenth Amendment; Republican William McKinley defeats Democrat William Jennings Bryan to become the twenty-fifth president

1900 Gold Standard Act places the nation on the gold standard

7 of the 9 contests between 1896 and 1928, and controlled both houses of Congress 17 of the next 20 sessions. One basic reason for the Republican victory of 1896 was the bad luck of the Democrats to be in power when the depression came. Republicans gleefully noted in 1894, "We were told in the old times that the rich were getting richer and the poor were getting poorer. To cure that imaginary ailment our political opponents have brought on a time when everybody is getting poorer."

The Populists, of course, suffered the most from the election results: Their party disappeared. Their attempt to unite farmers and labor, blacks and whites, failed. Like the Socialists and other radicals, the Populists were never able to recruit organized labor to forge a broadly based working-class movement. American Federation of Labor president Samuel Gompers and other labor leaders argued that farmers were capitalists, not wage earners, and that their goals were not compatible with labor's interests. For example, the inflation that farmers wanted would raise food prices to the detriment of workers already living close to the margin. In the South race proved to be more important than class, and many disillusioned white Populists such as Tom Watson became anti-black activists following their defeat. They joined gladly with the Bourbons to curtail black suffrage. Ironically, the Bourbons stirred up racism to defeat the Populists and then proved to be unable to put the genie back into the bottle. In many states they were replaced by less elitist, bigoted demagogues.

Americans had come to a turning point in 1896 and chose the conservative path. The Republican administration quickly raised duties with the Dingley Tariff of 1897. Three years later the Gold Standard Act officially put the nation on the gold standard by requiring all money to be redeemable in gold. Ironically, new discoveries of gold and more efficient extracting methods brought the inflation that farmers had sought from silver. Prosperity began to return, and the Republicans could point with pride to their slogan, "The Full Dinner Pail." That prosperity also emasculated the agrarian movement as rising prices eased farmers' economic distress. And such inventions and services as the telephone and rural free delivery of the mail de-

creased the isolation and boredom of their lives—especially after mail-order catalogs began to arrive from Montgomery Ward's and Sears, Roebuck.

CONCLUSION

After Reconstruction, national politics entertained the masses rather than solved the emerging problems of industrialization. The two major parties differed little in their laissez-faire support of business and seemed more concerned with the spoils of office than with the suffering of farmers, workers, and minorities. Political inertia bred crises as problems remained unresolved. Finally, a challenge to unrestrained capitalism arose from the losers in the race toward economic modernization. Led by disgruntled farmers, the Populists sought to unite large segments of the American population on the basis of class interest. As a result, the election of 1896 provided a real choice for American voters.

The conservative victory brought about the death of Populism, but many of the problems the farmers addressed in the 1890s continued into the twentieth century. Time vindicated their demands. A large number of their rejected solutions were adopted in the first two decades of the new century; most of their remaining agenda was enacted in modified form during the New Deal of the 1930s.

SUGGESTIONS FOR FURTHER READING

OVERVIEWS AND SURVEYS

Sean Dennis Cashman, *America in the Gilded Age* (1984); Vincent P. DeSantis, *The Shaping of Modern America, 1877–1916* (1973); Harold U. Faulkner, *Politics, Reform, and Expansion, 1890–1900* (1959); John A. Garraty, *The New Commonwealth, 1877–1890* (1968); Ray Ginger, *The Age of Excess* (1965); Alan Trachtenberg, *The Incorporation of America: Culture and Society in the Gilded Age* (1982).

EQUILIBRIUM AND INERTIA: THE NATIONAL POLITICAL SCENE

John Allswang, *Bosses, Machines, and Urban Voters* (1977); John M. Dobson, *Politics in the Gilded Age* (1972); J. Rogers Hollingsworth, *The Whirligig of Politics: The Democracy of Cleveland and Bryan* (1963); Richard Jensen, *The Winning of the*

Midwest (1971); Morton Keller, *Affairs of State: Public Life in Nineteenth Century America* (1977); Paul Kleppner, *The Cross of Culture: A Social Analysis of Midwestern Politics, 1850–1900* (1970), and *The Third Electoral System, 1853–1892* (1979); Michael E. McGerr, *The Decline of Popular Politics: The American North, 1865–1928* (1986); Robert D. Marcus, *GOP: Political Structure in the Gilded Age, 1880–1896* (1971); Horace S. Merrill, *Bourbon Democracy in the Middle West, 1865–1896* (1953); H. Wayne Morgan, *From Hayes to McKinley* (1969); David J. Rothman, *Politics and Power: The United States Senate, 1869–1901* (1966); Leonard D. White, *The Republican Era, 1869–1901* (1958); R. Hal Williams, *Years of Decision: American Politics in the 1890s* (1978).

STYLE OVER SUBSTANCE: GOVERNMENT IN THE GILDED AGE, 1877–1892

Mary R. Dearing, *Veterans in Politics* (1952); Vincent P. DeSantis, *Republicans Face the Southern Question, 1877–1897* (1959); Justus D. Doenecke, *The Presidencies of James A. Garfield & Chester A. Arthur* (1981); Eleanor Flexner, *Century of Struggle: The Women's Rights Movement in the United States*, rev. ed. (1975); Margaret Forster, *Significant Sisters: The Grassroots of Active Feminism, 1839–1939* (1984); Lewis L. Gould, *The Presidency of William McKinley* (1980); Stanley P. Hirshson, *Farewell to the Bloody Shirt: Northern Republicans and the Southern Negro* (1962); Ari A. Hoogenboom, *Outlawing the Spoils: The Civil Service Reform Movement* (1961); Aileen Kraditor, *The Ideas of the Woman's Suffrage Movement, 1890–1920* (1965); Gerald W. McFarland, *Mugwumps, Morals, and Politics 1884–1920* (1975); Michael McGerr, *The Decline of Popular Politics* (1986); Walter T. K. Nugent, *Money and American Society* (1968); Arnold M. Paul, *Conservative Crisis and the Rule of Law: Attitudes of Bar and Bench, 1887–1895* (1969); John G. Sproat, *The Best Men: Liberal Reformers in the Gilded Age* (1968); Tom E. Terrill, *The Tariff, Politics, and American Foreign Policy, 1874–1901* (1973); Allen Weinstein, *Prelude to Populism: Origins of the Silver Issue, 1867–1878* (1970).

THE FARMERS REVOLT

Peter H. Argersinger, *Populism and Politics: William Alfred Peffer and the People's Party* (1974); Allan G. Bogue, *Money at Interest: The Farm Mortgage on the Middle Border* (1955); Paul W. Glad, *McKinley, Bryan, and the People* (1964); Lawrence Goodwyn, *Democratic Promise: The Populist Moment in America* (1976); Sheldon Hackney, *Populism to Progressivism in Alabama* (1969); Steven Hahn, *The Roots of Southern Populism* (1983); John D. Hicks, *The Populist Revolt* (1931); Richard Hofstadter, *The Age of Reform* (1955); Robert McMath, Jr., *Populist Vanguard: A History of the Southern Farmers' Alliance* (1975); Walter T. K. Nugent, *The Tolerant Populists* (1963); Bruce Palmer, *Man over Money: The Southern Populist Critique of American Capitalism* (1980); Norman Pollack, ed., *The Populist Mind* (1967), and *The Populist Response to Industrial America* (1962); Barton C. Shaw, *The Wool-Boys: Georgia's Populist Party* (1984).

DEPRESSION AND TURBULENCE IN THE 1890s

John P. Diggins, *The American Left in the Twentieth Century* (1973); Robert F. Durden, *The Climax of Populism: The Election of 1896* (1965); Charles Hoffmann, *The Depression of the Nineties: An Economic History* (1970); Stanley L. Jones, *The Presidential Election of 1896* (1964); J. Morgan Kousser, *The Shaping of Southern Politics: Suffrage Restriction and Establishment of the One-Party South, 1880–1910* (1974); Paul Krause, *The Battle for Homestead, 1880–1892* (1992); Charles Lofgren, *The Plessy Case: A Legal-Historical Interpretation* (1987); Donald L. McMurry, *Coxey's Army* (1929); Samuel T. McSeveney, *The Politics of Depression* (1972); Howard N. Rabinowitz, *Race Relations in the Urban South, 1865–1890* (1978); C. Vann Woodward, *The Strange Career of Jim Crow*, rev. ed. (1974).

BIOGRAPHIES

Paolo Coletta, *William Jennings Bryan: Political Evangelist* (1964); Ray Ginger, *Bending Cross: A Biography of Eugene Victor Debs* (1949); Paul W. Glad, *The Trumpet Soundeth: William Jennings Bryan and His Democracy* (1960); Louis Koenig, *Bryan* (1971); Allan Nevins, *Grover Cleveland: A Study in Courage* (1932); Allan Peskin, *Garfield* (1978); Thomas Reeves, *Gentlemen Boss: The Life of Chester Alan Arthur* (1975); Martin Ridge, *Ignatius Donnelly* (1962); Nick Salvatore, *Eugene V. Debs: Citizen and Socialist* (1982); Charles Morrow Wilson, *The Commoner: William Jennings Bryan* (1970); C. Vann Woodard, *Tom Watson: Agrarian Rebel* (1938).

Fig. 16

THE FIRST DIVISION
OF THE
SAINT PAUL & PACIFIC RAILROAD.
WINTER TIME TABLE.
Taking effect Sunday, November the 16th, 1873.
MAIN LINE.   BRANCH LINE.

Miles from St. Paul	STATIONS.	Going West	Going East	Miles from St. Paul	STATIONS.	Going North	Going South
0	ST. PAUL..........	Le. 8.35 a.m	Ar. 5.00 p.m	0	ST. PAUL..........	Le. 7.30 a.m	Ar. 1.00 p.m

CHAPTER 22

The Progressive Struggle

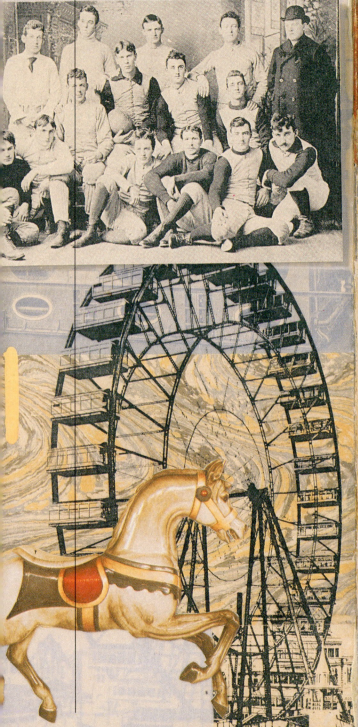

Times had changed by 1902 when George F. Baer declared "anthracite mining is business and not a religious, sentimental or academic proposition." Those tough-minded words might have won public approval at an earlier time, but many believed that Baer, spokesperson for mine owners in Pennsylvania, was merely pig-headed. His words were in response to a request by John Mitchell of the United Mine Workers (UMW) for arbitration of a labor dispute. There was an unusual amount of support for the coal miners' position. Exposés had increased popular awareness of miserable working conditions, and the union's demands seemed reasonable: a 9-hour day, recognition of the union, a 10 to 20 percent increase in wages, and a fair weighing of the coal mined. Mitchell repeatedly stated the miners' willingness to accept arbitration, both before and after 50,000 miners walked out of the pits in May 1902.

Skillfully led, the coal miners stood firm month after month. By September, coal reserves were running short and prices were rising. With winter approaching, empty coal bins began multiplying, even in schools and hospitals. Baer remained stubborn. "The rights and interests of the laboring man," he declared, "will be protected and cared for—not by the labor agitators, but by the Christian men to whom God in his infinite wisdom has given the control of property interests in this country." This proclamation of the Gospel of Wealth fell on deaf ears. Newspaper after newspaper expressed disgust with the mine owners, and some tentatively suggested government ownership of the mines.

On October 3, President Theodore Roosevelt, temporarily in a wheelchair as a result of an accident, presided over a conference in the White House. Attending were Mitchell, Baer, Attorney General Philander C. Knox, and other labor leaders and mine operators. Baer was not in a mood to be cooperative. "We object to being called here to meet a criminal," he told a reporter, "even by the President of the United States." Refusing to speak directly to Mitchell, Baer urged Roosevelt to prosecute UMW leaders under the Sherman Antitrust Act and to use federal troops to break the strike, just as Cleveland had done in the 1894 Pullman strike. While Mitchell "behaved like a gentleman" according to Roosevelt, Baer was obstinate, concluding one diatribe against unions by calling "free government . . . a contemptible failure if it can only protect the lives and property and secure comfort of the people by compromise with violators of law and instigators of violence and crime."

Irritated with Baer, Roosevelt declared, "If it wasn't for the high office I hold I would have taken him by the seat of the breeches and the nape of the neck and chucked him out of that window." When the owners returned to Pennsylvania, they took actions that indicated they might use force to break the strike. Roosevelt's response was to begin preparations to send 10,000 federal troops to take over and operate the mines. This action jolted opponents of state socialism, who induced banker J. P. Morgan to get involved. Serving as a broker, Morgan was able to patch together a compromise under which the miners returned to work and Roosevelt appointed a commission to arbitrate the dispute.

The commission and its findings illustrate a number of aspects of the turn-of-the-century reforms labeled "progressivism." Originally, the commission was to consist of an army engineer, a mining engineer, a businessperson "familiar with the coal industry," a federal judge, and an "eminent sociologist"—reflecting a progressive tendency to call upon "experts" to conduct public affairs. Its composition was also decidedly probusiness, and even the addition of two other members and the appointment of a labor leader as the "eminent sociologist" did not redress this imbalance. As a result, its findings were essentially conservative: a 10 percent wage increase and reduction of working hours to 8 a day for a handful of miners and to 9 for most. The union did not receive recognition, and the traditional manner of weighing coal was continued. The commission also suggested a 10 percent increase in the price of coal. Business influence on other progressive responses to social problems generally produced similar moderate solutions that frequently brought industrialists as many benefits as losses.

Nevertheless, Roosevelt's actions did add some new rules to the game. For the first time, a president did not give kneejerk support to business. Government became not merely a

President Roosevelt, surrounded here by coal miners after their 1902 strike, set a precedent by threatening the use of force against management rather than labor.

champion of the status quo, but also an arbiter of change. This retreat from laissez-faire was motivated by the demands of the middle class and workers. By 1902 many middle-class citizens had rejected the heavy-handed tactics of management, which often ended in chaos and conflict. They sought a more orderly, stable, and just society through government intervention. Workers also began to flex their political muscles, electing sympathetic mayors in a number of cities. Like the coal miners, Americans of all classes were learning the limits of individualism and joining together in organizations to accomplish their goals. National leaders such as Roosevelt began to recognize the need for change in order to preserve stable government and the capitalistic system. Roosevelt justified his actions in 1902 to save "big propertied men . . . from the dreadful punishment which their folly would have brought upon them." He stood, he declared, "between them and socialistic action." For a variety of motives, a plethora of legislation was enacted—sometimes with unintended results.

THE PROGRESSIVE IMPULSE

Americans exalted progress as a basic characteristic of their nation's distinctiveness. Technology was reshaping the human environment in dramatic ways. The pace of change was dizzying. Then in the late 1890s, people seemed to stop, catch their breath, and look around at their brave, new world. Much filled them with pride, but some of what they saw seemed outmoded or disruptive. Problems, however, appeared eminently solvable. Modern minds were explaining and harnessing natural forces. Could they not also understand and control human behavior? Could they not eliminate conflict and bring harmony to competing interests through some simple adjustments in the system? Americans increasingly answered "Yes" and called themselves "progressives." Many agreed with Thomas Edison's observation, "We've stumbled along for awhile, trying to run a new civilization in old ways, but we've got to start to make this world over."

America in 1901

The twentieth century opened with a rerun of the 1896 election between William Jennings Bryan and William McKinley. Although the outcome was the same, much was different. "I have never known a Presidential campaign so quiet," Senator Henry Cabot Lodge noted. By 1900 the crises of the 1890s had largely passed. Prosperity had returned and was shared by many. The nation also reveled in its new-found international power following the Spanish-American War. The social fabric seemed to be on the mend, but memories of the depression still haunted Americans, and society's blemishes appeared more and more intolerable to many.

As the nation reached adulthood, a number of ugly moles and warts had indeed erupted. Unequal distribution of wealth and income persisted. One percent of American families possessed nearly seven-eighths of its wealth. Four-fifths of Americans lived on a subsistence level, while a handful lived in incredible opulence. In

Breaker boys employed by the mines worked in dirty, dismal, and dangerous surroundings that robbed them of their childhood.

1900, Andrew Carnegie's income was $23 million; the average working man earned $500. The wealth of a few was increased by the exploitation of women and children. One out of five women worked to earn money for food, rather than for personal fulfillment, earning wages as low as $6 a week. The sacrifice of the country's young to the god of economic growth was alarming. One reporter undertook to do a child's job in the mines for one day and wrote, "I tried to pick out the pieces of slate from the hurrying stream of coal, often missing them; my hands were bruised and cut within a few minutes; I was covered from head to foot with coal dust, and for many hours afterwards I was expectorating some of the small particles of anthracite I had swallowed."

Working conditions were equally horrifying in other industries, and for many Americans housing conditions were as bad or worse. One investigator described a Chicago neighborhood, remarking on the "filthy and rotten tenements, the dingy courts and tumble down sheds, the foul stables and dilapidated outhouses, the broken sewer pipes, the piles of garbage fairly alive with diseased odors." At the same time the Vanderbilts summered in a "cottage" of 70 rooms, and wealthy men partied in shirts with diamond buttons worth thousands of dollars.

The middle class experienced neither extreme. Its members did have their economic grievances, however. Prosperity increased the cost of living by 35 percent in less than a decade, while many middle-class incomes remained fairly stable. Such people were not poor, but they believed they were not getting a fair share of the prosperity. Many came to blame the monopolies and watched with alarm as trusts, proving to be immune from the Sherman Act, proliferated rapidly. Nearly three-fourths of all trusts in 1904 had been created since 1898. Decreasing competition seemed to threaten America's status as the land of opportunity.

People came to believe that they had to find political solutions to the nation's problems. To achieve that goal they had to wrestle government from the hands of a few and return it to the "people." The great democratic experiment seemed to have run afoul. Wealthy industrialists bought state and federal legislators; urban political machines paid for votes with money from bribes; southern elections had become both bloody and corrupt.

Most problems were not new in 1901; neither were the proposed solutions. What came to be called progressivism was rooted in the Gilded Age. Whereas reform had been a sideshow earlier, it now became a national preoccupation. Progressivism was more broadly based and enjoyed greater appeal than any previous reform movement. The entire nation had experienced war or depression, never reform. One reason it did so was the diversity and pervasiveness of the voices calling for change.

Voices for Change

By 1900, Americans had done nothing less than reinterpret their understanding of their world. Under the old, classical interpretation, the universe was governed by absolute and unchangeable law. There was divine logic to all and truth was universal—the same at all times and in all places. Humanity's chore was to discover these truths, not to devise new ones. Under this vision, public policy should be aligned with natural laws; to attempt to change the course of those laws through man-made law was to court disaster. Such logic justified the concentration of wealth as well as the lack of governmental regulation of business and assistance to the poor and weak.

Social Darwinism, laissez-faire economics, and the Gospel of Wealth never enjoyed total acceptance. Throughout the Gilded Age, challenges and alternative visions had chipped away at their bases of support. The earlier challengers offered rather radical or simplistic alternatives. In 1879 Henry George wrote *Progress and Poverty*. As the title implies, he early recognized the unequal distribution of the fruits of economic growth. His solution was a "single tax" on what he called the "unearned increment" of land values. He wanted to tax those who benefited from land speculation and rising property values without producing anything. In essence he attacked the premise of capitalism that one could use money to make more money without providing other goods or services. In *Looking Backward* (1888) Edward Bellamy provided a

glimpse of a utopian society based upon a state-controlled economy propelled by cooperation rather than competition. The writings of such people profoundly influenced the Populists, the Socialists, and many who called themselves progressive.

Although critics dismissed the likes of George as crackpots, some respectable voices arose from the arts and literature, academia, the legal world, organized religion, and journalism. Realist writers described the world as it was, not as it should be. Instead of romantic heroes battling for abstract ideals, their characters were ordinary people dealing with concrete problems. The naturalists portrayed the powerlessness of the individual against the uncaring forces of urbanization and industrialization. Artists of the "ashcan" school painted urban scenes teeming with problems as well as life. Thus art and literature became mirrors of social concerns (see Chapter 19).

A revolution was also taking place in the academic world. Two of the most important changes were the democratization of higher education and the revolt against formalism. From 1870 to 1910 the number of colleges and universities nearly doubled, and their enrollment grew from 52,000 in 1870 to 600,000 in 1920. Higher education became less elitist, white, religious, and male, as women came to account for 47.3 percent of students in 1920 and black enrollment grew to over 20,000. Their professors became increasingly middle class as well. Such students and teachers had less interest in supporting the status quo.

Also undermining the status quo was the revolt against formalism. Previous academics had sought to explain the world by formulating abstract, universal theories. The new scholars, especially in the emerging social sciences, turned this approach on its head. They began instead by collecting concrete data. In field after field that data did not support the so-called natural laws propounded by their predecessors. Knowledge, philosopher and educator John Dewey proclaimed, was "no longer an immobile solid; it has been liquefied."

Theories had prescribed limits to human action; facts became weapons for change. Classical economists asserted that self-interested

These women in a physics class illustrate the growing presence of women in college during the Progressive Era.

economic decisions by individuals in a freely competitive economy provided natural regulation of markets through the laws of supply and demand. The new economists, calling themselves "institutional economists," conducted field research to learn how the economy actually worked. Their findings challenged the laissez-faire doctrines of the classicists on two levels: that free competition existed and that human decisions were based on purely economic motivations. To continue policies based on competition was absurd in an economy dominated by monopolies. In *Theory of the Leisure Class* (1899) and *The Instinct of Workmanship* (1914), economist Thorstein Veblen demonstrated the power of noneconomic motives. For example, vanity prompted the newly rich to indulge in "conspicuous consumption" well beyond their economic needs. For many economists "natural laws" were, in the words of Richard T. Ely, "used as a tool in the hands of the greedy."

A group of sociologists called themselves "Reform Darwinists" and rejected Spencer's Social Darwinism as another tool of exploitation. They accepted evolutionary principles and the influence of environment but denied that

people were merely pawns manipulated by natural forces. Human intelligence was an active factor that could control and change the environment, especially when people worked together. A leading Reform Darwinist, Lester Frank Ward, thus proclaimed, "The individual has reigned long enough. The day has come for society to take its affairs into its own hands and shape its own destinies."

Ward's call for "rational planning" and "social engineering" in his *Dynamic Sociology* (1883) was echoed by Frederick W. Taylor, an efficiency advisor to management. His time and motion studies led to lowered production costs, and he asserted, "The fundamental principles of scientific management are applicable to all kinds of human activities." The goal of most such social scientists was a more orderly society, as was expressed by Walter Lippmann, who called on society "to introduce plan where there has been clash, and purpose into the jungles of disordered growth."

Legal scholars joined the assault on formalism in both books and court decisions. During the Gilded Age, courts had read laissez-faire principles into their interpretation of the Constitution. Decisions striking down regulatory and reform legislation invoked such abstract principles as the sanctity of property rights and contracts. In theory all such rights were equal before the law; reality was a different matter. For example, in *Lochner* v. *New York* (1905) the Supreme Court struck down a New York law limiting bakers' working hours. The law, the Court ruled, violated the bakers' rights to bargain freely and to make contracts. Most workers, however, had no real power to bargain and maintaining that myth merely increased management's already overwhelming advantage.

A new breed of jurist, many of whom were disciples of Dean Roscoe Pound of the Harvard Law School, challenged laissez-faire justice. Pound advocated "sociological jurisprudence," calling for "the adjustment of principles and doctrines to the human conditions they are to govern rather than assumed first principles." Supreme Court Justice Oliver Wendell Holmes, Jr., agreed. He rejected the idea that laws had ever been the logical result of pure, universal principles. "The life of the law has not been logic;" he wrote, "it has been experience." Laws had been and should be based on "the felt necessities of the time." Lawyer Louis D. Brandeis successfully argued these ideas in 1908. That year the Supreme Court upheld a ten-hour law for women working in Oregon laundries in *Muller* v. *Oregon*, primarily because of social research documenting the damage done to women's health by long hours.

As Americans began to reject absolute truths and universal principles, the question remained of how to determine right from wrong and good from bad. The answer came from philosopher William James with his doctrine of pragmatism. Ideas, he argued, were to be judged by their results. An idea that produced a socially desirable end was right and good. Philosophical thought was useless unless it was directed at solving problems. Pragmatism was a distinctly American philosophy and found many adherents. One of them, John Dewey, applied its principles to education. Earlier schools that stressed rote memorization of a static body of facts, he believed, were unable to meet the needs of individuals in a dynamic, changing environment. Instead, education should be based on experience and directed toward personal growth. In schools modeled after Dewey's Lab-

oratory School at the University of Chicago, students engaged in activities that taught problem solving by doing rather than reading.

The literary and intellectual currents of the era helped to set the stage for reform by combining optimism, idealism, and a tough-minded practicality. Yet the educated elite were probably reflecting rather than shaping public opinion. Priests and preachers influenced far more people than professors. The impact of organized religion on progressivism was profound. It was no coincidence that Teddy Roosevelt's supporters marched around the hall singing "Onward Christian Soldiers" at their 1912 convention.

The confrontation between the church and the city produced the Social Gospel movement. The impact of environment was brought home to urban clergymen who saw bodies ravaged before souls could be saved. As a young Baptist minister in the dismal New York neighborhood "Hell's Kitchen," Walter Raushenbusch described the poor coming to his church for aid. "They wore down our threshold, and they wore away our hearts . . . one could hear human virtue cracking and crunching all around."

For Raushenbusch and many others like him, there was no conflict between science and religion. "Translate the evolutionary theses into religious faith," he declared, "and you have the doctrine of the Kingdom of God." Following the lead of William Graham Taylor at the Chicago Theological Seminary, theology schools added courses in Christian sociology to teach "the application of our common Christianity to . . . social conditions." The Social Gospelers used the tools of scientific inquiry to root out and solve human problems in order to usher in the "Kingdom of God on Earth." Many settlement house workers, such as Jane Addams, sought to put their faith into action for "the joy of finding the Christ that lieth in man, but which no man

In 1889 Jane Addams founded Hull House, a social settlement in Chicago. A "Social Gospeler," Addams turned to Christian ideals to solve social problems.

can unfold save in fellowship." The Social Gospelers advocated a kind of sacred humanism.

Progressivism was dominated by, but not limited to, Protestantism. The 1891 encyclical, *Rerum Novarum*, by Pope Leo XIII inspired such Catholic priests as Father John A. Ryan to declare "a small number of very rich men have been able to lay upon the masses of people a yoke little better than slavery itself" and "no practical solution of this question will ever be found without the assistance of the church." Such Catholics as Alfred E. Smith and Robert F. Wagner became prominent progressive politicians. Others such as Jewish lawyer Louis Brandeis illustrated that the reform sentiment was not exclusively Christian either.

The Muckrakers

A final spark that ignited public interest in reform was popular journalism. The expansion of education and cities provided a mass audience for low-priced magazines. Such journals as *Collier's* and *McClure's* sold for only 10 cents and could only succeed if large numbers of people bought them. Their editors quickly rediscovered people's fascination with evil and launched series of exposés. Investigative reporters peeked beneath all sorts of rocks and brought to light corruption in almost every facet of society. Their vivid, indignant accounts sold magazines, but appalled some of the elite such as Teddy Roosevelt, who compared the writers to the character in John Bunyan's *The Pilgrim's Progress*, who was too engrossed in raking muck to look up and accept a celestial crown. Thus these chroniclers came to be called muckrakers.

Most of the exposés came out serially in magazines. Others were published as books, but all titillated the public. John Spargo wrote on child labor, "Statistics cannot express the withering of child lips in the poisoned air of factories; the tired strained look of child eyes that never dance to the glad music of souls tuned to Nature's symphonies." The U.S. Senate, according to David Graham Phillips, "betrayed the public to that cruel and vicious spirit of Mammon [money] which has come to dominate the nation." Further, he argued, "The United States Senate is a larger factor than your labor and in-

telligence, you average American, in determining your income. And the Senate is a traitor to you!" State legislatures were little better, as was shown by William Allen White's investigation in Missouri. "The legislature met biennially, and enacted such laws as the corporations paid for and such as were necessary to fool the people." In *Following the Color Line* Ray Stannard Baker exhorted, "Whether we like it or not the whole nation . . . is tied by unbreakable bonds to its Negroes, its Chinamen, its slum-dwellers, its thieves, its murderers, its prostitutes. We cannot elevate ourselves by driving them back either with hatred, violence or neglect; but only by bringing them forward: by service." Ida Tarbell called Standard Oil "one of the most gigantic and dangerous conspiracies ever attempted." In similar, stirring words Lincoln Steffens denounced urban politics in *The Shame of the Cities*, and the socialist Upton Sinclair described the horrifying conditions in the meat-packing industry in *The Jungle*.

One might believe these men and women were cynical mudslingers, but that was not how they saw themselves. "We muckraked," said Baker, "not because we hated our world, but because we loved it. We were not hopeless, we

Ida Tarbell became one of the most influential muckrakers after the 1904 publication of her *History of the Standard Oil Company*.

were not cynical, we were not bitter." The public sometimes missed the intended message. Sinclair's goal in *The Jungle* was a socialist critique of the exploitation of labor in the meatpacking industry, but as he ruefully noted, "I aimed at the nation's heart and hit it in the stomach." After a few years, muckraking tended to degenerate into sloppy research and wild, unsubstantiated charges. Yet the publishers of the more than 2000 muckraking books and articles who aimed at the nation's pocketbooks hit a number of Americans in the heart.

PROGRESSIVES IN ACTION

Voices of change echoed a genuine transformation of popular sentiment. Americans of all classes began calling themselves "progressives" and sought to reform whichever social evil captured their attention. Most believed problems could be legislated away; their typical response to injustice or sin was "There ought to be a law." At the same time they rejected the individualism of Social Darwinism and believed that progress would come through cooperation rather than competition. Thus they organized themselves by droves into groups that shared their own particular vision of human progress.

The diversity of the organizations founded reflects the breadth of reform activity. Indeed, so varied were the aims of people calling themselves progressive that to call progressivism a movement is a mistake. There was little unity except in the idea that people could improve society. Most progressives, however, were middle-class moderates who abhorred radical solutions. Motivated by a fear and hatred of class conflict, such progressives sought to save the capitalists from their own excesses and thereby salvage the system. Their goal was an orderly and harmonious society.

The Drive to Organize

Organizing was a major activity at the turn of the century. Such professional groups as the American Medical Association (AMA) and the American Historical Association began to emerge in modern form. These groups reflected the rise of a new professionalism that helped to create a body of "experts" to be tapped by progressives wanting to impose order and efficiency on social institutions. The organizations themselves also acted to bring change. The AMA was reorganized in 1901, and by 1910 its membership had increased from 8400 to more than 70,000. Its major goal was to improve professional standards. The government assisted by enacting laws that required licenses to practice medicine. In 1910 a Carnegie Foundation study recommended minimum standards for medical education. The widespread acceptance of its report closed the doors of dozens of marginal medical schools, several of which trained minority doctors. The result of the new professionalism in most fields was to limit the number of practitioners. Although this did help weed out incompetents, it also increased the incomes of the remaining practitioners and often reduced minority participation. In other words, order, stability, and improved standards were achieved at the cost of decreased opportunity.

Given the religious bent of progressive thought, a number of church-related organizations also arose. One of the most important was the Federal Council of Churches of Christ in America. Founded in 1908, it was an interdenominational group that advocated safer working conditions, the abolition of child labor, shorter work weeks and higher wages, workmen's compensation, old-age pensions, and "the most equitable division of the products of industry that can ultimately be devised."

To a large extent, middle-class women led in the organization of reform. Technology and domestic help lessened the burdens of running a home for these women, but a stigma remained on paid employment. Women's clubs provided an outlet for the energies and abilities of many competent and educated women. Local organizations flourished and, in 1890 joined to form the General Federation of Women's Clubs. In the next two decades, reform groups founded and led mainly by women sprang up.

The majority of activist, middle-class women became involved in movements closely linked to their assigned social roles as guardians of morality and nurturers of the family. Many worked through such religious groups as the

(Text continues on p. 732)

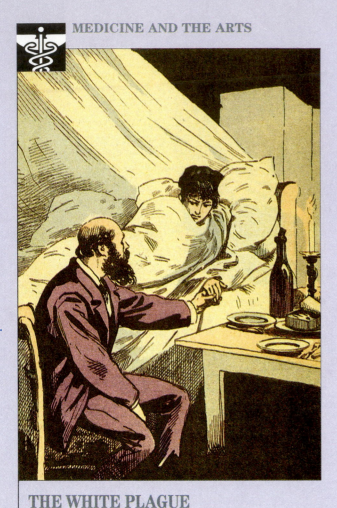

THE WHITE PLAGUE

During the Progressive Era, the rise of scientific ways of thinking cleared the way for reformers and health officers to launch a campaign against the disease most identified with industrialization—tuberculosis (TB). During the nineteenth century, TB was aptly called "the Captain of All the Men of Death." It killed more people and caused more sickness than any other disease in the western world. Its very name conjures up images of fetid sweatshops and sulfurous mills where men, women, and children had their

health broken by long working hours and physical exhaustion; of urban slums and overcrowded tenements rotten with disease; and, finally, of emaciated, ghostlike wretches, feverish with infection, gasping for breath, coughing up mouthfuls of blood, and staring hollow-eyed into space waiting for death.

In a sense, TB mirrors the complexity of the industrial revolution, for just as the transformation of the economy was multifaceted, TB is not one but many diseases. TB is merely the generic name for a host

of infections caused by tubercle bacilli, isolated in 1882 by Robert Koch, the famous German scientist. The most common (and most feared) is pulmonary tuberculosis, a chronic, debilitating disease of the lungs; it can kill its victims in a few months but usually requires several years to complete the task. Other common forms of the disease include meningeal TB, which produces an inflammation of the membranes surrounding the brain; TB of the spine, which causes a hunchback deformity of the spine; lupus, TB of the skin; and miliary TB, a generalized infection that occurs when the tubercle bacilli are distributed by the bloodstream throughout the body, producing small nodules on most organs.

Because the term "tuberculosis" did not appear in print until around 1840, most Americans knew the disease as consumption, which seemed the perfect metaphor for describing how the victims of the disease gradually wasted away from debilitating fever, weight loss, night sweats, chronic cough, and copious sputum, decorated toward the end with the bright red blood spots that denoted advanced pulmonary tuberculosis.

In less polite society, "consumptives" were called "lungers," a term of derision. Throughout the nineteenth century, many people associated TB with poverty and attached a social stigma to the disease. Others believed that TB was caused by some hereditary defect. For them, the perplexing problem was why the disease hit some families harder than others. In Ralph Waldo Emerson's family, for example, he and three of his brothers suffered from the disease, while his fellow transcendentalist, Henry David Thoreau, lost a father, a sister, and a grandfather to TB before dying from the disease himself.

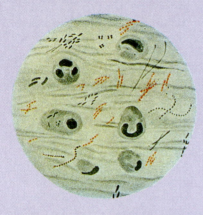

Paradoxically, despite its dreadful symptoms and terrifying ability to wipe out entire families, TB was romanticized on both sides of the Atlantic. For many writers, it became a metaphor for comparing decay in nature to disease in man. Thus, Henry Thoreau, upon seeing the first splashes of red in the green maple leaves of autumn, could write in 1852 in his *Journal Intime*: "Decay and disease are often beautiful, like ... the hectic glow of consumption."

In fact, the Age of Romanticism's much heralded "doom and gloom" may have derived at least in part from the sadness and melancholy caused by the deaths of loved ones from TB—especially the death of young adults for whom the disease had a special affinity. John Keats, the quintessential romantic poet, succumbed to TB at 26; Emily Brontë, author of the powerful *Wuthering Heights*, was cut down tragically at 30. The novels of the day, Charles Dickens's *David Copperfield*, for one, are positively littered with the corpses of people killed in the bloom of youth by the "White Plague."

The disease also broke its share of hearts in the theater and at the opera. Alexander Dumas lamented the death from TB of a beautiful heroine in *La Dame aux Camelias*, which in its English translation became the play, *Camille, or the Fate of a Coquette*, later adapted by Verdi for the opera as *La Traviata*. An identical fate befell the heroine in the play, *La Boheme*, which inspired Puccini's opera of the same name.

Under the spell of this heartwrenching romanticism, writers, poets, and artists created a new and profoundly twisted ideal of feminine beauty: the dying angel, smitten by consumption, whose physical appeal was somehow enhanced by her malady. One gravely ill woman confided to her diary, "I cough continually! But for a wonder, far from making me look ugly, this gives me an air of languor that is very becoming." As depicted by writers, the dying female consumptive was, to her fingertips, an exquisitely fragile creature, the very embodiment of both the romantic and the Victorian ideal of frail feminine beauty. Her languid pallor was rendered even more pale by the generous application of whitening powders; and her slender body, with its swanlike neck and elongated limbs, was adorned in thin, sheer white clothing of cotton or linen, giving her appearance an ethereal quality, as a spirit not quite of this earth.

Numerous artists struggled to capture this image on canvas, including Gabriel Rossetti of the Pre-Raphaelite school, who idealized tall, slender women "with cadaverous bodies and sensual mouths." Reducing this image to a word portrait, Henry James described

Janet Burden, one of the leading Pre-Raphaelite models, as "strange, pale, livid, gaunt, silent, and yet in a manner graceful and picturesque." To another observer the same woman looked "as if she had walked out of an Egyptian tomb at Luxor."

As the nineteenth century drew to a close, however, the romantic view of life gradually lost its hold on the public's imagination. Instead of celebrating TB, writers, joined by health reformers, saw TB through the lens of realism. They linked the disease to poverty, unsafe working conditions, overcrowded housing, poor diet, and the failure of government to safeguard the public's health. Rather than glorifying consumptives, this change in attitude depicted them as the victims of a cruel, punishing illness. TB was no longer something to spark the artistic imagination; it was now a microbial insult to mankind and an indictment against the society that tolerated it.

Young Women's Christian Association. Numerous others joined in a resurgence of prohibitionism. Americans had always drunk a lot of alcohol, and consumption had been increasing since the Civil War. By the 1890s, earlier movements to control consumption had faded, leaving only three states with prohibition laws. After a quarter of a century of inactivity, the Woman's Christian Temperance Union revived and by 1898 had 10,000 local branches. It was assisted by the Anti-Saloon League (organized in 1893) and such church organizations as the Temperance Society of the Methodist Episcopal church.

Some of the prohibitionists were Protestant fundamentalists who considered the consumption of alcohol a sin; others were concerned with its social impact. Urban reformers constantly saw the consequences of alcohol abuse in domestic violence, accidents, and pauperism. Alcohol was the root of so many social problems that to ignore it was like "bailing water out of a tub with the tap turned on; letting the . . . liquor traffic run full blast while we limply stood around and picked up the wreckage." The AMA reported the physically devastating effects of alcoholism. Many in the Anti-Saloon League were also dismayed by the part played by drinking establishments in machine politics.

The idea of legislating morality for the good of society spilled over into the sexual sphere. A major area of concern was prostitution, and its opponents had a variety of motivations. Some stressed its role in the spread of venereal disease. Others deplored the exploitation of women and the double standard that allowed only men sexual freedom. For some it was morally wrong; to others it was just one more social evil—a product of environment rather than original sin. Many linked it with immigration as they did alcohol abuse. The crusade against this age-old problem had deep roots, but at the turn of the century it followed a typically progressive path. Muckraking journalists enraged the public with lurid accounts of "white slavery" rings that kidnapped young women and forced them into prostitution. The first step toward eliminating the problem was to pressure local governments to establish commissions to study the issue. Most reports stressed the economic roots. One prostitute asked an investigator, "Do you suppose I am going back to earn five or six dollars

a week in a factory, when I can earn that amount any night and often much more?"

Some people believed prostitution was merely a symptom of a larger disease, and they became "purity crusaders." Dr. Will K. Kellogg wrote "The exorbitant demands of the sexual appetites encountered among civilized people are not the result of a normal instinct, but are due to the incitements of an abnormally stimulating diet, including alcohol, the seduction of prurient literature and so-called art, and the temptations of impure associations." After a national Purity Congress in 1895, the purity crusaders lobbied not only for the prohibition of alcohol and prostitution but also for such things as censorship and the regulation of narcotics.

Progressive social reform had two aims: control and justice. Women were deeply involved in social justice as well as control movements like prohibition. Middle-class women had long dominated humanitarian work, but during the 1890s their work took on a new aggressiveness. Women came to believe that aid to the poor was an inadequate response to society's ills; they wanted to attack the causes of poverty. They sought to improve wages and working conditions, especially for women, and to protect children from exploitation. To this end, they started several organizations. The National Consumers League, led by former Illinois factory inspector Florence Kelly, lobbied for protective legislation for women and children as well as better working and living conditions for all. Kelly became a leading advocate of child labor laws and was joined in this cause by Alabama clergyman Edgar Gardner Murphy, who proposed the formation of the National Child Labor Committee in 1904. Like most progressives, child labor reformers gathered data and photographs to document horrors for legislators at the local, state, and finally federal level.

A similar path was followed by many organizations that studied various urban problems and proposed solutions. The National Municipal League (1895) was a forum for improving city government. The National Housing Association (1910), seeking to obtain building codes with at least minimum health and safety standards, proposed federally subsidized housing. The American Association for Labor Legislation and the American Association for Old-Age Security lob-

Alarmed by the unhealthy child-care practices of many immigrants, visiting nurses went to immigrant homes to teach such things as the proper bathing of babies.

bied for protective legislation for labor and pension plans.

Some reformers were not content to be merely advocates for the poor and the weak; they wanted to become directly involved with such people in an effort to educate them and organize them to help themselves. Here again middle-class women played a key role. Foremost among such activities was the settlement house movement. Following the lead of Jane Addams of Hull House in Chicago, many young college-educated women moved into slum neighborhoods to live and work with those they sought to help. "From the first," Addams wrote, "it seemed understood that we were ready to perform the humblest neighborhood services. We were asked to wash the newborn babies, and to prepare the dead for burial, to nurse the sick, and to 'mind the children.' "

More than unselfishness motivated such women. One worker confessed that settlement houses gratified her "thirst to know how the other half lives." Some educated women wanted more freedom than marriage and part-time volunteer work seemed to offer. One appeal of settlement work was that men did not control it.

The result was a growing social feminism that cut across class lines. An example was the founding of the National Women's Trade Union League in 1905. Through it, wealthy supporters organized women workers, joined their strikes, and trained leaders.

At first such activity seemed to draw attention away from the suffrage movement. Women's roles in progressive reforms, however, convinced many people that women not only deserved the right to vote but also that their political participation would be socially beneficial. Jane Addams asserted, "If women have in any sense been responsible for the gentler side of life which softens and blurs some of its harsher conditions may they not have a duty to perform in our American cities?" Arguments based on women's "special role," however, cut both ways. In articles with such titles as "Famed Biologist's Warning on the Peril in Votes to Women," writers charged that voting was so "unnatural" for women that pregnant women would miscarry and nursing mothers' milk would cease to flow. As during the fight for ratification of the Equal Rights Amendment in the 1970s, not all opponents were male. Mrs. A. J. George of the National Association Opposed to Woman Suffrage declared, "The Woman-suffrage movement is an imitation-of-man movement, and as such, merits the condemnation of every normal man and woman."

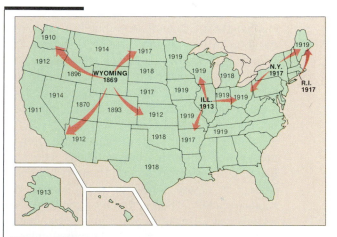

Women's Suffrage
Between 1869 and 1919, states gradually allowed women to vote in presidential elections, foreshadowing the Nineteenth Amendment.

Women employed a variety of tactics in their fight for the vote. Here Dr. Anne Shaw and Carrie Chapman Catt lead 20,000 marchers down Fifth Avenue in New York City.

In the face of such opposition, suffragists began to escalate their demands for the vote. Many became convinced that only national action could be effective. Thus the National American Woman Suffrage Association, led by Carrie Chapman Catt after 1915, began a broad-based campaign for a federal amendment to the Constitution. More militant women followed the young Quaker, Alice Paul, who founded the National Woman's party in 1914. She preferred the tactics of British suffragists who had picketed, gone on hunger strikes, and actively confronted both politicians and police.

Another group in the social justice movement sought to improve relations between blacks and whites. White Southerners had continued to devise forms of racial control to replace slavery. Their solution became a three-legged stool: legal segregation, disfranchisement, and violence. From the beginning, blacks resisted white efforts to suppress them. In city after city, African-Americans utilized almost every tool and tactic that would prove success-

ful in the 1960s. They marched, they lobbied legislative bodies, they petitioned, they challenged discriminatory legislation in courts, and they boycotted segregated streetcars. Under the leadership of Booker T. Washington, they also tried conciliation. Nothing stemmed the rising tide of racism.

As conditions grew worse, Booker T. Washington seemed to grow even more accommodating, at least in public. Behind the scenes, however, he supported protest activities, using code names and secret funds. Educated African-Americans, however, became increasingly disenchanted with his public performance. They also resented his suppression of dissent by his fellow blacks. His influence with white politicians and philanthropists as well as his control of much of the black press gave him incredible power, which he used ruthlessly on occasion. The so-called anti-Bookerite radicals found their spokesperson in W. E. B. Du Bois. Unlike Washington, who had been born into slavery and educated at an industrial school, Du

Bois was born to free parents in Massachusetts and became the first African-American to receive a doctorate from Harvard.

Gifted with staggering intellectual brilliance, Du Bois expressed the frustrations and dreams of his fellow blacks in *The Souls of Black Folks* (1903). Of being black in America, he wrote, "one ever feels his twoness—an American, a Negro, two souls, two thoughts, two unreconciled strivings, two warring ideals in one dark body." In that book he also penned a polite but devastating critical analysis of Washington's leadership. Among other things, he objected to Washington's failure to recognize the importance of the vote, his emphasis on industrial education at the expense of higher education, his reluctance to criticize as well as praise white actions, and his willingness to give up previously won rights.

Relations between the two men deteriorated steadily after 1903, even though only immediate methods and not ultimate goals separated them. Both wanted the full acceptance of African-Americans as first-class citizens. To Washington, the best route was self-help and educating the masses. To these ends, he made Tuskegee Institute into an impressive institution staffed entirely by blacks. Du Bois, on the other hand, was more integrationist and believed the key to black advancement was in cultivating what he called the "Talented Tenth." To him, more of the limited education funds should go to train the ablest 10 percent of African-Americans for leadership through liberal arts and professional schooling.

By 1905 their differences were so great that Du Bois joined William Monroe Trotter in forming the Niagara Movement, an organization devoted to two main objectives: opposition to Washington's leadership and demands for "full manhood rights." Only about 50 educated African-Americans—mainly Northerners—joined, and the movement struggled to exist in the face of unrelenting sabotage by Washington. It played an important role, however, in convincing northern white progressives that an alternative to Washington was desirable. When a white mob in Springfield, Illinois, went on a rampage against African-Americans, concerned whites joined with Du Bois to found the National

Association for the Advancement of Colored People (NAACP) in 1909. At first the group was led and dominated by whites; Du Bois was the only African-American to hold a responsible position, as editor of its journal *The Crisis*. The organization became more black over time, but the focus of its activities remained essentially the same: education and propaganda, court challenges to discrimination, and lobbying for such legislation as a federal antilynching law.

Immigration policy became another source of organizational activity. The American Protective Association (1887) sought to control and limit the access of the "teeming masses yearning to breathe free." Members lobbied for literacy tests and quotas. One described a boatload of immigrants, saying "in every face there was something wrong—lips thick, mouth coarse, upper lip too long, cheek bones too high, chin poorly formed, the bridge of the nose hollowed, the base of the nose tilted, or else the whole face prognathous." While many Americans recoiled from the nation's pluralistic nature, others welcomed it. One wrote, "our dream of the United States ought not to be a dream of monotony," but instead an "orchestration of mankind." Thus some progressives formed the North American League for Immigrants to "protect the newcomers from unscrupulous bankers, steamship captains and fellow countrymen."

Even if most were middle class, progressives obviously came from all classes, and within classes there was a diversity of responses to the modernization of society and the economy. Many businesspeople organized to fight regulatory and labor legislation in such groups as the National Association of Manufacturers and the American Anti-Boycott Association. Others, however, joined such moderate reform groups as the Reform Municipal Voters League and the Chamber of Commerce. Some viewed labor unionism as more desirable than government regulation. The National Civic Federation was founded in 1901 with wealthy Republican politician Mark Hanna as president and labor leader Samuel Gompers as vice president. The group accepted unionization and sought to bring together employers, employees, and the general public to discuss industrial problems.

W. E. B. Du Bois, shown here in the editorial offices of the *Crisis* at the New York headquarters of the NAACP, was at first the only African-American to hold a significant office in the organization.

The drive to organize pervaded all of society, creating such diverse groups as the Boy Scouts of America (1910), the Rotary Club (1915), the National Collegiate Athletic Association (1906), the National Birth Control League (1915), and even the Aero Club of America (1905) to popularize "ballooning as a sport, especially among the more wealthy class." Americans came to believe in cooperative efforts to reach goals. In unprecedented numbers they also began to look to government for answers—starting at the city level and moving up to Washington.

Urban Beginnings

Progressivism was largely a response to modernization, and it first confronted the most visible problems, most of which were found in the cities. Incredibly rapid increases in urban populations outpaced the ability of "small-town" governments to meet the challenges. Political machines provided needed services but came under attack in the 1890s as inefficient and corrupt. Progressivism began to emerge in cities even while most attention was still focused on the rural-based Populists. Middle- and upper-class reformers demanded that governments operate "on a strict business basis" and be run "not by partisans, either Republican nor Demo-

cratic, but by men who are skilled in business management and social service."

Urban reformers' victories included the secret ballot and voter registration in some cities. Then in 1900, a model for efficient, nonpartisan city government emerged from the chaos created when a devastating hurricane killed more than 6000 people in Galveston, Texas. Local government broke down and the state legislature appointed a five-man commission to run the city. The idea spread to over 400 cities by World War I. A refinement was added in 1913, when in the wake of a disastrous flood, the government of Dayton, Ohio, hired a city manager to run the city on a day-to-day basis.

The cost of efficiency was decreased democracy. Indeed, some urban reformers were openly antidemocratic. One wrote in 1901, "Ignorance should be excluded from control. City business should be carried on by trained experts selected on some other principle than popular suffrage." The ward system, under which aldermen were elected by district, was seen as a problem because, as a Chicago businessman noted in 1911, "Men of successful experience and ability large enough to do justice to public affairs will seldom live and bring up families in the poorer wards." Such reformers naively sought to take "politics" out of government, but by "politics" they often meant the voice of people not like themselves. Nevertheless, these goals contradicted broader support for democracy, and by 1914 most city commissioners were required to run for election—often, however, in at-large elections rather than by district.

Middle-class progressives sometimes found their will thwarted by lower-class voters. Breaking up urban machines often destroyed the informal welfare networks that met the needs of the poor. When that happened, the poor rejected the new efficiency. In 1901, the Tammany Hall machine recaptured New York with the campaign slogan "To hell with reform." Poor immigrants did not accept that their ignorance and "foreign ways" were at the root of urban problems. "It is not so much the under crust," one declared, "as the upper crust that endangers the interests of the people."

In a number of cities, voters elected mayors who sympathized with working-class desires. Tom L. Johnson, elected mayor of Cleveland in 1901, rejected Americanization efforts to impose middle-class morality on the poor. "I am not trying to enforce Christianity," he proclaimed, "only make it possible." To this end he expanded social services and brought about the public ownership of the waterworks, gas and electric utilities, and public transportation, thereby reducing their costs to the poor. After his election 1899, Mayor Samuel "Golden Rule" Jones sought to establish the "Cooperative Commonwealth, the Kingdom of Heaven on Earth," in Toledo, Ohio. Until his death in 1904, he worked to provide free kindergartens, free playgrounds, free golf courses, and free concerts. He also reformed the police department, substituting light canes for the heavy clubs carried by patrolmen and prohibiting the jailing of people without charges. He made some powerful enemies and once declared, "Everyone is against me but the people." Most urban liberals depended on working-class voters.

The move toward public ownership of utilities was most avidly supported by the Socialists, who showed growing strength on the local level. In 1910 a Socialist was elected mayor of Milwaukee, and in the next year 70 others were elected in towns and cities across the nation. By 1912 about 1000 held offices in 33 states and 160 cities. Their rising power, however, helped trigger a backlash by middle-class voters, who favored regulatory commissions to public ownership of utilities.

Urban progressivism was obviously not a coherent, unified movement. Different groups at different times succeeded in different cities. Social services were cut to lower business taxes in some cities and expanded in others. In most cities the evils of overcrowded, unhealthy tenements were attacked with varying degrees of success with such measures as building codes. By the turn of the century, however, more and more people began to look to the states to solve problems.

Reform Reaches the State Level

Regardless of their objectives, many urban reformers eventually dabbled in state politics. The city had little power and the federal government seemed too remote. Thus the states became major battlegrounds for reform. The form and leadership of state progressivism were as diverse and complex as urban progressivism. In the South, most progressives worked through the Democratic party; in the Midwest and on the Pacific Coast, progressives captured the Republican party. In the industrial Northeast, progressives emerged in both major parties, but the Democrats were the more successful. In some cases progressive governors, such as Al Smith of New York, were the products of urban machines that embraced reform to hold onto their electorates. Others, such as Robert La Follette of Wisconsin, were Republican regulars who bypassed party leaders to ride reform to power. In the South, reform governors were elected by startlingly diverse constituencies. In Mississippi, small-town lawyer and editor James K. Vardaman was elected by the "redneck" vote of poor farmers. In Georgia, the urban middle class was the main supporter of Hoke Smith, publisher of the *Atlanta Journal*.

State progressives pursued four major goals: establishing "direct democracy," protecting the public by regulating the economy, increasing state services, and social control. Reformers passed many laws, but the impact of legislation was not always what they expected.

One progressive creed was dramatically stated by William Allen White: "The voice of the people is indeed the will of God." By World War I many states had adopted political procedures designed to give the people a more direct say in running the government. An initiative allowed voters to propose legislative changes, usually by petition; a referendum gave the public a mechanism for voting directly on controversial legislation; recall provided a way to remove elected officials. Many states also established direct primaries. Other states adopted measures to cleanse electoral procedures, including the secret ballot, voter registration, and corrupt practices legislation. The drive for direct democracy culminated in the Seventeenth Amendment to the Constitution (1913), which substituted the popular election of senators for their election by state legislatures.

The victories of women suffragists at the state level also expanded democracy. After the 1890s their efforts seemed to stall, and no new state gave women the vote until Washington did so in 1910. California acted the next year, and four other western states followed suit by 1916.

Born on a Montana ranch in 1880 and graduated from the University of Montana in 1902, Jeannette Rankin was elected to Congress in 1916.

That year Jeannette Rankin was elected to Congress from Montana. These victories encouraged the efforts to obtain a constitutional amendment allowing women to vote.

Clearly, progressive actions to protect the public and regulate the economy took many forms. In the West, especially, the emphasis was on regulating railroads and utilities, reflecting the region's Populist heritage. Legislatures created commissions to regulate the rates charged by both. At the same time, taxes on corporations were increased. For example, after La Follette's election in Wisconsin in 1900, state revenues from taxes on railroads grew from $1.9 million to $3.4 million.

In the industrialized states, workmen's compensation became a major goal. Horror stories about industrial accidents had long abounded, and muckrakers further inflamed the public. Then in 1911 a major tragedy chilled the hearts of Americans. A fire broke out at the Triangle Shirtwaist Company in New York just 30 minutes before closing time. The doors were locked to prevent the women who worked there from leaving early, and many fire escape ladders were either broken or missing. By the time the flames were doused, 147 workers, mainly women and girls, had lost their lives—47 had jumped to their deaths, littering the street with bodies. The Triangle fire was the worst example of escalating industrial accident rates. The only recourse for most maimed workers or their widowed spouses was to sue the company, which for many was not a realistic option. Some did get large settlements, however, which represented an unpredictable cost to businesses. Thus, the idea of mandatory insurance grew in popularity with support of many factory owners. Between 1910 and 1916, 32 states enacted workmen's compensation laws.

The work of the National Child Labor Committee and other organizations moved states to legislate protection for women and children. Progressives gathered evidence of the harm done to both by long working hours and unsafe, unhealthy conditions. State action was necessary, they argued, for two reasons: Women and children could not protect themselves and the nation's future depended on the health of both. By 1916, 32 states had laws regulating the hours worked by women and children, 11 had specified minimum wages for women, and every state regulated child labor in some manner. Other protective legislation included building and sanitary codes.

A number of states also expanded social services. Because of lobbying by settlement house workers, by 1914 some 20 states had provided mother's pensions to widows or abandoned wives with dependent children. The sums paid were meager, ranging from $2 to $15 a month for the first child and lesser amounts for the rest.

Funding for education also increased. A major area of reform was the expansion of compulsory education to the high school level. Support often came from businesses, which saw public education as a means of preparing individuals for life in an industrial society. As a result, very few public schools were modeled on John Dewey's progressive educational doctrines. Instead of promoting personal development, education, in the industrialists' minds, should inculcate discipline and punctuality. Hence school bells trained one for factory whistles and letter grades taught the value of individual initiative. Governments also made school organization more businesslike with increased power given to school superintendents and principals, who were expected to be trained in management techniques.

The flip side of state social justice legislation was increased efforts at social control. Prohibitionists won many victories in the states, especially in the South. That region provided fertile soil because of the strength of Protestant fundamentalism and the so-called race problem. One southern prohibitionist argued that blacks were "a child race in the South, and if drunkenness causes three-fourths of the crime ascribed to it, whiskey must be taken out of the Negro's hands," and that it was the duty "of the stronger race to forego its own personal liberty for the protection of the weaker race." Between 1907 and 1909 Georgia, Mississippi, North Carolina, Tennessee, and Alabama adopted state prohibition, and 14 other states had joined them by 1916.

The move toward social control infected all regions. Between 1907 and 1917, 16 states passed laws authorizing sterilization of various categories of allegedly unfit individuals. Social control measures were usually directed at minorities, so the South naturally offered the most extreme examples, but California progressives excluded Asians almost as ruthlessly. Southern whites trumpeted segregation as a reform, and they had the approval of many northern progressives. Even race relations muckraker Ray Stannard Baker wrote, "As for the Jim Crow laws in the South, many of them, at least, are at present necessary to avoid clashes between the ignorant of both races." Segregation was often enacted under progressive governors—a paradox only if the general progressive tendency toward social control is ignored.

In most ways, southern progressivism was for whites only. Increased school funding was common, but the bulk went to educating white children. The discrepancies between the amounts spent accelerated, making even more of a lie of the *Plessy* v. *Ferguson* (1896) formula of "separate but equal" facilities. In 1919 southern states spent an average of $12.16 per white student and $3.29 per black student. Racism remained a potent force. As governor of Mississippi from 1903 to 1907, James K. Vardaman pursued progressive reforms in such areas as convict-lease, school funding, and railroad regulation. At the same time he defended lynching, saying "We would be justified in slaughtering every Ethiopian on earth to preserve unsullied the honor of one Caucasian home."

The legacy of progressivism in the states was mixed, as were the motives of reformers. Regardless of their goals, most came to look to the federal government for help. One reformer expressed their frustration. "When I was in the city council . . . fighting for a shorter work day, [my opponents] told me to go to the legislature; now [my fellow legislators] tell me to go to Congress for a national law. When I get there and demand it, they will tell me to go to hell."

PROGRESSIVISM MOVES TO THE NATIONAL LEVEL

When McKinley was reelected in 1900, few expected a national reform leader; but for a quirk of fate they would have been right. As the 1900 Republican convention rolled around, party leaders realized they had a problem. Theodore Roosevelt had become a national hero in the wake of the Spanish-American War, but he had angered party regulars by supporting regulatory legislation as governor of New York. When they decided to "bury" Roosevelt in the vice presidency, Mark Hanna warned, "Don't you realize that there's only one life between that madman and the White House?" On September 6, 1901, anarchist Leon Czolgosz shot McKinley. Eight days later that one life was gone, and Roosevelt was president. It was not immediately apparent, however, that he would usher in reform. Many remembered that during the Pullman strike Roosevelt had suggested shooting the strikers. Most therefore did not expect the action he took in the 1902 coal strike. That year, however, became the first in a decade and a half of snowballing reform that would result in a massive amount of legislation and four constitutional amendments by 1920.

Roosevelt and New Attitudes Toward Government Power

Roosevelt became the most forceful president since Lincoln, but few men have looked or sounded less presidential. He was short, nearsighted, beaver-toothed, and talked in a high-pitched voice. A frail, asthmatic child, he seemed intent on proving his manliness. Thus his life became a robust adventure of sports, hunting, and camping. Once while president he took a foreign diplomat skinny-dipping in the Potomac. His exuberance, vitality, and wit captivated most Americans. They called him "Teddy" and named a stuffed bear after him. To understand him, an observer declared, one had to remember "the president is really only six years old." He was not a simple man, however. His hobbies included writing history books, and he displayed a keen intellect that he had honed at Harvard.

Born into an aristocratic Dutch family in New York, Roosevelt rejected a leisurely life for the rough and tumble world of politics, which his friends declared was an occupation for saloonkeepers and such. "I answered," he wrote in his autobiography, "that if this were so it merely meant that the people I knew did not belong to the governing class, and that I intended to be one of the governing class." His privileged background made him an unlikely candidate for a reformer, yet he ended up making reform both fun and respectable. He saw himself as a conservative, but declared, "The only true conservative is the man who resolutely sets his face toward the future." To preserve what was vital, one had to reform. The conservatives of his time, however, rejected his call for change and continued to insist on laissez-faire policies and limited government.

Roosevelt, on the other hand, shared two progressive sentiments. One was that government should be efficiently run by able, competent people. The other was that industrialization had created the need for expanded governmental action. "A simple and poor society," he observed, "can exist as a democracy on the basis of sheer individualism. But a rich and complex society cannot so exist." As a result of these two sentiments, Roosevelt reorganized and revitalized the executive branch, modernized the army command structure and the consular service, and pursued the federal regulation of the economy that has characterized twentieth-century America.

Although he was later remembered more for his "trust-busting" and "Square Deal," Roosevelt considered conservation his greatest domestic accomplishment. It was the topic of his first presidential address. "We are prone to think of the resources of this country as inexhaustible; this is not so," he later warned Congress. In 1902 he backed the Newlands Reclamation Act, which set aside the proceeds from public land sales for irrigation and reclamation projects. He also used presidential power to add almost 150 million acres to national forests and to preserve valuable coal and water sites for national development. With his ally, chief forester, Gifford Pinchot, he sponsored a National Conservation Congress in 1908.

Some businesspeople already disliked Roosevelt for his conservation policies, but he aggravated others by two actions in 1902. The first was his handling of the coal strike, which served notice that the government could no longer be counted on to come automatically to the aid of management in labor disputes. The

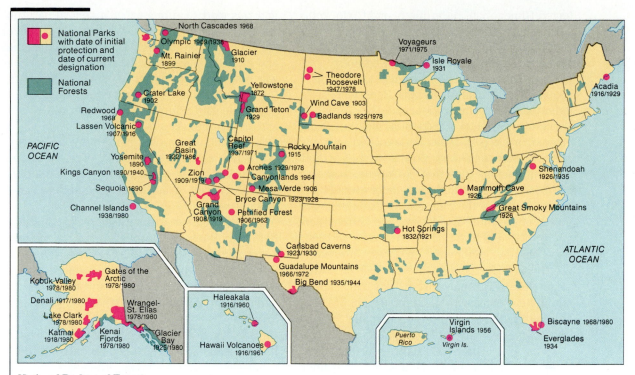

National Parks and Forests

Under the presidency of Theodore Roosevelt, who considered conservation his most important domestic achievement, millions of acres of land were set aside for national parks and forests.

second was a suit against Northern Securities Company under the Sherman Antitrust Act. Roosevelt's trust-busting was an answer to progressive prayers. Antimonopoly was a strong component of progressivism. Most agreed with Louis Brandeis that "If the Lord had intended things to be big, he would have made men bigger—in brains and character." Antitrust action had not been undertaken on a large scale in the cities and states only because federal action seemed necessary.

Northern Securities was a wise choice for action. It was a highly unpopular combination of northwestern railroad systems engineered by such heavyweights as James J. Hill and J. P. Morgan. The suit infuriated Hill, who complained, "It seems hard that we should be compelled to fight for our lives against the political adventurers who have never done anything but pose and draw a salary." In 1904 the Supreme Court ordered the company's dissolution. That same year, in a case against the major meat

packers, the Court also reversed the *E. C. Knight* ruling that exempted manufacturing from federal antitrust law.

The rulings pleased Roosevelt, who rejected the Court's earlier narrow, strict interpretations of the Constitution. Instead, he believed that the Constitution "must be interpreted not as a straight-jacket . . . but as an instrument designed for the life and healthy growth of the Nation." In his desire to expand federal power, he was once credited with asking "What's the Constitution between friends?" Yet Roosevelt was not a true convert to trust-busting.

"This is an age of combination," he wrote, "and any effort to prevent all combination will be not only useless, but in the end vicious." At the same time he believed "of all the forms of tyranny the least attractive and the most vulgar is the tyranny of mere wealth." Thus he attacked trusts that abused their power and left alone trusts that acted responsibly. He preferred to negotiate differences, and to do so he established in 1904 a Bureau of Corporations within the Department of Commerce and Labor, which had been created the year before.

Campaigning on the promise to provide a "Square Deal" to all Americans, Roosevelt easily defeated the Democratic candidate Alton B. Parker in the 1904 presidential election. Now elected in his own right, he launched into expanding the regulatory power of the federal government. His top priority over the objection of conservative Republican senators was effectively to control the railroads by expanding the power of the Interstate Commerce Commission (ICC). Although the Elkins Act, passed in 1903, had already eliminated rebates, Roosevelt wanted to go further and give the ICC the power to set rates. Through shrewd political maneuvering he got this with the Hepburn Act of 1906, although he had to give up his demand for limited court review of rate decisions.

The publication of Upton Sinclair's *The Jungle* in that same year caused a consumer uproar for regulation of the food and drug industries. A chemist in the Agriculture Department, Harvey W. Wiley had long been analyzing food products for chemical adulteration by testing additives on volunteers known as the "Poison Squad." His data were supplemented by an investigation of the meat-packing industry ordered by Roosevelt, which proved the truth of Sinclair's charges of filth and contamination. As a result, Congress passed the Pure Food and Drug Act and the Meat Inspection Act on the same day in 1906. By 1908 Roosevelt had left his indelible mark on the nation and decided not to run for reelection. He cast his support to William Howard Taft, who easily defeated William Jennings Bryan, the Democratic nominee and loser for the third time. Roosevelt then retired and went to hunt lions in Africa, a move that led J. P. Morgan to toast "Health to the Lions."

Taft and Quiet Progressivism

William Howard Taft brought to the presidency a distinguished record of public service. An Ohio lawyer, he had served as a federal judge, the first civil governor of the Philippines, and secretary of war. He did not, however, look presidential; he weighed more than 350 pounds

and this lead to rumors that a special bathtub was to be installed in the White House. Unlike his predecessor, he was far from charismatic and indeed quite shy. Legalistic and precise, he was neither a fiery writer nor speaker. In short, he was incapable of rallying public support for any cause, and reformers were especially skeptical about him. As a judge he had been called the "injunction standard bearer" by labor leaders. When soldiers shot into the crowd at the Haymarket riot, he confided, "they have only killed six as yet. This is hardly enough to make an impression."

Indeed Taft was essentially more conservative than Roosevelt, especially in his view of governmental power. "The lesson must be learned," he argued, "that there is only a limited zone within which legislation and governments can accomplish good." Further, he declared, "We can, by passing laws which cannot be enforced, destroy that respect for laws . . . which has been the strength of people of English descent everywhere." On the other hand, his respect for the law extended to the Sherman act.

Without federal regulation, meat packers exploited workers and allowed rats and other contaminants to be processed with meat to make sausage.

"We are going to enforce that law or die in the attempt," he promised, and far more cases were prosecuted in his administration than during the so-called trust-buster Roosevelt's tenure.

In his own quiet way Taft was as sympathetic to reform as Roosevelt. He supported the eight-hour day and favored legislation to improve mine safety. He also urged passage of the Mann-Elkins Act of 1910, which increased the rate-setting power of the ICC and extended its jurisdiction to telephone and telegraph companies. The Sixteenth and Seventeenth amendments were initiated under his presidency. Purity crusaders also won a victory in 1910 with the passage of the Mann Act, which made it illegal to transport women across state lines for "immoral purposes."

Nevertheless, Taft was not forceful enough to preside effectively over the growing divisions within the Republican party. The conservatives, led by the powerful Senator Nelson W. Aldrich, were determined to draw the line against further reform. At the same time, progressive Republicans such as Robert La Follette and George Norris were growing rebellious. Conflict came on several fronts. The first was the tariff. In his campaign Taft had promised a lower tariff, but in the end he accepted the much compromised Payne-Aldrich Tariff. While placing many nonessential items on the duty-free list, it actually raised some key duties. It disappointed reformers immensely. Listing such duty-free items as silkworm eggs, canary birdseed, hog bristle, leeches, and skeletons, the political humorist Finley Peter Dunne had his fictional bartender, Mr. Dooley, proclaim, "The new tariff puts these familyer commodyties within the reach iv all." Taft had suffered a defeat, but foolishly did not admit it. He called the tariff the "best" ever passed. In reality he backed down on his pledges because he believed the president should not interfere unduly with the legislative branch. He also simply had an accommodating personality. One Republican griped, "The trouble with Taft is that if he were Pope he would think it necessary to appoint a few Protestant Cardinals."

Caught in the middle of several conflicts, Taft eventually alienated the progressive wing of his party as well as Teddy Roosevelt. He first supported and then abandoned party insur-

At his inauguration in 1909, William Howard Taft did not realize the challenges he would face in Congress from a divided Republican party.

gents who challenged the power of conservative Speaker of the House "Uncle Joe" Cannon. Later, when Gifford Pinchot protested a sale of public lands by Secretary of the Interior Richard A. Ballinger, Taft fired him. That action infuriated both conservationists and Roosevelt, who was also irritated by Taft's antitrust prosecutions. Roosevelt believed that a case had been pursued against U.S. Steel to embarrass him. The investigation exposed a deal he made with J. P. Morgan in 1907 in return for the banker's aid in stemming a financial panic.

By 1912 progressive Republicans were ready to bolt the party if Taft were renominated, and Roosevelt declared his intention to run. The fight for the nomination became bitter. Taft called Roosevelt's supporters "political emotionalists or neurotics." Roosevelt labeled Taft's people as "men of cold heart and narrow mind, who believe we can find safety in dull timidity and dull inaction." As president, Taft was able to control the convention. The defeated Roosevelt walked out with his supporters and formed a third party, known as the Progressive or Bull Moose party.

Robert La Follette in Cumberland, Wisconsin, in 1897. La Follette, known for progressive reforms as governor of and U.S. senator from Wisconsin, was part of the split in the Republican party between progressives rebelling against Taft and conservatives opposing further reforms.

As soon became apparent, the real battle was between Wilson and Roosevelt. It was marked by an unusually high level of debate over the proper role of government in a modern, industrialized society. Wilson declared, "What this country needs above everything else is a body of laws which will look after the men who are on the make rather than the men who are already made." Labeling his program "New Freedom," his aim was the restoration of competition and his tool was to be trust busting. Roosevelt, on the other hand, believed that big business was not necessarily bad, but proclaimed, "Somehow or other we shall have to work out methods of controlling the big corporations without paralyzing the energies of the business community." His answer was "New Nationalism"—the expansion of federal regulatory activities to control rather than dismantle the trusts. Big government would offset the power of big business. Their rhetoric differed sharply, but in their presidencies each practiced a little of both "New Freedom" and "New Nationalism."

Many leading reformers attended the Progressive convention, which often resembled a religious revival with hymn singing and marches. Its platform endorsed such wide-ranging reforms as abolition of child labor; federal old-age, accident, and unemployment insurance programs; an eight-hour day; and women's suffrage. At Roosevelt's request, however, a plank supporting black equality was deleted. Calling the major parties "husks with no real soul," he accepted its nomination.

With the Republicans divided, Democratic chances of recapturing the White House increased. A former Republican senator lamented that the only unanswered question was "Which corpse gets the most flowers?" The scent of victory led to a hard fight for the Democratic nomination, which New Jersey's progressive governor, Woodrow Wilson, won on the forty-sixth ballot. The Socialist party nominated Eugene V. Debs, making it a four-way race.

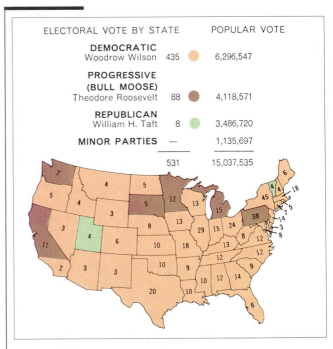

ELECTORAL VOTE BY STATE		POPULAR VOTE
DEMOCRATIC Woodrow Wilson	435	6,296,547
PROGRESSIVE (BULL MOOSE) Theodore Roosevelt	88	4,118,571
REPUBLICAN William H. Taft	8	3,486,720
MINOR PARTIES	—	1,135,697
	531	15,037,535

Election of 1912
Woodrow Wilson did not receive a majority of the popular vote, but the split in the Republican party gave him the majority of the votes in the Electoral College.

The split in the Republican party enabled the Democrats to capture not only the White House but also the Senate. Democrats also consolidated their control of the House, so Wilson entered the presidency with his party solidly in power. Nevertheless, Wilson did not receive a majority of the popular vote. He got 6.3 million votes, Roosevelt 4.1 million, Taft 3.5 million, and Debs nearly 1 million. In the Electoral College, however, Wilson won an impressive 435 votes to Roosevelt's 88 and a mere 8 for Taft.

Wilson and Moral Progressivism

As the third Progressive-Era president, Woodrow Wilson differed from his predecessors in both appearance and leadership style. He looked very much like the moralistic professor he was. The son and grandson of Presbyterian ministers, Wilson was raised in the South and practiced law in Atlanta before receiving his doctorate from Johns Hopkins University in Baltimore. His book *Congressional Government* was published in 1895, and he became president of Princeton University in 1902 before being elected governor of New Jersey. His religion was an important factor in his personality. "My life would not be worth living," he declared, "if it were not for the driving power of religion."

Wilson was not the kind of man whom people named stuffed animals after or gave nicknames. His self-righteousness was not endearing. One politician noted that when Wilson "said something to me . . . I didn't know whether God or him was talking." Although much less charismatic, Wilson did resemble Roosevelt in being a better speaker than Taft and in his view of the role of the president. Roosevelt had called the presidency a "bully pulpit," and Wilson agreed that the president should be the "political leader of the nation" because "his is the only national voice in politics." Unlike Taft, he argued that the president must be "as much concerned with the guidance of legislation as with the just and orderly execution of the laws."

Wilson's activism coincided with growing demands for further reform. Investigations and amendments launched earlier came to fruition during his presidency. The result was an outpouring of legislation. In 1913, his first year in office, the Sixteenth Amendment was ratified,

A distinguished professor, Woodrow Wilson brought both competence and a grim moral determination to the presidency.

allowing the imposition of a federal income tax. It appeared as a provision of the Underwood Tariff, which was passed in a special session of Congress that year. Wilson called the session to redeem a campaign pledge to lower duties as part of the New Freedom goal of restoring competition. During the tariff hearings, lobbyists were so plentiful Wilson complained, "a brick wouldn't be thrown without hitting one of them." This time, however, they did not all prevail. Congress significantly lowered duties for the first time since the Civil War. To recoup lost revenues, a graduated tax of from 1 to 6 percent was placed on personal incomes of $3000 and over.

Congress passed banking reform the same year. Following the panic of 1907, congressional investigations were launched into its causes. Everyone, including bankers, had come to believe the nation's banking system needed to be stabilized by governmental action. The question was *how* to do it. Wall Street wanted a centralized system owned and controlled by bankers. Others wanted a more decentralized system owned or controlled by the government. The Federal Reserve Act of 1913 was a compromise. It established the Federal Reserve System of 12 regional banks owned by bankers but under the control of a presidentially appointed Federal Reserve Board.

Prohibitionists won their first national victory with the Webb-Kenyon Act of 1913. It allowed dry states to interfere with the transportation of alcohol across their state lines. The next year those concerned with the large amounts of narcotics in patent medicines rejoiced over the passage of the Harrison Narcotic Act. It required a doctor's prescription for the sale of a list of controlled substances. Congress also compelled manufacturers of these drugs to register with the government and maintain sales records.

In 1914 Congress also took actions to deal with monopolies and to regulate business. In September it established the Federal Trade Commission to replace the Bureau of Corporations. The five-person body was charged with investigating alleged violations of antitrust law and could issue "cease and desist" orders against corporations found guilty of unfair trade practices. The next month the Clayton Antitrust Act sought to close some of the loopholes of the Sherman act and prohibited a number of business practices such as price discrimination. One provision declared that labor unions were not to be considered illegal combinations in restraint of trade—a move designed to undermine the use of court injunctions against strikers.

At that point Wilson believed he had accomplished his agenda. He was not a supporter of further labor legislation or farm-credit plans. A firm opponent of paternalism, he said, "The old adage that God takes care of those who take care of themselves is not gone out of date. No federal legislation can change that thing. The minute you are taken care of by the government you are wards, not independent men." As the election of 1916 approached, however, progressives reminded Wilson of the importance of the farm and labor vote. Legislation to win those votes soon followed. Farmers were given the Federal Farm Loan Act, which provided low-interest credit, and legislation giving federal supplemental funding for agricultural specialists in each county. Labor got the Keating-Owen Child Labor Act, which barred goods made by children under 16 from interstate commerce; the Adamson Act, which established an eight-hour day for railroad workers; and the Workman's Compensation Act, which provided protection to federal employees. Progressives were also pleased by Wilson's appointment of Louis Brandeis to the Supreme Court. All of these actions helped to ensure victory over the Republican nominee Charles Evans Hughes in 1916.

PROGRESSIVISM IN THE INTERNATIONAL ARENA

Many progressives did not believe that progress was limited by national boundaries. In their eyes, human beings had the capacity to create a more just and orderly society both at home and abroad. The progressive spirit was optimistic, and progressive victories on the home front merely expanded Americans' confidence in their ability to solve problems—even on the international level. This confidence was further bolstered by the nation's economic growth and victory in the Spanish-American War.

Everyone agreed that by 1900, America's status in the world had changed. How to respond to those changes was the unanswered question. Just as people differed over what alterations, if any, were required in domestic policies, various visions of a new American foreign policy also emerged. For some, progressivism simply redefined and reinvigorated the old ideas of manifest destiny. The United States would solve its problems at home and then remake the world in its own image. Such a new world order would also open up new markets for America's industrial and agricultural surpluses. Other progressives believed that democratic principles required that all people, even foreigners, be free to determine their own destinies. Order and justice were two progressive goals that sometimes conflicted. The conflict was also apparent in the international arena.

Big Stick Diplomacy

The first Progressive-Era president was Theodore Roosevelt, and his foreign policy reflected the same kind of vigor he displayed in everything else. His "macho" foreign policy followed his belief that a man's mission was to "work, fight, and breed." He believed progress and order could benefit the world as well as the nation. He also asserted Congress was "not well fitted for the shaping of foreign policy" and expanded presidential power in the conduct of diplomacy. It was his destiny to deal with the legacies of increased power and influence from the Spanish-American War. Order having been restored in Cuba and Philippines by 1903, Roosevelt launched the United States into the role of policeman. His doctrine was to "speak softly and carry a big stick," but he really only lived up to the second half of the slogan.

Possession of the Philippines brought with it concern over turbulent Asian politics. Most alarming was the emergence of Japan after its unexpected victories in the Russo-Japanese War (1904–1905). Often playing the role of arbiter at home, Roosevelt now shifted his arena and mediated the crisis at the Portsmouth, New Hampshire, conference in August 1905—an action that won him a Nobel Peace Prize. Japan remained a formidable rival, however, and agreements were reached to respect each other's Asian interests. In the Pacific, Roosevelt's "big stick" was displayed by conspicuous stops there during a 1907–1909 tour of America's "Great White Fleet." He meant to intimidate the Japanese, but he failed to halt their growing power.

Within the Western Hemisphere, Roosevelt was even less reluctant to threaten or use force. In 1906 he responded to Cuban demonstrations against the Platt Amendment and insurrection by sending in marines, who stayed until 1909. "I am doing my best," he declared, "to persuade the Cubans that if only they will be good, they will be happy. I am seeking the very minimum of interference necessary to make them good." The marines could be very persuasive.

Progress and strategic considerations also demanded that a canal in Central America link the Atlantic and Pacific oceans. Roosevelt was determined to make it happen. There were two possible routes: one through Nicaragua and one across the Panamanian isthmus, which belonged to Colombia. A start had been made in Panama by a French company, which ran out of funds and was reorganized as the New Panama

Canal Company. The new company's major asset was its concession from Colombia that extended to 1904.

Three commissions appointed to determine the route recommended Nicaragua, primarily because the New Panama Canal Company demanded $190 million for its rights, property, and previous work. Its stockholders, mainly Americans, were frantic to convince Congress to choose the Panamanian route. They dropped their demand to $40 million, contributed profusely to campaign funds, and hired a full-time lobbyist—Philippe Bunau-Varilla, the French chief engineer of the original company. In June 1902, Congress authorized efforts to secure the rights to a Panamanian canal. The Hay-Herran Treaty provided the United States with rights to a 6-mile-wide zone in return for a $10 million payment to Colombia and an annual rental fee of $250,000 to begin 9 years after the ratification of the treaty. As in America, ratification required the consent of the Colombian senate, which in August 1903 rejected the treaty unanimously. Its motive was probably to delay the treaty until 1904, when the New Panama Canal Company's concession expired and Colombia might receive some of the $40 million originally earmarked for the company.

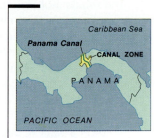

Panama Canal
The Panama Canal provided a strategic link between the Atlantic and the Pacific oceans.

Roosevelt was furious. "The blackmailers of Bogota," he roared, should not be allowed "permanently to bar one of the future highways of civilization." He drafted a message to Congress proposing to take the canal zone by force, but never delivered it. A different solution was found. Bunau-Varilla engineered a Panamanian revolution by providing people with a national constitution, flag, and anthem as well as assurances that the United States would not let their revolt fail. He was right. Most Colombian troops were prevented from even getting to the so-called revolution by the USS *Nashville*. Three days after its start, Roosevelt recognized the independence of the Republic of Panama. The

American secretary of state and the French citizen Bunau-Varilla, who had demanded to be made ambassador to the United States, then quickly drafted the Hay-Bunau-Varilla Treaty with essentially the same terms as the Hay-Herran Treaty—only now the payment went to the rebels, not Colombia.

American actions enraged people all over the world. At first Roosevelt denied any part in the revolution, but he eventually admitted, "I took the Canal Zone and let Congress debate; and while the debate goes on the Canal does also." In 1914, the canal, a monument to both progress and Yankee imperialism, was completed. It was a big investment, one that required protection from foreign military vessels.

At the same time, Latin American countries sometimes fell behind in debt payments to such European powers as Britain and Germany. As a result those two nations blockaded Venezuela in 1902–1903. A year later, Roosevelt announced that the United States would assume the responsibility of seeing that the nations of the Caribbean behaved themselves and paid their debts. European intervention, therefore, would not be necessary. Known as the Roosevelt Corollary to the Monroe Doctrine, this policy justified U.S. intervention in such places as the Dominican Republic, Nicaragua, and Haiti. Roosevelt's "big stick" diplomacy established America as the "police of the Western Hemisphere"—a role that would last long into the twentieth century.

Dollar Diplomacy

Before becoming president, William Howard Taft had served as governor-general in the Philippines and as Roosevelt's troubleshooter in Cuba. These experiences convinced Taft of two principles. The first was the need for order and stability. The second was the limited capacity of armed force for solving problems. He also realized that the United States had a new source of power—its economic clout. From 1898 to 1909, American overseas investments had risen from about $800 million to more than $2.5 billion.

Called "dollar diplomacy," Taft's approach was to use dollars instead of bullets to ensure stability and order. He wanted American capital to replace European capital in Latin America in order to increase U.S. influence there. When British bondholders wanted to collect their debts from Honduras in 1909, Taft asked American financiers to assume the debt. In 1910 he convinced New York bankers to take over the assets of the National Bank of Haiti. When needed, however, Taft also wielded a big stick. He refused to recognize a revolution in Nicaragua until the leaders agreed to accept American credits to pay off British debts and sent marines to punctuate his point.

Missionary Diplomacy

As in domestic policies, Woodrow Wilson's foreign policy differed more in style than substance from his predecessors. Wilson's moralism did not stop at national boundaries. Indeed his sermonistic foreign policy has sometimes been called "missionary diplomacy." His gospel was American-style democracy. "When properly directed," he declared, "there is no people not fitted for self-government." That direction was to come from the United States. He spoke of "releasing the intelligence of America for the service of mankind" and proclaimed "every nation needs to be drawn into the tutelage of America."

The rhetoric was different from his predecessors, but the results were the same. Renouncing both big stick and dollar diplomacy, Wilson continued to maintain stability and order in the Caribbean by similar measures. He sent marines to the Dominican Republic and Haiti, and kept them in Nicaragua. His interventionism ran into more trouble in Mexico, where the overthrow of long-time dictator Porfirio Diaz in 1911 began a cycle of revolution. Just before Wilson entered office Victoriano Huerta came to power through assassination—an action that repulsed the moralistic Wilson. To the surprise of many, Wilson refused to extend diplomatic recognition to Huerta's government. Such recognition was generally routine whenever a government could demonstrate control; it did not imply approval.

Wilson simply refused to accept what he

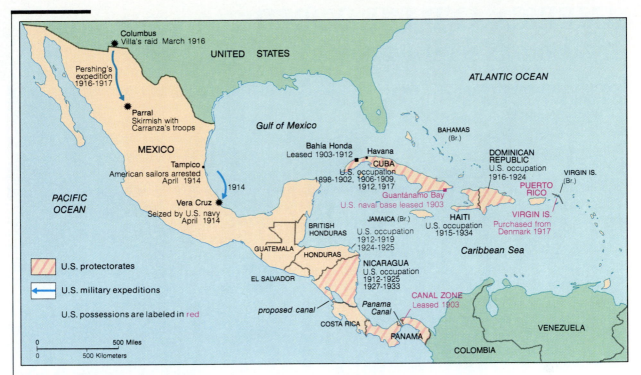

American Interventions in the Caribbean

Early in the twentieth century, the United States policed the Western Hemisphere and often took action when it judged Latin American countries were not running their affairs properly.

called a "government of butchers." He wrote one diplomat, "The United States intends not merely to force Huerta from power but to exert every influence it can to secure Mexico a better government under which all contracts and business concessions will be safer than they have ever been." Americans considered protection of contracts and concessions very important, and they controlled 75 percent of Mexico's mines, 60 percent of its oil, and 70 percent of its rubber. Wilson's tactics escalated from diplomatic pressure to landing troops at Veracruz, a move that infuriated Mexicans more than Huerta's despotism. Even after Huerta was overthrown, civil war continued between the government forces of Venustiano Carranza and rebels led by Pancho Villa.

In an attempt to draw America into the fracas, Villa launched a raid into New Mexico in March 1916. The tactic worked, and Wilson sent an expedition to capture Villa. Led by General John Pershing, American troops failed to find him. Soon they were 300 miles deep into Mexican territory, and as a result, on the brink of war with Carranza's government in January 1917. By then, however, America was being drawn into World War I, and Wilson decided to withdraw the troops. In the end he got basically the kind of government he wanted for Mexico, but Mexicans continued to believe that their government was their business and deeply resented the American intervention.

American involvement in World War I diverted attention from more than Mexico. Domestic reform took a backseat to "making the world safe for democracy." Yet war always brings changes on the home front. Thus the nation shifted gears, but progressivism did not entirely die. Indeed prohibitionists, woman suffragists, and immigration restrictionists won their greatest victories in the wake of war.

(Text continues on p. 752)

AMERICA AND THE WORLD
VERACRUZ: AN AFFAIR OF HONOR

U.S. Marines march into Veracruz to occupy the city while at the same time U.S. warships blockade the port to prevent delivery of weapons shipments from Europe. The occupation forces withdrew from Veracruz in November 1914, but U.S. troops remained in Mexico until 1917, when the United States finally recognized the new Mexican government established by Venustiano Carranza.

"It would be the irony of fate if my administration had to deal chiefly with foreign affairs," Woodrow Wilson remarked a few days before his inauguration as president in 1913. Wilson spoke the truth, as his own background had been limited almost exclusively to domestic affairs. In his career as a scholar, he had devoted years to the study of congressional government, and during his two-year stint as governor of New Jersey he had acquired first-hand knowledge of domestic affairs; but prior to entering the White House Wilson had evinced only a casual interest in international relations and knew very little about the workings or history of foreign affairs. As president, Wilson would face the ultimate test of his skills as a diplomatist in World War I, but his first challenge in foreign affairs came in revolution-torn Mexico, where he confronted warring political factions that demanded his attention from the day he entered office.

The problems in Mexico were as old as the nation. After winning independence from Spain in 1821, Mexico entered a period of profound political instability. More than a hundred governments came and fell during Mexico's first 50 years as a nation, as two factions, one conservative, the other liberal, fought for power. In broad terms, the conservative faction was composed of wealthy landowners who were aligned with the Catholic church and favored an aristocratic oligarchy (or even monarchy), and the liberal faction represented Mexico's nascent middle class and various peasant groups who favored democratic government and land reform.

Out of the constant clashes between these factions emerged General Porfirio Díaz, who ruled Mexico with an iron hand from the early 1870s to 1910. Díaz was a political strong man (*caudillo*) who drew his support from the military, wealthy landowners, and the Catholic church. As dictator, Díaz ended the political chaos and brought order to his nation, and he proved extremely adept at capitalizing on Mexico's new-found stability. He opened Mexico to foreign investors. Under his protective hand a flood of foreign businesspeople rushed in to tap Mexico's rich mineral wealth, to build railroads, and to exploit the agricultural sector of its economy. On the eve of World War I, American businesspeople valued their holdings in Mexico at one billion dollars. Yet only a handful of wealthy Mexicans benefited from the economic development of their nation, and the political stability Díaz brought to Mexico came at the expense of individual liberties. He crushed political opposition and turned a deaf ear to pleas for land reform.

In 1910, liberal opponents revolted and to the world's amazement Díaz proved to be a paper tiger. Unable to extinguish a series of small revolts that sprang up across Mexico, he fled the country and went into exile in France. Mexico's new leader was Francisco I. Madero, an idealist who championed the middle class's aspirations for democracy and the peasant class's demands for land reform. Madero had hardly settled into the presidency before new revolts broke out, plunging Mexico into political chaos. On February 22, 1913, less than two weeks before William Howard Taft's term as president ended, Madero and his vice president were assassinated by federal troops under the command of General Victoriano Huerta, who immediately proclaimed himself Mexico's new ruler. Despite the urgent recommendations of his ambassador to Mexico, Henry Lane Wilson, who was strongly identified with the Republican administration's "dollar diplomacy," President Taft did not extend diplomatic recognition to Huerta's government, leaving the issue to be resolved by the president-elect, Thomas Woodrow Wilson.

President Wilson refused to recognize Huerta's government. Wilson regarded Mexico's new strong man as a murderer and a usurper, a ruler who symbolized all that was wrong with Latin American governments. To Wilson's legalistic mind, diplomatic recognition implied moral approval, and he could never sanction a government that had seized power by substituting bullets for ballots. Moreover, no less than his claims to legitimacy, Huerta's claims to power were shaky. Following Madero's assassination, several political factions in Mexico revolted against Huerta. Emiliano Zapata led an army against federal troops in Morelos, a mountainous state in southern Mexico. In the north, Venustiano Carranza, the governor of Coahuila, declared himself the first chief of the Constitutionalist forces and won the allegiance of several powerful regional leaders, including Pancho Villa, Alvaro Obregon, and Pablo Gonzalez.

Because Huerta was not able to defeat his opponents in battle, his claim to controlling Mexico was suspect; and his apparent weakness only strengthened President Wilson's decision to withhold diplomatic recognition. In truth, Wilson wanted Huerta's government to fall, and American policy was designed to aid Huerta's opponents, particularly Carranza. As the self-proclaimed first chief of the Constitutionalist forces, Carranza appealed strongly to Wilson, who was anxious to find a tool for restoring democracy to Mexico. As Wilson confided to a British diplomat, "I am going to teach the South American republics to elect good men."

However noble his ambition, Wilson allowed his animus against Huerta to trigger an American invasion of Mexico. In April 1914, Mexican officials arrested several American sailors in Tampico, detained a mail courier, and delayed an official Department of State dispatch. Wilson used these minor incidents to precipitate a showdown with Huerta's government, and less than two weeks later American troops invaded the port city of Veracruz. At least 200 Mexicans died in the fighting that followed and another 300 were wounded, most of whom were noncombatant civilians. American troops remained in Veracruz for six months.

None of Mexico's warring factions approved the invasion and subsequent occupation of Veracruz. In fact, no issue has produced more bitterness in Mexico against the United States—not even the Mexican War. To Mexicans their defeat in the 1840s inflicted a serious wound to their national pride, but they saw the war as a lesson in power politics. Manifest destiny was a harsh policy, but Mexicans could understand the motives from which it sprang. Americans wanted American land, and they took it. What made the invasion of Veracruz so galling was that President Wilson clothed American aggression, in the words of one historian, "with the sanctimonious rainment of idealism." Because he insisted his acts were moral, Wilson "aroused both the hatred and the scorn of the Mexicans—hatred over the invasion but a deep scorn for what they saw as his hypocrisy."

In one sense, Wilson got what he wanted in Mexico. Huerta's government collapsed in 1915, and Carranza became the new president. In the larger sense, however, the United States was the big loser in Mexico. Mexicans deeply resented Wilson's arrogant assumption that he had the right to intervene in their internal affairs. Perhaps the ultimate lesson to be learned from Wilson's Mexican policy was that good intentions are no substitute for respecting the territorial integrity and independence of other nations.

PROGRESSIVE ACCOMPLISHMENTS, PROGRESSIVE FAILURES

The twentieth century began with great optimism about the power of human beings to shape their destinies. Progress, people believed, could be legislated. Efficient, noncorrupt government could provide order and stability, promote social justice, and improve personal morals. Groups organized to promote their goals, and more and more of them began to win their objectives. In the 1920s, however, some realized that legislation had not always had its desired effect, that not everyone had benefited equally, and that change had been far from radical.

The Impact of Legislation

Measured by direct results most progressive reforms proved disappointing. In some cases unintended consequences actually worked against the intended goals of laws. This often occurs when ideals confront reality. Solving one problem frequently creates another. Nevertheless, progressives established important precedents that opened doors to later, more effective reform.

Attempts to promote direct democracy were among the least effective. Direct election of senators did not seem to alter the kinds of people elected. Initiative, referendum, and recall were rarely used, and then not by people in general. The expense and organization needed for petition drives were beyond the reach of any but well-financed pressure groups. An unintended result of democratization was to increase the power of urban machines. Bosses may have had to work a little harder, but most were still able to dominate primaries as well as elections. The move toward popular voting increased the political power of populous cities and the machines that controlled them. The greatest failing of the movement was a dramatic drop in voter participation. Nevertheless, in some states, such as Wisconsin, government did become more responsive to public needs, and urban machines often adopted reform measures to maintain power.

Other kinds of urban reforms had varying results. In some, government did indeed become more efficiently and economically run. The competency and honesty of officials generally increased. An occasional consequence, however, was cuts in social services in less affluent neighborhoods. This was more likely to happen where the commissioner-manager system was adopted—usually in midsize cities without a tradition of machine politics. In other cities municipally owned utilities lowered rates, which provided real relief for the poor.

Attempts to regulate the railroads on either the state or national level rarely produced dramatic benefits for the general public. The chief advocates and beneficiaries of railroad regulation were frequently large shipping interests that did not share lower costs with consumers. With the Hepburn Act, Roosevelt did accomplish his primary goal of giving the ICC the power to set rates. The provision allowing court review of its decisions, however, made the act more significant as a precedent for expanded governmental power than as an immediate solution to problems. The courts ruled in favor of the railroads in most rate disputes.

Antimonopoly actions also did not always produce the intended results. For example, the breakups of Standard Oil and the American Tobacco Company did not increase competition or lower prices. Perhaps the only legislation to fulfill the promise of New Freedom was the Underwood Tariff, and it was reversed by the tariff legislation of the 1920s. The Clayton Antitrust Act was widely, and correctly, considered too vague for effective enforcement. The general counsel of the American Anti-Boycott Association analyzed the provision to exempt labor organizations from antitrust legislation and declared that the law "makes few changes in existing law as relating to labor unions, injunctions and contempts of court, and those are of slight practical importance." Later, the court decisions proved his assessment accurate.

The Federal Trade Commission (FTC) did not become an aggressive watchdog either. One of Wilson's cabinet members reported that the president viewed it as "a counsellor and friend to the business world," rather than as a "policeman to wield a club over the head of the business community." His appointments were fairly probusiness, and the appointments of the 1920s were even more so. In the end, the FTC proved beneficial to big business by protecting firms from unexpected suits and by outlawing many "unfair trade practices," many of which had promoted competition at the expense of stability. On the other hand, the FTC was also an important precedent.

Proclaimed victories for labor frequently turned out to be more symbolic than real. In the arbitration of the 1902 coal strike, for example, what the United Mine Workers did not receive is very significant: The union did not win recognition. As the 1920s would show, organized labor did not emerge from the progressive era any stronger. Yet the symbolism can be important. The precedent that the government would not automatically support the demands of management was later built upon during the New Deal of the 1930s.

Some labor legislation brought benefits but also produced unintended results. Child labor laws in combination with compulsory education legislation decreased the number of children from ages 10 to 15 who were working for wages from 1 in 5 in 1900 to 1 in 20 by 1930. During those same years, the number of students enrolled in secondary education increased by 800 percent. Both were desirable results, but in the short run at least, the poor received a mixed blessing. The incomes of a family's children were often crucial to its welfare, and no alternatives were provided. As one historian noted, "Child labor laws treated the symptoms and made the disease—poverty—worse." Much the same can be said about limits imposed on women's working hours. Laws establishing minimum wages for women helped somewhat to offset earning losses resulting from child labor legislation. In any event, laws such as the Child Labor Act were declared unconstitutional in the 1920s.

Workmen's compensation laws were an improvement over existing procedures but were not an unqualified victory of labor over management. Indeed, businesspeople eventually welcomed the relief from the growing number of suits instituted by hungry lawyers on a contingency fee basis. By agreeing to take a percentage of any damage awards and to charge no fee for lost cases, attorneys made it possible for poor workers to take legal action. The award schedule in most compensation plans provided payments far below what some lawyers had been winning in court. Workers, however, were guaranteed at least some compensation. For the industrialists, a predictable premium replaced the uncertainty of court actions, decreasing the risks and increasing stability in the cost of doing business.

The establishment of the Federal Reserve System also enhanced order and stability. Everyone benefited from the maintenance of cash reserves for emergencies, a more flexible currency, and national check clearing facilities. The banking system became more resistant to panics but, as 1929 would prove, not immune to them. Wall Street was not a big loser. Three of the five seats on the Federal Reserve Board went to large bankers, and the New York Federal Reserve bank quickly came to dominate the system. The new system, in other words, was a significant improvement, but far from a radical change.

From the consumer's point of view, the Pure Food and Drug Act and the Meat Inspection Act were great victories. After the rise of mass production and mass marketing, only federal action could provide adequate protection from adulteration of the nation's foodstuffs. Unintended beneficiaries, however, were the large drug and meat-packing companies that could more easily afford the increased expenses of meeting required production standards. Thus the effect was anticompetitive. Lobbying by the big meat packers also affected the final form of the legislation. Their victories included government payment of inspection costs and the deletion of the requirement to date canned meat. Like much progressive legislation, the final act did provide protection for consumers, but in a way agreeable to big business. Swift, one of the largest meat packers, even endorsed its passage in an advertisement declaring, "It is a wise law."

Other progressive legislation left mixed legacies. Roosevelt's conservation measures prevented wanton squandering of resources, but also aided the larger lumber companies. Morality legislation made undesirable activities illegal but at the same time more profitable for organized crime. It also fostered widespread disrespect for the law. With a maximum rate of 6 percent, the income tax did little to redistribute the huge fortunes of such men as J. P. Morgan but did establish an important tool for later use. A significant precedent was set by the Adamson Act, through which the federal government first dabbled in wage and in hour legislation. Many other progressive reforms were illusory or short lived. In the 1920s, lax enforcement and hostile court decisions reversed many of them. Nevertheless, laissez-faire had suffered an irreversible blow. That was a major accomplishment and perhaps as much as many progressives wanted.

Winners and Losers

Before the era was ended, people from almost every class and occupation had sought to take advantage of the climate of change to promote their interests. Obviously not all were equally successful. Few were unqualified winners or losers, but some gained far more than others, and some lost more than they gained. Clearly, large corporations were among the biggest winners. One historian labeled the movement "the triumph of conservatism." Given the basic moderation of all three presidents and most congressmen, as well as the resources and influence of big business, this may have been inevitable. It was not, however, the original intention of all legislation. To label most progressives as conservative is a gross mistake. They rejected the strict laissez-faire principles of nineteenth-century conservatives and embraced a vision of a more activist government.

Other winners included members of the growing body of middle-class technocrats. At all levels of government the search for orderly, efficient management created new job opportunities for engineers, health professionals, trained managers, and other experts. Reforms that diminished the influence of political parties also increased the power of special interest groups working for particular social and economic goals. Consumers of all classes shared benefits from government regulation.

In general most of the winners were white, urban, Protestant, and middle class. This was true even though working-class ethnics won victories in some cities and states. They and small businesspeople were among those who both lost and gained. African-Americans came closest to being unqualified losers. For them, the only lasting advances came from establishing organiza-

tions. The NAACP survived to become an important force later in the century, and self-help organizations provided aid to many. Other victories were mainly token; the defeats were concrete.

In the South, and often in the North as well, African-Americans were clearly losers on the local level. At the same time black relations with the federal government also deteriorated. Of the three presidents, Roosevelt was the most sympathetic to blacks. In 1901, he invited Booker T. Washington to dine at the White House, consulted with him on some southern appointments, and named a few African-Americans to federal positions. His actions hardly reflected an acceptance of black equality, however. He believed, "as a race and in the mass they are altogether inferior to whites." One of his speeches to Congress seemed to condone lynching. Most disturbing to African-Americans

Theodore Roosevelt gave the appearance of supporting African-Americans when he invited Booker T. Washington to the White House, but like many white leaders, he did not promote equality between blacks and whites.

CHRONOLOGY
OF KEY EVENTS

1879 Henry George's *Progress and Poverty* proposes a tax on land as a means of controlling illegitimate profits

1888 Edward Bellamy's *Looking Backward* depicts a utopian society guided by cooperation rather than competition

1889 Jane Addams founds Hull House

1901 President William McKinley is assassinated; Theodore Roosevelt becomes the twenty-sixth president

1902 Oregon, South Dakota, and Utah become first states to adopt initiative and recall; Roosevelt threatens to use troops to run coal mines when owners refuse to negotiate; Roosevelt charges Northern Securities with violating the Sherman Antitrust Act—in 1904, the U.S. Supreme Court orders the company's breakup

1903 In *The Souls of Black Folks*, W. E. B. Du Bois attacks Booker T. Washington for abandoning the goal of equal rights; Wisconsin becomes the first state to adopt primary elections; Elkins Act bars railroad rebates

1904 Lincoln Steffins's *Shame of the Cities* exposes corruption in city government; United States obtains right to build the Panama Canal; announcement of Roosevelt Corollary to the Monroe Doctrine, asserting the right of the United States to exercise international police power in the Caribbean

1905 Roosevelt helps negotiate an end to a war between Russia and Japan—he wins the Nobel Peace Prize for his efforts

1906 Upton Sinclair's *The Jungle* exposes unsanitary conditions in the meat-packing industry; Meat Inspection Act enforces health and sanitary standards in meat-packing industry; Pure Food and Drug Act prohibits the use of harmful additives and misleading advertisements of drugs; Hepburn Act gives the Interstate Commerce Commission the right to set maximum freight rates

1907 Roosevelt dispatches 16 battleships ("the great white fleet") on an around-the-world cruise

1908 Staunton, Virginia, hires the first city manager

1909 National Association for the Advancement of Colored People (NAACP) is founded to protect the rights of black Americans

1910 Mann-Elkins Act allows Interstate Commerce Commission to regulate railroad rates even without complaints from shippers

1912–1917 12 states adopt minimum wage laws for women; 30 states adopt industrial accident insurance

1912 Roosevelt and his supporters launch the Progressive party; Democrat Woodrow Wilson is elected the twenty-eighth president

1913 Sixteenth Amendment gives Congress the power to levy an income tax; Underwood-Simmons Tariff substantially lowers duties on imports and imposes a graduated income tax; Seventeenth Amendment requires direct election of senators; Federal Reserve System is created to supervise banking system and regulate money supply

1914 Federal Trade Commission is established to preserve economic competition by preventing unfair business practices; Clayton Antitrust Act prohibits interlocking corporate directorates and predatory pricing policies; U.S. Navy captures Mexican port of Veracruz

1915 U.S. marines are dispatched to Haiti

1916 U.S. troops enter Mexico to search for Pancho Villa; U.S. marines are sent to Dominican Republic

1919 Eighteenth Amendment prohibits manufacture and sale of liquor

1920 Nineteenth Amendment grants women the right to vote

was his handling of an incident in Brownsville, Texas, in 1906. There, a shoot-out occurred between white townspeople and black soldiers. No one could determine exactly what happened, but that did not deter Roosevelt from ordering dishonorable discharges for 167 black soldiers without court martial.

When Taft became president, he approved of southern disfranchisement and appointed white-supremacist Republicans to federal jobs. These actions by the two Republicans convinced some African-Americans, including W. E. B. Du Bois, to support Wilson in 1912. They made a mistake. The influence of Wilson's southern upbringing and advisors became apparent when he allowed his cabinet to segregate federal employees and to demote black office-holders, especially those "who boss white girls." Jim Crow moved to Washington, and Wilson's defense of these actions indicated the blindness and paternalism of many white progressives on race:

> It is true that the segregation of the colored employees in the several departments was begun upon the initiative and at the suggestion of the heads of departments, but as much in the interest of the negroes as for any other reason, with the approval of some of the most influential negroes I know, and with the idea that the friction, or rather the discontent and uneasiness, which had prevailed in many departments would thereby be removed. It is as far as possible from being a movement against the negroes. I believe it to be in their interest.

It seems that white progressives often seemed to feel they knew the best interests of those not like them, at home and abroad.

CONCLUSION

At the start of the new century, Americans confronted the urban squalor, poverty, powerful monopolies, corrupt and inefficient government, disorder, and despair that had accompanied the forces of modernization. They were determined to do something to achieve more social justice and stability. Numerous solutions were proposed and victories won. In the end, however, Americans rejected radicalism and ignored major problems.

Once again the nation resolutely refused to come to terms with its ethnic and cultural diversity. Rather than protect minorities, most actions infringed on their personal liberties and sought to control rather than accommodate their differences. Women won some victories, but the majority of Americans did not accept the radical feminists' vision of true equality. Socialists' dreams of a peaceful, democratic redistribution of the country's wealth fell on deaf ears. In the end, there was no significant change in the distribution of either wealth or power. The United States had weeded and tidied up its social garden, not replanted it. Although that garden produced bitter fruit for some people, many Americans benefited. Also, the vigor and diversity of progressive actions brought to light many problems and provided later generations with a body of experience in dealing with them.

SUGGESTIONS FOR FURTHER READING

OVERVIEWS AND SURVEYS

John W. Chambers, *The Tyranny of Change: America in the Progressive Era* (1980); Robert M. Crunden, *Ministers of Reform: The Progressives' Achievement in American Civilization* (1982); Arthur Ekrich, *Progressivism in America* (1974); Richard Hofstadter, *Age of Reform* (1955); Arthur S. Link and Richard L. McCormick, *Progressivism* (1983); Robert Wiebe, *The Search for Order* (1967).

THE PROGRESSIVE IMPULSE

Richard Abrams, *The Burdens of Progress* (1978); Jerold S. Auerbach, *Unequal Justice: Lawyers and Social Change in Modern America* (1976); Robert M. Crunden, *Ministers of Reform: The Progressives' Achievement in American Civilization, 1889–1920* (1982); Harold U. Faulkner, *The Quest for Social Justice, 1898–1914* (1931); Louis Filler, *The Muckrakers*, rev. ed. (1976); Samuel Haber, *Efficiency and Uplift: Scientific Management in the Progressive Era* (1964); Thomas Haskell, *The Emergence of Professional Social Science* (1977); William R. Hutchison, *The Modernist Impulse in American Protestantism* (1976); James T. Kloppenberg, *Uncertain Victory: Social Democracy and Progressivism in European and American Thought, 1870–1920* (1986); Samuel Konefsky, *The Legacy of Holmes and Brandeis* (1956); David W. Marcell, *Progress and Pragmatism* (1974); David W. Noble, *The Progressive Mind*, rev. ed. (1981);

Frank Tariello, *The Reconstruction of American Political Ideology* (1982); John L. Thomas, *Alternative America: Henry George, Edward Bellamy, Henry Demarest Lloyd, and the Adversary Tradition* (1983); Laurence Veysey, *The Emergence of the American University* (1970); James Weinstein, *The Corporate Ideal in the Liberal State, 1900–1918* (1968); Morton White, *Social Thought in America: The Revolt Against Formalism* (1975); Harold S. Wilson, *McClure's Magazine and the Muckrakers* (1970).

PROGRESSIVES IN ACTION

John D. Buenker, *Urban Liberalism and Progressive Reform* (1973); Norman H. Clark, *Deliver Us From Evil: An Interpretation of Prohibition* (1976); Allen F. Davis, *Spearheads for Reform: The Social Settlements and the Progressive Movement, 1890–1914* (1967); Rene J. Dubos, *The White Plague: Tuberculosis, Man, and Society* (1952); Nancy S. Dye, *As Equals and Sisters: Feminism, the Labor Movement, and the Women's Trade Union League of New York* (1980); Dewey Grantham, *Southern Progressivism: The Reconciliation of Progress and Tradition* (1983); Sheldon Hackney, *Populism to Progressivism in Alabama* (1969); Melvin G. Holli, *Reform in Detroit: Hazen S. Pingree and Urban Politics* (1969); Charles F. Kellogg, *NAACP* (1967); Ellen Condliffe Lagemann, *A Generation of Women: Education in the Lives of Progressive Reformers* (1979); Roy Lubove, *The Progressives and the Slums, 1890–1917* (1962); Richard L. McCormick, *From Realignment to Reform: Political Change in New York State, 1893–1910* (1981); August Meier, *Negro Thought in America, 1880–1915* (1963); George E. Mowry, *California Progressives* (1951); Bradley R. Rice, *Progressive Cities: The Commission Government Movement* (1977); Ruth Rosen, *The Lost Sisterhood: Prostitution in America, 1900–1918* (1982); Bruce M. Stave, *Urban Bosses, Machines, and Progressive Reformers*, 2d ed. (1984); David P. Thelen, *The New Citizenship: Origins of Progressivism in Wisconsin* (1972); James H. Timberlake, *Prohibition and the Progressive Movement* (1963); Walter I. Trattner, *Crusade for the Children* (1970); Irwin Yellowitz, *Labor and the Progressive Movement in New York State* (1965).

PROGRESSIVISM MOVES TO THE NATIONAL LEVEL

John D. Buenker, *The Income Tax and the Progressive Era* (1985); Paolo E. Coletta, *The Presidency of William Howard Taft* (1973); Lewis L. Gould, *Reform and Regulation: American Politics from Roosevelt to Wilson* (1986); James Holt, *Congressional Insurgents and the Party System* (1969); James Penick, Jr., *Progressive Politics and Conservation: The Ballinger-Pinchot Affair* (1968); James Oliver Robertson, *No Third Choice: Progressives in Republican Politics, 1916–1921* (1983).

PROGRESSIVISM IN THE INTERNATIONAL ARENA

P. Edward Haley, *Revolution and Intervention: The Diplomacy of Taft and Wilson with Mexico, 1910–1917* (1970); Walter LaFeber, *The Panama Canal*, rev. ed. (1989); Lester Langley, *The United States and the Carribean* (1980); Dana G. Munro, *Intervention and Dollar Diplomacy in the Caribbean, 1900–1921* (1964); Whitney Perkins, *Constraints of Empire: The United States and Caribbean Interventions* (1981); Robert E. Quirk, *An Affair of Honor: Woodrow Wilson and the Occupation of Veracruz* (1962); John Womack, *Zapata and the Mexican Revolution* (1968).

PROGRESSIVE ACCOMPLISHMENTS, PROGRESSIVE FAILURES

Paul D. Casdorph, *Republicans, Negroes, and Progressives in the South, 1912–1916* (1981); John Dittmer, *Black Georgia in the Progressive Era, 1900–1920* (1977); Jack Temple Kirby, *Darkness at the Dawning: Race and Reform in the Progressive South* (1972); Gabriel Kolko, *The Triumph of Conservatism* (1963); Robert Wiebe, *Businessmen and Reform* (1962).

BIOGRAPHIES

Howard K. Beale, *Theodore Roosevelt and the Rise of America to World Power* (1956); John M. Blum, *The Republican Roosevelt*, 2d ed. (1977), and *Woodrow Wilson and the Politics of Morality* (1956); John Milton Cooper, Jr., *The Warrior and the Priest: Woodrow Wilson and Theodore Roosevelt* (1983); Allen F. Davis, *American Heroine: Jane Addams* (1973); William Harbaugh, *The Life and Times of Theodore Roosevelt*, rev. ed. (1963); Louis R. Harlan, *Booker T. Washington: The Making of a Black Leader, 1856–1901* (1972), and *The Wizard of Tuskegee, 1901–1915* (1983); Arthur S. Link, *Wilson*, 5 vols. (1947–1965), and *Woodrow Wilson and the Progressive Era* (1954); Daniel Nelson, *Frederick W. Taylor and the Rise of Scientific Management* (1980); David Riesman, *Thorstein Veblen* (1953); Elliott M. Rudwick, *W. E. B. Du Bois* (1960); David P. Thelen, *Robert LaFollette and the Insurgent Spirit* (1976).

126

a

Fig. 55

4

New

900 Die as
400 Ameri
Washing

EUROPE VIA LIVERPOOL
LUSITANIA

1914

1918

Production Possibility
Curve 2

0   1914   1918

Guns

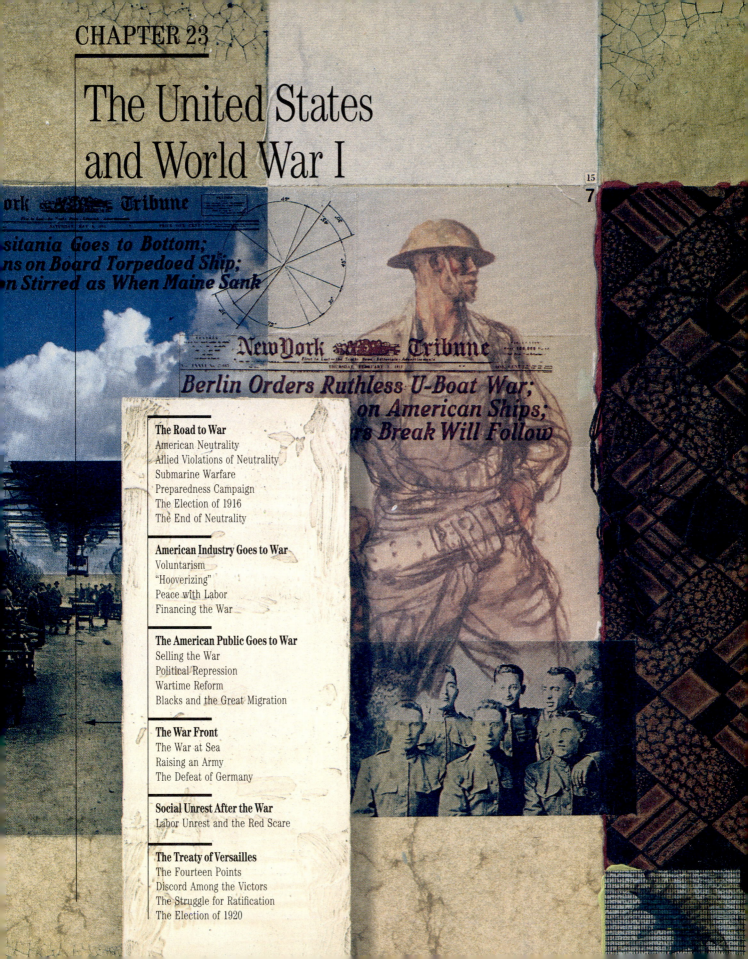

CHAPTER 23

The United States and World War I

The Road to War
American Neutrality
Allied Violations of Neutrality
Submarine Warfare
Preparedness Campaign
The Election of 1916
The End of Neutrality

American Industry Goes to War
Voluntarism
"Hooverizing"
Peace with Labor
Financing the War

The American Public Goes to War
Selling the War
Political Repression
Wartime Reform
Blacks and the Great Migration

The War Front
The War at Sea
Raising an Army
The Defeat of Germany

Social Unrest After the War
Labor Unrest and the Red Scare

The Treaty of Versailles
The Fourteen Points
Discord Among the Victors
The Struggle for Ratification
The Election of 1920

*D*isillusioned writers of the 1920s honored Randolph Bourne as "the intellectual hero of World War I," yet his appearance was anything but heroic. Theodore Dreiser called Bourne "as frightening a dwarf as I had ever seen." An unusually messy forceps delivery crushed one side of Bourne's skull at birth, leaving him with a misshapen ear, a partially paralyzed face, and a mouth permanently askew in a horrible grimace. Then, when he was four, an attack of spinal tuberculosis twisted his frame and left him a hunchback dwarf.

Bourne's brain, however, was razor sharp. He started reading at the age of 2, and by the time he entered school, he had devoured entire books, including the Bible. A brilliant student, Bourne attended Columbia University where he studied under Franz Boaz, the father of cultural anthropology; John Dewey, the famed educator and apostle of pragmatism; and Charles A. Beard, the historian who stressed the economic motives of the founding fathers.

Bourne left college on the eve of World War I determined to become a writer. Drawn by the intense intellectual ferment of the day, he settled in New York's Greenwich Village, where self-styled literary radicals had declared war on the smugness and the optimism of American culture. Bourne contributed to new magazines, such as *The New Republic*, *The Seven Arts*, and *The New Masses*. While his interests ranged wide and far, he made his reputation as a critic of America's entrance into World War I.

Bourne loathed President Woodrow Wilson, whom he labeled "an indubitably intellectualized president," but he directed his choicest barbs at fellow intellectuals who supported Wilson's policies. In effect, he accused them of not doing their job as thinkers—of not subjecting the president's high-sounding rhetoric to the fierce scrutiny required to sharpen public debate. Instead of questioning Wilson's policies, they had betrayed their duty by "opening the sluices and flooding the public with the sewage of the war spirit." When his colleagues accused Bourne of not understanding the realities of war, he replied: "In a time of faith, skepticism is the most intolerable of all insults."

Bourne refused to endow the war with lofty purposes. Hardly a knee-jerk pacifist, he knew that some wars were unavoidable, perhaps even necessary. In his judgment, however, World War I was not a struggle to make the world safe for democracy; it was nothing more than "frenzied mutual suicide." To those who argued that this war would be different, that this war could somehow be converted into an instrument of progress and democracy, Bourne replied that World War I would unleash "all the evils that are organically bound up with it." America's allies would reject Wilson's call for a "peace without victory," Bourne cautioned, because "war determines its own end—victory." Eschewing a just peace, they would try to win the war and "then grab what they can."

On the home front there would be "clumsily levied taxes and the robberies of imperfectly controlled private enterprises," warned Bourne, and the suppression of civil liberties and the growth of big government. "War is the health of the State," he declared in one of his most famous lines. "It automatically sets in motion

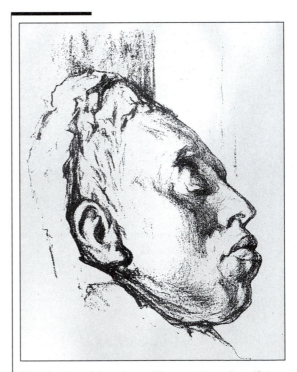

This drawing of American critic, essayist, and pacifist Randolph Silliman Bourne was done by Arthur G. Dove from the death mask by James Earle Fraser.

throughout society those irresistible forces for uniformity, for passionate cooperation with the Government in coercing into obedience the minority groups and individuals which lack the larger herd sense."

Like many of his contemporaries, Bourne feared the state. During wartime the state's power grew exponentially, making it "the inexorable arbiter and determinant of men's businesses and attitudes and opinions." The individual would lose every conflict with the state. Bourne denied that America could rely on "individual offerings of good will and enterprise" to conduct the war. "It will be coercion from above that will do the trick rather than patriotism from below," he warned.

Most alarming of all, the war would kill reform by diverting public attention from the unfinished work of progressivism. It would "leave the country spiritually impoverished because of the draining away of sentiment into the channels of war." Finally, Bourne rejected the charge that opposition to the war was unpatriotic. Patriotism, he opined, was "merely the emotion that fills the herd when it imagines itself engaged in massed defense or massed attack."

A few days after the Armistice was signed in 1918, Bourne died, a victim of the influenza epidemic that killed 500,000 Americans that winter. Although he had no visible impact on Wilson's administration, Bourne raised important questions about the relationship between the individual and the state during wartime, and many of his fears proved prophetic. In the end, the United States had little choice but to enter the conflict on the side of the Allies, but the war itself was a terrible human tragedy. World War I did not make "the world safe for democracy" or serve as the "war to end all wars" as President Wilson promised. Rather, World War I sowed the seeds of World War II.

THE ROAD TO WAR

On June 28, 1914, terrorists assassinated the heir to the Austro-Hungarian throne, Archduke Franz Ferdinand, in Sarajevo, the provincial capital of Bosnia in the Balkans. A complicated system of alliances pitting the Triple Entente of France, Russia, and Great Britain against the

Within weeks of the assassination of Archduke Franz Ferdinand, Germany, Turkey, Italy, and Austria-Hungary were at war with England, France, and Russia.

Central Alliance of Germany, Austria-Hungary, Italy, and Turkey triggered a chain reaction that started World War I. Austria blamed Serbian nationalists for the killing. After consulting with its ally Germany, Austria declared war on Serbia, ally to both Russia and France. When Russia and France mobilized to support Serbia, Germany immediately declared war on them. After Germany invaded Belgium, England entered the war on the side of France and Russia. In the Far East, Japan, England's ally since 1902, also declared war on Germany. Soon after the fighting began, Italy switched sides and joined the fight against Germany.

World War I caught most people by surprise. Lulled by a century of peace (Europeans had not seen a large-scale war since the defeat of Napoleon in 1815), many observers had come to regard armed conflict as an anachronism, a dead relic rendered unthinkable by human progress. Convinced that the major powers had

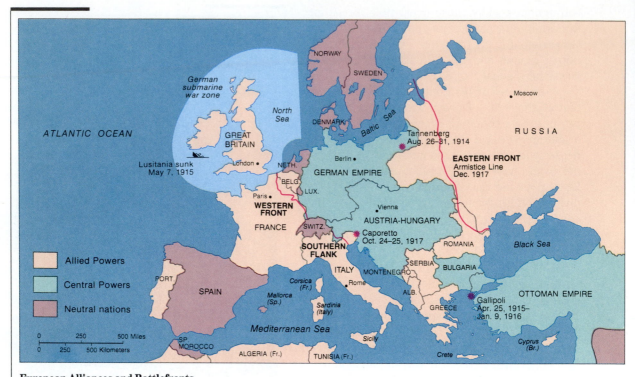

European Alliances and Battlefronts
Some Americans wanted Wilson to choose sides in World War I.

advanced too far morally and materially to fight, these optimists believed that nation states would settle disputes through diplomacy. And for a time, it looked as though the world had outgrown war. By the end of the century, peace societies abounded on both sides of the Atlantic, nurturing visions of a world without war, and the Hague Conferences of 1899 and 1907 seemed to bear out these hopes by codifying international law in order to establish procedures for the peaceful resolution of conflict. World War I shattered these dreams, demonstrating that death and destruction had not yet been banished from human affairs.

Both sides expected a swift victory; both sides miscalculated. After the Allies halted Germany's massive offensive through France and Belgium at the Marne River in September 1914, the Great War bogged down into trench warfare and a ghastly stalemate ensued. Congealed lines of men, stretching from the English Channel to the Swiss border, formed an unmovable battle front across northern France. There they remained throughout 1915: Four million men burrowed into the ground, ravaged by tuberculosis, plagued with lice and rats, staring at each other across barren expanses called "no man's land" and fighting pitched battles over narrow strips of blood-soaked earth.

Airplanes, tanks, hand grenades, and poison gases distinguished the Great War from earlier conflicts, but the machine gun did most of the killing. Aware that one machine gunner possessed the firepower of hundreds of soldiers, the German high command called this new weapon "the essence of concentrated infantry." The grim cycle repeated itself countless times: officers cried "Attack!"; men rose in waves; and the opposing forces opened fire with machine guns, spewing out death at the rate of eight bullets per second. In minutes, thousands of men lay wounded or dead, savage evidence of how efficiently military technology and insane tactics could slaughter a generation of young men. When the war ended, Germany had lost 1,800,000 men; Russia, 1,700,000; France, 1,385,000; Austria-Hungary, 1,200,000; and Great Britain, 947,000.

American Neutrality

Like the combatants, Americans did not see the war coming. As one North Carolinian wrote in November 1914, the war struck "as lightning out of a clear sky." Most Americans felt relieved when President Woodrow Wilson issued an official declaration of neutrality on August 4. Many citizens did not believe their nation's interest and security hinged on the war's outcome. Mindful of the wisdom embodied in Washington's Farewell Address, steeped in a long tradition of isolation from Europe's wars, and shielded from the hostilities by the Atlantic Ocean, they hoped to escape this insanity. As a *New York Sun* editorial declared, "It would be folly for the country to sacrifice itself to the frenzy of dynastic politics and the clash of ancient hatreds which is urging the Old World to destruction."

Two weeks after the official declaration of neutrality Wilson asked his countrymen to remain impartial "in thought as well as in action." Yet the president himself could not meet this standard. Privately, his sympathies lay with the Allies, especially Great Britain, whose culture and government he had long admired. "England is fighting our fight," he told his private secretary shortly after the war erupted; "she is fighting for her life and the life of the world." Moreover, with the notable exception of William Jennings Bryan, his first secretary of state, Wilson's closest advisors all favored Great Britain. Robert Lansing, who succeeded Bryan as secretary of state; Walter Hines Page, ambassador to the Court of St. James; and Colonel Edward House, Wilson's alter ego, pushed the president to side with England and her Allies. Yet Wilson saw the war's causes as complicated and obscure; simple prudence dictated that the United States must avoid taking sides.

Internal divisions underscored the wisdom of neutrality. Wilson knew his countrymen felt deeply divided over the war. Ties of language and culture prompted many Americans to side with the Allies, and, as the war progressed, the British adeptly exploited these bonds. After the German invasion of neutral Belgium, for exam-

Life in the trenches, as depicted by these British soldiers in 1916, was often cramped, uncomfortable, and miserable. Many men tried to make the best of it by surrounding themselves with personal effects.

ple, British propagandists had a field day depicting the Germans as sadistic brutes who committed atrocities against civilians. Yet the Central Powers had their sympathizers, too. Approximately one-third of the nation, 32 million people, were either foreign born or the children of immigrants, and more than 10 million derived from the nations of the Central Powers. Furthermore, millions of Irish-Americans sided with the Central Powers because they hated the English.

Domestic politics reinforced Wilson's determination to remain neutral. In 1914 the United States stood at the end of two decades of bitter social and political debate. Labor unrest, corporate growth, trust-busting, and the arrival of 12 million new immigrants since the turn of the century had opened deep fissures in American society. As Wilson struggled to correct these problems through legislation, he feared his domestic program would be endangered if neutrality failed. "Every reform we have won will be lost if we go into this war," declared Wilson in 1914.

Allied Violations of Neutrality

Because German armies held the edge in the land war, Great Britain had no choice but to press her naval superiority. Like Thomas Jefferson and James Madison a century earlier, President Wilson confronted a Great Britain bent upon ruling the waves, and no less than his predecessors in the White House, Wilson fought to protect neutral rights. During the early part of the war, British efforts to control the seas posed repeated threats to Anglo-American relations.

Immediately after war erupted, the British navy swept the sea lanes, attempting to blockade Europe. In February 1915 British ships mined the North Sea and started seizing American vessels bound for neutral countries, often without offering compensation. The British captured not only contraband of war (weapons, munitions, and the like), but noncontraband items, including food and cotton, bound for neutral nations such as Holland for reshipment to Germany. In 1916 Britain "blacklisted" some 87 American companies accused of trading with

Germany and censored the mail coming from Europe to the United States.

These actions, coupled with England's ruthless suppression of the Irish Rebellion in 1916, infuriated Wilson, who privately denounced the English as "poor Boobs." In retaliation, the State Department bombarded England with a flurry of firm (but polite) protests. These objections were consistently undermined, however, by Walter Hines Page, the pro-British American ambassador at the Court of St. James. On one occasion, for example, Page delivered a long dispatch to Sir Edward Grey, the British foreign secretary, and declared: "I have now read the dispatch but I do not agree with it; let us consider how it should be answered."

Wilson's protests left the British cold. They interpreted his ardent defense of neutral rights as petty, legalistic quibbling. England was fighting for its life. What did a few confiscated cargoes matter in comparison? Still, the British realized they could not push Wilson too far. Since they needed American trade to survive, they tried to enforce the blockade as tightly as possible without rupturing relations with the United States.

Wilson could have ended the controversy over neutral rights by clamping an embargo on trade with the belligerents, but he refused to take this action because wartime trade was stimulating the American economy. The United States had been in a recession when Wilson entered office in 1913, and the war had increased the volume of trade with the Allies from $824 million in 1914 to $3.2 billion in 1916. Commerce with the Central Powers, by contrast, declined from $169 million to $1.15 million.

The huge volume of trade quickly exhausted the Allies' cash reserves, forcing them to ask the United States for credit. Secretary of State William Jennings Bryan, a near pacifist and the only member of Wilson's cabinet who supported strict neutrality, opposed their requests, declaring: "Money is the worst of contrabands—it commands all other things." In truth, Bryan spoke for large groups within the Democratic party who regarded Wilson's version of neutrality as pro-British.

The peace Democrats had Wilson pegged. After hesitating several months, he agreed in

October 1915 to permit loans to belligerents, a decision that favored Great Britain and France far more than Germany. By 1917 American loans to the Allies had soared to $2.25 billion; loans to Germany stood at a paltry $27 million. The United States became a creditor nation for the first time, giving Americans a strong economic interest in an Allied victory.

Yet the marketplace did not drive America into the Allies' waiting arms. Ultimately, submarines broke the peace between the United States and Germany.

Submarine Warfare

Given Britain's overwhelming naval superiority, Germany had no chance of winning a conventional sea war. Therefore, Germany decided to rely on a new weapon, the submarine, and on February 4, 1915 Germany proclaimed a "war zone" around the British Isles. Henceforth all enemy merchant ships that entered the zone would be torpedoed without warning, and neutral ships would not be guaranteed safe passage. Germany was bluffing. It had only four submarines in the area, but Germany intended to use the threat of submarine warfare to terrorize and intimidate its enemies until it could build enough ships to enforce its threats.

A new development in naval technology, the submarine posed serious challenges to international law. The law required ships that attacked other vessels on the high seas to warn their intended victims, allow time for passengers to reach lifeboats and clear the area, and then rescue survivors after the sinking. Moreover, merchant vessels suspected of transporting contraband had to be "visited and searched" before being attacked. By its very nature, the submarine could not abide by these regulations. A silent assassin whose effectiveness depended on the element of surprise, it had to strike from below the surface. Therefore, Germany ignored international law and authorized its submarines to kill without warning.

Nothing in President Wilson's makeup prepared him to accept submarine warfare. He was not a student of naval history or international affairs. His own experience as a scholar and as a progressive governor had been limited to do-

The German U-boat (*Unterseeboot*) violated an international law that required a warship to warn a passenger or merchant vessel before attacking. The U-boat struck silently and without warning.

mestic politics, and he wanted to apply the same principles of liberal reform to foreign affairs. Wilson's approach to foreign affairs was both legalistic and moralistic. He expected nation-states to behave like gentlemen; and, above all, that meant living up to the letter of international law and respecting the rights of every nation.

To Wilson's legalistic mind, German submarines committed criminal acts. In contrast to British violations of American neutrality, which merely resulted in property losses, submarine warfare threatened to kill innocent civilians. In unusually blunt language, he warned Berlin that it would be held "strictly accountable" for American lives lost to submarine attacks. While international law did not guarantee the safety of neutrals who traveled on belligerent ships, Wilson acted as though it did. With the United States demanding that Germany treat a single

American passenger as a shield for an entire merchant ship, a German diplomat in Washington warned "there will be hell to pay."

On March 28, 1915, a German submarine torpedoed the *Falaba*, a British liner, killing 104 passengers, including one American. "PIRACY," "SHOCKING BLOODTHIRSTINESS," "BARBARISM RUN MAD," screamed the American press in banner headlines. Wilson was outraged, but Secretary of State Bryan reminded the president of numerous British violations of American neutrality in her attempt to blockade Germany. "Why be shocked at the drowning of a few people," asked Bryan, "if there is no objection to the starving of a nation?"

While Wilson and Bryan debated America's response, the German Embassy on May 1 took out ads in New York newspapers warning Americans not to travel on Allied ships. Undeterred, 197 Americans sailed for the British Isles on board the *Lusitania*, the queen of the British-owned Cunard fleet. On May 7, 1915, a German submarine torpedoed the *Lusitania* off the coast of Ireland. She sank in 18 minutes, killing 1198 persons, 128 of them Americans. The public was shocked and outraged. The *New York Nation* called the sinking "wholesale murder on the high seas," and a small minority of Americans, led by Theodore Roosevelt, demanded war. It did not seem to matter that the *Lusitania* (like the *Falaba*) was transporting munitions in her hull and had secret orders to ram submarines on sight.

Here was a harsh test of America's neutrality, and the president rose to the challenge. In a sharply worded dispatch, Wilson ordered Germany to apologize for the sinking, compensate the victims, and pledge to stop attacking merchant ships. When Berlin equivocated, Wilson sent a second *Lusitania* note repeating his demands. This time the Germans met him halfway. In February 1916 they expressed regret over the *Lusitania* and agreed to pay an indemnity. However, the Imperial Government refused to stop sinking merchant ships without warning, explaining that Germany's survival depended on full use of the submarine.

Though Wilson's handling of the *Lusitania* crisis had been far from bellicose, Bryan resigned from the cabinet on June 8 to protest what he saw as a dangerous tilt toward Great Britain in American policy. From the outset, he had urged the president to try to end the war through mediation and arbitration; but, as the war progressed, Bryan had become convinced that Wilson's policies would lead to war with Germany. While Bryan's resignation permitted the president to replace him as secretary of state with Robert Lansing, who shared Wilson's views, it also freed Bryan to plead his case for strict neutrality before the public.

For his part, Wilson felt relieved to put the *Lusitania* incident behind him, Bryan's resignation notwithstanding. Still, Wilson knew that the issue of submarine warfare had not been resolved. "I can't keep the country out of war," he admitted privately. "Any little German lieutenant can put us into war at any time by some calculated outrage."

Events soon showed how right he was. On March 24, 1916, a submarine attacked the *Sussex*, an unarmed French passenger ship. The *Sussex* reached port, but more than 80 people died in the attack and 7 Americans sustained severe wounds. While Secretary Lansing insisted that the time for writing notes had ended, Wilson tempered his response. He threatened to sever diplomatic relations unless Germany promised to stop sinking all merchant and passenger ships without warning. Anxious to keep the United States neutral, Berlin agreed. The so-called *Sussex* pledge reduced tensions between the United States and Germany for the remainder of 1916, but the fragile peace depended solely on German restraint.

Preparedness Campaign

As the submarine threatened to draw the United States into the fighting, the American people and their leaders debated whether or not to make ready for war. Initially, Wilson's policy toward preparedness reflected cautious hostility. In December 1914 he told Congress, "We never have had, and while we retain our present principles and ideals we never shall have, a large standing army."

Many Americans saw the issue differently. Wilson increasingly found himself assailed by prominent and highly vocal critics who insisted that the best way to preserve peace was to prepare for war. The pugnacious Theodore Roosevelt called the president "the popular pacifist hero," while another critic sneered that the Germans were "standing by their torpedoes, the British by their guns, and Wilson by strict accountability." As Tin Pan Alley produced songs with titles such as "I Did Not Raise My Boy to Be a Coward," the National Security League, headed by General Leonard Wood, organized volunteer military training programs across the country.

Yet Wilson felt pressured by groups opposed to war. Socialists such as Eugene V. Debs and Morris Hillquit dismissed the war as a struggle for assets among capitalist nations. Radicals such as anarchist Emma Goldman and "Big Bill" Haywood, head of the Industrial Workers of the World, shared this view and advocated violent resistance to preparedness. Liberal reformers such as Randolph Bourne and Oswald Garrison Villard feared that war would destroy the spirit of progressivism. Pacifists such as social worker Jane Addams and Hamilton Holt, head of the League to Enforce Peace, opposed the war on moral grounds. And most troubling of all, Wilson had to worry about groups within his own party that wanted no part of Europe's war. Speaking for the peace Democrats, former Secretary of State William Jennings Bryan warned that a preparedness campaign would transform the United States into "a vast armory with skull and crossbones above the door."

In the end, Wilson shifted ground and threw his support behind a moderate preparedness program. Throughout January and February 1916, he stumped the country pleading for a military force powerful enough to protect the nation's honor. In June 1916 Congress passed the National Defense Act (Hay Act), increasing the army from 90,000 to 175,000 men. A few months later Congress passed the Naval Construction Act, appropriating more than $500 million for new ships. Though of small importance militarily (Teddy Roosevelt dismissed the measures as a "shadow program" of "half preparedness"), both acts drew fire from the antipreparedness forces in Congress who predicted that armaments would lead to war.

At the height of the preparedness controversy, Wilson had to beat back a serious challenge to his control of American foreign policy. During the early months of 1916, Congress con-

sidered separate resolutions sponsored by Senator Thomas Gore of Oklahoma and Representative Jeff McLemore of Texas. Fearing that Wilson's defense of neutral rights would draw the United States into the conflict, the Gore-McLemore resolutions sought to prevent future incidents by prohibiting Americans from traveling on ships owned by belligerent nations and by prohibiting American vessels or neutral vessels from transporting American citizens and contraband "at one and the same time." Both resolutions enjoyed strong support in Congress, and for a while their passage appeared inevitable, but Wilson threw his power and prestige into a furious attack on both measures, insisting that if the United States accepted any abridgment of neutral rights "many other humiliations would follow." In the end, Congress accepted his argument and the Gore-McLemore resolutions went down to defeat.

The Election of 1916

Foreign affairs dominated the election of 1916. The Republicans chose Charles Evans Hughes as their candidate over the fiery Theodore Roosevelt. A member of the progressive wing of the GOP, Hughes was a former governor of New York and a Supreme Court justice who had earned a solid reputation as a liberal. His nomination demonstrated the GOP's determination to regain progressive support and avoid the split that had put Wilson in the White House four years earlier. Though his campaign speeches criticized the president soundly, Hughes had a hard time explaining how his policies differed.

Wilson, by contrast, ran squarely on his record. The Democratic platform, which Wilson wrote in advance of the convention, stressed the president's legislative victories for progressive reform, his patient handling of the Mexican crisis, and his steadfast insistence on American neutrality. While the delegates responded warmly to the first two items, they burst into thunderous applause as they heard speakers praise the president for keeping the nation at peace.

Profoundly influenced by the demonstrations, Wilson decided to make peace the key issue in 1916. For the remainder of the campaign, he labeled the Republicans the party of war and charged that Hughes' election would plunge the United States into Europe's madness. Despite his support for military preparedness and his battles with Congress, Wilson ran as the peace candidate in the election of 1916, and "He kept us out of war" became the Democrats' rallying cry.

The race was extremely close. On election eve the *New York Times* and the *New York World* both awarded victory to Hughes, who went to bed believing he had won. He ran well in traditional Republican strongholds such as the Midwest (he won Illinois, Indiana, and Michigan) and the large eastern states. However, Wilson won in the Electoral College by a vote of 277 to 254, with a popular vote margin of 9.1 million to Hughes's 8.5 million.

A careful analysis of Wilson's victory reveals that the Democrats won because they managed to fuse progressivism with the cause of peace. Wilson carried the Solid South, Ohio, Maryland, and New Hampshire, but he owed his victory to voters west of the Mississippi River, where he took every state except Oregon, Iowa, South Dakota, and Minnesota. This was the section of the country where peace sentiment ran high and the opposition to preparedness was the strongest. Moreover, the Democratic party's strength in 1916 clearly rested on an ethnic-worker-farmer coalition. Wilson captured the Solid South, the labor vote in the Northeast and Midwest, the old-line progressives, and substantial numbers of western farmers.

The End of Neutrality

Interpreting his reelection as a vote for peace, Wilson attempted to mediate. On December 18, 1916, he asked the belligerents to list their war aims and state their terms for peace. The following month he called for both sides to embrace his call for "peace without victory." Neither side welcomed his overtures. The Germans announced they would not permit neutrals at the conference table, while the British politely rejected Wilson's offer. Privately, a high-ranking British official confided to Walter Hines Page, the American ambassador: "Everybody is mad as hell," and called Wilson an "ass." Randolph Bourne was right. Above all else, the belligerents wanted victory.

Any hope for a negotiated settlement ended when Germany announced that after February 1, 1917, all vessels caught in the war zone, neutral or belligerent, armed or unarmed, would be sunk without warning. Driven to desperation by the British blockade and unable to break the impasse on land, Germany had decided to risk everything on a furious U-boat campaign designed to starve Britain into submission. The German high command expected the United States to declare war in retaliation, but they believed their submarines could deliver a knockout blow before America could mobilize.

Here, then, was the ultimate test of "strict accountability." Members of his cabinet pressed Wilson to declare war, but he broke diplomatic relations instead. Though critics accused the president of shaking first his fist and then his finger, Wilson refused to budge. Viewing war as the defeat of reason, he could not bring himself to act. For weeks he seemed indecisive and confused, unable to accept the fact that "strict accountability" demanded war once the Germans started sinking American ships.

The Zimmermann telegram snapped Wilson out of his daze. On January 16 British cryptographers intercepted a secret message from Arthur Zimmermann, the German foreign minister, to the German ambassador to Mexico, proposing an alliance between Germany and Mexico in the event Germany went to war with the United States. Germany promised to help Mexico recover the territory it had lost in the 1840s, roughly the present-day states of Texas, New Mexico, California, and Arizona. The British revealed the scheme to Wilson on February 24, hoping to draw the United States into the war.

The Zimmermann telegram convinced Wilson that German militarism threatened American security. For years the United States had been concerned about Germany's economic penetration of world markets, as well as her strong military tradition. The Zimmermann telegram persuaded millions of Americans that Germany would stop at nothing to satisfy her ambitions and that those ambitions posed a serious danger to America's rights and security.

Late in February Wilson asked Congress for permission to arm American merchant ships. The House approved, but 11 pacifists in the Senate filibustered against the bill. Dismissing his Senate opponents as "a little band of willful men, representing no opinion but their own," Wilson issued an executive order on March 12, arming merchant ships and instructing them to shoot submarines on sight.

At this critical juncture, with the United States and Germany virtually at war, the Russian Revolution erupted. Suddenly, the czar's government was swept away, and in its place stood the provisional government of a Russian Republic, complete with a representative parliament. Given his penchant for framing issues in moral terms, Wilson could now view the Allies in a new light: With the only autocratic regime among the Allies transformed overnight into a fledgling democracy, the war now truly seemed to pit the forces of democracy against the forces of despotism.

Pale and solemn, Wilson delivered his war message to Congress on April 2. The United States "had no quarrel with the German people," he insisted, but their "military masters" had to be defeated in order to make the world "safe for democracy." Congress interrupted his address several times with thunderous applause. The next day the Senate approved the war resolution, 82 to 6; the House followed on April 6, 373 to 50. The president signed the declaration on April 7, 1917, and America was at war.

For more than two years Wilson had worked frantically to keep the United States at peace: Why did he now lead the nation to war? True, cultural ties with Great Britain predisposed the United States to favor the Allies, and enormous volumes of trade and loans strengthened those ties. Yet cultural bonds and money did not decide the issue. Wilson drew the sword, although reluctantly, because of his devotion to the rule of law.

In the end, Wilson concluded that German submarines violated international law and made a mockery of America's long-standing commitment to freedom of the seas. Therefore, his strong defense of neutral rights left him no choice but to declare war once Germany resumed its attacks on American ships.

One additional factor weighed heavily on Wilson—his desire to help shape the peace. By entering the war, the United States would be guaranteed a place at the peace table. "I hate this war," an anguished Wilson confided to one of his aides, "and the only thing I care about on earth is the peace I am going to make at the end of it."

Most Americans supported Wilson's call to arms. John Dewey, the famed educator, spoke for progressives when he described war as an ugly reality that had to be converted into an instrument for benefiting mankind. Randolph Bourne disagreed. "If the war is too strong for you to prevent," he asked pointedly, "how is it going to be weak enough for you to control and mould to your liberal purposes?"

AMERICAN INDUSTRY GOES TO WAR

At first administration officials believed America's major contribution to the war would be economic, not military. Production had to be raised to supply the Allies. Yet no one, in or out of government, had a thorough understanding of the economy. Wilson looked skeptical when a leading economist at Columbia University estimated the war might cost as much as $10 billion in its first year. Wilson badly underestimated both the size and the cost of the task at hand.

Voluntarism

Thanks to the strength of the peace forces, the United States entered the Great War unprepared. The problems went far beyond the puny size of the military forces. Americans themselves had no idea of what the war would ask of them as a society. Decisions had to be made about mobilization, but the public had not formed a consensus on the proper role of government in society. One group of progressives demanded more government regulation, but another group simply wanted to break up the large industrial monopolies and then let market forces govern the economy. Conservatives opposed any growth of government power at the expense of business. Caught between these differing views, Wilson hesitated to mobilize by decree. Instead, he tried to create a system of economic incentives that would encourage Americans to support the war in a spirit of voluntarism.

It took nearly a year to organize an effective war administration. Wilson established a war cabinet with six key boards, conferring broad power on the central government. The War Industries Board (WIB), organized early in 1918 under the leadership of Bernard M. Baruch, a Wall Street financier, assumed the task of managing the economy. Baruch's team of 100 businessmen (many of them volunteer "Dollar-A-Year" men) fixed prices, set priorities, and reduced waste. To increase production, they appealed to the profit motive. Baruch reasoned that "you could be forgiven if you paid too much to get the stuff, but you could never be forgiven if you did not get it, and lost the war." The WIB set prices artificially high, permitting profits to triple during the war. One steel executive confessed: "We are all making more money out of this war than the average human being ought to."

The Fuel Administration, the War Trade Board, the Shipping Board, and the U.S. Railroad Administration adopted similar policies. Under the slogan "Mine More Coal," the Fuel Administration increased production by two-fifths and conserved supplies through voluntary "lightless nights" and "gasless Sundays." The Railroad Administration ended the chaos that had snarled the rail system during the early months of the war, spending more than $500 million on equipment and repairs. By offering large profits to railroads and high wages to workers, it established a rail system under national control.

"Hooverizing"

Agricultural production came under the jurisdiction of the Food Administration, headed by Herbert Hoover, a mining engineer and self-made millionaire who had served with distinction as director of relief operations in Belgium. Appealing to the spirit of patriotism, he preached "the gospel of the clean plate." Americans "Hooverized" with wheatless Mondays and Wednesdays, meatless Tuesdays, and porkless Thursdays and Saturdays.

No foe of profits, Hoover set farm prices at high levels to encourage production. He stabilized the grain market by guaranteeing farmers a minimum price, and he purchased raw sugar

and then sold it to refineries at a fixed rate. The policies worked. Overall, real farm incomes rose 30 percent during the war; and, despite bad wheat crops in 1916 and 1917, food production increased by one-quarter, domestic food consumption fell, and America's food shipments to the Allies tripled.

Peace with Labor

The government also made concessions to labor. At his own request, Wilson addressed the American Federation of Labor (AFL) convention in November 1917, the first time a president had so honored the trade union movement. Flanked by a guard of soldiers to dramatize the solemnity of the occasion, he delivered an eloquent plea for industrial peace. Important policy shifts followed. Gradually, Wilson recognized labor's right to organize and engage in collective bargaining, and he sanctioned other key demands, including the eight-hour workday. To settle labor disputes, Wilson created the National War Labor Board (WLB), with ex-president William Howard Taft and Frank B. Walsh, a liberal lawyer, as its chairmen. Though it lacked legal authority, the WLB had the president's backing and a commitment from industry and labor to accept its decisions. During the war the WLB heard 1241 cases affecting 711,500 workers.

While Wilson embraced the AFL, his administration opposed militant unions like the Industrial Workers of the World (IWW or the "Wobblies"). From the textile mills of New England to the logging camps of the Pacific Northwest, the Wobblies demanded higher wages and better working conditions, and they went out on strike to win them. Because the Wobblies frequently employed the rhetoric of class warfare to dramatize their demands, their strikes frightened many Americans who feared social revolution. Warning that strikes would cripple the war effort, shrewd businessmen played upon these fears to demand suppression of the so-called radical unions. The Wobblies were "traitors," they sneered, and the IWW stood for "I Won't Work."

Samuel Gompers, president of the AFL, shrewdly separated his union from the militant workers. He seized Wilson's olive branch and

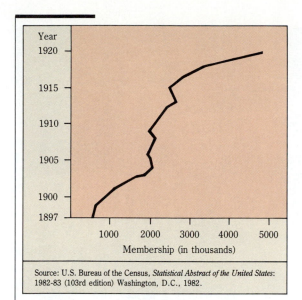

Figure 23.1
Labor union membership, 1897–1920

Source: U.S. Bureau of the Census, *Statistical Abstract of the United States:* 1982-83 (103rd edition) Washington, D.C., 1982.

pledged not to strike for the duration of the war. The AFL supported the war like superpatriots and joined the administration's attack on socialist critics. Gompers's policies paid handsome dividends. The AFL won a voice in homefront policy, and union men occupied seats in wartime agencies where they pushed for the 8-hour day and staved off pressure from employers bent on preserving the open shop. Real income of manufacturing workers and coal miners rose by one-fifth between 1914 and 1918. By 1919 almost half of the American labor force had achieved a 48-hour week (compared to one-eighth in 1915). Finally, the AFL expanded its membership from 2.7 million in 1916 to 4 million in 1919.

Financing the War

While business and labor both profited from the war, neither group could agree on how it should be financed. By 1920 the war had cost $33.5 billion—33 times the federal government's revenues in 1916. Conservatives favored a regressive tax policy—consumption taxes, borrowing, and, if necessary, a slight increase in income taxes. Reformers and radicals demanded a progressive tax policy—inheritance and excess

profits taxes coupled with higher income taxes. Wilson walked the middle ground, but the heaviest burdens fell on the wealthy through taxes on large incomes, corporate profits, and estates. By 1919 the tax burden in the highest income brackets had risen to 77 percent.

World War I brought an important change in the sources of federal tax revenues. Before the war nearly three-quarters of federal revenues had come from excise and customs taxes; the remainder came from a modest income tax and from other duties on wealth such as estate taxes. After the war, the ratios were reversed. America's tax structure shifted from taxing consumption to taxing wealth, proof that progressives had won an important victory in the struggle to make upper-income groups pay a large share of the cost of government. On the tax issue Randolph Bourne was wrong.

THE AMERICAN PUBLIC GOES TO WAR

Wilson opposed any action that might alter the nation's economic system. A fiscal conservative at heart, he wanted to keep the government's hands off the economy. Like most of his contemporaries, he preferred to see real authority and control exercised by the private sector. In the end, however, Wilson presided over the expansion of federal powers during World War I.

Selling the War

Wilson's decision to substitute voluntarism for state controls had profound social consequences. By refusing to impose statutory controls on industry, he placed the burden of supporting the war on the profit motive and the public's sense of patriotism. To be sure, this policy avoided the clash between Wilson and industry that would have resulted from strict government control over the economy, but it did so at a huge cost to civil liberties.

Throughout the war the government directed its coercion at people rather than industries. Because he doubted the loyalty of many ethnic Americans, Wilson established the Committee on Public Information (CPI) to mobilize public support for the war. Its chairman, George

Wilson's administration opposed militant labor unions like the Industrial Workers of the World (IWW), shown here striking against Oliver Steel in Pennsylvania. Such strikes did little to help the war effort at home. Samuel Gompers, who wanted to separate members of the American Federation of Labor (AFL) from more militant workers, pledged not to strike until the war was over.

W. Creel, an able and energetic journalist, created America's first propaganda agency. Creel immediately drafted a voluntary censorship agreement with newspapers that permitted them to cover the war but kept sensitive military information out of print. The CPI hired hundreds of musicians, writers, and artists to stage a patriotic campaign, and it sponsored 75,000 speakers who delivered 4-minute war pep talks in vaudeville and movie theaters across the country. During the war, Americans could not watch a movie without being told to love their country and hate the enemy.

Indeed, the CPI found a powerful ally in Hollywood. Quick to perceive the link between patriotism and profits, studio moguls cranked out scores of war films with titles such as *The Prussian Cur*, *The Claws of the Hun*, and *To Hell with the Kaiser*. Crude propaganda pieces all, these films reduced World War I to a conflict between good and evil, with the Allies cast as heroes and the Central Powers as villains. Moreover, movie stars such as Douglas Fairbanks, Mary Pickford, and Charlie Chaplin toured the country selling war bonds, while songwriters did their best to foster patriotism by pumping out a series of catchy tunes with titles like "Keep the Home Fires Burning" and "Over There."

Popular culture reflected the CPI's influence. Truth became the first casualty; language lost meaning, and stereotypes abounded. Suddenly, dissent meant treason, Germans devolved into Huns, and German-Americans all spied for the fatherland. It did not matter that the vast majority of German-Americans supported the United States; the CPI consistently attacked their loyalty. At its best the CPI may have sold war bonds, discouraged war stoppages, and convinced the public to support the war; at its worst the CPI fostered a witch-hunt.

As passions rose, Americans lashed out at all things German. In the name of patriotism, musicians no longer played Bach and Beethoven, and schools stopped teaching the German language. Americans renamed sauerkraut "liberty cabbage"; dachshunds, "liberty hounds"; and German measles, "liberty measles." Cincinnati, with its large German-American population, even removed pretzels from the free lunch counters in saloons. More alarming, vigilante groups attacked anyone suspected of being unpatriotic. German-speaking families feared talking on the street, and not without reason; many became the victims of mob violence. Workers who refused to buy war bonds often suffered harsh retribution, and attacks on labor protesters were nothing short of brutal. The legal system backed the suppression. Juries routinely released defendants accused of violence against individuals or groups critical of the war.

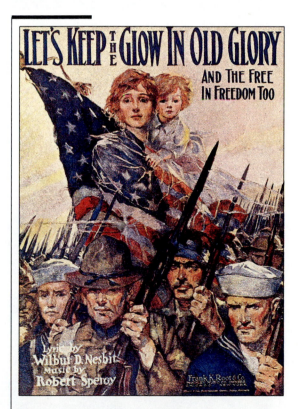

Hollywood and Tin Pan Alley did their parts to encourage patriotism by putting out scores of war films and a large number of music pieces like the one shown here.

Political Repression

The government fueled the hysteria. In June 1917 Congress passed the Espionage Act, which gave postal officials the authority to ban newspapers and magazines from the mails and threatened individuals convicted of obstructing the draft with $10,000 fines and 20 years in jail. The following year, Congress clamped down harder. The Sedition Act of 1918 made it a federal offense to use "disloyal, profane, scurrilous, or abusive language" about the Constitution, the government, the American uniform, or the flag. The government prosecuted over 2100 people under these acts. Randolph Bourne's prediction that civil rights would fall victim to the power of the state rang true.

Political dissenters bore the brunt of the repression. Eugene V. Debs, who urged socialists to resist militarism, went to prison for nearly three years. The IWW never recovered from government attacks during World War I. In September 1917 the Justice Department staged massive raids on IWW officers, arresting 169 of its veteran leaders. The administration's purpose was, as one attorney put it, "very largely to put the IWW out of business." Many observers thought the judicial system would protect dissenters, but the courts handed down stiff prison sentences to the Wobblies.

The Supreme Court later approved the attacks on civil liberties. Oliver Wendell Holmes, the court's leading champion of civil liberties, upheld the Espionage Act in *Schenck* v. *United States* (1919) by comparing the denial of free speech during the war to the prohibition against "a man falsely shouting fire in a theater and causing panic." In a second case, *Abrams* v. *United States* (1919), Holmes reversed himself and argued against the Sedition Act, returning to his support for "free trade in ideas." He was outvoted seven to two.

World War I did not cause repression; it merely intensified old fears. Many Americans clung to the image of the United States as a strong, isolated country, inhabited by old stock, white, middle-class Protestants. Their vision no longer reflected reality, but the war offered them a chance to lash out at those who had changed America. Immigrants, radical labor organizers, socialists, anarchists, Communists, and critics of any kind became victims of intolerance.

Wartime Reform

The war hysteria bred a curious alliance between superpatriots and old style reformers. Prohibitionists had little difficulty turning World War I to their advantage. They had been winning victories at the state level since the middle of the nineteenth century, but they did not enjoy any success at the federal level until 1917 when Congress prohibited the use of grain for the production of alcoholic beverages, insisting that foodstuffs must be used to feed America's soldiers and Allies. To supply an additional push, prohibitionists joined the anti-German craze, portraying America's enemies as beer-guzzling Huns and warning that German-Americans controlled the nation's breweries. Congress passed the Eighteenth Amendment in 1917 and the final state ratified the amendment two months after the Armistice. The Volstead Act, which banned the manufacture, transportation, and sale of alcoholic beverages, took effect one year later.

Like prohibition, women's suffrage benefited from the emergency atmosphere of World War I. Although radical suffragists, led by Alice Paul of the National Woman's Party, refused to back the war as long as women could not vote, most women's organizations supported the war effort. Wilson appointed suffragists Carrie Chapman Catt and Anna Howard Shaw as directors of the Women's Committee of the Council of National Defense. As blue-collar female workers started pouring into defense industries, middle-class women showed support for the war by volunteering to help the sick and the wounded. Thousands of women joined the Red Cross and the American Women's Hospital Service and served overseas as nurses, physicians, clerks, and ambulance drivers, and thousands more enlisted in the military after the army established the Army Corps of Nurses in 1918.

Suffragists demanded the vote in return for their support of the war. Wilson had long opposed women's suffrage, but political reality ultimately forced his hand. Most western states had granted women the vote before he entered

Members of the National Woman's Party, led by Alice Paul (on the balcony), celebrate their right to vote at their headquarters in Washington, D.C., in 1920.

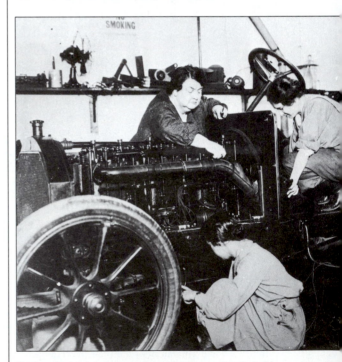

During the war, many women took jobs previously held by men. Here a group of women assemble an automobile in a factory.

the White House. When Illinois fell in line in 1914, followed by Rhode Island and New York in 1917, pressure started building for national action. Alice Paul, head of the National Woman's Party, pressed the issue by organizing around-the-clock picketing in front of the White House. Determined to prevent women's suffrage from becoming a political issue in the congressional elections of 1918, Wilson told the Senate that the vote for women "is vital to the winning of the war." In 1919, shortly after the Armistice, Congress passed the Nineteenth Amendment, granting women the right to vote. Ratification followed in the summer of 1920.

Apart from voting rights, World War I brought few permanent changes for women. Women had hoped the war would open new jobs for them. Instead, employment opportunities proved meager and brief. Of the one million women who found work in war-related industries, the majority had held jobs before the war. Labor unions opposed hiring women and tolerated their presence solely as a wartime necessity. Industrial jobs, the unions insisted, belonged to men and should be returned to them as soon as the war ended. As the Central Federated Union of New York put it: "the same patriotism which induced women to enter industry during the war should induce them to vacate their positions after the war." Fewer than half of the women who took jobs in heavy industry during the war still held them in 1919, and the number of women who remained in the work force in 1920 dropped below the 1910 figures.

Blacks and the Great Migration

Like women, blacks wanted to use the war to improve their status. While the government had given blacks little reason to shed their blood, most black newspapers backed the war. The militant black intellectual W. E. B. Du Bois urged blacks to "close ranks" with whites, declaring, "If this is our country, then this is our war." Du Bois hoped that blacks, by demonstrating patriotism and bravery, could win public respect and earn better treatment after the war.

At first military leaders even denied blacks the right to fight for their country. The marines accepted no blacks; the navy used them only as mess boys; and the army planned to make them

laborers and stevedores. When the National Association for the Advancement of Colored People (NAACP) and other black organizations protested, however, the army agreed to compromise. Following the Civil War example, the army created black regiments commanded almost exclusively by white officers. Black regiments committed to battle fought bravely, but most black soldiers in Europe never got the chance to prove their valor. Instead, they were assigned to move supplies. While two-thirds of the American Expeditionary Force saw combat, only one-fifth of the black troops did so.

Back home the record was equally mixed. In the decades following the Civil War a steady trickle of blacks had left the South to search for jobs in northern cities. During World War I the trickle became a flood. Plagued by the boll weevil, low cotton prices, and unrelenting white repression, sharecroppers longed for change. When labor agents appeared in 1916 promising jobs in the North, blacks responded eagerly. By November 1918 the "Great Migration" had brought half a million southern blacks to the "Land of Hope."

Many found jobs in northern factories and packing houses. The labor force in Chicago's packing houses had been 97 percent white in 1901, but by 1918 they employed 10,000 blacks—over 20 percent of the work force. The labor force in the northern steel industry had been virtually all white in 1900, but by 1920 blacks held 10 percent of those jobs. Still, regardless of the industry, discrimination forced blacks to the bottom of the ladder, where they took over the menial, backbreaking jobs that had been vacated by Slavic and Italian workers, the most recent wave of immigrants.

The Great Migration angered southern whites. The price of cotton tripled during the war; southern planters, fearing the loss of their labor force, resorted to intimidation and mob violence to stop the exodus. A mob in Mississippi, for example, derailed a train to prevent blacks from leaving. Like their ancestors who had taken the underground railroad to freedom, many blacks who moved to the North during World War I had to travel under cover of darkness.

Northern whites opposed the Great Migration, too. Manufacturers welcomed cheap black

The 369th Infantry Regiment returned from the war in February 1919. They were awarded the *Croix de Guerre* (war cross) for bravery in the Meuse-Argonne.

labor (especially as strikebreakers), but most Northerners felt threatened by the newcomers. Middle-class whites feared changes in the racial composition of their society, while immigrants resented the competition for jobs and housing. Increasingly, Northerners turned to segregation, discrimination, and violence; and blacks, hoping for a better life in the North, fought back. Race riots erupted in 26 cities in 1917, with the most serious violence occurring in East St. Louis, where at least 39 blacks died in the fighting.

Clearly, World War I meant different things to different groups: for the administration, a test of the limits of voluntarism; for businessmen and technocrats, a chance to pull the levers of government; for nativists and superpatriots, an excuse to lash out at "undesirable" elements; for radicals and dissenters, repression and hardship; for manufacturers and farmers, high profits; for reformers, victories on women's suffrage and prohibition; for trade unions, the right to organize for better pay; and for blacks, a chance to escape from southern poverty.

THE WAR FRONT

The United States entered World War I without a large army or the ships to transport one to Europe. Six weeks before Congress declared war, the army had not even drafted plans to organize a large military force. Confident the Allies were winning, Wilson hoped to limit America's contribution to supplies, financial credits, and moral support. In truth, the Allies were ready to collapse. The French army was in the throes of mutiny. Soldiers were tired of suicidal assaults ordered by inept generals, and the submarine offensive had reduced Britain to a six-week supply of food. (Allied losses for 1917 stood at 6.5 million tons of shipping.)

The War at Sea

Faced with a desperate situation, Wilson ordered the United States Navy to act immediately. American ships relieved the British of patrolling the Western Hemisphere while another portion of the fleet steamed to the north Atlantic to combat the submarine menace. Six destroyers reached Ireland on May 4; 35 ships had arrived by July; and 343 ships patrolled the seas surrounding England by the war's end.

American and British commanders disagreed sharply on how best to defend merchant ships. The British believed in the "needle in the haystack" theory—dispersing individual vessels widely at sea and then shooting them through carefully patrolled channels for the last leg of the journey. The policy had not worked. In April alone shipping losses totaled 881,027 tons. The Americans proposed a convoy system—using warships to escort merchant ships to Great Britain. The British reluctantly agreed, and by December the convoy system had cut losses in half.

Raising an Army

Wilson responded more cautiously to the Allies' cries for land forces. His choice to lead the American Expeditionary Force (AEF) was Major General John J. "Black Jack" Pershing. Despite urgent requests from Allied commanders, Pershing refused to send raw recruits to the front. He also rejected demands that American units be integrated as replacements into British and French regiments. Instead, Pershing insisted on keeping American troops as independent units under his command. To bolster Allied morale while the army trained, the War Department hurriedly dispatched the First Division to France, where it marched through Paris on July 4, 1917, to the cheers of thousands.

A bitter debate erupted over how to raise the troops. Confronted with heavy pressure from Theodore Roosevelt and others who favored a volunteer army, Wilson insisted on conscription. Critics opposed the draft as unnecessary and undemocratic. Responding to the selective service bill, Congressman Champ Clark of Missouri spoke for many when he declared: "There is precious little difference between a conscript and a convict." Despite widespread fears that the draft threatened democracy, Congress passed the Selective Service Act on May 18, 1917. (Unlike the Civil War, no draft riots followed.) More than 23 million men registered during World War I, and 2,810,296 draftees served in the armed forces.

To assign soldiers to the right military tasks, the army launched an ambitious program of psychological testing. The man who developed and presided over this effort was Robert M. Yerkes, a Harvard-trained psychologist and former president of the American Psychological Association. Yerkes was a brilliant organizer and a forceful promoter of his profession. Since most scientists regarded psychology as a "soft" discipline (most universities placed psychology in the philosophy department), Yerkes saw the war as an opportunity to establish the academic legitimacy of psychology by providing a vital service to the nation. "If the Army machine is to work smoothly and efficiently," he declared, "it is as important to fit the job to the man as to fit the ammunition to the gun."

Yerkes and his associates all believed intelligence was hereditary and quickly developed two separate tests designed to separate smart people from the masses. Army Alpha was for those who could read English; Army Beta was for men who failed the Alpha test or could not read English. The Alpha test included questions that became the stock and trade of mental testing—untangling sentences, supplying the next number of a sequence, making analogies, and so forth. The Beta test used pictures to examine the same skills. Both tests could be completed in less than an hour, and both could be administered to large groups of men. During the war, 1.75 million recruits took the tests.

Though Yerkes insisted his tests measured native intelligence, they did not. They favored men who possessed academic skills. Men who knew their way around a school room scored higher than those who did not. "It was touching," one examiner observed, "to see the intense effort . . . put into answering questions, often by men who had never held a pencil in their hands." Still, the army needed some means of sorting out its huge number of draftees, and mental testing appeared to be fair and democratic. Actually, it reinforced the class structure of American society. Native-born whites achieved the highest scores, while blacks and recent immigrants consistently scored lower.

Apart from selecting officers, the army made little use of the test data. Ordinary soldiers were not assigned tasks on the basis of test scores. After the war, however, Yerkes boldly proclaimed that mental testing had "helped to win the war." All it really accomplished was to sell the public on the idea of mental testing and lay the groundwork for a thriving peacetime industry. After the war, numerous businesses adopted mental tests to screen personnel, and many colleges began requiring them for admission. Few legacies of the war had a more lasting or widespread impact on American society.

The Defeat of Germany

As the American army trained, the situation in Europe deteriorated. The mutiny within the French army was spreading (ten divisions were now in revolt); the eastern front dissolved in March when the Bolsheviks, who had seized power in Russia in November, accepted Germany's peace terms; and German and Austrian forces had all but routed the Italian armies. In fact, by late 1917 the war had come down to a race between American mobilization and Germany's war machine.

(Text continues on p. 780)

THE FIRST DAY OF THE SOMME

During the American Civil War Richard J. Gatling hoped to become wealthy by selling the Union army his hand-cranked machine gun. His weapon could unleash up to 200 rounds a minute, as compared to the 2 to 3 rounds a minute from a rifled musket being loaded and fired by a well-trained soldier. Gatling considered his weapon "providential," the ultimate device, he wrote to Abraham Lincoln, for "crushing the rebellion." After the war Gatling even spoke of social benefits. His machine gun would ease the pain and suffering of war. Only one soldier would be needed "to do as much battle duty as a hundred" because of his gun's "rapidity of fire." His weapon would "supersede the necessity of large armies, and consequently exposure to battle and disease would be greatly diminished."

Hiram Maxim, another inventor, offered a major improvement in

1884 when he demonstrated a mechanism that would permit a machine gun to fire automatically, simply by depressing the trigger. Because of such technological breakthroughs, water-cooled machine guns capable of shooting 600 rounds a minute were commonplace in the arsenal of weapons used by the armies engaged in World War I. These Maxim guns, as they were generically known, could spray an area with bullets and easily destroy companies of soldiers trained well enough to fire their breechloading rifles 15 times a minute. The machine gun proved to be an effective killing weapon.

More sophisticated weapons did not, as Richard Gatling had assured his customers, result in any reduction in the size of wartime armies. During Europe's Age of Industrialization the major powers built up ever larger military forces, as if only huge masses of troops could defeat

the enhanced firepower of new weapons such as the machine gun.

When the armies of Europe first collided in August 1914 after Germany's penetration through Belgium, a stark reality became clear. Firepower, both in the form of small arms and large artillery, was so overwhelming that neither side could defeat the other without virtual annihilation. What emerged were opposing lines of trenches along the western front, running without interruption south from the North Sea all the way through France to the border of Switzerland. For the next three years combat became a horrible contest in which one or the other side tried to break through these trench lines.

The Battle of the Somme was in many ways typical. Up until June 1916 this sector in northeastern France was inactive. German divisions had been present since September 1914 and had constructed three defensive lines of trenches running back from "no man's land," an area some 500 to 1000 yards wide on the other side of which were trenches manned by the Allies—the British to the north and the French to the south of the Somme River. Because of a fearsome struggle occurring far to the south at Verdun, the Allied high command, after preliminary planning, decided in May 1916 to mount a massive offensive in the Somme sector.

If German lines could be permanently ruptured, then it would be possible to roll up enemy divisions on their flanks. German soldiers would face surrender or retreat, thus breaking the military deadlock in favor of the Allies. To breech the German trenches in coordinated fashion along 50 miles involved detailed planning, considering the thousands of troops and massive firepower that the Allies faced. Further, surprise attacks were impossible. German artillery and machine gun operators had the capacity to obliterate waves of soldiers trying to cross no man's land, even before they reached the barbed wire placed in front of the German trenches. The alternative was to prepare the way with an extended artillery bombardment.

The Battle of the Somme erupted with a seven-day cannonade. During the last week of June some 50,000 British artillerists fired 2,960,000 rounds at the German trenches. By evening of the second day, wrote an observer, "some sectors of the German front line were already unrecognizable and had become crater fields." The next day the British started releasing clouds of chlorine gas, hoping that it would seep down into dugouts 20 or more feet below ground where German soldiers were living, surviving, and listening carefully for the climactic fury of the bombardment, the sure sign that the infantry assault was to begin.

At 6:30 A.M., on July 1, 1916, one hour before infantry troops were to advance, the cannonade reached "an intensity as yet unparalleled . . . along the whole front." German soldiers noticed the difference and knew that the moment of reckoning was near. The whole course of the battle would depend on their ability to get back above ground, set up their machine guns, and begin firing before enemy infantry overran them. It was a moment for which they had repeatedly trained.

As zero hour approached, thousands of British and French soldiers made final preparations in their trenches. Their assignment was to secure control of the second German

line by the end of the day. Soon they would be climbing up scaling ladders and jumping over the top, then listening for the sounds of whistles from their platoon leaders to guide them across no man's land. Most found themselves "sweating at zero hour," supposedly from "nervous excitement." Many had attended church services the previous day. Explained one British soldier, "I placed my body in God's keeping, and I am going into battle with His name on my lips." Everyone received a warm breakfast and a healthy ration of rum to settle their jittery nerves.

Promptly at 7:30 A.M., the race began. Over the top went hundreds of thousands of British and French troops. Up out of their dugouts came German soldiers. In most areas the Germans were ready with time to spare. Their machine gun and artillery fire cut one-third of the British battalions to shreds before they reached what remained of the first German trenches.

British soldiers who survived witnessed unbelievable sights. One watched as "two men suddenly rose into the air vertically, 15 feet perhaps," as a German shell hit the ground ahead of him. "They rose and fell with the easy, graceful poise of acrobats," he noted, as they died. Another saw men "falling forward," stating that it was "some time before I realized they were hit." In one company only three soldiers made it to the German barbed wire. Their leader, a lieutenant, looked around in amazement and said: "God, God, where's the rest of the boys?"

Hardly over the top, a British sergeant heard the "patter, patter" of German machine guns. "By the time I'd gone another ten yards," he explained, "there seemed to be only

a few men left around me; by the time I had gone twenty yards, I seemed to be on my own. Then I was hit myself." This sergeant was among the fortunate. In some sectors, British soldiers who evaded machine gun fire and reached the other side "were burned to death by [German] flame throwers."

From the British perspective, the fighting went poorly that day. By evening they had not captured the German second line, but they had suffered 60,000 casualties, including 21,000 dead. The Germans, who got most of their machine guns up and operating, experienced only 6000 casualties by comparison.

The battle, however, had just begun. It would rage in fits and starts until November 18, 1916, when the Allies decided that a breakthrough in the Somme sector was not attainable. By that time the British had suffered 420,000 casualties, the French an estimated 200,000. No one knows exactly how many soldiers the Germans lost, but a fair guess would be in the 500,000 to 600,000 range. Yet virtually no ground had been lost or gained.

It is not surprising, then, that the Allies rejoiced when the Americans finally entered the war. They needed more than loans and war goods to achieve total victory. Field Marshal Joseph Joffre, the former French commander-in-chief, said it all when he arrived in the United States after Congress declared war in April 1917. Declared Joffe with his usual bluntness: "We want men, men, men."

On March 21, 1918, General Erich Ludendorff launched a massive offensive on the western front in the Valley of the Somme. Committing more than 600 artillery guns to the attack, the Germans struck the British and then the French. Germany's strategy was obvious: Split the French and British forces, drive the British into the sea, and win the war. For a time, it looked as though the Germans would succeed. Badly bloodied, the Allied forces lost ground. With German troops barely 50 miles from Paris, Marshal Ferdinand Foch, the leader of the French army, assumed command of the Allied forces.

On July 15, 1918, Germany mustered its forces for one last drive on Paris. After three days of heated battle, Foch's Allied troops, aided by 85,000 American soldiers, turned them back. Foch then launched a furious counteroffensive that lasted until August 6. Allied troops, strengthened by American divisions, hit the Germans hard in a series of bloody assaults, pushing them back to the Belgian border by the end of October.

During the final months of fighting, American troops hit Europe like a tidal wave. In June 279,000 American soldiers crossed the Atlantic; in July over 300,000; in August, 286,000. By mid-August, "Yanks" occupied the southern tip of the western front, and the American First Army, under the command of General Pershing, began its first independent action on September 12, capturing 16,000 Germans in three days. By the end of September, Pershing commanded an army of 1.2 million and the American forces manned about one-fourth (approximately 85 miles) of the western front.

All told, 1.5 million American troops arrived in Europe during the last six months of the war. Fresh and battle ready, Pershing's forces made the crucial difference in the war. Germany enjoyed numerical superiority when American troops first arrived, but by the end of the war the Allies could field 600,000 more men than the Germans.

Buoyed by the fresh manpower, the Allies pressed their advantage. Their furious offensive in the summer of 1918 broke the opposition, and within a few months the Central Powers faced certain defeat. The Austro-Hungarian Empire asked for peace; Turkey and Bulgaria stopped fighting; and Germany requested an armistice, hoping Wilson would give them enough time to withdraw to a more defensible position. Instead, he insisted that the German forces leave France and Belgium and surrender all arms. In a direct slap at the kaiser, Wilson announced he would negotiate only with a democratic regime in Germany. Though the military leaders and the kaiser wavered, the German people had suffered enough. A brief revolution forced the kaiser to abdicate, and a civilian regime assumed control of the government.

Germany's new government immediately accepted the armistice and agreed to negotiate a treaty. At 11:00 A.M., November 11, 1918, the guns stopped. At the moment of peace, German

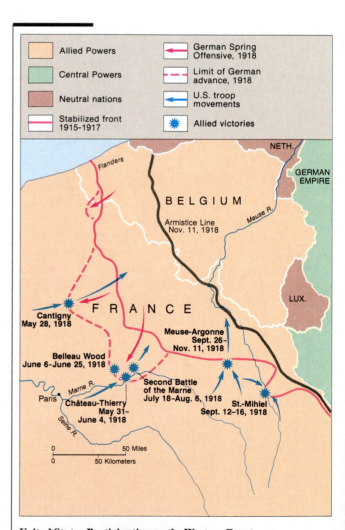

United States Participation on the Western Front

and Allied soldiers entered no man's land to gossip and trade souvenirs. Throughout the Western world, crowds filled the streets to celebrate peace.

SOCIAL UNREST AFTER THE WAR

Peace did not restore stability to the United States. Jubilation over the Armistice quickly dissolved into fear, unleashing the forces of conformity, vigilantism, and repression. Attacks centered on blacks, organized labor, and political dissidents—the very groups old-stock citizens blamed for the changes in American society they found most threatening. The Wilson administration either led the attacks or did nothing to stop them as government officials found new enemies at home to replace those abroad. Echoing Bourne's earlier warnings, Frederick Howe, the commissioner of immigration under President Wilson, later confided: "I became distrustful of the state. It seemed to want to hurt people; it showed no concern for innocence; it aggrandized itself and protected its powers by unscrupulous means."

Race relations deteriorated badly after the war. Tensions rose in the North because of competition between whites and blacks for jobs and housing. In the South, whites felt threatened by the return of 400,000 black veterans, many of whom had been trained in the use of firearms, even if many had not seen actual combat. Moreover, many black veterans had served in France where they were treated as equals, and southern whites feared they would demand the same treatment at home. Determined to keep blacks repressed, southern whites instituted a reign of terror. In 1919 10 black veterans were lynched (several still in uniform); 14 were burned at the stake. All told 70 lynchings occurred in the first year of peace.

As the heat of summer brought tensions to a boil, race riots broke out in 25 cities. The worst violence erupted on a Chicago beach where 17-year-old Eugene Williams strayed into waters claimed by whites. A rock-throwing mob kept him from reaching shore, and Williams drowned. Fighting broke out when police refused to arrest his killers. Thirteen days of

On November 11, 1918, American troops celebrated the news of the Armistice on the western front, while the Western world rejoiced at home.

street violence followed, leaving 38 dead, 578 injured, and 1000 families homeless.

The growing violence dismayed black and white liberals. In Atlanta, they established the Commission on Interracial Cooperation to promote better race relations. The NAACP, which had emerged from the war as the leading representative of black Americans, advised blacks to defend themselves until a solution could be found that combined peace with justice. W. E. B. Du Bois urged black veterans to put their military training to use, exhorting them to "return fighting." The sad truth, however, was that the black masses could not defend themselves from white attacks any more than civil rights organizations could destroy segregation, end discrimination, or abolish lynch law. Racial injustice remained a defining feature of American life throughout the Progressive Era.

Labor Unrest and the Red Scare

Labor was another trouble spot. Most workers demonstrated their patriotism by not striking during the war, but the Armistice ended their truce with management. High inflation, job competition from returning veterans, and government policies all contributed to labor's discontent. Of the three, inflation hit workers the hardest. Food prices more than doubled between 1915 and 1920; clothing costs more than tripled. Wilson had made peace with trade unions only as a wartime necessity. After the fighting stopped, he removed wartime controls on industry. Correctly interpreting this as a green light from the White House, business leaders closed ranks to roll back wartime concessions to workers.

The first strike came four days after the Armistice. In New York the Amalgamated Clothing Workers walked out for a 15 percent wage hike and a 44-hour week. To the surprise of most observers, the workers won. In the months that followed textile workers, actors, and telephone operators went out; a general strike paralyzed Seattle; the bituminous miners struck; 365,000 steelworkers staged the biggest strike the nation had ever seen; and the Boston police force even walked out. By the end of 1919 more than 4 million workers (a staggering 20 percent of the work force) had staged over 3600 strikes nationwide.

The strikes left the labor movement in shambles. Well-established unions affiliated with the AFL came through the turmoil in good shape, but unions of unskilled workers in the mass production industries, such as the United Mine Workers or the steelworkers, went down for the count. Overall, labor unions lost 1.5 million members by 1920. The message was clear: Without government backing, organized labor could not win against the united strength of the antiunion employers.

The strikes frightened middle- and upper-class Americans, who feared the country might be swept by revolution. The government made matters worse by blaming the strikes on Communists. The Bolshevik revolution had taken Russia out of the war by 1918, angering large numbers of Americans. Then in March 1919, the Bolsheviks organized the Third International and called for socialists and workers in Europe and the United States to seize their governments and join the worldwide revolution. When Communist revolts erupted in eastern Europe, Americans braced themselves for trouble at home.

A bomb scare brought public fears to a head. On the eve of May 1 (May Day), 1919, authorities discovered 20 bombs in the mail of prominent capitalists, including John D. Rockefeller and J. P. Morgan, Jr., as well as government officials like Postmaster General Albert S. Burleson and Justice Oliver Wendell Holmes. A month later, bombs exploded in eight American cities. Anarchists were probably responsible, but the public blamed the Communists. Ironically, most American radicals denounced the violence.

Fear sparked by the labor unrest, communism, and the bombings plunged the United States into the "Red Scare" of 1919 and early 1920. Every threat to national security, real or imagined, fed the public's anxiety. The nation had lost confidence in its ability to survive without police state tactics. Civil liberties became the first victim of the hysteria, for the Bill of Rights was all but suspended. Again, Randolph Bourne's warnings hit the mark.

Vigilantism flourished as juries across the country acquitted individuals accused of violent acts against Communists. In the Washington lumber town of Centralia, American Legionnaires stormed the IWW office on Armistice Day. Four attackers died in the fight, and townspeople lynched an IWW member in reprisal. Four other Wobblies received long prison sentences for murder. Following the Centralia raid, government officials went after IWW members across the state, arresting over 1000 Wobblies. Federal authorities then moved to break the IWW's back by prosecuting 165 Wobblie leaders, who received prison sentences ranging up to 25 years.

Congress joined the attack. In May 1919 the House refused to seat Victor Berger, a Milwaukee Socialist, after he was convicted of sedition. The House again denied him his seat following a special election in December 1919. Not until his reelection in 1922, after the government dropped its charges, did Congress seat him.

Attorney General A. Mitchell Palmer led the attack on radicalism. Determined to become president in 1920, Palmer hoped to ride a wave of public hysteria against radicalism into the White House. To root out sedition, he created a General Intelligence Division (the precursor of the FBI) in the Justice Department under the direction of J. Edgar Hoover. Hoover collected the names of thousands of known or suspected Communists and made plans for a coordinated government attack on their headquarters.

In November 1919 Palmer struck with lightning speed at radicals in 12 cities. The raids netted 250 arrests, a small taste of what followed. A second series of raids in 33 cities came in January. This time Palmer's men arrested more than 4000 alleged Communists, many of whom were jailed without bond, beaten, and denied food and water for days. Local authorities freed most of them in a few weeks, except for 600 aliens, who were deported.

Palmer insisted he was ridding the country of the "moral perverts and hysterical neurasthenic women who abound in communism." To cooler heads, however, his tactics gave off the unmistakable odor of a police state. Charles Evans Hughes denounced the raids as "violations of personal rights which savor of the worst practices of tyranny." Suddenly on the defensive, Palmer tried to rally public support by predicting a second wave of terrorist attacks on May Day, 1920. Federal troops went on alert, and police braced themselves in cities across the country, but May Day came and went with-

out incident. Suddenly Palmer looked more like dead wood than presidential timber. His bid for the White House fizzled, and the Red Scare faded into memory.

THE TREATY OF VERSAILLES

The Fourteen Points

Long before the war's military outcome became clear, the Allies started planning for peace. As early as 1915 Britain and France signed secret treaties plotting harsh peace terms for Germany. Their plans made a mockery of Wilson's call for "peace without victory." Wilson felt a punitive treaty would sow the seeds of future wars. Repeatedly during the war, he elaborated his ideas on the interdependence of democracy, free trade, and liberty, and on January 8, 1918, he unveiled the Fourteen Points, his personal peace formula.

Five of the points were general. Wilson called for "open covenants openly arrived at," freedom of the seas, free trade, arms reduction, and self-determination. Other points demanded partial or full independence for minorities and a recognition of the rise of nationalist senti-

TABLE 23.1

Woodrow Wilson's Fourteen Points, 1918: Success and Failure in Implementation

1. Open covenants of peace openly arrived at	Not fulfilled
2. Absolute freedom of navigation upon the seas in peace and war	Not fulfilled
3. Removal of all economic barriers to the equality of trade among nations	Not fulfilled
4. Reduction of armaments to the level needed only for domestic safety	Not fulfilled
5. Impartial adjustment of colonial claims	Not fulfilled
6. Evacuation of all Russian territory; Russia to be welcomed into the society of free nations	Not fulfilled
7. Evacuation and restoration of Belgium	**Fulfilled**
8. Evacuation and restoration of all French lands; return of Alsace-Lorraine to France	**Fulfilled**
9. Readjustment of Italy's frontiers along lines of Italian nationality	Compromised
10. Self-determination for the former subjects of the Austro-Hungarian Empire	Compromised
11. Evacuation of Rumania, Serbia, and Montenegro; free access to the sea for Serbia	Compromised
12. Self-determination for the former subjects of the Ottoman Empire; secure sovereignty for Turkish portion	Compromised
13. Establishment of an independent Poland, with free and secure access to the sea	**Fulfilled**
14. Establishment of a League of Nations affording mutual guarantees of independence and territorial integrity	Not fulfilled

Source: Data from G. M. Gathorne-Hardy, *The Fourteen Points and the Treaty of Versailles* (Oxford Pamphlets on World Affairs, no. 6, 1939), pp. 8–34; Thomas G. Paterson et al., *American Foreign Policy, A History Since 1900*, 2d ed., Vol. 2, pp. 282–93.

ments. The fourteenth point, which Wilson considered the heart of his plan, called for a League of Nations, an international organization to promote world peace by guaranteeing the territorial integrity of all nations. The fairness of the terms, Wilson hoped, would command the support of the Allies and strengthen the hand of peace advocates within Germany.

Economically, the Fourteen Points projected Wilson's vision of liberal capitalism, the New Freedom, onto a world stage. His call for freedom of the seas and free trade was designed to protect free market capitalism from monopolistic restrictions and open huge markets to booming American industries. Self-determination would offer independence to Europe's minorities and thereby delight millions of recent immigrants back in the United States, most of whom were drifting into the Democratic party. The League of Nations would enable the world to police aggression and relieve the United States of that responsibility. From Wilson's standpoint, the Fourteen Points were perfect: They offered peace, freedom, and profits.

When the tide of war turned in favor of the Allies in 1918, peace forces within Germany agreed to surrender on the basis of the Fourteen Points. They overthrew the kaiser's regime, paving the way for Wilson to make good on his promise of peace without victory.

Wilson's personal prestige peaked with the Armistice. During the war, Democrats and Republicans had closed ranks behind his leadership under the slogan, "politics is adjourned." Europeans saw Wilson as the moral leader of the Western democracies, and his authority rested not only on words but on might. Economically, the United States was now the most powerful nation on earth. It had been spared the devastation of war; its economy was booming; and its armed forces, in sharp contrast to Europe's exhausted armies, had barely geared up for battle.

Yet Wilson proved to be his own worst enemy in marshaling support for his peace plans. His first mistake was the "October Appeal," in which he asked voters to support Democratic candidates at the polls in 1918 if they wished him to continue as their "unembarrassed spokesman." His request offended Republicans who had faithfully supported the ad-

ministration throughout the war. When voters gave Republicans a narrow majority (primarily reflecting local issues), Wilson looked as if he had lost a national referendum on his leadership.

The American Peace Commission's composition further alienated Congress. Instead of allowing Secretary of State Robert Lansing to head the American commission, Wilson elected to take personal responsibility for negotiating the peace, a role no previous president had assumed. In addition, he named only one Republican to the five-man commission; the other three men were loyal Democrats and personal associates. The failure to include a prominent Republican senator, such as Henry Cabot Lodge of Massachusetts, the newly elected chairman of the powerful Senate Committee on Foreign Relations, was a serious tactical error. The treaty had to be approved by two-thirds of the Senate, and Republicans picked up five new Senate seats in the congressional elections of 1918, giving them a two-vote majority.

Discord Among the Victors

The delegates, who arrived in Europe early in January 1919, confronted three basic issues: territory, reparations, and future security. On each of these issues, Wilson and the Allies disagreed. Early in the war the Allies decided to divide Germany's territorial possessions among themselves, but the Fourteen Points called for self-determination. Devastated by the war, the Allies (especially France) wanted to saddle Germany with huge reparations to pay for the war. The Fourteen Points rejected punishment, arguing it would only lead to future wars. On the issue of security, France wanted Germany dismembered while the other Allies favored treaties and alliances.

Only five nations played an important role in the proceedings. Prime Minister David Lloyd George of Great Britain proved to be Wilson's staunchest ally. Yet he also defended Britain's colonial ambitions and insisted on reparations. Premier Georges Clemenceau, the "Tiger" of France, was determined to break up the German empire and bleed the German people dry in order to rebuild France. He wryly remarked, "God gave us the Ten Commandments and we

At the January peace conference in Paris, Wilson met with Prime Minister David Lloyd George, Premier Vittorio Orlando, and Premier Georges Clemenceau.

broke them. Wilson gave us his Fourteen Points—we shall see."

Premier Vittorio Orlando of Italy, the most urbane of the delegates, was bent on pressing Italy's territorial ambitions in the Tyrol and on the Adriatic. When Wilson refused to sanction Italy's sovereignty over the largely Yugoslav population near Fiume, Orlando stormed out of the peace conference in disgust. The final important negotiator was Count Nobuaki Makino, the ambitious spokesman for Japan, who demanded control over German interests in the Far East. In addition, he complicated peace negotiations by insisting upon a statement of racial equality in the League of Nations charter.

The Russians were conspicuously absent at Versailles. Allied leaders, furious at the Bolsheviks for negotiating a separate peace with Germany at Brest-Litovsk in March 1918, refused to assign V. I. Lenin's "Red" government a place at the peace conference. Indeed, the Allies had earlier decided to intervene militarily in the Russian Revolution, and even as their spokesmen met in Versailles, Allied armies were fighting in Russia on the side of the "White," or anti-Communist, forces.

Personally, Wilson despised the Bolsheviks (too undemocratic), and, in keeping with his response to Huerta's regime in Mexico, he refused to extend diplomatic recognition to Lenin's government. Moreover, much as he had with Mexico, Wilson did not stop to ponder how Russians would react to finding American soldiers on their soil. To help rescue Czech troops trapped by the Germans in northern Russia, Wilson sent 5000 American soldiers to the Soviet Union in 1918, where they joined British troops. The following year Wilson sent 9000 American troops to Siberia to help evacuate Czech troops through Vladivostok. Wilson hoped American troops in Russia would save the Czechs and discourage any Japanese designs on Siberia. In addition, he wanted this show of force to bolster the anti-Communist forces in Russia by weakening the Bolsheviks' claims to power. Consequently, the United States dragged its feet and did not withdraw its last troops from Russia until 1920.

American Military Forces in Russia, 1918

The Bolsheviks deeply resented these heavy-handed efforts to undermine their regime. Yet the invasion of Russian soil by American troops was not the only reason for the intense hatred that developed between Lenin and Wilson. As the architect of the Bolshevik Revolution, Lenin emerged as Wilson's chief rival for world leadership. Where Wilson offered liberal democracy and limited social change, Lenin championed communism, social revolution, and swift changes. Wilson was determined to see his vision of the future, not Lenin's, carry the day at Versailles.

To achieve any treaty at all, Wilson had to compromise. Though he fought gallantly, he could not overcome the combined strength of his opponents. In the end he tried to scale down their demands and pinned his hopes on the League of Nations. Under the territorial compromise, the Allies gained control of Germany's colonies as "mandates" under the League of Nation's supervision. Japan acquired Germany's Pacific islands under mandate and assumed Germany's economic interest in China's Shantung peninsula. In eastern Europe, the delegates created the nation states of Poland, Yugoslavia, Czechoslovakia, Estonia, Latvia, Lithuania, and Finland. Europe's political map for the first time roughly resembled its linguistic and cultural map.

Security proved more difficult to negotiate. Over the misgivings of most delegates, Wilson insisted on making the League of Nations an integral part of the final treaty. France remained dubious that any international organization could protect French borders and demanded a buffer zone. To satisfy Clemenceau, the delegates gave France control over Alsace-Lorraine for 10 years and placed the coal-rich Saar Basin under the League of Nations for 15 years. After Wilson and Lloyd George both signed security treaties guaranteeing these arrangements, France grudgingly agreed to join the League of Nations.

Despite promises of a just peace, the treaty imposed a harsh settlement on Germany, burdening the country with a $34 billion reparations bill, far more than Germany could pay. In addition, Germany lost territories that contained German people: Alsace-Lorraine to France, the Saar Basin to a League protectorate, a corridor containing the port of Danzig to Poland, and Upper Silesia to Czechoslovakia. Moreover, under the terms of the war guilt clause in the reparations bill, Germany accepted the blame for World War I, agreed to dismantle its war machine, and pledged not to rearm in the future.

Germany felt betrayed. Clearly, this was not a peace based upon the Fourteen Points. Rather, it brought to life Bourne's prediction of victors who "grab what they can."

Wilson derived no joy from the Treaty of Versailles. He accepted the treaty's territorial and punitive provisions in order to ensure the adoption of the League of Nations, which he hoped would secure world peace and eventually redress the treaty's inequities. The League consisted of an assembly that included all member states and an executive council composed of the United States, Great Britain, France, Italy, Japan, and four other states to be elected by the assembly. But the heart of the League was clearly Article 10, which pledged all members "to respect and uphold the territorial integrity and independence of all members of the

Europe after World War I

League." It embodied Wilson's dream of an international organization that would keep the peace by giving all nations (large and small) equality and protection.

The Struggle for Ratification

Wilson knew the treaty faced stiff opposition back home. In February 1919, 39 Senate Republicans had signed a petition warning they would not approve the League in its present form. To court domestic support, Wilson persuaded the delegates in Europe to acknowledge the Monroe Doctrine, omit domestic issues from the League's purview, and permit member states to withdraw after two years' notice. Though he worked to include provisions the Senate wanted, Wilson refused to separate the League from the treaty. In March he warned: "When the treaty comes back, the gentlemen on this side will find the covenant not only in it, but so many threads of the treaty tied to the covenant that you cannot dissect the covenant from the treaty without destroying the whole vital structure."

Senate opposition broke into three groups, each reflecting different visions of the future role the United States should play in world affairs. The first, the 14 "irreconcilables," were staunch isolationists who wanted the United States to remain unaligned and uninvolved. Led by Senator William Borah of Idaho, they were opposed to a League of Nations in any form. Though their attack was broad-based, they concentrated their fire on Article 10, which called for the mutual protection of the territorial integrity of all member states.

Henry Cabot Lodge of Massachusetts spoke for the second group of critics known as the "strong reservationists." Parodying Wilson's "Fourteen Points," Lodge offered 14 amendments, called the "Lodge" reservations. Of these the second reservation was the most important, as it struck at Article 10, the heart of the proposed League of Nations. The second Lodge reservation decreed that the United States "assumes no obligation" to protect the independence or territory boundaries of any other nation, or to send American troops for such purposes unless Congress should so order. Yet Lodge and his followers were basically in favor of the treaty

and could have been won over if Wilson agreed to their modifications.

The third group of opponents, the "limited reservationists," in all probability spoke for the majority of Americans. Steeped in the diplomatic legacy of the nineteenth century, these limited reservationists favored a middle ground between Senator Borah's acute isolationism and President Wilson's ardent internationalism. They instinctively approached international affairs as cautious nationalists, favoring an independent foreign policy as the best tool for protecting American interests. They, too, had doubts about Article 10 but could have been won over by relatively minor alterations. With their backing and the support of Senate Democrats, the treaty would have passed easily.

As Wilson sailed back to the United States, polls suggested that most Americans favored the League in some form. All he had to do was compromise and the treaty would pass. Instead, Wilson descended on Washington in July itching for a fight, and he grew more stubborn and frustrated as the summer wore on. He made little effort to mask his contempt for critics who questioned the treaty.

Wilson was determined to make the United States assume a leading role in world affairs. Dismissing his opponents as "blind and little provincial people," he declared that the "Senate must take its medicine." His use of a medical metaphor was telling, for Wilson's health had deteriorated under the strain of the war. In fact, in Paris he had suffered what doctors diagnosed as a severe bout of indigestion. In all probability, however, the attack was a mild stroke.

Fearing Senate debate had eroded popular support for the treaty, Wilson decided to take his case directly to the people. Against his doctor's advice, he launched a nationwide tour in September 1919, covering 8000 miles in 33 days and delivering 32 major addresses. He started in the Midwest where opposition to the treaty was strongest, gradually moving west where he met cheering crowds. Totally exhausted, Wilson collapsed on September 25 in Pueblo, Colorado. Four days after returning to Washington, he suffered a severe stroke that paralyzed the left side of his body. In all probability, Wilson sustained enough neurological damage to warp his personality and impair his judgment. Unable to

The refusal of the Senate to ratify the Treaty of Versailles and join the League of Nations is satirized in this cartoon.

work, he did not meet his cabinet for more than six months. Since the law made no provision for removing an incapacitated president, Wilson's second wife, Edith Bolling Wilson, assisted by a few close aides, ran the government, operating under a cloak of silence about the president's condition.

As the Senate vote on the treaty drew near, Wilson remained adamant, telling his wife: "Better a thousand times to go down fighting than to dip your colours to dishonorable compromise." He ordered all Democrats to vote against the treaty if it contained any changes. The treaty came to a vote one year, one week, and one day after the Armistice. The Senate defeated the revised version of the treaty, 55 to 39; a few minutes later the Senate defeated the treaty without changes, 39 to 53. The "irreconcilables" were delighted.

The Senate's failure to reach a compromise must be blamed on Wilson. When the treaty's supporters tried again in March, many of the Democrats disobeyed the president and voted for a revised version of the treaty. But 23 Democrats followed Wilson's orders, and the treaty fell 7 votes short of adoption. Elated by their

victory, Republicans proclaimed (in a parody of Wilson's 1916 slogan), "He kept us out of peace." Yet it would be wrong to interpret the treaty's defeat as an endorsement of isolationism. In essence, the Senate rejected both isolationism and Wilsonian internationalism in favor of preserving a nationalistic foreign policy that would allow the United States to act independently.

An admirer of the British parliamentarian system, Wilson then hatched a bizarre scheme that showed how badly he had lost contact with reality. He asked his Senate opponents to resign and stand immediately for reelection. If pro-League senators replaced them, Wilson would have his ratification; if a majority won reelection, Wilson would resign the presidency. At the urging of advisors, Wilson finally dropped the proposal.

The Election of 1920

Unable to accept defeat, Wilson decided to make the election of 1920 a "solemn referendum" on the League: The election of a Democrat would signify approval of the treaty; a Republican victory would mean the treaty's death. At best the president's proposal offered a dubious test of the public's support for the treaty. National elections rarely turn on a single issue. Instead, they involve a myriad of issues, most of which are quite local in character.

When the Democratic convention met in San Francisco, the delegates ignored Wilson's pathetic anglings for a third term and nominated Governor James M. Cox of Ohio. To round out the ticket, they selected the assistant secretary of the navy, Franklin D. Roosevelt, for vice president, largely to capitalize on the magic Roosevelt name. The Republicans nominated Senator Warren G. Harding of Ohio. A stalwart party regular on domestic issues, Harding had voted for the Treaty of Versailles with the Lodge reservations.

While Cox barnstormed the country, Harding campaigned from his front porch in Ohio. His campaign managers refused to turn him loose on the election circuit for fear of what he might say. As one wag put it, "Thank God only one of them can be elected." Cox campaigned unequivocally for the League of Nations and the

Treaty of Versailles. Harding, by contrast, waffled shamelessly, announcing that he opposed the League but favored an "association of nations." Thus, the election of 1920 did not provide a "solemn referendum" on the League because the issue was hopelessly confused.

Indeed, the League had become a dead issue. Most voters wished to preserve America's options in the coming decades by pursuing an independent foreign policy. Tired of foreign crusades, they wanted to repudiate Wilson's ardent internationalism, and they did just that, giving Harding the largest electoral victory (61 percent of the popular vote) since Washington's election. Harding received 16,152,200 votes to Cox's 9,147,353. Eugene V. Debs, the Socialist candidate, won 919,799 votes (at the time he was serving a prison term in the Atlanta federal penitentiary for opposing American involvement in the war). In the Electoral College, Harding trounced Cox 404 to 127.

The Republicans won because Wilson's fragile coalition of 1916 fell apart. Many Democrats, disillusioned by the costs of the war, either stayed at home or switched parties. Angered by the Treaty of Versailles, ethnic Americans (Germans, Italians, and the Irish in particular) abandoned the Democrats in droves. Their defection cost Democrats the nation's urban centers. Western states and the Midwest went Republican as well, for despite their wartime prosperity, many farmers believed that Wilson's agricultural policies had favored cotton growers in the South over grain producers of the Midwest. The Solid South remained a bastion of Democratic strength, but it did not have nearly enough votes to elect a president.

Harding interpreted his victory as a mandate to reject the League. America never joined the League of Nations, opening the way for those who later blamed the United States for the rise of fascism in Italy and Nazism in Germany. Critics went so far as to claim that America's failure to join the League caused World War II. If the United States had only joined, they insisted, the League would have been able to deter German and Japanese aggression by presenting a united front.

But what good was a united front if its members refused to fight? Critics failed to realize that the French and the English were not willing to use force to impose collective security. Neither was the United States, in or out of the League. Congress played the dominant role in foreign policy until the very eve of World War II, and it was determined to prevent the United States from being drawn into another European war. The war's main legacy, then, was not peace without victory, but bitterness and suspicion.

CONCLUSION

World War I made Randolph Bourne a prophet. The changes in American life between 1914 and 1919 bore out his fear that war obliterates idealism and brings out the dark side of the human spirit. Before the war, the United States had been an isolated, Western Hemisphere country, preoccupied with life on this side of the Atlantic. The industrial revolution had largely transformed the economic landscape, but many Americans still farmed their own land for a living. Although the progressive movement had attempted to use government to eliminate gross economic abuses, federal power remained miniscule compared to the private sector. And while it is true that many old-stock Americans felt threatened by cultural pluralism, they still thought they lived in a country that had more consensus than confusion, more accord than conflict.

World War I altered everything. It accelerated social and economic changes, unleashing extraordinary fears that led to attacks on labor unions, blacks, immigrants, Socialists, and Communists. Similar confusion gripped America's foreign policy. The United States emerged from the Great War as the premier economic power on earth, with global interests requiring protection. Those responsibilities terrified a country that had been lulled into a sense of security by three centuries of geographic isolation. Tired and disillusioned, Americans attempted to flee their responsibilities. Rather than make global political commitments commensurate with their new economic interests, they refused to ratify the Treaty of Versailles or join the League of Nations.

The result was an upsurge in isolationist sentiment in the United States during the 1920s and 1930s that made it very difficult for Amer-

CHRONOLOGY OF KEY EVENTS

1914 World War I begins in Europe

1915 U.S. marines are dispatched to Haiti; German submarine sinks the British passenger ship *Lusitania*, killing 1198 passengers including 128 Americans

1916 Germany suspends unannounced submarine attacks

1917 Germany resumes submarine attacks; Zimmermann telegram, secret note to German minister in Mexico, urges Mexico and Japan to join Central Powers if the United States enters the war in Europe; United States enters the war; Espionage Act passed, imposing fines and jail sentences for aiding the enemy or obstructing recruitment; Russian Revolution begins; War Industries Board is created to coordinate industrial production

1918 Wilson's Fourteen Points outline a plan for peace; National War Labor Board is created to arbitrate disputes between labor and management; Sedition Act passes, punishing any expression of disloyalty to the American government or flag; Germany surrenders

1919 Treaty of Versailles ends World War I

1920 Palmer raids arrest suspected Communists; Senate rejects Treaty of Versailles; Nineteenth Amendment grants women the right to vote; Republican Warren Harding is elected twenty-ninth president

---

ica's leaders to respond strongly to the rise of despotic governments in Europe and the Far East. The Great War did not make the world "safe for democracy." It left humankind a legacy of bitterness, hatred, and suspicion, creating rich soil for the seeds of future conflicts.

In 1920, however, most Americans felt too tired and too disillusioned to give much thought to the future. When Harding promised a return to "normalcy," he struck a responsive chord. Millions of Americans thought he meant resurrecting rural villages and a small farm economy, restoring Anglo-Protestant culture, and forgetting about the rest of the world. The 1920s proved they were in for a surprise.

SUGGESTIONS FOR FURTHER READING

OVERVIEWS AND SURVEYS

Randolph S. Bourne, *War and the Intellectuals: Collected Essays, 1915–1919* (1964); Foster R. Dulles, *America's Rise to World Power, 1898–1954* (1955); Robert H. Ferrell, *Woodrow Wilson and World War I, 1917–1921* (1985); Lloyd C. Gardner, *Safe for Democracy: The Anglo-American Response to*

Revolution, 1913–1923 (1984); Otis L. Graham, Jr., *The Great Campaigns: Reform and War in America, 1900–1928* (1971); Ellis W. Hawley, *The Great War and the Search for a Modern Order: A History of the American People and Their Institutions, 1917–1933* (1979); William E. Leuchtenburg, *The Perils of Prosperity, 1914–32* (1958); Emily S. Rosenberg, *Spreading the American Dream: American Economic and Cultural Expansion 1890–1945* (1982); Bernadotte Schmitt and Harold C. Vedeler, *The World in the Crucible: 1914–1919* (1984); Daniel M. Smith, *The Great Departure: The United States and World War I, 1914–1920* (1965).

THE ROAD TO WAR

John M. Cooper, Jr., *The Vanity of Power: American Isolationism and the First World War, 1914–1917* (1969) and *The Warrior and the Priest: Woodrow Wilson and Theodore Roosevelt* (1983); Patrick Devlin, *Too Proud to Fight: Woodrow Wilson's Neutrality* (1974); Ross Gregory, *The Origins of American Intervention in the First World War* (1971); George F. Kennan, *The Decision to Intervene* (1958) and *Russia Leaves the War* (1956); N. Gordon Levin, Jr., *Woodrow Wilson and World Politics: America's Response to War and Revolution* (1968); Arthur S. Link, *Woodrow Wilson:*

Revolution, War and Peace (1979); Ernest R. May, *The World War and American Isolation, 1914–1917* (1959); Barbara Tuchman, *The Guns of August* (1962).

AMERICAN INDUSTRY GOES TO WAR

Valerie Jean Conner, *The National War Labor Board: Stability, Social Justice, and the Voluntary State in World War I* (1983); Robert D. Cuff, *The War Industries Board: Business-Government Relations During World War I* (1973); Charles Gilbert, *American Financing of World War I* (1970); Maurine Weiner Greenwald, *Women, War, and Work: The Impact of World War I on Women Workers in the United States* (1980); Stephen Skowronek, *Building a New American State: The Expansion of National Administrative Capacities, 1877–1920* (1982); Neil A. Wynn, *From Progressivism to Prosperity: World War I and American Society* (1986).

THE AMERICAN PUBLIC GOES TO WAR

Rodolfo Acuña, *Occupied America*, 3d ed. (1988); Allan M. Brandt, *No Magic Bullet: A Social History of Venereal Disease in the United States Since 1880* (1985); Wayne Cornelius, *Building the Cactus Curtain: Mexican Migration and U.S. Responses from Wilson to Carter* (1980); James R. Grossman, *Land of Hope: Chicago, Black Southerners, and the Great Migration* (1989); David M. Kennedy, *Over Here: The First World War and American Society* (1980); K. Austin Kerr, *Organized for Prohibition: A New History of the Anti-Saloon League* (1985); Daniel J. Kevles, *In the Name of Eugenics: Genetics and the Uses of Human Heredity* (1985); Frederick C. Luebke, *Bonds of Loyalty: German-Americans and World War I* (1974); Carole Marks, *Farewell—We're Good and Gone: The Great Black Migration* (1989); John F. McClymer, *War and Welfare: Social Engineering in America, 1890–1925* (1980); Paul L. Murphy, *World War I and the Origin of Civil Liberties in the United States* (1979); H. C. Peterson and Gilbert C. Fite, *Opponents of War 1917–1918* (1957); William Preston, Jr., *Aliens and Dissenters: Federal Suppression of Radicals, 1903–1933* (1963); John A. Thompson, *Reformers and War: American Progressive Publicists and the First World War* (1987); Stephen Vaughn, *Holding Fast the Inner Lines: Democracy, Nationalism, and the Committee on Public Information* (1980).

THE WAR FRONT

Arthur E. Barbeau and Florette Henri, *The Unknown Soldiers: Black American Troops in World War I* (1974); Edward M. Coffman, *The War to End Wars: The American Military Experience in World War I* (1968); Harvey DeWeerd, *President Wilson Fights His War: World War I and the American Intervention* (1968); Russell F. Weigley, *The American Way of War: A History of United States Military Strategy and Policy* (1973).

SOCIAL UNREST AFTER THE WAR

Wesley M. Bagby, *The Road to Normalcy: The Presidential Campaign and Election of 1920* (1962); David Brody, *Labor in Crisis: The Steel Strike of 1919* (1965); Richard C. Cortner, *A Mob Intent on Death: The NAACP and the Arkansas Riot Cases* (1988); Paul Fussell, *The Great War and Modern Memory* (1975); Christine A. Lunardini, *From Equal Suffrage to Equal Rights: Alice Paul and the National Woman's Party, 1910–1928* (1986); Robert K. Murray, *The Red Scare: A Study in National Hysteria, 1919–1920* (1955); Burl Noggle, *Into the Twenties: The United States from Armistice to Normalcy* (1974); Francis Russell, *A City in Terror: 1919, the Boston Police Strike* (1975); Arthur M. Schlesinger, Jr., *The Crisis of the Old Order, 1919–1933* (1957); William Tuttle, Jr., *Race Riot: Chicago and the Red Summer of 1919* (1970).

THE TREATY OF VERSAILLES

Thomas A. Bailey, *Woodrow Wilson and the Great Betrayal* (1945), and *Woodrow Wilson and the Lost Peace* (1944); Warren F. Kuehl, *Seeking World Order* (1969); N. Gordon Levin, Jr., *Woodrow Wilson and World Politics: America's Response to War and Revolution* (1968); Herbert F. Margulies, *The Mild Reservationists and the League of Nations Controversy in the Senate* (1989); Arno J. Mayer, *Politics and Diplomacy in Peacemaking: Containment and Counterrevolution at Versailles, 1918–1919* (1967) and *Wilson vs. Lenin: Political Origins of the New Diplomacy, 1917–1918* (1959); Ralph A. Stone, *The Irreconcilables: The Fight Against the League of Nations* (1970); William C. Widenor, *Henry Cabot Lodge and the Search for an American Foreign Policy* (1980).

BIOGRAPHIES

Robert W. Cherny, *A Righteous Cause: The Life of William Jennings Bryan* (1985); Kendrick A. Clements, *William Jennings Bryan, Missionary Isolationist* (1982); Stanley Coben, *A. Mitchell Palmer: Politician* (1963); Lawrence W. Levine, *Defender of the Faith: William Jennings Bryan, The Last Decade, 1915–1925* (1965); Arthur S. Link, *Wilson* (5 vols., 1947–1965); James R. Vitelli, *Randolph Bourne* (1981); Edwin A. Weinstein, *Woodrow Wilson: A Medical and Psychological Biography* (1981).

a

EU
L

Fig. 55

1914

1918

1914   1918

Guns

F

D

4   8

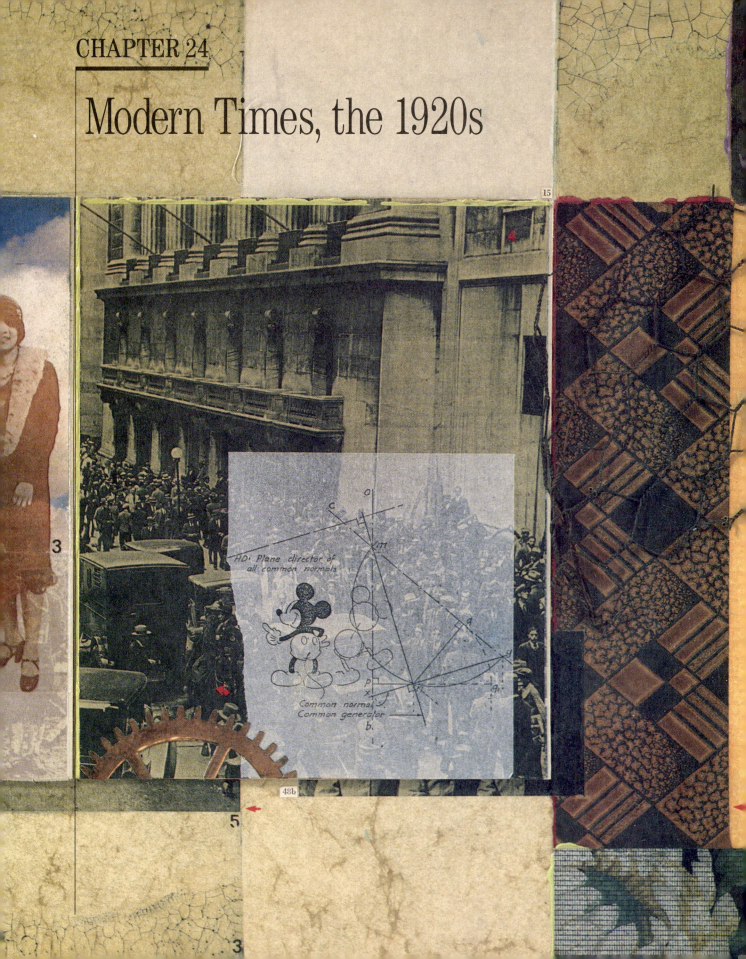

CHAPTER 24

Modern Times, the 1920s

In 1898 the Physicians Club of Chicago held a symposium on "sexual hygiene" to give its members some practical tips on marriage counseling. Confronted by an increasing number of married women who wanted information on birth control, Chicago physicians offered this advice: "Get a divorce and vacate the position for some other woman, who is able and willing to fulfill all a wife's duties as well as to enjoy her privileges."

Most Americans shared this view. They did not believe sex should be separated from procreation. To the male custodians of morality, birth control challenged patriarchy. It would lead to sexual promiscuity and an epidemic of venereal diseases, they charged, while others feared it would weaken the family by raising the divorce rate. Many women condemned birth control just as soundly. Taught from childhood to embrace the cult of domesticity, they accepted childbearing as their "biological duty" and rejected birth control as immoral and radical.

Yet by 1950 most Americans regarded birth control as a public virtue rather than a private vice. The person most responsible for this amazing transformation was Margaret Sanger (1879–1966), a tireless crusader who possessed an iron will and the soul of a firebrand. From 1914 to 1937 Sanger campaigned to make birth control morally acceptable. She built a network of clinics where women could get accurate information about contraception and obtain inexpensive, reliable birth control devices. After World War II, she helped organize the international planned parenthood movement and played a key role in the development of "the pill." Through her birth control work, Margaret Sanger probably had a greater influence on the world than any other American woman of her day.

Sanger's mother, Margaret Higgins, bore 11 children, all 10 pounders or more. Michael Higgins, her father, was a free-thinking Irishman who worked as a stonecutter but preferred to hang around pubs proclaiming his faith in socialism and doubts about God. Her mother died of pulmonary tuberculosis at 43; her father lived to 84. For the rest of her life, Sanger blamed her mother's suffering on the absence of effective family planning.

An unhappy marriage also pushed Sanger toward reform. While still in nursing school, she married William Sanger, an architect and would-be artist, and they set up housekeeping in Greenwich Village, a bohemian colony in New York City. After bearing three children in rapid succession, Sanger overcame her own struggle with tuberculosis, finished school, and began a nursing career. Through her husband, she met an amazing group of radicals in New York, including the anarchist Emma Goldman and the Wobbly William D. "Big Bill" Haywood. Feeling trapped by married life and determined to achieve her own identity, Margaret plunged into New York's labor movement. As her marriage to William slowly dissolved, she devoted herself to the working poor.

Convinced large families placed a terrible economic burden on poor people, Sanger sympathized with the countless women, rich and poor, who desperately wanted to control their fertility. After watching several working-class women bleed to death from back-alley abortions, she came to regard family planning as the most important issue of her day because birth control would make abortion, as well as unwanted babies, unnecessary. When male labor leaders refused to add contraception to their reform agenda, Sanger left the labor movement, resolving to make birth control her life's work.

On the eve of World War I, Sanger launched a one-woman crusade. She lectured to anyone who would listen and offered birth control devices to anyone in need. In 1921 she organized the American Birth Control League, which opened scores of clinics in major American cities. Next Sanger recruited physicians and social workers to agitate for repeal of the Comstock Act of 1873, a federal law making it illegal to send birth control information or devices through the mail. In addition, she attracted several wealthy feminists to the birth control movement and used their support to finance research on the relative safety and effectiveness of different kinds of contraceptives.

Sanger played a key role in the transition to modern times. Her career illustrates how the reform spirit of the Progressive Era survived the conservative climate of the 1920s to touch the lives of future generations. Whereas most reforms pursued political agendas, birth control

Margaret Sanger, a nurse who had watched many women suffer from unwanted births and die from illegal abortions, was one of the founders of the modern American birth control movement. After spending a year studying medical literature and learning about contraceptives, Sanger began publishing the journal *The Woman Rebel*.

developed into a social movement that involved feminists, philanthropists, social workers, physicians, and scientists. No legacy of progressivism was more far-reaching. The birth control movement reformed sexual mores, redefined women's role in society, and redistributed power within the family. But the birth control movement represented just one symptom of a society in flux, one in which urban growth, ethnic diversity, and economic development set the stage for controversy on almost every imaginable topic—race, sex, religion, alcohol, even the family automobile.

THE CLASH OF VALUES

Many Americans found the 1920s a confusing decade. In the wake of the Great War's carnage and failed promises, they disagreed on a host of issues. Wets battled drys, atheists ridiculed fundamentalists, white, Anglo-Saxon Protestants (WASPs) denounced the "new immigrants," whites lashed out against blacks, and practically everyone sensed a decline in morality. Rural folks debated the dubious morals of city dwell-

ers, while farmers glowered at industrialists. Midwesterners and Southerners voiced their skepticism about the Golden East, with its sprawling cities teeming with immigrants.

Yet none of these disputes was new. Each was a continuing, if sharpening, controversy that had been building for decades. At bottom these conflicts reflected more uncertainty than rancor, as a society in transition debated which of its traditional values to preserve and which to modify or abandon. Because the choices seemed so disconcerting, few Americans recognized these conflicts for what they were—unavoidable growing pains of a nation struggling to come to grips with cultural pluralism and changing values.

The Growth of Cities

Cities underwent dramatic and visible changes. According to the census of 1920, more Americans dwelled in cities than in the country for the first time in the nation's history. Most urbanites lived in small towns and cities, but a surprising number resided in metropolitan areas—large cities with 50,000 or more people. During the 1920s nearly 15 million Americans moved to cities. The South remained largely rural, but its rate of urbanization outstripped other areas, rising from 25 percent in 1920 to 32 percent in 1930, a clear indication of what the future held in store for the "Sun Belt."

Most new city dwellers came from the country. Farms lost over 10 million residents between 1920 and 1940. Even people who remained on the land did not escape the city's influence. Electrical power scattered industries over broad areas, and as the automobile increased labor's mobility, many rural folk commuted to jobs in nearby mill towns and cities.

Urban growth drove up land values and reshaped the skyline of America's cities, especially in central business districts. In New York and Chicago, office space more than doubled during the 1920s. Skyrocketing land prices forced architects to build "up" instead of "out," launching the first great era of skyscrapers. Builders completed New York's ornate Woolworth Building, rising 55 stories and 760 feet above ground level, in 1913, offering the prototype for the new "Woolworth Gothic" sky-

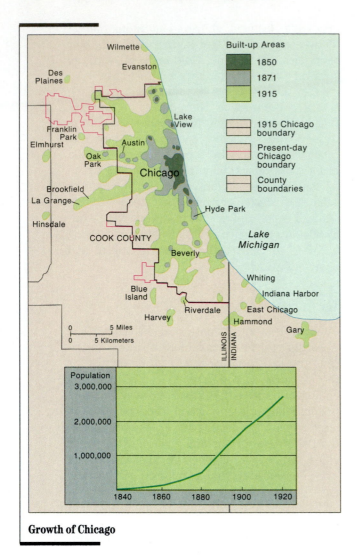

Growth of Chicago

migrants included large numbers of Roman Catholics, Jews, and members of the Greek Orthodox faith. Old-stock Americans had grown accustomed to immigrants from Ireland and Scandinavia, but they felt threatened by the arrival of Poles, Lithuanians, Czechs, Slovaks, Magyars, Ukrainians, Russians, Serbians, Croatians, Italians, Greeks, and Armenians.

The new immigrants poured into the industrial cities of the Northeast and Midwest, filling them with new sights, sounds, and smells that many old-stock Americans found offensive. World War I briefly stopped the flow of immigrants, but in 1919 the trickle again became a flood. Between 1919 and 1926, more than 3.2 million immigrants poured into the United States. Protestants resented the influx of Catholics and Jews; labor unions feared the competition for jobs; and eugenicists feared old-stock Americans would be outbred by the newcomers, with disastrous consequences for the nation.

Urban Segregation

In 1910 three out of every four black Americans lived on farms, and nine out of ten lived in the South. World War I changed that profile. Hoping to escape the tenant farming, sharecropping, and peonage of the South, 1.5 million blacks moved to cities in the 1920s. Some went to southern cities such as Houston, Memphis, Atlanta, and Birmingham, but most settled in major northern metropolises such as New York, Philadelphia, Cleveland, and Chicago. By 1930, one of five black Americans lived in the North.

Black migration intensified housing shortages, making competition for limited housing a source of friction between blacks and whites. In city after city, whites closed ranks against blacks, blocking access to white neighborhoods. Cities passed municipal residential segregation ordinances, white realtors refused to show blacks houses in white areas, and white property owners formed "neighborhood improvement associations." Above all, these associations stressed keeping blacks out. After the Supreme Court declared municipal residential segregation ordinances unconstitutional in 1917, however, whites resorted to the restrictive convenant, a formal deed restriction binding white property owners in a given neighbor-

scrapers that quickly dominated Manhattan's skyline. Soon Chicago had its 34-story, Gothic-topped Tribune Tower on Michigan Avenue, and other skyscrapers dotted the landscapes in Pittsburgh, Cleveland, Kansas City, and San Francisco. Cities throughout the United States were starting to look alike.

The New Immigration

America's cities attracted large numbers of new immigrants. Immigration patterns to the United States began to change in the 1880s, with fewer and fewer people arriving from northern and western Europe and more and more coming from southern and eastern Europe. Instead of bringing more Protestants, the new waves of im-

hood not to sell to blacks. Whites who broke these agreements could be sued by "damaged" neighbors. Not until 1948 did the Supreme Court strike down restrictive covenants, rendering them impossible to enforce, even if their language survived in many deeds.

Zoning laws offered a more subtle means of segregating blacks. Originally designed to keep businessmen and industries out of residential neighborhoods, zoning laws were upheld by the Supreme Court in 1926. By 1930, 981 American cities had adopted zoning ordinances. These new zoning laws addressed not only land usage but the height and shape of buildings, specifying rigid construction requirements that precluded low-income groups from building or buying homes in well-to-do neighborhoods. By the 1930s zoning restrictions had become the tool of choice for segregating people on the basis of wealth.

Racial animosity, restrictive covenants, and zoning restrictions confined blacks to certain neighborhoods. Between World War I and World War II, scores of American cities developed black cores. By 1930 New York and Chicago, the cities with the largest black populations, had wards that registered 95 percent black. Cities within cities, these "black metropolises" resembled ethnic ghettos of the late nineteenth and early twentieth centuries, with one major difference: Racial prejudice made it all but impossible for their residents to escape to the suburbs.

Black Protests

Black protests heightened the fears of many old-stock Americans. In the 1920s several black organizations stepped up their protests against discrimination. Closely identified with Booker T. Washington's conciliatory approach to race relations, the National Urban League, organized in 1911 by social workers, white philanthropists, and conservative blacks, concentrated on finding jobs for urban blacks. During the 1920s the League touted the new opportunities increased prosperity would bring to urban blacks, but a report from the Atlanta League on training blacks to become better janitors revealed the true employment picture. Blacks made scant progress on the job front during the 1920s.

Leaving economic issues to the Urban League, the National Association for the Advancement of Colored People (NAACP), formed in 1909, concentrated on civil rights and legal action. The NAACP won important Supreme Court decisions against the grandfather clause (1915) and restrictive covenants (1917). Except for W. E. B. Du Bois, who became the director of publicity, white liberals served as the NAACP's top officers during its early years. After World War I, however, the leadership gradually shifted to blacks.

Under the capable direction of James Weldon Johnson, its first black secretary, the NAACP fought school segregation in northern cities during the 1920s, and lobbied hard,

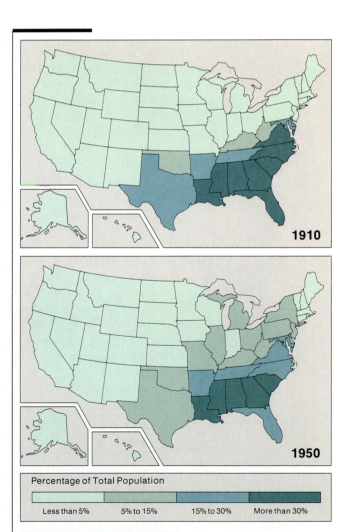

1910

1950

Percentage of Total Population

Less than 5%   5% to 15%   15% to 30%   More than 30%

Black Population, 1910 and 1950

though unsuccessfully, for a federal antilynching bill. Though progress on these fronts did not come until after World War II, the NAACP consolidated its position between the wars as the nation's leading civil rights organization.

Black radicals dismissed the Urban League and the NAACP as too conservative. A. Philip Randolph, the brilliant editor of the militant Socialist monthly, the *Messenger*, saw prejudice as the inevitable consequence of a capitalist system that drove a wedge between black and white workers. To end discrimination and achieve racial equality, he called for a "New Negro" who would meet violence with violence. Randolph also urged blacks to seek admission into trade unions. To promote this goal he organized the Brotherhood of Sleeping Car Porters in the 1920s. After years of bitter opposition, the Pullman Company recognized the Brotherhood in 1937 as the porters' bargaining agent. Though Randolph addressed the black masses, he appealed to the college educated, black elite. Most blacks neither read nor understood his intellectual theories.

Marcus Garvey, a charismatic Jamaican, encouraged black pride. His Universal Negro Improvement Association (UNIA) included one million members worldwide.

Marcus Garvey spoke for the black masses. A flamboyant and charismatic figure from Jamaica, Garvey rejected integration and preached racial pride and black separatism. He declared that God and Jesus were both black men and exhorted his followers to glorify their African heritage and to revel in the beauty of their black skin.

In 1914 Garvey organized the Universal Negro Improvement Association (UNIA) to promote black migration to Africa. Under the slogan, "Africa for the Africans, at home and abroad," the UNIA opened branches in many American cities and in several foreign countries after World War I. Its Black Star Steamship Line sold stock to thousands of members, promising to help blacks migrate to Africa. Garvey also advocated economic self-sufficiency for blacks who remained in the United States. To enable his followers to buy only from black-owned businesses, the UNIA opened a chain of laundries, groceries, restaurants, a hotel, a doll factory (whose products all had black bodies), and a printing plant.

The UNIA collapsed in the mid-1920s after the Black Star Line went bankrupt. Garvey was charged with mail fraud, jailed, and finally deported, but this "Black Moses" left behind a rich legacy. At a time when magazines and newspapers overflowed with advertisements for hair straighteners and skin lightening cosmetics, Garvey's message of racial pride struck a responsive chord in many black Americans.

The Harlem Renaissance

The movement for black pride found its cultural expression in the Harlem Renaissance. Located in New York's upper Manhattan, Harlem attracted black intellectuals who migrated from small towns or rural areas where they had felt stifled and oppressed. Langston Hughes, poet laureate of the Harlem Renaissance, captured the exhilaration of arriving in Harlem: "I can never put on paper the thrill of the underground ride to Harlem. I went up the steps and out into the bright September sunlight. Harlem! I stood there, dropped my bags, took a deep breath, and felt happy again."

By the 1920s the Harlem Renaissance was in bloom. Langston Hughes probed the past in his elegant poem, "The Negro Speaks of Rivers," while Countee Cullen struck an ironic note in "Yet Do I Marvel," where he pondered God's ways and declared: "Yet do I marvel at this curious thing: To make a poet black and bid him sing." In *Cane*, a compilation of short stories, poems, and vignettes, Jean Toomer, perhaps the most gifted prose writer of the renaissance, explored the lives of blacks who toiled in Georgia's sawmills in the 1880s.

Yet for all its artistic promise, the Harlem Renaissance had little influence on the black masses, most of whom never knew it existed. "The ordinary Negroes hadn't heard of the Negro Renaissance," Hughes later lamented. "And

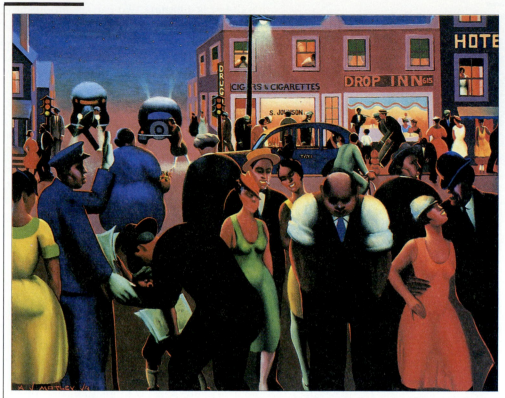

Artist Archibald Motley, Jr., one of the black painters of the 1920s Harlem Renaissance, celebrated the energy and excitement of the era in *Black Belt* (1934).

if they had, it hadn't raised their wages any." Moreover, the Harlem Renaissance often reflected the stereotypes of its white patrons, who wished to dabble in the cult of the primitive, which came into vogue during the 1920s. White liberals underwrote the Harlem Renaissance by providing scholarships, prizes, and grants to aspiring young black artists who all too often felt pressured to reinforce white stereotypes of black culture. Leaders of the Harlem Renaissance shied away from controversial social issues such as "passing" and all but ignored jazz, one of the most important black contributions to American popular culture.

The New Woman and the Sex Debate

"If all girls at the Yale prom were laid end to end, I wouldn't be surprised," sighed Dorothy Parker, the official wit of New York's smart set. Parker's quip captured the public's perception that America's morals had taken a nose-dive. As

early as 1913 an editor for *Current Opinion* complained that America had struck "Sex O' Clock," and a few years later a writer for *The Atlantic* warned of the "obsession of sex which has set us all a-babbling about matters once excluded from the amenities of conversation." Practically every newspaper featured articles on prostitution, venereal disease, sex education, birth control, and the rising divorce rate—not to mention somber warnings against "racial suicide" by eugenicists who feared "inferior stocks of people" might take over the country by outbreeding their social betters.

City life nurtured new sexual attitudes. With its crowded anonymity, urban culture eroded sexual inhibitions by relaxing community restraints on individual behavior. Cities also promoted secular, consumer values, and city people seemed to tolerate, if not welcome, many forms of diversity.

If cities spawned a new environment for sexual values, the new psychology of Sigmund

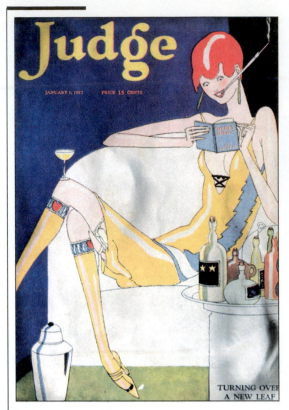

The image of the "flapper," who bobbed her hair, bared her knees, and smoked and drank in public, alarmed a public still clinging to Victorian codes of morality.

Freud provided the ideas. A Vienna physician, Freud revolutionized academic and popular thinking about human behavior by arguing that unconscious sexual anxieties cause much of human behavior. Freud also explained how sexual fears develop in infancy and stay with people throughout their lives. During the 1920s, Freud precipitated countless arguments as physicians, academics, advice columnists, women's magazines, and preachers debated his theories.

The image of the "flapper" said it all—the liberated woman who bobbed her hair, painted her lips, raised her hemline, and danced the Charleston. The public's anxiety about "fast" women reached all the way down to adolescent girls. One fretful mother told sociologists Robert and Helen Lynd, "My son has been asked to a dance by three different girls and there is no living with him," while another complained,

"It's the girls' clothing. We can't keep our boys decent when girls dress that way."

Women's behavior raised more eyebrows than hemlines. When Lewis Terman, a distinguished psychologist at Stanford University, questioned 777 middle-class women in 1938, he discovered that 74 percent of those born between 1890 and 1900 remained chaste until marriage, while the figure dropped to 32 percent among those born after 1910. Alfred C. Kinsey's research revealed a similar pattern. Between 1938 and 1956 Kinsey and his co-workers at Indiana University interviewed 5940 white females from all social classes. Women born after 1900 were twice as likely to have had premarital sex as their mothers, with the most pronounced changes occurring in the generation reaching maturity at the end of World War I and in the early 1920s.

Sexual permissiveness had eroded Victorian values, but the "new woman" posed less of a challenge to traditional morality than her critics feared. Far from being promiscuous, her sexual experience before marriage was limited (a woman usually had no more than one or two partners, one of whom she married), and she shared the older generation's commitment to marriage. In practice, this narrowed the gap between men and women and moved society toward a single standard of morality. Instead of turning to prostitutes, men made love with their sweethearts, who in many instances became their wives.

Moreover, the sexual revolution did not redefine gender roles for women. The "new woman" embraced the traditional roles of wife and mother. In fact, the most striking theme of women's history in the 1920s was its continuity with the past. Whether one looked at politics, the workplace, or the home, the status of women remained much the same.

Nowhere was the absence of change more evident than in politics. Most feminists had viewed politics as the key to ending discrimination against women, arguing the vote would bring other reforms in its train. After the Nineteenth Amendment passed, reformers talked about female voters uniting to clean up politics, improve society, and end discrimination in the marketplace.

None of these dreams came true during the 1920s. Women failed to organize into a bloc vote, and apart from a few state and local elections where the female vote did prove decisive, women did not vote differently than men. Even more galling to feminists, substantial numbers of women failed to vote at all. Throughout the 1920s significantly fewer women showed up at the polls than men.

Nor did women win new opportunities in the marketplace. According to the census of 1920, the American work force included over 8 million women (the figure rose to more than 10 million by 1930), employed in 437 different types of jobs. But black and foreign-born women comprised 57 percent of the female work force, and domestic service remained the largest occupation, followed by secretaries, typists, and clerks—all low-paying jobs. Though female workers made significant progress in organizing the garment industry, they failed to make inroads in other industries. The American Federation of Labor (AFL) remained openly hostile to women because it did not want females competing for male jobs.

Female professionals, too, made little progress. They consistently received less pay than their male counterparts. Moreover, while the proportion of women in the professions rose from roughly 12 to 14 percent between 1920 and 1930, three-quarters of female professionals concentrated in "female" occupations—teaching and nursing. The percentage of female lawyers and architects remained constant between 1910 and 1930 (about 3 percent), while the total number of female doctors declined from 9015 to 6825. The United States had only 60 female certified public accountants and 151 female dentists in the late 1920s.

Most Americans regarded working women as an anomaly. Young women could work during the interlude between leaving home and marriage, but they were expected to make homemaking their career after marriage. While economic necessity forced many poor women to continue working after marriage, most middle-class women of the 1920s abandoned any hope of combining careers with marriage. If anything, the 1920s saw feminism decline and domesticity surge. As one article put it, "the office woman,

no matter how successful, is a transplanted posey." The proper role for women, one college president advised, was "to strengthen and beautify and sanctify the home."

America had not resolved the basic conflict between equal rights for women and the sexual division of labor that continued to confine women to the domestic sphere. Feminists had secured the vote, not true equality.

THE REVOLT OF THE TRADITIONALISTS

Teeming cities, crowded ghettos, unfamiliar immigrants, black migration, civil rights protests, and new sexual mores all proved deeply threatening to traditional white Protestants. During

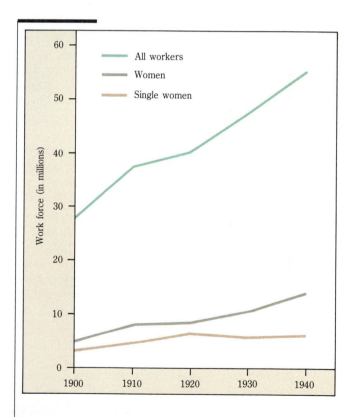

Figure 24.1

Women in the work force, 1900–1940. Although the number of women in the workplace rose from 1900 to 1940, they were concentrated in low-paying and traditionally "female" jobs.

(Text continues on p. 804)

THE SEXUAL REVOLUTION OF THE EARLY 1900s

During the 1800s, public sexual attitudes in the United States were rooted in a moral code known as "civilized sexual morality." This sexual code condemned public discussion of sexual matters, held that sexual relations outside marriage were the blackest of sins, and declared that the only legitimate purpose of sexual relations was reproduction. Foreign travelers were invariably struck by Americans' sexual prudery. In the United States, they reported, a chicken breast was called a bosom and a piano leg was called a limb and was covered with lace trousers.

This strict sexual code drew support from a large medical literature that declared that any violation of the tenets of civilized morality would be detrimental to a person's health. Respected physicians insisted that loss of semen through masturbation or excessive sexual intercourse would produce "urinary difficulties, disorders of the genital organs, spinal diseases, weakness of the brain, loss of memory, epilepsy, insanity, apoplexy, abortions, premature births, and extreme feebleness, morbid predispositions, and an early death of offspring." Medical authorities also

warned that women were too frail physically and too sensitive spiritually to engage in frequent intercourse and that "the majority of women (happily for them) are not very much troubled with sexual feelings of any kind." Above all, physicians warned that individuals who had sexual relations outside of marriage ran a high risk of contracting incurable venereal diseases.

The Victorian sexual code was a public ideal, not an accurate description of reality. Prostitution flourished in turn-of-the-century America. Every large city had at least one red-light district. In New York, there was the Tenderloin; in Chicago, the Levee; in New Orleans, Storyville; in San Francisco, the Barbary Coast. Early twentieth-century vice commissions estimated that there were "not less" than a quarter of a million prostitutes in the country. In Chicago, an estimated quarter of the city's males visited prostitutes annually, and paid them $15 million a year. Pornography was also widespread.

Nor were nineteenth-century women necessarily the prudish, asexual, sexually ignorant figures popularized in Victorian mythology.

An early sexual survey of the attitudes of 45 well-educated women, mainly born before 1870, reported that most enjoyed intercourse and experienced orgasm.

Nevertheless, the values of civilized sexual morality dominated polite society and received strong public backing from the broad-based crusade to suppress vice. A "purity crusade" had arisen in the 1860s and 1870s in response to proposals to legalize and regulate prostitution. In almost every major city in the country, former abolitionists like William Lloyd Garrison, feminists like Susan B. Anthony, temperance advocates, and ministers joined forces to defeat legalized prostitution. Prostitution, they argued, was a menace "to the chastity of our women and the sanctity of the home." It exploited poor women to satisfy male lust and endangered respectable women, who were often infected with syphilis and gonorrhea by their husbands.

In later years, the purity forces broadened their aims. In addition to fighting prostitution, they also sought to protect the family by outlawing abortion, restricting the sale of alcohol, stamping out pornography, censoring nudity in the arts, enforcing the Sabbath through enactment of "blue laws," suppressing the use of narcotics, and stopping the flow of birth control information through the mails.

The self-appointed leader of the purity forces was a staunch crusader named Anthony Comstock. Born on a farm in New Canaan, Connecticut, Comstock, as a youth, had been so upset by an impulse to masturbate that he feared he might be driven to commit suicide. While serving with a Connecticut regiment in the Civil War he had been appalled by the pornographic French postcards circulated among soldiers. After the war he moved to New York, where he became active in the Young Men's Christian Association and was shocked by the prevalence of prostitutes and of vendors selling obscene books.

In 1873, Comstock persuaded Congress to pass a federal law banning from the mails "every obscene lewd, lascivious or filthy book, pamphlet, paper, letter, writing, print or other publication of an indecent character." Comstock was then appointed special agent of the Post Office and made responsible for arresting those who used the mail in violation of the law. "Morals, not art or literature," was Comstock's motto. He took credit for hounding 16 persons to their deaths.

By 1910, Comstock and the purity forces had achieved many of their legislative goals. They had successfully pushed for state laws to restrict divorce; raised the age of consent for sexual intercourse (from 7, in some states, to 18); imposed tests for venereal disease prior to marriage; and criminalized abortion. The purity crusaders also won passage of a federal statute that defined the mailing of birth control information a felony.

The years just before World War I witnessed a series of sharp challenges to the nineteenth-century code of sexual purity. Radical new ideas about marriage were publicized and debated. Swedish feminist Ellen Key preached a scheme of "unwed motherhood"; Edith Ellis, wife of British sex researcher Havelock Ellis, advocated trial marriage and "semi-detached marriage" in which each spouse occupied a separate domicile; still others advocated "serial marriage" and easier divorce. Greenwich Village bohemians and political radicals advocated, and to some extent practiced, free love. Psychologists, including Havelock

Ellis, G. Stanley Hall, and Sigmund Freud, attacked the notion that women lacked sexual impulses.

Sexual conduct was also changing rapidly. The first scientific sex surveys indicated that women who came to maturity after the turn of the century were much more likely than their mothers to engage in sex before marriage and outside it. Women who were born around 1900 were two to three times as likely to have premarital intercourse compared to women born before 1900. They were also more likely to experience orgasm. Among men, premarital sexual experience did not increase, but it occurred less often with prostitutes and more frequently with other women.

Public alarm over the changes occurring in American sexual experience culminated in the first decade of the 1900s in an explosion of concern over "white slavery"—prostitution—and the "black plague"—venereal disease. Many lurid books appeared—with such titles as *The Traffic in Souls*, *The House of Bondage*, and *The Shame of a Great Nation*—which explained how innocent young girls were seduced by panderers and, through the use of a chloroformed cloth, a hypodermic needle, or a drugged drink, forced into prostitution. Congress attacked the problem of "white slavery" in 1910 by adopting the Mann Act, which made it a crime to transport women across state lines for immoral purposes. During World War I, Congress provided states with federal funds to set up facilities to detain and rehabilitate women apprehended as prostitutes. Fifteen thousand women were detained during the war. Sex was becoming a subject of open public debate and direct government involvement.

During the 1920s, the drift toward sexual liberalization continued.

Journalists wrote in bewilderment about a new social phenomenon, the flapper, the independent assertive, pleasure-hungry young woman, "making love lightly, boldly, and promiscuously." Systematic sex surveys showed that the incidence of premarital intercourse was continuing to rise and that an increasing number of young women had slept with men other than their future husband. Half of those women born in the first decade of the twentieth century and two-thirds of those born in the second decade had engaged in intercourse before marriage. Meanwhile, contraceptive practices were also changing dramatically. Instead of relying heavily on douching or coitus interruptus as a form of birth control, younger women were using the more effective and less disruptive diaphragms.

Growing sexual permissiveness evoked a sharp reaction. Purity forces renewed their crusade to discourage indecent styles of dancing, immodest dress, and impure books and films. Religious journals denounced popular dance styles as "impure, polluting, corrupting, debasing, destroying spirituality, [and] increasing carnality." A bill was introduced in the Utah state legislature to fine and imprison women who wore skirts on the streets "higher than three inches above the ankle." In the Ohio legislature it was proposed that cleavage be limited to two inches and that the sale of any "garment which unduly displays or accentuates the lines of the female figure" be prohibited. Four states and many cities established censorship boards to review films, and many other cities broke up red-light districts and required licenses for dance halls. But despite these efforts, a sexual revolution had begun that has continued until this day.

the 1920s, old-stock Americans vented their fears and frustrations by attacking alcohol, smoking, evolution, immigrants, and radicals.

Prohibition

Like the sex debate, prohibition exposed deep fissures in American society. The issue turned on the class, ethnic, and religious makeup of individual communities, not merely on whether the community was rural or urban.

At first prohibition's apparent success muted its critics. Distilleries and breweries shut down, saloons locked their doors, arrests for drunkenness declined, and alcohol-related deaths all but disappeared. Compliance, however, had less to do with piety and public support than the law of supply and demand: Since illegal liquor remained in short supply, its price rose beyond the average worker's means.

Private enterprise filled the void. Smugglers supplied wealthy imbibers who could afford the best liquor and wine, but the less affluent had to rely on small-time operators who produced for local consumption. Due to high shipping and storage charges, it cost more to produce beer or wine, so the price of liquor, relative to other alcoholic beverages, dropped. Drinking habits shifted accordingly: The consumption of hard liquor rose, while beer and wine sales declined.

Much of this booze ran the gamut from swill to poison. According to one widely circulated story, a potential buyer who sent a liquor sample to a laboratory for analysis was shocked when the chemist replied: "Your horse has diabetes." For others the problem of "killer batches" was no laughing matter. Hundreds, perhaps thousands, died from drinking concoctions with names like "Jackass Brandy" and "Soda Pop Moon."

Neither federal nor state authorities had enough funds to enforce prohibition. The Federal Prohibition Bureau began the 1920s with 1520 agents, and by 1930 the number had grown to only 2836. Lax enforcement, coupled with huge profits, enticed large-scale operators to enter bootlegging. Organized crime, of course, had long been a fixture of urban life, with gambling and prostitution as its base, but small-time, local operators managed these vices. Liquor demanded production plants, distribution networks, and sales forces, attracting large-scale operators with the capital and business skills to tackle big-time bootlegging.

Bootlegging turned into a gold mine for organized crime. By the late 1920s syndicates sold 150 million quarts of liquor each year, generating revenue in excess of $2 billion annually (more than 2 percent of the gross national product). Chicago's Al Capone had a gross income of $60 million in 1927 and employed an army of workers. A ruthless figure accused of ordering numerous gangland killings, he preferred to think of himself as a businessman. "All I do is supply a public demand," he insisted. "I do it in the best and least harmful way I can."

From the outset, cynics insisted prohibition could not be enforced. They were right. Where the public backed prohibition, it had teeth; where it lacked support, particularly in large cities, people openly flaunted it. On more than one occasion journalists saw President Warren Harding's bootlegger drive to the back door of the White House and unload cases of liquor in broad daylight.

In 1923 New York became the first state to repeal its enforcement law, and by 1930 six more states had followed suit. Others remained firmly committed to prohibition, prompting Walter Lippmann to conclude: "The high level of lawlessness is maintained by the fact that Americans desire to do so many things which they also desire to prohibit." Not until the 1930s, when the Great Depression gave the country something really serious to worry about, did prohibition lose steam. After a presidential commission reported prohibition could not be enforced, Congress finally repealed it in 1933, making liquor control a state and local matter, precisely the jurisdictions where many Americans thought it belonged.

The Antismoking Campaign: The Forgotten Reform

"Prohibition is won," exclaimed the evangelist Billy Sunday in 1920, "Now for tobacco!" Sunday's challenge became the battle cry for religious groups, educators, moral crusaders, and health advocates who wanted to follow up their victory over demon rum with a crusade against "our Lady Nicotine."

Opposition to tobacco was hardly new. King James I denounced smoking in 1603 as "a custom loathsome to the eye, hateful to the nose, harmful to the brain, dangerous to the lungs." During the nineteenth century, the antitobacco campaign remained an appendage of the temperance movement, and critics of the "vile weed" denounced pipes, cigars, plugs, and snuff with equal venom. After the introduction of machine-made cigarettes in the 1880s, however, opponents concentrated their fire on the "little white slavers," insisting cigarettes damaged the public's health more than previous forms of tobacco because smokers inhaled fumes filled with poison.

As early as the Civil War, a few cities had banned smoking in restaurants, theaters, public buildings, trolleys, and railway cars. After antismokers organized the National Anti-Cigarette League in 1903, scores of prominent leaders joined the crusade, including David Starr Jordan, the president of Stanford University, who told audiences, "Boys who smoke cigarettes are like wormy apples"; and the lecturer Elbert Hubbard who declared, "Cigarette smokers are men whose future lies behind them." Between 1896 and 1923, 14 states, mainly in the Midwest, outlawed the sale of cigarettes, prompting calls for a constitutional amendment for national prohibition.

Smokers had little to fear. By the end of the 1920s every state had repealed its law against cigarette sales. The crusade against tobacco was the last hurrah of the prohibition movement, and it failed because prohibition devolved into a legal fiasco and because the public considered smoking the lesser vice. Nor did the style of the antismokers help their cause. Many Americans dismissed them as moral zealots and opponents of individual liberty who wanted to expand the power of the state over private behavior.

Largely because a national consensus had not formed against tobacco, smokers had no difficulty defending their right to smoke. The tobacco industry supported them by opposing every effort to restrict the sale of cigarettes and by spending millions of dollars on advertisements to reassure the public smoking was sophisticated, sexy, and even healthy. Industry spokesmen hammered home the message that smoking should be left to individuals to decide, with no interference from the state. Not until the 1950s, when scientists linked smoking to lung cancer, did reformers win public support for their war against what one scholar has called "slow motion suicide."

The Scopes Trial

Many custodians of small-town morality also fretted over the teaching of evolution in public schools, and they got their day in court in the celebrated "Monkey Trial." In 1925 the Tennessee legislature passed a bill that prohibited the teaching of evolution in public schools. Immediately after the new law took effect, the officers of the American Civil Liberties Union offered to challenge the law in court, and George Rappelyea, a young mining engineer in Dayton, Tennessee, decided to accept the offer. He persuaded the town's 24-year-old science teacher, John Scopes, to provoke a test case by declaring publicly he taught biology from an evolutionary standpoint.

GATHERING DATA FOR THE TENNESSEE TRIAL

When biology teacher John Scopes taught evolutionary theory to his class, the state of Tennessee brought him to trial. The well-publicized trial emphasized the split between religious fundamentalists and those who advocated scientific and academic freedom.

Scopes was brought to trial in the summer of 1925. At the request of the World's Christian Fundamentals Association, William Jennings Bryan, rural America's defender of the faith, agreed to join the team of prosecutors, and Clarence Darrow, the celebrated trial lawyer and self-proclaimed agnostic, volunteered his services to the legal team retained by the American Civil Liberties Union to defend Scopes.

The trial opened on July 10, 1925, with the Honorable John T. Raulston, a fundamentalist judge from Gizzard's Cove, Tennessee, presiding. As Holy Rollers from the surrounding regions held revivals and as religious zealots carried signs telling people to read their Bibles and escape damnation, more than a thousand people jammed into the stifling courthouse to watch Bryan and Darrow do combat. Following a week of testimony, the judge grew concerned the building might collapse beneath the weight of all those spectators and conducted the final day of trial on the courthouse lawn, where the cries of hot dog vendors added to the carnival atmosphere.

The outcome was never in doubt. Scopes admitted he had broken the law. He was convicted and fined $100. (Tennessee's supreme court later upheld the case but rescinded the fine on a technicality.) What gave the trial its drama was the clash between Bryan and Darrow and the opposite images of America they represented. As one observer remarked, the trial "was a battle between two types of mind—the rigid, orthodox, accepting, unyielding narrow, conventional mind, and the broad liberal critical, cynical, skeptical and tolerant mind."

Near the end of testimony the defense surprised everyone by asking Bryan to take the stand as an expert witness on the Bible. Bryan's simple, direct answers to Darrow's sarcastic questions revealed an unshakable faith in the literal truth of the Bible. Though Darrow sought to belittle his testimony as "fool ideas that no intelligent Christian on earth believes," Bryan insisted "it is better to trust in the Rock of Ages than to know the ages of rocks." At one point tempers flared and both men leaped to their feet shaking their fists at one another.

Throughout the trial Eastern journalists ridiculed Bryan, but he defied their scorn. Bryan, who died five days after the trial ended, left the courtroom believing he had carried the day, and many fundamentalists for whom he spoke agreed. Bryan's opponents, however, thought he had been humiliated and proclaimed the Scopes trial a victory for academic freedom. In the end, the Scopes trial merely illustrated how little tolerance secular and fundamentalist groups had for each other.

Xenophobia and Restricting Immigration

Cultural fears unleashed a new wave of nativism in the 1920s. A broad band of Americans believed the new immigrants posed a grave threat to the United States: Organized labor, bent upon protecting high wages, resented competition from cheap labor; staunch nativists and superpatriots warned that foreign influences would corrupt the American character; social workers argued that their caseload of disadvantaged people was already at the breaking point; eugenicists made grave predictions about "racial suicide"; and assorted businessmen denounced immigrants as dangerous radicals.

To protect the United States these groups demanded drastic changes in the nation's immigration policy. After a stopgap immigration law in 1921 failed to halt the flow, Congress passed the National Origins Act of 1924. It established an annual immigration quota of 2 percent of each national group counted in the 1890 census. Since southern and eastern Europeans did not begin arriving in large numbers until the turn of the century, the law gave western and northern Europeans a big edge over the "new immigrants." Great Britain and Ireland, for example, could send 65,731 a year, but Italy only 5802.

Asians suffered the harshest treatment. Bowing to pressure from the West Coast, Congress excluded them entirely, even though earlier agreements with China and Japan had virtually stopped immigration from the Far East. (For example, the quota system would have allowed fewer than 150 Japanese to enter the United States annually.) The Japanese people deeply resented the insult. Japan boycotted American goods, a patriotic Japanese committed hara-kiri in front of the American Embassy in Tokyo, and the Japanese ambassador in Washington resigned in protest.

Hostility to immigrants also surfaced in the Sacco and Vanzetti case. On April 15, 1920, two unidentified gunmen robbed a payroll messenger from a shoe factory in South Braintree, Massachusetts, murdering a paymaster and a guard. The crime occurred at the peak of the Red Scare in the United States when the Justice Department was investigating two Italian immigrants, Nicola Sacco and Bartolomeo Vanzetti, both avowed anarchists, for distributing leaflets calling for a rally to protest the infamous Palmer raids. Justice Department officials worked hand-in-glove with local authorities in Massachusetts, and on May 5 police arrested the men, charging them with robbery and murder. Although the state failed to prove its case, it did present strong evidence against one of the defendants and prosecutors succeeded in parading the political views of both men before the jury. On July 14, 1921, Sacco and Vanzetti were convicted and sentenced to death.

The trial brought a storm of protest from Italian-Americans, liberals, and civil rights advocates. Sacco-Vanzetti defense funds sprang up in the United States and Europe, attracting distinguished supporters such as Albert Einstein, Felix Frankfurter, H. G. Wells, and George Bernard Shaw. Protesters demanded a review of the case, claiming Sacco and Vanzetti had been convicted not with facts but with their political views.

For six years the state granted stays of execution. Early in July 1927 Governor Alvan T. Fuller of Massachusetts appointed a blue-ribbon commission, headed by Harvard University president Abbott Lawrence Lowell, to investigate the case. After a month's work, the commission upheld the conviction. Sacco and Vanzetti, asserting their innocence to the end, went to the electric chair on August 23, 1927, with the words, "This is our career, and our triumph." Following their deaths, mobs attacked American embassies across Europe. Nor did the controversy fade with time. The debate about their guilt or innocence has reverberated down to this day.

The Ku Klux Klan

Fear of political radicals and ethnic minorities found its most strident voice during the 1920s in the Ku Klux Klan, a secret organization that stood for "100 percent pure Americanism" and limited its membership to white, native-born

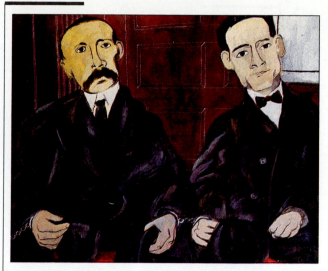

Many people felt that Sacco and Vanzetti, Italian-born admitted anarchists, were persecuted for their immigrant status and radical views rather than for any real crime. Their trial, shown here in a painting by Ben Shahn, became an important symbol in the fight for civil liberties and brought about violent protest in America and abroad.
(Ben Shahn, *Bartolomeo Vanzetti and Nicola Sacco* (1931–32). Tempera on paper over composition board, $10\frac{1}{2} \times 14\frac{1}{2}''$. Gift of Mrs. John D. Rockefeller, Jr./The Museum of Modern Art, New York.)

Protestants. Organized on Thanksgiving night, 1915, in a ceremony beneath a burning cross on a mountaintop in Georgia, the revived Klan was, in the words of its founder and imperial wizard, Colonel William Joseph Simmons, a "living memorial" to the Klan of Reconstruction days. An insurance salesman, part-time Methodist minister, and perennial booster of fraternal societies, Simmons had no political agenda. Under his inept leadership, the Klan attracted fewer than 5000 members during its first few years and remained a small southern organization teetering on the edge of bankruptcy.

That changed in 1920 when Simmons hired two advertising specialists, Edward Young Clark and Elizabeth Tyler, to market the Klan. They did nothing to change the product. The Klan remained, as before, a loosely knit web of vigilante groups, with no national program. Klan policy was set at the local level, varying from community to community to accommodate local prejudices, be they directed at blacks, Catho-

The Ku Klux Klan exploited postwar confusion and fear of things "un-American." Although the Klan had flourished in small, rural towns across the South, during the 1920s it spread to working-class and middle-class neighborhoods of large cities, where people felt threatened by the influx of African-American and immigrant workers.

lics, Jews, Mexicans, Orientals, foreigners, or "Reds." Clark and Tyler hired an army of organizers to canvas the country selling memberships in the Klan. (Membership cost $10; the sheet was $4 extra.) Working on commission and molding their pitch to match their clientele, they enjoyed astounding success. By 1921 the Klan had become a national organization with over 90,000 paying members; by 1925 it claimed a membership of 5 million! An amazed southern newspaper editor called the "idea of selling people their own prejudices almost equal to the old bunco game of selling a hick the Capitol."

Yet the Klan's membership was not limited to rednecks. True, the Klan was strongest (and most violent) in the South, but the Klan had a large following in the Southeast, the Far West, and the Midwest. Moreover, the Klan showed considerable strength in several large urban areas, including Chicago, Indianapolis, and Detroit. Its natural habitat was not the countryside, but middling towns and small cities. Most members were not "poor white trash," but members of the lower middle class from old-stock, respectable families.

In its heyday (1921–1926), the Klan was a political force to reckon with. At the state level, it controlled or influenced the election of governors and legislators in Alabama, Georgia, Arkansas, Texas, Oklahoma, California, Oregon, Indiana, and Ohio. In fact, the Klan's strength extended into Pennsylvania, New York, and parts of New England. Regardless of where it rose to power, however, the Klan's vision was essentially negative. Except for an Oregon statute requiring Catholic children to attend public schools (later declared unconstitutional), the Klan did not inspire a single law.

Night ridings, cross burnings, tar and featherings, public beatings, and lynchings formed the Klan's stock in trade, but the Klan did not limit its wrath to ethnic and religious offenders. The Klan's victims reflected the public's anxieties about the decline in private behavior. The Klan lashed out against wife beaters, drunkards, bootleggers, gamblers—anyone who violated time-honored standards of morality.

In the end, poor leadership and the absence of a political program destroyed the Klan. Once they attained office, Klan-supported officials offered no constructive legislation. Even more damaging, several Klan leaders became involved in sex scandals, and several more were indicted for corruption. By 1930 voters had turned Klansmen out of office, Klan membership had fallen to 50,000, and the forces of nativism were in full retreat. The country had abandoned a grass-roots movement that purported to stand for Americanism but smacked of fascism. The white sheets and cross burnings vanished from public view, to return again in a few decades when the civil rights movement challenged white supremacy.

THE RISE OF URBAN CULTURE

Despite all the upheavals, a new force for social cohesion was drawing Americans together during the 1920s. The United States was rapidly evolving a consumer culture that blunted regional differences and imposed similar tastes and life-styles. Centered in the cities and propelled by revolutions in transportation, advertising, communications, and entertainment, a new consumer society emerged during the 1920s, enshrining materialism and self-indulgence as the dominant cultural motifs of prosperity's decade.

The Automobile

"Why on earth do you need to study what's changing this country," a Midwesterner asked the sociologists Robert and Helen Lynd in 1924. "I can tell you what's happening in just four letters: A-U-T-O!" The man was right. In 1900 only 8000 motor vehicles were registered in the United States and the automobile was little more than a rich man's toy; by 1920 Americans owned more than 9 million automobiles. By 1925 Henry Ford had lowered the price of his sturdy Model Ts to less than $300, about three-months pay for the average urban worker. That year registrations reached 19,940,724, and by 1930 registrations had risen to 26,531,999 (more than one automobile for every five people).

No previous form of transportation (except walking) had been so widely available. In Muncie, Indiana, a town of 11,000, only 125 families owned a horse and carriage in 1890. Most people walked. By the time of the Lynds' study in 1924, however, two out of three families in Muncie owned an automobile. The great American love affair with the automobile had begun. One working-class housewife told the Lynds, "I'll go without food before I'll see us give up the car."

Enthusiasts claimed the automobile promoted family togetherness through evening rides, picnics, and weekend excursions. Critics decried family squabbles between parents and teenagers over use of the automobile, an apparent decline in church attendance resulting from all-day Sunday outings, and budget pressures working families faced to support their automobile habit. Others felt uneasy about the blurring of class lines (blue-collar families riding around just like rich folks). Worst of all, charged critics, automobiles gave young people freedom and privacy. Enclosed sedans constituted nearly 90 percent of the automobiles sold in the United States by 1927. These "portable bedrooms" removed courtship from the family parlor and gave couples a private room they could take anywhere.

Critics also blamed the automobile for undermining the public's devotion to thrift. In the past, people had been taught to live within their means. That meant paying cash for consumer goods or doing without. The automobile eroded this thrift ethic. An ad in a midwestern newspaper showed a kindly banker advising a young couple to buy an automobile on time, predicting the purchase would raise their horizons, which, in turn, would boost their earning power. Long before New Dealers started quoting John Maynard Keynes, Madison Avenue was telling Americans to spend themselves rich.

Appliances

Madison Avenue struck another bonanza in appliances, and electricity offered the key to this vast new market. Prior to World War I only one-fifth of America's households had electricity, but by 1929 the proportion had risen to two-thirds, and by 1940, to over four-fifths. Electric refrigerators, washing machines, vacuum cleaners, and toasters quickly took hold. By 1929 one in four homes had electric vacuum cleaners; one in five had toasters.

Appliances eased the sheer physical drudgery of housework, but they did not shorten the average housewife's work week. Women had to do more because the standards others told them to meet kept rising. In the 1920s and 1930s housewives fell under the spell of advice columnists, the ads of soap manufacturers who brought their favorite "soap" operas into their homes, and the precepts of appliance manufacturers. All equated cleanliness with motherly love, hoping to make women who did not keep spotless homes feel like failures. Sheets had to be changed weekly; the house had to be vacuumed daily.

In short, social pressure expanded household chores to keep pace with the new technology. Nor did the irony stop there. Touted as labor-saving devices, household appliances actually stopped the trend toward the centralization of certain jobs, like laundry and baking. Far from liberating women, appliances imposed new standards and pressures.

The Lost Generation

While most Americans embraced the consumer culture, others found it thoroughly disgusting. Disillusioned by the collapse of Wilsonian idealism, the hypocrisy of prohibition, and the upsurge of nativism, a new generation of American writers felt alienated. To these cultural critics, America had become a nation of conspicuous consumption, awash in materialism and devoid of spiritual vitality. Writers of the so-called Lost Generation despised the narrow-mindedness of small town life, with its complacency, its conformity, and, above all, its devotion to the all-mighty dollar.

No author captured these themes better than Sinclair Lewis, the first American to win the Nobel Prize for literature (1930). In *Main Street* (1920), he mingled satire with caricature when he declared: "Main Street is the climax of civilization. That this Ford might stand in front of the Bon Ton Store, Hannibal invaded Rome and Erasmus wrote in Oxford cloisters." In *Babbitt* (1922), a biting portrait of America's businessmen, Lewis attacked the spiritual conformity that drove Americans to follow the crowd.

H. L. Mencken mounted a scathing attack on his countrymen. As editor of *Mercury* maga-

zine, he wrote hundreds of essays mocking practically every aspect of American life. He called the South "the Sahara of the Bozart," a "gargantuan paradise of the fourth rate," and the middle class the "booboisie." Mencken directed his choicest barbs at reformers, whom he blamed for the bloodshed of World War I and the gangsters of the 1920s. "If I am convinced of anything," he snarled, "it is that Doing Good is in bad taste."

F. Scott Fitzgerald and Ernest Hemingway made the same points more obliquely. In novels such as *The Great Gatsby* (1925) and *Tender Is the Night* (1929), Fitzgerald exposed the decadence and materialism of American culture. Hemingway lionized toughness and "manly virtues" as a counterpoint to the softness of American life. In *The Sun Also Rises* (1926) and *A Farewell to Arms* (1929), he emphasized meaningless death and the importance of facing stoically the absurdities of the universe.

The Communication Revolution

In 1897 the United States had less than one telephone for every hundred residents, by 1914 the number had risen to one in ten, and by 1930 it stood at one in six. Americans averaged over 64 million calls per day in 1929, and a person in New York could talk with someone in London

Members of the "Lost Generation" of writers felt disillusioned with an American culture obsessed with money and devoid of spiritual vitality. Two of the Lost Generation's most prominent members were Ernest Hemingway (left) and F. Scott Fitzgerald (right).

for about $10 a minute that same year. The telephone hastened the transition from the written to the electronically transmitted word, brought the home in closer contact with the outside world, and reduced household visiting among neighbors as friends picked up the phone instead of dropping in.

Radio had an even greater impact. It drew the nation together by bringing news, entertainment, and advertisements to millions of listeners. With the organization of the National Broadcasting Corporation (NBC) in 1926 and the Columbia Broadcasting System (CBS) the following year, radio developed into a national industry, offering the same programs from coast to coast. In 1929 over 10 million households owned radios (well over one-third of the families in the country), and in that same year Americans spent a staggering $85 million on radio equipment.

The radio offered something for everyone. Not only did it report news events minutes after they happened, it brought politics to life as Americans listened to the voices of their political leaders and heard Will Rogers poke gentle fun at them. Serial adventures such as "The Green Hornet" and "The Lone Ranger" appealed to the entire family, while producers pitched sports broadcasts at male audiences. The "soaps" dominated weekday programming as millions of housewives listened to "Portia Faces Life" and "Life Can Be Beautiful."

Radio programs helped create mass culture by blunting regional differences. Listeners heard the same news reporters, serial shows, and sporting events delivered in the same dialect. They heard the same advertisements telling them what to buy, when to buy it, and how much to pay for it. Moreover, no other media had the power to create folk heroes so quickly. When Charles Lindbergh, the "Lone Eagle," became the first person to fly nonstop across the Atlantic from New York to Paris in 1927, the radio brought this incredible feat into American homes and made him a celebrity overnight.

Yet radio waves also brought the nation decidedly unheroic images. "Amos and Andy," which first aired in 1929, was one of the most popular shows of the depression. Its portrait of black life spread vicious racial stereotypes into homes whose white occupants knew little about black people. Other minorities fared no better. The Italian gangster, the bloodthirsty Indian, the Mexican with the sing-song voice, the tight-fisted Jew, and the Irish thug became stock characters in radio programming.

The Rise of Suburbs

Americans who bought the same products and listened to the same programs also shared new housing arrangements. The 1920s saw a spectacular growth in suburbs. Havens for the wealthy and upper middle class and home to a variety of white ethnic groups, suburbs expanded at a much faster rate than inner cities. Between 1920 and 1930 the population of Beverly Hills, a Los Angeles suburb, increased 2485 percent; Shaker Heights, a Cleveland suburb, 1000 percent; and Elmwood Park, a Chicago suburb, 717 percent.

New forms of transportation made the suburbs possible. For much of the nation's history, cities could not grow larger because workers had to live within walking distance of their jobs. Public transportation simply did not exist. After the Civil War, however, trolleys and streetcars greatly expanded labor's mobility, permitting workers to move beyond the walking radius surrounding factories. Metropolitan growth followed the trolley tracks as suburbs sprang up along the commuter lines. The automobile opened up vast new regions for housing, giving workers numerous options about where to live. Though suburbs had once been the exclusive domain of the well-to-do, the automobile enabled working-class families to move there, too.

Yet optimists who hoped to escape the city's congestion by moving to the suburbs got fooled. The sharp rise in road construction following the Federal Highway Act of 1916 produced complicated lateral traffic flows within cities and traffic congestion became worse. City planners counterattacked with traffic circles, synchronized stoplights, divided dual highways, and grade separation of highways from city streets, but nothing could free motorists from rush hour and holiday traffic jams. Whether one looked at the size and shape of cities or the flow of people within them, automobile tracks could be seen on virtually every inch of America's urban landscape.

Leisure Time: Games, Books, Sports, and Movies

Thanks to the unprecedented prosperity of the 1920s, Americans had more money for leisure activities than ever before. Spending for entertainment more than doubled during the 1920s, reaching $4.3 billion in 1929. The average worker devoted seven hours a week to play. Much of the time and money went for parlor games—mahjong sets, crossword puzzles, and the like. Contract bridge became the most durable of the new pastimes, followed closely by photography. Americans hit golf balls, played tennis, and bowled. Dance crazes swept the country. The fox trot made way for the Charleston, which in turn gave way to the jitterbug.

While Lewis, Mencken, Fitzgerald, and Hemingway found a wide audience, millions of Americans preferred the new popular literature, largely because it resolved rather than explored cultural tensions. In 1914, Edgar Rice Burroughs published *Tarzan of the Apes*, which immediately became a runaway bestseller. During the next 20 years, he wrote 40 other novels, most about Tarzan. For readers who felt concerned about urbanization and industrialization, the adventures of a lone white man in "dark Africa" revived the spirit of the frontier and individualism.

Zane Grey's novels enjoyed even greater popularity. His *Riders of the Purple Sage* appealed to readers who wished to celebrate their frontier heritage as a time when life seemed simple. Grey used a tried but true formula: romance, action, and a moralistic struggle between good and evil, all put in a western setting. Between 1918 and 1934, Grey wrote 24 books and became the best-known writer of popular fiction in the country.

While many readers demanded virtuous heroes and old-time values in their fiction, others wanted to be titillated. The 1920s saw a boom in "confession magazines." Urban values, liberated women, and Hollywood films had all relaxed Victorian standards, and confession magazines rushed to fill the vacuum, purveying stories of romantic success and failure, divorce, fantasy, and adultery. Of this genre, the most successful magazine was *True Story*, whose subscriptions soared from 10,000 in 1919 to more than 2 million in 1926. Writers survived the censors' cuts by placing moral tags at the end of their stories, advising readers to avoid similar mistakes in their own lives.

Spectator sports attracted vast audiences in the 1920s. The country yearned for heroes in an increasingly impersonal, organized society, and sports provided them. Prizefighting enjoyed a huge following, especially in the heavyweight division, where hard punchers like Jack Dempsey became national idols. Team sports flourished in colleges and high schools, but Americans focused on individual superstars, people whose talents or personalities made them appear larger than life. While Notre Dame emerged as a college football powerhouse in the 1920s, it was head coach Knute Rockne, with his "pep talks" on dedication and persistence, who got woven into the fabric of American popular culture. Harold "Red" Grange, the "Galloping Ghost" halfback for the University of Illinois, raised professional football to new heights when he signed a contract with the Chicago Bears in 1926.

Baseball drew even bigger crowds than football. George Herman "Babe" Ruth, the "Sultan of Swat," ruled as the sport's undisputed superstar. The public loved Ruth for his fabulous skills. As a member of the Boston Red Sox, Ruth set the major league record for the most scoreless innings pitched in a World Series. Ruth then went on to lead the New York Yankees to victory in four World Series by setting four home run records, hitting 60 in his best year. Yet quite apart from his pitching and hitting, the public adored Ruth for his gargantuan appetite and for his capacity to drink himself into a stupor. Die hard fans admired his beer belly almost as much as his swing.

Ruth transformed baseball in the 1920s because the public wanted change. Until the 1920s, Ty Cobb's brand of baseball dominated the sport—defense, base hits, and stolen bases. Ruth revolutionized the game in 1919 when he hit 29 home runs, the most ever in a single season, followed by an astonishing 54 in 1920. Between 1915 and 1930, the total number of home runs in major league baseball increased from 384 a year to 1565. Stolen bases dropped by one-half. Baseball became the game of the big hitter, the superstar, and no hitter was bigger,

Spectator sports became popular in the 1920s: Heroes of the day included men like "Red" Grange of the University of Illinois and "Babe" Ruth of the New York Yankees.

literally or figuratively, than Babe Ruth: He made baseball the "national pastime" as fans spent countless hours calculating, memorizing, and quizzing one another on baseball statistics.

Despite the mania for athletics, Americans shelled out ten times more money on movies than on spectator sports. By 1929, 90 million Americans went to the movies every week, out of a population of 120 million. Movies had become big business, and Hollywood could afford to produce huge spectacles. Cecil B. DeMille's *Ten Commandments* with its "cast of thousands" and dazzling special effects, demonstrated the new medium's ability to hold audiences spellbound. Comedies enjoyed great popularity as well, whether highly sophisticated pieces such as *Sinners in Silk*, featuring young men and women sharing in new sexual freedom, or slapstick masterpieces starring Charlie Chaplin, Buster Keaton, or Harold Lloyd. Ironically, slapstick comedies delivered the most significant social commentary of the 1920s, spoofing the pretensions of the wealthy and presenting sympathetic portraits of the poor.

Like radio and sports, movies helped create a new popular culture, with common speech, dress, behavior, and heroes. And like radio, Hollywood did its share to reinforce vicious racial stereotypes by denigrating minority groups. Mexicans appeared as sleepyeyed peasants, while the only parts for blacks went to actors like Stepin Fetchit, who got rich playing superstitious, blithering idiots. The wooden box and the silver screen both molded and mirrored mass culture.

THE REPUBLICAN RESTORATION

National politics looked backward during the 1920s. When Republican leaders promised to restore prosperity, most Americans embraced the conservative rhetoric, hoping to find in politics the stability they found lacking in their culture.

Talk about trust-busting and regulating big business gave way in "New Era" politics to calls for a partnership between government and industry, one that would promote the interests of American corporations at home and abroad. Politicos of the 1920s saw themselves as managers who understood economic growth. In place of government regulation, they put their faith in cooperation through the exchange of information among voluntary associations in every segment of the economy.

The Republican party dominated American politics in the 1920s, and its victories rested squarely on the votes of traditional Republicans. Though strongest in the rural states of the Midwest, Republicans enjoyed firm support in the Far West and in much of New England. Socially, the GOP remained the choice of old-stock, Protestant, middle-, upper-middle-, and upper-class Americans; occupationally, it drew its strength from bankers, professionals, business managers, and large farmers.

Handsome Harding

By and large the presidents of the New Era were mediocre figures. Senator Warren G. Harding of Ohio, who led off the decade, suited the times perfectly. Handsome enough to be a movie star, he not only looked great, but told the voters what they wanted to hear. Harding promised a return to "normalcy," which meant "not heroism but healing, not agitation but adjustment, not surgery but serenity." Democrat William McAdoo, the son-in-law of Woodrow Wilson and former secretary of the treasury, derided Harding's speeches as "an army of pompous phrases moving over the landscape in search of an idea," but McAdoo missed the point: Americans listened to Harding's words and felt reassured. He appeared to be a moderate, responsible leader who would avoid extremes and guide the country into a decade of prosperity. Harding trounced the Democratic candidate, Governor James M. Cox of Ohio, 16,143,407 to 9,130,328, carrying every state outside the Democratic South.

Harding remained in office what he had been before, a fun-loving man who liked to hit golf balls, play poker, drink whiskey, and shoot the breeze with old pals. He left government to his cabinet members and the Supreme Court, staffed by political conservatives all. They approached public service as managers, equating the people's interests with those of big business. Secretary of State Charles Evans Hughes championed American business interests abroad with unbridled enthusiasm; Andrew Mellon, secretary of the treasury, denounced government regulation and slashed taxes on the rich; and

Henry Wallace, the secretary of agriculture, organized conferences between farmers and bureaucrats under the Bureau of Agricultural Economics.

Business leaders had contributed $8 million to the GOP's campaign chest in 1920; in return they expected the federal government to roll back the gains organized labor had made during World War I. The courts led the attack. In 1921 Harding named William Howard Taft as chief justice of the Supreme Court. Taft's judicial philosophy embraced the sanctity of private property as the highest ideal of the republic. Under Taft, the Court took a narrow view of federal power, assigning the responsibility for protecting individual citizens to the states. During the 1920s the Court outlawed picketing, upheld the yellow-dog contract, overturned national child labor laws, and abolished minimum wage laws for women.

The decade's most capable figure was Herbert Hoover, secretary of commerce under both Harding and his successor, Calvin Coolidge. A world-famous engineer and self-made millionaire, Hoover abhorred destructive competition and waste in the economy, which he proposed to eliminate through "associationism." Hoover called for voluntary trade associations to foster cooperation in nearly every major industry and agricultural commodity through educational conferences, research commissions, trade practice controls, and ethical standards. By 1929 more than 2000 trade associations were busily at work implementing Hoover's vision of a stable and prosperous economy. Hoover also converted the Commerce Department into a planning agency for businesspeople. Working in cooperation with private groups, such as the National Bureau of Economic Research, the Commerce Department conducted studies and compiled statistics to aid corporate planning. No other Harding appointment matched Hoover's talent and vision.

In fact, several of Harding's appointees proved to be disasters. His own father once chided Harding: "It's a good thing you weren't born a girl. Because you'd be in a family way all the time. You can't say no." Harding found it especially hard to say no to old friends and cronies, members of the so-called Ohio Gang, when they asked for government jobs. In the end, this motley assortment of political hacks and hangers-on plunged his administration into disgrace.

Within two years after Harding assumed office, major scandals (involving bribes and kickbacks) erupted in the Justice Department and in the Veterans Bureau. Shortly after these disclosures, Harding died of a cerebral embolism on August 2, 1923. Immediately after his death, more misdeeds came to light, including the infamous Teapot Dome oil scandal. Albert B. Fall, a wealthy senator from New Mexico whom Harding had appointed as secretary of the interior, was convicted of accepting $360,000 in bribes in exchange for leasing drilling rights on federal naval oil reserves. He became the first cabinet member in American history convicted for crimes in office. Nor did the corruption in high places end there. After authorities accused Attorney General Harry Daugherty of accepting payoffs for selling German chemical patents controlled by the Alien Property Office, Daugherty resigned in disgrace.

In retrospect, two facts stand out about the scandals. First, none involved partisan attacks on private individuals or on political opponents, tactics associated with the Watergate scandal that brought down the presidency of Richard Nixon half a century later. Harding simply appointed men who were personally corrupt. Second, the public seemed indifferent to the scandals. Harding's successor, Calvin Coolidge, managed to convert the scandals into a political asset by convincing the public he had moved swiftly to punish the wrongdoers.

The Election of 1924

The election of 1924 symbolized, in a variety of ways, the tensions and concerns of the 1920s. Despite the Harding scandals, President Calvin Coolidge remained extremely popular, largely because the nation was awash in prosperity. Meeting in New York to nominate their candidate, the Democrats split their support between Alfred Smith, the governor of New York, and William Gibbs McAdoo. McAdoo represented the southern, rural wing of the party, which opposed immigration and evolution and supported prohibition, Protestantism, and the Ku Klux Klan. Smith spoke for the northern urban wing, which opposed immigration restriction, prohi-

Harding's administration was fraught with scandals involving bribes and kickbacks within his cabinet and inner circle.

bition, and the Ku Klux Klan. After 102 ballots in the sweltering heat of Madison Square Garden, the Democrats nominated a compromise candidate, John W. Davis, a Wall Street attorney. But by that time, the Democrats were so badly divided they had no chance for victory, at least not in 1924.

A coalition of labor leaders, social workers, and former progressives bolted both major parties and formed the Progressive party, which nominated Wisconsin Senator Robert La Follette for president. Their platform called for government ownership of natural resources, abolition of child labor, elimination of monopolies, and increased taxes on the rich. In the end, no issue could match the GOP's prosperity crusade. Coolidge won the election with 15,725,016 votes to Davis's 8,385,586 and La Follette's 4,822,856.

Silent Cal

Coolidge was a stern-faced, tight-lipped New Englander, whom Alice Roosevelt Longworth (Theodore Roosevelt's daughter) said looked like he had been "weaned on a pickle." Born in Plymouth Notch, Vermont, where five generations of Coolidges had worked the same family farm, he epitomized the rural values threatened by immigration, urbanization, and industrialization. After graduating from Amherst College, Coolidge opened a law office in Northampton, Massachusetts, where he embarked on a political career that led to the governorship of the Bay State. After crushing the Boston police strike in 1919 by calling out the National Guard, Coolidge gained a reputation as a staunch conservative. His reward came in 1920 when Republicans gave him the number two slot on their ticket.

Coolidge had no desire to be a strong president in the tradition of a Teddy Roosevelt or a Woodrow Wilson. In the words of Irving Stone, "He aspired to become the least President the country had ever had; he attained his desire." Coolidge went to bed early, slept ten hours a night, napped every afternoon, and seldom worked more than four hours a day. In part his sloth stemmed from a metabolic need for rest, but it also derived from a deep philosophical belief in the wisdom of inactivity. "Four-fifths of all our troubles in this life would disappear," sighed Coolidge, "if we would only sit down and keep still."

Harding and Coolidge both idealized rich businessmen, but Coolidge was positively consumed by his reverence for the corporate elite. "The man who builds a factory builds a temple," said Coolidge. "The man who works there, worships there." It followed, then, that government should do everything in its power to promote business interests. While Coolidge set the tone for his administration, he left it to his cabinet members, the courts, and Congress to devise strategies for consummating the marriage between business and government.

The Twilight of Progressivism

The government's tilt toward business signaled a retreat from progressivism. With the Democrats in disarray and Teddy Roosevelt's wing of the GOP all but dead, conservative Republicans were riding high. Still, the reform impulse did not disappear entirely during the 1920s. A small band of beleaguered reformers, led by Robert La Follette of Wisconsin and George Norris of Nebraska, kept progressivism alive in Congress, where they worked for farm relief, child labor laws, and regulation of wages and working hours for women.

In 1922, Congress passed the Capper-Volstead Act, which exempted farm cooperatives from antitrust prosecution, clearing the way for production restrictions and price-fixing. Yet the farm bloc failed to enact the McNary-Haugen Bill, which would have raised farm prices by having the government purchase farm surpluses and then sell them in foreign markets. Congress passed the bill twice, but Coolidge vetoed it both times. Progressives did manage to defeat an attempt by private investors (led by Henry Ford) to build a hydroelectric dam across the Tennessee River at Muscle Shoals, Alabama, thus preserving the task of developing electricity in the region for the federal government.

Welfare advocates won a few temporary victories at the national level. In 1912 President William Howard Taft created the Children's Bureau in the Department of Labor to compile information on a variety of problems involving the nation's youth. In 1918 the bureau reported that 16,000 women had died in childbirth that year and 250,000 children had failed to survive their first year. Armed with these figures, reformers demanded federal action to improve prenatal and neonatal care. Social workers, joined by Margaret Sanger and other birth control advocates, supported the idea, and although the American Medical Association opposed it, Harding backed it. In 1921 Congress passed the Sheppard-Towner Act, which appropriated $1.5 million in 1922 for state hygiene instruction programs. The program died seven years later when Coolidge refused to renew its funding.

In keeping with their historic pattern, progressives had better luck at the state and local level. Once again, social workers and women's groups spearheaded the campaigns, sponsoring a broad range of welfare legislation. By 1930, 43 states had passed laws providing assistance to women with dependent children, and 34 states had adopted workers' compensation laws. Under the leadership of Governor Alfred Smith, New York granted women a 41-hour work week and instituted the nation's first public housing program.

Welfare opponents counterattacked, arguing labor reforms would increase production costs and leave states that passed welfare legislation at a competitive disadvantage with states without such laws. Asked to choose between social welfare programs and jobs, Congress, along with most states, opted for jobs. Moreover, the public did not seem to care. As one coed told a pollster: "We're not out to benefit society . . . or to make industry safe. We're not going to suffer over how the other half lives."

The Election of 1928

Coolidge announced his retirement from politics in 1928 with the terse statement, "I do not choose to run." Following his exit, the Republicans nominated Herbert Hoover, while the Democrats turned to Alfred E. Smith. Since both parties adopted nearly identical platforms, the election turned on personalities and images. Few elections have pitted opponents who better defined the two faces of America—one rural, the other urban.

A native of Iowa, Hoover depicted himself as a simple farmboy who, through hard work and pluck, had grown up to become wealthy and famous. During the campaign he told folksy tales of an idyllic boyhood spent in rural America, replete with nostalgic glimpses of swimming holes, hunting and fishing trips, and moonlit romps in fresh snow. In truth, his childhood had been far from perfect. Orphaned as a boy, Hoover was shuttled back and forth among a variety of relatives until he went to Stanford University. After graduating with a degree in mining engineering in 1893, Hoover labored in the mines during the depression that year before landing an engineering job with an international firm. Brilliant, hard working, and focused, he was a millionaire 12 years later. As

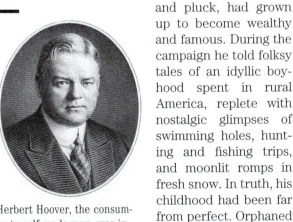

Herbert Hoover, the consummate self-made man, was in office only a few months when the stock market crashed.

a self-made man, Hoover presented a portrait of a safe, reassuring world.

Yet Hoover was also a spokesman for the future. A leading advocate of scientific progressivism, he accepted the reality of industrialization, technology, governmental activism, and global markets. In contrast to Harding and Coolidge, Hoover believed the president should lead the nation. He thought the federal government had a responsibility to coordinate the competing interests of a modern economy. According to Hoover, technology, logic, and expertise, in both the public and private sectors, would make economic prosperity a permanent feature of American life.

Smith offered voters a clear choice. The son of immigrants, he was an Irish Catholic from Hell's Kitchen in New York City who had started public life with nothing and had climbed the political ladder as a faithful son of Tammany Hall. Smith sported his eastern accent and mannerisms with the same pride that he tipped his brown derby hat. A foe of prohibition, he spoke for urban, ethnic Americans. Yet Smith, too, represented the future, not so much in terms of science, technology, and organization, but in terms of cultural pluralism and urbanization. America's future lay with her cities, and the cities contained large groups of ethnic Americans struggling for acceptance and their share of the good life. Trapped between its past and the future, the Democratic party might be badly divided between its rural and urban wings, but Smith made no bones about his loyalties.

Not that it made much difference who the Democrats ran. Thanks to the booming economy, the Republicans were unbeatable in 1928. Smith was hurt by his failure to bridge the North-South, urban-rural split in the party; by anti-Catholic sentiment; and by his own attacks on prohibition. Aided by prosperity, religious bigotry, and the dry vote, Hoover coasted to an easy victory, swamping Smith by 21,392,190 votes to 15,016,443. The Democrats were so divided that six states from Dixie abandoned the Solid South and defected to Hoover.

Yet even in defeat, Smith's campaign revealed the most significant political change of the 1920s—the growing power of urban and ethnic voters within the Democratic party. Smith carried the 12 largest cities in the United

States by a margin of 38,000 votes. Equally important, many voters cast ballots for the first time in the election, as total voter turnout rose from 49 percent in 1924 to 57 percent in 1928. In large measure, the new voters came from industrial, urban communities in the North. This meant that hyphenated Americans were rapidly acquiring the habit of voting, and they were voting Democratic, shrinking the influence of the rural element in the party, as well as in the nation.

Herbert Hoover's election marked the climax of New Era politics. As president he advocated total cooperation between government and business. "Given a chance to go forward with the policies of the last eight years," he declared shortly after entering the White House, "we shall soon with the help of God be in sight of the day when poverty will be banished from this nation." Optimistic businesspeople, bankers, and stockbrokers applauded Hoover's promises, predicting a future of prosperity and progress. Ironically, the stock market crashed before their cheers had stopped echoing.

THE GREAT CRASH

Economic historians have been hard pressed to explain why "prosperity's decade" ended in financial disaster. Employment was high, prices were stable, and production was soaring. Manufacturing output nearly doubled between 1921 and 1929, and the real wages of industrial workers rose by about 17 percent. Not everyone prospered, to be sure. Strapped with long-term debts, high taxes, and a sharp drop in crop prices, farmers lost ground throughout the decade, never matching their income of 1920. Most blacks and Hispanics lived in poverty, large numbers of poor whites haunted southern Appalachia, and virtually every large American city had its ghetto. Still, more people were comfortable, well-to-do, or rich during the 1920s than ever before in American history.

The upper income groups included many Americans who became downright greedy, displaying what the economist John Kenneth Galbraith called an "inordinate desire to get rich quickly with a minimum of physical effort."

Many speculators sought to make their fortune in the Florida land boom of 1925–1926, the most spectacular monument to investment irresponsibility of the decade. Land prices in Florida rose exponentially until two devastating hurricanes in 1926 showed, in the words of Frederick Lewis Allen, "what a Soothing Tropic Wind could do when it got a running start from the West Indies." After the wind and the rain washed away the land boom, prices fell back to earth, bringing financial disaster to those who thought providence had selected Florida's marshlands as the perfect instrument for making them wealthy.

The Great Bull Market offered even more Americans the chance to vent their passion for speculation. Beginning in the last six months of 1924 the price of securities began to rise. While there were periodic dips over the next few years, the stock market continued to climb upward until 1928 when the rate of increase switched from measured steps to vaulting leaps. In March of 1928 alone, the value of stocks shot up more than ten percent. With the price of individual stocks rising as much as 20 percent in a single day and 5 million shares changing hands, the ticker tapes often ran 2 hours behind.

Credit provided the yeast for the Great Bull Market. Margin buying allowed the purchaser of securities to pay only a fraction of their face value. The actual securities would then be left with the broker as collateral for the loan that paid for them, but the purchaser retained full title to them at their face value, including the right to sell them at a profit as the market rose. Speculators could get all the benefits of ownership without paying the full purchase price. In 1926 trading in the stock market stood at $451 million; by 1929 it had leaped to $1.1 billion. Brokers' loans stood at $3.5 billion in 1926; by 1929 they had jumped to $8.5 billion, showing how investment borrowing had transmuted itself into an orgy of speculation. Contrary to later mythology, the masses did not join in the fun. Most speculators were wealthy people or members of the upper middle class. Most working-class Americans did not own stocks, let alone play the market.

While the Federal Reserve Board was supposed to prevent such shenanigans, board members found themselves in a real dilemma. If they raised interest rates to stifle speculation, they risked slowing down the economy and creating unemployment. If they lowered interest rates to stimulate the economy, they risked making securities speculation worse. Confused and uncertain, the Federal Reserve Board pursued contradictory policies. Between 1927 and 1929 the board raised and lowered interest rates several times in a futile attempt to slow Wall Street down without harming the economy. In the end, private greed and government impotence combined to create a catastrophe.

A few days before he left office in 1929, Coolidge reassured the public stocks were "cheap at current prices." Critics disagreed. Financial analysts for the *New York Times* warned investors that the huge gap between stock prices and the rate of economic growth was bound to end in disaster. The bubble burst in September and October of 1929 when the market finally crashed. By November the value of the average stock had dropped 50 percent, reducing private wealth in the United States by an estimated $30 billion. Following a brief flirtation with stability in 1931, the market continued its downward spiral for the next several years. Overall, the index of common stocks dropped from a high of 26 points in 1929 to a low of 6.9 points in 1932.

But the Great Crash did not cause the Great Depression. Whole segments of the American economy, including agriculture, banking, manufacturing, and foreign trade, were shaky long before the stock market collapsed. Farm prices had been depressed ever since the end of World War I. Burdened by the heavy debts needed to finance wartime production increases, farmers could not compete on the world market when European agriculture revived. Following World War I, global farm production rose and commodity prices dropped. Caught with declining incomes, farmers tried to recover their losses and make their debt payments by increasing production. The collective result of millions of farmers raising output was larger surpluses and lower prices, a vicious cycle that persisted throughout the decade. Moreover, the decline in farm income reverberated throughout the economy: Rural consumers stopped buying farm implements, tractors, automobiles, furniture, and consumer goods from the mail order houses.

Millions of farmers defaulted on their debts, placing tremendous pressure on the banking system. Between 1920 and 1929 more than 5000 of the country's 30,000 banks failed. Afraid to put their money in banks, large numbers of people began hoarding cash, which by 1930 removed more than $1 billion from circulation. Following the stock market crash in 1929 and the continued downward spiral through 1933, the banking system saw more of its assets destroyed. Between 1929 and 1933, when the entire banking system collapsed, another 5000 banks went under. Small wonder many bankers became frightened and cautious, refusing to make loans even to worthy borrowers.

Thanks to the banking crisis, thousands of small businesspeople failed because they could not secure working capital loans. Thousands more failed because they had lost their working capital in the stock market. Instead of plowing some of their profits during the 1920s back into

This newspaper headline from October 25, 1929, tried to reassure the public that the economy was fundamentally sound, but the downward spiral continued through 1932, when prices were 80 percent below their 1929 highs.

their businesses and expanding capacity, many gambled on the securities markets. When the crash came in 1929, they lost money that should have gone into new factories, technologies, and distribution systems. Unable to raise their own cash or borrow funds, these small businesses shut their doors and laid off workers.

Labor formed another weak link in the chain. Because wage increases during the 1920s failed to keep pace with rising corporate profits, purchasing power could not absorb the supply of consumer goods. While business leaders promoted the consumer culture through advertising, they refused to give workers the wage increases needed to buy products. Like farmers, workers did not have enough purchasing power to sustain the economy.

Installment buying also weakened the economy. Between 1919 and 1927 term debt increased from $100 million to $7 billion. Consumers went on a spending binge, encouraged by "buy now and pay later" advertising. As demand for automobiles and furniture rose higher and higher, those industries expanded rapidly in the early 1920s. Later in the decade, consumer demand for cars and furniture reached the saturation point. By 1927 both industries found themselves with excess capacity and had to lay off workers.

Finally, Republican tariff policies damaged the economy by depressing foreign trade. Anxious to protect American industries from foreign competitors after World War I, Congress passed the Emergency Tariff Act of 1921, the Fordney-McCumber Tariff of 1922, and the Hawley-Smoot Tariff of 1930, each of which raised tariff rates to unprecedented levels. Along with serious weaknesses in the European economies, American tariffs stifled international trade and deepened the economic malaise, making it difficult for European nations to pay off their debts to creditor nations such as the United States.

Declining purchasing power created a vicious cycle. Drops in consumer spending led inevitably to reductions in production and worker layoffs. Unemployed workers then spent less and the cycle repeated itself. Business bankruptcies increased and even healthy firms postponed investment.

All these factors sapped the economy, leaving it ripe for disaster. Yet the depression did not strike instantly; it infected the country gradually, like a slow-growing cancer. From Maine to California, in numbers that seemed incredible, businesses failed, banks folded, and corporations slashed production, cut wages, and laid off employees. The national income dropped from $88 billion in 1929 to $40 billion in 1933, by which time 13 million Americans (25 percent of the work force) had lost their jobs.

Measured in human terms, the Great Depression was the greatest economic catastrophe in American history. It hit urban and rural areas, blue- and white-collar families alike. In the nation's cities, unemployed men took to the streets to sell apples or shine shoes. By the end of 1930, New York City had 33 soup kitchens, serving lines of hungry families that stretched for blocks. Thousands of men, many of whom deserted their wives and children, hopped freight trains and wandered from town to town looking for jobs or handouts.

Unlike most of western Europe, the United States had no federal system of unemployment insurance. The relief burden fell on state and municipal governments working in cooperation with private charities, such as the Red Cross and the Community Chest. Created to handle temporary emergencies, these groups lacked the resources to alleviate the massive suffering created by the Great Depression. The rural South had virtually no relief funds. A social worker in Alabama considered herself fortunate when the county appropriated $300 to serve 5000 unemployed, starving people.

Urban centers in the North fared little better. Most city charters did not permit public funds to be spent on work relief. Philadelphia provided relief to only one needy family in five, and those families lucky enough to receive assistance got less than $20 a month. New York paid less than $10 a month per family. Relative to the cost of living, these subsidies were meager, yet most small and medium-sized cities offered no assistance. By the fall of 1931 relief programs had collapsed in most cities. Adding insult to injury, several states disqualified relief clients from voting, while other cities forced them to surrender their automobile license plates. "Prosperity's decade" ended in economic disaster.

CHRONOLOGY OF KEY EVENTS

1914 Marcus Garvey organizes the Universal Negro Improvement Association (UNIA) to promote black migration to Africa

1915 Ku Klux Klan is revived and claims 4 million members by 1924

1917–1925 Some 600,000 black Americans migrate to northern industrial cities

1919 Labor unrest includes a nationwide steel strike, a coal miners strike, a general strike in Seattle, and a police strike in Boston; Race riots erupt in over 20 cities; Eighteenth Amendment bans the manufacture and sale of alcoholic beverages

1920 Palmer raids arrest suspected Communists; Massachusetts trial of two Italian anarchists, Nicola Sacco and Bartolomeo Vanzetti, begins on charges of murder and results in their execution in 1927; Sinclair Lewis's *Main Street* exposes the complacency of small-town life

1921 Warren Harding's inauguration as the twenty-ninth president begins 12 years of Republican control of the presidency; Revenue Act slashes taxes on higher incomes; European immigration is restricted to a quota of 3 percent of the population of a nationality living in the United States in 1910

1922 Fordney-McCumber Tariff raises duties on imports

1923 President Harding dies; Calvin Coolidge becomes the thirtieth president

1924 Congress reduces immigration quota to 2 percent of the population of a nationality living in the United States in 1890; Senate committee begins an investigation of Teapot Dome oil-leasing scandal

1925 Scopes trial, the celebrated "Monkey Trial," attacks the teaching of evolution in public schools; F. Scott Fitzgerald's *The Great Gatsby* criticizes the American success ethic

1926 New revenue act further reduces tax rates on high incomes

1929 Herbert Hoover is inaugurated as the thirty-first president; annual quota of immigrants is reduced to about 152,000; stock market crashes

1930 Hawley-Smoot Tariff raises import duties to unprecedented levels

CONCLUSION

Janus, the two-faced god of antiquity, offers an intriguing symbol for America in the 1920s. The nation's image was divided, with one profile looking optimistically to the future and the other staring longingly at the past. Caught between the disillusionment of World War I and the economic malaise of the Great Depression, the 1920s witnessed a gigantic struggle between an old and a new America, a time when the past was visibly, almost palpably laboring to give birth to the future.

No longer a land of farms and villages, the United States had become a nation of factories and cities. The Protestant culture of rural America was threatened by the secular values of urban society. Yet throughout the 1920s tradition gave way to accommodation as a modern society began to take shape. Country against city, native against immigrant, worker against farmer, Protestant against Catholic and Jew, fundamentalist against liberal, conservative against progressive, wet against dry, Victorian against libertarian—all these issues reflected different images of the same battle: a colossal identity crisis that saw the United States struggling to come to terms with secular values and cultural pluralism. But what World War I started, the Great Depression interrupted. The intense cultural upheavals of the 1920s gave way to the equally intense economic debates of the 1930s as cultural politics took a backseat to the politics of survival.

SUGGESTIONS FOR FURTHER READING

OVERVIEWS AND SURVEYS

Frederick Lewis Allen, *Only Yesterday: An Informal History of the Nineteen-Twenties* (1931); Paul A. Carter, *Another Part of the Twenties* (1977) and *The Twenties in America*, 2d ed. (1975); Ellis Hawley, *The Great War and the Search for Modern Order* (1979); John D. Hicks, *Republican Ascendancy, 1921–1933* (1960); William E. Leuchtenburg, *The Perils of Prosperity, 1914–32* (1958); Geoffrey Perrett, *America in the Twenties: A History* (1982).

THE CLASH OF VALUES

Houston A. Baker, Jr., *Modernism and the Harlem Renaissance* (1987); Albert Camarillo, *Chicanos in a Changing Society: From Mexican Pueblos to American Barrios in Santa Barbara and Southern California, 1848–1930* (1979); William H. Chafe, *The American Woman: Her Changing Social, Economic, and Political Role* (1972); Mark Thomas Connelly, *The Response to Prostitution in the Progressive Era* (1980); John D'Emilio and Estelle B. Freedman, *Intimate Matters: A History of Sexuality in America* (1988); Peter G. Filene, *Him/Her/Self: Sex Roles in Modern America* (1986); David H. Fischer, *Growing Old In America* (1978); Ellen Fitzpatrick, *Endless Crusade: Women Social Scientists and Progressive Reform* (1990); Penina Migdal Glazer and Miriam Slater, *Unequal Colleagues: The Entrance of Women into the Professions, 1890–1940* (1987); Linda Gordon, *Woman's Body, Woman's Right: A Social History of Birth Control in America* (1976); John B. Holway, *Black Diamonds: Life in the Negro Leagues From the Men Who Lived It* (1989); Nathan Huggins, *Harlem Renaissance* (1971); Ira Katznelson, *Black Men, White Cities* (1973); Kenneth Kusmer, *A Ghetto Takes Shape: Black Cleveland, 1870–1930* (1976); J. Stanley Lemons, *The Woman Citizen: Social Feminism in the 1920s* (1973); David Levering Lewis, *When Harlem Was in Vogue* (1981); Gilbert Osofsky, *Harlem: The Making of a Ghetto: Negro New York, 1890–1930*, 2d ed. (1971); James Reed, *From Private Vice to Public Virtue: The Birth Con-*

trol Movement and American Society Since 1830 (1978); Ricardo Romo, *East Los Angeles: History of a Barrio* (1983); Ruth Rosen, *The Lost Sisterhood: Prostitution in America, 1900–1918* (1982); Leslie W. Tentler, *Wage-Earning Women: Industrial Work and Family Life in the United States, 1900–1930* (1979); Theodore Vincent, *Black Power and the Garvey Movement* (1971); Winifred D. Wandersee, *Women's Work and Family Values, 1920–1940* (1981); Nancy Weiss, *The National Urban League, 1910–1940* (1974).

THE REVOLT OF THE TRADITIONALISTS

David Chalmers, *Hooded Americans: The First Century of the Ku Klux Klan, 1865–1965* (1965); Robert A. Divine, *American Immigration Policy, 1924–1952* (1957); Norman Furniss, *The Fundamentalist Controversy, 1918–1931* (1954); Ray Ginger, *Six Days or Forever? Tennessee v. John Thomas Scopes* (1958); Vivian Gornick, *The Romance of American Communism* (1977); John Higham, *Strangers in the Land: Patterns of American Nativism, 1860–1925* (1955); Kenneth T. Jackson, *The Ku Klux Klan in the City, 1915–1930* (1967); Don S. Kirshner, *City and Country: Rural Responses to Urbanization in the 1920s* (1970); Andrew Sinclair, *Prohibition* (1962); William Young and David E. Kaiser, *Postmortem: New Evidence in the Case of Sacco and Vanzetti* (1985).

THE RISE OF URBAN CULTURE

Loren Baritz, ed., *The Culture of the Twenties* (1970); Erik Barnouw, *A Tower of Babel: A History of Broadcasting in the United States to 1933* (1966); Robert Crunden, *From Self to Society: 1919–1941* (1972); Paula Fass, *The Damned and the Beautiful: American Youth in the 1920s* (1977); James J. Flink, *The Car Culture* (1975); Lewis F. Fried, *Makers of the City* (1990); Frederick Hoffman, *The Twenties: American Writing in the Postwar Decade*, rev. ed. (1962); Kenneth T. Jackson, *Crabgrass Frontier: The Suburbanization of the United States* (1985); Peter J. Ling, *America and the Automobile: Technology, Reform, and Social Change* (1990); Fred J. MacDonald, *Don't Touch That Dial!* (1979); Roderick Nash, *The Nervous Generation: American Thought, 1917–1930* (1970); Daniel Pope, *The Making of Modern Advertising* (1983); John B. Rae, *The Road and the Car in American Life* (1971); Robert Sklar, *Movie-Made America: A Cultural History of American Movies* (1975).

THE REPUBLICAN RESTORATION

LeRoy Ashby, *The Spearless Leader: Senator Borah and the Progressive Movement in the 1920s* (1972); Gary Dean Best, *The Politics of American Individualism: Herbert Hoover in Transition, 1918–1921* (1976); David Burner, *The Politics of Provincialism: The Democratic Party in Transition, 1918–1932* (1968); Clarke Chambers, *Seedtime of Reform, 1918–1932* (1963); Paula Eldot, *Governor Alfred E. Smith: The Politician as Reformer* (1983); John D. Hicks and Theodore Saloutos, *Twentieth Century Populism: Agricultural Discontent in the Midwest, 1900–1939* (1951); Allan Lichtman, *Prejudice and the Old Politics: The Presidential Election of 1928* (1979); Robert K. Murray, *The Harding Era: Warren G. Harding and His Administration* (1969) and *The Politics of Normalcy* (1973); Burl Noggle, *Teapot Dome: Oil and Politics in the 1920s* (1962); Robert H. Zieger, *Republicans and Labor, 1919–1929* (1969).

THE GREAT CRASH

William J. Barber, *From New Era to New Deal: Herbert Hoover, the Economists, and American Economic Policy, 1921–1933* (1985); Irving Bernstein, *The Lean Years: A History of the American Worker, 1920–1933* (1960); David Brody, *Workers in Industrial America: Essays on the Twentieth Century Struggle* (1980); Alfred Chandler, *Strategy and Structure: Chapters in the History of the Industrial Enterprise* (1962); Martin L. Fausold, *The Presidency of Herbert Hoover* (1985); John Kenneth Galbraith, *The Great Crash, 1929* (1955); Ellis W. Hawley, *The Great War and the Search for a Modern Order* (1979); Sanford M. Jacoby, *Employing Bureaucracy: Managers, Unions, and the Transformation of Work in American Industry, 1900–1945* (1985); David C. Jones, *Empire of Dust: Settling and Abandoning the Prairie Dry Belt* (1987); C. P. Kindleberger, *The World in Depression, 1929–1939* (1973); Jim Potter, *The American Economy Between the World Wars*, rev. ed. (1985); James Prothro, *The Dollar Decade: Business Ideas in the 1920s* (1954); Albert U. Romasco, *The Poverty of Abundance: Hoover, the Nation, and the Depression* (1965); Jordan A. Schwarz, *Interregnum of Despair: Hoover, Congress, and the Depression* (1970); Robert Sobel, *The Great Bull Market* (1968); George Soule, *Prosperity Decade: From War to Depression, 1917–1929* (1947); Peter Temin, *Did Monetary Forces Cause the Great Depression?* (1976).

BIOGRAPHIES

David Burner, *Herbert Hoover: A Public Life* (1979); Ellen Chesler, *Woman of Valor; Margaret Sanger and the Birth Control Movement in America* (1992); William Harbaugh, *Lawyer's Lawyer: The Life of John W. Davis* (1973); Matthew Josephson and Hannah Josephson, *Al Smith: Hero of the Cities* (1969); David Kennedy, *Birth Control in America: The Career of Margaret Sanger* (1970); Lawrence Levine, *Defender of the Faith: William Jennings Bryan, the Last Decade, 1915–1925* (1965); Richard Lowitt, *George W. Norris* (1971); Manning Marable, *W. E. B. Du Bois: Black Radical Democrat* (1986); Donald R. McCoy, *Calvin Coolidge: The Quiet President* (1967); George Nash, *The Life of Herbert Hoover—the Engineer*, vol. 1 (1983); Randy Roberts, *Jack Dempsey, the Manassa Mauler* (1979); Francis Russell, *The Shadow of Blooming Grove: Warren G. Harding in His Times* (1968); Andrew Sinclair, *The Available Man: The Life Behind the Masks of Warren Gamaliel Harding* (1965); Richard N. Smith, *An Uncommon Man: The Triumph of Herbert Hoover* (1984); David P. Thelen, *Robert M. La Follette and the Insurgent Spirit* (1976); William Allen White, *A Puritan in Babylon: The Story of Calvin Coolidge* (1938).

CHAPTER 25

The Age of Roosevelt

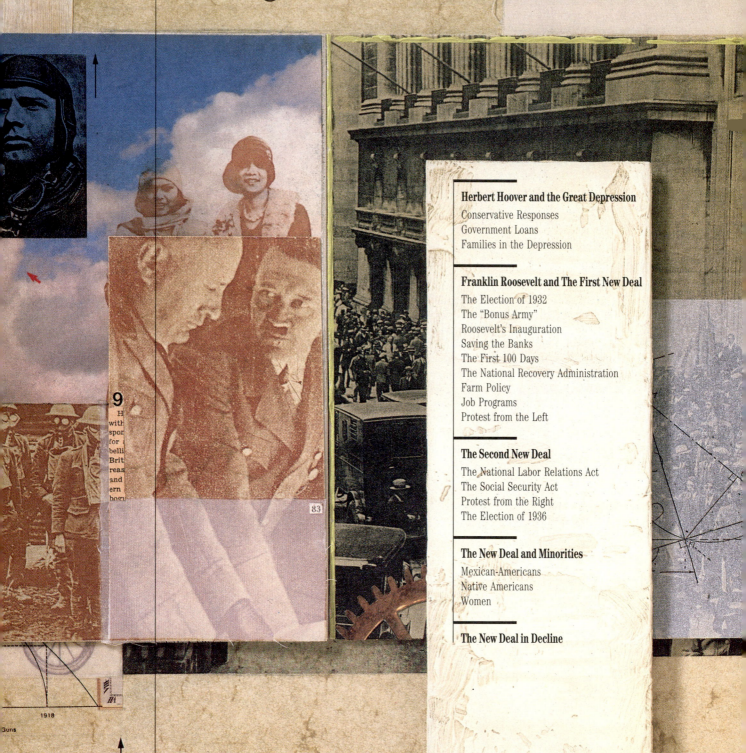

Locust.

52

2

Fig. 113(b)

true form

Fig. 113(bb)

To fans of authentic folk music, Woodrow Wilson "Woody" Guthrie was a "Shakespeare in overalls," the finest American frontier balladeer of the twentieth century. Yet Guthrie himself downplayed his importance, insisting "All you can write is what you see." He must have seen plenty, for according to Alan Lomax, the distinguished musicologist, Guthrie knew America's plain folk better than anyone. His singing voice (droning, nasal, and high-pitched) was definitely an acquired taste, but the words of Guthrie's songs spun pure poetry. In lyrics at once simple and penetrating, he sang of vagabonds who wandered the land in search of work, of union men who saw their comrades on the picket lines knocked to the ground by company goons, and of farmers who watched with horror as their land dried up, blew away, and turned the skies of the Southwest into a dust bowl. In short, he put to music the hardships and struggles of working-class Americans trapped in the Great Depression.

Guthrie drew his material from his life. Born in 1912, Woody (his mother named him after Woodrow Wilson who won the Democratic nomination a week before his birth) grew up in Oklahoma and the Texas Panhandle in a family star-crossed by disasters. When he was still a boy his older sister died from setting herself on fire after an argument with their mother; his father, once a prosperous land speculator, sank into alcoholism as land prices plummeted following the collapse of the oil boom; and his mother slipped slowly into madness and had to be committed to the state mental hospital where she died of Huntington's chorea, the illness that later claimed Woody.

In the face of these tragedies the Guthrie household simply dissolved, leaving Woody pretty much on his own. By nature shy and a bit of a loner, he passed the time by learning to play the guitar and harmonica. Guthrie soon discovered he had a natural talent for music and for making people laugh, and he started playing on street corners for the small change people tossed into his cigar box. Eventually, he dropped out of school and became a drifter, driven by an internal restlessness that kept him on the road for the rest of his life.

Guthrie spent the Great Depression riding the rails, playing his music on a revolving stage of one-night stands and visiting "his" people, the "Okies" and "Arkies" along the boxcars, hobo jungles, and squalid migrant camps from Oklahoma to California. As he crisscrossed the country, he saw families sleeping on the ground and children with distended bellies who cried from hunger while guards hired to protect the orchards prevented them from eating fruit that lay rotting on the ground. Over time a quiet anger began to eat at him and he blamed the nation's "polli-Tish-uns" for not doing more to relieve the people's suffering. In private he even spoke of strapping on six-guns, robbing banks, and giving the money to the poor, like the Robin Hood figure, "Pretty Boy Floyd," in one of his ballads.

By 1940, Guthrie had made his debut in New York City, where he recorded several albums and quickly became a cult figure. By this time his repertoire of Dust Bowl ballads had grown to include a variety of protest ballads, including an endless assortment of union songs. His home-grown radicalism made him an instant hit with Socialist and Communist intellectuals and entertainment figures who saw his music as a powerful weapon in the class struggle. They saw Guthrie as an authentic folk hero, the very embodiment of the proletarian artist.

In truth, Guthrie held more radical political views than most Americans. Nevertheless, he

Woody Guthrie often inscribed the phrase, "This machine surrounds hate and destroys it" on his guitars.

aptly fulfilled his role as the "voice of the people" by putting to music the most important themes to emerge in American life during the 1930s—the common man's defiant pride, his will to survive in the face of adversity, and the extraordinary love Americans felt for their country. In the opening verse of "Dust Can't Kill Me," for example, Guthrie has an anguished mother proclaim:

> That old dust storm killed my baby,
> But it won't kill me, lord.
> No, it won't kill me.

In "God Blessed America" (which later generations of Americans would recognize by its first line, "This land is your land, this land is my land"), Guthrie sang of "endless skyways," "golden valleys," "diamond deserts," and "wheat fields waving," evoking the country's grandeur with a poet's sense of beauty. What gave the song its power, however, was the idea that America belonged to the people: Every verse closed with the refrain, "God blessed America for me."

Thus, even in the depths of the Great Depression, Guthrie found much of enduring value in America. Somehow the nation was surviving without blowing itself apart, and he gave much of the credit to America's plain folks. In ballad after ballad, he celebrated their fortitude, dignity, and strength. Woody Guthrie was right to praise the people. They provided the glue that held things together while President Franklin D. Roosevelt experimented with policies and programs designed to promote relief, recovery, and reform.

HERBERT HOOVER AND THE GREAT DEPRESSION

When the Great Depression struck, most political and economic leaders regarded recessions as inevitable. The prevailing economic theory held that government intervention was both unnecessary and unwise. Periodic dips, economists argued, formed a natural part of the business cycle. Financial panics in 1837, 1857, 1873, 1893, and 1907 had failed to elicit much response from government; and many economists

in 1929 continued to extol the virtues of inaction. Left to itself, they counseled, the economy would recover. President Hoover disagreed. Though Hoover saw the Great Crash as a temporary slump in a fundamentally healthy economy, he believed the president should try to facilitate economic recovery.

Conservative Responses

First, Hoover resorted to old-fashioned "jawboning." Shortly after the stock market crashed, he summoned business and labor leaders to the White House for a series of meetings. In response to the president's pleas to sustain prices, wages, and employment, industrial leaders promised to maintain prices and wages, and labor spokesmen pledged not to strike or demand higher wages. While Hoover remained hopeful voluntary measures would suffice, businesspeople could not maintain employment.

Next, the president tried cheerleading. The contrast between Hoover's speeches and conditions in the country was jarring. In the spring of 1930, just before unemployment figures rose sharply, he assured Americans: "The worst effects of the crash upon unemployment will have passed during the next sixty days." According to Hoover, the economy was fundamentally sound, hard times were nearly over, and recovery was just around the corner. After listening to his rosy pronouncements, critics accused Hoover of being insensitive to the unemployed and the dispossessed, and the public gradually came to share this view. Cynics called the shantytown slums on the edges of cities "Hoovervilles." Newspapers became "Hoover blankets" and empty pockets turned inside out, "Hoover flags."

Neither cruel nor insensitive, Hoover was a humane man who felt tormented by poor people's suffering. Yet he could not bring himself to sanction large-scale federal public works programs because he honestly believed recovery depended on the private sector, because he wanted to maintain a balanced budget, and because he feared the "dole" (his derisive term for federal relief programs) would undermine individual character by making the recipient dependent on the state. He did not realize the sheer size and complexity of the nation's economic problems rendered meaningless old shibboleths like "self-reliance" and "rugged individualism."

Government Loans

When jawboning and cheerleading failed to revive the economy, Hoover reluctantly adopted other measures. In 1932 Congress created the Reconstruction Finance Corporation (RFC) and authorized it to loan $2 billion to banks, savings and loan associations, railroads, and life insurance companies. Blaming the depression on tight credit, Hoover believed federal loans would "trickle down" through the money markets to businesses, enabling them to increase production and hire workers. The same principle applied to the Federal Home Loan Bank System (FHLBS), created by Congress in July 1932 to lend up to $500 million to savings and loan associations to revive the construction industry.

Yet by early 1933 Hoover's antidepression agencies had exhausted their resources without making a dent in the Great Depression. The money from the RFC and FHLBS had not trickled down because the real problem was not tight credit but the soft demand for goods, a problem that flowed both from the chronic low wages paid to the bulk of American workers and the massive layoffs following the Great Crash. It was a vicious cycle. Unemployed workers could not buy goods, so businesspeople cut back production and laid off additional workers. Businesspeople did not ask banks for working capital loans because they had no interest in increasing production. Therefore, government-sponsored loans, which Hoover had hoped would revive the economy, simply rotated back and forth between financial institutions and the RFC and FHLBS. In the meantime, thousands of banks across the country went bankrupt, the unemployment rate climbed to 25 percent, and life got worse for millions of people.

Down to the bitter end, Hoover refused to admit people were starving in America, even though his opponents placed the responsibility squarely at the White House door. Here was proof Hoover was a great engineer, sneered one

Bank failures wiped out the life savings of many prudent Americans.

critic, for "in a little more than two years he has drained, ditched, and damned the United States."

Families in the Depression

The Great Depression did not affect people equally. Many rich people, insulated by their wealth, maintained their opulent life-styles, and perhaps as many as 40 percent of Americans made it through these years without experiencing real hardships. Still, the majority of Americans saw the Great Depression as a wolf at the door. "Mass unemployment," as one journalist observed, "is both a statistic and an empty feeling in the stomach." The unemployment figures reveal how many Americans felt these hunger pains: When Franklin D. Roosevelt took office in 1933, one-quarter of the nation's families had no breadwinner. That figure fluctuated during the 1930s, but it did not drop below 14.3 percent until 1941.

For all but the most fortunate, the Great Depression reduced family income. In 1929 the average American family earned $2300; by 1933 the figure had declined to $1500, a 35 percent drop. Most of the loss resulted from unemployment, but it also reflected reduced wages for those who kept their jobs. By 1933 nine out of ten companies had cut wages (some by as much as 50 percent), and more than half of all employers had converted their work force from full- to part-time jobs, averaging roughly 60 percent of the normal work week.

These reductions devastated workers. As late as 1870, half the work force was self-employed (on farms, for the most part), but by 1923 three out of four Americans worked for salaries or wages, leaving them vulnerable to economic changes. The depression forced Americans to develop a new category of poor people. In addition to the traditional poor, who included single parents, the elderly, tenant farmers, and the disabled, officials now spoke of the "new" poor—middle- and working-class people who had lost their jobs and slid into poverty as a result of the depression.

The depression had a powerful impact on families. It forced couples to delay marriage, lowered the divorce rate (many couples could not afford to maintain separate households or pay legal fees to obtain divorces), and drove the birthrate below the replacement level for the first time in American history.

The depression also altered traditional roles within the family. Many unemployed fathers saw their status lowered by the Great Depression. With no wages to punctuate their authority, they lost power as primary decision makers. In fact, large numbers of men who could not fulfill their roles as breadwinners lost self-respect, became immobilized, and stopped looking for work, while others turned to alcohol and became self-destructive or abusive to their families. Still others walked out the door, never to return. A survey in 1940 revealed that more than 1.5 million married women had been deserted by their husbands.

In contrast to men, many women saw their status rise during the depression. Despite the historic opposition to outside employment for wives, married women entered the work force in large numbers. (Black women, in particular, found it easier than black men to find jobs.) Most women worked as domestic servants, clerks, secretaries, salespersons, textile workers, and the like. But regardless of their jobs, the fact they were employed elevated their po-

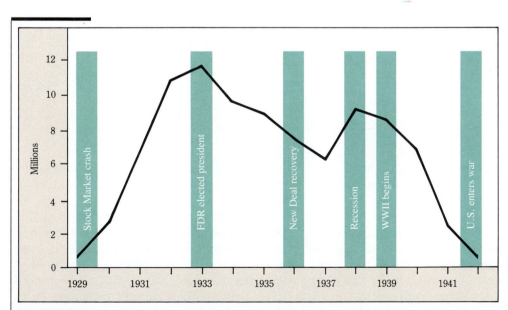

Figure 25.1
Unemployment, 1929–1942

TABLE 25.1

Depression Shopping List: 1932–1934

Automobiles		Household Items		Toys	
Pontiac Coupe	$585.00	Silverplate flatware,		Doll carriage	$ 4.98
Chrysler Sedan	995.00	26 pieces	$ 4.98	Sled	1.45
Dodge	595.00	Double-bed sheets	.67	Tricycle	3.98
Studebaker	840.00	Bath towel	.24	Bicycle	10.95
Packard	2150.00	Wool blanket	1.00	Fielder's glove and ball	1.25
Chevrolet ½-ton pick-up truck	650.00	Wool rug (9′ × 12′)	5.85		
				Food	
Clothing		**Appliances**			
				Sirloin steak/lb	$ .29
Women's		Electric iron	$ 2.00	Rib roast/lb	.22
		Electric coffee percolator	1.39	Bacon/lb	.22
Mink coat	$585.00	Electric mixer	9.95	Ham/lb	.31
Leopard coat	92.00	Vacuum cleaner	18.75	Chicken/lb	.22
Cloth coat	6.98	Electric washing machine	47.95	Pork chops/lb	.20
Wool dress	1.95	Gas stove	23.95	Salmon (16 oz can)	.19
Wool suit	3.98	Electric sewing machine	24.95	Milk (quart)	.10
Wool sweater	1.69			Butter/lb	.28
Silk stockings	.69	**Furniture**		Eggs (dozen)	.29
Leather shoes	1.79			Bread (20 oz loaf)	.05
		Dining room set, 8-piece	$46.50	Coffee/lb	.26
Men's		Lounge chair	19.95	Sugar/lb	.05
		Double bed and mattress	14.95	Rice/lb	.06
Overcoat	$ 11.00	Mahogany coffee table	10.75	Potatoes/lb	.02
Wool suit	10.50	Chippendale sofa	135.00	Tomatoes (16 oz. can)	.09
Trousers	2.00	Louis XV walnut dining table	124.00	Oranges/dozen	.27
Shirt	.47	Wing chair	39.00	Cornflakes (8 oz. box)	.08
Pullover sweater	1.95	Grand piano	395.00		
Silk necktie	.55			**Air Travel**	
Stetson hat	5.00				
Shoes	3.85			New York to Chicago,	
				round trip	$86.31
				Chicago to Los Angeles,	
				round trip	207.00

sition within the family. Bringing home paychecks gave women economic power and this, in turn, strengthened their voices in family decisions.

The depression hit older Americans especially hard. The number of senior citizens had increased sharply since the Civil War. In 1860, for example, only 1 American in 40 was 65 or older; by 1940, the figure had risen to 1 in 15. For most senior citizens, a longer life span meant financial dependency. According to a government survey in 1937, less than 35 per-

cent of elderly Americans enjoyed financial security; nearly half had to rely upon relatives for support.

Despite the hardships it inflicted, the Great Depression drew some families closer together. As one observer noted, "Many a family has lost its automobile and found its soul." Families had to devise strategies for getting through hard times because their survival depended on it. Their stories, as Woody Guthrie knew instinctively, shed as much light on the Great Depression as anything that happened in Washington.

Consider the case of the Jewell Jones family of Bauxite, Arkansas, a small mining town near the center of the state. Though they never went hungry, the Joneses depended on contributions from each family member. The father brought home $3 a week for one day's work in the mines, while the mother earned $2 a week scrubbing floors in the company hospital. The couple's two sons added a few extra dollars by working as caddies at a nearby golf course, and their three daughters helped tend the family garden, can produce, and slaughter chickens and a calf each year.

The family's meager income supported few luxuries. The father made toys for the children, and the mother sewed most of their clothes, which were carefully mended and handed down from child to child. Shoes were an exception. The Jones children each got a pair of "store-bought" shoes when school began in the fall (plenty large so they would fit all year). When the soles wore out, they continued to wear the tops even though their bare feet touched the ground. Looking back on those hard times 50 years later, Cornelia, one of the daughters, recalled:

> One year there came a terrible snowstorm and Mamma wouldn't let me go to school because my shoes were worn out and my feet would freeze. I cried and cried because I had a perfect attendance that year. So I was just bawling when Winfred [the older brother] took Mamma into the kitchen, talked to her, and then came out smiling. "Don't cry, Sissy," he said. "You can go to school." He carried me the whole way [about three miles round trip] on his back. You see, he was a football star in high school, and the company had bought him football shoes. So he could walk on the snow.

Like many other American families, the Joneses made it through the depression by pulling together.

In a sense, the Joneses were lucky because they managed to hold their own. Others, like Benjamin Isaac's family of Chicago, Illinois, lost ground. Prior to the depression, Ben had earned a comfortable living selling clothing door-to-door on credit, collecting by the week. Most of his customers, he recalled, were middle-class folks who bought freely and paid their bills promptly. After the depression struck, however, Ben watched his weekly collections drop from $400 to $15. Suddenly, he could not pay the rent and had to move his wife and three children out of their spacious apartment into a $15 a month flat. "I'm telling you," he lamented, "today a dog wouldn't live in that place. Such a dirty, filthy, dark place."

Shortly after they moved in, their landlord abandoned the building and the city turned off the water. For the next two months, his wife had to carry water from another building to cook, wash, bathe, and flush the toilet. Their diet suffered, too. Though they managed to buy a good cut of meat on occasional Sundays, their meat ration for the rest of the week was half a pound of baloney.

Ben's most painful memory was going on relief. Over time they lost all their family resources, including their car, which had to be sold to buy food. Unemployed and destitute, Ben finally asked for help:

> I didn't want to go on relief. Believe me, when I was forced to go to the office . . . the tears were running out of my eyes. I couldn't bear myself to take money from anybody for nothing. If it wasn't for those kids I tell you the truth—many a time it came to my mind to go commit suicide [rather] than go ask for relief. But somebody had to take care of those kids.

Ben did not find a steady job for the remainder of the depression. After their public assistance ran out, he turned to selling razor blades and shoe laces door-to-door. Some days his total earnings did not exceed 50 cents. Yet somehow the Isaac family held together and survived.

Like the Joneses and the Isaacs, other families pooled their incomes, moved in with relatives in order to cut expenses, bought day-old bread, ate in souplines, and did without. Many families drew comfort from their religion, sustained by the hope things would turn out well in the end, while others placed their faith in themselves, in their own dogged determination to survive that so impressed observers like Woody Guthrie. But many Americans no longer believed the problems could be solved by people acting alone or through voluntary associations. Increasingly, they looked to the federal government for help.

FRANKLIN ROOSEVELT AND THE FIRST NEW DEAL

The Election of 1932

Franklin D. Roosevelt won the Democratic nomination in June 1932. At first glance he did not look like a man who could relate to other peoples' suffering, for Roosevelt had spent his entire life in the lap of luxury. A fifth cousin of Teddy Roosevelt, he was born in 1882 to a wealthy family in Dutchess County, New York. Roosevelt enjoyed a privileged youth. He attended Groton, an exclusive private school, Harvard (where his professors did not regard him as a serious student), and Columbia Law School. Blessed with a famous political family name, Roosevelt entered public service in 1910 as a state senator in New York. President Wilson appointed him as assistant secretary of the navy in 1913, and his status as the rising star of the Democratic party was confirmed when James Cox chose Roosevelt as his running mate in the presidential election of 1920.

Roosevelt was charming and charismatic, and many people felt he was genuinely interested in their concerns. Here Roosevelt meets with a miner during his 1932 campaign.

Handsome and outgoing, Roosevelt seemed to have a bright political future. Then disaster struck. In 1921 he was stricken with polio. The disease left him paralyzed from the waist down and confined to a wheelchair for the rest of his life. Instead of retiring, however, Roosevelt threw himself into a rehabilitation program and labored diligently to return to public life. "If you had spent two years in bed trying to wiggle your toe," he later declared, "after that anything would seem easy."

Buoyed by an exuberant optimism and devoted political allies, Roosevelt won the governorship of New York in 1928, one of the few Democrats to survive the Republican landslide. As governor, he surrounded himself with able advisors, including several college professors and social workers who had spent their lives fighting urban poverty. Together they converted New York into a laboratory for testing political reforms, involving conservation, old age pensions, public works projects, and unemployment insurance—reforms that presaged how Roosevelt would later attack the depression as president.

In his acceptance speech before the Democratic convention in Chicago, Roosevelt promised "a New Deal for the American people." As the band struck up "Happy Days Are Here Again," the delegates cheered wildly. In truth, Roosevelt had not given them much to yell about, for his speech contained few concrete proposals. Many intellectuals remained suspicious. Walter Lippmann described Roosevelt as "a pleasant man who, without any important qualifications for the office, would very much like to be President."

The people saw Roosevelt differently. During the campaign, he calmed their fears, raised their spirits, and gave them hope. A member of Hoover's administration admitted: "The people seem to be lifting eager faces to Franklin Roosevelt, having the impression that he is talking intimately to them." Charismatic and utterly charming, Roosevelt radiated confidence. He even managed to turn his lack of a blueprint into an asset. Instead of offering plans, he advocated the experimental method. "It is common sense to take a method and try it," he declared, "if it fails, admit it frankly and try another."

The Republicans stuck with Hoover. Dejected and embittered, he projected despair and failure. (One observer quipped that "if you put a rose in Hoover's hand, it would wilt.") Advocating the same measures that had failed to bring relief since 1929, Hoover's campaign slogan was "It could have been worse." No doubt this was true, but it did not reassure the public that Hoover had any idea how to make things better. At any rate, when Hoover challenged Roosevelt to a debate, Roosevelt remained silent and watched Hoover end what little chance he had for reelection by his callous treatment of the "Bonus Army."

The "Bonus Army"

The "Bonus Army" was a bedraggled collection of unemployed veterans and their families who marched on Washington in the spring of 1932. Calling themselves the Bonus Expeditionary Force (BEF), a parody of the American Expeditionary Force (AEF), they asked Congress for immediate payment of their war service bonuses, which did not come due until 1945. More than 15,000 strong, they erected a shantytown, camped out in vacant lots, and occupied empty government buildings. Though the House gave them what they wanted, the Senate killed the bill after Hoover lobbied against it, prompting one angry veteran to shout in disgust, "We were heroes in 1917, but we're bums today."

Most of the veterans then left Washington, D.C., but a few thousand stayed behind because they had no place to go. At Hoover's request, Congress appropriated $100,000 to help pay their expenses home. Late in July, however, the District of Columbia police tried to evict some bonus marchers from government buildings and a riot broke out in which two policemen and two marchers died.

Secretary of War Patrick Hurley urged Hoover to declare martial law, but he refused. Hoover did not want to harm the veterans. Instead, he told Hurley to order General Douglas MacArthur to use federal troops to remove them from the government buildings. MacArthur exceeded these orders badly. Using tanks, tear gas, rifle fire, sabers, and torches, he attacked and drove the veterans from the city.

Bonus army recruits poured into Washington, D.C., from every part of the country during the spring and summer of 1932.

Newsmen captured the melee in vivid photographs papers carried the next day.

Hoover was appalled by what happened. Privately, he blamed both Hurley and MacArthur; publicly, he accepted the responsibility but endorsed MacArthur's charge that the bonus marchers included dangerous radicals who wanted to overthrow the government. Yet most Americans felt outraged by the government's harsh treatment of the Bonus Army, and Hoover encountered bitter resentment everywhere he campaigned. In Detroit crowds of unemployed auto workers chanted, "Down with Hoover, Slayer of Veterans." Upon learning of the Bonus Army incident, Franklin D. Roosevelt remarked: "Well, this will elect me."

Roosevelt buried Hoover in November. He won 22,809,638 votes to Hoover's 15,758,901, and 472 to 59 electoral votes. In addition, the Democrats swept Congress: 311 to 119 seats in the House (including 131 freshmen Democrats from Republican districts) and 60 to 35 in the Senate.

Roosevelt appealed to a wide range of voters. A Protestant, he returned the South to the Democratic fold. In addition, he attract-

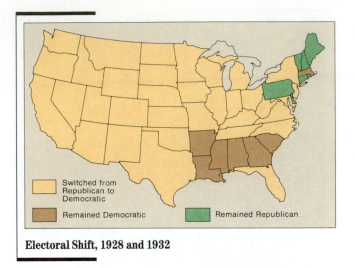

Electoral Shift, 1928 and 1932

Switched from Republican to Democratic

Remained Democratic

Remained Republican

ed new groups of voters, including young people, women, and ethnic Americans. Moreover, Roosevelt carried every state but seven in the Northeast (Pennsylvania was the only large state he lost). Here careful analysis reveals that Roosevelt's support was strongly non-Protestant. Urban Catholics, Jews, and members of the Eastern Orthodox Church voted overwhelmingly for Roosevelt, the first of many elections to come in which the Democratic party's fortunes would be strongly affected by these groups.

While many Republicans apparently boycotted the election, the vast majority of Americans stayed within the two-party system, despite their disdain for Hoover. The Socialist nominee received only 880,000 votes; the Communist party's candidate, only 100,000.

Roosevelt's Inauguration

The New Deal was a jumble of hastily improvised legislation and executive orders, which in the words of one historian somehow added up to "more than the sum of its parts." Most of the legislation was economic and came in three spurts: the first in 1933, the second in 1935, and the last in 1938. From beginning to end, the New Deal represented an intensely personal enterprise unified only by Roosevelt's personality. The ideas behind particular measures came from his advisors, for Roosevelt never pretended to be an original thinker. In place of a

well-defined political philosophy, he pursued a vague commitment to moderate reform, leavened with keen political instincts and a desire to help people.

Roosevelt's greatest asset was his ability to persuade, and no president has ever encountered a Congress so eager to follow. As one representative confessed, "I had as soon start a mutiny in the face of a foreign foe as . . . [go] against the program of the President." Even Senator Arthur H. Vandenberg, a leading Republican conservative, insisted the situation called for a "dictator." No one knew what Roosevelt should do, but the country preferred anything to inaction. On inauguration day Will Rogers exclaimed: "If he burned down the Capitol we would cheer and say, 'Well, at least he got a fire started anyhow.'"

In his inaugural address on March 4, 1933, Roosevelt told the public, "the only thing we have to fear is fear itself." Promising decisive action, he called Congress into special session and demanded "broad executive power to wage a war against the emergency, as great as the power that would be given me if we were in fact invaded by a foreign foe." His ringing speech summoned the nation to battle, and across the nation people held their breaths waiting to see what the new president would do.

Saving the Banks

Roosevelt attacked the banking crisis first. In the months before he took office, America's banking system had all but disintegrated. Hundreds of banks had collapsed, wiping out the life savings of nearly 10 million people. Thirty-eight states had closed their banks, while banks in the remaining states operated on reduced schedules. On March 5 Roosevelt declared a national bank holiday, stopping all banking transactions. A few days later he sent Congress the Emergency Banking Relief Bill, a conservative set of reforms drafted with the assistance of Hoover's advisors. Immediately approved by Congress, the new law permitted solvent banks to reopen under government supervision. More important, it allowed the RFC to buy the stock of troubled banks and keep them open until they could be reorganized. Fi-

(Text continues on p. 839)

PRIMARY SOURCE ESSAY
THE FIRST "FIRESIDE CHAT"

On the eve of Franklin D. Roosevelt's inauguration America's banking system was in shambles. In the first three years following the Great Crash some 5500 banks had closed, and only a handful of those that remained open were solvent. With less than $6 billion in cash against $41 billion in deposits, banks were vulnerable to a wholesale run. If depositors demanded their money, banks would be forced to sell their assets (securities and mortgages) at a fraction of their former value to raise funds.

In the weeks before Roosevelt took office, the run began. Warned that Detroit's Union Guardian Trust Company was about to collapse and drag other banks down with it, Governor William A. Comstock declared a banking moratorium throughout Michigan on February 14, 1933. As news of Michigan's horrors spread, long lines of depositors demanding their money appeared in banks across the land. Banks in Indiana, Ohio, and Kentucky tried to weather the storm by limiting withdrawals to five percent of balances, but many states followed Michigan's lead. By March 1, 17 states had declared so-called "banking holidays." During the next two days every bank in Kansas and Minnesota closed its doors, and the closings quickly spread into North Carolina and Virginia. On the eve of Roosevelt's inauguration, rumors spread that the largest banks in New York City and Chicago were teetering. With its two most important financial strongholds in jeopardy, the nation's financial system was truly on the brink of disaster.

Within days after taking office, Roosevelt moved to restore the public's confidence in banks. The first bill he sent to Congress addressed the nation's banking crisis, and on March 12, 1933, Roosevelt held his first "Fireside Chat" to explain his actions directly to the American people. He spoke not as some remote politician on high but as a straightforward man who understood the public's concerns and could relate to their fears. Above all, he spoke with simple language and profound confidence. When the banks reopened the following morning, the long lines disappeared, as people demonstrated their confidence by returning far more money to their accounts than they withdrew. In the Federal Reserve districts alone, deposits outstripped withdrawals by more than $10 million dollars in a single day.

President Franklin Delano Roosevelt, Jr., used the relatively new broadcast medium of radio to deliver a message of reassurance to the American public.

The following are excerpts from the president's speech. Notice his word choice, his gift for simplifying complicated issues, and his ability to banish "the phantom of fear" from peoples' hearts:

I want to talk for a few minutes with the people of the United States about banking—with the comparatively few who understand the mechanics of banking but more particularly with the overwhelming majority who use banks for the making of deposits and the drawing of checks. I want to tell you what has been done in the last few days, why it was done, and what the next steps are going to be. . . .

First of all, let me state the simple fact that when you deposit money in a bank the bank does not put the money into a safe deposit vault. It invests your money in many different forms of credit—bonds, commercial paper, mortgages and many other kinds of loans. . . . In other words, the total amount of all

the currency in the country is only a small fraction of the total deposits in all of the banks.

What, then, happened during the last few days of February and the first few days of March? Because of undermined confidence on the part of the public, there was a general rush by a large portion of our population to turn bank deposits into currency or gold—a rush so great that the soundest banks could not get enough currency to meet the demand. . . .

By the afternoon of March 3d scarcely a bank in the country was open to do business. . . .

It was then that I issued the proclamation providing for the nationwide bank holiday and this was the

The threat of bank runs, like that pictured here, in which depositors demanded their funds from banks unable to produce their money, prompted FDR's first fireside chat.

bank puts your money to work to keep the wheels of industry and of agriculture turning around.   A comparatively small part of the money you put into the bank is kept in currency--an amount which in normal times is wholly sufficient to cover the cash needs of the average citizen.   In other words the total amount of all the currency in the country is only a ~~comparatively~~ small ~~proportion~~ fraction of the total deposits in all of the banks.

What, then, happened during the last few days of February and the first few days of March?   Because of undermined confidence on the part of the public, there was a general rush by a large portion of our population to turn bank deposits into currency or gold. --- A rush so great that the soundest banks could not get enough currency to meet the demand.   The reason for this was that on the spur of the moment it was, of course,

This page is a reproduction of the actual radio script FDR used in his fireside chat of March 12, 1933. Note the handwritten changes made to simplify the address even further.

first step in the Government's reconstruction of our financial and economic fabric.

The second step was the legislation promptly and patriotically passed by the Congress confirming my proclamation and broadening my power so that it became possible in view of the requirement of time to extend the holiday and lift the ban of that holiday gradually. . . .

The third stage has been the series of regulations permitting the banks to continue their functions to take care of the distribution of food and household necessities and the payment of payrolls. . . .

A question you will ask is this: why are all the banks not to be reopened at the same time? The answer is simple. Your Government does not intend that the history of the past few years shall be repeated. We do not want and will not have another epidemic of bank failures.

As a result, we start tomorrow, Monday, with the opening of banks in the twelve Federal Reserve bank cities—those banks which on first examination by the treasury have already been found to be all right.

This will be followed on Tuesday by the resumption of all their functions by banks already found to be sound in cities where there are recognized clearing houses. . . .

On Wednesday and succeeding days banks in smaller places all through the country will resume business, subject, of course, to the Government's physical ability to complete its survey. . . .

The success of our whole great national program depends, of course, upon the cooperation of the public—on its intelligent support and use of a reliable system. . . .

It has been wonderful to me to catch the note of confidence from all over the country. . . .

. . . Confidence and courage are the essentials of success in carrying out our plan. You people must have faith; you must not be stampeded by rumors or guesses. Let us unite in banishing fear. We have provided the machinery to restore our financial system; it is up to you to support and make it work.

It is your problem no less than it is mine. Together we cannot fail.

Few political speeches have enjoyed more success than President Roosevelt's first "Fireside Chat." Before he addressed the nation, there were over $7.5 billion in circulation; the figure declined by $1.25 billion during the remainder of March and an additional $2 billion by the end of August. The money returned to banks derived from hoarded funds rather than general circulation, as most deposits came in the larger bills ($50 or over) not generally used in day-to-day transactions.

The flow of money back into banks saved them. Three days after the banking holiday ended, 4507 national banks and 567 state banks reopened for business, an impressive 76 percent of all the member banks of the Federal Reserve System. By the middle of April, 7400 nonmember banks (approximately 72 percent of the total of such banks) had been licensed by state authorities. By the end of 1933, the banks that had reopened had been strengthened with new capital, either from local interests or funds supplied by the Reconstruction Finance Corporation. The U.S. banking system had survived its greatest challenge in history, thanks in no small part to the superb communication skills and resolute action of President Roosevelt.

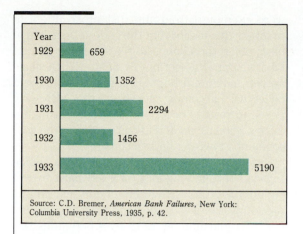

Year		
1929	659	
1930	1352	
1931		2294
1932	1456	
1933		5190

Source: C.D. Bremer, *American Bank Failures*, New York: Columbia University Press, 1935, p. 42.

Figure 25.2
Bank failures, 1929–1933

nally, the law gave the president broad powers over the Federal Reserve System.

To generate support for his programs, Roosevelt appealed directly to the people. On March 12, he conducted the first of many "fireside chats" over a national radio network heard by 60 million Americans. Using the radio the way later presidents exploited television, he explained what he had done in plain, simple terms and told the public to have "confidence and courage." Roosevelt's serene assurance paid handsome dividends. When the banks reopened the following day, people demonstrated their faith by making more deposits than withdrawals. One of Roosevelt's key advisors did not exaggerate when he later boasted, "Capitalism was saved in eight days."

Three months later Congress passed the Glass-Steagall Banking Act of 1933. The law gave the federal reserve banks greater power to curb the lending practices of member banks. To protect depositors from risky projects, the law separated investment banking from commercial banking. It also established the Federal Deposit Insurance Corporation (FDIC), which addressed a chronic problem in America's banking system. During the 1920s and early 1930s, panic-stricken depositors made numerous "runs" on banks, forcing bankers to liquidate assets or default. By guaranteeing all deposits up to $2500 (raised to $5000 in 1934, to $10,000 in 1950, to $15,000 in 1966, to $20,000 in 1969, and

most recently to $100,000), the FDIC hoped to restore the public's confidence in banks.

The First 100 Days

Banking reform was just the beginning. During the first "100 Days" of Roosevelt's term, Congress rammed through 15 major bills, more legislation than any preceding session had passed in history. Most of the early bills were conservative and deflationary. During his first days in office, Roosevelt opposed deficit spending to finance government programs. Cutting federal spending, placing a consumer tax on beer, and helping large bankers at the expense of small bankers—these were measures that Hoover could have supported. In fact, no less than his predecessor, Roosevelt hoped to maintain a balanced budget.

The later bills of the 100 Days marked a change in direction. Distancing himself from Hoover's tight-money policies, Roosevelt provided relief to debtors and exporters by devaluing the dollar, abandoning the gold standard, and ordering the Federal Reserve System to ease credit. This shift reflected the declining clout within his administration of conservatives like Lewis Douglas, the budget director, and the growing influence of advisors who came to be known as the "brain trust."

TABLE 25.2

Legislation Enacted During the Hundred Days, March 9–June 16, 1933

March 9	Emergency Banking Relief Act
March 20	Economy Act
March 22	Beer-Wine Revenue Act
March 31	Unemployment Relief Act
March 31	Civilian Conservation Corps Act
May 12	Agricultural Adjustment Act
May 12	Federal Emergency Relief Act
May 18	Tennessee Valley Authority Act
May 27	Securities Act of 1933
June 5	Gold Repeal Joint Resolution
June 13	Home Owners' Refinancing Act
June 16	Farm Credit Act
June 16	Banking Act of 1933
June 16	Emergency Railroad Transportation Act
June 16	National Industrial Recovery Act

Drawing upon the talents of a bright young group of economists and college professors whose members included Rexford G. Tugwell (generally regarded as the architect of the first New Deal), Raymond Moley, and Adolph A. Berle, Jr., the brain trust supplied Roosevelt with economic ideas and oratorical ammunition. Harking back to the position of Theodore Roosevelt, they saw "bigness" as the natural product of a mature industrial economy. Instead of busting trusts, they believed government should accept consolidation, impose national economic planning on private corporations, and enforce regulations designed to promote open and fair competition. Under their tutelage, Roosevelt launched two major reforms, one directed at industry, the other at agriculture.

The National Recovery Administration

Roosevelt called the National Recovery Administration (NRA), established by the National Industrial Recovery Act (NIRA), "the most important and far-reaching legislation ever passed by the American Congress." The NRA distilled three decades of federal efforts to define a working relationship between government and industry. Philosophically, the NRA had much in common with Teddy Roosevelt's "New Nationalism"; it rejected Woodrow Wilson's "New Freedom" because the New Dealers thought Wilson had attempted to regulate industry too closely; it copied its labor policies from Bernard Baruch's experiences with the War Industries Board of World War I; and it embraced Hoover's trade association movement, although he opposed the NRA because it replaced voluntary cooperation with government coercion.

The NRA proposed to resolve the major causes of economic instability (ruinous competition, overproduction, labor-management confrontations, and price fluctuations) through economic planning. Under the NRA, boards of industrial leaders, labor representatives, and government officials would draft codes of competition to limit production, assign quotas among individual producers, and impose strict price guidelines. Participation in the NRA was purely voluntary, but businesses that joined were exempted from antitrust prosecution. In practice, this meant that the codes offered businesspeople the chance to fix prices. To attract labor's support, Section 7A of the NIRA guaranteed maximum hours, minimum wages, and collective bargaining. In short, the NRA proposed to restore economic health by letting industry regulate itself and by conferring the government's blessing on labor unions.

General Hugh Johnson, Roosevelt's choice to head the new agency, worked hard to win support for the NRA, and under his tireless prodding, the new agency got off to a promising start. By midsummer 1933, over 500 industries had signed codes covering 22 million workers. By the end of the summer the nation's ten largest industries had been won over, as well as hundreds of smaller businesses ranging from dog food producers to burlesque houses. All across the land businesses displayed the "Blue Eagle," the insignia of the NRA, in their windows, and General Johnson remained confident the public would boycott businesses that refused.

The NRA's success was short-lived. Johnson proved to be an overzealous leader who alienated many businesspeople by attacking NRA critics as "chiselers." Instead of creating a smooth-running corporate state, Johnson presided over a chorus of endless squabbling. Since representatives of big business dominated the boards, the boards drafted codes that favored their interests over those of small competitors. Aware the NRA lacked the staff to monitor compliance with the codes, many small businesses simply ignored them. Moreover, even though they controlled the new agency from the outset, many leaders of "big business" opposed the NRA. At bottom, the NRA allowed government to tell businesspeople what to do and they resented it.

For labor the NRA was a mixed blessing. On the positive side, the codes abolished child labor and established the precedent of federal regulation of minimum wages and maximum hours. In addition, the NIRA boosted the labor movement by drawing large numbers of unskilled workers into unions. For example, John L. Lewis of the United Mine Workers (UMW), which merged with the garment trade unions in 1938

John L. Lewis, one of the nation's most influential labor leaders, expanded the membership of the United Mine Workers Union (UMW) under the National Industrial Recovery Act.

to form the Congress of Industrial Organizations (CIO), pointed to Section 7A as proof of Roosevelt's support for organized labor. During the NRA's first year, Lewis expanded the UMW's membership from 150,000 to 500,000. On the negative side, however, the NRA codes set wages in most industries well below what labor demanded, and large occupational groups, such as farm workers, fell outside the codes' coverage. In the end, the "National Run Around" pleased no one.

The NIRA also tried to promote industrial recovery through "pump-priming," a favorite scheme of the "brain trusters." They advocated large public works construction projects to stimulate the economy. Title II of the NIRA appropriated $3.3 billion for public projects, but the administration moved too slowly. A cautious administrator who insisted upon meticulous planning, Harold Ickes, secretary of the interior and director of the Public Works Administration (PWA), was obsessed with eliminating waste and political influence from the public projects. While the PWA eventually pumped $3 billion into the economy, Ickes's prudence prevented the funds from being spent fast enough to have any measurable impact.

Backing Ickes fully, Roosevelt allowed public construction to lag because he wanted to return unspent PWA funds to the federal budget. As late as 1936 federal spending on new construction reached only 60 percent of its predepression level. Other New Deal agencies followed the same pattern as the PWA. While the New Deal was remarkably scandal free, the government often worked at cross purposes with itself, permitting concern for potential corruption to hamper prompt and decisive action.

Farm Policy

The Great Depression all but destroyed America's farmers. Between 1929 and 1933 farmers saw their income fall 60 percent, leaving them with crops they could not sell and mortgages they could not pay. To make matters worse, their current woes followed a decade of hard times in the 1920s. Small wonder farmers looked back wistfully to the brief period of prosperity they had enjoyed on the eve of World War I and tried to regain it through their repeated calls for "parity," a pricing policy that would have allowed farm prices to occupy the same position relative to industrial prices that had existed in 1914.

The New Deal attacked farm problems through a variety of programs. As late as 1935 more than 6 million of America's 6.8 million farms had no electricity. Unlike their sisters in the city, farm women had no washing machines, refrigerators, or vacuum cleaners. As one historian has noted, farm wives "performed their backbreaking chores like peasant women in a preindustrial age." Nor did private utility companies intend to change things. Estimating it would cost as much as $5000 per mile to build power lines to individual farms, private companies insisted electrical service could never be brought to rural areas.

Roosevelt disagreed. Aware that hydroelectric power generated most of America's electricity, he agreed with the critic who asked, "Who and what should own a river, if not the people as a whole?" Roosevelt wanted to break the private monopoly of electric power in rural areas, and he envisioned a future in which electric power would serve broader goals, including flood control, soil conservation, reforestation, diversification of industry, and a general improvement in the quality of life for rural Americans. Settling on the 40,000 square-mile valley of the Tennessee River as his test site, Roosevelt decided to put the government into the electric business.

Two months after he took office, Congress passed a bill creating the Tennessee Valley Authority (TVA). The bill authorized the TVA to build 21 dams to generate electricity for tens of thousands of farm families. In 1935 Roosevelt signed an executive order creating the Rural Electrification Administration (REA) to bring electricity generated by government dams to America's hinterland. As the poles with their silvery lines paralleled county roads, as lines stretched from poles to homes, and as homes got wired, the sense of anticipation became almost unbearable while people waited for the electricity to be turned on. In the Texas hill country, for example, a family returned home after dark one evening and the mother exclaimed, "Oh my God, the house is on fire." "No Mamma," her daughter replied. "The lights are on." Between 1935 and 1942 the lights came on for 35 percent of America's farm families.

Nor was electricity the only benefit the New Deal bestowed on farmers. The Soil Conservation Service helped farmers battle erosion; the Farm Credit Administration provided some relief from farm foreclosures; and the Commodity Credit Corporation permitted farmers to use stored products as collateral for loans. Roosevelt's most ambitious farm program, however, was the Agriculture Adjustment Act (AAA).

Like the NRA, the AAA sought a partnership between the government and major producers. Together the new allies would raise prices by reducing the supply of farm goods. Secretary of Agriculture Henry Wallace borrowed the idea from farmers in the Midwest who had experimented with "farm holidays," hoping to boost prices by holding goods off the market. Under the AAA, the large producers, acting through farm cooperatives, would agree upon a "domestic allotment" plan that would set total output by assigning acreage quotas to each producer. Participation would be voluntary. Farmers who thought they could make it without government subsidies could go their own way, but those who cut production to comply with the quotas would be paid for land left fallow. These payments, in turn, would be financed by a tax on middlemen and processors, making the AAA largely self-supporting.

Unfortunately for its backers, the AAA got off to a horrible start. Because the 1933 crops had already been planted by the time Congress established the AAA, the administration ordered farmers to plow their crops under. Farmers collected over $100 million for mowing down

10 million acres of cotton. To forestall a glut in the hog market, the government purchased and slaughtered 6 million shoats and 200,000 pregnant sows, burying over 9 million pounds of pork. True, the government salvaged one million pounds for the needy, but the public neither understood nor forgave the waste. While future reductions came from planning rather than destruction, the AAA's image never recovered. The AAA remained a public relation's disaster, as most Americans never forgave the agency for destroying food while jobless people went hungry.

Overall, the AAA's record was mixed. Farm income doubled between 1933 and 1936, but large farmers reaped most of the profits. The AAA did little to help sharecroppers and tenant farmers, the groups hardest hit by the agricultural crisis. The South had more than 700,000 sharecroppers and tenant farmers who rented land in return for money or a share of the harvest. After they signed acreage reduction contracts, landlords threw more than 50,000 tenant families off the land. Between 1932 and 1935, 3 million Americans abandoned farming and moved to the city.

Nor did the AAA succeed in solving overproduction. Thanks to technological breakthroughs, such as the widespread use of chemical fertilizers and the increased mechanization of farm tasks, dramatic increases in crop yields per acre more than offset reductions produced by allotment plans. The pattern of subsidy and surplus so familiar to post-World War II America was already in place by the late 1930s.

Job Programs

Even the most optimistic New Dealers knew the NRA and the AAA would not end the depression overnight. To provide short-term assistance for the unemployed, Roosevelt reluctantly turned to welfare programs. In March 1933 Congress created the Civilian Conservation Corps (CCC) to offer young people jobs in national parks. By midsummer, the government had hired 300,000 young men between the ages of 18 and 25 who went to work planting saplings, building fire towers, stocking depleted streams, and restoring historic battlefields. All told, the CCC built 2650 camps and by 1942, 2.5 million men had served in Roosevelt's "Tree Army."

No New Deal program enjoyed greater popularity. The CCC offered young men fresh air, exercise, healthy food, and educational programs. In addition to room and board, they received a modest wage, most of which went home to their families or got set aside in savings accounts to help finance college. Though clearly a public relations triumph, the CCC's economic impact was small. It excluded women, imposed rigid quotas on blacks, and offered employment to only a small number of the young people who needed work.

The Civil Works Administration (CWA), established in November 1933, sponsored truly ambitious relief programs. At its helm stood Harry Hopkins, the unorthodox social worker who had headed Roosevelt's relief program in New York State. Hopkins did not fit the traditional "Jane Addams" image of the social worker. He was divorced, played the horses, and cursed fluently, but even his critics admitted Hopkins knew how to get things done. When he arrived for work and found his office under construction, he set up a desk in the hallway and spent $5 million dollars in two hours channeling relief funds through state and local agencies. Within a month, the CWA put 2.6 million men to work, and within two months it employed 4 million men building 250,000 miles of road, 40,000 schools, 150,000 privies, and 3700 playgrounds.

In March 1934, however, Roosevelt scrapped the CWA because he (like Hoover) did not wish to create a permanent dependent class. In a rare display of poor judgment, Roosevelt blithely observed: "No one is going to starve during warm weather." Official statistics later revealed that 110 Americans starved to death in 1934.

Roosevelt badly underestimated the crisis. As government funding slowed down and economic indicators leveled off, the depression deepened in 1934, triggering a series of violent strikes. Communists agitated among farm workers from coast to coast; a general strike closed down San Francisco for four days; and a British correspondent reported that Toledo was "in the

For $30 a month, workers in the Civilian Conservation Corps (CCC) planted trees and dug drainage ditches. Such federal work relief programs helped many retain their self-respect.

grip of civil war." On Labor Day, 1934, garment workers launched the single largest strike in the nation's history. All across the land, critics attacked Roosevelt for not doing enough to combat the depression, charges that did not go unheeded in the White House.

The congressional elections of 1934 put more pressure on the president. The Democrats won 13 new House seats and 9 new Senate seats, a clear mandate for bolder action. After the elections, the Republicans controlled less than one-third of the seats in Congress and a paltry 7 governorships. Many newly elected Democrats had campaigned as reformers, prompting an elated Harry Hopkins to exclaim: "Boys—this is our hour. We've got to get everything we want—a works program, social security, wages and hours, everything—now or never."

Following the elections, Roosevelt abandoned his hopes for a balanced budget. He had lost faith in government planning and the proposed alliance with business, which left only one other road to recovery—government spending. Privately, he called the dole "a narcotic, a subtle destroyer of the human spirit." Yet no other choice seemed possible. Encouraged by the CCC's success, he decided to create more federal jobs for the unemployed.

In January 1935 Congress created the Works Progress Administration (WPA), Roosevelt's program to employ 3.5 million workers at a "security wage"—twice the level of welfare payments but well below union scales. To head the new agency, Roosevelt again turned to Harry Hopkins. Since the WPA's purpose was to employ men quickly, Hopkins opted for labor-intensive tasks, creating jobs that were often makeshift and inefficient. Jeering critics said the WPA stood for "We Piddle Along," but the agency built many worthwhile projects. In its first five years alone, the WPA constructed or improved 2500 hospitals, 5900 schools, 1000 airport fields, and nearly 13,000 playgrounds. By 1941 it had provided jobs to 40 percent of the nation's unemployed, pumping $11 billion into the economy.

The WPA sponsored several cultural programs. With the economy in shambles, America seemed all the more precious, and the public wanted to preserve it. While folksingers like Woody Guthrie honored the nation in ballads, other artists were hired to catalog it, photograph it, paint it, record it, and write about it. In photojournalism, for example, the Farm Security Agency (FSA) employed scores of talented photographers, including Dorothea Lange, Walker Evans, and Ben Shahn, to create a pictorial record of the land and its people. They produced a raft of "I've seen America" books, and among the 27,000 photographs they shot, only a handful showed people who appeared broken in health or in spirit. Most of the faces belonged to survivors, people in whom determination had triumphed over despair.

In fact, the celebration of "the people" became the New Deal's dominant cultural motif. Under the auspices of the WPA, the Federal Writers Project sponsored an impressive set of state guides and dispatched an army of folklorists into the backcountry in search of tall tales and other "American Stuff." Oral historians collected slave narratives, and musicologists compiled an amazing collection of folk music. (Woody Guthrie was the subject of an extensive interview and three-album recording session.)

Other WPA programs included the Theatre Project, which produced the "living newspaper," a running commentary on everyday affairs, and the Art Project, which decorated the nation's libraries and post offices with murals of muscular workmen, bountiful wheatfields, and massive machinery. Since their subject matter had to be approved by local authorities, these murals reveal how communities saw themselves and how they wished to be seen by others. This was especially true in the South, where local leaders, sensitive to the image of their region as a benighted land, forced artists to paint murals that presented sympathetic portraits of southern life, promoting what one historian has called "a gentle reconstruction."

Valuable in their own right, the WPA's cultural programs had the added benefit of providing work for thousands of writers, artists, actors, and other creative people. In addition, these programs established the precedent of federal support to the arts and the humanities, laying the groundwork for future federal programs to promote the life of the mind in America.

Protest from the Left

The WPA marked the zenith of Roosevelt's influence over Congress. Following its passage, Congress dallied for several months over the remainder of his program. Opposition came from both the right and the left. Conservatives attacked the NRA and New Deal labor policy, while liberals accused Roosevelt of not doing enough to help poor people. Not one but three figures stepped forward to challenge Roosevelt: Huey Long, a Louisiana senator; Father Charles Coughlin, a Catholic priest from Detroit; and Francis Townsend, a retired California physician.

Of the three, Huey Long attracted the widest following. For those who insisted America needed a dictator, Louisiana's self-styled "Kingfish" was the man of the hour. Long took his nickname from one of the characters on the hit radio show, "Amos and Andy." Rotten with ambition, endowed with supernatural energy, and totally devoid of scruples, Long was a fiery, spellbinding orator in the tradition of southern populism. As governor and then senator, he ruled Louisiana with an iron hand. Yet the people of Louisiana loved him because he attacked the big oil companies, increased state spending on public works, and improved public schools. Although he backed Roosevelt in 1932, Long quickly abandoned the president and opposed the New Deal as too conservative.

Early in 1934 Long announced his "Share Our Wealth" program. Vowing to make "Every Man a King," he promised to soak the rich by imposing a stiff tax on inheritances over $5 million and by levying a 100 percent tax on annual incomes over $1 million. The confiscated funds, in turn, would be distributed to the people, guaranteeing every American family an annual income of no less than $2000, in Long's words more than enough to buy "a radio, a car, and a home." By February 1935 Long's followers had organized over 27,000 "Share Our Wealth" clubs. Roosevelt had to take him seriously, for a Democratic poll revealed the "Kingfish" could attract three to four million voters to an independent presidential ticket.

Like Long, Father Charles Coughlin was an early supporter who turned sour on the New Deal. Known as the "radio priest," he spoke to the nation from his Catholic parish in Royal Oak, Michigan, a Detroit suburb. By 1934 Coughlin's weekly mail was larger than the president's and his radio audience was estimated at 30 million. In a rich, warm voice, he blamed the depression on greedy bankers and challenged Roosevelt to solve the crisis by nationalizing banks and inflating the currency. When Roosevelt refused to heed his advice, Coughlin stopped referring to the New Deal as "Christ's Deal" and denounced it as the "Pagan Deal." In 1934 he broke with Roosevelt and formed the National Union for Social Justice.

Roosevelt's least strident opponent was Dr. Francis Townsend, a decent man whose opposition to the New Deal flowed less from personal ambition than from honest disagreements. As a public health officer in Long Beach, California, he found himself unemployed at the age of 67, with only $100 in savings. Townsend saw many people in similar straits in California, el-

The WPA program employed artists like Jackson Pollock, Willem de Kooning, and Ben Shahn to decorate public buildings with murals that celebrated American culture.

derly migrants from the Midwest with no jobs and no resources. What finally drove him to act, however, was the sight of three old women rummaging through garbage cans for scraps of food. Their plight, coupled with his own financial difficulties, made Townsend embrace old age relief as the key to ending the depression.

In January 1934 Townsend announced his plan for "Old Age Revolving Pensions, Limited," demanding a $200 monthly pension for every citizen over the age of 60. In return, recipients had to retire and spend their entire pension every month within the United States. As explained by Townsend, younger adults would inherit the jobs vacated by senior citizens, and the economy would be stimulated by the increased purchasing power of the elderly. Critics lambasted Townsend, arguing it was ludicrous to spend $24 billion out of a national income of only $40 billion to benefit a mere 9 percent of the population. Yet those Americans who found his plan refreshingly simple no doubt agreed with Townsend when he replied, "I'm not in the least interested in the cost of the plan." By 1936 Townsend claimed to have 3.5 million followers.

Roosevelt could not afford to ignore his critics. Acting alone, Long, Coughlin, and Townsend might not have enough support to defeat Roosevelt, but their challenge was real. In a close election, they commanded more than enough votes to tip the scales in favor of a Republican candidate. To remain in office, Roosevelt had to shift policies.

THE SECOND NEW DEAL

Alarmed by his critics, Roosevelt slowly abandoned his dream of building a coalition that would unite all Americans behind the New Deal. Previously, he had seen himself as an honest broker attempting to reconcile the conflicting demands of widely diverse interest groups. Now Roosevelt stopped trying to please everyone and started inching toward the left.

The Supreme Court shoved Roosevelt further in this direction. On May 26, 1935, the Court struck down the NRA in *Schechter* v. *United States*—the famous "sick chicken" case. In *Schechter* the Court held unanimously the federal government did not have the power to regulate the sale of poultry in Brooklyn, delivering a stinging rebuke both to Roosevelt and the Congress for expanding federal authority where it did not belong. Denying the transaction could be deemed interstate commerce, the Court ruled the sale a purely local transaction that Congress could not regulate without violating the separation of powers. Roosevelt was furious. He accused the court of returning the nation "to the horse-and-buggy definition of interstate commerce." In June Roosevelt refused to dismiss Congress for summer vacation, vowing to make its members swelter in the Washington heat until they passed his new legislative agenda. The result was the "Second Hundred Days."

The National Labor Relations Act

The National Labor Relations Act (Wagner Act) came first. Senator Robert F. Wagner of New York, the bill's sponsor, seized the opportunity to replace Section 7A of the NIRA with what he called "labor's Magna Carta." Down to this point Roosevelt had resisted any drastic change in government labor policy, but once the Wagner Act's passage seemed assured he gave it his belated blessing. The bill passed overwhelmingly, delivering the government's most important concession to labor to date. It guaranteed labor's right to organize by creating the National Labor Relations Board (NLRB), which had the power to conduct labor elections, determine bargaining units, and restrain business from "unfair labor practices."

The Wagner Act inspired an unprecedented burst of labor organizing. Philip Murray of the United Mine Workers (UMW) organized the Steel Workers' Organizing Committee; Sidney Hillman established the Textile Workers' Organizing Committee; and late in 1936 Walter Reuther and the United Automobile Workers (UAW) launched their famous "sit-down" strikes in which workers occupied factories but refused to work. The automobile companies responded with violence, but the union prevailed. In February 1937 General Motors recognized the union, and UAW membership increased from 30,000 members to more than 400,000 in less than a year.

Union organizers made inroads in other industries as well. When the Steel Workers' Organizing Committee signed up 350,000 workers by 1937, the United States Steel Corporation capitulated to the union's demands. The new umbrella organization for the UMW, the UAW, the Steel Workers' Organizing Committee, the Textile Workers' Organizing Committee, and the Amalgamated Clothing Workers (and other unions) was the Congress of Industrial Organizations (CIO), formed in 1938 under the leadership of John L. Lewis, who was active in drafting labor legislation and in promoting industrial unionism. The Wagner Act had put the full force of the federal government behind labor's right to bargain collectively.

The Social Security Act

The Social Security bill came next. A goal of reformers since the Progressive Era, the bill was aimed at alleviating the plight of America's visible poor—dependent children, the elderly, and the handicapped. Senator Robert Wagner of New York and Congressman David Lewis of Pennsylvania, both of whom had firsthand knowledge of poverty, sponsored the bill, and Roosevelt signed it on August 15, 1935.

A major political victory for Roosevelt, the Social Security Act was a triumph of social legislation. It stole Francis Townsend's thunder by offering workers 65 or older monthly stipends based on previous earnings (with payments due to start in 1940), and it gave the indigent elderly small relief payments, financed by the federal government and the states. In addition, the act provided assistance to blind Americans and those with other handicaps, and to dependent children who did not have a wage-earning parent. The act also established the nation's first federally sponsored system of unemployment insurance. Mandatory payroll deductions levied equally on employees and employers financed both the retirement system and the unemployment insurance.

Yet the Social Security Act was profoundly disappointing to reformers who demanded "cradle to grave" protection as the birthright of every American. According to its critics, the new system authorized pitifully small payments (initially, they ranged from $10 to $85 a month); its retirement system left huge groups of workers uncovered, as it excluded such occupations as migrant workers, civil servants, domestic servants, merchant seamen, day laborers, and employees of charitable, religious, and educational institutions; its budget came from a regressive tax scheme that placed a disproportionate tax burden on the poor; and, most troubling of all, it failed to provide health insurance. According to conservatives, however, the act placed the United States on the road to socialism by making the government responsible for duties that belonged to individuals or to their families.

Despite criticisms from the left and the right, the Social Security Act introduced a new era in American history. It committed the government to a social welfare role by providing the first federally sponsored "floor" for elderly, disabled, dependent, and unemployed Americans. By so doing, the act greatly expanded the public's sense of entitlement, the support people expected the government to give all citizens. Defending the compromises he made as "politics all the way through," Roosevelt boasted that because the program was financed by both employers and employees through payroll deductions, "no damn politician can ever scrap my social security program." He was right. Over the next few decades, the Social Security system assumed the status of a "sacred cow" in American politics.

The remaining "must legislation" of the Second Hundred Days included utilities regulation, banking reform, and a new tax proposal. Yet none of these measures represented a drastic change in American politics. On the whole, the Second New Deal merely sought to make capitalism more humane. William Allen White, a distinguished American journalist, described these measures as a "belated attempt to bring the American people up to the modern standards of

TABLE 25.3

Later New Deal Legislation	
1934	Farm Mortgage Refinancing Act
	Gold Reserve Act
	Civil-Works Emergency Relief Act
	Home Owners' Loan Act
	Farm Mortgage Foreclosure Act
	Bank Deposit Insurance Act
	Silver Purchase Act
	Securities Exchange Act
	Labor Dispute Joint Resolution
	Railway Pension Act
	Communication Act
1935	Emergency Relief Appropriation Act
	National Labor Relations Act
	Social Security Act
	Public Utility Holding Company Act
	Work Relief Act
1937	National Housing Act
	Bankhead-Jones Farm Tenancy Act
1938	Fair Labor Standards Act

English-speaking countries." Roosevelt never contemplated, much less achieved, a social revolution. He made no attacks on private property; the well-to-do retained their privileges; wealth was not redistributed; the poor remained poor.

The majority of Americans did not want dramatic changes. Despite severe economic hardships, they still supported capitalism. How else can one explain the phenomenal success of Monopoly, the new board game introduced in 1935 by the Parker Brothers? In the true spirit of rapacious capitalism, this new real estate game required players to acquire private property, convert their property into monopolies, and then drive their competitors to the wall through exorbitant rents. An instant hit, Monopoly went on to become the most popular board game in American history.

Protest from the Right

To hear many wealthy conservatives tell it, however, Roosevelt was a wild-eyed radical who threatened the very foundation of capitalism. William Randolph Hearst ordered his newspapers to substitute the words "Raw Deal" for "New Deal." Firmly committed to a balanced budget, conservatives viewed heavy government spending as sacrilege, and they were appalled by the growth of the bureaucracy in Washington, D.C. In 1932 the number of civilian federal employees in the nation's capital stood at 73,445, but by 1936 the number had climbed to 122,937. (By 1940 it had risen to 139,770, nearly double what it had been in 1932.) Conservatives feared government's growth would increase federal power at the expense of states' rights and individual liberties, and they believed Roosevelt would raise rich people's taxes to finance his relief programs for the poor.

Viewing Roosevelt as a traitor to his class, many wealthy Americans saw the election of 1936 as their chance to save the country. Mark Sullivan, a conservative journalist, warned his readers that 1936 might be "the last presidential election America may ever have," and confessed his despair over the public's failure "to see that the New Deal is to America what the early phase of Nazism was to Germany."

The Election of 1936

To carry its banner in 1936, the GOP picked Alfred M. Landon of Kansas, the only Republican governor who survived the 1934 elections. As their campaign song, the Republicans chose Stephen Foster's "Oh! Susanna." Clearly, nostalgia was the primary appeal of the soft-spoken, sincere "Kansas Coolidge." Yet Landon was far more liberal than many of his backers. He had opposed the KKK, backed business regulation, and supported many New Deal programs. A poor public speaker, Landon offered few alternatives to Roosevelt's programs.

To win in 1936 the GOP needed help from a third party. Assistance from this quarter never arrived. Huey Long's organization fell apart following his assassination in 1935, and Roosevelt's swift reconciliation with Louisiana Democrats became known as the "Second Louisiana Pur-

"Mother, Wilfred wrote a bad word!"

Some Americans felt capitalism was threatened under Roosevelt's New Deal. This 1938 *Esquire* cartoon captures the mood of disapproval prevalent among many at the time.

chase." Francis Townsend's campaign, already weakened by passage of the Social Security Act in 1935, collapsed in the spring of 1936 under charges of corruption; and by 1936 Father Coughlin had been reduced to an abusive name-caller who had been publicly rebuked by the Catholic church. By the time the remnants of their followers formed the Union party and nominated William Lemke, the farm radical from North Dakota, as their candidate, Roosevelt's critics on the left no longer posed a threat.

Always a brilliant campaigner, Roosevelt enjoyed the race. Embracing the rhetoric of the left, he lashed out at "economic royalists" who opposed the New Deal. Economic indicators supported the Democrats. In 1936 industrial output more than doubled its 1933 figures, and the national income rose half again as much. When Landon heard the third-quarter economic report he privately conceded defeat.

On election night Roosevelt's inner circle gathered at Hyde Park to hear the news: Approximately 61 percent of the eligible voters had cast ballots—27,752,869 for the president, 16,674,665 for Landon, and 882,479 for Lemke. Roosevelt carried every state but Maine and Vermont. James A. Farley, the president's political manager, joked, "As Maine goes, so goes Vermont," while another New Dealer boasted: "If Roosevelt had given one more speech he would have carried Canada." Democrats won an equally lopsided victory in the congressional races: 331 to 89 in the House and 76 to 16 in the Senate. The election swept so many Democrats into Congress that 12 freshman senators had to sit on the Republican side.

The Democrat's victory rested on a broad base of support. Roosevelt's backers included poor people, organized labor, urban ethnics, the Democratic South, blacks, and many intellectuals. A formidable alliance of diverse groups, Roosevelt's New Deal coalition would shape the contours of American politics for decades to come.

THE NEW DEAL AND MINORITIES

Among Roosevelt's supporters, blacks benefited least from the New Deal. From a purely political standpoint, Roosevelt at first had little reason to reward blacks. In the election of 1932 he received only 21 percent of the black vote; the overwhelming majority of black voters showed their traditional loyalty to the party of Lincoln. By the end of Roosevelt's first administration, however, one of the most dramatic voter shifts in American history had occurred, and in 1936, 75 percent of black voters supported the Democrats.

Blacks turned to Roosevelt in part because his spending programs gave them a measure of relief from the depression and in part because the GOP had done little to repay their earlier support. Still, Roosevelt's record on civil rights must have made many blacks wonder why they bothered to change. Instead of using New Deal programs to promote civil rights, the administration consistently bowed to discrimination. Neither major party placed a high priority on equal rights for blacks; and the vast majority of white Americans did not think race relations required any changes. In that sense Roosevelt reflected his times.

Politics shaped Roosevelt's approach to the race issue. In order to pass major New Deal legislation, he needed the support of southern Democrats. Vigorous promotion of civil rights for blacks, Roosevelt feared, would alienate southern whites. Time and time again, he backed away from equal rights to avoid antagonizing southern whites, although his wife, Eleanor, did take a public stand in support of civil rights.

Most New Deal programs discriminated against blacks. The NRA, for example, not only offered whites the first crack at jobs but authorized separate and lower pay scales for blacks. To disillusioned blacks, the NRA stood for "Negroes Ruined Again." The Federal Housing Authority (FHA) refused to guarantee mortgages for blacks who tried to buy in white neighborhoods, and the CCC maintained segregated camps. Furthermore, the Social Security Act excluded precisely those job categories blacks traditionally filled. One NAACP writer became so disgruntled with Roosevelt's record he dismissed the New Deal as "the same raw deal."

The story in agriculture was particularly grim. Since 40 percent of all black workers made

(Text continues on p. 852)

THE TUSKEGEE SYPHILIS STUDY

The South in the 1930s was the section of the United States that most resembled the underdeveloped nations of the world. Its people (white and black) remained mostly rural; they were less well-educated than other Americans; and they made decidedly less money.

As a group, black Americans in the South were among the poorest of the poor—virtual paupers, chronically unemployed, without benefit of sanitation, adequate diet, or the rudiments of hygiene. They suffered from a host of diseases, including tuberculosis, syphilis, hookworm, pellagra, rickets, and rotting teeth; and their death rate far exceeded that of whites.

Despite their need, few blacks received proper medical care. In fact, many black Americans lived outside the world of modern medicine, going from cradle to grave without ever seeing a doctor. There

was a severe shortage of black physicians, and many white physicians refused to treat black patients. In addition, there were only a handful of black hospitals in the South, and most white hospitals either denied blacks admission or assigned them to segregated wings that were often overcrowded.

But poverty was as much to blame as racism for the medical neglect of black Americans. Medical care in the United States was offered on a fee-for-services basis, and the simple truth was that many blacks were too poor to be able to afford medical care.

To combat these and other problems, the federal government in 1912 united all its health-related activities under the Public Health Service (PHS). Over the next few decades, the PHS distinguished itself by launching attacks on hookworm, pellagra, and a host of other

illnesses. In no field was it more active than in its efforts to fight venereal diseases.

Health reformers knew that syphilis was a killer, and that it was also capable of inflicting blindness, deafness, and insanity on its victims. Furthermore, they saw the disease as a serious threat to the family because they associated it with prostitution and with loose morals in general, which added a moral dimension to their medical concerns.

Taking advantage of the emergency atmosphere of World War I, progressive reformers pushed through Congress in 1918 a bill to create a special Division of Venereal Diseases within the PHS. The PHS officers who launched this new offensive against syphilis began with high motives, and their initial successes were impressive. By 1919, they had established over 200 health clinics, which treated over 64,000 patients who could not otherwise have afforded health care.

In the late 1920s, the PHS joined forces with the Rosenwald Fund (a private philanthropic foundation based in Chicago) to develop a syphilis control program for blacks in the South. Most doctors assumed that blacks suffered a much higher infection rate than whites because blacks abandoned themselves to sexual promiscuity. And once infected, the argument went, blacks remained infected because they were too poor and too ignorant to seek medical care.

To test these theories, PHS officers selected communities in six different southern states, examined the local black populations to ascertain the incidence of syphilis, and offered free treatment to those who were infected. This pilot program had hardly gotten underway, however, when the stock market collapse forced the Rosenwald Fund to terminate its support, and the PHS was left without sufficient funds to follow up its syphilis control work among blacks in the South.

Macon County, Alabama, was the site of one of those original pilot programs. Its county seat, Tuskegee, was the home of the famed Tuskegee Institute. It was in and around Tuskegee that the PHS had discovered an infection rate of 35 percent among those tested, the highest incidence in the six communities studied. In fact, despite the presence of the Tuskegee Institute, which boasted a well-equipped hospital that might have provided low-cost health care to blacks in the region, Macon County was home to the worst poverty and the most sickly residents the PHS uncovered anywhere in the South. It was precisely this ready-made laboratory of human suffering that prompted the PHS to return to Macon County in 1932. Since they could not afford to treat syphilis, the PHS officers decided to document its damage on its victims by launching a scientific study of the effects of untreated syphilis on black males. Many white Southerners (including physicians) believed that although practically all blacks had syphilis, it did not harm them as severely as it did whites. PHS officials knew that syphilis was a serious threat to the health of black Americans, and they intended to use the results of the study to pressure southern state legislatures into appropriating funds for syphilis control work among rural blacks.

Armed with these good motives, the PHS launched the Tuskegee Study in 1932. It involved approximately 400 black males, who tested positive for the disease, and 200 nonsyphilitic black males to serve as controls. In order to secure cooperation, the PHS told the local residents that they had returned to Macon County to treat people who were ill. The PHS did not inform them that they had syphilis. Instead, the men were told that they had "bad blood," a catch-all phrase rural blacks used to describe a host of ailments.

While the PHS had not intended to treat the men, state health officials demanded, as the price of their cooperation, that the men be given at least enough medication to render them noninfectious. Consequently, all of the men received a little treatment. No one worried much about the glaring contradiction of offering treatment in a study of untreated syphilis because the men had not received enough treatment to cure them. Thus, the experiment was scientifically flawed from the outset.

Although the original plan called for a one-year experiment, the Tuskegee Study continued until 1972—partly because many of the health officers became fascinated by the scientific potential of a long-range study of syphilis. No doubt others rationalized the study by telling themselves that the men were too poor to afford proper treatment, or that too much time had passed for treatment to be of any benefit. The health officials, in some cases, may have seen the men as clinical material rather than human beings.

At any rate, the Tuskegee Study killed approximately 100 black men who died as a direct result of syphilis, scores went blind or insane, and still others endured lives of chronic ill health from syphilis-related complications. Throughout their suffering, the PHS made no effort to treat the men, and on several occasions took steps to prevent them from getting treatment on their own. As a result, the men did not receive penicillin when that "wonder drug" became widely available after World War II.

During those same four decades, however, civil protests raised America's concern for the rights of black people, and the ethical standards of the medical profession changed dramatically. These changes had no impact on the Tuskegee Study. PHS officials published no fewer than 13 scientific papers on the experiment (several of which appeared in the nation's leading medical journals), and the PHS routinely presented sessions on it at medical conventions. The Tuskegee Study ended in 1972 because a "whistle-blower" in the PHS named Peter Buxtun leaked the story to the press. At first health officials tried to defend their actions, but public outrage quickly silenced them, and they agreed to end the experiment. As part of an out-of-court settlement, the survivors were finally treated for syphilis. In addition, the men, and the families of the deceased, received small cash payments.

The 40-year deathwatch had finally ended, but its legacy can still be felt today. In the wake of its hearings, Congress enacted new legislation to protect the subjects of human experiments. The Tuskegee Study left behind a host of unanswered questions about the social and racial attitudes of the medical establishment in the United States. It served as a cruel reminder of how class distinctions and racism could negate ethical and scientific standards.

their living as sharecroppers and tenant farmers, the AAA acreage reduction hit blacks hard. White landlords could make more money by leaving land untilled than by putting land into production. As a result, the AAA's policies forced more than 100,000 blacks off the land in 1933 and 1934. Moreover, many black sharecroppers and tenants who remained on the land received no AAA payments because the money had to pass through the hands of white landlords before it reached them. In 1934 white liberals and black leaders organized the Southern Tenant Farmers Union (STFU) to protest the plight of sharecroppers, including blacks, but when the STFU demanded direct AAA payments to tenants, white commercial farmers protested and the administration backed down.

Even more galling to black leaders, the president failed to support an antilynching bill and a bill to abolish the poll tax. When questioned by Walter White, head of the NAACP, about the antilynching bill, Roosevelt pleaded political necessity, telling critics "I just can't take that risk." Conservative southern Democrats had seniority in Congress and controlled many committee chairmanships, he explained, and if he tried to fight them on the race question, they would block his bills.

Yet the New Deal did record a few gains in civil rights. Roosevelt named Mary McLeod Bethune, a black educator, to the advisory committee of the National Youth Administration (NYA), and thanks to her efforts, blacks received a fair share of NYA funds. The WPA was color-blind, and blacks in northern cities benefited from its work relief programs. Harold Ickes, a strong supporter of civil rights, poured federal funds into black schools and hospitals in the South. True, black leaders would have preferred integrated facilities, but most agreed that separate facilities beat no facilities. Ickes's department quickly became the home of the much publicized "Black Cabinet," including Clark Foreman as his personal assistant and Robert C. Weaver and William H. Hastie, two bright young lawyers. Together they lobbied the administration at every turn (if unsuccessfully) to end segregation.

Still, most blacks appointed to New Deal posts served in token positions as advisors on

Mary McLeod Bethune, a member of the advisory committee for the National Youth Administration, meets here with Eleanor Roosevelt.

black affairs in one department or another. At best they achieved a new visibility in government. No longer called in from the outside for consultations and then sent home, they now had permanent positions within the administration.

Mexican-Americans

During the 1930s most Mexican-Americans lived in California or the Southwest. Like blacks, they reaped few benefits from the New Deal. AAA acreage reduction programs affected migrant workers in much the same way as sharecroppers and tenant farmers. Many Mexican-Americans lost their jobs due to acreage reductions or competition in the fields from unemployed whites.

Still, the New Deal offered Mexican-Americans a little help. The Farm Security Administration established camps for migrant farm workers in California, and the CCC and WPA hired unemployed Mexican-Americans on relief jobs. Yet many Mexican-Americans did not qualify for relief assistance because they worked as migrant workers and did not live in the same place long enough to meet residency requirements. Furthermore, agricultural workers were not eligible for benefits under workers' compensation, Social Security, and the National Labor Relations Act.

Mexican-Americans also faced serious opposition from organized labor. As unemployment rose, labor unions resented competition from Mexican workers. Unions demanded deportation, and federal, state, and local authorities surrendered to the pressure. Los Angeles deported Mexicans and Mexican-Americans alike to prevent them from applying for relief. "The Mexicans are trash," declared one California official. "They have no standard of living. We herd them like pigs." All told, the United States deported more than 400,000 people of Mexican descent during the 1930s. Since this group included many citizens of the United States (American-born husbands, wives, and children of Mexican aliens), the deportations constituted a gross violation of civil liberties.

Native Americans

The so-called "Indian New Deal" was the only bright spot in the administration's treatment of minorities. In 1933 Roosevelt appointed John Collier as commissioner of Indian affairs. At Collier's request, Congress created the Indian Emergency Conservation Program (IECP), a CCC-type project for the reservations. By the time World War II broke out, the IECP had employed more than 85,000 Indians, building 1742 dams and reservoirs, 12,230 miles of fence, 91 lookout towers, and 9737 miles of fire trails. In addition, Indian workers conducted pest control projects on 1,315,870 acres of land and removed poisonous weeds from 263,129 acres of reservation farm and grazing land. Collier also made certain that the PWA, WPA, CCC, and NYA hired Native Americans.

Collier had long been an opponent of the 50-year-old government allotment program, in which tribal lands had been broken up and distributed to individual Native Americans and whites. In 1934 Congress passed the Indian Reorganization Act, which terminated the allotment program of the Dawes Severalty Act of 1887; provided funds for tribes to purchase new land; offered government recognition of tribal constitutions; and repealed prohibitions on the use of Native American languages, tribal ceremonies, and traditional dress on reservations. That same year, the Johnson-O'Malley Act provided federal grants to local school districts, hospitals, and social welfare agencies to assist Native Americans.

Women

Women achieved measured progress under the New Deal. Prior to the depression, women had dominated both social work and the voluntary associations that provided charity for the poor and unemployed. Since the same skills were needed to combat the depression, women joined the throngs of professionals who rushed to Washington to work in the New Deal.

Once there, women formed a tightly knit network of professionals who supported each other's careers. Frances Perkins, the secretary of labor and the first woman in American history to hold a cabinet appointment, brought many women into government; and Molly Dewson, the director of the Women's Division of the Democratic Committee, helped place women throughout the administration. By 1939 women held one-third of all positions in the independent agencies and almost one-fifth of the jobs in the executive departments.

Eleanor Roosevelt deserves much of the credit for the progress made by minorities. The first president's wife to stake out an independent public position, she provided the social conscience of the New Deal. Few people knew how much she hated making public appearances. She had to overcome an almost pathological shyness to voice her sympathies and convictions, but overcome it she did. In 1933 alone the First Lady traveled 40,000 miles, visiting families, investigating work conditions, and checking welfare programs. In fact, she seemed to pop up everywhere: a *New Yorker* cartoon of the 1930s showed a startled coal miner at the bottom of a pit exclaiming: "For gosh sakes, here comes Mrs. Roosevelt!"

The First Lady worked tirelessly to persuade her husband and the heads of government agencies to hire well-qualified women and blacks. More courageous than her husband and less restricted politically, she did not hesitate to take a public stand on civil rights. When the Daughters of the American Revolution refused in 1939 to grant the black contralto Marian Anderson permission to sing in Constitution Hall, Mrs. Roosevelt arranged for a concert on the steps of the Lincoln Memorial on Easter Sunday.

Philosophically, the president appeared to move closer to his wife's vision of society after the election of 1936. In his second inaugural address, he promised to press for new social legislation. "I see one-third of a nation ill-housed, ill-clad, ill-nourished," he told the country. Yet instead of pursuing new reforms, Roosevelt allowed his second term to bog down in political squabbles. He wasted his energies on an ill-conceived battle with the Supreme Court and an abortive effort to purge the Democratic party.

THE NEW DEAL IN DECLINE

As Roosevelt's first term drew to a close, the Supreme Court turned on the New Deal. In 1935 the Court ruled the NRA unconstitutional in *Schechter* v. *United States*; and in 1936 it struck down the AAA in *Butler* v. *United States*. Hitting as they did at the heart of the New Deal, these decisions convinced Roosevelt the Supreme Court was at odds with the other two branches of government. The president therefore decided to make his opponents on the Supreme Court resign so he could replace them with justices more sympathetic to his policies. On February 5, 1937, Roosevelt announced a plan to add one new member to the Supreme Court for every judge who had reached the age of 70 without retiring (six justices were over 70). To offer a carrot with the stick, Roosevelt also outlined a generous new pension program for retiring federal judges.

The court-packing scheme was a political disaster. Conservatives and liberals alike de-

nounced Roosevelt for attacking the separation of powers, and critics accused him of trying to become a dictator. Fortunately, the Court itself ended the crisis by shifting ground—"the switch in time that saved nine," as one wit quipped. In two separate cases, each decided by five-to-four votes, the Court upheld the Wagner Act and approved a Washington state minimum wage law (much like the one it had overthrown in New York). Two more close decisions (one upholding compulsory unemployment insurance, the other old age pensions) furnished added proof the Court had softened its opposition to the New Deal.

Yet Roosevelt remained too obsessed with the battle to realize he had won the war. He lobbied for the court-packing bill until the end of July, squandering his strength on a struggle that had long since become a political embarrassment. In the end, the only part of the president's plan to gain congressional approval was the pension program. Once it passed, Justice Willis Van Devanter, the most obstinate New Deal opponent on the Court, resigned. By 1941 Roosevelt had named five justices to the Supreme Court, including Hugo Black and William O. Douglas. Few legacies of the president's leadership proved more important, for the new "Roosevelt Court" significantly expanded the government's role in the economy and in civil liberties.

Roosevelt's second blunder in 1937 involved fiscal policy. One group within his administration, led by Secretary of the Treasury Henry Morganthau, demanded severe spending cuts to balance the federal budget and to restore business confidence. A second group, led by WPA head Harry Hopkins, wanted the administration to follow the teachings of the British economist, John Maynard Keynes. A proponent of vigorous government action, Keynes recommended tax cuts and new spending programs to combat the depression. Reassured by good economic news in 1936, Roosevelt sided with the budget balancers. Late in 1937 he slashed government spending.

The budget cuts knocked the economy into a tailspin. By early 1938 economic indicators dipped nearly as low as they had been in 1932, and just as he had reaped credit for the recovery of 1936, Roosevelt got blamed for the depression of 1937–1938. Republicans, bone-sick of hearing about "Hoover's depression," relished the chance to decry "Roosevelt's depression." Finally, on April 14, 1938, Roosevelt reversed himself and asked Congress to resume spending. Congress responded with huge appropriations for the PWA and increased welfare funds for the states. As before, public spending blunted the worst effects of the troubled economy, but it took the massive federal budgets of World War II to end the depression and restore economic health to the nation.

The third (and final) mistake of Roosevelt's second term was the president's futile attempt to purge the Democratic party of conservative senators who had opposed the New Deal. In the congressional elections of 1938, Roosevelt campaigned against five southern senators, all of whom won reelection. The abortive purge intensified the conservative-liberal split within the Democratic party by showing conservatives they could defy the president with impunity. It also weakened the Democratic coalition at a time when Roosevelt badly needed conservative support for military preparedness to meet the growing threat from Europe.

By the end of 1938 the reform spirit was gone. Even Harry Hopkins admitted Americans had become "bored with the poor, the unemployed, and the insecure." In Congress a conservative alliance of southern Democrats and northern Republicans blocked all efforts to expand the New Deal. Yet if Roosevelt could not pass any new measures, neither could his opponents dismantle his programs. The New Deal ended in stalemate, but with several reforms ensconced as permanent features of American politics.

CONCLUSION

From a purely economic perspective, the New Deal barely made a dent in the Great Depression. Roosevelt's programs suffered from poor planning and moved with considerable caution. By 1939 national productivity had barely reached 1929 levels, and 10 million men and

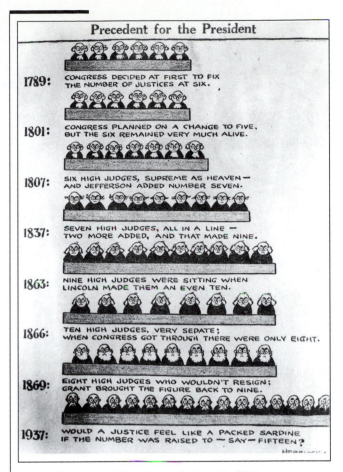

Roosevelt's court-packing scheme, designed to fill the court with justices sympathetic to his policies, outraged both liberals and conservatives because it seemed to attack the separation of powers doctrine.

women remained unemployed. Roosevelt simply could not bring himself to support huge federal budgets. Government expenditures stayed below $10 billion a year, with annual deficits on the scale of $4 billion. Indeed, despite the handwringing and wailing of conservatives, huge deficits did not become a feature of the federal budget until World War II, when federal spending leaped to $95 billion a year, with deficits over half that amount. World War II, not the New Deal, snapped America out of the depression, for then and only then did the economy recover and unemployment disappear.

Yet whatever its economic shortcomings, the New Deal blunted the worst effects of the

CHRONOLOGY OF KEY EVENTS

1928 Herbert Hoover is elected thirty-first president

1929 Stock market crashes

1930 Hawley-Smoot Tariff raises import duties to unprecedented levels

1932 Congress creates Reconstruction Finance Corporation to lend money to banks, railroads, and insurance companies; to revive the construction industry, Congress creates the Federal Home Loan Bank System to lend money to savings and loan associations; Bonus Army, a group of veterans demanding immediate payment of World War I bonuses, is dispersed by federal troops in Washington, D.C.; Franklin Roosevelt is elected thirty-second president

1933 Emergency Banking Relief Act addresses banking crisis; Roosevelt conducts the first of many "fireside chats" over national radio; Civilian Conservation Corps puts young people to work conserving natural resources; Federal Emergency Relief Act provides relief payments to the unemployed through local and state welfare agencies; Civil Works Administration offers employment to over 4 million people; Agricultural Adjustment Act sets up a system of farm price supports and production limits; National Industrial Recovery Act authorizes industrial codes regulating production, prices, and working conditions and provides funds for public works projects; Tennessee Valley Authority constructs dams and hydroelectric plants in the Tennessee River valley; Twenty-first Amendment repeals prohibition; Glass-Steagall Act creates the Federal Deposit Insurance Corporation to insure savings accounts against bank failure; Farm Credit Administration and Home Owners' Loan Corporation provide low-interest loans to farmers and home owners

1934 Dr. Francis Townsend proposes a $200 monthly pension for every citizen over 60; the "radio priest" Father Charles Coughlin breaks with Roosevelt and forms the National Union for Social Justice; Senator Huey Long of Louisiana announces his "Share Our Wealth Program" to provide every American family with a guaranteed annual income; Indian Reorganization Act provides funds for tribes to purchase land, offers recognition of tribal constitutions, and repeals prohibitions on Native American customs

1935 *Schechter* v. *United States* declares National Industrial Recovery Act unconstitutional; Emergency Relief Appropriation Act creates Works Progress Administration and National Youth Administration; National Labor Relations Act guarantees workers' right to organize and bargain collectively; Public Utility Holding Company Act is passed to prevent monopolies in gas and electricity distribution; Social Security Act creates a federal system of old age pensions and state-run unemployment compensation programs

1937 Roosevelt proposes his "court-packing" scheme

1938 Fair Labor Standards Act bans child labor and establishes minimum wages and maximum hours

Great Depression. Through economic reforms and public works projects Roosevelt managed to preserve the public's faith in capitalism and in democratic government at a time when both seemed on the verge of destruction. Most of the New Deal's economic reforms were modest in scope, but they strengthened the public's faith in the government as their agency of action and reform. Roosevelt accomplished this, in large measure, by reaching out to groups that Washington had largely neglected in the past. The Social Security program, while it ignored many, made the government responsible for old age pensions and welfare payments to citizens who could not support themselves. The NIRA and the Wagner Act encouraged the growth of unions; minimum wage laws put an economic floor under many workers; and child labor was finally abolished in industry (though it remained in agriculture). While the New Deal stopped far short of providing equal treatment under the law for black Americans, it offered them a measure of relief from the depression and a new visibility in government.

The New Deal encouraged Americans to look to the White House for strong executive leadership. When Roosevelt took office the situation required decisive action, and he responded in kind. A compassionate man and a bold leader, Roosevelt had little difficulty persuading Congress to pass his programs. More and more, the public expected the other branches of government to support presidential initiatives. Roosevelt's administrative style, creating special agencies to handle specific problems and placing people in charge who answered directly to him, further enhanced presidential power. Moreover, on a purely partisan level, the New Deal benefited the Democratic party mightily by forging the Roosevelt coalition, a powerful alliance of labor, blacks, urban ethnics, intellectuals, and southern whites that helped shape American politics for the next several decades.

Above all the New Deal made the federal government responsible for safeguarding the nation's economic health. Prior to the 1930s if people were asked how the government affected them, they probably thought in terms of the state government, or even their local government. Federal policies simply did not impinge that much on the public. The New Deal changed all that. FDR's alphabet soup of programs and agencies made the federal government such a daily presence in people's lives they now expected Washington to involve itself in everything from farm subsidies to the sale of stocks and securities.

Finally, there is the question of federal fiscal policy. Anyone comparing the political economy of 1920 and 1940 notices two dramatic changes. First, by 1940 the federal government had claimed responsibility for stable prices and full employment, and second, Keynesian fiscal policies had largely replaced older theories on how the government should approach the economy. For better or for worse, the New Deal had dramatically altered the government's fiscal policy.

SUGGESTIONS FOR FURTHER READING

OVERVIEWS AND SURVEYS

James M. Burns, *Roosevelt: The Lion and the Fox* (1956); Sean Dennis Cashman, *America in the Twenties and Thirties: The Olympian Age of Franklin Delano Roosevelt* (1989); Paul K. Conkin, *The New Deal*, 2d ed. (1975) and *The Southern Agrarians* (1988); Otis L. Graham, Jr., *The New Deal: The Critical Issues* (1971); Robert L. Heilbroner and Aaron Singer, *The Economic Transformation of America* (1977); Jack Temple Kirby, *Rural Worlds Lost: The American South, 1920–1960* (1987); William E. Leuchtenburg, *Franklin D. Roosevelt and the New Deal* (1963) and *The Perils of Prosperity, 1914–32* (1958); James T. Patterson, *America's Struggle Against Poverty* (1981); Albert U. Romasco, *The Politics of Recovery: Roosevelt's New Deal* (1983); Studs Terkel, *Hard Times: An Oral History of the Great Depression* (1970).

HERBERT HOOVER AND THE GREAT DEPRESSION

William J. Barber, *From New Era to New Deal; Herbert Hoover, the Economists, and American Economic Policy, 1921–1933* (1985); Andrew Bergman, *We're in the Money: Depression America and Its Films* (1971); Roger Daniels, *The Bonus March: An Episode of the Great Depression* (1971); Glen H. Elder, Jr., *Children of the Great Depression: Social Change in Life Experience* (1974); Martin L.

Fausold, *The Presidency of Herbert Hoover* (1985); Donald J. Lisio, *The President and Protest: Hoover, Conspiracy, and the Bonus Riot* (1974); Albert U. Romasco, *The Poverty of Abundance: Hoover, the Nation, the Depression* (1965); Jordan A. Schwarz, *Interregnum of Despair: Hoover, Congress, and the Depression* (1970); Winifred D. Wandersee, *Women's Work and Family Values, 1920–1940* (1981).

FRANKLIN ROOSEVELT AND THE FIRST NEW DEAL

Sue Bridwell Beckham, *Depression Post Office Murals and Southern Culture: A Gentle Reconstruction* (1989); Bernard Bellush, *The Failure of the NRA* (1975); Donald R. Brand, *Corporatism and the Rule of Law: A Study of the National Recovery Administration* (1988); David E. Conrad, *The Forgotten Farmers: The Story of the Sharecroppers in the New Deal* (1965); Frank Freidel, *Launching the New Deal* (1973); Robert F. Himmelberg, *The Origins of the National Recovery Administration* (1976); R. Douglas Hurt, *The Dust Bowl: An Agricultural and Social History* (1981); Jerre Mangione, *The Dream and the Deal: The Federal Writers' Project, 1935–1943* (1972); Robert S. McElvaine, *The Great Depression: America, 1929–1941* (1984); David Milton, *The Politics of U.S. Labor: From the Great Depression to the New Deal* (1982); Michael Parrish, *Securities Regulation and the New Deal* (1970); John Salmond, *The Civilian Conservation Corps, 1933–1942: A New Deal Case Study* (1967); Ronald W. Schatz, *The Electrical Workers: A History of Labor at General Electric and Westinghouse, 1923–1960* (1983).

THE SECOND NEW DEAL

Alan Brinkley, *Voices of Protest: Huey Long, Father Coughlin, and the Great Depression* (1982); Robert F. Burk, *The Corporate State and the Broker State: The Du Ponts and American National Politics, 1925–1940* (1990); Keith Dix, *What's a Coal Miner to Do? The Mechanization of Coal Mining* (1988); Sidney Fine, *Sit-Down: The General Motors Strike of 1936–1937* (1969); Philip J. Funigiello, *Toward a National Power Policy: The New Deal and the Electric Utility Industry, 1933–1941* (1973); Ellis Hawley, *The New Deal and the Problem of Monopoly: A Study in Economic Ambivalence* (1966); James A. Hodges, *New Deal Labor Policy and the Southern Cotton Textile Industry, 1934–1941* (1986); Harvey Klehr, *The Heyday of American Communism: The Depression Decade* (1984); Roy

Lubove, *The Struggle for Social Security, 1900–1935*, 2d ed. (1986); Thomas McCraw, *TVA and the Power Fight, 1933–1939* (1971); James T. Patterson, *Congressional Conservatism and the New Deal* (1967); Richard Polenberg, *Reorganizing Roosevelt's Government, 1936–1939* (1966).

THE NEW AND MINORITIES

Dan T. Carter, *Scottsboro: A Tragedy of the American South*, rev. ed. (1979); William H. Chafe, *The American Woman: Her Changing Social, Economic, and Political Role, 1920–1970* (1972); Cletus E. Daniel, *Bitter Harvest: A History of California Farmworkers, 1870–1941* (1981); Sara M. Evans, *Born for Liberty: A History of Women in America* (1989); Suzanne Forrest, *The Preservation of the Village: New Mexico's Hispanics and the New Deal* (1989); Mario T. García, *Mexican Americans: Leadership, Ideology, & Identity, 1930–1960* (1989); Nancy L. Grant, *TVA and Black Americans: Planning for the Status Quo* (1990); William H. Harris, *Keeping the Faith: A. Philip Randolph, Milton P. Webster, and the Brotherhood of Sleeping Car Porters, 1925-1937* (1977); Abraham Hoffman, *Unwanted Mexican Americans in the Great Depression, Repatriation Pressures, 1929–1939* (1974); James H. Jones, *Bad Blood: The Tuskegee Syphilis Experiment, A Tragedy of Race and Medicine*, rev. ed. (1992); Lawrence C. Kelly, *The Assault on Assimilation: John Collier and the Origins of Indian Policy Reform* (1983); Harry A. Kersey, Jr., *The Florida Seminoles and the New Deal, 1933–1942* (1989); Alice Kessler-Harris, *Out to Work: A History of Wage-Earning Women in the United States* (1982); Kenneth Philp, *John Collier's Crusade for Indian Reform, 1920-1954* (1977); Mark Reisler, *By the Sweat of Their Brow: Mexican Immigrant Labor in the United States, 1900–1940* (1976); Lois Scharf, *To Work and to Wed: Female Employment, Feminism, and the Great Depression* (1980); Susan Ware, *Beyond Suffrage: Women in the New Deal* (1981); Nancy J. Weiss, *Farewell to the Party of Lincoln: Black Politics in the Age of FDR* (1983); Raymond Wolters, *Negroes and the Great Depression: The Problem of Economic Recovery* (1970); Robert L. Zangrando, *The NAACP Crusade Against Lynching, 1909–1950* (1980).

BIOGRAPHIES

John Barnard, *Walter Reuther and the Rise of the Auto Workers* (1983); David Burner, *Herbert Hoo-*

ver: *A Public Life* (1979); Melvyn Dubofsky and Warren Van Tine, *John L. Lewis: A Biography* (1977); Steven Fraser, *Labor Will Rule: Sidney Hillman and the Rise of American Labor* (1991); Thomas Kessner, *Fiorello H. La Guardia and the Making of Modern New York* (1989); Joe Klein, *Woody Guthrie: A Life* (1980); Joseph Lash, *Eleanor and Franklin* (1971); Arthur Schlesinger, Jr., *The Age of Roosevelt*, 3 vols. (1957–1960); Richard N. Smith, *An Uncommon Man: The Triumph of Herbert Hoover* (1984); Geoffrey C. Ward, *A First-Class Temperament: The Emergence of Franklin Roosevelt* (1989); T. Harry Williams, *Huey Long* (1969).

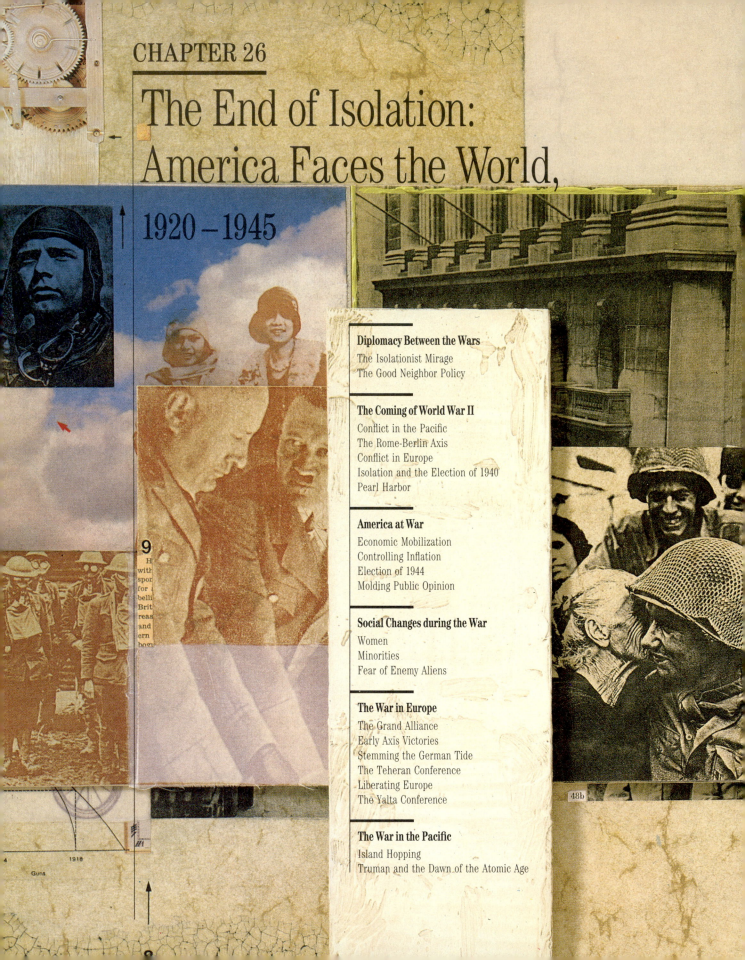

CHAPTER 26

The End of Isolation: America Faces the World, 1920–1945

hen he saw the production figures on American industry during World War II, Winston Churchill smiled broadly and exclaimed, "Nothing succeeds like excess!" Great Britain's bulldog of a prime minister was right: Allied armies won the decisive battles of World War II, but the Allied victory rested squarely on America's economic might. The gross national product rose from $91 billion in 1939 to $166 billion in 1945, and industrial production soared by an astonishing 96 percent. By 1943 America's productivity outstripped all its enemies combined; by 1944 it was twice as great.

No one symbolized this economic miracle better than Henry J. Kaiser. A man of stout frame, formidable jowls, and a pronounced paunch, Kaiser excelled at making money. Before the war his Six Companies consortium built Boulder Dam and sank the piers for the Golden Gate Bridge. Spectacular feats of engineering such as these more than supported the boasts of his son, Edgar, who proudly declared: "We are building an empire." When World War II erupted, Kaiser immediately used his experience with government contracts and officials to become one of the leading industrial architects of the Allied victory.

Kaiser built ships—tankers, small aircraft carriers, troop ships, and Liberty ships, the basic cargo carrier of the war. Speed was his watchword, and he would not tolerate delays in production schedules. In 1941 it took 355 days to build a Liberty ship. With prefabricated parts and assembly-line methods, Kaiser trimmed that time down to 56 days in 1943. By 1945 his 10 shipyards feasted on more than $3 billion in government contracts and turned out a ship a day. With enemy submarines sinking everything in sight, Kaiser stressed speed and large-scale production, not efficiency, cost, or quality.

Kaiser's shipyards formed a microcosm of American society. Teeming with migrants from farms and small towns, they employed 125,000 men and women who faced problems ranging from overcrowded housing to nonexistent child care. Kaiser devised ingenious ways to attract workers. He paid good wages, built a modern hospital or clinic near every shipyard, enrolled workers and their families in an excellent health plan, and experimented with round-the-clock nurseries and child-care centers.

After the war Kaiser praised himself as the embodiment of rugged individualism and dynamic capitalism, but in truth his success derived from "welfare capitalism." Government loans financed his shipyards, and cost-plus government contracts guaranteed his profits. In that sense, he was a charter member of the military-industrial complex. Yet his concern for workers and their families tempered capitalism with compassion, creating a model of corporate management that survived long after the last of his ships went into mothballs.

DIPLOMACY BETWEEN THE WARS

World War I's horrible casualties, disappointments over the Treaty of Versailles, the United States' failure to join the League of Nations, and the Red Scare left the public suspicious of foreign crusades. Americans wanted to retreat from world affairs. "The people have had all the

One of the biggest producers of war goods was Henry Kaiser. Almost one quarter of America's entire wartime output of merchant shipping came from his shipyards.

war, all the taxation, and all the military service they want," declared President Calvin Coolidge in 1925. During the 1920s and much of the 1930s, the United States concentrated on improving its status in the Western Hemisphere and on avoiding European entanglements.

The Isolationist Mirage

Throughout the 1920s, Republican leaders debated and ultimately refused to join the League of Nations or the World Court. Such commitments, they feared, might involve the United States too deeply in global politics. Yet Washington remained keenly interested in preserving international stability and tried to promote world peace through diplomatic means.

In December 1921 Secretary of State Charles Evans Hughes convened a disarmament conference in Washington, D.C., which produced the Five-Power Naval Treaty the following year. The treaty established a ten-year moratorium on the construction of battleships and set current tonnage for battleships at a ratio of 5:5:3 for the United States, Great Britain, and Japan; 1.75 for France and Italy. To win support for what the Japanese delegates called a ratio of "Rolls-Royce, Rolls-Royce, Ford," the United States and Great Britain agreed not to improve their fortifications in the Far East, especially in the Philippines. In 1922 the United States also signed the Nine-Power Treaty, an agreement to preserve the "Open Door" in China, and the Four-Party Treaty, which committed the United States, Great Britain, France, and Japan to consult before going to war in Asia.

Several years later the United States and France launched an international crusade to banish war from world affairs. In 1928 the French foreign minister, Aristide Briand, and Secretary of State Frank B. Kellogg negotiated the Kellogg-Briand Pact, which renounced war as an instrument for resolving international disputes and symbolized the post–World War I era's disillusionment with naked force. If attacked, however, the signatories, 62 in all, could defend themselves by force. While it raised hopes for peace and earned Kellogg the Nobel Peace Prize, the Kellogg-Briand Pact had no chance of preventing future bloodshed. Since the pact was without an enforcement mechanism, the pledges it rested upon were like pie crusts—easily formed and easily broken.

The Good Neighbor Policy

During the 1920s Republican administrations inched away from gunboat diplomacy and tried to develop better relations with Latin America. True, progress was uneven and Washington's policies occasionally reverted to heavy-handed interventions, but the thrust of Republican diplomacy during the 1920s clearly anticipated the shift toward improved relations with Latin America, which the Democrats dubbed the "Good Neighbor Policy" in the 1930s.

In 1924, for example, the United States pulled the marines out of the Dominican Republic, and the following year American troops left Nicaragua, only to be sent back a few months later when a revolution broke out. But the real test of the United States' desire for improved relations came in Mexico.

Following Alvaro Obregon's election as president of Mexico in 1920, the Mexican government threatened to expropriate American-owned oil properties. The oil companies demanded government intervention, but in 1927 President Calvin Coolidge appointed Dwight Morrow, a partner in the firm of J. P. Morgan and Company, as ambassador. Mexicans expected the worst; one newspaper declared, "after Morrow come the marines." They were wrong. Morrow liked Mexico. One of his first actions was to change the sign on the embassy to read "United States Embassy" rather than "American Embassy." It was a small gesture, but it was not lost on the Mexicans, who had long resented the United States' arrogance in appropriating a continental adjective. Morrow's diplomacy paid handsome dividends, and in 1927 Mexico once again recognized American-owned oil properties.

President Herbert Hoover continued the diplomacy of reconciliation. He announced plans to withdraw marines from Nicaragua and Haiti, and he resisted pressure from Congress to establish a customs receivership in El Salvador when the government there defaulted on its bonds. In 1930 Hoover approved a document

(Text continues on p. 866)

AMERICA AND THE WORLD
MARTIANS, WIZARDS, AND THE BATTLE OVER ISOLATIONISM

In *The Great Dictator*, his first talking film, Charlie Chaplin appeared as both the ranting "furore," a parody of Adolf Hitler, and the well-known little tramp character in the guise of a Jewish banker who pleads with the dictator for decency.

In 1938 Halloween came one day early. At 8 P.M. on Sunday, October 30, Orson Welles's Mercury Theater went on the air as usual to the strains of the Tchaikovsky Piano Concerto in B Flat Minor. Perhaps a million Americans listened to the opening of the CBS radio show. Far more—around 11 million—had their radios tuned to NBC's "Chase and Sanborn Hour," featuring the popular comedian and ventriloquist Edgar Bergen and his wooden, red-headed dummy Charlie McCarthy. At 8:12—right after Bergen finished his first skit, Chase and Sanborn began its first commercial, and listeners across

America started to fidget with their dials to see what else was on the radio—something strange happened on CBS's Mercury Theater. Breaking from the music of Ramon Raquello at the Meridian Room in New York's Hotel Park Plaza, the show shifted to the town of Groves Mills, New Jersey, for a special bulletin.

Something strange, terribly strange, was going on. Announcer Carl Phillips and Professor Pierson of Princeton were examining an object of unknown origin that had plummeted to earth from outer space. As they debated whether the smooth, cylindrical object was a meteorite or something totally new, the top of the object began to rotate. Tentacles, "wriggling out of the shadow like a gray snake," appeared, followed by a creature of sinister ugliness. Sobbing and retching, Phillips announced: "There, I can see the thing's body. It's large as a bear and it glistens like wet leather. But the face. It ... it's indescribable. I can hardly force myself to keep looking at it. The eyes are black and gleam like a serpent. The mouth is V-shaped with saliva dripping from its rimless lips that seem to quiver and pulsate. . . ."

The monster was followed by others, "the vanguard of an invading army from planet Mars." Equipped with flame throwers and poison gases, the Martians destroyed the New Jersey state police and National Guard and march on New York City. Each lightning strike was covered live by CBS radio. At 9:45 when CBS took a commercial break, the regular announcer informed his audience that it was listening to the Mercury Theater's production of H. G. Wells's *War of the Worlds*. But for many Americans the announcement came too late, for gripped in panic they had already left their radio sets. They had taken to the streets, fleeing the phantom invaders. They crammed churches and city halls, imploring God and politicians for help. A study conducted after the broadcast estimated that 1.7 million people believed the broadcast. Listeners who had not completed grammar school and who had been out of work for more than three years were the most vulnerable. But rich and well-educated Americans also fell under the show's spell.

Why? Part of the answer was radio itself. Americans had grown accustomed to radio announcers interrupting a broadcast with a special bulletin. And studies indicated that most Americans trusted radio commentators more than print journalists. Edward R. Murrow, Raymond Gram Swing, Elmer Davis, H. V. Kaltenborn, and other radio commentators were familiar, trusted voices. Part of the answer was the times. It was an uncertain age. Hitler was on the move in Europe. Talk of bombs and invasions, wars and crises, filled the air waves. Only a month before the broadcast, the Munich Pact was signed, ending the tense Czechoslovakian crisis that most Americans had believed would lead to another European war. But even with the Munich Pact, millions of Americans believed that the United States was headed toward a war. The *War of the Worlds* broadcast was made all the more believable because Americans had come to expect a crisis.

If world events could color the way Americans listened to and interpreted a radio show, mass media could influence the way Americans understood world events. During the 1930s, movies dominated the mass media. Eighty million Americans—two-thirds of the nation's population—went to the movies each week.

Throughout most of the 1930s the film industry ignored the rise of fascism in Europe, ignored the violent anti-Semitism and expansionist foreign policies of Hitler and Mussolini. The primary reason for this was that 40 to 50 percent of the industry's revenues came from foreign distribution and exhibition. If Germany, Italy, or any major country prohibited Hollywood's only product, the film industry would suffer. When Hollywood did touch, however obliquely, on foreign policy matters, it suggested that isolationism was the best solution for the United States. Released in 1939, the year Europe went to war, *The Wizard of Oz* underscored the theme, "There's no place like home."

Economic changes in the film industry, however, soon silenced such isolationist impulses. By the end of 1940 Hollywood's European market had all but vanished. Germany and Italy banned all American films in the areas they controlled. Only Great Britain remained as a solid market for American films, and Great Britain was at war with Germany. In short, the economic motive *not* to offend the Fascist dictatorships was removed.

Hollywood responded with a series of films emphasizing internationalism. One of the earliest internationalist films, *Blockade*, articulated the new position in Hollywood. The film tells of the barbarities committed by the Fascists during the Spanish Civil War. *Confessions of a Nazi Spy* (1939) condemned Nazi aggression and brutality and identified Germany as a real threat to the United States. Charlie Chaplin's *The Great Dictator* (1940) poked fun at Hitler and fascism. *Pastor Hall* (1940) vividly portrayed the brutality of Nazi Germany. Other anti-Nazi films followed—*The Mortal Storm* (1940), *Four Sons* (1940), *Escape* (1940), *I Married a Nazi* (1940), and *Man Hunt* (1941). All condemned Germany, Hitler,

and Nazism. Still other films glorified America's own military traditions. *Sargeant York* (1941), perhaps the most stirring of the latter group, reminded Americans that there were issues worth fighting for. This story of America's most publicized World War I hero amplified the theme of aggressive internationalism.

The power of Hollywood's newly found internationalism was not lost on politicians in Washington. President Roosevelt, who was working in support of Britain's war efforts, applauded films that cast Britain in the best possible light. Isolationists in Congress, however, charged that Hollywood had become a propaganda mill determined to push America into another European war. Senator Gerald P. Nye of North Dakota, one of the country's most vocal isolationists, told a national radio audience that Hollywood had "ceased to be an instrument of entertainment" and had become the home of propaganda and warmongers whose motive was to "rouse the war fever in America." The films glorified and sanitized war, Nye maintained. Instead of showing men "crouching in the mud . . . English, Greek, and German boys disemboweled, blown to bit," the films showed soldiers "marching in their bright uniforms, firing the beautiful guns at distant targets."

Isolationists in Congress demanded an investigation of Hollywood. In the late summer of 1941 a special subcommittee of the Senate Interstate Commerce Committee held hearings stemming from the charge that Hollywood had "been extensively used for propaganda purposes designed to influence the public mind in the direction of participation in the European war." Chaired by isolationist Bennett C. Clark of Missouri and stacked with other isolationists, the subcommittee had its sights set on changing the internationalist mood in Hollywood.

Hollywood fought back. The film industry hired Wendell L. Willkie, who had run for the presidency in 1940 on the Republican ticket, as their chief legal counsel. Willkie and such witnesses from Hollywood as Harry Warner, one of the Warner brothers, argued that the anti-Nazi films were factually accurate and that Hitler *was* a threat to the United States. "The motion picture industry and its executives are opposed to the Hitler regime," Willkie said. Nazism is "an evil force," Warner added. Hollywood's vigorous defense silenced the isolationists. The subcommittee adjourned the hearings on September 26 without issuing a report.

Two and a half months later the isolationists' charges became moot. The Japanese bombed Pearl Harbor and America went to war. And Hollywood was quickly enlisted to support the war effort. Movies had helped prepare America for war. Now they would help win the war.

written by Undersecretary of State J. Reuben Clark. The Clark Memorandum repudiated the Roosevelt Corollary to the Monroe Doctrine, which for 25 years had justified U.S. intervention in Latin America.

In his first inaugural address, President Franklin D. Roosevelt dedicated the United States "to the policy of the good neighbor," bestowing a name on the new relationship with Latin America. Secretary of State Cordell Hull stunned Latin America in December 1933 at the Seventh Pan-American Conference by declaring, "no state has the right to intervene in the international or external affairs of another." The marines left Nicaragua in 1933 and Haiti in 1934. In the Hull-Alfara Treaty of 1934, the United States finally gave Panama its political independence and surrendered the right to intervene in its affairs. Furthermore, when Mexico finally expropriated foreign oil properties in 1938, Roosevelt rejected calls to send in troops and let the action stand. The Good Neighbor Policy did not solve all the problems with Latin America. Fears of Yankee military power and economic might still remained, but the Good Neighbor Policy promoted better relations just when the United States needed hemispheric solidarity to meet the threat of global war.

THE COMING OF WORLD WAR II

Conflict in the Pacific

The first major threat to international stability following World War I came in the Far East, with Japan as the aggressor. Chronically short of raw materials and desperate to establish political and cultural hegemony in Asia, the Japanese looked enviously at Manchuria, China, Indochina, and the East Indies, where they could find iron ore, coal, rice, rubber, and petroleum. In September 1931 Japan invaded Manchuria, reducing the province to a puppet state, renamed Manchukuo in 1932. While Japan's aggression violated the League of Nations, the Treaties of Washington (1921–1922), and the Kellogg-Briand Pact, President Hoover, a peaceful man, refused to take strong actions in the Far East, explaining his policy was not to

allow "under any circumstances anybody to deposit that baby in our lap."

Having rejected military intervention, Hoover also refused to impose economic sanctions against Japan, fearing such reprisals might hurt American exports or, worse yet, lead to war. Instead, Hoover applied the Stimson Doctrine (named after Secretary of State Henry L. Stimson), which revived the Wilsonian policy of refusing to recognize governments based on force. Expecting bolder measures, Japan ignored this slap on the wrist and concluded the United States would not use military might to oppose her designs on the Far East, a misapprehension for which Japan paid dearly in the next decade.

In 1933 the League of Nations condemned Japan's aggression in Manchuria. Determined to rival the colonial powers of Europe, Japan responded by withdrawing from the League of Nations. Justifying this action, one Japanese leader complained that Europe's leaders had taught Japan the game of poker but, having acquired all the chips, Europe now condemned poker as immoral and proposed to take up contract bridge.

Japan preferred to gamble. The following year, 1934, Japan terminated the Five-Power Naval Treaty of 1922, which had limited its naval power in the Pacific. When Japan walked out of the London Naval Conference in 1935, naval disarmament was dead, leaving Japan free to build an Asian empire, confident the Western powers, including the United States, would not use force to oppose her actions.

At first President Roosevelt seemed to follow Hoover's Far Eastern policy. The new administration continued to withhold recognition from Manchukuo, and Roosevelt's secretary of state, Cordell Hull, peppered Japan with diplomatic notes on the sanctity of treaties. Yet these measures obscured subtle policy changes. Instead of concentrating on Japan, the United States attempted to strengthen China, largely through technical and financial aid. The idea was to build China into an effective counterweight to Japan. By 1935, however, the United States acknowledged Japan's overwhelming superiority in the Far East and adopted a neutral posture toward China.

In 1937 Japan invaded China, a clear violation of the Nine-Power Treaty, the Kellogg-Briand Pact, and the Four-Party Treaty. The fighting erupted in the north and then spread quickly to the south where Japan attacked Shanghai, China's largest port. Furious fighting followed in Nanking, where Japanese troops routed the Chinese in less than a month, after which the Japanese occupied the city and perpetrated the "rape of Nanking," an orgy of looting and murder. In response to Japan's renewed aggression, the League of Nations sponsored a conference of the Nine-Power Treaty members (and others) at Brussels in November 1937. As the delegates debated whether or not to impose economic sanctions against Japan, the United States announced it would not support sanctions. The conference adjourned after passing a report that mildly criticized Japan for violating the Nine-Power Treaty.

Any doubts regarding the U.S. desire to avoid war vanished a few weeks later. In December 1937 Japanese aircraft bombed the *Panay*, a U.S. gunboat stationed on the Yangtze River near Nanking, killing 3 Americans and injuring 43 more. While the attack angered the public, few calls for war rang out similar to those following the sinking of the *Maine* or the *Lusitania*. If anything, Americans remained pensive and calm, as though they were determined to avoid what they regarded as earlier mistakes. Senator William E. Borah, chairman of the Foreign Relations Committee, called the incident "just one of those regrettable things," while Senator Henrik Shipstead of Minnesota thought Americans should "get the hell out of China war zones." Secretary Hull sent sharply worded protests to Tokyo, but the United States quickly accepted Japan's "profound apology," which included indemnities for the injured and relatives of the dead, promises against future attacks, and punishment of the pilots responsible for the bloodshed. In short, by the end of 1937, as one historian has noted, "America's Far Eastern Policy had retreated to inaction."

The Rome-Berlin Axis

The modern world had never known a leader like Adolf Hitler. Of course, he was a charismatic personality and a spellbinding orator, but history had seen such men before. What made Hitler unique was his ability to articulate a nation's darkest fears and hatreds and then turn them to his own twisted purposes. Winston Churchill offered a profound truth when he described Hitler as the "monstrous product of former wrongs and shame."

Hitler exploited the psychological injuries inflicted on Germans by World War I. Rare indeed was the German who did not feel stunned by his country's sudden, unexpected defeat or who did not seethe with anger over the harsh peace imposed by the victors. In truth, most Germans felt humiliated by their defeat and despised the Treaty of Versailles. Hitler's great genius (and history's great tragedy) was his ability to tap into his countrymen's anger and resentment. Exploiting the ugly strain of anti-Semitism in German culture, he blamed many of the nation's economic woes on German Jews, reducing them to scapegoats. In addition, he attacked the Treaty of Versailles, telling his countrymen they would regain their national honor only if they repudiated the war's verdict and abrogated the treaty. Purged of so-called Jewish traitors, cleared of the blame for causing the war, freed from onerous reparation payments, and rescued from emasculating disarmament, Germany would rise anew and reclaim her position as a world leader.

The 1920s had prepared Germans to embrace any leader who promised to restore national pride. The Treaty of Versailles had saddled Germany with a reparations bill of $34 billion in 1921. Unable to make the interest payments, let alone the principal, Germany staggered beneath the burden until its economy dissolved into severe unemployment and hyperinflation.

Confronted by Germany's imminent economic collapse, the United States offered a measure of relief. In 1924 Charles Dawes, a prominent American banker, worked out a proposal (the Dawes Plan) that reduced the reparations bill and provided Germany with an American loan. In 1929 the so-called Young Plan, developed by another American banker, Owen D. Young, cut reparations to $2 billion, but even that proved too much when the Great

Depression struck. Germany entered the 1930s with its economy in shambles. Poverty-stricken and chafing under the blame for World War I, Germans desperately wanted to reclaim their self-respect. Adolf Hitler vowed to restore this and more.

Hitler came to power in 1933, promising to repudiate the Treaty of Versailles and reassert German military might in Europe. True to his word, he immediately pulled Germany out of the League of Nations. In 1935 he rearmed Germany and started a peacetime draft, clear violations of the Treaty of Versailles. Recognizing Germany's right to rearm, Great Britain and France did not oppose Hitler's actions.

Next Hitler concentrated on forging alliances. When Benito Mussolini, whose Fascist party had won control of Italy in 1922, attacked helpless Ethiopia in 1935, Hitler recognized a kindred spirit and made overtures to Italy. As these negotiations went forward, Germany and Japan signed the Anti-Comintern Pact (forerunner of a full-scale military alliance) in 1936. Shortly thereafter Germany and Italy formed the Rome-Berlin Axis. That same year German troops reoccupied the Rhineland, the German-speaking region between the Rhine River and France. Once again, France and Great Britain

did not oppose Hitler's bold advance, for they believed (or wanted to believe) the Rhineland would satisfy his ambitions.

But the Rhineland only whetted Hitler's appetite. Intent on reuniting all German-speaking peoples of Europe under the "Third Reich," Hitler annexed Austria in 1938. Once again, the British and the French acquiesced, hoping Austria would be Hitler's last stop. Later that year he seized the Sudentenland, the German-speaking region of western Czechoslovakia.

This time France and Great Britain felt compelled to act. In September 1938 Edouard Daladier, the premier of France, and Neville Chamberlain, Britain's prime minister, met with Hitler in Munich, Germany, to demand whether he had further designs on Europe. Fearing they could not count on each other to use force, British and French leaders eagerly accepted Hitler's promises not to seek additional territory in Europe. Upon arriving in England, Chamberlain told his anxious countrymen he had returned with an agreement that guaranteed "peace in our time." In less than a year, Munich would become synonymous with shameful appeasement and Chamberlain would be vilified for believing Hitler's lies.

By 1938, then, Hitler had kept his promise to avenge the humiliations Germans had suffered at Versailles. Germany's frontiers were larger than they had been in 1914, Germany was rearmed, and German national pride had been restored. In addition, Germany had acquired powerful allies in Japan and in Italy, whose military forces had demonstrated their taste for aggression by attacking China and Ethiopia.

All this had transpired virtually unopposed by the victors of World War I. The League of Nations had failed to act and its member states had offered only feeble protests. Their caution reflected the mood of a war-weary world. Everyone hoped the Germans, Italians, and Japanese would be satisfied with their acquisitions and stop expanding. In retrospect, such hopes were clearly wrong, but at the time they did not appear unfounded. Western leaders assumed they were dealing with reasonable and responsible men: They had no way of knowing appeasement would only fuel the Axis dictators' appetites for expansion.

Benito Mussolini and Adolf Hitler share their diplomatic triumph over France and England in Munich in 1938.

Axis Takeovers in Europe, 1936–1939

The United States responded to Europe's turmoil with caution. Preoccupied with the Great Depression, President Roosevelt had little time or energy to deal with foreign affairs. Yet America's timidity also reflected the strength of isolationist sentiment. Congress, not the president, played the dominant role in foreign affairs for much of the 1930s, and Congress was determined to keep the United States out of another European conflict.

Roosevelt's first diplomatic initiative involved the Soviet Union. Hoping to expand foreign trade and to use the Soviet Union to balance Japan in the Far East, he formally recognized the Soviet Union in 1933, provoking the wrath of isolationists and anti-Communists alike. In addition, Roosevelt raised eyebrows by refusing to cooperate with international efforts to combat the global depression. Instead of supporting the London Economic Conference of 1933, which tried to stabilize international currencies, Roosevelt shocked Western leaders by taking the United States off the gold standard. Outraged by Roosevelt's economic nationalism, the British accused the United States of under-

mining international efforts to restore economic stability to the world's markets.

Meanwhile, isolationist forces were gaining strength in the Senate. In 1934 Gerald P. Nye, a Republican from North Dakota, accused international bankers and weapons manufacturers of manipulating the United States into World War I in order to increase profits. While Nye never substantiated his charges, he held hearings for three years, feeding the public's fears the United States had been suckered into World War I by "merchants of death" who put profits above the national interest. If only Wilson's government had withheld foreign loans, clamped an embargo on trade with the belligerents, and kept Americans off ships in war zones, the argument went, the United States could have remained at peace.

Privately, Roosevelt opposed the retreat into isolation. In his view, the United States, like it or not, had to play an important role in world affairs because it had become a major power. But Roosevelt's freedom to act was severely limited by isolationists in Congress. Unlike Wilson, who had successfully resisted the challenge to his control over foreign affairs embodied in the Gore-McLemore resolutions, Roosevelt could not prevent Congress from converting its own commitment to peace into binding legislation.

Between 1935 and 1937, Congress passed three separate neutrality laws that clamped an embargo on arms sales to belligerents, forbade American ships from entering war zones and prohibited them from being armed, barred Americans from traveling on belligerent ships, and restricted trade with belligerents on non-embargoed exports to a "cash and carry" basis. Clearly, Congress was determined not to repeat what it regarded as the mistakes that had plunged the United States into World War I.

The neutrality laws troubled Roosevelt. Convinced these laws posed a serious threat to presidential power, he looked for opportunities to reassert his leadership. In a speech delivered in Chicago in October 1937, Roosevelt spoke of the need to "quarantine the aggressors," but he immediately retreated into silence when it became clear the public did not support vigorous action. This was where matters stood when Hitler decided to take advantage of the world's indecisiveness.

Conflict in Europe

On August 24, 1939, Germany and the Soviet Union signed the Nazi-Comintern Pact, a non-aggression treaty. In exchange for the pact, Hitler agreed to grant the Soviet Union a sphere of influence over eastern Poland, Estonia, Latvia, Finland, and Bessarabia (northeastern Romania), while Stalin approved Germany's designs on western Poland and Lithuania. His eastern flank protected, Hitler invaded Poland on September 1, 1939. Two days later, France and Great Britain honored their treaty obligations to defend Poland and declared war on Germany. World War II had formally begun.

Poland was no match for Germany. Though its people fought bravely, Poland fell in a few weeks, and then the land fighting in Europe stopped for several months. The Sitzkrieg (Phony War or Bore War) ended in April 1940, when German tanks swept through Denmark and Norway. Hitler's next victim was the Netherlands, which fell in five days.

Most observers expected Germany to stop there. If German troops marched again, they would have to confront France, with her army of 3 million men poised behind the Maginot line, a military engineering feat of miles of concrete underground installations. Undeterred, Germany attacked France in May. Hitler outflanked the supposedly invincible Maginot line by slicing his tank divisions through the Ardennes Forest. France surrendered in June, and only the heroic boatlift at Dunkirk saved 300,000 British and French troops from capture. With his homeland now controlled by pro-German sympathizers who installed a new government called Vichy France, Charles de Gaulle fled to London, declared himself the leader of Free France, and established a government in exile.

Following France's defeat, Great Britain braced herself for invasion. To soften her up, Hitler ordered his Luftwaffe (air force) to bomb Britain mercilessly. British fighter pilots ultimately won the Battle of Britain, establishing control of the air space over the British Isles; and as 1940 ended, Great Britain, though knocked to her knees and badly bloodied, had survived.

Americans watched the bloodshed with the gravest concern. During the first year of the war

Hitler's armies devastated Poland with their tremendous force and firepower. Here soldiers drive through a town battered by repeated bombings.

bookstores sold out their entire stock of Rand McNally's European maps as people tried to keep abreast of the German Blitzkrieg (lightning war). Throughout the fall of 1940, CBS's Edward R. Murrow, speaking from the rooftops of London, kept Americans glued to their radios with stirring reports of the dog fights.

Like Wilson before him, Roosevelt responded to Europe's war by declaring America's neutrality. Unlike the idealistic Wilson, however, he did not ask his countrymen to be "neutral in thought as well as in action." After France fell, Roosevelt feared a German victory would threaten America's future security, and he resolved to save England at all costs—including war.

Before he could rescue Britain, however, Roosevelt first had to regain control of American foreign policy. Soon after Germany invaded Poland, he pushed a fourth Neutrality Act through Congress. It modified the earlier legislation by permitting belligerents to purchase war materials, provided they paid cash and carried the goods away in their own ships. This act was pro-British because England controlled the Atlantic. Using private companies as go-betweens and acting on his own authority, Roosevelt then rushed thousands of planes and guns to Britain. In September 1940 he persuaded Congress to pass the first peacetime draft in American history and signed an executive agreement with Great Britain transferring 50 destroyers in exchange for 99 year leases on eight British bases in the Western Hemisphere. Most Americans supported the destroyers-for-bases deal. When the first ships slipped out of Boston harbor, motorists on the Charleston Bridge blew their horns, while pedestrians cheered from the shore.

Fearing Roosevelt was duplicating Wilson's mistakes, isolationists opposed the tilt toward Britain. Strongest in the Midwest, they represented the entire spectrum of political thought, including Republicans such as Senators Arthur Vandenberg of Michigan and Robert Taft of Ohio; Democrats such as Joseph Kennedy, ambassador to Great Britain; and progressives such as Wisconsin's Senator Robert La Follette. Isolationists offered several antiwar arguments, some compelling, others specious. Betraying a deep strain of anti-Semitism, aviator Charles Lindbergh accused Jews of trying to push the United States into war with Germany. Vandenberg warned against the growth of executive power, anticipating later concerns about the "imperial presidency." Yet their most powerful argument was that Europe's war did not threaten "fortress America." Germany had no designs on the Western Hemisphere, they insisted. Therefore, the United States should sit this war out because Germany did not endanger America's security.

Isolation and the Election of 1940

The war dominated the election of 1940. Roosevelt easily won renomination for an unprecedented third term and proceeded to dump Vice President John Garner, who had opposed a third term for the president. As his new running mate, Roosevelt picked Secretary of Agriculture Henry A. Wallace. The Republicans passed over their front runners (isolationists all) to nominate a dark horse candidate, Wendell L. Willkie of Indiana. Head of a large public utilities holding company, Willkie was a liberal Republican who had been a Democrat most of his life.

Few American elections have been so dirty. Willkie faced such a barrage of missiles when he spoke in the big Democratic cities the *New York Times* issued daily reports of the objects thrown and the hits registered. (The projectiles ranged from rotten eggs to a five-pound steel wastebasket that split open the head of a teenage girl.) At first Willkie tried to attract voters by saying the New Deal amounted to socialism; but when this charge failed, he accused Roosevelt of trying to maneuver the United States into war. Stung by these attacks, Roosevelt assured American parents on the eve of the election: "I have said this before, but I shall say it again and again: Your boys are not going to be sent into any foreign wars."

Not since 1916 had a presidential election been decided by such a narrow popular vote. Roosevelt defeated Willkie 27 million votes to 22 million votes, and 449 electoral votes to 82. Democrats gained 7 seats in the House, but Republicans picked up 5 in the Senate. As New York City Mayor Fiorello La Guardia put it, Americans preferred "Roosevelt with his known faults to Willkie with his unknown virtues."

After the election, Churchill informed Roosevelt that England had run out of money and no longer could purchase war supplies. Consequently, the president replaced "cash and carry" with "lend-lease." In a press conference, he compared lend-lease to offering a garden hose to a neighbor whose house was on fire, explaining that after the fire had been extinguished, the neighbor would return the hose. Isolationists saw things differently. "Lending war equipment is a good deal like lending chewing gum," snarled Senator Taft of Ohio. "You don't want it back."

Roosevelt submitted the lend-lease bill to Congress in January 1941, setting off months of debate. The nastiest comment came from Senator Burton Wheeler, who called lend-lease a "Triple A foreign policy that would plow under every fourth American boy." Americans argued about lend-lease in barber shops, board meetings, and grocery stores across the country. Early in March, Congress passed the bill and Roosevelt signed it on March 11, 1941. With "this legislation," he declared, "our country has determined to do its full part in creating an adequate arsenal of democracy."

To cement the Anglo-American bond, Roosevelt met with Churchill in August 1941 on board the USS *Augusta* off the coast of Newfoundland. There they negotiated the Atlantic Charter, which pledged mutual support for democracy, freedom of the seas, arms reductions, and a just peace. In everything but name the United States and Great Britain were now allies.

While the public strongly supported aid for Great Britain, many Americans balked at helping the Russians. After Hitler invaded Russia in June 1941, the Soviet Union had no choice but to join the Grand Alliance against Germany. Roosevelt immediately offered lend-lease aid to the Soviet Union. While critics denounced Roosevelt, Churchill, who knew wars often made strange bedfellows, supported the decision wholeheartedly. "If Hitler invaded Hell," declared Churchill, "I would make at least a favorable reference to the Devil in the House of Commons." In November 1941, the United States allocated $1 billion in lend-lease to the Soviets. By 1945 America's allies had received $50 billion, four times the amount loaned to the allies in World War I.

In April 1941 the United States went beyond financial assistance by constructing bases in Greenland. During the summer American destroyers began escorting convoys as far as Iceland. To protect convoys the rest of the way, the American navy started tracking German submarines and signaling their locations to British destroyers. In September a German submarine attacked the *Greer*, the American destroyer that had been shadowing it. Assuring the public the *Greer* had been on an innocent mail run to Iceland, Roosevelt then ordered the navy to "shoot on sight" any German ships in the waters surrounding Iceland. Yet the president stopped short of asking Congress for a for-

Kneeling in prayer near the Capitol in Washington, D.C., members of the "Mother's Crusade" against the lend-lease bill plead for Congress not to pass the measure.

mal declaration of war; for a few more months the United States maintained the fiction of neutrality.

Pearl Harbor

Thanks to the public's preoccupation with Europe, Roosevelt had a relatively free hand in the Far East. Here the problem centered on Japan's march to acquire colonies. Japan wanted to build what it called the Greater East Asia Co-Prosperity Sphere, an empire that would encompass large parts of China, Southeast Asia, and the western Pacific. Yet Japan's dream of expansion clashed with the two main pillars of America's Far Eastern policy—preserving the "Open Door" for trade, and protecting China's territorial integrity.

After Japan invaded China in 1937, relations between Washington and Tokyo deteriorated rapidly. The United States pressured Japan to withdraw, but Tokyo refused, insisting the United States must drop all aid to Chiang Kai-shek, the leader of the Chinese government. In July 1939 Secretary of State Cordell Hull, aware American exports fueled Japan's war machine, threatened to impose economic sanctions. While Hull also considered clamping an embargo on all war materials, Roosevelt held back, fearing Japan would attack the Dutch East Indies to secure the oil it needed.

Events quickly forced Roosevelt's hand. After Germany defeated France in 1940, Vichy France "invited" Japan to occupy northern Indochina, an obvious step toward the Dutch East Indies. Roosevelt now believed Japan wanted to bring all of Asia under its control, threatening America's quest for free markets. Late in September he placed an embargo on scrap iron and steel, hoping economic sanctions would strengthen moderates in Japan who wished to avoid conflict with the United States. Following the embargo, however, Japan promptly negotiated the Tripartite Pact with Germany and Italy. To protect its northern flank, Japan then signed a five-year nonaggression pact in April 1941 with the Soviet Union. Japan punctuated these diplomatic maneuvers by occupying bases in southern Indochina.

Roosevelt's response was swift and decisive. As Japan tightened the noose around the Dutch East Indies, the Philippines, and British Malaya, Roosevelt retaliated in July 1941 by freezing Japanese assets in the United States and cutting off steel, oil, and aviation fuel exports to Japan.

The sanctions hurt Japan. Striving to secure the materials her military needed, Japan negotiated with the United States throughout 1941. Instead of compromising, however, the United States asked Japan to withdraw immediately from Indochina and China, concessions that would have ended Japan's dream of economic and military hegemony in Asia.

In a last ditch effort to avoid war, Japan promised not to march further south, not to attack the Soviet Union to the north, and not to declare war against the United States if Germany and America went to war. In return, Japan asked the United States to abandon Chiang Kai-shek. Roosevelt refused. In October 1941 the Japanese government fell and General Hideki Tojo, the leader of the militants, seized power. War was imminent.

In November 1941 Tokyo offered to compromise if Washington would soften its demands, but Secretary of State Hull remained adamant. Having already decided on war if the United States rejected this last olive branch, Japan issued the final order on December 2 for an air strike on Pearl Harbor. More than a year earlier American cryptographers had broken Japan's highest diplomatic code (the Purple Cipher), though not the military code. In early December the volume of diplomatic cables increased, raising American suspicions, and on December 6 the United States intercepted a hostile sounding message from Tokyo to Japan's ambassador in Washington.

Most military experts expected Japan to attack the Dutch East Indies to secure oil and rubber. Before striking there, however, Japan moved to neutralize American power in the western Pacific. At 8:00 A.M. on Sunday morning, December 7, 1941, Japanese planes hit Pearl Harbor, executing the most daring surprise attack in military history. In less than two hours, Japan reduced the base to flames, sank two battleships, and heavily damaged six others. The remainder of the fleet was either damaged or destroyed. The United States lost more than 2400 dead, while Japan's sustained minimal losses.

Yet Japan had won a costly victory. Her planes failed to destroy America's aircraft carriers, as routine maneuvers had taken the flattops out to sea before the attack. More important, the attack united the American public as nothing else could have. Opposition to Roosevelt simply evaporated. Speaking for his fellow isolationists, Senator Wheeler shouted: "The only thing to do now is to lick the hell out of them." On December 8 Congress declared war on Japan with but one dissenting vote. Germany declared war on the United States on December 11.

AMERICA AT WAR

Practically everyone agreed what had to be done: Jump-start the economy, raise an army, and win the war. Yet the economic challenges facing the United States were truly mind-boggling. New plants had to be built and existing ones expanded; raw materials had to be procured and distributed where needed; labor had to be kept on the job; production had to be raised; and all this had to be accomplished without producing soaring inflation.

Economic Mobilization

Following Pearl Harbor, Roosevelt made the switch from reformer to war leader with ease, telling reporters that "Dr. New Deal" had to be replaced by "Dr. Win-the-War." Like Wilson before him, Roosevelt wished to avoid government controls. He, too, would fail. World War II created a huge (and apparently permanent) federal bureaucracy.

In January 1942 Roosevelt created the War Production Board (WPB) to "exercise general responsibility" over the economy. To lead the agency, he selected Donald Nelson, the highly respected head of Sears, Roebuck and Company. Yet Roosevelt refused to make Nelson the "czar" of American industry, reserving real power for himself.

Business leaders responded coolly to Nelson's call for economic conversion. With profits already booming because of the war in Europe, many industrialists did not wish to jeopardize their position in the domestic market by converting factories to military production. Others worried about getting stuck with inflated capacity after the war ended. As one executive cautioned, "Guns are not windshield wipers."

Detroit provided the test case for economic conversion. Not only did automobile makers possess the capacity to produce badly needed tanks and planes, their assembly lines consumed 80 percent of the nation's rubber, 18 percent of its steel, and 14 percent of its copper. Yet when Roosevelt called for 50,000 airplanes a year, Detroit ran for cover. Automotive sales had shot up by 40 percent in 1941, and industry executives did not want to risk profits.

To gain their support, Washington offered even greater returns. The armed services suspended competitive bidding, offered cost-plus contracts, guaranteed low-cost loans for retooling, and paid huge subsidies for plant construction and equipment. Lured by huge profits, Detroit made the switch. Aircraft production leaped from 6000 planes in 1940 to 47,000 in 1942; by 1943 production had jumped to 86,000; and by the end of the war it exceeded 100,000, more than doubling Roosevelt's goal. Secretary of War Henry Stimson defended Detroit's huge profits, explaining "in a capitalist country, you have to let business make money out of the process or business won't work."

Consumer industries prospered, too. Robert W. Woodruff of Coca-Cola made his 5-cent drink the most widely distributed consumer product in the world by convincing the army that soldiers needed Coke to refresh their fighting spirit. Backed by government subsidies, Woodruff built an international network of plants, and then purchased them at a fraction of their cost after the war, ensuring Coca-Cola's postwar supremacy in the soft drink industry.

Most military contracts went to big businesses because large-scale production simplified buying. At Roosevelt's insistence the Justice Department stopped prosecuting antitrust violators shortly after Pearl Harbor, despite clear evidence international cartels (particu-

In a little more than an hour, the surprise attack at Pearl Harbor had killed more than 2400 American sailors and damaged or sunk eight battleships, including the USS *Arizona* pictured here.

larly those involved in developing synthetic rubber) had impeded the war effort. Not until 1944 did Roosevelt allow the Justice Department to resume antitrust prosecutions. Moreover, he did so not to protect small businesspeople or consumers but to block business arrangements that might endanger national defense in the future.

Government policies accelerated business consolidations. Overall, industrial profits doubled, but small industries got crowded away from the federal trough. In 1940 the top 100 companies had produced 30 percent of America's industrial output; by 1943, they produced 70 percent and the other 175,000 companies the rest. After congressional hearings, chaired by Senator Harry S Truman from Missouri, accused conglomerates of squeezing out small businesses, Congress established the Smaller War Plants Corporation in 1943, but small companies simply lacked the capital to convert to war production and the political connections to borrow enough money to retool.

Research, supported by government grants, developed into a major new industry during World War II. When the war began, Germany enjoyed scientific and technological superiority, especially in tanks and artillery. To counter this advantage, Roosevelt created the Office of Scientific Research and Development (OSRD) in 1942. Its most ambitious project was the the atomic bomb. Alerted by Albert Einstein of Hitler's interest in developing nuclear weapons, Roosevelt put over $2 billion and 500,000 workers into the Manhattan Project, the atomic bomb's code name.

Federal funds also supported the development of radar, flame throwers, antiaircraft artillery, rockets, and penicillin. New blood plasma techniques permitted 13 million pints of blood to be collected. Moreover, antimalarial drugs and insecticides, including DDT, dramatically reduced the incidence of mosquito-carried diseases among troops in the Mediterranean and Pacific. Thanks to these advances, the death rate of wounded soldiers who reached medical installations was half that of World War I. Even more amazing, the noncombat-related death rate among troops was virtually the same as the domestic death rate.

No less than industry, American agriculture performed impressively during World War II. To encourage production, Roosevelt allowed farmers to make large profits by setting crop prices at 110 percent of parity, defined as the ratio between agricultural prices and manufactured goods prices during the agricultural boom years of 1910 to 1914. Good weather, mechanization, and a dramatic increase in the use of fertilizers did the rest. Cash income for farmers jumped from $2.3 billion in 1940 to $9.5 billion in 1945.

The distribution of profits in agriculture followed the same pattern as industry: The "big guys" flourished, while the "little guys" floundered. Most profits went to large-scale operators who could afford expensive machinery and fertilizers. Many small farmers, saddled with huge debts from the depression, abandoned their farms for jobs in defense plants or the armed services. Over 5 million farm residents (17 percent of the total) left rural areas during the war.

Overall, the war brought unprecedented prosperity to Americans. Per capita income rose from $373 in 1940 to $1074 in 1945, and total personal income went from $81 billion to $182 billion during the same years. Workers never had it so good. The total income of families increased dramatically as large numbers of women joined the work force, creating millions of two-income families.

In fact, World War II brought Americans more money than they could spend, for the production of consumer goods could not keep pace with the new buying power. During 1942 the gap between disposable income and available goods approached $17 billion. Hair curlers, toaster, dishes, diapers, spoons—everything was in short supply. As early as 1943 many manufacturers started accepting postwar orders. General Electric's ad the month of the Normandy invasion announced, "Now we'll be glad to put your name down for earliest available data on postwar air conditioning and refrigeration equipment."

Steeped in the values of a consumer society, Americans emerged from the depression with a backlog of desires only to face empty shelves. Most people accepted the deprivations stoically, but others hoarded what they could— shoes, canned goods, used tires, and other scarce products. If stores did not have what they wanted, some customers grabbed anything. On December 7, 1944, the third anniversary of Pearl Harbor, Macy's set a new sales record as many of its stores sold down to the bare shelves.

Controlling Inflation

The shortages led to inflation. Prices rose 18 percent between 1941 and the end of 1942, with an increase of 11 percent in food prices alone in 1942. Fearing inflation would destroy the economy, Congress created the Office of Price Administration (OPA) in January 1942 to control prices. The OPA quickly defined the ceiling for individual merchants as the highest price they had charged for a particular item in March 1942.

Since the success of price controls depended on the rationing of scarce goods, the OPA also introduced ten major rationing programs in 1942. For staple products in short supply, the OPA issued ration cards and coupons to more than 120 million people. To purchase sugar, meat, butter, bacon, cheese, alcohol, canned goods, and shoes, shoppers had to hand coupons to retailers, who found the whole system hopelessly cumbersome. The government rationed gasoline, too, allowing drivers a mere three gallons a week. To a society intoxicated with the automobile, three gallons a week posed a real hardship.

Relying on voluntarism and patriotism, the OPA extolled the virtues of self-sacrifice, telling people to "Use it up, wear it out, make it do, or do without." Yet the response to rationing often reflected old-fashioned Yankee ingenuity. When the OPA ordered a 10 percent cut in the cloth for women's bathing suits, manufacturers introduced the two-piece bathing suit. A bare midriff had suddenly become patriotic.

In addition to rationing, Washington attacked inflation by reducing the public's purchasing power. The administration targeted war bond sales directly at working-class families. Secretary of the Treasury Henry Morgenthau rejected a poster that showed a woman in a mink coat buying war bonds. He told the artist to draw a woman in overalls. The plan worked. War bonds not only helped finance the war; by 1944 they absorbed more than 7 percent of the real personal income of Americans.

The government also attacked inflation through tax reforms. Fewer than four million Americans had filed tax returns in 1939, and most blue-collar workers that year had paid no income taxes at all. To cool off consumer purchasing power, Congress passed the Revenue Act of 1942, which raised corporate taxes, increased the excess profits tax from 60 to 90 percent, and levied a flat 5 percent withholding tax on anyone who earned more than $642 a year. By mid-1943 most American workers had taxes deducted weekly from wages, and the number of tax returns at the end of the year leaped to 30 million. Tax reform during World War II reduced the public's buying power, forced citizens to pay more than 40 percent of the war's total cost as the war progressed, and laid the foundation for postwar tax policies.

Wage controls offered another tool for controlling inflation. The War Labor Board (WLB), established in 1942, had the power to set wages, hours, and working conditions. Because it had to proceed on a case-by-case basis, however, wage disputes quickly swamped the WLB. The government needed a test case to establish national guidelines, and steel workers provided such a case.

In the summer of 1942, workers in several steel mills demanded a dollar-a-day raise. In response, the WLB adopted what came to be called the "Little Steel" formula. Using January 1, 1941, as the starting point, the Little Steel formula permitted wages to rise by 15 percent to compensate for the cost of living increases up to May 1942, but additional pay increases were prohibited for the duration of the war. This meant the steel workers received only a 5.5 percent raise (about 44 cents a day) because they had already won pay hikes earlier in the year. The Little Steel formula was not inflationary because workers in other industries had already secured the maximum increase.

In practice, however, the Little Steel formula did not freeze wages. It applied only to hourly wages, not weekly totals. Thus, while

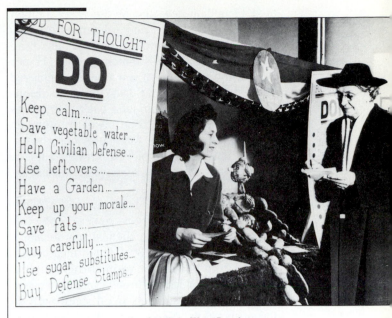

At a consumer conservation booth in West Dundee Township, Illinois, women offered "food for thought" in an attempt to help the war effort.

wage rates increased a modest 24 percent during the war, the weekly paychecks of workers, thanks to overtime, rose 70 percent.

Though price controls offered another effective weapon against inflation, the government refused to use them until labor demanded action. In October 1942 Roosevelt appointed James F. Byrnes, his chief all-purpose advisor, head of the Office of Economic Stabilization, later renamed the Office of War Mobilization. Byrnes instituted broad price freezes in the spring, and by the summer prices had stopped climbing. To placate consumers still further, Byrnes rolled back prices 10 percent on selected agricultural products, including meat and butter.

Working together, these programs brought inflation under control. After 1942 the annual inflation rate did not exceed 1.5 percent. Still, the administration's methods pleased no one. Everyone groused about taxes; manufacturers and farmers denounced price controls as an attack on their profits; and labor officials condemned wage freezes as an assault on their incomes.

Yet American workers clearly reaped a bonanza from World War II. Because the war created 17 million new jobs at the exact moment when 15 million men and women entered the armed services, unemployment virtually disappeared. In 1939 over 8 million people (17 percent of the work force) remained unemployed, but between 1939 and 1941 most traditional breadwinners got their jobs back. After Pearl Harbor, labor soared to an absolute premium, drawing into the work force previously unemployed and underemployed groups such as women, teenagers, blacks, senior citizens, and the handicapped.

The war also gave labor unions a lift. Under the benevolent hand of government protection, unions rebounded from their sharp decline of the 1920s and early 1930s. Union membership jumped from 10.5 million to 14.75 million during the war. The WLB enforced "maintenance of membership" agreements in all shops with defense contracts. Newly hired workers had 15 days to resign from the union. If they did not, the company had to collect their union dues. This represented a compromise between management's insistence upon an open shop (workers could join or drop the union at will) and labor's demand for a closed shop (all employees had to belong to the union).

Despite these gains, labor unrest increased throughout the war. After Pearl Harbor union officials pledged not to strike until the war ended, but inflation and wage restrictions quickly eroded their goodwill. Work stoppages rose from 2960 in 1942 to 4956 in 1944, though most ended quickly and did not harm the war effort. In 1943, however, coal miners went on strike and railroad workers threatened to follow. According to John L. Lewis, the fiery president of the United Mine Workers, the reason for the strike was simple: The average mine worker earned only $1700 in 1942 (well below the national average) and deserved a raise.

Lewis won a hefty pay increase for his men. By 1944 their wages averaged $2535 a year, the first time in American history coal miners earned more than most manufacturing workers. Yet labor's victory did not come cheaply. Most Americans condemned strikes as unpatriotic, and Roosevelt considered drafting or jailing the strikers. Lewis had supported Wendell Willkie in 1940, so there was no love lost between the president and the union leader. Privately,

Roosevelt offered to resign as president if Lewis promised to commit suicide, but publicly Roosevelt was a model of restraint with labor leaders. After all, labor formed a vital element of the New Deal coalition.

In contrast to the president, Congress took a hostile stand toward labor. Over Roosevelt's veto, it passed the Smith-Connally Act, which banned strikes in war industries, authorized the president to seize plants useful to the war effort, and limited political activity by unions. "In doing so," declared *Time* magazine, "it dealt Franklin Roosevelt the most stinging rebuke of his entire career, his worst domestic defeat of World War II." The Smith-Connally Act failed to end labor unrest. The bill's supporters blamed strikes on a handful of unruly labor barons, but in reality the pressure for strikes came from rank-and-file workers.

The Smith-Connally Act reflected a resurgence of conservatism, both in Congress and in the country at large. Democratic voters failed to turn out in large numbers in the congressional elections of 1942, as full employment seemed to weaken blue-collar voting. In addition, Congress did not allow soldiers away from home to vote. Though the Democrats continued to maintain a thin majority in both houses of Congress throughout the war, a coalition of Republicans and conservative Democrats after 1942 could defeat any measure. Secretary of the Treasury Morgenthau spoke the truth when he complained: "I can get all my New Dealers in the bathtub now."

Beginning in 1943 Roosevelt's opponents led a successful attack against the New Deal, refusing to fund the Civilian Conservation Corps, the Works Progress Administration, the National Youth Administration, and the National Resources and Planning Board. According to conservatives, these agencies had dangerously expanded federal power and deserved to die.

Election of 1944

With reform in retreat, the Republicans expected to win the election of 1944. Thomas E. Dewey, the dapper young governor of New York, won his party's nomination on the first ballot. (Harold Ickes quipped that the 42-year-old Dewey had thrown his diaper into the ring.)

While Dewey accepted the New Deal as part of American life, he opposed its expansion. No distance separated the two major candidates on foreign affairs: Dewey supported Roosevelt's foreign policy initiatives.

Despite his declining health, Roosevelt easily captured his party's nomination for a fourth term. In March 1944 doctors discovered he suffered from high blood pressure, creating special concern about his choice of a running mate. He dumped Vice President Henry Wallace, the ardent internationalist who promised to build "the Century of the Common Man" after the war ended. As his replacement, Roosevelt selected Harry S Truman, the little known senator from Missouri who had chaired the Senate hearings on wartime industrial profits.

The campaign revitalized Roosevelt. After delivering a flurry of vague speeches about ending poverty at home, he unveiled plans for a "GI Bill of Rights," promising liberal unemployment benefits, educational support, medical care, and housing loans for veterans. Congress approved it overwhelmingly in 1944. Fearing a Democratic windfall, Republicans again rallied their forces to defeat a federal voting bill permitting soldiers to cast absentee ballots. A Bill Mauldin cartoon aptly captured the disappointment of GIs, as Willie consoled his buddy by saying, "That's okay, Joe, at least we can take bets."

The smart money backed FDR, as the president easily won reelection. Unwilling to switch leaders while at war, the public stuck with Roosevelt to see the crisis through. The president received 25,611,936 votes to Dewey's 22,013,372, and he won in the Electoral College by 432 to 99.

Molding Public Opinion

Having witnessed the mistakes of World War I, Roosevelt did not want government propaganda to arouse or fuel false hopes. Shortly before Pearl Harbor, he created the Office of Facts and Figures under Archibald MacLeish, the Librarian of Congress. A gentle poet, MacLeish became embroiled in bureaucratic struggles with government agencies, the armed services, and the Office of Strategic Services. By 1944 the government had all but abandoned its efforts to shape public opinion about the war.

Private enterprise filled the void. Movies, comic strips, newspapers, books, and advertisements reduced the war to a struggle between good and evil as the Allies engaged in mortal combat with Japan and Germany. The Japanese bore the brunt of the propaganda, especially during the first two years of fighting. Caricatured with thick glasses and huge buck teeth, public portraits of the Japanese grew more ugly and vicious as deeply ingrained racism fed the stereotypes, reviving old fears of the "yellow peril."

Germans, by contrast, elicited more complex attitudes in Americans, largely because racism did not inflame passions. At first, Americans blamed Hitler for the war. As eyewitness accounts of German atrocities began to filter back from the front, however, the public's views shifted. Gradually, Americans came to blame not just the Nazis, but all Germans for the war.

Motion pictures emerged as the most important instrument of propaganda during World War II, but Hollywood made little effort to confront the war's complexities. Instead, the industry churned out a series of simple morality plays. War films featured exhausted, shell-shocked troops who battled the enemy to the end. Movies such as *Back to Bataan, Thirty-Seconds over Tokyo,* and *Guadalcanal Diary* showed a few Americans outfighting Japanese hordes. Hollywood also produced sympathetic portraits of America's allies, including the sentimental *Mrs. Miniver,* which won seven Academy Awards in 1942. Hollywood produced 982 movies during the war, enough for three new movies each week at the neighborhood theater.

Popular culture both fed and reflected the public's desire to win the war and get the boys back. Soldiers abroad wanted to return to Mom, and, as one GI told cartoonist Bill Mauldin, to a "piece of blueberry pie." Mauldin's characters, Willie and Joe, fought because they had to. They did not talk about building a new world; all they wanted was to go home to the good life in America—baths, steaks, and wives.

SOCIAL CHANGES DURING THE WAR

World War II produced important changes in American life, some subtle, others profound.

"Joe, yestiddy ya saved my life an' I swore I'd pay ya back. Here's my last pair of dry socks."

Bill Mauldin's cartoon characters, Willie and Joe, were popular not only at home but also among soldiers abroad.

Above all it set families in motion, pulling them off farms, out of small towns, and packing them into large urban areas. Urbanization had virtually stopped during the depression, but the war saw the number of city dwellers leap from 46 to 53 percent.

War industries sparked the urban growth. Detroit's population exploded as the automotive industry switched to war vehicles. Washington, D.C., became another boomtown, as tens of thousands of new workers staffed the swelling ranks of the bureaucracy. The most dramatic growth occurred in California. Of the 15 million civilians who moved across state lines during the war, over 2 million went to California to work in defense industries.

Women

The war had a dramatic impact on women. Easily the most visible change involved the sudden appearance of large numbers of women in uni-form. The military organized women into auxiliary units with special uniforms, their own officers, and, amazingly, equal pay. By 1945 over 140,000 women had joined the Women's Army Corps (WAC); 60,000 the Army Nurses Corps; 100,000 the Women Accepted for Voluntary Emergency Service (WAVES); 14,000 the Navy Nurses Corps; 23,000 the marines; and 13,000 the Coast Guard. Most women who joined the armed services either filled traditional women's roles, such as nursing, or replaced men in noncombat jobs.

Women also substituted for men on the home front. For the first time in history married working women outnumbered single working women as 6.3 million women entered the work force during the war. Yet the majority of married women still did not work outside the home. Though women composed 37 percent of the civilian work force in 1945, only 22 percent of married women worked for wages. Nevertheless, the war challenged the conventional image of female behavior, as "Rosie the Riveter" became the popular symbol of women who abandoned traditional female occupations to work in defense industries.

Most observers expected women to retreat to the kitchen when the men returned home. Yet when the Women's Bureau surveyed working women in 1943, 70 percent said they hoped to keep their jobs after the war. Many women liked the economic freedom wages brought (sales of women's clothing doubled during the war), while others insisted they had to work to improve their family's standard of living, anticipating arguments for the two-income family after the war.

Women paid a high price for their economic independence. Outside employment did not free wives from domestic duties. The same women who put in full days in offices and factories went home to cook, clean, shop, and care for children. They had not one job, but two, and the only way they could fill both was to become "superwomen" who sacrificed relaxation, recreation, and sleep.

Yet not even a "superwoman" could be two places at once, which raised the question that troubled many Americans, "Who's minding the children?" A few industries, such as Kaiser Steel, offered day-care facilities, but most women had to make their own arrangements. Whether relatives or babysitters filled the void, child-care problems often arose, with a corresponding rise in the incidence of "latchkey" children.

Social critics had a field day attacking women. Social workers blamed working mothers for the rise in juvenile delinquency during the war, while other critics condemned women for their immodesty, self-indulgence, drinking, dress standards, and sexual promiscuity. "Choose any set of criteria you like," wrote the famous anthropologist Margaret Mead in 1946, "and the answer is the same: women and men are confused, uncertain and discontented with the present definition of women's place in America."

Amid this confusion, many women elected to cling to the familiar by embracing the traditional roles of housewives and mothers. From 1941 to 1945, the marriage rate oscillated between 93 and 105 per 1000 women between the ages of 17 and 29, well above the 89.1 for women of that age group during the "normal" years of 1925 to 1929. The birthrate increased, too, rebounding sharply from the all-time low of 18 to 19 per 1000 people during the depression. In 1943 the birthrate jumped to 22.7, and by 1946 it reached 25, where it remained with modest fluctuations for the rest of the decade. Overall, the "baby boom" did not signal a return to large families; rather, the birthrate rose because women married at younger ages and had their families earlier in life.

Hasty marriages between young partners often proved brittle. Wartime separations forced newlyweds to develop new roles and become self-reliant, and many couples later found it difficult to reestablish their relationships. Rather than remain in unhappy marriages, they often opted for divorce. In 1946 the American courts granted a record 600,000 divorces. By 1950 the divorce rate stood at one-quarter of the marriages, well above the prewar levels.

Yet Americans had not soured on marriage. The divorce rate had been climbing steadily (except during the depression years when many people could not afford to get married or divorced) since 1900. Furthermore, most Americans who divorced during the 1940s promptly remarried. They had rejected their mates, not marriage.

During the war, a growing number of women not only joined the armed services, but also helped out in the labor force at home by filling jobs normally held by men.

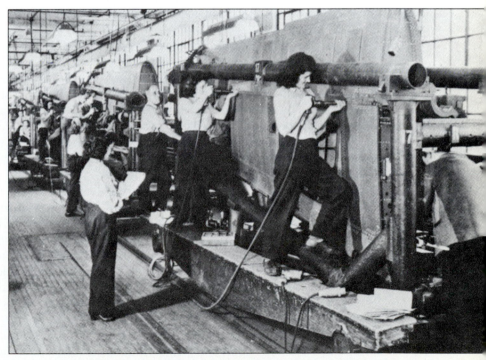

Minorities

World War II accelerated long-developing social trends for blacks. The war changed where many blacks lived and worked, as they moved to cities and found jobs in factories. Indeed, more than one million blacks migrated to the North during the war (twice the number who did so in World War I), and more than two million found work in defense industries. Yet blacks continued to be the last hired and the first fired, and other forms of discrimination remained blatant, especially in housing and employment.

Black leaders fought discrimination vigorously. In the spring of 1941 (months before America entered the war), the president of the Brotherhood of Sleeping Car Porters, A. Philip Randolph, with strong backing from the National Association for the Advancement of Colored People (NAACP), called for 150,000 blacks to march on Washington to protest discrimination in defense industries. Embarrassed and concerned, Roosevelt issued an executive order prohibiting discrimination in defense industries and creating the Fair Employment Practices Commission (FEPC). But the FEPC's tiny staff lacked the power and resources to enforce its decisions. During the war the FEPC did not even process most complaints, and contractors ignored 35 of the 45 compliance orders it issued.

Blacks fared no better in the public sector. Most blacks in the federal bureaucracy worked as janitors, and the armed services treated blacks as second-class citizens. The marines excluded blacks; the navy used them as servants; and the army created separate black regiments commanded mostly by white officers. The Red Cross even segregated blood plasma.

Not surprisingly, racial tensions deepened during the war. The number of black GIs rose from 100,000 in 1941 to 700,000 in 1944. Many joined the armed services hoping to find social mobility. Instead, they encountered segregation and discrimination. They resented white officials who denounced Nazi racism but remained silent about discrimination against blacks. Northern blacks stationed in the South found race relations shocking. Signs on buses in Charleston, South Carolina, read: "Avoid Friction. Be Patriotic. White passengers will be seated from front to rear, colored passengers from rear to front."

Conditions in the civilian sector were no better. As urban areas swelled with defense workers, housing and transportation shortages exacerbated racial tensions. In 1943 a riot broke out in Detroit in a federally sponsored housing project. Polish-Americans wanted blacks barred from the new apartments named, ironically, in honor of Sojourner Truth, the black abolitionist and poet. White soldiers from a nearby base joined the fighting, and other federal troops had to be brought in to disperse the mobs. The violence left 35 blacks and 9 whites dead.

Similar conflicts erupted across the nation, exposing in each instance the same jarring contradiction: White Americans espoused equality abroad but practiced discrimination at home. One black soldier told Swedish social scientist Gunnar Myrdal, "just carve on my tombstone, here lies a black man killed fighting a yellow man for the protection of a white man." A 1942 survey showed many black Americans sympathized with the Japanese struggle to expel white colonialists from the Far East. Significantly, the same survey revealed a majority of white industrialists in the South preferred a German victory to racial equality for blacks.

Many blacks responded to the rising tensions by joining civil rights organizations. During World War II, the NAACP intensified its legal campaign against discrimination, and its membership grew from 50,000 to 500,000 as large numbers of blacks and middle-class whites demanded racial equality.

Some blacks, however, considered the NAACP too slow and too conciliatory. Rejecting legal action, the Congress of Racial Equality (CORE), founded in 1942, organized a series of "sit-ins." Civil disobedience produced a few victories in the North, but the South's response was brutal. In Tennessee, for example, angry whites savagely beat Bayard Rustin, who became a prominent civil rights leader in the 1950s, for refusing to move to the back of the bus. While black activists won few gains during World War II, they forged new demands and tactics that shaped the civil rights movement after the war.

Federal officials did little to advance civil rights. Personally, Roosevelt sympathized with blacks, but he feared losing the Solid South's support if he moved too rapidly on the race issue. Thus, while he admitted black leaders to the White House to hear their grievances, Roosevelt seldom took action. Eleanor Roosevelt remained the conscience of the administration, voicing her sympathy for civil rights at every juncture, but the president refused to take the political risks needed to end discrimination and promote racial equality.

World War II affected Mexican-Americans no less than blacks. Almost 400,000 Mexican-Americans served in the armed forces. As soldiers, they expanded their contacts with Anglo society, visiting new parts of the country and meeting for the first time large groups of people who held few prejudices against them. For Mexican-Americans in the civilian sector, jobs in industry provided an escape hatch from the desperate poverty of migratory farm labor. In New Mexico, for example, about one-fifth of the rural Mexican-American population left for war-related jobs.

The need for farm workers rose dramatically after Pearl Harbor. To meet the demand, the United States established the *bracero* (work hands) program in 1942, and by 1945 several hundred thousand Mexican workers had immigrated to the Southwest. Commercial farmers welcomed them, but labor unions resented the competition, leading to animosity and discrimination against Mexicans and Mexican-Americans alike.

In Los Angeles, ethnic tensions erupted into violence. Anglo society both feared and resented newly formed Mexican-American youth gangs, whose members celebrated their ethnicity by wearing flamboyant "zoot suits" and by tattooing their left hands. In June 1943 hundreds of Anglo sailors on liberty from nearby naval bases invaded downtown Los Angeles. Eager to put down the Mexican-American youths, they attacked the "zooters" and riots broke out for several nights. The local press blamed Mexican-American gangs, and the riots did not end until military police ordered sailors back to their ships.

Despite the outbursts of violence and discrimination, World War II benefited the poor of all races. Thanks to full employment and progressive taxation, people at the bottom saw income redistributed in their favor. Americans who occupied the top 5 percent economically saw their share of disposable income fall from 23 percent in 1939 to 17 percent in 1945. Before the war there were 12 families with an income under $2000 for every family with an income over $5000; after the war the ratio was almost even. Still, the gains made by poor people came from the state of the economy (the need for soldiers and workers), not from federal policies or the efforts of organized labor.

Fear of Enemy Aliens

On December 8, 1941, Roosevelt issued an executive order regarding enemy aliens. It suspended naturalization proceedings for Italians, Germans, and Japanese immigrants, required them to register, restricted their mobility, and prohibited them from owning items that might be used for sabotage, such as cameras and shortwave radios. In practice, however, the government did not accord enemy aliens the same treatment: Italian and German aliens received lenient treatment, while Japanese aliens suffered gross injustices.

Approximately 600,000 Italian aliens lived in the United States in 1940. In general, the government treated them well throughout the war, administering the enemy alien laws with compassion. On Columbus Day, 1942 (just before the congressional elections), Roosevelt lifted the enemy alien designation for Italians and established simplified naturalization procedures. Moreover, German aliens received similar treatment. Though less numerous (264,000) and not as politically important to the Democrats, Roosevelt's administration treated them fairly throughout the war.

Jewish refugees complicated the German question. Reflecting a nasty strain of anti-Semitism, Congress in 1939 refused to raise immigration quotas to admit 20,000 Jewish children fleeing Nazi oppression. As the wife of the U.S. commissioner of immigration remarked at a cocktail party, "20,000 children would all too soon grow up to be 20,000 ugly adults."

Instead of relaxing immigration quotas, American officials worked in vain to persuade Latin American countries and Great Britain to admit Jewish refugees. Other officials, such as

Assistant Secretary of State Breckinridge Long, the chief administrator for immigration policy, insisted that winning the war offered the best means for rescuing European Jews. Bitterly anti-Semitic in his private views, Long argued that any relaxation of the quota system would permit Nazi spies to slip into the country along with legitimate refugees.

While the futile debates dragged on, Hitler's death camps killed helpless victims at the rate of 2000 an hour. As late as 1944, American officials who knew the ghastly truth publicly downplayed reports of genocide in the press. Air reconnaissance missions had taken scores of photographs of the death camp at Auschwitz, and military intelligence officers had learned the locations of several other concentration camps.

Nazi Concentration Camps

Finally, in January 1944, Secretary of the Treasury Henry Morgenthau, forced the issue to a head. The only Jew in the Cabinet, Morgenthau presented to Roosevelt the "Report to the Secretary on the Acquiescence of this Government in the Murder of the Jews." Shamed into action, Roosevelt created the War Refugee Board, which, in turn, set up refugee camps in Italy, North Africa, and the United States. But America's response offered too little, too late. During the 18 months of the War Refugee Board's existence, Hitler killed far more Jews than the War Refugee Board saved.

Like Jews, Japanese-Americans got a bitter taste of discrimination during World War II. Barred from immigrating to the United States by the Immigration Act of 1924, they comprised a tiny portion of the population in 1941, totaling no more than 260,000 people, of whom 150,000 lived in Hawaii, with the remaining 110,000 concentrated on the West Coast, where they worked mostly as small farmers or businesspeople serving the Japanese community. After Pearl Harbor, rumors spread about Japanese troops preparing to land in California, where

they allegedly planned to link up with Japanese-Americans and Japanese aliens poised to strike as a fifth column for the invasion.

On February 19, 1942, Roosevelt authorized the Department of War to designate military areas and to exclude any or all persons from them. Armed with this power, military authorities immediately moved against Japanese aliens. In Hawaii, where residents of Japanese ancestry formed a large portion of the population and where the local economy depended on their labor, the military did not force Japanese-Americans to relocate. On the West Coast, however, military authorities ordered the Japanese to leave, drawing no distinction between aliens and citizens. Forced to sell their property for pennies on the dollar, most Japanese-Americans suffered severe financial losses. Relocation proved next to impossible, as no other states would take them. The governor of Idaho opposed any migration, declaring: "The Japs live like rats, breed like rats and act like rats. We don't want them."

When voluntary measures failed, Roosevelt created the War Relocation Authority. It resettled 100,000 Japanese-Americans in ten camps scattered across seven western states. Called relocation camps, they resembled minimum security prisons. In these concentration camps, American citizens who had committed no crimes were locked behind barbed wire, crowded into ramshackle wooden barracks where they lived one family to a room furnished with nothing but cots and bare light bulbs, forced to endure bad food, inadequate medical care, and poorly equipped schools.

Japanese-American Internment Camps

Nearly 18,000 Japanese-American men won release from those camps to fight for the United States Army. Most served with the 100th Infantry Battalion and the 442nd Regimental Combat Team. In Italy, the 442nd sustained nearly 10,000 casualties, with 3600 Purple Hearts, 810 Bronze Stars, 342 Silver Stars, 123 divisional citations, 47 Distinguished Service Crosses, 17 Legions of Merit, 7 Presidential Unit Citations, and 1 Congressional Medal of Honor. In short, they fought heroically, emerging as the most decorated military unit in World War II. In one of the most painful scenes in American history, Japanese-American parents, still locked inside concentration camps, received posthumous Purple Hearts for their sons.

Japanese-Americans protested their treatment, claiming numerous civil rights violations. Citing national security considerations, the Supreme Court backed the government six to three in *Korematsu* v. *U.S.* (1944). But in a dissenting opinion, Frank Murphy admitted federal policy had fallen "into the ugly abyss of racism." On December 18, 1944, in the *Endo* case, the Supreme Court ruled a civilian agency, the War Relocation Authority, had no right to incarcerate law-abiding citizens. Two weeks later the federal government began closing down the camps, ending one of the most shameful chapters in American history.

THE WAR IN EUROPE

The Grand Alliance

Following Pearl Harbor, the Axis Powers of Germany, Japan, and Italy faced the Grand Alliance, composed of the United States, Great Britain, Free France, and the Soviet Union. Yet from the beginning the Grand Alliance was an uneasy coalition, born of necessity and filled with tension. Apart from the need to defeat the enemy, the Allies found it difficult to agree on anything.

Great Britain's gaze fell on Europe, where Churchill approached international affairs in spheres-of-influence, balance-of-power terms. He wanted the war to weaken all the other continental powers, allowing Great Britain to play a major role in redrawing the postwar map of Europe, especially in Poland and the Balkans, where the British hoped to erect a barrier against Soviet expansion. In addition, Churchill intended for Britain to emerge from the war with her empire intact.

France's goals reflected the vision of one man—General Charles de Gaulle. Above all, de Gaulle wanted to restore France to greatness. By nature aloof, enigmatic, suspicious, and

Japanese-Americans of all ages, tagged like pieces of luggage, awaited their relocation to one of ten detention camps in seven western states. This family was from Hayward, California.

stubborn, he was equally charismatic and forceful. Like Churchill, he fought to retain his country's empire, and as the war progressed American officials came to regard de Gaulle as a political extremist. In policy disputes, he often sided with Britain to oppose American and Soviet demands.

Joseph Stalin spoke for the Soviet Union. The son of a cobbler, Stalin rose to power by crushing all political rivals during the turbulent years following the Bolshevik revolution. Iron-willed, deeply paranoid, and bold as a thief, "Uncle Joe" enjoyed a well-deserved reputation as a formidable negotiator. Throughout World War II, he pressed for a postwar settlement that would guarantee the Soviet Union's future security and open new lands for communism. To protect the Soviet Union from future attacks, Stalin insisted upon Germany's total destruction. As additional insurance, he demanded parts of Poland and Finland and all of the Baltic states. Eastern Europe would then form a buffer against future aggression from the West, provide colonies for rebuilding the Soviet economy, and add new territory to the communist world map.

Roosevelt had his own ideas about how the world should look after the war. In broad terms, he opposed colonialism and the spread of communism; and he supported open markets, democratic elections to counter spheres of influence, and a new League of Nations to promote world peace. Among these objectives, anticolonialism and support for free markets were his top priorities, and both goals reflected Roosevelt's remarkable ability to join political principle with economic advantage.

No less than his counterparts, Roosevelt's personality shaped his policies. Of all the Allied leaders he had the most exaggerated sense of his abilities as a diplomat. The basic problem was his temperament. Because he disliked the rough and tumble of hard bargaining, Roosevelt tried to avoid clashes with other leaders by postponing difficult decisions and by relying too heavily on his personal charm. In addition, Roosevelt's pragmatic approach to problem solving made him seek compromises whenever possible, which meant that he often sacrificed principles in order to preserve Allied cooperation.

From the outset, then, dissent riddled the Grand Alliance. In pursuit of its own national interest, each ally had a separate agenda, its own set of demands, and its own vision of the how the world map should look when the war ended. Given these conflicts, the Allies could look forward not to harmony but to clashes over military strategy throughout the war, bitter debates over peace terms at the war's end, and decades of international strife in the postwar era.

Early Axis Victories

After Pearl Harbor, the United States had to prepare for global war. Before the conflict ended, the United States had troops and supplies scattered around the world. The war would cost America one million casualties, and over 300,000 deaths. The financial price was equally high: $350 billion in all—about $250 million a day at the peak of the fighting.

During the first six months of combat Japan looked unbeatable. Japanese forces captured Guam, Wake Island, the Philippines, Hong Kong, and Malaya and slashed deep into Burma, cutting the Burma Road, China's lifeline to the West. General Douglas MacArthur, though vowing to return, was driven from the Philippines

in March 1942. In a matter of months Japanese troops had conquered a vast expanse extending from the Gilbert Islands through the Solomons and from New Guinea to Burma, leaving India and Australia vulnerable to attack.

Nor did the Allied cause look any brighter in Europe. During the first ten months of 1942, German submarines sank over 500 American merchant ships. With its lend-lease supplies threatened, Great Britain stood in danger of collapsing before the United States could mobilize. On the Russian front, German troops pressed toward Stalingrad, making short work of Stalin's divisions in their path. The news from North Africa was equally bleak. On May 26, 1942, German Field Marshal Erwin Rommel, the famous "Desert Fox," began his sweep toward the Suez Canal. A brilliant strategist, he slashed almost to Alexandria before the British managed to halt him.

In short, World War II opened badly for the Allies. Axis victories in the Pacific, Europe, and Africa served notice the war would be long and costly.

Stemming the German Tide

Roosevelt decided to assign Germany top priority for two reasons: First, he doubted Hitler could be dislodged from Europe if Britain fell; and, second, Roosevelt wanted to placate Stalin. Throughout the war, Stalin remained suspicious, fearing his allies planned to let Germans and Russians kill one another off so both nations would emerge from the war as second-rate powers. As the Germans drove deep into Soviet territory in 1942, Stalin demanded a second front in France to force Germany to divide her armies, thereby relieving some of the pressure on the Soviet Union. As one observer remarked, Soviet Foreign Minister V. M. Molotov knew only four words of English: "yes," "no," and "second front."

By the autumn of 1942 the tide was beginning to turn on the eastern front. In September Germany lost 12 divisions at Stalingrad, and in November the Red Army launched a furious counterattack, beginning the long drive to push the Germans back across the Ukraine. Despite Soviet victories and Stalin's repeated pleas for a second front, the Allies, at Churchill's insistence, decided to attack the Germans in North

World War II, European Theater

Map legend:
- Axis Powers before World War II
- Extent of Axis control early Nov. 1942
- Allies
- Neutral nations
- Allied troop movements
- Major battles

Africa instead of France. Stalin saw this as a betrayal and his suspicions deepened.

Allied victories in Africa seemed to confirm Churchill's wisdom. British Field Marshal Sir Bernard Montgomery drove the Germans back to Tunis in October, and in November 1942 General Dwight David Eisenhower led a force of 400,000 Allied soldiers in a full-scale invasion of North Africa (Operation TORCH). The German and Italian forces fought bravely. By the end of the campaign the Axis armies had lost 349,000 soldiers killed or captured, while the Allies had suffered only 70,000 casualties. Complete victory in North Africa came on May 12, 1943, when the remnants of the Axis armies surrendered. Germany and Italy had suffered a major defeat and Allied shipping could now cross the Mediterranean in safety.

Cheered by the North African victory, Allied leaders paused to select the next target. In January 1943 Churchill and Roosevelt met in Casablanca, French Morocco, without Stalin, who was invited but refused to attend, explaining he could not leave the Soviet Union at this critical juncture of the war. Haunted by ghastly memories of World War I and fearing a premature invasion of France might bog down into trench-style warfare, Churchill pushed hard for an attack on Sicily and then Italy. The United States initially opposed the plan (Operation HUSKY), arguing it would delay the invasion of France without accomplishing any decisive results, but Churchill prevailed. As one American military advisor remarked at the time: "We came, we listened, and we were conquered."

With the promised invasion of France again put on hold, Churchill and Roosevelt moved to reassure Stalin. The Casablanca conference yielded a renewed pledge for a second front in Europe, and Roosevelt and Churchill vowed to make peace with the Axis powers only on the basis of unconditional surrender. While the two leaders announced their "unconditional surrender" agreement to the public on the last day of the conference, they kept Stalin in the dark for several months about other agreements reached at Casablanca, including their decision to postpone the second front.

Sicily fell in August 1943 after a campaign of slightly more than a month. Shortly before its surrender, Italian dissidents, anticipating an Allied invasion of their homeland, deposed Mussolini and placed him under arrest. (German paratroopers later rescued Mussolini in a daring assault and installed him as head of the Italian government in German-occupied Italy.) To head Italy's new government, King Victor Emmanuel III then appointed Marshal Pietro Badoglio, an old fascist who had led the Italian invasion of Ethiopia. Under Badoglio, Italy promptly surrendered on September 8, 1943, immediately switched sides, and declared war on Germany.

The Allied victory in Italy did not come cheaply. The terrain was mountainous, and the Germans offered savage resistance. Though the Italian campaign secured the Mediterranean,

depleted German troops, and secured air bases for flights over central Europe, Stalin deeply resented the commitment of Allied troops there instead of France. Furthermore, he held Badoglio in contempt and opposed his sudden rehabilitation as an ally. Did Churchill and Roosevelt intend to allow other former Fascists to head Allied-dominated governments?

Stalin's protests fell on deaf ears. Since Soviet troops had not fought in the Italian campaign, Roosevelt and Churchill refused to permit Stalin to participate in organizing an occupation government in Italy. Stalin learned his lesson well. The next time he wanted a voice in a region he made certain to have his armies on site.

Meanwhile, Soviet troops were winning the war on the eastern front. By October 1943 they had recorded stunning victories at Leningrad and Stalingrad. American aid did not arrive in time to help win these victories, but American weapons, vehicles, clothing, and food contributed mightily to subsequent Soviet offensives. Keeping the Soviets supplied was no longer a problem because the Allies had won the Battle of the Atlantic. Radar, air patrols, and destroyer escorts neutralized the German submarines, lowering shipping losses from 514,744 tons in March 1943 to 199,409 tons in May.

The Teheran Conference

In November 1943 Roosevelt, Churchill, and Stalin held their first face-to-face conference, meeting in Teheran, the capital of Iran. Buoyed by military success, Stalin sounded conciliatory as they discussed the long-awaited second front and the shape of the postwar world. In response to Stalin's demands, the leaders set May 1944 as the target date for Operation OVERLORD, the code name for the invasion of France. To increase the odds for success, Stalin promised to coordinate Russia's spring offensive with the invasion.

Once the leaders turned to postwar issues, however, the conference dissolved into bitter controversy. Stalin demanded Soviet control over Eastern Europe and insisted Germany be divided into several weak states. Opposing both demands, Churchill proposed democratic governments for Eastern Europe, especially in Poland, for which England had gone to war. He wanted no part of dismembering Germany, arguing the balance of power in postwar Europe required a united Germany. Moreover, while he fought Stalin over Eastern Europe, Churchill bristled at any criticism of Britain's plans to retain her colonies.

Roosevelt played the conciliator at Teheran. He agreed to the partition of Germany, and he did not press Stalin over Eastern Europe. Though he supported Churchill's position, Roosevelt knew Stalin had the inside track in Eastern Europe. Convinced he could handle "Uncle Joe," Roosevelt decided to leave territorial questions to a postwar international organization dominated by the victors. Apart from reaching agreement on the second front, the Teheran Conference merely aired the leaders' conflicting demands.

Liberating Europe

In preparation for the invasion, the Allies instituted saturation bombing, dropping 2,697,473 tons of bombs on German territory, killing 305,000 civilians, and damaging over 5.5 million homes. The Allies paid a high price for these air raids. In a single week in February 1944 the Americans lost 226 bombers and 2600 crewmen. All told, Allied airmen suffered 158,000 fatalities. While the air raids were supposed to wipe out the German war machine and break the people's will to resist, the bombs often missed military targets and killed innocent civilians. Missions such as the firebombing of Dresden, which killed 100,000 people, made many Germans believe Hitler's ravings about the evil Allies. In truth, the air raids stiffened Germany's will to fight.

As the bombers pounded Germany the Allies prepared for the invasion. Over 3 million soldiers massed in England under the command of General Dwight D. Eisenhower, a careful strategist who had a gift for soothing the sensitive egos of other Allied commanders. D-Day came on June 6, 1944. After two weeks of desperate fighting on the beaches of Normandy, the Allies began to push inland. Quickly achieving air mastery, they broke out of the bottleneck on the Normandy peninsula at the end of June. A month later Allied troops were sweeping across

Europe in a race for Berlin. They liberated Paris in August, and by mid-September Allied forces had crossed the German border.

True to his word, Stalin synchronized his spring offensive with the invasion. Soviet troops engaged the Germans in furious combat all across Eastern Europe, tying up men and materials that otherwise could have been hurled against the Allies. Indeed, Stalin's forces battled three German divisions for every single German division that opposed the invasion from the west.

On December 16, 1944, German troops launched a massive counteroffensive. Allied commanders had concentrated their forces north and south of the Ardennes Forest in eastern France, leaving the forest itself lightly defended. The Battle of the Bulge opened with German armored divisions slashing 60 miles through the gap to the Franco-Belgian border. The American 101st Airborne Division, joined by other units, held them off at Bastogne until General George Patton's Third Army moved in for the kill. When the battle ended, the Americans had suffered 77,000 casualties while inflicting 120,000 on the Germans.

Meanwhile, the eastern front had turned into a rout. By January 1945 Soviet troops had captured Warsaw, and by February they were within 45 miles of Berlin.

The Yalta Conference

With victory in Europe at hand, Roosevelt, Churchill, and Stalin met in February 1945 at Yalta, a resort on the Russian Black Sea, to settle the shape of the postwar world. They quickly concurred on the partition of Germany, including a zone for French occupation, but there the agreement stopped. They clashed bitterly over Soviet demands for the dismemberment of Germany and stiff reparation payments. Stalin wanted $20 billion in reparations, half of which would go to Russia. Churchill opposed him, rejecting any plan that would leave Germany financially prostrate after the war.

Eastern Europe was the most divisive issue at Yalta. As early as December 1941, Stalin had told the British he would join an anti-German alliance only if England would sanction Soviet control over the Baltic states (Estonia, Lithuania, and Latvia), as well as portions of Finland, Poland, and Romania. In October 1944 Stalin and Churchill met secretly in Moscow to strike a deal on Eastern Europe. Unbeknownst to Roosevelt, they agreed to divide Eastern Europe into British and Soviet spheres for the duration of the war. The Soviet Union would dominate Romania, Great Britain would control Greece, and the two great powers would exercise joint authority over Yugoslavia.

Stalin kept his part of the bargain. In December 1944, amid fierce street fighting in Athens to drive out Axis troops, British and Greek troops suddenly turned their guns on the Greek Communists who had been their allies. Stalin did not lift a finger to prevent the slaughter. No doubt he expected Churchill to repay his restraint over Greece by supporting his designs on Eastern Europe.

At Yalta Stalin laid claim to eastern Poland. To compensate Poland and to weaken Germany, he demanded a large chunk of Germany for Poland. Reminding Churchill and Roosevelt of how he had been barred from playing any role in Italy, Stalin served notice the shoe was now on the other foot. He would not tolerate any interference in Eastern Europe.

Confronted by Roosevelt's and Churchill's bitter opposition, however, Stalin grudgingly agreed to a face-saving compromise: Poland would hold free elections, and any new government formed there would include democratic elements. Yet as one of Roosevelt's chief military advisors warned the president, Stalin tacked so many amendments onto the Polish agreement the Soviets "could stretch it all the way from Yalta to Washington without technically breaking it." Moreover, the three leaders agreed to consult and make unanimous decisions before taking any action in Eastern Europe. In other words, Stalin won a veto over the Western powers in Eastern Europe.

The remaining issues at Yalta proved less troublesome. Stalin promised to enter the war against Japan within three months after Germany surrendered, and he renewed his pledge to join the United Nations. Roosevelt considered both concessions important victories because he wanted Soviet help in defeating Japan and because he remained hopeful the United Nations could negotiate peaceful solutions to the

(Text continues on p. 892)

LANDINGS ON D-DAY:
The Longest Day

For the Allies in World War II, the D-Day landing of June 6, 1944, was the long-planned, long-anticipated blow against Nazi Germany. Originally scheduled for 1942, it had been pushed back first to 1943 and finally to 1944. Although both the Soviet Union and impatient Americans had clamored for an earlier invasion, Prime Minister Winston Churchill of Great Britain, who remembered the difficulties of Dunkirk, counseled caution.

The cross-channel invasion was a risky proposition and an immense undertaking. During early 1944 the Allies moved thousands of aircraft, tanks, trucks, jeeps, and men into southeastern England, moving soldiers to joke that if the invasion was long postponed, England would tilt and sink into the Channel. Then there were the imponderables that defied careful planning: weather, visibility, the state of the Channel.

As much as possible General Dwight D. Eisenhower, who was the overall commander of the invasion, tried to deceive the Germans into believing that the invasion would take place at the Pas de Calais, around Boulogne, Calais, and Dunkirk. It appears that Hitler did believe that the Allies would strike at the Pas de Calais. Instead, Ike centered his attack further to the west, along the French coast between Cherbourg and Le Havre. Altogether, the Allies assaulted five beaches and dropped paratroopers and airborne infantry into three sites.

Further east, British paratroopers were given the task of securing the left flank by gaining control of the Orne River. American paratroopers were given the job of securing the right flank along the Merderet River. In between these two points, the Allies landed on five beaches: Sword (British), Juno (Canadian), Gold (British), Omaha (American), and Utah (American). All totaled, 2,876,000 soldiers, sailors, and airmen; 11,000 aircraft; and over 2000 vessels played a role in the invasion.

At several beaches, especially Utah, the Allies met little opposition. At others, notably Omaha, the story was different and losses were heavy. More than 2000 Americans were killed or wounded securing Omaha beach on June 6. But by the end of that "longest day" the Allies had accomplished their goal. They were back in France and ready to move east toward Germany.

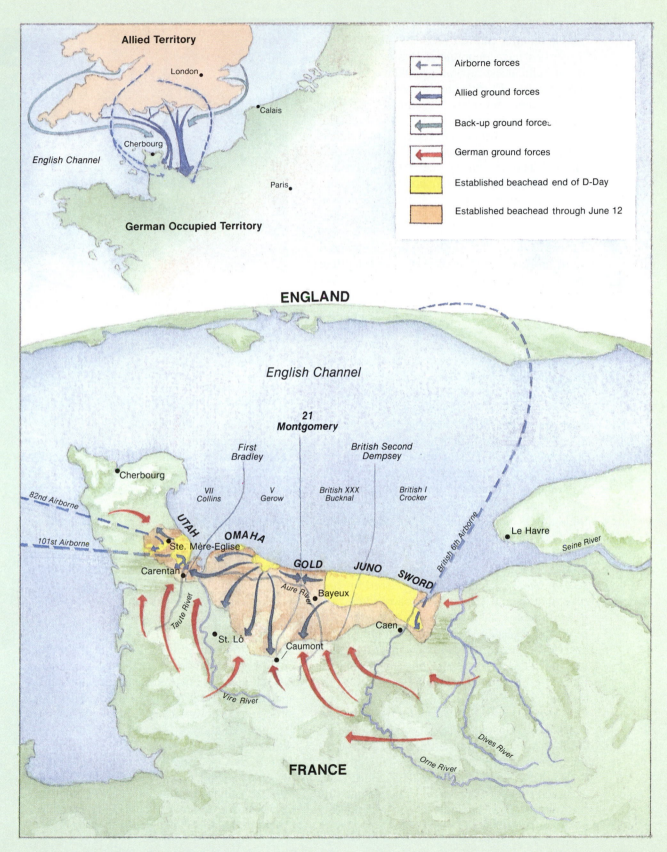

Allied Territory

London

Calais

Cherbourg

English Channel

German Occupied Territory

Paris

Airborne forces

Allied ground forces

Back-up ground forces

German ground forces

Established beachhead end of D-Day

Established beachhead through June 12

ENGLAND

English Channel

21
Montgomery

First
Bradley

British Second
Dempsey

VII
Collins

V
Gerow

British XXX
Bucknal

British I
Crocker

Cherbourg

82nd Airborne

101st Airborne

British 6th Airborne

Le Havre

Seine River

UTAH

OMAHA

Ste. Mère-Eglise

GOLD

JUNO

SWORD

Carentan

Aure River

Bayeux

Caen

Taute River

St. Lô

Caumont

Vire River

Dives River

Orne River

FRANCE

disputes between the United States and the Soviet Union after the war ended.

Critics have denounced Roosevelt for his role at Yalta, insisting Stalin would have surrendered Eastern Europe had Roosevelt held firm. This argument seriously discounts the strength of Stalin's commitment to future security. In the words of one psychologist, the Soviets reduced all reality to the "searing experience of World War II." The war destroyed 1700 towns and 70,000 villages; it left 25 million Soviets homeless. The Soviet military sustained 7.5 million casualties, and another 10 million civilians died in the fighting. More than 600,000 Soviets starved to death during the siege of Leningrad alone, and more Soviets died at Stalingrad than the United States lost in all theaters of the war combined.

When Stalin arrived at Yalta, Soviet troops (not American troops) had occupied Eastern Europe, and he refused to lose at the conference table what he had won on the battlefield. Given his obsession with protecting his homeland from future attacks, Stalin was not about to vacate Eastern Europe without a fight, and most Americans did not want to declare war on the Soviet Union. Looking back at Yalta, Churchill remarked, "Our hopeful assumptions were soon to be falsified. Still, they were the only ones possible at the time."

Allied victories came rapidly after the Battle of the Bulge. On March 4, American troops reached the Rhine River, and in April they joined forces with the Soviet army 60 miles south of Berlin. After Roosevelt's death on April 12, however, Stalin immediately tested the new president, Harry S Truman. Stalin ordered the execution of democratic leaders in Eastern Europe and replaced them with Communist governments. Truman deplored Stalin's disregard for the Yalta agreements, but like Roosevelt he refused to fight the Soviets to save Eastern Europe.

Despite his anger, Truman ignored Churchill's pleas to occupy Prague and Berlin before the Red Army. Instead, he followed General Eisenhower's advice about finishing off Germany. On April 22 Soviet troops reached Berlin and occupied the city after house-to-house fighting. On April 30 Hitler committed suicide, and Germany surrendered one week later. On May 8,

Stalin, Roosevelt, and Churchill met at Yalta in February 1945 to discuss the state of the postwar world.

1945, the Allies celebrated V-E (Victory in Europe) Day.

THE WAR IN THE PACIFIC

Though Europe received top priority, American forces managed to halt Japanese advances in the Pacific by late summer of 1942. Two decisive naval battles, Coral Sea and Midway, turned the tide. In May, a Japanese troop convoy sailed into the Coral Sea between New Guinea and Australia to capture Port Moresby. The U.S. Navy intercepted and destroyed the convoy, preventing the attack and forcing Japan to shelve her plans for invading Australia.

Island Hopping

In June 1942, at Midway Island in the Central Pacific, the Japanese launched an aircraft carrier offensive to cut American communications and isolate Hawaii to the east. American naval intelligence, however, had finally broken the Japanese military code and Admiral Chester Nimitz's ships were ready. The battle began on June 3, and by June 6, the Japanese had lost three destroyers, a heavy cruiser, and four carriers. The Americans lost one carrier (the *Yorktown*) and a destroyer. The Battle of Midway broke the back of Japan's navy.

On August 7, 1942, the 1st Marine Division attacked Guadalcanal in the Solomon Islands. Marines captured the air strip on Guadalcanal, and in February, following months of bloody fighting, they drove the Japanese troops into the sea, securing the Allied supply line to Australia. In addition, the victory at Guadalcanal protected the Allies' eastern flank, allowing General Douglas MacArthur, commander of southwest Pacific forces, to continue his march through New Guinea back to the Philippines.

Japanese advances in China proved more difficult to halt. While Allied troops had to cut a new road through the mountainous terrain of Burma to supply Chiang Kai-shek's army, the real problems stemmed from China's civil war. Chiang fought harder against the Communist forces headed by Mao Tse-tung than he did against the Japanese. Lieutenant General Joseph W. Stilwell ("Vinegar Joe"), the head of Allied forces in China, became so disillusioned he nicknamed Chiang "Peanut," but Roosevelt continued to regard Chiang as a strong ruler, destined to lead a powerful country.

Despite setbacks in China, the Allies won major victories in the South Pacific, where they squeezed Japan from two directions. In the southwest Pacific, General MacArthur seized Lae on the northern coast of New Guinea in September 1943. Then, instead of assaulting Japanese strong points head-on, he leapfrogged up the coast, capturing isolated positions and forcing Japanese troops to abandon their fortifications to attack. Japanese commanders ex-

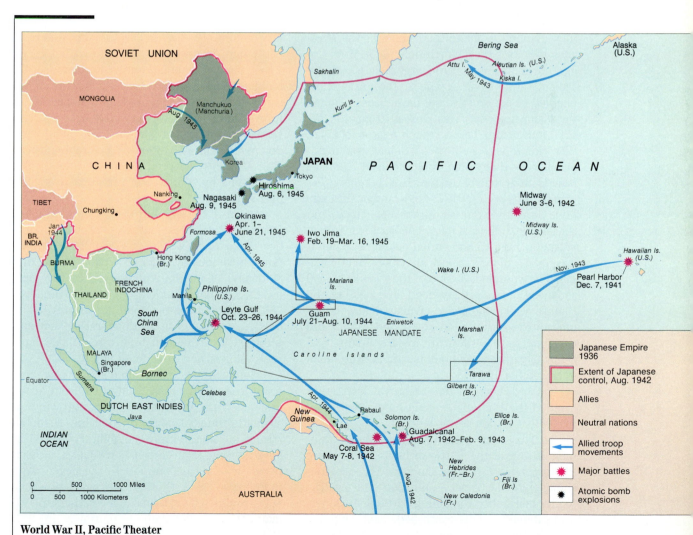

World War II, Pacific Theater

pected MacArthur to assault their impregnable 100,000-man fortress at Rabaul on New Britain. Instead, he cut its supply lines and bypassed it. By July 1944 MacArthur's forces controlled all of New Guinea.

Meanwhile, Admiral Chester Nimitz's naval and marine forces in the Central Pacific were "island hopping" toward Japan, capturing important positions, building airstrips, and then moving on to the next island. Their first target was the Gilbert Islands. In late November 1943, the marines attacked Tarawa, a tiny island 3 miles long and 600 yards wide. In the bloody 3-day battle that followed, Japanese troops fought to the death, inflicting 3301 casualties on American marines.

With the Gilberts secured, Nimitz invaded the Marshall Islands in February 1944. The Japanese offered only light resistance because they planned to make their stand at the Marianas Islands, prizes worth defending. Here the fighting centered on three large islands, Saipan, Tinian, and Guam, which the Americans planned to use as advance naval bases. Saipan, the major objective, was closest to Japan. Only 1200 miles from Tokyo (much nearer to Japan than Hawaii is to California), Saipan could supply airbases that would bring the main Japanese islands into range of the new B-29 bombers. Determined to protect their homeland against airraids, Japanese commanders resolved to defend the islands to the last man. The battle for Saipan began on June 15 and ended on July 9. When it was over, 14,000 American troops had been killed or wounded, 30,000 of the island's 32,000 Japanese defenders lay dead, and 6000 of the island's 12,000 Japanese civilians had committed suicide rather than surrender. Tinian and Guam fell to the Americans in early August, and B-29s began regular bombing raids over Japan in November 1944.

On October 21, 1944, General MacArthur invaded the Philippines, splashing ashore with the 96th Division for the benefit of photographers. That same month the navy won a stunning victory at the Battle of Leyte Gulf, where the Japanese lost four carriers, three battleships, eight destroyers, and nine cruisers, virtually their entire remaining battle fleet. American submarines now controlled Pacific shipping lanes, sealing the Japanese Islands off from mil-itary and food supplies. In January, Allied forces invaded Luzon, the main island of the Philippines, and Allied troops claimed victory five months later. All told 240,000 Japanese soldiers died in the fighting.

While MacArthur was reclaiming the Philippines, Nimitz was bearing down on Iwo Jima. Its capture would enable fighter planes to link up with B-29s heading out of the Marianas, providing fighter escorts for their raids on Japan. The 3d, 4th, and 5th Marine Divisions attacked Iwo Jima in February 1945, and by early March the island fell into American hands. Four thousand marines died in the battle.

With Iwo Jima safely under American control, fighter planes joined the B-29s over Japan, allowing bomber squadrons to reduce armaments and increase bombloads. American commanders made a strategic decision to shift to firebombing. By the end of the war American pilots had dropped 160,000 tons of bombs on Japan. Japan's population density, combustible building materials, and limited industrial capacity made firebombing more effective than in Europe. Bombs killed over 330,000 civilians (86,000 in the firebombing of Tokyo alone) and destroyed over 40 percent of the buildings in 65 cities. Japan's war production fell dramatically: oil refining by 83 percent and aircraft engines by 75 percent.

On April 1, 1945, American troops attacked Okinawa, 350 miles southwest of Japan. Japanese resistance was fierce. Kamikaze attacks (suicide flights by Japanese pilots) rose dramatically. Of the 4000 planes lost by the Japanese at Okinawa, kamikaze missions numbered 2800. Japan's soldiers fought just as bravely. Indeed, many fought to the death rather than surrender. Okinawa fell in June, after 70,000 Japanese soldiers had died defending it.

Confronted with certain defeat, many moderate leaders in Japan wanted to avoid an invasion. With the peace party growing in strength, Hideki Tojo resigned in July 1944, but strong factions within the military vowed to keep fighting. In an effort to save Japan, the Emperor switched his support to the peace party in February 1945. He then sent out peace feelers to Stalin, who in turn conveyed them to Truman at the Potsdam Conference in July 1945.

Truman and the Dawn of the Atomic Age

Few presidents have been asked to conduct diplomacy with less preparation than Harry S Truman. He had risen to power as a loyal machine politician in Kansas City. As vice president and former senator from Missouri he knew next to nothing about foreign affairs. Roosevelt had kept Truman largely in the dark, neither seeking his counsel nor confiding in him. When Roosevelt's death elevated him to the White House, Truman told reporters: "I felt like the moon, the stars, and all planets had fallen on me." Yet Truman brought certain assets to the challenge. A man who possessed the courage of his convictions, he fully intended to be a strong president and to make decisions resolutely.

Truman's first test came at Potsdam, a suburb of Berlin, where the Allied leaders convened in July 1945 for their last wartime meeting. Though new to the job, Truman had been in office long enough to believe Roosevelt had been too soft on Stalin. Truman viewed Stalin as a liar and a bully who only understood force. Yet like his predecessor Truman did not wish to risk a showdown over Eastern Europe, largely because his military advisors insisted the United States still needed the Soviet Union's help against Japan.

While Truman stopped short of picking a fight over Eastern Europe, he pushed Stalin hard at Potsdam. During the negotiations, Truman received word American scientists had successfully tested the first atomic bomb. Hoping to impress Stalin, Truman told him in a conversation one evening the United States now possessed a new weapon of awesome power. Stalin blithely replied he trusted the United States would make good use of it against Japan. Thus, Truman's first effort at "nuclear diplomacy" ended in failure. Far from being intimidated, Stalin had stood his ground.

Deadlocked on Eastern Europe, Truman and Stalin turned their attention to Japan. The Potsdam Declaration of July 26 (the conference's sole accomplishment) demanded immediate "unconditional surrender," warning that any other action would lead to "prompt and utter destruction."

Despite its apocalyptic tone, the Potsdam Declaration failed to give Japan ample warning,

On October 21, 1944, General MacArthur, commander of the Southeast Pacific forces, splashed ashore in the Philippines with the 96th Division.

and over the next several days, opponents of nuclear warfare pleaded with Truman not to use the bomb. Many scientists who had helped develop the bomb, joined by several key political figures, opposed the bomb because they foresaw its implications for a postwar arms race with the Soviet Union. Others, arguing from a moral position, wanted the United States to warn the Japanese about the bomb's terrifying power, giving them a chance to surrender. As a compromise, others advised Truman to conduct a demonstration. The United States could drop the bomb on an uninhabited Pacific island, before an audience of neutral observers (at a safe distance) who would tell Japan's leaders what they had witnessed.

Truman rejected these alternatives. The atomic bomb was the most jealously guarded secret of World War II, and Truman had no intention of divulging it to the enemy. Moreover, he rejected a test demonstration because his scientists could not guarantee the bomb would explode and because the United States had only three bombs in its nuclear arsenal. In the end, Truman decided to drop the bomb.

(Text continues on p. 899)

HIROSHIMA AND NAGASAKI

On July 16, 1945, the Atomic Age became reality. The place was Alamogordo Air Force Base in the southern desert region of New Mexico. The occasion was the first successful detonation of an atomic bomb. Observers witnessed "a blinding flash that lighted the entire northwestern sky." Next came "a huge billow of smoke," followed by "an enormous ball of what appeared to be fire and closely resembled a rising sun." Dr. J. Robert Oppenheimer, the chief scientist in charge of the team that designed the weapon, was so astonished by the scale of the blast that he recalled the Hindu quotation: "I am become death, shatterer of worlds."

Back in 1939 two brilliant scientists, Albert Einstein and Enrico Fermi, both of whom had fled fascism and anti-Semitism in Europe, warned President Roosevelt that German nuclear physicists under

Adolf Hitler's control might well be trying to develop such a bomb. Roosevelt realized the implications; he set in motion what became the "Manhattan Project," a top-secret effort involving civilian scientists and army engineers to apply the theory of nuclear fission to a bomb. Hitler's scientists never succeeded, but in July 1945, with the war over in Europe, the United States now had a weapon with the potential to threaten civilization itself. The question was whether the bomb would be used against Japan, the last of the Axis powers still at war.

The Japanese were a formidable foe. Since 1942 U.S. troops had been rolling back their empire, all the way to the shores of Japan and the Chinese mainland by the summer of 1945. The toll in casualties was horrendous. Japanese soldiers fought with a sense of personal honor that struck Americans as

fanatical. They would not surrender when beaten but would fight to their death. To do otherwise would be to disgrace themselves, their families, and their emperor, whom they considered a god.

At first, in defending Pacific islands such as Guadalcanal (August 1942–February 1943), Japanese soldiers mounted suicidal *banzai* charges. They ran forward in waves at U.S. troops, inflicting massive damage before being shot down. Later, on islands such as Iwo Jima (February–March 1945), they used elaborate networks of underground bunkers to wreak havoc, so much so that U.S. casualties started to reach the 50 percent range. By 1945 the Japanese were unleashing kamikaze raids in which pilots sacrificed themselves for the glory of the empire by dive bombing their planes into U.S. naval vessels. In the bloody battle of Okinawa (April–June 1945), kamikaze pilots flew some 2800 planes into American ships, inflicting 10,000 casualties and sinking 28 vessels, besides damaging 325 other ships.

American soldiers, as well as the U.S. public at large, neither understood nor respected Japanese martial values. Explained a Marine Corps general, to shoot "a Jap . . . was like killing a rattlesnake." A Guadalcanal veteran stated that the Japanese soldier "possessed considerable cleverness; he could not be classified as an intellectual. He was more of an animal. He could live on a handful of rice." Almost universally Americans used terms of racial derision to describe an enemy that had not only mounted the "sneak attack" on Pearl Harbor but now refused to surrender when beaten.

Such attitudes affected the development of a comprehensive U.S.

war plan, known as Operation DOWNFALL, constructed on the assumption that only a full-scale invasion of Japan would bring total victory in the Pacific. The first phase of the plan, called Operation OLYMPIC, involved an assault on Kyushu, the southernmost island of Japan, to begin in November 1945. The Joint Chiefs of Staff presented OLYMPIC to President Truman in June and stated that American casualties could reach 268,000 (out of 767,000 participants). The Japanese still had 2.3 million soldiers ready to fight and another 4 million citizens trained in the use of arms. If they battled to the death, as they had so far, American casualties, the Joint Chiefs predicted, would exceed 1 million by the time U.S. troops conquered the main island of Honshu in 1946 or 1947.

Because of the bloody price everyone expected to pay, high-ranking American officials were anxious to involve Russia—to attack through Manchuria and Korea—in the final crushing of Japan. At Yalta in February 1945 President Roosevelt secured pledges of Soviet assistance. Then at Potsdam in July, President Truman seemed much less interested. Having just learned of the test results in New Mexico, Truman told Joseph Stalin of "a new weapon of unusual destructive force." Stalin, however, would not be cast aside. He still wanted the territory (the lower half of Sakhalin Island, the Kurile islands, and certain considerations in Manchuria) promised at Yalta. The Soviet leader thus "hoped" the United States "would make good use" of the weapon "against the Japanese"; but the Russians would not be denied their part in the invasion or the promised territory.

Meanwhile, a committee of American scientists and military officers were at work in selecting possible targets. Some advocated a demonstration at a preannounced neutral site as a way of cajoling the Japanese into surrender, but others feared what might happen should the bomb prove to be a dud. All leverage would then be lost. Finally, with great reluctance, these advisors agreed that there was "no acceptable alternative to direct military use" of the bomb.

In public, Truman never admitted to any qualms about the decision to employ the new weapon, but in private he wondered how "we as the leader of the world for the common welfare" could drop "this terrible bomb." Still, he accepted the responsibility for many reasons. He hoped to save thousands of American lives by avoiding a full invasion of Japan against soldiers who fought like "savages, ruthless, merciless, and fanatic." Likely, too, Truman and his advisors feared the expansionism of the Communist regime of Joseph Stalin. Using the bomb might prove a great point of leverage in dealing with the Soviets in the days ahead.

While Truman and others considered the alternatives, a select unit of the Army Air Force, flying B-29s, made a series of practice bomb runs over Japan. Since these planes did not attack, as they had so often before in firebombing cities like Tokyo, no one paid much attention. Then on August 6, 1945, at a few minutes past 8:00 A.M., three B-29s at 31,600 feet of altitude appeared over Hiroshima. Colonel Paul Tibbets, piloting the lead bomber, *Enola Gay*, turned the controls over to Major Thomas Ferebee, the bombardier officer, who completed the run. It took 45 seconds, as *Enola Gay* banked away quickly, for the atomic bomb to reach the ground. As the fireball erupted toward the sky, nearly 100,000 people, including thousands of soldiers at the headquarters of Japan's Second General Army just 2000 yards from ground zero, died instantly. Three days later, in the absence of a firm willingness to surrender, a second bomb flattened Nagasaki and killed about 35,000 people. Thousands more perished later from serious burns, radiation poisoning, and other devastating effects of the two bombings.

Dropping the atomic bombs gave peace advocates in Japan the muscle they needed to overcome the militarists. When on August 10 Emperor Hirohito agreed to seek peace terms, the war faction reluctantly acceded, but only after General Anami Korechika, the war minister, upheld his honor on August 14 by committing suicide. He could not bear hearing Hirohito's proclamation of surrender.

When American troops training for Operation OLYMPIC heard about the surrender, they rejoiced. "We would not be obliged to run up the beaches near Tokyo assault-firing while being mortared and shelled," wrote one soldier. "We are going to live. We are going to grow up to adulthood after all." They did not realize how different the world would be with nuclear weapons in the hands of the two superpowers to emerge from World War II. For a moment, however, General Douglas MacArthur understood. After the Japanese surrender ceremony on September 2, 1945, he stated: "We have had our last chance. If we do not devise some greater and more equitable system, Armageddon will be at our door."

1921 Washington Naval Conference places limits on construction of large warships

1922 Mussolini seizes power in Italy

1924 Dawes Plan to help Germany pay reparations

1928 Kellogg-Briand Pact renounces war "as an instrument of national policy"; Clark Memorandum states that the United States does not have a right to intervene militarily in the affairs of Latin American nations

1931 Japan invades Manchuria

1932 Stimson Doctrine declares that the United States would not recognize Japanese territorial gains in China

1933 Adolf Hitler is appointed chancellor of Germany; Roosevelt announces Good Neighbor Policy, withdraws marines from Haiti, and nullifies Platt Amendment

1935 Neutrality Act allows president to bar arms sales to nations at war; is extended in 1936 to bar loans to belligerents and in 1937 to bar shipments of nonmilitary goods

1936 German troops reoccupy the Rhineland; Spanish Civil War begins

1937 Japan invades China

1938 Germany annexes Austria; Munich Pact hands over a third of Czechoslovakia to Nazi Germany

1939 Soviet Union and Germany sign a non-aggression pact; World War II begins following Germany's invasion of Poland

1940 United States transfers 50 destroyers to Britain in exchange for bases in Newfoundland and the Caribbean; United States institutes first peacetime military draft; Roosevelt is elected to third term

1941 Lend-Lease Act allows United States to lend war materials to Britain; Roosevelt issues order prohibiting discrimination in defense industries; Hitler's army invades USSR; United States sets embargo on scrap metal, oil, and fuel to Japan; Japan attacks Pearl Harbor, killing over 2400 U.S. soldiers and sailors; United States enters World War II

1942 Congress creates the Office of Price Administration to control prices and ration scarce goods; President Roosevelt authorizes internment of 112,000 West Coast Japanese-Americans; Philippine Islands surrender; U.S. navy wins a major victory at Midway Island in the central Pacific; British and U.S. forces land in French North Africa

1943 British and U.S. forces defeat Axis forces in North Africa; U.S. marines secure control of Guadalcanal in the Solomon Islands; Soviets halt German drive into Soviet Union; Allies invade Italy; Mussolini is overthrown and new Italian government surrenders to Allies

1943–1944 U.S. marines and navy seize islands of Tarawa, Kwajalein, Wake, and Guam in Central Pacific and New Guinea in the South Pacific

1944 U.S. Supreme Court upholds the legality of the forced relocation of Japanese-Americans; D-Day: Allies launch amphibious invasion of northern France; U.S. forces begin an invasion of Philippine Islands and aerial attacks on Japan; Bretton Woods conference draws up plans for International Monetary Fund and International Bank to finance postwar economic recovery; Dumbarton Oaks conference makes plans for creation of United Nations; German troops launch counteroffensive in the Ardennes Forest along Belgium-Luxembourg border

1945 At Yalta, Roosevelt, Churchill, and Stalin discuss Soviet entry into the war against Japan, the postwar division of Europe, and plans for the United Nations; Roosevelt dies; Harry S Truman becomes thirty-third president; Germany surrenders; Potsdam conference plans postwar settlement in Europe and final attack on Japan; United States drops atomic bombs on Hiroshima and Nagasaki; Japan surrenders

Military considerations played a large role in his decision. According to the best intelligence reports, an invasion of the Japanese Islands might cost one million Allied casualties, with the Japanese suffering several times that figure. Ironically, the bomb had the potential to save countless lives on both sides by ending the war immediately. Yet Truman's decision to drop the bomb also reflected his growing frustration with the Soviet Union. He wanted to demonstrate the bomb's awesome power to impress Stalin so the Soviets would be easier to deal with after the war.

Following Japan's rejection of the Potsdam Declaration, Truman gave the final order. On August 6 three B-29s flew over Hiroshima and the lead bomber, the *Enola Gay*, dropped an atomic bomb that destroyed 4.4 square miles and killed 100,000 people instantly. Two days later the Soviets entered the war against Japan, making good on Stalin's promise at Yalta. Because Japan failed to surrender immediately, Truman ordered a second atomic strike. On August 9 Nagasaki was obliterated, killing another 35,000 Japanese. The following day Japan asked for peace.

The news that peace negotiations were going forward triggered spontaneous celebrations in the United States as tens of millions of Americans filled the streets in mass demonstrations of joy and relief. V-J Day (Victory in Japan) came on September 2, 1945, when Japanese officials surrendered unconditionally to General MacArthur aboard the battleship *Missouri* in Tokyo Bay. Truman refused to permit the Soviets to attend the ceremony or to play any role in creating an occupation government for Japan.

World War II was over. The fascist governments had been destroyed, their military machines crushed, their economies shattered, their major cities reduced to rubble, and their people ravaged by disease and starvation. Yet the war left the Allies hardly less devastated, except for the United States, which emerged from the fighting stronger than ever. Much of the world had to be reordered and rebuilt, but the conflicts between the United States and the Soviet Union that festered throughout the war raised grave doubts about the prospects for future cooperation.

This photo of the remains of the Nagasaki Medical College shows the almost total destruction by the atomic blast. The buildings that remained standing were made of reinforced concrete.

CONCLUSION

When World War II erupted in Europe, Roosevelt knew most Americans supported the Allies. So did he, but isolationists in Congress severely limited his freedom to act. For more than two years, Roosevelt struggled to preserve the fiction of neutrality while constructing programs to assist the Allies. After the attack on Pearl Harbor, isolationist opposition crumbled and the public united behind the war. The United States joined the Grand Alliance with Great Britain, Free France, and the Soviet Union to defeat the Axis Powers—Germany, Japan, and Italy. Yet apart from the need to crush the enemy, the Allies agreed upon little. Throughout the war, they clashed over military strategy and peace terms, disagreements that foreshadowed the conflicts of the postwar era.

World War II had an immediate and spectacular impact on the economy: It ended the Great Depression. Fueled by government contracts, the economy expanded dramatically, soaring to full employment and astounding the world with its productivity. The war accelerated corporate mergers and the trend toward large-scale units in agriculture. Labor unions also grew during the war as the government adopted pro-union policies, continuing the New Deal's sympathetic treatment of organized labor. Moreover, Keynesian economic principles took root as public policy during World War II, presaging the postwar growth of a large federal bureaucracy.

The Democrats reaped a political windfall from the war. Roosevelt rode the wartime emergency to unprecedented third and fourth terms, preserving the New Deal coalition so effectively that many people wondered if the Republicans would ever elect another president. Despite political victories, however, the Democrats could not rekindle congressional support for liberal reforms. The reform spirit had waned, a victim, it seemed, of the country's unmistakable swing to the right in politics.

The war's social effects varied from group to group. For most people, it had a disruptive influence—separating families, overcrowding housing, and creating a shortage of consumer goods. The war also set people in motion, accelerating the movement from the countryside to the cities; and it challenged gender and racial roles, opening new opportunities for women and minority groups. Yet sexual and racial barriers remained, highlighting reforms left unfinished at home even as American troops fought totalitarian forces abroad.

Presidential power expanded enormously during World War II, anticipating the rise of what postwar critics termed the "imperial presidency." Much of the president's energy went into formulating and directing a revolution in American foreign policy. Gone forever was the notion of fortress America, isolated and removed from world affairs. In its place stood a strong internationalist state, determined to exercise power on a global scale. Second only to the victory the Allies won for freedom, the war's most important legacy was the end of isolation and the rise of America's commitment to international security.

SUGGESTIONS FOR FURTHER READING

OVERVIEWS AND SURVEYS

Selig Adler, *The Uncertain Giant: American Foreign Policy Between the Wars* (1969); Albert R. Buchanan, *The United States and World War II*, 2 vols. (1964); Sean Dennis Cashman, *America, Roosevelt and World War II* (1989); Martha Hoyle, *A World in Flames: A History of World War II* (1970); Robert Leckie, *The Wars of America*, rev. ed., 2 vols. (1981); Studs Terkel, ed., *"The Good War"? An Oral History of World War Two* (1984); Russell F. Weigley, *The American Way of War: A History of United States Military Strategy and Policy* (1973); Gordon Wright, *The Ordeal of Total War 1939–1945* (1968).

DIPLOMACY BETWEEN THE WARS

Charles Chatfield, *For Peace and Justice: Pacifism in America 1914–1941* (1971); Charles DeBenedetti, *Origins of the Modern American Peace Movement, 1915–1929* (1978); Michael Dunne, *The United States and the World Court, 1920–1935* (1988); Robert H. Ferrell, *Peace in Their Time* (1953); Irwin F. Gellman, *Good Neighbor Diplomacy: United States Policies in Latin America, 1933–1945* (1979); Manfred Jonas, *Isolationism in America, 1935-1941* (1966); Joan Hoff-Wilson, *American Business and Foreign Policy, 1920–1933* (1971); John E. Wiltz, *In Search of Peace: The Senate Munitions Inquiry, 1934–36* (1963); Bryce Wood, *The Making of the Good Neighbor Policy* (1961).

THE COMING OF WORLD WAR II

Thomas A. Bailey and Paul B. Ryan, *Hitler vs. Roosevelt: The Undeclared Naval War* (1979); Robert J. Butow, *Tojo and the Coming of the War* (1961); Warren I. Cohen, *America's Response to China: A History of Sino-American Relations*, 3d ed. (1990); Wayne S. Cole, *America First: The Battle Against Intervention, 1940–1941* (1953), and *Roosevelt and the Isolationists, 1932–45* (1983); James V. Compton, *The Swastika and the Eagle: Hitler, the United States, and the Origins of World War II* (1967); Robert Dallek, *Franklin D. Roosevelt and American Foreign Policy, 1932–1945* (1979); Robert A. Divine, *Illusion of Neutrality* (1962), and *Second Chance: The Triumph of Internationalism During World War II* (1967); Herbert Feis, *The Road to Pearl Harbor: The Coming of the War Between the United States and Japan* (1950); Robert Edwin Herzstein, *Roosevelt & Hitler: Prelude to War* (1989); Akira Iriye, *After Imperialism: The Search for a New Order in the Far East, 1921–1931* (1965); Warren F. Kimball, *The Most Unsordid Act: Lend-Lease, 1939–1941* (1982); William L. Langer and S. Everett Gleason, *The Challenge to Isolation: The World Crisis of 1937–1940 and American Foreign Policy* (1952); Joseph P. Lash, *Roosevelt and Churchill, 1939–1941: The Partnership that Saved the West* (1976); Martin V. Melosi, *The*

Shadow of Pearl Harbor: Political Controversy over the Surprise Attack, 1941–1946 (1977); Keith L. Nelson, Victors Divided: America and the Allies in Germany, 1918–1923 (1975); Gordon W. Prange, At Dawn We Slept: The Untold Story of Pearl Harbor (1981); David Reynolds, The Creation of the Anglo-American Alliance, 1937–41: A Study in Competitive Co-operation (1982); Bruce Russett, No Clear and Present Danger: A Skeptical View of the United States Entry into World War II (1972); Michael Schaller, The U.S. Crusade in China, 1938–1945 (1979); John E. Wiltz, From Isolation to War, 1931–1941 (1968); Roberta Wohlstetter, Pearl Harbor: Warning and Decision (1962).

AMERICA AT WAR

John Morton Blum, V Was for Victory: Politics and American Culture During World War II (1976); Eliot Janeway, Struggle for Survival (1951); William K. Klingaman, 1941: Our Lives in a World on the Edge (1988); Paul A. C. Koistinen, The Hammer and the Sword: Labor, the Military, and Industrial Mobilization, 1920-1945 (1979); Nelson Lichtenstein, Labor's War at Home: The CIO in World War II (1982); Richard Lingeman, Don't You Know There's a War On? The American Home Front, 1941–1945 (1970); Richard Polenberg, The War and Society: The United States, 1941–1945 (1972); Harold G. Vatter, The U.S. Economy in World War II (1985); Gerald T. White, Billions for Defense: Government Financing by the Defense Plant Corporation During World War II (1980).

SOCIAL CHANGES DURING THE WAR

Karen Anderson, Wartime Women: Sex Roles, Family Relations, and the Status of Women During World War II (1981); Allan Berube, Coming Out under Fire: The History of Gay Men and Women in World War Two (1990); A. Russell Buchanan, Black Americans in World War II (1977); Dominic J. Capeci, Jr., Race Relations in Wartime Detroit: The Sojourner Truth Housing Controversy of 1942 (1984); Richard M. Dalfiume, Desegregation of the U.S. Armed Forces: Fighting on Two Fronts, 1939–1953 (1969); Roger Daniels, Concentration Camps USA: Japanese Americans and World War II (1971); Richard Drinnon, Keeper of Concentration Camps: Dillon S. Myer and American Racism (1987); Charity Adams Earley, One Woman's Army: A Black Officer Remembers the WAC (1989); Audrie Girdner and Anne Loftig, The Great Betrayal: The Evacuation of the Japanese-Americans During World War II (1969); Sherna Berger Gluck, Rosie the Riveter Revisited: Women, the War, and Social Change (1987); Anne Bosanko Green, One Woman's

War: Letters Home from the Women's Army Corps, 1944–1946 (1989); Chester W. Gregory, Women in Defense Work During World War II: An Analysis of the Labor Problem and Women's Rights (1974); Susan M. Hartmann, The Home Front and Beyond: American Women in the 1940s (1982); Peter H. Irons, Justice at War: The Story of the Japanese American Internment Cases (1983); Mauricio Mazón, The Zoot-Suit Riots: The Psychology of Symbolic Annihilation (1984); August Meier and Elliot Rudwick, CORE, 1942–1968 (1973); Gunnar Myrdal, An American Dilemma (1944); Robert Shogan and Thomas Craig, The Detroit Race Riot (1964); Neil Wynn, The Afro-American and the Second World War (1976).

THE WAR IN EUROPE

James MacGregor Burns, Roosevelt: Soldier of Freedom (1970); Diane Shaver Clemens, Yalta (1970); Kent Roberts Greenfield, American Strategy in World War II: A Reconsideration (1963); Eric Larrabee, Commander in Chief: Franklin Delano Roosevelt, His Lieutenants, and Their War (1987); Ronald Schaffer, Wings of Judgment: American Bombing in World War II (1985); Bradley F. Smith, The Shadow Warriors: O.S.S. and the Origins of the C.I.A. (1983); Gaddis Smith, American Diplomacy During the Second World War, 1941–1945 (1965); John Snell, Illusion and Necessity: The Diplomacy of Global War, 1939–1945 (1963); Mark A. Stoler, The Politics of the Second Front: American Military Planning and Diplomacy in Coalition Warfare, 1941–1943 (1977).

THE WAR IN THE PACIFIC

Gar Alperovitz, Atomic Diplomacy: Hiroshima and Potsdam, rev. ed. (1985); Robert Butow, Japan's Decision to Surrender (1954); Herbert Feis, The Atomic Bomb and the End of World War II (1966); Gregg Herkin, The Winning Weapon: The Atomic Bomb in the Cold War; 1945–1950 (1980); Robert Jungk, Brighter than a Thousand Suns: A Personal History of the Atomic Scientists (1958); Dan Kurzman, Day of the Bomb: Countdown to Hiroshima (1986); Martin J. Sherwin, A World Destroyed: The Atomic Bomb and the Grand Alliance (1975); Ronald H. Spector, Eagle Against the Sun: The American War with Japan (1985).

BIOGRAPHIES

Saul Alinsky, John L. Lewis (1949); Mark S. Foster, Henry J. Kaiser: Builder in the Modern American West (1989); Michael Schaller, Douglas MacArthur: The Far Eastern General (1989); Barbara Tuchman, Stilwell and the American Experience in China, 1911–45 (1971).

4

Containing the Russian Bear

The Containment Policy

The Cold War at Home

The Paranoid Style

43b

CHAPTER 27

Waging Peace and War

*I*t was Sunday, August 27, 1948. Whittaker Chambers appeared calm as he answered questions on "Meet the Press," a weekly radio news show. The appearance, like most of Chambers's life, was a deception. He knew he was on enemy ground and that questions were the ammunition of the war. "I sought not to let myself be crowded," he later recalled, "not to lose my temper during the baiting." Chambers sat very still, waiting for the inevitable question. He didn't have to wait long. Edward T. Folliard, a reporter for the *Washington Post*, asked, "Are you willing to say now that Alger Hiss is or ever was a Communist?" Chambers paused a second before answering, for the answer could open him up to a slander or libel suit. Then came his terse, important reply: "Alger Hiss was a Communist and may be now." Like his questioners, Chambers also knew how to use words as weapons.

The road to "Meet the Press" had begun for Chambers a generation and a lifetime before 1948. It was paved with unhappiness. His father, Jay, was almost a stranger in his own house. For a time Jay left his wife Laha; after three years he returned. He demonstrated no love or affection for his wife or children. Whittaker remembers that Jay—who never allowed his children to call him "Papa"—dined alone and seldom spoke, except perhaps to say "don't." Home experiences left Chambers rebellious and feeling unwanted. He was forced to withdraw from Columbia for writing a mildly sacrilegious play, and he flirted with radical political philosophies, moved through a succession of love affairs, and kicked about Europe. In 1926 his brother Richard committed suicide. It was the most painful event in Chambers's life. For several months he was inconsolable. Almost as a form of therapy, he committed himself fully to another family— the Communist party. During his time of troubles, it gave his life a direction and a purpose.

During the late 1920s and early 1930s, as the United States sank deeper and deeper into the Great Depression, other Americans joined Chambers in the Communist party. Feeling betrayed by the capitalist order, they looked toward the Soviet Union for economic and political inspiration. Under Joseph Stalin, the Soviet Union appeared less affected by the depression than the capitalist West. Still more Americans joined the Communist party because only the Soviets seemed to be standing up against the Fascist threat posed by Hitler, Mussolini, and Franco. For Chambers and his comrades, then, the Red Star represented the future and the best hope of the world.

Chambers met Alger Hiss in 1934, when they both belonged to the same Communist "cell" in Washington, D.C. In appearance and personality they were almost perfect opposites. Chambers was overweight and sloppy; his clothes always seemed rumpled, and his face had a sleepy, slightly disinterested cast. Hiss was cut from different cloth. Handsome, thin, aristocratic looking, Hiss's career was marked by ambition and achievement. He was an honors student at Johns Hopkins and Harvard Law School; he was a favorite of future Supreme Court justice Felix Frankfurter; he clerked for the legendary Oliver Wendell Holmes. Popular with influential superiors and his co-workers, Hiss obviously had been singled out as one of the best and brightest, as one who would succeed. And he did. He acted as a counsel for the Agricultural Adjustment Administration, worked for the Senate committee investigating the munitions industry, went to the Yalta Conference with President Roosevelt, helped to organize the United Nations, and served as the president of the Carnegie Endowment for International Peace.

During his impressive career, Hiss worked with Whittaker Chambers for the Communist party. While Hiss served as a legal assistant for the Senate committee investigation of the munitions industry, he became close friends with Chambers. Hiss allowed Chambers to use his Washington, D.C., apartment for two months, gave him an automobile, and even permitted him to stay in his home on several occasions. Although Hiss would later deny that he knew Chambers—and then admit that he knew him slightly under a different name—the evidence is clear on one point: The bureaucrat and spy had formed a close friendship. It was during that period of friendship in the mid-1930s, Chambers later testified, that Hiss began to give him secret government documents.

Like many of his American comrades, Chambers abandoned the ideology of communism and lost faith in the Soviet Union during

Alger Hiss (left), accused of being a Communist spy by Whittaker Chambers (right), was convicted of perjury. This episode helped heighten American fear of communism at home.

the late 1930s. There were sound reasons for his break with the Communist party. For the true believers of the early 1930s, the Soviet Union was the light that failed. By 1938 news of Stalin's purges, which would eventually lead to the death of millions of Soviets, had reached the West. Such gross disregard for humanity shook many American Communists. In addition, in 1939 Stalin signed a nonaggression pact with Hitler's Germany. Once seen as the bulwark against Nazi expansion, the Soviet Union now joined Germany in dividing Poland. Although during World War II the United States and the Soviet Union were forced together as allies, Communist ideology ceased to attract many American followers.

Chambers not only quit the Communist party, he turned against it with vengeful wrath. As an editor for *Time* magazine, he openly criticized Communist tactics and warned about the evils of the Soviet Union. Time only increased his rage. Finally in 1948 he went before the House Un-American Activities Committee (HUAC) and told his life story, carefully naming all his former Communist party friends and associates. Of all the people he named, the one who attracted the most attention was the brilliant young New Dealer Alger Hiss.

Of course, Hiss denied Chambers's allega-

tions. He too appeared before HUAC. Well-dressed and relaxed despite a too tight collar, he testified, "I am not and never have been a member of the Communist Party . . . I have never followed the Communist Party line, directly or indirectly. To the best of my knowledge, none of my friends is a Communist." As he answered questions, he smiled and confidently stood on his record of public service. Unlike his nervous, rumpled accuser, Hiss was the picture of placid truthfulness. His testimony satisfied most of the committee members, even the Republicans.

He satisfied most, but not all. After hearing both Chambers and Hiss, Richard Nixon, a junior congressman from California, still was not sure Hiss was as innocent as he seemed. As one psycho-historian bluntly put it, Hiss "was everything Nixon was not." Nixon's struggling background contrasted sharply with Hiss's career, and Nixon believed Hiss treated him "like dirt." At Nixon's insistence, Hiss and Chambers were brought together face to face before HUAC. At that meeting, Chambers demonstrated his encyclopedic knowledge about Hiss, his family, and his life. He discussed the furniture in Hiss's house and Hiss's hobbies. He showed beyond any doubt that he had been close to Hiss. For once Hiss's confident equanimity vanished. He challenged Chambers to make his accusations in public, where he would not be protected against a libel suit.

Chambers accepted the challenge, and on "Meet the Press" he repeated his charges. Hiss hesitated for a month and then sued Chambers for defamation. During the involved trials that followed, Chambers proved his case. He even produced a series of classified, microfilmed documents he had stored in a hollowed-out pumpkin on his Maryland farm. Experts testified that the classified documents had been written in Hiss's hand or typed on Hiss's Woodstock typewriter. Hiss was indicted for perjury by a federal grand jury. Although the first trial ended in a hung jury, the second trial was far less satisfactory for Hiss. In January 1950 he was found guilty of perjury and sentenced to five years in prison.

The Hiss-Chambers affair was one of the major episodes of the late 1940s. It was a time of momentous changes. America took an active and aggressive stand in world affairs and accepted the responsibilities and problems of world leadership. Across the globe it clashed with the Soviet Union over a series of symbolic and real issues. Labeled the Cold War, these ideological and economic battles affected American domestic and foreign policy. During the late 1940s and early 1950s Americans attacked the Communist threat inside as well as outside the United States. In an atmosphere charged with fear, anxiety, paranoia, and hatred, the United States waged peace and war with equal emotional intensity.

CONTAINING THE RUSSIAN BEAR

During World War II, when the United States and the Soviet Union were allies, Joseph Stalin was known as Uncle Joe. The media portrayed him as a stern but fair leader and pictured communism as strikingly like capitalism. Even Hollywood cooperated in this image-making process. Warner Brothers's *Mission to Moscow* (1943), Sam Goldwyn's *North Star* (1943), MGM's *Song of Russia* (1943), and Frank Capra's *Battle of Russia* all emphasized pro-Soviet themes. *Mission to Moscow* was partic-

ularly kind to Stalin, who appeared on screen as a gentle, pipe-smoking, sad-eyed friend of America.

In reality Stalin was a determined, ruthless leader who had over the years systematically eliminated his actual and suspected political rivals. Between 1933 and 1938 he violently eliminated over 850,000 members of the Communist party, and perhaps one million more died in labor camps. He was apparently suspicious of almost everyone inside and outside of the Soviet Union. If his attitude was extreme, it was not totally irrational. Twice in his lifetime Russia had been invaded from the West. Twice Germans had pushed into his country, killing millions upon millions of Russians. Russia suffered almost 4 million military and civilian deaths in World War I, and the Soviet Union more than 20 million killed in World War II. For Stalin, the West stood unalterably opposed to communism. He would take what he could from the West, but he would never trust westerners.

Stalin, however, was not the only suspicious world leader. The newest Western leader, President Harry Truman, was wary of Stalin, but did not exactly regard him as the enemy, at least not in 1945. After all, the Soviet Union and America had been allies during World War II. When Truman took office on April 12,1945, he assumed he could deal with Stalin. Advisors told him that Stalin was a tough, no-nonsense leader. These were characteristics that the tough, no-nonsense Truman could appreciate. His first meeting with Stalin at Potsdam confirmed his initial assessment of the Soviet leader. "I like Stalin," Truman wrote his wife Bess. "He is straightforward. Knows what he wants and will compromise when he can't get it."

Potsdam was the light before the long dark tunnel. Truman was overly optimistic about his ability to work with Stalin. Totally different backgrounds and philosophies separated the two leaders from the start, and the directions in which they led their countries drove them further apart. The United States and the Soviet Union emerged from World War II as the two most powerful countries in the world, even though the Soviet Union had suffered tremendous industrial, agricultural, and human losses

The onset of the Cold War was due in part to the growing divergence between the United States and the Soviet Union after World War II. At Potsdam, Britain's Prime Minister Clement Attlee, President Truman, and Stalin tried unsuccessfully to decide the future of Poland and Germany.

during the war. Both countries were inexperienced as world leaders, but both knew exactly what they wanted, and what they wanted guaranteed future conflicts. The Cold War was the result.

Origins of the Cold War

For Western leaders and their diplomats, World War II had a successful but not a neat ending. Too many questions were left unanswered, too many issues unresolved. At Yalta and then at Potsdam the leaders of the Soviet Union, Great Britain, and the United States discussed the future of Poland and Germany, but they arrived at no firm conclusions. Afraid of further straining the already uneasy wartime alliance, they decided to leave such thorny issues to the future. The future arrived in August 1945 after America dropped two atomic bombs on Japan. The fates of Eastern Europe and Germany were as yet undetermined as was the relationship between the United States and the Soviet Union.

When Germany invaded Poland in early September 1939, England and France came to the aid of Poland. The Soviet Union did not. Instead, the Soviets invaded Poland from the east and gobbled up a large section of the country. In 1941, however, Germany invaded the Soviet Union and forced Stalin to join the Grand Alliance against Hitler. For the remainder of World War II, the Soviets battled heroically against Germany on the eastern front. The West contributed massive amounts of weapons and supplies in this theater of war; but it was the Red Army working alone that drove the Germans out of Eastern Europe. When the war ended, the Soviets controlled all of Eastern Europe from Stettin on the Baltic Sea to Trieste on the Adriatic Sea.

Had the Soviet Union liberated Eastern Europe, or simply replaced Germany as the master of the region? That was the crucial question of 1945. The debate centered on the fate of Poland. Truman insisted that the Soviets allow free and democratic elections in Poland. Certainly, Truman conceded, the Soviets had the right to expect any Polish government to be friendly toward the Soviet Union, but he expected Stalin to give Poland its complete freedom. In America

Poland's fate was no abstract diplomatic issue. Millions of Americans of Eastern European origins pressed Truman to take a tough stand. Truman complied. He told Soviet Foreign Minister V. M. Molotov that America would not tolerate Poland being made into a Soviet puppet state. His speech was salted with profanity—"words of one syllable," Truman described them—and Molotov remarked, "I have never been talked to like that in my life."

Truman's mule-skinner language, however, did not impress Stalin. The Soviet leader had survived a harsh youth, a brutal prison term, a lonely exile, a revolution, and two world wars. He was not now about to give away Poland or any other territory the Red Army occupied simply because of Truman's colorful phrases. Twice during the twentieth century Germany had invaded Russia through Poland. Stalin was determined it would never happen again. As he had bluntly stated at Yalta, "For the Russian people, the question of Poland is not only a question of honor but also a question of security . . . of life and death for the Soviet Union."

Confronted by an inflexible opponent, Truman played his trump card. He threatened to cut off economic aid to the Soviet Union. Devastated by World War II, the Soviet Union needed the aid, but Stalin believed Poland was even more important. Rather than abandon Poland, Stalin accepted the loss of American money. In the end, Truman was powerless. Americans would certainly not accept a war with the Soviet Union to reliberate Poland, and in 1945 the Soviet Union was not about to leave Poland voluntarily. Although there was no war, there was one important casualty: Relations between America and the Soviet Union were strained to the breaking point.

A World Divided

The controversy over Poland indicated the direction of postwar Soviet-American relations. The two countries were divided by substantial issues, the most important of which was the degree of control over other nations. At the end of the war both nations occupied large areas of land. America's control was based on the strength of its economy as much as its military position. Even as the country demobilized,

American leaders were confident that they could use foreign aid to exert influence on the future development of the world. They were also confident that what was good for America would indeed be good for the world. The Soviet Union's control in all of Eastern Europe—Hungary, Romania, Bulgaria, and Czechoslovakia, as well as Poland—depended on the physical presence of the Red Army. Stalin freely granted America and England their spheres of influence, but he wanted the West to recognize his own.

Truman refused. A believer in free trade, national self-determination, and the virtues of democracy, he opposed Stalin's use of military force as a diplomatic weapon. As he told Averell Harriman, America's ambassador to the Soviet Union, the United States might not expect to obtain 100 percent of what it wanted, but "we should be able to get eighty-five percent." The irony of the United States' position was clearly seen by political commentator Walter Lippmann: "While the British and the Americans held firmly . . . the whole position in Africa and the Mediterranean . . . and the whole of Western Germany . . . they undertook by negotiation and diplomatic pressure to reduce Russia's position in Eastern Europe."

Approaching issues from different perspectives, the Soviet Union and America arrived at different conclusions. After World War II ended, they agreed on very little. The fate of Germany illustrates the basic conflict between the two powers. The Soviets wanted to punish Germany by stripping the country of its industry and imposing harsh reparation payments. Only a prostrate Germany, unarmed and unthreatening, would satisfy Stalin. As Truman lost confidence in the Soviet Union, he came to believe in the need for a strong Germany to act as a block against Soviet expansion. The result of these conflicting approaches was a divided Germany. Occupied by the Red Army, East Germany became a Soviet satellite. West Germany fell under the American, British, and French spheres of influence and soon became part of the postwar democratic alliance.

Control over atomic weapons also divided the two powers. America developed and used the first atomic bomb—demonstrating to the world that it possessed not only the scientific knowledge to construct the bomb but also the

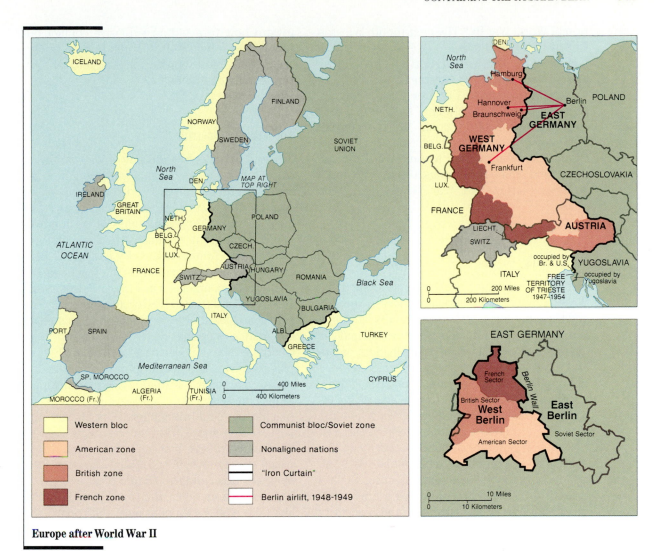

Europe after World War II

will to use the weapon—but realized that future world safety depended on some plan to control the awesome potential of the weapon. Publicly Truman seemed favorable to international control of the world's fissionable materials. Yet privately he used the threat of the bomb in his negotiations with the Soviet Union. America, Secretary of War Henry L. Stimson commented, wore the "weapon rather ostentatiously on our hip." Stalin reacted with suspicion and bitterness to this contradictory policy, distrusting any atomic control plan that originated in the United States. Rather than make Stalin more manageable, America's atomic diplomacy stiffened his resolve, heightened his suspicions, and made him cling even more firmly to Eastern Europe

as a buffer. At a high-level meeting in the Kremlin he announced his own plan: "A single demand of you, comrades: Provide us with atomic weapons in the shortest possible time. You know that Hiroshima has shaken the whole world. The equilibrium has been destroyed. Provide the bomb. It will remove a great danger from us." The result was an atomic arms race, not international cooperation.

By early 1946 U.S.-Soviet relations were irreparably strained. In February 1946, Stalin warned all Soviet citizens that there would never be a lasting peace with the capitalistic West. Economic sacrifices and perhaps more warfare lay ahead. Supreme Court Justice William Douglas labeled the speech "the declaration of World War III." The next month Winston Churchill traveled to Fulton, Missouri, to give a lecture of his own. With Truman by his side, he announced that "from Stettin in the Baltic to Trieste in the Adriatic, an iron curtain has descended across the continent." Only a combined Anglo-American effort could lift the curtain. Fortunately, Churchill emphasized, "God has willed" the atomic bomb to America. Dramatic words and ominous warnings, threats and counterthreats—the Cold War clearly had been declared.

Tough Talk

Although real issues divided America and the Soviet Union, the emotionally charged rhetoric and the emergence of Cold War myths hardened the battle lines. Truman lacked the skill and the language of a diplomat, and like leaders before and after him he was trying to avoid the mistakes of the immediate past. Truman's advisors encouraged the president to take a hard line toward the Soviet Union. Remembering how the British and the French had given in to Hitler at the Munich Conference of 1938, American foreign policy makers were determined not to allow history to repeat itself. Equating Stalin's goals with Hitler's, however, was a grave mistake. Stalin was concerned more with security than expansion; he wanted to protect his country from a future attack, not initiate World War III. As George Kennan, America's leading expert on the Soviet Union, later observed, "The image of a Stalinist Russia poised and yearning to attack the West, and deterred only by our possession of atomic weapons, was largely a creation of the Western imagination."

The Munich example and the get-tough talk turned American public opinion against the Soviet Union. Leading American diplomat Dean Acheson warned, "I think it is a mistake to believe that you can, at any time, sit down with the Russians and solve problems." Comments of this sort were aired over and over in public as the media formed a new, more menacing image of Stalin. The pipe in hand and sad, soft eyes of Uncle Joe quickly faded in late 1945 and early 1946. News stories emphasized confrontation, conflict, and controversy. Talk turned no longer

toward how to avoid an explosive conflict but rather how to win it. In the mind of the public, the Soviet Union soon became the once and future enemy of America.

The Truman Doctrine

America's rise as a world power was paralleled by Britain's decline. England, like much of the rest of Europe, suffered terribly during World War II. The war shattered its economy, and burned-out buildings and miles of fresh graveyards gave silent testimony to the country's physical and human losses. By early 1947 Britain could no longer stand as the leader of the Western democracies. On Friday, February 21, 1947, England passed the torch to America. The British ambassador in Washington requested an emergency meeting with Secretary of State George C. Marshall. He had "a piece of blue paper" to deliver. The quaint phrase meant in diplomatic parlance a formal and important message. Simply put, the ambassador announced that Britain could no longer economically support Greece and Turkey in their fight against Communist rebels. If these two vital countries, which stood between the Soviet Union and the Mediterranean and the Middle East, were to be kept as Western allies, the United States had to aid their cause. Emphasizing this point, the message concluded, "Unless urgent and immediate support is given to Greece, it seems probable that the Greek Government will be overthrown and a totalitarian regime of the extreme left will come into power."

Truman was prepared to assume the burden, but there were doubts whether the country was. Republicans had regained control of Congress in the November 1946 elections, and they were not anxious to shoulder expensive new foreign programs. In addition, rapid demobilization after World War II had drastically reduced the size and effectiveness of the American military forces. Still, something had to be done. Truman's advisors and congressional leaders recommended that he speak directly to the American people. But as Republican Senator Arthur Vandenberg warned, to win public support the president would have to "scare the hell out of the American people."

On March 12, 1947, Truman appeared before a joint session of Congress and described the Greek and Turkish situations as battles between the forces of light and the legions of darkness. "At the present moment in world history nearly every nation must choose between alternative ways of life," he said. "One way of life is based upon the will of the majority, and is distinguished by free institutions, representative government, free elections, guarantees of individual liberty, freedom of speech and religion, and freedom from political oppression. The second way of life is based upon the will of a minority forcibly imposed upon the majority. It relies upon terror and oppression." Congress sounded its approval as Truman came to his climactic sentence: "I believe that it must be the policy of the United States to support free peoples who are resisting attempted subjugation by armed minorities or outside pressures." Labeled the Truman Doctrine, the statement set the course U.S. foreign policy would follow during the next generation.

Specifically, Truman called for economic and financial aid to "save" Greece and Turkey.

Congress responded by appropriating $400 million. By later standards it was a paltry sum, but it was a significant beginning. In the future, America would send billions of dollars in economic and military aid to countries fighting communism, even though the leaders of some of those nations were themselves dictators. In Truman's morality play, however, "anti-Communists" and "free peoples" became synonymous.

Although Truman succeeded in getting aid for Greece and Turkey and in arousing the American public, a few foreign policy experts believed that his scare tactics did more harm than good. George Kennan deplored the sweeping language of the Truman Doctrine, which placed U.S. aid to Greece "in the framework of a universal policy rather than in that of a specific decision addressed to a specific set of circumstances."

The Marshall Plan: "Saving Western Europe"

The millions of dollars sent to Greece and Turkey stabilized the pro-American governments of the two countries. But at the same time America was losing support in Western Europe, a far more vital region. Although the war had ended in the spring of 1945, Europe's problems continued. It lacked the money to rebuild its war-torn economies and scarred cities. To make matters worse, the winters of 1946 and 1947 were brutally cold. News reports from early 1947 told the sad story. Snow buried thousands of sheep in northern England; between December 1 and February 8, 40 residents of Berlin and 68 of Hamburg died from the cold; Holland was short of food; Italy was inundated by floods; and across the continent the weather report was always the same: "cold or very cold." The winter hardships fueled the Communist party, which made marked gains. American leaders assumed that economic distress would continue to breed political extremism. Anne O'Hare McCormick told Americans in the *New York Times:* "The extent to which democratic government survives on [the] continent depends on how far this country is willing to help it survive." Truman concurred, and so did his advisors. They were

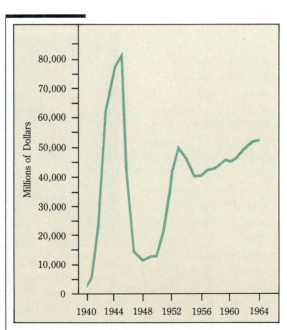

Figure 27.1
National defense budgets, 1940–1964

upset by the growth of anti-Americanism in Europe, an area that figured prominently in their postwar economic plans. The image of America had changed from loyal ally to selfish exploiter. Describing the typical occupation soldier in Germany, an army chaplain wrote, "There he stands in his bulging clothes, fat, overfed, lonely, a bit wistful, seeing little, understanding less—the Conqueror, with a chocolate bar in one pocket and a package of cigarettes in the other. . . . The chocolate bar and the cigarettes are about all that he, the Conqueror, has to give the conquered."

At the Harvard University commencement on June 5, 1947, Secretary of State George C. Marshall announced a plan to give Europe more. After describing the severe problems facing Europe, Marshall suggested that America could not afford to send a Band-Aid to cover the deep European wounds. "A cure rather than a mere palliative" was in order. Europe needed massive economic blood transfusions. He told his audience that the cost might seem high. Without America's help, however, "economic, social, and political deterioration of a very grave character" would result. And from a more selfish point of view, America needed a strong democratic Europe to provide rich markets for American goods and to act as a check against Soviet westward expansion.

In early 1948 Congress appropriated $17 billion to be spent over the next four years for the European Recovery Program (ERP), more popularly called the Marshall Plan. The program put food in the mouths of hungry children, coal in empty furnaces, and money in near-empty banks. More importantly, it rebuilt the economic infrastructure of Western Europe and restored economic prosperity to the region. In the process it created stable markets for American goods. Americans were proud of the Marshall Plan, and Europeans were moved by it. Winston Churchill judged it "the most unsordid act in history." And Hugh Gaitskell, British chancellor of the exchequer, noted: "We are not an emotional people . . . and not very articulate, but these characteristics should not . . . hide the real and profound sense of gratitude toward the American people." All told, the Marshall Plan greatly restored America's prestige abroad.

The Marshall Plan also fostered the economic integration of Western Europe by curbing nationalistic economic policies. American policy makers believed that only by functioning as a single economic unit could Western Europe enjoy real prosperity. "A healthy Europe," John Foster Dulles remarked, could not be "divided into small compartments." Although the process toward economic integration was slow and occasionally painful, it did move forward. The European Payments Union was created in 1950, the European Coal and Steel Authority in 1951, and the European Economic Community (Common Market) in 1958. In the final analysis, the Marshall Plan served both America's Cold War strategy and plans for a economic internationalism.

THE CONTAINMENT POLICY

Money, even billions of dollars, could not substitute for a concrete foreign policy to guide U.S. actions: an explicit policy that mixed the international idealism of the Truman Doctrine and the economic realism of the Marshall Plan with the will to meet the real or perceived Soviet threat. The policy was not long in coming. In July 1947, the journal *Foreign Affairs* contained an article entitled "The Sources of Soviet Conduct" by "Mr. X." The article provided a blueprint for the policy of containment, which would influence American foreign policy for at least the next generation.

"Mr. X" was George Kennan, the government's foremost authority on Russian history. Educated at Princeton University, Kennan had spent his adult life in the U.S. foreign service where he carefully stud-

George Kennan's analysis of United States-Soviet relations encouraged U.S. "containment" of the Russians and played a major role in the intensification of the Cold War.

ied the Soviet scene. During World War II he was stationed in Moscow, and was able to observe Soviet political behavior. Although he believed Russians were a "great and appealing people," he distrusted the Soviet government. In February 1946, he expressed his views of the Soviet Union in an 8000-word telegram to his superiors in Washington, and in the 1947 *Foreign Affairs* article, Kennan made his views public. He believed that Soviet communism was driven by two engines: the need for a repressive dictatorship at home and the belief there could never be any sense of community or true accord with the capitalist West. In fact, the Kremlin used the supposed threat from capitalism to justify its continued dictatorship. But, Kennan argued, Stalin and the leaders in the Kremlin were more interested in security than expansion. Soviets would only expand when allowed by American weakness. It could be *contained* to its present borders by a politically, economically, and militarily active United States. What was needed was "the adroit and vigilant application of counter-force at a series of constantly shifting geographical and political points, corresponding to the shifts and maneuvers of Soviet policy." Kennan even suggested that if the United States was firm in its resolve to contain Soviet expansion, "the possibility remains . . . that Soviet power . . . bears within it the seeds of its own decay." In short, Kennan held out the hope of complete victory in the Cold War.

Although Kennan later remarked that he was talking about the political containment of a political threat, in 1947 his article was read as primarily a military blueprint. As such, it satisfied hard-liners but was challenged by many other politicians and respected political commentators. Walter Lippmann challenged Kennan's policy in a series of newspaper articles later published as *The Cold War: A Study in U.S. Foreign Policy* (1947). Containment, Lippmann commented, allowed the Soviet Union largely to decide when and where its battles against America would take place, and it promised to tie the United States to small unstable "client" countries that would be a political, economic, and military drain on America. Seeing that the plan was primarily focused on Western European problems, Lippmann suggested that if followed it might well lead America into a land war in Asia where the idea of victory would be a cruel delusion. America, Lippmann maintained, was not in the military, economic, or strategic position to implement containment. Lippmann found it "hard to understand how Mr. X could have recommended such a strategic monstrosity."

Containment involved confronting the spread of communism across the globe and as Americans soon learned, it came with a heavy price. It meant supporting our allies around the world with billions of dollars in military and economic aid, and it meant thousands of Americans dying in foreign lands. Since containment was a defensive policy, it involved permanent Cold War without any hope of ultimate victory. Unlike World War I and World War II, the Cold War emphasized the doctrine of limited wars fought for limited goals. And in this arrangement, Kennan noted, "Man would have to recognize . . . that the device of military coercion would have . . . only relative—never an absolute—value in the pursuit of political objectives." It was a policy bound to breed frustration and anxiety—certain to influence domestic as well as foreign policy.

Berlin Test

During the late 1940s containment seemed to fit American needs. American-Soviet tensions centered particularly on the future of Germany. The United States maintained that the economic revival of Western Europe depended on a reindustrialized and prosperous Germany. The Soviets believed that a reindustrialized Germany was a dangerous Germany. An early test of the two different viewpoints came in Berlin, a divided city located in the heart of East Germany, deep within the Soviet zone. Future Soviet Premiere Nikita Khrushchev called democratic West Berlin a "bone in the throat" of Russia. In June 1948, Stalin decided to remove the bone by stopping all road and rail traffic between West Germany and Berlin. It was a crisis tailor-made for the containment policy. Stalin had picked the time and place. Now Truman had to decide upon a response.

He chose the sky. Stalin could close highways and railways, but he could not effectively close the skyways. For almost one year America and Britain kept West Berlin alive and democratic by a massive airlift. Food, coal, clothing, and all other essentials were flown daily into Berlin. It was an heroic feat, a triumph of technology. Western pilots logged 277,264 flights into West Berlin; they hauled in 2,343,315 tons of food, fuel, medicine, and clothing. Finally on May 12, 1949, Stalin lifted his blockade of West Berlin. For Stalin, the success of the airlift had become an embarrassment for the Soviet Union. In the West, containment had passed an important test.

Troubling Times

Truman scored a series of triumphs during 1947 and 1948. The Truman Doctrine, the Marshall Plan, and the Berlin Airlift strengthened his popularity at home and U.S. prestige abroad. In the election of 1948 Truman won a remarkable upset victory over Thomas E. Dewey. Then in 1949 eleven of the Western democracies joined the United States in signing the North Atlantic Treaty Organization (NATO), a mutual defense pact. NATO signified America's position as the leader of the Western Alliance, and it con-

formed to the containment policy. But difficult times for Truman, containment, and America lay ahead. In late August 1949, American scientists detected traces of radioactive material in the Soviet atmosphere. The cause was as clear as a mushroom-shaped cloud. The Soviets had the bomb—a full decade before American intelligence expected it.

On September 22 Truman told the public: "We have evidence that an atomic explosion occurred in the USSR." Although the press tried to downplay the story, a wave of anxiety swept the country. Physicist Harold C. Urey told reporters, "There is only one thing worse than one nation having the atomic bomb—that's two nations having it." There was another thing even worse: One of the nations that had the bomb also had the Red Army.

Between 1945 and 1949 the threat of the bomb had given teeth to American policy. It was America's check to the Red Army, and U. S. policy makers seldom allowed Soviet leaders to forget it. In 1945 then Secretary of State James F. Byrnes told his Soviet counterpart V. M. Molotov, "If you don't cut out all this stalling and let us get down to work, I am going to pull an atomic bomb out of my hip pocket and let you have it." Now Molotov had one in his hip pocket.

During 1948 and 1949, an American and British airlift brought close to 7000 tons of food and fuel each day to Soviet-blockaded West Berlin.

Truman responded by asking his scientists to accelerate the development of a hydrogen bomb; and Congress responded by voting appropriations for Truman's latest defense requests. Of such events and decisions arms races have their humble origins.

On the heels of the Soviet bomb came more unwelcome news—the establishment of the Communist government in China after a bitter civil war. The war between Mao Zedung's (Mao Tse-tung) and Chou En-lai's Communists and Jiang Jieshi's (Chiang Kai-shek) Nationalists had been raging since the 1930s. The United States had strongly backed Jiang during the civil war, providing him with more than $3 billion in aid between 1945 and 1949. But the aid was unable to prop up a government that was structurally unsound, inefficient, and corrupt. In the first week of May 1949, Jiang fled across the Formosa Strait to Taiwan, and on September 21, Mao proclaimed Red China's sovereignty. With Jiang in Taiwan and Mao on the mainland, China became a tale of two countries.

The Truman administration tried to put the best face possible on the turn of events. Secretary of State Dean Acheson issued a thousand-page White Paper explaining how Mao had won the civil war. It detailed the rampant corruption in the Nationalist government and Jiang's many mistakes. Assessing the role of the United States in the outcome of the conflict Acheson concluded, "Nothing that this country did or could have done within the reasonable limits of its capabilities could have changed that result . . . it was the product of internal Chinese forces, forces which this country tried to influence but could not."

For the American public, however, that explanation was not good enough. The China most Americans knew, as one historian put it, was associated with novelist "Pearl Buck's peasants, rejoicing in the good earth . . . dependable, democratic, warm, and above all pro-American." It was an image that American missionaries confirmed during the 1920s and 1930s and one that journalists supported during World War II. Americans were told that there were two types of Asians—the good Chinese and the evil Japanese. In 1941 *Time* magazine even ran an article entitled "How to Tell Your Friends From the Japs." It confidently reported, "the Chinese

The celebration of the first anniversary of Mao Zedung's rule in 1950 brought many to the streets of Peking.

expression is likely to be more placid, kindly, open; the Japanese more positive, dogmatic, arrogant."

Republicans and supporters of Jiang in America blamed Truman for "losing" China. Led by Henry Luce, the influential publisher of *Time* and *Life* who was the China-born son of American missionaries, an informal group known as the China Lobby blasted the Truman administration. They claimed "egg-sucking phony liberals" had "sold China into atheistic slavery." The China Lobby believed that America had far more influence than it actually had, that a country that contained 6 percent of the earth's population could control the other 94 percent. They were wrong, but millions of Americans took their loud cries seriously.

"China lost itself," Acheson countered. "We picked a bad horse," Truman admitted. But given the political pressure at home, Truman was not about to change mounts in the middle of the race. Reversing America's traditional policy of recognizing de facto governments whether approved or not, Truman refused to recognize the Communist People's Republic of China. Instead he insisted that Jiang's Nationalist government on Taiwan was the legitimate government of China. It was an unrealistic policy, but one that future presidents found politically difficult to reverse. The United States and the People's Republic of China did not establish formal relations until 1979.

The Korean War

The rhetoric of the Truman administration tended to simplify complex issues, intensify the Cold War rivalry, and tie foreign policy to domestic politics. Failure abroad could have calamitous consequences for politicians at home. "If you can't stand the heat, get out of the kitchen," Truman often said. By 1950 the kitchen had become hotter. After "China fell," Truman was more than ever determined to contain communism.

The mood of the Truman administration is clearly evident in National Security Council Paper Number 68 (NSC-68), one of the most important documents of the Cold War. Completed in April of 1950, it expressed the views of foreign policy planner Paul Nitze and Dean Acheson that communism is a monolithic world movement directed from the Kremlin; it advocated "an immediate and large-scale build-up in our military and general strength of our allies with the intention of righting the power balance and in the hope that through means other than all-out war we could induce a change in the nature of the Soviet system." NSC-68 extended the Truman Doctrine and called for America to protect the world against the spread of communism. The cost would be great—NSC-68 estimated it at 20 percent of the gross national product or over a 300 percent increase in military appropriations—but planners warned that without the commitment America faced the prospect of a world moving toward communism.

Truman realized that NSC-68 "meant a great military effort in time of peace. It meant doubling or tripling the budget, increasing taxes heavily, and imposing various kinds of economic controls." And he doubted whether Congress would accept such a peacetime buildup. He never got a chance to find out, for in June 1950 America went to war in Korea.

Korea, like Germany, was a divided country. When the Japanese surrendered its forces in Korea after World War II, Soviet troops accepted the surrender north of the 38th parallel, American troops south of that line. With the deepening of the Cold War, the temporary division line became permanent. North of the 38th parallel, Communist Kim Il Sung governed North Korea. Supported by the Soviet Union, Kim forged a modern, disciplined army during the late 1940s. In South Korea, 75-year-old President Syngman Rhee, who received strong aid and support from the United States, opposed any reconciliation with Communist North Korea. But, as Secretary of State Acheson noted in an unfortunate speech before the National Press Club on January 12, 1950, South Korea lay outside America's primary "defense perimeter." As far as military security of South Korea was concerned, Acheson emphasized, should "an attack occur the initial resistance" must come from "the people attacked."

On June 25, 1950, the attack occurred. In an orderly, coordinated offensive, North Korea sent 90,000 men across the 38th parallel into South Korea. They faced a weak, disorderly South Korean army, aptly described as "little more than a constabulary." It was a mismatch of epic proportions, and South Korean troops quickly mounted an all-out retreat. As the monsoon rains drenched the rice paddies and mountains, Korea moved swiftly toward unification under Kim's Communist government.

Why did North Korea attack? At the time, the Truman administration believed that the Soviets directed the assault. It regarded Kim as little more than a puppet whose strings were manipulated in Moscow. There is little evidence, however, to support this contention. More likely internal Korean politics dictated the course of events. Kim's position in North Korea was by no means secure. He faced organized opposition from a Democratic Front for the Unification of the Fatherland. The invasion of South Korea, therefore, may have been launched to undercut that movement. Certainly Kim informed Stalin of the impending invasion, but the idea and the timing were probably his own.

Truman had just finished a Saturday dinner in Independence, Missouri, when Acheson telephoned him with news of the invasion. His reaction was as rapid and as certain as North Korea's attack. Since both Koreas were technically wards of the United Nations, the Truman administration took the matter to the Security Council. With the Soviet Union absent (it was boycotting the United Nations over the refusal of the organization to seat the People's Republic of China), the Security Council by a 9 to 0 vote condemned the North Korean assault and demanded an immediate cease-fire. Encouraged by the United Nations's prompt action and without consulting Congress, Truman pledged American support to South Korea and strengthened the military position of the United States in Asia.

Truman termed the conflict a "UN police action" and, in fact, a number of UN members sent troops, but for all practical purposes it was a war that initially matched the United States and South Korea against North Korea. Air force advisors told Truman that they could stop the North Korean advance by bombing the Communist supply line. They convinced Truman that ground forces would not be needed. Truman's advisors seemed convinced that the Asians would turn and run at the first show of Western force. Although the bombs destroyed miles of roads and bridges, they did not slow the North Korean advance.

On June 30, Truman took the fateful step of ordering American occupation troops sta-

tioned in Japan to proceed to Korea. They soon joined their South Korean allies in a headlong retreat. For six weeks the allies fell steadily back until they stabilized a perimeter in southeast Korea around the port city of Pusan. With their offensive halted, North Korean troops mounted a seige. To the surprise of the world, the Pusan perimeter held firm.

For American soldiers it had been a painful and disappointing two months. They were fighting in an unfamiliar country for an unsatisfactory objective. Truman's announced goal was simply to restore the 38th parallel as the border between the two Koreas. Victory then was defined as a stalemate. Corporal Stephen Zeg of Chicago expressed the feeling of other soldiers when he commented, "I'll fight for my country, but I'll be damned if I see why I'm fighting to save this hellhole."

But fighting they were, and General Douglas MacArthur was determined to reverse the military situation of the war. A bold, even arrogant man, firmly fixed in his opinions and certain of his ability to command in battle, MacArthur decided to split his forces and launch a surprise attack against the North Koreans' rear. On the morning of September 15, 1950, American marines began an amphibious attack on In-

American occupation troops stationed in Japan joined South Korean allies in a retreat to the southeast area of Korea, where they managed to hold off the North Korean forces.

chon, a port city, wrote one historian, "about as large as Jersey City, as ugly as Liverpool, and as dreary as Belfast." MacArthur's military advisors warned him against the move, noting that Inchon possessed every natural and geographic handicap. MacArthur, however, was confident of victory. It was a bold, risky maneuver—a bold, risky, successful maneuver.

Faced with an enemy to their front and their rear, North Korean troops retreated across the border. By the beginning of October those North Korean soldiers who were not captured or killed were above the 38th parallel. Truman had achieved his stated objective. But the warrior in MacArthur wanted more—he wanted

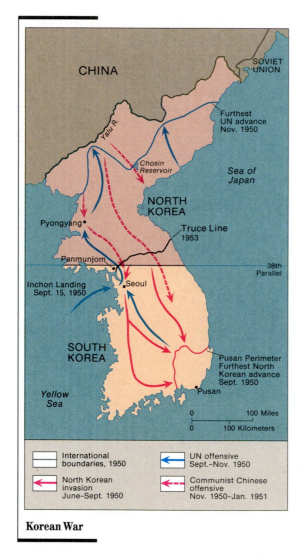

Korean War

victory on the battlefield. And he said so, loudly and publicly. In private the Truman administration was moving toward MacArthur's position. Containment was giving way to a policy of liberation. After receiving MacArthur's reassurances at a private meeting on Wake Island, Truman decided to allow U.S. forces to move across the 38th parallel and "liberate" North Korea. Like MacArthur's Inchon landing, it was a bold plan, predicated on the widely held American belief that Red China would not intervene in the conflict.

This time boldness failed. North Korea was a difficult country to invade. The American army had no reliable maps and mountainous terrain rendered traditional military tactics impossible. In addition, as MacArthur's forces moved recklessly north toward Manchuria, Chinese officials sent informal warnings to the United States that unless the advance stopped, their country would enter the fray. MacArthur ignored Chinese warnings and his own intelligence reports and kept moving.

Communist China struck in late November. Over 300,000 troops poured across the border and attacked unprepared American forces. An advance force of marines near the Chosin Reservoir was cut off from the main army. They made the best of a bad situation. "The enemy is in front of us, behind us, to the left of us, and to the right of us," Colonel Lewis B. "Chesty" Puller told his regiment. "They won't escape *this* time." Puller's bravado, however, could not hide the terrible truth. The entry of Communist China into the conflict had radically altered the nature of the war.

Victory was now out of the question. Only MacArthur continued to talk about an absolute victory. If a nation was going to fight a war, he sermonized, it should fight to win. In Washington, however, the Truman administration was shifting back to the pre-Inchon policy of containment. When MacArthur publicly criticized the administration's newest approach, an angry Truman recalled him and replaced him with General Matthew B. Ridgway. In America Truman's sacking of Mac raised a firestorm of protest. An April 1951 Gallup poll reported that 66 percent of Americans disapproved of Truman's firing of the general, and then in October, 56 percent indicated that they believed Korea was a "useless war."

The Korean War dragged on until July 10, 1951, when formal peace negotiations began, but it proved to be a long, difficult process. While diplomats talked, American soldiers fought and died. Altogether, 34,000 Americans were killed and 103,000 wounded during the Korean War. When Truman left office in early 1953 the carnage still continued. Finally on July 26, 1953, the war ended as it began, with North Koreans above the 38th parallel and South Koreans below it. It was a victory for Truman's containment policy, but for millions of Americans it somehow tasted like defeat.

THE COLD WAR AT HOME

Commie for a day. It was a theme idea. It answered the question, "What would it be like to live under a Soviet-type, communist dictatorship?" On May Day 1950, at Mosinee, Wisconsin, American Legionnaires disguised themselves as Soviet soldiers and staged a mock Communist takeover of their town. They arrested and summarily locked up the mayor and clergymen, nationalized all businesses, confiscated all firearms, and rid the library of rows of objectionable books. They even forced Mosinee residents to alter their eating habits. The local restaurants served only potato soup, dark bread, and black coffee, and only Young Communist Leaguers were permitted to eat candy. Eventually Mosinee patriots "liberated" their town, and at dusk they held a mass democratic rally amidst much patriotic music and the burning of Communist literature.

For most of Mosinee's citizens it was an edifying experiment. "We really learned about what 100 percent communism would be like," one resident observed. They concluded that life under communism was hardly worth living. Many found intolerable the lack of such basic freedoms as privacy, speech, press, religion, and decent food. One participant confessed, "I know some people who even drove to [neighboring] Wausau to get something to eat. In Russia I guess you wouldn't be able to get anything else anywhere."

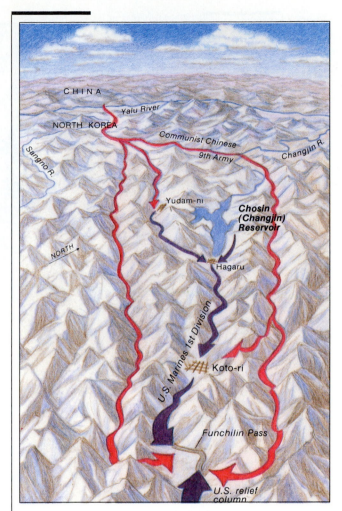

Marine Breakout from Chosin Reservoir
The Communist Chinese forces (100,000) had set a trap for the Marines (20,000) at Chosin Reservoir. The Marines doggedly fought their way out of the mountains in weather that ranged from −30°F at night to about 0° during the day.

There is an element of humor to Mosinee's Red May Day. But behind the events was a national mood that was far from funny. As Truman waged the Cold War abroad, Cold War issues gradually came to dominate the American domestic scene. During the ensuing Red Scare, the fear of communism disrupted American life, and the freedoms that Americans took for granted came under attack. At home as well as abroad, Americans battled real and imagined Communist enemies.

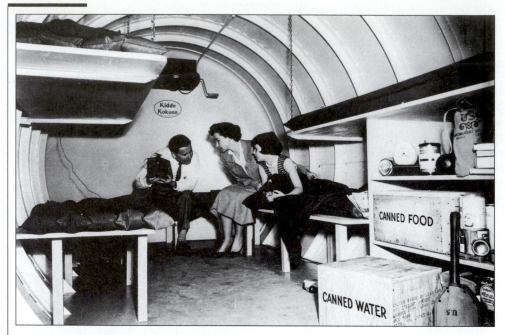

H-bomb shelters could take care of a family for three to five days and were big selling items in the 1950s. This deluxe model came equipped with five bunks and air mattresses.

Adjusting to Peace

Truman and his advisors approached the end of World War II with their eyes on the past. They were uneasy about the future. Memories of the Great Depression and the painful social and economic adjustment after World War I clouded their thinking. They knew that massive wartime spending, not the New Deal, had ended the decade of depression, and they worried that peace might bring more economic suffering. Peace with prosperity was their goal.

The solution to the problems of converting back to a peacetime economy, Truman believed, lay in the continuation, at least for a time, of wartime government economic controls. During the war the Office of Price Administration (OPA) had controlled prices and held inflation in check. After Japan surrendered, Truman asked Congress to continue price controls and outlined a program for economic reconversion. To ensure future prosperity, Truman advocated such economic measures as a 65-cents-an-hour minimum wage, nationalization of the housing industry, and stronger fair employment practices legislation.

Congress responded half-heartedly. It did pass the Employment Act of 1946. Although it was less than Truman had requested, it did provide the institutional framework for more government control over the economy. The act created the Council of Economic Advisors to help "promote free competitive enterprise, to avoid economic fluctuations . . . and to maintain employment, production, and purchasing power." During the decades after 1946, the council exerted a powerful influence over economic policy.

On the other hand, Republicans and southern Democrats balked against a return to more "New Dealism." One influential congressman even accused Truman of "out-dealing the New Deal." Instead, Congress destroyed the OPA by relaxing its controls, a policy that created immediate inflation. Congress's refusal to pass Truman's economic package did not tumble America into another depression. In truth, the American economy was basically sound. Wartime employment and wartime saving had created a people whose money was burning holes in their pockets. They wanted peacetime goods—automobiles, houses, Scotch whiskey, nylon stockings, and red meat. Given the demand and the short supply, inflation was inevitable. In addition, the short supply of consumer goods increased black market activities. Americans offered bribes for preferential treatment from car salesmen, butchers, and landlords. But as industries converted to peacetime production, consumer supplies rose to meet the new demands.

Confronting the Demands of Labor

The death of the OPA led to demands for higher wages as well as higher prices. During the war labor unions had taken "no strike" pledges, and through their efforts America became the "arsenal of democracy." Workers labored long and hard, agreeing to speedups and higher production quotas. Virtually no production time was lost to strikes.

The end of the war signaled the start of the strike season as workers demanded rewards for their wartime efforts and their loss of overtime pay. During 1946 over 4.5 million laborers struck, and 107,476,000 workdays were lost to strikes. If labor's cause was just, its timing was disastrous. After clashing repeatedly with an obstreperous Congress, Truman was in no mood to coddle labor. When two national railway brotherhoods threatened to disrupt the transportation system, Truman proposed to draft the workers. On national radio he announced, "The crisis at Pearl Harbor was the result of action by a foreign enemy. The crisis tonight is caused by a group of men within our country who place their private interests above the welfare of the nation." Confronted by hostile public opinion and an unsympathetic president, the brotherhoods went back to work.

Labor was angry. United Mine Workers leader John L. Lewis told reporters, "You can't mine coal with bayonets." As winter approached, Lewis took his men out on strike. The prospect of a cold winter created anxiety, and Truman reacted angrily. He threatened to take over the mines and lashed out publicly at the defiant Lewis. Finally Truman appealed directly to the miners, asking them to go back to work for the good and warmth of the nation. It worked. Lewis called off the strike. Truman's prestige and confidence soared.

Truman's gains were labor's losses. The congressional elections of 1946, which brought the conservative Republican-controlled Eightieth Congress, added to labor's problems. Led by Robert Taft, Congress pushed through the Labor-Management Relations Act of 1947 (better known as the Taft-Hartley Act), which was passed over Truman's veto. It outlawed the closed shop (a business or industry in which all the employees were required to join a union), gave presidents power to delay strikes by declaring a "cooling-off" period, and curtailed the political and economic power of organized labor. The act signified the conservative mood of the country.

It was a bad period for all workers, but for female workers it was especially hard. During the war they had filled a wide range of industrial jobs, but returning soldiers quickly displaced them. Some accepted the change and returned to their prewar occupations. Others resented the loss of their relatively high-paying jobs. What was worse, when new jobs opened employers hired and trained younger males rather than rehire the experienced females. Thus while male workers complained about the antilabor mood of the country, many unemployed women laborers lamented the antifemale prejudices among employers.

Failure of the Fair Deal

Political experts expected America to vote Republican in the 1948 presidential elections. Truman's policies had angered liberals, labor, Southerners, and most of Congress. Moreover, Democrats had occupied the White House since 1933. Republicans reasoned that it was time for a change. They nominated Thomas E. Dewey of New York, the GOP candidate in 1944. The Democrats stayed with Truman, even though large numbers of Southerners and liberals deserted the party to follow third-party movements. Southerners, angered by Truman's support of civil rights, formed the States' Rights Democratic party—better known as the Dixiecrats—and nominated Governor J. Strom Thurmond of South Carolina for president. Liberals joined with Communists to form the Progressive party, which nominated FDR's former vice president Henry A. Wallace for president.

SAID SOMETHING!

Most pollsters predicted that Republican candidate Thomas E. Dewey would win the 1948 presidential election, but in a stunning political upset the voters re-elected President Truman.

An underdog from the start, Truman rolled up his sleeves and took his cause to the people. His train was the 17-car "Presidential Special." The rear car was the *Ferdinand Magellan,* the bulletproof, steel-and-concrete reinforced presidential car that had been made for Roosevelt during the war. It weighed 285,000 pounds—enough to crush every other car in the train had the engineer stopped suddenly. It moved across the country, and at each stop Truman blasted the "do-nothing" Eightieth Congress. "If you send another Republican Congressman to Washington, you're a bigger bunch of suckers than I think you are," he lectured. "Give 'em hell, Harry!" was the popular refrain. By contrast, Dewey sat tight, seemingly more concerned with his fastidious appearance than his bland speeches. His cold personality failed to move American voters. "I don't know which is

the chillier experience—to have Tom ignore you or shake your hand," noted a Truman supporter. "You have to get to know Dewey to dislike him," added another.

By election day Truman had closed the gap. The old Roosevelt coalition—midwestern farmers, urban ethnics, organized labor, blacks, and Southerners—remained sufficiently strong to send Truman back to the White House. Neither the Dixiecrats nor the progressives hurt Truman in any substantial way. Most Democrats chose to remain in the center of the party with Truman rather than drift toward the radical fringes. The election was a testimony to the legacy of FDR as well as Truman's scrappiness, and to the often overlooked fact that Democrats outnumbered Republicans in the nation.

"Keep America Human With Truman," read one of his campaign posters. In 1949 he announced a plan to do just that. Known as the Fair Deal, the legislative package included an expansion of Social Security, federal aid to education, a higher minimum wage, federal funding for public housing projects, a national plan for medical insurance, civil rights legislation for minorities, and other measures to foster social and economic justice. As Truman explained, "I expect to give every segment of our population a fair deal." At the core of the Fair Deal was the belief that government-controlled economic expansion blunts extremism from the right and left and ensures prosperity.

Congress took Truman's package, stripped off the wrapping, threw away some of the contents, and sent it back to the president for his signature. Congress did extend Social Security, raise the minimum wage to 75 cents an hour, and further develop several New Deal programs. But the more original proposals of the Fair Deal—civil rights legislation, a national health insurance program, an imaginative farm program, and federal aid to education—were rejected by a Congress that opposed anything defined as "creeping socialism."

Truman, as well as Congress, contributed to the ultimate failure of the Fair Deal to achieve its objectives. To be sure, Republicans and Southerners joined forces in opposition to civil rights and government spending programs. But on domestic issues Truman demonstrated an almost total inability to work with Congress. In addition, by 1949 foreign policy dominated the president's attention and claimed an increasing share of the federal budget.

Searching for the Enemy Within

While Congress removed the heart from Truman's Fair Deal, Cold War winds were chilling the country's political landscape. The tough diplomatic rhetoric of Truman, Acheson, and other policymakers encouraged Americans to view the rivalry between the Soviet Union and the United States in simplistic terms. America became the "defender of free people," the Soviet Union the "atheistic enslaver of millions." Every time a world event did not go America's way, it was seen as a Soviet victory. In this world of black-and-white thinking, the suspicion that "enemies within" America were secretly aiding the Soviet cause took shape. Soon talk of American "atomic spies" giving information to the Soviets and State Department officials sabotaging U.S. foreign policy became common.

Were spies working against American interest to further the Soviet cause? Unquestionably, yes. In 1945 Igor Gouzenko, a Soviet embassy official in Ottawa, defected to the West, carrying with him documents that detailed a Communist spy ring working in Canada and the United States. The evidence led to the arrests of two British physicists, Dr. Alan Munn May and Dr. Klaus Fuchs, who had worked on the Manhattan Project. Fuchs implicated a group of American radicals—Harry Gold, David Greenglass, Morton Sobell, and Julius and Ethel Rosenberg. Clearly these individuals had passed atomic secrets to the Soviets during the war. Whether or not this information helped the Soviet Union to develop an atomic bomb is largely conjecture.

The damage done by British spies Kim Philby, Guy Burgess, and Donald Maclean is more certain. All these men held high British diplomatic and intelligence posts and were privy to sensitive American CIA and British Secret Intelligence Service (SIS) information. In 1951 Burgess and Maclean defected to the Soviet Union. In 1963 Philby joined them. There is considerable circumstantial evidence that the information they passed to the Soviet Union severely compromised American Cold War intelligence and perhaps may have been influential in the Chinese intervention into the Korean War.

There were certainly spies; but the issue soon outgrew the question of mere espionage and became an instrument of partisan politics. Republicans accused Democrats of being "soft" on communism—in fact, of harboring spies in the State Department and other government agencies. Richard M. Nixon, who was elected to Congress in 1946, announced that Democrats were responsible for "the unimpeded growth of the communist conspiracy in the United States." As proof Republicans pointed to the "fall" of China, the atomic bomb in the Soviet Union, and Alger Hiss in the State Department.

Truman reacted to such criticism as early as 1947 by issuing Executive Order 9835 establishing the Federal Employee Loyalty Program, a federal employee loyalty program that authorized the FBI to investigate all government employees. Although the search disclosed no espionage or treason, thousands of employees were forced to resign or were fired because their personal lives or past associations did not meet government inspection. Homosexuality, alcoholism, unpaid debts, contribution to left-wing causes, support of civil rights—all became grounds for dismissal.

Truman also used the anti-Communism issue to drum up support for his foreign policy. At the end of World War II public opinion polls revealed that few Americans regarded communism as a serious problem. Republican charges and Truman's loyalty program, however, encouraged citizens to profess 100 percent Americanism. In 1947 the president sent a special "Freedom Train" across the country to exhibit important national documents, including the Truman Doctrine. By 1950 communism had become a more visible issue at home as well as abroad.

Ethel and Julius Rosenberg paid the supreme price. They were Communists, and at least one—Ethel—may have been a spy, but the death penalty was not mandatory for their crime. Judge Irving R. Kaufman, nevertheless, made an example of them. Their "diabolical conspiracy to destroy a God-fearing nation,"

Widespread protesting, both for and against Julius and Ethel Rosenberg, was common after their conviction for treason in 1951 and subsequent execution in 1953.

Kaufman charged, had given the Soviets the bomb "years before our best scientists predicted." He ordered the couple's execution for treason. On June 19, 1953, the Rosenbergs, parents of two young sons, died in the electric chair.

The Rise and Fall of Joseph McCarthy

More than any other person, Wisconsin Senator Joseph McCarthy capitalized on the anti-Communism issue. Although he did not start the crusade or even join it until 1950, the entire movement bears the name "McCarthyism." His career, which caused so much suffering for so many, illuminated the price the country had to pay for temporarily placing anti-Communism above the Constitution.

Elected to the Senate in 1946, McCarthy spent four years in relative obscurity, all the while demonstrating his incompetency and angering his colleagues. Then on February 9, 1950,

he gave a Lincoln's Birthday address in Wheeling, West Virginia. Warning his audience about the threat of communism to America, he boldly announced, "While I cannot take the time to name all of the men in the State Department who have been named as members of the Communist Party and members of a spy ring, I have in my hand a list of 205 . . . a list of names that were known to the Secretary of State and who nevertheless are still working and shaping the policy of the State Department." McCarthy had no real list; he had no names. Simply put, he was lying. But within days he became a national sensation.

McCarthy dealt in simple solutions for complex problems. He told Americans that the United States could control the outcome of world affairs if it would get the Communists out of the State Department. It was those "State Department perverts," those "striped-pants diplomats" who "gave away" Poland, "lost" China, and allowed the Soviet Union to develop the bomb. It was the "bright young men who are born with silver spoons in their mouths" who were "selling the Nation out." His arguments found receptive ears among Catholics who had relatives in Eastern Europe, political outsiders in this country who resented the power of the "Ivy League Eastern Establishment," supporters of Jiang, and pragmatic Republicans who wanted to return to the White House in 1952. And with the outbreak of the Korean War in the early summer of 1950, Joseph McCarthy's support grew.

McCarthy's origins were humble; he worked his way through high school and a Catholic college and intentionally cultivated the image of a bull in a china closet. With his beetle brow, he looked the part of a movie villain. He was in all ways the opposite of Secretary of State Dean Acheson, whose Ivy League degrees, waxed mustache, and aristocratic accent were a flapping red flag to McCarthy. Throughout the early 1950s McCarthy bitterly attacked "Red Dean" and the State Department. But in the end, McCarthy ferreted out no Communists, espionage agents, or traitors.

McCarthy's basic tactic was never defend. Caught in a lie, he told another; when one case dissolved, he created another. He attacked Truman and Eisenhower, Acheson and Marshall, the State Department and the U.S. Army. No authority or institution frightened him. In 1954 his campaign against the army became so bitter that the Senate arranged special hearings. Televised between April 22 and June 17, the Army-McCarthy hearings attracted a high audience rating. It was the first time that most Americans saw McCarthy in action—the bullying of witnesses, the cruel innuendo, the tasteless humor. At one point he attempted to ruin a young lawyer's career in order to discredit the lawyer's associate, Joseph Welch, the army's chief counsel. Welch tried to stop McCarthy but couldn't. Appalled, the chief counsel interrupted, "Until this moment, Senator, I think I never really gauged your cruelty or your recklessness. . . . If it were in my power to forgive you for your reckless cruelty, I would do so. I like to think I am a gentle man, but your forgiveness will have to come from someone other than me. . . . Have you no sense of decency, sir, at long last?"

He didn't, and a large television audience saw that he didn't. McCarthy's downfall was as rapid as his rise. When the polls showed that his popularity had swung sharply downward, his colleagues mounted an offensive. On December 2, 1954, the Senate voted to "condemn" McCarthy for his unsenatorial behavior. Newspapers stopped printing his outlandish charges. He sank back into relative obscurity, and died on May 2, 1957.

The end of the Korean War and McCarthy's downfall signaled the end of the Red Scare. The Cold War remained, but most Americans soon realized that there was no significant domestic Communist threat. They learned that an occasional spy was part of the price that free societies pay for their personal freedom, and that "McCarthyism" can be the result of a curtailment of that freedom.

THE PARANOID STYLE

The Cold War mentality left its imprint on politics and culture during the late-1940s and early 1950s. A certain "paranoid style" permeated the early Cold War years. Defining the term historian Richard Hofstadter wrote:

Senator Joseph McCarthy's downfall came about as a result of his unsubstantiated charges of Communist infiltration throughout the country.

(Text continues on p. 928)

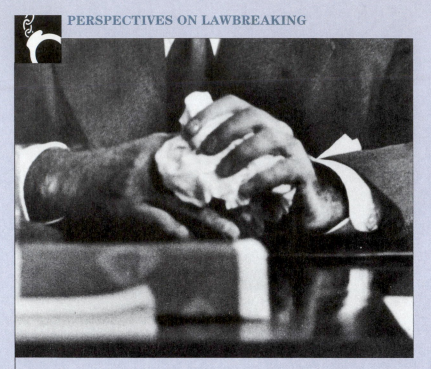

THE KEFAUVER CRIME COMMITTEE

In May 1950, at the very moment that Senator Joseph McCarthy was beginning his crusade against the domestic political threat posed by communism, the U.S. Senate created a special committee to investigate another "enemy within": organized crime. The nation appeared to be in the midst of an unprecedented wave of lawlessness. A memorandum to the president reported that a serious crime was committed in the United States every 18.7 seconds. Aggravated assault was up 68.7 percent over prewar averages; rape was up 49.9 percent. Burglary, murder, robbery, prostitution, gambling, and racketeering all were on the increase. Criminologists attributed the postwar crime wave to such factors as the wartime disruption of families, shortages of goods during

and after the war, and a continuing public demand for illicit gambling. But journalists, citizen crime commissions, and the Federal Bureau of Narcotics identified another villain, organized crime.

Estes Kefauver, an ambitious 47-year-old first-term Tennessee Democratic senator, originally proposed a congressional investigation of organized crime in January 1949. The Truman administration, already rocked by charges of fiscal mismanagement, financial irregularities, and favors to businessmen, feared that any inquiry might link urban Democratic political machines to criminal activities. For a time, the administration succeeded in blocking a potentially embarrassing investigation. But on April 6, 1950, the bodies of two gangsters were

found in a Kansas City, Missouri, Democratic political club under a photograph of President Truman. The Democratic-controlled Senate quickly authorized the investigation of organized crime.

For the next 15 months, the committee held hearings in 14 major cities and took testimony from more than 800 witnesses. The committee immediately attracted national attention by linking individuals close to Florida's Democratic governor, Fuller Warren, to a bookmaking syndicate controlled by Al Capone's mob in Chicago. Subsequent hearings in Kansas City and Chicago revealed widespread examples of political corruption and influence peddling.

Television made the Kefauver committee's hearings among the most influential in American history. While the Kefauver committee did not hold the first televised congressional hearings (it was actually the fifth congressional committee to allow TV cameras into a hearing room), it was the first to attract a massive number of viewers. As many as 20 to 30 million Americans watched spellbound as crime bosses, bookies, pimps, and hitmen appeared on their television screen. They listened intently as the committee's chairman informed them that "there is a secret international government-within-a-government" in the United States, controlling gambling, vice, and narcotics traffic and infiltrating legitimate businesses, protected by corrupt police officers, prosecutors, judges, and politicians.

The high point of the investigation occurred in New York City, where the committee held televised hearings beginning on March 12, 1951 and lasting eight days. Over 50 witnesses testified before the committee, but public interest centered on the alleged boss of the New York underworld Frank Costello, alias Francisco Castaglia, alias Frank Severio. Costello was purportedly head of the organized crime family previously run by Vito Genovese and Charles Luciano.

In his initial appearance before the committee, Costello's lawyer objected to having his client's face televised. Technicians proceded to focus the cameras on Costello's hands. The result was television at its most powerful. As committee counsel Rudolph Halley fired questions, Costello was seen nervously ripping sheets of paper to shreds, drumming his fingers on the table top, and clenching his fist.

During the New York hearings, the daytime television audience grew from a miniscule 1.5 percent of homes to a phenomenal 26.2 percent. In the New York metropolitan area an average of 86.2 percent of all individuals watching television watched the hearings, twice the number that had watched the World Series the previous October. The New York City electric company had to add a generator to supply power for all the television sets in use. Commented *Life* magazine: "The week of March 12, 1951, will occupy a special place in history.... [People] had suddenly gone indoors into living rooms, taverns and clubrooms, auditoriums and backoffices. There, in eerie half-light, looking at millions of small frosty screens, people sat as if charmed.... Never before had the attention of the nation been riveted so completely on a single matter."

The Kefauver committee failed to produce effective crime fighting legislation, but it did heighten public awareness of the problem of political corruption and organized crime and generated pressure to enforce existing law. In the aftermath of the committee's investigation, more than 70 local crime commissions were established. The Special Rackets Squad of the FBI launched 46,000 investigations, and by 1957, federal prosecutors had won 874 convictions and recovered $336 million. The committee's hearings were largely responsible for the defeat of proposals to legalize gambling in Arizona, California, Massachusetts, and Montana.

The investigation was important in one other respect. The Kefauver committee played a vital role in popularizing the myth that organized crime in the United States was an alien import, brought to the United States by Italian, and especially by Sicilian, immigrants in the form of the Mafia, a highly centralized, secret organization, which used violence and deceit to prey on the weaknesses and vices of the public. In its report, the committee asserted that much of the responsibility for gambling, loan sharking, prostitutions, and narcotics trafficking lay in two major syndicates.

In fact, the committee's conclusion—that organized crime was rooted in a highy centralized ethnic conspiracy—was in error. Most organized crime in the United States is organized on a municipal and regional, rather than a national, basis. And despite the image portrayed in such epics as Mario Puzo's *The Godfather*, diverse ethnic groups have participated in such sophisticated crimes as large-scale gambling, loan sharking, narcotics trafficking, and labor racketeering.

Today, the power of the nation's traditional Mafia families appears to be dwindling. Since the mid-1980s, more than 100 top Cosa Nostra leaders have been sentenced to long prison terms. In Detroit, Kansas City, Milwaukee, New England, New Jersey, Philadelphia, and St. Louis, where Mafia gangs once influenced the construction, trucking, trash collection, and garment manufacturing industries, Mafia strength has sharply declined. Nevertheless, the decline of the mob does not mean the end of organized crime; rival crime groups have stepped in and taken over activities such as illegal gambling and drug trafficking.

It is, above all, a way of seeing the world and of expressing oneself. . . . The distinguishing thing about the paranoid style is . . . that its exponents see . . . a "vast" or "gigantic" conspiracy as *the motive force* in historical events. . . . The paranoid spokesman sees the fate of this conspiracy in apocalyptic terms—he traffics in the birth and death of whole worlds, whole political orders, whole systems of human values. . . . Since what is at stake is always a conflict between absolute good and absolute evil, the quality needed is not a willingness to compromise but the will to fight things out to the finish.

The nature of the fight against communism contributed to the paranoid style. Politicians warned Americans that communism silently and secretly destroyed a country from within. Although directed from Moscow, its aim was subversion through the slow destruction of a country's moral fiber. No one knew which institution it would next attack, or when. It might be the State Department or the YMCA; it might be the presidency, the army, the movie industry, or the Cub Scouts. Politicians counseled vigilance. They told Americans to watch for the unexpected, to suspect everyone and everything. As a result, between 1945 and 1955 a broad spectrum of institutions, organizations, and individuals came under suspicion. Whether it was the Mafia or the fluoridation of drinking water, Americans sought the answers to complex problems in the workings of conspiracies.

HUAC Goes to Hollywood

The House of Representatives established the Un-American Activities Committee (HUAC) in the late 1930s to combat subversive right-wing and left-wing movements. Its history was less than distinguished. From the first it tended to see subversive Communists everywhere at work in American society. HUAC even announced that the Boy Scouts were Communist infiltrated. During the late 1940s and the early 1950s HUAC picked up the tempo of its investigations, which it conducted in well-publicized sessions. Twice during this period HUAC traveled to Hollywood to investigate Communist infiltration in the film industry.

HUAC first went to Hollywood in 1947. Al-though it didn't find the party line preached in the movies, it did call a group of radical screen writers and producers into its sessions to testify. Asked if they were Communists, the "Hollywood Ten" refused to answer questions about their political beliefs. As Ring Lardner, Jr., one of the ten, said, "I could answer . . . but if I did, I would hate myself in the morning." They believed that the First Amendment protected them. In the politically charged late 1940s, however, their rights were not protected. Those who refused to divulge their political affiliations were tried for contempt of Congress, sent to prison, and blacklisted.

HUAC went back to Hollywood in 1951. This time it called hundreds of witnesses from both the political right and the political left. Conservatives told HUAC that Hollywood was littered with "Commies." Walt Disney even recounted attempts to have Mickey Mouse follow the party line. Of the radicals, some talked but most didn't. To cooperate with HUAC entailed "naming names"—that is, informing on one's friends and political acquaintances. Again, those who refused to name names found themselves unemployed and unemployable.

The House Un-American Activities Committee conducted an investigation of Communist activities in Hollywood that included testimony by such notable actors as Ronald Reagan.

The HUAC hearings and blacklisting convinced Hollywood producers to make strongly anti-Communist films. Between 1947 and 1954 they released more than 50 such films. Most were second-rate movies, starring third-rate actors. The films assured Americans that Communists were thoroughly bad people—they didn't have children, they exhaled cigarette smoke too slowly, they murdered their "friends," and they went berserk when arrested. As one film historian has commented, the Communists in these anti-Communist films even looked alike; most were "apt to be exceptionally haggard or disgracefully pudgy," and there was certainly "something terribly wrong with a woman if her slip straps showed through her blouse."

If the films were bad civics lessons, they did have an impact. They seemed to confirm HUAC's position that Communists were everywhere, that subversives lurked in every shadow. They reaffirmed the paranoid style and helped to justify McCarthy's harangues and Truman's Cold War rhetoric.

Movies like *Rebel Without a Cause*, starring James Dean, depicted the futility and hopelessness of American youth in the 1950s.

"What's Wrong with Our Kids Today?"

At the same time it turned out films about serious but bumbling Communists, Hollywood produced movies that contributed to the fear that something was terribly wrong with the youth of America. Films such as *The Wild One* (1954), *Blackboard Jungle* (1955), and *Rebel Without a Cause* (1955) portrayed adolescents as budding criminals, emerging homosexuals, potential Fascists, and pathological misfits—everything but perfectly normal kids. On close inspection, cultural critics concluded that something was indeed wrong with American youth, who like Tony in *I Was a Teenage Werewolf* (1957) seemed closer to uncontrollable beasts than civilized adults. As Tony tells a psychiatrist, "I say things, I do things—I don't know why."

FBI reports and congressional investigations reinforced the theme of adolescent moral decline. J. Edgar Hoover, head of the FBI, linked the rise in juvenile delinquency to the decline in the influence of family, home, church, and local community institutions. Youths had moved away from benign authority toward temptations of popular culture, which, Hoover said, "flout indecency and applaud lawlessness."

Frederic Wertham, a psychiatrist who studied the problem extensively, agreed, emphasizing particularly the pernicious influence of comic books. He believed that crime and horror comic books fostered racism, fascism, and sexism in their readers. In his book *Seduction of the Innocent* (1954), Wertham even linked homosexuality to the reading of comics. Describing how the comic *Batman* could lead to homosexuality, Wertham quoted one of his male patients: "I remember the first time I came across the page mentioning the 'secret bat cave.' The thought of Batman and Robin living together and possibly having sex relations came to my mind . . . I felt I'd like to be loved by someone like Batman or Superman." Far from being an unheard voice, Wertham's attack generated congressional investigations of and local attacks against the comic book industry. In response, the comic book industry passed several self-regulatory codes designed to restrict the violent and sexual content of comic books.

For a number of critics, sports were an antidote to the ills of wayward youths. "Organized sport is one of our best weapons against juvenile delinquency," remarked J. Edgar Hoover. Youths who competed for championship trophies felt no inclination to compete for "wrist watches, bracelets and automobiles that belong to other people." Nor would they turn to communism. As Senator Herman Welker of Idaho bluntly put it, "I never saw a ballplayer who was a Communist."

Given these widespread beliefs, the sports scandals of the early 1950s shocked the nation and raised fresh questions about the morality of American adolescents. In February 1951 New York authorities disclosed that players for the City College of New York (CCNY) basketball team had accepted money to fix games. By the time the investigations ended, Long Island University, New York University, Manhattan College, St. John's, Toledo, Bradley, and Kentucky were implicated in the scandal, which involved forging transcripts and paying players as well as fixing games.

In August 1951 the scandal moved to football. This one involved academic cheating, not point shaving, and was confined to one school—the United States Military Academy at West Point. Altogether, academy officials dismissed 90 cadets, half of them football players, for violations of the school's honor code. "These acts," said Senator Harry F. Byrd of Virginia, "have struck a blow at the morals of the youth of the country which will last for a long time."

The West Point scandal especially struck at the nation's heart, for half a world away in Korea American soldiers were battling to contain communism. What of their moral fiber? They too had read comics, watched films written by left-wing screen writers, and been exposed to the "subversive" influences. Did they have the "right stuff"? These questions swirled around the Korean prisoner of war (POW) controversy. Early reports suggested the American POWs in Korea were different from, and inferior to, those of World War II. Journalists portrayed them as undisciplined, morally weak, susceptible to "brainwashing," uncommitted to traditional American ideals, and prone to collaborate with their guards. POW experiences seemed to confirm that something indeed was wrong with the kids of America.

What was wrong? Who was corrupting the youth of America? The Republican *Chicago Tribune* blamed the affair on the New Deal. The Communist *Daily Worker* said it was the fault of Wall Street, bankers, and greedy politicians. The paranoid style, after all, had no party affiliation. Other Americans, without being too specific, simply felt that there was some ominous force working within America against America.

Adherents to the paranoid style dealt more with vague perceptions than concrete facts. They reacted more to what seemed to be true than to what actually was true. In fact, sociologists and historians have demonstrated that Korean POWs behaved in much the same way as POWs from earlier wars. And during the late 1940s and 1950s juvenile delinquency was not on an upswing. Alien subversive forces were not undermining American morality. In retrospect, we know this. But the rhetoric of the Cold War and McCarthyism created a political atmosphere that proved fertile for the paranoid style.

CONCLUSION

By 1953 and 1954 there were indications of a thaw in the Cold War. First came the death of Joseph Stalin, which was officially announced on March 5, 1953. Shortly thereafter Georgi Malenkov told the Supreme Soviet, the highest legislative body of the Soviet Union: "At the present time there is no disputed or unresolved question that cannot be settled peacefully by mutual agreement. . . . This applies to our relations with all states, including the United States of America." That summer the Korean War ended in a stalemate that allowed both the United States and the Communist forces to save face. In America, 1954 saw the fall of McCarthy. Certainly these events did not end the paranoid style in either America or the Soviet Union, but they did ease the tension.

In addition, by 1954 both the United States and the Soviet Union had become more comfortable in their positions as world powers. Leaders in both countries had begun to realize that neither side could readily win the Cold War. Between 1945 and 1954 each had carved out

CHRONOLOGY
OF KEY EVENTS

1938 House Un-American Activities Committee (HUAC) is created to investigate Fascist or Communist subversion

1945 United Nations is founded

1947 Truman Doctrine declares that the United States will provide military and economic aid to allies faced by external aggression or internal subversion; Truman establishes a federal program to investigate the loyalty of government employees; Marshall Plan provides $17 billion over four years to aid Western Europe's economic recovery; Taft-Hartley Act passed over President Truman's veto bans the closed shop, restricts union political contributions, and allows courts to delay strikes threatening health or safety; HUAC investigates Communist infiltration of the film industry

1948 State of Israel proclaimed; United States, Britain, and France merge their zones of occupation in Germany to form an independent nation, West Germany; Soviet Union blockades Berlin; ex-Communist Whittaker Chambers charges former State Department official Alger Hiss of giving him secret government documents

1949 NATO is founded; Berlin blockade ends; Mao Tse-tung's Communist forces win China's civil war; Soviet Union successfully tests an atomic bomb

1950 NSC-68 argues that the United States must commit itself to whatever military steps are necessary to stop the spread of communism; Senator Joseph McCarthy claims he has the names of 205 State Department employees who were members of the Communist party; North Korean troops cross the 38th parallel, beginning the Korean War; UN forces invade North Korea; Chinese troops enter North Korea and force UN troops to retreat across the 38th parallel

1951 Negotiations to work out a cease-fire in Korea begin; HUAC conducts a second investigation of Communist subversion in Hollywood; Ethel and Julius Rosenberg are sentenced to death for atomic espionage

1953 Dwight D. Eisenhower is inaugurated thirty-fourth president; cease-fire in Korean War

1954 Army-McCarthy hearings; U.S. Senate censures McCarthy for "conduct unbecoming a member"

spheres of influence. The Soviet Union and its sometime-ally China dominated most of Eastern Europe and the Asian mainland. America and its allies controlled Western Europe, North and South America, most of the Pacific, and to a lesser extent Africa, the Middle East, and Southeast Asia. Throughout much of the Third World, however, emerging nationalistic movements challenged both U.S. and Soviet influences.

In the United States, the containment policy was seldom even debated. The Truman Doctrine and muscular internationalism governed foreign policy decisions, but economic and political questions lingered. How much would containment cost? Where would the money come from? Which Americans would pay the most? Would it mean the end of liberal reform? During the next decade American leaders would wrestle with these and other questions.

SUGGESTIONS FOR FURTHER READING

OVERVIEWS AND SURVEYS

Stephen E. Ambrose, *Rise to Globalism: American Foreign Policy since 1938*, 5th ed. (1988); H. W. Brands, *Inside the Cold War* (1991); William H. Chafe, *The Unfinished Journey*, 2d ed. (1991), and *The American Woman* (1972); Alexander DeConde, *A History of American Foreign Policy* (1963); Robert H. Ferrell, *American Diplomacy* (1959); John Lewis Gaddis, *The United States and the Cold War* (1992); Alonzo Hamby, *The Imperial Years* (1976); Godfrey Hodgson, *America in Our Time* (1976); Michael J. Lacey, ed., *The Truman Presidency* (1989); Walter LaFeber, *America, Russia, and the Cold War*, 5th ed. (1985); R. W. Leopold, *The Growth of American Foreign Policy* (1962); William Leuchtenburg, *A Troubled Feast*, rev. ed. (1983); William Manchester, *The Glory and the Dream* (1974); Thomas J. McCormick, *America's Half-Century* (1989); Thomas G. Paterson et al., *American Foreign Policy*, 3d ed., 2 vols. (1988), and with Robert J. McMahon, *The Origins of the Cold War*, 3d ed. (1991); Richard Polenberg, *One Nation Divisible* (1980); Emily and Norman Rosenberg, *In Our Times*, 4th ed. (1991); Frederick F. Siegel, *A Troubled Journey* (1984); William A. Williams, *The Tragedy of American Diplomacy*, 2d ed. (1972), and *The Roots of the Modern American Empire* (1969); Lawrence Wittner, *Cold War America*, rev. ed. (1978); Howard Zinn, *Postwar America, 1945–1971* (1973).

CONTAINING THE RUSSIAN BEAR

Gar Alperovitz, *Atomic Diplomacy*, rev. ed. (1985); Terry H. Anderson, *The United States, Great Britain and the Cold War, 1944–1947* (1981); James Aronson, *The Press and the Cold War* (1970); Stanley D. Bachrack, *The Committee of One Million: "China Lobby" Politics, 1953–1971* (1976); Richard J. Barnet, *The Giants: Russia and America* (1977); Ronald J. Caridi, *The Korean War and American Politics* (1969); Gordon H. Chang, *Friends and Enemies: The United States, China, and the Soviet Union, 1948–1972* (1990); Bernard C. Cohen, *The Public's Impact on Foreign Policy* (1972); Bruce Cumings, *The Origins of the Korean War*, 2 vols. (1981–1990); Lynn Etheridge Davis, *The Cold War Begins: Soviet-American Conflict over Eastern Europe* (1974); A. W. DePorte, *Europe Between the Superpowers: The Enduring Balance*, 2d ed. (1986); Herbert Feis, *From Trust to Terror: The Onset of the Cold War* (1970); Richard B. Finn, *Winners in Peace: MacArthur, Yoshida, and Postwar Japan* (1992); D. F. Fleming, *The Cold War and Its Origins*, 2 vols. (1961); John L. Gaddis, *The United States and the Origins of the Cold War, 1941–1947* (1972), and *Strategies of Containment: A Crucial Appraisal of Postwar American National Security Policy* (1982); Lloyd C. Gardner, *Architects of Illusion: Men and Ideas in American Foreign Policy, 1941–1949* (1970); Marshall I. Goldman, *Detente and Dollars: Doing Business with the Soviets* (1975); Michael Hogan, *The Marshall Plan* (1987); Akira Iriye, *The Cold War in Asia* (1974); Howard Jones, *A New Kind of War: America's Global Strategy and the Truman Doctrine in Greece* (1989); Burton Kaufman, *Trade and Aid* (1982); Joyce and Gabriel Kolko, *The Limits of Power: The World and U.S. Foreign Policy, 1945–1954* (1972); Bennett Kovrig, *The Myth of Liberation; East-Central Europe in U.S. Diplomacy and Politics Since 1941* (1973); Bruce Kuklick, *American Policy and the Division of Germany* (1972); Melvyn P. Leffler, *A Preponderance of Power: National Security, the Truman Administration, and the Cold War* (1991); Ralph B. Levering, *The Public and American Foreign Policy, 1918–1978* (1978), and *The Cold War, 1945–1987*, 2d ed. (1988); Louis Liebovich, *The Press and the Origins of the Cold War, 1944–1947* (1988); Vojtech Mastny, *Russia's Road to the Cold War, 1941–1945* (1979); Ernest R. May, *The Truman Administration and China, 1945–1949* (1975); Thomas Paterson, *On Every Front: The Making and Unmaking of the Cold War*, rev. ed. (1992); David Rees, *Korea: The Limited War* (1964); Martin Sherwin, *A World Destroyed: The Atomic Bomb and the Grand Alliance* (1975); John W. Spanier, *The Truman-MacArthur Controversy and the Korean War* (1959); Hugh Thomas, *Armed Truce: The Beginnings of the Cold War* (1986); Adam B. Ulam, *Expansion and Coexistence: The History of Soviet Foreign Policy, 1917–73*, 2d ed. (1974); William Welch, *American Images of Soviet Foreign Policy* (1970); Allen S. Whiting, *China Crosses the Yalu: The Decision to Enter the Korean War* (1960); Lawrence Wittner, *American Intervention in Greece, 1943–1949* (1982); Daniel Yergin, *Shattered Peace* (1977).

THE COLD WAR AT HOME

Edwin R. Bayley, *Joe McCarthy and the Press* (1981); Jeff Broadwater, *Eisenhower and the Anti-Communist Crusade* (1992); David Brody, *Workers in Industrial America* (1980); David Caute, *The Great Fear: The Anti-Communist Purge under Truman and Eisenhower* (1978); Alistair Cooke, *A Generation on Trial* (1950); Richard Freeland, *The Truman Doctrine and the Origins of McCarthyism*

(1972); Richard M. Fried, *Men Against McCarthy* (1976), and *Nightmare in Red* (1990); Walter Goodman, *The Committee* (1968); Robert Griffith, *The Politics of Fear*, 2d ed. (1987); Alonzo Hamby, *Beyond the New Deal: Harry S. Truman and American Liberalism* (1973); Susan M. Hartmann, *Truman and the 80th Congress* (1971); Fred Inglis, *The Cruel Peace: Everyday Life and the Cold War* (1991); Richard S. Kirkendall, *Harry S. Truman, Korea, and the Imperial Presidency* (1975); Stanley I. Kutler, *The American Inquisition: Justice and Injustice in the Cold War* (1982); R. Alton Lee, *Truman and Taft-Hartley* (1966); Samuel Lubell, *Future of American Politics* (1952); Maeva Marcus, *Truman and the Steel Seizure Case* (1977); Allen J. Matusow, *Farm Policies and Politics in the Truman Years* (1967); Michael Rogin, *The Intellectuals and McCarthy* (1967); Athan Theoharis, *Seeds of Repression: Harry S. Truman and the Origins of McCarthyism* (1971); Allen Weinstein, *Perjury: The Hiss-Chambers Case* (1978); Theodore Wilson, "The Kefauver Committee" in *Congress Investigates,* vol. 5, Arthur M. Schlesinger, Jr., and Roger Bruns, eds. (1975).

THE PARANOID STYLE

Larry Ceplair and Steven Englund, *The Inquisition in Hollywood* (1980); Stephen Fox, *Blood and Power: Organized Crime in Twentieth Century America* (1990); Eric Goldman, *The Crucial Decade and After* (1961); Richard Hofstadter, *The Paranoid Style in American Politics and Other Essays* (1965); William Howard Moore, *The Kefauver Committee and the Politics of Crime* (1974); Victor Navasky, *Naming Names* (1980); Nora Sayre, *Running Time: Films of the Cold War* (1982); Stephen J. Whitfield, *The Culture of the Cold War* (1991).

BIOGRAPHIES

Dean Acheson, *Present at the Creation: My Years in the State Department* (1969); Charles E. Bohlen, *Witness to History, 1929-1969* (1973); Robert J. Donovan, *Conflict and Crisis* (1977), and *Tumultuous Years* (1982); Robert H. Ferrell, *George C. Marshall* (1966), and *Harry S Truman and the Modern American Presidency* (1983); Charles L. Fontenay, *Estes Kefauver* (1980); Joseph Bruce Gorman, *Kefauver* (1971); Walter L. Hixson, *George F. Kennan* (1989); David S. McLellan, *Dean Acheson* (1976); David M. Oshinsky, *A Conspiracy So Immense: The World of Joe McCarthy* (1983); James T. Patterson, *Mr. Republican: A Biography of Robert A. Taft* (1972); Thomas C. Reeves, *The Life and Times of Joe McCarthy* (1982); Richard R. Rovere, *Senator Joe McCarthy* (1959); Edward L. and Frederick H. Schapsmeier, *Prophet in Politics: Henry A. Wallace and the War Years, 1940–1965* (1971); Gaddis Smith, *Dean Acheson* (1972); Ronald Steel, *Walter Lippmann and the American Century* (1980); Anders Stephanson, *Kennan and the Art of Foreign Policy* (1989); Mark A. Stoler, *George C. Marshall* (1989); Harry S Truman, *Memoirs*, 2 vols. (1955–1956).

Fig. 287

103

COMPANY

CHAPTER 28

Ike's America

A

Figure 1-3. Equator, Latitude, and Parallels of Latitude

20c

ose Wright stood and surveyed the courtroom. Most of the faces he saw were white. The two accused men were white. The 12 jurors were white. The armed guards were white. Slowly, Wright, a 64-year-old black sharecropper, extended his right arm. "Thar he," Wright answered, pointing at J. W. Milam. He then pointed at Roy Bryant, the second defendant. In essence, Wright was accusing the two whites of murdering Emmett Till, his 14-year-old nephew—accusing them in a segregated courtroom in Sumner, Mississippi. Wright later recalled that he could "feel the blood boil in hundreds of white people as they sat glaring in the courtroom. It was the first time in my life I had the courage to accuse a white man of a crime, let alone something as terrible as killing a boy. I wasn't exactly brave and I wasn't scared. I just wanted to see justice done."

It was 1955, but the march of racial justice in the South had been painfully slow. In 1954 the Supreme Court of the United States in the landmark *Brown* v. *Board of Education of Topeka* decision had ruled that segregated schooling was "inherently unequal." News of the *Brown* decision drew angry comments and reactions from all corners of the Jim Crow South. Mississippi Senator James Eastland told his constituents that the decision destroyed the Constitution of the United States and counseled, "You are not obliged to obey the decisions of any court which are plainly fraudulent." Throughout Dixie, Klansmen burned crosses while other white leaders hastily organized Citizens' Councils. Self-proclaimed protectors of white America vowed "to make it difficult, if not impossible, for any Negro who advocates desegregation to find and hold a job, get credit, or renew a mortgage."

Into this racially charged atmosphere came Emmett Till in August 1955. Taking a summer vacation from his home on the South Side of Chicago, he rode a train to visit relatives living near Money, Mississippi. Emmett had known segregation in Chicago, but nothing like what he discovered in Money, where shortly before his arrival a black girl had been "flogged" for "crowding white people" in a store.

Emmett's mother told him what to expect and how to act: "If you have to get on your knees and bow when a white person goes past, do it

willingly." But Emmett had a mind and a mouth of his own. In Chicago, he told his cousins, he was friends with plenty of white people. He even had a picture of a white girl, *his* white girl, he said. "Hey," challenged a listener, "there's a [white] girl in that store there. I bet you won't go in there and talk to her."

Emmett accepted the challenge. He entered Bryant's Grocery and Meat Market, browsed about, and bought some bubble gum. As he left, he said, "Bye, Baby" to Carolyn Bryant and gave a "wolf call" whistle. Outside an old black man told Emmett to scat before the woman got a pistol and blew "his brains out." The advice sounded sage enough, so Emmett beat a hasty retreat.

A few days later Roy Bryant returned to Money after hauling shrimp from Louisiana to Texas. What his wife told him is unknown, but it was enough to make him angry. After midnight that Saturday night, he and his half-brother, J. W. "Big" Milam, drove to Mose Wright's unpainted cabin. They demanded the "boy who done the talkin'." Mose tried to explain that Emmett was from "up nawth," that he "ain't got good sense" and was unfamiliar with southern ways. The logic of the argument was lost on the two white men, one of whom told Mose that if he caused trouble he would never see his next birthday.

Various stories have been told about what happened during the next few hours. One thing is for certain: Emmett Till did not live much past daybreak. According to Milam and Bryant's account, they had only meant to scare the northern youth. But Emmett did not beg for mercy. Therefore they *had* to kill him. "What else could we do?" Milam asked. "He was hopeless. I'm no bully; I never hurt a nigger in my life. I like niggers in their place. I know how to work'em. But I just decided it was time a few people got put on notice."

Three days later Emmett's badly beaten body was found in the Tallahatchie River. A gouged out eye, crushed forehead, and bullet in his skull gave evidence to the beating he took. Around his neck, attached by barbed wire, was a 75-pound cotton gin fan. At the request of his mother, the local sheriff sent the decomposing body to Chicago for burial.

Mamie Bradley, Emmett's mother, grieved

openly and loudly. Contrary to the wishes of Mississippi authorities, she held an open casket funeral. Thousands of black Chicagoans attended the viewing, and the black press closely followed the episode. *Jet* magazine even published a picture of the mutilated corpse. In the black community the Till murder case became a cause célèbre. In a land that valued justice, would any be found in Mississippi?

In Money, white Southerners rallied to Bryant and Milam's side. Supporters raised a $10,000 defense fund, and southern editorials labeled the entire affair a "Communist plot" to destroy southern society. By the time the trial started, American interest seemed focused on Mississippi. Few people, however, expected that Bryant and Milam would be judged guilty because few expected any blacks would testify against white men in Mississippi.

Mose Wright proved the folly of common wisdom. He dramatically testified against the white men. So did several other relatives of Emmett Till. But in his closing statement, John C. Whitten, one of the five white attorneys, told the all-white, all-male jury: "Your fathers will turn over in their graves if [Milam and Bryant are found guilty] and I'm sure that every last Anglo-Saxon one of you has the courage to free these men in the face of that [outside] pressure."

The jury returned a "not guilty" verdict in one hour and seven minutes. "If we hadn't stopped to drink a pop, it wouldn't have taken that long," one juror commented. On that day in 1955 there was no justice in Sumner, Mississippi. Michigan Congressman Charles Diggs, who sat with other blacks in the rear section of the segregated courtroom, recalled, "I certainly was angered by the decision, [but] I was not surprised by it. And I was strengthened in my belief that something had to be done about the dispensation of justice in that state." Roy Wilkins of the NAACP remarked that "there is in the entire state no restraining influence of decency, not in the state capital, among the daily newspapers, the clergy, not among any segment of the so-called lettered citizens."

But if there was no justice that day, there were clear signs of change. A black man had demanded justice in white-controlled Mississippi. Soon—very soon—other voices would

Mose Wright and his three boys, seated in the "colored" section of the courtroom, attended the trial of Bryant and Milam, accused of killing Emmett Till in Mississippi.

join Mose Wright's. Their peaceful but insistent cries would be heard over the surface quiet of Dwight Eisenhower's America. They would force America to come to terms with its own ideology. After an heroic struggle against fascism and during a cold conflict against communism, Americans no longer could ignore racial injustice and inequality at home.

It was time for a change. During the late 1940s and the 1950s the process began. Slow, painful, poignant, occasionally uplifting—the march toward justice moved forward. It was part of other significant social and economic changes taking place in America. Against the backdrop of Eisenhower's calm assurances, a new country was taking shape.

QUIET CHANGES

Most white Americans during the late 1940s and the early 1950s were unconcerned about the struggles of their black compatriots. Perhaps some admired Jackie Robinson's efforts on the baseball field, but few made the connection between integration in sports and civil rights throughout society. Other concerns seemed more urgent. In November 1952 the Korean War was dragging into its third year, and the chances for a satisfactory peace were fading. Joseph McCarthy was still warning Americans about the Communist infiltration of the U.S. government. Political corruption had stained the Truman administration. At the polls Americans were ready to vote for change.

I Like Ike

Republicans certainly felt it was time for change. The Democrats had occupied the White House for the previous 20 years. In 1952 they ran Governor Adlai Stevenson of Illinois for the presidency. A political moderate and a vocal anti-Communist, the witty, sophisticated Stevenson was burdened by Truman's unpopularity. His Republican opponent was Dwight David Eisenhower, a moderate, anti-Communist war hero. The Republican campaign strategy was summarized in a formula—K_1C_2. Eisenhower promised that if elected he would first end the war in Korea then battle communism and corruption at home. The nation responded. Eisenhower was swept into office. He even carried several southern states and cut into the urban-ethnic coalition of the Democrats.

The country responded to Eisenhower. "I Like Ike" campaign buttons and posters captured the public sentiment. And there was much to like. Few people had advanced so far while making so few enemies. Ike's was the classic Horatio Alger success story. Although born in Texas, he was raised in Abilene, Kansas, the northern terminus of the Chisholm Trail. An accomplished athlete and a good student, Ike earned an appointment to West Point, where he graduated in 1915 among "the class on which the stars fell." (Fifty-nine of the 164 graduates of the class would rise to the rank of brigadier general or higher.)

As an army officer, Eisenhower demonstrated rare organizational abilities and a capacity for complex detail work. If by 1939 he had only risen to the rank of lieutenant colonel, he had impressed his superiors. With the outbreak of World War II, he was promoted with startling rapidity. In fact, in 1942 General George Mar-

shall passed over 366 more senior officers to promote Eisenhower to major general and appoint him commander of the European Theater of Operations. It was Ike who planned and oversaw America's invasions of North Africa, Sicily, and Italy and who led the combined British-American D-Day invasion of France. By the end of the war, Ike was a four-star general and an international hero.

Ike's ability to win the loyalty of others and work with people of diverse and difficult temperaments would serve him well as a politician. But during the early postwar years, he expressed no interest in holding political office. "I cannot conceive of any set of circumstances that could drag out of me permission to consider me for any political post from dog catcher to Grand High Supreme King of the Universe," he told a reporter in 1946. And indeed there is no evidence that Ike had ever voted or had any party affiliation before running for the presidency on the Republican ticket in 1952.

Eisenhower did have strong beliefs concerning America's domestic and foreign policies. His fiscal conservativism led him to the Republican party, and his internationalism convinced him to run for the presidency. He did not want to see an isolationist Republican elected in 1952, and the early front-runner was isolationist Robert Alphonso Taft, the powerful Ohio senator. Once Ike had defeated Taft for the nomination, his victory over Stevenson was almost anticlimactic.

Almost overnight the image of Eisenhower was transformed from one of a master military organizer to one of mumbling, bumbling, smiling incomprehensibility. Reporters commented on his friendly smile, engaging blue eyes, and his mangled syntax. As a young officer he wrote striking speeches for Douglas MacArthur, and as a World War II general he impressed reporters with the precision of his thought. Commenting on Ike's speaking style, FDR's press secretary said, "He knows his facts, he speaks freely and frankly, and he has a sense of humor, he has poise, and he has command."

Had Eisenhower somehow sunk into senility on taking office? Certainly not. He sensed that the country needed a rest from 20 years of active presidents. Rather than an earth shaker, the country needed a "dirt smoother." The result was the "hidden hand leadership" of Ike. In public he seemed everyone's favorite grandfather and golfing buddy, friendly, outgoing, quick to please, but only slightly interested in being president. Although he had read widely in both military history and the classics, he insisted publicly that he only read westerns, and those not too closely. But throughout his eight years in office, Eisenhower focused closely on his two major priorities: U.S.-Soviet relations and a balanced budget. These issues, not civil rights or other important social concerns, occupied most of his attention.

"Dynamic Conservativism"

Eisenhower brought the military chain of command system to the White House. He was in charge, and he kept the major decisions of his administration in his own hands. But he left the detail work and the political battling to his subordinates. The most important person after Eisenhower in this command structure was Sherman Adams, the former governor of New Hampshire who served as Ike's chief of staff. Adams determined who got to see the president and what issues were placed before him. Although forced to resign in 1958 for influence peddling (he had accepted an Oriental rug and a vicuña coat from a New England textile magnate), Adams pioneered modern White House administration.

Ike saw himself as a forward-looking Republican. He called himself a conservative, "but an extremely liberal conservative," one who was concerned with fiscal prudence but not at the expense of human beings. Ike termed his approach "modern Republicanism" and "dynamic conservativism," by which he meant, "conservative when it comes to money matters and liberal when it comes to human beings." In practice this approach led the Eisenhower administration to cut spending but not to attempt any rollback of New Deal social legislation.

George Humphrey, a conservative Ohio industrialist, served as Eisenhower's treasury secretary. More conservative than Eisenhower, Humphrey believed that the federal government should shift more fiscal responsibilities to the state and private sectors. He did succeed in getting Congress to abolish the Reconstruction

Finance Corporation (see Chapter 24) and turn over off-shore oil rights to the seaboard states. The *New York Times* called this latter piece of legislation, the Submerged Land Act, "one of the greatest and surely the most unjustified give-away programs in all the history of the United States." On the whole, however, Eisenhower's domestic programs were hardly reactionary.

During Ike's two terms the country made steady and at times spectacular economic progress. In 1955 the minimum wage was raised from 75 cents to $1 per hour, and during the 1950s the average family income rose 15 percent and real wages were up 20 percent. And work was plentiful. During the decade, unemployment averaged only 4.5 percent per year, a figure close to the magical 4 percent economists considered "full employment." Stable prices, full employment, and steady growth were the economic hallmarks of the 1950s. "American labor has never had it so good," AFL-CIO chief George Meany told his associates in 1955. Although the population increased by 28 million people, the country was on the whole better housed and fed than ever before. The output of goods and services rose 15 percent. Especially for white Americans, "modern Republicanism" seemed a viable alternative to New Dealism.

A Country of Wheels

If Eisenhower labored to curtail the role of the federal government in some areas, he expanded it in other places. As an expert on military logistics, Ike frequently expressed concern about the sad state of the American highway system. During World War II he had been impressed by Hitler's system of *Autobahnen*, which allowed the German dictator to deploy troops to different parts of Germany with incredible speed. From his first days in office, Eisenhower worked for legislation to improve America's highway network.

The highway lobby agreed. A loose collection of pressure groups formed the lobby, including representatives from the automobile, trucking, bus, oil, rubber, asphalt, and construction industries. Following the philosophy that what was good for General Motors was good for the country, the highway lobby pushed for a new federally subsidized interstate highway system. Not only would such a project provide millions of new jobs, it would contribute to a safer America by making it easier to evacuate major cities in the event of a nuclear attack.

As a result of presidential and lobby pressure, in 1956 Congress passed the National System of Interstate and Defense Highways Act, the most significant piece of domestic legislation enacted under Eisenhower. As planned, the system would cover 41,000 (later expanded to 42,500) miles, cost $26 billion, and take 13 years to construct. Although it took longer to complete and cost far more than Congress projected, it did provide the United States with the world's most extensive superhighway system. Secretary of Commerce Sinclair Weeks estimated that the act would create 150,000 new construction jobs and rank as "the greatest public works program in history."

More than any other piece of legislation, it also changed America. After Congress passed the 1956 bill, cultural critic Lewis Mumford wrote, "When the American people, through their Congress, voted . . . for a $26 billion highway program, the most charitable thing to assume is that they hadn't the faintest notion of what they were doing." Mumford realized that this commitment to internal combustion engines would alter the culture and landscape of America; and it has. It accelerated the decline of the inner city and the flight to the suburbs. The downtown portions of cities, once thriving with commerce and excitement, rapidly turned into ghost towns. As downtown businesses, hotels, and theaters closed, suburban shopping malls with multi-screen cinemas and roadside motels began to dot the American highway landscape. Drive-in theaters, gasoline service stations, mobile homes, and multicar garages signified the birth of a new extended society, one without center or focus. Indeed, highway construction was simply one expression of Americans' obsession with the automobile during the 1950s and 1960s. After being deprived of new cars during the war—when the maximum speed limit was 35 miles per hour—Americans adopted the new automobile philosophy of bigger is better and the biggest and fastest is the best. In 1952 over 52 million cars crowded American roads, and that number doubled during the next 20 years.

Home architecture exemplified America's mobile-minded culture. The garage, once separated from and located behind the house, achieved a new position. By the 1960s the average home devoted more space to the family automobiles than to individual family members. With access to the house itself—usually through the kitchen—the garage had become an integrated part of the house and the car an important member of the family. Home architects in the 1960s and 1970s showed the growing importance of the automobile by placing the garage in a prominent position in the front of the house.

America's commitment to highways and cars created numerous problems. Mass transportation suffered most conspicuously. Street cars and commuter railroads languished, as did the country's major interstate railroads. Since highway construction was financed by a nondivertible gasoline tax, government often ignored mass transit. In the years since the end of World War II, 75 percent of government expenditures for transportation have gone for highways as opposed to 1 percent for urban mass transit. As a result, those without the use of automobiles—the old, the very young, the poor, the handicapped—became victims of America's automobile obsession.

Ike, Dulles, and the World

For Eisenhower, "modern Republicanism" was more than simply a domestic economic credo. It also implied an internationalist foreign policy. As with domestic policy, in foreign policy Ike preferred to operate behind the scenes. But he did make all major foreign policy decisions.

The point man for Ike's foreign policy was Secretary of State John Foster Dulles. When Eisenhower asked Dulles to head the State Department, he remarked, "You've been training yourself to be Secretary of State ever since you were nine years old." And so he had. An interest in foreign affairs was part of the Dulles heritage. Dulles's maternal grandfather had served as Benjamin Harrison's secretary of state, and one of his uncles, Robert Lansing, had occupied the

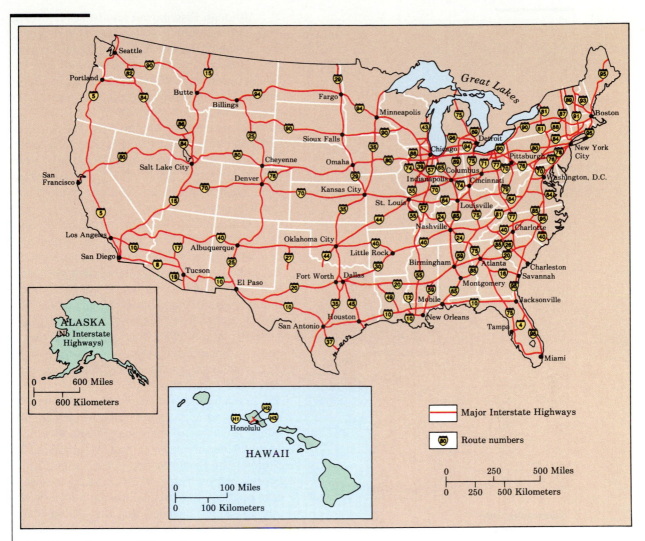

United States Interstate Highway System

The 1956 plan to create an interstate highway system drastically changed America's landscape and culture.

same post under Woodrow Wilson. In 1919 as a young man, Dulles had been part of the American delegation to the Versailles Peace Conference, and later, as a member of the prestigious Wall Street law firm of Sullivan and Cromwell, he represented clients with international interests. After World War II, he helped organize and then served as a delegate to the United Nations. In addition, throughout his life Dulles was a careful student of foreign affairs and international politics. Eisenhower noted, there was "only one man I know who has seen *more* of the world and talked with more people and *knows* more than [Dulles] does—and that's me."

Dulles's experience and knowledge were somewhat offset by his rigidity and excessive moralism. If Americans felt comfortable calling President Eisenhower "Ike," not even close friends called Dulles "Jack." Plain and as unpolished as granite, Dulles took himself, his Presbyterian religion, and the world seriously. "His face," commented an associate, "was permanently lined with an expression of unhappiness mingled with faint distaste—the kind of

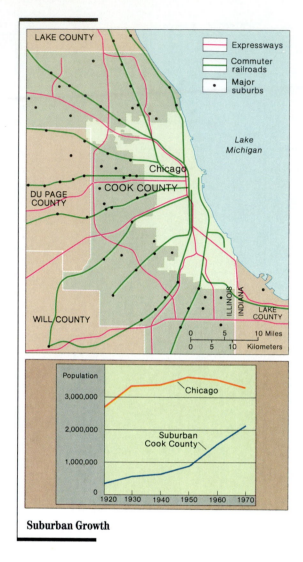

LAKE COUNTY

Expressways

Commuter
railroads

Major
suburbs

*Lake
Michigan*

Chicago

COOK COUNTY

DU PAGE
COUNTY

WILL COUNTY

ILLINOIS
INDIANA
LAKE
COUNTY

0   5   10 Miles

0   5   10   Kilometers

Population

3,000,000

Chicago

2,000,000

Suburban
Cook County

1,000,000

0

1920 1930 1940 1950 1960 1970

Suburban Growth

Although Eisenhower and Dulles had strikingly different public styles, they shared a common vision of the world. Both were internationalists and cold warriors who believed that the Soviet Union was the enemy and that the United States was and should be the protector of the free world. Peace was their objective—but never a peace won by appeasement. To keep honorable peace, both were willing to consider the use of nuclear weapons and go to the brink of war. As Dulles said in 1956, "You have to take some chances for peace, just as you must take chances in war."

Occasionally Dulles's impassioned anti-Communist rhetoric obscured the actual policies pursued by the Eisenhower administration. In public Dulles rejected the containment doctrine as a "negative, futile and immoral policy" and advocated the "liberation" of Eastern Europe. It was time to "roll back" the Iron Curtain, he said, and if nuclear weapons were needed to achieve America's objectives—well, then, so be it. In public Dulles constantly flexed his—and America's— muscles.

In reality, Eisenhower's objectives were far more limited and his approach toward foreign policy much more cautious. Eisenhower supported containment, but not as practiced by Truman. In Eisenhower's eyes, Truman's approach was unorganized and far too expensive. Like political journalist Walter Lippmann in the late-1940s, Ike believed that the United States could not support every country that claimed to be fighting communism. As historian Charles C. Alexander noted, "The chief lesson Eisenhower and his associates drew from Korea was that limited wars, fought with conventional weaponry on the periphery of the Communist world, only drained the nation's resources and weakened its allies' resolve." If America continued Truman's shotgun policies, the costs would soon become higher than Americans would be willing to pay. A change, Ike maintained, was needed.

Eisenhower termed his adjustments of the containment doctrine the "New Look." Ike's program began with the idea of saving money. To do this he decided to emphasize nuclear weapons over conventional weapons, assuming that the next major war would be a nuclear conflict. This "more bang for the buck" program

face that, on those rare occasions when it was drawn into a smile, looked as though it ached in every muscle to get back into its normal shape." One Washington correspondent described him as "a card-carrying Christian," and he frequently delivered lectures on the evils of "atheistic, materialistic Communism." He tended to see opposition to communism in religious terms. A friend recalled a conversation in which China's Jiang Jieshi (Chiang Kai-shek) and South Korea's Syngman Rhee were criticized. Offended, Dulles announced: "No matter what you say about them, those two gentlemen are modern-day equivalents of the founders of the church. They are Christian gentlemen who have suffered for their faith."

drew angry criticism. Congressional hawks claimed that Eisenhower was "putting too many eggs in the nuclear basket," and liberals suggested that the program would inevitably lead to nuclear destruction.

Whatever the criticisms, the New Look did save money. While air and missile forces were expanded, the army's budget was trimmed of all of its fat and much of its bone. In fact, if Eisenhower had had his way, the army would have been completely reorganized. The results of Eisenhower's approach were dramatic. In 1953 defense cost $50.4 billion. By 1956 Eisenhower had reduced the defense budget to $35.8 billion. In addition, during the same period troop levels were reduced by almost one-third.

Future presidents did not so much reverse Eisenhower's approach as enlarge it. They continued the nuclear buildup started by Eisenhower, and at the same time insisted on increased spending on conventional weapons. The result was an ever escalating defense budget.

The New Look took an unconventional approach to conventional warfare. Ike had learned from Truman's mistakes in Korea. America could not send weapons and men to all corners of the world to contain communism. It was a costly, deadly policy. Instead, the New Look emphasized the threat of massive retaliation to keep order, and reinforced America's position with a series of foreign alliances that encouraged indigenous troops and peoples to resist Communist expansion. Finally, Eisenhower used the CIA as a covert foreign policy arm. Through timely assassinations and political coups engineered by the CIA, Eisenhower was able to prevent—or at least forestall—the emergence of anti-America regimes. While historians argue about the morality of the CIA's covert operations, they were very much a part of the New Look.

A New Face in Moscow

The world changed dramatically a few months after Eisenhower took office. On March 5, 1953, Joseph Stalin, the Soviet dictator whom Ike knew personally, died. Always fearful of rivals, Stalin did not groom a successor. The result was

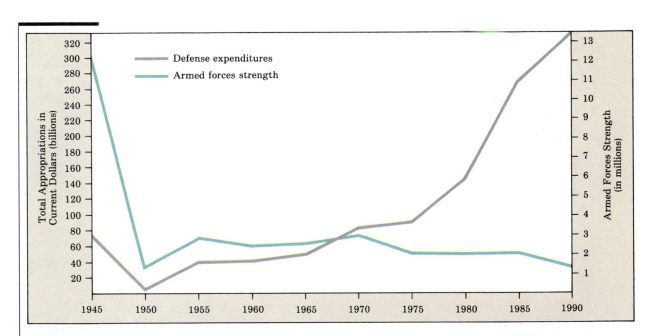

Figure 28.1
Defense expenditures, armed forces strength, 1945–1990

a power struggle within the Kremlin, from which Nikita Khrushchev emerged as the winner.

Khrushchev looked like a cross between a Russian peasant and Ike himself. Short, rotund, and bald, he had a warm smile and alert eyes. Unlike Stalin, Khrushchev enjoyed meeting people, making speeches, and traveling abroad. If occasionally he lost his temper and uttered belligerent remarks—he once even took off his shoe and pounded it on a table at the United Nations—Khrushchev did try to lessen the tensions between the Soviet Union and the United States.

Ike shared Khrushchev's dream for peaceful coexistence between the two world leaders. In fact, Eisenhower used Stalin's death as an opportunity to extend an olive branch. The Soviet Union peacefully responded. During 1955 the nations resolved several thorny issues: the Soviets repatriated German prisoners of war who had been held in the Soviet Union since World War II, established relations with Greece and Israel, and gave up claims to Turkish territory. The Soviet Union's most significant action was to withdraw from its occupation zone of Austria. Until the massive changes in Eastern Europe in 1990 and 1991, it was the only time that the Soviet Union withdrew from territory that it had seized during the war.

The cold winter of the Cold War seemed to be over. Khrushchev condemned Stalin's excesses, and Eisenhower talked guardedly about a new era of cooperation. In July 1955, the two leaders met in Geneva, Switzerland, for a summit conference. During the meeting, Eisenhower suggested that the United States and the Soviet Union allow aerial surveillance and photography of each other's nations to lessen the chance of a possible surprise attack. Khrushchev rejected this "open skies" proposal, calling it "a very transparent espionage device." Actually, the meeting achieved few tangible results, but the two leaders seemed to be working toward the same peaceful ends. Against Dulles's advice, Eisenhower even smiled when posing for pictures with the Soviets. "A new spirit of conciliation and cooperation" had been achieved, Ike announced. Unfortunately, "the Spirit of Geneva" would not survive the confrontations ahead.

At the Twentieth Congress of the Communist party in the Soviet Union, a worker from the Kiev region greets Soviet Premier Nikita Khrushchev.

1956: The Dangerous Year

Neither Eisenhower nor Khrushchev was completely candid. While working for "peaceful coexistence," both still had to satisfy critics at home. In Washington, Dulles continued to call for the "liberation" of Eastern Europe and to hint that the United States would rally behind any Soviet-dominated country that struck a blow for freedom. In reality, Eisenhower was not about to risk war with the Soviet Union to come to the defense of Poland, Hungary, or Czechoslovakia.

At the same time, Khrushchev's speeches often promised more than he would or could deliver. On February 24, 1956, for example, Khrushchev delivered a remarkable speech before the Twentieth Party Congress. For four hours in his "Crimes of Stalin" speech, he condemned the former dictator's domestic crimes and foreign policy mistakes, endorsed "peaceful coexistence" with the West, and indicated that he was willing to allow greater freedom behind the "iron curtain." Although the speech was supposed to be secret, the CIA obtained copies and distributed them throughout Eastern Europe.

Poland took Khrushchev at his word and moved in a more liberal, anti-Stalinist direction. Wladyslaw Gomulka, who represented the nationalistic wing of the Polish Communist party, gained power in Poland and moved his country away from complete Soviet domination. Claiming that "there is more than one road to socialism," Gomulka announced that Poles would defend with their lives their new freedoms. Since Poland did not attempt to withdraw from the Soviet bloc, Khrushchev allowed Poland to move along its more liberal course.

What Poland had won, Hungary wanted—and perhaps a bit more. On October 23, 1956, students and workers took to the streets in Budapest loudly demanding changes. They knocked over a gigantic statue of Stalin and desecrated it with freedom slogans and graffiti. As in Poland, they forced a political change. Independent Communist Imre Nagy replaced a Stalinist leader. The Soviets peacefully recognized the new government. Pressing his luck, Nagy then announced that he planned to pull Hungary out of the Warsaw Pact—the Soviet-dominated defense community that was created in response to the signing of the NATO Pact—and allow opposition political parties.

Khrushchev sent Soviet tanks and soldiers into Budapest to crush what he now termed a "counterrevolution" and the work of "fascist reactionary elements." Students with bricks and hastily made Molotov cocktails were no match for the Red Army. The Soviets kidnapped Nagy (and later executed him), killed hundreds of demonstrators, and brutally restored their control over Hungary. All the while, the Eisenhower administration just watched, demonstrating that the notion of "liberation" was mere rhetoric, not policy. Ike even refused a CIA request to parachute weapons and supplies to the Hungarian freedom fighters. Hungary, said Ike, was "as inaccessible to us as Tibet."

Actually, at the time of the Soviet move into Budapest, Eisenhower was more concerned with the troubled Western alliance. The source of the problem was Egypt, whose nationalistic leader, President Gamal Abdel Nasser, was struggling to remain neutral in the Cold War.

The United States had attempted to win Nasser's favor by promising to finance the construction of the Aswan High Dam on the Nile. But when Nasser recognized the People's Republic of China and pursued amicable relations with the Soviet Union, the Eisenhower administration withdrew the proposed loan. Neither Dulles nor Eisenhower was happy with Nasser's fence-sitting diplomacy.

Nasser struck back. On July 26, he nationalized the Suez Canal, the waterway linking the oil rich Gulf of Suez and the Mediterranean. Half of Western Europe's oil came through the Suez Canal, which Ike believed was essential to the security of Western Europe. "And it will be run by Egyptians," Nasser added in an emotional message to the world. If Eisenhower was upset, British and French leaders were outraged, loudly claiming that the seizure threatened their Middle Eastern oil supplies. Eisenhower counseled caution, but Britain, France, and Israel resorted to "drastic actions." On October 29, Israel invaded Egypt and Britain and France used the hostilities as a pretext to seize the Suez Canal.

Eisenhower was furious. He interrupted his reelection campaign to return to Washington. One observer reported, "The White House crackled with barracks-room language." Ike told Dulles to inform the Israelis that "goddamn it, we're going to apply sanctions, we're going to the United Nations, we're going to do everything that there is so we can stop this thing." And in a severe "tongue-lashing" he reduced British Prime Minister Anthony Eden to tears.

Eisenhower stood on the high ground, where he was uncomfortably aligned with the Soviet Union. Without law there can be no peace, he claimed, adding, "and there can be no law—if we were to invoke one code of international conduct for those who oppose us—and another for our friends." Cut off from American support and faced with angry Soviet threats, Britain, France, and Israel halted their operations on November 6, the same day Eisenhower overwhelmingly defeated Adlai Stevenson and was reelected for a second term.

Taken together, the Hungarian and the Suez crises strained America's relations with both the Soviet Union and Western Europe. "The spirit of Geneva" was being replaced by a

Before the crushing Soviet onslaught on November 4, 1956, Hungarian freedom fighters rushed toward Budapest in an attempt to fight off Soviet forces.

more hostile mood. Nowhere was this better seen than in the 1956 Olympic Games, held in Melbourne, Australia, only two weeks after the November incidents. Egypt, Lebanon, and Iraq refused to take part in any Games that included Britain, France, and Israel. And in the water polo competition, a match between the Soviet Union and Hungary quickly deteriorated into a form of aquatic warfare. The pool ran red with blood and the contest had to be halted before its official end.

The Troubled Second Term

In foreign affairs, Eisenhower's second term was less successful than his first. Although he restrained military spending and shrewdly utilized information gathered by U-2 spy missions, his actions received more criticism at home and abroad. Age and health may have contributed to this turn of events. During his first four years in office, Ike suffered a heart attack and a bout with ileitis, which entailed a serious operation. During his second term, he was more apt to take vacations and play golf and bridge with his close friends. John Foster Dulles's health was also declining. During the Suez crisis doctors discovered that he had cancer. Acute physical pain punctuated his last years as secretary of state and he died in 1959.

Sputnik and Sputtering Rockets

More than ill health plagued Ike's foreign policy. Soviet technological advances created a mood of edginess in American foreign policy and military circles. In 1957 the Soviet Union successfully placed a tiny transmitter encased in a 184-pound steel ball into an orbit around earth. They called the artificial satellite *Sputnik*—Russian for "fellow traveler of Earth"—but the humor of the name was lost on most Americans, who were too concerned about Soviet rocket advances to laugh.

Less than one month later, the Soviet Union launched its second *Sputnik*, this one built on a larger and grander scale. It weighed 1120 pounds, contained instruments for scientific research, and carried a small dog named Laika who was wired with devices to gauge the effects of extragravitational flight on animal functions. If the first *Sputnik* demonstrated that the Soviets had gained the high ground, the second indicated that they intended to go higher and to place men in space.

Before the end of 1957, the United States tried to respond with a satellite launch of its own. Code-named *Vanguard*, the satellite was placed on the top of a three-stage navy rocket that was ignited on December 6. Describing the "blast off," a historian wrote, "It wobbled a few feet off the pad and exploded. The grapefruit-sized American rival to *Sputnik* fell to the ground and beeped its last amid geysers of smoke." It was the first of a series of highly publicized American rocket launches that ended with the sputtering sound of failure.

Sputnik forced Americans to question themselves and their own values. Had the country become soft and overly consumer oriented? While Soviet students were studying calculus, physics, and chemistry, had American students spent too much time in shop, home economics, and driver education classes? More importantly, did *Sputnik* give the Soviet Union a military superiority over the United States? If a Soviet rocket could put a thousand-pound ball in orbit could the same rocket armed with nuclear warhead hit a target in the United States? Such questions disturbed ordinary Americans and U.S. policymakers alike.

In truth, Americans overrated the importance of *Sputnik*. It was not all that it seemed. As Wernher von Braun, one of America's leading German rocket scientists, would later demonstrate, launching a satellite was no great accomplishment. It simply took rockets with great thrust. Delivering a warhead to a specific target was quite another matter. That entailed sophisticated guidance systems, which the Soviet Union had certainly not developed.

Sputnik then did not demonstrate Soviet technological superiority. It did, however, indi-cate the willingness of Soviet leaders to place military advancement ahead of the physical well-being of their citizens. As a French journalist noted, the price of *Sputnik* was "millions of pots and shoes lacking." Then, as well as today, the Soviet Union lagged behind the West in diet, health care, education, housing, clothing, and transportation.

American policymakers reacted to the illusion of Soviet success. Congress appropriated more money for "defense-related" research and funneled more dollars into higher education in the United States. In fact, *Sputnik* was a tremendous boon for education. In an attempt to improve science and mathematics skills, Con-

U.S. efforts to compete with the Soviet Union's space advances suffered a major setback when the *Vanguard* exploded two seconds after takeoff on December 6, 1957.

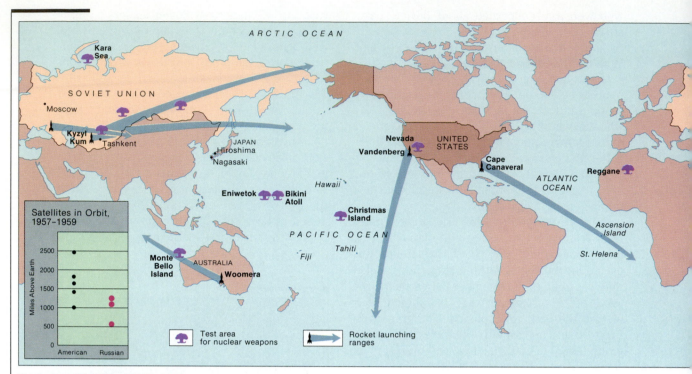

Rockets and Satellites, 1957–1959
The U.S. reaction to *Sputnik* led to a proliferation of rockets and satellites in both the USSR and the
United States in the late 1950s.

gress passed the National Defense Education Act (1958) to help finance the undergraduate and graduate educations of promising students. The Eisenhower administration jumped into the "space race" determined to be the swiftest. A leading historian of space measured the success of Eisenhower's effort by noting, "more new starts and technical leaps occurred in the years before 1960 than in any comparable span. Every space booster and every strategic missile in the American arsenal, prior to . . . the 1970s, date from these years."

Third World Challenges

If *Sputnik* was largely an illusionary challenge, nationalist movements in the Third World created more serious problems. Eisenhower's response to such movements varied from case to case. On the one hand, he opposed Britain and France's efforts to use naked physical aggression to whip Egypt into line. On the other hand, Ike employed covert CIA operations to achieve

his foreign policy goals. In 1953 the CIA planned and executed a coup d'état which replaced a popularly elected government in Iran with a pro-American regime headed by Shah Mohammad Reza Pahlavi. The reason for the coup was that the elected government had taken over Iranian oil resources that the British had been exploiting. One year later the CIA masterminded the overthrow of a leftist government in Guatemala and replaced it with an unpopular but strongly pro-American government.

To keep order in what he believed were areas vital to American interests, Eisenhower would even resort to armed intervention. In 1958, Lebanese Moslems backed by Egypt and Syria, threatened a revolt against the Beirut government dominated by the Christian minority. President Camille Chamoun appealed to Eisenhower for support. Concerned with Middle Eastern oil, Ike ordered marines from America's Sixth Fleet into Lebanon. Watching from the beaches of Beirut, sunbathers and ice-cream vendors cheered the American show of force.

Once order was restored and Lebanese politicians had agreed on a successor to Chamoun, Ike withdrew American troops from Lebanon. But like the CIA activities in Guatemala and Iran, short-term benefits came with long-term costs. Increasingly, the United States became identified with unpopular, undemocratic, and intolerant right-wing regimes. Such actions tarnished America's image in the Third World.

The problems of Eisenhower's approach toward the Third World were clearly seen in his handling of the Cuban Revolution. In 1959, revolutionary Fidel Castro overthrew Fulgencio Batista, a right-wing dictator who had encouraged American investments in Cuba at the expense of the Cuban people. Before the revolution, in fact, American companies owned 90 percent of Cuban mining operations, 80 percent of its utilities, and 40 percent of its sugar operations. Castro quickly set about to change the situation. He confiscated land and properties in Cuba owned by Americans, executed former Batista officials, built hospitals and schools, ended racial segregation, improved workers' wages, and moved leftward. Before long, Castro had begun to jail writers and critics, hold public executions, postpone elections, and condemn the United States as the "vulture . . . feeding on humanity."

Instead of waiting for Cuba's anti-American feelings to subside, Eisenhower decided to move against Castro. He gave the CIA permission to plan an attack on Cuba by a group of anti-Castro exiles, a plan that would culminate with the disastrous Bay of Pigs invasion (see Chapter 29). As one of his last acts as president, in 1961 Eisenhower severed diplomatic relations with Cuba. Such actions only increased Castro's anti-American resolve and further drove him into the arms of the Soviet Union.

Ultimately, the Truman and Eisenhower brands of containment were unsuccessful in dealing with nationalistic independence movements. Such movements dominated the post–World War II world. Between 1944 and 1974, for example, 78 countries won their independence. These included more than one billion people, or close to one-third of the world's population. By using a political yardstick to evaluate these movements, American presidents since Truman have made critical mistakes that have lowered the image of the United States in the Third World and given ammunition to Third World politicians who have pandered to anti-American emotions.

Not with a Bang, But a Whimper

Going into his last year in office, Eisenhower hoped to improve on the foreign policy record of his second term. Since his last meeting with Khrushchev in Geneva, the Cold War had intensified. In particular, the Soviets were once again threatening to cut off Western access to West Berlin, an action Eisenhower feared might lead to a nuclear war. To solve the problem—or at least to neutralize it—Khrushchev visited the United States. He toured Iowa farms, visited Hollywood, and was generally warmly received by the American people. His biggest disappointment was that for security reasons he could not visit Disneyland. Turning to politics, he spent two days in private talks with Eisenhower at Camp David, where the two agreed to a formal summit meeting set for May 1960 in Paris.

The two world leaders never again had serious talks. Just before the meeting the Soviets shot down an American U-2 spy plane over their territory. So sophisticated was the plane's surveillance equipment, it could read a newspaper headline from 10 miles above the earth's surface or take pictures of the earth's surface 125 miles wide and 3000 miles long. During the previous few years, U-2 missions had kept Eisenhower abreast of Soviet military developments and convinced him that *Sputnik* posed no military threat to the United States. Nevertheless, the existence of such planes was a military secret, and U-2 pilots had strict orders to self-destruct their planes rather than be forced down in enemy territory. (For crash landings in neutral countries, the pilots carried a silk banner with the same statement in 14 languages: "I bear no malice toward your people. If you help me you will be rewarded.")

Assuming that the pilot had followed orders, Eisenhower responded to the Soviet charges of spying by publicly announcing that the Soviets had shot down a weather plane that had blown off course. Unfortunately for Ike, the pilot, Francis Gary Powers, had not followed orders, and the Soviets had him and the wreckage of his plane. Trying to save the summit, Khrushchev offered Eisenhower a way to save face. The Soviet leader indicated that he was sure that Eisenhower had not known about the flights. Eisenhower, however, accepted full personal responsibility and refused to apologize for actions he deemed were in defense of America. Rather than appear soft himself, Khrushchev refused to engage in the Paris summit.

Eisenhower's presidency ended on this note of failure. A chance to improve Soviet-American relations had been lost. But the end of his presidency should not obscure his positive accomplishments. He had ended one war, kept America out of several others, limited military spending, and presided over seven and a half years of relative peace. Like George Washington, when Eisenhower left office he issued warnings to America about possible future problems. In particular, he noted, the "military-industrial complex"—an alliance between government and business—could threaten the democratic process in the country. As Eisenhower remarked early in his presidency, "Every gun that is made, every warship launched, every rocket fired signifies, in the final sense, a theft from those who hunger and are not fed, those who are cold and are not clothed."

WE SHALL OVERCOME

When Dwight Eisenhower took office in early 1953 almost everywhere in the United States racism—often institutionalized, sometimes less formal—was the order of the day. Below the Mason-Dixon line it reached its most virulent form in the Jim Crow laws that governed the everyday existence of southern blacks. Whites framed the Jim Crow laws to separate the races and to demonstrate to all white superiority and black inferiority. Jim Crow dictated that whites and blacks eat in separate restaurants, drink from separate water fountains, sleep in separate hotels, and learn in separate schools. In some states, the separate schoolbooks of black and white children were stored in separate closets so as to avoid contamination by touch.

Jim Crow subjected blacks to daily bouts of degradation and soul-destroying humiliation. Blacks had to give way on sidewalks to whites, tip their hats, and speak respectfully. Blacks addressed whites of all ages as Mr., Mrs., or Miss; whites addressed blacks of all ages by their first names. Although the underpinning of the Jim Crow laws was the "separate but equal" doctrine enunciated in *Plessy* v. *Ferguson* (1896), both blacks and whites realized that subjuga-

The U-2 spy plane's sophisticated surveillance equipment kept President Eisenhower informed about Soviet military developments including nuclear testing.

tion, not equality, was the object of the laws. And Jim Crow leaped over national boundaries. When a waitress at a Howard Johnson's in Dover, Delaware, refused to serve a glass of orange juice to the finance minister of Ghana because of his color, America's image abroad suffered.

Segregation affected whites as well as blacks. Melton A. McLaurin, a historian who grew up in Wade, North Carolina, recalled that race relations in the South in the mid-1950s were much as they had been in the 1890s. Jim Crow etiquette touched all relations between both races. "Blacks who had to enter our house," McLaurin noted, "for whatever reason, came in the back door. Unless employed as domestic servants, blacks conducted business with my father or mother on the back porch or, on rare occasions, in the kitchen. Blacks never entered our dining or living areas . . . except as domestics. . . . When a black person approached a doorway at the same time as a white adult, the black stepped back and sometimes even held the door open for the white to enter. The message I received from hundreds of such signals was always the same. I was white; I was different; I was superior. It was not a message with which an adolescent boy was apt to quarrel."

North of Dixie the situation was not much better. To be sure, rigid Jim Crow laws did not exist, but informally blacks were excluded from the better schools, neighborhoods, and jobs. Whites argued that the development of ghettos was a natural process, not some sort of racist agreement between white realtors. Such, however, was not the case. William Levitt, the most famous post–World War II suburban housing developer, attempted to keep blacks out of his developments. A passage in the New York Levittown covenant read: "No dwelling shall be used . . . by members of other than the Caucasian race, but the employment and maintenance of other than Caucasian domestic servants shall be permitted." Even after the courts struck down such restrictions, Levitt instructed his realtors not to sell to blacks. Indeed, *Shelley* v. *Kraemer* (1948), the court case that stated that state courts could not uphold housing restrictions, only declared such restrictions legally unenforceable; it did not outlaw such practices per se. To break a racially motivated housing

Jim Crow laws were not limited only to restaurants or hotels in cities. This roadside sign shows that segregation was common outside southern metropolitan areas.

restriction, a black had to take the initiative and force a court test.

When Ike left office in 1961, segregation remained largely unchanged. In that year, John Howard Griffin's best-selling book *Black Like Me* gave white America a stark look at the daily life of millions of black Americans. After shaving his head and darkening his skin chemically, Griffin traveled about the South to experience what it was like to live as a black in Jim Crow America. He described the humiliating search for hotels, restaurants, and rest rooms in a land where for blacks unequal facilities was a constant and no facilities always a real possibility. He also described how blacks came to each other's aid and support. A national best-seller that sold over five million copies, Griffin's tale shocked and shamed many whites who never realized—or even considered—the plight of black Americans.

During Eisenhower's years in office, however, blacks did make significant strides in their

(Text continues on p. 954)

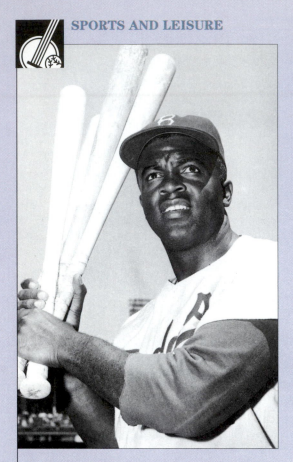

INTEGRATION IN SPORTS

On April 18, 1946, the sports world focused on a baseball field in Jersey City, an industrial wasteland on the banks of the Passaic River. It was the opening day for the Jersey City Giants of the International League. Their opponents were the Montreal Royals, the Brooklyn Dodgers' leading farm team. Playing second base for the Royals was Jackie Roosevelt Robinson, a pigeon-toed, highly competitive, marvelously talented black athlete. The stadium was filled with curious and excited spectators, and in the press box sportswriters from New York,

Philadelphia, Baltimore, and cities further west fidgeted with their typewriters. It was not just another season opening game. Professional baseball, America's national game, was about to be integrated.

Since the late-nineteenth century professional baseball and most other professional team sports had prohibited competition between whites and blacks. White athletes played for the highest salaries, in the best stadiums, before the most spectators. During the same years black teams barnstormed the country playing where they could and ac-

cepting what was offered. For blacks, the pay was low, the stadiums rickety, and the playing conditions varied between bad and dangerous. The *Plessy* v. *Ferguson* ideal of "separate but equal" was a cruel joke.

During the period of forced segregation whites stereotyped black athletes. Since colonial times whites had maintained that blacks were instinctive rather than thoughtful, physical rather than intellectual, complacent rather than ambitious. As athletes, whites believed blacks were physically gifted but lazy, undisciplined, and wholly lacking in competitive drive. Disregarding the success of black athletes in individual sports whites clung to the racist theory that nature had fashioned blacks to laugh and sing and dance and play, but not to sacrifice, train, work, compete, and win.

The most successful black athletes and teams catered to these stereotypes. The Harlem Globetrotters, for example, played the role of Sambo in sweats. Started in 1927 by white Chicago entrepreneur Abe Saperstein, the all-black Harlem Globetrotters basketball team presented black athletes as wide-eyed, toothy, camera-mugging clowns. White audiences loved their antics—Marques Haynes dribbling circles around his hopeless white opponents while the rest of the Trotters stretched out on the floor feigning sleep; Meadowlark Lemon hiding the basketball under his jersey and sneaking down the court to make a basket; Goose Tatum slam-dunking while reading a comic book; all of them cavorting around with deflated, lopsided, or balloon balls, throwing confetti-filled water buckets on an indulgent crowd, and deviously getting away with every conceivable infraction of the rules.

Saperstein insisted that "his boys" conform off as well as on the court. As a Trotter veteran told new teammate Connie Hawkins, "Abe don't care what you do with colored, but don't let him catch you with no white broads . . . And don't let him see you with a Cadillac. He don't stand for that either." Nor did Saperstein allow his players to contradict whites. He wanted only "happy darkies," not "uppity niggers," on his team.

The Indianapolis Clowns were the Harlem Globetrotters of baseball. They played in grass skirts and body paint and engaged in comedy as much as baseball. Pregame routines included acrobatics and dancing, exaggerated black English, minstrel slapstick, and grinning, always lots of grinning. How could any reasonable person expect major league performances out of people playing baseball in grass skirts and war paint?

Jackie Robinson came to bat in the first inning. His very presence had ended segregation in "organized baseball." Now he wanted to strike a blow against the racist stereotyping. Nervous, he later recalled that his palms seemed "too moist to grip the bat." He didn't even swing at the first five pitches. On the sixth pitch he hit a bouncing ball to the shortstop who easily threw him out. It was a start of sorts.

In the third inning Robinson took his second at bat. With runners on first and second, he lashed out at the first pitch and hit it over the left field fence 330 feet away. In the press box Wendell Smith and Joe Bostic, two black reporters for the *Amsterdam News*, "laughed and smiled . . . Our hearts beat just a

little faster and the thrill ran through us like champagne bubbles." According to another account, among the white sportswriters "there were some very long faces."

Robinson wasn't through for the day. In the fifth inning he had a bunt single, stole second, advanced to third on a ground ball, and, faking an attempt to steal home, forced a balk and scored. It was a virtuoso performance. During the remainder of the game he had two more hits, another stolen base, and forced a second balk. In the field he was tough, intense, and smart, a reverse image of the stereotypical black athlete. It was a fine day for Robinson and his supporters. "Baseball took up the cudgel of democracy," Bostic wrote, "and an unassuming, but superlative Negro boy ascended the heights of excellence to prove the rightness of the experiment. And prove it in the only correct crucible for such an experiment— the crucible of white hot competition."

The success of Jackie Robinson in baseball led to the integration of the other major professional sports. In 1946 the Cleveland Rams moved their football franchise to Los Angeles and to boost ticket sales signed blacks Kenny Washington and Woody Strode, both of whom had played football with Robinson at UCLA. Professional football thus became integrated. In 1950 the Boston Celtics of the National Basketball Association signed Chuck Cooper of Duquesne to a professional contract, and the New York Knicks signed Nat "Sweetwater" Clifton away from the Harlem Globetrotters, despite Abe Saperstein's bitter protests. The same year the United States Lawn Tennis Association allowed blacks to compete at Forest Hills.

In a relatively short time integration came to American professional sports.

The process was not without individual pain. Robinson especially became the object of hate mail, death threats, and racial slurs. Opposition runners spiked him and pitchers threw at him. Off the field he faced a life of segregated restaurants, clubs, theaters, and neighborhoods. Patient, witty, and quick to forgive, he endured extraordinary humiliation. He became an American hero, but he paid dearly. Throughout the 1946 and 1947 seasons Robinson was plagued by headaches, bouts of depression, nausea, and nightmares. Talking about the pressures on her husband, Rachel Robinson recalled, "There were the stresses of just knowing that you were pulling a big weight of a whole lot of people on your back . . . I think Jackie felt . . . that there would be serious consequences if he didn't succeed and that one of them would be that nobody would try again for a long time." Of course, the other black players also confronted trials on and off the field, but as Robinson's teammate Roy Campanella said, "nothing compared to what Jackie was going through."

Integration in sports preceded integration in society at large. But whether in sports or the civil rights movement, racial gains were paid for by individuals willing to risk serious hardships. Change seldom came easily and the struggle never ended quickly. In baseball, for example, as late as 1988 many white bureaucrats still resisted the idea of black managers, resorting to the same racial stereotyping that had plagued blacks for over 350 years in America.

quest for civil rights. In particular, during the decade after 1954 blacks won a series of legal victories that in theory if not always in practice buried Jim Crow. They were years of joy and years of sadness, when the best as well as the worst aspects of the American character were clearly visible.

Taking Jim Crow to Court

World War II underscored the yawning gap between the promise and reality of life in America. Fighting against Nazi racist theories helped to draw attention to real racial problems at home. At the start of the war defense industry managers refused to hire blacks, and the races were segregated in the armed services. The war and a threat by black leader A. Philip Randolph to organize a protest march on Washington led to some changes. Executive Order 8802 prohibited discrimination in the war industries. But the outbreak of the Detroit race riot during the hot summer of 1943 demonstrated that blacks were dissatisfied with racial conditions at home. "Our war is not against Hitler and Europe," claimed one black columnist, "but against the Hitlers in America." And blacks drafted to fight against Japan foresaw the irony of many of their fates: "Here lies a black man killed fighting a yellow man for the glory of a white man."

After the war conditions improved at a snail's pace. With an eye on black Democratic northern voters, Truman established the President's Committee on Civil Rights, which issued a report that most white politicians ignored. While Truman called for "fair employment throughout the federal establishment" and ordered the racial desegregation of the armed services, southern politicians proclaimed the need to return to the embrace of Jim Crow. "No Negro will vote in Georgia for the next four years," Eugene Talmadge promised after he was elected governor of Georgia. And in Congress, Southerners like Senator Theodore G. Bilbo railed against Truman's moderate racial reforms. Opposing Truman's plan for universal military training, Bilbo exhorted, "If you draft Negro boys into the army, give them three good meals a day and let them shoot craps and drink liquor around the barracks for a year, they won't be worth a tinker's dam thereafter."

By the late 1940s blacks realized that they would have to lead the fight against racial injustice. In the early years of the battle, the NAACP spearheaded the struggle. But the organization faced a number of problems, both within and outside the black community. For example, many blacks believed the NAACP was racist and elitist. The organization was staffed by educated middle-class blacks who seemed out of touch with the majority of their race. Worse yet, many blacks agreed with radical Marcus Garvey and continued to charge that the NAACP was staffed by light-skinned blacks because it accepted the theory that mulattos were more aggressive, enterprising, and ambitious than their pure-blooded counterparts.

Outside of the black community, the NAACP encountered a hostile white society. In Congress, southern Democrats—there were few southern Republicans—opposed any assault on segregation—the prevailing form of institutionalized racism.

Given this racial climate, the NAACP moved cautiously. Instead of attacking segregation head on and demanding full equality, the organization chose to chip away at the legal edges of Jim Crow. The separate but equal doctrine was particularly vulnerable. In *Missouri ex rel Gaines* (1938), *Sweatt* v. *Painter* (1950), and *McLaurin* v. *Board of Regents* (1950), the NAACP lawyers demonstrated the impossibility, even the absurdity, of applying the separate but equal yardstick to graduate education and law schools. In all three cases, the Supreme Court agreed. If, the court implied, separate but equal educational systems were to be continued, then states had to pay more than lip service to equality.

In grade school and high school education, just as in graduate education, the South translated separate but equal to read "separate and highly unequal." In South Carolina's Clarendon County, for example, 75 percent of the students were black, but the white minority received 60 percent of the educational funds. On the average, the county spent $179 per year on each white student and $43 per year on each black student. Where were the separate but equal standards, asked NAACP lawyers.

Intellectual and financial considerations were not the only factors that precluded equal-

While some children attended segregated schools, others such as these black children in West Memphis, Arkansas, were crammed into the sanctuary of a church for their classes.

ity. Psychologists argued that segregation instilled feelings of inferiority among black children. Black psychologist Kenneth Clark conducted a simple test with black children attending segregated schools. He showed the children two dolls, one black and the other white. In one case, of the 16 children tested, 10 said they liked the white doll better, 11 added that the black doll looked "bad," and 9 remarked that the white doll looked "nice." Recalling the tests, Clark noted, "The most disturbing question—and the one that really made me, even as a scientist, upset—was the final question: 'Now show me the doll that's most like you.' Many of the children became emotionally upset when they had to identify with the doll they had rejected. These children saw themselves as inferior, and they accepted the inferiority as part of reality." When asked that question, one child even smiled and pointed to the black doll: "That's a nigger. I'm a nigger."

It was inhumane to continue such psychological damage, the NAACP concluded. In 1952

the NAACP consolidated a series of cases under the name of the first case—*Brown* v. *Board of Education of Topeka*—which challenged the very existence of the separate but equal doctrine. The Supreme Court listened to the arguments and began its extended deliberation. Then in September 1953 Chief Justice Fred M. Vinson, who seemed to be leaning against ending segregation, died of a heart attack.

President Eisenhower named Earl Warren to take Vinson's place. It was a political, not an ideological, appointment. Formerly governor of California, Warren had helped Ike win the Republican nomination in 1952. Appointment as Chief Justice of the United States was a fine reward. On the surface, minorities had little reason to suspect that Warren would be on their side. During World War II he had been active in the relocation of 100,000 Japanese-Americans into internment camps; but in the years after that action, Warren realized that it had been a mistake. The *Brown* case offered him a second chance.

After working to achieve unanimity in the court, Warren read the Court's decision on May 17, 1954. "Does segregation of children in public schools solely on the basis of race, even though the physical facilities and other tangible factors may be equal, deprive children of the minority group of equal educational opportunities?" Warren asked. "We believe it does," he answered. "To separate them from others of similar age and qualifications solely because of their race generates a feeling of inferiority as to their status in the community that may affect their hearts and minds in a way very unlikely ever to be undone." In public education, he concluded, the "separate but equal" doctrine has no place. "Separate educational facilities are inherently unequal."

The *Chicago Defender* labeled the *Brown* decision "a second emancipation proclamation," and the *Washington Post* called it "a new birth of freedom." But such Court decisions have to be enforced. As Charles Houston, a leading NAACP lawyer, remarked, "Nobody needs to explain to a Negro the difference between the law in the books and the law in action."

A Failure of Leadership

A year after the *Brown* decision, the Supreme Court ruled that schools should desegregate "with all deliberate speed." It was a vague phrase, a cautious phrase, a legally meaningless phrase. Perhaps it was the price Warren had to pay for the previous year's unanimous verdict. In any case, the second decision placed the burden of desegregation into the hands of local, state, and national leaders. If the process was to be accomplished with the minimum amount of conflict, those leaders would have to be firm in their resolve to see justice done. Such, however, would not be the case.

On the national level, Eisenhower moved uncomfortably and cautiously on the issue of civil rights and desegregation. Born in Texas and reared in the white Midwest, Ike spent most of his life in a segregated army. He did not see racism as a great moral issue, and he was unresponsive to the black demand for equality. In truth, Eisenhower believed that the *Brown* decision had been a mistake, for which he blamed

Earl Warren. He later asserted that the appointment of Warren had been the "biggest damn fool mistake" he had ever made. When questioned about the decision in 1954, he claimed, "I don't believe you can change the hearts of men with laws or decisions."

The brand of Ike's leadership and his ambitions for the Republican party further weakened his response. His behind-the-scenes approach—the "hidden hand" style—led him to avoid speaking out clearly and forcefully on the subject. Moral outrage was not his style. In addition, he was popular in the South and harbored hopes of bringing that section of the country into the Republican party. Finally, his commitment to integration was lukewarm at best, and he placed controlling military spending above desegregating the South. Therefore, instead of deploring the killing of Emmett Till and other atrocities by southern whites against blacks, Eisenhower kept quiet.

In the South, Eisenhower's silence was often as deadly as bullets. If Eisenhower had acted decisively in support of the *Brown* v. *Board of Education* decision—if he had placed the full weight of his office behind desegregation—there is some evidence that the South would have complied peacefully with the verdict. By not acting forcefully, however, Eisenhower strengthened the position of Southerners who equated desegregation with death. "Ending segregation," Governor James F. Byrnes of South Carolina said, "would mark the beginning of the end of civilization in the South as we have known it." Governor Herman Talmadge agreed, adding that integration would also inevitably lead to intermarriage and the "mongrelization of the races."

The Little Rock crisis demonstrated the failure of national and state leadership. In 1957 in Little Rock, Arkansas, school officials were ordered to desegregate. As they prepared to do so, Governor Orval Faubus, locked in a reelection fight, intervened. He announced that any integration attempt would disrupt public order and sent in the National Guard to prevent black children from entering Central High. While Eisenhower quietly tried to maneuver behind the scenes, a crisis brewed. On the morning of September 23, 1957, when black children attempted to attend school, they were inhospitably greeted by an angry mob chanting, "two, four, six, eight, we ain't going to integrate."

Television turned the ugly episode into a national drama. Millions of Americans for the first time witnessed violent racism as angry whites moved around the defenseless black children like hungry sharks. Television gave a face to racism, a concept that for many white Americans was still an abstraction. It showed the reality of hate and racism in the South. For the first but not last time, television aided the cause of civil rights by conveying the human suffering caused by racism.

To restore order, Eisenhower federalized the Arkansas National Guard and sent one thousand paratroopers from the 101st Airborne Division to Little Rock. It was the first time since Reconstruction that a president ordered troops to the South. Although their presence desegregated Central High in 1957, the following year Faubus closed Little Rock's public schools, declaring "I stand now and always in opposition to integration by force or at bayonet point." Taken together, Faubus's shortsighted political moves and Eisenhower's refusal to take action until public order had been disrupted created a crisis that more thoughtful leadership might have avoided.

The Word from Montgomery

The failure of white leaders convinced blacks that court orders would not magically produce equal rights. The fight would be difficult, the march long. Many blacks realized this even before the Little Rock crisis. On a cold afternoon in 1955 in Montgomery, Alabama, Rosa Parks, a well-respected black seamstress who was active in the NAACP, took a significant stride toward equality. She boarded a bus and sat in the first row of the "colored" section. The white section of the bus quickly filled, and according to Jim Crow rules, blacks were expected to give up their seats rather than force whites—male or female—to stand. The time came for Mrs. Parks

Paratroopers escorted black students to and from school in Little Rock, Arkansas, after violence erupted when the schools were instructed to desegregate.

to give up her seat. She stayed seated. When told by the bus driver to get up or he would call the police, she said, "You may do that." Later she recalled that the act of defiance was "just something I had to do." The bus stopped, the driver summoned the police, and Rosa Parks was arrested.

Rosa Parks's arrest for refusing to move to the back of a bus led to citywide bus boycotts throughout 1956. Martin Luther King, Jr., was one of the first to ride the buses when the bus systems were integrated.

Black Montgomery rallied to Mrs. Parks's side. Like her, they were tired of riding in the back of the bus, tired of giving up their seats to whites, tired of having their lives restricted by Jim Crow. Local black leaders decided to organize a boycott of Montgomery's white-owned and white-operated bus system. They hoped that economic pressure would force changes that court decisions could not. For the next 381 days, more than 90 percent of Montgomery's black citizens participated in a heroic and successful demonstration against racial segregation. The common black attitude toward the protest was voiced by an elderly black woman when a black leader offered her a ride. "No," she replied, "my feets is tired, but my soul is rested."

To lead the boycott, Montgomery blacks turned to the new minister of the Dexter Avenue Baptist Church, a young man named Martin Luther King, Jr. Reared in Atlanta, the son of a respected and financially secure minister, King had been educated at Morehouse College, Crozier Seminary, and Boston University, from which he earned a doctorate in theology. King was an intellectual, excited by ideas and deeply influenced by the philosophical writings of Henry David Thoreau and Mahatma Gandhi as well as the teachings of Christ. They believed in the power of nonviolent, direct action.

King's words as well as his ideas stirred people's souls. At the start of the Montgomery boycott he told his followers:

> There comes a time when people get tired. We are here this evening to say to those who have mistreated us so long that we are tired—tired of being segregated and humiliated, tired of being kicked about by the brutal feet of oppression . . . We've come here tonight to be saved from the patience that makes us patient with anything less than freedom and justice . . . If you protest courageously and yet with dignity and Christian love, in the history books that are written in future generations, historians will have to pause and say "there lived a great people—a black people—who injected a new meaning and dignity into the veins of civilization."

In King, civil rights had found a genuine spokesman, one who preached a doctrine of change guided by Christian love not racial hatred. "In our protest," he observed, "there will be no cross burnings. No white person will be taken from his home by a hooded Negro mob and brutally murdered. There will be no threats and no intimidation."

The success of the Montgomery boycott inspired nonviolent black protests elsewhere in the South. Increasingly, young blacks took the lead. Violence and biased law enforcement did not stop the protesters. Indeed, within a few months of the successful conclusion of the Montgomery boycott, demonstrations erupted in 54 cities in 9 states. The protesters were arrested, jailed, beaten, and even knocked off their feet by high-pressure fire hoses, but still they protested.

The protests were widely reported in the country's newspapers and televised nightly on the news shows. They confronted Americans everywhere with the stark reality of segregation. Ignorance of the situation became an impossibility; and as the violence continued, pressure mounted on white national politicians to take decisive action. By the early 1960s the word from Montgomery had reinforced the *Brown* decision. It was time for freedom to become a reality. (See Chapter 30 for fuller treatment of civil rights.)

THE SOUNDS OF CHANGE

Beginning in the 1970s, American advertisers started to market a new commodity—the fifties. They marketed it as a Golden Decade, a carefree time before the assassination of John F. Kennedy, the Vietnam War, and Watergate. According to the popular myth, kids in the 1950s thought "dope" referred to a dull-witted person, parents married for life, and major family problems revolved around whether or not sis had a date for the prom. This image of the decade has taken different forms. "Happy Days" presented it on television; *American Grafitti* and *Diner* (set in the early sixties) detailed it on the silver screen. It was an age of innocence, tranquility, and static charm. In truth, however, that carefully packaged Golden Decade never

Television programs of the 1950s often centered around a happy, well-adjusted suburban family with two or three children.

existed. Instead, the decade was alive with dynamic, creative tensions.

Father Knows Best

The stock television situation comedy of the 1950s centered on a white family with a happily married husband and wife and two—or sometimes three—well-adjusted children. Most often, the family lived in a white, two-story suburban home, from which the father ventured daily to his white-collar job. The wife did not work outside the house—there was no need since the husband made a comfortable living. In any case, the shows emphasized, wives were also mothers, and mothers were supposed to stay home and tend the children. "Father Knows Best" was the classic example of this genre. It ran from 1954 to 1962 and signaled an optimistic outlook through its title song, "Just Around the Corner There's a Rainbow in the Sky."

The picture these sitcoms presented of America was not entirely inaccurate. Starting after World War II, Americans moved steadily toward the suburbs, which during the 1950s grew six times faster than cities. Several factors contributed to this migration. The high price of urban real estate had driven industries out of the cities, and as always in American history, the population followed the jobs. By 1970 suburban areas had more manufacturing jobs than the central cities. In addition, developers built abundant, inexpensive homes, which newly married couples, aided by VA and FHA loans, purchased. Of the 13 million homes constructed during the 1950s, 11 million were built in the suburbs.

Nor was the television image of predominantly white suburban families misleading. A far greater percentage of whites than blacks moved to the suburbs. In 1950 blacks comprised 12.5 percent of America's urban population and 4.9 percent of the country's suburban population. By 1970 the urban figure had climbed to 20.5 percent and the suburban number declined modestly to 4.8 percent. Housing and job restrictions worked to keep blacks in the central cities while allowing whites to fill the suburban areas.

Even the image of the suburban housewife preoccupied with her husband and her family was socially sanctioned. American women in the 1950s had babies as never before. The population of the United States increased by under 10 million in the 1930s, 19 million in the 1940s, and a staggering 30 million in the 1950s. During the 1950s the nation's growth rate approached that of India. The best-sellers list even indicated America's concern with children. Between 1946 and 1976 the pocket edition of Dr. Benjamin Spock's *Baby and Child Care* sold over 23 million copies, ranking it behind only the Bible and the combined works of Mickey Spillane and Dr. Seuss.

During the age of remarkable fertility, popular writers glorified the role of the mother. The best-seller *Modern Woman: The Lost Sex* went as far as to say that an independent woman was "a contradiction in terms." The ideal woman, writers observed, was content being a wife and a mother or, in a word, a homemaker. "Women must boldly announce," wrote novelist Sloan Wilson, "that no job is more exacting, more necessary, or more rewarding than that of housewife and mother." In the 1950s women married younger and had children sooner than they had in the previous two decades.

The Other Side of the Coin

"Father Knows Best" and other shows portrayed an ideal world where serious problems seldom intrude and where life lacks complexity. In fact, the move to suburbia and the changes in family life forced Americans to reevaluate many of their beliefs.

Cultural critics, for example, claimed that life in suburbia fostered mindless conformity. Lewis Mumford described suburbs as "a multitude of uniform, unidentifiable houses, lined up inflexibly, at uniform distances, on uniform roads, in a treeless communal wasteland, inhabited by people of the same class, the same income, the same age group." And a popular song called the suburban homes:

> Little boxes on the hillside,
> Little boxes made of ticky tacky
> Little boxes on the hillside,
> Little boxes all the same.

Some writers feared the United States had become a country of unthinking consumers driven by advertisers to desire only the latest gadget. Americans bought automobiles, houses,

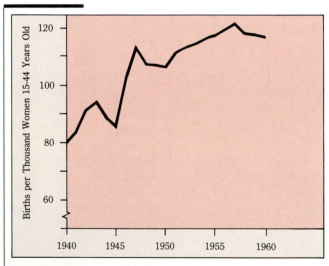

Figure 28.2
American birthrate, 1940–1960

(Text continues on p. 964)

PRIMARY SOURCE ESSAY

EDWARD R. MURROW AND
THE FUNCTION OF TELEVISION

During the 1940s and the 1950s, Edward R. Murrow (1908–1965) was the soul of radio and television news. His crisp, laconic style was as familiar to American listeners as his darting eyes and ever-present cigarette were to American viewers. Murrow entered the radio news business in the mid-1930s and he helped to determine its course and development. In 1938 when Hitler's determination to take the Sudetenland threatened war in Europe, Murrow and his roving reporter William L. Shirer brought the crisis to the American people with a series special broadcasts. During World War II Murrow—with his familiar "This . . . is London"—broadcast reports from rooftops, streets, and air-raid shelters, amid falling bombs and flying debris. After the war Murrow took his professional news skills to television. In 1951 his "See It Now" aired for the first time. This weekly half-hour show probed the important issues, policies, and personalities of the day. In 1954 "See It Now" even took on Senator Joseph McCarthy. From 1953 to 1959 Murrow also hosted the popular "Person to Person," an entertainment program that featured interviews with Hollywood celebrities and world leaders. But Murrow was always first a journalist and only second an entertainer. He deplored the shift in television from education to entertainment. Defeated by the forces of escapism and profit, he left broadcasting in 1961.

Edward R. Murrow at the microphone of his CBS-TV program, September 1957. Murrow believed in the instructional value of television and deplored the fact that most televised entertainment insulated the viewing public from reality.

REPRINTED IN *THE REPORTER* (NOV. 13, 1958), PP. 32–36

Our history will be what we make it. And if there are any historians about fifty or a hundred years from now, and there should be preserved the kinescopes for one week of all three networks, they will there find recorded in black-and-white, or color, evidence of decadence, escapism, and insulation from the realities of the world in which we live. I invite your attention to the television schedules of all networks between the hours of eight and eleven P.M. Eastern Time. Here you will find only fleeting and spasmodic reference to the fact that this nation is in mortal danger. There are, it is true, occasional informative programs presented in that intellectual ghetto on Sunday afternoons. But during the daily peak viewing periods, television in the main insulates us from the realities of the world in which we live. If this state of affairs continues, we may alter an advertising slogan to read: "Look Now, Pay Later." For surely we shall pay for using this most powerful instrument of communication to insulate the citizenry from the hard and demanding realities which must be faced if we are to survive. I mean the word—"survive"—literally. If there were to be a competition in indifference, or perhaps in insulation from reality, then Nero and his fiddle, Chamberlain and his umbrella, could not find a place on an early-afternoon sustaining show. If Hollywood were to run out of Indians, the program schedules would be mangled beyond all recognition. Then some courageous soul with a small budget might be able to do a documentary telling what, in fact, we have done—and are still doing—to the Indians in this country. But that would be unpleasant. And we must at all costs shield the sensitive citizens from anything that is unpleasant.

One of the basic troubles with radio and television news is that both instruments have grown up as an incompatible combination of show business, advertising, and news. Each of the three is a rather bizarre and demanding profession. And when you get all three under one roof, the dust never settles. The top management of the networks, with a few notable exceptions, has been trained in advertising, research, sales, or show business. But by the nature of the corporate structure, they also make the final and crucial decisions having to do with news and public affairs. Frequently they have neither the time nor the competence to do this. It is not easy for the same small group of men to decide whether to buy a new station for millions of dollars, build a new building, alter the rate card, buy a new Western, sell a soap opera, decide what defensive line to take in connection with the latest Congressional inquiry, how much money to spend on promoting a new program, what additions or deletions should be made in the existing covey or clutch of view-presidents, and at the same time—frequently on the same long day—to give mature, thoughtful consideration to the manifold problems that confront those who are charged with the responsibility for news and public affairs.

Edward R. Murrow addresses news reporters at a special press conference following Senator Joseph McCarthy's filmed rebuttal to Murrow's exposé of the senator on the journalist's "See It Now" program. Murrow gave up "See It Now" airtime to allow McCarthy to respond to the exposé.

In 1958 the Radio-Television News Directors Association (RTNDA) invited Murrow to address their annual meeting. The organization did not care about the subject of his address; they wanted Murrow for his name not for his thoughts on any particular subject. To the surprise of the organization, Murrow accepted the invitation. His speech "may do neither of us any good," he told RTNDA's program chairman. But he did have something that needed saying.

Murrow was the most famous television and radio journalist in America. No one else was even close. On CBS, "See It Now" had made as well as reported the news. In 1954 "See It Now" had courageously and successfully defended Lieutenant Milo Radulovich, an officer in the Air Force Reserve, who had been dismissed because of his associations with suspected radicals. The suspected radicals were his father and his sister. After Murrow's show on the case, the air force reinstated Radulovich. That same year, Murrow had taken on Joe McCarthy, and the show helped to break the grip of terror McCarthy had on America. Ending the show, Murrow told his viewers, "We proclaim ourselves—as indeed we are—the defenders of freedom, . . . but we cannot defend freedom abroad by deserting it at home. The actions of the junior Senator from Wisconsin have caused alarm and dismay amongst our allies abroad and given considerable comfort to our enemies, and whose fault is it? Not really his. He didn't create this situation of fear; he merely exploited it, and rather successfully. Cassius was right: 'The fault, dear Brutus, is not in the stars but in ourselves . . .'"

But with fame came controversy and problems, especially with the management of CBS. Television is a commercial medium. It depends on advertising by sponsors for its revenues. And sponsors fear shows that generate controversy, for controversy can create a negative image that might defeat the objective of advertising itself. Alcoa, the sponsor of "See It Now," worried about the impact of the show, and this in turn concerned CBS president Frank Stanton and chairman of the board William S. Paley. In short, CBS was caught in the classic conflict of commercial television: programming freedom versus the demands of the sponsor. Murrow believed that the news division should not be constrained editorially by the profit motive. Stanton and Paley were not so sure. By 1958 Murrow could see that he was losing the fight, and he wanted to warn America before the contest was completely over.

Murrow's speech before RTNDA had a sense of urgency. "We are currently wealthy, fat, comfortable, and complacent," he said. "We have currently a built-in allergy to unpleasant or disturbing information. Our mass media reflect this. But unless we get up off our fat surpluses and recognize that television in the main is being used to distract, delude, amuse, and insulate us, then television and those who finance it, those who look at it and those who work at it, may see a totally different picture too late." He believed in the possibilities of television, but he knew that it could only be as good as the people who controlled the networks and stations: "This instrument can teach, it can illuminate; yes, it can even inspire. But it can do so only to the extent that humans are determined to use it to those ends. Otherwise it is merely wires and lights in a box."

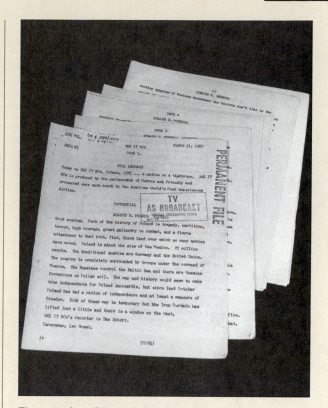

The script from Edward R. Murrow's "See It Now" broadcast, March 31, 1957.

Murrow lost the fight. In less than three years he was gone from CBS. But what he said was as true in 1958 as it is today. When asked why he criticized the industry that brought him fame and fortune, Murrow responded, "I've always been on the side of the heretics against those who burned them because the heretics so often proved right in the long run. Dead—but right." Murrow, the heretic, lost his electronic pulpit because he told the truth.

TABLE 28.1

Population of Metropolitan Areas by Region, Size, and Race, 1950–1970

Year		Inner City	Suburbs	Black Population as Percent of Inner City	Black Population as Percent of Suburbs
1950	White	43,001,634	33,248,836		
	Black	6,194,948	1,736,521	12.5	4.9
	Other	216,210	102,531		
1970	White	49,430,443	71,148,286		
	Black	13,140,331	3,630,279	20.5	4.8
	Other	1,226,169	843,303		

Historical Statistics of the United States, Bicentennial Edition, vol. 1, p. 40.

and electrical appliances as never before. Thirty percent more Americans owned homes in 1970 than in 1940. Between 1945 and 1960 the number of cars in the country increased by 133 percent and the use of electricity tripled. Perhaps the symbol of this consumerism was the Barbie doll. Introduced to the American public in 1958, Barbie cost only $3 dollars, but her full wardrobe cost over $100. Indeed, the buying of homes, cars, televisions, and electrical appliances fueled the tremendous economic growth between 1945 and 1970. Clearly buying was good for the American economy, but was it beneficial to the individuals who spent more and more of their time in their cars and watching their televisions? Cultural observers despaired.

Some women also expressed frustration about their roles as wives and mothers. One poll of the 1934 graduates of the best women's colleges reported that one out of every three women felt unfulfilled. Although many women worked, cultural stereotyping prevented most of them from rising to the higher paying, more prestigious positions. In addition, Betty Friedan, a leader in the women's rights movement, noted that those women who did place a career above marriage or family were regarded as abnormal.

The problems of suburban life were explored in numerous films, novels, articles, and advice books. The film *Invasion of the Body Snatchers* (1956) is an outstanding example of the fear that suburbia had created a nation of conformists. In the movie, the inhabitants of the town Santa Mira are turned into emotionless shells by giant pods from outer space. Like abusers of Miltown or Thorazine—the most popular adult drugs of the 1950s—the pod-people utterly lack individuality. As one explains, podism means being "reborn into an untroubled world, where everyone's the same." In that world, "there is no need for love or emotion." For such cultural critics as David Riesman, author of *The Lonely Crowd* (1955), America's acceptance of conformity threatened to make podism a form of reality.

The critics, however, overreacted to the "suburban threat." If the houses looked the same, the people were individuals—even if they often banded together to try to form suburban communities. In the suburbs, white working-class families could afford for the first time to purchase homes and live middle-class lives. This was a real accomplishment. The problems that critics observed in the suburbs—the tendency toward conformity, cultural homogeneity, materialism, and anxiety over sex roles—were urban problems as well.

The Meaning of Elvis

The harshest critics of "suburban values" were American youths. Their criticism took different forms. Some of it was thoughtful and formalized, the result of the best efforts of young intellectuals. At other times it took a more visceral form, a protest that came from the gut rather than the mind. Of the second type of protest, none was more widely embraced by youths—or roundly attacked by adults—than rock and roll.

Rock and roll was the bastard mulatto child of a heterogeneous American culture. It combined black rhythm and blues with white country music. It was made possible by the post–World War II demographic changes. The movement of southern blacks and whites to the cities of the upper South and North threw together different musical traditions and forged an entirely new sound. Its lyrics and heavy beat challenged the accepted standards of "good taste" in music. Giving voice to this challenge, black rock-and-roll artist Chuck Berry sang:

> Well, I'm gonna write a little letter, gonna mail it to my local D.J.
> Yes, it's a jumpin' little record I want my jockey to play
> Roll over Beethoven, I gotta hear it again today
> You know my temp'rature's risin' and the jukebox blowin' a fuse
> My heart's beatin' rhythm and my soul keeps singin' the blues
> Roll over Beethoven and tell Tchaikovsky the news.

Confronting conventional morality, rock and roll was openly vulgar. The very term—"rock 'n' roll"—had long been used in blues songs to describe lovemaking, and early black rock-and-roll singers glorified physical relationships. Little Richard sang:

> Well, Long Tall Sally she's built for speed, she got
> Everythin' that Uncle John needs.

And in another song, he boasted:

> I'm gonna RIP IT UP!
> I'm gonna rock it up!
> I'm gonna shake it up. I'm gonna ball it up!
> I'm gonna RIP IT UP and ball tonight.

From its emergence in the early 1950s, rock and roll generated angry criticism. In the South, white church groups attacked it as part of an NAACP plot to corrupt the morals of southern youths and foster integration. In Hartford, Connecticut, Dr. Francis J. Braceland described rock and roll as "a communicable disease, with

Elvis Presley, one of the great pioneers of rock-and-roll music, was the target of much controversy throughout his life.

music appealing to adolescent insecurity and driving teenagers to do outlandish things . . . It's cannibalistic and tribalistic." Particularly between 1954 and 1958, there were numerous crusades to ban rock and roll from the airways.

Most of the critics of rock and roll focused on Elvis Presley, who more than any other artist most fully fused country music with rhythm and blues. In his first record, he gave the rhythm-and-blues song "That's All Right Mama" a country feel and the country classic "Blue Moon over Kentucky" a rhythm-and-blues swing. It was a unique exhibition of genius. In addition, Presley exuded sexuality. When he appeared on the Ed Sullivan Show, network executives instructed cameramen to avoid shots of Elvis's suggestive physical movements. Finally, Presley upset segregationists by performing "race music." Head of Sun Records Sam Phillips had once claimed, "If I could find a white man who had the Negro sound and the Negro feel, I could make a million dollars." Presley was that white man.

In the end, however, the protests implicit in Elvis Presley and rock and roll were largely coopted by middle-class American culture. Record producers, most of whom were white, smoothed the jagged edges of rock and roll. Sexually explicit black recordings were rewritten and rerecorded—a process known as "covering"—by white performers and then sold to white youths. Black singer Joe Turner, for example, recorded "Shake, Rattle and Roll" for a black audience. Its lyrics ran:

> Get out of that bed,
> And wash your face and hands.
> Get into the kitchen,
> Make some noise with the pots and pans.
> Well you wear low dresses,
> The sun comes shinin' through.
> I can't believe my eyes,
> That all of this belongs to you.

The white group Bill Haley and the Comets "covered" the song for a white audience. The new version stated:

> Get out in that kitchen,
> And rattle those pots and pans.
> Roll my breakfast
> 'Cause I'm a hungry man.
> You wear those dresses,
> Your hair done up so nice.
> You look so warm,
> But your heart is cold as ice.

In the second recording all references to beds and bodies have been eliminated; by 1959 rock and roll had become an accepted part of mainstream American culture.

A Different Beat

Rock-and-roll artists never rejected the idea of success in America. If they challenged conventional sexual mores and tried to create a unique sound, they accepted the rewards of success in a capitalistic society. Elvis Presley translated success into a steady stream of Cadillacs and conventional, unchallenging films. Not all youth protests, however, were so easily absorbed into middle-class culture. The Beat movement, for example, questioned the values at the heart of that culture.

The Beat Generation extolled the very thing that ˙conventional Americans abhorred, and

they rejected what the others prized. Beats scorned materialism, traditional family life, religion, sexuality, and politics. They renounced the American Dream. Instead, they valued spontaneity and intuition, searching for truth through Eastern mysticism and drugs. Although whites formed the rank and file of the Beat Generation, they glorified the supposedly "natural" life of black Americans, a life representing (at least for whites) pure instinctual drives. They adopted black music and the jive words of the black lexicon. *Cat, solid, chick, Big Apple, square,* were all absorbed into the Beat vocabulary.

Allen Ginsberg was the leading poet of the Beat Generation. A graduate of Columbia University, where he was influenced by the lifestyle of New York City lowlifes and artists, Ginsberg moved to San Francisco in the mid-1950s. There, surrounded by kindred souls, Ginsberg came to accept his homosexuality and preached a life based on experimentation. He also developed an authentic poetic voice. In 1955 he wrote "Howl," the prototypical Beat poem. Written under the influence of drugs, "Howl" is a literary kaleidoscope, a breathless succession of stark images and passionate beliefs. In a unique but soon to be widely imitated style, Ginsberg declared,

Allen Ginsberg was educated at the University of California, Berkeley, and at Columbia University. His poems expressed the Beat Generation's dissatisfaction with conventional middle-class values.

CHRONOLOGY OF KEY EVENTS

1944 GI Bill of Rights grants veterans financial aid for education and government loans for building houses and starting businesses

1947 25-year-old Jackie Robinson becomes the first black player in major league baseball

1948 President Truman bans segregation in armed forces

1953 Dwight D. Eisenhower becomes thirty-fourth president; Stalin dies; Nikita Khrushchev emerges as leader of the Soviet Union; CIA helps bring Shah Mohammad Reza Pahlavi to power in Iran

1954 CIA masterminds overthrow of leftist government of Guatemala; *Brown* v. *Board of Education of Topeka* decision holds that "separate educational facilities are inherently unequal"

1955 Emmett Till murder; black residents of Montgomery, Alabama, organize a bus boycott to protest segregation; Eisenhower and Khrushchev hold summit in Geneva, Switzerland

1956 Soviet troops crush Hungarian uprising; Suez crisis; United States begins interstate highway system

1957 Eisenhower sends troops to Little Rock, Arkansas, to allow black students to enroll in formerly all-white public schools; Soviet Union launches the first satellite, *Sputnik*

1958 U.S. marines intervene in Lebanon; Congress passes the National Defense Education Act to provide federal aid to schools and colleges

1959 Fidel Castro leads Cuban Revolution against the regime of Fulgencio Batista

1960 U-2 spy plane is shot down over the Soviet Union

> I saw the best minds of my generation destroyed
> by madness, starving hysterically naked,
> dragging themselves through the negro streets
> at dawn looking for an angry fix . . .

Ginsberg even questioned accepted Cold War beliefs. He wrote:

> America you don't really want to go to war.
> America it's them bad Russians.
> Them Russians them Russians and them China-
>   men. And them Russians.
> Them Russians want to eat us alive.
> America this is quite serious.
> America this is the impression I get from looking
>   in the television set.
> America is this correct?

Ginsberg and Jack Kerouac, the leading Beat novelist, outraged adults but discovered followers on college campuses and in cities across America. They tapped an underground dissatisfaction with the prevailing blandness of conventional culture. In this their appeal was similar to that of rock and roll. Both were scattering seeds that would bear fruit during the next decade.

CONCLUSION

Ike's America was both more and less than what it seemed. In foreign and domestic affairs, Eisenhower appeared to allow his subordinates to run the country, when in reality he made the important decisions. Whether it was national highways or the Middle East, Eisenhower's vision of order helped shape American policy. He was more influential than most Americans during the 1950s realized.

If Eisenhower was more active than he appeared, then the country was more dynamic than it seemed on the surface. Although critics railed against the conformity of suburban America, everywhere there were signs of change. During the 1950s blacks quickened the pace of their struggle for equality and youths experimented with alternatives to traditional behavior. And increasingly these two rebellions merged to form a distinct subculture. During the 1960s, the war in Vietnam would give a political edge to that subculture.

SUGGESTIONS FOR FURTHER READING

OVERVIEWS AND SURVEYS

Stephen E. Ambrose, *Rise to Globalism: American Foreign Policy Since 1938*, 5th ed. (1988); William H. Chafe, *The Unfinished Journey*, 2d ed. (1991), and *The American Woman* (1972); Alexander DeConde, *A History of American Foreign Policy* (1963); Robert H. Ferrell, *American Diplomacy* (1959); Alonzo Hamby, *The Imperial Years* (1976); Godfrey Hodgson, *America in Our Time* (1976); Walter LaFeber, *America, Russia, and the Cold War*, 5th ed. (1985); R. W. Leopold, *The Growth of American Foreign Policy* (1962); William Leuchtenburg, *A Troubled Feast*, rev. ed. (1983); William Manchester, *The Glory and the Dream* (1974); Thomas G. Paterson et al., *American Foreign Policy*, 3d ed., 2 vols. (1988); Richard Polenberg, *One Nation Divisible* (1980); Emily and Norman Rosenberg, *In Our Times*, 4th ed. (1991); Frederick F. Siegel, *A Troubled Journey* (1984); William A. Williams, *The Tragedy of American Diplomacy*, 2d ed. (1972), and *The Roots of the Modern American Empire* (1969); Lawrence Wittner, *Cold War America*, rev. ed. (1978); Howard Zinn, *Postwar America, 1945–1971* (1973).

QUIET CHANGES

Charles Alexander, *Holding the Line: The Eisenhower Era, 1952–1961* (1975); Chester L. Cooper, *The Lion's Last Roar: Suez, 1956* (1978); Robert A. Divine, *Eisenhower and the Cold War* (1981); Fred I. Greenstein, *The Hidden-Hand Presidency: Eisenhower as Leader* (1982); Peter L. Hahn, *The United States, Great Britain, and Egypt, 1945–1956* (1991); Richard Immerman, *The CIA in Gua-*

temala (1982); Madeleine Kalb, *The Congo Cables: The Cold War in Africa—from Eisenhower to Kennedy* (1982); Richard Melanson and David Mayers, eds., *Reevaluating Eisenhower: American Foreign Policy in the 1950s* (1987); John B. Rae, *The Road and the Car in American Life* (1971); Mark H. Rose, *Interstate: Express Highway Politics, 1939–1989*, rev. ed. (1990); Walt W. Rostow, *The Stages of Economic Growth: A Non-Communist Manifesto*, 2d ed. (1971); Stephen Schlesinger and Steven Kinzer, *Bitter Fruit: The Untold Story of the American Coup in Guatemala* (1982); James Sundquist, *Politics and Policy: The Eisenhower, Kennedy, and Johnson Years* (1968); Richard Welch, Jr., *Response to Revolution: The United States and the Cuban Revolution, 1959–1961* (1985).

WE SHALL OVERCOME

Numan V. Bartley, *The Rise of Massive Resistance: Race and Politics in the South During the 1950s* (1969); Jack Bass, *Unlikely Heroes: The Dramatic Story of the Southern Judges of the Fifth Circuit* (1981); Sally Belfrage, *Freedom Summer* (1965); William Berman, *The Politics of Civil Rights in the Truman Administration* (1970); Albert Blaustein and Clarence Clyde Ferguson, Jr., *Desegregation and the Law*, 2d ed. (1962); William H. Chafe, *Civilities and Civil Rights: Greensboro, North Carolina, and the Black Struggle for Equality* (1980); Robert Conot, *Rivers of Blood, Years of Darkness* (1967); Richard Dalfiume, *Desegregation of the U.S. Armed Forces: Fighting on Two Fronts, 1939–1953* (1969); David Garrow, *Protest at Selma* (1978); Richard Kluger, *Simple Justice: The History of Brown v. Board of Education and Black America's Struggle for Equality* (1976); Steven Lawson, *Black Ballots: Voting Rights in the South, 1944–1969* (1976), and *Running for Freedom: Civil Rights and Black Politics in America since 1941* (1991); Manning Marable, *Race, Reform, and Rebellion: The Second Reconstruction in Black America, 1945-1990* (1991); Donald R. McCoy and Richard T. Ruetten, *Quest and Response: Minority Rights and the Truman Administration* (1973); Melton A. McLaurin, *Separate Pasts: Growing Up White in the Segregated South* (1987); Neil R. McMillen, *The Citizens' Council: Organized Resistance to the Second Reconstruction, 1954–64* (1971); August Meier and Elliott Rudwick, *CORE: A Study in the Civil Rights Movement, 1942–1968* (1973); Benjamin Muse, *The American Negro Revolution* (1968); Gunnar Myrdal, *An American Dilemma*, 2 vols. (1944); William L. O'Neill, *American High: The Years of Confidence, 1945–1960* (1986);

James Peck, *Freedom Ride* (1962); Howell Raines, *My Soul Is Rested: Movement Days in the Deep South Remembered* (1977); Harvard Sitkoff, *The Struggle for Black Equality* (1981); Morton Sosna, *In Search of the Silent South: Southern Liberals and the Race Issue* (1977); Howard Zinn, *The Southern Mystique* (1964).

THE SOUNDS OF CHANGE

Kent Anderson, *Television Fraud* (1978); Erik Barnouw, *Tube of Plenty*, 2d ed. (1990); Carl Belz, *The Story of Rock*, 2d ed. (1972); Paul A. Carter, *Another Part of the Fifties* (1983); William H. Chafe, *Women and Equality* (1977); Bruce Cook, *The Beat Generation* (1971); Marcus Cunliffe, *The Literature of the United States*, 4th ed. (1986); John D'Emilio and Estelle Freedman, *Intimate Matters: A History of Sexuality in America* (1988); Scott Donaldson, *The Suburban Myth* (1969); James Flink, *The Car Culture* (1975); Betty Friedan, *The Feminine Mystique* (1963); John Kenneth Galbraith, *The Affluent Society*, 4th ed. (1984); Herbert Gans, *The Levittowners* (1967); Charlie Gillett, *The Sound of the City: The Rise of Rock and Roll*, rev. ed. (1984); Michael Harrington, *The Other America: Poverty in the United States* (1962); Molly Haskell, *From Reverence to Rape: The Treatment of Women in the Movies*, 2d ed. (1987); Will Herberg, *Protestant, Catholic, Jew* (1955); Jerry Hopkins, *The Rock Story* (1970); Kenneth Jackson, *The Crabgrass Frontier: The Suburbanization of the United States* (1985); Pauline N. Kael, *I Lost It at the Movies* (1965); Marcus Klein, comp., *The American Novel since World War II* (1969); W. T. Lhamon, Jr., *Deliberate Speed: The Origins of a Cultural Style in the American 1950s* (1990); David Marc, *Demographic Vistas: Television in American Culture* (1984), Greil Marcus, *The Mystery Train*, 3d ed. (1990); Douglas Miller and Marion Nowak, *The Fifties: The Way We Really Were* (1977); James T. Patterson, *America's Struggle Against Poverty, 1900–1980* (1981); Ned Polsky, *Hustlers, Beats, and Others* (1967); David M. Potter, *People of Plenty: Economic Abundance and the American Character* (1954); David Riesman, *The Lonely Crowd* (1950); Stephen M. Rose, *The Betrayal of the Poor: The Transformation of Community Action* (1972); Lynn Spigel, *Make Room for TV: Television and the Family Ideal in Postwar America* (1992); I. F. Stone, *The Haunted Fifties* (1963); Michael Wood, *America in the Movies* (1975).

BIOGRAPHIES

Stephen E. Ambrose, *Eisenhower*, 2 vols. (1983–1984); Jervis Anderson, *A. Philip Randolph* (1973); Robert A. Caro, *The Power Broker: Robert Moses and the Fall of New York* (1974); Robert J. Donovan, *Eisenhower* (1956); David Garrow, *Bearing the Cross: Martin Luther King, Jr., and the Southern Christian Leadership Conference* (1986); Peter Goldman, *The Death and Life of Malcolm X*, 2d ed. (1979); Alex Haley, *Autobiography of Malcolm X* (1965); Townsend Hoopes, *The Devil and John Foster Dulles* (1973); David L. Lewis, *King*, 2d ed. (1978); Peter Lyon, *Eisenhower: Portrait of the Hero* (1974); Anne Moody, *Coming of Age in Mississippi* (1968); Stephen B. Oates, *Let the Trumpet Sound: The Life of Martin Luther King, Jr.* (1982).

CHAPTER 29

Vietnam and the Crisis of Authority

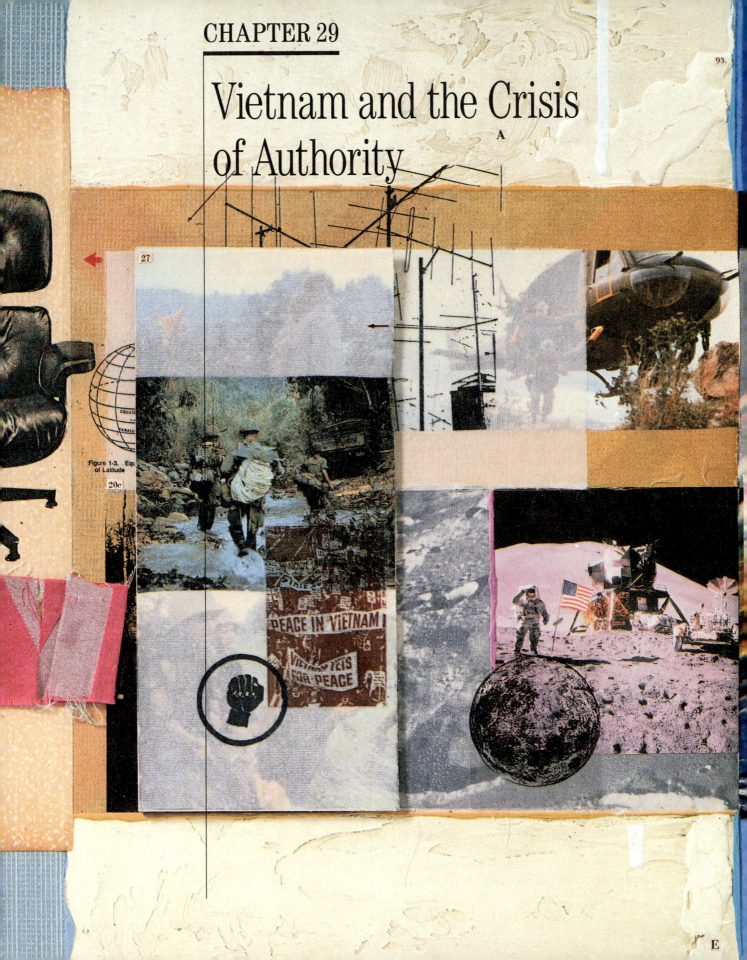

Ho Chi Minh was born roughly 9000 miles from America, but he might as well have come from a different planet. Ho was a tiny man, a frail, thin splinter of a man. He was gentle, and in public always deferential. Even after he had come to sole power in North Vietnam, he steadfastly avoided all the trappings of authority. Instead of uniforms or the white sharkskin suit of the mandarin, Ho favored the simple shorts and sandals worn by the Vietnamese peasants. He was sure of who he was—certain of his place in Vietnamese history—and he had no desire to impress others with his position. To his followers, he was "Uncle Ho," the kind, bachelor relative who treated all Vietnamese citizens like the children he never had. But in the pursuit of Vietnamese independence and the realization of a Communist nation, Ho could be cold-blooded and ruthless.

Ho was born in 1890 in a village in a central province of Vietnam and originally named Nguyen Sinh Cung. In 1912 Ho left Vietnam and began a generation-long world odyssey. Signing aboard a French freighter, he moved from one port to the next. For a time he stayed in the United States, visiting Boston, New York City, and San Francisco. He was amazed not only by America's skyscrapers but also by the fact that immigrants in the United States enjoyed the same legal rights as American citizens. He was also struck by the impatience of the American people, their expectations of immediate results. (Later, during the Vietnam War, Ho would say to his military leaders, "Don't worry, Americans are an impatient people. When things begin to go wrong, they'll leave.")

After three years of almost constant travel, Ho settled in London, where he worked at the elegant Carlton Hotel. He lived in squalid quarters and learned that poverty existed even in the wealthiest, most powerful countries. Then it was on to Paris, where he came in contact with the French left. There he studied, and his nationalist ambitions became tinged with revolutionary teachings. He was still in Paris when the Great War ended and the world leaders came to Versailles for the Peace Conference. Inspired by Woodrow Wilson's call for national self-determination, Ho wrote that "all subject peoples are filled with hope by the prospect that an era of right and justice is opening to them . . . in the struggle of civilization against barbarism." Ho wanted to meet Wilson; he wanted to plead for independence for his country. Wilson ignored his request; Vietnam remained France's colony. Ho moved on—farther east and further left.

Disillusioned with France and socialism, Ho traveled to Moscow, where Lenin had declared war against imperialism. In the Soviet Union Ho embraced communism. In the ideology he saw a road to his ultimate goal, the liberation of Vietnam. By the early 1920s he was actively organizing Vietnamese exiles into a revolutionary force. He continued to travel—to Western Europe, back to Russia, to China, back to Russia, to Thailand, back to the West. He lived a life of secrecy, moving from place to place, changing his name, renouncing anything even remotely resembling a personal life. No wife, no children, few friends—only a cause. As he advised one Vietnamese returning to the homeland, "The colonialists will be on your trail. Keep away from our friends' homes and don't hesitate to pose as a degenerate if it will help put the police off the scent."

In 1941 Ho returned to Vietnam. The time was right, he believed, to free Vietnam from colonial domination. During the early part of World War II, the Japanese had won control of the country from the French; now Ho and his followers would force out the Japanese. Once again Ho allied himself with the United States. Working alongside American Office of Strategic Services (OSS) agents, Ho proved his mettle. He impressed the OSS agents with his bravery, intelligence,

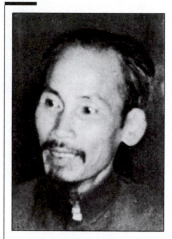

Ho Chi Minh was influenced by French socialism and Soviet communism in his goal to liberate Vietnam from the French.

and unflagging devotion to his cause. On September 2, 1945, borrowing passages from the American Declaration of Independence, Ho declared Vietnamese independence.

THE ILLUSION OF GREATNESS 973

The French, who returned to Vietnam after the war, had different plans for Vietnam, but Ho's struggle continued. In candid moments he admitted that he didn't expect to live to see Vietnam fully independent. Yet he knew that the struggle of others would eventually secure independence. Ho had patience. It was a quality that the West—first France and then the United States—found difficult to understand.

That was only one of the qualities of Ho and of the Vietnamese that the West did not understand. A deep intellectual chasm divided Vietnam and the West. The West viewed history as a straight line in which progress was the governing principle. Emphasizing technological advancements and material improvements, Westerners glorified change and prized individualism.

The Vietnamese were products of different beliefs. Notions of competition, individualism, and technological change were anathema to traditionbound Vietnamese. For a thousand years they had survived using the same rice cultivating methods. Often, however, the margin between survival and death was a razor's edge. Unlike the United States, Vietnam did not have fertile frontier areas to settle. To make do with the land they had, the Vietnamese organized life around villages and practiced cooperative existence. Rich people were considered selfish because their wealth *had* to be gained at the direct expense of others. As one authority explained, "the idea remains with the Vietnamese that great wealth is antisocial, not a sign of success but a sign of selfishness."

Like wealth, individualism threatened the corporate nature of village life, based on duties, not individual rights, and on social harmony more than individual justice. Even their language excluded the idea of individualism. Vietnamese has no personal pronoun equivalent to the Western *I, je, ich*. A person speaks of oneself in relationship to the person being addressed—for example, as "your teacher," "your brother," "your wife."

Nor did Vietnamese believe in intellectual freedom, which fostered debate and discord, rather than community stability. Americans considered Soviet communism evil because it discouraged the exchange of free ideas; Ho Chi Minh was drawn to the doctrine because it provided a set of answers not subject to questioning. Ho Chi Minh was the product of that closed world. America was the prophet of an open world. Motivated by the Cold War, during the period between 1954 and 1973, U.S. officials became convinced that they had to "save" Vietnam from Ho Chi Minh and his Communist brand of nationalism. Given Vietnamese leadership, traditions, and desire for independence, the American intervention in Vietnam was almost certain to fail.

THE ILLUSION OF GREATNESS

Television's President

John Fitzgerald Kennedy was made for television. His tall, thin body gave him the strong vertical line that cameras love, and his weatherbeaten good looks appealed to women without intimidating men. He had a full head of hair, and even in the winter he maintained a tan. Complementing his appearance was his attitude. He was always "cool" in public. This too was tailormade for the "cool medium" television. Wit, irony, and understatement, all delivered with a studied nonchalance, translate well on television. Table thumping, impassioned speech, and even earnest sincerity often just do not work on television.

In the 1960 presidential race Kennedy challenged his Republican opponent Richard M. Nixon to a series of television debates. At the time, Kennedy faced an uphill battle. Young, handsome, and wealthy, Kennedy was considered by many too young, too handsome, and too wealthy to make an effective president. His undistinguished political record stood in stark contrast to Nixon's work in Congress and eight years as Eisenhower's vice president. In addition, Kennedy was Catholic, and Americans had never elected a Catholic president. Behind in the polls, Kennedy needed a dramatic boost. Thus the challenge. Against the advice of his campaign manager, Nixon accepted.

The first debate was held in Chicago on September 26, 1960, only a little more than a month before the election. Nixon arrived looking ill and weak. During the previous six weeks he had banged his kneecap, which became infected, spent several weeks at the Walter Reed

During the Kennedy-Nixon debates, John F. Kennedy demonstrated that for television politics, style was as important as substance.

Nixon fought back. He perspired, scored debating points, produced memorized facts, and struggled to win; but his efforts were "hot"—bad television. Instead of hearing a knowledgeable candidate, viewers saw a nervous, uncertain man, one whose clothes did not fit and whose face looked pasty and white. In contrast, what Kennedy said sounded statesmanlike, and he *looked* very good. Kennedy was the clear winner. Only later did Nixon realize that the telecast had been a production, not a debate.

The polls registered the results. For the first time during the campaign, Kennedy inched ahead of Nixon in a Gallup poll. Republicans realized the impact of the debate. Republican Senator Barry Goldwater called it "a disaster." Most of the people who were undecided before watching the debate voted for Kennedy. That proved to be the margin of victory. Only one-tenth of one percent separated the two candidates. Perhaps the most important result of the election, however, was not Kennedy's victory but the demonstration of the power of television. It came into its own in 1960.

The "Macho" Presidency

In his inaugural address Kennedy issued threats and challenges as well as making promises. Proud to be the first American president born in the twentieth century, proud to be the torchbearer for "a new generation," Kennedy wanted the world to know where he stood: "Let every nation know, whether it wishes us well or ill, that we shall pay any price, bear any burden, meet any hardship, support any friend, oppose any foe to assure the survival and the success of liberty." And who would pay, bear, meet, support, and oppose? On this point too Kennedy was clear: "And so, my fellow Americans: ask not what your country can do for you—ask what you can do for your country."

After the blandness and mangled syntax of Eisenhower's addresses, here was a speaker of rare ability, here were speeches beautifully phrased. Kennedy probably asked for more sacrifice and promised more rewards than any other president since Woodrow Wilson. Only years after his death did people begin to ask if he was serious or if he was more concerned with

Hospital, and then caught a bad chest cold that left him hoarse and weak. All and all, by the day of the debate he looked like a nervous corpse—pale, 20 pounds underweight, and haggard. Makeup experts offered to hide his heavy beard and soften his jowls, but Nixon accepted only a thin coat of Max Factor's "Lazy Shave," a pancake cosmetic.

Kennedy looked better, very much better. He didn't need makeup to appear healthy, nor did he need special lighting to hide a weak profile. He did, however, change suits. He believed that a dark blue rather than a gray suit would look better under the bright lights. Kennedy was right, of course, as anyone who watches a nightly news program must realize.

The debate started. Kennedy spoke first. Although he was nervous, he intentionally slowed down his delivery. His face was controlled and cool. He smiled with his eyes and perhaps the corners of his mouth, and his laugh was a mere suggestion of a laugh. His body language was perfect. As for what he said, Kennedy disregarded the prearranged ground rules and shifted what was supposed to be a debate on domestic issues to one on foreign policy.

how he said something than what he said. Indeed, he and his speech writers were attracted to verbal sleight-of-hand tricks: "If a free society cannot help the many who are poor, it cannot save the few who are rich. . . . Let us never negotiate out of fear, let us never fear to negotiate." Like the television debates, such statements emphasized style over substance.

Who was the speaker? Competition and an aggressively masculine view of the world ran through the life of John F. Kennedy. He was the son of a multimillionaire who demanded excellence of all his sons and who believed that as Boston Irish Catholics they had to try harder and be tougher than their Protestant neighbors. This was particularly difficult for John Kennedy, who suffered throughout his life from a series of illnesses and physical problems, including Addison's disease and chronic back trouble. His brother Bobby recalled, "At least one-half of the days that he spent on this earth were days of intense physical pain."

But he never used—and his father never accepted—pain as an excuse for inactivity. At Harvard University he played football, boxed, swam, and ran, and during vacations at the family home in Hyannis Port he roughhoused with his brothers and sisters. Throughout his life, Kennedy maintained this physical view of life. To impress the Kennedys, one associate remembered, you had to "show raw guts, fall on your face now and then. Smash into the house once in a while going after a pass. Laugh off twisted ankles or a big hole torn in your best suit."

Kennedy's macho ethos extended to his attitude toward women. Like his father, he regarded sexual conquests as a sign of manhood and considered females first and foremost as sexual objects. During his Washington years as a U.S. senator, he moved from one affair to the next. He did not even bother to learn the names of his one-night-stands, referring to them by such generic names as "Kiddo" or "Sweetie." Nor did Kennedy's affairs end after he was married and elected president. When he wanted companionship and conversation he turned to his male friends.

Kennedy brought this masculine attitude to his presidency. He surrounded himself with advisors who shared his energetic approach to work and play. He seemed charged with a sense of urgency and was fond of the Churchill quote, "Come then—let us to the task, to the battle and toil—each to our part, each to our station. Let us go forward together in all parts of the [land]. There is not a week, nor a day, nor an hour to be lost." In his own speeches Kennedy stressed the theme that America was entering a period of crisis: "In the long history of the world, only a few generations have been granted the role of defending freedom in its maximum danger. I do not shrink from this responsibility—I welcome it." Without crisis, Kennedy believed, no person could achieve greatness, and he desired greatness. As was expressed in his Pulitzer-Prize-winning *Profiles in Courage*, "Great crises produce great men, and great deeds of courage."

Something Short of Camelot

From the very first, journalists associated the Kennedy administration with Camelot. According to the popular legend, King Arthur and his Knights of the Round Table established in the realm of Camelot a period of unparalleled peace and prosperity. Although Kennedy himself encouraged the Camelot comparisons, the record of his administration and personal behavior fell short of the ideal.

Several factors worked to limit the success of Kennedy's domestic programs. To begin with, Kennedy lacked both political support in Congress and a firm commitment to push for liberal reforms. Ideologically, he was a centrist Democrat. In addition, although his party held a solid majority in the House, 101 of 261 Democratic representatives came from southern and border states, and they normally voted with conservative Republicans. Added to this problem was Kennedy's distaste for legislative infighting and his poor working relations with many senators. He limited his domestic agenda to such traditional Democratic proposals as a higher minimum wage, increased Social Security benefits, and modest housing and educational programs. In his inaugural address he did not even mention poverty or race. In the final analysis, Kennedy was so concerned with the "crises abroad" that he did not want to risk any of his political capital on unpopular domestic reforms. Nor, as one biographer of Kennedy has commented,

(Text continues on p. 978)

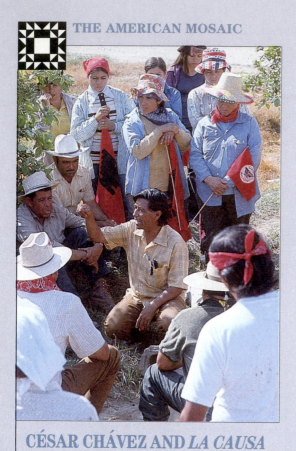

CÉSAR CHÁVEZ AND *LA CAUSA*

In early April 1962, a 35-year-old community organizer named César Estrada Chávez set out single-handedly to organize impoverished migrant farm laborers in the California grape fields. He, his wife, and their eight children packed their belongings into a dilapidated nine-year-old station wagon, and moved to Delano, California, a town of 12,000, which was the center of the nation's table grape industry. Over the next two years, Chávez spent his entire lifetime savings of $1200 creating a small social service organization for Delano's field laborers, which offered immigration counseling, citizenship classes, funeral benefits, credit to buy cars and homes, assistance with voter registration, and a cooperative to buy tires and gasoline. As the emblem of his new organization, the National Farm Workers Association, Chávez chose a black Aztec eagle inside a white circle on a red background.

Chávez's sympathy for the plight of migrant farm workers came naturally. He was born in Yuma, Arizona in 1927, one of five children of Mexican immigrants. When he was 10 years old, his parents lost their small farm, and the family was forced to become migrant laborers, picking peas, lettuce, tomatoes, figs, prunes, grapes, and apricots in Arizona and California. There were times when the family had to sleep in its car or camp under bridges. When young César was able to attend school (he attended more than 30 mostly segregated schools), he was often shunted into special classrooms set aside for Mexican-American children.

In 1944, when he was 17, Chávez joined the navy, and served for two years on a destroyer escort in the Pacific. After World War II was over, he married and spent two-and-a-half years as a sharecropper raising strawberries. That was followed by work in apricot and prune orchards and in a lumber camp. Then in 1952 his life took a fateful turn. He joined a social service organization, known as the Community Service Organization (CSO), during a voter registration drive. The Community Service Organization wanted to educate and organize the poor so that they could solve their own social and economic problems. After founding CSO chapters in Madera, Bakersfield, and Hanford, California, Chávez was named the organization's general director in 1958. Four years later, he broke with the organization when it rejected his proposal to establish a farm workers union.

Most labor leaders considered Chávez's goal of creating the first successful union of farm workers in U.S. history an impossible dream. Not only did farm laborers suffer from high rates of illiteracy and poverty (average family earnings were just $2000 in 1965), they also experienced persistently high rates of unemployment (traditionally around 19 percent) and were divided into a variety of ethnic groups (Mexican, Arab, Filipino, and Puerto Rican). Making unionization even more difficult were the facts that farm laborers rarely remained in one locality for very long and were easily replaced by inexpensive Mexican day laborers, known as *braceros*, who were trucked into California and the Southwest at harvest time.

Moreover, farm workers were specifically excluded from the protection of the National Labor Relations Act of 1935 (the Wagner Act). Unlike other American workers, farm workers were not guaranteed the right to organize, had no guarantee of a minimum wage, and had no federally guaranteed standards of work in the fields. State laws requiring toilets, rest periods, and drinking water in the fields were largely ignored.

In September 1965 Chávez was drawn into his first important labor controversy. The Filipino grape pickers went on strike. "All right, Chávez," asked one of the Filipino grape pickers' leaders, "are you going to stand beside us, or are you going to scab against us?" Despite his fear that the National Farm Workers Association was not sufficiently well organized to support a strike (it had less than $100 in its strike fund), he assured the Filipino workers that members of his association would not go into the field as strikebreakers. *Heulga!*—the Spanish word for strike—became the grape pickers' battle cry.

Within weeks, the labor strike began to attract national attention. Unions, church groups, and civil rights organizations offered financial support for *La Causa*, as the farm workers' movement became known. In March 1966, Chávez led a 250-mile Easter march from Delano to Sacramento to dramatize the plight of migrant farm laborers. That same year, Chávez's National Farm Workers Association merged with an AFL-CIO affiliate to form the United Farm Workers Organizing Committee.

A staunch apostle of nonviolence,

Chávez was deeply troubled by the violent incidents that marred the strike. Some growers raced tractors along the roadside, covering the strikers with dirt and dust. Others drove spraying machines along the edges of their fields, spraying insecticide and fertilizer on the picketers. Local police officers arrested a minister for reading Jack London's definition of a scab ("a two-legged animal with a corkscrew soul, a water-logged brain, and a combination backbone made of jelly and glue"). Some strikers, in turn, intimidated strikebreakers by pelting them with marbles fired from slingshots and by setting fire to packing crates. One striker tried to drive a car into a group of growers.

In an effort to quell the escalating violence and to atone for the militancy of some of his union's members, Chávez began to fast on February 14, 1968. For 5 days he kept the fast a secret. Then, in an hour-long speech to striking workers, he explained that continued violence would destroy everything the union stood for. He said that the "truest act of courage, the strongest act of manliness, is to sacrifice ourselves for others in a totally nonviolent struggle for justice." For 21 days he fasted; he lost 35 pounds and his doctor began to fear for his health. He finally agreed to take a small amount of bouillon and grapefruit juice and medication. On March 11, he ended his fast by taking communion and breaking bread with Senator Robert F. Kennedy.

The strike dragged on for three years. To heighten public awareness of the farm workers' cause, Chávez in 1968 initiated a boycott of table grapes. It was the boycott that pressured many of the growers into settling the strike. An estimated

17 million American consumers went without grapes in support of the farm workers bargaining position. By mid-1970, two-thirds of California grapes were grown under contract with Chávez's union. Later that year, Chávez launched a nationwide boycott of lettuce produced by ununionized farm laborers.

In the years following its 1970 victory, Chávez's union has been beset by problems from within and without. Union membership dwindled from a high of more than 60,000 in 1972 to a low of 5000 in 1974 (it has since climbed back to around 30,000), and many of Chávez's top lieutenants resigned or were fired. Meanwhile, public concern for the plight of migrant farm workers declined.

Whatever his union's current problems, Chávez's achievements remain nothing short of remarkable. As a result of his efforts, the most backbreaking tool used by farm workers, the short hoe, was eliminated and the use of many dangerous pesticides in the grape fields was prohibited. His efforts also brought about a 70 percent increase in real wages from 1964 to 1980, and establishment of health care benefits, disability insurance, pension plan, and standardized grievance procedures for farm workers. He helped secure passage of the nation's first agricultural labor relations act in California in 1975, which prohibited growers from firing striking workers or engaging in bad-faith bargaining. Thanks to his efforts, migrant farm laborers won a right held by all other American workers: the right to bargain collectively.

was the electorate "crying out for social justice legislation in the early 1960s."

There were small successes. Congress raised the minimum wage, expanded Social Security, and appropriated a few billion dollars for public housing and aid to economically depressed areas. But such legislation hardly amounted to the "new frontier" Kennedy promised. These gains were offset by the setbacks, which Kennedy accepted perhaps too stoically. Congress defeated the president's plan for federal aid to education, a health insurance plan for the aged, and programs to help migrant workers, unemployed youths, and urban commuters.

Black Americans were especially disappointed with Kennedy's performance. They had, after all, supplied Kennedy's margin of victory in the 1960 election. But once elected JFK was slow in using his office to further the cause of civil rights.

For blacks, the early 1960s were difficult, violent years that tested their resolve. White segregationists confronted blacks' nonviolent desegregation efforts with unprovoked ferocity. In city after city violence erupted. NAACP organizer Medgar Evers was shot down outside his home in Jackson, Mississippi. Four black girls were killed when a Birmingham church was bombed. Police authorities sprayed black protesters with high-pressure fire hoses and unleashed attack dogs on them. (See Chapter 30 for a fuller treatment of the fight for civil rights.)

Through his first two years in office, Kennedy remained largely silent. To win southern congressional support he even backed the nomination of a Mississippi jurist who had once referred to blacks as "chimpanzees" for a seat on the federal bench. Although Attorney General Robert Kennedy aided protesters when federal laws were violated, JFK and the FBI staked out a conservative position. As one historian noted, "Civil rights workers were assaulted and shot at—systematically, often openly, frequently by law enforcement officials themselves. And through it all, in virtually every case, federal authorities did nothing."

In 1963 Kennedy changed his position. In part this about-face was the result of Robert Kennedy's prodding. In part it was the result of television, which daily showed shocking examples of brutality in the South and accelerated the demand for change. In late May 1963, Kennedy eloquently announced his new position. It should be possible, he said, "for American students of any color to attend any public institution without having to be backed up by troops. . . . But this is not the case. . . . We preach freedom around the world . . . but are we to say to the world . . . that we have no second-class citizens except Negroes, that we have no class or caste system, no ghettos, no master race except with respect to Negroes?"

Perhaps Kennedy was convinced that the time had come for "the nation to fulfill its promise." Perhaps, as his supporters claim, in 1963 Kennedy was beginning to fulfill his own promise. His death in late 1963 left questions unanswered, potential unrealized. Judged by his accomplishments, however, Kennedy's Camelot, like King Arthur's, existed largely in the realm of myth. Although he could inspire people to follow, too often on domestic issues he chose not to lead.

Cuba Libre Revisited

Foreign affairs consumed Kennedy's interest. Unlike domestic politics, international conflicts were more clear-cut, and the divisions between "us" and "them" more certain. Foreign affairs also allowed Kennedy to express his masculine view of the world. They permitted JFK to employ the Kennedy approach to difficult decisions, which he once described as calculate the odds, make your choice, and "grab [your] balls and go."

In his approach to the world, Kennedy generally continued the essentially Cold War policies of Truman and Eisenhower. He accepted the strategy of containment and the notion that the Soviet Union would take advantage of any sign of weakness by the United States. He was also suspicious of conventional diplomatic channels, preferring to listen to his young advisors rather than seasoned State Department officials.

Kennedy's handling of Cuban relations revealed his bellicose tendencies. Like Eisenhower, Kennedy was dismayed by the success of Fidel Castro. Just as Americans during the 1890s had cried "Cuba Libre," on taking office

Kennedy began to search for a way to "free" Cuba, this time from Castro's communism rather than Spain's colonialism. His desire to strike a blow against communism led him to embrace a CIA plan to overthrow Castro. If the CIA had successfully planned coups in Guatemala, Iran, and Laos, Kennedy reasoned, then perhaps it could do the job in Cuba.

The CIA plan, which was hatched during the Eisenhower administration, entailed the assassination of Castro and the training and transporting of a force of Cuban exiles to Cuba, where they would launch a counterrevolution. It was a plan that even the joint chiefs of staff believed would probably fail. Even worse, the plan was one of the worst kept secrets in the Western Hemisphere. One historian noted, "Washington knew because the CIA had to drum up broad support in the government for it. Miami knew because the CIA had done everything but take out classified ads to get volunteers. Guatemala knew because the exile brigade was training there, as a local newspaper pointed out. And Castro knew because everyone else did—except the American people." Pierre Salinger, Kennedy's press secretary, later called the plan "the least covert military operation in history," and Kennedy bitterly complained before the invasion, "I can't believe what I'm reading! Castro doesn't need agents over here. All he has to do is read our papers. It's all laid out for him."

The invasion on April 17, 1961, at the Bay of Pigs was an unmitigated disaster. Several attempts to assassinate Castro failed, and the Cuban people did not rise up to join the invaders, who were trapped on the beaches. Nor would Kennedy authorize U.S. air support for the exile forces. As a result, all but 300 of the 1500 invaders were killed or captured. If anything, the Bay of Pigs fiasco strengthened Castro's position in Cuba.

The Bay of Pigs invasion, however, did not end Kennedy's problems with Cuba. In the fall of 1962 a more serious crisis arose when the Soviet Union began to install intermediate-range ballistic missiles (IRBMs) in Cuba. Instead of trying to work through proper diplomatic avenues—a process that would have taken time and might have hurt the Democrats in the upcoming election—Kennedy announced the alarming news to an anxious television audience. After showing the public the American cities that the missiles could destroy, Kennedy said he would not permit Soviet ships transporting the weapons to enter Cuban waters. "The people were assured," a scholar commented, "that he would run any risk, including thermonuclear war, on their behalf." Such assurances created a genuine mood of crisis in the country.

Behind the scenes, Kennedy and Soviet Premier Nikita Khrushchev searched for a way to defuse the crisis. During the entire affair Bobby Kennedy counseled level-headed restraint and Khrushchev eschewed any shoe-pounding antics. In the end, the world leaders achieved a solution. Khrushchev agreed to remove the missiles under United Nations inspection in return for an American pledge not to invade Cuba. The Kennedy administration interpreted the result as a victory. "We're eyeball to eyeball and I think the other fellow just blinked," Secretary of State Dean Rusk observed during the episode. And, indeed, the Soviet Union could hardly disagree. The missile crisis provided the ammunition to force Khrushchev out of power.

The two "superpowers" had stood at the brink, gazed into the abyss, and stepped back. And for what? "When all is said and done," observed one historian, "it seems that President Kennedy had risked ultimate disaster in service to a crisis that was more illusory than real, at least in military terms."

Again, the unsatisfactory "perhaps" reappeared. Perhaps Kennedy learned more from the Cuban missile crisis than he had from the Bay of Pigs invasion. Friends of Kennedy claimed that he reached maturity during the crisis and that it motivated him to move toward détente—an easing of tensions—with the Soviet Union. In several 1963 speeches he called for "not merely peace in our time but peace for all time" and a "world safe for diversity." And he did support a treaty banning all atmospheric testing of nuclear weapons. Perhaps Kennedy had come to a new maturity.

The tragedy is that nobody can ever know. On November 22, 1963, Lee Harvey Oswald assassinated Kennedy in Dallas, Texas. (Later investigations, however, questioned whether Oswald acted alone.) The event moved the nation.

Shocked and saddened, Americans everywhere shared the loss felt by President Kennedy's widow and two young children.

Newsman Walter Cronkite cried on television, and millions of Americans cried in their homes. Once again, television gave the event a mythical quality—showing his grieving wife, his barely understanding children, his solemn funeral. Americans mourned together, eyes fixed on their television sets; and immediately commentators began to evaluate Kennedy's presidency in terms of not what was but what might have been.

VIETNAM: AMERICA'S LONGEST WAR

Vietnam and Southeast Asia

How did it start? And when? Even while the war in Vietnam tore at the heart of America in the 1960s most Americans, including some foreign policy experts, were not exactly sure of the answers to such basic questions. Johnson said he was con-

tinuing Kennedy's policy, who had continued Eisenhower's, who had continued Truman's, who had acted as he believed Roosevelt would have acted. The answers stretch back into time.

A Small Corner of a Bigger Picture

Struggle, like a mighty river, runs through the history of Vietnam. Ironically, part of Vietnam's troubles was the result of the richness of its own land. Its agricultural products (especially rice) and mineral deposits lured invaders from the East and West. China, the giant to its north, came first. For almost 2000 years Vietnam battled China for its own independence. The French came next. During the seventeenth, eighteenth, and nineteenth centuries, French traders and missionaries penetrated Vietnam, establishing their control over the country in the name of *la mission civilisatrice*. This "civilizing mission," however, robbed the Vietnamese of the wealth of their land and their independence. France's rules of governing Vietnam—described as "a lot of subjugation, very little autonomy, a dash of assimilation"—created discontent among the Vietnamese, some of whom welcomed the Japanese who took over the country during World War II.

In 1945 the Vietnamese declared their independence, but the same year the French returned, bent on the resubjugation of the country. The struggle continued, with the Communist Vietminh under Ho Chi Minh controlling the north of the country and the French the south. Between 1945 and 1954 both sides suffered terrible losses in the bitter guerrilla warfare.

The United States faced a difficult decision. During World War II, Franklin Roosevelt had favored Vietnamese independence and aided Ho's fight against the Japanese. He recognized that the age of colonialism was doomed, and he wanted the United States identified with anti-colonialism. At the same time, however, Roosevelt believed that a strong postwar Western Europe was essential to American security, and he did not want to alienate Britain or France by pressing too hard for an end to empires.

On Roosevelt's death, Harry Truman inherited FDR's problems. Even more than his former boss, he advocated a strong Western Europe, even if that strength had to be based on the continuation of empires. It was a Cold War decision. The United States, Truman maintained, "had no interest" in "championing schemes of international trusteeship" that would weaken the "European states whose help we need to balance Soviet power in Europe."

In the game of Cold War politics, Vietnam became a pawn. Truman wanted French support against the Soviet Union. France wanted Vietnam. Truman willingly agreed to aid France's ambitions in exchange for France's support. The success of Mao Zedong's Communist revolution in China strengthened America's support of the French in Vietnam. Obsessed with the idea of an international Communist conspiracy, Truman and his advisors contended that Stalin, Mao, and Ho were united by the single ambition of world domination. They overlooked the historical rivalries that pulled Russia, China, and Vietnam apart. As Ho Chi Minh once told his people, "It is better to sniff French dung for a while than eat China's all our life."

By the late 1940s, the United States had as-

sumed a large part of the cost of France's effort to regain its control over Vietnam. The price escalated during the early 1950s. By 1952 the United States was shouldering roughly one-third of the cost of the war, and between 1950 and 1954 America contributed $2.6 billion to France's war effort. But it was not enough. France was unable to defeat Ho's Vietminh.

In 1954 the war reached a crisis stage. In an effort to lure the Vietminh into a major engagement, the leading French commander moved more than 13,000 soldiers to Dien Bien Phu, a remote outpost in a river valley in northwest Vietnam. The Vietminh surrounded the fort and moved artillery pieces to the hills above the French airstrip. From there they mounted a siege of Dien Bien Phu. As the months passed, French manpower and prestige suffered punishing blows. Inside Dien Bien Phu, latrines overflowed, food supplies ran out, water spoiled, and unburied bodies fouled the air. Finally, on May 7, 1954, the last French commander surrendered.

During the siege the French continually asked President Eisenhower for military support, but he refused to act without the consent of Congress and Britain. Neither favored American military intervention. Senator Lyndon Johnson of Texas expressed the majority view in Congress when he opposed "sending American G.I.s into the mud and muck of Indochina on a blood-letting spree to perpetuate colonialism and white man's exploitation in Asia." As a result, France gave up its attempt to recolonize Vietnam. At the peace talks in Geneva, the countries involved agreed to temporarily divide Vietnam at the 17th parallel into two countries and hold elections in the summer of 1956 to reunify Vietnam.

Although Eisenhower would not militarily aid France, he quickly supported the independent government established in South Vietnam under the leadership of Ngo Dinh Diem. In America, where he spent several years in a Catholic seminary, Diem was known as an anti-Communist and a nationalist. In Vietnam, where he had not been for 20 years, he was hardly known at all. As a popular leader, he had no appeal. Imperious, often paranoid, overly reliant on his own family, Diem, a Catholic in an overwhelmingly Buddhist nation, successfully alienated almost everyone who came into contact with him. Even United States intelligence sources rated his chances of establishing order in South Vietnam as "poor."

Diem, nevertheless, was America's man. Why? Because he was an anti-Communist and a nationalist, and, as John Foster Dulles said, "because we know of no one better." Lyndon Johnson put it more bluntly in 1961: "Diem's the only boy we got out there." And even Eisenhower supported Diem militarily and politically. Vietnam became a test case, an opportunity for the U.S. to battle communism in Asia with dollars instead of Americans. When the time came to hold the unification election, Diem, with American backing, refused. Instead, to show his popularity he held "free" elections in South Vietnam, where he received an improbable 98.2 percent of the popular vote. The dishonesty of the elections was underscored by the Saigon returns where Diem received 605,000 votes although there were only 405,000 registered voters.

The United States supported Ngo Dinh Diem because of his anti-Communist views, but he alienated the Vietnamese people, who rejected his rule.

Diem's absolutist policies created problems. By the end of 1957, Vietminh guerrillas in South Vietnam—often called the Vietcong—were in open revolt. Two years later, North and South Vietnam resumed hostilities. The United States increased its aid, most of which went to improving the South Vietnamese military or into the pockets of corrupt officials. The United States spent little money on improving the quality of life of the peasants. Nor did the United States object strongly to Diem's dictatorial methods. Diem once said that the sovereign was "the mediator between the people and heaven," and he demanded absolute obedience.

By the end of Eisenhower's second term America had become fully committed to Diem and South Vietnam. To be sure, problems in Vietnam were not America's major concern. In fact, most Americans were unaware of their country's involvement there. More than anything, Vietnam was a small corner of a bigger picture. U.S. policy there was determined by larger Cold War concerns. America's presence in Vietnam, however, would soon be expanded.

Kennedy's Testing Ground

On taking office, John Kennedy reaffirmed his country's commitment to Diem and South Vietnam. He announced his intention to be even more aggressive than Truman or Eisenhower. In Vietnam Kennedy saw an opportunity to "prove" his nation's resolve and strength. In the end, South Vietnam as a country was less important to Kennedy than the challenge it presented.

Kennedy believed that the United States needed a fresh military approach. Eisenhower's "massive retaliation" was too limited. It was of no use in a guerrilla war like Vietnam. Kennedy labeled his approach "flexible response," and it entailed the development of conventional and counterinsurgency (antiguerrilla) forces as well as a nuclear response. Vietnam rapidly became the laboratory for counterinsurgency activities, a place for Special Forces (Green Berets) units to develop their own tactics. To achieve this end, Kennedy expanded the Special Forces from 2500 to 10,000 men.

To "win" in Vietnam, Kennedy realized that he would have to strengthen America's presence there. In November of 1961 he decided to deploy American troops to South Vietnam. By the end of 1961, 3205 American "advisors" were in Vietnam. Kennedy increased this force to 11,300 in 1962 and 16,300 in 1963. Although several of his advisors questioned this military escalation, arguing that once the United States committed troops it would be more difficult to pull out of the conflict, Kennedy remained firm in his desire to "save" South Vietnam.

As the American involvement deepened, Diem's control over South Vietnam declined. He alienated peasants by refusing to enact meaningful land reforms and Buddhists by passing laws to restrict their activities. Responding to Diem's pro-Catholic policies, Buddhists began organized protests. They conducted hunger strikes and nonviolent protests. Several Buddhist monks engaged in self-immolation. In full view of American reporters and cameras, one burned himself to death on a busy, downtown Saigon intersection. Although the gruesome sight shocked Americans, Diem's sister-in-law, Madame Nhu, laughed at the "barbecues," offering gasoline and matches for more fiery deaths.

More fiery deaths followed. Protests mounted. Outside of Saigon, Diem exerted little influence. Such insightful American reporters as Davis Halberstam, Neil Sheehan, Peter Arnett, and Stanley Karnow argued that the Diem regime was isolated and paranoid, that a stable democracy would never develop as long as Diem held power. Rather than talk with reporters, Diem delivered five-, six-, even ten-hour monologues. One reporter recalled that during these sessions Diem's "face seemed to be focused on something beyond me. . . . The result was an eerie feeling that I was listening to a monologue delivered at some other time and in some other place—perhaps by a character in some allegorical play."

The Kennedy administration soon reached the conclusion that without Diem South Vietnam had serious problems, with Diem the country was doomed. In sum, Diem had to go. Behind the scenes, Kennedy encouraged Vietnamese generals to overthrow Diem. On November 1, 1963, Vietnamese army officers arrested and murdered Diem and his brother. Although Kennedy did not approve of the assassination, the United States quickly aided the new government.

Three weeks later Kennedy was assassinated in Dallas. Several friends of Kennedy have suggested that he had begun to reevaluate his Vietnam policy and that after the 1964 election he would have started the process of American disengagement. In a moment of insight, Kennedy himself had observed, "The troops will march in; the bands will play; the crowds will cheer; and in four days everyone will have forgotten. Then we will be told we have to send more troops. It's like taking a drink. The effect wears off, and you have to take another." But whatever Kennedy's plans or insights, he had increased U.S. involvement in Vietnam.

Unfortunately for Kennedy's successor, the prospects for South Vietnam's survival were less than they had been in 1961. By 1963 South Vietnam had lost the fertile Mekong Delta to the Vietcong and with it most of the country's rural population. From the peasants' perspective, the Saigon government stood for heavy taxes, no services, and military destruction; and increasingly they identified the United States with Saigon. Such was the situation Lyndon Johnson inherited.

Texas Tough in the Gulf of Tonkin

Lyndon Baines Johnson was a complex man—shrewd, arrogant, intelligent, sensitive, vulgar, vain, and occasionally cruel. He loved power, and he knew where it was, how to get it, and how to use it. "I'm a powerful sonofabitch," he told two Texas congressmen in 1958 when he was the most powerful legislator on Capitol Hill. Everything about Johnson seemed to emphasize or enhance his power. He was physically large, and seemed even bigger than he was, and he used his size to persuade people. The "Johnson treatment" involved "pressing the flesh"—a backslapping, hugging sort of camaraderie. He also used symbols of power adroitly, especially the telephone, which had replaced the sword and pen as the symbol of power. "No gunman," remarked one historian, "ever held a Colt .44 so easily" as Johnson handled a telephone.

A legislative genius, Johnson had little experience in foreign affairs. Reared in the poverty of the Texas hill country, educated at a small teachers' college, and concerned politically with domestic issues, before becoming president LBJ had expressed little interest in foreign affairs. "Foreigners are not like the folks I am used to," he often said, and whether it was a joke or not he meant it. He was particularly uncomfortable around foreign dignitaries and ambassadors, often receiving them in groups and scarcely paying attention to them. "Why do I have to see them?" he once asked. "They're [Secretary of State] Dean Rusk's clients, not mine."

Yet to say Johnson had little experience in foreign affairs is not to suggest that he did not have strong opinions on the subject. Like most politicians of the period, Johnson was an unquestioning Cold Warrior. In addition, along with accepting the domino theory—the idea that if Vietnam fell, other nations would also fall to communism—and a monolithic view of communism, Johnson cherished a traditionally southern notion of honor and masculinity. It was his duty, he maintained, to honor commitments made by earlier presidents. "We are [in Vietnam] because . . . we remain fixed on the pursuit of freedom, a deep and moral obligation *that will not let us go.*" Leaving Vietnam, Johnson believed, would be a dishonorable act, dangerous for the nation's future. Raised in an area where the frontier was still visible, Johnson approached foreign policy like a frontier sheriff. To show weakness and back down was worse than cowardly—it was unmanly. As he often said, "If you let a bully come into your front yard one day, the next day he will be up on your porch and the day after that he will rape your wife in your own bed."

Furthermore, Johnson believed that any retreat from Vietnam would destroy him politically. Soon after becoming president, he told America's ambassador to Vietnam, "I am not going to be the President who saw Southeast Asia go the way China went." No, he would not "lose" Vietnam and allow Republican critics to attack him as they had Truman. "I knew," LBJ later noted, "that Harry Truman and Dean Acheson had lost their effectiveness from the day the communists took over China." Johnson was determined to win the war, to "nail the coonskin to the wall."

Before winning in Vietnam, however, he had to win in the United States. The presidential election in 1964 was his top priority. He was pitted against Barry Goldwater, the powerful Arizona senator from the Republican Right. "Extremism in the defense of liberty is no vice," Goldwater said, and if elected he promised to defend South Vietnam at any cost. He also preached against the welfare state, Social Security, the Nuclear Test Ban Treaty of 1963, and any rapprochement with the Soviet Union or China. Democrats transformed his campaign slogan "In Your Heart, You Know He's Right," to "In Your Heart, You Know He Might," by which they meant that Goldwater might start a nuclear war. Goldwater did little to discourage such thinking. In his campaign he labored to make "nukes" socially acceptable, even coining the

In the presidential campaign of 1964, Republican candidate Barry Goldwater, a U.S. senator from Arizona, promised to defend South Vietnam regardless of the price.

uncomfortably comforting phrase "conventional nuclear weapon."

Johnson's campaign strategy was to appear as the thoughtful, strong moderate. He would not lose Vietnam, he told voters, but neither would he use nuclear weapons or "send American boys nine or ten thousand miles from home to do what Asian boys ought to be doing themselves." Johnson promised that if elected he would create a "Great Society" at home and honor American commitments abroad. As usual, he knew what the voters wanted to hear, and they rewarded him with a landslide victory in the November election.

Behind the scenes, however, the Johnson administration was maneuvering to obtain a free hand for conducting a more aggressive war in Vietnam. He did not want a formal declaration of war, which might frighten voters. Rather he desired a quietly passed resolution giving him the authority to deploy American forces. Such a resolution would allow him to act without the consent of Congress. Johnson and his advisors were planning to escalate American involvement in the Vietnam War, but they hoped it would go unnoticed.

Johnson used two reported North Vietnamese attacks on the American destroyer *Maddox* as a pretext for going before Congress to ask for the resolution. Actually, he was less than truthful about the circumstances of the attack. The first incident occurred in the Gulf of Tonkin in early August 1964 when the North Vietnamese suspected the *Maddox* of aiding a South Vietnamese commando raid into North Vietnam, a violation of that country's sovereignty. When North Vietnamese patrol boats approached the *Maddox*, the American ship and supporting navy jets opened fire, sinking one of the North Vietnamese ships and crippling two others. Although the North Vietnamese ships had launched several torpedoes, the *Maddox* was not hit and suffered only superficial machine gun damage and a loss of ammunition. The second of the Gulf of Tonkin incidents probably never occurred. Assaulted by high waves, thunderstorms, and freak atmospheric conditions, the *Maddox's* sonar equipment apparently malfunctioned registering 22 invisible enemy torpedoes. No enemy ships were visually sighted, and none of the electronically sighted torpedoes hit the Maddox or its accompanying ship the

In this photo, a North Vietnamese torpedo boat attacks the American destroyer USS *Maddox*. The attack took place in the Gulf of Tonkin on August 2, 1964, but the incident was not explored fully until publication of the Pentagon Papers in 1971.

C. Turner Joy. Soon after the incident the commander of the *Maddox* reached the conclusion that no attack had ever taken place.

Johnson realized the dubious nature of the second attack. He told an aide, "Hell, those dumb stupid soldiers were just shooting at flying fish." Nevertheless, he went on national television and announced, "Aggression by terror against peaceful villages of South Vietnam has now been joined by open aggression on the high seas against the United States of America." Reassuring the country, he continued, "We know, although others appear to forget, the risks of spreading conflict. We seek no wider war." A few days later he pressed Congress for a resolution. American ships, he emphasized, had been repeatedly attacked, and he wanted authorization to "take all necessary measures" to repel attacks, prevent aggression, and protect American security. It was a broad resolution; Johnson said that it was "like Grandma's nightshirt—it covered everything." Almost without debate, the Senate passed the resolution on August 7 with only two dissenting votes, and the House of Representatives endorsed it unanimously. You "will live to regret it," Wayne Morse, who voted against it in the Senate, told the resolution's supporters. In the years that followed, as Johnson used his new powers to escalate the war, Morse's vote and prediction were vindicated, for the Gulf of Tonkin Resolution allowed Johnson to act in an imperial fashion.

Lyndon's War

Lyndon Johnson liked to personalize things. Once a military aide tried to direct Johnson to the correct helicopter, saying "Mr. President, that's not your helicopter." "Son, they're all my helicopters," Johnson replied. So it was with the Vietnam War. He did not start the war, but once reelected he quickly made it "his war." Over the war he exercised complete control. One authority on the war described Johnson's role:

He made appointments, approved promotions, reviewed troop requests, determined deployments, selected bombing targets, and restricted aircraft sorties. Night after night, wearing a dressing gown and carrying a flashlight, he would descend into the White House basement "situation room" to monitor the conduct of the conflict . . . often, too, he would doze by his bedside telephone, waiting to hear the outcome of a mission to rescue one of "my pilots" shot down over Haiphong or Vinh or Thai Nguyen. It was his war.

When he became president it was still a relatively obscure conflict for most Americans. Public opinion polls showed that 70 percent of the American public paid little attention to U.S. activities in Vietnam. At the end of 1963 only 16,300 U.S. military personnel were in Vietnam; the number rose to 23,300 by the end of 1964. Most of the soldiers there, however, were volunteers. Only a few people strongly opposed America's involvement. All this would change dramatically during the next four years.

With the election behind him, in early 1965 Johnson started to reevaluate the position of the United States. In Saigon crisis followed crisis as one unpopular government gave way to the next. Something had to be done, and Johnson's advisors suggested two courses. The military and most of LBJ's foreign policy experts called for a more aggressive military presence in Vietnam, including bombing raids into North Vietnam and more ground troops. Other advisors, notably Under Secretary of State George Ball, believed the United States was making the same mistakes as the French had made. Ball believed that a land war in Indochina was not in America's best strategic interests and that bombing North Vietnam would only stiffen the resolve of the Communists. Thus escalation of the war could create serious problems. "Once on the tiger's back," Ball noted, "we cannot be sure of picking the place to dismount."

Johnson chose the first course, claiming it would be dishonorable not to come to South Vietnam's aid. In February 1965 Vietcong troops attacked the American base in Pleiku, killing several soldiers. Johnson used the assault as a pretext to commence air raids into the North. Code-named ROLLING THUNDER, the operation was designed to use American technological superiority to defeat North Vietnam. At first, Johnson limited U.S. air strikes to enemy radar and bridges below the 20th parallel. But as the war dragged on, he ordered "his pilots" to hit military targets in metropolitan areas. Between 1965 and 1973, American pilots flew more than 526,000 sorties and dropped 6,162,000 tons of bombs on enemy targets. (As a point of contrast, the total tonnage of explosives dropped in World War II by all the belligerent countries was 2,150,000 tons.) As a result, much of the landscape of South and North Vietnam took on a lunar look.

However, the bombs did not lead to victory. Ironically, as Ball had predicted, the bombing missions actually strengthened the Communist government in North Vietnam. As a U.S. intelligence report noted, the bombing of North Vietnam "had no significantly harmful effects on popular morale. In fact, the regime has apparently been able to increase its control of the populace and perhaps even to break through the political apathy and indifference which have characterized the outlook of the average North Vietnamese in recent years."

The massive use of air power also undermined U.S. counterinsurgency efforts. Colonel John Paul Vann, an American expert on counterinsurgency warfare noted, "The best weapon 'for this type of war' . . . would be a knife. . . . The worst is an airplane. The next worst is artillery. Barring a knife, the best is a rifle—you know who you're killing." By using bombing raids against the enemy in both the North and South, U.S. forces inevitably killed large numbers of civilians, the very people they were there to help. For peasants everywhere in Vietnam, U.S. jets, helicopters, and artillery "meant more bombing, more death, and more suffering."

A larger air war also led to more ground troops. As Johnson informed Ambassador Maxwell Taylor, "I have never felt that this war will be won from the air, and it seems to me what is much more needed and will be more effective is a larger and stronger use of rangers and special forces and marines." Between 1965 and 1968 the escalation of American forces was dramatic. When George Ball warned in 1965 that 500,000 American troops in Vietnam might not be able to win the war, other members of the Johnson administration laughed. By 1968 no one was laughing. Ball's prediction was painfully accurate. Escalation of American troops and deaths went hand in hand. The year-end totals for the United States between 1965 and 1968 were:

1965: 184,300 troops; 636 killed.
1966: 385,300 troops; 6644 killed.
1967: 485,600 troops; 16,021 killed.
1968: 536,000 troops; 30,610 killed.

But still there was no victory.

To Tet and Beyond

Throughout the escalation Johnson was less than candid with the American people. He argued that there had been no real change in American policy and that victory was in sight. Any reporter who said otherwise, he roundly criticized. Increasingly he demanded unquestioning loyalty from his close advisors. Such demands led to an administration "party line." As the war ground on, the "party line" bore less and less similarity to reality.

In late 1967, General William Westmoreland returned to America briefly to assure the public that he could now see the "light at the end of the tunnel." In his annual report Westmoreland commented, "The year ended with the enemy increasingly resorting to desperation tactics; . . . and he has experienced only failure in these attempts." At the time, the American press focused most of its attention on the battle of Khe Sanh, and Westmoreland assured everyone that victory there was certain.

Then with a suddenness that caught all America by surprise, North Vietnam struck into the very heart of South Vietnam. On the morning of January 30, 1968, North Vietnam launched the Tet offensive. "Tet," the Vietnamese holiday that celebrates the lunar new year, traditionally is supposed to determine family fortunes for the rest of the year. Certainly the Tet offensive boded well for North Vietnam. A Vietcong suicide squad broke into the U.S. embassy in Saigon, and Vietnamese Communists mounted offensives against every major target in South Vietnam, including 5 cities, 64 district capitals, 36 provincial capitals, and 50 hamlets.

For what it was worth, the United States repelled the Tet offensive. For a few days the fighting was ferocious and bloody, as the rivals fought in highly populated cities and almost evacuated hamlets. In order to retake Hue, the ancient cultural center close to the border between North and South Vietnam where the fighting lasted for several weeks, allied troops had to destroy part of the city. One observer recorded that the city was left a "shattered, stinking hulk, its streets choked with rubble and rotting bodies." When United States and South Vietnamese troops finally recaptured Hue, they discovered that North Vietnamese and Vietcong soldiers had killed several thousand political leaders, teachers, and other civilians, many of whom had been buried alive in one mass grave. In another village, where victory came at a high price, the liberating American general reported, "We had to destroy the town to save it." Both sides suffered terribly. But after the allies cleared the cities of enemy troops, General Westmoreland judged the episode a great allied victory. In the end, American and South Vietnamese troops recaptured lost areas and South Vietnamese civilians did not rally to the Vietcong cause. Indeed the Vietcong was so decimated by the Tet offensive that it never regained its full fighting strength.

If technically the Tet offensive was a military defeat for North Vietnam, it was also a profound psychological victory. Johnson, his advisors, and his generals had been proclaiming that the enemy was on the run, almost defeated, tired of war, ready to quit. Tet demonstrated that the contrary was true. Upset and confused, CBS anchorman Walter Cronkite, the national voice of reason, expressed the attitude on his nightly newscast: "What the hell is going on? I thought we were winning the war?" The Tet offensive, more than any other single event, turned the media against the war and exposed the widening "credibility gap" between official pronouncements and public beliefs. NBC anchorman Frank McGee reported that the time had come "when we must decide whether it is futile to destroy Vietnam in the effort to save it."

After Tet, Americans stopped thinking about victory and turned toward thoughts of how best to get out of Vietnam. "Lyndon's planes" and "Lyndon's boys" had been unable to achieve Lyndon's objectives. For Johnson this fact was politically disastrous. In the polls his popularity plummeted, and in the New Hampshire primary Democratic peace candidate Eugene McCarthy received surprisingly solid support. On CBS's the *Smothers Brothers Comedy Hour* folk singer Pete Seeger openly criticized Johnson in the song "Waist Deep in the Big Muddy" about a "Big Fool [who] says to push on." Too intelligent a politician not to realize what was happening, on the night of March 31, LBJ went on television and made two important announcements. First, he said that the United States would limit its bombing of North Vietnam and would enter into peace talks any time and at any place. And second, Johnson surprised the nation by saying, "I will not seek, and I will not accept, the nomination of my party for another term as your President." A major turning point had been reached. The gradual escalation of the war was over. The period of deescalation had started. Even in official government circles, peace had replaced victory as America's objective in Vietnam.

The Politics of a Divided Nation

If Johnson's fall seemed remarkably swift, and if it seemed as if he were surrendering power without a fight, it was because he knew that his policies had badly divided the nation. LBJ honestly believed he had pursued the only honorable course in Vietnam, that he had had America's best interests at heart. His problem, however, was *not* that his intentions were dishonorable but that his *modus operandi*—the style of his leadership—involved great duplicity. Instead of fully committing the United States by calling up the reserves and National Guardsmen and by pushing for higher taxes to pay for the war, Johnson gambled that a slow, steady escalation would be enough to force North Vietnam to accept a negotiated peace. All during the buildup, LBJ assured the American people that he was not drastically changing policy and, besides, victory was in sight. But he could not fool all the people all the time, and after the Tet offensive he knew that he could not even fool most of the people any more.

Dissatisfaction with Johnson's policy surfaced first among the young, the very people who were being asked to fight and die for the cause. Most of the young men who were drafted

(Text continues on p. 990)

LOGISTICS IN A GUERRILLA WAR: The Longest War

The Vietnam War was a logistical nightmare for the United States. Fought 9000 miles from America's shores, the United States had to ship hundreds of tons of supplies daily from the United States to bases in the Pacific and finally to fortified positions along the coast of Vietnam. Once the supplies were in Vietnam, they had to be protected from Vietcong guerrillas, who blended into the civilian population and often obtained jobs on U.S. bases. As a result, although American forces established defense perimeters around their bases, the areas were never totally secure. Bombs in U.S. movie theaters or even mess halls were haunting reminders of the unpredictability of guerrilla warfare.

North Vietnam sent much of its supplies south along the Ho Chi Minh Trail. Following a traditional series of trails through mountains and jungles from North Vietnam into Laos and Cambodia and finally emptying into South Vietnam, the Ho Chi Minh Trail was widened into a road capable of handling heavy trucks and thousands of troops. Along the trail, support facilities, often built underground to escape American detection and air strikes, included operating rooms, fuel storage tanks, and supply coaches. Throughout the war, United States forces tried but failed to effectively disrupt the flow of supplies and soldiers south.

The Vietcong tunnel complex created even more problems for American troops. The tunnels allowed Vietcong troops to appear and disappear almost by magic. The most famous tunnel complex was under Cu Chi, approximately 25 miles northeast of Saigon. It contained conference rooms, sleeping chambers, storage halls, and kitchens. U.S. forces bombed, gassed, and defoliated the Cu Chi area, but failed to destroy the tunnels. The "tunnel rats"—South Vietnamese soldiers and short, wiry GI combat engineer SWAT teams—fought heroically in the tunnels, but they too were unable to destroy the complexes. In the end, the unconventional nature of the Vietnam War guaranteed frustration and made it America's longest war.

Map: From *The Tunnels of Cu Chi* by Tom Mangold and John Penycate. Copyright © 1985 by Tom Mangold and John Penycate. Reprinted by permission of Random House, Inc.

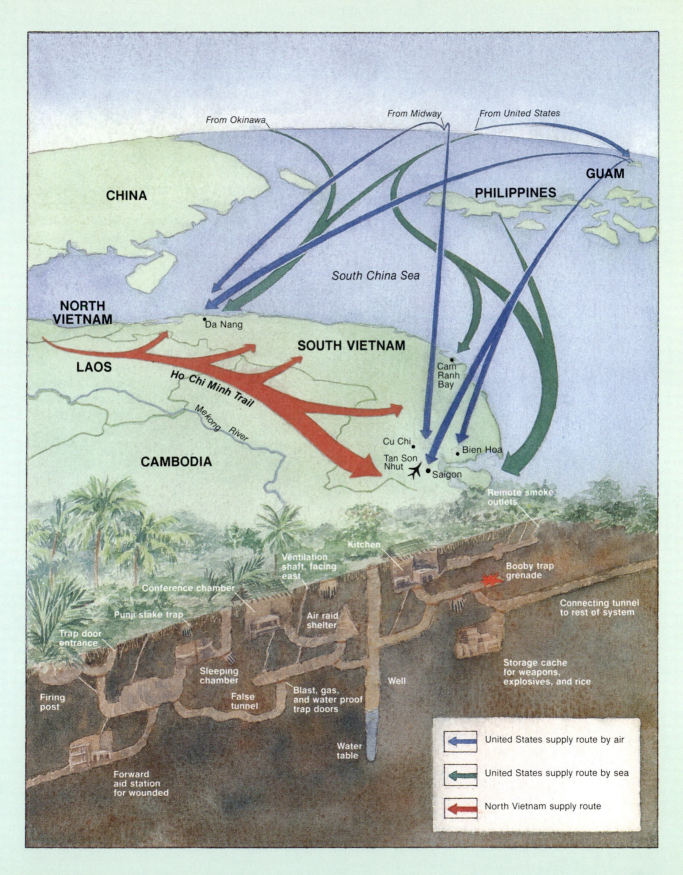

CHINA

NORTH VIETNAM

LAOS

Da Nang

Ho Chi Minh Trail

SOUTH VIETNAM

CAMBODIA

Mekong River

From Okinawa

From Midway

From United States

GUAM

PHILIPPINES

South China Sea

Cam Ranh Bay

Cu Chi

Tan Son Nhut

Bien Hoa

Saigon

Remote smoke outlets

Kitchen

Ventilation shaft, facing east

Conference chamber

Booby trap grenade

Punji stake trap

Air raid shelter

Connecting tunnel to rest of system

Trap door entrance

Sleeping chamber

False tunnel

Blast, gas, and water proof trap doors

Well

Storage cache for weapons, explosives, and rice

Firing post

Water table

Forward aid station for wounded

United States supply route by air

United States supply route by sea

North Vietnam supply route

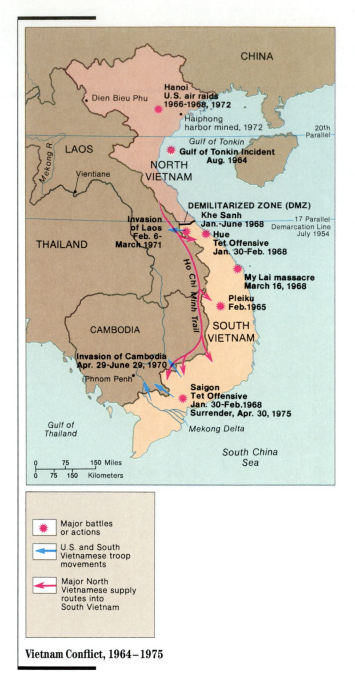

Vietnam Conflict, 1964–1975

provements in South Vietnamese village life. But by his last tour, in 1970, his idealism had died. As he told a friend, "I'm still ready to serve—any time. But as a killing machine, not a humanitarian."

As the war lengthened, an ever growing number of soldiers shared in this disillusionment. The disillusionment took different forms. Some soldiers turned to drugs to relieve the constant stress and fear that the war engendered. Journalist Michael Herr has written eloquently about the horrors of the war: "Satchel charges and grenades blew up jeeps and movie houses, the VC (Vietcong) got work inside all the camps as shoe shine boys and laundresses, . . . they'd starch your fatigues . . . then go home and mortar your area. Saigon and Cholan and Danang held such hostile vibes that you felt that you were being dry sniped every time someone looked at you." Drugs and sex helped some soldiers—many just boys away from home for the first time—to cope with the nature of a guerrilla war. One GI recalled that R&R—the traditional rest and recreation leave—was really I&I—"intoxication and intercourse." A 1969 Pentagon study estimated that nearly two of every three American soldiers in Vietnam were using marijuana and that one of every three or four had tried heroin. In 1970 CBS News televised a "smoke-in," in which GIs smoked marijuana through the barrel of a combat rifle. In such an atmosphere boys became men, fast. "How do you feel," Herr asked, "when a nineteen-year-old kid tells you from the bottom of his heart that he has gotten too old for this kind of shit?"

Other soldiers reacted by viewing all Vietnamese as the enemy. In part the nature of the war against the Vietcong caused this attitude. In a village of "civilians" any man, woman, or child *might* be the enemy. "Vietnam was a dark room full of deadly objects," wrote Herr, "and the VC were everywhere all at once like spider cancer." Tension and anxiety were as ever present as olive drab.

Empty government phrases, however, also contributed to the problem. How could soldiers win the "hearts and minds" of villagers one day and rain napalm on them the next? Reacting to the surface idealism of U.S. policy, one experienced soldier commented, "All that is just a *load* man. We're here to kill gooks, period." The

did serve, and most served bravely. In the early years of "Lyndon's war," many soldiers sincerely believed that they were fighting—and dying— to preserve freedom and nourish democracy in Southeast Asia. One career soldier, who did his first tour in Vietnam in 1966, recalled the idealism of his experience. He talked enthusiastically about American contributions to the im-

My Lai massacre, which saw American soldiers kill more than 100 (the official figure was 122 but it was probably many more) South Vietnamese civilians, was the sad extension of this attitude.

As the war lengthened, morale of American soldiers plummeted. Desertion and absent-without-leave (AWOL) rates skyrocketed. In 1966 the army desertion rate had been 14.9 men per thousand; by 1971 it had risen to 73.5. In 1966 there were 57.2 AWOL incidents per thousand; that figure leaped to 176.9 in 1971. Even worse, "fragging"—the term soldiers used to describe the assassination of overzealous officers and noncommissioned officers (NCOs) by their own troops—increased at an alarming rate. The army claimed that at least 1011 officers and NCOs were killed or wounded by their own men during the Vietnam War.

At home, university students, most of whom had draft exemptions, also reacted to the war and Johnson's policies. They were the earliest and most vocal critics of the Vietnam War. If they lacked a coherent ideology, they were strong in numbers and energy. Between 1946 and 1970 enrollments in institutions of higher education had climbed from 2 million to 8 million. Although not all the students protested against the war, the most politically active ones did. As politicians they formed a curious breed—segregated from society as a whole, freed from adult responsibilities, bound to no real constituency, and encouraged by their teachers to think critically. Most student protesters were from upper middle-class families and could afford the intellectual luxury of being political idealists. (Youth culture as a whole will be discussed in greater detail in Chapter 30.)

Led by such leftist groups as Students for a Democratic Society (SDS), university students called for a more just society in which political life was governed by morality, not greed. During the early 1960s they focused on the civil rights movement, participating in freedom rides and voter registration drives. By the mid-1960s, however, they were increasingly shifting their attention to America's "unjust and immoral" war in Southeast Asia; and with the shift their numbers swelled. In 1962 only ten universities had SDS chapters, and each chapter had only a handful of members. By 1968 the organization

boasted more than 100,000 members. By then, too, older voices had joined the student chorus of condemnation.

It was the older voices, energized by the idealism of youth, that led to Johnson's decision not to seek reelection in 1968. For many, it seemed as if the future of American politics belonged to the proponents of peace and morality. Students flocked to presidential candidate Gene McCarthy's peace cause. They cut their long hair, shaved their beards ("be clean for Gene"), put on coats and ties, and worked for McCarthy's campaign. After Johnson pulled his hat out of the ring, Robert Kennedy announced his candidacy. Although McCarthy supporters saw Kennedy as a political op-

In 1968, Democrat Eugene McCarthy ran for his party's presidential nomination as a peace candidate.

portunist, he spoke eloquently for the cause of humanity and peace. When students at a Catholic university called for more bombings, RFK asked, "Do you understand what that means? It means you are voting to send people, Americans and Vietnamese to die. . . . Don't you understand that what we are doing to the Vietnamese is not very different than what Hitler did to the Jews." Kennedy, who enjoyed midnight bull sessions on the meaning of existence and looked at ease with his tie loosened and his shirt sleeves rolled above his elbows, spoke a language that radical students understood. He exhibited the passion and commitment that McCarthy lacked. By the conclusion of the campaign, Kennedy had become the foremost peace candidate, and representative of young liberals.

At the celebration party after his narrow victory in the California primary, Kennedy said, "We are a great country, an unselfish country, and a compassionate country. I intend to make that my basis for running." Moments later a fanatic Palestinian shot him in the head. With Kennedy died the dreams of many Americans

Although he was slow to declare his candidacy, Robert Kennedy soon became the darling of the anti-war movement.

for a moral society. Columnist Murray Kempton spoke for many people: "I have liked many public men immensely, but I guess [RFK] is the only one I have ever loved." Although RFK had started in political life as a committed, aggressive anti-Communist and Cold Warrior, by the time of his death he had radically reevaluated his earlier beliefs.

The Democratic party went to the Chicago convention without a candidate. There they battled among themselves—young and old; radical, liberal, and conservative. In the streets, outside the convention hall, police beat protesters in full view of television cameras. An official commission later termed it a "police riot." Inside the convention hall the fighting was largely verbal, but it was just as intense and bitter. Abraham Ribicoff, a senator from Connecticut, accused Chicago's mayor Richard Daley of allowing the police to use "Gestapo tactics" in the street; Daley accused Ribicoff of having unnatural re-

lations with his mother. In the end, the Democratic party chose Hubert Humphrey, Johnson's liberal vice president, as their presidential candidate. Instead of change, the Democratic party chose a representative of the "old politics."

In a more tranquil convention in Miami, the Republican party endorsed Richard M. Nixon, who promised when elected to honorably end the Vietnam War, move against forced busing of black children to white schools, and restore "law and order." More calm and relaxed than ever before, the "new Nixon" claimed to speak for the great majority of Americans who obeyed the nation's laws, paid their taxes, regularly attended church, and loved their country. It was the same message Alabama's Governor George Wallace used as the foundation of his third-party candidacy. Running on the American Independent ticket, Wallace spoke for millions of working-class white Americans, young and old alike, who opposed forced integration of schools and neighborhoods, radical college students, and what they believed was the country's drift toward the left. Although Humphrey finished the campaign strong, Nixon's and Wallace's appeal to traditional values had an undeniable attraction. And on election day, Nixon received 43.4 percent of the popular vote, Humphrey 42.7 percent, and Wallace 13.5 percent. Given the combined votes for Nixon and Wallace—57 percent—it was clear that the country was moving right rather than left.

THE TORTUOUS PATH TOWARD PEACE

During the presidential campaign of 1968, Richard Nixon expected the American voter to accept certain things on faith. First, he asked them to believe that he had a plan to honorably end the war in Vietnam. Second, he hoped that they would "buy" his new public image—the "new Nixon," experienced, statesmanlike, mature, secure, and ever so well adjusted. Most Americans probably did not believe either in the "new Nixon" or his pledge to "bring us to-

gether." On election day only 27 percent of eligible voters cast their ballot for him, but in 1968 that proved enough votes to win the election.

Outsiders on the Inside

If Nixon had developed "new" characteristics, those qualities had not forced out the "old." Richard Nixon still considered himself something of an outsider, a battler against an entrenched political establishment. Reared on the West Coast in humble circumstances, he had to overcome considerable obstacles in his rise to power. In the process certain character traits emerged. He was a hard worker—careful, studious with a tendency toward perfectionism. No detail was too small for his consideration. In addition, he did not shy away from an unpopular task. During his years as Eisenhower's vice president, Nixon had proved particularly adept as a political hatchet man. He was also a loner—shy, introverted, humorless, uncomfortable in social situations. He was essentially a man of action, one who for most of his career carried a list of things to do in the inside pocket of his suit coat. Journalist Tom Wicker noted that the new Nixon was not very different from the old.

At the Democratic convention in Chicago, police attacked thousands of unarmed, middle-class, antiwar college students in what was later termed a "police riot."

Writing of the new Nixon, Wicker observed: "He is, if anything, more reserved and inward, as difficult as ever to know, driven still by deep inner compulsion toward power and personal vindication, painfully conscious of slights and failures, a man who had imposed upon himself a self-control so rigid as to be all but visible."

As a restless outsider, Nixon harbored a heightened suspicion of political insiders. Throughout his career he had been an outspoken critic of State Department officials and other establishment bureaucrats. On taking office he therefore surrounded himself with close advisors who held noncabinet titles. Cabinet appointees, and particularly his secretary of state, William Rogers, had almost no voice in key decisions. Personal aides H. R. Haldeman and John Ehrlichman—called the "Germans" by the White House press corps—advised Nixon on domestic political issues. Vice President Spiro Agnew assumed the role of the administration's hatchet man so well that he became known as "Nixon's Nixon." He attacked the establishment with the ferocity of a professional wrestler verbally abusing an archrival. The "sniveling, handwringing power structure," he said, "deserves the violent rebellion it encourages." As for foreign affairs, Nixon relied on his national security advisor, Henry Alfred Kissinger.

Most commentators regarded Kissinger as a strange ally for Nixon. Kissinger, after all, taught at Harvard, was a close associate of Nelson Rockefeller—Nixon's longtime Republican opponent—and had even offered to work for Nixon's Democratic opponent Hubert Humphrey. "Look," Kissinger said in 1968, "I've hated Nixon for years." Yet even while Kissinger was courting Humphrey, he was secretly working for Nixon's election. No matter who won in 1968, Kissinger would be on the victorious side. It was a piece of Machiavellian maneuvering that Nixon might have appreciated.

Beneath Kissinger's sophisticated exterior, he shared with Nixon fundamental characteristics and beliefs. Like Nixon, Kissinger's path to power was not a traditional one. A German Jew, he had lived for five years (between the ages of 10 and 15) in Nazi Germany; he had been verbally and physically abused by his Aryan classmates. With the rest of his family, he fled to the United States during the late 1930s.

After serving as an army translator-interrogator during World War II, he enrolled as a scholarship student at Harvard, from where he was graduated *summa cum laude* in 1950 and was awarded his Ph.D. in 1954. His dissertation, later published as *A World Restored*, examined the ideas and policies of the conservative world leaders and diplomats who reconstructed Europe after the social and political upheavals caused by the Napoleonic Wars. During the late 1950s and 1960s, Kissinger wrote, taught, and emerged as a leading expert on foreign affairs. Kissinger viewed himself as a political realist, and he resisted rigid ideological or moral stands. Successful diplomacy, he believed, demanded flexible and creative leaders.

Vain, irreverent, articulate, and intellectual, Kissinger shared Nixon's desire to alter the very nature of the country's foreign relations and to make history. Neither particularly enjoyed being part of a committee process, and the diplomacy of secrecy and intrigue attracted both. For all their surface differences, the shy politician and the flamboyant scholar were kindred spirits who combined to form an impressive team. As one historian observed, "each filled a vital gap in the other's abilities. Kissinger had no gift for American politics; he needed to serve a president who could manipulate the electorate into supporting his policies. Nixon benefited from Kissinger's good press contacts since his own were disastrous."

Vietnamization: The Idea and the Process

During his campaign Nixon had promised "peace with honor" and suggested that he had a secret plan to achieve those ends. Controversy surrounded just what that plan entailed. Several historians have suggested that Nixon's plan was an updated version of Eisenhower's plan to end the Korean War. In 1953 when Ike took office, he publicly called for peace while secretly sending a message to Chinese and North Korean leaders that if they stalled at the peace talks, he was prepared to use nuclear weapons to end the war. Nixon told his White House aide H. R. Haldeman that his plan was similar to Eisenhower's. He wanted North Vietnam to believe that he was a "madman." "I want the North Vietnamese to believe I've reached the point where I might do anything to stop the war," Nixon told Haldeman. "We'll just slip the word to them that 'for God's sakes, you know Nixon is obsessed about communists. We can't restrain him when he's angry—and he has his hand on the nuclear button'—and Ho Chi Minh himself will be in Paris in two days begging for peace." The "madman theory" helps to explain Nixon's dramatic shifts during his first four years in office as he moved between the poles of peacefully concluding the war and violently expanding the conflict.

One thing was certain, however, Nixon knew that he could not continue Johnson's policy. "I'm not going to end up like LBJ," he remarked, "holed up in the White House afraid to show my face on the street." The country needed something new. Whatever else he did, Nixon realized that to ensure some semblance of domestic tranquility he would have to begin to remove American troops from Vietnam. In May 1969 he announced, "The time is approaching when the South Vietnamese forces will be able to take over some of the fighting fronts now being manned by Americans." That summer he drummed harder on the idea of the South Vietnamese fighting their own war. In what has become known as the "Nixon Doctrine," the president insisted that Asian soldiers must carry more of the combat burden. Certainly the United States would continue to materially aid any anti-Communist struggle, but the aid would not include the wholesale use of American troops.

The Nixon Doctrine formed the foundation of Nixon's Vietnamization policy. Working from the questionable premise that the government of Nguyen Van Thieu was stable and prepared to assume greater responsibility for fighting the war, Nixon announced that he planned to gradually deescalate American military involvement. Increasingly U.S. aid would be limited to war matériel, military advice, and air support. He coupled Vietnamization with a more strenuous effort to move along the peace talks.

Actually, the idea of Vietnamization was hardly new. In 1951 the French had called it *jaunissement*, or "yellowing." Advisors for Eisenhower, Kennedy, and Johnson had suggested one variation or another of the plan as the solution to the war. The major problem was

that the South Vietnamese could not successfully fight the war—not in 1951 or 1961 or 1971. But faced with angry criticism at home, Nixon had no choice but to implement the policy.

At the same time as he extended the olive branch, he expanded the nature of the conflict. Hoping to slow down the flow of North Vietnamese supplies and soldiers into South Vietnam, Nixon ordered American B-52 pilots to bomb the Ho Chi Minh Trail both in Vietnam and in Cambodia. He kept this violation of Cambodian neutrality secret from the American public. It was a bold move, but not very productive. The bombs only reduced the flow of men and supplies by approximately 10 percent.

When both increased bombings of North Vietnam and Kissinger's peace talks with North Vietnamese officials failed to end the war, Nixon resorted to harsher military efforts. After watching *Patton*, his favorite movie, on board the presidential yacht *Sequoia*, he decided to "go for all the marbles" and send American ground forces to Cambodia to destroy Communist supply bases. On the night of April 30, 1970, he went on television and told the American people of his plan. Ignoring previous American violations of Cambodia neutrality, he said that U.S. policy had been "to scrupulously respect the neutrality of the Cambodian people," while North Vietnam had used the border areas for "major base camps, training sites, logistics facilities, weapons and ammunition factories, airstrips and prisoner-of-war compounds," as well as their chief military headquarters. As a result, Nixon announced a joint American and South Vietnamese "incursion" into Cambodia's border regions to be limited to 60 days. In an attempt to rally American support, Nixon emphasized that the country's honor and even manhood were at stake: "We will not be humiliated, we will not be defeated. If when the chips are down the U.S. acts like a pitiful helpless giant, the forces of totalitarianism will threaten free nations and free institutions throughout the world. It is *not our power but our will* that is being tested tonight."

Militarily the "incursion" fell far short of success. Although American forces captured large stockpiles of weapons and supplies, the operation did not force North Vietnam to end the war. But the "incursion" had dangerously enlarged the battlefield. More importantly, the invasion of Cambodia reignited the fires of the peace movement at home. Throughout the country, colleges and universities shut down in protest. Students raged at what they believe was an "immoral, imperialist policy." At Kent State University in Ohio a volley of gunshots fired by Ohio National Guardsmen broke up a peaceful demonstration. The shots killed 4 students and wounded 11 others. Less than two weeks later, policemen shot 2 more innocent students at Jackson State University in Mississippi. Instead of victory or even peace, Nixon's efforts had further divided America.

As an effective policy for ending the war, Vietnamization was a failure. To be sure, the policy allowed Nixon to bring home American combat troops. When Nixon took office 540,000 American troops were in Vietnam; four years later only 70,000 remained. But American reductions were not accompanied by a marked improvement in the South Vietnamese army. This was clearly illustrated by the unsuccessful 1971 South Vietnamese invasion into Laos. If anything, South Vietnam became more dependent on the United States during the years of Vietnamization. By 1972 South Vietnam's only product and export was war, and even this commodity was of inferior quality.

A "Decent Interval"

By 1972 Nixon simply wanted to end the war with as little embarrassment as possible. As a viable country, South Vietnam was hopeless. Without an active U.S. military presence, the country's demise was a forgone conclusion. Negotiations presented the only way out. Nixon and Kissinger hoped to arrange for a peace that would permit the United States and South Vietnam to save face and allow a "decent interval" of time to ensue between the American departure and the collapse of the government in Saigon. In the pursuit of the goal, Nixon changed the character of American foreign policy.

The Soviet Union and the People's Republic of China aided and advised North Vietnam. Yet the two large Communist nations were hardly allies themselves. In fact, the Sino-Soviet split demonstrated to American leaders the fallacy of

In the spring of 1970, Ohio National Guardsmen fired into a group of protesting students at Kent State University, killing four.

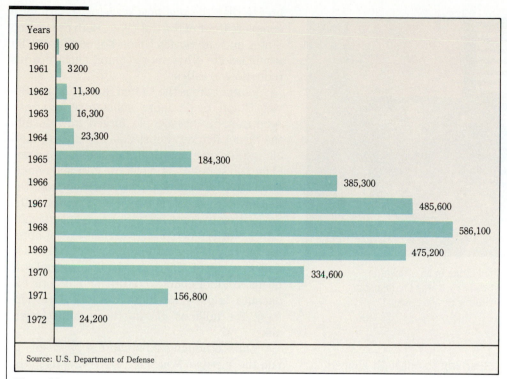

Years	
1960	900
1961	3 200
1962	11,300
1963	16,300
1964	23,300
1965	184,300
1966	385,300
1967	485,600
1968	586,100
1969	475,200
1970	334,600
1971	156,800
1972	24,200

Source: U.S. Department of Defense

Figure 29.1
U.S. troop levels in Vietnam

the old Cold War theme of a monolithic Communist movement. Nixon and Kissinger were astute enough to use the Sino-Soviet rift to improve U.S. relations with both countries. Improved relations, they believed, would move the United States several steps closer to an "honorable" peace in Vietnam. Unfortunately, Nixon and Kissinger greatly overestimated the influence of the Soviet Union and China on North Vietnam.

From his first days in office, Nixon had his eyes on the People's Republic of China, a nation that the United States had refused to recognize. One Nixon aide reported in 1969, "You're not going to believe this, but Nixon wants to recognize China." It seemed remarkable, for Nixon's Cold War record—his opposition to any concession to the Communists—was well known. But Nixon understood that his very record would protect him from public cries of being soft on communism; Nixon knew that unlike Truman, Kennedy, and Johnson, he did not have a Nixon to worry about.

Nixon approached China like a man holding a vase from the Ming dynasty, mixing caution with slow careful movements. In fact, both China and the United States walked on egg shells. Mao Zedung told reporter Edgar Snow that he "would be happy to talk with [Nixon] either as a tourist or as President." And Mao ended China's athletic isolation in 1971 by sending a table tennis team to the world championships in Nagoya, Japan, and then inviting an American team to compete in Beijing. Capitalizing on the success of Ping-Pong diplomacy, in the summer of 1971 Kissinger made a very secret trip to China. Kissinger's mission paved the way for Nixon's own very public trip to China in February 1972. American television cameras recorded Nixon's every move as he toured the Great Wall, the Imperial Palace, and the other sites of historic China. For the White House, one reporter noted, "It was the social event of the year." Constantly smiling and bubbling with excitement, Nixon thoroughly enjoyed the event, going so far as quoting Chairman Mao at an of-

In 1972 Richard Nixon visited China in an attempt to improve relations with that country. It was the first step toward achieving détente with the Soviet Union.

ficial toast and learning to eat with chopsticks. Although full diplomatic relations would not be established until 1979 under Jimmy Carter, Nixon's trip to China was the single most important event in the history of the relations between the United States and the People's Republic of China. It bridged, as Chinese foreign minister Chou En-lai remarked, "the vastest ocean in the world, twenty-five years of no communication."

Concerned about the growing rapprochement between China and America, the Soviet Union sought to move closer to the United States. Once again, Nixon and Kissinger were pleased to oblige. In late May 1972, after many months of preparatory talks, Nixon traveled to Moscow to sign an arms control treaty with Soviet leader Leonid Brezhnev. The Strategic Arms Limitation Treaty of 1972 (SALT I) certainly did not preclude a future nuclear war between the superpowers. Although it froze intercontinental ballistic missile (ICBM) deployment, it did not alter the buildup of the more dangerous multiple independent reentry vehicles (MIRVs), which, according to one historian "was about as meaningful as freezing the cavalry of the European nations in 1938 but not the tanks." As so often has been the case during the Cold War, SALT I provided more a warm

breeze than the real heat wave necessary for a complete thaw of the Cold War. Both the United States and the Soviet Union hoped the SALT I would lead to other, more comprehensive, arms reductions treaties.

In other areas the United States and the Soviet Union made more substantial progress. American businesspeople forged inroads into the Soviet market. Pepsi-Cola executives, metallurgy and ammonia dealers, computer and machine tools traders, and electric gear and mining equipment salespersons all benefited from the improved relations between America and the Soviet Union. Some farmers also reaped significant rewards when disastrous harvests at home led the Soviet Union to purchase several billion dollars worth of American wheat, corn, and soybeans. And, of course, cultural and athletic exchanges and competition provided entertainment for millions of Americans and Soviets alike.

Thus although Nixon had not been able to end the Vietnam War, his 1972 triumphs in the Soviet Union and China gave him more influence with North Vietnam's major allies. His visits to Beijing and Moscow also dazzled American voters. In 1972 Nixon easily defeated Democratic candidate George McGovern, capturing 61 percent of the popular vote and 521 of the 538 votes of the Electoral College. Nixon's success with blue-collar workers, conservative Catholics, and Southerners signified the end of the New Deal coalition.

Once reelected, Nixon again focused on Vietnam. A month before the election, Kissinger had announced, "Peace is at hand," but no sooner was Nixon safely reelected than the peace talks broke down once again. Nixon's response was more and heavier bombing of North Vietnam. Starting on December 18 and continuing for the next ten days, the Christmas bombings—code-named Operation LINEBACKER II—attacked military targets in Hanoi and Haiphong and killed more than 1500 civilians, leveled a hospital, and destroyed large parts of Hanoi. Critics charged that Nixon was attempting to "wage war by tantrum" and that the bombings served no military purpose. Some even suggested that Nixon had become mentally unbalanced. Military authorities, however, maintained that the bombings quickened the pace of the peace process. When the bombings concluded, the warring nations resumed peace talks.

In a week North Vietnam and the United States hammered out a peace, one that was strikingly similar to the October proposal. On January 27, 1973, America ended its active participation in the Vietnam War. The peace treaty provided for the release of all prisoners of war and America's military withdrawal from Vietnam. It also established a monitored cease-fire between North and South Vietnam and set up procedures aimed at solving the differences between the two countries. Nixon quickly claimed that he had won an honorable peace, that his "secret plan" had worked, even if it had taken four years and claimed the lives of 21,000 American, 107,000 South Vietnamese, and more than 500,000 North Vietnamese soldiers. And, of course, the lives of many thousands of Vietnamese civilians. Informing the American people of the peace, Nixon claimed, "South Vietnam has gained the right to determine its own future. . . . Let us be proud that America did not settle for a peace that would have betrayed our ally . . . that would have ended the war for us but continued the war for the fifty million people of Indochina." But as one historian commented, "In all likelihood, the peace accords that were finally signed in January 1973 could have been negotiated four years earlier. In the name of credibility, honor, and patriotism, hundreds of thousands of lives had been lost."

America left the war in 1973, but the war did not end then. All the peace provided for was a "decent interval" between America's withdrawal and North Vietnam's complete victory. When the South Vietnamese leader Nguyen Cao Ky heard Nixon's peace speech, he commented, "I could not stomach [it], so nauseating was its hypocrisy and self-delusion . . . there is no reason why they [the Communists] should stop now. . . . I give them a couple of years before they invade the South." He was right. Almost as soon as the ink on the "peace treaty" was dry, North Vietnam and the Vietcong were once again engaged in a war with the government in South Vietnam. Finally, in the spring of 1975 South Vietnamese forces collapsed. In March North Vietnam forces took Hue and Da Nang; by late April they were close to Saigon. On April

21 President Nguyen Van Thieu publicly lambasted the United States, resigned, and beat a hasty retreat from his country. On April 30 South Vietnam formally announced its unconditional surrender. Vietnam was finally unified. Free elections in 1956 might have accomplished the same results.

The Legacy of the War

Although America's active military participation in the Vietnam War ended in 1973, the controversy engendered by the war raged on long after the firing of the last shot. Much of the controversy centered on the returning veterans. Reports of drug use and fragging frightened many Americans who had come no closer to the war than their television sets. And veterans—most of whom had served their country faithfully and to the best of their abilities—were shocked by the cold, hostile reception they received when they returned to the United States. In *First Blood* (1982), John Rambo, played by Sylvester Stallone, captured the pain of the returning veterans: "Nothing is over. Nothing! You just don't turn it off. It wasn't my war—you asked me, I didn't ask you . . . and I did what I had to do to

The Vietnam War inspired a number of movies dealing with the conflict of veterans on their return home. Some of these movies portrayed the veterans as victims of a tragic war; others like *Rambo: First Blood II* (shown here) made the veteran a hero and transformed the conflict into a noble crusade.

win. . . . Then I came back to the world and I see all those maggots at the airport, protesting me, spitting on me, calling me a baby-killer and all kinds of vile crap. . . . Back there I could fly a gunship, I could drive a tank, I was in charge of million dollar equipment. Back here I can't even hold down a job parking cars. . . . Back here there's nothing!"

During the 1970s and 1980s the returning Vietnam War veteran loomed large in American popular culture. He was first portrayed as a dangerous killer, a deranged ticking time bomb that could explode at any time and in any place. He was Travis Bickle in *Taxi Driver* (1976), a veteran wound so tight that he seemed perpetually on the verge of snapping. Travis Bickle, wrote one film historian, "is the prototypical movie vet: In ways we can only imagine, the horror of the war unhinged him. He's lost contact with other human beings. . . . He's edgy: he can't sleep at night." He waits to explode. Or he was Colonel Kurtz in *Apocalypse Now* (1979), who adjusted to a mad war by going mad himself. Or he was Lieutenant Howard Hunter of the popular "Hill Street Blues" television series. A Vietnam War veteran, Hunter was portrayed as a misfit, a competent policeman but lonely and antisocial.

Not until the late 1970s did popular culture begin to treat the Vietnam War veteran as a victim of the war rather than a madman produced by the war. *Coming Home* (1978) and *The Deer Hunter* (1978) began the popular rehabilitation of the veteran, and such films as *First Blood* (1982), *Rambo: First Blood II* (1985), and *Missing in Action* (1984) transformed the veteran into a hero. On television, "Magnum, P.I.," "The A-Team," and "Air Wolf" also presented the veteran as a misunderstood hero.

The transformation of the veteran that took place in the late 1970s and 1980s indicated a fundamental shift in America's attitude toward the war. Millions of Americans began once again to see the war in terms of a noble crusade that could have been won. As John Rambo said in *Rambo: First Blood II*, "Do we get to win this time?" His former commander replied: "This time it's up to you." This message fit well with the political message of Ronald Reagan's America.

As American filmmakers "Ramboized" the conflict, Vietnam labored to reconstruct a viable nation out of the rubble of war. It was a difficult struggle. Roads and bridges, power plants and factories lay in ruins. Ports suffered from damage and neglect. Raw materials and investment capital were in short supply. If peace brought hope, it also brought the spector of economic ruin.

The recovery of the Socialist Republic of Vietnam has been slow. One of the poorest countries in the world, it has suffered from high inflation and unemployment, food shortages and starvation, and government inefficiency and corruption. In addition, military adventures— such as the 1978 invasion of Kampuchea (formerly Cambodia)—has siphoned off money needed to rebuild the country. Finally, the Soviet Union, Vietnam's closest ally, has not solved Vietnam's economic problems. "Americans without dollars," the Vietnamese have called the Soviets. One Vietnamese joke reflected the new relationship with the Soviet Union. After appealing to the Soviets for loans, Vietnam receives the cable: "Tighten your belts." Vietnam replies: "Send belts."

In 1986 Vietnam committed itself to radical change. A new generation of leaders turned to increased democracy and capitalism to solve their country's problems. They also turned to the West, and particularly the United States, for help. American leaders during the late 1980s and early 1990s, however, rejected Vietnam's pleas for aid. Although Vietnam has weakened its ties to the Soviet Union, withdrawn from Kampuchea, and tried to resolve the prisoners of war–missing in action (POW–MIA) issue, official American policy continues to regard the Socialist Republic of Vietnam as a country untouchable. Vietnam may have won the war, but it has not won peace.

CONCLUSION

The Vietnam War confused and divided the nation. Tim O'Brien captured something of this confusion in his acclaimed novel *Going after Cacciato* (1978). After fighting in the war, his protagonist "didn't know who was right, or what was right; he didn't know if it was a war of self-determination or self-destruction, outright aggression or national liberation; he didn't know which speeches to believe, which books, which

CHRONOLOGY
OF KEY EVENTS

1954 The French garrison at Dien Bien Phu falls to Vietnamese nationalists led by Ho Chi Minh; Geneva conference divides Vietnam into two regions with the promise to hold elections to reunify the country in 1956; North Vietnam is led by the Communist government of Ho Chi Minh and South Vietnam by the government of Ngo Dinh Diem

1956 South Vietnam refuses to participate in elections to unify the two Vietnams

1961 John F. Kennedy is inaugurated thirty-fifth president; Alliance for Progress pledges $20 billion in U.S. aid to Latin America over a ten-year period; Cuban exiles stage abortive invasion of Cuba at Bay of Pigs; East Germans erect Berlin Wall; Soviet Union breaks a three-year moratorium on nuclear tests

1962 Cuban missile crisis: In response to Khrushchev's decision to build missile bases in Cuba, President Kennedy imposes a naval blockade of Cuba; Khrushchev orders the bases dismantled; President Kennedy increases the number of American advisors in South Vietnam to approximately 16,000

1963 United States and Soviet Union agree to ban nuclear tests in atmosphere; South Vietnamese army officers arrest and murder President Diem; President Kennedy is assassinated; Lyndon Johnson becomes thirty-sixth president

1964 North Vietnamese torpedo boats attack the U.S. destroyers *Maddox* and *C. Turner Joy* in the Gulf of Tonkin off the North Vietnamese coast; Gulf of Tonkin Resolution gives the president authority to retaliate against North Vietnamese aggression

1965 United States begins regular bombing missions over North Vietnam and sends first American ground combat troops into South Vietnam

1968 Tet offensive: During Tet, the Vietnamese lunar new year, the Viet Cong stage attacks on major South Vietnamese cities; President Johnson suspends the bombing of North Vietnam and announces that he will not run for reelection; Democratic presidential candidate Robert F. Kennedy is assassinated; Richard M. Nixon is elected thirty-seventh president

1969 Nixon announces "Vietnamization" policy; South Vietnam will take increased responsibility for fighting the war

1970 32,000 U.S. troops join the South Vietnamese army in invading Cambodia; in antiwar protests, 4 students are killed and 11 injured at Kent State University in Ohio; and 2 students die and 12 are injured at Jackson State University in Mississippi; Congress repeals Gulf of Tonkin Resolution

1972 Nixon travels to China, ending 25 years of nonrecognition of the People's Republic of China; Strategic Arms Limitation Treaty with the Soviet Union freezes intercontinental ballistic missile deployment

1973 United States ends active participation in the Vietnam War

1975 North Vietnamese forces enter Saigon; North and South Vietnam are reunited; the former South Vietnamese capital is renamed Ho Chi Minh City

politicians; he didn't know if nations would topple like dominos or stand separate like trees; he didn't know who started the war, or why, or when, or with what motives; he didn't know if it mattered."

Richard Nixon promised in 1968 that if he were elected president, he would end the war honorably and bring Americans together again. Instead, he enlarged the scope of the war before ending it and further divided the country. So, too, Johnson had divided the nation. His vision of a better, more just society—the Great Society (see Chapter 30)—was dashed on the rocks of Vietnam. There was in Johnson's position the essence of tragedy. As he later explained to biographer Doris Kearns, "I knew from the start that I was bound to be crucified either way I moved. If I left the woman I really loved—the Great Society—in order to get involved with the bitch of a war on the other side of the world, then I would lose everything at home . . . but if I left that war and let the communists take over South Vietnam, then I would be seen as a coward and my nation would be seen as an appeaser and we would both find it impossible to accomplish anything for anybody anywhere on the entire globe." In Johnson's view he was like a Puritan wrestling with the question of his own salvation:

> Damned if you do,
> Damned if you don't.
> Damned if you will
> Damned if you won't.

Of course, both Nixon and LBJ further injured their cause by using conscious deception in dealing with the American people.

Vietnam, then, destroyed Johnson's presidency, and it helped to undermine Nixon's. It was a war that left scars—on the people who fought in it and on the people who opposed and supported it; on Americans and on Vietnamese; and on U.S. foreign policy and its position in the world. For almost 35 years the United States had been actively involved in Indochina, but its influence in the region effectively ended in 1975. The Vietnam War, like the Communist victory in China in 1949, undercut America's position in Asia.

The most constructive outcome of the war was the lessons it taught. Congress learned that it had to take a more active role in foreign af-

fairs. The War Powers Act (1973), which requires the president to account for his actions within 48 hours of committing troops in a foreign war, demonstrated that the Gulf of Tonkin Resolution had taught Congress a painful lesson. Ho Chi Minh's nationalism taught policymakers that communism was not a monolithic movement and that not all small nations are dominos. Perhaps politicians, policymakers, and citizens alike even learned that national policy should be based on the realities of individual situations and not Cold War stereotypes.

SUGGESTIONS FOR FURTHER READING

OVERVIEWS AND SURVEYS

Stephen E. Ambrose, *Rise to Globalism: American Foreign Policy Since 1938*, 5th ed. (1988); William H. Chafe, *The Unfinished Journey*, 2d ed. (1991), and *The American Woman* (1972); Mario T. García, *Mexican Americans: Leadership, Ideology, Identity, 1930–1960* (1989); Juan Gómez-Quiñones, *Chicano Politics: Reality and Promise, 1940–1990* (1990); Alonzo Hamby, *The Imperial Years* (1976); Godfrey Hodgson, *America in Our Time* (1975); Walter LaFeber, *America, Russia, and the Cold War*, 5th ed. (1985); William Leuchtenburg, *A Troubled Feast*, rev. ed. (1983); Kim McQuaid, *The Anxious Years* (1989); Matt Meier and Feliciano Rivera, *The Chicanos* (1972); James S. Olson and Randy Roberts, *Where the Domino Fell: America in Vietnam, 1945–1990* (1991); Thomas G. Paterson et al., *American Foreign Policy*, 3d ed., 2 vols. (1988); Richard Polenberg, *One Nation Divisible* (1980); Emily and Norman Rosenberg, *In Our Times*, 4th ed. (1991); Julian Samora, *Los Mojados* (1971); Frederick F. Siegel, *A Troubled Journey* (1984); Ronald B. Taylor, *Chavez and the Farm Workers* (1975); Lawrence Wittner, *Cold War America*, rev. ed. (1978).

THE ILLUSION OF GREATNESS

Irving Bernstein, *Promises Kept: John F. Kennedy's New Frontier* (1991); James G. Blight and David A. Welch, *On the Brink: Americans and Soviets Reexamine the Cuban Missile Crisis* (1989); Carl M. Brauer, *John F. Kennedy and the Second Reconstruction* (1977); David Detzer, *The Brink: Cuban Missile Crisis, 1962* (1979); Herbert S. Dinerstein, *The Making of a Missile Crisis: October 1962* (1976); Louise FitzSimons, *The Kennedy Doctrine* (1972); Trumbull Higgins, *The Perfect Failure: Kennedy, Eisenhower, and the C.I.A. at the Bay of Pigs* (1987); Richard D. Mahoney, *JFK: Ordeal in Africa* (1983); Allen Matusow, *The Unraveling of America:*

A History of Liberalism in the 1960s (1984); Bruce Miroff, *Pragmatic Illusions: The Presidential Politics of JFK* (1976); Victor Navasky, *Kennedy Justice* (1971); Jack M. Schick, *The Berlin Crisis, 1958–1962* (1971); Richard Walton, *Cold War and Counterrevolution: The Foreign Policy of John F. Kennedy* (1972); Peter Wyden, *Bay of Pigs* (1979).

VIETNAM: AMERICA'S LONGEST WAR

David L. Anderson, *Trapped by Success: The Eisenhower Administration and Vietnam, 1953–1961* (1991); Larry Berman, *Planning a Tragedy: The Americanization of the War in Vietnam* (1982), and *Lyndon Johnson's War* (1989); Peter Braestrup, *Big Story: How the American Press and Television Reported and Interpreted the Crisis of Tet 1968 in Vietnam and Washington* (1978); Larry E. Cable, *Conflict of Myths: The Development of American Counterinsurgency Doctrine and the Vietnam War* (1986), and *Unholy Grail: The United States and the Wars in Vietnam* (1991); Philip Caputo, *A Rumor of War* (1977); Harry Caudill, *Night Comes to the Cumberlands* (1963); Chester L. Cooper, *The Lost Crusade: America in Vietnam* (1970); Robert A. Divine, ed., *Exploring the Johnson Years* (1981); Bernard Fall, *Street Without Joy: Insurgency in Indochina, 1946–63* (1964), and *The Two Vietnams*, 2d ed. (1967); Frances FitzGerald, *Fire in the Lake* (1972); Todd Gitlin, *The Whole World Is Watching: Mass Media in the Making & Unmaking of the New Left* (1980); Sherry Gershon Gottlieb, *Hell No, We Won't Go: Evading the Draft During Vietnam* (1992); David Halberstam, *The Making of a Quagmire: America and Vietnam During the Kennedy Era*, rev. ed. (1988), and *The Best and the Brightest* (1972); Michael Herr, *Dispatches* (1977); George C. Herring, *America's Longest War: The United States and Vietnam, 1950–1975*, 2d ed. (1986); Seymour Hersh, *My Lai 4: A Report on the Massacre and Its Aftermath* (1970); Stanley Karnow, *Vietnam, A History* (1983); Christopher Lasch, *The Agony of the American Left* (1969); David Levy, *The Debate over Vietnam* (1991); Guenter Lewy, *America in Vietnam* (1978); Abraham Lowenthal, *The Dominican Intervention* (1972); Roger Morris, *Uncertain Greatness: Henry Kissinger and American Foreign Policy* (1977); Don Oberdorfer, *Tet!* (1971); George Reedy, *The Twilight of the Presidency*, rev. ed. (1987); Neil Sheehan, ed., *The Pentagon Papers* (1971); Kathleen J. Turner, *Lyndon Johnson's Dual War: Vietnam and the Press* (1985); Brian VanDeMark, *Into the Quagmire: Lyndon Johnson and the Escalation of the Vietnam War* (1991); Tom Wicker, *JFK and LBJ: The Influence of Personality upon Politics* (1968); Marilyn Young, *The Vietnam Wars: 1945–1990* (1991).

THE TORTUOUS PATH TOWARD PEACE

Carl Bernstein and Robert Woodward, *All the President's Men* (1974); John Dean, *Blind Ambition: The White House Years* (1976); Lloyd C. Gardner, ed., *The Great Nixon Turn-around: America's New Foreign Policy in the Post-Liberal Era* (1973); Stephen Graubard, *Kissinger: Portrait of a Mind* (1973); Robert T. Hartmann, *Palace Politics: An Inside Account of the Ford Years* (1980); Seymour Hersh, *The Price of Power: Kissinger in the Nixon White House* (1983); Leon Jaworski, *The Right and the Power: The Prosecution of Watergate* (1976); J. Anthony Lukas, *Nightmare: The Underside of the Nixon Years* (1976); Richard Nixon, *RN: The Memoirs of Richard Nixon*, 2 vols. (1978); Thomas Powers, *The Man Who Kept the Secrets: Richard Helms & the CIA* (1979); William Safire, *Before the Fall: An Inside View of the Pre-Watergate White House* (1975); Jonathan Schell, *The Time of Illusion* (1975); Arthur M. Schlesinger, Jr., *The Imperial Presidency* (1973); William Shawcross, *Sideshow: Kissinger, Nixon, and the Destruction of Cambodia*, rev. ed. (1987); Edward R. F. Sheehan, *The Arabs, Israelis, and Kissinger* (1976); John Sirica, *To Set the Record Straight: The Break-in, the Tapes, the Conspirators, the Pardon* (1979); Theodore H. White, *Breach of Faith: The Fall of Richard Nixon* (1975).

BIOGRAPHIES

Fawn Brodie, *Richard Nixon* (1981); David Burner, *John F. Kennedy and a New Generation* (1988); Robert Caro, *The Years of Lyndon Johnson: The Path to Power* (1982), and *Means of Ascent* (1990); Warren Cohen, *Dean Rusk* (1980); Paul K. Conkin, *Big Daddy from the Pedernales: Lyndon Baines Johnson* (1986); Ronnie Dugger, *The Politician: The Life and Times of Lyndon Johnson* (1982); Henry Fairlie, *The Kennedy Promise: The Politics of Expectation* (1973); Eric Goldman, *The Tragedy of Lyndon Johnson* (1969); Doris Kearns, *Lyndon Johnson and the American Dream* (1976); Bruce Mazlish, *In Search of Nixon* (1972); Jack Newfield, *Robert Kennedy* (1969); Herbert S. Parmet, *Jack: The Struggles of John F. Kennedy* (1980), and *JFK: The Presidency of John F. Kennedy* (1983); Thomas C. Reeves, *A Question of Character: A Life of John F. Kennedy* (1991); Arthur Schlesinger, Jr., *A Thousand Days: John F. Kennedy in the White House* (1965); Winthrop Yinger, *Cesar Chavez* (1975).

The Struggle for a Just Society

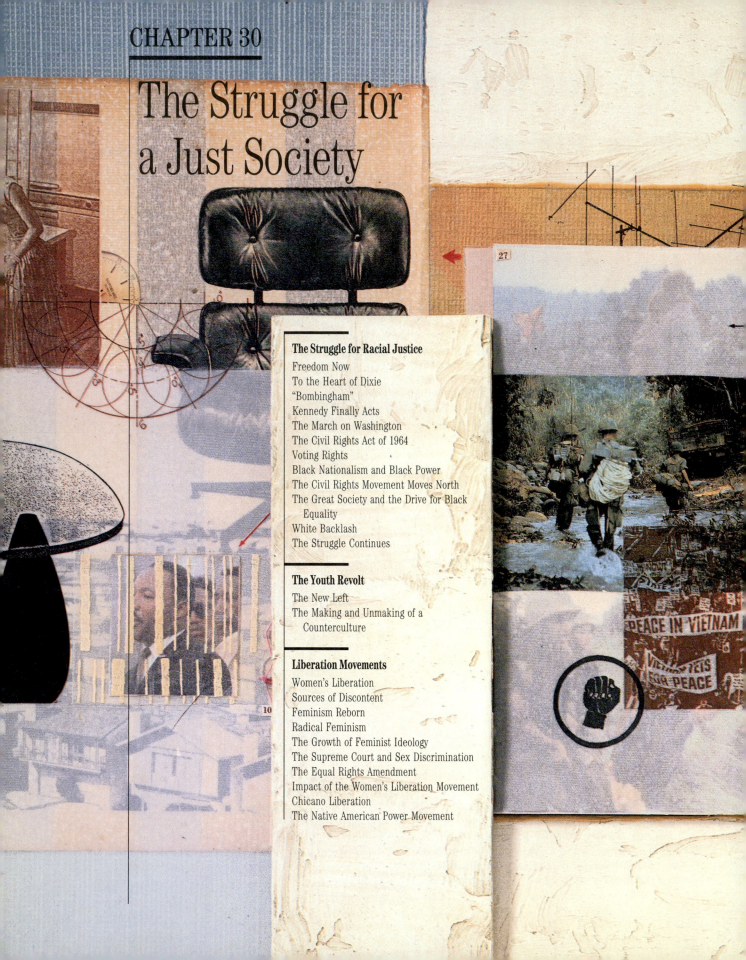

He has been called the nation's nag. He denounced soft drinks for containing excessive amounts of sugar (more than nine teaspoons a can). He warned Americans about the health hazards of red dyes used as food colorings and of nitrates used as preservatives in hot dogs. He even denounced high heels: "It is part of the whole tyranny of fashion, where women will inflict pain on themselves . . . for what, to please men." His name is Ralph Nader and since the mid-1960s he has been the nation's leading consumer advocate.

An extraordinarily frugal and committed crusader on behalf of the nation's consumers, Nader lived for years in an $80-a-month rooming house on about $15,000 a year. He eats in cheap restaurants, has never owned a car, has almost no social life, avoids all junk food, and dresses plainly. In 1983 he was still wearing shoes he had bought while he was in the army in 1959.

His parents came to the United States from Lebanon and settled in Winsted, Connecticut, where they ran a restaurant. Nader credits his parents with instilling the sense of justice and civic duty that has inspired his career.

He was born on February 27, 1934, and speaks at least five foreign languages, including Arabic, Chinese, Portuguese, Spanish, and Russian. He received his bachelor's degree from Princeton (he once wore a bathrobe to class to protest conformity in dress) and earned a law degree at Harvard. At law school, he found his initial cause: automobile safety. After learning that auto accidents were the fourth leading cause of death (behind heart disease, cancer, and strokes), he launched a study of auto injury cases. His research convinced him that the law placed too much emphasis on driver mistakes and not enough on the unsafe design of cars.

In 1963, Nader hitchhiked from Hartford, Connecticut, where he had practiced law, to Washington, D.C., to devote his life to consumer protection. In 1965, he published a best-seller, entitled *Unsafe at Any Speed*, which charged that automakers stressed styling, comfort, speed, power, and a desire to cut costs at the expense of safety. The book sold 60,000 copies in hardcover and 400,000 copies in paperback.

Nader gained public celebrity when the General Motors Corporation hired a detective to investigate his politics, religion, and sex life. General Motors's chairman was forced to apologize for this invasion of privacy before a Senate subcommittee, and eventually paid Nader a $425,000 settlement. Nader used the money to establish more than two dozen public interest groups. The people who work for these groups are known as "Nader's Raiders."

During the 1960s and 1970s, Nader was the driving force behind the passage of more than two dozen landmark consumer protection laws, including the National Traffic and Motor Vehicle Safety Act (which set up a federal agency to establish auto-safety standards and order recalls of cars that failed to meet them), the Occupational Safety and Health Act (which established another agency to set standards for on-the-job safety), the Consumer Products Safety Act, and the Freedom of Information Act (which allows citizens to request and see government records). His efforts have been instrumental in attaining job protection for whistleblowers (employees who expose corrupt or abusive business practices), federal financing of presidential elections, and the creation of the Environmental Protection Agency. Few Americans have ever compiled such a long and impressive list of legislative accomplishment.

But his ultimate goal was not simply to protect consumers from shoddy or dangerous products. It was to reinvigorate the nation's ideal of democracy by encouraging active grass-roots citizen participation in politics. The best answer to society's problems, he believed, was for ordinary citizens to campaign for safer consumer products, better schools, a cleaner environment, and safer workplaces.

During the late 1970s and 1980s, his influence seemed to wane. In 1978, Congress defeated his proposal for a Consumer Protection Agency. Critics dismissed him as a "scold." Said *Newsweek* magazine: "An optimistic society wearies of his endless discontents." In a decade of deregulation, Nader's call for greater regulations seemed out of step with the beat of the times.

As the 1980s ended and the 1990s began, however, it was clear that Nader remained a ma-

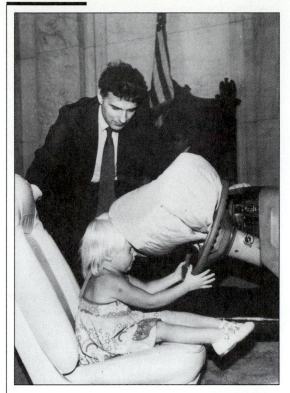

Ralph Nader is the best-known advocate of consumer protection laws in the United States. His group of attorneys, nicknamed "Nader's Raiders," have investigated such wide-ranging problems as automobile safety, the rights of the handicapped, tax reform, the environment, and public health. Here, Nader looks on during a demonstration showing the operation of an automobile air bag safety restraint.

jor force in American politics. He played a central role in passing a California initiative that rolled back the cost of auto insurance. He led a bitter fight against a proposed 51 percent congressional pay raise. And his long campaign for auto safety achieved an important breakthrough when the major automobile manufacturers agreed to install air bags in most of their cars.

Ralph Nader illustrates in vivid terms the difference that one person's life can make. His life also epitomizes the idealism and activism of the 1960s—a decade when hundreds of thousands of ordinary Americans gave new life to the nation's democratic ideals by pressing for racial justice, peace, and improvements in the quality of American life. Black Americans used sit-ins, freedom rides, and protest marches to fight segregation, poverty, and unemployment. Feminists demanded equal employment opportunities and an end to sexual discrimination. Mexican-Americans protested discrimination in voting, education, and employment. Native Americans demanded that the government recognize their land rights and the right of tribes to govern themselves.

Although consumerists, environmentalists, civil rights workers, feminists, and other grassroots activists seemed to fade from public view during the 1980s, they—like Ralph Nader—never abandoned their causes and today remain a powerful force in American life. Indeed, the success of their very efforts has led to a conservative grass-roots reaction, one in which equally committed Americans have denounced busing, affirmative action, quotas, and abortion.

THE STRUGGLE FOR RACIAL JUSTICE

For black Americans in 1960 the statistics were grim. Their average life span in 1960 was seven years less than white Americans'. Their children had only half the chance of completing high school, only a third the chance of completing college, and a third the chance of entering a profession when they grew up. On average, black Americans earned half as much as white Americans and were twice as likely to be unemployed.

Despite a string of court victories during the late 1950s, many black Americans were still second-class citizens. Six years after the landmark *Brown* v. *Board of Education* decision, just 49 southern school districts had desegregated and less than 1.17 percent of black schoolchildren in the 11 states of the old Confederacy attended public school with white classmates. Less than a quarter of the South's voting age black population could vote, and in certain southern counties blacks could not vote, serve on grand juries and trial juries, or frequent all-white beaches, restaurants, barber shops, hotels, and apartments.

TABLE 30.1

High School Graduates
(Percentage of Population Age 25–29)

	1960	1966	1970
Blacks			
Male	36	49	54
Female	41	47	58
Whites			
Male	63	73	79
Female	65	79	76

In the North, too, black Americans suffered humiliation, insult, embarrassment, and discrimination. Many neighborhoods, businesses, and unions almost totally excluded blacks. Just as black unemployment had increased in the South with the mechanization of cotton production, so too in northern cities black unemployment soared as labor-saving technology eliminated many semiskilled and unskilled jobs that historically provided many blacks with work. Black families experienced severe strain; the proportion of black families headed by women jumped from 8 percent in 1950 to 21 percent in 1960. "If you're white, you're right," a black folk saying went; "if you're brown stick around; if you're black, stay back."

During the 1960s, however, a growing hunger for full equality arose among black Americans. The Rev. Dr. Martin Luther King, Jr., gave voice to the new mood: "We're through with tokenism and gradualism and see-how-far-you've-comeism. We're through with we've-done-more-for-your-people-than-anyone-else-ism. We can't wait any longer. Now is the time."

TABLE 30.2

Income Distribution 1960, 1969 (Percentage)

	Blacks and Other Nonwhites		Whites	
	1960	1969	1960	1969
Under $3000	38	20	14	~8
$3000–4999	22	19	14	10
$5000–6999	16	17	19	12
$7000–9999	14	20	26	22
$10,000 and over	~9	24	27	49

Freedom Now

"Now is the time." It became the credo and rallying cry for a generation. On Monday, February 1, 1960, four black freshmen at North Carolina Agricultural and Technical College—Ezell Blair, Jr., Franklin McClain, Joseph McNeill, and David Richmond—walked into the F.W. Woolworth store in Greensboro, North Carolina, and sat down at the lunch counter. They asked for a cup of coffee. A waitress told them that she would only serve them if they stood.

Instead of walking away, the four college freshmen stayed in their seats until the lunch counter closed—giving birth to the "sit-in." The next morning, the 4 college students reappeared at Woolworth's, accompanied by 25 fellow students. On Wednesday, student protests filled 63 of the lunch counter's 66 seats. By the end of the week protesters filled Woolworth's and other lunch counters in town. Now was their time, and they refused to end their nonviolent protest against inequality. Six months later, white city officials granted blacks the right to be served in a restaurant.

Although the student protesters ascribed to King's doctrine of nonviolence, their opponents did not. One black student described a confrontation with white youths at the lunch counter: "Curiously, there were no police inside the store when the white teenagers and others stood in the aisles insulting us, blowing smoke in our faces, grinding out cigarette butts on our backs and finally pulling us off our stools and beating us. Those of us pulled off our seats tried to regain them as soon as possible, but none of us fought back in anger." When the police finally arrived, they arrested black protesters, not the white tormenters.

By the end of February, lunch counter sit-ins had spread through 30 cities in 7 southern states. In Charlotte, North Carolina, a storekeeper unscrewed the seats from his lunch counter. Other stores roped off seats so that every customer had to stand. Alabama, Georgia, Mississippi, and Virginia, hastily passed anti-trespassing laws to stem the outbreak of sit-ins. Despite these efforts, the nonviolent student protests spread across the South. Students attacked segregated libraries, lunch counters, and other "public" facilities.

In April, 142 student sit-in leaders from 11 states met in Raleigh, North Carolina, and voted to set up a new group to coordinate the sit-ins, the Student Nonviolent Coordinating Committee (SNCC). The Rev. Dr. Martin Luther King, Jr., told the students that their willingness to go to jail would "be the thing to awaken the dozing conscience of many of our white brothers." The president of Fisk University echoed King's judgment: "This is no student panty raid. It is a dedicated universal effort, and it has cemented the Negro community as it has never been cemented before."

In the summer of 1960, sit-ins gave way to "wade-ins" at segregated public beaches. In Atlanta, Charlotte, Greensboro, and Nashville, black students lined up at white-only box offices of segregated movie theaters. Other students staged pray-ins (at all-white churches), study-ins (at segregated libraries), and apply-ins (at all-white businesses).

By the end of 1960, 70,000 people had taken part in sit-ins in over 100 cities in 20 states. Police arrested and jailed more than 3600 protesters, and authorities expelled 187 students from college because of their activities. Nevertheless, the new tactic worked. On March 21, 1960, lunch counters in San Antonio, Texas, were integrated. By August 1, lunch counters in 15 states had been integrated. By the end of the year, protesters had succeeded in integrating eating establishments in 108 cities.

The Greensboro sit-in initiated a new, activist phase in black America's struggle for equal rights. Fed up with the slow, legalistic approach that characterized the civil rights movement in the past, southern black college students began to attack segregation directly. Instead of relying on court decisions or federal intervention to bring equal rights, students used nonviolent direct action to win civil rights for black Americans.

In the upper South, federal court orders and student sit-ins successfully desegregated lunch counters, theaters, hotels, public parks, churches, libraries, and beaches. But in three states—Alabama, Mississippi, and South Carolina—segregation in restaurants, hotels, and bus, train, and airplane terminals remained intact. In those states, young civil rights activists launched new assaults against segregation.

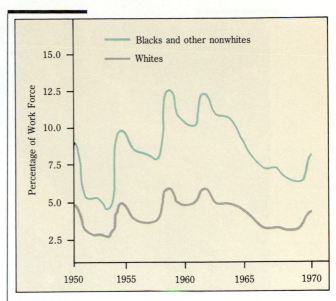

Figure 30.1
Unemployment, 1950–1970

To the Heart of Dixie

In early May 1961 13 men and women, black and white, set out from Washington, D.C., on two buses. They called themselves "freedom riders," and they wanted to demonstrate that despite a federal ban on segregated travel on interstate buses, segregation prevailed throughout much of the South. The freedom riders' trip was sponsored by the Congress of Racial Equality (CORE), a civil rights group dedicated to breaking down racial barriers through nonviolent protest. Inspired by the nonviolent, direct action ideals incorporated in the philosophy of Indian nationalist Mahatma Gandhi, the freedom riders were willing to endure jail and suffer beatings to achieve integration. "We can take anything the white man can dish out," said one black freedom rider, "but we want our rights . . . and we want them now."

In Virginia and North Carolina, the freedom riders met little trouble. Black freedom riders were able to use white restrooms and sit at white lunch counters. But in Winnsboro, South Carolina, police arrested two black freedom riders, and outside Anniston, Alabama, a white hurled a bomb through one of the bus's windows, setting the vehicle on fire. Waiting white

Lunch counter sit-ins in 1960 sparked an advance in the crusade against southern segregation. Such passive resistance tactics proved very effective.

thugs beat the freedom riders as they tried to escape the smoke and flames. Eight other whites boarded the second bus and assaulted the freedom riders before police restrained the attackers.

In Birmingham, Alabama, another mob attacked the second bus with blackjacks and lengths of pipe. In Montgomery, a club-swinging mob of 100 whites attacked the freedom riders; and a group of white youths poured an inflammable liquid on one black man and ignited his clothing. Local police arrived ten minutes later, state police an hour later. Explained Montgomery's police commissioner: "We have no intention of standing police guard for a bunch of troublemakers coming into our city."

In Washington, President Kennedy was appalled by the violence. He hastily deputized 400 federal marshals and Treasury agents and flew them to Alabama to protect the freedom riders' rights. The president publicly called for a "cooling-off period," but conflict continued. When freedom riders arrived in Jackson, Mississippi, 27 were arrested for entering a "white-only" washroom and were sentenced to 60 days on the state prison farm.

The threat of racial violence in the South led the Kennedy administration to pressure the Interstate Commerce Commission to desegregate air, bus, and train terminals. In more than 300 southern terminals, signs saying "white" and "colored" were taken down from waiting room entrances and lavatory doors.

Civil rights activists' next major aim was to open state universities to black students. Many southern states opened their universities to black students without incident. Other states were stiff-backed in their opposition to integration. The depth of hostility to integration was apparent in an incident that took place in February, 1956. A young woman named Autherine Lucy became the first black student ever admitted to the University of Alabama. A mob of 1000 greeted the young woman with chant, "Keep 'Bama White!" Two days later, rioting students threw stones and eggs at the car she was riding to class. Lucy decided to withdraw from school, and for the next seven years no black students attended the University of Alabama.

A major breakthrough occurred in September, 1962, when a federal court ordered the state of Mississippi to admit James Meredith—

a nine-year veteran of the air force—to the University of Mississippi in Oxford. Ross Barnett, the state's governor, promised on statewide television that he would "not surrender to the evil and illegal forces of tyranny" and would go to jail rather than permit Meredith to register for classes. Barnett flew into Oxford, named himself special registrar of the university, and ordered the arrest of federal officials who tried to enforce the court order.

James Meredith refused to back down. A "man with a mission and a nervous stomach," Meredith was determined to get a higher education. "I want to go to the university," he said. "This is the life I want. Just to live and breathe—that isn't life to me. There's got to be something more." Meredith arrived at the Ole Miss campus in the company of police officers, federal marshals, and lawyers. Angry white students waited, chanting, "Two, four, six, eight—we don't want to integrate."

Four times James Meredith tried unsuccessfully to register at Ole Miss. He finally succeeded on the fifth try, escorted by several hundred federal marshals. The ensuing riot left 2 people dead and 375 injured, including 166 marshals. Ultimately, President Kennedy sent 16,000 troops to put down the violence.

"Bombingham"

By the end of 1961, protests against segregation, job discrimination, and police brutality had erupted from Albany and Atlanta, Georgia, to Jackson, Mississippi; from Nashville, Tennessee, to Birmingham, Alabama. Staunch segregationists responded by vowing to defend segregation. The symbol of unyielding resistance to integration was George C. Wallace, a former state judge and a onetime state Golden Gloves featherweight boxing champion, who won the Alabama governorship on an extreme segregationist platform. Promising that he would refuse to obey "any order to mix races in our schools," Wallace offered to "stand in the schoolhouse door" and if need be go to jail before permitting integration. At his inauguration in January 1963, Wallace declared: "I draw the line in the dust and toss the gauntlet before the feet of tyranny, and I say segregation now, segregation tomorrow, segregation forever."

It was in Birmingham, Alabama, that civil rights activists faced the most determined resistance. A sprawling steel town of 340,000 known as the "Pittsburgh of the South," Birmingham had a long history of racial acrimony. In open defiance of Supreme Court rulings, Birmingham had closed its 38 public playgrounds, 8 swimming pools, and 4 golf courses rather than integrate them. Calling Birmingham "the most thoroughly segregated city in the United States," the Rev. Dr. Martin Luther King, Jr., announced in early 1963 that he would lead demonstrations in the city until "Pharaoh lets God's people go." King and his followers demanded fair hiring practices, an end to segregation, and amnesty for previously arrested civil rights demonstrators.

Day after day, well-dressed and carefully groomed men, women, and children marched against segregation—only to be jailed for demonstrating without a permit. On April 12 King himself was arrested—and while in jail wrote a scathing attack on those who asked black Americans to wait patiently for equal rights. A group of white clergymen had publicly criticized King for staging "unwise and untimely" demonstrations. King wrote out his reply on pieces of toilet paper and newspaper margins. "I am convinced," King wrote in his "Letter from Birmingham Jail," "that if your white brothers dismiss us as 'rabble rousers' and 'outside agitators'—those of us who are working through the channels of nonviolent direct action—and refuse to support our nonviolent efforts, millions of Negroes, out of frustration and despair, will seek solace and security in black nationalist ideologies, a development that will lead inevitably to a frightening racial nightmare."

For two weeks, all was quiet, but in early May demonstrations resumed with renewed vigor. On May 2 and again on May 3, more than a thousand of Birmingham's black children marched for equal rights. In response, Birmingham's police chief, Theophilus Eugene ("Bull") Connor, unleashed police dogs on the children and sprayed them with fire hoses with 700 pounds of pressure. Watching the naked brutality on television, millions of Americans, white and black, were shocked by the face of segregation. CBS commentator Eric Sevareid later wrote, "A newspaper or a television picture of a snarling police dog set upon a human being is recorded in the permanent photoelectric file of every human brain."

Tension mounted as police arrested 2543 blacks and whites between May 2, 1963 and May 7, 1963. Under intense pressure, the Birmingham Chamber of Commerce reached an agreement on May 9 with black leaders to desegregate public facilities in 90 days, hire blacks as clerks and salespersons in 60 days, and release demonstrators without bail in return for an end to the protests.

King's goal was nonviolent social change—but the short-term result of protest was violence and confrontation. On May 11, white extremists firebombed an integrated motel. That same night, a bomb destroyed the home of King's brother. Shooting incidents and racial confrontations quickly spread across the South. Over the next 10 weeks there were more than 750 riots in 186 cities and towns. In June, an assassin, armed with a Springfield rifle, ambushed

37-year-old Medgar Evers, the NAACP field representative in Mississippi, and shot him in the back. "I'm not afraid of dying," Evers had once said. "It might do some good."

In September, an explosion destroyed Birmingham's Sixteenth Street Baptist Church, killing 4 black girls and injuring 14 others. Segregationists had planted 10 to 15 sticks of dynamite under the steps of the 50-year-old church building. That same day, a 16-year-old black Birmingham youth was shot from behind by a police shotgun, and a 13-year-old boy was shot while riding his bicycle. All told, 10 people died during racial protests in 1963, 35 black homes and churches were firebombed, and 20,000 people were arrested during civil rights protests.

Kennedy Finally Acts

The eruption of violence in Birmingham and elsewhere finally forced the Kennedy administration to introduce legislation to guarantee black civil rights. Twice before, in 1957 and 1960, the federal government had adopted weak civil rights acts designed to provide federal protection for black voting rights. Now Kennedy responded to the racial violence by proposing a new stronger civil rights bill that required the desegregation of public facilities, outlawed discrimination in employment and voting, and allowed the attorney general to initiate school desegregation suits.

Kennedy's record on civil rights inspired little confidence. He had voted against the 1957 Civil Rights Act, and in the 1960 campaign many black leaders, including the Rev. Martin Luther King, Sr., and Jackie Robinson backed Richard Nixon. During the 1960 campaign, however, Kennedy worked hard to court the black vote. He promised new civil rights legislation and declared that as president he would end housing discrimination with a "stroke of the pen." A few weeks before the 1960 election, Kennedy broadened his black support by helping to secure the release of the Rev. Dr. Martin Luther King, Jr., from an Atlanta jail, where he had been imprisoned for leading an antisegregation demonstration.

Once in office, however, Kennedy moved slowly on civil rights issues both because he

Police used dogs, high-pressure water hoses, clubs, and electric cattle prods to break up the nonviolent civil rights demonstration in Birmingham, Alabama, in May 1963. Scenes such as this one, broadcast on television to millions of viewers, aroused public indignation and sympathy for the civil rights movement.

(Text continues on p. 1016)

PRIMARY SOURCE ESSAY

MARTIN LUTHER KING, JR., AND THE "LETTER FROM BIRMINGHAM CITY JAIL"

During the Montgomery bus boycott, Martin Luther King, Jr. (1929–1968) first pricked the conscience of white America. He was unjustly arrested and walked out of jail to solemnly speak of the power of love. His house was bombed, and he calmed the angry crowd and then faced the cameras to quietly assure reporters that violence could never cause him to leave his path of nonviolence. King's dignity and dedication impressed many people, but he still had not become the larger-than-life leader of later years. He was only 26 years old. He had not organized the boycott and had only reluctantly agreed to assume its leadership. After the Montgomery success, King received many invitations to speak and was invited to attend two conferences of southern ministers in 1957. As a result of those meetings the Southern Christian Leadership Conference (SCLC) was organized the following year in Atlanta with King as its president. During this time, King was being legally harassed in both Alabama and Georgia. Especially after the student-led sit-in movement began in 1960, he and the SCLC mainly responded to calls for help from campaigns already underway. He joined movements in Atlanta and Albany, Georgia. He was jailed in both cities, but neither campaign met with the dramatic success of Montgomery. By 1963, King was seeking a site for a victory by nonviolent direct action.

The five-week-long civil rights demonstrations in Birmingham, Alabama, in the spring of 1963, which included a boycott of all white-owned stores in that city, culminated with the arrest of Dr. Martin Luther King, Jr., and other protest leaders. Here, the police force Dr. King, wearing old clothes to dramatize the store boycott, into the police paddy wagon.

LETTER FROM BIRMINGHAM CITY JAIL

We know through painful experience that freedom is never voluntarily given by the oppressor; it must be demanded by the oppressed. Frankly I have never yet engaged in a direct action movement that was "well timed," according to the timetable of those who have not suffered unduly from the disease of segregation. For years now I have heard the word "Wait!" It rings in the ear of every Negro with a piercing familiarity. This "wait" has almost always meant "never." It has been a tranquilizing Thalidomide, relieving the emotional stress for a moment, only to give birth to an ill-formed infant of frustration. We must come to see with the distinguished jurist of yesterday that "justice too long delayed is justice denied." We have waited for more than 340 years for our constitutional and God-given rights. The nations of Asia and Africa are moving with jetlike speed toward the goal of political independence, and we still creep at horse and buggy pace toward the gaining of a cup of coffee at a lunch counter.

I guess it is easy for those who have never felt the stinging darts of segregation to say wait. But when you have seen vicious mobs lynch your mothers and fathers at will and drown your sisters and

Dr. King's message to white Alabama clergymen has been called 'a modern classic'

MY dear Fellow Clergymen,

While confined here in the Birmingham City Jail, I came across your recent statement calling our present activities "unwise and untimely." . . . since I feel that you are men of genuine goodwill and your criticisms are sincerely set forth, I would like to answer your statement in what I hope will be patient and reasonable terms.

I think I should give the reason for my being in Birmingham, since you have been influenced by the argument of "outsiders coming in." . . . I am here, along with several members of my staff, because we were invited here. I am here because I have basic organizational ties here.

Beyond this, I am in Birmingham because injustice is here. Just as the eighth century prophets left their little villages and carried their "thus saith the Lord" far beyond the boundaries of their home towns; and just as the Apostle Paul left his little village of Tarsus and carried the gospel of Jesus Christ to practically every hamlet and city of the Graeco-Roman world, I, too, am compelled to carry the gospel of freedom beyond my particular home town. Like Paul, I must constantly respond to the Macedonian call for aid. . . .

You deplore the demonstrations that are presently taking place in Birmingham. But I am sorry that your statement did not express a similar concern for the conditions that brought the demonstrations into being. . . . I would not hesitate to say that it is unfortunate that so-called demonstrations are taking place in Birmingham at this time, but I would say in more emphatic terms that it is even more unfortunate that the white power structure of this city left the Negro community with no other alternative.

In any nonviolent campaign there are four basic steps: 1) Collection of the facts to determine whether injustices are alive. 2) Negotiation. 3) Self-purification and 4) Direct Action. We have gone through all of these steps in Birmingham. There can be no gainsaying of the fact that racial injustice engulfs this community. Birmingham is probably the most thoroughly segregated city in the United States. Its ugly record of police brutality is known in every section of this country. Its unjust treatment of Negroes in the courts is a notorious reality. There have been more unsolved bombings of Negro homes and churches in Birmingham than any city in this nation. These are the hard, brutal and unbelievable facts. On the basis of these conditions Negro leaders sought to negotiate with the city fathers. But the political leaders consistently refused to engage in good faith negotiation.

Then came the opportunity last September to talk with some of the leaders of the economic community. In these negotiating sessions certain promises were made by the merchants—such as the promise to remove the humiliating racial signs from the stores. On the basis of these promises Rev. Shuttlesworth and the leaders of the Alabama Christian Movement for Human Rights agreed to call a moratorium on any type of demonstrations. As the weeks and months unfolded we realized that we were the victims of a broken promise. The signs remained. Like so many experiences of the past we were confronted with blasted hopes, and the dark shadow of a deep disappointment settled upon us. So we had no alternative except that of preparing for direct action, whereby we would present our very bodies as a means of laying our case before the conscience of the local and national community. We were not unmindful of the difficulties involved. So we

The "Letter from Birmingham City Jail," published in the August 1963 issue of *Ebony* magazine, stands as an eloquent statement of Dr. King's vision of racial equality and of his philosophy of nonviolent civil disobedience. This photograph is of the first page of the letter as it appeared in *Ebony*.

brothers at whim; when you have seen hate-filled policemen curse, kick, brutalize, and even kill your black brothers and sisters with impunity; when you see the vast majority of your 20 million Negro brothers smothering in an airtight cage of poverty in the midst of an affluent society; when you suddenly find your tongue twisted and your speech stammering as you seek to explain to your six-year-old daughter why she can't go to the public amusement park that has just been advertised on television, and see the tears welling up in her little eyes when she is told that Funtown is closed to colored children, and see the depressing clouds of inferiority begin to form in her little mental sky, and see her begin to distort her little personality by unconsciously developing a bitterness toward white people; when you have to concoct an answer for a five-year-old son who is asking in agonizing pathos: ''Daddy, why do white people treat colored people so mean?''; when you take a cross country drive and find it necessary to sleep night after night in the uncomfortable corners of your automobile because no motel will accept you; when you are humiliated day in and day out by nagging signs reading ''white'' men and ''colored''; when your first name becomes ''nigger'' and your middle name becomes ''boy'' (however old you are) and your last name becomes ''John,'' and when your wife and mother are never given the respected title of ''Mrs.''; when you are harried by day and haunted by night by the fact that you are a Negro, living constantly at tip-toe stance, never quite knowing what to expect next, and plagued with inner fears and outer resentments; when you are forever fighting a degenerating sense of ''nobodiness''—then you will understand why we find it difficult to wait. There comes a time when the cup of endurance runs over, and men are no longer willing to be plunged into an abyss of injustice where they experience the bleakness of corroding despair. I hope, sirs, you can understand our legitimate and unavoidable impatience.

Martin Luther King, Jr., came to Birmingham in 1963 at the request of the Reverend Fred Shuttlesworth. This time, however, King was to be involved in the movement from the start. He and his staff met with Birmingham leaders to painstakingly plan every detail before launching sit-ins and demonstrations. Organization was thorough and successful. However, Police Commissioner Eugene "Bull" Connor employed tactics to prevent the movement from gaining national attention, thereby limiting its effectiveness. King decided he must once again go to jail and was arrested on April 12. While there he received a newspaper containing a statement by eight white Alabama clergymen critical of King and the Birmingham campaign. They argued that King was an "outsider" and that the movement was ill-timed, lawless, extremist, and designed to provoke violence when negotiation was a better path.

In his jail cell King drafted a reply on the margins of the newspaper. He continued to write on scraps of paper provided by a black trustee until he finally got a pad of paper from his lawyers. Point by point he answered his fellow clergymen's charges. The result of his efforts was called the "Letter from Birmingham City Jail." It was later polished and reprinted in King's *Why We Can't Wait*. Like his "I Have a Dream" speech, the letter was an eloquent statement of his vision and was widely quoted.

Some of the letter answered criticisms specific to Birmingham. Most of it, however, explained the aspirations of African Americans and the doctrines of nonviolence and civil disobedience. Few of King's ideas were original. Because the letter was addressed to the clergy, he cited the Bible and theologians to make his points. The document was also intended for the American public, so King also drew examples from U.S. history. He noted the Boston Tea Party as an act of civil disobedience. To answer charges of extremism he listed others similarly accused: Jesus, Saint Paul, Martin Luther, John Bunyan, Abraham Lincoln, and Thomas Jefferson. In other words, he utilized widely believed and cherished ideals to define his movement. He sought to make whites understand and feel the frustrations of African Americans by recounting everyday experiences with which they could relate.

King had his human weaknesses. He did not single-handedly initiate, organize, or lead the civil rights movement. The real unsung heroes are probably the countless men and women in cities and small towns all over the South who risked everything to desegregate places like Winona, Mississippi. Nevertheless, King was the most effective propagandist of the black cause. He served extremely well in the role of chief interpreter and translator of the movement to white America. It was a crucial role for which he has been justly honored.

Arrested during the Birmingham protests, Dr. King was held in the city jail for eight days, the first 24 hours of which were in solitary confinement.

feared alienating white southern Democrats and because he had no real commitment to or passion for the cause. In his inaugural address and first State of the Union Address, he barely mentioned civil rights. And although Kennedy's administration filed 28 suits to protect black voting rights (compared to 10 suits filed during the Eisenhower years), it was not until November, 1963, that Kennedy took steps to end housing discrimination with a "stroke of a pen"—after he had received hundreds of pens from frustrated civil rights leaders.

Violence in Birmingham finally forced Kennedy to act. A hundred years after the Emancipation Proclamation, Kennedy declared, American blacks are still not "fully free. They are not yet freed from the bonds of injustice, they are not yet freed from social and economic oppression." As a result, "fires of frustration and discord are burning in every city, North and South." New laws against discrimination "are needed at every level."

The March on Washington

The violence that erupted in Birmingham and elsewhere in 1961 and 1962 alarmed many veteran civil rights leaders. In December, 1962, two veteran fighters for civil rights—A. Philip Randolph and Bayard Rustin—met at the office of the Brotherhood of Sleeping Car Porters in Harlem. Both men were pacifists, eager to rededicate the civil rights movement to the principle of nonviolence. Both men wanted to press Kennedy and Congress to enact a civil rights bill, school desegregation, federal job training programs, and a ban on job discrimination. Thirty-two years before, Randolph had threatened to lead a march on Washington unless the federal government ended job discrimination against black workers in war industries. Now Rustin revived the idea of a massive march for civil rights and jobs.

On August 28, 1963, over 200,000 people gathered around the Washington Monument and marched eight-tenths of a mile to the Lincoln Memorial. As they walked, the marchers carried placards reading: "Effective Civil Rights Laws—Now! Integrated Schools—Now! Decent Housing—Now!" and sang the civil rights an-

them, "We Shall Overcome." At the Lincoln Memorial, folk singers Joan Baez, Bob Dylan, and Peter, Paul, and Mary sang spirituals and civil rights songs.

Ten speakers addressed the crowd, but the event's highlight was an address by the Rev. Dr. Martin Luther King, Jr. "It would be fatal," King warned, "for the nation to overlook the urgency of the moment and to underestimate the determination of the Negro. This sweltering summer of the Negro's legitimate discontent will not pass until there is an invigorating autumn of freedom and equality." King finished his prepared text and launched into his legendary closing words. "I have a dream," he declared, "that one day on the red hills of Georgia the sons of former slaves and the sons of former slaveowners will be able to sit down together at the table of brotherhood. . . . I have a dream that one day even the state of Mississippi, a state sweltering with people's injustices, sweltering with the heat of oppression, will be transformed into an oasis of freedom and justice." As his audience roared their approval, King continued to describe his dream, a dream of a color-blind nation united by a belief in equality achieved through nonviolent methods: "I have a dream that one day this nation will rise up and live out the true meaning of its creed: 'We hold these truths to be self-evident; that all men are created equal.' "

The Civil Rights Act of 1964

For seven months, debate raged in the halls of Congress. In a futile effort to delay the Civil Rights Bill's passage, opponents proposed over 500 amendments and staged a protracted filibuster in the Senate. On July 2, 1964—a little over a year after President Kennedy had sent it to Congress—the Civil Rights Act was enacted into law. It had been skillfully pushed through Congress by President Lyndon Johnson, who took office after Kennedy was assassinated in November 1963. As finally passed, the act prohibited discrimination in voting, employment, and public facilities such as hotels and restaurants, and it established the Equal Employment Opportunity Commission to prevent discrimination in employment on the basis of race, religion, or sex. Ironically, the provision barring sex discrimination had been added by opponents of the civil rights act in an attempt to kill the bill.

Although most white Southerners accepted the new federal law without resistance, many violent incidents occurred. Angry whites vented their rage in shootings and beatings. But despite such incidents, the Civil Rights Act was a success. In the first weeks under the 1964 civil rights law segregated restaurants and hotels from Dallas to Charleston and from Memphis to Tallahassee opened their doors to black patrons. Over the next ten years, the Justice Department would bring legal suits against more than 500 school districts charged with racial discrimination and more than 400 suits against hotels, restaurants, taverns, gas stations, and truck stops.

Voting Rights

The 1964 Civil Rights Act prohibited discrimination in employment and public accommodations. But many blacks were denied an equally fundamental constitutional right, the right to vote. The most effective barriers to black voting were state laws requiring prospective voters to read and interpret sections of the state constitution. In Alabama, voters had to provide written answers to a 20-page test on the Constitution and state and local government. Questions included: Where do presidential electors cast ballots for president? Name the rights a person has after he has been indicted by a grand jury?

In an effort to bring the issue of voting rights to national attention, Martin Luther King, Jr., in early 1965 launched a voter registration drive in Selma, Alabama, a city of 29,500 people—14,400 whites, 15,100 blacks. Despite the fact that the federal government had filed a voting rights suit in 1961, Selma's voting rolls were 99 percent white and 1 percent black.

For seven weeks, King led hundreds of Selma's black residents to the county courthouse to register to vote. In the first attempt to register black voters, more than 400 blacks marched to the county courthouse. They were stopped by County Sheriff James Clark, armed with a billy club and a cattle prod, who herded the marchers into a nearby alleyway. In suc-

On August 28, 1963, over 200,000 African-Americans and whites gathered for a day-long rally at the Lincoln Memorial to demand an end to racial discrimination. The highlight of the event was Martin Luther King, Jr.'s inspiring "I Have a Dream" speech.

ceeding weeks, Clark jailed nearly 2000 black demonstrators for contempt of court, juvenile delinquency, and parading without a permit. When King himself was arrested, he could accurately state that "there are more Negroes in jail with me than there are on the voting rolls." After a federal court ordered Clark not to interfere with orderly registration, the sheriff forced black applicants to stand in line for up to five hours before being permitted to take a "literacy" test. Not a single black voter was added to the registration rolls.

The demonstrations spread to nearby Marion, where 50 state troopers and white toughs attacked 400 black demonstrators. During the attack a young black man named Jimmie Lee Jackson was shot in the stomach; he died eight days later. King responded by calling for a march from Selma to the state capitol of Montgomery, 50 miles away.

On Sunday, March 7, 1965, black voting-rights demonstrators prepared to march. "I can't promise you that it won't get you beaten," King told them, ". . . but we must stand up for what is right!" Led by John Lewis, head of the Student Nonviolent Coordinating Committee (SNCC), and Hosea Williams, an official of King's Southern Christian Leadership Conference, the demonstrators, marching double file, headed toward the Edmund Pettus Bridge, across the Alabama River. As they crossed the bridge, 200 state police with tear gas, night sticks, and whips attacked them.

The five day march from Selma to Montgomery finally resumed on March 21, with protection from over 100 federal marshals, 1000 military police, and 1900 federalized Alabama National Guardsmen. The marchers chanted: "Segregation's got to fall . . . you never can jail us all." On March 25, a crowd of 25,000 gathered at the state capitol to celebrate the march's completion. Martin Luther King, Jr., addressed the crowd and called for an end to segregated schools, poverty, and voting discrimination. "I know you are asking today, 'How long will it take?' . . . How long? Not long, because no lie can live forever."

Still, the violence continued. Within hours of the march's end, four Ku Klux Klan members shot and killed a 39-year-old white civil rights volunteer from Detroit named Viola Liuzzo. President Johnson expressed the nation's shock and anger. "Mrs. Liuzzo went to Alabama to serve the struggle for justice," the President said. "She was murdered by the enemies of justice who for decades have used the rope and the gun and the tar and the feather to terrorize their neighbors."

Two measures adopted in 1965 helped safeguard the voting rights of black Americans. On January 23, the states completed ratification of the Twenty-fourth Amendment to the Constitution barring a poll tax in federal elections. At the time, five southern states still had a poll tax. On August 6, President Johnson signed the Voting Rights Act, which prohibited literacy tests and sent federal examiners to seven southern states to register black voters. Within a year, 450,000 southern blacks registered to vote.

Black Nationalism and Black Power

At the same time that such civil rights leaders as the Rev. Dr. Martin Luther King, Jr., fought for racial integration, other black leaders emphasized separatism and identification with Af-

After nearly 2000 blacks were arrested for trying to register to vote in Selma, Alabama, demonstrators (including Martin Luther King, Jr.) began a protest march from Selma to Montgomery.

rica. Black nationalist sentiment was not something new. During the early nineteenth century, black leaders such as Paul Cuffe and Martin Delaney, convinced that blacks could never achieve true equality in the United States, advocated migration overseas. At the turn of the century, Booker T. Washington and his followers emphasized racial solidarity, economic self-sufficiency, and black self-help, and at the end of World War I, millions of black Americans were attracted by Marcus Garvey's call to drop the fight for equality in America and instead "plant the banner of freedom on the great continent of Africa."

One of the most important expressions of the separatist impulse during the 1960s was the rise of the Black Muslims, which attracted 100,000 members. Founded in 1931, in the depths of the depression, the Nation of Islam drew its appeal from among the growing numbers of urban blacks living in poverty.

The Black Muslims elevated racial separatism into a religious doctrine and declared that whites were doomed to destruction. "The white devil's day is over," Black Muslim leader Elijah Muhammad cried. "He was given six thousand years to rule . . . He's already used up most trapping and murdering the black nations by the hundreds of thousands. Now he's worried, worried about the black man getting his revenge." Unless whites acceded to the Muslim demand for a separate territory for themselves, Muhammad said, "Your entire race will be destroyed and removed from this earth by Almighty God. And those black men who are still trying to integrate will inevitably be destroyed along with the whites."

The Black Muslims did more than vent anger and frustration. The organization was also a vehicle of black uplift and self-help. The Black Muslims called upon black Americans to "wake up, clean up, and stand up" in order to achieve true freedom and independence. To root out any behavior that conformed to racist stereotypes, the Muslims forbade eating pork and cornbread, drinking alcohol, and smoking cigarettes. Muslims also emphasized the creation of black businesses.

The most controversial exponent of black nationalism was Malcolm X. The son of a Baptist minister who had been an organizer for Marcus

TABLE 30.3

Black Voter Registration Before and After the Voting Rights Act of 1965

State	1960	1966	Percent Increase
Alabama	66,000	250,000	278.8
Arkansas	73,000	115,000	57.5
Florida	183,000	303,000	65.6
Georgia	180,000	300,000	66.7
Louisiana	159,000	243,000	52.8
Mississippi	22,000	175,000	695.4
North Carolina	210,000	282,000	34.3
South Carolina	58,000	191,000	229.3
Tennessee	185,000	225,000	21.6
Texas	227,000	400,000	76.2
Virginia	100,000	205,000	105.0

U.S. Bureau of the Census, *Statistical Abstract of the United States: 1982–83* (103d edition) Washington, D.C., 1982.

Garvey's United Negro Improvement Association, he was born Malcolm Little in Omaha, Nebraska, and grew up in Lansing, Michigan. A reformed drug addict and criminal, Malcolm X learned about the Black Muslims in a high security prison. After his release from prison in 1952, he adopted the name Malcolm X to replace "the white slave-master name which had been imposed upon my paternal forebears by some blue-eyed devil." He quickly became one of the Black Muslims' most eloquent speakers, denouncing alcohol, tobacco, and extramarital sex.

Condemned by some whites as a demagogue for such statements as "If ballots won't work, bullets will," Malcolm X was a popular speaker on college campuses. He gained widespread public notoriety by attacking the Rev. Dr. Martin Luther King, Jr., as a "chump" and an Uncle Tom, by advocating self-defense against white violence, and by emphasizing black political power.

Malcolm X's main message was that discrimination led many black Americans to despise themselves. "The worst crime the white man has committed," he said, "has been to teach us to hate ourselves." Self-hatred caused black Americans to lose their identity, straighten their hair, and become involved in crime, drug addiction, and alcoholism.

In March 1964 (after he violated an order from Elijah Muhammad and publicly rejoiced at the assassination of President John F. Kennedy), Malcolm X withdrew from Elijah Muhammad's organization and set up his own Organization of Afro-Americans. Less than a year later, his life ended in bloodshed. On February 21, 1965, in front of 400 followers, he was shot and killed, appparently by followers of Black Muslim leader Elijah Muhammad, as he prepared to give a speech in New York City.

Malcolm X, frustrated with moderate civil rights advocates, spoke sharply against racism and called for African-American self-defense against white violence. In 1964, he founded the Organization of Afro-American Unity, which was socialist in its philosophy.

Inspired by Malcolm X's example, young black activists increasingly challenged the traditional leadership of the civil rights movement and its philosophy of nonviolence. Several factors contributed to a new spirit of nationalism and radicalism. Many young blacks lost faith in white liberals and interracial political activity when the 1964 Democratic party presidential convention refused to unseat an all-white delegation from Mississippi. A white backlash against civil rights also contributed to an upsurge of militancy. In 1964 Alabama Governor George Wallace, an avowed segregationist, entered three northern democratic presidential primaries and gained between a third and half of the vote. Between mid-1964 and mid-1965, the Ku Klux Klan made its largest membership gains ever.

The single greatest contributor to the growth of militancy was the violence perpetrated by white racists. One of the most publicized incidents took place in June, 1964, in Philadelphia, Mississippi, and led many young black civil rights workers to lose faith in nonviolence. On June 21, 1964, three civil rights workers—two whites, Andrew Goodman and Michael Schwerner, and one black, James Cha-

ney—disappeared in the murky, snake-infested swamps of eastern Mississippi, where the charred shell of their station wagon was found. Earlier that day, the three had been stopped by police on the outskirts of Philadelphia, on a charge of driving 65 m.p.h. in a 30 m.p.h. zone. Six weeks later, the badly decomposed bodies of the three young men were found buried in a dam six miles southwest of Philadelphia. All three had been beaten, then shot. In December, the sheriff and deputy sheriff of Neshoba County, Mississippi, along with 19 others, were arrested on charges of violating the three men's civil rights, but just six days later the charges were dropped. At the funeral of the three civil rights workers, black leader David Dennis angrily declared: "I'm sick and tired of going to the funerals of black men who have been murdered by white men. . . . I've got vengeance in my heart."

In 1966 two key civil rights organizations—SNCC and CORE (the Congress of Racial Equality)—embraced black nationalism. In May, Stokely Carmichael, who had been born in Trinidad, was elected chairman of SNCC. He proceeded to transform SNCC from an interracial organization committed to nonviolence and integration into an all-black organization committed to "black power." "Integration is irrelevant," declared Carmichael. "Political and economic power is what the black people have to have." Although Carmichael initially denied that "black power" implied racial separatism, he eventually called on blacks to form their own separate political organizations. "To ask Negroes to get in the Democratic party," he declared, "is like asking Jews to join the Nazi party." One SNCC leader, James Forman, demanded that white churches and synagogues pay black Americans $3 billion in "reparations."

In July 1966—one month after James Meredith, the black air force veteran who had integrated the University of Mississippi, was ambushed and shot while marching for voting rights in Mississippi—CORE also endorsed black power and repudiated nonviolence. In 1967, the organization deleted the word "multiracial" from its constitution and the next year, the CORE's national chairman, Roy Innis, announced that the group had become "once and for all . . . a Black Nationalist Organization" committed to "separation" of the races.

Of all the groups advocating racial separatism and black power, the one that received the widest publicity was the Black Panther party. Formed in October 1966, in Oakland, California, the Black Panther party was an armed revolutionary socialist organization advocating self-determination for black ghettoes. "Black men," declared one party member, must unite to overthrow their white "oppressors," becoming "like panthers—smiling, cunning, scientific, striking by night and sparing no one!" The Black Panthers gained public notoriety by entering the gallery of the California State Assembly brandishing guns and by following police to prevent police harrassment and brutality toward blacks.

Separatism and black nationalism attracted no more than a small minority of black Americans. Public opinion polls indicated that only about 15 percent of black Americans identified themselves as separatists and that the overwhelming majority of blacks considered Martin Luther King, Jr., their favored spokesperson. The older civil rights organizations such as the NAACP rejected separatism and black power. To veteran civil rights workers, black power meant abandonment of nonviolence and integration and the embracing, in King's words, of "a nihilistic philosophy." Since blacks comprised just 10 percent of the nation's population, said King, "we can't win violently. We have neither the instruments nor the techniques at our disposal, and it would be totally absurd for us to believe we could do it."

Yet despite their relatively small following, black power advocates exerted a powerful and positive influence upon the civil rights movement. In addition to giving birth to a host of community self-help organizations, supporters of black power spurred the creation of black studies programs in universities and encouraged black Americans to take pride in their racial background and recognize that "black is beautiful." A growing number of black Americans began to wear "Afro" hairstyles and take African or Islamic surnames. Singer James Brown captured the new spirit: "Say it loud—I'm black and I'm proud."

In an effort to maintain support among more militant blacks, civil rights leaders began to address the problems of the black lower classes who lived in the nation's cities. The civil

rights movement, Martin Luther King, Jr., declared, had made only "surface changes" in the lives of black Americans. By the mid-1960s he had begun to move toward the political left. He said it did no good to be allowed to eat in a restaurant if you had no money to pay for a hamburger. King denounced the Vietnam War as "an enemy of the poor," described the United States as "the greatest purveyor of violence in the world today," and predicted that "the bombs that [Americans] are dropping in Vietnam will explode at home in inflation and unemployment." He urged a radical redistribution of wealth and political power in the United States in order to provide medical care, jobs, and education for all of the country's people. And he spoke of the need for a second "March on Washington" by "waves of the nation's poor and dis-

A major achievement of the black power movement was to increase educational opportunities for minorities in universities across the country.

inherited," who would "stay until America responds . . . [with] positive action." The time had come for radical measures "to provide jobs and income for the poor."

The Civil Rights Movement Moves North

On August 11, 1965, five days after President Lyndon Johnson signed the Voting Rights Act, the arrest of a 21-year-old for drunk driving ignited a riot in Watts, a predominantly black section of Los Angeles. The violence lasted five days and resulted in 34 deaths, 3900 arrests, and the destruction of over 744 buildings and 200 businesses in a 20-square-mile area. Rioters smashed windows, hurled bricks and bottles from rooftops, and threw Molotov cocktails into buildings. Looters stripped store shelves of clothing, liquor, groceries, and furniture and burned credit records.

Over the next four summers, more than 150 major urban riots erupted in such cities as Buffalo, Chicago, Cincinnati, Des Moines, Detroit, Milwaukee, Newark, and Washington, D.C. The worst violence occurred during the summer of 1967, when riots occurred in 127 cities. In Newark 26 persons lost their lives, over 1500 were injured, and 1397 were arrested. In Detroit 43 people died, over 2000 were injured, 5000 arrested, 5000 left homeless, and 14 square miles gutted by fire. Damage estimates reached $500 million.

The assassination of Martin Luther King, Jr., in Memphis, Tennessee, on April 4, 1968, while supporting a sanitation workers' strike, touched off the last major wave of rioting. Violence erupted in 168 cities, leaving 46 dead, 3500 injured, and $40 million worth of damage. Altogether, 5117 fires were set, 1928 homes and businesses were wrecked or ransacked, and 23,987 people arrested. In Washington, D.C., fires burned within three blocks of the White House.

In 1968 President Johnson appointed a commission to examine the causes of the race riots of the preceding three summers. Led by Illinois Governor Otto Kerner, the commission attributed racial violence to "white racism" and its heritage of discrimination and exclusion. Joblessness, poverty, a lack of political power, decaying and dilapidated housing, police bru-

tality, and poor schools bred a sense of frustration and rage that had exploded into violence. The commission warned that unless major steps were taken, the United States would inevitably become "two societies, one black, one white— separate and unequal."

Until 1964 most white Northerners regarded race as a peculiarly southern problem that could be solved by extending voting rights to southern blacks and desegregating southern schools, buses, and lunchrooms. After 1964 the nation learned that discrimination and racial prejudice were nationwide problems, that black Americans were demanding not just desegregation in the South but equality in all parts of the country. The nation also learned that resistance to black demands for equal rights was not confined to the Deep South, but existed in the North as well.

Beginning in early 1964 northern blacks pressed for an end to discrimination. On February 3, 1964, 460,000 New York City students boycotted classes, staging a one-day protest against school segregation. A month later, black demonstrators staged a sit-in on New York City's Triborough bridge, blocking traffic. In Cleveland demonstrators chained themselves together at construction sites to protest job discrimination, and a thousand demonstrators in San Francisco staged a sit-in at the Sheraton-Palace Hotel. In all these protests northern blacks were reminding northern whites that racism and discrimination existed *everywhere* in America.

During the 1950s and early 1960s many northern cities had passed new laws and strengthened old ones forbidding discrimination in housing and employment. Nevertheless, prejudice and job discrimination existed in the North as well as in the South. A 1963 Louis Harris public opinion poll found that "whites, North and South, do not want the Negro living next door" and that "the white image of the Negro is . . . an implausible and contradictory caricature, half Stepin Fetchit—lazy, unwashed, shiftless, unambitious, slow-moving—and half Sportin' Life—cunning, lewd, flashy, strong, fearless, immoral, and vicious."

In the North, however, blacks suffered primarily not from de jure (legal) segregation, but from de facto discrimination in housing, schooling, and employment—discrimination that lacked the overt sanction of law. "De facto segregation," wrote James Baldwin, "means that Negroes are segregated but nobody did it." The most obvious example of de facto segregation was the fact that the overwhelming majority of northern black schoolchildren attended predominantly black inner-city schools while most white children attended schools with an overwhelming majority of whites. In 1968—fourteen years after the *Brown* v. *Board of Education* decision—federal courts began to order busing as a way to deal with de facto segregation brought about by housing patterns. In April 1971 in the case of *Swann* v. *Charlotte-Mecklenburg Board of Education*, the Supreme Court upheld "bus transportation as a tool of school desegregation."

Before becoming the first black Supreme Court justice in 1967, Thurgood Marshall presented the legal arguments against school segregation that resulted in the *Brown* v. *Board of Education of Topeka* decision.

The Great Society and the Drive for Black Equality

No American president ever showed a stronger commitment to improving the position of black Americans than Lyndon Baines Johnson, the first Southerner to reside in the White House in half a century. As president he prodded Congress to pass a broad spectrum of civil rights laws, ranging from the Civil Rights Act of 1964 and the Voting Rights Act of 1965 to the 1968 Fair Housing Act barring discrimination in the sale or rental of housing. LBJ also took direct steps to require employers to take "affirmative action" to ensure that black Americans were not discriminated against in employment or promotions. Executive Order 11246, issued in 1965, required government contractors to ensure that job applicants and employees are not discriminated against. It required all contractors to prepare an "affirmative action plan" to achieve these goals.

Johnson broke many other color barriers. In 1966, he named the first black cabinet member, Secretary of Housing and Urban Development Robert Weaver. That same year, he appointed the first black woman, Constance Baker Motley, to the federal bench. In 1967 he appointed Thurgood Marshall to become the first black American to serve on the Supreme Court. But Johnson's most lasting legacy was a battery of domestic antipoverty programs.

LBJ had a vision for America. During the 1964 campaign he often spoke about it. He envisioned an America "where no child will go unfed and no youngster will go unschooled; where every child has a good teacher and every teacher has good pay, and both have good classrooms; where every human being has dignity and every worker has a job; where education is blind to color and employment is unaware of race." Johnson called his vision the Great Society. In a 1964 speech at the University of Michigan, LBJ decisively declared that problems of housing, income, employment, and health were ultimately a federal responsibility. When Johnson left the presidency in 1969, his Great Society program had transformed the federal government. At the end of the Eisenhower presidency in 1961, there were only 45 domestic social programs. By the end of the Johnson administration, the number had climbed to 435. Federal spending on social programs, excluding Social Security, had risen from $9.9 billion in 1960 to $25.6 billion in 1968.

To combat poverty, the federal government raised the minimum wage and enacted programs to train poorer Americans for new and better jobs, including the 1964 Manpower Development and Training Act and the Economic Opportunity Act, which established such programs as the Job Corps and the Neighborhood Youth Corps. To assure adequate housing, in

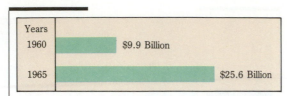

Figure 30.2
Federal spending on social programs, excluding social security

1966 Congress adopted the Model Cities Act to attack urban blight, set up a cabinet-level Department of Housing and Urban Development, and began a program of rent supplements.

To promote education, Congress passed the Higher Education Act in 1965 providing student loans and scholarships, the Elementary and Secondary Schools Act of 1965 to pay for textbooks, and the Educational Opportunity Act of 1968 to help the poor finance college educations. To address the nation's health needs, the Child Health Improvement and Protection Act of 1968 provided for prenatal and postnatal care, the Medicaid Act of 1968 paid for the medical expenses of the poor, and Medicare, established in 1965, extended medical insurance to older Americans under the Social Security system.

When President Johnson announced his Great Society program in 1964, he promised substantial reductions in the number of Americans living in poverty. When he left office, he could legitimately argue that he had delivered on his promise. In 1960, 40 million Americans, 20 percent of the population, were classified as poor. By 1969, their number had fallen to 24 million, 12 percent of the population. Johnson also pledged to qualify the poor for new and better jobs, to extend health insurance to the poor and elderly to cover hospital and doctor costs, and to provide better housing for low-income families. Here too Johnson could say he had delivered. Infant mortality among the poor, which had barely declined between 1950 and 1965, fell by one-third in the decade after 1965 as a result of expanded federal medical and nutritional programs. Before 1965, 20 percent of the poor had never seen a doctor; by 1970 the figure had been cut to 8 percent. The proportion of families living in houses lacking indoor plumbing also declined steeply, from 20 percent in 1960 to 11 percent a decade later.

Despite the widespread view that "in the war on poverty, poverty won," substantial progress had in fact been made. Although critics argued that Johnson took a shotgun approach to reform and pushed poorly thought-out bills through Congress without a coordinated strategy, supporters responded that at least Johnson tried to move toward a more compassionate society. During the 1960s median black family income rose 53 percent; black employment in professional, technical, and clerical occupations doubled; and average black educational attainment increased by four years. The proportion of blacks below the poverty line fell from 55 percent in 1960 to 27 percent in 1968. The black unemployment rate fell 34 percent. The country had taken major strides toward extending equality of opportunity to black Americans. In addition, the number of whites below the poverty line dropped dramatically, and such poverty-plagued regions as Appalachia made significant economic strides.

White Backlash

Ghetto rioting, the rise of black militancy, and resentment over Great Society social legislation combined to produce a backlash among many

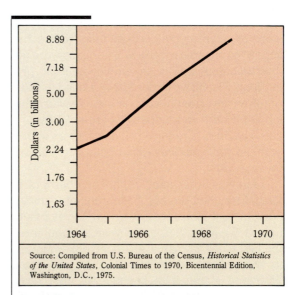

Source: Compiled from U.S. Bureau of the Census, *Historical Statistics of the United States*, Colonial Times to 1970, Bicentennial Edition, Washington, D.C., 1975.

Figure 30.3
Federal aid to education, 1964–1970

whites. In the wake of the riots, many whites fled the nation's cities. The Census Bureau estimated that 900,000 whites moved each year from central cities to the suburbs between 1965 and 1970.

Commitment to bringing black Americans into full equality declined. In 1968 Alabama Governor George Wallace ran for president on the newly formed American Independent party ticket, declaring he would repeal "so-called civil rights laws." Wallace drew nearly 10 million votes in the election, 13.5 percent of the total votes cast, and won sufficient support in such northern states as Illinois and Ohio to swing these states to Republican candidate Richard Nixon.

During his 1968 campaign for the White House, Nixon promised to eliminate "wasteful" federal antipoverty programs and to name "strict constructionists" to the Supreme Court. Once in office, Nixon moved quickly to keep his commitments. In an effort to curb Great Society social programs, Nixon did away with the Model Cities program and the Office of Economic Opportunity. "The time may have come," declared a Nixon aide, "when the issue of race could benefit from a period of benign neglect." The number of investigations to determine whether communities were in compliance with school desegregation fell off sharply, from 16 in 1969, the year Nixon took office, to zero in 1974. The administration urged Congress not to extend the Voting Rights Act of 1965 and to end a fair housing enforcement program.

President Nixon also made a series of Supreme Court appointments that brought to an end the liberal activist era of the Warren Court. During the 1960s, the Supreme Court greatly increased the ability of criminal defendants to defend themselves. In *Mapp* v. *Ohio* (1961), the high court ruled that evidence secured by the police through unreasonable searches must be excluded from trial. In *Gideon* v. *Wainwright* (1963), it declared that indigent defendants have a right to a court-appointed attorney. In *Escobedo* v. *Illinois* (1964), it ruled that suspects being interrogated by police have a right to legal counsel.

As president, Nixon promised to alter the balance between the rights of criminal defendants and society's rights. He selected Warren Burger, a moderate conservative, to replace Earl Warren as chief justice of the Supreme Court and then nominated two convervative white Southerners for a second court vacancy, only to have both nominees rejected (one for financial improprieties, the other for alleged insensitivities to civil rights). He eventually named four justices to the high court: Burger, Harry Blackmun, Lewis Powell, and William Rehnquist.

Under Chief Justice Burger and his successor William Rehnquist, the Supreme Court clarified the remedies that can be used to correct past racial discrimination. In 1974 the Court limited the use of school busing for purposes of racial desegregation by declaring that busing could not take place across school district lines. In 1978 in the landmark *Bakke* case, the Court held that educational institutions could take race into account when screening applicants, but could not use rigid racial quotas. In 1979 in the controversial *Weber* "reverse-discrimination" case, the court ruled that employers and unions could legally establish voluntary programs, including the use of quotas, to aid minorities and women in employment.

The Struggle Continues

Over the past quarter century, black Americans have made impressive social and economic gains, yet full equality remains an unrealized dream. State-sanctioned segregation in restaurants, hotels, courtrooms, libraries, drinking fountains, and public washrooms was eliminated and many barriers to equal opportunity were shattered. In political representation, educational attainment, and representation in white-collar and professional occupations, black Americans have made striking gains. Between 1960 and 1988 the number of black officeholders swelled from just 300 to nearly 6600 and the proportion of blacks in professional positions quadrupled. Black mayors have governed many of the nation's largest cities, including Chicago, Detroit, Los Angeles, Philadelphia, and Washington, D.C. Respect for black culture has also grown. The number of black performers on television and in film has grown, though most still appear in comedies or crime stories. Today, the most popular television performers (Bill Cosby and Oprah), the most popular movie star (Eddie Murphy), and many of the most popular musicians and sports stars are black.

Nevertheless, millions of black Americans still do not share fully in the promise of American life. According to census figures, blacks still suffer twice the unemployment rate of whites and earn only about half as much. The poverty rate among black families is three times that of whites, the same ratio as in the 1950s. Forty percent of black children are raised in fatherless homes and almost half of all black children are born into families earning less than the poverty level.

Separation of the races in housing and schooling remains widespread. Nationally, less than a quarter of all black Americans live in integrated neighborhoods and only about 38 percent of black children attend racially integrated schools. And despite great gains in black political clout, blacks still do not hold political offices in proportion to their share of the population. In 1990 there were only 400 black legislators (state and federal), against 7335 white legislators, and altogether blacks still make up less than two percent of the nation's officeholders.

Although the United States has eliminated many obstacles to black progress, reformers maintain that much remains to be done before the country attains Martin Luther King's dream of a nation where "all of God's children, black man and white man, Jew and Gentile, Protestant and Catholic, will be able to join hands and sing in the words of the old Negro spiritual, 'Free at Last, Free at Last, Thank God Almighty, I'm Free at Last.'"

Tom Bradley, the son of a sharecropper, became the first black mayor of Los Angeles in 1973, winning more than 56 percent of the total vote.

THE YOUTH REVOLT

During the 1960s, one age group of Americans loomed larger than any other: youth. Their skepticism of corporate and bureaucratic authority, their strong emotional identification with the underprivileged, and their intense desire for stimulation and instant gratification shaped the nation's politics, dress, music, and film. Unlike their parents, who had grown up amid the hardships of the depression and the patriotic sacrifices of World War II, young people of the 1960s grew up during a period of rapid economic growth. Feeling a deep sense of economic security, they sought personal fulfillment and tended to dismiss their parents generation's success-oriented lives. "Never trust anyone over 30," went a popular saying.

Never before had young people been so numerous or so well-educated. During the 1960s, there was a sudden explosion in the number of teenagers and young adults. As a result of the depressed birthrates during the 1930s and the postwar baby boom, the number of young people aged 14 to 25 jumped 40 percent in a decade, until they constituted 20 percent of the nation's population. The nation's growing number of young people received far more schooling than their parents. Over 75 percent graduated high school and nearly 40 percent went on to higher education.

At no earlier time in American history had the gulf between the generations seemed so wide. Blue jeans, long hair, psychedelic drugs, casual sex, hippie communes, campus demonstrations, and rock music all became symbols of the distance separating youth from the world of conventional adulthood.

The New Left

Late in the spring of 1962, five dozen college students gathered at a lakeside camp near Port Huron, Michigan, to discuss politics. For four days and nights the members of an obscure student group known as Students for a Democratic Society (SDS) talked passionately about such topics as civil rights, foreign policy, and the quality of American life. At 5 o'clock in the morning of June 16 the gathering ended. The participants had agreed on a political platform that expressed their sentiments. This manifesto, one of the pivotal political documents of the 1960s, became known as the Port Huron Statement.

The goal set forward in the Port Huron Statement was the creation of a radically democratic political movement in the United States that rejected hierarchy and bureaucracy. In its most important paragraphs, the document called for "participatory democracy"—direct individual involvement in the decisions that affected their lives. This notion would become the battle cry of the student movement of the 1960s—a movement that came to be known as the New Left.

The Port Huron Statement's chief author was Tom Hayden. Hayden had been born on December 11, 1939, in Royal Oak, Michigan, a predominantly Catholic working-class suburb of Detroit. From an early age, Hayden had been unusually politically conscious and questioning of established authority. In high school, his idols were critics of conventional society, such as J. D. Salinger's Holden Caulfield and *Mad Magazine's* Alfred E. Neuman. He then attended the University of Michigan, where he edited the university's student newspaper. He read Jack Kerouac's beat novel *On the Road*, hitchhiked across the country, and witnessed student protests at the University of California at Berkeley. He spent much of 1961 in the South, worked with the SNCC, and was once badly beaten by local whites in McComb, Mississippi.

During the 1960s, Tom Hayden became one of the key figures in the New Left. In 1968 he flew to North Vietnam as a protest against the Vietnam War. The next year he gained further notoriety as one of the Chicago Seven defendants who were acquitted of charges of conspiring to disrupt the 1968 Democratic presidential convention. Briefly, Hayden dropped out of politics, moved to Venice, California, and lived under a pseudonym. Later, he married actress Jane Fonda and became a member of the California legislature.

During the 1960s, thousands of young college students, like Tom Hayden, became politically active. The first issue to spark student radicalism was the impersonality of the modern university. Many students criticized the bureaucratic, impersonal nature of the modern "megaversity." Students questioned university requirements, restrictions on student political activities, and dormitory rules that limited the hours that male and female students could socialize with each other. Restrictions on students handing out political pamphlets on university property led to the first campus demonstrations that broke out at the University of California at

Tom Hayden (right) was a key figure in student activism in the 1960s. Here Hayden and fellow activists Abbie Hoffman (left) and Jerry Rubin (center) address a crowd in Chicago on the day conspiracy indictments were handed down to the Chicago Seven.

Berkeley and soon spread to other campuses. Mario Savio, leader of the Berkeley Free Speech Movement, succinctly summarized the feelings of many student radicals:

> The university is well structured, well tooled, to turn out people with all the sharp edges worn off, the well-rounded person. . . . This means that the best among the people who enter must for four years wander aimlessly much of the time questioning why they are on campus at all, doubting whether there is any point in what they are doing, and looking forward toward a very bleak existence afterward in a game in which all of the rules have been made up, which one cannot really amend.

Involvement in the civil rights movement in the South initiated many students into radical politics. In the early 1960s, many white students from northern universities began to participate in voter registration drives, freedom schools, sit-ins, and freedom rides in order to help desegregate the South. For the first time, many witnessed poverty, discrimination, and violence first hand.

Student radicalism also drew inspiration from a literature of social criticism that flourished in the 1950s. During that decade, many of the most popular films, novels, and writings aimed at young people criticized conventional middle class life. Popular films, like *Rebel Without a Cause*, and popular novels, like J. D. Salinger's *Catcher in the Rye*, celebrated sensitive, directionless, alienated youths unable to conform to the conventional adult values of suburban and corporate America. Sophisticated works of social criticism, by such maverick sociologists, psychologists, and economists as Herbert Marcuse, Norman O. Brown, Paul Goodman, Michael Harrington, and C. Wright Mills, documented the growing concentration of power in the hands of social elites, the persistence of poverty in a land of plenty, and the stresses and injustices in America's social order.

Above all, student radicalism owed its support to student opposition to the Vietnam War. SDS held its first antiwar march in 1965, which attracted at least 15,000 protestors to Washington, and commanded wide press attention. Over

In the late summer of 1964 the first major student demonstrations took place at the University of California at Berkeley. Student protests against war, racism, and poverty continued throughout the country into the 1970s.

the next three years, oppposition to the war brought thousands of new members to SDS. The organization grew phenomenally, from fewer than a thousand members in 1962 to at least 50,000 in 1968. In addition to its antiwar activities, members of SDS also tried to organize a democratic "interracial movement of the poor" in northern city neighborhoods.

Many members of SDS quickly grew frustrated by the slow pace of social change and began to embrace violence as a tool to transform society. "I'm a nihilist! I'm proud of it, proud of it!" shouted a delegate at a 1967 SDS meeting in Princeton. "Tactics? It's too late. . . . Let's break what we can. Tear them apart." An underground newspaper, the *Berkeley Barb*, proclaimed that the "university cannot be reformed" and called for guerrilla bands to sweep through "college campuses, busting up classrooms, and freeing our brothers from the prison of the university."

After 1968 SDS rapidly tore itself apart as an effective political force. The Marxist-Leninist Progressive Labor party infiltrated the organization. SDS's final convention in 1969 degenerated into a shouting match, as factions tried to shout each other down with chants of "Ho, Ho, Ho Chi Minh!" and "Mao, Mao, Mao Tse-tung!" In 1969 the Weathermen, a surviving faction of SDS, attempted to launch a guerrilla war in the streets of Chicago—an incident known as the "Days of Rage"—to "tear pig city apart." Finally, in 1970 three members of the Weathermen blew themselves up in a Greenwich Village brownstone trying to make a bomb out of a stick of dynamite and an alarm clock.

Throughout the 1960s the SDS and other radical student organizations claimed to speak for the nation's youth, and in thousands of editorials and magazine articles, journalists accepted this claim. In fact, the SDS represented only a small minority of college students, who themselves composed a minority of the country's youth. Far more young Americans voted for George Wallace in 1968 than joined SDS, and most college students during the decade spent far more time studying and enjoying the college experience than protesting. Nevertheless, radical students did help to draw the nation's attention to the problem of racism in American so-

ciety and the moral issues involved in the Vietnam War. In that sense, their impact far exceeded their numbers.

The Making and Unmaking of a Counterculture

The New Left had a series of heroes—ranging from Marx, Lenin, Ho, and Mao to Fidel, Che, and other revolutionaries. It also had its own uniforms, rituals, and music. Faded blue work shirts and jeans, wire-rimmed glasses, and work shoes were de rigueur even if the dirtiest work the wearer performed was taking notes in a college class. The proponents of the New Left emphasized their sympathy with the working class—an emotion that was seldom reciprocated—and listened to labor songs that once fired the hearts of unionists. The political protest folk music of Greenwich Village—of Phil Ochs, Bob Dylan, and their crowd—inspired the New Left.

But the New Left was only one part of youth protest during the 1960s. While the New Left labored to change the world and remake American society, other youths attempted to alter themselves and reorder consciousness. Variously labeled the counterculture, hippies, or flower children, they had their own heroes, music, dress, and approach to life.

In theory, supporters of the counterculture rejected individualism, competition, and capitalism. Adopting rather unsystematic ideas from oriental religions, they sought to become one with the universe. "The solution to the problem of identity is, get lost," wrote Norman O. Brown, whose books influenced the counterculture. All humanity, Brown believed, was part of a single entity, and man existed not as an individual but as part of the whole. As one interpreter of Brown explained, "Body existed, not as location or flesh, but as a field of energy; ego, character, personality were mere illusion. . . . Indeed, knowledge of the unity could be attained only by breaking the bonds of the ego, by having 'no self.' "

But how could one lose oneself? The process began with the act of rejection—of such liberal values as progress, order, reason, achievement, social responsibility; of competition, materialism, the work ethic, and other bourgeois "hang-ups." Rejection of monogamy and releasing one's sexual energy also aided the process. If the counterculture did not invent sex, it claimed to have improved the patent. As in other aspects of the movement, the emphasis was on sharing. The traditional nuclear family gave way to the tribal or communal ideal, where members renounced individualism and private property and shared food, work, and sex. In such a community, love was a general abstract ideal rather than a focused emotion.

The quest for openness with the universe led many youths to experiment with hallucinogenic drugs. LSD had a particularly powerful allure. Under its influence, poets, musicians, politicians, and thousands of other Americans claimed to have tapped into an all-powerful spiritual force. After taking LSD, Henry Luce, founder and president of Time-Life, Inc., claimed that God told him all was right with America. Timothy Leary, the Harvard professor who became the leading prophet of LSD, asserted that the drug would unlock the universe. Picking up on Kennedy's New Frontier theme, Leary told LSD takers "You are venturing out (like the Portuguese sailors, like the astronauts) on uncharted margins. But be assured—it is an old human custom." Poet Allen Ginsberg agreed that LSD led to new insights—after taking the drug he tried to get Kennedy and Khrushchev on the telephone to "settle all this about the bomb once and for all."

Although LSD was outlawed in 1966, the drug continued to spread. Perhaps some takers discovered profound truths, but by the late 1960s drugs had done more harm than good. The history of the Haight-Ashbury section of San Francisco illustrated the problems caused by drugs. In 1967 Haight was the center of the "counterculture," the home of the "flower children." During that "summer of love" the song "Are You Going to San Francisco?" soared to the top of the pop chart, and in the "city of love" hippies ingested LSD, smoked pot, listened to "acid rock," and proclaimed the dawning of a new age. Even the Hell's Angels, an outlaw motorcycle group, temporarily joined the act, serving as the hippies' private police force. But even as *Time* magazine described Haight as "the vibrant epicenter of the hippie movement," the

area was suffering from severe problems. High levels of racial violence, venereal disease, rape, drug overdoses, and poverty ensured more bad trips than good. "No doubt real love existed somewhere in the Haight," noted one historian. "But the case of the sixteen-year-old girl who was shot full of speed and raffled off in the streets was closer to the dominant reality."

Even music, which along with drugs and sex formed the counterculture trinity, failed to alter human behavior. In 1969 journalists hailed the Woodstock Music Festival as a symbol of love. But a few months later a group of Hell's Angels violently interrupted the Altamont Raceway music festival. As Mick Jagger sang "Sympathy for the Devil" an Angel stabbed to death a black man.

Like the New Left, the counterculture fell victim to its own excesses. Sex, drugs, and rock and roll did not solve the problems facing the United States. And by the end of the 1960s the counterculture had lost its force.

LIBERATION MOVEMENTS

The struggle of black Americans for racial justice inspired a host of other groups to seek full equality. Women, Mexican-Americans, Native Americans, and many other deprived groups protested against discrimination and organized to promote social change.

Women's Liberation

Hosted by Jack Bailey, a gravel-voiced former carnival barker, it was one of the most popular daytime television shows of the 1950s. Five times a week, three women, each with a hard-luck story, recited their tales of woe—diseases, retarded children, poverty—and the studio audience, with the aid of an applause meter, decided which woman was the most miserable. She became "Queen for a Day." Bailey put a crown on her head, wrapped her in a mink coat (which she got to keep for 24 hours), and told her about the new Cadillac she would get to drive (also for the next 24 hours). And then came gifts for the queen; a year's supply of Helena Rubinstein cosmetics; a Clairol permanent and once-over by a Hollywood makeup art-

The popular television show "Queen for a Day" reinforced established female sex roles by providing winners with everything they needed to be better housewives. Here, host Jack Bailey crowns the "Queen for a Day."

ist; and the electric appliances necessary for female happiness—a toaster oven, automatic washer, automatic dryer, and an iron. Altogether, everything a woman needed to be a prettier and better housewife.

One woman in the television audience was Betty Friedan. A 1942 honors graduate of Smith College and former psychology Ph.D. candidate at the University of California at Berkeley, Friedan had quit graduate school, married, moved to the New York suburbs, and bore three children in rapid succession. American culture told her that husband, house, children, and electric appliances were true happiness. But Friedan was not happy. And she was not alone.

In 1957 Friedan sent out a questionnaires to fellow members of her college graduating class. The replies amazed her. Again and again, she found women suffering from "a sense of dissatisfaction." Over the next five years, Friedan

interviewed other women at PTA meetings and suburban cocktail parties, and she repeatedly found an unexplainable sense of melancholy and incompleteness. "Sometimes a woman would say 'I feel empty somehow . . . incomplete.' Or she would say, 'I feel as if I don't exist.' " Friedan was not the only observer to detect a widespread sense of discontent among American women. Doctors identified a new female malady, the housewife's syndrome, characterized by a mixture of frustration and exhaustion. CBS broadcast a television documentary entitled "The Trapped Housewife." *Newsweek* magazine noted that the nation's supposedly happy housewife was "dissatisfied with a lot that women of other lands can only dream of. Her discontent is deep, pervasive, and impervious to the superficial remedies which are offered at every hand." *The New York Times* editorialized, "Many young women . . . feel stifled in their homes." *Redbook* magazine ran an article entitled "Why Young Mothers Feel Trapped" and asked for examples of this problem. It received 24,000 replies.

Why, Friedan asked, were American women so discontented? In 1963 she published her answer in a book entitled *The Feminine Mystique*. This book, one of the most influential books ever written by an American, helped to launch a new movement for women's liberation. The book touched a nerve, but the origins of the movement lay in the role of females in American society.

Sources of Discontent

During the 1950s, many American women reacted against the poverty of the depression and the upheavals of World War II by placing renewed emphasis on family life. Young women married earlier than had their mothers, and had more children and bore them faster. The average marriage age of American women dropped to 20, a record low. The fertility rate rose 50 percent between 1940 and 1950—producing a population growth rate approaching that of India. Growing numbers of women decided to forsake higher education or a full-time career and achieve emotional fulfillment as wives and mothers. A 1952 advertisement for Gimbel's department store expressed the prevailing point of view. "What's college?" the ad asked. "That's where girls who are above cooking and sewing go to meet a man so they can spend their lives cooking and sewing." By "marrying at an earlier age, rearing larger families," and purchasing a house in the suburbs, young women believed, in the words of *McCall's* magazine, that they could find their "deepest satisfaction."

Politicians, educators, psychologists, and the mass media all echoed the view that women would find their highest fulfillment managing a house and caring for children. Adlai Stevenson, the Democratic presidential nominee in 1952 and 1956, told the graduating women at Smith College in 1955 that their role in life was to "influence us, men and boys" and "restore valid, meaningful purpose to life in your home." Many educators agreed with the president of Barnard College, who argued that women could not compete with men in the workplace because they "had less physical strength, a lower fatigue point, and a less stable nervous system." Women's magazines pictured housewives as happy with their tasks and depicted career women as neurotic, unhappy, and dissatisfied.

Already, however, a series of dramatic social changes was underway that would contribute to a rebirth of feminism. A dramatic upsurge took place during the 1950s in women's employment and education. More and more married women entered the labor force, and by 1960 the proportion of married women working outside the home was one in three. The number of women receiving college degrees also rose. The proportion of bachelor's and master's degrees received by women rose from just 24 percent in 1950 to over 35 percent a decade later. Meanwhile, beginning in 1957 the birthrate began to drop as women elected to have fewer children. A growing discrepancy had begun to appear between the popular image of women as full-time housewives and mothers and the actual realities of many women's lives.

Feminism Reborn

Women in 1960 played a limited role in American government. Although women comprised about half of the nation's voters, there were no female Supreme Court justices, federal appeals court justices, governors, cabinet officers, or

ambassadors. Only 2 of 100 U.S. senators and 15 of 435 representatives were women. Of 307 federal district judges, 2 were women. Of 7700 members of state legislatures, 234 were women. Nor were these figures atypical. Only 2 American women had ever been elected governor, only 2 had ever served in a president's cabinet, and only 6 had ever served as ambassador.

Economically, women workers were concentrated in low-paying service and factory jobs. The overwhelming majority worked as secretaries, waitresses, beauticians, teachers, nurses, and librarians. Only 3.5 percent of the nation's lawyers were women, 10 percent of the nation's scientists, and less than 2 percent of the nation's leading business executives.

Lower pay for women doing the same work as men was commonplace. One out of every three companies had separate pay scales for

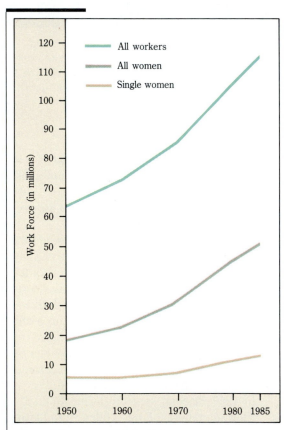

Figure 30.4
Women in the work force, 1950–1985

male and female workers. A female bank teller typically made $15 a week less than a man with the same amount of experience, and a female laundry worker made 49 cents an hour less than her male counterpart. Altogether, the earnings of women working full-time averaged only about 60 percent of those of men.

In many parts of the country, the law discriminated against women. In three states—Alabama, Mississippi, and South Carolina—women could not sit on juries. Many states restricted married women's right to make contracts, sell property, engage in business, control their own earnings, and make wills. Six states gave fathers preference in the custody of young children after a divorce. In practically every state, men had a legal right to have intercourse with their wives and to administer an unspecified amount of physical punishment.

Women were often portrayed in the mass media in an unrealistic and stereotyped way. Popular magazines like *Reader's Digest* and popular television shows like "I Love Lucy" often depicted women as stupid or foolish, jealous of other women, irresponsible about money, and overanxious to marry.

In December 1961 President John F. Kennedy placed the issue of women's rights on the national political agenda. Eager to fulfill a debt to women voters—he had not named a single woman to a policymaking position—Kennedy established a President's Commission on the Status of Women, the first presidential panel ever to examine the status of American women. Chaired by Eleanor Roosevelt, the commission was to recommend ways to combat "the prejudices and outmoded customs [that] act as barriers to the full realization of women's rights."

In 1963, the year that Betty Friedan published *The Feminine Mystique*, the commission issued its report. The report's recommendations included a call for an end to all legal restrictions on married women's right to own property, to enter into business, and to make contracts; equal opportunity in employment; and greater availability of child-care services.

The most important reform to grow out of the commission's investigations was the 1963 Equal Pay Act, which required equal pay for men and women who performed the same jobs under equal conditions. The Equal Pay Act was

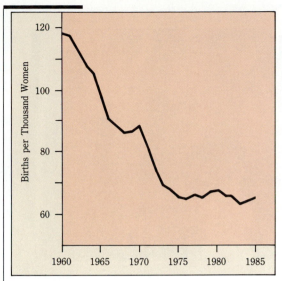

Figure 30.5
American birthrate, 1960–1985

the first federal law to prohibit discrimination on the basis of sex.

The next year, Congress enacted a new weapon in the fight against sex discrimination. Title VII of the 1964 Civil Rights Act prohibited discrimination in hiring or promotion based on race, color, religion, national origin, or sex by private employers and unions. As originally proposed, the bill only outlawed racial discrimination; but in a futile effort to block the measure, Representative Howard Smith of Virginia amended the bill to prohibit discrimination on the basis of sex. Some liberals including Representative Edith Green of Oregon, a cosponsor of the 1963 Equal Pay Act, opposed the amendment on the grounds that it diverted attention from racial discrimination. But it passed in the House of Representatives 168 to 133. "We made it! God Bless America!" shouted a female voice from the House gallery when the amendment passed.

The Civil Rights Act made it illegal for employers to discriminate against women in hiring and promotion unless the employer could show that sex was a "bona fide occupational qualification" (for example, hiring a man as an attendant for a men's restroom). To investigate complaints of employment discrimination, the

(Text continues on p. 1036)

THE MODERN FAMILY

Does a father have the right to give his children his last name even if his wife objects? Can an expectant mother obtain an abortion without her husband's permission? Should a teenager, unhappy with her parents' restrictions on her smoking, dating, and choice of friends, be allowed to have herself placed in a foster home? Should a childless couple be permitted to hire a "surrogate mother" to be artificially inseminated and carry a child to delivery? These are among the questions that the nation's courts have had to wrestle with as the nature of American family life has, in the course of a generation, been revolutionized.

During the 1950s, the Cleavers on the television show "Leave It to Beaver" epitomized the American family. In 1960, over 70 percent of all American households were like the Cleavers: made up of a breadwinner father, a homemaker mother, and their kids. Today, "traditional" families with a working husband, an unemployed wife, and one or more

children make up less than 15 percent of the nation's households. And as America's families have changed, the image of the family portrayed on television has changed accordingly. Recent television families run the gamut from two-career families like the Huxtables on "The Cosby Show" to two single mothers and their children on "Kate and Allie," and an unmarried couple who cohabit in the same house on "Who's the Boss."

Profound changes have reshaped American family life in recent years. In a decade, divorce rates doubled. The number of divorces today is twice as high as in 1966 and three times higher than in 1950. The rapid upsurge in the divorce rates contributed to a dramatic increase in the number of single-parent households—or what used to be known as broken homes. The number of households consisting of a single woman and her children has tripled since 1960. A sharp increase in female-headed homes has been ac-

companied by a startling increase in the number of couples cohabitating outside of marriage. The number of unmarried couples living together has quadrupled since 1970.

What accounts for these upheavals in family life? One of the most far-reaching forces for change has been a sexual revolution far more radical than the early twentieth century "revolution in morals and manners." Contemporary Americans are much more likely than their predecessors to postpone marriage, to live alone, and to engage in sexual intercourse outside of marriage. Today, over 80 percent of all women say that they were not virgins when they married, compared to less than 20 percent a generation ago. Extramarital sex has also increased sharply. Back in the 1940s, just 8 percent of married women under the age of 25 had committed adultery. Today the estimated figure is 24 percent. Meanwhile, the proportion of children born to unmarried mothers has climbed from just 5 percent in 1960 to over 20 percent today.

The roots of these developments were planted during the early 1960s, when a new openness about sexuality swept the nation's literature, movies, theater, advertising, and fashion. In 1960, the birth control pill was introduced, offering a highly effective method of contraception. Two years later, Grossinger's resort in New York State's Catskill Mountains introduced the first singles-only weekend, thereby acknowledging couples outside marriage. In 1964, the first "singles bar" opened in New York City; the musical *Hair* introduced nudity to the Broadway stage; California designer Rudi Gernreich created the first topless bathing suit; and bars sprouted featuring topless waitresses and dancers. Sexually oriented magazines began to display pubic hair and filmmakers began to show simulated sexual acts on the screen. A new era of public sexuality was ushered in and as a result it became far easier and more acceptable to have an active social life and sex life outside of marriage.

At the same time, the nation's courts and state legislatures liberalized laws governing sex and contraception. In 1957, the Supreme Court narrowed the legal definition of obscenity, ruling that the portrayal of sex in art, literature, and film was entitled to constitutional protections of free speech, unless the work was utterly without redeeming social value. In 1962, Illinois became the first state to decriminalize all forms of private sexual conduct between consenting adults. In succeeding years, the Supreme Court struck down a series of state statutes that prohibited the prescription or distribution of contraceptives, and in 1973, in the case of *Roe* v. *Wade*, the high court decriminalized abortion. These legal decisions, to a large extent, took government out of the business of regulating private heterosexual behavior and defining the sexual norms according to which citizens were supposed to live.

Another factor reshaping family life has been a massive influx of mothers into the work force. As late as 1940, less than 12 percent of white married women were in the work force; today the figure is nearly 60 percent and over half of all mothers of preschoolers work outside the home. The major forces that have propelled women into the work force include a rising cost of living, which spurred many families to seek a second source of income; increased control over fertility through contraception and abortion, which allows women to work without interruption; and rising educational levels, which lead many women to seek employment for intellectual stimulation and fulfillment.

As wives have assumed a larger role in their family's financial support, they have felt justified in demanding that husbands perform more child care and housework. At the same time, fewer children have a full-time mother and as a result an increasing number of young children are cared for during the day by adults other than their own parent. Today, over two-thirds of all 3- to 5-year-olds take part in a day-care, nursery school, or prekindergarten program, compared to a fifth in 1970.

Feminism has been another major force that has transformed American family life. The women's liberation movement attacked the societal expectation that women defer to the needs of spouses and children as part of their roles as wives and mothers. Militant feminist activists like Ti-Grace Atkinson denounced marriage as "slavery" and "legalized rape." The larger mainstream of the women's movement articulated a powerful critique of the idea that child care and housework were the apex of a woman's accomplishments or her sole means of fulfillment.

The feminist movement awakened American women to what many viewed as one of the worst forms of social and political oppression: sexism. The introduction of this awareness would go far beyond the feminists themselves. Although only a small minority of American women openly declared themselves to be feminists, the arguments of the women's movement drastically altered women's attitudes toward family roles, child care, and housework. As a result of feminism, a substantial majority of women now believe that both husband and wife should have jobs, do housework, and take care of children.

The changes that have taken place in family life have been disruptive and troubling and have transformed the family into a major political battleground. Both liberals and conservatives have offered their own proposals about how the American family can best be strengthened. Conservative activists, fearful that climbing rates of divorce, single parenthood, and working mothers represent a breakdown of family values, launched a politically influential "profamily movement" during the 1970s. They sought to restrict access to abortion, block ratification of the proposed Equal Rights Amendment to the Constitution, restrict eroticism on television, and limit teenagers' access to contraceptive information. Liberals have approached family issues from a different tack. Unlike conservatives, they are more willing to use government social policies to strengthen family life. Some of the proposals they have made to strengthen families include expanded nutritional and health programs for pregnant women, federal subsidies for day-care services for low-income families, uniform national standards for child-care centers, and a requirement that employers give parents unpaid leave to take care of a newborn or seriously ill child. Without a doubt, the family will remain one of the hottest political issues in the years to come.

act set up the Equal Employment Opportunity Commission (EEOC).

At first, the EEOC focused its enforcement efforts on racial discrimination and largely ignored sex discrimination. The commission's director considered the provision prohibiting sex discrimination "a fluke . . . conceived out of wedlock," and the EEOC rejected a proposal that separate want ads for men and women be outlawed.

To pressure the EEOC to enforce the law prohibiting sex discrimination, Betty Friedan and 300 other women formed the National Organization for Women (NOW) in 1966, with Friedan as president. The organization pledged "to take action to bring women into full participation in the mainstream of American society now, exercising all the privileges and responsibilities thereof in truly equal partnership with men." NOW filed suit against the EEOC "to force it to comply with its own government rules." It also sued the country's 1300 largest corporations for sex discrimination, lobbied President Johnson to issue an executive order that would include women within federal affirmative action requirements, and challenged airline policies that required stewardesses to retire after they married or reached the age of 32.

At its second national conference in November 1967, NOW drew up an eight-point bill of rights for women. It called for adoption of an Equal Rights Amendment (ERA) to the Constitution, prohibiting sex discrimination; equal educational, job training, and housing opportunities for women; and repeal of laws limiting access to contraceptive devices and abortion.

Two proposals produced fierce dissension within the new organization. One source of disagreement was the Equal Rights Amendment. The amendment consisted of two dozen words: "Equality of rights under the law shall not be denied or abridged by the United States or by any state on account of sex." It had originally been proposed in 1923 to mark the seventy-fifth anniversary of the Seneca Falls Women's Rights Convention and was submitted to Congress at almost every session. For over 40 years, professional women, who favored the amendment, battled with organized labor and the Women's Bureau of the Labor Department, which opposed the amendment on the ground that it en-

dangered "protective" legislation that set minimum wages and maximum hours for less-skilled women workers. At NOW's convention, women from the United Automobile Workers (UAW) opposed inclusion of the ERA in the Bill of Rights. When they lost, the UAW stopped providing NOW with office space and clerical services.

The other issue that generated controversy was the call for reform of abortion laws. In 1967 only one state—Colorado—had reformed nineteenth-century legal statutes that made abortion a criminal offense. Dissenters believed that NOW should avoid controversial issues that would divert attention away from economic discrimination.

Despite internal disagreements, NOW's membership grew rapidly, reaching 40,000 by 1974 and 175,000 by 1988. The group broadened its attention to include such issues as the plight of poor and nonwhite women, domestic violence, rape, sexual harrassment, the role of women in sport, and the rights of lesbians. At the same time, the organization claimed a number of achievements. Two victories were particularly important. In 1967, NOW persuaded President Lyndon Johnson to issue Executive Order 11375, which prohibited government contractors from discriminating on the basis of sex and required them to take "affirmative action" to ensure that women are properly represented in their work force. The next year, the EEOC ruled that separate want ads for men and women were a violation of Title VII of the 1964 Civil Rights Act.

Radical Feminism

Alongside the National Organization for Women, other more radical feminist groups emerged during the 1960s among college students involved in the civil rights movement and the New Left. Women within these organizations for social change often found themselves treated as "second-class citizens," responsible for kitchen work, typing, and serving "as a sexual supply for their male comrades after hours." "We were the movement secretaries and the shit-workers," one woman recalled; "we were the earth mothers and the sex-objects for the movement's men." In 1964 Ruby Doris Smith

Women have been involved in protest movements throughout the years. Here women march in support of the Equal Rights Amendment. Failure to achieve ratification by the required three-fourths of states sent the amendment to its final defeat in 1982.

Robinson presented an indignant assault on the treatment of women civil rights workers in a paper entitled "The Position of Women in SNCC," to a SNCC staff meeting. Stokely Carmichael reputedly responded, "The only position for women in SNCC is prone."

Women in the New Left also expressed unhappiness. "You are allowed to participate and to speak," noted one woman, "only the men stop listening when you do . . . How many times have you seen men get up and actually walk out of a room while a woman speaks, or begin to whisper to each other as she starts?" When women tried to raise the "woman question" at SDS's 1965 convention, men responded with "catcalls, storms of ridicule and verbal abuse, 'She just needs a good screw,' or . . . 'She's a castrating female.'"

In cities across the country, independent women's groups sprouted up in 1967. In the fall, at the first national gathering of women's groups at the National Conference for New Politics, women demanded 51 percent of all committee seats in the name of minority rights. When men refused to meet their demand, the women walked out—signaling the beginning of a critical split between the New Left and the women's movement. The next year, radical women's groups appeared on the front pages of the nation's newspapers when they staged a protest of the Miss America pageant and provided a "freedom trash can," in which women could throw "old bras, girdles, high heeled shoes, women's magazines, curlers, and other instruments of torture to women." They concluded their rally by crowning a sheep Miss America.

Over the next three years the number of women's liberation groups rapidly multiplied, bearing such names as the Redstockings, WITCH (the Women's International Terrorist Conspiracy from Hell), and the Feminists. By 1970 there were at least 500 women's liberation groups, including 50 in New York, 25 in Boston, 30 in Chicago, and 35 in San Francisco. Women's liberation groups established the first feminist book stores, battered women's shelters, rape crisis centers, and abortion counseling centers. In 1971 Gloria Steinem and others published *Ms.*, the first national feminist magazine. The first 300,000 copies were sold out in eight days.

Radical new ideas began to fill the air. One women's liberation leader, Ti-Grace Atkinson, denounced marriage as "slavery," "legalized rape," and "unpaid labor." Meanwhile, a host of new words and phrases entered the language, such as "consciousness raising," "Ms.," "bra burning," "sexism," "male chauvinist pig."

On August 26, 1970, the fiftieth anniversary of the ratification of the Nineteenth Amendment, the women's liberation movement dramatically demonstrated its growing strength by mounting a massive Strike for Equality. In New York City, 50,000 women marched down Fifth Avenue; in Boston, 2000 marched; in Chicago, 3000. Members of virtually all feminist groups joined together in a display of unity and strength.

The Growth of Feminist Ideology

Feminists subscribe to no single doctrine or set of goals. All are united, however, by a belief that women have historically occupied a subordinate position in politics, education, and the economic system. Modern feminist thought traces its roots to a book published by a famous French philosopher Simone de Beauvoir in 1949. Entitled *The Second Sex*, the book traced the assumptions, customs, educational practices, jokes, laws, and modes of speech that socialize young women to believe that they are inferior beings.

A decade and a half later, Betty Friedan made another important contribution to the development of feminist ideology. In *The Feminine Mystique*, she analyzed and criticized the role of educators, psychologists, sociologists, and the mass media in conditioning women to believe that they could only find fulfillment as housewives and mothers. By requiring women to subordinate their own individual aspirations to the welfare of their husbands and children, the "feminine mystique" prevented women from achieving self-fulfillment and inevitably left women unhappy.

In the years following the publication of *The Feminine Mystique*, feminists developed a large body of literature analyzing the economic, psychological, and social roots of female subordination. It was not until 1970, however, that the more radical feminist writings reached the broader reading public with the publication of Shulamith Firestone's *The Dialectic of Sex*, Germaine Greer's *The Female Eunuch*, and Kate Millett's *Sexual Politics*. These books argued that gender distinctions structure virtually every aspect of individual lives, not only in such areas as law and employment, but also in personal relationships, language, literature, religion, and an individual's internalized self-perceptions. Even more controversially, these works attributed female oppression to men and an ideology of male supremacy. "Women have very little idea how much men hate them," declared Greer. As examples of misogyny these authors cited pornography, grotesque portrayals of women in literature, sexual harrassment, wife abuse, and rape.

Since 1970 feminist theory has exploded into many different directions. Today, there are more than 30 national feminist news and opinion magazines along with an additional 20 academic journals dealing with women's issues. Women's historians, feminist literary and film critics, and physical and social scientists have begun to take insights derived from feminism and ask new questions about women's historical experience, the sex and status differences between women and men, sex role socialization, economic and legal discrimination, and the depiction of women in literature.

The Supreme Court and Sex Discrimination

Despite its conservative image, the Supreme Court under chief justices Warren Burger and William Rehnquist has been active in the area of sex discrimination and women's rights. In contrast to the Warren Court, which ruled on only one major sex discrimination case—upholding a law that excluded women from serving on juries—the Burger and Rehnquist Courts have considered numerous cases involving women's rights.

The Burger Court issued its first important discrimination decision in 1971. In its landmark decision, *Griggs* v. *Duke Power Company*, the Court established the principle that regardless of an employer's intentions, any employment practice is illegal if it has a "disparate" impact on women or minorities and "if it cannot be shown to be related to job performance." In subsequent cases, the Court legitimized the use of statistics in measuring employment discrimination and approved the use of back pay in compensating discrimination victims.

In 1975 the Burger Court reversed the Warren Court by striking down a Louisiana statute calling for all-male juries. In subsequent decisions, the high court ruled against a Utah law setting different ages at which men and women became adults and overturned an Alabama law setting minimum height and weight requirements for prison guards, standards that meant that almost no woman would qualify.

The Court has not yet set an absolute rule that laws and employment practices must treat men and women the same. In 1976 the Court adopted its current standard for sex discrimination. The Court's test is that to be constitutional, a policy that discriminates on the basis of sex must be "substantially related to an important government objective."

The Court's most controversial decision involving women's rights was delivered in 1973 in the case of *Roe* v. *Wade*. A single, pregnant Texas waitress, assigned the pseudonym Jane Roe in order to protect her privacy, brought suit against Dallas district attorney Henry Wade, to prevent him from enforcing a nineteenth-century Texas statute prohibiting abortion. The Court ruled on the woman's behalf and struck down the Texas law and all similar laws in other states. In its ruling, the Court declared that the decision to have an abortion is a private matter of concern only to a woman and her physician, and that only in the last three months of pregnancy could the government limit the right to abortion.

Many Americans—including many Catholic lay and clerical organizations—bitterly opposed the Supreme Court's *Roe* v. *Wade* decision and banded together to form the "right to life" movement, which ran Ellen MacCormack as a presidential candidate in the 1976 presidential primaries. Like feminist and civil rights organizations, the right to life movement drew on a broad base of popular discontent, and it often employed direct, nonviolent protests to demonstrate its belief that the nation's laws were unjust. The major legislative success of the right to life movement was adoption by Congress of the so-called Hyde Amendment, which permitted states to refuse to fund abortions for indigent women.

The Equal Rights Amendment

In March 1972 the Congress passed an Equal Rights Amendment (ERA) to the United States Constitution, prohibiting sex discrimination, with only 8 dissenting votes in the Senate and 24 in the House. Before the year was over, 22 state legislatures ratified the ERA. Ratification by 38 states was required before the amendment would be added to the Constitution. Over the next 5 years, only 13 more states ratified the amendment—and 5 states rescinded their ratification. In 1978, Congress gave proponents of the amendment 39 more months to complete ratification, but no other state gave its approval.

The ERA had been defeated, but why? Initially, opposition came largely from organized labor, which feared that the amendment would eliminate state "protective legislation," that established minimum wages and maximum hours for women workers. Increasingly, however, resistance to the amendment came from women of lower economic and educational status, whose self-esteem and self-image were bound up with being wives and mothers and who wanted to ensure that women who devoted their lives to their families were not accorded lower status than women who worked outside the home.

The leader of the anti-ERA movement was Phyllis Schlafly, a Radcliffe-educated mother of six from Alton, Illinois. A larger than life figure, Schlafly earned a law degree at the age of 54, wrote nine books (including the 1964 best-seller *A Choice Not an Echo*), and created her own

Right-to-life groups, backed by Protestant fundamentalists, conservatives, and the Catholic church, scored a victory with the Hyde amendment. However, prochoice groups helped organize privately funded agencies and clinics to allow women a choice.

lobbying group, the Eagle Forum. Schlafly argued that the ERA was unnecessary because women were already protected by the Equal Pay Act of 1963 and the Civil Rights Act of 1964, which barred sex discrimination, and that the amendment would outlaw separate public restrooms for men and women and deny wives the right to financial support. She also raised the "women in combat" issue by suggesting that the passage of the ERA would mean that woman would have to fight alongside men during war.

Impact of the Women's Liberation Movement

Since 1960 women have made enormous social gains. Gains in employment have been particularly impressive. During the 1970s, the number of working women climbed 42 percent and much of the increase was in what traditionally was considered "men's" work and professional work. The percentage of lawyers who were women increased by 9 percentage points; the percentage of professors by 6 points; of doctors by 3.6 points. By 1986, women made up 15 per-

cent of the nation's lawyers, 40 percent of all computer programmers, and 29 percent of the country's managers and administrators.

Striking gains have been made in undergraduate and graduate education. Today, for the first time in American history, women constitute a majority of the nation's college students and nearly as many women as men receive master's degrees. In addition, the number of women students receiving degrees from professional schools—including dentistry, law, and medicine—has shot upward, from just 1425 in 1966 to over 20,000 by the early 1990s. Women comprise nearly a third of the students attending law school and medical school.

Women have also made impressive political gains. In 1988 over two dozen women served in Congress, over 80 served as mayors of large cities, and over a thousand served in state legislatures. In 1984, for the first time, a major political party nominated a woman, Geraldine Ferraro, for the vice presidency. Ten percent of the top appointed offices during the Reagan administration went to women and Sandra Day

TABLE 30.4

Occupation by Sex, 1972, 1980 and 1989 (Percentage)

Occupation	1972/Female	1980/Female	1989/Female
Professional/technical	39.3	44.3	45.2
Accountants	21.7	36.2	48.6
Computer specialists	16.8	25.7	35.7
Engineers	0.8	4.0	7.6
Lawyers and judges	3.8	12.8	22.3
Life/physical scientists	10.0	20.3	26.9
Physicians/dentists	9.3	12.9	16.5
Professors	28.0	33.9	38.7
Engineering/science technicians	9.1	17.8	19.2
Writers/artists/entertainers	31.7	39.3	46.0
Sales	41.6	45.3	49.3
Real estate agents/brokers	36.7	50.7	51.0
Clerks, retail	68.9	71.1	81.8
Clerical	75.6	80.1	80.0
Bookkeepers	97.9	90.5	91.7
Clerical supervisors	57.8	70.5	58.2
Office machine operators	71.4	72.6	62.6
Secretaries	99.1	99.1	98.3
Crafts workers	3.6	6.0	8.6
Blue-collar supervisors	6.9	10.8	n/a*
Machinists and jobsetters	0.6	4.0	n/a*
Tool and die makers	0.5	2.8	n/a*
Mechanics (except automobile)	1.0	2.6	3.1

*n/a, not available.

U.S. Bureau of the Census, *Statistical Abstract of the United States: 1982–83* (103d edition), *1991* (111th edition), Washington, D.C., 1982, 1991.

O'Connor was named the first woman to sit on the Supreme Court. Three women held cabinet posts and the president appointed a woman ambassador to the United Nations. By 1988 over 15,000 women held elective office.

In spite of all that has been achieved, however, problems remain. Most women today continue to work in a relatively small number of traditional "women's" jobs and a full-time female worker earned only 68 cents for every $1 paid to men. Even more troubling is the fact that large numbers of women live in poverty. The "feminization of poverty" was one of the growing trends of the 1970s and 1980s. Today, nearly half of all marriages end in divorce and many others end in legal separation and desertion—and the economic plight of these women is often grave. Families headed by women are four and a half times as likely to be poor as families headed by males. Although female-headed families constitute only 15 percent of the U.S. population, they account for over 50 percent of the poor population.

Chicano Liberation

On election day, 1963, hundreds of Mexican-Americans in Crystal City, Texas, the "spinach capital of the world," gathered near a statue of Popeye the Sailor to do something that many had never done before: vote. Although Mexican-Americans outnumbered Anglos two to one, Anglos controlled all five seats on the Crystal City council. For three years, organizers struggled to register Mexican-American voters. When the election was over, Mexican-Americans had won

TABLE 30.5

Ratio of Divorces to Marriages, 1890–1987	
1890	1–17
1900	1–12
1910	1–11
1920	1–7
1930	1–5
1940	1–6
1950	1–4.3
1960	1–3.8
1970	1–3.5
1980	1–2
1987	1–2.1

control of the city council. "We have done the impossible," declared Albert Fuentes, who led the voter registration campaign. "If we can do it in Crystal City, we can do it all over Texas. We can awaken the sleeping giant."

As the 1960s began, Mexican-Americans shared problems of poverty and discrimination with other minority groups. The median income of a Mexican-American family was just 62 percent of the median income of the general population, and over a third of Mexican-American families lived on less than $3000 a year. Unemployment was twice the rate among non-Hispanic whites and four-fifths of employed Mexican-Americans were concentrated in semi-skilled and unskilled jobs, a third in agriculture.

Educational attainment lagged behind other groups (Mexican-Americans averaged less than nine years of schooling as recently as 1970), and Mexican-American pupils were concentrated in predominantly Mexican-American schools, less well staffed and supplied than non–Mexican-American schools, with few Hispanic or Spanish-speaking teachers. Gerrymandered election districts and restrictive voting legislation resulted in the political underrepresentation of Mexican-Americans. They were underrepresented or excluded from juries by requirements that jurors be able to speak and understand English.

During the 1960s, a new Mexican-American militancy arose. In 1962 César Chávez began to organize California farm workers, and three years later, in Delano, California, he led his first strike. At the same time that Chávez led the struggle for higher wages, enforcement of state labor laws, and recognition of the farm worker union, Reies Lopez Tijerina fought to win compensation for the descendants of families whose lands had been seized illegally. In 1963 Tijerina founded the Alianza Federal de Mercedes (the Federal Alliance of Land Grants) in New Mexico to restore the legal rights of heirs to Spanish and Mexican land grants that had been guaranteed under the treaty ending the Mexican War.

In Denver, Rodolfo ("Corky") Gonzales formed the Crusade for Justice in 1965 to protest school discrimination; provide legal, medical, and financial services and jobs for Chicanos; and foster the Mexican-American cultural heritage. La Raza Unida political parties arose in a number of small towns with large Mexican-American populations. On college campuses across the Southwest, Mexican-Americans formed political organizations.

In 1968 Congress responded to the demand among Mexican-Americans for equal educational opportunity by enacting legislation encouraging school districts to adopt bilingual education programs to instruct non-English speakers in both English and their native language. In a more recent action, Congress moved in 1986 to legalize the status of many immigrants, including many Mexicans, who entered the United States illegally. The Immigration Reform and Control Act of 1986 provided permanent legal residency to undocumented workers who had lived in the United States since before 1982 and prohibits employment of illegal aliens.

Since 1960 Mexican-Americans have made impressive political gains. During the 1960s four Mexican-Americans—Senator Joseph Montoya of New Mexico and representatives Eligio de la Garza and Henry B. Gonzales of Texas and Edward R. Roybal of California— were elected to Congress. In 1974 two Chicanos were elected governors—Jerry Apodaca in New Mexico and Raul Castro in Arizona—becoming the first Mexican-American governors since early in this century. In 1981 Henry Cisneros of San Antonio became the first Mexican-American mayor of a large city.

Today, the 10.5 million Mexican-Americans, the nation's second largest minority group, continue to struggle to expand their political influence, improve their economic position, and preserve their distinctive culture.

The Native American Power Movement

In November 1969, 200 Native Americans seized the abandoned federal penitentiary on Alcatraz Island in San Francisco Bay. For 19 months Indian activists occupied the island in order to draw attention to conditions on the nation's Indian reservations. Alcatraz, the Native Americans said, symbolized conditions on reservations: "It has no running water; it has inadequate sanitation facilities; there is no industry, and so unemployment is very great; there are no health care facilities; the soil is rocky and unproductive." The activists, who called themselves Indians of All Tribes, offered to buy Alcatraz from the federal government for "$24 in glass beads and red cloth."

On Thanksgiving Day, 1970, 350 years after the Pilgrims' arrival, Wampanoag Indians, who had taken part at the first Thanksgiving, held a National Day of Mourning at Plymouth, Massachusetts. A tribal representative declared, "We forfeited our country. Our lands have fallen into the hands of the aggressor. We have allowed the white man to keep us on our knees." Meanwhile, another group of Native Americans established a settlement at Mount Rushmore, to demonstrate Indian claims to the Black Hills.

During the late 1960s and early 1970s, a new spirit of political militancy arose among the first Americans, just as it had among black Americans and women. No other group, however, faced problems more severe than Native Americans. Throughout the 1960s, American Indians were the nation's poorest minority group, worse off than any other group according to virtually every socioeconomic measure. In 1970 the Indian unemployment rate was 10 times the national average, and 40 percent of the Native American population lived below the poverty line. In that year, Native American life expectancy was just 44 years, a third less than that of the average American. In one Apache town of 2500 on the San Carlos reservation in

Henry Cisneros, elected mayor of San Antonio in 1981, was interviewed by Walter Mondale in 1984 as a potential Democratic vice-presidential nominee.

Arizona, there were only 25 telephones and most homes had outdoor toilets and relied on wood-burning stoves for heat.

Conditions on many of the nation's reservations were not unlike those found in underdeveloped areas of Latin America, Africa, and Asia. The death rate among Native Americans exceeded that of the U.S. population as a whole by a third. Deaths caused by pneumonia, hepatitis, dysentery, strep throat, diabetes, tuberculosis, alcoholism, suicide, and homicide were 2 to 60 times higher than the entire U.S. population. Half a million Indian families lived in unsanitary dilapidated dwellings, many in shanties, huts, or even abandoned automobiles.

On the Navajo reservation in Arizona, which is roughly the size of West Virginia, most families lived in the midst of severe poverty. The birthrate was very high; two-and-a-half times the overall U.S. rate and the same as India's. Living standards were low; the average family's purchasing power was about the same as a family in Malaysia. The typical house had just one or two rooms, and 60 percent of the reservation's dwellings had no electricity and 80 percent had no running water or sewers. Educational levels were low. The typical resident had completed just five years of school, and fewer than one adult in six had graduated high school.

During World War II Native Americans began to revolt against such conditions. In 1944 Native Americans formed the National Congress of American Indians (NCAI), the first major intertribal association. Among the group's primary concerns were protection of Indian land rights and improved educational opportunities for Native Americans. When Congress voted in 1953 to allow states to assert legal jurisdiction over Indian reservations without tribal consent and the federal government sought to transfer federal Indian responsibilities for a dozen tribes to the states (a policy known as "termination") and to relocate Indians into urban areas, the NCAI led opposition to these measures. "Self-determination rather than termination!" was the NCAI slogan. Earl Old Person, a Blackfoot leader, commented, "It is important to note that in our Indian language the only translation for termination is to 'wipe out' or 'kill off' . . . how can we plan our future when the Indian Bureau threatens to wipe us out as a race? It's like trying to cook a meal in your tipi when someone is standing outside trying to burn the tipi down."

By the late 1950s a new spirit of Indian nationalism had arisen. In 1959 the Tuscarora tribe, which lived in upstate New York, successfully resisted efforts by the state power authority to convert reservation land into a reservoir. In 1961 a militant new Indian organization appeared, the National Indian Youth Council, which began to use the phrase "Red Power" and sponsored demonstrations, marches, and "fish-ins" to protest state efforts to abolish Indian fishing rights guaranteed by federal treaties. Native Americans in the San Francisco Bay area in 1964 established the Indian Historical Society to present history from the Indian point of view, while the Native American Rights Fund brought legal suits against states that had taken Indian land and abolished Indian hunting, fishing, and water rights in violation of federal treaties. Many tribes also took legal action to prevent strip mining or spraying of pesticides on Indian lands.

The best known of all Indian Power groups was AIM, the American Indian Movement, formed by a group of Chippewas in Minneapolis in 1966 to protest alleged police brutality. In the fall of 1972, AIM led urban Indians, traditionalists, and young Indians along the "Trail of Broken Treaties" to Washington, D.C., seized the offices of the Bureau of Indian Affairs in Washington, D.C., and occupied them for a week in order to dramatize Indian grievances. In the spring of 1973, 200 heavily armed Indians took over the town of Wounded Knee, South Dakota, site of an 1890 massacre of 300 Sioux by the U.S. army cavalry, and occupied the town for 71 days.

Indians are no longer a vanishing group of Americans. The 1980 census recorded an Indian population of 1.38 million in the United States, 72 percent over the figure reported in 1970 and four times the number recorded in 1950. About half of these people live on reservations, which cover 52.4 million acres in 27 states, while most others live in urban areas. The largest Native American populations are located in Alaska, Arizona, California, New Mexico, and Oklahoma. As the Indian population has grown in size, individual Indians have claimed many accomplishments, including receipt of the Pulitzer Prize for fiction by N. Scott Momaday, a Kiowa.

Although Native Americans continue to face severe problems of employment, income, and education, they have demonstrated conclusively that they will not abandon their Indian identity and culture or be treated as dependent wards of the federal government.

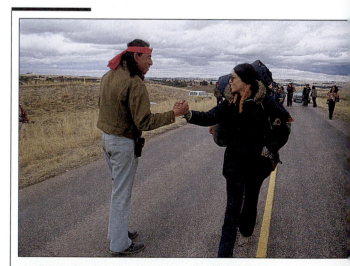

Members of the American Indian Movement occupied the town of Wounded Knee, South Dakota, for over two months to focus attention on Native American grievances.

CHRONOLOGY
OF KEY EVENTS

1960 Four black freshman at North Carolina Agricultural and Technical College in Greensboro, North Carolina, stage the first sit-in to protest segregation; Student Nonviolent Coordinating Committee (SNCC) is founded

1961 Congress of Racial Equality (CORE) stages freedom rides to expose segregation in transportation; *Mapp* v. *Ohio* holds that evidence obtained by unreasonable searches must be excluded at trial

1962 James Meredith enrolls at the University of Mississippi; Students for a Democratic Society (SDS) issue Port Huron Statement; Cesar Chavez begins to organize California farm workers

1963 George C. Wallace is inaugurated Alabama governor; Martin Luther King, Jr., leads demonstrations against segregation in Birmingham, Alabama; racial violence in the South leaves 10 people dead, 35 black homes and churches firebombed; Betty Friedan publishes *The Feminine Mystique*, helping launch a new feminist movement; Equal Pay Act, first federal law to prohibit sex discrimination, requires equal pay for identical work; *Gideon* v. *Wainright* holds that indigent defendants have a right to a court-appointed attorney; March on Washington, D.C., for civil rights and jobs; John F. Kennedy is assassinated; Lyndon Johnson becomes thirty-sixth president

1964 President Johnson announces War on Poverty; Manpower Development and Training Act and Economic Opportunity Act establish the Job Corps and Neighborhood Youth Corps; in *Escobedo* v. *Illinois*, Supreme Court rules that suspects being interrogated by police have a right to legal counsel; Civil Rights Act prohibits discrimination in employment and public facilities; Twenty-fourth Amendment prohibits poll taxes in federal elections

1965 Malcolm X is assassinated; Martin Luther King, Jr., leads demonstrations in Selma, Alabama, to bring issue of voting rights to national attention; Voting Rights Act prohibits literacy tests and sends federal examiners to seven southern states to register black voters; riot in Watts, predominantly black section of Los Angeles, results in 34 deaths; Medicare extends medical insurance to older Americans; Executive Order 11246 requires government contractors to prepare affirmative action plans; Ralph Nader publishes *Unsafe at Any Speed*

1966 SNCC and CORE embrace black nationalism; Black Panther party is organized; National Organization for Women is formed; Congress passes Model Cities Act to attack urban blight

1967 Riots take place in 127 cities

1968 Medicaid expanded to cover the medical expenses of the poor; assassination of Martin Luther King, Jr., in Memphis, Tennessee, is followed by riots in 168 cities

1971 In *Swann* v. *Charlotte-Mecklenburg Board of Education*, U.S. Supreme Court upholds school busing as a tool of racial integration

1973 *Roe* v. *Wade* decision legalizes abortion

1979 *Weber* "reverse-discrimination" case rules that employers could establish voluntary programs including quotas to aid minorities and women

1986 Immigration Reform and Control Act provides permanent legal residency to undocumented workers who have lived in United States since 1982

CONCLUSION

During the l960s, many groups, including black Americans, women, Mexican-Americans, and Native Americans, struggled for equal rights. Early in the decade, black college students, impatient with the slow pace of legal change, staged sit-ins, freedom rides, and protest marches to challenge legal segregation in the South. Passionately committed to a philosophy of nonviolent direct action, these students suffered beatings and went to jail to achieve integration. Their efforts led the federal government to pass the Civil Rights Act of 1964, prohibiting discrimination in public facilities and employment, and the Twenty-fourth Amendment to the Constitution and the Voting Rights Act in 1965, guaranteeing black voting rights.

Despite significant legal gains, many black Americans felt a growing sense of frustration and anger. The violence perpetrated by white racists and a growing white backlash against civil rights led black nationalists to downplay the goal of integration and instead emphasize black political power, community control of schools, creation of black businesses, and black pride. Frustration also grew in urban ghettoes, where the black poor faced problems of poverty, unemployment, and de facto segregation that were not addressed by civil rights legislation. In the summer of 1965, black frustration erupted into violence in Watts, a predominantly black district of Los Angeles, and over the next three years, over 150 major riots occurred.

In a farreaching effort to reduce poverty, alleviate hunger and malnutrition, extend medical care, provide adequate housing, and enhance the employability of the poor, black and white, President Johnson launched his Great Society program in 1964. Although critics charged that federal public assistance food subsidies, health programs, and child care programs contributed to welfare dependence, family breakup, and an increase in out-of-wedlock births, the programs did succeed in cutting the proportion of families living in poverty in half.

The example of the civil rights movement inspired other groups to press for equal opportunity. The women's movement fought for passage of antidiscrimination laws, equal educational and employment opportunities, and a transformation of traditional views about women's place in society. Mexican-Americans battled for bilingual education programs in schools, unionization of farm workers, improved job opportunities, and increased political power. Native Americans pressed for control over Indian lands and resources, the preservation of Indian cultures, and tribal self-government.

SUGGESTIONS FOR FURTHER READING

OVERVIEWS AND SURVEYS

Taylor Branch, *Parting the Waters: America in the King Years* (1988); Wiliam H. Chafe, *Unfinished Journey*, 2d ed. (1991); Richard N. Goodwin, *Remembering America: A Voice from the Sixties* (1988); Godfrey Hodgson, *America in Our Time* (1976); Allen Matusow, *The Unraveling of America: A History of Liberalism in the 1960s* (1984); William O'Neill, *Coming Apart* (1971).

THE STRUGGLE FOR RACIAL JUSTICE

Sally Belfrage, *Freedom Summer* (1965); Michel Belknap, *Federal Law and Southern Order: Racial Violence and Constitutional Conflict in the Post-Brown South* (1987); Derrick Bell, *And We Are Not Saved: The Elusive Quest for Racial Justice* (1987); Jack Bloom, *Class, Race, and the Civil Rights Movement* (1987); Carl Brauer, *John F. Kennedy and the Second Reconstruction* (1977); Clayborne Carson, *In Struggle: SNCC and the Black Awakening of the 1960s* (1981); William H. Chafe, *Civilities and Civil Rights* (1980); Ronald P. Formisano, *Boston Against Busing: Race, Class, and Ethnicity in the 1960s and 1970s* (1991); David Garrow, *Bearing the Cross: Martin Luther King, Jr. and the Southern Christian Leadership Conference* (1986), and *The FBI and Martin Luther King* (1981); David R. Goldfield, *Black, White, and Southern: Race Relations and Southern Culture* (1990); Hugh Davis Graham, *The Civil Rights Era: The Origins and Development of National Policy* (1990); Vincent Harding, *There is a River: The Black Struggle for Freedom in America* (1981); Walter A. Jackson, *Gunnar Myrdal and America's Conscience: Social Engineering and Racial Liberalism* (1990); Richard Kluger, *Simple Justice: The History of the Brown v. Board of Education and Black America's Struggle for Equality* (1975); Steven Lawson, *Black Ballots* (1976), and *Running for Freedom: Civil Rights and Black Politics*

(1991): Nicholas Lemann, *The Promised Land: The Great Black Migration and How It Changed America* (1991); Doug McAdam, *Freedom Summer* (1988); August Meier and Elliot Rudwick, *CORE: A Study in the Civil Rights Movement, 1942–1968* (1973); Stephen Oates, *Let the Trumpet Sound: The Life and Times of Martin Luther King, Jr.* (1982); Frank R. Parker, *Black Votes Count: Political Empowerment in Mississippi* (1990); Thomas R. Peake, *Keeping the Dream Alive: A History of the Southern Christian Leadership Conference* (1987); Armstead L. Robinson and Patricia Sullivan, eds., *New Directions in Civil Rights Studies* (1991); Bernard Schwartz, *Inside the Warren Court* (1983); Howard Sitkoff, *The Struggle for Black Equality* (1981); Melvin I. Urofsky, *A Conflict of Rights: The Supreme Court and Affirmative Action* (1991), and *The Continuity of Change: The Supreme Court and Individual Liberties, 1953–1986* (1990); Nancy J. Weiss, *Whitney M. Young, Jr., and the Struggle for Civil Rights* (1989); John White, *Black Leadership in America*, 2d ed. (1990); Juan Williams, *Eyes on the Prize: America's Civil Rights Years* (1987); Eugene Wolfenstein, *The Victims of Democracy: Malcolm X and the Black Revolution* (1980); C. Vann Woodward, *Strange Career of Jim Crow*, 3d ed. (1974).

THE YOUTH REVOLT

Paul Buhle, *History and the New Left* (1990); Morris Dickstein, *Gates of Eden: American Culture in the Sixties* (1977); Todd Gitlin, *The Sixties* (1987), and *The Whole World Is Watching: The Mass Media in the Making & Unmaking of the New Left* (1980); Maurice Isserman, *. . . If I Had a Hammer: The Death of the Old Left and the Birth of the New Left* (1987); W. J. Rorabaugh, *Berkeley at War: The 1960s* (1989); Theodore Roszak, *The Making of a Counter Culture* (1969); Stanley Rothman and S. Robert Lichter, *Roots of Radicalism* (1982); Kirkpatrick Sale, *SDS* (1973); Jon Wiener, *Come Together: John Lennon in His Time* (1984).

LIBERATION MOVEMENTS

Rodolfo Acuña, *Occupied America*, 3d ed. (1988); Mary Jo Bane, *Here to Stay: American Families in the Twentieth Century* (1978); Mario Barrera, *Race and Class in the Southwest* (1979); Judith Barwick, *In Transition: How Feminism, Sexual Liberation, and the Search for Self-Fulfillment Have Altered America* (1979); Mary Frances Berry, *Why ERA Failed* (1986); Albert Camarillo, *Hispanics in a Changing Society* (1979); William H. Chafe, *Women and Equality* (1977); Andrew J. Cherlin, ed., *The Changing American Family and Public Policy* (1988); Sara Evans, *Personal Politics: The Roots of Women's Liberation in the Civil Rights Movement and the New Left* (1979); Victor R. Fuchs, *How We Live* (1983); Mario T. García, *Mexican Americans: Leadership, Ideology and Identity* (1989); Juan Gómez-Quiñones, *Chicano Politics* (1990); Hazel W. Hertzberg, *The Search for an American Identity* (1971); Judith Hole and Ellen Levine, *Rebirth of Feminism* (1971); Peter Iverson, *The Navajo Nation* (1981); Virginia Sánchez Korrol, *From Colonia to Community* (1983); Sar A. Levitan et al., *What's Happening to the American Family? Tensions, Hopes, Realities* (1988); Matt S. Meier and Feliciano Rivera, *The Chicanos* (1972); Steven Mintz and Susan Kellogg, *Domestic Revolutions: A Social History of American Family Life* (1988); Joan Moore and Harry Pachon, *Hispanics in the United States* (1985); Roger Nichols, *The American Indian: Past and Present*, 3d ed. (1985); David Popenoe, *Disturbing the Nest: Family Change and Decline in Modern Societies* (1988); Leila Rupp and Verta Taylor, *Survival in the Doldrums: The American Women's Rights Movement, 1945 to the 1960s* (1987).

A

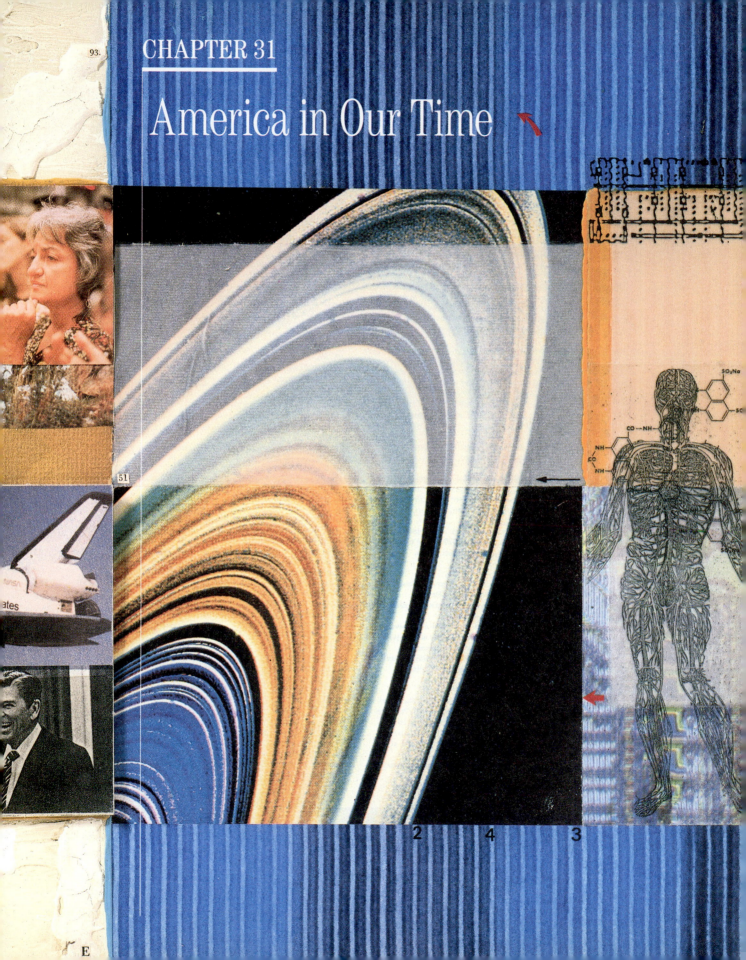

CHAPTER 31

America in Our Time

Shortly after 1 A.M. on the morning of June 17, 1972, Frank Wills, a security guard at the Washington, D.C., Watergate office complex, spotted a strip of masking tape covering the lock of a basement door. He removed it. A short while later, he found the door taped open again. He called the police, who found two more taped locks, and a jammed door leading into the offices of the Democratic National Committee. Inside they discovered five men carrying cameras and electronic eavesdropping equipment.

The White House press secretary soon dismissed the incident as a "third-rate burglary attempt," but the identities of the burglars suggested something more serious. One, James McCord, was chief security coordinator and electronics expert of the Committee for the Reelection of the President. Others had links to the CIA. Two of the burglars carried papers bearing the name Howard Hunt, a special White House consultant, and $6500, which was traced to President Nixon's campaign committee.

At first, the Watergate break-in seemed like a minor incident. But it set in motion a chain of events that eventually forced Richard Nixon to resign the presidency. Over the course of the next year, it became clear that the break-in was one of a series of secret operations coordinated by the White House and financed by illegal campaign contributions, operations which posed a threat to America's constitutional system of government.

The Watergate break-in had its roots in Richard Nixon's obsession with secrecy and political intelligence. In July 1970 he approved a plan to use the FBI, CIA, National Security Agency, and Defense Intelligence Agency to gather information on campus demonstrators, antiwar protestors, and other radicals, which involved opening personal mail and breaking and entering into offices and residences. FBI Director J. Edgar Hoover called the Huston plan (named after the plan's originator, Nixon aide Tom Huston) "clearly illegal," and it was rescinded. But the Nixon administration subsequently established a secret unit to carry out similar illegal activities.

To stop leaks of information to the press, in 1971 the Nixon White House assembled a team of "plumbers," consisting of former CIA operatives. This private police force, paid for in part by illegal campaign contributions, engaged in a wide range of criminal acts such as tapping the phones of officials and journalists suspected of handling leaked information; burglarizing the office of a psychiatrist consulted by Daniel Ellsberg, who had leaked the Pentagon Papers, a secret Pentagon history of the Vietnam War, to the press; and fabricating a State Department cable linking the Kennedy administration to the assassination of South Vietnam's President Diem.

In 1972 when President Nixon was running for reelection, his campaign committee authorized another series of illegal activities. It hired Donald Segretti to stage "dirty tricks" against potential Democratic candidates, which included mailing letters that falsely accused Senator Henry Jackson of homosexuality and fathering an illegitimate child. It considered a plan to use call girls to blackmail Democrats at their national convention and to kidnap anti-Nixon radical leaders. The committee also authorized $250,000 for intelligence gathering operations. Four times the committee sent burglars to break into Democratic headquarters.

The Watergate scandal led to the downfall of Richard Nixon. Here the Senate Watergate Committee questions Nixon aide H. R. Haldeman.

Precisely what the campaign committee hoped to learn from these intelligence-gathering activities remains a mystery. It seems likely that it was seeking information about the Democratic party's campaign strategies and any information the Democrats had about illegal campaign contributions to the Republican party.

As early as June 23—six days after the botched break-in—President Nixon sought to impede the investigation of the Watergate break-in. He ordered aides to block an FBI investigation into White House involvement into the break-in on grounds that an investigation would endanger national security. He also counseled his aides to lie under oath, if necessary: "I don't give a [expletive deleted] what happens," he told his former attorney general, John Mitchell, who was then his campaign manager, "I want you all to stonewall it, let them plead the Fifth Amendment, cover-up, or anything else."

The Watergate break-in did not hurt Nixon's reelection campaign. Between the activities of the burglars and the president were layers of officials that had to be carefully peeled away. That would take time and energy. *Washington Post* reporters Bob Woodward and Carl Bernstein had both. They sensed that the break-in was only part of a larger scandal. Slowly they pieced together part of the story. Federal judge John Sirica helped the ends of justice by sentencing the uncooperative burglers to long jail terms. To lessen their time in prison, some of the burgers began to tell the truth, and the truth illuminated a path leading to the White House.

If Nixon had few political friends, he had legions of enemies. Over the years he had offended or attacked many of the Democrats—and a number of the prominent Republicans. His detractors latched onto the Watergate issue with the tenacity of bulldogs. House Majority Leader Tip O'Neill told a congressional ally in early 1973, "All my years tell me what's happening. They did so many bad things during that campaign that there is no way to keep it from coming out. . . . The time is going to come when impeachment is going to hit this Congress."

The Senate appointed a special committee to investigate the Watergate scandal. Most of Nixon's top aides continued the cover-up. John Dean, the president's counsel, did not.

Throughout the episode he had kept careful notes, and in a quiet precise voice he told the Senate Watergate Committee that the president was deeply involved in the cover-up. The matter was still not solved. All the committee had was Dean's word against the other White House aides.

On July 16, 1973, Alexander Butterfield, a former White House employee, dropped a bombshell by testifying that Nixon had recorded all Oval Office conversations. Whatever Nixon and his aides had said about Watergate in the Oval Office, therefore, was faithfully recorded on tape.

Nixon tried to keep the tapes from the committee by invoking executive privilege and interpreting that doctrine to imply that a president had a right to keep confidential any White House communication, whether or not it involved sensitive diplomatic or national security matters. When Archibald Cox, a special prosecutor investigating violations of criminal law in the Watergate affair, persisted in demanding the tapes, Nixon ordered his attorney general, Elliot Richardson, to fire him; Richardson refused and resigned; Richardson's assistant, William Ruckelshaus also resigned. Ruckelshaus's assistant, Robert Bork, finally fired Cox, but Congress forced Nixon to name a new special prosecutor, Houston attorney Leon Jaworski. Ultimately, a unanimous Supreme Court ordered Nixon to turn over the tapes.

In the midst of the Watergate investigations, another scandal broke. Federal prosecutors accused Vice President Spiro Agnew of extorting payoffs from engineers and road building contractors while he was Maryland's governor and Baltimore County executive. In a plea bargain, Agnew pleaded no contest to a relatively minor charge—that he had falsified his income tax in 1967—in exchange for a $10,000 fine. Agnew was succeeded as vice president by Gerald Ford, whom Nixon appointed.

The word "Watergate" gradually ballooned well beyond the break-in and cover-up and came to encompass a wide range of presidential wrongdoings, including political favors to ITT and milk producers in exchange for campaign contributions; the offer of the job of FBI director to a judge to influence his decision in a pending case; questionable deductions on Nixon's income taxes and misuse of public funds to improve his houses. This list of crimes and misdeeds Nixon was charged with also included deceiving Congress and the public about the secret bombing of Cambodia in 1969 and 1970; authorization of illegal domestic political surveillance, military spying on civilians, and espionage against dissidents, political opponents, and journalists; and attempts to use FBI investigations and income tax audits by the Internal Revenue Service to harass political enemies.

On July 24, 1974, the House Judiciary Committee recommended that the House of Representatives impeach Nixon for obstruction of justice, abuse of power, and refusal to relinquish the tapes. The end was near. On August 5 Nixon obeyed the Supreme Court ruling and released the tapes, which confirmed Dean's detailed testimony. Nixon had been involved in a cover-up; he had obstructed justice. On August 9, in a tearful farewell Nixon became the first American president to resign from office. The following day, Gerald Ford became the new president. "Our long national nightmare," he said, "is over."

CRISIS OF POLITICAL LEADERSHIP

The Vietnam War and the Watergate scandal had a profound effect on the presidency. The office suffered a dramatic decline in public respect, and Congress became increasingly unwilling to defer to presidential leadership. Congress enacted a series of reforms that would make future Watergate-type abuses of presidential authority less likely. In the process Congress recaptured constitutional powers that had been ceded to an increasingly dominant executive branch.

Restraining the Imperial Presidency

Over the course of the twentieth century, the presidency gradually supplanted Congress as the center of federal power. Presidential powers increased, presidential staff grew in size, and the executive branch gradually acquired a dominant relationship over Congress.

Beginning with Theodore Roosevelt's Square Deal program, the president, and not Congress, established the nation's legislative agenda. Increasingly, Congress ceded its budget-making authority to the president. Lacking its own budget bureau to analyze specific funding needs, Congress was reluctant to depart from the budget put forward by the president and create its own priorities. Presidents even found a way to make agreements with foreign nations without congressional approval. After World War II, presidents moved away from treaty-making procedures, substituting executive agreements for treaties that require Senate approval. Even more important, presidents gained the power to wage undeclared war, despite the fact that Congress is the sole branch of government empowered by the Constitution to "declare" war.

No president went further than Richard Nixon in concentrating powers in the presidency. He refused to spend funds that Congress had appropriated for specific purposes, undercutting Congress's power of the purse. He claimed executive privilege against disclosure of information on administration decisions, hindering Congress's ability to see that programs were being properly carried out. He refused to allow key decision makers to be questioned before congressional committees. He reorganized the executive branch and broadened the authority of new cabinet positions without congressional approval. And during the Vietnam War, Nixon ordered harbors mined and bombing raids launched without consulting Congress.

Watergate brought an end to the "imperial presidency"—the growth of presidential power that dates from Theodore Roosevelt's accession to the White House in 1901. In the wake of Watergate, Congress enacted a series of reforms designed to curb abuses of presidential power.

Over the president's veto, both houses of Congress enacted limitations on the power of U.S. presidents to wage war. The War Powers Act (1973) required future presidents to win specific authorization from Congress to engage U.S. forces in foreign combat for more than 90 days. Under the law, a president who orders troops into action abroad must report the reason for this action to Congress within 48 hours.

Disclosures during the Watergate investigations of money laundering, blatant influence peddling, and briefcases stuffed with $100 bills, led Congress to reform the way elections are financed. Congress enacted legislation calling for public financing of presidential elections, public disclosure of sources of funding, limits on private campaign contributions and spending, and enforcement of campaign finance laws by an independent Federal Election Commission. The law limited the amount individuals could give to a single candidate to $1000. In addition, political action committees (PACs) were allowed to give only $5000 to a candidate.

The Watergate scandal revealed how difficult it is for the Justice Department to investigate crimes in the executive branch, because it operates under the authority of the president. Congress responded by requiring the attorney general to appoint a special prosecutor to investigate accusations of illegal activities within the executive branch.

To reassert its budget-making authority, Congress created a Congressional Budget Office and specifically forbade a president to impound funds without congressional approval. To open government to public scrutiny, Congress opened more committee deliberations and enacted the Freedom of Information Act, which allows the public and press to request declassification of government documents.

To reduce the authority of arbitrary and aging committee chairmen, the House of Representatives weakened the seniority system. In addition, the Senate modified the filibuster rule, allowing debate to be cut off with the consent of 60 senators instead of the previous requirement of two-thirds present and voting. The end result was to streamline the workings of Congress.

Some of the post-Watergate reforms have not been as effective as reformers anticipated. The War Powers Act has never been invoked and while various administrations have attempted to comply with the spirit of the law, no president has accepted its constitutional validity.

Campaign financing reform did not curb the power of special interests to curry favor with politicians or the ability of the very rich to outspend opponents. The Supreme Court struck down laws that forbade candidates to give more

On August 9, 1974, Richard Nixon resigned the presidency after the release of secret tapes revealed that he had been involved in a cover-up of the Watergate affair.

than $50,000 to their own presidential campaign and, more importantly, barred any limitations on unauthorized "independent expenditures" by individuals on behalf of a candidate. A further weakness of campaign financing reform was its limited applicability to congressional races. It established spending ceilings but provided no government subsidies for campaigns.

Bringing the FBI and CIA to Heel

During the 1970s, congressional investigators discovered that the Federal Bureau of Investigation and the Central Intelligence Agency, in defiance of their charters and federal law, broke into the homes, tapped the phones, and opened the mail of American citizens; illegally infiltrated antiwar groups and black radical organizations; accumulated dossiers on 7200 dissidents; and had been used by presidents for political purposes. Investigators also found that the CIA had been involved in assassination plots against foreign leaders, and had tested the effects of radiation, electric shock, and drugs (such as LSD) on unsuspecting people. Congress was outraged to learn that the CIA and organized crime plotted to assassinate Fidel Castro by supplying him with poison cigars, giving him drugs that would make his beard fall out, and shooting him with a weapon disguised as a pen.

The FBI, CIA, army, and National Security Agency violated civil liberties by opening some 380,000 first-class letters, infiltrating suspected subversive organizations, and developing lists of 26,000 Americans to be detained during a national emergency. A Senate report concluded: "Too many people have been spied upon by too many Government agencies and too much information has been collected."

As a result of these investigations, the government severely limited CIA operations in the United States and laid down strict guidelines for FBI activities. To tighten congressional control over the CIA, Congress established a joint committee to supervise CIA operations.

New Style Presidents

In the wake of Nixon's abuses of presidential power, the next two presidents, Gerald Ford and Jimmy Carter, cultivated reputations as modest, honest, forthright men. The first important public image of Ford's presidency was of Ford stepping outside his front door in his pajamas to pick up his newspaper. The first important image of Carter's presidency was of the new president carrying his own bags into the White House. Both Ford and Carter sought to project the appearance of ordinariness in order to symbolically reduce the presidency to a more human size. As Gerald Ford put it, "I am a Ford not a Lincoln." Both were men of decency and integrity, but neither established reputations as strong, dynamic leaders.

An Eagle scout, college football hero, and 13-term congressman from Grand Rapids, Michigan, Gerald Ford never aspired to the presidency. During his 25 years in the House, he established a reputation as a moderate Republican who voted against federal aid to education, Medicare, and antipollution programs and staunchly supported the Vietnam War. When Spiro Agnew resigned the vice presidency, Nixon turned to Ford, who had a reputation for intense personal loyalty. Nixon's resignation made Ford president.

Ford's successor as president was Jimmy Carter, a deeply intelligent and caring man, but, like Ford, wholly lacking in foreign policy experience. Carter, the first president from the Deep South since Zachary Taylor, grew up on a humble Georgia farm that lacked running water and electricity. He won an appointment to the Naval Academy in 1942, then joined the Navy's atomic submarine program. After his father's death, he reluctantly left the navy and returned home to run the family peanut farm. He was elected to the Georgia state senate in 1962 and won the state's governorship in 1970. Two years later he began planning his presidential campaign, which involved spending months in states with early primaries and caucuses in order to create the momentum that he needed to win the Democratic nomination.

By virtue of his southern birth and firm religious beliefs (he was a born-again Christian), Carter temporarily restored the New Deal Democratic coalition, the broad-based voter coalition that consisted of an unlikely mixture of minorities: southern whites, Jews, ethnic blue-collar workers, blacks, and intellectuals. Many blue-collar voters and white Southerners had been angered in 1972 by Democratic presidential nominee George McGovern's support of legalized abortion, benign attitude toward drugs, advocacy for the unilateral American withdrawal from Vietnam and amnesty for draft evaders, as well as his liberal stand on welfare, busing, and other civil rights issues. Carter's conservative demeanor reassured these voters and helped him narrowly defeat Ford in the 1976 presidential election.

While many Americans admired their honesty and sincerity, neither Ford nor Carter succeeded in winning the confidence of the American people. Both of their administrations were likened to ships without rudders, veering from one problem to another, without a clear sense of direction. Both Ford and Carter were viewed as waffling on major issues of public policy. As a result, both came to be regarded as unsure, vacillating presidents.

At the beginning of his presidency, Ford dismissed the possibility of pardoning Richard Nixon for his Watergate misdeeds. "I do not think the public would stand for it," he said. But he did pardon Nixon. In the realm of economic policy, he began by urging tax increases and budget cuts and then called for a large tax cut. His energy policy was crippled by the same indecision. At first, he tried to raise prices by imposing import fees on imported oil and ending domestic price controls, then he abandoned that position in the face of severe political pressure.

Carter, too, suffered from the charge that he modified his stances in the face of political pressure. He came to office determined to cut military spending, calling for the abolition of nuclear weapons and the withdrawal of American troops from South Korea. By the end of his term, after Soviet forces occupied Afghanistan and Iran took several hundred American hostages, Carter spoke of the need for sustained growth in defense spending, upgrading nuclear forces in Europe, and developing a new strategic bomber.

Critics accused both Ford and Carter of substituting slogans for concrete policies—for Ford, WIN ("Whip Inflation Now"); for Carter, energy conservation as the "moral equivalent of war" ("meow" to the program's critics). Both were described as "passionless presidents," who failed to project a clear vision of where they wanted to lead the country. But in their defense, both faced serious problems, ranging from dealing with rising oil prices to confronting third-world terrorists.

On the domestic front, both lacked the political skills and the base of popular support necessary to get a coherent program through Congress. Both alienated the activist wings of their parties. Ford failed to win the support of Republican right wingers, who supported Ronald Reagan in the 1976 primaries; Carter failed to win over Democratic liberals, who favored Edward Kennedy in the 1980 primaries. Carter ran for the presidency by running against the Washington establishment, but once elected he seemed to lack the political acumen necessary to get his programs enacted, most notably SALT II, a second strategic arms agreement with the Soviet Union.

By the end of their presidencies, a growing number of Americans doubted that Ford and Carter had come to grips with the burdens of their office. Their triumphs did not inspire the nation; their failures provoked scorn. During his two-and-a-half years in office, Ford succeeded in healing the deep political divisions produced by Watergate, but his record in office failed to win the nation's confidence. During his single term, Carter negotiated peace between Israel and Egypt, normalized relations with China, improved American relations with Latin America, and placed a new emphasis on human rights in American foreign policy; but Americans were more concerned about double-digit inflation, interest rates approaching 20 percent, and Carter's failure to secure release of American diplomats held hostage in Iran.

WRENCHING ECONOMIC TRANSFORMATIONS

He is the personification of American business. His autobiography stood on the top of the best-seller list for years. A thick, powerful slab of a man, Lee Iacocca is the picture of a successful, confident American businessman. The irony of the picture is, of course, that Lee Iacocca is also the most visible symbol of the American automobile industry, which is in turn the most prominent example of the failure of American industry to compete in a changing world economy.

At one time, the car makers in Detroit produced automobiles that mirrored America's strength and power. They were big, heavy, powerful cars, with such expensive options as power windows, power brakes, and power steering. When an engineer at Chrysler designed a smaller, low-slung car, K. T. Keller, the

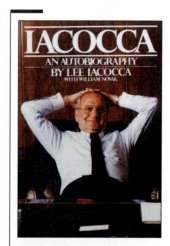

The cover of Lee Iacocca's autobiography portrays him as the consummate successful businessperson. Despite the decline in the American automobile industry, he put the ailing Chrysler company back on its feet.

company's top executive, remarked in disgust, "Chrysler builds cars to sit in, not to piss over." So what if they weren't energy efficient. So what if they only traveled 10 to 13 miles on a gallon of gas. Until 1973, gas was cheap; just 37 cents a gallon that year.

Detroit—the land of big cars, of General Motors, Ford, and Chrysler—was Iacocca's world. From 1946 to 1978 he worked for Ford, climbing the corporate ladder from salesman to zone manager, to district manager, to divisional head, to president of Ford. He was the driving force behind Ford's most popular car—the Mustang.

In 1978, Henry Ford II, the grandson of the company's founder, fired Iacocca. Iacocca lashed back: "Your timing stinks," he told Ford. "We've just made a billion eight for the second year in a row. That's three and a half billion in the past two years. But mark my words, Henry. You may never see a billion eight again. And do you know why? Because you don't know how the _____ we made it in the first place!"

In Iacocca's angry words there was more truth than perhaps he even realized. In the late 1970s, the American automotive industry had crashed into new economic realities. Although Middle Eastern oil had been inexpensive during the period between 1945 and the early 1970s, economic realities dictated that the price *must* eventually rise dramatically. Each year more and more nations entered the industrial ranks; each year the consumption of oil increased; each year the limited supplies of oil decreased. These simple economic facts combined with emerging Arab nationalism and the solidarity of the Organization of Petroleum Exporting Countries (OPEC) were bound to drive up the price of oil. As the price of a gallon of gas charged toward the dollar mark, American drivers purchased smaller, better engineered, fuel-efficient cars from Japan and Europe. By 1982, Japanese cars had captured 30 percent of the U.S. market.

Men like Iacocca looked to the government for help. After being fired from Ford, Iacocca accepted the top position at Chrysler. With the help of a $1.2 billion loan from Washington, he put the ailing company on its feet again.

Since 1973, the American economy has undergone a series of wrenching economic transformations. Economic growth slowed; productivity flagged; inflation rose; and major industries faltered in the face of foreign competition. Despite a massive influx of women into the work force, family wages stagnated. A quarter century of rapid post–World War II economic growth ended.

This economic slowdown was not confined to the United States; all major industrialized nations experienced slower economic growth. Annual growth in America's real national output per employed person averaged 1.8 percent between 1960 and 1973; it dropped to 0.1 percent between 1974 and 1978. Japan's rate fell from 8.9 percent during the first period to 3.2 percent in the second; West Germany's fell from 4.7 to 3 percent.

The causes of worldwide economic decline are hotly contested. It has been attributed to surges in world oil prices during the 1970s; to the growing expense of government policies designed to protect public health, safety, and the environment and to aid the poor; to alleged foreign "dumping" of products at prices below their cost of production; to demands of organized labor for higher wages; to low productivity increases in the expanding service sector; and to excessive government deficits.

If the causes of economic stagnation remain unclear, the social and political consequences have been profound—evident in a sharp influx of wives into the work force, tax revolts and demands for tax reform, and calls for protection of American industry.

The Age of Inflation

In 1967, the average price of a three-bedroom house was $17,000. A brand new Cadillac convertible went for $6700 and a new Volkswagen $1497. A portable typewriter cost $39 and a man's gray flannel suit $60. A Hershey chocolate bar sold for a nickel; a pound of sirloin for 89 cents; and a gallon of regular gasoline cost 39 cents. Two decades later, the prices of these products had quadrupled.

The upsurge in inflation started when Lyndon Johnson decided to fight the Vietnam War without raising taxes enough to pay for it. By 1968 the war was costing the United States $3 billion dollars a month, and the federal budget

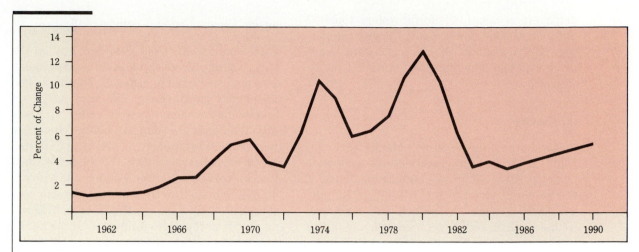

Figure 31.1
Consumer price index, 1960–1990

skyrocketed to $179 billion. With hundreds of thousands of Americans in the military service and even more working in defense-related industries, unemployment fell, wages rose, demand mushroomed, and government deficits increased. Inflation accelerated in the early 1970s as a result of a series of crop failures and sharp rises in commodities, especially oil.

High inflation had many negative effects on the American economy. It wiped out many families' savings. It provoked labor turmoil, as teachers, sanitation workers, auto workers, and others went on strike to try to win wage settlements ahead of inflation. It encouraged speculation in tangible assets—like art, antiques, precious metals, and real estate—rather than productive investment in new factories and technology. Above all, the effects of inflation seemed extremely unfair. Certain organized interest groups were able to keep up with inflation, while other less powerful groups, such as welfare recipients, saw the value of their benefits decline significantly.

This surge of inflation contributed to an abrupt reversal of a 20-year period of steady income growth. Inflation reduced the purchasing power of most Americans and pushed many into higher tax brackets.

Inflation raised the prices of virtually all goods and services, but it had a particularly large impact on two areas of the economy: health care and housing, which experienced price rises far above the inflation rate. One result was a sharp increase in the number of Americans unable to afford health insurance. Another consequence was a sharp increase in the proportion of income that Americans spent on housing. For most of the post–World War II period, a family expected to spend 25 percent of its total income on housing, but by the 1980s six million American households were paying more than half their income on rent. An increase in homelessness was the most graphic symbol of this mounting housing problem.

For over a decade, family wages remained flat. The hourly wages of American workers peaked in 1973, the year of the first OPEC oil embargo. Wages flattened between 1973 and 1977, then fell sharply in 1978, 1979, and 1980. During the 1980s, real wages rose at a modest rate, but by the end of the decade they had climbed to just $36 over 1973 levels.

One consequence of shrinking paychecks was a rash of tax revolts. Traditionally Americans paid a much lower level of taxes than people in the rest of the industrialized world. After World War II, however, the level of taxation rose steadily. Between 1955 and 1988, taxes grew at twice the rate of household income. In 1955, a median family of four paid an average federal tax rate of 9 percent. By 1988, the rate was 24 percent. With paychecks squeezed by inflation, taxpayers revolted. California voters touched off the national tax revolt in 1978 with the passage of Proposition 13, which cut state taxes, capped public spending, and curtailed public services.

Oil Embargo

Political unrest in the oil-rich Middle East contributed significantly to America's economic troubles. After suffering a humiliating defeat at the hands of Israel in the 1973 "Yom Kippur" war, Arab leaders unsheathed a new political weapon: oil. In order to pressure Israel out of territory conquered in the 1967 and 1973 wars, Arab nations cut oil production 25 percent and embargoed all oil exports to the United States. Leading the struggle was OPEC, which had been founded by Iran, Saudi Arabia, and Venezuela in 1960 to fight a reduction in prices by oil companies.

Because Arab nations controlled 60 percent of the proven oil reserves in the non-Communist world, they had the western nations over a barrel. Production cutbacks produced an immediate global shortage. The United States imported a third of its oil from Arab nations; western Europe imported 72 percent from the Middle East; Japan, 82 percent.

Gas prices rose, and long lines formed at gas pumps. President Nixon asked Americans to forego outdoor Christmas displays and to reduce thermostats to 68 degrees. Some factories shortened the work week and some shopping centers restricted business hours.

The Arab struggle for higher oil prices began in 1970, when the ruler of Libya, Col. Muammar Qaddafi, launched a bitter, ten-month battle for high oil royalties. As a result, he was able to increase Libya's oil royalties by 120 percent within two years—from $1 a barrel to $2.20 a barrel.

The oil crisis brought to an end an era of cheap and ample energy. Americans had to learn to live with smaller cars and less heating and air conditioning. But the crisis did have a positive side effect. It increased public consciousness about the environment and stimulated awareness of the importance of conservation. But for millions of Americans the lessons were painful to learn.

Foreign Competition and Deindustrialization

It was January 17, 1949. Standing idly on the dock, waiting for work to begin, several longshoremen snickered in disbelief. The car looked ridiculously un-American. Tiny and ugly, it resembled half a walnut shell with wheels, or better yet, an insect, a "bug," a "beetle." Ben Pon, the official Volkswagen agent to the United States, was aboard the Dutch freighter *Westerdam* in New York Harbor, holding a press conference to introduce the VW to American consumers. He called the car the "Victory Wagon," but skeptical reporters dubbed it "Hitler's car." It was. A generation of American moviegoers remembered seeing it in 1930s newsreels touting Germany's economic recovery. But how could it ever appeal to Americans? The Volkswagen was slow, dull, small, and fuel efficient, just when Americans were lusting after fins, scoop grilles, and chrome—lots of chrome. In 1949 Americans purchased 6,250,000 new automobiles. Two were VWs. The longshoremen were right, but not for long. They were laughing at the future.

In 1947, the United States was truly the world's factory. Half of all the world's manufacturing took place in the United States. Americans made 57 percent of the world's steel and 80 percent of the world's cars. It was inevitable that other countries would eventually challenge American manufacturers. Still, the experience was painful for millions of Americans. During the early 1960s, foreign manufacturers produced 6 percent of the cars purchased by Americans. That figure climbed to 10.6 percent in the late 1960s, 15 percent in the early 1970s, and 20 percent in the late 1970s. The decline in the American share of the market meant fewer jobs in the American automobile, steel, and rubber industries.

The foreign penetration extended far beyond the market for compact cars. Foreign countries began to dominate the highly profitable, technologically advanced fields, such as consumer electronics, luxury automobiles, and machine tools. Americans discovered that technologies their country had pioneered—such as semiconductors, color televisions, and video cassette recorders—were now produced almost exclusively by foreign manufacturers.

Few economic developments aroused as much public concern during the 1970s as the loss of American jobs in basic industry. Between mid-1975 and early 1981, 24 tire plants shut down in the United States, resulting in 20,000 lost jobs. Since the early 1970s, the steel industry eliminated the jobs of over 120,000 steelworkers. During the 1970s General Electric reduced its U.S. employment by 25,000; RCA cut its U.S. employment by 14,000. According to one estimate, 30 million jobs disappeared during the 1970s as the direct result of plant, store, and office shutdowns.

The decline of basic industry had a high human cost. Displaced workers saw their savings depleted, mortgages foreclosed, and health and pension benefits lost. Even when they found new jobs, they typically had to settle for wages substantially below what they had earned before. Plant shutdowns and closings had profound effects on entire communities, which lost their tax bases at the time that they needed to fund health and welfare services.

American jobs were lost in basic industry principally because the same goods could be produced in foreign countries at a far lower cost. American and even Japanese companies shifted low-skill production work to such places as South Korea, Taiwan, Hong Kong, Singapore, and Indonesia where they paid much lower wages.

The decline of the nation's major industries also had profound political consequences. It has led to demands for protective tariffs, quotas, and voluntary limitations on imported goods, including steel, autos, and shoes. It has also led to proposals to restrict foreign investment by American companies, and to ensure that goods sold domestically contain a certain minimum proportion of American-produced components. The steel industry received protection from foreign competition beginning in 1969. Japanese automakers agreed to voluntarily restrict exports to the United States in 1981.

Whipping Stagflation

During the 1960s, the primary goal of economic policy was to encourage growth and keep unemployment low. Inflationary pressures were successfully tamed through "jawboning" industry leaders and unions to keep prices and wages stable. But by the early 1970s the economy started to suffer from *stagflation*—high unemployment and inflation coupled with stagnant economic growth. This presented economic policymakers with a new and perplexing problem. Stagflation contradicted the last 40 years of Keynesian economic experience. Unemployment and inflation usually did not coexist. When unemployment was high, prices had been stable or even declining. Policymakers could increase government spending, reduce taxes, and expand the money supply—all of which augmented consumer purchasing power and created jobs—without having to worry about creating an inflation problem. When inflation had been the problem, jobs were plentiful. Policymakers could raise taxes, trim government spending, and contract the money supply, reducing consumer demand and the upward pressure on prices without producing a recession. The object was to maintain full employment (defined as 96 percent employment) and keep inflation under 2 percent a year. But how to attack both inflation and unemployment at the same time? This was the question that presidents Nixon, Ford, and Carter had to address.

The problem with stagflation was the pain of its options. To attack inflation by reducing consumer purchasing power only made unemployment worse. The other choice was no better. Stimulating purchasing power and creating jobs also drove prices higher. Not surprisingly, economic policy during the 1970s was a nightmare of confusion and contradiction.

By 1971, pressures produced by the Vietnam War and federal social spending, coupled with increase in foreign competition, pushed the inflation rate to 5 percent and unemployment to 6 percent. President Richard Nixon responded by increasing federal budget deficits and devaluing the dollar. These policies were an attempt to stimulate the economy and to make American goods more competitive overseas. Nixon also imposed a 90-day wage and price freeze to curb inflation. The freeze was followed by a mandatory set of wage-price guidelines, and then by voluntary controls. Inflation stayed at about 4 percent during the freeze, but once controls were lifted, inflation resumed its up-

(Text continues on p. 1062)

AMERICA AND THE WORLD
THE POLITICS OF OIL

This photo of a mass of derricks, typical of early oil drilling operations, in the Spindletop oil fields of Texas was taken during the heyday of oil production in the early twentieth century. When consumption outpaced production, the search for new reserves led to offshore sites. The oil platform pictured here is in the Gulf of Mexico off the coast of Louisiana.

The modern era of oil production began on August 27, 1859, when Edwin L. Drake drilled the first successful oil well—69 feet deep—near Titusville in northwestern Pennsylvania. Just 5 years earlier, the invention of the kerosene lamp had ignited an intense demand for oil. By drilling an oil well, Drake had hoped to meet the growing demand for oil for lighting and lubrication.

Drake's success inspired hundreds of small companies to explore for oil. In 1860, world oil production reached 500,000 barrels; by the 1870s production soared to 20 million barrels annually. In 1879, the first oil well was drilled in California; and in 1887, in Texas. But as production boomed, prices fell and oil industry profits declined.

In 1882, John D. Rockefeller devised a solution to the problem of unbridled competition in the oil fields: the Standard Oil trust, which brought together 40 of the nation's leading refiners. Through its control of refining, Standard Oil was temporarily able to control the price of oil.

During the early twentieth century, oil production continued to climb. By 1920, oil production reached 450 million barrels annually—prompting fear that the nation was about to run out of oil. Government officials predicted that the nation's oil reserves would last just 10 years.

Up until around 1910, the United States produced between 60 and 70 percent of the world's oil supply. As fear grew that American oil reserves were dangerously depleted, the search for oil turned worldwide. Oil was discovered in Mexico at the beginning of the twentieth century, in Iran in 1908, in Venezuela during World War I, and in Iraq in 1927. Many of the new oil discoveries occurred in areas dominated by Britain and the Netherlands: in the Dutch East Indies, Iran, and British mandates in the Middle East. By 1919, Britain controlled 50 percent of the world's proven oil reserves.

After World War I, a bitter struggle for control of world oil reserves erupted. The British, Dutch, and French excluded American companies from purchasing oil fields in territories under their control. Congress retaliated in 1920 by adopting the Mineral Leasing Act, which denied access to American oil reserves to any foreign country that restricted American access to its reserves. The dispute was ultimately resolved during the 1920s, when American oil companies were finally allowed to drill in the British Middle East and the Dutch East Indies.

The fear that American oil reserves were nearly exhausted ended abruptly in 1924, with the discovery of enormous new oil fields in Texas, Oklahoma, and California. These discoveries, along with production from new fields in Mexico, the Soviet Union, and Venezuela, combined to drastically depress oil prices. By 1931, with crude oil selling for 10 cents a barrel, domestic oil producers demanded restrictions on production in order to raise prices. Texas and Oklahoma passed state laws and stationed militia units at oil fields to prevent drillers from exceeding production quotas. Despite these measures, prices continued to fall.

In a final bid to solve the problem of overproduction, the federal government stepped in. Under the National Recovery Administration (NRA), the federal government imposed production restraints, import restrictions, and price regulations. After the Supreme Court declared the NRA unconstitutional, the federal government imposed a tariff on foreign oil.

During World War II, the oil surpluses of the 1930s quickly disappeared. Six billion of the seven billion barrels of petroleum used by the allies during the war came from the United States. Public officials again began to worry that the United States was running out of oil.

It seemed imperative that the United States secure access to foreign oil reserves. Increasingly, policymakers and the oil industry focused their attention on the Middle East, particularly the Persian Gulf, which they believed would become the center of postwar oil production. As early as the 1930s, Britain had gained control over Iran's oil fields and the United States discovered oil reserves in Kuwait and Saudi Arabia. After World War II ended, Middle Eastern oil production surged upward. Gradually, American dependence on Middle Eastern oil increased.

During the 1950s, a combination of cheap fuel and a burgeoning consumer culture led to an orgy of consumption. With only 6 percent of the world's population, the United States accounted for one-third of global oil consumption. Foreign oil was so cheap that coal-burning utilities made the expensive shift to oil and natural gas. World oil prices were so low that Iranian, Venezuelan, and Arabian oil producers banded together in 1960 to form OPEC, the Organization of Petroleum Exporting Countries, a producers' cartel, to negotiate for higher oil prices.

By the early 1970s, the United States depended on the Middle East for one-third of its oil. Foreign oil producers were finally in a position to raise world oil prices. The oil embargo of 1973 and 1974, during which oil prices quadrupled, and the oil crisis of 1978 and 1979, when oil prices doubled, graphically illustrated how vulnerable the nation had become to foreign producers.

The oil crises of the 1970s had an unanticipated side effect. Rising oil prices stimulated conservation and exploration for new oil sources. As a result of increasing supplies and declining demand, oil prices fell from $35 a barrel in 1981 to $9 a barrel in 1986. This sharp slide in world oil prices was one of the factors that led Iraq to invade neighboring Kuwait in 1990, in a bid to gain control over 40 percent of Middle Eastern oil reserves.

In the century-and-a-half since Edwin L. Drake drilled the first oil well, the history of the oil industry has been a story of vast swings between periods of overproduction, when low prices and profits led oil producers to devise ways to restrict output and thereby raise prices, and periods when oil appeared to be on the brink of exhaustion, stimulating a global search for new sources. This cycle may now be approaching an end, as world oil supplies may truly be reaching their natural limits. With proven world oil reserves anticipated to last fewer than 40 years, the era of oil production that began near Titusville may be coming to an end. In the years to come, the search for new sources of oil will be transformed into a quest for entirely new sources of energy.

ward climb, leading Nixon to impose another 60-day wage and price freeze in June 1973.

In 1974 during the first oil embargo, inflation hit 12 percent. Gerald Ford, the new president, initially attacked the problem in a traditional Republican fashion, tightening the money supply by raising interest rates and limiting government spending. He also unveiled in 1975 his WIN ("Whip Inflation Now") program and urged Americans to wear WIN lapel buttons. In the end, WIN proved to be no more than a series of ineffectual wage and price guidelines monitored by the federal government. In the subsequent recession, unemployment reached 9 percent.

When Jimmy Carter took office in January, 1977, 7.4 percent of the work force was unemployed. Carter responded with an ambitious spending program and called for the Federal Reserve (the Fed) to expand the money supply. Within two years, inflation had accelerated to 13.3 percent.

With inflation getting out of hand, Paul Volcker, the chairman of the Federal Reserve Board, announced that the Fed's primary goal would be to fight inflation by restraining the growth of the money supply. Unemployment increased and interest rates moved to their highest levels in the nation's history. Volcker was convinced that wringing inflation out of the economy required a prolonged period of substantial unemployment. In November 1982 the so-called Volcker recession reached a painful climax. Unemployment hit 10.8 percent, the highest since 1940. One out of every five American workers went some time without a job and poverty had increased from 13 percent of the population (or 29.3 million in 1980) to 15 percent in 1982 (34.4 million). But interest rates had fallen, inflation was down, and the stock market was bullish.

Along with high interest rates, the Carter administration adopted another weapon in the battle against stagflation: deregulation. Convinced that rather than protecting consumers, regulators too often protected the industries they were supposed to oversee, the Carter administration deregulated air and surface transportation and the savings and loan industry (the Reagan administration would deregulate telecommunications).

Declines in exports and increases in imports continue to trouble U.S. industry in the 1990s.

The effects of deregulation are hotly contested. Rural towns suffered cutbacks of bus, rail, and air service. Truckers and rail workers lost economic benefits of regulation. Travelers complained about rising air fares and congested airports. Cable TV viewers resented rising rates. Champions of deregulation argued that the policy increased competition, stimulated new investment, and forced inefficient firms either to become more efficient or shut down.

A NEW AMERICAN ROLE IN THE WORLD

In his inaugural address in 1961, John Kennedy made a famous pledge: "Let every nation know, whether it wishes us well or ill, we shall pay any price, bear any burden, meet any hardship, support any friend or oppose any foe to assure the survival and the success of liberty."

By 1973, in the wake of the Vietnam War, American foreign policymakers regarded Kennedy's stirring pledge as unrealistic. The Vietnam War offered a lesson about the limits of American power. It underscored the need to distinguish between vital national interests and peripheral interests, and to balance America's military commitments with its limited resources. Above all, the Vietnam War appeared to illustrate the dangers of obsessive anti-Communism. Such a policy failed to recognize the fact that the world was becoming more complex, that power blocs were shifting, and that the interests of Communist countries and the United States could sometimes overlap. Too often, American policy seemed to have driven nationalists and reformers into Communist hands and to have led the United States to support corrupt, unpopular authoritarian regimes.

The great challenge facing American foreign policy makers was how to preserve the nation's international prestige and influence in the face of declining defense budgets and mounting congressional opposition to direct overseas intervention.

Détente

As president, Richard Nixon radically redefined America's relationship with its two foremost adversaries, China and the Soviet Union. In a remarkable turnabout from his record of staunch anti-Communism, he opened relations with China and began strategic arms limitation talks with the Soviet Union. The goal of this policy, known as *détente* (the easing of tensions between nations), was to continue to resist and deter Soviet adventurism while striving for "more constructive relations" with the Communist world.

Nixon and Henry Kissinger, the German-born former Harvard professor who served as assistant for national security affairs and later secretary of state, believed that it was necessary to curb the arms race, improve great power relationships, and learn to coexist with Communist regimes. In Kissinger's view, American foreign policy of the 1950s and 1960s rested on "an outmoded foreign policy concept": an ideological commitment to contain communism. His goal was to shift the focus of American policy away from a moralistic anti-Communism to issues of national interest. The Nixon administration sought to use the Chinese and Soviet need for western trade and technology as a way to extract foreign policy concessions.

The new direction of American foreign policy was inaugurated in 1971 when the Nixon Administration made the first overtures to China. Since 1949 U.S. policy recognized the Jiang Jieshi regime on Taiwan as the legitimate government of China and refused to recognize the Chinese Communist government. In 1972 Nixon took part in a summit meeting in Beijing, walked the Great Wall, and slowly expanded American trade with China (see Chapter 29 for a fuller discussion of Nixon's foreign policy).

Less dramatic, but no less important, was the beginning of a détente with the Soviet Union, culminating in a massive trade pact and strategic arms limitation talks. In a 1972 summit meeting in Moscow, the United States and Soviet Union vowed not to seek "unilateral advantages" against each other.

Recognizing that one of the legacies of Vietnam was a reluctance on the part of the American public to risk overseas interventions, Nixon and Kissinger also sought to build up regional powers that shared American strategic interests, most notably China, Iran, and Saudi Arabia.

By the late 1970s, an increasing number of Americans regarded the Nixon-Kissinger strategy of détente, strategic arms limitation, and support of regional superpowers as a failure. A growing number of Americans believed that the Soviet hardliners viewed détente as a mere tactic to lull the West into relaxing its vigilance. Soviet Communist party chief Leonid Brezhnev reinforced this view in 1976 when he told the Twenty-fifth Communist Party Congress: "We make no secret of the fact that we see détente as the way to create more favorable conditions for peaceful socialist and Communist construction." He also announced what came to be known as the "Brezhnev Doctrine," that the Soviet Union was prepared to intervene anywhere if "bid by our revolutionary conscience, our Communist convictions" and that it was the Soviet Union's right to support "the struggle of other peoples for freedom and progress." The Soviet leader boasted of gains that his country had made at the United States's expense—in Vietnam, Angola, Cambodia, Ethiopia, and Laos.

An alarming Soviet arms buildup contributed to the sense that détente was not working.

By 1975, the Soviet Union had 50 percent more intercontinental ballistic missiles (ICBMs) than the United States, 30 times as many antiaircraft missile launchers, 3 times as many army personnel, 3 times as many attack submarines, and 4 times as many tanks. The United States continued to have a powerful strategic deterrent, holding a 9000 to 3200 advantage in deliverable nuclear bombs and warheads. But the gap between the countries was narrowing.

Superpower Battlegrounds

By the end of the 1970s détente had been overcome by a revived cold war. During the late 1970s the Middle East, Africa, and the Near East all emerged as arenas for superpower conflict. In southern Africa, a major problem was the unwillingness of whites to yield power to their countries' black majorities. In Rhodesia Henry Kissinger succeeded in persuading 274,000 whites to peacefully transfer majority rule to the nation's 6.1 million blacks. In

Angola, a former Portuguese colony, 13,000 Cuban troops helped install a Communist government.

In the Middle East the United States achieved a tremendous diplomatic success by negotiating peace between Egypt and Israel. Since the founding of Israel in 1948, Egypt's foreign policy had been built around destroying the Jewish state. The two countries seemed to divide their time between fighting wars and planning to fight wars. The fighting resulted in an enlarged Israel and a weakened Egypt. Then in 1977, Anwar el-Sadat, the practical and farsighted leader of Egypt, decided to seek peace with Israel. To demonstrate that his intentions were sincere, he even traveled to Israel and spoke with the Israeli Knesset. It was an act of rare political courage, for Sadat risked alienating Egypt from the rest of the Arab world without a firm commitment for a peace treaty with Israel.

Although both countries wanted peace, major obstacles had to be overcome. Sadat wanted

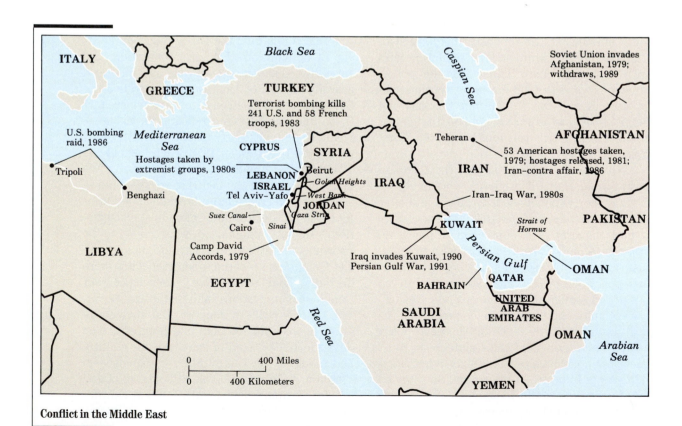

Conflict in the Middle East

Israel to retreat from the West Bank of the Jordan River and from the Golan Heights (which it had taken from Jordan in the 1967 war), recognize the Palestine Liberation Organization (PLO), provide a homeland for the Palestinians, relinquish its unilateral hold on the city of Jerusalem, and return the Sinai to Egypt. Such conditions were unacceptable to Israeli Prime Minister Menachem Begin, who refused to consider recognition of the PLO or the return of the West Bank. By the end of 1977, Sadat's peace mission had run aground.

Enter Jimmy Carter. He invited both men to Camp David, the presidential retreat in Maryland's Catoctin Mountains, for face-to-face talks. It was almost like a working holiday. They negotiated, played tennis, negotiated, watched movies, and negotiated. The world leaders and their teams of experts worked through the chilly autumn nights and beautiful days. In the end they hammered out a peace.

To be sure, the peace was not perfect. It did not settle such important territorial issues as the West Bank, the Golan Heights, Jerusalem, and recognition of the PLO. But Begin did agree to return the Sinai to Egypt, Egypt agreed to recognize Israel, and Egypt became a staunch American ally. For Carter it was a proud moment. No American president, Begin claimed, "has ever so involved himself in our problems." Unfortunately, the Camp David Accords were denounced by the rest of the Arab Middle East, and in 1981 Sadat paid for his vision with his life when anti-Israeli Egyptian soldiers assassinated him.

Carter's success at Camp David was soon overshadowed by other events. The single greatest source of superpower tension at the end of the 1970s was Afghanistan. Just six months after a summit in Vienna at which he pledged his hope for peace, in late 1979 Communist party leader Leonid Brezhnev sent Soviet tanks into Afghanistan. In response, the Carter administration embargoed grain and high-technology exports to the Soviet Union and boycotted the 1980 Olympics in Moscow. During the 1980s, the Reagan administration provided arms to Afghan rebels, arms which aided the Afghans in their fight against the Soviet Union and ultimately helped to convince the Soviets to withdraw its troops.

Jimmy Carter's greatest triumph as president came with the signing of the Camp David Accords between Egypt and Israel.

No Islands of Stability

One of the tragic unfortunate aspects of American foreign policy is that the United States historically has supported many countries that hold power through murder, torture, and other violations of human rights. In the mid-1970s, torture was practiced by such U.S. allies as Argentina, Brazil, Chile, El Salvador, Iran, Nicaragua, Paraguay, the Philippines, South Korea, and Uruguay. Such practices are an affront to basic American values. As Henry Kissinger put it, "A government that tramples on the rights of its citizens denies the purpose of its existence."

During the 1970s, and particularly during the presidency of Jimmy Carter, the United States began to show a growing regard for the human rights practices of its allies. Carter was convinced that American foreign policy should embody the country's basic moral beliefs. In 1977 Congress began to require reports on human rights conditions in countries receiving American aid.

Of the nations accused of practicing torture, one of the most frequently cited was Iran. Estimates of the number of political prisoners in Iran ranged from 25,000 to 100,000. It was widely believed that most of them had been tortured by SAVAK, the secret police. Tortures included electric shock, beatings, insertions of bottles in the rectum, hanging weights from the testicles, and rape. Writers, artists, and intellectuals were often targets of torture.

Since the end of World War II, Iran had been a valuable friend of the United States in the troubled Middle East. In 1953 the CIA had worked to ensure the power of the young shah, Mohammad Reza Pahlavi. And between 1953 and 1978, the shah had oftentimes repaid the debt. He allowed the United States to establish electronic listening posts in northern Iran along the border of the Soviet Union, and during the 1973–1974 Arab oil embargo the shah continued to sell oil to the United States. In addition, the shah bought arms from the United States with, as one historian noted, "the abandon of an alcoholic using a credit card in a liquor store." These purchases helped ease the American balance-of-payments problem. All things considered, few world leaders were more loyal to the United States.

Like previous American presidents, Carter was willing to overlook the Shah's violations of human rights. To demonstrate America's support of the shah, Carter visited Iran in late December 1977 for a New Year's Eve celebration. After being entertained at a lavish banquet, Carter made a toast, which crammed a series of mistaken assumptions into very few words. He spoke of Iran as "an island of stability in one of the most troubled areas of the world" and of the shah as a great leader who had won "the respect and the admiration and love" of his people.

The shah was popular among wealthy Iranians and Americans. In the slums of the southern section of Teheran and in the poverty-stricken villages of Iran, however, there was little respect, admiration, or love for the shah. Led by a fundamentalist Islamic clergy and emboldened by want, the masses of Iranians turned against the shah and his westernization policy. And as Carter spoke, revolutionary sentiment stirred.

In early fall the revolutionary surge in Iran gained force. The shah, who had once seemed so powerful and secure, was paralyzed by indecision, alternating between ruthless suppression and attempts to liberalize his regime. In Washington, Carter was almost as indecisive as the shah, uncertain whether to stand firmly behind the shah or to cut losses and prepare to deal with a new government in Iran. One diplomatic historian commented, "President Carter inherited an impossible situation—and he and his advisors made the worst of it."

On January 16, 1979, the shah left Iran for an extended "vacation" in Egypt. He never returned to his native land. In his wake, however, exiled religious leader Ayatollah Ruholla Khomeini did return to Iran, preaching the doctrine that the United States was the "Great Satan" behind the shah. Relations between America and the new Iranian government were terrible, but Iranian officials warned that they would become infinitely worse if the shah were admitted to the United States. Yet that was exactly what Henry Kissinger and others were advising Carter to do. When Carter learned that the shah needed to come to the United States for treatment of lymphoma, he extended a humanitarian invitation.

"You're opening a Pandora's box," the Iranian prime minister remarked when he heard the news. On November 4, 1979, Iranian supporters of Khomeini invaded the American embassy in Teheran and captured 66 Americans, 13 of whom were freed several weeks later. The rest were held hostage for 444 days and were the objects of intense political interest and media coverage. Between 1972 and 1977 the three major networks had devoted only an average of five minutes per year to coverage of Iran; during the hostage crisis Iran coverage appeared every night.

Carter was helpless. Because Iran was not a stable country in any recognizable sense, it was impossible to pressure. "The powerless, with little to lose," noted historian Gaddis Smith, "have a special power." Carter devoted far too much attention to the almost insoluble problem. Iran's demands—the return of the shah to Iran and admission of U.S. guilt in supporting the shah—were unacceptable. The hos-

After 444 days the Iranian hostage crisis ended, but not before it had virtually paralyzed Carter's administration and destroyed his chances for reelection.

tages stayed in the public spotlight because Carter kept them there.

Some Carter advisors advocated the use of force to free the hostages. At first, Carter disagreed, saying "The problem with all of the military options is that we could use them and feel good for a few hours—until we found out they had killed our people. And once we started killing people in Iran, where will it end?" But eventually Carter authorized a rescue attempt. It failed and Carter's position became even worse. Negotiations finally brought the hostages' release, but not until Ronald Reagan had been president for half an hour.

When Carter left office in January 1981 many Americans judged his presidency a failure. Although in 1978 he had pushed through Congress the Panama Canal Treaty, which pro-

vided for the return of the Canal Zone to Panama and improved the image of the United States in Latin America, and although in 1979 he consummated the process of recognizing Communist China, the prolonged hostage crisis undermined his presidency. Instead of being remembered for the good he accomplished for the Middle East at Camp David, he was remembered for what he failed to accomplish. But like his relations with Iran, often the failures of his presidency were paved with good intentions.

A Sense of Failure

The Iranian hostage crisis became the emblem of America's declining role in the world. During the 1970s, the United States did not enjoy a major unqualified military success. The bungled attempt in April, 1980, to free the Iranian hostages was only one example of the apparent ineffectiveness of the American military. Earlier, North Korea had seized the USS *Pueblo*; it took months for the Nixon administration to secure the crew's release. During the Ford administration, Cambodia hijacked another American ship, the *Mayaguez*, resulting in an abortive American assault on Koh Tang Island in an attempt to free the sailors.

Compounding Americans' sense of frustration was the realization that U.S. nuclear superiority over the Soviet Union had eroded. The modernization of Soviet ground, naval, and tactical air forces, which began in the late 1960s, while American resources were diverted to Vietnam, allowed the Soviet Union to achieve parity. During the 1970s, U.S. defense expenditures, after inflation, declined by almost 25 percent. The share of gross national product (a measure of the nation's total output) devoted to defense fell from 8.2 to 5.2 percent. The size of the U.S. Navy shrank from 752 warships to 473. The army lost 3 of its 16 divisions. The number of air force tactical combat aircraft fell from almost 3300 to less than 2400. America's nuclear forces were not being modernized. As an air deterent, the country depended on a deteriorating fleet of B-52s. Ronald Reagan, the 1980 Republican presidential nominee, asserted that the United States faced a "window of vulnerability" that might tempt the Soviet Union to launch an attack.

THE REAGAN REVOLUTION

The traumatic events of the 1970s—Watergate, stagflation, the energy crisis, the defeat of South Vietnam, and the Iranian hostage crisis—produced a severe loss of confidence among the American people. Americans were deeply troubled by the relative decline of American strength in the world; the decline of the productivity and innovation in American industry; and the dramatic growth of lobbies and special-interest groups that seemed to have paralyzed the legislative process. Many worried that too much power had been stripped from the presidency, that political parties were so weakened

and Congress so splintered that it was impossible to enact a coherent legislative program.

Ronald Reagan capitalized on frustration over double-digit inflation, a gasoline crisis, and failure to rescue the hostages. When he ran for the presidency against Carter in 1980, he asked Americans, "Are you better off than you were four years ago?" With inflation at 18 percent, the answer was obvious: "No." Reagan won a landslide victory, carrying 43 states and almost 51 percent of the popular vote compared to Carter's 41 percent. Reagan became the first candidate to defeat an elected incumbent president since Franklin Roosevelt in 1932. In addition, the Democrats lost the Senate for the first time since 1954.

The Gipper

As the nation's fortieth president, Ronald Reagan could claim an extraordinary string of accomplishments. He doubled the defense budget, named the first woman to the Supreme Court, launched an economic boom of unprecedented length, and created a heightened sense of national unity.

And yet Reagan was also one of the most controversial presidents in American history. His supporters said that he restored vigor to the national economy and psyche, rebuilt America's military might, regained the nation's place as the world's preeminent power, and proved the workability of the American political system after a series of failed presidencies. They argued that he restored American pride and patriotism and championed traditional family values.

His detractors criticized him for reckless use of military power, breaking a bipartisan consensus on civil rights, and violating congressional prohibitions on aid to the Nicaraguan contras and of trying to trade arms for Middle Eastern hostages. They accused Reagan of fostering greed, chauvinism, and intolerance, and they charged that his administration, in its zeal to cut waste from government, ripped the social safety net and skimped on the government's regulatory functions. Yet, however one evaluates his presidency, there can be no doubt that he dramatically altered the nation's mood and its political agenda.

Ronald Reagan is a man of many paradoxes. A staunch conservative, he is the only American president to have served as president of a union; he was also a founding member of such liberal organizations as Americans for Democratic Action and United World Federalists. A strong defender of traditional family values, he was the first divorced person to become president. A leading opponent of abortion, he signed one of the nation's first laws legalizing abortion while governor of California.

When he was elected president in 1980, he was already well known to the American people as a movie actor and radio and television announcer. He had risen to celebrity from extremely modest beginnings. His shoe-salesman father drank and gambled, and young Reagan grew up in a succession of small Illinois towns—Tampico, where he was born on February 6, 1911, Galesburg, Monmouth, and Dixon. To help support his family, he worked as a lifeguard, and is credited with rescuing 70 drowning people. In order to attend Eureka College, a 250-student Disciples of Christ school, he washed dishes. As a freshman he led a weeklong student strike that forced college officials to rescind cuts in the educational program.

He graduated in 1932, in the depths of the depression, and eventually became a sportscaster at radio station WHO in Des Moines. His ultimate goal, however, was Hollywood, and in 1937 he received a screen test at Warner Brothers and landed a $200 a week contract. He eventually made 50 movies but never became a major star. "I became the Errol Flynn of the B's," he said. He became identified with one role: George Gipp, the Notre Dame halfback, in *Knute Rockne, All American* (1940), whose dying words were "win one for the gipper." After World War II, with his movie career winding down, he was elected to six terms as president of the Screen Actors Guild. In 1954, he turned to television, hosting "GE Theater" and "Death Valley Days."

In politics, he started out as a self-described "hemophiliac bleeding-heart liberal," who staunchly supported Franklin D. Roosevelt and the New Deal. As head of the Screen Actors Guild, however, he became concerned about Communist infiltration of the labor movement in Hollywood. "Then I discovered at first hand the cynicism, the brutality, the complete lack of morality of their positions and the cold-bloodedness of their attempt, at any cost, to gain control of that industry." In 1948 he supported Harry Truman, but in 1952 and 1956, he voted for Dwight Eisenhower and in 1960 he led Democrats for Nixon.

Reagan was catapulted into the national political spotlight in 1964 when he gave an emotional television speech in support of Republican nominee Barry Goldwater, denouncing big government, foreign aid, welfare, urban renewal, and high taxes. Two years later, he successfully ran for governor of California as a "citizen politician." Declaring that there are simple answers to the state's problems, he took office in 1967 promising to cut state spending by ten percent, reduce welfare costs, and crack down on student protesters. In fact, during his eight years as governor, state spending and taxes nearly doubled and state aid to schools and local services rose substantially. But he did slow the growth of state employment, required able-bodied welfare recipients to take job training courses or perform public service work, and left his successor a $500 million budget surplus.

In the 1980 presidential campaign, Reagan drew strong support from white Southerners, suburban Catholics, the nation's 40 million evangelical Christians, and particularly the New Right, a confederation of disparate political and religious groups bound together by their concern over what they considered the erosion of values in America. He truly captured the nation's imagination in March 1981 when an assassin's bullet nearly killed him. Reagan responded to the shooting with remarkable courage. From his hospital bed, he sent a message to his wife Nancy, "Honey, I forgot to duck."

Reaganomics

When President Reagan took office he promised to cut inflation, rebuild the nation's defenses, restore economic growth, and trim the size of the federal government by limiting its role in welfare, education, and housing. He pledged to end exorbitant union contracts to make American goods competitive again, to drastically cut taxes to stimulate investment and purchasing power, and to decontrol businesses strangled by federal regulation in order to restore competition. If in his eight years in office Reagan did not achieve his complete agenda—his policies trimmed little from the size of the federal government, failed to make American goods competitive in the world market, and led to increased consolidation rather than competition—many Americans believed that his ecomonic policies had improved the country's many economic problems.

Reagan blamed the country's economic ills on declining capital investment and a tax structure biased against work and productive investment. To stimulate the economy, he persuaded Congress to slash tax rates. In 1981, he pushed a bill through Congress cutting taxes 5 percent in 1981 and 10 percent in 1982 and 1983. In 1986, the administration pushed through another tax bill, which substantially reduced tax rates on the wealthiest Americans to 28 percent, while closing a variety of tax loopholes.

In a symbolic attack on inflationary wage increases, Reagan, in August 1981, dismissed 15,000 striking air traffic controllers, breaking their union and dealing a devastating blow to organized labor. Union leaders condemned the firings, but in an antiunion atmosphere most

Americans backed Reagan. His popularity ratings soared.

To strengthen the nation's defenses, the Reagan administration doubled the defense budget, even with adjustments for the rate of inflation. Between 1981 and 1987, the defense budget jumped from $165 billion a year to more than $330 billion. Reagan believed that a militarily strong America would not have been humiliated by Iran and would have discouraged Soviet adventurism.

To "liberate free enterprise from fifty years of liberal Democratic restraints," Reagan expanded the Carter administration's efforts to decontrol and deregulate the economy. In 1982, Congress deregulated the banking industry and lifted ceilings on interest rates. Federal price controls on airfares were lifted as well. In 1983, Congress deregulated the natural gas industry. The Department of Transportation postponed the application of federally mandated passive restraint systems and fuel efficiency standards for automobiles; the Environmental Protection Agency relaxed its interpretation of the Clean Air Act; and the Department of the Interior opened up large areas of the federal domain, including offshore oil fields, to private development.

The results of deregulation were mixed. Bank interest rates became more competitive, but smaller banks found it difficult to hold their own against larger institutions. Natural gas prices increased once decontrol set in, but so did production, easing some of the country's dependence on foreign fuel. Airfares on high-traffic routes between major cities dropped dramatically in the 1980s when price controls were lifted, but fares for short, low-traffic flights skyrocketed. Most critics agreed, however, that deregulation had restored some short-term competition to the marketplace. Yet in the long term, competition also led to increased business failures and consolidation.

The urge for deregulation carried over to Reagan's social programs. Convinced that federal welfare programs promoted "acceptance of indolence, promiscuity, easy abortion, casual attitudes toward marriage and divorce, and maternal indifference to child-rearing responsibilities," Reagan halted the growth of social welfare programs and limited benefits to those

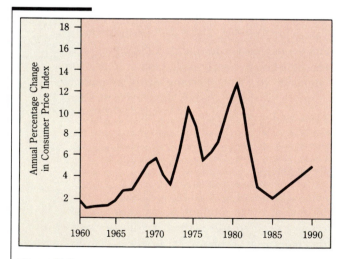

Figure 31.2
Inflation, 1960–1990

he considered the "truly needy." The Reagan administration curtailed spending on a variety of social welfare programs. Between 1981 and 1984, spending on Aid to Families with Dependent Children was reduced 13 percent; food stamps, 13 percent; child nutrition, 28 percent; job training for young people, 53 percent; programs to prevent child abuse, 12 percent; and mental health services, 26 percent. The Reagan administration also eliminated cash welfare assistance for the working poor, reduced federal subsidies for child care services for low-income families, and cut grants used to pay for the regulation of child care programs. A symbol of Reagan social service cuts was an attempt by the Agriculture Department in 1981 to allow ketchup to be counted as a vegetable in school lunches.

Reagan left office with the economy in the midst of its longest post–World War II expansion. The economy was growing faster, with less inflation, than any time since the mid-1960s. Adjusted for inflation, disposable personal income per person rose 20 percent after 1980. Inflation fell to less than 4 percent. Unemployment was down to around 5 percent. These figures compared favorably to January 1981, the month Reagan became president, when inflation was running at 13 percent a year and unemployment stood at 7.4 percent.

Reagan's critics, however, charged that Reagan had only created the illusion of prosperity. They denounced the massive federal budget deficit, which increased $1.5 trillion during the Reagan presidency, three times the debt accumulated by all 39 of Reagan's presidential predecessors. They decried the growing income gap between rich and poor, as well as the expensive consequences of reduced government regulation, such as cleaning up federal nuclear weapons facilities, and, especially, bailing out the nation's savings and loans industry. This last problem, however, would fall to Reagan's successor as president, George Bush.

The Celebration of Wealth

In 1981, the year Ronald Reagan was inaugurated as president, ABC television introduced the smash hit "Dynasty," a show celebrating glamour and greed. It was, in the eyes of many

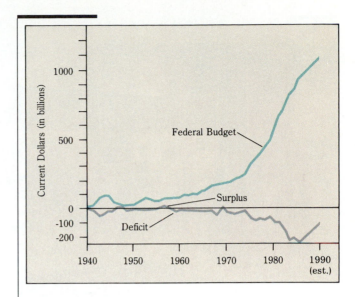

Figure 31.3
U.S. budget deficits, 1940–1990

social commentators, an appropriate beginning for the 1980s—a decade of greed, selfishness, and an anything-goes attitude. It was a decade when financier Ivan Boesky claimed, "Greed is not a bad thing. You shouldn't feel guilty"; when Nancy Reagan spent $25,000 on her inaugural wardrobe and $209,508 on new White House china; when the circulation of *Money* magazine climbed from 800,000 to 1.85 million; when the prime-time soap opera about the super-rich, "Dallas," reached number one in the ratings; and when Madonna had a pop music hit entitled "Material Girl." On television advertisers told consumers, "Yes, you can have it all, you deserve it all, all for you, yes . . ." President Reagan's message was similar. Americans could have it all—low taxes, a strong defense, and middle-class entitlements.

Michael Milken, a financial wizard at the investment banking firm of Drexel Burnham Lambert, personified the "go-go" spirit of the "roaring eighties." After graduating from the Wharton School in 1969, Milken joined Drexel at a salary of $25,000 a year. Milken was convinced that the stock market valued many corporations for far less than the worth of the company's assets. By using low-grade, risky "junk bonds" to finance corporate acquisitions, cor-

(Text continues on p. 1074)

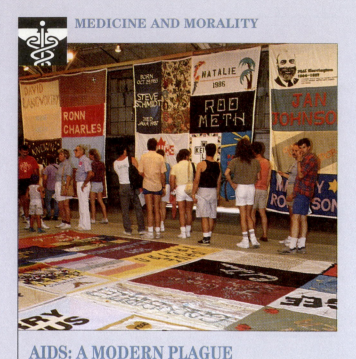

AIDS: A MODERN PLAGUE

Americans have long debated what to do about sexually transmitted disease (STD). Health officials have insisted that STD is a medical problem that should be handled like any other communicable disease: through research, treatment, public education, and the vigorous application of modern techniques of epidemiology. Others have argued that STD is primarily a moral problem.

World War I brought the issue to a head. Army planners debated whether to concentrate on trying to prevent STD through educational propaganda against extramarital sex (accompanied by a crackdown on red-light districts), or whether to sanction the use of condoms and focus on medical treatment to cure infection. In the end, they elected to combine both approaches. Moreover, when the identical problem

reappeared in World War II, the government promptly adopted the same solution: scary propaganda against extramarital sex, followed by condoms and treatment for soldiers who surrendered to temptation. Even the debate over treatment sounded like an echo. The discovery of penicillin precipitated another round of arguments over whether this new "wonder drug" should be given to soldiers who contracted STD, and the dispute was settled exactly as it had been in World War I: Wayward souls received treatment.

Following World War II, public funding for STD work rose and the number of cases fell. The victory over STD, however, proved to be short-lived, for the infection rates tripled between 1950 and 1975. What happened? In part, health officials were victims of their own

success. Given the power of new antibiotics, doctors stopped worrying as much about the social behavior that led to transmission, and they became less vigilant in their efforts to track down the partners of infected patients. Yet the doctors were not solely to blame. The public's apathy was reflected in reduced health budgets for STD work.

The lull ended in the 1980s with the appearance of acquired immune deficiency syndrome (AIDS), the most terrifying disease of modern times. As early as 1980, physicians began reporting a strange medical phenomenon among gay men. Patients from these groups were falling prey to fatigue, a puzzling combination of infections, a rare skin cancer known as Kaposi's sarcoma, and eventual death. No one recovered from the disease.

After prolonged and ill-funded research, AIDS was finally linked to a retrovirus, which scientists named the "human immunodeficiency virus," or HIV. Additional research soon revealed AIDS cases among heterosexuals, Haitians, hemophiliacs, and intravenous drug users, indicating that the disease was not limited to a single group; rather, it threatened everyone. But why did it take so long to mobilize research efforts and public awareness? The explanation lies in long-standing attitudes about STD.

First and foremost, AIDS was widely regarded as a "gay" disease, and homosexuals were a favorite target of the "new right" and the "moral majority," whose political clout had helped put Ronald Reagan in the White House. Patrick Buchanan, White House director of communications, proclaimed that homosexuals had "declared war on nature, and now nature is extracting an awful retribution." By the time the United States finally took notice of AIDS in 1987, more than 21,000 Americans had died from the disease. Part of the reason lay in President Reagan's cutbacks in domestic programs: AIDS became another casualty of Reaganomics, another victim of the administration's hostility to social services. In the end, however, a series of shocking events forced the government to act: These included the discovery of AIDS-contaminated hospital blood supplies; the appearance of AIDS in heterosexuals; and the surprisingly bold anti-AIDS campaign of Surgeon General C. Everett Koop.

Koop recommended AIDS education for school children "at the earliest date possible," and he further advocated the promotion and use of condoms. Conservatives were outraged and charged the government with attempting to promote immorality. But Koop and other public health officials held firm. The government sponsored television and radio commercials warning the public against "unsafe sex" and mailed an explicit brochure on AIDS to every household in America.

As the public's concern rose, various groups demanded that AIDS sufferers be quarantined. Though health authorities repeatedly stressed that casual contacts could not spread the disease, many people feared the worst. The objections of civil libertarians, who opposed quarantine, left them cold, as did the arguments of those who rejected quarantine on practical grounds. (Where were tens of thousands of AIDS sufferers to be kept? Who was to pay for their care during this forced isolation?) While these arguments kept any serious movement for quarantine from developing, the public remained edgy. Some parents withdrew their children from schools where AIDS patients were enrolled, and AIDS sufferers found that many of their co-workers wanted them removed from their jobs.

Yet some of the reactions to AIDS within the gay community were no less extreme. Granted, most gay leaders struggled from the outset to publicize AIDS and to promote safe sex and monogamous relationships. But other gays reacted with denial. Some initially believed (or chose to believe) that AIDS was a heterosexual propaganda tactic designed to crush the nascent gay movement. To many, gay liberation meant not merely toleration of homosexuality but a celebration of sexuality, a reordering of values with greater emphasis on the long-suppressed pleasure principle. Multiple and unprotected contacts were the final necessary step to political freedom. Others proclaimed that AIDS could never hit them. And still others became resigned and carried on as usual. In the gay community they became known as Doris Days, after the actress famous for singing "*Que será, será*."

The end of the AIDS story cannot be written, for no one can predict the impact this deadly disease will have on American society. To date (1992), more than 60,000 Americans have been diagnosed with the disease, more than 33,000 have died from it, and another 1.5 million are believed to be infected. With a cure nowhere in sight, medical authorities expect to be confronted by literally hundreds of thousands of AIDS patients by the turn of the century. Their care will be both protracted and expensive. Who will pay for it?

Despite these grim realities, sex researchers report few changes in the public's private behavior, especially in those groups that are at high risk for contracting the disease. Though hard data are lacking, the experts agree that "unsafe sex" remains a common practice among adolescents and young adults, and the same holds true for many gays, particularly those who are just becoming sexually active. Thus, even in the midst of this terrifying plague, modern-day health authorities, like their progressive ancestors, have found it difficult to modify behavior in order to prevent venereal infections. And like the progressives, many Americans today will no doubt continue to place their hopes on education and on the search for new medical advances with which to eradicate AIDS, debating all the while whether those who contract the disease should be pitied or condemned.

porate raiders or takeover artists purchased and then dismantled companies for a huge profit. In 1987, Milken earned $550 million by financing acquisitions.

The Reagan years witnessed a corporate merger and takeover boom of unprecedented proportions. In one Milken-backed raid, Texas oilman T. Boone Pickens threatened to acquire Gulf Oil in 1984. To get rid of Pickens, Gulf paid the oilman $400 million. The culmination of the boom occurred when Kohlberg, Kravis, Roberts and Co. purchased RJR Nabisco for $24.9 billion.

During the 1980s, 100,000 Americans became millionaires every year and the average earnings of the top 20 percent of the population rose $9000 a year after inflation. The earnings of the bottom 20 percent, however, fell $576 to $8800. In addition, many of the new jobs created during the Reagan years were in the low-wage service industries.

By the early 1990s, there were signs that the time had come to pay for the financial excesses of the 1980s. Following a 508-point fall in the Dow Jones industrial average on October 19, 1987—a 22.6 percent plunge—many Wall Street stock brokerage firms began to lay off employees, cutbacks which continued despite the market's recovery. In 1989, Milken, his brother Lowell, and a former Drexel employee were indicted on 98 counts of criminal racketeering, securities fraud, and other crimes. The next year, Drexel Burnham Lambert agreed to pay a fine of $650 million and filed for bankruptcy. Wall Street speculator Ivan Boesky was fined $100 million for insider trading and sentenced to jail. Those Americans who had participated in the ambition, greed, vanity, and excess of the eighties seemed to be getting their comeupance. Capturing the popular mood, the 1989 film *Wall Street* follows the downfall of Gordon Gekko, a figure based on men like Milken and Boesky. At his height of power, Gekko asserts, "Greed . . . is good. Greed is right. . . . Greed—mark my words—will save . . . the U.S.A." In the film's end, however, greed landed Gekko in prison.

The Reagan Doctrine

During the early years of the Reagan presidency, Cold War tensions between the Soviet Union and the United States intensified. Reagan entered office deeply suspicious of the Soviet Union. During the 1980 presidential campaign he described communism as "a form of insanity [that] is contrary to human nature" and said that détente "has been a one-way street that the Soviets have used to continue moving toward the Marxist goal of a socialist, one world state."

In September 1983, a few months after President Reagan had described the Soviet Union as "an evil empire" and called for a space-based missile defense system—Star Wars—a Soviet fighter shot down Korean Airlines flight 007 that had strayed into Soviet airspace, killing all 269 passengers on board. This incident intensified superpower conflict and set the stage for other confrontations.

Reagan and his advisors tended to view every regional conflict through a Cold War lens. Nowhere was this more true than in the Caribbean and Central America. He was determined not to allow a Communist government to take power in the Caribbean, Mexico, or Central America. Fidel Castro's successful revolution in Cuba in 1959, and his subsequent alignment

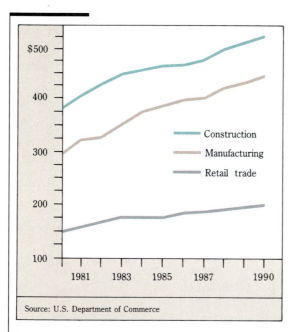

Source: U.S. Department of Commerce

Figure 31.4
Weekly earnings, 1980–1990

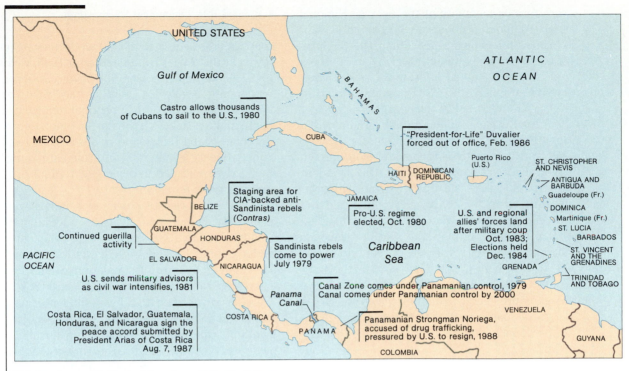

U.S. Involvement in Central America and the Caribbean

with the Soviet Union, had created serious problems for the United States, and Reagan was not about to allow it to happen again.

In October 1983 Prime Minister Maurice Bishop of Grenada, a small island nation in the Caribbean, was assassinated and a more radical Marxist government took power. Soviet money and Cuban troops came to Grenada, and when they began constructing an airfield capable of landing large military aircrafts, the Reagan administration decided to overthrow the Communists and restore a pro-American regime. On October 25 American troops invaded Grenada, killed or captured 750 Cuban soldiers, and established a new government. Although most Latin American nations condemned the invasion as "Yankee imperialism," the Grenadans themselves approved the American humbling of the "Marxist thugs." The invasion, however, sent a clear message throughout the region that the Reagan administration would not tolerate communism in its hemisphere.

In his 1985 state of the union address, President Reagan spelled out the "Reagan Doctrine" in foreign policy: American support for anti-

Communist revolutions. "We must not break faith with those who are risking their lives on every continent from Afghanistan to Nicaragua to defy Soviet-supported aggression."

In Afghanistan, the United States provided aid to anti-Soviet freedom fighters, ultimately helping to force Soviet troops to withdraw. It was in Nicaragua, however, that the Reagan doctrine received its most controversial application.

In 1979 Nicarguans revolted against the corrupt Somoza regime. A new junta took power, dominated by young Marxists known as Sandinistas. The Sandinistas insisted that they favored free elections, nonalignment, and a mixed economy, but once in power they postponed elections, forced opposition leaders into exile, and turned to the Soviet bloc for arms and advisors. For the Reagan administration, Nicaragua looked "like another Cuba," a clearinghouse for the exportation of Marxism and revolution to El Salvador, Guatemala, and Honduras.

In his first months in office, President Reagan approved covert training of anti-Sandinista rebels (called "contras"), some of whom were former members of the Somoza National Guard. While the contras waged war on the Sandinistas from camps in Honduras, the CIA provided assistance, mining Nicaraguan harbors and issuing a manual offering ways of assassinating Sandinistas. In 1984 Congress ordered an end to all covert aid to the contras.

The Reagan administration circumvented Congress by soliciting contributions for the contras from private individuals and from foreign governments seeking U.S. favor. The president also permitted the sale of arms to Iran, with profits diverted to the contras. The arms sale and transfer of funds to the contras were handled surreptitiously through the CIA intellegence network, apparently with the full support of CIA director William Casey. Exposure of the Iran-Contra Affair in late 1986 threatened the Reagan presidency and provoked a major congressional investigation. The ensuing scandal seriously weakened the influence of the president.

The American preoccupation with Nicaragua began to subside in 1987, after President Oscar Arias Sanches of Costa Rica proposed a regional peace plan. In national elections in 1990, the Nicaraguan opposition routed the Sandinistas, bringing an end to ten turbulent years of Sandinista rule.

Controversy and unrest arose in the Reagan administration when no one would accept responsibility for the Iran-contra affair.

A Remarkable Ideological Turnaround

Following the accession of Mikhail Gorbachev to power in the Soviet Union in March 1985, Cold War tensions began to ease. Only five years after denouncing the Soviet Union as "the focus of evil in the modern world," President Reagan began to make peace with the Soviet Union, offering concessions that made it possible to conclude a treaty eliminating intermediate range nuclear weapons and to begin negotiations on a strategic arms reduction treaty.

It was the rise to power of a new Soviet leader that helped ease Reagan's visceral anti-Communism. In 1982, 75-year-old Soviet party leader Leonid Brezhnev died. His regime had been marked by growing stagnation, corruption, and a huge military buildup. His successor, Yuri V. Andropov, former KGB head, died after only 15 months in power and was replaced by Konstantin U. Chernenko, a Brezhnev loyalist, who died just a year later. His successor was Mikhail S. Gorbachev, a 54-year-old agricultural specialist with little formal experience in foreign affairs.

Gorbachev pledged to continue his predecessors' policies, but within weeks he called for sweeping political liberalization—*glasnost*—and economic reform—*perestroika*. Within a year of his election as Communist party general secretary, Gorbachev solidified control over the Soviet state by removing almost half of the directors of ministries and state commissions and top leaders in Central Committee politics.

During the late 1980s, Mikhail Gorbachev reshaped world politics. East-West confrontations were replaced by negotiations. The arms race slowed down and there was a trend toward arms control and disarmament. In 1989, old-style rulers were deposed in Eastern Europe in a wave of revolutions. For his accomplishments, he was awarded the 1990 Nobel Peace Prize.

Within the Soviet Union Gorbachev brought, in George Bush's words, "historically significant change, both political and economic." He allowed wider freedom of press, assembly, travel, and religion, and permitted churches across the country to reopen. He persuaded the Communist party leadership to end its constitutionally guaranteed monopoly on power; created the Soviet Union's first working legislature; allowed the first nationwide competitive elections in 1989; and freed hundreds of political prisoners, largely ending persecution for political views.

In an effort to boost the sagging Soviet economy, he legalized small private business cooperatives, won parliamentary approval for the leasing of lands to individuals with the right of inheritance, and approved foreign investment within the Soviet Union.

In foreign policy, he abandoned the traditional Soviet aim of parity with the United States, the commitment to a protective chain of satellite nations in Eastern Europe, and the Brezhnev doctrine of military intervention in Communist countries. He cut the Soviet defense budget, withdrew 115,000 Soviet troops from Afghanistan, unilaterally pulled 500,000 Soviet troops and 10,000 tanks out of Europe, agreed to let a unified Germany become a member of NATO, and agreed with the United States to destroy short-range and medium-range nuclear weapons.

He stimulated settlement of conflicts in Angola, Namibia, Cambodia, and Nicaragua. Most dramatically, Gorbachev actively promoted the democratization of the countries of Eastern Europe, easing their transformation from satellite states into budding new democracies.

The Reagan Revolution in Perspective

Ronald Reagan was the first president since Andrew Jackson to complete two terms in office and then hand power over to a successor from his own political party. He dampened inflation, restored public confidence in government, and presided over the beginning of the end of the Cold War. He left office more popular than he arrived.

His critics, however, derided him as a "Dr. Feelgood" who reassured Americans with a "narcotic of cheerfulness" while problems accumulated. Reagan's critics were particularly concerned about his economic legacy. While inflation eased, unemployment fell, and the gross national product doubled from $2.7 trillion to $5.3 trillion, the national debt tripled, from $909 billion to almost $2.9 trillion, soaking up savings, causing interest rates to rise, depressing local economies, and forcing the federal government

In order to stimulate the Soviet economy, Mikhail Gorbachev launched his program of *perestroika*, or economic restructuring, which welcomed foreign investment and encouraged joint ventures with foreign businesses. *Perestroika* permitted U.S. businesses, like this American pizzeria, to operate in Moscow.

to shift more and more expensive responsibilities onto the states. During Reagan's years in office, interest on the federal debt doubled to 14 percent of the federal budget—more than the combined budgets of the Agriculture, Commerce, Education, Energy, Interior, Justice, Labor, State, and Transportation departments. Corporate and individual debt also soared. During the 1990s, the American people consumed $1 trillion more goods and services than they produced. The United States also became the world's biggest debtor, as a result of a weak dollar, a low level of exports, and the need to borrow abroad to finance budget deficits. By 1990 foreign holdings in the United States amounted to $1.5 trillion, compared with $1.2 trillion in U.S. assets abroad.

President Reagan's critics also charged that he starved vital social welfare programs for funds and was insensitive on racial issues. On national television, he had disparaged civil rights leaders for "doing very well [by] keeping alive the feeling that they're victims of prejudice." He had also opposed extending the scope of the 1965 Voting Rights Act, and in 1982 he approved tax-exempt status for private schools accused of racial discrimination (a practice overruled by the Supreme Court a year later).

The Last Presidential Campaign of the Cold War

In the presidential election of 1984, Ronald Reagan and Vice President George Bush won in a landslide over Walter Mondale and Geraldine Ferraro, the first woman nominated for vice president on a major party ticket. In 1988, however, the Democrats seemed to have a good shot at winning the White House, with the Soviet threat diminishing and the militant antigovernment, antitax sentiment of the late 1970s subsiding.

The Republican candidate, Vice President George Bush, was said to have the best resume in Washington. The son of a Connecticut banker and senator, Bush attended prep school at Andover and joined the military on his eighteenth birthday, winning the Distinguished Service Cross during World War II. After the war, he made a fortune in the Texas oil business, and then he went to Washington where he served as a representative, ambassador to the United Nations, envoy to China, and director of the CIA. His Democratic opponent, Massachusetts governor Michael Dukakis, was a serious, hardworking son of Greek immigrants.

Mudslinging and personal invective are nothing new in American politics, but the 1988 campaign was unusually vacuous and cynical. There were real differences between the candidates—over health care, housing policy, foreign policy, and defense spending—but these differences were submerged in a battle over character, abortion, prison furloughs, school prayer, and patriotism. The most emotional issue of the campaign involved the Pledge of Allegiance. Seizing on Governor Dukakis's veto of a 1977 Massachusetts bill requiring teachers to lead their classes in the pledge, Vice President

Bush suggested that his opponent's liberalism led him to place civil liberties above patriotism. "Should public-school teachers be required to lead our children in the Pledge of Allegiance?" Bush asked his audience at the Republican convention. "My opponent says no—but I say yes."

The 1988 presidential campaign dramatized a development that had been reshaping American politics since the late 1960s: the growing power of media consultants and pollsters, who market candidates much as cigarette manufacturers or soap companies sell their products, by emphasizing imagery and symbolism. Republican handlers portrayed the Democrats as fiscally irresponsible, soft on defense, and purveyors of the notion that America was in decline, while picturing the GOP as the party of patriotism, low taxes, and vigilant anti-Communism. Democrat strategists, in turn, argued that the Republicans reduced taxes for the wealthy while transferring responsibility for national problems like drugs, homelessness, education, pollution, and a decaying infrastructure to the states. At the end of a race that saw both candidates use negative campaigning, Bush was elected the forty-first president of the United States, with 56 percent of the popular vote.

THE BUSH PRESIDENCY

Presidents' inaugural addresses often set the tone for their entire terms in office. At his inauguration, Jimmy Carter stressed the limits of American power in the world: "We have learned that 'more' is not necessarily 'better,' that even our great nation has its recognized limits." Ronald Reagan set an entirely different tone in his inaugural address, in which he voiced his desire to reduce government's social welfare role: "Government is not the solution to our problem; government is the problem."

In his inaugural address, Bush signaled a departure from the avarice and greed of the Reagan era by calling for a "new engagement in the lives of others." He promised to be more of a "hands on" administrator than President Reagan, and he committed his presidency to creating a "kindler, gentler" nation, more sensitive and caring to the poor and disadvantaged.

In his first state of the union address, Bush

repeated his call for new initiatives to address the nation's social problems. His vision for America was a society where "there's a job for everyone who wants one;" where "women working outside the home can be confident their children are in safe and loving care." He called for new legislation to ensure a clean environment, equal opportunity for the disabled, aid to the homeless, and drug-free streets and schools. The challenge he confronted as president was to address many long-ignored problems in the face of a deficit-ridden federal budget and a $3 trillion federal debt.

A Kindler, Gentler Nation

During his first years in office, President Bush and the Democratic-controlled Congress addressed many issues ignored during the Reagan years. For the first time in eight years, the federal government raised the minimum wage from $3.35 to $4.25 an hour. Between 1981, when it was last raised, and 1989, inflation had eroded the value of the minimum wage by 27 percent. For the first time in 13 years, Congress amended federal air pollution laws in order to reduce noxious emissions from smokestacks and tailpipes and reduce acid rain. For the first time since 1971, Congress considered child care legislation, and ultimately voted to provide subsidies to low-income families to defray the costs of child care. In other actions, Congress prohibited job discrimination against the disabled, required nutrition labeling on processed foods, and expanded immigration into the United States.

In two areas critics accused President Bush of reneging on his promise of a "kindler, gentler" nation. He vetoed a new civil rights bill bolstering protections for minorities and women against job discrimination, on the grounds that it would lead to quotas, and he also vetoed a bill that would have provided up to six months of unpaid family leave for workers with newly born or adopted children or emergencies. In November 1991, however, Bush signed a compromise Civil Rights Act, which made it easier for workers to win antidiscrimination lawsuits.

Economic Policy

Many Americans believed that the end of the Cold War would bring a huge peace dividend, which could be used to reduce the federal budget deficit and fund domestic social programs. Soon after Bush took office, however, Americans learned that much of the peace dividend would have to be spent to clean up nuclear wastes produced at federal facilities and to bail out the nation's troubled savings and loan industry—at an estimated cost between $325 billion and $500 billion.

The roots of the savings and loan crisis were planted during the presidency of Jimmy Carter, when high inflation and high interest rates threatened to bankrupt savings institutions. With their resources tied up in long-term home mortgages, the savings institutions could not compete with other financial institutions permitted to pay high interest rates.

A 1980 law lifted limits on the interest rates savings institutions could pay and allowed them to make a limited amount of investments in commercial real estate. In 1982 and 1983, when President Reagan was in the White House, Congress broadened the institutions's capacity to make unsecured commercial loans and investments in commercial real estate. In the mid-1980s, falling oil prices led to a collapse of land values especially in Texas, California, and the Southwest, creating huge losses for savings institutions invested in real estate. By the end of the decade these institutions began to fail in large numbers. The mounting bills for the savings and loan bailout propelled President Bush in 1990 to violate his 1988 "no new taxes" campaign pledge.

Foreign Policy

Every president since John F. Kennedy—with the single exception of Jimmy Carter—has felt it necessary early in his administration to assert American interests with the unilateral use of force. George Bush was no exception. The first important foreign policy act of the Bush administration was an invasion of Panama, which the Pentagon called Operation JUST CAUSE. The origins of the conflict stretched back to 1987 when a high Panamanian military official accused strong-man General Manuel Antonio Noriega of committing fraud in the 1984 presidential election and of drug trafficking. Violent street demonstrations broke out in Panama. Angry Panamanians called for Noriega's overthrow. Noriega responded by declaring a state of emergency. The crisis escalated when two Florida grand juries indicted the general on charges that he protected and assisted the Medellín drug cartel.

U.S.-Panamanian relations deteriorated further when Noriega voided results of the 1989 presidential election and sent paramilitary forces into the streets of Panama City where they beat up opposition candidates. Conflict grew imminent when Noriega declared his country in a "state of war" against the United States. A day later four unarmed American military personnel were fired on at a roadblock by Panamanian troops, and one American was killed. Bush dispatched a force of 10,000 troops to safeguard the lives of Americans and protect the integrity of the Panama Canal treaties. It is estimated that between 300 and 800 Panamanian civilians and military personnel died during the invasion. There were 23 American casualties. In the end, however, Noriega was forced out of power and deported to the United States to stand trial for drug trafficking.

Collapse of Communism

The collapse of Communist regimes in Eastern Europe dominated the world scene as the 1990s began. On New Year's Day, 1989, Communist parties held power in Czechoslovakia, East Germany, Hungary, Poland, Bulgaria, and Romania. Czechoslovakia was run by an aging brutal dictatorship that imprisoned noted writers like Vaclav Havel and stripped dissidents of their jobs. Romania was ruled by dictator Nicolae Ceausescu, perhaps the most corrupt and brutal of the Eastern European dictators. For 28 years, the Berlin Wall had stood as the symbol of the division of Europe, a reinforced concrete and barbed-wire scar that separated the East from the West. By the year's end, the Berlin Wall had been smashed and Eastern European Communist parties had collapsed.

Across Eastern Europe, citizens took to the streets and overthrew 40 years of Communist rule. Like a series of falling dominos, from Poland and East Germany in the north to Hungary and Czechoslovakia in the middle to Romania and Bulgaria in the south, Communist parties

United States troops patrol the streets of Panama City during the U.S. invasion of Panama in December 1989.

fell from power. In Poland, Solidarity, a party and union founded by shipyard workers, won a landslide victory over Communists in parliamentary elections and established Poland's first non-Communist government since World War II. In Hungary, the Communist party disbanded, reconstituting itself as a Socialist party, and rewrote the Hungarian constitution to allow independent parties to contest free elections.

Tens of thousands of East Germans, seeking passage to West Germany, escaped across the Hungarian-Austrian border, while protestors demanded reforms in the largest antigovernment demonstrations in that nation's history. As a result East German Communist party chief Erich Honecker was ousted. Almost exactly a year later, East and West Germany were reunified.

Popular protests in East Germany and Hungary inspired 30,000 Czechoslovakians to demonstrate in Prague. Riot police brutally crushed the peaceful demonstration, clubbing and teargassing hundreds of people. This led more than 200,000 people to take to the streets in Prague and other cities, demanding free elections and resignations of hard-line Communist leaders. As a result, Czechoslovakia's top Communist leadership resigned, and on December 29, 1989, Vaclav Havel was elected president.

In Bulgaria, hard-liner Todor Zhivkov, long-time Communist party chief, was ousted and replaced by a moderate, Petar Mladenov. Then, in the largest protest since Bulgaria became a Communist nation, 50,000 people in Sofia demanded free elections, respect for human rights, and an end to 45 years of police repression.

In Timisoara, Romania, thousands of people were killed in protests against the Communist government. Then, in what appears to have been more of a coup than a revolution, Romanian Communist leader Nicolae Ceausescu was executed and a new government took power, promising free elections.

The speed and the success of the Eastern European revolutions surprised Westerners. To be sure, millions of Eastern Europeans had long hoped for fundamental changes. Poles and Hungarians had fought and died for change in 1956, as had Czechs in 1968. Throughout the 1980s Solidarity had pressed for change in Poland. The economic failure of communism was clear to millions of people living in Eastern Europe. They realized that each year they fell further behind the West economically. But the political leaders in Eastern Europe ruled confidently, knowing that the Soviet Union, backed by the Red Army, would always send in the tanks when the forces for change became too great.

Mikhail Gorbechev changed the 40-year pattern. At the same time as he moved toward reform within the Soviet Union and détente with the West, he pushed the conservative regimes of Eastern Europe outside his protective umbrella. No more Red Army, no more tanks to the rescue. Eastern European leaders had long expected the unexpected, but they had never bargained on a liberal Soviet leader. One authority on the region observed, "Eastern European leaders were left on their own with nothing between them and their subjects except the most incriminating thing of all: their own record." And it was a record on which no leader would care to run for office.

Gorbachev, who had wanted to reform communism, had not anticipated the swift swing toward democracy in Eastern Europe. Nor had he fully foreseen the impact that democracy in Eastern Europe would have on the Soviet Union. By 1990 leaders of several Soviet republics began to demand independence or greater autonomy within the Soviet Union. The Baltic republics of Lithuania, Latvia, and Estonia wanted to leave the Soviet Union. The republic of Russia, led by its president Boris Yeltsin, also demanded greater autonomy, if not outright independence. The republics of the Ukraine and Moldavia, as well as several of the southern republics, similarly voiced discontent with the traditional political arrangement of the Soviet Union.

Gorbachev had to balance the growing demand for radical political change within the Soviet Union with the demand by Soviet hardliners that he dam the new democratic currents and turn back the clock. It was a near impossible task. Faced with dangerous political opposition

For nearly three decades the Berlin Wall was the most visible symbol of the Cold War and of the division between East and West. The most dramatic incident marking the end of the Cold War was the destruction of the Wall in November 1989.

(Text continues on p. 1084)

AMERICA AND THE WORLD
THE END OF TWO ERAS

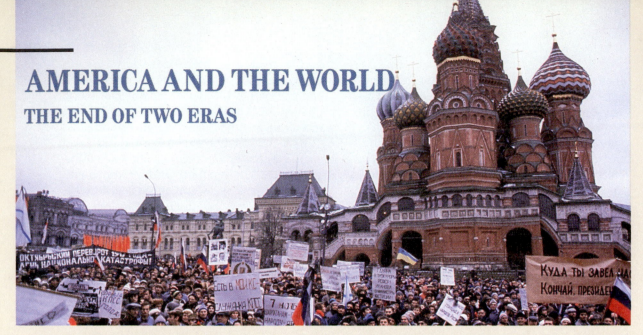

On November 7, 1990, on the anniversary of the 1917 revolution that brought Lenin to power, demonstrators in Moscow gathered to protest Communist rule.

The dates on the obituary read 1922 to 1991. When the death was duly recorded in newspapers and magazines throughout the world only a handfull of bureaucrats mourned the corpse. That body—the Union of Soviet Socialist Republics (USSR)—was the light that failed. Born in the cold and ice of a late Russian December, the USSR promised equality and justice. Driven by the belief in communism, Vladimir Lenin, the leader of the Bolsheviks who came to power in Russia in 1917 and founded the USSR five years later, announced that Russia was only the first step. Eventually, he said, communism would free the entire world and introduce a new epoch of peace, prosperity, and happiness for all people. The epoch never arrived. It remained only in the minds of the true believers. Instead of liberating the world, Soviet leaders suppressed freedom inside the Soviet Union. As one journalist noted in his obituary of the Soviet Union, "There is no reason to mourn the death of a country that killed millions of its own citizens in the collectivization campaign, the purges and the famines that were used as an instrument of government policy."

Born in a brutal Russian winter, the USSR died in an equally severe winter. About the death there was a singular note of irony. The Soviet leader who had done the most to reform and humanize the country caused its death. Mikhail Gorbachev became the leader of the Soviet Union in 1985. He was relatively young—in 1980 he had become the youngest full member of the Politburo, the ruling body in the USSR—and very well educated. He knew that every year his country was falling further and further behind the west in every material sense. Determined to correct the slide, he introduced measures to restructure the Soviet economy (*perestroika*) and to create a new political openness (*glasnost*). His economic measures never worked, but his political initiatives worked all too well. First, Eastern Europe used the new openness to break away from the Soviet orbit. Then, the USSR's Baltic republics of Lithuania, Latvia, and Estonia demanded and received independence. Finally, the remaining 12 republics of the Soviet Union decided that the union was unworkable and undesirable. Gorbachev attempted to hold the republics together but failed. On Christmas Day, 1991, he faced the reality that the Soviet Union no longer existed and resigned from office.

The Soviet newspaper *Tzvestia* commented that Gorbachev "did all he could." Perhaps no leader could have kept the Soviet Union from breaking apart once liberalization had started. Political freedom was singularly out of step with Soviet political traditions. But Gorbachev did fail in several areas. A man who had risen through the Soviet bureaucracy, Gorbachev failed to significantly reform or abolish that bureaucracy even though it became clear that that very bureaucracy was the primary obstacle to *perestroika*. In addition, he never devised a plan to allow enough freedom in the individual republics, and he even tacitly permitted Soviet security forces to use tanks and guns to suppress the Baltic independence movements. But most importantly, Gorbachev's *perestroika* did not work because it did not bring a new era of prosperity to the Soviet Union. Gorbachev admitted that "the old system fell apart even before the new system began to work," but as one authority commented, "there was no new system." Like every Soviet leader since Lenin, Gorbachev promised far more than he delivered.

The death of the Soviet Union posed immense problems both for the newly independent republics and the United States. Even before Gorbachev's resignation, 11 of the 12 remaining republics—only the republic of Georgia was excluded—joined together into a new confederation called the Commonwealth of Independent States. Led by the republics of Russia, Belorussia, and Ukraine, the new entity was more an alliance than a state. The republics agreed to cooperate in economic reforms aimed at moving them toward a free enterprise system and maintain at least temporarily the ruble as the common currency. Further, and without being very specific, they announced that the Commonwealth would coordinate economic, military, and foreign policies of its independent members. Central to the Commonwealth, however, was the idea that each member was and remained a sovereign nation. To underscore this idea, the Commonwealth located its capital in Minsk rather than Moscow, the seat of Soviet power, or St. Petersburg, the capital of czarist Russia.

From the first, the Commonwealth faced a difficult task. Disputes quickly arose over how to divide the military and economic resources of the old Soviet Union. The sovereign republics had to decide how to divide the forces and equipment of the Red Army and the Soviet Navy as well as the Soviet state treasury, central television network, space infrastructure, and the hundreds of other assets once controlled by the Soviet Union. As a symbol of the great change, in February 1992 the Commonwealth Olympic team competed in the Albertville Winter Games under the Olympic flag and their victories were marked by the playing of the Olympic anthem.

Even more pressing than the decision on how to divide Soviet property was the conversion to a limited free-market system. In early 1992 the Commonwealth lifted most price controls and the cost of goods shot upward. The prices of such basic commodities as bread and gasoline, over which some controls still existed, tripled or quadrupled literally overnight. The prices of noncontrolled items increased much more. A kilo of *kolbasa* sausages was 2.20 rubles in January 1991; the price rose to 43.75 rubles (and as high as 200 rubles in particularly hard-pressed St. Petersburg) in January 1992. The ruble iteself experienced the shock. The official exchange used to be 1.8 per dollar; in January 1992 the exchange rate rose to well over 100 rubles per dollar. The economic changes created severe hardships for people whose monthly income averaged 400 rubles. Many citizens of the Commonwealth considered the winter of 1992 as the worst in their lives.

The death of the Soviet Union also had a profound effect on the United States. On one level the United States had to redirect its foreign policy. The era of the Cold War was over. The Soviet Union, America's Cold War rival, no longer existed. President George Bush responded to the changes by announcing victory in the Cold War, recognizing the new independent republics, and sending aid to the beleaguered members of the Commonwealth. Although Americans continued to worry about who controlled the Commonwealth's nuclear weapons, there was no longer the fear of war between the Soviet Union and the United States.

On another level, the end of the Cold War undermined one of the organizing principles of American culture. American mass culture in particular revolved around the idea of "us" and "them." Throughout the Cold War era Hollywood made successful movies that played on this theme. From such movies as *I was a Communist for the FBI*, *My Son John*, *Dr. Strangelove*, *Fail Safe*, *Red Alert*, and *On the Beach* to the James Bond action pictures and John Wayne westerns, Cold War issues provided the explicit or implicit basis for the films. Not to be outdone, popular writers capitalized on Cold War themes. John Le Carre, William F. Buckley, Jr., and Tom Clancy wrote best-sellers that centered on Cold War plots. Television also pitted "us" against "them" on numerous programs. During the 1960s "The Man from U.N.C.L.E.," "Mission Impossible," and "I Spy" were popular programs that featured Cold War stories. Even sports were influenced by the Cold War. In particular, the Olympic Games reflected Cold War tension and anxieties. American cheers of "U.S.A., U.S.A." at Olympic events became ritualistic Cold War chants.

American education and science similarly were partial hostages to the Cold War. After the success of the Soviet *Sputnik* in 1957, Congress appropriated funds for the establishment of the National Aeronautics and Space Administration (N.A.S.A.) and passed the National Defense Education Act. In the Cold War the space race and education became highly political issues. President John F. Kennedy's decision to push America's space program toward putting a person on the moon—a decision that many of America's leading scientists opposed—was more a response to the Cold War than the needs of science. And Neil Armstrong's July 21, 1969, moon walk was confirmation of America's victory in the space race.

The death of the Soviet Union, then, ended two eras. How citizens of both the United States and the Commonwealth of Independent States will respond to that death will be one of the most important issues in the 1990s and the twenty-first century.

from the right and the left and with economic failure throughout the Soviet Union, Gorbachev tried to satisfy everyone and in the process satisfied no one.

Gorbachev's unsuccessful balancing act ended on August 18, 1991. On that day elements of the Soviet army and the KGB, attempted a right-wing political coup. They confronted Gorbachev at his vacation retreat on the Black Sea and demanded that he effectively transfer his power to them. After Gorbachev told the coup members to "go to hell," he was placed under house arrest.

From the first, however, the coup faced problems. It did not have the cooperation of all of the important generals and little of the sympathy of the average soldier. In addition, it lacked popular support. Boris Yeltsin, the most popular leader in the Soviet Union, denounced the coup and rallied public support against it. On August 21, the coup fell apart. Several conspirators committed suicide and most of the rest were arrested. Gorbachev returned to power.

The failure of the right to grasp power strengthened the left. The Baltic republics quickly announced their independence, and the Soviet Union formed a new confederation that granted far greater freedom and autonomy to the individual republics. In the end, what the right had hoped to prevent, it accelerated.

The move away from dictatorship was not confined to Eastern Europe and the Soviet Union. It also swept Latin America. In 1983, a year-and-a-half after defeat in a war with Britain over the Falkland Islands, Argentina returned to democratic rule. In 1986, Jean-Claude Duvalier of Haiti fled into exile, ending his family's 28-year dictatorship. At the end of the 1980s, Brazil, Chile, Costa Rica, Honduras, and Nicaragua inaugurated elected presidents committed to a market economy and free elections.

The winds of change blew across countries as disparate as the Philippines and South Africa. In 1973 Philippines President Ferdinand Marcos imposed martial law and made himself a virtual dictator. He jailed 6000 political prisoners. In 1986, Ferdinand Marcos was forced into exile after he tried to steal an election from Corazon C. Aquino. Riding the crest of "people power," she became president of her island nation. In South Africa, there were signs that minority white rule might be coming to an end, as Nelson Mandela was released from a South African prison after 27 years and the government legalized the African National Congress, lifted a 30-year ban on black political demonstrations, and ordered municipalities to integrate their beaches.

The First Crisis of the Post–Cold War Era

At 2 A.M., August 2, 1990, 80,000 Iraqi troops invaded and occupied Kuwait, a small, oil-rich emirate on the Persian Gulf, touching off the first major international crisis of the post–Cold War era. Days later, Iraq annexed Kuwait as the country's nineteenth province. Iraq's leader, Saddam Hussein, justified the invasion on the grounds that Kuwait, which he accused of intentionally depressing world oil prices, was a historic part of Iraq.

Iraq's invasion caught the United States off guard. The Hussein regime was a brutal military dictatorship that ruled by secret police and used poison gas against Iranians, Kurds, and Shiite Moslems. For years the United States and other countries had tried to moderate Iraq's leader Saddam Hussein. During the 1970s and 1980s, the United States—and Britain, France, the Soviet Union, West Germany—sold Iraq an awesome arsenal of weapons, including missiles, tanks, and the equipment needed to produce biological, chemical, and nuclear weapons. During Baghdad's eight-year-long war with Iran, the United States, which opposed the growth of Moslem fundamentalist extremism, tilted toward Iraq.

On August 6, 1990, President Bush dramatically declared, "This aggression will not stand." With Iraqi forces poised near the Saudi Arabian border, the Bush administration dispatched 180,000 troops to protect the Saudi kingdom. In a sharp departure from American foreign policy during the Reagan presidency, Bush also organized an international coalition against Iraq, convincing Turkey and Syria to close Iraqi oil pipelines, winning Soviet support for an arms embargo, and establishing a multinational army to protect Saudi Arabia, with contingents from western and Arab nations, including Britain,

Lacking public and popular support, the attempted right-wing coup in the Soviet Union collapsed within days. Here, protestors cheer the soldiers who have withdrawn their tanks from the coup.

Egypt, France, Italy, and Syria. In the United Nations, the administration succeeded in persuading the Security Council to adopt a series of resolutions condemning the Iraqi invasion, demanding restoration of the Kuwaiti government, and imposing an economic blockade.

Bush's decision to draw "a line in the sand" grew naturally out of his personal experience and his vision of the role of the United States in world affairs. As a 16-year-old high school student, Bush heard Franklin D. Roosevelt's Secretary of War Henry L. Stimson declare that it was the obligation of the United States to protect less-powerful countries against aggression. Inspired by Stimson's words, Bush dropped out of school to enlist as a naval pilot, flying Avenger torpedo and dive bombers. At 19, he was the navy's youngest pilot. On September 2, 1944, Bush's airplane was shot down and two crewmen died. Bush landed in the sea and managed to find a life raft. Later a submarine picked him up.

The decision to resist Iraqi aggression also reflected the president's assessment of vital national interests. Iraq's invasion gave Saddam Hussein direct control over a significant portion of the world's oil supply. It disrupted the Middle East balance of power and placed Saudi Arabia and the Persian Gulf emirates in jeopardy. Iraq's battle-hardened war machine—consisting of 545,000 troops, 5000 tanks, 500 fighter aircraft, and chemical and biological weapons—threatened the security of such valuable U.S. allies as Egypt and Israel.

On November 8, 1990, two days after midterm elections, the crisis took a dramatic turn when President Bush surprised the nation by doubling the 150,000 American troops deployed in the Persian Gulf. Iraqi forces in Kuwait had climbed to 430,000 and coalition forces had to increase if it hoped to eject Iraq from Kuwait by force. The troop increase produced a strong reaction from Congress. Many members demanded that Bush receive prior approval from Congress for any use of force against Iraq. Before going to Congress, the president went to the United Nations for a resolution permitting the use of force against Iraq after January 15, 1991. Then, after a heated debate, Congress gave the president authority to wage war.

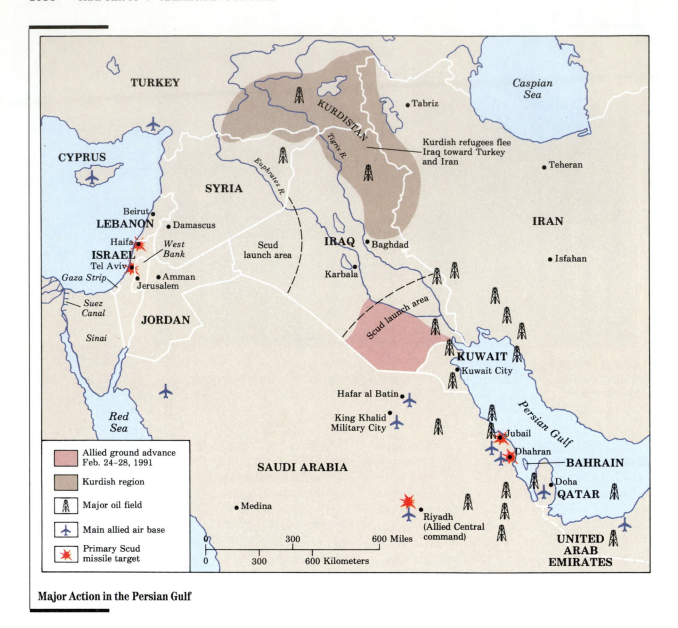

Major Action in the Persian Gulf

In a last-ditch effort to avert war, U.S. Secretary of State James Baker and Iraq's Foreign Minister Tariq Aziz met in Geneva for more than six hours. The talks failed. Aziz told Baker: "Your Arab allies will desert you. They will not kill other Arabs. Your alliance will crumble and you will be left lost in the desert." On January 15, Bush signed a national security directive authorizing the liberation of Kuwait.

President Bush's decision to reverse Iraqi aggression and liberate Kuwait was an enormous political and military gamble. The

545,000-strong Iraqi army, the world's fourth largest, was equipped with antiship Exocet missiles, top-of-the-line Soviet T-72 tanks, and long-range artillery capable of firing nerve gas. The Iraqi leader tried to break up the allied coalition by launching Scud missiles at Israeli cities in order to bring Israel into the war. This strategy was thwarted by Israeli restraint and the American decision to send Patriot antimissile missiles to the Jewish state. Iraq also engaged in what some environmentalists called "eco-terrorism"—setting fire to Kuwaiti oil wells and deliberately spewing oil into the Persian Gulf.

A month of allied bombing gave the coalition forces air supremacy and destroyed thousands of Iraqi tanks and artillery pieces, supply routes and communications lines, command-and-control bunkers, and limited Iraq's ability to produce nuclear, chemical, and biological weapons. Iraqi troop morale suffered so badly under the bombing that an estimated 30 percent of Baghdad's forces deserted before the ground campaign started.

The allied ground campaign relied on deception, mobility, and overwhelming air superiority to defeat a larger Iraqi army. The allied strategy was to mislead the Iraqis into believing that the allied attack would occur along the Kuwaiti coastline and Kuwait's border with Saudi Arabia. Meanwhile, General H. Norman Schwarzkopf, American commander of coalition forces, shifted more than 300,000 American, British, and French troops into western Saudia Arabia, allowing them to strike deep into Iraq and trap Iraqi forces deep in southern Iraq and Kuwait. Only 100 hours after the ground war started, the war ended.

The end of the war did not mean the end of suffering or even hostilities. Saddam Hussein remained in power, and in the war's aftermath he brutally suppressed independence movements by two minority groups—the Shiites and the Kurds—in his own country. Nor did the liberated Kuwait move toward a more liberal nation. But Saddam's power in the region was dramatically limited.

The Significance of the Persian Gulf Conflict

The Persian Gulf conflict was the most popular American war since World War II, restoring American confidence in its position as the world's sole superpower and helping to exorcise the ghost of Vietnam that had haunted American foreign policy debates for more than a decade—a time of doubt, drift, and demoralization that began with the Vietnam War and the Watergate scandal appeared to have ended.

Public debate over the Persian Gulf conflict was also haunted by the specter of Vietnam. Antiwar protesters, some of whom waved banners proclaiming "No Blood for Oil," questioned whether the war would advance U.S. interests in the Arab world and whether it would bring stability and security to the Perisan Gulf. Some critics argued that the Iraqi takeover of Kuwait was a product of a maldistribution of Arab oil wealth between poorly populated, rich oil producers like Kuwait and Saudi Arabia and large, poor Arab states. Others questioned the wisdom of defending countries like Kuwait that deny such basic personal freedoms as the right of women to drive a car.

The Vietnam War exerted a powerful influence on the thinking of American military and political leaders. During the 1970s and 1980s a consensus gradually emerged that the United States should not fight a war that did not involve vital American interests, that lacked clearly defined objectives, and that failed to have broad public and congressional support.

The war with Iraq illustrated many of the lessons that Americans had learned from the nation's unhappy experience in Vietnam—an inconclusive, unpopular war. In stark contrast to the Vietnam War, which was fought without a clear definition of victory, the Persian Gulf War had a clearly designated goal: to force Iraq to leave Kuwait. Even after the United States had routed the Iraqi army and could easily have carried the ground war to the Iraqi capital of Baghdad, Bush made it clear that the United States was eager to withdraw its forces as soon as possible.

Also, unlike Vietnam, which was fought without clear congressional authority or international support, the Persian Gulf War received strong support from Congress, the United Nations, and an international coalition that included some 30 nations. And finally, unlike Vietnam, the Persian Gulf War was fought without half measures. The United States agreed to no cease-fire until its adversary's army was routed.

Years may have to pass before historians will be able to conclusively evaluate the consequences of the Persian Gulf War. Only the future will tell whether America's success against Iraq made future wars less likely by deterring aggression and whether the war brought stability to the Middle East.

In a scene recalling the antiwar protests of the 1960s, demonstrators in San Francisco show their disapproval of U.S. military involvement in the Persian Gulf.

Assessing the Bush Presidency

In January 1991 *Time* magazine placed George Bush on its cover. It pictured him with two faces, because his presidency seemed to have two very different images. "One was a foreign policy profile that was a study in resoluteness," the magazine said, "the other a domestic visage just as strongly marked by wavering and confusion."

In the Persian Gulf War, Bush acted from clear, unequivocal principles. Convinced that it was necessary to humiliate Saddam Hussein and prove that America would resist aggression, Bush demonstrated that a determined and skillful president has the power to move a reluctant nation. Throughout the Persian Gulf crisis, Bush repeatedly convinced the American people that resolute action was necessary. In early August, 1990, a Gallup poll found that 56 percent of the American people opposed sending troops to defend Saudi Arabia; yet Bush succeeded in mobilizing overwhelming public support for his decision to deploy troops in the kingdom. Just ten days before he launched the ground war, a poll

found only 11 percent of American people favored such a step. The day after the ground war began, 75 percent approved.

In domestic affairs, in stark contrast, Bush's leadership was less decisive. On such issues as taxes, abortion, and civil rights, he adopted a flexible, pragmatic approach that led some critics to describe him as a political chameleon. Unlike Ronald Reagan, who brought a series of fixed philosophical principles to domestic issues, Bush appeared less interested in domestic affairs and more willing to flip-flop on his pledge not to raise taxes.

A New Covenant

Bush's failure to alter the downward slide of the American economy played the crucial role in the 1992 presidential election. In a bitter three-way contest, marked by intense assaults on the candidates' records and characters, Arkansas Governor Bill Clinton defeated George Bush and Texas businessman Ross Perot to become the first Democratic president in 12 years. President Bush, whose popularity soared to 90

1970 President Nixon approves Huston plan to use the government intelligence agencies to gather information on domestic "radicals"; plan is later rescinded

1971 A secret tape-recording system is installed in the White House; Nixon authorizes establishment of plumbers unit to "stop security leaks and investigate other sensitive matters"

1972 Five burglars arrested breaking into Democratic national headquarters at Washington's Watergate Office Complex; President Nixon takes part in summit in China; President Nixon is reelected with 61 percent of the vote

1973 Televised Senate hearings on Watergate begin; Spiro Agnew pleads no contest to a charge of income tax evasion and resigns as vice president

1974 Federal grand jury indicts Nixon aides for perjury and obstruction of justice and names the president as an unindicted coconspirator; House Judiciary Committee adopts three articles of impeachment against President Nixon; Nixon becomes the first president to resign from office; Ford becomes thirty-eighth president; Federal Campaign Reform Act sets limits on private campaign contributions and provides tax funds to presidential candidates

1975 Cambodia seizes American merchant ship *Mayaguez*

1976 Jimmy Carter is elected thirty-ninth president; Soviet Premier Leonid Brezhnev announces the "Brezhnev Doctrine"

1978 President Carter mediates Egyptian-Israeli peace settlement; Iranian revolution begins

1979 United States formally recognizes China; Iranian militants seize American hostages; Soviet Union invades Afghanistan; Somoza regime in Nicaragua is overthrown; Sandinistas take power

1980 Ronald Reagan is elected fortieth president

1981 American hostages are released from Iran; Reagan is shot in assassination attempt; Reagan approves covert training of anti-Sandinista contras; Reagan tax cuts are approved

1982 Congress deregulates banking industry and lifts controls on air fares

1983 Reagan proposes "Star Wars" missile defense system; United States topples Communist government on the Caribbean island of Grenada; Soviet fighter shoots down Korean Airlines flight 007

1984 Congress orders an end to all covert aid to Nicaraguan contras

1985 United States begins secret arms-for-hostages negotiations with Iran; Mikhail Gorbachev becomes leader of the Soviet Union

1986 Profits from Iranian arms sales are diverted to Nicaraguan contras

1987 Iran-Contra hearings; stock market plunges 508 points in a single session

1988 George Bush is elected forty-first president

1989 Opposition defeats Sandinistas in Nicaraguan elections; Communist regimes collapse in Eastern Europe

1990 Iraqi troops invade and occupy Kuwait

1991 U.S., Western, and Arab forces eject Iraq from Kuwait by force; failed coup in Soviet Union results in a shift in power to the Soviet republics and in independence for Lithuania, Latvia, and Estonia; confirmation hearings for Clarence Thomas to the U.S. Supreme Court focus national attention on the issue of sexual harassment; United States and Soviet Union host peace talks between Israelis, Palestinians, and Arab states

1992 Bill Clinton is elected forty-second president

percent after the Persian Gulf War, received 38 percent of the vote, to Clinton's 43 percent and Perot's 19 percent.

The central issue in the election was the nation's sluggish economy. During the Bush presidency, fewer new jobs were created than in any other presidential term since World War II. Indeed, fewer Americans were on private payrolls at the end of this term than when he took office. Unemployment reached the highest level in eight years; personal incomes stagnated; businesses failed in record numbers; the federal debt surpassed $4 trillion; and medical care absorbed 15 percent of the nation's output, while a quarter of the population lacked health insurance. Poverty rose to the highest rate in over two decades—a fact dramatically underscored by the outbreak of the deadliest riot in America's history, in Los Angeles in April 1992.

President Clinton pledged a "new covenant" for America: a new approach to government between the unfettered free market championed by the Republicans and the welfare state economics that the Democratic party had represented in the past. He called for higher taxes on the wealthiest Americans, reduced defense spending, college aid for all qualified students, and expanded job training programs. A new era in the nation's history, Clinton promised, had begun.

CONCLUSION

As the twentieth century draws to a close, America's ideals of democracy and personal freedom are ascendant across the world. From Tiananmen Square—where Chinese students erected a goddess of liberty modeled on the Statue of Liberty—to the Philippines, popular protests and demonstrations have called for "government of the people, for the people, and by the people." In Eastern Europe, the former Soviet Union, and across Latin America, people demand free speech, freedom of religion, freedom of the press, and free markets.

Yet paradoxically, as American ideals and values flourish abroad, Americans are anxious about their economy and their country's future. Many are angry, expressing cynical contempt toward their government.

The American economy remains the world's most productive. Nevertheless, many fear that American competitiveness and inventiveness are declining. The economic picture is mixed. The American economy today is almost three times as large as Japan's and nearly twice as large as the combined economies of Germany, France, and Britain. The average American worker still produces a third more than the average Japanese worker. The proportion of national income invested in research and development is as large as in Europe and Japan.

Yet at the same time other nations save more and invest more than the United States, and are increasing the productivity of their industries faster than America. Except for a few areas of trade—such as high-tech products, financial services, and aircraft—foreign countries dominate the most technologically advanced fields, such as consumer electronics, luxury automobiles, and machine tools.

Other economic problems also prompt concern. The national debt and federal deficit stand at record levels. Foreign ownership of American factories, real estate, and stocks and bonds is actually greater than American ownership of foreign assets. No longer does the United States possess the world's highest level of per capita income.

Americans also worry about crime, the state of their central cities, and the level of health and education in their society. The level of crime and violence in the United States is the highest in the industrialized world. No one, not even presidents, has been immune from the threat of violence. Four of the last eight presidents have been targets of assassins' bullets. The nation's infant death rate is higher than that of 19 other nations and is twice as high as Japan's. Schooling is a particular source of dismay. Standardized tests indicate that America's schoolchildren lag behind those in other advanced societies in almost every branch of learning—foreign languages, geography, mathematics, natural sciences. America's rates of drug use, juvenile delinquency, teenage pregnancy, and teen suicide are the highest in the industrialized world.

At the end of World War II, many commentators referred to the twentieth century as the "American century." Today, the United States remains the mightiest, most productive nation in the world, a model of freedom and pluralism that people across the globe still strive to emulate. The great question Americans ask as the "American century" comes to an end is whether the people who have reached the moon and routed the Iraqi army have the commitment and will to solve the down-to-earth problems that confront their cities, their schools, and their physical environment.

SUGGESTIONS FOR FURTHER READING

OVERVIEWS AND SURVEYS

Michael Barone, *Our Country: The Shaping of America from Roosevelt to Reagan* (1990); Peter N. Carroll, *It Seemed Like Nothing Happened: The Tragedy and Promise of the 1970s* (1990); William H. Chafe, *The Unfinished Journey: America Since World War II*, 2d ed. (1991); Frederick F. Siegel, *Troubled Journey: From Pearl Harbor to Ronald Reagan* (1984).

CRISIS OF POLITICAL LEADERSHIP

Terry Deibel, *Presidents, Public Opinion, and Power: The Nixon, Carter, and Reagan Years* (1986); Stanley I. Kutler, *The Wars of Watergate: The Last Crisis of Richard Nixon* (1990); J. Anthony Lukas, *Nightmare: The Underside of the Nixon Years* (1976); Kim McQuaid, *The Anxious Years: America in the Vietnam-Watergate Era* (1989); Richard E. Neustadt, *Presidential Power and Modern Presidents*, rev. ed. (1990); James Reichley, *Conservatives in an Age of Change: The Nixon and Ford Administrations* (1981); Edward L. and Frederick H. Schapsmeier, *Gerald R. Ford's Date with Destiny: A Political Biography* (1989); Jonathan Schell, *The Time of Illusion* (1975); Arthur M. Schlesinger, Jr., *The Imperial Presidency* (1973).

WRENCHING ECONOMIC TRANSFORMATIONS

Barry Bluestone and Bennett Harrison, *The Deindustrialization of America* (1982); David Calleo, *The Imperious Economy* (1982); Emmett Dedmon, *Challenge and Response: A Modern History of the Standard Oil Company* (1984); Thomas Edsall, *The New Politics of Inequality* (1984); Michael Goldfield, *The Decline of Organized Labor in the United States* (1987); Frank Levy, *Dollars and Dreams: The Changing American Income Distribution* (1987); Martin V. Melosi, *Coping with Abundance: Energy and Environment in Industrial America* (1985); Norman E. Nordhauser, *The Quest for Sta-bility: Domestic Oil Regulation* (1979); Bernard Nossiter, *Fat Years and Lean Years: The American Economy Since Roosevelt* (1990); Michael Piore, *The Second Industrial Divide* (1984); Stephen G. Rabe, *The Road to OPEC* (1982); Herbert Stein, *Presidential Economics: The Making of Economic Policy from Roosevelt to Reagan*, 2d ed. (1988); Michael Stoff, *Oil, War, and Security* (1980); Daniel Yergin, *The Prize: The Epic Quest for Oil, Money, and Power* (1990).

A NEW AMERICAN ROLE IN THE WORLD

James A. Bill, *The Eagle and the Lion: The Tragedy of American-Iranian Relations* (1988); Gordon H. Chang, *Friends and Enemies: The United States, China, and the Soviet Union* (1990); Mark Gasiorowski, *U.S. Foreign Policy and the Shah* (1991); J. Michael Hogan, *The Panama Canal in American Politics* (1986); Nikki R. Keddie, *Iran, the United States, and the Soviet Union* (1991); Walter La-Feber, *The Panama Canal*, rev. ed. (1989); Joseph Lepgold, *The Declining Hegemon: The United States and European Defense, 1960–1990* (1990); Richard A. Melanson, *Reconstructing Consensus: American Foreign Policy Since the Vietnam War* (1990); Kuross A. Samii, *Involvement by Invitation: American Strategies of Containment in Iran* (1987); Robert D. Schulzinger, *Henry Kissinger* (1989); Gaddis Smith, *Morality, Reason and Power: American Diplomacy in the Carter Years* (1986); Seth Tillman, *The United States in the Middle East* (1982); Marvin Zonis, *Majestic Failure: The Fall of the Shah* (1991).

THE REAGAN REVOLUTION

Norman C. Amaker, *Civil Rights and the Reagan Administration* (1988); Cynthia J. Arnson, *Crossroads: Congress, the Reagan Administration, and Central America* (1989); Coral Bell, *The Reagan Paradox: American Foreign Policy in the 1980s* (1989); Sidney Blumenthal, *Our Long National Daydream: A Political Pageant of the Reagan Era* (1988); Paul Boyer, ed., *Reagan as President* (1990); Lou Cannon, *President Reagan: The Role of a Lifetime* (1991); Robert Dallek, *Ronald Reagan: The Politics of Symbolism* (1984); Theodore Draper, *A Very Thin Line: The Iran-Contra Affairs* (1991); Thomas Ferguson and Joel Rogers, *Right Turn: The Decline of the Democrats and the Future of American Politics* (1986); Steve Fraser and Gary Gerstle, *The Rise and Fall of the New Deal Order* (1990); Fred Halliday, *From Kabul to Managua: Soviet-American Relations in the 1980s* (1989); J. David Hoeveler, Jr., *Watch on the Right: Conservative Intellectuals in the Reagan Era*

(1991); Haynes Johnson, *Sleepwalking Through History: America in the Reagan Years* (1991); David E. Kyvig, ed., *Reagan and the World* (1990); Jane Mayer and Doyle McManus, *Landslide: The Unmaking of the President, 1984–1988* (1988); John L. Palmer, ed., *Perspectives on the Reagan Years* (1986); Robert Pastor, *Condemned to Repetition: The United States and Nicaragua* (1987); Martin Wattenberg, *The Decline of American Political Parties, 1952–1988* (1990), and *The Rise of Candidate-Centered Politics: Presidential Elections of the 1980s* (1991); Garry Wills, *Reagan's America* (1987).

THE BUSH PRESIDENCY

Sidney Blumenthal, *Pledging Allegiance: The Last Campaign of the Cold War* (1990); Kevin Buckley, *Panama: The Whole Story* (1991); Jill Crystal, *Oil and Politics in the Gulf* (1990); E. J. Dionne, Jr., *Why Americans Hate Politics* (1991); Alan Ehrenhalt, *The United States of Ambition: Politicians, Power, and the Pursuit of Office* (1991); Robert O. Freedman, *Moscow and the Middle East* (1991); Moshe Lewin, *The Gorbachev Phenomenon* (1991); Martin Mayer, *The Greatest Ever Bank Robbery: The Collapse of the Savings and Loan Industry* (1990); Henry R. Nau, *The Myth of America's Decline* (1990); William Pfaff, *Barbarian Sentiments: How the American Century Ends* (1989); Stephen Pizzo, et al., *Inside Job: The Looting of America's Savings and Loans* (1989); Gail Sheehy, *The Man Who Changed the World: The Lives of Mikhail S. Gorbachev* (1990); Lawrence J. White, *The S&L Debacle* (1991); Garry Wills, *Under God: Religion and American Politics* (1990); Bob Woodward, *The Commanders* (1991).

Appendix

The Declaration of Independence

In Congress, July 4, 1776

The Unanimous Declaration of the thirteen United States of America

When, in the course of human events, it becomes necessary for one people to dissolve the political bonds which have connected them with another, and to assume, among the powers of the earth, the separate and equal station to which the laws of nature and of nature's God entitle them, a decent respect to the opinions of mankind requires that they should declare the causes which impel them to the separation.

We hold these truths to be self-evident: That all men are created equal; that they are endowed by their Creator with certain unalienable rights; that among these are life, liberty, and the pursuit of happiness; that, to secure these rights, governments are instituted among men, deriving their just powers from the consent of the governed; that whenever any form of government becomes destructive of these ends, it is the right of the people to alter or to abolish it, and to institute new government, laying its foundation on such principles, and organizing its powers in such form, as to them shall seem most likely to effect their safety and happiness. Prudence, indeed, will dictate that governments long established should not be changed for light and transient causes; and accordingly all experience hath shown that mankind are more disposed to suffer, while evils are sufferable, than to right themselves by abolishing the forms to which they are accustomed. But when a long train of abuses and usurpations, pursuing invariably the same object, evinces a design to reduce them under absolute despotism, it is their right, it is their duty, to throw off such government, and to provide new guards for their future security. Such has been the patient sufferance of these colonies; and such is now the necessity which constrains them to alter their former systems of government. The history of the present King of Great Britain is a history of repeated injuries and usurpations, all having in direct object the establishment of an absolute tyranny over these states. To prove this, let facts be submitted to a candid world.

He has refused his assent to laws, the most wholesome and necessary for the public good.

He has forbidden his governors to pass laws of immediate and pressing importance, unless suspended in their operation till his assent should be obtained; and when so suspended, he has utterly neglected to attend to them.

He has refused to pass other laws for the accommodation of large districts of people, unless those people would relinquish the right of representation in the legislature, a right inestimable to them, and formidable to tyrants only.

He has called together legislature bodies at places unusual, uncomfortable, and distant from the depository of their public records, for the sole purpose of fatiguing them into compliance with his measures.

He has dissolved representative houses repeatedly, for opposing with manly firmness, his invasions on the rights of the people.

He has refused for a long time, after such dissolutions, to cause others to be elected; whereby the legislative powers, incapable of annihilation, have returned to the people at large for their exercise; the state remaining, in the mean time, exposed to all the dangers of invasions from without and convulsions within.

He has endeavored to prevent the population of these states; for that purpose obstructing the laws for naturalization of foreigners; refusing to pass others to encourage their migration hither, and raising the conditions of new appropriations of lands.

He has obstructed the administration of justice, by refusing his assent to laws for establishing judiciary powers.

He has made judges dependent on his will alone, for the tenure of their offices, and the amount and payment of their salaries.

He has erected a multitude of new offices, and sent hither swarms of officers to harass our people and eat out their substance.

He has kept among us, in times of peace, standing armies, without the consent of our legislatures.

He has affected to render the military independent of, and superior to, the civil power.

He has combined with others to subject us to a jurisdiction foreign to our constitution, and unacknowledged by our laws, giving his assent to their acts of pretended legislation:

For quartering large bodies of armed troops among us;

For protecting them, by a mock trial, from punishment for any murders which they should commit on the inhabitants of these states;

For cutting off our trade with all parts of the world;

For imposing taxes on us without our consent;

For depriving us, in many cases, of the benefits of trial by jury;

For transporting us beyond seas, to be tried for pretended offenses;

For abolishing the free system of English laws in a neighboring province, establishing therein an arbitrary government, and enlarging its boundaries, so as to render it at once an example and fit instrument for introducing the same absolute rule into these colonies;

For taking away our charters, abolishing our most valuable laws, and altering fundamentally the forms of our governments;

For suspending our own legislatures, and declaring themselves invested with power to legislate for us in all cases whatsoever.

He has abdicated government here, by declaring us out of his protection and waging war against us.

He has plundered our seas, ravaged our coasts, burned our towns, and destroyed the lives of our people.

He is at this time transporting large armies of foreign mercenaries to complete the works of death, desolation, and tyranny already begun with circumstances of cruelty and perfidy scarcely paralleled in the most barbarous ages, and totally unworthy the head of a civilized nation.

He has constrained our fellow-citizens, taken captive on the high seas, to bear arms against their country, to become the executioners of their friends and brethren, or to fall themselves by their hands.

He has excited domestic insurrection among us, and has endeavored to bring on the inhabitants of our frontiers the merciless Indian savages, whose known rule of warfare is an undistinguished destruction of all ages, sexes, and conditions.

In every stage of these oppressions we have petitioned for redress in the most humble terms; our repeated petitions have been answered only by repeated injury. A prince, whose character is thus marked by every act which may define a tyrant, is unfit to be the ruler of a free people.

Nor have we been wanting in our attentions to our British brethren. We have warned them, from time to time, of attempts by their legislature to extend an unwarrantable jurisdiction over us. We have reminded them of the circumstances of our emigration and settlement here. We have appealed to their native justice and magnanimity; and we have conjured them, by the ties of our common kindred, to disavow these usurpations, which would inevitably interrupt our connections and correspondence. They,

too, have been deaf to the voice of justice and of consanguinity. We must, therefore, acquiesce in the necessity which denounced our separation, and hold them, as we hold the rest of mankind, enemies in war, in peace friends.

We, therefore, the representatives of the United States of America, in General Congress assembled, appealing to the Supreme Judge of the world for the rectitude of our intentions, do, in the name and by the authority of the good people of these colonies, solemnly publish and declare, that these United Colonies are, and of right ought to be, FREE AND INDEPENDENT STATES; that they are absolved from all allegiance to the British crown, and that all political connection between them and the state of Great Britain is, and ought to be, totally dissolved; and that, as free and independent states, they have full power to levy war, conclude peace, contract alliances, establish commerce, and do all other acts and things which independent states may of right do. And for the support of this declaration, with a firm reliance on the protection of Divine Providence, we mutually pledge to each other our lives, our fortunes, and our sacred honor.

JOHN HANCOCK

BUTTON GWINNETT	THS. NELSON, JR.	RICHD. STOCKTON
LYMAN HALL	FRANCIS LIGHTFOOT LEE	JNO. WITHERSPOON
GEO. WALTON	CARTER BRAXTON	FRAS. HOPKINSON
WM. HOOPER	ROBT. MORRIS	JOHN HART
JOSEPH HEWES	BENJAMIN RUSH	ABRA. CLARK
JOHN PENN	BENJA. FRANKLIN	JOSIAH BARTLETT
EDWARD RUTLEDGE	JOHN MORTON	WM. WHIPPLE
THOS. HEYWARD, JUNR.	GEO. CLYMER	SAML. ADAMS
THOMAS LYNCH, JUNR.	JAS. SMITH	JOHN ADAMS
ARTHUR MIDDLETON	GEO. TAYLOR	ROBT. TREAT PAINE
SAMUEL CHASE	JAMES WILSON	ELBRIDGE GERRY
WM. PACA	GEO. ROSS	STEP. HOPKINS
THOS. STONE	CAESAR RODNEY	WILLIAM ELLERY
CHARLES CARROLL OF CARROLLTON	GEO. READ	ROGER SHERMAN
GEORGE WYTHE	THO. M'KEAN	SAM'EL. HUNTINGTON
RICHARD HENRY LEE	WM. FLOYD	WM. WILLIAMS
TH. JEFFERSON	PHIL. LIVINGSTON	OLIVER WOLCOTT
BENJA. HARRISON	FRANS. LEWIS	MATTHEW THORNTON
	LEWIS MORRIS	

The Constitution of the United States of America

PREAMBLE

We the people of the United States, in order to form a more perfect union, establish justice, insure domestic tranquility, provide for the common defense, promote the general welfare, and secure the blessings of liberty to ourselves and our posterity, do ordain and establish this Constitution for the United States of America.

ARTICLE I

Section 1   All legislative powers herein granted shall be vested

Passages no longer in effect are printed in italic type.

in a Congress of the United States, which shall consist of a Senate and a House of Representatives.

Section 2   The House of Representatives shall be composed of members chosen every second year by the people of the several States, and the electors in each State shall have the qualifications requisite for electors of the most numerous branch of the State Legislature.

No person shall be a Representative who shall not have attained to the age of twenty-five years, and been seven years a citizen of the United States, and who shall not, when elected, be an inhabitant of that State in which he shall be chosen.

Representatives and direct taxes shall be apportioned among the several States which may be included within this Union, according to their respective numbers, *which shall be determined by adding to the whole number of free persons, including those bound to service for a term of years and excluding Indians not taxed, three-fifths of all other persons.* The actual enumeration shall be made within three years after the first meeting of the Congress of the United States, and within every subsequent term of ten years, in such manner as they shall by law direct. The number of Representatives shall not exceed one for every thirty thousand, but each State shall have at least one Representative, *and until such enumeration shall be made, the State of New Hampshire shall be entitled to choose three, Massachusetts eight, Rhode Island and Providence Plantations one, Connecticut five, New York six, New Jersey four, Pennsylvania eight, Delaware one, Maryland six, Virginia ten, North Carolina five, South Carolina five, and Georgia three.*

When vacancies happen in the representation from any State, the Executive authority thereof shall issue writs of election to fill such vacancies.

The House of Representatives shall choose their Speaker and other officers; and shall have the sole power of impeachment.

Section 3   The Senate of the United States shall be composed of two Senators from each State, *chosen by the legislature thereof,* for six years; and each Senator shall have one vote.

Immediately after they shall be assembled in consequence of the first election, they shall be divided as equally as may be into three classes. The seats of the Senators of the first class shall be vacated at the expiration of the second year, of the second class at the expiration of the fourth year, and of the third class at the expiration of the sixth year, so that one-third may be chosen every second year; and if vacancies happen by resignation or otherwise, during the recess of the legislature of any State, the Executive thereof may make temporary appointments until the next meeting of the legislature, which shall then fill such vacancies.

No person shall be a Senator who shall not have attained to the age of thirty years, and been nine years a citizen of the United States, and who shall not, when elected, be an inhabitant of that State for which he shall be chosen.

The Vice-President of the United States shall be President of the Senate, but shall have no vote, unless they be equally divided.

The Senate shall choose their other officers, and also a President *pro tempore*, in the absence of the Vice-President, or when he shall exercise the office of President of the United States.

The Senate shall have the sole power to try all impeachments. When sitting for that purpose, they shall be on oath or affirmation. When the President of the United States is tried, the Chief Justice shall preside: and no person shall be convicted without the concurrence of two-thirds of the members present.

Judgment in cases of impeachment shall not extend further than to removal from the office, and disqualification to hold and enjoy any office of honor, trust or profit under the United States: but the party convicted shall nevertheless be liable and subject to indictment, trial, judgment and punishment, according to law.

Section 4   The times, places and manner of holding elections for Senators and Representatives shall be prescribed in each State by the legislature thereof; but the Congress may at any time by law make or alter such regulations, except as to the places of choosing Senators.

The Congress shall assemble at least once in every year, and such meeting *shall be on the first Monday in December, unless they shall by law appoint a different day.*

Section 5   Each house shall be the judge of the elections, returns and qualifications of its own members, and a majority of each shall constitute a quorum to do business; but a smaller number may adjourn from day to day, and may be authorized to compel the attendance of absent members, in such manner, and under such penalties, as each house may provide.

Each house may determine the rules of its proceedings, punish its members for disorderly behavior, and with the concurrence of two-thirds, expel a member.

Each house shall keep a journal of its proceedings, and from time to time publish the same, excepting such parts as may in their judgment require secrecy; and the yeas and nays of the members of either house on any question shall, at the desire of one-fifth of those present, be entered on the journal.

Neither house, during the session of Congress, shall, without the consent of the other, adjourn for more than three days, nor to any other place than that in which the two houses shall be sitting.

Section 6   The Senators and Representatives shall receive a compensation for their services, to be ascertained by law and paid out of the treasury of the United States. They shall in all cases except treason, felony and breach of the peace, be privileged from arrest during their attendance at the session of their respective houses, and in going to and returning from the same; for any speech or debate in either house, they shall not be questioned in any other place.

No Senator or Representative shall, during the time for which he was elected, be appointed to any civil office under the authority of the United States, which shall have been created, or the emoluments whereof shall have been increased during such time; and no person holding any office under the United States shall be a member of either house during his continuance in office.

Section 7   All bills for raising revenue shall originate in the House of Representatives; but the Senate may propose or concur with amendments as on other bills.

Every bill which shall have passed the House of Representatives and the Senate, shall, before it become a law, be presented to the President of the United States; if he approve he shall sign it, but if not he shall return it with objections to that house in which it originated, who shall enter the objections at large on their journal, and proceed to reconsider it. If after such reconsideration two-thirds of that house shall agree to pass the bill, it shall be sent, together with the objections, to the other house, by which it shall likewise be reconsidered, and, if approved by two-thirds of that house, it shall become a law. But in all such cases the votes of both houses shall be determined by yeas and nays, and the names of the persons voting for and against the bill shall be entered on the journal of each house respectively. If any bill shall not be returned by the President within ten days (Sundays excepted) after it shall have been presented to him, the same shall be a law, in like manner as if he had signed it, unless the Congress by their adjournment prevent its return, in which case it shall not be a law.

Every order, resolution, or vote to which the concurrence of the Senate and House of Representatives may be necessary (except on a question of adjournment) shall be presented to the President of the United States; and before the same shall take effect, shall be approved by him, or being disapproved by him, shall be repassed by two-thirds of the Senate and House of Representatives, according to the rules and limitations prescribed in the case of a bill.

Section 8   The Congress shall have power

To lay and collect taxes, duties, imposts, and excises, to pay the debts and provide for the common defense and general welfare of the United States; but all duties, imposts and excises shall be uniform throughout the United States;

To borrow money on the credit of the United States;

To regulate commerce with foreign nations, and among the several States, and with the Indian tribes;

To establish an uniform rule of naturalization, and uniform laws on the subject of bankruptcies throughout the United States;

To coin money, regulate the value thereof, and of foreign coin, and fix the standard of weights and measures;

To provide for the punishment of counterfeiting the securities and current coin of the United States;

To establish post offices and post roads;

To promote the progress of science and useful arts by securing for limited times to authors and inventors the exclusive right to their respective writings and discoveries;

To constitute tribunals inferior to the Supreme Court;

To define and punish piracies and felonies committed on the high seas and offenses against the law of nations;

To declare war, grant letters of marque and reprisal, and make rules concerning captures on land and water;

To raise and support armies, but no appropriation of money to that use shall be for a longer term than two years;

To provide and maintain a navy;

To make rule for the government and regulation of the land and naval forces;

To provide for calling forth the militia to execute the laws of the Union, suppress insurrections, and repel invasions;

To provide for organizing, arming, and disciplining the militia, and for governing such part of them as may be employed in the service of the United States, reserving to the States respectively the appointment of the officers, and the authority of training the militia according to the discipline prescribed by Congress;

To exercise exclusive legislation in all cases whatsoever, over such district (not exceeding ten miles square) as may, by cession of particular States, and the acceptance of Congress, become the seat of government of the United States, and to exercise like authority over all places purchased by the consent of the legislature of the State, in which the same shall be, for erection of forts, magazines, arsenals, dock-yards, and other needful buildings—and

To make all laws which shall be necessary and proper for carrying into execution the foregoing powers, and all other powers vested by this Constitution in the government of the United States, or in any department or officer thereof.

Section 9 *The migration or importation of such persons as any of the States now existing shall think proper to admit shall not be prohibited by the Congress prior to the year 1808; but a tax or duty may be imposed on such importation, not exceeding $10 for each person.*

The privilege of the writ of habeas corpus shall not be suspended, unless when in cases of rebellion or invasion the public safety may require it.

No bill of attainder or ex post facto law shall be passed.

No capitation, or other direct, tax shall be laid, unless in proportion to the census or enumeration herein before directed to be taken.

No tax or duty shall be laid on articles exported from any State.

No preference shall be given by any regulation of commerce or revenue to the ports of one State over those of another; nor shall vessels bound to, or from, one State be obliged to enter, clear, or pay duties in another.

No money shall be drawn from the treasury, but in consequence of appropriations made by law; and a regular statement and account of the receipts and expenditures of all public money shall be published from time to time.

No title of nobility shall be granted by the United States; and no person holding any office of profit or trust under them, shall, without the consent of the Congress, accept of any present, emolument, office, or title, or any kind whatever, from any king, prince, or foreign state.

Section 10 No State shall enter into any treaty, alliance, or confederation; grant letters of marque and reprisal; coin money; emit bills of credit; make anything but gold and silver coin a tender in payment of debts; pass any bill of attainder, ex post facto law, or law impairing the obligation of contracts, or grant any title of nobility.

No State shall, without the consent of Congress, lay any imposts or duties on imports or exports, except what may be absolutely necessary for executing its inspection laws: and the net produce of all duties and imposts, laid by any State on imports or exports, shall be for the use of the treasury of the United States; and all such laws shall be subject to the revision and control of the Congress.

No State shall, without the consent of Congress, lay any duty of tonnage, keep troops or ships of war in time of peace, enter into any agreement or compact with another State, or with a foreign power, or engage in war, unless actually invaded, or in such imminent danger as will not admit of delay.

ARTICLE II

Section 1 The executive power shall be vested in a President of the United States of America. He shall hold his office during the term of four years, and, together with the Vice-President, chosen for the same term, be elected as follows:

Each State shall appoint, in such manner as the legislature thereof may direct, a number of electors, equal to the whole number of Senators and Representatives to which the State may be entitled in the Congress; but no Senator or Representative, or person holding an office of trust or profit under the United States, shall be appointed an elector.

The electors shall meet in their respective States, and vote by ballot for two persons, of whom one at least shall not be an inhabitant of the same State with themselves. And they shall make a list of all the persons voted for, and of the number of votes for each; which list they shall sign and certify, and transmit sealed to the seat of government of the United States, directed to the President of the Senate. The President of the Senate shall, in the presence of the Senate and House of Representatives, open all the certificates, and the votes shall then be counted. The person having the greatest number of votes shall be the President, if such number be a majority of the whole number of electors appointed; and if there be more than one who have such majority, and have an equal number of votes, then the House of Representatives shall immediately choose by ballot one of them for President; and if no person have a majority, then from the five highest on the list said house shall in like manner choose the President. But in choosing the President the votes shall be taken by States, the representation from each State having one vote; a quorum for this purpose shall consist of a member or members from two-thirds of the States, and a majority of all the States shall be necessary to a choice. In every case, after the choise of the President, the person having the greatest number of votes of the electors shall be the Vice-President. But if there should remain two or more who have equal votes, the Senate shall choose from them by ballot the Vice-President.

The Congress may determine the time of choosing the electors and the day on which they shall give their votes; which day shall be the same throughout the United States.

No person except a natural-born citizen, *or a citizen of the United States at the time of the adoption of this Constitution,* shall be eligible to the office of President; neither shall any person be eligible to that office who shall not have attained to the age of thirty-five years, and been fourteen years a resident within the United States.

In case of the removal of the President from office or of his death, resignation, or inability to discharge the powers and duties of the said office, the same shall devolve on the Vice-President, and the Congress may by law provide for the case of removal, death, resignation, or inability, both of the President and Vice-President, declaring what officer shall then act as President, and such officer shall act accordingly, until the disability be removed, or a President shall be elected.

The President shall, at stated times, receive for his services a compensation, which shall neither be increased nor diminished during the period for which he shall have been elected, and he shall not receive within that period any other emolument from the United States, or any of them.

Before he enter on the execution of his office, he shall take the following oath or affirmation:—"I do solemnly swear (or affirm) that I will faithfully execute the office of the President of the United States, and will to the best of my ability preserve, protect and defend the Constitution of the United States."

Section 2   The President shall be commander in chief of the army and navy of the United States, and of the militia of the several States, when called into the actual service of the United States; he may require the opinion, in writing, of the principal officer in each of the executive departments, upon any subject relating to the duties of their respective offices, and he shall have power to grant reprieves and pardons for offenses against the United States, except in cases of impeachment.

He shall have power, by and with the advice and consent of the Senate, to make treaties, provided two-thirds of the Senators present concur; and he shall nominate, and by and with advice and consent of the Senate, shall appoint ambassadors, other public ministers and consuls, judges of the Supreme Court, and all other officers of the United States, whose appointments are not herein otherwise provided for, and which shall be established by law: but Congress may by law vest the appointment of such inferior officers, as they think proper, in the President alone, in the courts of law, or in the heads of departments.

The President shall have power to fill up all vacancies that may happen during the recess of the Senate, by granting commissions which shall expire at the end of their next session.

Section 3   He shall from time to time give to the Congress information of the state of the Union, and recommend to their consideration such measures as he shall judge necessary and expedient; he may, on extraordinary occasions, convene both houses, or either of them, and in case of disagreement between them, with respect to the time of adjournment, he may adjourn them to such time as he shall think proper; he shall receive ambassadors and other public ministers; he shall take care that the laws be faithfully executed, and shall commission all the officers of the United States.

Section 4   The President, Vice-President and all civil officers of the United States shall be removed from office on impeachment for, and on conviction of, treason, bribery, or other high crimes and misdemeanors.

ARTICLE III

Section 1   The judicial power of the United States shall be vested in one Supreme Court, and in such inferior courts as the Congress may from time to time ordain and establish. The judges, both of the Supreme and inferior courts, shall hold their offices during good behavior, and shall, at stated times, receive for their services a compensation which shall not be diminished during their continuance in office.

Section 2   The judicial power shall extend to all cases, in law and equity, arising under this Constitution, the laws of the United States, and treaties made, or which shall be made, under their authority;—to all cases affecting ambassadors, other public ministers and consuls;—to all cases of admiralty and maritime jurisdiction;—to controversies to which the United States shall be a party;—to controversies between two or more States;—*between a State and citizens of another State;*—between citizens of different States;—between citizens of the same State claiming lands under grants of different States, and between a State, or the citizens thereof, and foreign states, citizens or subjects.

In all cases affecting ambassadors, other public ministers and consuls, and those in which a State shall be party, the Supreme Court shall have original jurisdiction. In all the other cases before mentioned, the Supreme Court shall have appellate jurisdiction, both as to law and fact, with such exceptions, and under such regulations, as the Congress shall make.

The trial of all crimes, except in cases of impeachment, shall be by jury; and such trial shall be held in the State where said crimes shall have been committed; but when not committed within any State, the trial shall be at place or places as the Congress may by law have directed.

Section 3   Treason against the United States shall consist only in levying war against them, or in adhering to their enemies, giving them aid and comfort. No person shall be convicted of treason unless on the testimony of two witnesses to the same overt act, or on confession in open court.

The Congress shall have power to declare the punishment of treason, but no attainder of treason shall work corruption of blood, or forfeiture except during the life of the person attainted.

ARTICLE IV

Section 1   Full faith and credit shall be given in each State to the public acts, records, and judicial proceedings of every other State. And the Congress may by general laws prescribe the manner in which such acts, records, and proceedings shall be proved, and the effect thereof.

Section 2   The citizens of each State shall be entitled to all privileges and immunities of citizens in the several States.

A person charged in any State with treason, felony, or other crime, who shall flee from justice, and be found in another State, shall on demand of the executive authority of the State from which he fled, be delivered up, to be removed to the State having jurisdiction of the crime.

No person held to service or labor in one State under the laws thereof, escaping into another, shall, in consequence of any law or regulation therein, be discharged from such service or labor, but shall be delivered up on claim of the party to whom such service or labor may be due.

Section 3   New States may be admitted by the Congress into this Union; but no new State shall be formed or erected within the jurisdiction of any other State; nor any State be formed by the junction of two or more States, or parts of States, without the consent of the legislatures of the States concerned as well as of the Congress.

The Congress shall have power to dispose of and make all needful rules and regulations respecting the territory or other property belonging to the United States; and nothing in this Constitution shall be so construed as to prejudice any claims of the United States, or of any particular State.

Section 4 The United States shall guarantee to every State in this Union a republican form of government, and shall protect each of them against invasion; and on application of the legislature, or of the executive (when the legislature cannot be convened), against domestic violence.

ARTICLE V

The Congress, whenever two-thirds of both houses shall deem it necessary, shall propose amendments to this Constitution, or, on the application of the legislatures of two-thirds of the several States, shall call a convention for proposing amendments, which, in either case, shall be valid to all intents and purposes, as part of this Constitution, when ratified by the legislatures of three-fourths of the several States, or by conventions in three-fourths thereof, as the one or the other mode of ratification may be proposed by the Congress; provided *that no amendments which may be made prior to the year one thousand eight hundred and eight shall in any manner affect the first and fourth clauses in the ninth section of the first article*; and that no State, without its consent, shall be deprived of its equal suffrage in the Senate.

ARTICLE VI

All debts contracted and engagements entered into, before the adoption of this Constitution, shall be as valid against the United States under this Constitution, as under the Confederation.

This Constitution, and the laws of the United States which shall be made in pursuance thereof; and all treaties made, or which shall be made, under the authority of the United States, shall be the supreme law of the land; and the judges in every State shall be bound thereby, anything in the Constitution or laws of any State to the contrary notwithstanding.

The Senators and Representatives before mentioned, and the members of the several State legislatures, and all executive and judicial officers, both of the United States and of the several States, shall be bound by oath or affirmation to support this Constitution; but no religious test shall ever be required as a qualification to any office or public trust under the United States.

ARTICLE VII

The ratification of the conventions of nine States shall be sufficient for the establishment of this Constitution between the States so ratifying the same.

Done in Convention by the unanimous consent of the States present, the seventeenth day of September in the year of our Lord one thousand seven hundred and eighty-seven and of the Independence of the United States of America the twelfth. In witness whereof we have hereunto subscribed our names.

GEORGE WASHINGTON,
President and Deputy from Virginia

New Hampshire
JOHN LANGDON
NICHOLAS GILMAN

Massachusetts
NATHANIEL GORHAM
RUFUS KING

Connecticut
WILLIAM S. JOHNSON
ROGER SHERMAN

New York
ALEXANDER HAMILTON

New Jersey
WILLIAM LIVINGSTON
DAVID BREARLEY
WILLIAM PATERSON
JONATHAN DAYTON

Pennsylvania
BENJAMIN FRANKLIN
THOMAS MIFFLIN
ROBERT MORRIS
GEORGE CLYMER
THOMAS FITZSIMONS
JARED INGERSOLL
JAMES WILSON
GOUVERNEUR MORRIS

Delaware
GEORGE READ
GUNNING BEDFORD, JR.
JOHN DICKINSON
RICHARD BASSETT
JACOB BROOM

Maryland
JAMES MCHENRY
DANIEL OF ST. THOMAS JENIFER
DANIEL CARROLL

Virginia
JOHN BLAIR
JAMES MADISON, JR.

North Carolina
WILLIAM BLOUNT
RICHARD DOBBS SPRAIGHT
HU WILLIAMSON

South Carolina
J. RUTLEDGE
CHARLES C. PINCKNEY
PIERCE BUTLER

Georgia
WILLIAM FEW
ABRAHAM BALDWIN

Amendments to the Constitution

AMENDMENT I

Congress shall make no law respecting an establishment of religion, or prohibiting the free exercise thereof; or abridging the freedom of speech, or of the press; or the right of the people peaceably to assemble, and to petition the government for a redress of grievances.

AMENDMENT II

A well-regulated militia being necessary to the security of a free State, the right of the people to keep and bear arms shall not be infringed.

AMENDMENT III

No soldier shall, in time of peace, be quartered in any house without the consent of the owner, nor in time of war but in a manner to be prescribed by law.

AMENDMENT IV

The right of the people to be secure in their persons, houses, papers, and effects, against unreasonable searches and seizures, shall not be violated, and no warrants shall issue but upon probable cause, supported by oath or affirmation, and particularly describing the place to be searched, and the persons or things to be seized.

AMENDMENT V

No person shall be held to answer for a capital, or otherwise infamous crime, unless on a presentment or indictment of a grand jury, except in cases arising in the land or naval forces, or in the militia, when in actual service in time of war or public danger; nor shall any person be subject for the same offense to be twice put in jeopardy of life or limb; nor shall be compelled in any criminal case to be a witness against himself, nor be deprived of life, liberty, or property, without due process of law; nor shall private property be taken for public use without just compensation.

AMENDMENT VI

In all criminal prosecutions, the accused shall enjoy the right to a speedy and public trial, by an impartial jury of the State and district shall have been previously ascertained by law, and to be informed of the nature and cause of the accusation; to be confronted with the witnesses against him; to have compulsory process for obtaining witnesses in his favor, and to have the assistance of counsel for his defense.

AMENDMENT VII

In suits at common law, where the value in controversy shall exceed twenty dollars, the right of trial by jury shall be preserved, and no fact tried by a jury shall be otherwise reexamined in any court of the United States, than according to the rules of the common law.

AMENDMENT VIII

Excessive bail shall not be required, nor excessive fines imposed, nor cruel and unusual punishments inflicted.

AMENDMENT IX

The enumeration in the Constitution, of certain rights, shall not be construed to deny or disparage others retained by the people.

AMENDMENT X

The powers not delegated to the United States by the Constitution, nor prohibited by it to the States, are reserved to the States respectively, or to the people.

AMENDMENT XI
[Adopted 1798]
The judicial power of the United States shall not be construed to extend to any suit in law or equity, commenced or prosecuted against one of the United States by citizens of another State, or by citizens or subjects of any foreign state.

AMENDMENT XII
[Adopted 1804]
The electors shall meet in their respective States, and vote by ballot for President and Vice-President, one of whom, at least, shall not be an inhabitant of the same State with themselves; they shall name in their ballots the person voted for as President, and in distinct ballots the person voted for as Vice-President, and they shall make distinct lists of all persons voted for as President, and of all persons voted for as Vice-President, and of the number of votes for each, which lists they shall sign and certify, and transmit sealed to the seat of government of the United States, directed to the President of the Senate;—the President of the Senate shall, in the presence of the Senate and House of Representatives, open all the certificates and the votes shall then be counted;—the person having the greatest number of votes for President shall be the President, if such number be a majority of the whole number of electors appointed; and if no person have such majority, then from the persons having the highest number not ex-

ceeding three on the list of those voted for as President, the House of Representatives shall choose immediately, by ballot, the President. But in choosing the President, the votes shall be taken by States, the representation from each State having one vote; a quorum for this purpose shall consist of a member or members from two-thirds of the States, and a majority of all the States shall be necessary to a choice. And if the House of Representatives shall not choose a President whenever the right of choice shall devolve upon them, before *the fourth day of March* next following, then the Vice-President shall act as President, as in the case of the death or other constitutional disability of the President.

The person having the greatest number of votes as Vice-President shall be the Vice-President, if such number be a majority of the whole number of electors appointed; and if no person have a majority, then from the two highest numbers on the list the Senate shall choose the Vice-President; a quorum for the purpose shall consist of two-thirds of the whole number of Senators, and a majority of the whole number shall be necessary to a choice. But no person constitutionally ineligible to the office of President shall be eligible to that of Vice-President of the United States.

AMENDMENT XIII

[Adopted 1865]

Section 1 Neither slavery nor involuntary servitude, except as a punishment for crime whereof the party shall have been duly convicted, shall exist within the United States, or any place subject to their jurisdiction.

Section 2 Congress shall have power to enforce this article by appropriate legislation.

AMENDMENT XIV

[Adopted 1868]

Section 1 All persons born or naturalized in the United States, and subject to the jurisdiction thereof, are citizens of the United States and of the State wherein they reside. No State shall make or enforce any law which shall abridge the privileges or immunities of citizens of the United States; nor shall any State deprive any person of life, liberty, or property, without due process of law; nor deny to any person within its jurisdiction the equal protection of the laws.

Section 2 Representatives shall be apportioned among the several States according to their respective numbers, counting the whole number of persons in each State, excluding Indians not taxed. But when the right to vote at any election for the choice of Electors for President and Vice-President of the United States, Representatives in Congress, the executive and judicial officers of a State, or the members of the legislature thereof, is denied to any of the male inhabitants of such State, being twenty-one years of age and citizens of the United States, or in any way abridged, except for participation in rebellion, or other crime, the basis of representation therein shall be reduced in the proportion which the number of such male citizens shall bear to the whole number of male citizens twenty-one years of age in such State.

Section 3 No person shall be a Senator or Representative in Congress, or Elector of President and Vice-President, or hold any office, civil or military, under the United States, or under any State, who, having previously taken an oath, as a member of Congress, or as an officer of the United States, or as a member of any State legislature, or as an executive or judicial officer of any State, to support the Constitution of the United States, shall have engaged in insurrection or rebellion against the same, or given aid or comfort to the enemies thereof. Congress may, by a vote of two-thirds of each house, remove such disability.

Section 4 The validity of the public debt of the United States, authorized by law, including debts incurred for payment of pensions and bounties for services in suppressing insurrection or rebellion, shall not be questioned. But neither the United States nor any State shall assume or pay any debt or obligation incurred in aid of insurrection or rebellion against the United States, or any claim for the loss of emancipation of any slave; but all such debts, obligations, and claims shall be held illegal and void.

Section 5 The Congress shall have power to enforce, by appropriate legislation, the provisions of this article.

AMENDMENT XV

[Adopted 1870]

Section 1 The right of citizens of the United States to vote shall not be denied or abridged by the United States or by any State on account of race, color, or previous condition of servitude.

Section 2 The Congress shall have power to enforce this article by appropriate legislation.

AMENDMENT XVI

[Adopted 1913]

The Congress shall have power to lay and collect taxes on incomes, from whatever source derived, without apportionment among the several States, and without regard to any census or enumeration.

AMENDMENT XVII

[Adopted 1913]

Section 1 The Senate of the United States shall be composed of two Senators from each State, elected by the people thereof, for six years; and each Senator shall have one vote. The electors in each State shall have the qualifications requisite for electors of [voters for] the most numerous branch of the State legislatures.

Section 2 When vacancies happen in the representation of any State in the Senate, the executive authority of such State shall issue writs of election to fill such vacancies: Provided, that the Legislature of any State may empower the executive thereof to make temporary appointments until the people fill the vacancies by election as the Legislature may direct.

Section 3 This amendment shall not be so construed as to affect the election or term of any Senator chosen before it becomes valid as part of the Constitution.

AMENDMENT XVIII

[Adopted 1919; Repealed 1933]

Section 1 After one year from the ratification of this article the manufacture, sale, or transportation of intoxicating liquors within, the importation thereof into, or the exportation thereof from the United States and all territory subject to the jurisdiction thereof, for beverage purposes, is hereby prohibited.

Section 2 The Congress and the several States shall have concurrent power to enforce this article by appropriate legislation.

Section 3   This article shall be inoperative unless it shall have been ratified as an amendment to the Constitution by the legislatures of the several States, as provided by the Constitution, within seven years from the date of the submission thereof to the States by the Congress.

AMENDMENT XIX

[Adopted 1920]

Section 1   The right of citizens of the United States to vote shall not be denied or abridged by the United States or by any State on account of sex.

Section 2   The Congress shall have power to enforce this article by appropriate legislation.

AMENDMENT XX

[Adopted 1933]

Section 1   The terms of the President and Vice-President shall end at noon on the 20th day of January, and the terms of Senators and Representatives at noon on the 3d day of January, of the years in which such terms would have ended if this article had not been ratified; and the terms of their successors shall then begin.

Section 2   The Congress shall assemble at least once in every year, and such meeting shall begin at noon on the 3d day of January, unless they shall by law appoint a different day.

Section 3   If, at the time fixed for the beginning of the term of the President, the President-elect shall have died, the Vice-President-elect shall become President. If a President shall not have been chosen before the time fixed for the beginning of his term, or if the President-elect shall have failed to qualify, then the Vice-President-elect shall act as President until a President shall have qualified; and the Congress may by law provide for the case wherein neither a President-elect nor a Vice-President-elect shall have qualified, declaring who shall then act as President, or the manner in which one who is to act shall be selected, and such persons shall act accordingly until a President or Vice-President shall have qualified.

Section 4   The Congress may by law provide for the case of the death of any of the persons from whom the House of Representatives may choose a President whenever the right of choice shall have devolved upon them, and for the case of the death of any of the persons from whom the Senate may choose a Vice-President whenever the right of choice shall have devolved upon them.

Section 5   Sections 1 and 2 shall take effect on the 15th day of October following the ratification of this article.

Section 6   This article shall be inoperative unless it shall have been ratified as an amendment to the Constitution by the Legislatures of three-fourths of the several States within seven years from the date of its submission.

AMENDMENT XXI

[Adopted 1933]

Section 1   The eighteenth article of amendment to the Constitution of the United States is hereby repealed.

Section 2   The transportation or importation into any State, Territory, or Possession of the United States for delivery or use therein of intoxicating liquors, in violation of the laws thereof, is hereby prohibited.

Section 3   This article shall be inoperative unless it shall have been ratified as an amendment to the Constitution by conventions in the several States, as provided in the Constitution, within seven years from the date of submission thereof to the States by the Congress.

AMENDMENT XXII

[Adopted 1951]

Section 1   No person shall be elected to the office of President more than twice, and no person who has held the office of President, or acted as President, for more than two years of term to which some other person was elected President shall be elected to the office of President more than once. But this article shall not apply to any person holding the office of President when this article was proposed by the Congress, and shall not prevent any person who may be holding the office of President, or acting as President, during the term within which this article becomes operative from holding office of President or acting as President during the remainder of such term.

Section 2   This article shall be inoperative unless it shall have been ratified as an amendment to the Constitution by the legislatures of three-fourths of the several States within seven years from the date of its submission to the States by the Congress.

AMENDMENT XXIII

[Adopted 1961]

Section 1   The District constituting the seat of Government of the United States shall appoint in such manner as the Congress may direct:

A number of electors of President and Vice-President equal to the whole number of Senators and Representatives in Congress to which the District would be entitled if it were a State, but in no event more than the least populous State; they shall be in addition to those appointed by the States, but they shall be considered for the purposes of the election of President and Vice-President, to be electors appointed by a State; and they shall meet in the District and perform such duties as provided by the twelfth article of amendment.

Section 2   The Congress shall have the power to enforce this article by appropriate legislation.

AMENDMENT XXIV

[Adopted 1964]

Section 1   The right of citizens of the United States to vote in any primary or other election for President or Vice-President, for electors for President or Vice-President, or for Senator or Representative in Congress, shall not be denied or abridged by the United States or any State by reason of failure to pay any poll tax or other tax.

Section 2   The Congress shall have the power to enforce this article by appropriate legislation.

AMENDMENT XXV

[Adopted 1967]

Section 1   In case of the removal of the President from office or of his death or resignation, the Vice-President shall become President.

Section 2   Whenever there is a vacancy in the office of the Vice President, the President shall nominate a Vice President who shall take office upon confirmation by a majority vote of both Houses of Congress.

Section 3   Whenever the President transmits to the President pro tempore of the Senate and the Speaker of the House of Representatives his written declaration that he is unable to discharge the powers and duties of his office, and until he transmits to them a written declaration to the contrary, such powers and duties shall be discharged by the Vice-President as Acting President.

Section 4   Whenever the Vice President and a majority of either the principal officers of the executive departments or of such other body as Congress may by law provide, transmit to the President pro tempore of the Senate and the Speaker of the House of Representatives their written declaration that the President is unable to discharge the powers and duties of his office, the Vice President shall immediately assume the powers and duties of the office as Acting President.

Thereafter, when the President transmits to the President pro tempore of the Senate and the Speaker of the House of Representatives his written declaration that no inability exists, he shall resume the powers and duties of his office unless the Vice President and a majority of either the principal officers of the executive department[s] or of such other body as Congress may by law provide, transmit within four days to the President pro tempore of the Senate and the Speaker of the House of Representatives their written declaration that the President is unable to discharge the powers and duties of his office. Thereupon Congress shall decide the issue, assembling within forty-eight hours for that purpose if not in session. If the Congress, within twenty-one days after receipt of the latter written declaration, or if Congress is not in session, within twenty-one days after Congress is required to assemble, determines by two-thirds vote of both Houses that the President is unable to discharge the powers and duties of his office, the Vice President shall continue to discharge the same as Acting President; otherwise, the President shall resume the powers and duties of his office.

AMENDMENT XXVI

[Adopted 1971]

Section 1   The right of citizens of the United States, who are eighteen years of age or older, to vote shall not be denied or abridged by the United States or by any State on account of age.

Section 2   The Congress shall have power to enforce this article by appropriate legislation.

AMENDMENT XXVII

[Adopted 1992]

No law varying the compensation for the services of the Senators and Representatives shall take effect, until an election of Representatives shall have intervened.

Presidential Elections

Year	Candidates	Parties	Popular Vote	Electoral Vote	Voter Participation
1789	**GEORGE WASHINGTON**		*	69	
	John Adams			34	
	Others			35	
1792	**GEORGE WASHINGTON**		*	132	
	John Adams			77	
	George Clinton			50	
	Others			5	
1796	**JOHN ADAMS**	Federalist	*	71	
	Thomas Jefferson	Democratic-Republican		68	
	Thomas Pinckney	Federalist		59	
	Aaron Burr	Dem.-Rep.		30	
	Others			48	
1800	**THOMAS JEFFERSON**	Dem.-Rep.	*	73	
	Aaron Burr	Dem.-Rep.		73	
	John Adams	Federalist		65	
	C. C. Pinckney	Federalist		64	
	John Jay	Federalist		1	

*Electors selected by state legislatures.

Year	Candidates	Parties	Popular Vote		Electoral Vote	Voter Participation
1804	**THOMAS JEFFERSON**	Dem.-Rep.	*		162	
	C. C. Pinckney	Federalist			14	
1808	**JAMES MADISON**	Dem.-Rep.	*		122	
	C. C. Pinckney	Federalist			47	
	George Clinton	Dem.-Rep.			6	
1812	**JAMES MADISON**	Dem.-Rep.	*		128	
	De Witt Clinton	Federalist			89	
1816	**JAMES MONROE**	Dem.-Rep.	*		183	
	Rufus King	Federalist			34	
1820	**JAMES MONROE**	Dem.-Rep.	*		231	
	John Quincy Adams	Dem.-Rep.			1	
1824	**JOHN Q. ADAMS**	Dem.-Rep.	108,740	(30.5%)	84	26.9%
	Andrew Jackson	Dem.-Rep.	153,544	(43.1%)	99	
	William H. Crawford	Dem.-Rep.	46,618	(13.1%)	41	
	Henry Clay	Dem.-Rep.	47,136	(13.2%)	37	
1828	**ANDREW JACKSON**	Democratic	647,286	(56.0%)	178	57.6%
	John Quincy Adams	National Republican	508,064	(44.0%)	83	
1832	**ANDREW JACKSON**	Democratic	687,502	(55.0%)	219	55.4%
	Henry Clay	National Republican	530,189	(42.4%)	49	
	John Floyd	Independent			11	
	William Wirt	Anti-Mason	33,108	(2.6%)	7	
1836	**MARTIN VAN BUREN**	Democratic	765,483	(50.9%)	170	57.8%
	W. H. Harrison	Whig			73	
	Hugh L. White	Whig	739,795	(49.1%)	26	
	Daniel Webster	Whig			14	
	W. P. Magnum	Independent			11	
1840	**WILLIAM H. HARRISON**	Whig	1,274,624	(53.1%)	234	80.2%
	Martin Van Buren	Democratic	1,127,781	(46.9%)	60	
	J. G. Birney	Liberty	7069		—	
1844	**JAMES K. POLK**	Democratic	1,338,464	(49.6%)	170	78.9%
	Henry Clay	Whig	1,300,097	(48.1%)	105	
	J. G. Birney	Liberty	62,300	(2.3%)	—	
1848	**ZACHARY TAYLOR**	Whig	1,360,967	(47.4%)	163	72.7%
	Lewis Cass	Democratic	1,222,342	(42.5%)	127	
	Martin Van Buren	Free-Soil	291,263	(10.1%)	—	
1852	**FRANKLIN PIERCE**	Democratic	1,601,117	(50.9%)	254	69.6%
	Winfield Scott	Whig	1,385,453	(44.1%)	42	
	John P. Hale	Free-Soil	155,825	(5.0%)	—	
1856	**JAMES BUCHANAN**	Democratic	1,832,955	(45.3%)	174	78.9%
	John C. Frémont	Republican	1,339,932	(33.1%)	114	
	Millard Fillmore	American	871,731	(21.6%)	8	
1860	**ABRAHAM LINCOLN**	Republican	1,865,593	(39.8%)	180	81.2%
	Stephen A. Douglas	Democratic	1,382,713	(29.5%)	12	
	John C. Breckinridge	Democratic	848,356	(18.1%)	72	
	John Bell	Union	592,906	(12.6%)	39	
1864	**ABRAHAM LINCOLN**	Republican	2,213,655	(55.0%)	212	73.8%
	George B. McClellan	Democratic	1,805,237	(45.0%)	21	
1868	**ULYSSES S. GRANT**	Republican	3,012,833	(52.7%)	214	78.1%
	Horatio Seymour	Democratic	2,703,249	(47.3%)	80	
1872	**ULYSSES S. GRANT**	Republican	3,597,132	(55.6%)	286	71.3%
	Horace Greeley	Democratic; Liberal Republican	2,834,125	(43.9%)	66	
1876	**RUTHERFORD B. HAYES**	Republican	4,036,298	(48.0%)	185	81.8%
	Samuel J. Tilden	Democratic	4,300,590	(51.0%)	184	

Year	Candidates	Parties	Popular Vote		Electoral Vote	Voter Participation
1880	**JAMES A. GARFIELD**	Republican	4,454,416	(48.5%)	214	79.4%
	Winfield S. Hancock	Democratic	4,444,952	(48.1%)	155	
1884	**GROVER CLEVELAND**	Democratic	4,874,986	(48.5%)	219	77.5%
	James G. Blaine	Republican	4,851,981	(48.2%)	182	
1888	**BENJAMIN HARRISON**	Republican	5,439,853	(47.9%)	233	79.3%
	Grover Cleveland	Democratic	5,540,309	(48.6%)	168	
1892	**GROVER CLEVELAND**	Democratic	5,556,918	(46.1%)	277	74.7%
	Benjamin Harrison	Republican	5,176,108	(43.0%)	145	
	James B. Weaver	People's	1,041,028	(8.5%)	22	
1896	**WILLIAM McKINLEY**	Republican	7,104,779	(51.1%)	271	79.3%
	William J. Bryan	Democratic People's	6,502,925	(47.7%)	176	
1900	**WILLIAM McKINLEY**	Republican	7,207,923	(51.7%)	292	73.2%
	William J. Bryan	Dem.-Populist	6,358,133	(45.5%)	155	
1904	**THEODORE ROOSEVELT**	Republican	7,623,486	(57.9%)	336	65.2%
	Alton B. Parker	Democratic	5,077,911	(37.6%)	140	
	Eugene V. Debs	Socialist	402,283	(3.0%)	—	
1908	**WILLIAM H. TAFT**	Republican	7,678,908	(51.6%)	321	65.4%
	William J. Bryan	Democratic	6,409,104	(43.1%)	162	
	Eugene V. Debs	Socialist	420,793	(2.8%)	—	
1912	**WOODROW WILSON**	Democratic	6,293,454	(41.9%)	435	58.8%
	Theodore Roosevelt	Progressive	4,119,538	(27.4%)	88	
	William H. Taft	Republican	3,484,980	(23.2%)	8	
	Eugene V. Debs	Socialist	900,672	(6.0%)	—	
1916	**WOODROW WILSON**	Democratic	9,129,606	(49.4%)	277	61.6%
	Charles E. Hughes	Republican	8,538,221	(46.2%)	254	
	A. L. Benson	Socialist	585,113	(3.2%)	—	
1920	**WARREN G. HARDING**	Republican	16,152,200	(60.4%)	404	49.2%
	James M. Cox	Democratic	9,147,353	(34.2%)	127	
	Eugene V. Debs	Socialist	919,799	(3.4%)	—	
1924	**CALVIN COOLIDGE**	Republican	15,725,016	(54.0%)	382	48.9%
	John W. Davis	Democratic	8,386,503	(28.8%)	136	
	Robert M. La Follette	Progressive	4,822,856	(16.6%)	13	
1928	**HERBERT HOOVER**	Republican	21,391,381	(58.2%)	444	56.9%
	Alfred E. Smith	Democratic	15,016,443	(40.9%)	87	
	Norman Thomas	Socialist	267,835	(0.7%)	—	
1932	**FRANKLIN D. ROOSEVELT**	Democratic	22,821,857	(57.4%)	472	56.9%
	Herbert Hoover	Republican	15,761,841	(39.7%)	59	
	Norman Thomas	Socialist	881,951	(2.2%)	—	
1936	**FRANKLIN D. ROOSEVELT**	Democratic	27,751,597	(60.8%)	523	61.0%
	Alfred M. Landon	Republican	16,679,583	(36.5%)	8	
	William Lemke	Union	882,479	(1.9%)	—	
1940	**FRANKLIN D. ROOSEVELT**	Democratic	27,244,160	(54.8%)	449	62.5%
	Wendell L. Willkie	Republican	22,305,198	(44.8%)	82	
1944	**FRANKLIN D. ROOSEVELT**	Democratic	25,602,504	(53.5%)	432	55.9%
	Thomas E. Dewey	Republican	22,006,285	(46.0%)	99	
1948	**HARRY S TRUMAN**	Democratic	24,105,695	(49.5%)	304	53.0%
	Thomas E. Dewey	Republican	21,969,170	(45.1%)	189	
	J. Strom Thurmond	State-Rights Democratic	1,169,021	(2.4%)	38	
	Henry A. Wallace	Progressive	1,156,103	(2.4%)	—	
1952	**DWIGHT D. EISENHOWER**	Republican	33,936,252	(55.1%)	442	63.3%
	Adlai E. Stevenson	Democratic	27,314,992	(44.4%)	89	
1956	**DWIGHT D. EISENHOWER**	Republican	35,575,420	(57.6%)	457	60.6%
	Adlai E. Stevenson	Democratic	26,033,066	(42.1%)	73	
	Other	—	—		1	

Year	Candidates	Parties	Popular Vote		Electoral Vote	Voter Participation
1960	**JOHN F. KENNEDY**	Democratic	34,227,096	(49.9%)	303	62.8%
	Richard M. Nixon	Republican	34,108,546	(49.6%)	219	
	Other	—	—		15	
1964	**LYNDON B. JOHNSON**	Democratic	43,126,506	(61.1%)	486	61.7%
	Barry M. Goldwater	Republican	27,176,799	(38.5%)	52	
1968	**RICHARD M. NIXON**	Republican	31,770,237	(43.4%)	301	60.6%
	Hubert H. Humphrey	Democratic	31,270,533	(42.7%)	191	
	George Wallace	American Indep.	9,906,141	(13.5%)	46	
1972	**RICHARD M. NIXON**	Republican	47,169,911	(60.7%)	520	55.2%
	George S. McGovern	Democratic	29,170,383	(37.5%)	17	
	Other	—	—		1	
1976	**JIMMY CARTER**	Democratic	40,828,587	(50.0%)	297	53.5%
	Gerald R. Ford	Republican	39,147,613	(47.9%)	241	
	Other	—	1,575,459	(2.1%)	—	
1980	**RONALD REAGAN**	Republican	43,901,812	(50.7%)	489	52.6%
	Jimmy Carter	Democratic	35,483,820	(41.0%)	49	
	John B. Anderson	Independent	5,719,722	(6.6%)	—	
	Ed Clark	Libertarian	921,188	(1.1%)	—	
1984	**RONALD REAGAN**	Republican	54,455,075	(59.0%)	525	53.3%
	Walter Mondale	Democratic	37,577,185	(41.0%)	13	
1988	**GEORGE H. W. BUSH**	Republican	48,886,000	(53.4%)	426	57.4%
	Michael S. Dukakis	Democratic	41,809,000	(45.6%)	111	
1992	**BILL CLINTON**	Democratic	43,728,375	(43%)	370	55.0%
	George H. W. Bush	Republican	38,167,416	(38%)	168	
	Ross Perot	—	19,237,247	(19%)	—	

*Electors selected by state legislatures.

Vice Presidents and Cabinet Members by Administration

The Washington Administration (1789–1797)

Vice President	John Adams	1789–1797
Secretary of State	Thomas Jefferson	1789–1793
	Edmund Randolph	1794–1795
	Timothy Pickering	1795–1797
Secretary of Treasury	Alexander Hamilton	1789–1795
	Oliver Wolcott	1795–1797
Secretary of War	Henry Knox	1789–1794
	Timothy Pickering	1795–1796
	James McHenry	1796–1797
Attorney General	Edmund Randolph	1789–1793
	William Bradford	1794–1795
	Charles Lee	1795–1797
Postmaster General	Samuel Osgood	1789–1791
	Timothy Pickering	1791–1794
	Joseph Habersham	1795–1797

The John Adams Administration (1797–1801)

Vice President	Thomas Jefferson	1797–1801
Secretary of State	Timothy Pickering	1797–1800
	John Marshall	1800–1801
Secretary of Treasury	Oliver Wolcott	1797–1800
	Samuel Dexter	1800–1801
Secretary of War	James McHenry	1797–1800
	Samuel Dexter	1800–1801
Attorney General	Charles Lee	1797–1801
Postmaster General	Joseph Habersham	1797–1801
Secretary of Navy	Benjamin Stoddert	1798–1801

The Jefferson Administration (1801–1809)

Vice President	Aaron Burr	1801–1805
	George Clinton	1805–1809

Secretary of State	James Madison	1801–1809
Secretary of Treasury	Samuel Dexter	1801
	Albert Gallatin	1801–1809
Secretary of War	Henry Dearborn	1801–1809
Attorney General	Levi Lincoln	1801–1805
	Robert Smith	1805
	John Breckinridge	1805–1806
	Caesar Rodney	1807–1809
Postmaster General	Joseph Habersham	1801
	Gideon Granger	1801–1809
Secretary of Navy	Robert Smith	1801–1809

The Madison Administration (1809–1817)

Vice President	George Clinton	1809–d. 1812
	Elbridge Gerry	1813–d. 1814
Secretary of State	Robert Smith	1809–1811
	James Monroe	1811–1817
Secretary of Treasury	Albert Gallatin	1809–1813
	George Campbell	1814
	Alexander Dallas	1814–1816
	William Crawford	1816–1817
Secretary of War	William Eustis	1809–1812
	John Armstrong	1813–1814
	James Monroe	1814–1815
	William Crawford	1815–1817
Attorney General	Caesar Rodney	1809–1811
	William Pinkney	1811–1814
	Richard Rush	1814–1817
Postmaster General	Gideon Granger	1809–1814
	Return Meigs	1814–1817
Secretary of Navy	Paul Hamilton	1809–1813
	William Jones	1813–1814
	Benjamin Crowninshield	1814–1817

The Monroe Administration (1817–1825)

Vice President	Daniel Tompkins	1817–1825
Secretary of State	John Quincy Adams	1817–1825
Secretary of Treasury	William Crawford	1817–1825
Secretary of War	George Graham	1817
	John C. Calhoun	1817–1825
Attorney General	Richard Rush	1817
	William Wirt	1817–1825
Postmaster General	Return Meigs	1817–1823
	John McLean	1823–1825
Secretary of Navy	Benjamin Crowninshield	1817–1818
	Smith Thompson	1818–1823
	Samuel Southard	1823–1825

The John Quincy Adams Administration (1825–1829)

Vice President	John C. Calhoun	1825–1829
Secretary of State	Henry Clay	1825–1829
Secretary of Treasury	Richard Rush	1825–1829
Secretary of War	James Barbour	1825–1829
	Peter Porter	1828–1829
Attorney General	William Wirt	1825–1829
Postmaster General	John McLean	1825–1829
Secretary of Navy	Samuel Southard	1825–1829

The Jackson Administration (1829–1837)

Vice President	John C. Calhoun	1829–1832
	Martin Van Buren	1833–1837
Secretary of State	Martin Van Buren	1829–1831
	Edward Livingston	1831–1833
	Louis McLane	1833–1834
	John Forsyth	1834–1837
Secretary of Treasury	Samuel Ingham	1829–1831
	Louis McLane	1831–1833
	William Duane	1833
	Roger B. Taney	1833–1834
	Levi Woodbury	1834–1837
Secretary of War	John H. Eaton	1829–1831
	Lewis Cass	1831–1837
	Benjamin Butler	1837
Attorney General	John M. Berrien	1829–1831
	Roger B. Taney	1831–1833
	Benjamin Butler	1833–1837
Postmaster General	William Barry	1829–1835
	Amos Kendall	1835–1837
Secretary of Navy	John Branch	1829–1831
	Levi Woodbury	1831–1834
	Mahlon Dickerson	1834–1837

The Van Buren Administration (1837–1841)

Vice President	Richard M. Johnson	1837–1841
Secretary of State	John Forsyth	1837–1841
Secretary of Treasury	Levi Woodbury	1837–1841
Secretary of War	Joel Poinsett	1837–1841
Attorney General	Benjamin Butler	1837–1838
	Felix Grundy	1838–1840
	Henry D. Gilpin	1840–1841
Postmaster General	Amos Kendall	1837–1840
	John M. Niles	1840–1841
Secretary of Navy	Mahlon Dickerson	1837–1838
	James Paulding	1838–1841

The William Harrison Administration (1841)

Vice President	John Tyler	1841
Secretary of State	Daniel Webster	1841
Secretary of Treasury	Thomas Ewing	1841
Secretary of War	John Bell	1841
Attorney General	John J. Crittenden	1841
Postmaster General	Francis Granger	1841
Secretary of Navy	George Badger	1841

The Tyler Administration (1841–1845)

Vice President	None	
Secretary of State	Daniel Webster	1841–1843
	Hugh S. Legaré	1843
	Abel P. Upshur	1843–1844
	John C. Calhoun	1844–1845
Secretary of Treasury	Thomas Ewing	1841
	Walter Forward	1841–1843
	John C. Spencer	1843–1844
	George Bibb	1844–1845

Secretary of War	John Bell	1841
	John C. Spencer	1841–1843
	James M. Porter	1843–1844
	William Wilkins	1844–1845
Attorney General	John J. Crittenden	1841
	Hugh S. Legaré	1841–1843
	John Nelson	1843–1845
Postmaster General	Francis Granger	1841
	Charles Wickliffe	1841
Secretary of Navy	George Badger	1841
	Abel P. Upshur	1841
	David Henshaw	1843–1844
	Thomas Gilmer	1844
	John Y. Mason	1844–1845

The Polk Administration (1845–1849)

Vice President	George M. Dallas	1845–1849
Secretary of State	James Buchanan	1845–1849
Secretary of Treasury	Robert J. Walker	1845–1849
Secretary of War	William L. Marcy	1845–1849
Attorney General	John Y. Mason	1845–1846
	Nathan Clifford	1846–1848
	Isaac Toucey	1848–1849
Postmaster General	Cave Johnson	1845–1849
Secretary of Navy	George Bancroft	1845–1846
	John Y. Mason	1846–1849

The Taylor Administration (1849–1850)

Vice President	Millard Fillmore	1849–1850
Secretary of State	John M. Clayton	1849–1850
Secretary of Treasury	William Meredith	1849–1850
Secretary of War	George Crawford	1849–1850
Attorney General	Reverdy Johnson	1849–1850
Postmaster General	Jacob Collamer	1849–1850
Secretary of Navy	William Preston	1849–1850
Secretary of Interior	Thomas Ewing	1849–1850

The Fillmore Administration (1850–1853)

Vice President	None	
Secretary of State	Daniel Webster	1850–1852
	Edward Everett	1852–1853
Secretary of Treasury	Thomas Corwin	1850–1853
Secretary of War	Charles Conrad	1850–1853
Attorney General	John J. Crittenden	1850–1853
Postmaster General	Nathan Hall	1850–1852
	Samuel D. Hubbard	1852–1853
Secretary of Navy	William A. Graham	1850–1852
	John P. Kennedy	1852–1853
Secretary of Interior	Thomas McKennan	1850
	Alexander Stuart	1850–1853

The Pierce Administration (1853–1857)

Vice President	William R. King	1853–d. 1853
Secretary of State	William L. Marcy	1853–1857
Secretary of Treasury	James Guthrie	1853–1857
Secretary of War	Jefferson Davis	1853–1857
Attorney General	Caleb Cushing	1853–1857
Postmaster General	James Campbell	1853–1857
Secretary of Navy	James C. Dobbin	1853–1857
Secretary of Interior	Robert McClelland	1853–1857

The Buchanan Administration (1857–1861)

Vice President	John C. Breckinridge	1857–1861
Secretary of State	Lewis Cass	1857–1860
	Jeremiah S. Black	1860–1861
Secretary of Treasury	Howell Cobb	1857–1860
	Philip Thomas	1860–1861
	John A. Dix	1861
Secretary of War	John B. Floyd	1857–1861
	Joseph Holt	1861
Attorney General	Jeremiah S. Black	1857–1860
	Edwin M. Stanton	1860–1861
Postmaster General	Aaron V. Brown	1857–1859
	Joseph Holt	1859–1861
	Horatio King	1861
Secretary of Navy	Isaac Toucey	1857–1861
Secretary of Interior	Jacob Thompson	1857–1861

The Lincoln Administration (1861–1865)

Vice President	Hannibal Hamlin	1861–1865
	Andrew Johnson	1865
Secretary of State	William H. Seward	1861–1865
Secretary of Treasury	Samuel P. Chase	1861–1864
	William P. Fessenden	1864–1865
	Hugh McCulloch	1865
Secretary of War	Simon Cameron	1861–1862
	Edwin M. Stanton	1862–1865
Attorney General	Edward Bates	1861–1864
	James Speed	1864–1865
Postmaster General	Horatio King	1861
	Montgomery Blair	1861–1864
	William Dennison	1864–1865
Secretary of Navy	Gideon Welles	1861–1865
Secretary of Interior	Caleb B. Smith	1861–1863
	John P. Usher	1863–1865

The Andrew Johnson Administration (1865–1869)

Vice President	None	
Secretary of State	William H. Seward	1865–1869
Secretary of Treasury	Hugh McCulloch	1865–1869
Secretary of War	Edwin M. Stanton	1865–1867
	Ulysses S. Grant	1867–1868
	Lorenzo Thomas	1868
	John M. Schofield	1868–1869
Attorney General	James Speed	1865–1866
	Henry Stanbery	1866–1868
	William M. Evarts	1868–1869
Postmaster General	William Dennison	1865–1866
	Alexander Randall	1866–1869
Secretary of Navy	Gideon Welles	1865–1869

Secretary of Interior	John P. Usher	1865
	James Harlan	1865–1866
	Ovrille H. Browning	1866–1869

The Grant Administration (1869–1877)

Vice President	Schuyler Colfax	1869–1873
	Henry Wilson	1873–d. 1875
Secretary of State	Elihu B. Washburne	1869
	Hamilton Fish	1869–1877
Secretary of Treasury	George S. Boutwell	1869–1873
	William Richardson	1873–1874
	Benjamin Bristow	1874–1876
	Lot M. Morrill	1876–1877
Secretary of War	John A. Rawlins	1869
	William T. Sherman	1869
	William W. Belknap	1869–1876
	Alphonso Taft	1876
	James D. Cameron	1876–1877
Attorney General	Ebenezer Hoar	1869–1870
	Amos T. Ackerman	1870–1871
	G. H. Williams	1871–1875
	Edwards Pierrepont	1875–1876
	Alphonso Taft	1876–1877
Postmaster General	John A. J. Creswell	1869–1874
	James W. Marshall	1874
	Marshall Jewell	1874–1876
	James N. Tyner	1876–1877
Secretary of Navy	Adolph E. Borie	1869
	George M. Robeson	1869–1877
Secretary of Interior	Jacob D. Cox	1869–1870
	Columbus Delano	1870–1875
	Zachariah Chandler	1875–1877

The Hayes Administration (1877–1881)

Vice President	William A. Wheeler	1877–1881
Secretary of State	William M. Evarts	1877–1881
Secretary of Treasury	John Sherman	1877–1881
Secretary of War	George W. McCrary	1877–1879
	Alex Ramsey	1879–1881
Attorney General	Charles Devens	1877–1881
Postmaster General	David M. Key	1877–1880
	Horace Maynard	1880–1881
Secretary of Navy	Richard W. Thompson	1877–1880
	Nathan Goff, Jr.	1881
Secretary of Interior	Carl Schurz	1877–1881

The Garfield Administration (1881)

Vice President	Chester A. Arthur	1881
Secretary of State	James G. Blaine	1881
Secretary of Treasury	William Windom	1881
Secretary of War	Robert T. Lincoln	1881
Attorney General	Wayne MacVeagh	1881
Postmaster General	Thomas L. James	1881
Secretary of Navy	William H. Hunt	1881
Secretary of Interior	Samuel J. Kirkwood	1881

The Arthur Administration (1881–1885)

Vice President	None	
Secretary of State	F. T. Frelinghuysen	1881–1885
Secretary of Treasury	Charles J. Folger	1881–1884
	Walter Q. Gresham	1884
	Hugh McCulloch	1884–1885
Secretary of War	Robert T. Lincoln	1881–1885
Attorney General	Benjamin H. Brewster	1881–1885
Postmaster General	Timothy O. Howe	1881–1883
	Walter Q. Gresham	1883–1884
	Frank Hatton	1884–1885
Secretary of Navy	William H. Hunt	1881–1882
	William E. Chandler	1882–1885
Secretary of Interior	Samuel J. Kirkwood	1881–1882
	Henry M. Teller	1882–1885

The Cleveland Administration (1885–1889)

Vice President	Thomas A. Hendricks	1885–d. 1885
Secretary of State	Thomas F. Bayard	1885–1889
Secretary of Treasury	Daniel Manning	1885–1887
	Charles S. Fairchild	1887–1889
Secretary of War	William C. Endicott	1885–1889
Attorney General	Augustus H. Garland	1885–1889
Postmaster General	William F. Vilas	1885–1888
	Don M. Dickinson	1888–1889
Secretary of Navy	William C. Whitney	1885–1889
Secretary of Interior	Lucius Q. C. Lamar	1885–1888
	William F. Vilas	1888–1889
Secretary of Agriculture	Norman J. Colman	1889

The Benjamin Harrison Administration (1889–1893)

Vice President	Levi P. Morton	1889–1893
Secretary of State	James G. Blaine	1889–1892
	John W. Foster	1892–1893
Secretary of Treasury	William Windom	1889–1891
	Charles Foster	1891–1893
Secretary of War	Redfield Proctor	1889–1891
	Stephen B. Elkins	1891–1893
Attorney General	William H. H. Miller	1889–1891
Postmaster General	John Wanamaker	1889–1893
Secretary of Navy	Benjamin F. Tracy	1889–1893
Secretary of Interior	John W. Noble	1889–1893
Secretary of Agriculture	Jeremiah M. Rusk	1889–1893

The Cleveland Administration (1893–1897)

Vice President	Adlai E. Stevenson	1893–1897
Secretary of State	Walter Q. Gresham	1893–1895
	Richard Olney	1895–1897
Secretary of Treasury	John G. Carlisle	1893–1897
Secretary of War	Daniel S. Lamont	1893–1897
Attorney General	Richard Olney	1893–1895
	James Harmon	1895–1897
Postmaster General	Wilson S. Bissell	1893–1895
	William L. Wilson	1895–1897

Secretary of Navy	Hilary A. Herbert	1893–1897
Secretary of Interior	Hoke Smith	1893–1896
	David R. Francis	1896–1897
Secretary of Agriculture	Julius S. Morton	1893–1897

The McKinley Administration (1897–1901)

Vice President	Garret A. Hobart	1897–d. 1899
	Theodore Roosevelt	1901
Secretary of State	John Sherman	1897–1898
	William R. Day	1898
	John Hay	1898–1901
Secretary of Treasury	Lyman J. Gage	1897–1901
Secretary of War	Russell A. Alger	1897–1899
	Elihu Root	1899–1901
Attorney General	Joseph McKenna	1897–1898
	John W. Griggs	1898–1901
	Philander C. Knox	1901
Postmaster General	James A. Gary	1897–1898
	Charles E. Smith	1898–1901
Secretary of Navy	John D. Long	1897–1901
Secretary of Interior	Cornelius N. Bliss	1897–1899
	Ethan A. Hitchcock	1899–1901
Secretary of Agriculture	James Wilson	1897–1901

The Theodore Roosevelt Administration (1901–1909)

Vice President	Charles Fairbanks	1905–1909
Secretary of State	John Hay	1901–1905
	Elihu Root	1905–1909
	Robert Bacon	1909
Secretary of Treasury	Lyman J. Gage	1901–1902
	Leslie M. Shaw	1902–1907
	George B. Cortelyou	1907–1909
Secretary of War	Elihu Root	1901–1904
	William H. Taft	1904–1908
	Luke E. Wright	1908–1909
Attorney General	Philander C. Knox	1901–1904
	William H. Moody	1904–1906
	Charles J. Bonaparte	1906–1909
Postmaster General	Charles E. Smith	1901–1902
	Henry C. Payne	1902–1904
	Robert J. Wynne	1904–1905
	George B. Cortelyou	1905–1907
	George von L. Meyer	1907–1909
Secretary of Navy	John D. Long	1901–1902
	William H. Moody	1902–1904
	Paul Morton	1904–1905
	Charles J. Bonaparte	1905–1906
	Victor H. Metcalf	1906–1908
	Truman H. Newberry	1908–1909
Secretary of Interior	Ethan A. Hitchcock	1901–1907
	James R. Garfield	1907–1909
Secretary of Agriculture	James Wilson	1901–1909
Secretary of Labor and Commerce	George B. Cortelyou	1903–1904
	Victor H. Metcalf	1904–1906
	Oscar S. Straus	1906–1909
	Charles Nagel	1909

The Taft Administration (1909–1913)

Vice President	James S. Sherman	1909–d. 1912
Secretary of State	Philander C. Knox	1909–1913

Secretary of Treasury	Franklin MacVeagh	1909–1913
Secretary of War	Jacob M. Dickinson	1901–1911
	Henry L. Stimson	1911–1913
Attorney General	George W. Wickersham	1909–1913
Postmaster General	Frank H. Hitchcock	1909–1913
Secretary of Navy	George von L. Meyer	1909–1913
Secretary of Interior	Richard A. Ballinger	1909–1911
	Walter L. Fisher	1911–1913
Secretary of Agriculture	James Wilson	1909–1913
Secretary of Labor and Commerce	Charles Nagel	1909–1913

The Wilson Administration (1913–1921)

Vice President	Thomas R. Marshall	1913–1921
Secretary of State	Williams J. Bryan	1913–1915
	Robert Lansing	1915–1920
	Bainbridge Colby	1920–1921
Secretary of Treasury	William G. McAdoo	1913–1918
	Carter Glass	1918–1920
	David F. Houston	1920–1921
Secretary of War	Lindley M. Garrison	1913–1916
	Newton D. Baker	1916–1921
Attorney General	James C. McReynolds	1913–1914
	Thomas W. Gregory	1914–1919
	A. Mitchell Palmer	1919–1921
Postmaster General	Albert S. Burleson	1913–1921
Secretary of Navy	Josephus Daniels	1913–1921
Secretary of Interior	Franklin K. Lane	1913–1920
	John B. Payne	1920–1921
Secretary of Agriculture	David F. Houston	1913–1920
	Edwin T. Meredith	1920–1921
Secretary of Commerce	William C. Redfield	1913–1919
	Joshua W. Alexander	1919–1921
Secretary of Labor	William B. Wilson	1913–1921

The Harding Administration (1921–1923)

Vice President	Calvin Coolidge	1921–1923
Secretary of State	Charles E. Hughes	1921–1923
Secretary of Treasury	Andrew Mellon	1921–1923
Secretary of War	John W. Weeks	1921–1923
Attorney General	Harry M. Daugherty	1921–1923
Postmaster General	Will H. Hays	1921–1922
	Hubert Work	1922–1923
	Harry S. New	1923
Secretary of Navy	Edwin Denby	1921–1923
Secretary of Interior	Albert B. Fall	1921–1923
	Hubert Work	1923
Secretary of Agriculture	Henry C. Wallace	1921–1923
Secretary of Commerce	Herbert C. Hoover	1921–1923
Secretary of Labor	James J. Davis	1921–1923

The Coolidge Administration (1923–1929)

Vice President	Charles G. Dawes	1925–1929
Secretary of State	Charles E. Hughes	1923–1925
	Frank B. Kellogg	1925–1929
Secretary of Treasury	Andrew Mellon	1923–1929

Secretary of War	John W. Weeks	1923–1925
	Dwight F. Davis	1925–1929
Attorney General	Henry M. Daugherty	1923–1924
	Harlan F. Stone	1924–1925
	John G. Sargent	1925–1929
Postmaster General	Harry S. New	1923–1929
Secretary of Navy	Edwin Derby	1923–1924
	Curtis D. Wilbur	1924–1929
Secretary of Interior	Hubert Work	1923–1928
	Roy O. West	1928–1929
Secretary of Agriculture	Henry C. Wallace	1923–1924
	Howard M. Gore	1924–1925
	William M. Jardine	1925–1929
Secretary of Commerce	Herbert C. Hoover	1923–1928
	William F. Whiting	1928–1929
Secretary of Labor	James J. Davis	1923–1929

The Hoover Administration (1929–1933)

Vice President	Charles Curtis	1929–1933
Secretary of State	Henry L. Stimson	1929–1933
Secretary of Treasury	Andrew Mellon	1929–1932
	Ogden L. Mills	1932–1933
Secretary of War	James W. Good	1929
	Patrick J. Hurley	1929–1933
Attorney General	William D. Mitchell	1929–1933
Postmaster General	Walter F. Brown	1929–1933
Secretary of Navy	Charles F. Adams	1929–1933
Secretary of Interior	Ray L. Wilbur	1929–1933
Secretary of Agriculture	Arthur M. Hyde	1929–1933
Secretary of Commerce	Robert P. Lamont	1929–1932
	Roy D. Chapin	1932–1933
Secretary of Labor	James J. Davis	1929–1930
	William N. Doak	1930–1933

The Franklin D. Roosevelt Administration (1933–1945)

Vice President	John Nance Garner	1933–1941
	Henry A. Wallace	1941–1945
	Harry S Truman	1945
Secretary of State	Cordell Hull	1933–1944
	Edward R. Stettinius, Jr.	1944–1945
Secretary of Treasury	William H. Woodin	1933–1934
	Henry Morgenthau, Jr.	1934–1945
Secretary of War	George H. Dern	1933–1936
	Henry A. Woodring	1936–1940
	Henry L. Stimson	1940–1945
Attorney General	Homer S. Cummings	1933–1939
	Frank Murphy	1939–1940
	Robert H. Jackson	1940–1941
	Francis Biddle	1941–1945
Postmaster General	James A. Farley	1933–1940
	Frank C. Walker	1940–1945
Secretary of Navy	Claude A. Swanson	1933–1940
	Charles Edison	1940
	Frank Knox	1940–1944
	James V. Forrestal	1944–1945
Secretary of Interior	Harold L. Ickes	1933–1945

Secretary of Agriculture	Henry A. Wallace	1933–1940
	Claude R. Wickard	1940–1945
Secretary of Commerce	Daniel C. Roper	1933–1939
	Harry L. Hopkins	1939–1940
	Jesse Jones	1940–1945
	Henry A. Wallace	1945
Secretary of Labor	Frances Perkins	1933–1945

The Truman Administration (1945–1953)

Vice President	Alben W. Barkley	1949–1953
Secretary of State	Edward R. Stettinius, Jr.	1945
	James F. Byrnes	1945–1947
	George C. Marshall	1947–1949
	Dean G. Acheson	1949–1953
Secretary of Treasury	Fred M. Vinson	1945–1946
	John W. Snyder	1946–1953
Secretary of War	Robert P. Patterson	1945–1947
	Kenneth C. Royall	1947
Attorney General	Tom C. Clark	1945–1949
	J. Howard McGrath	1949–1952
	James P. McGranery	1952–1953
Postmaster General	Frank C. Walker	1945
	Robert E. Hannegan	1945–1947
	Jesse M. Donaldson	1947–1953
Secretary of Navy	James V. Forrestal	1945–1947
Secretary of Interior	Harold L. Ickes	1945–1946
	Julius A. Krug	1946–1949
	Oscar L. Chapman	1949–1953
Secretary of Agriculture	Clinton P. Anderson	1945–1948
	Charles F. Brannan	1948–1953
Secretary of Commerce	Henry A. Wallace	1945–1946
	W. Averell Harriman	1946–1948
	Charles W. Sawyer	1948–1953
Secretary of Labor	Lewis B. Schwellenbach	1945–1948
	Maurice J. Tobin	1948–1953
Secretary of Defense	James V. Forrestal	1947–1949
	Louis A. Johnson	1949–1950
	George C. Marshall	1950–1951
	Robert A. Lovett	1951–1953

The Eisenhower Administration (1953–1961)

Vice President	Richard M. Nixon	1953–1961
Secretary of State	John Foster Dulles	1953–1959
	Christian A. Herter	1959–1961
Secretary of Treasury	George M. Humphrey	1953–1957
	Robert B. Anderson	1957–1961
Attorney General	Herbert Brownell, Jr.	1953–1958
	William P. Rogers	1958–1961
Postmaster General	Arthur E. Summerfield	1953–1961
Secretary of Interior	Douglas McKay	1953–1956
	Fred A. Seaton	1956–1961
Secretary of Agriculture	Ezra T. Benson	1953–1961
Secretary of Commerce	Sinclair Weeks	1953–1958
	Lewis L. Strauss	1958–1959
	Frederick H. Mueller	1959–1961
Secretary of Labor	Martin P. Durkin	1953
	James P. Mitchell	1953–1961

Secretary of Defense	Charles E. Wilson	1953–1957
	Neil H. McElroy	1957–1959
	Thomas S. Gates, Jr.	1959–1961
Secretary of Health, Education, and Welfare	Oveta Culp Hobby	1953–1955
	Marion B. Folsom	1955–1958
	Arthur S. Flemming	1958–1961

The Kennedy Administration (1961–1963)

Vice President	Lyndon B. Johnson	1961–1963
Secretary of State	Dean Rusk	1961–1963
Secretary of Treasury	C. Douglas Dillon	1961–1963
Attorney General	Robert F. Kennedy	1961–1963
Postmaster General	J. Edward Day	1961–1963
	John A. Gronouski	1963
Secretary of Interior	Stewart L. Udall	1961–1963
Secretary of Agriculture	Orville L. Freeman	1961–1963
Secretary of Commerce	Luther H. Hodges	1961–1963
Secretary of Labor	Arthur J. Goldberg	1961–1962
	W. Willard Wirtz	1962–1963
Secretary of Defense	Robert S. McNamara	1961–1963
Secretary of Health, Education, and Welfare	Abraham A. Ribicoff	1961–1962
	Anthony J. Celebrezze	1962–1963

The Lyndon Johnson Administration (1963–1969)

Vice President	Hubert H. Humphrey	1965–1969
Secretary of State	Dean Rusk	1963–1969
Secretary of Treasury	C. Douglas Dillon	1963–1965
	Henry H. Fowler	1965–1969
Attorney General	Robert F. Kennedy	1963–1964
	Nicholas Katzenbach	1965–1966
	Ramsey Clark	1967–1969
Postmaster General	John A. Gronouski	1963–1965
	Lawrence F. O'Brien	1965–1968
	Marvin Watson	1968–1969
Secretary of Interior	Stewart L. Udall	1963–1969
Secretary of Agriculture	Orville L. Freeman	1963–1969
Secretary of Commerce	Luther H. Hodges	1963–1964
	John T. Connor	1964–1967
	Alexander B. Trowbridge	1967–1968
	Cyrus R. Smith	1968–1969
Secretary of Labor	W. Willard Wirtz	1963–1969
Secretary of Defense	Robert F. McNamara	1963–1968
	Clark Clifford	1968–1969
Secretary of Health, Education, and Welfare	Anthony J. Celebrezze	1963–1965
	John W. Gardner	1965–1968
	Wilbur J. Cohen	1968–1969
Secretary of Housing and Urban Development	Robert C. Weaver	1966–1969
	Robert C. Wood	1969
Secretary of Transportation	Alan S. Boyd	1967–1969

The Nixon Administration (1969–1974)

| Vice President | Spiro T. Agnew | 1969–1973 |
| | Gerald R. Ford | 1973–1974 |

Secretary of State	William P. Rogers	1969–1973
	Henry A. Kissinger	1973–1974
Secretary of Treasury	David M. Kennedy	1969–1970
	John B. Connally	1971–1972
	George P. Shultz	1972–1974
	William E. Simon	1974
Attorney General	John N. Mitchell	1969–1972
	Richard G. Kleindienst	1972–1973
	Elliot L. Richardson	1973
	William B. Saxbe	1973–1974
Postmaster General	Winton M. Blount	1969–1971
Secretary of Interior	Walter J. Hickel	1969–1970
	Rogers Morton	1971–1974
Secretary of Agriculture	Clifford M. Hardin	1969–1971
	Earl L. Butz	1971–1974
Secretary of Commerce	Maurice H. Stans	1969–1972
	Peter G. Peterson	1972–1973
	Frederick B. Dent	1973–1974
Secretary of Labor	George P. Shultz	1969–1970
	James D. Hodgson	1970–1973
	Peter J. Brennan	1973–1974
Secretary of Defense	Melvin R. Laird	1969–1973
	Elliot L. Richardson	1973
	James R. Schlesinger	1973–1974
Secretary of Health, Education, and Welfare	Robert H. Finch	1969–1970
	Elliot L. Richardson	1970–1973
	Caspar W. Weinberger	1973–1974
Secretary of Housing and Urban Development	George Romney	1969–1973
	James T. Lynn	1973–1974
Secretary of Transportation	John A. Volpe	1969–1973
	Claude S. Brinegar	1973–1974

The Ford Administration (1974–1977)

Vice President	Nelson A. Rockefeller	1974–1977
Secretary of State	Henry A. Kissinger	1974–1977
Secretary of Treasury	William E. Simon	1974–1977
Attorney General	William B. Saxbe	1974–1975
	Edward Levi	1975–1977
Secretary of Interior	Rogers Morton	1974–1975
	Stanley K. Hathaway	1975
	Thomas Kleppe	1975–1977
Secretary of Agriculture	Earl L. Butz	1974–1976
	John A. Knebel	1976–1977
Secretary of Commerce	Frederick B. Dent	1974–1975
	Rogers Morton	1975–1976
	Elliot L. Richardson	1976–1977
Secretary of Labor	Peter J. Brennan	1974–1975
	John T. Dunlop	1975–1976
	W. J. Usery	1976–1977
Secretary of Defense	James R. Schlesinger	1974–1975
	Donald Rumsfeld	1975–1977
Secretary of Health, Education, and Welfare	Caspar W. Weinberger	1974–1975
	Forrest D. Mathews	1975–1977
Secretary of Housing and Urban Development	James T. Lynn	1974–1975
	Carla A. Hills	1975–1977
Secretary of Transportation	Claude S. Brinegar	1974–1975
	William T. Coleman	1975–1977

The Carter Administration (1977–1981)

Vice President	Walter F. Mondale	1977–1981
Secretary of State	Cyrus R. Vance	1977–1980
	Edmund Muskie	1980–1981
Secretary of Treasury	W. Michael Blumenthal	1977–1979
	G. William Miller	1979–1981
Attorney General	Griffin Bell	1977–1979
	Benjamin R. Civiletti	1979–1981
Secretary of Interior	Cecil D. Andrus	1977–1981
Secretary of Agriculture	Robert Bergland	1977–1981
Secretary of Commerce	Juanita M. Kreps	1977–1979
	Philip M. Klutznick	1979–1981
Secretary of Labor	F. Ray Marshall	1977–1981
Secretary of Defense	Harold Brown	1977–1981
Secretary of Health Education, and Welfare	Joseph A. Califano	1977–1979
	Patricia R. Harris	1979
Secretary of Health and Human Services	Patricia R. Harris	1979–1981
Secretary of Education	Shirley M. Hufstedler	1979–1981
Secretary of Housing and Urban Development	Patricia R. Harris	1977–1979
	Moon Landrieu	1979–1981
Secretary of Transportation	Brock Adams	1977–1979
	Neil E. Goldschmidt	1979–1981
Secretary of Energy	James R. Schlesinger	1979–1979
	Charles W. Duncan	1979–1981

The Reagan Administration (1981–1989)

Vice President	George Bush	1981–1989
Secretary of State	Alexander M. Haig	1981–1982
	George P. Shultz	1982–1989
Secretary of Treasury	Donald Regan	1981–1985
	James A. Baker, III	1985–1988
	Nicholas Brady	1988–1989
Attorney General	William F. Smith	1981–1985
	Edwin A. Meese, III	1985–1988
	Richard Thornburgh	1988–1989
Secretary of Interior	James Watt	1981–1983
	William P. Clark, Jr.	1983–1985
	Donald P. Hodel	1985–1989
Secretary of Agriculture	John Block	1981–1986
	Richard E. Lyng	1986–1989
Secretary of Commerce	Malcolm Baldrige	1981–1987
	C. William Verity, Jr.	1987–1989

Secretary of Labor	Raymond Donovan	1981–1985
	William E. Brock	1985–1988
	Ann Dore McLaughlin	1988–1989
Secretary of Defense	Caspar W. Weinberger	1981–1988
	Frank Carlucci	1988–1989
Secretary of Health and Human Services	Richard Schweiker	1981–1983
	Margaret Heckler	1983–1985
	Otis R. Bowen	1985–1989
Secretary of Education	Terrel H. Bell	1981–1985
	William J. Bennett	1985–1988
	Lauro F. Cavazos	1988–1989
Secretary of Housing and Urban Development	Samuel Pierce	1981–1989
Secretary of Transportation	Drew Lewis	1981–1983
	Elizabeth Dole	1983–1987
	James L. Burnley, IV	1987–1989
Secretary of Energy	James Edwards	1981–1982
	Donald P. Hodel	1982–1985
	John S. Herrington	1985–1989

The Bush Administration (1989–1993)

Vice President	J. Danforth Quayle	1989–
Secretary of State	James A. Baker, III	1989–1992
Secretary of Treasury	Nicholas F. Brady	1988–
Attorney General	Richard Thornburgh	1989–1991
	William Barr	1991–
Secretary of Interior	Manuel Lujan, Jr.	1989–
Secretary of Agriculture	Clayton K. Yeutter	1989–1991
	Edward Madigan	1991–
Secretary of Commerce	Robert A. Mosbacher	1989–1991
	Barbara Hackman Franklin	1992–
Secretary of Labor	Elizabeth H. Dole	1989–1990
	Lynn Morley Martin	1991–
Secretary of Defense	Richard Cheney	1989–
Secretary of Health and Human Services	Louis W. Sullivan	1989–
Secretary of Education	Lauro F. Cavazos	1989–1990
	Lamar Alexander	1991–
Secretary of Housing and Urban Development	Jack F. Kemp	1989–
Secretary of Transportation	Samuel K. Skinner	1989–1991
	Andrew H. Card, Jr.	1992–
Secretary of Energy	James D. Watkins	1989–
Secretary of Veterans Affairs	Edward J. Derwinski	1989–1992

Supreme Court Justices

Name	Terms of Service[1]	Appointed by	Name	Terms of Service[1]	Appointed by
John Jay	1789–1795	Washington	Lucious Q. C. Lamar	1888–1893	Cleveland
James Wilson	1789–1798	Washington	**Melville W. Fuller**	1888–1910	Cleveland
John Rutledge	1790–1791	Washington	David J. Brewer	1890–1910	B. Harrison
William Cushing	1790–1810	Washington	Henry B. Brown	1891–1906	B. Harrison
John Blair	1790–1796	Washington	George Shiras, Jr.	1892–1903	B. Harrison
James Iredell	1790–1799	Washington	Howell E. Jackson	1893–1895	B. Harrison
Thomas Johnson	1792–1793	Washington	Edward D. White	1894–1910	Cleveland
William Paterson	1793–1806	Washington	Rufus W. Peckham	1896–1909	Cleveland
John Rutledge[2]	1795	Washington	Joseph McKenna	1898–1925	McKinley
Samuel Chase	1796–1811	Washington	Oliver W. Holmes	1902–1932	T. Roosevelt
Oliver Ellsworth	1796–1800	Washington	William R. Day	1903–1922	T. Roosevelt
Bushrod Washington	1799–1829	J. Adams	William H. Moody	1906–1910	T. Roosevelt
Alfred Moore	1800–1804	J. Adams	Horace H. Lurton	1910–1914	Taft
John Marshall	1801–1835	J. Adams	Charles E. Hughes	1910–1916	Taft
William Johnson	1804–1834	Jefferson	Willis Van Devanter	1911–1937	Taft
Brockholst Livingston	1807–1823	Jefferson	Joseph R. Lamar	1911–1916	Taft
Thomas Todd	1807–1826	Jefferson	**Edward D. White**	1910–1921	Taft
Gabriel Duvall	1811–1835	Madison	Mahlon Pitney	1912–1922	Taft
Joseph Story	1812–1845	Madison	James C. McReynolds	1914–1941	Wilson
Smith Thompson	1823–1843	Monroe	Louis D. Brandeis	1916–1939	Wilson
Robert Trimble	1826–1828	J. Q. Adams	John H. Clarke	1916–1922	Wilson
John McLean	1830–1861	Jackson	**William H. Taft**	1921–1930	Harding
Henry Baldwin	1830–1844	Jackson	George Sutherland	1922–1938	Harding
James M. Wayne	1835–1867	Jackson	Pierce Butler	1923–1939	Harding
Roger B. Taney	1836–1864	Jackson	Edward T. Sanford	1923–1930	Harding
Philip P. Barbour	1836–1841	Jackson	Harlan F. Stone	1925–1941	Coolidge
John Cartron	1837–1865	Van Buren	**Charles E. Hughes**	1930–1941	Hoover
John McKinley	1838–1852	Van Buren	Owen J. Roberts	1930–1945	Hoover
Peter V. Daniel	1842–1860	Van Buren	Benjamin N. Cardozo	1932–1938	Hoover
Samuel Nelson	1845–1872	Tyler	Hugo L. Black	1937–1971	F. Roosevelt
Levi Woodbury	1845–1851	Polk	Stanley F. Reed	1938–1957	F. Roosevelt
Robert C. Grier	1846–1870	Polk	Felix Frankfurter	1939–1962	F. Roosevelt
Benjamin R. Curtis	1851–1857	Fillmore	William O. Douglas	1939–1975	F. Roosevelt
John A. Campbell	1853–1861	Pierce	Frank Murphy	1940–1949	F. Roosevelt
Nathan Clifford	1858–1881	Buchanan	**Harlan F. Stone**	1941–1946	F. Roosevelt
Noah H. Swayne	1862–1881	Lincoln	James F. Byrnes	1941–1942	F. Roosevelt
Samuel F. Miller	1862–1890	Lincoln	Robert H. Jackson	1941–1954	F. Roosevelt
David Davis	1862–1877	Lincoln	Wiley B. Rutledge	1943–1949	F. Roosevelt
Stephen J. Field	1863–1897	Lincoln	Harold H. Burton	1945–1958	Truman
Salmon P. Chase	1864–1873	Lincoln	**Frederick M. Vinson**	1946–1953	Truman
William Strong	1870–1880	Grant	Tom C. Clark	1949–1967	Truman
Joseph P. Bradley	1870–1892	Grant	Sherman Minton	1949–1956	Truman
Ward Hunt	1873–1882	Grant	**Earl Warren**	1953–1969	Eisenhower
Morrison R. Waite	1874–1888	Grant	John Marshall Harlan	1955–1971	Eisenhower
John M. Harlan	1877–1911	Hayes	William J. Brennan, Jr.	1956–1990	Eisenhower
William B. Woods	1881–1887	Hayes	Charles E. Whittaker	1957–1962	Eisenhower
Stanley Matthews	1881–1889	Garfield	Potter Stewart	1958–1981	Eisenhower
Horace Gray	1882–1902	Arthur	Byron R. White	1962–	Kennedy
Samuel Blatchford	1882–1893	Arthur	Arthur J. Goldberg	1962–1965	Kennedy

Chief Justices in bold type

[1]The date on which the justice took his judicial oath is here used as the date of the beginning of his service, for until that oath is taken he is not vested with the prerogatives of his office. Justices, however, receive their commissions ("letters patent") before taking their oath—in some instances, in the preceding year.

[2]Acting Chief Justice; Senate refused to confirm appointment.

Name	Terms of Service[1]	Appointed by	Name	Terms of Service[1]	Appointed by
Abe Fortas	1965–1970	Johnson	Sandra Day O'Connor	1981–	Reagan
Thurgood Marshall	1967–1991	Johnson	**William H. Rehnquist**	1986–	Reagan
Warren E. Burger	1969–1986	Nixon	Antonin Scalia	1986–	Reagan
Harry A. Blackmun	1970–	Nixon	Anthony Kennedy	1988–	Reagan
Lewis F. Powell, Jr.	1971–1988	Nixon	David H. Souter	1990–	Bush
William H. Rehnquist	1971–1986	Nixon	Clarence Thomas	1991–	Bush
John Paul Stevens	1975–	Ford			

Chief Justices in bold type

[1]The date on which the justice took his judicial oath is here used as the date of the beginning of his service, for until that oath is taken he is not vested with the prerogatives of his office. Justices, however, receive their commissions ("letters patent") before taking their oath—in some instances, in the preceding year.

[2]Acting Chief Justice; Senate refused to confirm appointment.

Admission of States to the Union

State	Date of Admission	State	Date of Admission
1. Delaware	December 7, 1787	26. Michigan	January 26, 1837
2. Pennsylvania	December 12, 1787	27. Florida	March 3, 1845
3. New Jersey	December 18, 1787	28. Texas	December 29, 1845
4. Georgia	January 2, 1788	29. Iowa	December 28, 1846
5. Connecticut	January 9, 1788	30. Wisconsin	May 29, 1848
6. Massachusetts	February 6, 1788	31. California	September 9, 1850
7. Maryland	April 28, 1788	32. Minnesota	May 11, 1858
8. South Carolina	May 23, 1788	33. Oregon	February 14, 1859
9. New Hampshire	June 21, 1788	34. Kansas	January 29, 1861
10. Virginia	June 25, 1788	35. West Virginia	June 20, 1863
11. New York	July 26, 1788	36. Nevada	October 31, 1864
12. North Carolina	November 21, 1789	37. Nebraska	March 1, 1867
13. Rhode Island	May 29, 1790	38. Colorado	August 1, 1876
14. Vermont	March 4, 1791	39. North Dakota	November 2, 1889
15. Kentucky	June 1, 1792	40. South Dakota	November 2, 1889
16. Tennessee	June 1, 1796	41. Montana	November 8, 1889
17. Ohio	March 1, 1803	42. Washington	November 11, 1889
18. Louisiana	April 30, 1812	43. Idaho	July 3, 1890
19. Indiana	December 11, 1816	44. Wyoming	July 10, 1890
20. Mississippi	December 10, 1817	45. Utah	January 4, 1896
21. Illinois	December 3, 1818	46. Oklahoma	November 16, 1907
22. Alabama	December 14, 1819	47. New Mexico	January 6, 1912
23. Maine	March 15, 1820	48. Arizona	February 14, 1912
24. Missouri	August 10, 1821	49. Alaska	January 3, 1959
25. Arkansas	June 15, 1836	50. Hawaii	August 21, 1959

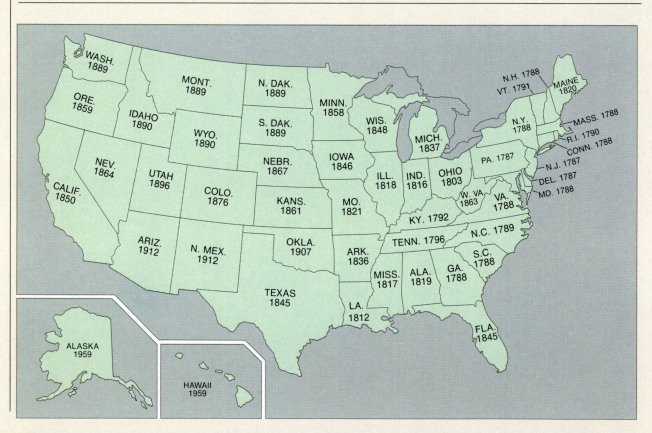

U.S. Population, 1790–1990

Year	Population	Percent Increase	Population Per Square Mile	Sex (rounded to nearest million) Male	Female	Median Age
1790	3,929,214		4.5	NA	NA	NA
1800	5,308,483	35.1	6.1	NA	NA	NA
1810	7,239,881	36.4	4.3	NA	NA	NA
1820	9,638,453	33.1	5.5	5	5	16.7
1830	12,866,020	33.5	7.4	7	6	17.2
1840	17,069,453	32.7	9.8	9	8	17.8
1850	23,191,876	35.9	7.9	12	11	18.9
1860	31,443,321	35.6	10.6	16	15	19.4
1870	39,818,449	26.6	13.4	19	19	20.2
1880	50,155,783	26.0	16.9	26	25	20.9
1890	62,947,714	25.5	21.2	32	31	22.0
1900	75,994,575	20.7	25.6	39	37	22.9
1910	91,972,266	21.0	31.0	47	45	24.1
1920	105,710,620	14.9	35.6	54	52	25.3
1930	122,775,046	16.1	41.2	62	61	26.4
1940	131,669,275	7.2	44.2	66	66	29.0
1950	150,697,361	14.5	50.7	75	76	30.2
1960	179,323,175	18.5	50.6	88	91	29.5
1970	203,302,031	13.4	57.4	99	104	28.0
1980	226,545,805	11.4	64.0	110	116	30.0
1985	237,839,000	5.0	64.0	117	123	31.3
1990	249,975,000	1.1	70.3	121	127	32.6

NA = Not available.

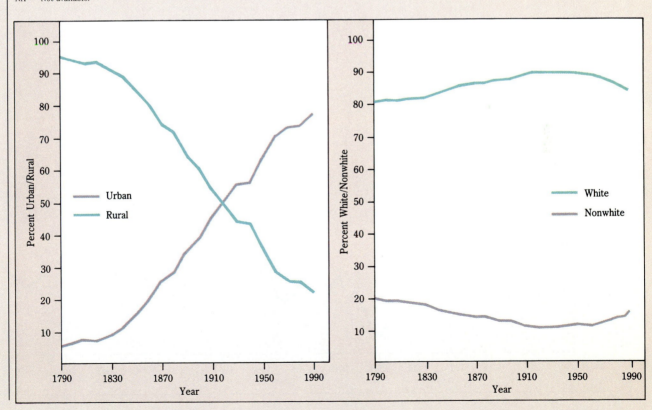

Employment, 1870–1990

Year	Number of Workers (in Millions)	Male/Female Employment Ratio	Percentage of Workers in Unions
1870	12.5	85/15	—
1880	17.4	85/15	—
1890	23.3	83/17	—
1900	29.1	82/18	3
1910	38.2	79/21	6
1920	41.6	79/21	12
1930	48.8	78/22	7
1940	53.0	76/24	27
1950	59.6	72/28	25
1960	69.9	68/32	26
1970	82.1	63/37	25
1980	108.5	58/42	23
1985	108.9	57/43	19
1990	126.4	55/45	16.4

Unemployment

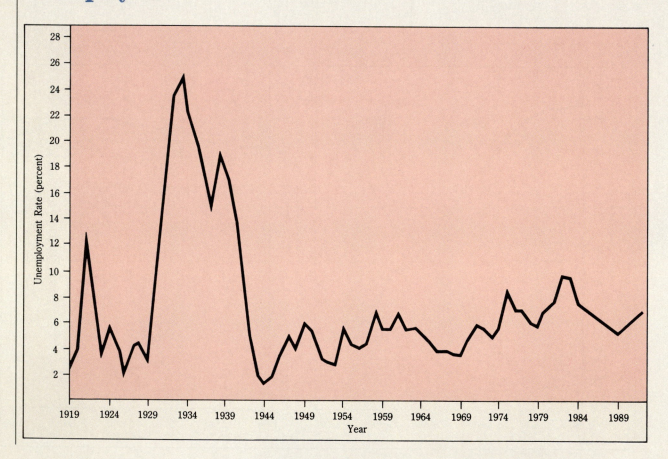

Regional Origins of Immigration

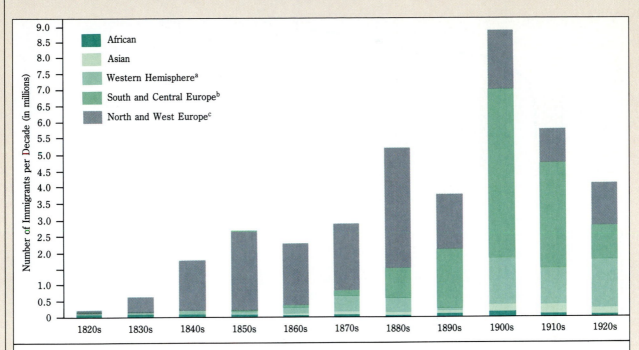

Number of Immigrants per Decade (in millions)

Legend:
- African
- Asian
- Western Hemisphere[a]
- South and Central Europe[b]
- North and West Europe[c]

Decades: 1820s, 1830s, 1840s, 1850s, 1860s, 1870s, 1880s, 1890s, 1900s, 1910s, 1920s

[a]Canada and all countries in South America and Central America.
[b]Italy, Spain, Portugal, Greece, Germany (Austria included, 1938-1945), Poland, Czechoslovakia (since 1920), Yugoslavia (since 1920), Hungary (since 1861), Austria (since 1861, except 1938-1945), U.S.S.R. (excludes Asian U.S.S.R. between 1931 and 1963), Latvia, Estonia, Lithuania, Finland, Romania, Bulgaria, Turkey (in Europe), and other European countries not classified elsewhere.
[c]Great Britain, Ireland, Norway, Sweden, Denmark, Iceland, Netherlands, Belgium, Luxembourg, Switzerland, France.
SOURCE: Stephan Thernstrom, ed., *Harvard Encyclopedia of American Ethnic Groups* (1980), p. 480; and U.S. Bureau of the Census, *Statistical Abstract of the United States, 1984* (1983), p. 9.

Total Federal Debt

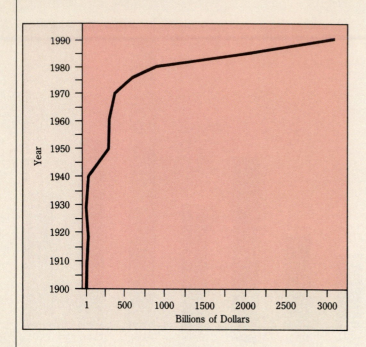

Credits

Contents

Chapter Openers

Chapters 14–16 Captured slave: Musée de l'Homme, Paris. Slave sale broadside: State Historical Society of Wisconsin. Slave nurse: Cook Collection/Valentine Museum, Richmond, Va. Robert E. Lee: Library of Congress. Union soldier: Chicago Historical Society. Pickett's Charge: Gettysburg National Military Park. Battle of the Crater: The Commonwealth Club, Richmond, Virginia. Ulysses S. Grant: Library of Congress. 1st Virginia Regiment: Cook Collection/Valentine Museum, Richmond, Va. Infantry at Fort Lincoln: Library of Congress. Ruins of Richmond, Virginia: Library of Congress. Elizabeth Cady Stanton: Culver Pictures. Susan B. Anthony: The Sophia Smith Collection (Women's History Archive), Smith College, Northampton, Mass.

Chapters 17–22 Chinese fire hose team: Library of Congress. Cowboys: Montana Historical Society, Helena. Cattle brands: From *We Pointed Them North*, copyright 1954, University of Oklahoma Press. Sitting Bull: Library of Congress. George Custer: Library of Congress. Golden spike ceremony: Union Pacific Railroad Museum Collection. Cowboy: © Charles J. Belden, Whitney Gallery of Western Art, Cody, Wyo. Football team: Steve Karchin Collection. Ferris wheel: Chicago Historical Society. Horse: *Treasury of American Design.* Skyscraper: The New-York Historical Society, New York City. Edison's electric light bulbs: Greenfield Village and Henry Ford Museum, Dearborn, Mich. Immigrants: International Museum of Photography/George Eastman House. Schoolroom: Brown Brothers.

Chapters 23–27 Immigrant: International Museum of Photography/George Eastman House. Jack Johnson: Bettmann Archive. Lusitania ad: Culver Pictures. Henry Ford in Model T: UPI/Bettmann. Shell casing factory: National Archives. WW I soldier: Smithsonian Institution. WW I soldiers: Charlotte Iglarsh Collection. FDR and Eleanor: UPI/Bettmann. Charles Lindbergh: Bettmann Archive. Flappers: Schomberg Collection/New York Public Library, Astor, Lenox and Tilden Foundations. Soldiers wearing gas masks: UPI/Bettmann. Wall Street, October 29, 1929: Brown Brothers. Mickey Mouse: © Walt Disney Productions. Hitler and Mussolini: National Archives. Woman kissing WW II soldier: U.S. Army. Blimp and bombers: U.S. Navy Photo. U.S. at War headline: *San Francisco Chronicle*, December 8, 1941. WW II poster: National Archives. Sailors: U.S. Navy Photo. Mushroom cloud over Nagasaki: U.S. Air Force photo.

Chapters 28–31 Dwight Eisenhower: Library of Congress. Woman in kitchen: Bettmann Archive. Suburban homes: FPG. Noguchi table, Eames chair: © Herman Miller, Inc., Zeeland, Mich. Fabric samples: Alexander Girard, © Herman Miller, Inc., Zeeland, Mich. Martin Luther King, Jr.: Costa Manos/Magnum Photos. Kennedy-Nixon debate: Wide World Photos. Missiles: Cornell Capa/Magnum Photos. Helicopter, Vietnam: UPI/Bettmann. March on Washington, 1963: Robert W. Kelley, LIFE Magazine © 1970 Time Inc. Saturn rings photographed from Voyager 2: NASA. Woodstock Festival: Elliot Landy/Magnum Photos. Soldiers, Vietnam: Philip Jones Griffiths/Magnum Photos. Antiwar demonstration: Jean-Claude Lejeune. Astronauts on moon: NASA. Betty Friedan: Michael Ginsburg/Magnum Photos. Sam Ervin, Senate Watergate Investigating Committee: Mark Godfrey/Archive Pictures. Richard Nixon: Hiroji Kubota/Magnum Photos. Student demonstration: Wayne Miller/Magnum Photos. Supreme Court Justice Sandra Day O'Connor: Owen Franken/Sygma. Space shuttle: UPI/Bettmann Newsphotos. Ronald Reagan and Mikhail Gorbachev: Sygma.

Chapter Photos

Unless otherwise acknowledged, all photographs are the property of Scott, Foresman and Company. Page abbreviations are as follows: (T)top, (C)center, (B)bottom, (L)left, (R)right, (Ins)inset.

Archive **727** The Bettmann Archive **728** The Lawrence Lee Pelletier Library, Allegheny College **730** The Granger Collection, New York **731** Centers for Disease Control, Atlanta, Center for Professional Development & Training, Still Pictures Archives **733T** Chicago Historical Society **734** AP/Wide World **735** NAACP **738** UPI/Bettmann **742** Brown Brothers **743** Library of Congress **744** State Historical Society of Wisconsin **745** Brown Brothers **750** The Granger Collection, New York **754** Library of Congress

Chapter 23
760 The Granger Collection, New York **761** UPI/Bettmann **763** Imperial War Museum, London **765** UPI/Bettmann **772** The Archives of Labor and Urban Affairs, Wayne State University **773** New York Public Library, Astor, Lenox and Tilden Foundations **774T** UPI/Bettmann **774B** The National Archives **775** The National Archives **778** Imperial War Museum, London **781** Robert Hunt Library **785** Brown Brothers **788** CHICAGO TRIBUNE-N.Y. News Syndicate

Chapter 24
795 Culver Pictures **798** AP/Wide World **799** Hampton University Museum, Hampton, Va. **800** Culver Pictures **802** The Granger Collection, New York **805** Rollin Kirby, *New York World*, May 19, 1925 **808** Brown Brothers **810L** *Vanity Fair* photograph by Breaker/ Copyright © 1928, 1956 by Conde Nast Publications, Inc. **810R** Brown Brothers **813L** Brown Brothers **813R** UPI/Bettmann **815** *LIFE*, June 8, 1920 **817** U.S. Bureau of Printing and Engraving **819** *New York Times*, Oct. 25, 1929

Chapter 25
826 Culver Pictures **828** UPI/Bettmann **832** AP/Wide World **833** Library of Congress **835** Brown Brothers **836** Brown Brothers **837** The Franklin D. Roosevelt Library **841** The Bettmann Archive **843** AP/Wide World **845** Culver Pictures **848** © 1938 by Esquire, Inc. **850** Courtesy Lou Erikson **852** Keystone/FPG

Chapter 26
862 Brown Brothers **864** Photofest **868** UPI/Bettmann **870** UPI/Bettmann **872** UPI/Bettmann **875** Official U. S. Navy Photograph **877** AP/Wide World **880** *Up front* by Bill Mauldin, published by Henry Holt & Co. **881L** Library of Congress **881R** Baker Library, Harvard Business School **885** Photograph by Dorothea Lange/The National Archives/War Relocation Authority **892** The Franklin D. Roosevelt Library **895** UPI/Bettmann **896** United States Air Force Photo **899** United States Air Force Photo

Chapter 27
905R James Whitmore/Life Magazine, Time Warner Inc. **905L** Thomas D. McAvoy **907** Acme/UPI/Bettmann **912** UPI/Bettmann **914** Ferro Jacobs/Black Star **915** Eastfoto/SOVFOTO **917** UPI/Bettmann **920** AP/Wide World **922** The Granger Collection, New York **924(All)** Elliot Erwitt/Magnum Photos **924** AP/Wide World **925** UPI/Bettmann **926** Alfred Eisenstaedt/Life Magazine, Time Warner Inc. **928** Wide World **929** Film Stills Archive/The Museum of Modern Art, New York

Chapter 28
937 AP/Wide World **944** SOVFOTO **946** UPI/Bettmann **947** UPI/Bettmann **950** United States Air Force Photo **951** Costa Manos/Magnum Photos **952** UPI/Bettmann **955** © 1949/Ed Clark/Life Magazine, Time Warner Inc. **957** AP/Wide World **958(All)** AP/Wide World **959** Life

Magazine, Time Warner Inc. **961** Brown Brothers **962** Brown Brothers **963** Courtesy CBS **965** Don Wright/Life Magazine, Time Warner Inc. **966** UPI/Bettmann

Chapter 29
972 UPI/Bettmann **974** UPI/Bettmann **976** Bob Fitch/Black Star **980** *New York Daily News* Photo **982** UPI/Bettmann **984** UPI/Bettmann **985** AP/Wide World **991** Roger Falconer/Black Star **992** Steve Schapiro/ Black Star **993** Paul Sequeira **996** Kent State University News Service **998** Magnum Photos **999** Kobal Collection/Superstock

Chapter 30
1007 AP/Wide World **1010** UPI/Bettmann **1012** Charles Moore/Black Star **1013** AP/Wide World **1015** Charles Moore/Black Star **1017** Fred Ward/Black Star **1018** Bob Adelman/Magnum Photos **1020** John Launois/Black Star **1021** Constantine Manos/Magnum Photos **1023** Yoichi Okomoto/Photo Researchers **1026** B. Bartholomew/Black Star **1027** Nacio Jan Brown/Black Star **1028** Wayne Miller/Magnum Photos **1031** PhotoFest **1034** David Strick/Onyx **1037** Arthur Grace/Sygma **1039L** Ira Wyman/Sygma **1039R** Kathleen Foster/Black Star **1043** Herman Kokojan/Black Star **1044** Michael Abramson/Black Star

Chapter 31
1050 Mark Godfrey/Archive Pictures Inc. **1053** Alex Webb/Magnum Photos **1055** Anthony Loew © 1984 **1060** Courtesy American Petroleum Institute **1060 (Ins)** Milt & Joan Mann/Cameramann International, Ltd. **1062** Locher/Reprinted by permission: Tribune Media Services **1065** Bill Fitzpatrick/The White House **1067** Special Features/SIPA-Press **1072** Bob Glaze/Artstreet **1076** Jack Higgins/© with permission of the *Chicago Sun-Times*, Inc. **1077** Laski/SIPA-Press **1080** Timothy Ross/Picture Group **1081** R. Bossu/Sygma **1082** Le Segretain/Sygma **1085** Klaus Reisinger/Black Star **1088** Patrick Forden/Sygma

Figure, Map, and Literary Permissions
783 Data from G. M. Gathorne-Hardy, *The Fourteen Points and the Treaty of Versailles*, Oxford Pamphlets on World Affairs, no. 6, 1939 and Thomas G. Paterson, et al., *American Foreign Policy, A History Since 1900*, 2d ed., vol. 2. **796** From *Chicago: Growth of a Metropolis* by Harold M. Mayer and Richard C. Wade. Copyright © 1969 by The University of Chicago. Reprinted by permission of The University of Chicago Press. **839** Data from C. D. Premer, *American Bank Failures*, Columbia University Press, 1935. **948** From *An Atlas of World Affairs* by Andrew Boyd. Reprinted by permission of Metheum & Co., Ltd. **960** From "Little Boxes," words and music by Malvina Reynolds. Copyright © 1962 by Schroder Music Co. (ASCAP). Used by permission. All rights reserved. **965** From "Long Tall Sally" by Richard Penniman, Enntris Johnson, and Robert A. Blackwell and "Rip It Up" by Robert A. Blackwell and John S. Marascalo. Copyright © 1956, renewed 1984 by Venice Music Inc. All rights controlled and administered by SBK Blackwood Music Inc. under license from ATV Music (Venice). All rights reserved. International copyright secured. Used by permission. From "Roll Over Beethoven" by Chuck Berry. Used by permission of Isalee Music Company. **966** From "Shake, Rattle and Roll" by Charles Calhoun. Copyright © 1954 by Unichappell Music Inc. All rights reserved. Used by permission. **967** Excerpt from "Howl" from *Collected Poems 1947–1980* by Allen Ginsberg. Copyright © 1955 by Allen Ginsberg. Excerpt from "America" from *Collected Poems 1947–1980* by Allen Ginsberg. Copyright © 1956, 1959 by Allen Ginsberg. Reprinted by permission of HarperCollins Publishers.

Index